Pearson Arab World Editions – Business & Economics

The Arab world's location between three continents ensures its place at the centre of an increasingly integrated global economy, as distinctive as any business culture. We think learning should be as dynamic, relevant and engaging as the business environment. Our new Arab World Editions for Business & Economics provide this uniquely Arab perspective for students in and of the Arab world.

Each Arab World Edition integrates cases, companies, research, people and discussions representing the diverse economic, political, and cultural situations across the nations that span the Arab world, whilst retaining the quality, research, and relevant global perspectives of the world's leading business thinkers.

We hope that you find this edition a valuable contribution to your teaching or business studies. We aim to set a new benchmark for contextualised learning with our adapted and new titles, and hope that they will prove a valuable contribution in the success of students and teachers along each step of their business programme.

Supplementary support includes P .... anuals, test bank generators and MyLab online tuto ....

T0342132

Titles span a range of subjects and disciplines, including:

- Management – Robbins & Coulter
- Strategic Management: Concepts and Cases – David
- Principles of Marketing – Kotler & Armstrong
- Statistics for Business – Benghezal
- Principles of Managerial Finance – Gitman
- Marketing Management – Kotler & Keller
- Organizational Behavior – Robbins & Judge
- Human Resource Management – Dessler
- Introductory Mathematical Analysis for Business, Economics and Life and Social Sciences – Haeussler

To find out more, go to www.pearson.com/middleeast/awe

ALWAYS LEARNING

PEARSON

PRINCIPLES OF MARKETING

Arab World Edition

PHILIP KOTLER
Northwestern University

GARY ARMSTRONG
University of North Carolina

AHMED TOLBA
American University in Cairo

ANWAR HABIB
Higher Colleges of Technology, UAE

Acquisitions Editor: Rasheed Roussan
Development Editor: Sarah Wightman
Project Editor: Kate Sherington
Editor: Fay Gibbons
Copy-editor: Jackie Mace
Proofreader: Jim Caunter
Design Manager: Sarah Fach
Permissions Editor: Rachel Thorne
Picture Researcher: Emily Taylor and Zohir Naciri
Indexer: Indexing Specialists (UK) Ltd
Marketing Manager: Sue Mainey
Production Controller: Christopher Crow
Cover Designer: Sarah Fach
Typesetter: Integra
Typeface: 9/12.5, Palatino

Printed in Malaysia (CTP-VVP)

Pearson Education Limited
Edinburgh Gate
Harlow
Essex CM20 2JE
England

and Associated Companies throughout the world

© Pearson Education Limited 2011

First published 2011

20 19
IMP 10 9 8

ISBN: 978-1-4082-5568-1

About the Authors

Gary
Armstrong is the Crist W. Blackwell Distinguished Professor of Undergraduate Education in the Kenan-Flagler Business School at the University of North Carolina at Chapel Hill. He holds undergraduate and master's degrees in business from Wayne State University in Detroit, and he received his PhD in marketing from Northwestern University. Professor Armstrong has contributed numerous articles to leading business journals. As a consultant and researcher, he has worked with many companies on marketing research, sales management, and marketing strategy.

But Professor Armstrong's first love has always been teaching. His Blackwell Distinguished Professorship is the only permanent endowed professorship for distinguished undergraduate teaching at the University of North Carolina at Chapel Hill. He has been very active in the teaching and administration of Kenan-Flagler's undergraduate program. His administrative posts have included Chair of Marketing, Associate Director of the Undergraduate Business Program, Director of the Business Honors Program, and many others. He has worked closely with business student groups and has received several campuswide and Business School teaching awards. He is the only repeat recipient of the school's highly regarded Award for Excellence in Undergraduate Teaching, which he has received three times. Most recently, Professor Armstrong received the UNC Board of Governors Award for Excellence in Teaching, the highest teaching honor bestowed by the 16-campus University of North Carolina system.

Philip
Kotler is the S. C. Johnson & Son Distinguished Professor of International Marketing at the Kellogg School of Management, Northwestern University. He received his master's degree at the University of Chicago and his PhD at MIT, both in economics. Professor Kotler is the author of *Marketing Management* (Pearson Prentice Hall), now in its thirteenth edition and the most widely used marketing text book in graduate business schools worldwide. He has authored dozens of other successful books and has written more than 100 articles in leading journals. He is the only three-time winner of the coveted Alpha Kappa Psi award for the best annual article in the *Journal of Marketing*.

Professor Kotler was named the first recipient of two major awards: the *Distinguished Marketing Educator of the Year Award*, given by the American Marketing Association and the *Philip Kotler Award for Excellence in Health Care Marketing*, presented by the Academy for Health Care Services Marketing. His numerous other major honors include the Sales and Marketing Executives International *Marketing Educator of the Year Award*; the European Association of Marketing Consultants and Trainers *Marketing Excellence Award*; the *Charles Coolidge Parlin Marketing Research Award*; and the *Paul D. Converse Award*, given by the American Marketing Association to honor "outstanding contributions to science in marketing." In a recent *Financial Times* poll of 1,000 senior executives across the world, Professor Kotler was ranked as the fourth "most influential business writer/guru" of the twenty-first century.

Professor Kotler has served as chairman of the College on Marketing of the Institute of Management Sciences, a director of the American Marketing Association, and a trustee of the Marketing Science Institute. He has consulted with many major U.S. and international companies in the areas of marketing strategy and planning, marketing organization, and international marketing. He has traveled extensively throughout Europe, Asia, and South America, advising companies and governments about global marketing practices and opportunities.

Ahmed
Tolba

is Assistant Professor of Marketing in the School of Business at the American University in Cairo. He is also Director of El-Khazindar Business Research and Case Center (KCC), which is the first center in the MENA region to focus on developing world-class refereed case studies. He was awarded his PhD from the George Washington University in 2006, and his MBA & BSc from the American University in Cairo in 1997 and 2001 respectively. His professional experience includes four years at Procter & Gamble Egypt; he also worked as a marketing consultant for several local firms.

His research focuses on brand equity, nation branding, branding strategies, and social marketing. His work has been published and presented in leading academic journals, such as the *Journal of Product and Brand Management*, the *Journal of Technology Marketing,* the *International Journal of Marketing Studies,* and the *Journal of International Business and Cultural Studies,* and presented at conferences for the American Marketing Association (AMA), the Academy of Marketing Science (AMS), the Society for Marketing Advances, the Academy of Management (SMA), the Thought Leaders International Conference on Brand Management, Frontiers in Services Conference, and the Association for Global Business, among others.

Anwar
Habib

is a faculty member at the Dubai Women's College, Higher Colleges of Technology in United Arab Emirates. He holds an MBA from the University of Dhaka, Bangladesh, and is currently completing his DBA at the Business School Laussane, Switzerland. He has been teaching marketing since 2006.

Anwar Habib has 20 years of practical marketing experience working for Unilever, Ciba-Geigy and Johnson & Johnson, in South Asia, Australia and the Middle East. He started out as a brand manager at Unilever, and gradually progressed through senior roles in marketing and sales. His last role before teaching was General Manager of Johnson & Johnson Vision Care for the Middle East and North Africa region.

Brief Contents

Contents

Feature matrix

Chapter 1	Chapter opening case	BBK, formerly known as The Bank of Bahrain and Kuwait B.S.C.	Regional
	Real Marketing 1.1	Etisalat: Delighting Customers	Regional
	Real Marketing 1.2	Media and Direct Communication Trends in the Arab World	Regional
	Company Case	Diwan: A Tale of Heart Over Matter	Egypt
Chapter 2	Chapter opening case	The London Olympics	United Kingdom
	Real Marketing 2.1	Mo'men Sandwich: A Recipe for Success	Egypt
	Real Marketing 2.2	Niching: Voluntourism, A New Way to See the World	Regional
	Company Case	Bahrain Bay: Building Customer Relations for the Future	Bahrain
Chapter 3	Chapter opening case	The Dubai property market	UAE
	Real Marketing 3.1	Niching: 'On the Run' in Egypt	Egypt
	Real Marketing 3.2	First National Bank: Now You Can Be a Movie Star	Lebanon
	Company Case	Al Jazirah: The Genius Inventor	Saudi Arabia
Chapter 4	Chapter opening case	Maktoob Research's 'Arab Eye' website	Regional
	Real Marketing 4.1	Collecting Brand Information in the Arab World	Regional
	Real Marketing 4.2	Luxury Brands in the UAE	UAE
	Company Case	Ariel in Egypt: The Value of Consumer Insight	Egypt
Chapter 5	Chapter opening case	Al-Ahly and Zamalek football teams	Egypt
	Real Marketing 5.1	How McDonald's Markets to the Arab Consumers	Regional
	Real Marketing 5.2	Lexus: Delighting Customers After the Sale to Keep Them Coming Back	UAE
	Company Case	Arabic BlackBerry: Adapting to the Language of the Market	Regional
Chapter 6	Chapter opening case	Advanced Electronics Company	Saudi Arabia
	Real Marketing 6.1	Aramex Partners with Business Customers	Regional
	Real Marketing 6.2	International Marketing Manners: When in Rome, Do as the Romans Do	Global
	Company Case	Boeing: Selling a Dream(Liner)	United States
Chapter 7	Chapter opening case	Damas Group	Regional
	Real Marketing 7.1	Ramadan Spirit in the Arab World	Regional
	Real Marketing 7.2	Islamic Banking	Regional
	Company Case	The Arab Online World—Microsoft Maren	Regional
Chapter 8	Chapter opening case	Bahrain Islamic Bank	Bahrain
	Real Marketing 8.1	Breakaway Brands: Connecting with Customers	Global
	Real Marketing 8.2	Fayrouz: An International Brand Built in the Region	Egypt
	Real Marketing 8.3	Service Marketing	Global
	Company Case	Alshaya: The House of Brands	Regional

Chapter 9	Chapter opening case	Apple	Global
	Real Marketing 9.1	Nasamat Al Riyadh: TMG's New Product in the Kingdom of Saudi Arabia	Saudi Arabia
	Real Marketing 9.2	Etisalat Challenges Different Stages of the Product Life Cycle	Regional
	Company Case	Activia in Egypt	Egypt
Chapter 10	Chapter opening case	Carrefour	Regional
	Real Marketing 10.1	Cheap Chinese Products Flood into Arab Markets	Regional
	Real Marketing 10.2	The World Wonder, Dubai	UAE
	Company Case	Flydubai Pricing Strategy	UAE
Chapter 11	Chapter opening case	Unilever Arabia	Regional
	Real Marketing 11.1	Economic Slowdown and the Digital Advertising Boom in the Arab World	Regional
	Real Marketing 11.2	Qatar Airways	Qatar
	Company Case	Burger King: Promoting a Food Fight	Global
Chapter 12	Chapter opening case	TBWA\RAAD	UAE
	Real Marketing 12.1	Dove: Championing Real Beauty in the Arab World	Regional
	Real Marketing 12.2	Qatar Automobiles Company	Qatar
	Company Case	Coca-Cola: Advertising Hits	Regional
Chapter 13	Chapter opening case	Amazon.com	Global
	Real Marketing 13.1	Online Business in the Arab World	Regional
	Real Marketing 13.2	Social Networks in the Arab World	Regional
	Company Case	Elsou2.com: The First Online Supermarket in the Arab World	Egypt
Chapter 14	Chapter opening case	Al Zaytoun	Palestine
	Real Marketing 14.1	Toys "R" Us	Regional
	Real Marketing 14.2	Orchestrating the Retail Experience	Global
	Company Case	Zara: The Technology Giant of the Fashion World	Global
Chapter 15	Chapter opening case	Bahrain Polytechnic	Bahrain
	Real Marketing 15.1	Middle Eastern Airlines Filling the Market Gaps	Regional
	Real Marketing 15.2	Ritz-Carlton: Creating Customer Intimacy	Global
	Company Case	Bose: Competing by Being Truly Different	Global
Chapter 16	Chapter opening case	McDonald's	Global
	Real Marketing 16.1	Oreos and Milk, Chinese Style	China
	Real Marketing 16.2	Ramadan Desserts	Regional
	Company Case	B-Tech: A Successful Regional Brand	Egypt
Chapter 17	Chapter opening case	CSR Middle East	Regional
	Real Marketing 17.1	Improving Society Via Cultural and Islamic Virtues	Regional
	Real Marketing 17.2	Takaful: A True Customer-Driven Product	Regional
	Company Case	ExxonMobil: Social Responsibility in a Commodity Market	United States

Foreword

We are very pleased to see the Arab World Edition of *Principles of Marketing*. The text was first published for the North America region and has been successfully adopted by hundreds of universities in the Middle East and in other parts of the world. This great edition for the Arab world demonstrates that this textbook, in its scope and depth, effectively meets the demands of educators for a book that offers a comprehensive focus on marketing as a tool for creating valuable customer experiences in various and changing cultural settings.

The Arab World Edition brings to the readers the local marketing scenario, perspectives, and practices through case studies and examples.

The book provides local insights into the exciting world of marketing in a region that has become a competing arena for increasing numbers of national and multinational corporations.

While maintaining the essence of the original U.S. edition, this Arab world version provides students with concepts, approaches, and examples relevant to the Arab culture and its business environment.

We are thrilled to see it available for educators and students in the Arab world and hope that they find it useful.

Philip Kotler

Gary Armstrong

Preface

The New Arab World Edition! Creating More Value for You!

The goal of every marketer is to create more value for customers. So it makes sense that our goal for the new Arab World Edition of Kotler & Armstrong's *Principles of Marketing* is to continue creating more value for you—*our* customer. Our goal is to introduce you to the fascinating world of modern marketing in an innovative yet practical and enjoyable way, incorporating relevant examples from across the Arab region and across the globe. In this way, the Arab World Edition has the advantage of offering the best of both the regional, as well as the global, worlds of marketing.

This Arab World Edition aims to help students in the region to understand and apply the concepts and practices of modern marketing, by relating marketing strategies and theory to students' experiences in daily life. We have tried to bring to life global marketing concepts by showcasing and analyzing regional marketing initiatives and practices from all over the Arab world. Of course, we have also retained global examples which demonstrate marketing theory and practice in an international context. In this way, the Arab World Edition has the advantage of offering the best of both the regional, as well as the global, worlds of marketing.

Marketing: Creating Customer Value and Relationships

A recent survey of top marketers showed that they all share a common goal: putting the consumer at the heart of marketing. Today's marketing is all about creating customer value and building profitable customer relationships. It starts with understanding consumer needs and wants, deciding which target markets the organization can serve best, and developing a compelling value proposition by which the organization can attract, keep, and grow targeted consumers. If the organization does these things well, it will reap the rewards in terms of market share, profits, and customer equity.

Five Major Value Themes

From beginning to end, the Arab World Edition of *Principles of Marketing* develops an innovative customer-value and customer-relationships framework that captures the essence of today's marketing. It builds on five major value themes:

1. *Creating value for customers in order to capture value from customers in return.* Today's marketers must be good at *creating customer value* and *managing customer relationships.* Outstanding marketing companies understand the marketplace and customer needs, design value-creating marketing strategies, develop integrated marketing programs that deliver customer value and delight, and build strong customer relationships. In return, they capture value from customers in the form of sales, profits, and customer loyalty.

   This innovative *customer-value framework* is introduced at the start of Chapter 1 in a five-step marketing process model, which details how marketing *creates* customer value and *captures* value in return. The framework is carefully explained in the first two chapters and then fully integrated throughout the remainder of the text.

2. *Building and managing strong, value-creating brands.* Well-positioned brands with strong brand equity provide the basis upon which to build customer value and profitable customer relationships. Today's marketers must position their brands powerfully and manage them well. They must build close brand relationships and experiences with customers.

3. *Measuring and managing return on marketing.* Marketing managers must ensure that their marketing budgets are being spent wisely. In the past, many marketers spent freely on big, expensive marketing programs, often without thinking carefully about the financial returns on their spending. But that has all been changing in recent years. 'Marketing

accountability'—measuring and managing return on marketing investments—has now become an important part of strategic marketing decision making. This emphasis on marketing accountability is addressed throughout this book.

4. *Harnessing new marketing technologies.* New digital and other high-tech marketing developments are dramatically changing how consumers and marketers relate to one another. The Arab World Edition thoroughly explores the new technologies impacting marketing, from 'Web 2.0' in Chapter 1 to new-age digital marketing and online technologies in Chapters 12 and 13 to the exploding use of online social networks and customer-generated marketing in Chapters 1, 5, 11, 13, and elsewhere.

5. *Sustainable marketing around the globe.* As technological developments make the world an increasingly smaller and more fragile place, marketers must be good at marketing their brands globally and in responsible and ethical ways. Material and examples throughout the Arab World Edition emphasize the concept of sustainable marketing—meeting the present needs of consumers and businesses while also preserving or enhancing the ability of future generations to meet their needs.

Adapted for Students in the Arab World

We've thoroughly adapted *Principles of Marketing* to meet the needs of students in the Arab region, by including examples which reflect the marketing environment and experience of businesses operating in the Arab region, while still retaining a global perspective overall. We have also included cultural and social insights which will be more familiar and relevant to our audience. We retain Kotler & Armstrong's successful formula: a sharp focus on how to create, communicate and deliver value to customers, and we discuss the major trends and forces impacting marketing in this era of customer value and relationships. Here are just some of the ways in which we've adapted the book to be ideal for students in the Arab world.

- Throughout each chapter, Arab businesses and familiar cultural examples are integrated into the text, making the whole book more relevant for our readers.

- In-depth case studies in each chapter show marketing principles and concepts in practice, at the Chapter Openers, the in-chapter "Real Marketing" boxes, and end-of-chapter Company Cases. These now feature a well-balanced spread of global examples alongside companies and examples from across the Arab region including Saudi Arabia, the United Arab Emirates, Egypt, Jordan, Palestine, Lebanon, Qatar, Bahrain, Kuwait, Northern Africa, and elsewhere.

- An English-Arabic Glossary has been added at the end of the book, providing a translation of the key terms found in each chapter.

- Each chapter has been carefully edited to adapt the English vocabulary to be sympathetic to students whose first language is not English. We have ensured that over-complicated words, sayings or idioms are replaced with straightforward language so that students can focus their energy on understanding the concepts.

- The book has been reduced in length to 17 focused chapters, to meet the demand for a resource which is easier to handle and cover in the time available.

Real Value Through Real Marketing

Principles of Marketing features in-depth, real-world examples and stories that show concepts in action and reveal the drama of modern marketing. In the Arab World Edition, every Chapter Opening case study, "Real Marketing" box and end-of-chapter Company Case has been reviewed for its relevance to you, our Arab world audience. We have replaced many of these case studies throughout the book with examples from the Arab region which will provide familiar, fresh and relevant insights into real marketing practices. We have deliberately retained many other examples from across the world to emphasize the global nature of modern day marketing. A selection of these examples include the following:

- BBK Bank (formerly The Bank of Bahrain and Kuwait) has grown to become a leading commercial bank in its markets, by focusing on client-driven customer service, employee development and brand building. (Chapter 1)

- The 'voluntourism' movement has sprung up to meet the needs of a particular niche – we explore voluntourism programmes operating in Jordan, Syria, Lebanon and elsewhere. (Chapter 2)
- Saudi Arabian company Al Jazirah has capitalized on environmental factors in successfully developing and marketing its evaporative coolers. (Chapter 3)
- Proctor & Gamble launched its Ariel product into Egypt, based on rigorous market research and a solid understanding of the current habits and needs of potential customers. (Chapter 4)
- The devoted and divided fan bases of the Egyptian football teams Al-Ahly and Zamalek show the importance of social and cultural interests such as football in shaping consumer behavior. (Chapter 5)
- Advanced Electronics Company (AEC), the Saudi-based company, has developed an international client base including Boeing, Lockheed Martin, Rockwell International, Saudi Ministry of Water & Electricity, Aramco, Siemens, Nokia. It has built an approach to business-to-business marketing based on deep relationships with clients, to become a strategic, problem-solving partner. (Chapter 6)
- Damas Group, the jewelry and watch retailer operating across the Arab world and beyond, uses segmentation wisely to target different customer groups. (Chapter 7)
- Microsoft developed its Maren product, which represented a leap forward in addressing the problem of using Arabic language online and with a QWERTY keyboard, by working to understand customer needs and responses in depth. (Chapter 7)
- Alshaya understands the importance of brands, and uses this knowledge to operate franchises of many international brands in the Arab world. (Chapter 8)
- Apple founder Steve Jobs used dazzling customer-driven innovation to first start the company and then to remake it again 20 years later. (Chapter 9)
- Flydubai used pricing strategy to meet the demand for low cost flights and launch as a new airline in the UAE. (Chapter 10)
- Coca-Cola combines music and advertising to appeal to its customers, with recent campaigns in the Middle East including Nancy Ajram to raise profile. (Chapter 12)
- Amazon.com has developed industry-leading expertise in using the internet as a tool for delivering customer value. (Chapter 13)
- Bahrain Polytechnic has created a clear competitive advantage for its target students by distinctly differentiating itself from its competitors. (Chapter 15)
- McDonald's, the quintessential all-American company, now sells more burgers and fries outside the United States than within. We explore its journey into the Russian market. (Chapter 16)
- CSR Middle East promotes corporate social responsibility across the region by working closely with a range of businesses, organizations and NGOs. (Chapter 17)

Each chapter is packed with countless real, relevant, and timely examples that reinforce key concepts and bring marketing to life.

Valuable Learning Aids

The Arab World Edition continues the hallmark approach to text design crafted in *Principles of Marketing*, to inspire students and present everything as clearly as possible. A wealth of chapter-opening, in-chapter, and end-of-chapter learning devices help students to learn, link, and apply major concepts:

- *Chapter Preview.* As part of an active and integrative chapter-opening design, a brief section at the beginning of each chapter previews chapter concepts, links them with previous chapter concepts, and introduces the chapter-opening story.
- *Chapter-opening marketing stories.* Each chapter begins with an engaging, deeply developed, illustrated, and annotated marketing story that introduces the chapter material and sparks student interest. Many relevant and inspiring examples from the Arab world have been added.
- *Objective outline.* This chapter-opening feature provides a helpful preview outline of chapter contents and learning objectives.
- *Author comments and figure annotations.* Throughout the chapter, author comments ease and enhance student learning by introducing and explaining major chapter sections. There are also comment bubbles on the figures to help explain concepts to students.

- *Real Marketing boxes.* Each chapter contains two boxed case study features that provide an in-depth look at real marketing practices of large and small companies, including a wide range of new examples from the Arab world.
- *Reviewing the Objectives and Key Terms.* A summary at the end of each chapter reviews major chapter concepts, chapter objectives, and key terms.
- *Discussing and Applying the Concepts.* Each chapter contains a set of discussion questions and application exercises covering major chapter concepts.
- *Focus on Technology.* Application exercises at the end of each chapter provide discussion of important and emerging marketing technologies in this digital age.
- *Focus on Ethics.* Situation descriptions and questions highlight important issues in marketing ethics at the end of each chapter.
- *Marketing by the Numbers.* An exercise at the end of each chapter lets students apply analytical and financial thinking to relevant chapter concepts and links the chapter to Appendix 2: Marketing by the Numbers.
- *Company Cases.* Company cases for class or written discussion are provided at the end of each chapter—many of these are now developed specifically for the Arab World Edition. These cases challenge students to apply marketing principles to real companies in real situations.
- *Video Cases.* Short cases and discussion questions appear at the end of every chapter, to be used with the set of 4- to 6-minute videos that accompany this edition.
- *Marketing Plan appendix.* Appendix 1 contains a sample marketing plan that helps students to apply important marketing planning concepts.
- *Marketing by the Numbers appendix.* An innovative Appendix 2 provides students with a comprehensive introduction to the marketing financial analysis that helps to guide, assess, and support marketing decisions.

More than ever before, the Arab World Edition of *Principles of Marketing* creates value for you—it gives you all you need to know about marketing in an effective and enjoyable total learning package!

A Valuable Learning Package

A successful marketing course requires more than a well-written book. A total package of resources extends this edition's emphasis on creating value for you. The following aids support *Principles of Marketing.*

Videos

The video library features exciting segments for this edition. All segments are available in mymarketinglab. Here are just a few of the videos offered:

Live Nation's Customer Relationships

TOMS Shoes' Marketing Environment

E*TRADE's Advertising and PR Strategies

Principle Financial Group's Personal Selling

Umpqua Bank's Competitive Advantage

PEARSON
mymarketinglab™

mymarketinglab (www.pearsoned.co.uk/kotler) gives you the opportunity to test yourself on key concepts and skills, track your own progress through the course, and use the personalized study plan activities—all to help you achieve success in the classroom.
Features include:

- **Personalized study plans**—Pre- and post-tests with remediation activities directed to help you understand and apply the concepts where you need the most help.
- **Self-assessments**—Prebuilt self-assessments allow you to test yourself.

- **Interactive elements**—A wealth of hands-on activities and exercises let you experience and learn firsthand. Whether it is with the online e-book where you can search for specific keywords or page numbers, highlight specific sections, enter notes right on the e-book page, and print reading assignments with notes for later review or with other materials including "Real People Real Choices Video Cases," online end-of-chapter activities, "Active Flashcards," and much more.
- **iQuizzes**—Study anytime, anywhere—iQuizzes work on any color-screen iPod and are comprised of a sequence of quiz questions, specifically created for the iPod screen.

Find out more at **www.pearsoned.co.uk/kotler.**

No book is the work only of its authors. We greatly appreciate the valuable contributions of several people who helped make this new edition possible.

Anwar Habib: I would like to acknowledge the continuous inspiration and support of my wife Fahmida in writing this text. I would also like to thank Nada Yaghi, my ex-student, for her valuable research and support in selecting appropriate regional examples for the text. Finally I would like to thank all the regional organizations, like MAF group, Unilever, Masafi, and Al Islami Foods, who have supported me with case study materials and other information. I'd also like to extend a special thanks to Sarah Wightman for her excellent editorial support.

Ahmed Tolba: I would like to dedicate this edition to my wife Nayla and my kids Ismail and Amina. I would also like thank Ahmed El Banhawy for his significant contribution to the completion of this textbook, and my teaching assistants Laila Yassin and Ali El Gendy for their remarkable efforts in finding appropriate regional case studies. Finally, I would like to thank everyone at Pearson for their significant efforts and professional support.

Anwar Habib

Ahmed Tolba

Acknowledgments

We would like to thank the following reviewers for their thoughtful comments and suggestions for this new Arab World Edition:

Dr Saleh AlShebil, King Fahd University of Petroleum & Minerals, Saudi Arabia

Dr Ibrahim Hegazy, American University of Cairo, Egypt

Professor Peter Mason, American University of Sharjah, UAE

Dr Ahmad Zamil, King Saud University, Saudi Arabia

Dr Abdullah Sultan, Kuwait University, Kuwait

Professor Hassan Naja, Lebanese American University, Lebanon

Dr Imad Baalbaki, American University of Beirut, Lebanon

Dr Jean Boisvert, American University of Sharjah, UAE

Dr Samaa Attia, British University in Egypt, Egypt

Professor Mariam Abou-Youssef, German University in Cairo, Egypt

Professor Abbas Abu Altimen, University of Sharjah, UAE

Dr Ahmed Ghoneim, Cairo University, Egypt

Dr Hani Al-Dmour, University of Jordan, Jordan

Dr Rania Hussein, Cairo University, Egypt

Dr Khaled Hanafy, Arab Academy for Science, Technology & Maritime Transport, Egypt

Dr Mohamed A. Radwan, American University in Cairo, Egypt

We would also like to thank contributors Dr. Mohamed A. Radwan, Adjunct Faculty at American University in Cairo and Managing Director of Platinum Partners, Mike Lewicki, Marketing Instructor at the University College of Bahrain, Annelie Moukaddem Baalbaki, Instructor at the Lebanese American University, Sarah Wightman and Owen Davies, who provided additional material for this text and for the supporting supplementary materials. Their excellent work has added real value to this edition.

Many reviewers and contributors have provided valuable comments and suggestions for previous editions of *Principles of Marketing*. We'd like to thank them all for their insights, which have informed our work on this adaptation.

PART 1

Defining Marketing and the Marketing Process

Chapter 1

Part 1   Defining Marketing and the Marketing Process (Chapters 1, 2)
Part 2   Understanding the Marketplace and Consumers (Chapters 3, 4, 5, 6)
Part 3   Designing a Customer-Driven Strategy and Mix (Chapters 7, 8, 9, 10, 11, 12, 13, 14)
Part 4   Extending Marketing (Chapters 15, 16, 17)

Marketing Creating and Capturing Customer Value

Chapter PREVIEW

In this chapter, we introduce you to the basic concepts of marketing. We start with the question, "What *is* marketing?" Simply put, marketing is managing profitable customer relationships. The aim of marketing is to create value *for* customers and to capture value *from* customers in return. Next, we discuss the five steps in the marketing process—from understanding customer needs, through designing customer-driven marketing strategies and programs, to building customer relationships and capturing value for the firm. Finally, we discuss the major trends and forces affecting marketing in this age of customer relationships. Understanding these basic concepts and forming your own ideas about what they really mean to you will give you a solid foundation for all that follows.

Let's start with a good story about marketing in action at the bank BBK. This example describes BBK's efforts to provide a unique, customer-driven service.

BK, formerly known as The Bank of Bahrain and Kuwait B.S.C., was established on March 16, 1971 and started business a year later. BBK has been the pioneer in commercial banking for 40 years in the Kingdom of Bahrain.

In 1972, BBK began operations with capital of 1 million Bahraini dinars (BD) (equivalent to US$2.6 million). Today, BBK has grown to become one of the largest commercial banks in Bahrain, with a capital base of 300 million BD (US$795 million).

BBK has been successfully building its name and reputation, and is respected locally as well as internationally. The bank has a strong local presence, with a nationwide network of financial malls, branches, and ATM cash machines strategically placed throughout Bahrain. In addition to domestic branches, BBK has operations in the State of Kuwait, the Republic of India, and a representative office in Dubai, in the United Arab Emirates.

As a market leader, in 2006 BBK conceived the revolutionary 'financial mall' concept, housing partners such as CrediMax Visa credit cards, telecommunication services, and travel and insurance needs under one roof, along with many other customer-oriented products and services. The financial malls provide customer-convenient services, personal financial advisors, and queue management automated systems that immediately show customers the expected waiting time until they will be served. The financial mall concept is a genuine effort to deliver exceptional customer service to a growing number of financial consumers seeking secured financial services. Each financial mall has a drive-up automated cash machine outside, two automated cash machines at the branch entrance, four teller stations, ample seating for BBK customers, a wealth management area where clients can meet with an advisor, a separate area for corporate clients and priority clients, a travel agent, a Western Union money transfer agent, and access to the BBK branch manager, whose office is visible from each area of the main floor of the BBK financial mall. The back-office functions are usually carried out from the second floor.

BBK is able to provide a full range of lending, deposit, treasury, and investment services to various sectors of the domestic and regional, as well as international, markets, using state-of-the-art technology. The bank plays a major role in Bahrain, financing infrastructure and industrial projects, and creating products and services that cater to the needs of individuals, investors, businesses, corporations, and the government of Bahrain.

The bank has made the marketing decision that its customers want online banking and banking technology to be user-friendly. As a result, it provides an easily accessible web-

> **BBK has grown to become a leading commercial bank in Bahrain by putting customer relationships first.**

2

site (www.bbkonline.com) where payments and transfers can be made, and the bank has recently linked each customer's mobile phone. This means that the bank can receive any out-of-branch transaction that occurs on the customer's account, such as a payment or transfer online, or a purchase of groceries using the BBK ATM debit card at the supermarket. Minutes after the transaction takes place, BBK customers receive a text message confirming the transaction. This effort reinforces the bank's capabilities to its customers and the priority it gives to customer concerns such as card security. The effort to link client transactions to the clients' ATM debit card is part of the larger SMART card process that the bank and the banking industry undertook in 2009 and 2010.

BBK segments its customer base to include wealthier individuals who seek priority banking and a higher level of service, as typically this level of customer is more active and has different and more varied needs compared with traditional retail-only customers. BBK provides a personal relationship officer designated to the priority banking customer to manage all banking enquiries and transactions. BBK also offers the opportunity for priority clients to have casual limits, which means that the priority banking client, as a higher-net-worth individual, has more flexibility. BBK also offers full confidentiality, especially with priority banking customers, ensuring that priority banking is built on trust and that all priority banking activities and transactions will be carefully handled and maintained as private between BBK and the customer. Finally, the priority banking client is provided with a level of service known as VIP Treatment. All BBK priority banking clients are VIPs, therefore all banking requirements of priority clients are fast-tracked and managed as quickly as possible.

From a corporate perspective, BBK has enforced high standards in corporate governance. Such efforts to be ethical and to operate with corporate responsibility as a strategic goal have been fundamental to BBK maintaining its position within the local and regional banking sector, and within the community that BBK serves. BBK regularly reviews and adheres to strong corporate governance practices, which help enhance compliance levels according to international standards and in line with the policies of regulatory authorities and statutory requirements in the Kingdom of Bahrain and other countries where BBK operates.

BBK believes that the bank's people are important assets, especially since employees deliver the bank's products and inter-act daily with BBK customers, both retail and corporate. BBK provides employees with an environment and with initial and ongoing training that brings the best out of each employee. This effort to empower employees is at the center of delivering the finest possible service to BBK customers. BBK is also active as a responsible corporate citizen, devoting time and resources to improving the lives of people in the communities where BBK operates. This includes initiatives such as donations and sponsorships.

BBK takes its brand very seriously. BBK selects appropriate locations for its financial malls, placing them within the market that the bank chooses to serve. Each financial mall is tall, colorful, and has ample parking so that customers may park their cars prior to entry. Each BBK financial mall has the www.bbkonline.com address printed in large letters on the building's outside wall, so citizens can see the letters as they drive by in their cars, and customers can see the letters as they park. The idea is that in today's online environment, many in-branch banking transactions can be completed online. Additionally, because BBK online services are rated so highly, the online product and service offerings are a part of the bank's brand and identity.

When you enter a BBK financial mall, each employee is dressed in blue, white, and yellow, and wears an orange tie as part of the colors that make up the BBK brand identity and corporate logo. Such efforts are a nice touch and really reinforce the level of customer experience delivered and felt at BBK.

> BBK's website was developed to deliver convenient service to customers.

> BBK's 'financial malls' concept is a genuine effort on the part of the bank to deliver exceptional customer service, specifically targeting a growing number of consumers who want all their banking needs in one place.

Source: *This case was provided by Mike Lewicki, University College of Bahrain.*

Today's successful companies have one thing in common: Like BBK, they are strongly customer-focused and heavily committed to marketing. These companies share a passion for understanding and satisfying customer needs in well-defined target markets. They motivate everyone in the organization to help build lasting customer relationships based on creating value. As Mohamed Helmy, general manager of Qatar-based Mannai Trading Company, puts it: "Great customer service is the heart and soul of Mannai Group."[1]

Objective Outline

Author Comment | Stop here for a second and think about how you'd answer this question before studying marketing. Then, see how your answer changes as you go through the chapter.

What Is Marketing? (pp 4–6)

Marketing, more than any other business function, deals with customers. Although we will soon explore more-detailed definitions of marketing, perhaps the simplest definition is this one: *Marketing is managing profitable customer relationships.* The twofold goal of marketing is to attract new customers by promising superior value and to keep and grow current customers by delivering satisfaction.

Wal-Mart has become the world's largest retailer—and the world's largest *company*—by delivering on its promise, "Save money. Live better." At Disney theme parks, imagineers work wonders in their quest to "make a dream come true today." Apple fulfills its motto to "Think Different" with dazzling, customer-driven innovation that captures customers' imaginations and loyalty. Its wildly successful iPod grabs more than 70 percent of the music player market; its iTunes music store captures nearly 90 percent of the song download business.[2]

Good marketing is critical to the success of every organization. Large for-profit firms such as Emirates, Etisalat, Saudi Aramco, Emaar, Masafi, Zain, NBK, Almarai, Sadafco, Unilever, Johnson & Johnson, Procter & Gamble, Google, Target, Toyota, Apple, and Marriott use marketing. But so do not-for-profit organizations such as colleges, hospitals, museums, aid agencies, and charities such as Dubai Cares, "a philanthropic establishment launched . . . with the aim of improving access to primary education for children in developing countries." The charity aims to eliminate underlying causes that prevent children from accessing quality primary education.[3]

You already know a lot about marketing—it's all around you. Marketing comes to you in the good old traditional forms: You see it in the abundance of products at your nearby shopping mall and in the advertisements that fill your television screen, flash up on your favorite websites, feature in your magazines, or clutter your mailbox. But in recent years, marketers have assembled a number of new marketing approaches, everything from imaginative websites, Internet chat rooms, and social networks to interactive television and your cellphone. These new approaches aim to do more than just blast out messages to the masses. They aim to reach you directly and personally. Today's marketers want to become a part of your life and to enrich your experiences with their brands—to help you *live* their brands.

At home, at school, where you work, and where you play, you see marketing in almost everything you do. Yet, there is much more to marketing than meets the consumer's casual eye. Behind it all is a massive network of people and activities competing for your attention and purchases. This book will give you a complete introduction to the basic concepts and practices of today's marketing. In this chapter, we begin by defining marketing and the marketing process.

Marketing Defined

What *is* marketing? Many people think of marketing only as selling and advertising. And no wonder—every day we are bombarded with television commercials, direct-mail offers, sales calls, and email pitches. However, selling and advertising are only the tip of the marketing iceberg.

Today, marketing must be understood not in the old sense of making a sale—'telling and selling'—but in the new sense of *satisfying customer needs*. If the marketer understands consumer needs; develops products that provide superior customer value; and prices, distributes, and promotes them effectively, these products will sell easily. In fact, according to management guru Peter Drucker, "The aim of marketing is to make selling unnecessary."[4] Selling and advertising are only part of a larger 'marketing mix'—a set of marketing tools that work together to satisfy customer needs and build customer relationships. The marketing mix should not undermine the importance of the sales function, but the unmarketed (or unplanned, from a marketing perspective) product or service, even with extended sales efforts, will continuously face market problems. Marketers can be seen as planners and designers of a complete product or a service, while salespeople close the deals.

Broadly defined, marketing is a social and managerial process by which individuals and organizations obtain what they need and want through creating and exchanging value with others. In a narrower business context, marketing involves building profitable, value-based exchange relationships with customers. Hence, we define **marketing** as the process by which companies create value for customers and build strong customer relationships in order to capture value from customers in return.[5]

Marketing
The process by which companies create value for customers and build strong customer relationships in order to capture value from customers in return.

The Marketing Process

Figure 1.1 presents a simple five-step model of the marketing process. In the first four steps, companies work to understand consumers, create customer value, and build strong

This important figure shows marketing in a nutshell! By creating value *for* customers, marketers capture value *from* customers in return. This five-step process forms the marketing framework for the rest of the chapter and the rest of the text.

Create value *for customers* and build customer relationships

Capture value *from customers* in return

| Understand the marketplace and customer needs and wants | Design a customer-driven marketing strategy | Construct an integrated marketing program that delivers superior value | Build profitable relationships and create customer delight | **Capture value from customers to create profits and customer equity** |

FIGURE | 1.1 A Simple Model of the Marketing Process

customer relationships. In the final step, companies reap the rewards of creating superior customer value. By creating value *for* consumers, companies in turn capture value *from* consumers in the form of sales, profits, and long-term customer equity.

In this chapter and the next, we will examine the steps of this simple model of the marketing process. In this chapter, we will review each step but focus more on the customer relationship steps—understanding customers, building customer relationships, and capturing value from customers. In Chapter 2, we'll look more deeply into the second and third steps—designing marketing strategies and constructing marketing programs.

> **Author Comment** | Marketing is all about creating value for customers. So, as the first step in the marketing process, the company must fully understand consumers and the marketplace in which it operates.

Understanding the Marketplace and Customer Needs (pp 6–9)

As a first step, marketers need to understand customer needs and wants and the marketplace within which they operate. We now examine five core customer and marketplace concepts: (1) *needs, wants, and demands*; (2) *market offerings (products, services, and experiences)*; (3) *value and satisfaction*; (4) *exchanges and relationships*; and (5) *markets*.

Customer Needs, Wants, and Demands

Needs
States of felt deprivation.

The most basic concept underlying marketing is that of human needs. Human **needs** are states of felt deprivation. They include basic *physical* needs for food, clothing, warmth, and safety; *social* needs for belonging and affection; and *individual* needs for knowledge and self-expression. These needs were not created by marketers; they are a basic part of the human makeup.

Wants
The form human needs take as they are shaped by culture and individual personality.

Demands
Human wants that are backed by buying power.

Wants are the form human needs take as they are shaped by culture and individual personality. A Muslim *needs* food to break the fast during Ramadan but *wants* dates, harees, and a laban drink. Children *need* food but *want* a Big Mac, French fries, and a soft drink. Wants are shaped by one's society and are described in terms of objects that will satisfy needs. When backed by buying power, wants become **demands**. Given their wants and resources, people demand products with benefits that add up to the most value and satisfaction.

When it comes to converting wants into needs, there are no limits to generating successful product ideas, as long as basic human needs are met. But since the basic needs of customers are determined by factors such as ethnicity, religion, and demography, as well as cultural heritage, ways to successfully meet human needs may differ in many respects.

At the basic level, marketers should discover customers' values and beliefs and tailor their message and actions to match those beliefs. If customers are concerned about price, marketers should attempt to sell their products and services at a low price. If customers want a product for a recreational activity, the marketer's task is to explain how the product will enhance that activity. On the broader level, some marketers tend to target certain personality types. Some customers become emotionally involved with a purchase and only buy a product or service if it 'feels' good. In these circumstances, marketers offer the customers the reassurance they need to make them feel they are doing the right thing. The most common approach of all is the limited time offer approach. This approach takes advantage of the customer's desire to buy a product and adds the product to the shopping basket at a lower price for a limited time, creating an urgent need for the customer to buy the product before missing out on the good deal.

Being successful in changing wants into needs is a vital ingredient for a booming and sustainable business, even in the worst economic conditions.

Outstanding companies go to great lengths to learn about and understand their customers' needs, wants, and demands. They conduct consumer research and analyze mountains of customer data. Their people at all levels—including top management—stay close to customers. For example, at Lulu hypermarket, senior managers spend time on the shop floor and mingle with customers to understand customer needs and wants. At Masafi, managers frequently make market visits, in addition to carrying out regular market research, to understand the needs and wants of their customers.

Market Offerings—Products, Services, and Experiences

Market offerings

Some combination of products, services, information, or experiences offered to a market to satisfy a need or want.

Consumers' needs and wants are fulfilled through **market offerings**—some combination of products, services, information, or experiences offered to a market to satisfy a need or want. Market offerings are not limited to physical *products*. They also include *services*—activities or benefits offered for sale that are essentially intangible and do not result in the ownership of anything. Examples include banking, airline, hotel, beauty parlor, and home repair services.

More broadly, market offerings also include other entities, such as *persons*, *places*, *organizations*, *information*, and *ideas*. For example, DestinationOman.com markets Oman as a tourist destination, highlighting the country's historic heritage, natural beauty, folklore, and traditional industries.[6]

Market offerings can include places: DestinationOman.com markets Oman as a tourist destination.

Many sellers make the mistake of paying more attention to the specific products they offer than to the benefits and experiences produced by these products. These sellers suffer from **marketing myopia**. They are so taken with their products that they focus only on existing wants and lose sight of underlying customer needs.[7] They forget that a product is only a tool to solve a consumer problem. A manufacturer of quarter-inch drill bits may think that the customer needs a drill bit. But what the customer *really* needs is a quarter-inch hole. These sellers will have trouble if a new product comes along that serves the customer's need better or less expensively. The customer will have the same *need* but will *want* the new product.

Smart marketers look beyond the attributes of the products and services they sell. By orchestrating several services and products, they create *brand experiences* for consumers. For example, you don't just watch a Formula 1 Grand Prix in Yas Marina, Abu Dhabi, you immerse yourself in the exhilarating Yas Marina Grand Prix experience and its festive atmosphere.[8] Similarly, Hewlett-Packard (HP) recognizes that a personal computer is much more than just a collection of wires and electrical components. It's an intensely personal user experience. As noted in an HP advert, "There is hardly anything that you own that is *more* personal. Your personal computer is your backup brain. It's your life.... It's your unique strategy, fantastic proposal, personal calculation. It's your autobiography, written in a thousand daily words."[9]

Marketing myopia

The mistake of paying more attention to the specific products a company offers than to the benefits and experiences produced by these products.

Customer Value and Satisfaction

Consumers usually face a broad array of products and services that might satisfy a given need. How do they choose among these many market offerings? Customers form expectations about the value and satisfaction that various market offerings will deliver and buy accordingly. Satisfied customers buy again and tell others about their good experiences.

Dissatisfied customers often switch to competitors and tell others about their less than satisfactory experiences.

Marketers must be careful to set the right level of expectations. If they set expectations too low, they may satisfy those who buy but fail to attract enough buyers. If they raise expectations too high, buyers will be disappointed. Customer value and customer satisfaction are key building blocks for developing and managing customer relationships. We will revisit these important concepts later in the chapter.

Exchanges and Relationships

Exchange

The act of obtaining a desired object from someone by offering something in return.

Marketing occurs when people decide to satisfy needs and wants through exchange relationships. **Exchange** is the act of obtaining a desired object from someone by offering something in return. In the broadest sense, the marketer tries to bring about a response to some market offering. The response may be more than simply buying or trading products and services. A political candidate, for instance, wants votes, a mosque wants a large jama'ah (number of worshipers), an orchestra wants an audience, and a social action group wants idea acceptance.

Marketing consists of actions taken to build and maintain desirable exchange *relationships* with target audiences involving a product, service, idea, or other object. Beyond simply attracting new customers and creating transactions, the goal is to retain customers and grow their business with the company. Marketers want to build strong relationships by consistently delivering superior customer value. We will expand on the important concept of managing customer relationships later in the chapter.

Markets

Market

The set of all actual and potential buyers of a product or service.

The concepts of exchange and relationships lead to the concept of a market. A **market** is the set of actual and potential buyers of a product. These buyers share a particular need or want that can be satisfied through exchange relationships.

Marketing means managing markets to bring about profitable customer relationships. However, creating these relationships takes work. Sellers must search for buyers, identify their needs, design good market offerings, set prices for them, promote them, and store and deliver them. Activities such as consumer research, product development, communication, distribution, pricing, and service are core marketing activities.

Although we normally think of marketing as being carried out by sellers, buyers also carry out marketing. Consumers do marketing when they search for products, interact with companies, and obtain information and make their purchases. In fact, today's digital technologies, from websites and blogs to cellphones and other wireless devices, have empowered consumers and made marketing a truly interactive affair. Marketers are no longer asking only "How can we reach our customers?" but also "How should our customers reach us?" and even "How can our customers reach each other?"

🔖 **Figure 1.2** shows the main elements in a marketing system. Marketing involves serving a market of final consumers in the face of competition. The company and its competitors research the market and interact with consumers to understand their needs. Then they create and send their market offerings and messages to consumers, either directly or through marketing intermediaries. All of the parties in the system are affected by major environmental forces (demographic, economic, physical, technological, political/legal, and social/cultural).

Each party in the system adds value for the next level. All of the arrows represent relationships that must be developed and managed. Thus, a company's success at building profitable relationships depends not only on its own actions but also on how well the entire system serves the needs of final consumers. The hypermarket retailer

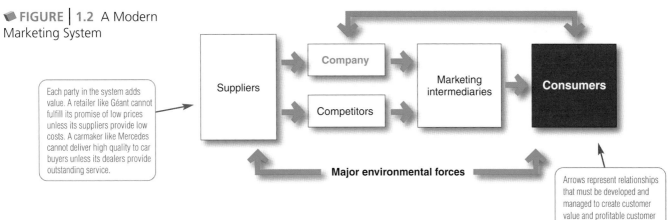

FIGURE | 1.2 A Modern Marketing System

Each party in the system adds value. A retailer like Géant cannot fulfill its promise of low prices unless its suppliers provide low costs. A carmaker like Mercedes cannot deliver high quality to car buyers unless its dealers provide outstanding service.

Major environmental forces

Arrows represent relationships that must be developed and managed to create customer value and profitable customer relationships.

Géant cannot fulfill its promise of high quality goods at attractive prices unless its suppliers provide merchandise at low costs. And Mercedes cannot deliver high quality to car buyers unless its dealers provide outstanding sales and service.

Author Comment | Now that the company fully understands consumers and the marketplace, it must decide which customers it will serve and how it will bring them value.

Designing a Customer-Driven Marketing Strategy (PP 9-13)

Once a company fully understands consumers and the marketplace, marketing management can design a customer-driven marketing strategy. We define **marketing management** as the art and science of choosing target markets and building profitable relationships with them. The marketing manager's aim is to find, attract, keep, and grow target customers by creating, delivering, and communicating superior customer value.

To design a winning marketing strategy, the marketing manager must answer two important questions: *What customers will we serve (what's our target market)?* and *How can we serve these customers best (what's our value proposition)?* We will discuss these marketing strategy concepts briefly here, and then look at them in more detail in the next chapter.

Marketing management
The art and science of choosing target markets and building profitable relationships with them.

Selecting Customers to Serve

The company must first decide *who* it will serve. It does this by dividing the market into segments of customers (*market segmentation*) and selecting which segments it will go after (*target marketing*). Some people think of marketing management as finding as many customers as possible and increasing demand. But marketing managers know that they cannot serve all customers in every way. By trying to serve all customers, they may not serve any customers well. Instead, the company wants to select only customers that it can serve well and profitably. For example, Jashanmal stores, which sell some of the world's top brands,[10] profitably target affluent professionals; the 5–10 Riyal/Dirham stores profitably target families with lower incomes.

Some marketers may even seek *fewer* customers and reduced demand. For example, government organizations, through campaigns that raise awareness of the effects that smoking has on health, seek to reduce the number of smokers. In this and other cases of excess demand, companies may practice *demarketing* to reduce the number of customers or to shift customer demand temporarily or permanently. For instance, many power companies sponsor programs that help customers reduce their power usage through peak-load control devices, better energy use monitoring, and heating system tune-up incentives. Progress Energy even offers an Energy Manager on Loan program that provides schools and other customers from the public sector with a free on-site energy expert to help them find energy-saving opportunities.

Ultimately, marketing managers must decide which customers they want to target and on the level, timing, and nature of their demand. Simply put, marketing management is *customer management* and *demand management.*

Choosing a Value Proposition

The company must also decide how it will serve targeted customers—how it will *differentiate and position* itself in the marketplace. A company's *value proposition* is the set of benefits or values it promises to deliver to consumers to satisfy their needs. BMW promises "the ultimate driving machine," whereas Land Rover lets you "Go Beyond"—to "get a taste of adventure, whatever your tastes." And with cellphones, Nokia is "Connecting People—anyone, anywhere," whereas with Apple's iPhone, "Touching is believing."

Such value propositions differentiate one brand from another. They answer the customer's question "Why should I buy your brand rather than a competitor's?" Companies must design strong value propositions that give them the greatest advantage in their target markets.

Value propositions: Land Rover lets you "Go Beyond"—to "get a taste of adventure, whatever your tastes."

Marketing Management Orientations

Marketing management wants to design strategies that will build profitable relationships with target consumers. But what *philosophy* should guide these marketing strategies? What weight should be given to the interests of customers, the organization, and society? Very often, these interests conflict.

There are five alternative concepts under which organizations design and carry out their marketing strategies: the *production, product, selling, marketing,* and *societal marketing concepts.*

The Production Concept

The **production concept** holds that consumers will favor products that are available and highly affordable. Therefore, management should focus on improving production and distribution efficiency. This concept is one of the oldest orientations that guides sellers.

The production concept is still a useful philosophy in some situations. For example, computer maker Lenovo dominates the highly competitive, price-sensitive Chinese PC market "through low labor costs, high production efficiency, and mass distribution."[11] However, although useful in some situations, the production concept can lead to marketing myopia. Companies adopting this orientation run a major risk of focusing too narrowly on their own operations and losing sight of the real objective—satisfying customer needs and building customer relationships.

The Product Concept

The **product concept** holds that consumers will favor products that offer the best quality, performance, and innovative features. Under this concept, marketing strategy focuses on making continuous product improvements.

Production concept
The idea that consumers will favor products that are available and highly affordable and that the organization should therefore focus on improving production and distribution efficiency.

Product concept
The idea that consumers will favor products that offer the best quality, performance, and features and that the organization should therefore devote its energy to making continuous product improvements.

Product quality and improvement are important parts of most marketing strategies. However, focusing *only* on the company's products can also lead to marketing myopia. For example, some manufacturers believe that if they can "build a better mousetrap, the world will beat a path to their door." But they are often rudely shocked. Buyers may be looking for a better solution to a mouse problem, but not necessarily for a better mousetrap. The better solution might be a chemical spray, an exterminating service, or something else that works even better than a mousetrap. Furthermore, a better mousetrap will not sell unless the manufacturer designs, packages, and prices it attractively; places it in convenient distribution channels; brings it to the attention of people who need it; and convinces buyers that it is a better product.

The Selling Concept

Selling concept

The idea that consumers will not buy enough of the firm's products unless it undertakes a large-scale selling and promotion effort.

Many companies follow the **selling concept**, which holds that consumers will not buy enough of the firm's products unless it undertakes a large-scale selling and promotion effort. The selling concept is typically practiced with unsought goods—those that buyers do not normally think of buying, such as insurance or blood donations. These industries must be good at tracking down prospects and selling them on product benefits.

Such aggressive selling, however, carries high risks. It focuses on creating sales transactions rather than on building long-term, profitable customer relationships. The aim often is to sell what the company makes rather than making what the market wants. It assumes that customers who are coaxed into buying the product will like it. Or, if they don't like it, they will possibly forget their disappointment and buy it again later. These are usually poor assumptions.

The Marketing Concept

Marketing concept

The marketing management philosophy that holds that achieving organizational goals depends on knowing the needs and wants of target markets and delivering the desired satisfactions better than competitors do.

The **marketing concept** holds that achieving organizational goals depends on knowing the needs and wants of target markets and delivering the desired satisfactions better than competitors do. Under the marketing concept, customer focus and value are the *paths* to sales and profits. Instead of a product-centered 'make and sell' philosophy, the marketing concept is a customer-centered 'sense and respond' philosophy. The job is not to find the right customers for your product but to find the right products for your customers.

Figure 1.3 contrasts the selling concept and the marketing concept. The selling concept takes an *inside-out* perspective. It starts with the factory, focuses on the company's existing products, and calls for heavy selling and promotion to obtain profitable sales. It focuses primarily on obtaining customers—getting short-term sales with little concern about who buys or why.

In contrast, the marketing concept takes an *outside-in* perspective. As Sam Barnett of MBC, the free-to-air television network broadcasting across the Arab world, says: "We will invest in content that people want to watch."[12] The marketing concept starts with a well-defined market, focuses on customer needs, and integrates all the marketing

FIGURE | 1.3 The Selling and Marketing Concepts Contrasted

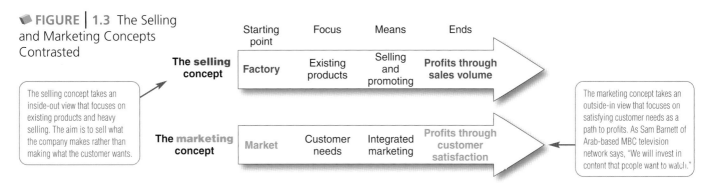

The selling concept takes an inside-out view that focuses on existing products and heavy selling. The aim is to sell what the company makes rather than making what the customer wants.

	Starting point	Focus	Means	Ends
The selling concept	Factory	Existing products	Selling and promoting	Profits through sales volume
The marketing concept	Market	Customer needs	Integrated marketing	Profits through customer satisfaction

The marketing concept takes an outside-in view that focuses on satisfying customer needs as a path to profits. As Sam Barnett of Arab-based MBC television network says, "We will invest in content that people want to watch."

Customer-driving marketing: Even 20 years ago, how many consumers would have thought to ask for now-commonplace products such as cellphones, personal digital assistants, notebook computers, iPods, and digital cameras? Marketers must often understand customer needs even better than the customers themselves do.

activities that affect customers. In turn, it yields profits by creating lasting relationships with the right customers based on customer value and satisfaction.

Implementing the marketing concept often means more than simply responding to customers' stated desires and obvious needs. *Customer-driven* companies research current customers deeply to learn about their desires, gather new product and service ideas, and test proposed product improvements. Such customer-driven marketing usually works well when a clear need exists and when customers know what they want.

In many cases, however, customers *don't* know what they want or even what is possible. For example, even 20 years ago, how many consumers would have thought to ask for now-commonplace products such as cellphones, notebook computers, iPods, digital cameras, 24-hour online buying, and satellite navigation systems? Such situations call for *customer-driving* marketing—understanding customer needs even better than customers themselves do and creating products and services that meet existing and latent needs, now and in the future. As an executive at 3M puts it, "Our goal is to lead customers where they want to go before *they* know where they want to go."

The Societal Marketing Concept

Societal marketing concept
The idea that a company's marketing decisions should consider consumers' wants, the company's requirements, consumers' long-run interests, and society's long-run interests.

The **societal marketing concept** questions whether the pure marketing concept overlooks possible conflicts between consumers' *short-run wants* and consumers' *long-run welfare*. Is a firm that satisfies the immediate needs and wants of target markets always doing what's best for consumers in the long run? The societal marketing concept holds that marketing strategy should deliver value to customers in a way that maintains or improves both the consumer's *and society's* well-being.

Consider today's flourishing bottled water industry. You may view bottled water companies as offering a convenient, tasty, and healthy product. Its packaging suggests 'green' images of clear springs, lakes, and snow-capped mountains. Yet making, filling, and shipping billions of plastic bottles generates huge amounts of carbon dioxide emissions that contribute substantially to global warming. Further, the plastic bottles pose a substantial recycling and solid waste disposal problem. Thus, in satisfying short-term consumer wants, the highly successful bottled water industry may be causing environmental problems that run against society's long-run interests.[13]

As ◖ **Figure 1.4** shows, companies should balance three considerations in setting their marketing strategies: company profits, consumer wants, *and* society's interests.

◖ **FIGURE** | 1.4

The Considerations Underlying the Societal Marketing Concept

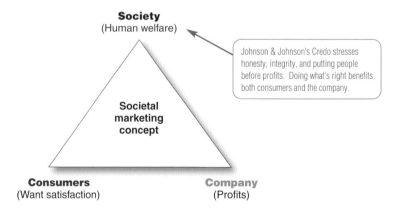

Our Credo

We believe our first responsibility is to the doctors, nurses and patients,
to mothers and fathers and all others who use our products and services.
In meeting their needs everything we do must be of high quality.
We must constantly strive to reduce our costs
in order to maintain reasonable prices.
Customers' orders must be serviced promptly and accurately.
Our suppliers and distributors must have an opportunity
to make a fair profit.

We are responsible to our employees,
the men and women who work with us throughout the world.
Everyone must be considered as an individual.
We must respect their dignity and recognize their merit.
They must have a sense of security in their jobs.
Compensation must be fair and adequate,
and working conditions clean, orderly and safe.
We must be mindful of ways to help our employees fulfill
their family responsibilities.
Employees must feel free to make suggestions and complaints.
There must be equal opportunity for employment, development
and advancement for those qualified.
We must provide competent management,
and their actions must be just and ethical.

We are responsible to the communities in which we live and work
and to the world community as well.
We must be good citizens — support good works and charities
and bear our fair share of taxes.
We must encourage civic improvements and better health and education.
We must maintain in good order
the property we are privileged to use,
protecting the environment and natural resources.

Our final responsibility is to our stockholders.
Business must make a sound profit.
We must experiment with new ideas.
Research must be carried on, innovative programs developed
and mistakes paid for.
New equipment must be purchased, new facilities provided
and new products launched.
Reserves must be created to provide for adverse times.
When we operate according to these principles,
the stockholders should realize a fair return.

Johnson & Johnson

The societal marketing concept: Johnson & Johnson's credo stresses putting people before profits.

Johnson & Johnson, a big provider of healthcare and other products, does this well. Its concern for societal interests is summarized in a company document called "Our Credo," which stresses honesty, integrity, and putting people before profits. Under this credo, Johnson & Johnson would rather take a big loss than ship a bad batch of one of its products.

Consider the tragic tampering case in which eight people died in 1982 from swallowing cyanide-laced capsules of Tylenol, a Johnson & Johnson brand. Although Johnson & Johnson believed that the pills had been altered in only a few stores, not in the factory, it quickly recalled all of its product and launched an information campaign to instruct and reassure consumers. The recall cost the company US$100 million in earnings. In the long run, however, the company's swift recall of Tylenol strengthened consumer confidence and loyalty, and today Tylenol remains one of the United States leading brands of pain reliever.

Johnson & Johnson management has learned that doing what's right benefits both consumers and the company. Says former CEO Ralph Larsen, "The Credo should not be viewed as some kind of social welfare program…it's just plain good business. If we keep trying to do what's right, at the end of the day we believe the marketplace will reward us." Thus, over the years, Johnson & Johnson's dedication to consumers and community service has made it one of America's most admired companies *and* one of the most profitable.[14]

As another example, The National Bank of Kuwait (NBK) focuses both on making profit and helping society by engaging in activities such as feeding the poor in the month of Ramadan and arranging a walkathon every year to increase health awareness.

Author Comment | The customer-driven marketing strategy discussed in the last section outlines which customers the company will serve (the target market) and how it will serve them (the value proposition). Now, the company develops marketing plans and programs—a marketing mix—that will actually deliver the intended customer value.

Preparing an Integrated Marketing Plan and Program (p 13)

The company's marketing strategy outlines which customers the company will serve and how it will create value for these customers. Next, the marketer develops an integrated marketing program that will actually deliver the intended value to target customers. The marketing program builds customer relationships by transforming the marketing strategy into action. It consists of the firm's *marketing mix*—the set of marketing tools the firm uses to implement its marketing strategy.

The major marketing-mix tools are classified into four broad groups, called the *four Ps* of marketing: product, price, place, and promotion. To deliver on its value proposition, the firm must first create a need-satisfying market offering (product). It must decide how much it will charge for the offering (price) and how it will make the offering available to target consumers (place). Finally, it must communicate with target customers about the offering and persuade them of its merits (promotion). The firm must blend all of these marketing mix tools into a comprehensive *integrated marketing program* that communicates and delivers the intended value to chosen customers. We will explore marketing programs and the marketing mix in much more detail in later chapters.

Author Comment | Doing a good job with the first three steps in the marketing process sets the stage for step four, building and managing lasting customer relationships.

Building Customer Relationships (pp 13–21)

The first three steps in the marketing process—understanding the marketplace and customer needs, designing a customer-driven marketing strategy, and constructing marketing programs—all lead up to the fourth and most important step: building profitable customer relationships.

Customer Relationship Management

Customer relationship management is perhaps the most important concept of modern marketing. Some marketers define customer relationship management narrowly as a customer data management activity (a practice called *CRM*). By this definition, it involves managing detailed information about individual customers and carefully managing customer 'touchpoints' in order to maximize customer loyalty. We will discuss this narrower CRM activity in Chapter 4 when dealing with marketing information.

Most marketers, however, give the concept of customer relationship management a broader meaning. In this broader sense, **customer relationship management** is the overall process of building and maintaining profitable customer relationships by delivering superior customer value and satisfaction. It deals with all aspects of acquiring, keeping, and growing customers.

Customer relationship management

The overall process of building and maintaining profitable customer relationships by delivering superior customer value and satisfaction.

Relationship Building Blocks: Customer Value and Satisfaction

The key to building lasting customer relationships is to create superior customer value and satisfaction. Satisfied customers are more likely to be loyal customers and to give the company a larger share of their business.

Customer Value.   Attracting and retaining customers can be a difficult task. Customers often face a wide array of products and services from which to choose. A customer buys from the firm that offers the highest **customer-perceived value**—the customer's evaluation of the difference between all the benefits and all the costs of a market offering relative to those of competing offers.

Customer-perceived value

The customer's evaluation of the difference between all the benefits and all the costs of a market offering relative to those of competing offers.

For example, consider why visitors may choose to stay at the Burj Al Arab hotel in Dubai, given its prices are so much higher than other hotels in the same area. In fact, it is one of the most expensive hotels in the world, with the lowest priced suites starting at AED 6,500 per night (US$1,750) and the most expensive being the Royal Suite, which is so luxurious that it includes its own cinema, marble bathrooms, and chauffeur-driven Rolls-Royce service, costing up to AED 100,000 (US$27,000) per night. The hotel is not just for the super rich—it is also used by ordinary visitors. The reason they are willing to pay such high prices is that they perceive a stay at the hotel as the ultimate luxury treat, a once-in-a-lifetime experience. Jumeirah, the company operating the hotel, markets it with the message "Arrive in absolute awe, stay individually inspired." Customers such as the guests at the Burj Al Arab hotel often do not judge values and costs 'accurately' or 'objectively.' They act on *perceived* value. Can the Burj Al Arab hotel possibly provide the superior quality of experience to justify the difference in the prices it charges compared with other hotels? It's all a matter of personal value perceptions, but for many guests the answer is yes. One visitor wrote: "Everything about this hotel said 'money'—an ultra luxury hotel with most attentive staff and fabulous surroundings… Yes, it is expensive, but well worth the money."[15]

Customer satisfaction

The extent to which a product's perceived performance matches a buyer's expectations.

Visitors to the spectacular Burj Al Arab hotel are willing to pay much more than standard hotel prices for the perceived value of a once-in-a-lifetime experience.

Customer Satisfaction.   **Customer satisfaction** depends on the product's perceived performance relative to a buyer's expectations. If the product's performance falls short of expectations, the customer is dissatisfied. If performance matches expectations, the customer is satisfied. If performance exceeds expectations, the customer is highly satisfied or delighted.

Outstanding marketing companies go out of their way to keep important customers satisfied. Most studies show that higher levels of customer satisfaction lead to greater customer loyalty, which in turn results in better company performance. Smart companies aim to delight customers by promising only what they can deliver, then delivering more than they promise. Delighted customers not only make repeat purchases, they become willing marketing partners and 'customer spokespersons' who spread the word about their good experiences to others (see **Real Marketing 1.1**).[16]

Real Marketing 1.1

Etisalat:
Delighting Customers

Etisalat is a company based in the UAE that provides telephone, television, and Internet services for business and individual customers. The company is one of the largest operators in the world, with subsidiaries and investments in 17 countries, and 80 million subscribers.

In June 2009 the company was named 'Best in Dubai' for customer service at the second annual ITP awards.[17] Winners of the award are determined, not by a panel of judges, but by public vote.

Zoe Cooper-Clark of ITP Publishing Group said: "It gives us great pleasure to award Etisalat as the winner of the Best in Dubai award for customer service. This category was created to recognise those companies that really care for the customer, and take efforts to exceed their expectations time and again. On behalf of the residents of Dubai, I congratulate Etisalat and wish them continued success."

Khalifa Al Shamsi, vice president, Marketing, Etisalat said: "Etisalat has always endeavored to provide the highest levels of customer service and we are very grateful to our customers for their loyalty. We wish to assure them that we will continue to serve them to the best of our capabilities."

Etisalat operates over 80 business centers and sales outlets across UAE. It has a 24-hour customer contact center that uses interactive voice response (IVR) technology, enabling

Etisalat aims to deliver customer "delight" through excellent customer service.

communication in four different languages. The company also provides customers with a choice of 11 different payment methods. These include online payments, credit card payments, payments by post, and payments through banks and Emirates Post, Etisalat payment machines, direct debit, check deposit drop boxes, and a Bizdirect service.

Customers can subscribe to new services through the website and can use the Internet to manage their accounts. They can view, manage, and pay their bills for all Etisalat services and also change their billing address or provide feedback on existing services.

The company also offers an eSupport service for its Internet customers. This aims to help customers to solve their basic Internet issues quickly and efficiently, without having to visit a business center or customer care center.

The 'Best in Dubai' customer service award adds to other titles that Etisalat has earned. The company received a Datamatix award at the Arab World Excellence Awards in 2009, and was named Best Operator in the Middle East six times in the three years up to 2009. Etisalat has also been named Best International Carrier at the World Communications Awards.

Source: "Dubai Residents Vote Etisalat's Customer Service—'Best in Dubai'," *AME Info*, June 2, 2009, www.ameinfo.com/198978.html.

For companies interested in delighting customers, exceptional value and service are more than a set of policies or actions—they are a company-wide attitude, an important part of the overall company culture. For example, in Lebanon and Syria, most restaurants and cafés offer an excellent customer experience, with staff members who are always friendly and very attentive. This has resulted in the talent exportation of Lebanese and Syrian service teams to all over the Arab world. The friendliness, tone of communication, and overall attitude of excellent customer experience has influenced the standard of service in the region. Most Lebanese and Syrian restaurants are now positioned to offer more than just food; they are all about the excellent dining experience.

However, although the customer-centered firm seeks to deliver high customer satisfaction relative to competitors, it does not attempt to *maximize* customer satisfaction. A company can always increase customer satisfaction by lowering its price or increasing its services. But this may result in lower profits. Thus, the purpose of marketing is to generate customer value profitably. This requires a very delicate balance: The marketer must continue to generate more customer value and satisfaction but not 'give away the house.'

Customer Relationship Levels and Tools

Companies can build customer relationships at many levels, depending on the nature of the target market. At one extreme, a company with many low-margin customers may seek to develop *basic relationships* with them. For example, Unilever does not telephone or call on all of its Dove consumers to get to know them personally. Instead, Unilever creates relationships through brand-building advertising, sales promotions, and its Dove website: www.unileverme.com/our-brands/personal-care/dove.asp. At the other extreme, in markets with few customers and high margins, sellers want to create *full partnerships* with key customers. For example, Unilever customer teams work closely with Carrefour, Géant, Watani, Union Coop, Lulu, and other large retailers. In between these two extreme situations, other levels of customer relationships are appropriate.

Today, most leading companies are developing customer loyalty and retention programs. Beyond offering consistently high value and satisfaction, marketers can use specific marketing tools to develop stronger bonds with consumers. For example, many companies now offer *frequency marketing programs* that reward customers who buy frequently or in large amounts. Airlines offer frequent-flyer programs, hotels give room upgrades to their frequent guests, and supermarkets give patronage discounts to 'very important customers.'

To build customer relationships, companies can add structural ties as well as financial and social benefits. A business marketer might supply customers with special equipment or online linkages that help them manage their orders, payroll, or inventory. For example, Aramex, the Arab-based global distribution and supply-chain management company, provides a range of services to help customers keep track of their orders, inventory, and freight. It also uses a warehouse management system, Optilog, which allows Aramex logistics customers to track their orders and stock, and to generate real-time reports.[18, 19]

The Changing Nature of Customer Relationships

Significant changes are occurring in the ways in which companies are relating to their customers. Yesterday's big companies focused on mass marketing to all customers at arm's length. Today's companies are building deeper, more direct, and more lasting relationships with more carefully selected customers. Here are some important trends in the way companies and customers are relating to one another.

Selective relationship management: Vodafone divides customers into prepaid and postpaid customers, with different offerings to each, so that it can profitably target two different types of customers.

Relating with More Carefully Selected Customers

Few firms today still practice true mass marketing—selling in a standardized way to any customer who comes along. Today, most marketers realize that they don't want relationships with every customer. Instead, they are targeting fewer, more profitable customers. Called *selective relationship management*, many companies now use customer profitability analysis to weed out losing customers and to target winning ones for pampering. Once they identify profitable customers, firms can create attractive offers and special handling to capture these customers and earn their loyalty.

But what should the company do with unprofitable customers? If it can't turn them into profitable ones, it may even want to 'fire' customers that are too unreasonable or that cost more to serve than they are worth.

Mobile operator Vodafone Egypt divides its telephone customers into prepaid customers and postpaid customers, amongst other groups of services. Prepaid customers have to top up their phone with pre-bought credit to be able to make a call, while postpaid customers are charged for their calls at the end of the month.

The postpaid customers have an overall consistent flow of calls throughout the month. There is no limit to the number of calls they can make, other than their own self-restraint about talking on the phone. The prepaid customers have to have their phones continuously topped up with credit to be able to make calls. For a large percentage of the prepaid customers, when their accounts are close to running out of credit, they find other ways to make calls: For example, they call their contact and hang up before their contact picks up the phone. Using the caller ID function, the person then calls them back. Catering to this need, Vodafone built a service for prepaid customers who are out of credit, called Call Me Please. A prepaid caller who is out of credit can send a fellow Vodafone customer an SMS message, for free, requesting a call back. That way Vodafone still makes money from the call, regardless of who initiated it.

Vodafone also initiated another new service called Give Me a Loan Please, where a limited credit is offered to the prepaid customer ahead of them crediting their phones. The amount they receive is deducted the next time they top up their phone with credit. With these two services, among other similar ones, the average usage of what had been less-revenue-generating customers began to trigger calls.

Relating More Deeply and Interactively

Beyond choosing customers more selectively, companies are now relating with chosen customers in deeper, more meaningful ways. Rather than relying only on one-way, mass-media messages, today's marketers are incorporating new, more interactive approaches that help build targeted, two-way customer relationships.

The deeper nature of today's customer relationships results in part from the rapidly changing communications environment. New technologies have profoundly changed the ways in which people communicate and relate to one another. For example, thanks to rapid advances in Internet and computer technology, people can now interact in direct and surprisingly personal ways with others, whether nearby or scattered around the world. New tools for communicating and relating include everything from email, blogs, websites, and video sharing to online communities and social networks such as MySpace, Facebook, Twitter, Fainak.com, Maktoob, YouTube, and Second Life.

This changing communications environment also affects how consumers relate to companies and products. Increasingly, marketers are using the new communications approaches in building closer customer relationships. The aim is to create deeper consumer involvement and a sense of community surrounding a brand—to make the brand a meaningful part of consumers' conversations and lives. "Becoming part of the conversation between consumers is infinitely more powerful than handing down information via traditional advertising," says one marketing expert. "It [makes] consumers...a part of the process, rather than being dumb recipients of the message from on high—and that is of huge potential value to brands."[20]

However, at the same time that the new communications tools create relationship-building opportunities for marketers, they also create challenges. They give consumers greater power and control. Today's consumers have more information about brands than ever before, and they have a wealth of platforms for airing and sharing their brand views with other consumers. And more than ever before, consumers can choose the brand conversations and exchanges in which they will participate. According to Mark Parker, chief executive of Nike, the new power of the consumer is "the most compelling change we've seen over the past four or five years. They are dictating what the dialogue is, how we're conducting it, and it's definitely a two-way conversation."[21]

Creating community with customers: Nike's new, more interactive media include in-person events and other activities designed to build brand community and deeper customer relationships.

Greater consumer control means that, in building customer relationships, companies can no longer rely on marketing by *intrusion*. They must practice marketing by *attraction*—creating market offerings and messages that involve consumers rather than interrupt them. Hence, most marketers now augment their mass-media marketing efforts with a rich mix of direct marketing approaches that promote brand–consumer interaction.

For example, many are participating in the exploding world of *online social networks* or creating online communities of their own. Toyota, the world's fifth-largest advertiser, spends US$3.1 billion a year on media advertising. But it also sells Scions at Second Life and maintains a Scion presence on MySpace, Gaia Online, and other cyber hangouts. And the company's Toyota.com/hybrids site creates a community in which more than 17,500 Prius, Camry, and Highlander hybrid 'believers' meet to share their reasons for buying hybrid vehicles and videos and messages on their experiences, both good and bad. "There's value in being totally authentic and transparent [with your customers]," says a manager of consumer-generated media at Toyota, "as much as it hurts sometimes."[22]

Similarly, Nike has recently shifted a bigger chunk of its media budget toward new, more direct interactions with consumers. It now spends just 33 percent of its almost US$700 million annual ad budget on television and other traditional media, down from 55 percent from 10 years ago. Nike's new media include not only the Internet, but also in-person events and other activities designed to build brand community and deeper customer relationships.[23]

In March 2010, Nike Middle East ran a region-wide football initiative designed to give young players the chance to train like their favorite stars. The scheme was open to all young footballers, with regional competition finals in Dubai. A select handful of winners from the competition finals won the opportunity to go to Juventus FC in Italy to continue their training.

The excitement was summed up by one young hopeful, Firas Hassan: "Last year, Nike Elite Training gave me the opportunity to play football with the best local coaches, connect with international players using Nike Football+ and master the game I love! My dream is to reach the World Cup in 2018 and I am certain that Nike will help me get there."[24]

As a part of the new customer control and dialogue, consumers themselves are now creating brand conversations and messages on their own. And increasingly, companies are even *inviting* consumers to play a more active role in shaping brand messages and ads. For example, Frito-Lay, Southwest, and Heinz have run contests for consumer-generated commercials that have been aired on national television. Other companies, including marketing heavyweights such as Coca-Cola, McDonald's, and Apple, have snagged brand-related consumer videos from YouTube and other popular video-sharing sites and turned them into commercial messages.

Consumer-generated marketing

Marketing messages, ads, and other brand exchanges created by consumers themselves—both invited and uninvited.

Consumer-generated marketing has become a significant marketing force. In fact, in 2006, *Advertising Age* magazine awarded its coveted Ad Agency of the Year designation to—you guessed it—the consumer. "The explosion of video, blogs, Web sites, [and consumer-generate ads] confirmed what we knew all along," says the magazine. When it comes to creative messages, "the consumer is king."[25]

Real Marketing 1.2

Media and Direct Communication Trends in the Arab World

Advertisers are testing the boundaries with an increasing variety of different media, including mobile marketing.

In a region dominated by subcultures, the consumer profile of someone in Jordan or Qatar, for example, is not the same as the consumer profile of someone in Saudi Arabia or the UAE. More and more industry participants plan to offer specialized communication services to clients in order to target niche subgroups. From a cultural standpoint, more people in the Arab world are embracing Western culture and hence encouraging advertisers to test boundaries with an increasing variety of different media, especially the Internet, mobile, and ambient marketing.

In terms of creative improvement, a budding young audience that is wealthy and media-aware is forcing advertisers to be more creative. Graduates returning from abroad are bringing back with them a wide range of creative insights and ideas that are quickly being adopted into the markets. Despite this positive outlook on future creativity, almost all Arab markets have been facing a recent downturn in the advertising employment sectors. Advertisers are also continually seeking alternative and more effective ways to reach and connect directly with their target audiences.

Direct marketing techniques range from simple direct-mail campaigns to more sophisticated relationship-based web promotions. In the United States and Europe, total expenditure on direct marketing can be as much as 20 percent of total advertising budgets. However, according to a recent Booz Allen Hamilton survey, direct marketing represents a mere 2 percent of total advertising spend in the Arab world. A key problem for direct marketing in the Arab world is the lack of reliable and efficient residential postal service delivery. In addition, the relatively low Internet penetrations in many Arab countries are limiting advertisers' appetites for online advertising. In 2003, total Internet advertising spend in the Arab world, excluding non-cash barter deals, did not exceed US$6 million.

The joining together of the telecoms and media industries is leading to new opportunities

in 'infotainment'-related value-added services, including mobile marketing. This development could prove to be an effective way to energize the historically underdeveloped direct marketing industry in the region and to open an attractive new option for advertisers.

The rise of the mobile phone value-added services industry is already evident from the proliferation of mobile ringtones and logos, and the emergence of services such as SMS breaking news from Al Jazeera. A wide range of media, technology, and telecoms players are involved at the various stages of the value-added services value chain in order for content to eventually reach the mobile phone screen. Content supplied by companies such as Disney and Rotana is delivered by service providers using specialized IT applications via mobile operator networks to be displayed and manipulated on mobile devices.

"The current market for value-added services in the Middle East is estimated at around US$350 million, which is distributed across the various players along the value chain according to a web of content fees and revenue sharing agreements," said Karim Sabbagh, partner and vice president with the communications, media, and technology practice at Booz Allen Hamilton, based in the firm's Riyadh and Dubai offices. "Half of the current market value is in the form of mobile personalization services such as ringtones, logos, wallpapers, etc. Operators, media owners, and independent value-added services providers are already tapping into this market. As a result, future growth is expected to come from value-added services categories

such as general entertainment, interactive media services, gaming, and information, bringing the total market to over US$1.7 billion by 2010."

Gabriel Chahine, principal with Booz Allen Hamilton and a member of the Global Communications, Media, and Technology Group based in Dubai, said, "[Extending] the mobile value-added services industry with the classical direct marketing activities of customer database management, creative, and campaign services management instantly creates an altogether new industry for mobile marketing. Mobile marketing seems to be one of the most attractive options for advertisers."

Ahmed Galal Ismail, associate with Booz Allen Hamilton and based in the firm's Dubai office, commented that, "The key success factors of mobile marketing hinge on multimedia creative services, access to advanced technology, and elaborate permission-based customer databases. The emerging players are challenged to build a sustainable operating model with the required core capabilities. Prime mover advantage is also likely to be a winning strategy for players needing to build capabilities, relationships, and market shares ahead of multiple new entrants in this exciting new market."

The rising use of mobile phones in the Arab world due to increased competition and falling prices—coupled with the overall underdeveloped state of direct marketing in the Arab world—underscores the potential of mobile marketing. In addition, current

Continued on next page ▼

Real Marketing 1.2 Continued ▼

and potential heavy users of mobile marketing in Europe, such as consumer-goods and automotive companies, are already well represented in the region with significant annual advertising budgets. As such, regional mobile marketing revenues are projected to grow by 52 percent annually.

Looking forward, mobile marketing could rejuvenate the vastly underdeveloped direct marketing industry in the Arab world. A sustainable business model for any mobile marketing service provider would have to rely

on a mix of in-house and partner capabilities along an emerging value chain that mixes elements from the advertising, media, and telecoms industries. A handful of independent players are already starting to shape the market across the region, but many operators and agencies have been less engaged.

Overall, the potential size of the mobile marketing prize in the region is significant. However, the market will only realize its full potential if players actively and co-operatively invest in developing the market and respect consumer privacy, instead of focusing on unsustainable short-term gains.

Based on extracts from: Imran Jaffrey, "Advertising Trends in the Middle East—A Look Towards 2009," *Business Insights*, Worldwide Partners Inc., November 10, 2008, www.worldwidepartners.com/news/view? article_id=36637; and "The Future of Mobile Marketing in the Middle East: Trends and Opportunities," *AME Info*, September 29, 2004, www.ameinfo.com/56541.html (pp. 1, 3).

> **Author Comment** | Marketers can't create customer value and build customer relationships by themselves. They need to work closely with other company departments and with partners outside the company.

Partner relationship management
Working closely with partners in other company departments and outside the company to jointly bring greater value to customers.

Partner Relationship Management

When it comes to creating customer value and building strong customer relationships, today's marketers know that they can't go it alone. They must work closely with a variety of marketing partners. In addition to being good at *customer relationship management*, marketers must also be good at **partner relationship management**. Major changes are occurring in how marketers partner with others inside and outside the company to jointly bring more value to customers.

Partners Inside the Company

Traditionally, marketers have been charged with understanding customers and representing customer needs to different company departments. The old thinking was that marketing is done only by marketing, sales, and customer-support people. However, in today's more connected world, every functional area can interact with customers, especially electronically. The new thinking is that every employee must be customer-focused. David Packard, late co-founder of Hewlett-Packard, wisely said, "Marketing is far too important to be left only to the marketing department."[26]

Today, rather than letting each department go its own way, firms are linking all departments in the cause of creating customer value. Rather than assigning only sales and marketing people to customers, they are forming cross-functional customer teams. For example, Procter & Gamble assigns customer development teams to each of its major retailer accounts. These teams—consisting of sales and marketing people, operations specialists, market and financial analysts, and others—co-ordinate the efforts of many P&G departments toward helping the retailer be more successful.

Marketing Partners Outside the Company

Changes are also occurring in how marketers connect with their suppliers, channel partners, and even competitors. Most companies today are networked companies, relying heavily on partnerships with other firms.

Marketing channels consist of distributors, retailers, and others who connect the company to its buyers. The *supply chain* describes a longer channel, stretching from raw materials to components to final products that are carried to final buyers. For example, the supply chain for personal computers consists of suppliers of computer chips and other components, the computer manufacturer, and the distributors, retailers, and others who sell the computers.

Through *supply-chain management*, many companies today are strengthening their connections with partners all along the supply chain. They know that their fortunes rest not just on how well they perform. Success at building customer relationships also rests on how well their entire supply chain performs against competitors' supply chains. These companies don't just treat suppliers as vendors and distributors as customers. They treat both as partners in delivering customer value. On the one hand, for example, Lexus works closely with carefully selected suppliers to improve quality and operations efficiency. On the other hand, it works with its franchise dealers to provide top-grade sales and service support that will bring customers in the door and keep them coming back.

> **Author** | Check back to
> **Comment** | Figure 1.1. In the first
> four steps of the marketing process,
> the company creates value for target
> customers and builds strong relation-
> ships with them. If it does that well,
> it can capture value from customers
> in return in the form of loyal custom-
> ers who buy and continue to buy the
> company's brands.

Capturing Value from Customers (pp 21–24)

The first four steps in the marketing process outlined in **Figure 1.1** involve building customer relationships by creating and delivering superior customer value. The final step involves capturing value in return in the form of current and future sales, market share, and profits. By creating superior customer value, the firm creates highly satisfied customers who stay loyal and buy more. This, in turn, means greater long-run returns for the firm. Here, we discuss the outcomes of creating customer value: customer loyalty and retention, share of market and share of customer, and customer equity.

Creating Customer Loyalty and Retention

Good customer relationship management creates customer delight. In turn, delighted customers remain loyal and talk favorably to others about the company and its products. Studies show big differences in the loyalty of customers who are less satisfied, somewhat satisfied, and completely satisfied. Even a slight drop from complete satisfaction can create an enormous drop in loyalty. Thus, the aim of customer relationship management is to create not just customer satisfaction, but customer delight.[27]

Companies are realizing that losing a customer means losing more than a single sale. It means losing the entire stream of purchases that the customer would make over a lifetime of patronage. For example, here is a dramatic illustration of **customer lifetime value**:

Customer lifetime value
The value of the entire stream of purchases that the customer would make over a lifetime of patronage.

> Stew Leonard, who operates a highly profitable four-store supermarket in the U.S. states of Connecticut and New York, says that he sees US$50,000 flying out of his store every time he sees an unhappy customer. Why? Because his average customer spends about US$100 a week, shops 50 weeks a year, and remains in the area for about 10 years. If this customer has an unhappy experience and switches to another supermarket, Stew Leonard's has lost US$50,000 in revenue. The loss can be much greater if the disappointed customer shares the bad experience with other customers and causes them to defect. To keep customers coming back, Stew Leonard's has created what the *New York Times* has dubbed the "Disneyland of Dairy Stores," complete with costumed characters, scheduled entertainment, a petting zoo, and animatronics throughout the store. From its humble beginnings as a small dairy store in 1969, Stew Leonard's has grown at an amazing pace. It has built 29 additions onto the original store, which now serves more than 300,000 customers each week. This crowd of loyal shoppers is largely a result of the store's passionate approach to customer service. Rule #1: at Stew Leonard's— The customer is always right. Rule #2: If the customer is ever wrong, reread rule #1![28]

> Stew Leonard is not alone in assessing customer lifetime value. Lexus, for example, estimates that a single satisfied and loyal customer is worth more than US$600,000 in lifetime sales.[29] Thus, working to retain and grow customers makes good economic sense. In

Customer satisfaction should be at the heart of the firm's strategy.

fact, a company can lose money on a specific transaction but still benefit greatly from a long-term relationship. This means that companies must aim high in building customer relationships. Customer delight creates an emotional relationship with a brand, not just a rational preference. And that relationship keeps customers coming back.

Emirates Airline recognized that it faced tough challenges when entering airline management, so it focused on customer delight and loyalty in pursuit of growth in the industry. Emirates is committed to the highest standards in order to achieve customer delight through each customer's relationship with the company. Accordingly, Skywards, which is Emirates' frequent flier reward and loyalty program, is different from any other similar programs. Emirates claims that Skywards is not just about earning and spending Skywards Miles. Emirates presents the program in terms of managing the customer's journey and also offering benefits beyond the journey itself. For example, members can earn and spend Skywards Miles with Emirates, and also with its prestigious global partners such as Le Meridien, Jumeirah, Citibank, Hertz, and Damas.

Growing Share of Customer

Share of customer

The portion of the customer's purchasing that a company gets in its product categories.

Beyond simply retaining good customers to capture customer lifetime value, good customer relationship management can help marketers to increase their **share of customer**—the share they get of the customer's purchasing in their product categories. Thus, banks want to increase 'share of wallet.' Supermarkets and restaurants want to get more 'share of stomach.' Car companies want to increase 'share of garage,' and airlines want greater 'share of travel.'

To increase share of customer, firms can offer greater variety to current customers. Or they can create programs to cross-sell and up-sell in order to market more products and services to existing customers. For example, Amazon.com is highly skilled at leveraging relationships with its 66 million customers to increase its share of each customer's purchases. Originally an online bookseller, Amazon.com now offers customers music, videos, gifts, toys, consumer electronics, office products, home improvement items, lawn and garden products, apparel and accessories, jewelry, tools, and even groceries. In addition, based on each customer's purchase history, the company recommends related products that might be of interest. This recommendation system may influence up to 30 percent of all sales.[30] In these ways, Amazon.com captures a greater share of each customer's spending budget.

Building Customer Equity

We can now see the importance of not just acquiring customers, but of keeping and growing them as well. One marketing consultant puts it this way: "The only value your company will ever create is the value that comes from customers—the ones you have now and the ones you will have in the future. Without customers, you don't have a business."[31] Customer relationship management takes a long-term view. Companies want not only to create profitable customers, but also to 'own' them for life, earn a greater share of their purchases, and capture their customer lifetime value.

What Is Customer Equity?

Customer equity

The total combined customer lifetime values of all of the company's customers.

The ultimate aim of customer relationship management is to produce high *customer equity*.[32] **Customer equity** is the total combined customer lifetime values of all of the company's current and potential customers. Clearly, the more loyal the firm's profitable customers, the higher the firm's customer equity. Customer equity may be a better measure of a firm's performance than current sales or market share. Whereas sales and market share reflect the past, customer equity suggests the future. Federal Express (now FedEx) realised that it had a great opportunity to improve customer equity in air delivery service, because a poor rate of on-time delivery had resulted in low repeat business for most delivery companies:

> Federal Express (now FedEx) entered the air delivery market in the mid-1970s at a time when packages delivered by air were handled by several different carriers and delays were frequent. Air delivery firms were dependent on scheduled airlines, and any delays

Customer equity: Federal Express (now FedEx) recognised the value of customer loyalty and retention, transforming the industry's approach to delivering packages by air.

or cancellations to those services resulted in late delivery. Typically only 43 percent of packages were actually delivered on time. Of course, this resulted in huge dissatisfaction among customers, and low retention rates for any delivery firm. Customers were frequently changing their delivery company and were rarely content.

Federal Express decided to tackle this problem and turn it into a business opportunity to win customer equity. The company looked at the actual process for handling freight, and turned it on its head. It developed a unique focus on distribution, with a central hub at Memphis which received all packages and then routed them to their final destinations. Crucially, Federal Express also purchased its own fleet of aircraft, giving it control over flight scheduling: it started flying its planes at night, resulting in minimal delays at airports. The company's marketing slogan captured attention: "When it absolutely, positively has to be there overnight."

Customer retention rates for Federal Express shot up to over 90 percent compared with just over 40 percent for the industry average. It didn't take too long before Federal Express became the industry leader, and its approach to placing value on customer equity enabled it to maintain that position. [33]

Building the Right Relationships with the Right Customers

Companies should manage customer equity carefully. They should view customers as assets that need to be managed and maximized. But not all customers, not even all loyal customers, are good investments. Surprisingly, some loyal customers can be unprofitable, and some disloyal customers can be profitable. Which customers should the company acquire and retain?

The company can classify customers according to their potential profitability and manage its relationships with them accordingly. 🖙 **Figure 1.5** classifies customers into one

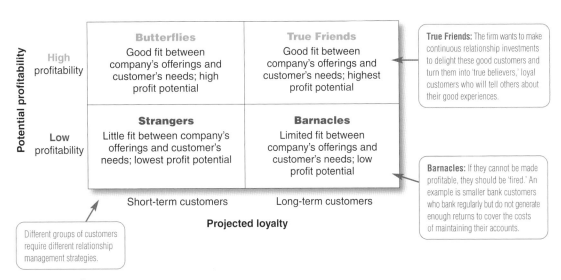

	Butterflies	**True Friends**
High profitability	Good fit between company's offerings and customer's needs; high profit potential	Good fit between company's offerings and customer's needs; highest profit potential
Low profitability	**Strangers** Little fit between company's offerings and customer's needs; lowest profit potential	**Barnacles** Limited fit between company's offerings and customer's needs; low profit potential

Potential profitability

Short-term customers   Long-term customers

Projected loyalty

True Friends: The firm wants to make continuous relationship investments to delight these good customers and turn them into 'true believers,' loyal customers who will tell others about their good experiences.

Barnacles: If they cannot be made profitable, they should be 'fired.' An example is smaller bank customers who bank regularly but do not generate enough returns to cover the costs of maintaining their accounts.

Different groups of customers require different relationship management strategies.

🖙 **FIGURE** | 1.5 Customer Relationship Groups

Source: Reprinted by permission of Harvard Business Review. Adapted from "Mismanagement of Customer Loyalty" by Werner Relnartz and V. Kumar, July 2002, p. 93. Copyright © by the president and fellows of Harvard College; all rights reserved.

of four relationship groups, according to their profitability and projected loyalty.[34] Each group requires a different relationship management strategy. 'Strangers' show low potential profitability and little projected loyalty. There is little fit between the company's offerings and their needs. The relationship management strategy for these customers is simple: Don't invest anything in them.

'Butterflies' are potentially profitable but not loyal. There is a good fit between the company's offerings and their needs. However, like real butterflies, we can enjoy them for only a short while and then they're gone. An example is stock market investors who trade shares often and in large amounts but who enjoy hunting out the best deals without building a regular relationship with any single brokerage company. Efforts to convert butterflies into loyal customers are rarely successful. Instead, the company should enjoy the butterflies for the moment. It should use promotional blitzes to attract them, create satisfying and profitable transactions with them, and then cease investing in them until the next time around.

'True friends' are both profitable and loyal. There is a strong fit between their needs and the company's offerings. The firm wants to make continuous relationship investments to delight these customers and nurture, retain, and grow them. It wants to turn true friends into 'true believers,' who come back regularly and tell others about their good experiences with the company.

'Barnacles' are highly loyal but not very profitable. There is a limited fit between their needs and the company's offerings. An example is smaller bank customers who bank regularly but do not generate enough returns to cover the costs of maintaining their accounts. Barnacles are perhaps the most problematic customers. The company might be able to improve their profitability by selling them more, raising their fees, or reducing service to them. However, if they cannot be made profitable, they should be 'fired.'

The point here is an important one: Different types of customers require different relationship management strategies. The goal is to build the *right relationships* with the *right customers.*

<table>
<tr><td>**Author**
Comment | Marketing doesn't take place in a vacuum. Now that we've discussed the five steps in the marketing process, let's examine how the ever-changing marketplace affects both consumers and the marketers who serve them. We'll look more deeply into these and other marketing environment factors in Chapter 3.</td></tr>
</table>

The Changing Marketing Landscape (pp 24–28)

Every day, dramatic changes are occurring in the marketplace. Richard Love of Hewlett-Packard observes, "The pace of change is so rapid that the ability to change has now become a competitive advantage." As the marketplace changes, so must those who serve it.

In this section, we examine the major trends and forces that are changing the marketing landscape and challenging marketing strategy. We look at four major developments: the digital age, rapid globalization, the call for more ethics and social responsibility, and the growth of not-for-profit marketing.

The Digital Age

The recent technology boom has created a digital age. The explosive growth in computer, communications, information, and other digital technologies has had a major impact on the ways companies bring value to their customers. Now, more than ever before, we are all connected to each other and to information anywhere in the world. Where it once took days or weeks to receive news about important world events, we now learn about them as they are occurring through live satellite broadcasts and news websites. Where it once took weeks to correspond with others in distant places, they are now only moments away by cellphone, email, or webcam.

The digital age has provided marketers with exciting new ways to learn about and track customers and to create products and services tailored to individual customer needs. It's helping marketers to communicate with customers in large groups or one-to-one. Through web videoconferencing, marketing researchers at a company's headquarters in

New York can look in on focus groups in Cairo or Dubai without ever stepping onto a plane. With only a few clicks of a mouse button, a direct marketer can tap into online data services to learn anything from what car you drive and what you read to what flavor of ice cream you prefer. Or, using today's powerful computers, marketers can create their own detailed customer databases and use them to target individual customers with offers designed to meet their specific needs.

Digital technology has also brought a new wave of communication, advertising, and relationship-building tools—ranging from online advertising, video-sharing tools, cellphones, and video games to web widgets and online social networks. The digital shift means that marketers can no longer expect consumers to always seek them out. Nor can they always control conversations about their brands. The new digital world makes it easy for consumers to take marketing content that once lived only in advertising or on a brand website with them wherever they go and to share it with friends. More than just add-ons to traditional marketing channels, the new digital media must be fully integrated into the marketer's customer relationship-building efforts. Says one marketer, "We're [now] building a network of experiences."[35]

Perhaps the most dramatic new digital technology is the Internet. The number of Internet users worldwide now stands at more than 1.7 billion and will reach an estimated 3.4 billion by 2015. A Nielsen online report indicated that about one-fifth of the Arab world populations have access to the Internet; however, there is great variation across countries, For example, growth in Internet usage has been much higher in some Arab countries than in others. A detailed analysis is provided in Chapter 4. Today's typical Internet users spend 47 percent of their time online looking at online content—watching video, reading the news, or getting the lowdown on friends and celebrities on MySpace or Facebook. They spend another 11 percent of their online time communicating with each other, 15 percent shopping, and 5 percent googling or using other search engines. Computers and the Internet have become an indispensable part of our lives.

What do we value most? Judging by how we spend our time, our computers. Most people spend more time with their computers than with their spouse or significant other. More than 80 percent report that they grow more dependent on their computer every year. Computers are also a growing source of stress. The average consumer experiences frustrating computer problems twice a month and wastes 12 hours a month due to computer problems. Eleven percent say they'd be willing to implant a device in their brains that would allow them to access the Internet. Twenty-four percent say the Internet can serve as a substitute for a significant other. Ten percent say the web brings them close to God.

Internet usage surged in the 1990s with the development of the user-friendly World Wide Web. During the overheated web mania of the late 1990s, dot-coms popped up everywhere. The mania cooled during the dot-com meltdown of 2000, when many poorly conceived e-tailers and other web start-ups went out of business. Today, a new version of the Internet has emerged—a 'second coming' of the web often referred to as *Web 2.0*. Web 2.0 involves a more reasoned and balanced approach to marketing online. It also offers a fast-growing set of new web technologies for connecting with customers, such as weblogs (blogs) and vlogs (video-based blogs), social-networking sites, and video-sharing sites. The interactive, community-building nature of these new technologies makes them ideal for relating with consumers.[36]

Electronic and online media offer new marketing opportunities for companies.

Online marketing is now the fastest-growing form of marketing. These days, it's hard to find a company that doesn't use the web in a significant way. In addition to the 'click-only' dot-coms, most traditional 'brick-and-mortar' companies have now become 'click-and-mortar' companies. They have ventured online to attract new customers and build stronger relationships with existing ones. Today, more than 65 percent of American online users use the Internet to shop.[37] Business-to-business online commerce is also booming. It seems that almost every business has set up shop on the web. Although e-commerce penetration in the Arab world has not grown at the same pace, it has certainly become more familiar in some specific industries such as airlines, hotels, and jewelry.

Thus, the technology boom is providing exciting new opportunities for marketers. We will explore the impact of the new digital marketing technologies in future chapters, especially Chapter 13.

Rapid Globalization

As they are redefining their relationships with customers and partners, marketers are also taking a fresh look at the ways in which they relate with the broader world around them. In an increasingly smaller world, many marketers are now connected *globally* with their customers and marketing partners.

Today, almost every company, large or small, is touched in some way by global competition. A large U.S. electronics manufacturer competes in its home markets with giant Korean rivals. An Internet retailer such as Amazon finds itself receiving orders from all over the world at the same time that an American consumer-goods producer introduces new products into emerging markets abroad. Arab world consumers are offered several choices of grocery retailer; from small, local stores to multinational hypermarkets. Products offered by these retailers are produced by a large number of local, regional and multinational firms.

American firms have been challenged at home by the skillful marketing of European and Asian multinationals. Companies such as Toyota, Nokia, Nestlé, Sony, and Samsung have often outperformed their U.S. competitors in American markets. Similarly, U.S. companies in a wide range of industries have developed truly global operations, making and selling their products worldwide. McDonald's now serves 52 million customers daily in 31,600 restaurants worldwide—some 65 percent of its revenues come from outside the United States. Similarly, Nike markets in more than 160 countries, with non-U.S. sales accounting for 53 percent of its worldwide sales. Even MTV Networks has joined the elite of global brands—its 150 channels worldwide deliver localized versions to 419 million homes in 164 countries around the globe. And it reaches millions more daily via the more than 5,000 mobile, console, and online games and virtual worlds that it shares on its more than 300 websites worldwide.[38]

Today, companies are not only trying to sell more of their locally produced goods in international markets, they are also buying more supplies and components from abroad. For example, Brilliance Auto in Egypt is one of the successful automotive manufacturers in China. In 2005, Brilliance Auto and Bavarian Auto Group—the sole importer and distributor of Rolls-Royce, BMW, and Mini Cooper brands in Egypt—signed an agreement to assemble Brilliance's top-end Galena luxury saloon in Egypt. The Brilliance Galena is designed by the chief Italian designers Giugiaro and Pininfarina, and is equipped with a 2.0 liter Japanese Mitsubishi engine and a chassis system certified by Porsche.

Thus, managers in countries around the world are increasingly taking a global, not just local, view of the company's industry, competitors, and opportunities.

McDonald's is one of the most popular fast food restaurants in Saudi Arabia.

They are asking: What is global marketing? How does it differ from domestic marketing? How do global competitors and forces affect our business? To what extent should we 'go global'? We will discuss the global marketplace in more detail in Chapter 16.

The Call for More Ethics and Social Responsibility

Marketers are reexamining their relationships with social values and responsibilities. As the worldwide consumerism and environmentalism movements mature, today's marketers are being called upon to take greater responsibility for the social and environmental impact of their actions. Corporate ethics and social responsibility have become hot topics for almost every business. And few companies can ignore the renewed and very demanding environmental movement. Every company action can affect customer relationships:[39]

> There is an unwritten contract today between customers and the brands they buy. First, customers expect companies to consistently deliver what they advertise. Secondly, they expect the companies they do business with to treat them with respect and to be honorable and forthright.... Everything a company does affects the brand in the eyes of the customer. For example, Google's decision to use solar energy for its server farms reinforces what Google stands for and strengthens the Google brand.

The social responsibility and environmental movements will place even stricter demands on companies in the future. Some companies resist these movements, acting only when forced by legislation or organized consumer protests. More forward-looking companies, however, readily accept their responsibilities to the world around them. They view socially responsible actions as an opportunity to do well by doing good. They seek ways to profit by serving the best long-run interests of their customers and communities.

Some Arab companies—such as SEKEM, Orascom, Aramex, Al Mansour Group, Abraaj Capital (Wamda Celebration of Entrepreneurship), and others—are practicing 'caring capitalism,' setting themselves apart by being civic-minded and responsible. They are building social responsibility and action into their company value and mission statements. For example, SEKEM was founded in Egypt in 1977, with the aim of achieving its vision of sustainable human development. Its work relates to the production and marketing of a range of organic products including spices, tea, wholefoods, and cotton. A number of specialized companies are involved, each working for sustainable development in relation to economics, organic agriculture, research and development, education, and health care. An important focus is on biodynamic farming, which restores and maintains soil as well as ensuring the biodiversity of nature. One typical initiative has been to create the Egyptian Biodynamic Association (EBDA), a non-governmental organization providing the findings of biodynamic research and training to Egyptian farmers.[40]

We will revisit the topic of marketing and social responsibility in greater detail in Chapter 17.

The Growth of Not-for-Profit Marketing

In the past, marketing has been most widely applied in the for-profit business sector. In recent years, however, marketing has also become a major part of the strategies of many not-for-profit organizations, such as colleges, hospitals, museums, zoos, symphony orchestras, and religious establishments. Not-for-profit organizations face stiff competition for support and membership. Sound marketing can help them to attract membership and support.[41] Consider the marketing efforts of Hospital 57357, the newly developed cancer hospital for childern in Egypt:

> Hospital 57357 was established in 2007 aiming to cure, free of charge, children diagnosed with cancer. Childhood cancer is a global problem. According to a report developed by the U.S. government, each year 150 children per million under 20 years are diagnosed with cancer. Further, the probability of developing cancer before the age of 20 years is 1 in 300.

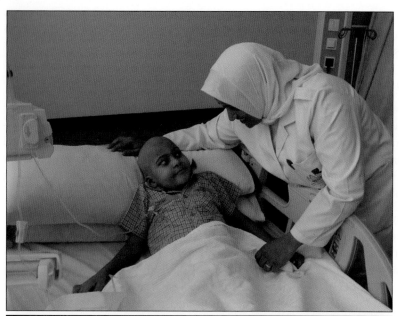

Children's Cancer Hospital Egypt: A result of individual and corporate donations.

According to the World Health Organization (WHO), each year over 160,000 children worldwide are diagnosed with cancer, and over 90,000 of these children die. Eighty percent of the children who die live in developing countries. In Egypt, for example, it is estimated that approximately 8,400 children will develop cancer in any year. Forty percent of these children will die due to lack of adequate treatment and facilities. This contrasts with 80–85 percent survival rates in the West, which occur because specialized pediatric oncology healthcare teams are able to offer intensive treatment programs in modern facilities. The Arab world and Africa needed a center of excellence dedicated only to children with cancer to achieve these rates.[42] An Egyptian organization, the Association of Friends of the National Cancer Institute (AFNCI), committed to constructing the first children's cancer hospital in this region. The Association also aimed to develop a comprehensive, sustainable healthcare system, where management and treatment utilized the most modern scientific approaches. It considered that only by following both programs would it ensure that survival rates improved.[43]

Obviously, the main challenge was to collect donations to realize this noble project. A national advertising campaign was initiated to build awareness and attract donations. Strategic partnerships were formed with different firms and institutions. Since 2002, over 40 companies and governmental departments have signed up to a creative campaign calling for a '1 Egyptian Pound donation' project, whereby employees agree to give a monthly donation to the hospital, to be sent as a group donation from the company. Some companies have also recognized the effort their employees are making for charity and are matching the total yearly donation. Further, celebrities volunteered to publicize the project. As a result, the project successfully collected the necessary funds to run a world-class hospital and started realizing its mission. A key success factor was gaining the trust of the Egyptian people. Salwa Serarfi, an Egyptian, said: "I'm very glad to see a hospital like that in our…country…. Thank you for all you do for these children."[44]

Government agencies have also shown an increased interest in marketing. For example, the Egyptian government designed a massive campaign aiming to gain people's trust of the tax-collection process. The campaign was successful and led to a significant increase in tax revenues. Various government agencies are now designing *social marketing campaigns* to discourage smoking, encourage birth control, and advise wise spending of money on important items. Such campaigns are considered crucial to increase the efficiency of governmental institutions and to improve the welfare of the people.[45]

Author Comment | Remember Figure 1.1 outlining the marketing process? Now, based on everything we've discussed in this chapter, we'll expand that figure to provide a road map for learning marketing throughout the rest of the text.

So, What is Marketing? Pulling It All Together (pp 28–30)

At the start of this chapter, **Figure 1.1** presented a simple model of the marketing process. Now that we've discussed all of the steps in the process, **Figure 1.6** presents an expanded model that will help you pull it all together. What is marketing? Simply put, marketing is the process of building profitable customer relationships by creating value for customers and capturing value in return.

The first four steps of the marketing process focus on creating value for customers. The company first gains a full understanding of the marketplace by researching customer needs and managing marketing information. It then designs a customer-driven marketing strategy based on the answers to two simple questions. The first question is "What consumers will we serve?" (market segmentation and targeting). Companies good at marketing know that they cannot serve all customers in every way. Instead, they need to focus their resources on the customers they can serve best and most profitably. The second marketing strategy question is "How can we best serve targeted customers?" (differentiation and positioning). Here, the marketer outlines a value proposition that spells out what values the company will deliver in order to win target customers.

With its marketing strategy decided, the company now constructs an integrated marketing program—consisting of a blend of the four marketing mix elements, or the four Ps—that transforms the marketing strategy into real value for customers. The company develops product offers and creates strong brand identities for them. It prices these offers to create real customer value and distributes the offers to make them available to target consumers. Finally, the company designs promotion programs that communicate the value proposition to target consumers and persuade them to act on the market offering.

Perhaps the most important step in the marketing process involves building value-laden, profitable relationships with target customers. Throughout the process, marketers

This expanded version of Figure 1.1 at the beginning of the chapter provides a good road map for the rest of the text. The underlying concept of the entire text is that marketing creates value *for* customers in order to capture value *from* customers in return.

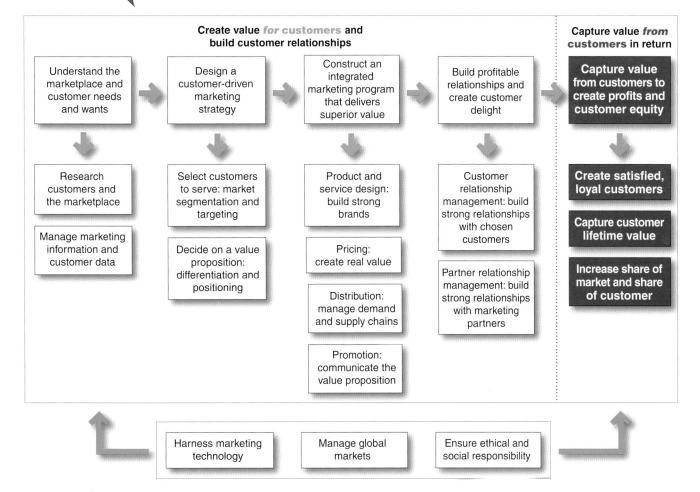

FIGURE | 1.6 An Expanded Model of the Marketing Process

practice customer relationship management to create customer satisfaction and delight. In creating customer value and relationships, however, the company cannot go it alone. It must work closely with marketing partners both inside the company and throughout the marketing system. Thus, beyond practicing good customer relationship management, firms must also practice good partner relationship management.

The first four steps in the marketing process create value *for* customers. In the final step, the company gains the rewards of its strong customer relationships by capturing value *from* customers. Delivering superior customer value creates highly satisfied customers who will buy more and will buy again. This helps the company to capture customer lifetime value and greater share of customer. The result is increased long-term customer equity for the firm.

Finally, in the face of today's changing marketing landscape, companies must take into account three additional factors. In building customer and partner relationships, they must harness marketing technology, take advantage of global opportunities, and ensure that they act in an ethical and socially responsible way.

Figure 1.6 provides a good road map to future chapters of the text. Chapters 1 and 2 introduce the marketing process, with a focus on building customer relationships and capturing value from customers. Chapters 3, 4, 5, and 6 address the first step of the marketing process—understanding the marketing environment, understanding consumer and business buyer behavior, and marketing research. In Chapter 7, we look more deeply into the two major marketing strategy decisions: selecting which customers to serve (segmentation and targeting) and deciding on a value proposition (differentiation and positioning). Chapters 8 through 14 discuss the marketing mix variables, one by one. Chapter 15 sums up customer-driven marketing strategy and creating a competitive advantage in the marketplace. Then, the final two chapters examine special marketing considerations: global and regional marketing, and marketing ethics and social responsibility.

REVIEWING Objectives AND KEY Terms

Today's successful companies—whether large or small, for-profit or not-for-profit, domestic or global—share a strong customer focus and a heavy commitment to marketing. The goal of marketing is to build and manage customer relationships. Marketing seeks to attract new customers by promising superior value and to keep and grow current customers by delivering satisfaction. To be successful, companies will have to be strongly market focused.

OBJECTIVE 1   Define marketing and outline the steps in the marketing process. (pp 4–6)

Marketing is the process by which companies create value for customers and build strong customer relationships in order to capture value from customers in return.

The marketing process involves five steps. The first four steps create value *for* customers. First, marketers need to understand the marketplace and customer needs and wants. Next, marketers design a customer-driven marketing strategy with the goal of getting, keeping, and growing target customers. In the third step, marketers construct a marketing program that actually delivers superior value. All of these steps form the basis for

the fourth step, building profitable customer relationships and creating customer delight. In the final step, the company reaps the rewards of strong customer relationships by capturing value *from* customers.

OBJECTIVE 2   Explain the importance of understanding customers and the marketplace, and identify the five core marketplace concepts. (pp 6–9)

Outstanding marketing companies go to great lengths to learn about and understand their customers' needs, wants, and demands. This understanding helps them to design want-satisfying market offerings and build value-laden customer relationships by which they can capture customer lifetime value and greater share of customers. The result is increased long-term customer equity for the firm.

The core marketplace concepts are needs, wants, and demands; market offerings (products, services, and experiences); value and satisfaction; exchange and relationships; and markets. Wants are the form taken by human needs when shaped by culture and individual personality. When backed by buying power, wants become demands. Companies address needs by putting forth a value proposition—a set of benefits that they promise to consumers to satisfy their needs. The value proposition is fulfilled through a market offering, which delivers customer value and satisfaction, resulting in long-term exchange relationships with customers.

OBJECTIVE 3 | Identify the key elements of a customer-driven marketing strategy and discuss the marketing management orientations that guide marketing strategy. (pp 9-13)

To design a winning marketing strategy, the company must first decide *who* it will serve. It does this by dividing the market into segments of customers (*market segmentation*) and selecting which segments it will cultivate (*target marketing*). Next, the company must decide *how* it will serve targeted customers (how it will *differentiate and position* itself in the marketplace).

Marketing management can adopt one of five competing market orientations. The *production concept* holds that management's task is to improve production efficiency and bring down prices. The *product concept* holds that consumers favor products that offer the most in quality, performance, and innovative features; thus, little promotional effort is required. The *selling concept* holds that consumers will not buy enough of the organization's products unless it undertakes a large-scale selling and promotion effort. The *marketing concept* holds that achieving organizational goals depends on determining the needs and wants of target markets and delivering the desired satisfactions more effectively and efficiently than competitors do. The *societal marketing concept* holds that generating customer satisfaction *and* long-run societal well-being are the keys to both achieving the company's goals and fulfilling its responsibilities.

OBJECTIVE 4 | Discuss customer relationship management and identify strategies for creating value for customers and capturing value from customers in return. (pp 13-24)

Broadly defined, *customer relationship management* is the process of building and maintaining profitable customer relationships by delivering superior customer value and satisfaction. The aim of customer relationship management is to produce high *customer equity,* the total combined customer lifetime values of all of the company's customers. The key to building lasting relationships is the creation of superior *customer value* and *satisfaction.*

Companies want not only to acquire profitable customers but also to build relationships that will keep them and grow share of customers. Different types of customers require different customer relationship management strategies. The marketer's aim is to build the *right relationships* with the *right customers.* In return for creating value *for* targeted customers, the company captures value *from* customers in the form of profits and customer equity.

In building customer relationships, good marketers realize that they cannot go it alone. They must work closely with marketing partners inside and outside the company. In addition to being good at customer relationship management, they must also be good at *partner relationship management.*

OBJECTIVE 5 | Describe the major trends and forces that are changing the marketing landscape in this age of relationships. (pp 24-30)

Dramatic changes are occurring in the marketing arena. The boom in computer, telecommunications, information, transportation, and other technologies has created exciting new ways to learn about and track customers, and to create products and services tailored to individual customer needs. It has also allowed new approaches by which marketers can target consumers more selectively and build closer, two-way customer relationships.

In an increasingly smaller world, many marketers are now connected *globally* with their customers and marketing partners. Today, almost every company, large or small, is touched in some way by global competition. Today's marketers are also reexamining their ethical and societal responsibilities. Marketers are being called upon to take greater responsibility for the social and environmental impact of their actions. Finally, in the past, marketing has been most widely applied in the for-profit business sector. In recent years, however, marketing has also become a major part of the strategies of many not-for-profit organizations, such as colleges, hospitals, museums, zoos, symphony orchestras, and religious establishments.

Pulling it all together, as discussed throughout the chapter, the major new developments in marketing can be summed up in a single word: *relationships.* Today, marketers of all kinds are taking advantage of new opportunities for building relationships with their customers, their marketing partners, and the world around them.

KEY Terms

OBJECTIVE 1

Marketing (p 5)

OBJECTIVE 2

Needs (p 6)
Wants (p 6)
Demands (p 6)
Market offering (p 7)
Marketing myopia (p 7)
Exchange (p 8)
Market (p 8)

OBJECTIVE 3

Marketing management (p 9)
Production concept (p 10)
Product concept (p 10)
Selling concept (p 11)
Marketing concept (p 11)
Societal marketing concept (p 12)

OBJECTIVE 4

Customer relationship management (p 14)

Customer-perceived value (p 14)
Customer satisfaction (p 14)
Consumer-generated marketing (p 18)
Partner relationship management (p 20)
Customer lifetime value (p 21)
Share of customer (p 22)
Customer equity (p 23)

DISCUSSING & APPLYING THE Concepts

Discussing the Concepts

1. What is marketing and what is its primary goal?

2. Compare and contrast customer needs, wants, and demands. Describe the need versus the want for the following products: Gatorade, Nike shoes, and iPod.

3. Explain how a company designs a customer-driven marketing strategy.

4. What are the five different marketing management orientations? Which orientation do you believe your school follows when marketing itself?

5. Explain the difference between *share of customer* and *customer equity*. Why are these concepts important to marketers?

6. How has the Internet changed consumers? Marketers?

Applying the Concepts

1. Ask five businesspeople from different industries (for example, food service, retailing, consumer-product manufacturing, industrial-product manufacturing, education, and so on) what they think marketing is. Evaluate their definitions and discuss whether or not they are consistent with the goal of creating customer value and managing profitable customer relationships.

2. In a small group, develop a marketing plan for a private student tutoring service. Who is your target market? How will you enable customers to get the best value? Define what you mean by value and develop the value proposition of your offering for this target market.

3. Define the different relationship levels companies can build with customers. Pick a company and describe the types of relationships you have with it.

FOCUS ON Technology

Embracing the marketing concept is one thing; implementing it is another. How do marketers know what consumers' needs and wants are so that they can develop a marketing strategy and mix to satisfy those needs and wants? Research, of course. But that takes time and resources, so many companies are turning to the Internet to get continuous, timely, and innovative information from customers. For example, software maker SAP developed its Business Process Expert (BPX) community by which customers share feedback in forums, blogs, and articles. Procter & Gamble wants you to 'Share Your Thoughts' at www.pg.com/getintouch/. But if you have a really good idea, perhaps you should look into licensing with P&G (see http://secure3.verticali.net/pg-connection-portal/ctx/noauth/PortalHome.do).

1. Explore the websites of other companies to learn how they get feedback from customers. Start by clicking on 'Contact Us,' then dig deeply to see if you can find a place where each company seeks or accepts feedback and ideas. Write a brief report of what you find.

2. Discuss other ways in which businesses can use the Internet to create greater customer value.

FOCUS ON Ethics

Did you drive a car today? Use a laptop computer? Buy a product in a store? If so, you emitted carbon dioxide (CO_2) and created a carbon footprint. All of us do that every day. Individuals and companies emit carbon dioxide in everyday activities. Many consumers feel bad about doing this; others expect companies to take action. What's the answer? Reducing carbon emissions is one solution, but another one is to offset your carbon emissions by purchasing carbon offsets and renewable energy certificates (RECs). Individual consumers do this, and companies are flocking to purchase carbon offsets for themselves or to offer to their customers, resulting in an estimated US$100 million market. And experts predict exponential growth over the next few years. Airlines routinely offer flyers the option of paying a few extra dollars to offset their carbon emissions. For example, JetBlue Airways introduced its *Jetting to Green* program that allows flyers to make their flight carbon-neutral for a very small fee. Flyers' donations will then support reforestation, wind, and waste management projects.

1. Learn more about carbon offsets and discuss four examples of how businesses are using them. In your opinion, are these companies embracing the societal marketing concept?

2. One criticism of carbon offsetting is that companies are not really helping the environment by changing their own behavior; instead they're merely buying 'environmental pardons.' Do you think carbon offsets are a responsible solution to environmental concerns? Write a brief essay debating this issue.

MARKETING BY THE Numbers

How much are you worth to a given company if you continue to purchase its brand for the rest of your life? Many marketers are grappling with that question, but it's not easy to determine how much a customer is worth to a company over his or her lifetime. Calculating customer lifetime value can be very complicated. Intuitively, however, it can be a fairly simple net present value calculation. To determine a basic customer lifetime value, each stream of profit is discounted back to its present value (PV) and then summed. The basic equation for calculating net present value (NPV) is as follows:

$$\mathrm{NPV} = \sum_{t=0}^{N} \frac{C_t}{(1 + r)^t}$$

Where,

t = time of the cash flow
N = total customer lifetime
r = discount rate

Ct = net cash flow (the profit) at time t (The initial cost of acquiring a customer would be a negative profit at time 0.)

NPV can be calculated easily on most financial calculators or by using one of the calculators available on the Internet, such as the one found at www.investopedia.com/calculator/NetPresentValue.aspx. For more discussion of the financial and quantitative implications of marketing decisions, see Appendix 2, Marketing by the Numbers.

1. Assume that a customer shops at a local grocery store and spends an average of US$150 a week and that the retailer earns a 5 percent margin. Calculate the customer lifetime value if this shopper remains loyal over a 10-year lifespan, assuming a 5 percent annual interest rate and no initial cost to acquire the customer.

2. Discuss how a business can increase a customer's lifetime value.

VIDEO Case

Harley-Davidson

Few brands engender such intense loyalty as that found in the hearts of Harley-Davidson owners. Long ago, Harley-Davidson realized that the best way to create lasting relationships with its customers was to understand them on their own terms. The company spends a great deal of time and money in pursuit of that goal. It wants to know who its customers are, how they think and feel, and why they buy a Harley. That customer-centric strategy has helped build Harley-Davidson into a multibillion-dollar company with the largest company-sponsored owner's group in the world.

Harley-Davidson has learned that it sells much more than motorcycles. The company sells a feeling of independence, individualism, and freedom. These strong emotional connections have made Harley-Davidson ownership much more of a lifestyle than merely a product consumption experience. To support that lifestyle, Harley-Davidson recognizes that its most important mar-

keting tool is the network of individuals who ride Harleys. For this reason, Harley-Davidson engages its customer base through company-sponsored travel adventures, events, and other things, such as clothes and accessories both for riders and for those who simply like to associate with the brand.

After viewing the video featuring Harley-Davidson, answer the following questions about managing profitable customer relationships:

1. How does Harley-Davidson build long-term customer relationships?

2. What is Harley-Davidson's value proposition?

3. Relate the concept of customer equity to Harley-Davidson. How does Harley-Davidson's strategy focus on the right relationships with the right customers?

COMPANY Case

Diwan: A Tale of Heart Over Matter

During their annual meeting on December 1, 2009, the managing partners of Al-Sharq for Bookstores—Diwan—examined the effects of their increased expansion over the last two years. The study of the financial statements revealed an unpredictable situation that jeopardized the partners' vision for the company. As a result of its fast expansion all over Egypt from December 2007 to December 2009, Diwan experienced a steep increase in costs which were not covered by the revenues generated. The execu-

tive board, Hind Wassef, Nihal Schawky, and Nadia Wassef, had to take several tough decisions before the end of January 2010 to save their business.

ENTREPRENEURS' BACKGROUND

Driven by their passion for reading and culture, Hind and Nadia Wassef graduated from the American University in Cairo (AUC) with a Bachelor of Arts in political science, and English and comparative literature in 1991 and 1994 respectively. Both sisters went on to get Master's degrees, in English and comparative literature, in 1994 and 1996. Afterwards, Nadia continued her education at the University of London, where she obtained another Master's degree in social anthropology in 2000. The start of the twenty-first century marked a shift in the sisters' interests away from social reform, especially women's rights, to an entrepreneurial pursuit that would not only re-shape their personal lives but also contribute to cultural reform in Egyptian society. Joined by their friends Ziad Bahaa El-Din, Nihal Schawky, and Ali Dessouki, they founded Diwan Bookstore.

The introduction of Diwan to the Egyptian market bridged the gap between book-starved customers and book retailers. Before the launch of Diwan, some bookstores in Egypt stocked only a limited selection of books, which were rarely current titles. In order to acquire their desired publications book-hungry individuals were forced to purchase them in other countries, where the book retailing industry is more developed, or to wait for the annual international book fair, which offers a great variety of new and used books. However, with the book fair held only once a year, individuals had to pay a lot of money in order to satisfy their yearlong book needs. For this reason, Diwan is considered a pioneer in the book retailing industry in Egypt.

Some fortunate coincidences guided the way: First was the availability of a retail space in Zamalek. Secondly, Alaa El Aswany, a prominent Egyptian author, had just published his most famous novel *Omaret Yacoubian* (The Yacoubian Building). This novel grabbed the attention of all sectors of Egyptian society as it addressed the social struggles currently facing the different segments of the society. The interest in reading and discussing this novel provided Diwan with an opportunity to capitalize on. Last but not least, some economic factors also affected Diwan, such as the devaluation of the Egyptian Pound, which meant that people preferred to spend their disposable income in local rather than foreign markets. These unplanned factors played a major role in Diwan's introduction to the Egyptian market.

DIWAN'S START-UP

The five friends wanted to create a recreational cultural experience for families with a disposable income. Until Diwan, the middle-class Egyptian family had to rely on restaurants for an outing. Motivated by their passion for books, the friends' idea of a boutique bookstore that sold niche products came to life. The first Diwan in Zamalek was launched on March 8, 2002.

Services offered by Diwan include, first, an extensive selection of books in Arabic, English, French, and German in many different categories, such as the arts, history, and fiction. Secondly, a multimedia section offers audio books, DVDs, educational CD-ROMs, music CDs, and PC games for both children and adults. In addition, Diwan offers more than just new multimedia releases; it also offers classics which aren't easily found in the Egyptian market. Also, Diwan has a stationery section in every branch that offers products from local and international suppliers, artistic calendars, bookmarks, and notebooks. Last, but not least, Diwan offers a variety of other services such as book binding, children's activities, corporate gifts and services, gift-wrapping, services for schools (including field trips, supplying books for school libraries), event hosting, and used book exchanges.

However, Diwan cannot be described as just another bookstore, for it has transformed the ordinary purchase of a book into a cultural retail experience. In addition, Diwan's priority as always has been customer service and satisfaction, which was one of the reasons why services such as delivery and loyalty cards were established. These loyalty cards allow customers to accumulate points based on their purchases. Upon reaching 100 points, customers

are rewarded with an LE 100 (US$20) voucher with which they can purchase any of the products offered by Diwan.

The success of Diwan wouldn't have come about without an exceptional management team, which has certain indispensable characteristics: they are strategic thinkers who have a long-term vision and are committed to the development of the organization. Hence, their main objective is to empower their teams in order to increase productivity and customer satisfaction. In addition, Diwan has partnered with several strategic partners who are equally passionate about the revolutionary transformation of the book culture in the Egyptian society. These partners include publishers, writers, local non-governmental organizations, and cultural centers. These partners not only aid Diwan in bringing books into the mainstream, they also diversify the services that Diwan has to offer as well as increase its target market.

DIWAN'S ORGANIZATIONAL CULTURE

Diwan's management culture is based on the passion that drives people to do what they do best while enjoying it. This culture can be felt as soon as one steps in one of Diwan's branches. One can see the values that have been set up from the beginning and which have played a gigantic role in the success that is witnessed today, such as passion, transparency, and sensitivity to the needs of the community. These values also emphasize teamwork instead of hierarchy. Trust, recognition, social responsibility, and innovation are also essential elements. Diwan's priority is customer satisfaction, with its welcoming, warm, and comforting atmosphere as well as its various services that seek customers' fulfillment.

Moreover, Diwan is constantly and relentlessly striving for innovation and the creation and implementation of new ideas that will further transform the concept of the traditional around-the-corner bookstore into a cultural center where intellectuals get together to improve the cultural status of the country and region. This innovativeness comes from constant learning in order to enrich and broaden customers' horizons. Consequently, Diwan has developed its own website in which it offers several features, such as discussion forums and book clubs, as well as insightful and inspirational daily entries on history, culture, and arts.

OVER-EXPENDITURE PROBLEM IN 2009

The success of their first branch in Zamalek encouraged Nadia and her partners to expand, in order to end the book retail famine all over Egypt. Citadel Capital, a private equity firm, supplied 40 percent of the initial investment capital, enabling Diwan to expand all over Cairo and the north coast. In a matter of two years, Diwan was able to revolutionize and change the concept of a traditional bookstore by opening the first book-retailing stations in huge shopping malls, such as the Diwan Station in Alexandria city center. Also, December 2007 witnessed the birth of the largest bookstore in Cairo: Diwan Heliopolis. Expansion continued to dominate Diwan's main business strategy until there were about 12 branches of Diwan eager to serve the awaiting market.

There are many costs to consider when opening a new branch. First, there's the rent, which varies according to the space and location. The refurbishment costs vary from LE 3000/m^2 (US$500) to LE 5000/ m^2 (US$850), with an average branch size of 120 m^2. In addition, there's the high cost of some essential parts such as the cashier unit and the décor that fits Diwan's culture and atmosphere. Needless to say, the merchandise and the books inventory, which includes some direct costs such as the purchase price and some other indirect costs such as shipping, custom duties, etc.

The idea in evaluating the breakeven point in Diwan's business model is to amortize the costs of all the branches on the sales of all of them. The amortization of the costs of each branch on its own sales would demonstrate that branches with the larger spaces are less costly than those with smaller spaces. Hence, the division of the costs on the total number of branches would lead to a breakeven and, from then on, the ability to estimate the percentage of the revenues compared to that of the costs.

For Diwan, the opening of its branches had negative impact that appeared during the analysis of the expenses and revenues. The analysis demonstrated a 60 percent deficit in the budget. And the revenues that were generated by the different outlets were covering only 40 percent of the costs. Therefore, an immediate decision had to be made in order to avoid further losses and to break even.

FUTURE OF DIWAN

In an effort to sustain its market share, Diwan's innovativeness is impeccable. By using the experiences of the more developed book cultures in other countries, where book retail has had a chance to mature, Diwan is able to bring in many new ideas to the Egyptian market, and hence, it is able to sustain its everlasting development. The next step for Diwan is to introduce e-books, making use of the spread of different technologies such as Apple's iPad and Kindle. Also to expand the range of social-related events, such as lectures given by prominent people on different subjects.

CONCLUSION

Diwan is more than just a book retailer; it offers lots of activities for the people of Egypt as a whole—for children and adults. As well as serving the book-hungry population, Diwan also meets the cultural and intellectual needs of Egyptian society. Diwan has revolutionized the book-buying experience in Egypt, but its success has come at a cost that threatens the company's profits and operations. The time has come for Diwan to re-shape its business model. According to Nadia Wassef, "The best business decisions are made at the worst of times and the worst business decisions are made at the best of times." One option is for Diwan to build a strong bond with its loyal customers—the ones that value the services offered and could potentially bring in new customers in the future.

Questions for Discussion

1. Give examples of needs, wants, and demands that Diwan's customers demonstrate, differentiating each of these three concepts.

2. In detail, describe all facets of Diwan's product offering.

3. Which of the five marketing management concepts best describes Diwan?

4. Discuss in detail the value that Diwan creates for its customers.

5. Is Diwan likely to be successful in continuing to build customer relationships? Why or why not?

Source: El-Khazindar Business Research and Case Center (KCC), School of Business, The American University in Cairo; Case authored by May M. Kamal.

Chapter 2

Part 1	Defining Marketing and the Marketing Process (Chapters 1, 2)
Part 2	Understanding the Marketplace and Consumers (Chapters 3, 4, 5, 6)
Part 3	Designing a Customer-Driven Strategy and Mix (Chapters 7, 8, 9, 10, 11, 12, 13, 14)
Part 4	Extending Marketing (Chapters 15, 16, 17)

Company and Marketing

Strategy Partnering to Build Customer Relationships

Chapter PREVIEW

In the first chapter, we explored the marketing process by which companies create value for consumers in order to capture value from them in return. We will now dig deeper into steps two and three of the marketing process—designing customer-driven marketing strategies and constructing marketing programs. First, we look at the organization's overall strategic planning, which guides marketing strategy and planning. Next, we discuss how, guided by the strategic plan, marketers partner closely with others inside and outside the firm to create value for customers. We then examine marketing strategy and planning—how

marketers choose target markets, position their market offerings, develop a marketing mix, and manage their marketing programs. Finally, we look at the important step of measuring and managing return on marketing investment.

But first, let's look at the Olympic brand. Staging an Olympic Games is an enormous challenge for any city or country. Venues and accommodation need to be constructed for the athletes, and the infrastructure of the host city needs to be transformed. In order to achieve success, these physical issues have to be addressed, along with the ability to market the spectacle to an ever-broadening world audience. None of this is possible unless sponsors are brought onboard at the earliest opportunity and they are able to see tangible benefits from their involvement.

The Olympic brand is a powerful worldwide symbol representing not only sports but also a celebration of the best in the world and an opportunity for nations to join together and compete for glory. The Beijing Olympics in 2008 was immensely popular worldwide and successful, delivering a quality experience for the athletes, spectators, and millions of viewers around the world. It was also vital in rebranding and repackaging China as a modern nation. China hoped that the Olympics would help it build business links that would push the country forward. The massive effort to deliver the Games was not without cost; billions were invested, and some of this funding came from sponsors and partners.

The London 2012 Olympic Games promises to be another tremendous spectacle, although the budget is only roughly half of what Beijing's was. Yet sponsors and partners including Visa, Coca-Cola, Adidas, and British Airways have already signed up. The purpose of the partnerships is not merely financial; it is about building customer relationships, both for the Games and for the businesses.

On a slightly less grand level, the Olympics provides smaller businesses with an opportunity to be involved, provide products and services, and promote the fact that they have an association with the 2012 Olympics. In June 2008, before the Beijing Olympics had even got underway, the latest London 2012 business-engagement figures were published. Business engagement refers to the numbers of companies registered with the Olympics to provide the event with products and services. Nearly 90 percent of the registered companies (18,000) were small-to-medium sized.

The Olympic Delivery Authority (ODA) and the London Organizing Committee (LOCOG) will allocate over US$9 bil-

lion of work to various businesses. There will be at least 75,000 business opportunities, including the direct contracts and the supply chains used to fulfill those contracts. John Armitt, ODA chairman, had been involved in numerous discussions with British businesses and had found that an enormous number were keen to be involved in the London 2012 Games. At this stage it was smaller businesses that were finding opportunities, many being able to establish themselves as key providers with experience in dealing with a project of this size. Armitt believed that this would put them in a prime position to compete with even larger contractors in the future. Armitt recognized it was a challenging project and it needed the best British businesses to keep it on track.

The Organizing Committee's chief executive, Paul Deighton, was suitably impressed with the British business response to the London 2012 Business Network. The London 2012 procurement team and business development partners had worked hard to encourage as many businesses as possible to become involved at some level in providing

The Olympic logo is one of the world's most powerful brands, attracting sponsorship deals from companies all over the world.

goods and services. The push would go on into 2009, with increasing numbers of U.K. businesses registering on the 'Compete For' system. By registering on this system Deighton was certain that the businesses would not regret getting involved in the Games, as it represented a "lifetime business opportunity."

Tessa Jowell, the former Olympics Minister, has discussed the potential business benefits of the Olympic Games for local enterprises, pointing out that, of the 650 companies supplying the games as of mid-2008, 70 were small- and medium-sized enterprises. In the first six months of 2008, 500 companies were signing up to supply the London Olympics each week, demonstrating the British business community's determination to make the most of the economic opportunities on offer. Jowell also explained that, besides their most obvious goal – working to deliver the Olympics on schedule and to budget – the London 2012 team also aimed to promote long-term economic growth in Britain, and foster a successful new generation of workers and businesses.

Lord Digby Jones, previously the U.K.'s Minister for Trade and Investment, also noted the opportunities that the Olympics represent for local businesses. He, too, pointed out that many small- and medium-sized businesses had won contracts for work around the 2012 London Olympic and Paralympics Games, and that those winning businesses would help to drive economic growth, as well as demonstrating the skills and capabilities of British businesses and the British workforce before an enormous international audience. The argument can be made that association with the Olympics is sure to be a positive for businesses, beyond the value of any contract that a business might be able to secure.

Clearly, the marketing opportunities are enormous for partner businesses and suppliers to the Olympics. However, one of the key concerns is the use of the Olympic logos by businesses that have nothing

to do with the event. According to intellectual property expert Tracey Huxley, "The outstanding success of Team Great Britain in China this summer [2008] is likely to encourage companies to use the growth of national pride and the gathering momentum of London 2012 in their marketing, both in the immediate future and throughout the next four years." Adidas, for example, sponsored the Beijing Games and is a partner with

Impossible is nothing: Adidas was one of the main sponsors of the Beijing Olympics in 2008. The company's ad campaign featured medal-hopeful athletes from countries across the globe, reflecting the aspirational nature of Adidas' target markets.

London 2012. The company ran a series of advertisements with medal-winning athletes that feature the phrase: "Impossible is Nothing." Visa's advertisements proudly announced "The Journey to London 2012 Starts Now."

> **The huge commercial possibilities of being associated with the Olympic brand cannot be underestimated. Businesses that sponsor the Olympics or those that provide products and services, or for that matter suppliers, make full use of their association with the Olympics. This consists of a full partnership approach aimed at securing and building customer relationships. Before the Beijing Games were even over, the push to be associated with the London 2012 Olympics Games had begun.**

Strategic planning
The process of developing and maintaining a strategic fit between the organization's goals and capabilities and its changing marketing opportunities.

Like Beijing 2008 and London 2012, outstanding marketing organizations employ strongly customer-driven marketing strategies and programs that create customer value and relationships. These marketing strategies and programs, however, are guided by broader companywide strategic plans, which must also be customer focused. Thus, to understand the role of marketing, we must first understand the organization's overall strategic-planning process.

Author Comment | Companywide strategic planning guides marketing strategy and planning. Like marketing strategy, the company's broad strategy must also be customer focused.

Companywide Strategic Planning: Defining Marketing's Role (pp 37–41)

Each company must find the game plan for long-run survival and growth that makes the most sense given its specific situation, opportunities, objectives, and resources. This is the focus of **strategic planning**—the process of developing and maintaining a

Objective Outline

strategic fit between the organization's goals and capabilities and its changing marketing opportunities.

Strategic planning sets the stage for the rest of the planning in the firm. Companies usually prepare annual plans, long-range plans, and strategic plans. The annual and long-range plans deal with the company's current businesses and how to keep them going. In contrast, the strategic plan involves adapting the firm to take advantage of opportunities in its constantly changing environment.

At the corporate level, the company starts the strategic-planning process by defining its overall purpose and mission (see ⬤ **Figure 2.1**). This mission is then turned into detailed supporting objectives that guide the whole company. Next, headquarters decides what portfolio of businesses and products is best for the company and how much support to give each one. In turn, each business and product develops detailed marketing and other departmental plans that support the companywide plan. Thus, marketing planning occurs at the business-unit, product, and market levels. It supports company strategic planning with more detailed plans for specific marketing opportunities.

FIGURE | **2.1** Steps in Strategic Planning

Defining a Market-Oriented Mission

An organization exists to accomplish something, and this purpose should be clearly stated. Developing an effective mission begins with the following questions: What is our business? Who is the customer? What do consumers value? What *should* our business be? These simple-sounding questions are among the most difficult the company will ever have to answer. Successful companies continuously raise these questions and answer them carefully and completely.

Many organizations develop formal mission statements that answer these questions. A **mission statement** is a statement of the organization's purpose—what it wants to accomplish in the larger environment. A clear mission statement acts as an 'invisible hand' that guides people in the organization. Studies have shown that firms with well-crafted mission statements have better organizational and financial performance.[1]

Some companies define their missions shortsightedly in product or technology terms ("We make and sell furniture" or "We are a chemical-processing firm"). But mission statements should be *market oriented* and defined in terms of satisfying basic customer needs. Products and technologies eventually become outdated, but basic market needs may last forever. Microsoft's mission isn't simply to sell software packages. Its mission is to "help people and businesses throughout the world realize their full potential."[2] Likewise, Spinneys in Dubai developed the following mission statement: "We are dedicated to consistent growth by providing our markets with distinct high quality products and services that meet & exceed the needs of our customers and principals. We will lead our respective fields into the future by creating customer loyalty and principal partnerships through a well trained and dedicated workforce."[3] ● **Table 2.1** provides several other examples of product-oriented versus market-oriented business definitions.

Mission statements should be meaningful and specific yet motivating. They should emphasize the company's strengths in the marketplace. Too often, mission statements are written for public relations purposes and lack specific, workable guidelines.[4]

As Jack Welch, former GE super-CEO, points out, there are not enough business leaders who understand how to craft mission statements which communicate real meaning and direction. He believes that most mission statements descend into jargon or are too vague to mean anything to anyone; too many are written along the lines of "our mission is to be the best company in our industry". He advises companies to make choices about how they will actually be successful and win. For example, Nike's old statement "Crush Reebok" certainly conveyed its direction. And Google avoids a generic statement such as "We will be the best search engine in the world." Instead it has crafted an inspiring and clear mission: "To organize the world's information and make it universally accessible and useful."

Finally, a company's mission should not be stated as making more sales or profits—profits are only a reward for creating value for customers. A company's employees need to feel that their work is significant and that it contributes to people's lives. For example, Microsoft's aim is to help people to "realize their potential." "Your potential, our passion," says the company. Target tells customers to "Expect more. Pay less."

Setting Company Objectives and Goals

The company needs to turn its mission into detailed supporting objectives for each level of management. Each manager should have objectives and be responsible for reaching them. For example, Procter & Gamble (P&G) makes and markets a diverse product mix that includes everything from detergents,

Mission statement
A statement of the organization's purpose—what it wants to accomplish in the larger environment.

Spinneys' mission statement expresses its commitment to providing "distinct high quality products and services that meet & exceed the needs of our customers."

● TABLE | 2.1   Market-Oriented Business Definitions

Company	Product-Oriented Definition	Market-Oriented Definition
Amazon.com	We sell books, videos, CDs, toys, consumer electronics, hardware, housewares, and other products online.	We make the Internet buying experience fast, easy, and enjoyable—we're the place where you can find and discover anything you want to buy online.
Aramex	We enable and facilitate regional and global trade and commerce.	We aim to be recognized as one of the top five global logistics and transportation companies.
Carrefour	We run discount stores.	We deliver the best prices and the best merchandise.
Disney	We run theme parks.	We create fantasies—a place where dreams come true and the world still works the way it's supposed to.
Google	We provide the world's best online search engine.	We help you organize the world's information and make it universally accessible and useful.
Nike	We sell athletic shoes and apparel.	We bring inspiration and innovation to every athlete* in the world. (*If you have a body, you are an athlete.)
Revlon	We make cosmetics.	We sell lifestyle and self-expression; success and status; memories, hopes, and dreams.
Ritz-Carlton Hotels	We rent rooms.	We create the Ritz-Carlton experience—one that enlivens the senses, instills well-being, and fulfills even the unexpressed wishes and needs of our guests.
SEKEM	We provide organic products.	We seek curing the environment via biodynamic agriculture methods while providing customers with a variety of organic and healthy products.
Zain	We provide mobile telecommunications services.	*World-class telecommunications services* is our business and innovation is how we achieve success.

P&G's overall objective is to build profitable customer relationships by developing better products.

baby care, and hair care products, among others. But P&G does more than just produce such products. Its mission includes to "improve the lives of the world's consumers."

> Companies should define themselves not in terms of what they do or make ("We sell athletic shoes") but in terms of how they create value for customers ("We bring inspiration and innovation to every athlete in the world").

This broad mission leads to a hierarchy of objectives, including business objectives and marketing objectives. P&G's overall objective is to build profitable customer relationships by developing better products. It does this by investing in research—P&G's principles state that "innovation is the cornerstone of our success."[5] Its R&D is expensive and requires improved profits to reinvest back into research programs. So improving profits becomes another major P&G objective. Profits can be improved by increasing sales or reducing costs. Sales can be increased by improving the company's share of domestic and international markets. These goals then become the company's current marketing objectives.

Marketing strategies and programs must be developed to support these marketing objectives. To increase its market share, P&G might increase its products' availability and promotion in existing markets. To enter new global markets, the company can create new local partnerships within targeted countries.

These are P&G's broad marketing strategies. Each broad marketing strategy must then be defined in greater detail. For example, increasing the product's promotion may require more salespeople, advertising, and public relations efforts; if so, both requirements will need to be spelled out. In this way, the firm's mission is translated into a set of objectives for the current period.

Zain, a pioneering mobile telecommunications provider, has well-defined objectives which are translated into its mission statement: "Ultimately, our mission can be distilled down to this: to cement Zain as a leading global mobile operator that provides professional, world-class mobile and data services to all our customers, wherever they are, worldwide. And we aim to achieve this by exceeding our customers' expectations, rewarding our employees, and providing returns beyond reasonable expectations for our shareholders."[6]

Author Comment Companies need to identify the attractiveness of each of its products in order to effectively allocate its resources.

Designing The Business Portfolio (pp 41–46)

Guided by the company's mission statement and objectives, management now must plan its **business portfolio**—the collection of businesses and products that make up the company. The best business portfolio is the one that best fits the company's strengths and weaknesses to opportunities in the environment. Business portfolio planning involves two steps. First, the company must analyze its *current* business portfolio and decide which businesses should receive more, less, or no investment. Secondly, it must shape the *future* portfolio by developing strategies for growth and downsizing.

Business portfolio
The collection of businesses and products that make up the company.

Analyzing the Current Business Portfolio

The major activity in strategic planning is business **portfolio analysis**, whereby management evaluates the products and businesses that make up the company. The company will want to put strong resources into its more profitable businesses and phase down or drop its weaker ones.

Portfolio analysis
The process by which management evaluates the products and businesses that make up the company.

Management's first step is to identify the key businesses that make up the company, called *strategic business unit* (SBUs). An SBU can be a company division, a product line within a division, or sometimes a single product or brand. The company next assesses the attractiveness of its various SBUs and decides how much support each deserves. When designing a business portfolio, it's a good idea to add and support products and businesses that fit closely with the firm's core philosophy and competencies.

The purpose of strategic planning is to find ways in which the company can best use its strengths to take advantage of attractive opportunities in the environment. So most standard portfolio analysis methods evaluate SBUs on two important dimensions—the attractiveness of the SBU's market or industry and the strength of the SBU's position in that market or industry. The best-known portfolio-planning method was developed by the Boston Consulting Group, a leading management consulting firm.[7]

Growth-share matrix
A portfolio-planning method that evaluates a company's strategic business units in terms of its market growth rate and relative market share. SBUs are classified as stars, cash cows, question marks, or dogs.

The Boston Consulting Group Approach. Using the now-classic Boston Consulting Group (BCG) approach, a company classifies all its SBUs according to the **growth-share matrix** as shown in ⬛ **Figure 2.2**. On the vertical axis, *market growth rate* provides a measure

⬛**FIGURE | 2.2**
The BCG Growth-Share Matrix

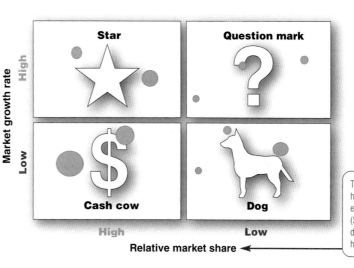

Under this classic Boston Consulting Group portfolio planning approach, the company invests funds from mature, successful products and businesses (cash cows) to support promising products and businesses in faster-growing markets (stars and question marks), hoping to turn them into future cash cows.

The company must decide how much it will invest in each product or business (SBU). For each SBU, it must decide whether to build, hold, harvest, or divest.

of market attractiveness. On the horizontal axis, *relative market share* serves as a measure of company strength in the market. The growth-share matrix defines four types of SBUs:

Stars. Stars are high-growth, high-share businesses or products. They often need heavy investments to finance their rapid growth. Eventually their growth will slow down, and they will turn into cash cows.

Cash cows. Cash cows are low-growth, high-share businesses or products. These established and successful SBUs need less investment to hold their market share. Thus, they produce a lot of cash that the company uses to pay its bills and to support other SBUs that need investment.

Question marks. Question marks are low-share business units in high-growth markets. They require a lot of cash to hold their share, let alone increase it. Management has to think hard about which question marks it should try to build into stars and which should be phased out.

Dogs. Dogs are low-growth, low-share businesses and products. They may generate enough cash to maintain themselves but do not promise to be large sources of cash.

The 10 circles in the growth-share matrix represent a company's 10 current SBUs. The company has two stars, two cash cows, three question marks, and three dogs. The areas of the circles are proportional to the SBU's dollar sales. This company is in fair shape, although not in good shape. It wants to invest in the more promising question marks to make them stars and to maintain the stars so that they will become cash cows as their markets mature. Fortunately, it has two good-sized cash cows. Income from these cash cows will help finance the company's question marks, stars, and dogs. The company should take some decisive action concerning its dogs and its question marks.

Once it has classified its SBUs, the company must determine what role each will play in the future. One of four strategies can be pursued for each SBU. The company can invest more in the business unit in order to *build* its share. Or it can invest just enough to *hold* the SBU's share at the current level. It can *harvest* the SBU, milking its short-term cash flow regardless of the long-term effect. Finally, the company can *divest* the SBU by selling it or phasing it out and using the resources elsewhere.

As time passes, SBUs change their positions in the growth-share matrix. Many SBUs start out as question marks and move into the star category if they succeed. They later become cash cows as market growth falls, then finally die off or turn into dogs toward the end of their lifecycle. The company needs to add new products and units continuously so that some of them will become stars and, eventually, cash cows that will help finance other SBUs.

Problems with Matrix Approaches.   The BCG and other formal methods revolutionized strategic planning. However, such centralized approaches have limitations: They can be difficult, time consuming, and costly to implement. Management may find it difficult to define SBUs and measure market share and growth. In addition, these approaches focus on classifying *current* businesses, but provide little advice for *future* planning.

Because of such problems, many companies have dropped formal matrix methods in favor of more customized approaches that better suit their specific situations. Moreover, unlike former strategic-planning efforts that rested mostly in the hands of senior managers at company headquarters, today's

Managing the business portfolio: Most people think of Disney as theme parks and wholesome family entertainment, but over the past two decades it has become a sprawling collection of media and entertainment businesses, even including cruises, that requires big doses of the famed 'Disney Magic' to manage.

strategic planning has been decentralized. Increasingly, companies are placing responsibility for strategic planning in the hands of cross-functional teams of divisional managers who are close to their markets.

For example, consider The Walt Disney Company. Most people think of Disney as theme parks and wholesome family entertainment. But in the mid-1980s Disney set up a powerful, centralized strategic-planning group to guide the company's direction and growth. Over the next two decades, the strategic-planning group turned The Walt Disney Company into a huge and diverse collection of media and entertainment businesses. The sprawling Disney grew to include everything from theme resorts and film studios (Walt Disney Pictures, Touchstone Pictures, Hollywood Pictures, and others) to media networks (ABC plus Disney Channel, ESPN, A&E, History Channel, and a half dozen others) to consumer products and a cruise line. The newly transformed company proved hard to manage and performed unevenly. Recently, Disney disbanded the centralized strategic-planning unit, decentralizing its functions to Disney division managers.

Developing Strategies for Growth and Downsizing

Beyond evaluating current businesses, designing the business portfolio involves finding businesses and products the company should consider in the future. Companies need growth if they are to compete more effectively, satisfy their stakeholders, and attract top talent. "Growth is pure oxygen," states one executive. "It creates a vital, enthusiastic corporation where people see genuine opportunity." At the same time, a firm must be careful not to make growth itself an objective. The company's objective must be to manage "profitable growth."[8] **Real Marketing 2.1** considers one company which is aiming to achieve profitable growth in its own way.

Marketing has the main responsibility for achieving profitable growth for the company. Marketing needs to identify, evaluate, and select market opportunities and lay down strategies for capturing them. One useful device for identifying growth opportunities is the **product/market expansion grid**, shown in **Figure 2.3**.[9] We apply it here to Orascom Group, an Egyptian business group with a wide portfolio of products. The group established in 1950 focusing on the construction industry, then it expanded into a variety of other industries, including telecommunications, hotels and development, and technology solutions.

First, Orascom considered whether the company could achieve deeper **market penetration**—making more sales by focusing on the construction industry. It generated growth through marketing mix improvements—primarily through adjustments to its product offerings and quality. For example, Orascom Construction Industries now offers a variety of services that satisfy customers' needs and which have helped to penetrate the market and build a positive image in the market.

Secondly, Orascom considered possibilities for **market development**—identifying and developing new markets for its current products. For instance, managers could review new *demographic markets* within Egypt. Managers could also explore new *geographical markets*. Orascom Construction Industries expanded swiftly into regional and international markets. The company has expanded its operations in Western Europe, Central and Eastern

Product/market expansion grid
A portfolio-planning tool for identifying company growth opportunities through market penetration, market development, product development, or diversification.

Market penetration
A strategy for company growth by increasing sales of current products to current market segments without changing the product.

Market development
A strategy for company growth by identifying and developing new market segments for current company products.

FIGURE | 2.3
Product/Market Expansion Grid

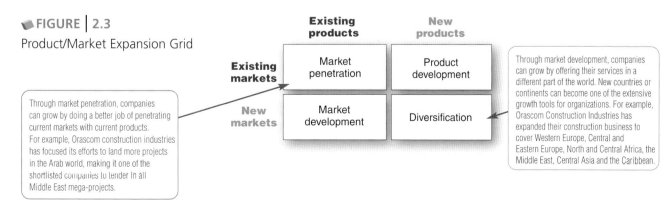

Through market penetration, companies can grow by doing a better job of penetrating current markets with current products. For example, Orascom construction industries has focused its efforts to land more projects in the Arab world, making it one of the shortlisted companies to tender In all Middle East mega-projects.

Through market development, companies can grow by offering their services in a different part of the world. New countries or continents can become one of the extensive growth tools for organizations. For example, Orascom Construction Industries has expanded their construction business to cover Western Europe, Central and Eastern Europe, North and Central Africa, the Middle East, Central Asia and the Caribbean.

	Existing products	**New products**
Existing markets	Market penetration	Product development
New markets	Market development	Diversification

Real Marketing 2.1

Mo'men Sandwich: A Recipe for Success

Mo'men, the sandwich company, launched its first branch in 1988 as a family-run business for sandwich takeaway and delivery. Today, Mo'men is the third biggest player in Egypt's fast-food market and has the third biggest market share, serving over 9.5 million customers a year. This transformation from a small family business to one of Egypt's leading fast-food players did not happen overnight; it is the result of a combination of ingredients which, when put together, created the perfect recipe for success.

When the three Mo'men brothers first launched Mo'men, their main focus was to define its brand identity and product offering. They succeeded in building a brand with a local and family feel. They also succeeded at differentiating Mo'men's product offering across three levels: product composition, product packaging, and product variety. Once brand identity and product offering were defined, the next challenge was to expand Mo'men's operations across Egypt without compromising the quality of its products or services. In order to do so, clearly defined operating standards had to be established and implemented. Accordingly, the Mo'men brothers developed the Mo'men standard review to audit the company's operations and ensure consistency across all branches.

The idea behind Mo'men was to offer innovative sandwiches for quick pick-up or delivery to customers. The first branch opened in Heliopolis and did not have a sit-in area for dining. The business started with a capital of EGP 12,000 (US$2,000) and no brand recognition. When the company launched, the main objective of the three brothers was to turn the store into a profitable, revenue-generating business; they successfully did so.

The first ingredient in Mo'men's success was finding a catchy, easy-to-remember name that set it apart from international and local brands that would enter the Egyptian market. The name Mo'men was initially chosen in reference to the last name of the three founding brothers. This name has built the foundation for Mo'men's brand image; it is a catchy, easy-to-remember name with a local ring to it. "'Mo'men', translating into 'faithful' or 'believer', has a differentiated proposition from international competitors. It is seen as a home-grown champion in the Egyptian market which offers a blend between local taste and culture with international branding and quality."

Building a brand based on a family name instiled the second ingredient in Mo'men's branding success: a strong sense of family culture. From the start of its operations in 1988 till today, Mo'men continues to value and emphasize the sense of family in its working culture. For instance, when Mo'men opened its second branch in Agamy, a popular summer destination in Egypt, its staff wore shorts and T-shirts to mirror the culture of its clients. The Agamy branch became an instant hit, and further expanded recognition of the Mo'men brand.

The second ingredient to Mo'men's success is differentiation of its products. Mo'men was able to differentiate its products on three levels: product composition, product variety, and product packaging. Its key competitive advantage was to offer innovative sandwiches that were not already present in the market. The ingredients used were available and well-known in the market. However, the Mo'men brothers succeeded in combining these ingredients to create sandwiches that had an extra twist to them. For instance, when Mo'men first started, it was renowned for its shawarma

Mo'men has expanded its fast-food operations from a small family-run branch in Cairo, to serving around 10 million customers a year. It has had to manage its growth strategy carefully in order to maintain its high quality standards.

sandwiches. The success of the shawarma sandwiches was due to the addition of extra spices that other shawarma sellers did not add. There was no research and development (R&D) department. Instead, the three Mo'men brothers would just try adding or removing ingredients until they found the perfect combination for the company's signature sandwiches. That is exactly how some of Mo'men's signature sandwiches, such as the Chicken Keuive, were developed.

Mo'men also provided its customers with a large variety of sandwiches, making it one of the few players in the Egyptian fast-food market to offer such a wide range of choices. For instance, Mo'men offers customers six categories of food: beef, chicken, seafood, salads, snacks, and deserts. This categorization is similar to other players in

---

Product development

A strategy for company growth by offering modified or new products to current market segments.

Europe, North and Central Africa, the Arab world, Central Asia, and the Caribbean with great success. Furthermore, the company's contracting services are offered in various public and private projects, primarily in the Arab world, North Africa, and Central Asia.

Thirdly, management could consider **product development**—offering modified or new products to current markets. Orascom Construction offered a variety of contracting services to support its current operations and to satisfy its current customers. It succeeded

the market. However, what is different is the large number of different products offered under each category. Mo'men offers 12 beef sandwiches, 12 chicken sandwiches, 6 seafood sandwiches, 6 types of salads, and 5 different deserts; thereby ensuring every customer's taste is met.

The Mo'men brothers then took an extra step in further differentiating their products. Not only did their sandwiches taste different, they were also packaged differently. All sandwiches are packed in a colorful, high-quality carton, which is color-coded according to type of sandwich. Beef sandwiches are packed in red cartons, chicken sandwiches are packed in warm yellow cartons, and seafood sandwiches are packed in golden yellow cartons.

As production of Mo'men sandwiches began to grow, the Mo'men brothers wanted to ensure that all Mo'men sandwiches looked and tasted the same, regardless of who assembled them and where they were served. In order to do so, the Mo'men brothers began to define operating standards. Operating standards included the exact amount of ingredients to be used in each sandwich, the amount of time each sandwich should be served in store, the exact way of communicating an order between staff, and so on. The Mo'men brothers recall that the starting point for defining operating standards began with defining the exact amount of condiments to be used in each sandwich. Condiment jars were weighed before and after each sandwich was made. The net weight became the set target for condiment use per sandwich. Today, each Mo'men store has identical menus and identical sandwiches. Clearly defined operating standards and operating processes have enabled Mo'men to grow without compromising the quality of its products or service.

Clear definition of operating standards and processes enabled Mo'men to deliver the same level of quality across its branches. However, in order to sustain this level of quality over time, a special ingredient needed to be present: the auditing of operating standards and processes. Auditing occurs in a cycle. It refers to the examination of each operating standard to ensure it is fully followed as well as the continuous identification of ways to improve each operating standard. For example, when it comes to auditing operating standards for Mo'men sandwich delivery, an auditor examines each step involved in delivering the Mo'men sandwich, sets a target for the time this process should take, and continuously looks for ways to exceed the target delivery time. These new ways become the basis for a new action plan to improve delivery time, which is then audited again. Accordingly, the company has developed the Mo'men standard review (MSR), which is a scoring system for each restaurant, designed specifically to audit Mo'men's level of service, quality, and cleanliness. Each branch has a quality team which is responsible for filling out the MSR and communicating it to the branch's staff. The MSR pinpoints critical areas of operational improvement. On reviewing the score, the branch's staff can identify operational strengths as well as development areas. These development areas form the basis of a new action plan to further improve operations.

This combination of ingredients has created the perfect recipe for Mo'men's local success. "Mo'men restaurants are serving more than double the number of customers and achieving double the sales per restaurant compared with any of the international brands operating in Egypt. Today, Mo'men restaurants are in the process of rapid expansion to open more restaurants, serving Mo'men sandwich lovers all over Egypt and Overseas."

Mo'men's next challenge is global expansion of its brand and products. It has set out on this path via a series of joint ventures and acquisitions. In October 2005, Mo'men opened its first branch in Sudan, which became an instant success, generating revenues four times those forecasted before its opening. Since then Mo'men has opened up branches across the Arab world and beyond, with eight branches in Bahrain, three in Libya, two in Sudan, one in Malaysia, and one in the UAE. The UAE expansion began in 2007 as a joint venture between Mo'men and Al Islami Food, with a 15-year span and a total investment of US$22 million. In Malaysia, Mo'men is looking at acquiring a chain of about 20 restaurants for approximately US$5 million. According to Mo'men's chairman, the company is looking to acquire various local firms working in food production outside of the meat and dairy sector, and has up to US$12.5 million to expand its market presence globally. Saudi Arabia, Kuwait, and the Emirates are among the markets in which the group is eyeing acquisitions.

Mo'men has gone from a small local takeaway and delivery business to Egypt's third largest fast-food player after McDonald's and KFC. The Mo'men brothers leveraged Mo'men's success in Egypt and aspired for global growth. Through a series of acquisitions and joint ventures, they were able to expand gradually throughout the Arab world. Mo'men's plans do not stop at global expansion. Mo'men Group is planning to sell a 40 percent stake in itself in an initial public offering (IPO) in late 2012, reveals Mohammad Mo'men, chairman of Mo'men. The IPO's value "would not be less than US$70 million and the preliminary date is the end of 2012," Mo'men says. If Mo'men moves in this direction, its main challenge will be to maintain a favorable environment for effective corporate governance, where each employee's role is clearly defined and communicated, starting from the chairman all the way to the cleaner. Corporate governance is the key ingredient in maintaining transparency to investors.

Sources: "Actis Announces a Significant Investment in Mo'men, A Leading Egyptian Consumer Business," Actis company press release, July 30, 2008, www.act.is; "Al Islami Foods Signs AED80 Million Joint Venture with Mo'men Group of Egypt," Al Bawaba, May 9, 2007, www1.albawaba.com; "Mo'men Group: Private Company Information," *Bloomberg BusinessWeek*, July 10, 2010, http://investing.businessweek.com; with additional information from sources including the Mo'men Group website, www.momen-chain.com/profile/; "Al Islami Foods Launches Mo'men Chain of Restaurant in UAE," *AMEInfo*, October 14, 2009, www.ameinfo.com/212249.html; Arabian Franchise website, www.arabianfranchise.com/?p=523.

This case was authored by Lina El-Hussamy, El-Khazindar Business Research and Case Center (KCC), School of Business, The American University in Cairo.

Diversification

A strategy for company growth through starting up or acquiring businesses outside of the company's current products and markets.

to offer comprehensive services that helped the company generate incremental sales by capitalizing on the trust of its existing customers.

Fourthly, Orascom might consider **diversification**—starting up or buying businesses outside of its current products and markets. Already Orascom Group has realized the opportunity for growing its business by venturing into new industries. Orascom Group introduced Orascom Telecom in 1998, followed by Orascom Hotels & Development, and

Orascom Technology Systems. The group's business realized significant growth as a result. The group's current capital investment exceeds US$3 billion and its annual revenues exceed US$1 billion.

Companies must not only develop strategies for *growing* their business portfolios, but also strategies for **downsizing** them. There are many reasons that a firm might want to abandon products or markets. The market environment might change, making some of the company's products or markets less profitable. The firm may have grown too fast or entered areas where it lacks experience. This can occur when a firm enters too many international markets without the proper research, or when a company introduces new products that do not offer superior customer value. Finally, some products or business units simply age and die.

When a firm finds brands or businesses that are unprofitable or that no longer fit its overall strategy, it must carefully cut, harvest, or divest them. Weak businesses usually require a disproportionate amount of management attention. Managers should focus on promising growth opportunities, not waste energy trying to salvage fading ones.

Downsizing

Reducing the business portfolio by eliminating products or business units that are not profitable or that no longer fit the company's overall strategy.

Author Comment | Marketing, alone, can't create superior customer value. Under the companywide strategic plan, marketers must work closely with other departments to form an effective company value chain and then must work with other companies in the marketing system to create an overall value delivery network that jointly serves customers.

Planning Marketing: Partnering to Build Customer Relationships (pp 46–48)

The company's strategic plan establishes what kinds of businesses the company will operate and its objectives for each. Then, within each business unit, more detailed planning takes place. The major functional departments in each unit—marketing, finance, accounting, purchasing, operations, information systems, human resources, and others—must work together to accomplish strategic objectives.

Marketing plays a key role in the company's strategic planning in several ways. First, marketing provides a guiding *philosophy*—the marketing concept—that suggests that company strategy should revolve around building profitable relationships with important consumer groups. Secondly, marketing provides *inputs* to strategic planners by helping to identify attractive market opportunities and by assessing the firm's potential to take advantage of them. Finally, within individual business units, marketing designs *strategies* for reaching the unit's objectives. Once the unit's objectives are set, marketing's task is to help carry them out profitably.

Customer value is the key ingredient in the marketer's formula for success. However, as we noted in Chapter 1, marketers alone cannot produce superior value for customers. Although marketing plays a leading role, it can be only a partner in attracting, keeping, and growing customers. In addition to *customer relationship management*, marketers must also practice *partner relationship management*. They must work closely with partners in other company departments to form an effective *value chain* that serves the customer. Moreover, they must partner effectively with other companies in the marketing system to form a competitively superior *value delivery network*. We now take a closer look at the concepts of a company value chain and a value delivery network.

Partnering with Other Company Departments

Value chain

The series of departments that carry out value-creating activities to design, produce, market, deliver, and support a firm's products.

Each company department can be thought of as a link in the company's **value chain**.[10] That is, each department carries out value-creating activities to design, produce, market, deliver, and support the firm's products. The firm's success depends not only on how well each department performs its work, but also on how well the various departments co-ordinate their activities.

For example, Carrefour's goal is to create customer value and satisfaction by providing shoppers with the products they want at the lowest possible prices. Marketers at Carrefour play an important role. They learn what customers need and stock the stores' shelves with the desired products at unbeatable low prices. They prepare advertising and merchandising programs and assist shoppers with customer service. Through these and other activities, Carrefour's marketers help deliver value to customers.

The value chain: Carrefour's promise to provide lower prices ("Thanks to our massive buying power, we guarantee to cut costs and keep our prices low") depends on the contributions of people in all of the company's departments.

However, the marketing department needs help from the company's other departments. Carrefour's ability to offer the right products at low prices depends on the purchasing department's skill in developing the needed suppliers and buying from them at low cost. Carrefour's information technology department must provide fast and accurate information about which products are selling in each store. And its operations people must provide effective, low-cost merchandise handling.

A company's value chain is only as strong as its weakest link. Success depends on how well each department performs its work of adding customer value and on how well the activities of various departments are co-ordinated. At Carrefour, if purchasing can't obtain the lowest prices from suppliers, or if operations can't distribute merchandise at the lowest costs, then marketing can't deliver on its promise of lowest prices.

Ideally then, a company's different functions should work in harmony to produce value for consumers. But, in practice, departmental relations are full of conflicts and misunderstandings. The marketing department takes the consumer's point of view. But when marketing tries to develop customer satisfaction, it can cause other departments to do a poorer job *in their terms*. Marketing department actions can increase purchasing costs, disrupt production schedules, increase inventories, and create budget headaches. Thus, the other departments may resist the marketing department's efforts.

Yet marketers must find ways to get all departments to 'think consumer' and to develop a smoothly functioning value chain. The idea is to "maximize the customer experience across the organization and its various customer touch points," says a marketing consultant. Jack Welch, the highly regarded former GE CEO, told his employees, "Companies can't give job security. Only customers can!" He emphasized that all GE people, regardless of their department, have an impact on customer satisfaction and retention. His message: "If you are not thinking customer, you are not thinking."[11]

"If you are not thinking customer, you are not thinking." Jack Welch, former GE CEO

Partnering with Others in the Marketing System

In its quest to create customer value, the firm needs to look beyond its own value chain and into the value chains of its suppliers, distributors, and, ultimately, its customers. Consider McDonald's. The company's nearly 30,000 restaurants in more than 100 countries serve more than 52 million customers daily, capturing over 40 percent of the burger market.[12] People do not come to McDonald's only because they love the chain's hamburgers. Consumers are attracted to the McDonald's *system*, not just to its food products. Throughout the world, McDonald's finely tuned system delivers a high standard of what the company calls QSCV—quality, service, cleanliness, and value. McDonald's is effective only to the extent that it successfully partners with its franchisees, suppliers, and others to jointly deliver exceptionally high customer value.

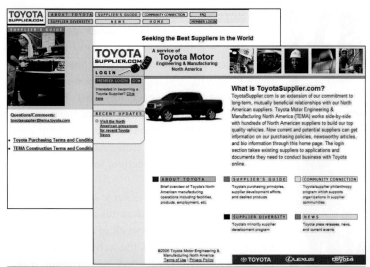

Toyota partners with its suppliers and helps them meet its very high expectations. Creating satisfied suppliers helps Toyota produce lower-cost, higher-quality cars, which in turn result in more satisfied customers.

Value delivery network
The network made up of the company, suppliers, distributors, and, ultimately, customers who 'partner' with each other to improve the performance of the entire system.

More companies today are partnering with the other members of the supply chain to improve the performance of the customer **value delivery network**. For example, Toyota knows the importance of building close relationships with its suppliers. In fact, it even includes the phrase "achieve supplier satisfaction" in its mission statement:

Achieving satisfying supplier relationships has been a cornerstone of Toyota's stunning success and has been crucial in helping the company to weather recent storms. In one survey of parts makers—which measured items such as degree of trust, open and honest communication, amount of help given to reduce costs, and the opportunity to make a profit—Toyota scored far higher than competitors. On a scale of 1 to 500, with an industry mean of 270, Toyota rated 415, whereas GM rated 174 and Ford rated just 162. U.S. competitors often alienate their suppliers through self-serving, heavy-handed dealings. "The [U.S. automakers] set annual cost-reduction targets [for the parts they buy]," says one supplier. "To realize those targets, they'll do anything. [They've created] an unfriendly atmosphere and it gets worse every year."

By contrast, rather than squeezing suppliers, Toyota partners with them and helps them to meet its very high expectations. Toyota learns about their businesses, conducts joint improvement activities, helps train supplier employees, gives daily performance feedback, and actively seeks out supplier concerns. It even recognizes top performers with annual performance awards. The high supplier satisfaction means that Toyota can rely on suppliers to help it improve its own quality, reduce costs, and develop new products quickly. And in times of crisis, this solid supplier foundation becomes a vital strength. In January 2010 Toyota hit the headlines worldwide in an emergency recall of vehicles due to faulty accelerator pedals and other problem parts. Toyota's president, Akio Toyoda, was clear in his position: "As the president of Toyota, I take personal responsibility. That is why I am personally leading the effort to restore trust in our word and in our products," he wrote. By showing leadership in taking full responsibility for the crisis, and by using the crisis as a reason to scrutinize and improve supplier relationships, Toyota gradually began to recover its reputation and rebuild customer trust.[13]

Increasingly in today's marketplace, competition no longer takes place between individual competitors. Rather, it takes place between the entire value delivery networks created by these competitors. Thus, Toyota's performance against Ford depends on the quality of Toyota's overall value delivery network versus Ford's. Even if Toyota makes the best cars, it might lose in the marketplace if Ford's dealer network provides more customer-satisfying sales and service.

Author Comment | Now that we've set the context in terms of companywide strategy, it's time to talk about customer-driven marketing strategy and programs!

Marketing Strategy and the Marketing Mix (pp 48–53)

The strategic plan defines the company's overall mission and objectives. Marketing's role and activities are shown in **Figure 2.4**, which summarizes the major activities involved in managing a customer-driven marketing strategy and the marketing mix.

Marketing strategy
The marketing logic by which the business unit hopes to create customer value and achieve profitable customer relationships.

Consumers stand in the center. The goal is to create value for customers and build profitable customer relationships. Next comes **marketing strategy**—the marketing logic by which the company hopes to create this customer value and achieve these profitable

FIGURE | 2.4

Managing Marketing Strategies and the Marketing Mix

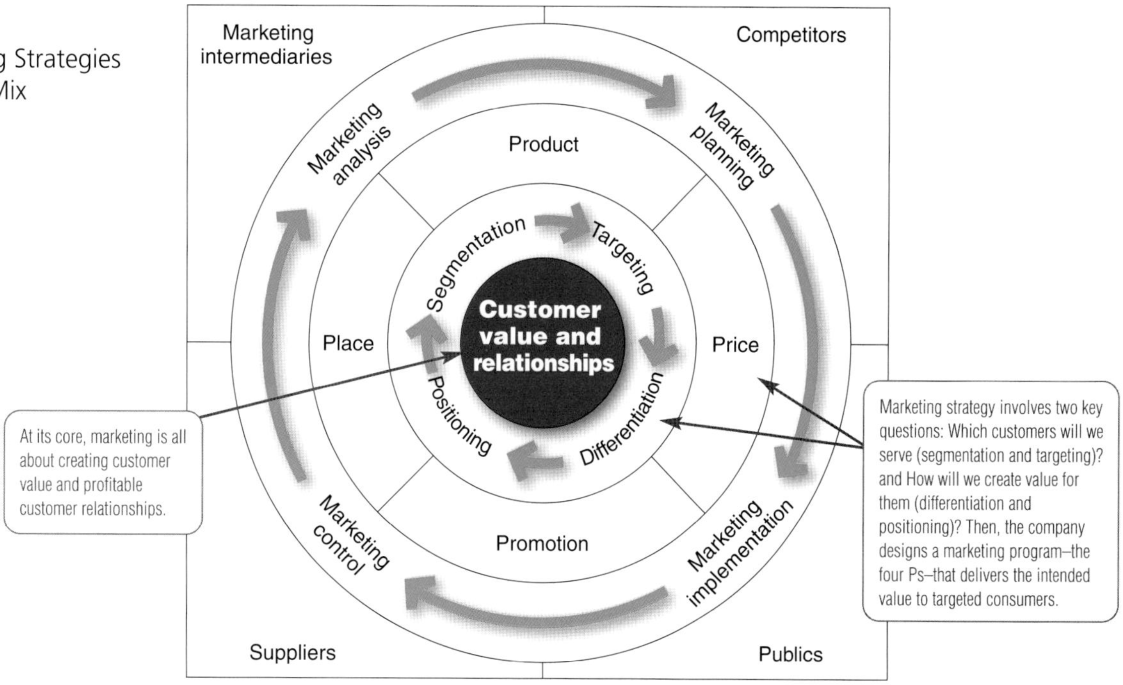

Marketing intermediaries

Competitors

Marketing analysis

Marketing planning

Product

Segmentation

Targeting

Customer value and relationships

Place

Price

Positioning

Differentiation

Marketing control

Promotion

Marketing implementation

Suppliers

Publics

At its core, marketing is all about creating customer value and profitable customer relationships.

Marketing strategy involves two key questions: Which customers will we serve (segmentation and targeting)? and How will we create value for them (differentiation and positioning)? Then, the company designs a marketing program—the four Ps—that delivers the intended value to targeted consumers.

relationships. The company decides which customers it will serve (segmentation and targeting) and how (differentiation and positioning). It identifies the total market, then divides it into smaller segments, selects the most promising segments, and focuses on serving and satisfying the customers in these segments.

Guided by marketing strategy, the company designs an integrated *marketing mix* made up of factors under its control—product, price, place, and promotion (the four Ps). To find the best marketing strategy and mix, the company engages in marketing analysis, planning, implementation, and control. Through these activities, the company watches and adapts to the actors and forces in the marketing environment. We will now look briefly at each activity. Then, in later chapters, we will discuss each one in more depth.

Customer-Driven Marketing Strategy

As we emphasized throughout Chapter 1, to succeed in today's competitive marketplace, companies need to be customer centered. They must win customers from competitors, then keep and grow them by delivering greater value. But before it can satisfy consumers, a company must first understand their needs and wants. Thus, sound marketing requires a careful customer analysis.

Companies know that they cannot profitably serve all consumers in a given market—at least not all consumers in the same way. There are too many different kinds of consumers with too many different kinds of needs. And most companies are in a position to serve some segments better than others. Thus, each company must divide up the total market, choose the best segments, and design strategies for profitably serving chosen segments. This process involves *market segmentation*, *market targeting*, *differentiation*, and *positioning*.

Market Segmentation

Market segmentation

Dividing a market into distinct groups of buyers who have different needs, characteristics, or behaviors, and who might require separate products or marketing programs.

The market consists of many types of customers, products, and needs. The marketer has to determine which segments offer the best opportunities. Consumers can be grouped and served in various ways based on geographic, demographic, psychographic, and behavioral factors. The process of dividing a market into distinct groups of buyers who have different needs, characteristics, or behaviors, and who might require separate products or marketing programs is called **market segmentation**.

Market segment
A group of consumers who respond in a similar way to a given set of marketing efforts.

Every market has segments, but not all ways of segmenting a market are equally useful. For example, Panadol would gain little by distinguishing between low-income and high-income pain reliever users if both respond the same way to marketing efforts. A **market segment** consists of consumers who respond in a similar way to a given set of marketing efforts. In the car market, for example, consumers who want the biggest, most comfortable car regardless of price make up one market segment. Consumers who care mainly about price and operating economy make up another segment. It would be difficult to make one car model that was the first choice of consumers in both segments. Companies are wise to focus their efforts on meeting the distinct needs of individual market segments.

Market Targeting

After a company has defined market segments, it can enter one or many of these segments. **Market targeting** involves evaluating each market segment's attractiveness and selecting one or more segments to enter. A company should target segments in which it can profitably generate the greatest customer value and sustain it over time.

Market targeting
The process of evaluating each market segment's attractiveness and selecting one or more segments to enter.

A company with limited resources might decide to serve only one or a few special segments or 'market niches.' Such 'nichers' specialize in serving customer segments that major competitors overlook or ignore. For example, Ferarri sells only 5,700 of its very high-performance cars each year, but at very high prices—from an eye-opening US$190,000 for its Ferrari F430 model to an astonishing US$2 million for its FXX super sports car, which can be driven only on race tracks (it sold 10 in the United States last year). Most nichers aren't quite so exotic. Isis, an Egyptian brand developed by SEKEM Group, offers a variety of organic products targeting a niche segment of health-conscious consumers—a relatively small but growing segment. **Real Marketing 2.2** describes an example of niche market targeting in the tourism industry.

Alternatively, a company might choose to serve several related segments—perhaps those with different kinds of customers but with the same basic wants. The Gap Inc., for example, targets different segments through its brands: Gap, Banana Republic, Old Navy, Piperlime, and Athleta. Similarly in Egypt, Mansour Group offers two different brands of grocery stores targeting different segments: Metro and Khair Zaman. Metro mainly targets A and upper B classes by providing its customers with high-quality products, imported goods, and products that may not be available elsewhere. Metro stores are concerned about the display, cleanliness, and presentation of the products. On the other hand, Khair Zaman targets lower B and C classes by providing the daily essentials that these segments need. Khair Zaman offers goods in economical sizes, discounted prices, and minimum standards of shelving and display in order to make the biggest savings for its customers.

Most companies enter a new market by serving a single segment, and if this proves successful, they add more segments. A large company might decide to offer a complete range of products to serve all market segments, eventually seeking full market coverage. It wants to be the General Motors of its industry. GM says that it makes a car for every "person, purse, and personality." The leading company normally has different products designed to meet the special needs of each segment.

Market Differentiation and Positioning

After a company has decided which market segments to enter, it must decide how it will differentiate its market offering for each targeted segment and what positions it wants to occupy in those segments. A product's *position* is the place the product occupies relative to competitors' products in consumers' minds. Marketers want to develop unique market positions for their products. If a product is perceived to be exactly like others on the market, consumers would have no reason to buy it.

Positioning
Arranging for a product to occupy a clear, distinctive, and desirable place relative to competing products in the minds of target consumers.

Positioning is arranging for a product to occupy a clear, distinctive, and desirable place relative to competing products in the minds of target consumers. As one positioning expert puts it, positioning is "why a shopper will pay a little more for your brand."[14] Thus, marketers plan positions that distinguish their products from competing brands and give them the greatest advantage in their target markets.

Real Marketing 2.2

Niching:

Voluntourism, A New Way to See the World

Voluntourism targets a niche segment of the tourism industry.

Tourism is one of the largest industries in the world. Countries like Cyprus and Egypt rely on tourism for employment and it is a major part of their economy. In 2010, international tourist arrivals worldwide were up by almost 7 percent to reach 935 million. The Arab world showed large growth in the tourism sector over the year 2010 to reach 60 million arrivals—this is double the figure for 2009. This boom in international tourism, following the economic downturn of 2008–9, is good news, especially for those developing countries that depend heavily on tourism for revenue and jobs.

When you look at an advertisement promoting a country, the chances are you will be faced with images of people relaxing on a sunny, sandy beach; people exploring an ancient ruin; people enjoying an active nightlife; or people shopping in extravagant malls. These images have been exhausted by so many different destinations trying to attract a wide range of customers looking for a traditional getaway.

In recent years, countries have started to market a different kind of tourism. They have tried to move away from the very competitive circles of traditional tourism into new niche markets where the atmosphere is less cut-throat. New kinds of tourism have started to evolve that target specific segments in society, such as medical tourism, adventure tourism, and voluntourism (volunteer tourism).

Voluntourism became part of the tourist industry in 1998 in Nevada, USA. Two years later, the concept grew to a substantial business model. Marketers started to see money in voluntourism. Voluntourism is defined as travel that includes volunteering for a charitable cause. In recent years, this niche market has grown in popularity and evolved in its definition, implementation, and suppliers. Today, voluntourism can vary from a simple model of going on a vacation and taking a day or two out of your time to meet the locals and do some light environmental work, to traveling to a disaster zone to help underprivileged individuals.

Voluntourism has now become themed, customized, and is promoted to individuals based on their areas of interest. Some websites offer a customized itinerary catering for different interests. The most popular volunteer service, based on 2008 statistics, is support of underage children. Another form of popular voluntourism is environmental cleanup.

When you take a look at the characteristics of the people who actively participate in voluntourism, one finds a thin segment of society with diverse backgrounds and interests but with one major thing in common, the desire to 'do something good.' By 2008 there were about 200 nonprofit organizations which facilitated such service opportunities.

In the Arab world, there are two programs especially that have capitalized on this niche market—the Abraham's Path and the Visit Jordan Voluntourism Program.

Abraham's Path (*Masar Ibrahim al Khalil*) is a blend of walking and cultural tourism that follows the footsteps of Abraham or Ibrahim through the Arab world. The path leads from Turkey down through Syria, Jordan, and Palestine. The path is just a set of directions and a route that people walk. There is no physical path; the road is not paved, neither is it altered. The path is actually created by people walking it.

Quoting the Abraham's Path organization: "The Masar ('Path' in Arabic) provides a place of meeting and connection for people of all faiths and cultures, inviting us to remember our common origins, to respect our cultural differences, and to recognize our shared humanity. The Masar also serves as a catalyst for sustainable tourism and economic development; a platform for the energy and idealism of young people; and a focus for positive media highlighting the rich culture and hospitable people of the Middle East."

In 2009, when the path was prepared for the travelers to trek, the communities living close to the path started benefiting from all the visiting tourists. Businesses were established and others grew.

The Jordan Tourism Board North America promotes the Visit Jordan Voluntourism Program as a way for people to explore Jordan beyond the traditional sites and nightlife. As part of the campaign, tourists are invited to take time out of their vacation to play with handicapped children, to read to the blind, to help paint old houses, or to visit nursing homes. This and similar initiatives are setting themselves apart from mainstream tourism in Jordan. The program is highly endorsed by the government and by local and international travel agencies. Jordan Tourism Board's North America director, Malia Asfour, said in a conference about voluntourism in Jordan, "It is a concept we're working on promoting as means of enriching the travel experience in Jordan, as visitors go beyond the adventures of sightseeing to more meaningful experiences of engaging with the community themselves."

To make the voluntourism market more lucrative, travel agencies have started promoting the mixed vacation plan—where travelers can enjoy their regular vacations, relax, have good wholesome fun, and devote as much time as they like volunteering for the service of their choice.

To develop the whole voluntourism concept, someone has to be making money. Both governments and travel agencies are benefiting. Governments are very glad to promote the concept, which ultimately increases the number of tourists that visit their country and thus helps to improve the economy. The travel agencies are taking the voluntourism concept and building programs, custom-made tours, special offers, and even competitions around it.

Travelocity.com organized a competition where competitors created videos based on one of their partner's signature trips and showed how they were inspired by the work done. The winner was awarded US$5,000.

Continued on next page ▼

Real Marketing 2.2 Continued ▼

Sources: UN News Centre (2011) "Global Tourism Posts Strong Recovery in 2010, Says UN Agency," January 17, 2011; "Abraham's Path Initiative," LinkedIn corporate profile, 2011, http://il.linkedin.com/company/abraham-path-initiative; "Voluntourism—A Whole New Dimension to the Travel Experience in Jordan," *The Jordan Times*, December 20, 2006; with additional information from sources including the United Nations World Tourism Organization, www.unwto.org; "Volunteer Journals," Travelocity, www.volunteerjournals.com; "Visit Jordan," The Jordan Tourism Board, www.visitjordan.com.

This case was provided by Mohamed Radwan, adjunct faculty member at the American University in Cairo and managing director for Platinum Partners.

Thus, Wal-Mart promises "Save Money. Live Better."; Target says "Expect More. Pay Less."; MasterCard gives you "priceless" experiences. Mobinil, the Egyptian mobile service provider, positions itself as the brand close to the people. Accordingly, it created the slogan of "Talk from the heart" to support this positioning. Such deceptively simple statements form the backbone of a product's marketing strategy. For example, Visa has designed its entire integrated marketing campaign around the "Life Takes Visa" slogan.

In positioning its product, the company first identifies possible customer value differences that provide competitive advantages upon which to build the position. The company can offer greater customer value either by charging lower prices than competitors, or by offering more benefits to justify higher prices. But if the company *promises* greater value, it must then *deliver* that greater value. Thus, effective positioning begins with **differentiation**—actually *differentiating* the company's market offering so that it gives consumers more value. Once the company has chosen a desired position, it must take strong steps to deliver and communicate that position to target consumers. The company's entire marketing program should support the chosen positioning strategy.

Differentiation
Actually differentiating the market offering to create superior customer value.

Developing an Integrated Marketing Mix

After deciding on its overall marketing strategy, the company is ready to begin planning the details of the marketing mix, one of the major concepts in modern marketing. The **marketing mix** is the set of controllable, tactical marketing tools that the firm blends to produce the response it wants in the target market. The marketing mix consists of everything the firm can do to influence the demand for its product. The many possibilities can be collected into four groups of variables known as 'the four Ps': *product, price, place*, and *promotion*. ◗ **Figure 2.5** shows the marketing tools under each *P*.

Product means the goods-and-services combination the company offers to the target market. Thus, a Ford Escape consists of nuts and bolts, spark plugs, pistons, headlights, and thousands of other parts. Ford offers several Escape models and dozens of

Marketing mix
The set of controllable tactical marketing tools—product, price, place, and promotion—that the firm blends to produce the response it wants in the target market.

◗ **FIGURE** | **2.5**
The Four Ps of the Marketing Mix

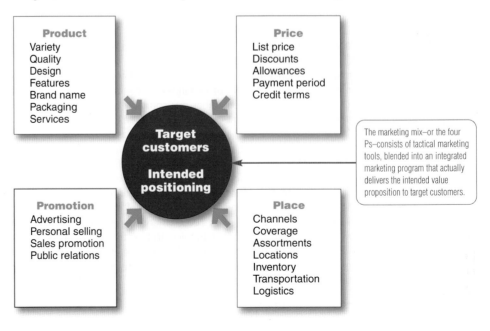

The marketing mix—or the four Ps—consists of tactical marketing tools, blended into an integrated marketing program that actually delivers the intended value proposition to target customers.

optional features. The car comes fully serviced and with a comprehensive warranty that is as much a part of the product as the tailpipe.

Price is the amount of money customers must pay to obtain the product. Ford calculates suggested retail prices that its dealers might charge for each Escape. But Ford dealers rarely charge the full sticker price. Instead, they negotiate the price with each customer, offering discounts, trade-in allowances, and credit terms. These actions adjust prices for the current competitive situation and bring them into line with the buyer's perception of the car's value.

Place includes company activities that make the product available to target consumers. Ford partners with a large body of independently owned dealerships that sell the company's many different models. Ford selects its dealers carefully and supports them strongly. The dealers keep an inventory of Ford automobiles, demonstrate them to potential buyers, negotiate prices, close sales, and service the cars after the sale.

Promotion means activities that communicate the merits of the product and persuade target customers to buy it. Ford Motor Company spends more than US$2.5 billion each year on U.S. advertising to tell consumers about the company and its many products.[15] Dealership salespeople assist potential buyers and persuade them that Ford is the best car for them. Ford and its dealers offer special promotions—sales, cash rebates, low-financing rates—as added purchase incentives.

An effective marketing program blends all of the marketing mix elements into an integrated marketing program designed to achieve the company's marketing objectives by delivering value to consumers. The marketing mix constitutes the company's tactical tool kit for establishing strong positioning in target markets.

Some critics think that the four Ps may omit or underemphasize certain important activities. For example, they ask, "Where are services?" Just because they don't start with a *P* doesn't justify omitting them. The answer is that services, such as banking, airline, and retailing services, are products too. We might call them *service products*. "Where is packaging?" the critics might ask. Marketers would answer that they include packaging as just one of many product decisions. All said, as **Figure 2.5** suggests, many marketing activities that might appear to be left out of the marketing mix are included under one of the four Ps. The issue is not whether there should be 4, 6, or 10 Ps so much as what framework is most helpful in designing integrated marketing programs.

There is another concern, however, that is valid. It holds that the four Ps concept takes the seller's view of the market, not the buyer's view. From the buyer's viewpoint, in this age of customer value and relationships, the four Ps might be better described as the four Cs:[16]

4Ps	4Cs
Product	Customer solution
Price	Customer cost
Place	Convenience
Promotion	Communication

Thus, whereas marketers see themselves as selling products, customers see themselves as buying value or solutions to their problems. And customers are interested in more than just the price; they are interested in the total costs of obtaining, using, and disposing of a product. Customers want the product and service to be as conveniently available as possible. Finally, they want two-way communication. Marketers would do well to think through the four Cs first and then build the four Ps on that platform.

Author Comment | So far we've focused on the *marketing* in marketing management. Now, let's turn to the *management*.

Managing the Marketing Effort (pp 53–58)

In addition to being good at the *marketing* in marketing management, companies also need to pay attention to the *management*. Managing the marketing process requires the four marketing management functions shown in **Figure 2.6**—*analysis, planning, implementation,*

📖 FIGURE | 2.6
Managing Marketing: Analysis,
Planning, Implementation,
and Control

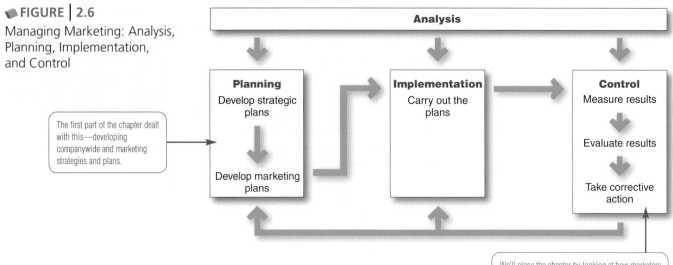

The first part of the chapter dealt with this—developing companywide and marketing strategies and plans.

We'll close the chapter by looking at how marketers manage those strategies and plans—how they implement marketing strategies and programs and evaluate the results.

and *control*. The company first develops companywide strategic plans and then translates them into marketing and other plans for each division, product, and brand. Through implementation, the company turns the plans into actions. Control consists of measuring and evaluating the results of marketing activities and taking corrective action where needed. Finally, marketing analysis provides information and evaluations needed for all of the other marketing activities.

Marketing Analysis

SWOT analysis

An overall evaluation of the company's strengths (S), weaknesses (W), opportunities (O), and threats (T).

Managing the marketing function begins with a complete analysis of the company's situation. The marketer should conduct a **SWOT analysis**, by which it evaluates the company's overall strengths (S), weaknesses (W), opportunities (O), and threats (T) (see 📖 **Figure 2.7**). Strengths include internal capabilities, resources, and positive situational factors that may help the company to serve its customers and achieve its objectives. Weaknesses include internal limitations and negative situational factors that may interfere with the company's performance. Opportunities are favorable factors or trends in the external environment that the company may be able to exploit to its advantage. And threats are unfavorable external factors or trends that may present challenges to performance.

The company should analyze its markets and marketing environment to find attractive opportunities and identify environmental threats. It should analyze company strengths and weaknesses as well as current and possible marketing actions to determine which opportunities it can best pursue. The goal is to match the company's strengths to attractive opportunities in the environment, while eliminating or overcoming the weaknesses and minimizing the threats. Marketing analysis provides inputs to each of the other marketing management functions. We discuss marketing analysis more fully in Chapter 3.

📖 FIGURE | 2.7
SWOT Analysis: Strengths (S),
Weaknesses (W),
Opportunities (O),
and Threats (T)

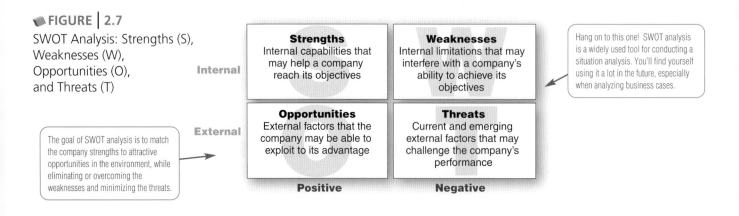

The goal of SWOT analysis is to match the company strengths to attractive opportunities in the environment, while eliminating or overcoming the weaknesses and minimizing the threats.

Hang on to this one! SWOT analysis is a widely used tool for conducting a situation analysis. You'll find yourself using it a lot in the future, especially when analyzing business cases.

Marketing Planning

Through strategic planning, the company decides what it wants to do with each business unit. Marketing planning involves deciding on marketing strategies that will help the company attain its overall strategic objectives. A detailed marketing plan is needed for each business, product, or brand. What does a marketing plan look like? Our discussion focuses on product or brand marketing plans.

● **Table 2.2** outlines the major sections of a typical product or brand marketing plan. (See Appendix 1 for a sample marketing plan.) The plan begins with an executive summary that quickly reviews major assessments, goals, and recommendations. The main section of the plan presents a detailed SWOT analysis of the current marketing situation as well as potential threats and opportunities. The plan next states major objectives for the brand and outlines the specifics of a marketing strategy for achieving them.

● TABLE | 2.2   Contents of a Marketing Plan

Section	Purpose
Executive summary	Presents a brief summary of the main goals and recommendations of the plan for management review, helping top management to find the plan's major points quickly. A table of contents should follow the executive summary.
Current marketing situation	Describes the target market and the company's position in it, including information about the market, product performance, competition, and distribution. This section includes: • a *market description* that defines the market and major segments, then reviews customer needs and factors in the marketing environment that may affect customer purchasing. • a *product review* that shows sales, prices, and gross margins of the major products in the product line. • a review of *competition* that identifies major competitors and assesses their market positions and strategies for product quality, pricing, distribution, and promotion. • a review of *distribution* that evaluates recent sales trends and other developments in major distribution channels.
Threats and opportunities analysis	Assesses major threats and opportunities that the product might face, helping management to anticipate important positive or negative developments that might have an impact on the firm and its strategies.
Objectives and issues	States the marketing objectives that the company would like to attain during the plan's term and discusses key issues that will affect their attainment. For example, if the goal is to achieve a 15 percent market share, this section looks at how this goal might be achieved.
Marketing strategy	Outlines the broad marketing logic by which the business unit hopes to create customer value and relationships and the specifics of target markets, positioning, and marketing expenditure levels. How will the company create value for customers in order to capture value from customers in return? This section also outlines specific strategies for each marketing mix element and explains how each responds to the threats, opportunities, and critical issues spelled out earlier in the plan.
Action programs	Spells out how marketing strategies will be turned into specific action programs that answer the following questions: *What* will be done? *When* will it be done? *Who* will do it? *How* much will it cost?
Budgets	Details a supporting marketing budget that is essentially a projected profit-and-loss statement. It shows expected revenues (forecasted number of units sold and the average net price) and expected costs of production, distribution, and marketing. The difference is the projected profit. Once approved by higher management, the budget becomes the basis for materials buying, production scheduling, personnel planning, and marketing operations.
Controls	Outlines the control that will be used to monitor progress and allow higher management to review implementation results and spot products that are not meeting their goals. It includes measures of return on marketing investment.

A *marketing strategy* consists of specific strategies for target markets, positioning, the marketing mix, and marketing expenditure levels. It outlines how the company intends to create value for target customers in order to capture value in return. In this section, the planner explains how each strategy responds to the threats, opportunities, and critical issues spelled out earlier in the plan. Additional sections of the marketing plan lay out an action program for implementing the marketing strategy along with the details of a supporting *marketing budget*. The last section outlines the controls that will be used to monitor progress, measure return on marketing investment, and take corrective action.

Marketing Implementation

Marketing implementation

The process that turns marketing strategies and plans into marketing actions in order to accomplish strategic marketing objectives.

Planning good strategies is only a start toward successful marketing. A brilliant marketing strategy counts for little if the company fails to implement it properly. **Marketing implementation** is the process that turns marketing *plans* into marketing *actions* in order to accomplish strategic marketing objectives. Whereas marketing planning addresses the *what* and *why* of marketing activities, implementation addresses the *who, where, when*, and *how*.

Many managers think that 'doing things right' (implementation) is as important as, or even more important than, 'doing the right things' (strategy). The fact is that both are critical to success, and companies can gain competitive advantages through effective implementation. One firm can have essentially the same strategy as another, yet win in the marketplace through faster or better execution. Still, implementation is difficult—it is often easier to think up good marketing strategies than it is to carry them out.

In an increasingly connected world, people at all levels of the marketing system must work together to implement marketing strategies and plans. At Black & Decker, for example, marketing implementation for the company's power tools, outdoor equipment, and other products requires day-to-day decisions and actions by thousands of people both inside and outside the organization. Marketing managers make decisions about target segments, branding, packaging, pricing, promotion, and distribution. They talk with engineering about product design, with manufacturing about production and inventory levels, and with finance about funding and cash flows. They also connect with outside people such as advertising agencies to plan ad campaigns, and the news media to obtain publicity support. The sales force urges its different retailers throughout the world to advertise Black & Decker products, provide ample shelf space, and use company displays.

Marketing Department Organization

The company must design a marketing organization that can carry out marketing strategies and plans. If the company is very small, one person might do all of the research, selling, advertising, customer service, and other marketing work. As the company expands, a marketing department emerges to plan and carry out marketing activities. In large companies, this department contains many specialists. They have product and market managers, sales managers and salespeople, market researchers, advertising experts, and many other specialists.

To head up such large marketing organizations, many companies have now created a *chief marketing officer* (or CMO) position. The CMO heads up the company's entire marketing operation and represents marketing on the company's top management team. The CMO position puts marketing on equal footing with other C-level executives, such as the chief executive officer (CEO) and the chief financial officer (CFO).[17]

Modern marketing departments can be arranged in several ways. The most common form of marketing organization is the *functional organization*. Under this organization, different marketing activities are headed by a functional specialist—a sales manager, advertising manager, marketing research manager, customer-service manager, or new-product manager. A company that sells across the country or internationally often uses a *geographic organization*. Its sales and marketing people are assigned to specific countries, regions, and districts. Geographic organization allows salespeople to settle into a territory, get to know their customers, and work with a minimum of travel time and cost.

Companies with many very different products or brands often create a *product management organization*. Using this approach, a product manager develops and implements a complete strategy and marketing program for a specific product or brand. Product management first appeared at Procter & Gamble in 1929. A new company soap, Camay, was not doing well and a young P&G executive was assigned to give his exclusive attention to developing and promoting this product. He was successful, and the company soon added other product managers.[18] Since then, many firms, especially consumer-products companies, have set up product management organizations.

For companies that sell one product line to many different types of markets and customers that have different needs and preferences, a *market* or *customer management organization* might be best. A market management organization is similar to the product management organization. Market managers are responsible for developing marketing strategies and plans for their specific markets or customers. This system's main advantage is that the company is organized around the needs of specific customer segments. Many companies develop special organizations to manage their relationships with large customers. For example, companies such as Procter & Gamble and Black & Decker have large teams, or even whole divisions, set up to serve large customers such as Wal-Mart, Target, Safeway, or Home Depot.

Marketers must continually plan their analysis, implementation, and control activities.

Large companies that produce many different products flowing into many different geographic and customer markets usually employ some *combination* of the functional, geographic, product, and market organization forms. This ensures that each function, product, and market receives its share of management attention. However, it can also add costly layers of management and reduce organizational flexibility. Still, the benefits of organizational specialization usually outweigh the drawbacks.

Marketing organization has become an increasingly important issue in recent years. As we discussed in Chapter 1, today's marketing environment calls for less focus on products, brands, and territories and more focus on customer relationships. More and more, companies are shifting their brand management focus toward *customer management*—moving away from managing just product or brand profitability and toward managing profitability and customer equity. They think of themselves not as managing portfolios of brands, but as managing portfolios of customers.

Marketing Control

Marketing control

The process of measuring and evaluating the results of marketing strategies and plans and taking corrective action to ensure that objectives are achieved.

Because many surprises occur during the implementation of marketing plans, marketers must practice constant **marketing control**—evaluating the results of marketing strategies and plans and taking corrective action to ensure that objectives are attained. Marketing control involves four steps. Management first sets specific marketing goals. It then measures its performance in the marketplace and evaluates the causes of any differences between expected and actual performance. Finally, management takes corrective action to close the gaps between its goals and its performance. This may require changing the action programs or even changing the goals.

Operating control involves checking ongoing performance against the annual plan and taking corrective action when necessary. Its purpose is to ensure that the company achieves the sales, profits, and other goals set out in its annual plan. It also involves determining the profitability of different products, territories, markets, and channels. *Strategic control* involves looking at whether the company's basic strategies are well matched to its opportunities. Marketing strategies and programs can quickly become outdated, and each company should periodically reassess its overall approach to the marketplace.

The marketing audit covers *all* major marketing areas of a business, not just a few trouble spots. It assesses the marketing environment, marketing strategy, marketing organization, marketing systems, marketing mix, and marketing productivity and profitability. The audit is normally conducted by an objective and experienced outside party. The findings may come as a surprise—and sometimes as a shock—to management. Management then decides which actions make sense and how and when to implement them.

Author Comment | Measuring ROI has become a major marketing emphasis recently. But it can be difficult. For example, during the holy month of Ramadan television ads reach their peak in terms of reach (viewership). As a result, during Ramadan, 30 seconds of airtime can cost more than 10 times that of a regular slot. How do you measure the specific return on such an investment in terms of sales, profits, and building customer relationships? We'll look into that question again in Chapter 12.

Measuring and Managing Return on Marketing Investment (pp 58–59)

Marketing managers must ensure that their marketing dollars are being well spent. In the past, many marketers spent freely on big, expensive marketing programs, often without thinking carefully about the financial returns on their spending. They believed that marketing produces intangible outcomes, which do not lend themselves readily to measures of productivity or return. But all that is changing:

> For years, corporate marketers have walked into budget meetings regularly asking for more money. They couldn't always justify how well they spent past handouts or what difference it all made. They just wanted more money—for flashy television ads, for big-ticket events, for, you know, getting out the message and building up the brand. But those heady days of blind budget increases are fast being replaced with a new mantra: measurement and accountability. Armed with a lot of data, increasingly sophisticated tools, and growing evidence that the old tricks simply don't work, there's hardly a marketing executive today who isn't demanding a more scientific approach to help defend marketing strategies in front of the chief financial officer. Marketers want to know the actual return on investment (ROI) of each dollar. They want to know it often, not just annually.... Companies... have become obsessed with mastering the science of measuring marketing performance. "Marketers have been pretty unaccountable for many years," notes one expert. "Now they are under big pressure to estimate their impact."[19]

Return on marketing investment (or marketing ROI)

The net return from a marketing investment divided by the costs of the marketing investment.

In response, marketers are developing better measures of *return on marketing investment*. **Return on marketing investment** (or *marketing ROI*) is the net return from a marketing investment divided by the costs of the marketing investment. It measures the profits generated by investments in marketing activities.

It's true that marketing returns can be difficult to measure. In measuring financial ROI, both the *R* and the *I* are uniformly measured in dollars. But there is as of yet no consistent definition of marketing ROI. "It's tough to measure, more so than for other business expenses," says one analyst. "You can imagine buying a piece of equipment... and then measuring the productivity gains that result from the purchase," he says. "But in marketing, benefits like advertising impact aren't easily put into dollar returns. It takes a high level of faith to come up with a number."[20]

One recent survey of CMOs from top marketing companies found that "make marketing accountable" emerged as a top strategic theme, second only to "put the consumer at the heart of marketing." However, another recent survey of top marketing executives found that although 58 percent of the companies surveyed have formal accountability programs, only 28 percent are satisfied with their ability to use marketing ROI measures to take action.[21]

A company can assess return on marketing in terms of standard marketing performance measures, such as brand awareness, sales, or market share. Many companies are assembling such measures into *marketing dashboards*—meaningful sets of marketing

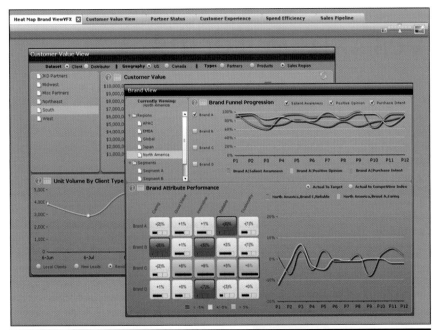

Many companies are assembling marketing dashboards—meaningful sets of marketing performance measures in a single display used to set and adjust their marketing strategies.

performance measures in a single display used to monitor strategic marketing performance. Just as automobile dashboards present drivers with details on how their cars are performing, the marketing dashboard gives marketers the detailed measures they need to assess and adjust their marketing strategies.[22]

Increasingly, however, beyond standard performance measures, marketers are using customer-centered measures of marketing impact, such as customer acquisition, customer retention, customer lifetime value, and customer equity. These measures capture not just current marketing performance but also future performance resulting from stronger customer relationships. **Figure 2.8** views marketing expenditures as investments that produce returns in the form of more profitable customer relationships.[23] Marketing investments result in improved customer value and satisfaction, which in turn increase customer attraction and retention. This increases individual customer lifetime values and the firm's overall customer equity. Increased customer equity, in relation to the cost of the marketing investments, determines return on marketing investment.

Regardless of how it's defined or measured, the return on marketing investment concept is here to stay. "Marketing ROI is at the heart of every business," says an AT&T marketing executive. "[We've added another P to the marketing mix]—for *profit and loss* or *performance*. We absolutely have to…quantify the impact of marketing on the business. You can't improve what you can't measure."[24]

FIGURE | 2.8

Return on Marketing Investment

Source: Adapted from Roland T. Rust, Katherine N. Lemon, and Valerie A. Zeithaml, "Return on Marketing: Using Consumer Equity to Focus Marketing Strategy," *Journal of Marketing*, January 2004, p. 112.

Beyond measuring return on marketing investment in terms of standard performance measures such as sales or market share, many companies are using customer-relationship measures such as customer satisfaction, retention, and equity. These are more difficult to measure, but capture both current and future performance.

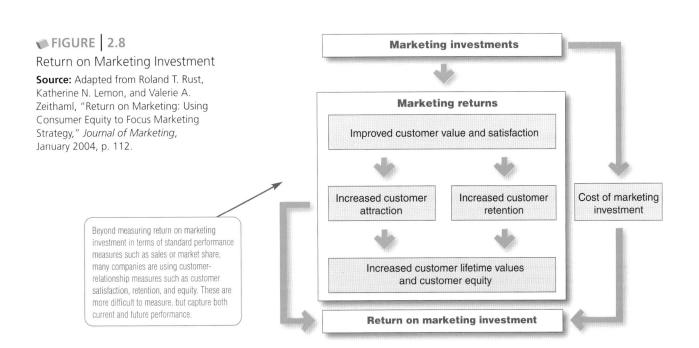

REVIEWING Objectives AND KEY Terms

In Chapter 1, we defined *marketing* and outlined the steps in the marketing process. In this chapter, we examined company-wide strategic planning and marketing's role in the organization. Then, we looked more deeply into marketing strategy and the marketing mix, and reviewed the major marketing management functions. So you've now had a pretty good overview of the fundamentals of modern marketing. In future chapters, we'll expand on these fundamentals.

OBJECTIVE 1 Explain companywide strategic planning and its four steps. (pp 37–41)

Strategic planning sets the stage for the rest of the company's planning. Marketing contributes to strategic planning, and the overall plan defines marketing's role in the company. Although formal planning offers a variety of benefits to companies, not all companies use it or use it well.

Strategic planning involves developing a strategy for long-run survival and growth. It consists of four steps: defining the company's mission, setting objectives and goals, designing a business portfolio, and developing functional plans. *Defining a clear company mission* with drafting a formal mission statement, should be market oriented, realistic, specific, motivating, and consistent with the market environment. The mission is then transformed into detailed *supporting goals and objectives* to guide the entire company. Based on those goals and objectives, headquarters designs a *business portfolio*, deciding which businesses and products should receive more or fewer resources. In turn, each business and product unit must develop *detailed marketing plans* in line with the companywide plan.

OBJECTIVE 2 Discuss how to design business portfolios and develop growth strategies. (pp 41–46)

Guided by the company's mission statement and objectives, management plans its *business portfolio*, or the collection of businesses and products that make up the company. The firm wants to produce a business portfolio that best fits its strengths and weaknesses to opportunities in the environment. To do this, it must analyze and adjust its *current* business portfolio and develop growth and downsizing strategies for adjusting the *future* portfolio. The company might use a formal portfolio-planning method. But many companies are now designing more customized portfolio-planning approaches that better suit their unique situations. The *product/market expansion grid* suggests four possible growth paths: market penetration, market development, product development, and diversification.

OBJECTIVE 3 Explain marketing's role in strategic planning and how marketing works with its partners to create and deliver customer value. (pp 46–48)

Under the strategic plan, the major functional departments—marketing, finance, accounting, purchasing, operations, information systems, human resources, and others—must work together to accomplish strategic objectives. Marketing plays a key role in the company's strategic planning by providing a *marketing concept philosophy* and *inputs* regarding attractive market opportunities. Within individual business units, marketing designs *strategies* for reaching the unit's objectives and helps to carry them out profitably.

Marketers alone cannot produce superior value for customers. A company's success depends on how well each department performs its customer value-adding activities and how well the departments work together to serve the customer. Thus, marketers must practice partner *relationship management*. They must work closely with partners in other departments to form an effective *value chain* that serves the customer. And they must partner effectively with other companies in the marketing system to form a competitively superior *value delivery network*.

OBJECTIVE 4 Describe the elements of a customer-driven marketing strategy and mix, and the forces that influence it. (pp 48–53)

Consumer value and relationships are at the center of marketing strategy and programs. Through market segmentation, targeting, differentiation, and positioning, the company divides the total market into smaller segments, selects segments it can best serve, and decides how it wants to bring value to target consumers. It then designs an *integrated marketing mix* to produce the response it wants in the target market. The marketing mix consists of product, price, place, and promotion decisions.

OBJECTIVE 5 List the marketing management functions, including the elements of a marketing plan, and discuss the importance of measuring and managing return on marketing investment. (pp 53–59)

To find the best strategy and mix and to put them into action, the company engages in marketing analysis, planning, implementation, and control. The main components of a *marketing plan* are the executive summary, current marketing situation, threats and opportunities, objectives and issues, marketing strategies, action programs, budgets, and controls. To plan good strategies is often easier than to carry them out. To be successful, companies must also be effective at *implementation*—turning marketing strategies into marketing actions.

Much of the responsibility for implementation goes to the company's marketing department. Marketing departments can be organized in one or a combination of ways: *functional marketing organization*, *geographic organization*, *product management organization*, or *market management organization*. In this age of customer relationships, more and more companies are now changing their organizational focus from product or territory management to customer relationship management. Marketing organizations carry out *marketing control*, both operating control and strategic control. They use *marketing audits* to determine marketing opportunities and problems, and to recommend short-run and long-run actions to improve overall marketing performance.

Marketing managers must ensure that their marketing dollars are being well spent. Today's marketers face growing pressures to show that they are adding value in line with their costs. In response, marketers are developing better measures of *return* *on marketing investment*. Increasingly, they are using customer-centered measures of marketing impact as a key input into their strategic decision making.

KEY Terms

OBJECTIVE 1

Strategic planning (p 37)
Mission statement (p 38)

OBJECTIVE 2

Business portfolio (p 41)
Portfolio analysis (p 41)
Growth-share matrix (p 41)
Product/market expansion grid (p 43)
Market penetration (p 43)
Market development (p 43)

Product development (p 44)
Diversification (p 45)
Downsizing (p 46)

OBJECTIVE 3

Value chain (p 46)
Value delivery network (p 48)

OBJECTIVE 4

Marketing strategy (p 48)
Market segmentation (p 49)

Market segment (p 50)
Market targeting (p 50)
Positioning (p 50)
Differentiation (p 52)
Marketing mix (p 52)

OBJECTIVE 5

SWOT analysis (p 54)
Marketing implementation (p 56)
Marketing control (p 57)
Return on marketing investment (p 58)

DISCUSSING & APPLYING THE Concepts

Discussing the Concepts

1. Define strategic planning and briefly describe the four steps that lead managers and the firm through the strategic-planning process. Discuss the role marketing plays in this process.

2. Describe the Boston Consulting Group approach to portfolio analysis. Briefly discuss why management may find it difficult to dispose of a 'question mark.'

3. Name and describe the four product/market expansion grid strategies. McDonald's is now rolling out a new McArabia line to add to its menu lineup. Which growth strategy does this represent?

4. Discuss the differences between market segmentation, targeting, differentiation, and positioning. What two simple questions do they address?

5. Define each of the four Ps. Does the four Ps framework do an adequate job of describing marketer responsibilities in preparing and managing marketing programs? Why? Do you see any issues with this framework in relation to service products?

6. What is return on marketing investment? Why is it difficult to measure?

Applying the Concepts

1. Explain what a SWOT analysis involves. Develop a SWOT analysis for a travel agency in your community.

2. In a small group, discuss whether the following statement from Olympic Group, manufacturers and pioneers of the household appliance industry in Egypt and the region, meets the five criteria of a good mission statement: "Enriching our customers' lives with unique innovative household appliances and electronic solutions at the fair value to our stakeholders. We will continue to grow by seizing opportunities that create synergies with our business."[25]

3. Explain the role of a chief marketing officer (CMO). Learn more about this C-level executive position and find an article that describes the importance of this position, the characteristics of an effective CMO, or any issues surrounding this position.

FOCUS ON Technology

Mobile marketing is touted as the next 'big thing,' offering the promise of connecting with consumers on the most personal medium—their cellphones. Technological advances are letting marketers send not only text messages to cellphones but also video messages. In Japan, QR codes (quick response codes), originally developed for manufacturing purposes, are now placed on outdoor, print, and other media advertisements so that consumers can snap pictures of them and be taken directly to mobile websites. Although not widely practiced yet, some U.S. marketers are now dabbling in mobile marketing. For example, Jaguar used a mobile campaign and sold over 1,100 XFs in one month. Visa used mobile marketing in China to encourage consumers to pass video commercials on to their friends via mobile phones. Even textbook publishers are using mobile marketing to send updated information to students and teachers. Although there are still technical roadblocks stifling rapid expansion of this marketing method, some experts claim that marketers had better jump on this bandwagon or risk being left behind.

1. Visit the Mobile Marketing Association's website at www. mmaglobal.com and click on "Resources" and then "Case

Studies" on the left. Discuss one case study and describe the factors you think made that application of mobile marketing a success.

2. Analysis is an important first step in the marketing management process. The rapid advance in mobile technology poses opportunities as well as threats for marketers. Discuss both the opportunities and threats for marketers.

FOCUS ON Ethics

Obesity is a serious problem in the Arab world as well as worldwide. Young people in the Arab world are facing problems caused by obesity for many reasons, such as a lack of outdoor sports owing to the high temperatures in many of the Arab world countries, and bad eating habits. Some companies have identified increasing levels of obesity as a business opportunity and have started to introduce many products with claims that consumers can lose more than 10 kg in a week. Many of these products are made from natural ingredients, and so companies claim that they have no unwanted side effects.

Many of these products are registered by the Health Ministry in some Arab world countries, which support product claims that customers will experience no side effects. Accordingly marketers are allowed to sell them.

1. Many of these products are offered by sellers of natural ingredients. What product-market growth strategy does this represent for these companies?

2. If these products do not deliver the benefits claimed, should marketers be allowed to continue selling them?

MARKETING BY THE Numbers

Appendix 2, Marketing by the Numbers, discusses other marketing profitability metrics beyond the return on marketing investment (marketing ROI) measure described in this chapter. The following is a profit-and-loss statement for a business. Review Appendix 2 and answer the following questions.

1. Calculate the net marketing contribution (NMC) for this company.

2. Calculate both marketing return on sales (or marketing ROS) and marketing return on investment (or marketing ROI) as described in Appendix 2. Is this company doing well?

Net sales		$800,000,000
Cost of goods sold		(375,000,000)
Gross margin		$425,000,000
Marketing Expenses		
Sales expenses	$70,000,000	
Promotion expenses	30,000,000	
		(100,000,000)
General and Administrative Expenses		
Marketing salaries and expenses	$10,000,000	
Indirect overheads	60,000,000	(70,000,000)
Net profit before income tax		$255,000,000

VIDEO Case

Live Nation

Live Nation may not be a household name. But if you've been to a concert in the past few years, chances are you've purchased a Live Nation product. In fact, Live Nation has been America's largest concert promoter for many years, promoting as many as 29,000 events annually. But through very savvy strategic planning, Live Nation is shaking up the structure of the music industry.

A recent US$120 million deal with Madonna illustrates how this concert promoter is diving into other businesses as well. Under this deal, Live Nation will become Madonna's record label, concert promoter, ticket vendor, and merchandise agent. Similar deals have been reached with other performers such as Jay-Z and U2.

But contracting with artists is only part of the picture. Live Nation is partnering with other corporations as well. A venture with Citi will expand its reach to potential customers through a leveraging of database technologies. Joining forces with ticket reseller powerhouses such as StubHub will give Live Nation a position in the thriving business of secondary ticket sales.

After viewing the video featuring Live Nation, answer the following questions about the role of strategic planning:

1. What is Live Nation's mission?

2. Based on the product/market expansion grid, provide support for the strategy that Live Nation is pursuing.

3. How does Live Nation's strategy provide better value for customers?

COMPANY Case

Bahrain Bay: Building Customer Relations for the Future

Bahrain Bay Development is a joint venture between Arcapita Bank and a Bahrain-based investment group. It is a US$2.5 billion development off the northeast coast of Manama in the Kingdom of Bahrain that included the creation of an entire island.

The project—a mix of commercial, residential, and retail units—is set around the Manama waterfront. The centerpiece? Bahrain's first Four Seasons hotel.

Construction of Bahrain Bay got underway in 2006 with land reclamation extending to 430,000 m². The global headquarters of Arcapita and the new hotel were completed in 2008. Phase Three of the operation involved the construction of residential, commercial, and retail units. The whole project will cover an area of some 1.1 million m².

The architectural and engineering firm Skidmore, Owings & Merrill LLP designed the ultra-modern site. In 2005, when the project had been given final approval, Atif A. Abdulmalik, CEO of Arcapita, said, "Just five months from the initial announcement of this project, the preparatory stages for design and planning considerations have progressed very well and Bahrain Bay BSC is able to launch Bahrain Bay ahead of schedule. A month from now, site work will commence on what we believe will be an outstanding addition to the Kingdom of Bahrain, as befits its place as a regional center for banking and finance. With its futuristic, urban designs, Bahrain Bay will be a stunningly presented collection of waterfront residential, retail, and commercial developments, representing a unique new focal point in Bahrain."

Abdulmalik went on to explain the importance of the project for Bahrain: "There are many aspects that make Bahrain Bay a particularly attractive opportunity. The demographic changes within Bahrain, its proximity to the rapidly growing Eastern Province of Saudi Arabia, and the location within Manama's prime northern corridor make this a compelling project. Added to these, the early commitment of the highly regarded Four Seasons Hotels and Resorts, the innovative architectural design, and the experience and track record of each of the companies involved in the development are among the many other components that make this a unique proposition."

The planning phase of the operation was not undertaken lightly; advice and support were sought from a variety of sources, Abdulmalik explained. "The project team has taken soundings from the marketplace throughout the planning stage. Response from every quarter has been excellent, and Bahrain Bay BSC is already in discussions with several interested parties to participate as developers of the other subprojects of Bahrain Bay."

By March 2008, the development had succeeded in selling 60 percent of the units to domestic and international companies. In the beginning, many analysts had believed that it was a mad scheme to make a new island and then try to sell the land on it at a premium to hotel developers and retailers. The analysts could not have been more wrong.

The project was able to release the news at the global property exhibition, MIPIM in Cannes, France, where the marketing teams for the project were attending the exhibition and seeking additional investors and developers. It was an ideal event, attracting nearly 26,000 property and investment professionals from around the world. In March 2008, Bob Vincent, chief executive of Bahrain Bay, said, "This news confirms that international and regional developers and investors are committed to our vision of creating a new waterfront community for the rapidly developing north short of Manama, the vibrant hub of Bahrain's business district. As the economy of Bahrain grows and diversifies, a new community will be created that will offer a way of living and working designed for the 21st century."

So successful was the project so far, that the investors and developers were already looking for other sites around the world where island-making projects could be launched.

Nothing so far had been left to chance with the project. Alloptic, a U.S.-based company that provides optical access networks, had been brought onboard in 2007. The intention was to provide Bahrain Bay with a next-generation access network together with a complete communications, entertainment, security, and building-management system. The idea was that Bahrain Bay would offer constant wireless broadband connectivity and would allow both residents and visitors total access to information and communications. Even the background music in public areas could be changed if required. Many of the facilities services would also be controlled and automated through the new network. Vincent said of this part of the project: "Bahrain Bay is committed to helping develop a commercially sound and ecologically viable approach to development. Our goal is to ensure that Bahrain Bay is a self-governing and self-sustaining community, supporting an exceptional quality of life for residents, businesses, and visitors alike. In developing the Bahrain Bay community, we recognized early on the importance that digital connectivity plays in both residential life and creating enhanced productivity for businesses. Identifying, locating, and deploying the right communications infrastructure has been an integral part of our development process. We believe that the Alloptic solution provides us with the world-class infrastructure Bahrain Bay demands."

By July 2008, the project had moved on even further in terms of sales and marketing. The managers of the project could now announce that they had sold 80 percent of the land. "We have been marketing the project for about 16 months now, and over the next 12–24 months, we will see the remaining parcels being sold," said Vincent. "That success has been built around willingness to take advice from key stakeholders within the project, including our shareholders and government, about what they would like to see as their final outcome, and following their advice and delivering their expectations. It has also been enhanced through our own initiatives, such as spending the time and effort to go offshore and exhibit the opportunity of Bahrain Bay. So far, we have attracted CapitaLand, one of Asia's largest developers, who will be developing a $800 million development within the project. We have also attracted developers from India, France, and the United States. Subregional developers from Kuwait, Saudi Arabia, the United Arab Emirates, and Bahrain have also committed and are progressing their design development process."

Bahrain Bay is not the only development taking place and firmly positioning Bahrain as a major financial and commercial center. Other key projects include the Bahrain Investment Wharf, Bahrain Financial Harbour, Bahrain City Center, Durrat Al Bahrain, and Amwaj Islands. Between them, they are contributing 27.4 percent average growth per annum to the country's real-estate sector.

In order to imbed the project into the community, Bahrain Bay decided to sponsor and make a substantial donation to the Busaiteen Football Club. Vincent explained why: "As Bahrain Bay develops a new waterfront community along the north shore of Manama, it is imperative that we take our philosophy of community development and support into the communities already present around Bahrain Bay. The community we are creating will affect not only the people and businesses who wish to live and operate in Bahrain Bay, but it will also touch those communities around it for a long time to come. By investing in and working with local activities now, we are creating the foundations for a long lasting partnership between Bahrain Bay and its wider community. Our support of Busaiteen represents how we are making our objective a reality. Sport is an important part of the social fabric of any community, and it's great to be part of the Busaiteen story, Bahrain Bay's local team, and we hope that our donation will help them along the way to great achievements in the league this year."

As far as the overall marketing plan is concerned, Bahrain Bay sees it as an evolving process. The key marketing messages are:

- Communicate a wide range of messages to the broadest range of audiences.
- Address challenges as they present themselves in the competitive marketplace.
- Ensure that all marketing messages conform to the highest possible standards.
- Support the brand name of Bahrain Bay as a vision of the business' future.

The Bahrain Bay website is an extensive one (www.bahrainbay. com). It is, understandably, very corporate. The international and Arab world press carry a large number of stories on the project; a testament that the first of the marketing issues are being addressed by the business.

Questions for Discussion

1. What are Bahrain Bay's four founding philosophies, and how might they be used as marketing tools?

2. What would you see as being Bahrain Bay's mission?

3. What is MIPIM, and why was it important for Bahrain Bay to target its potential customers, investors, developers, and retailers?

4. Why might the Kingdom of Bahrain be an attractive location for overseas investors?

5. What are Bahrain's closest competitors for inward foreign investment?

6. What part of the marketing mix is related to the football sponsorship, and what function does it perform?

Sources: "Bahrain Bay—$1.5 Billion Urban Development Set to Change the Face of Manama," *AMEInfo*, December 10, 2005, www. ameinfo.com/73637.html; "60pc Bahrain Bay Plots Sold Out," *Gulf Daily News*, March 12, 2008, www.gulf-daily-news.com/NewsDetails. aspx?storyid=211254; "Bahrain Bay Supports Busaiteen Football Club," *AMEInfo*, January 16, 2008, www.ameinfo.com/143928.html; additional information from Bahrain Bay Development B.S.C, www.bahrainbay.com; Arcapita, www.arcapita.com; Property Wire, www.propertywire.com.

PART 2

Understanding the Marketplace and Consumers

Chapter 3

Part 1   Defining Marketing and the Marketing Process (Chapters 1, 2)
Part 2   Understanding the Marketplace and Consumers (Chapters 3, 4, 5, 6)
Part 3   Designing a Customer-Driven Strategy and Mix (Chapters 7, 8, 9, 10, 11, 12, 13, 14)
Part 4   Extending Marketing (Chapters 15, 16, 17)

Analyzing the Marketing Environment

Chapter PREVIEW

In Part 1 (Chapters 1 and 2), you learned about the basic concepts of marketing and the steps in the marketing process for building profitable relationships with targeted consumers. In Part 2, we'll look deeper into the first step of the marketing process—understanding the marketplace and customer needs and wants. In this chapter, you'll discover that marketing operates in a complex and changing environment. Other *actors* in this environment—suppliers, intermediaries, customers, competitors, publics, and others—may work with or against the company. Major environmental *forces*—demographic, economic, natural, technological, political, and cultural—shape marketing opportunities, pose threats, and affect the company's ability to build customer relationships.

To develop effective marketing strategies, you must first understand the environment in which marketing operates. Let's start with a look at a business icon in the Arab world, Emaar.

Dubai real estate experienced the start of a freehold property revolution in May 2002. Before then, only UAE nationals could own property in Dubai, but in that month, Dubai Crown Prince General Sheikh Mohammed bin Rashid Al Maktoum issued a decree allowing foreigners to buy property freehold. This replaced the recently adopted policy of allowing 99-year leases for foreign purchase, a policy which had not been a great success.

The policy of allowing freehold tenure, and particularly allowing foreign ownership, created a boom in the Dubai residential property market.[1] The economy was growing rapidly, partly as a result of the growth in free trade cities, and partly because of the effect of strong oil prices. There was also the excitement of planned 'mega projects' like the Dubai International Financial Centre, Dubai Festival City, and the Dubai Metals and Commodities Centre.

Emaar Properties PJSC, a global real estate developer based in Dubai, first created the 3.5 km-long Dubai Marina, designed to be the focus of the New Dubai and home to more than 40,000 residents in a high-rise 'city within a city.' Following Emaar's subsequent development of 'The Meadows' villas, almost a thousand potential purchasers queued at the Emirates Towers hotel. A similar sell-out occurred when Emaar's competitor, Nakheel, put 2,000 'The Palm' villas up for sale. This 5 km-long, palm-shaped island off the Dubai coastline became an international sensation. The question then became how quickly new companies, in addition to Emaar and Nakheel, could develop their projects.

The main focus turned to the Burj Khalifa. This mid-town development was, at around 170 stories, planned to be the tallest building in the world. By 2005 more than 100 high-rise towers were being built in the area. The maturity of the Dubai real-estate market was confirmed when HSBC started to offer local mortgages.

By the end of 2008 the property prices in Dubai had peaked and prices started to show signs of weakness. *AME Info*, an online business magazine in the Middle East, reported: "It is clear to us that the landscape has changed significantly since the end of September. A new factor, namely a shortage of liquidity caused by the international financial crisis, has impacted the market. Over the past three quarters the rate of growth has slowed to the point where we expect overall price growth to enter negative territory in the fourth [quarter]." By the end of 2009, property prices on average had dropped by about 50 percent from the high of Q3 2008.[2]

What would this mean for Emaar? Emaar's signature developments had been at the heart of the Dubai 'economic miracle,' and had effectively changed the face of Dubai within seven years, and redefined lifestyles in the Emirate. Key to these developments had been the idea

> Emaar's rise and maturity is symbolized by the Burj Khalifa, the world's tallest building when it opened in 2010.

of self-contained communities with high-quality amenities. A range of schools, parks, landscaped grounds, and retail centers were integrated so that residents were offered lifestyles based around, for example, golf, equestrian, and marine activities.

The Emaar Group expanded by developing Emaar International (aiming to diversify into foreign markets, thus reducing the risks associated with a single market and sustaining growth for the future). Emaar Properties PJSC became one of the world's largest real-estate companies; in 2007, it entered the *Financial Times* Global 500 ranking of the world's largest companies.[3] But despite all this, Emaar was not immune to the economic downturn in the UAE, particularly the fall of property prices in Dubai. Its share price, normally hovering between US$2.72 and US$3.54, crashed to US$0.5 in February 2009.[4]

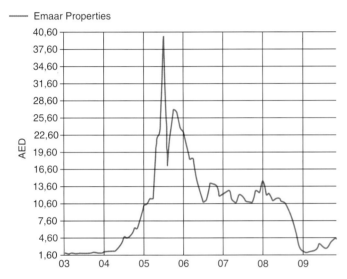

Emaar Properties

Source: Share Graph, data provided by Dubai Financial Market, supplied by Euroland.com. Accessed at www.emaar.com/index. aspx?page=investorrelations-shareprice-graph.html, October 2009.

Emaar attempted to turn the business around by refocusing its strategy. It recorded revenues of Dhs 5,429m (US$1,478m) in the first nine months of 2009, with net operating profits of Dhs 1,401m (US$381m).[5] This improvement occurred largely as a result of focusing on initiatives to support customers through property purchases and a commitment to project delivery. Chairman Mohamed Alabbar said the focus of the company for that period had been on completing announced projects and strengthening customer relationships. "Emaar successfully worked with its contractors and suppliers to achieve the project completion schedules as well as launched customer-oriented initiatives that have helped strengthen investor confidence," he said. "The city remains on track for sustained growth, despite the impact of the global

financial crisis, which will further boost the property sector," he added.[6]

Emaar's Dubai mall development contains over 1,000 stores, including a range of global brands represented for the first time in the Arab world. The mall's attractions include SEGA Republic, the Arab world's largest theme park; and Reel Cinemas, Dubai's largest cinema complex.

In other key international development plans, Emaar signed a management agreement to develop BeitMisk, a master-planned community in Lebanon. In Jordan, the company opened the second phase of 'The Apartments'—Mediterranean-style low-rise towers in the Samarah Dead Sea Resort.

By October 2010, Emaar Properties reported net operating profits of AED 2.343 billion (US$638 million) for the first nine months of the year. In other words, net operating profits were up over 67 percent on the previous year. The company claimed that this was largely because of strong recurring revenue from its hospitality and malls businesses. Chairman Alabbar commented that: "The solid results posted by Emaar during the first nine months of the year, marked by the delivery of our iconic tower Burj Khalifa, are testament to the strength of our diversified growth model. We have successfully focused on our strategy of geographic expansion in promising markets and delivered on our core competency of creating world-class real estate developments."[7]

In the early years of the millennium, Emaar had started with very rapid growth, resulting from the new property ownership laws and high oil prices. It then experienced the effects of the international economic downturn of 2009. However, by January 2010, Emaar was recovering well, as illustrated by its share price of US$0.95.

Dubai Marina is a sensationally ambitious project by Emaar to create a man-made marina and new waterfront along a 3.5 km stretch.

Even the successes of several major real-estate projects including Emirates Hills and the Dubai Marina were not enough to protect property development company Emaar from the global recession. But Emaar is a good example of how an awareness of the marketing environment can help a company navigate both the good times and the hard times.

Objective Outline

OBJECTIVE 1 Describe the environmental forces that affect the company's ability to serve its customers.

OBJECTIVE 2 Explain how changes in the demographic and economic environments affect marketing decisions.

OBJECTIVE 3 Identify the major trends in the firm's natural and technological environments.

OBJECTIVE 4 Explain the key changes in the political and cultural environments.

OBJECTIVE 5 Discuss how companies can react to the marketing environment.

Marketing environment
The actors and forces outside the marketing department that affect marketing management's ability to build and maintain successful relationships with target customers.

Microenvironment
The actors close to the company that affect its ability to serve its customers—the company, suppliers, marketing intermediaries, customer markets, competitors, and publics.

Macroenvironment
The larger societal forces that affect the microenvironment—demographic, economic, natural, technological, political, and cultural forces.

A company's **marketing environment** consists of the actors and forces outside the marketing department that affect marketing management's ability to build and maintain successful relationships with target customers. Like Emaar, companies constantly watch and adapt to the changing environment.

More than any other group in a company, marketers must be the environmental trend trackers and opportunity seekers. Although every manager in an organization needs to observe the outside environment, marketers have two special skills. They have disciplined methods—marketing research and marketing intelligence—for collecting information about the marketing environment. They also spend more time in customer and competitor environments. By carefully studying the environment, marketers can adapt their strategies to meet new marketplace challenges and opportunities.

The marketing environment is made up of a *microenvironment* and a *macroenvironment.* The **microenvironment** consists of the actors close to the company that affect its ability to serve its customers—the company, suppliers, marketing intermediaries, customer markets, competitors, and publics. The **macroenvironment** consists of the larger forces in society that affect the microenvironment—demographic, economic, natural, technological, political, and cultural forces.

We look first at the company's microenvironment.

Author Comment The microenvironment includes all of the actors close to the company that affect, positively or negatively, its ability to create value for and relationships with its customers.

The Company's Microenvironment (pp 68–71)

Marketing management's job is to build relationships with customers by creating customer value and satisfaction. However, marketing managers cannot do this alone. **Figure 3.1** shows the major actors in the marketer's microenvironment. Marketing success will require

■FIGURE | 3.1 Actors in the Microenvironment

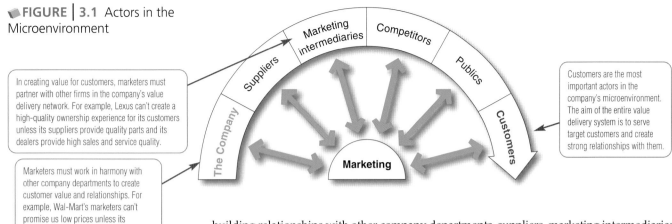

FIGURE | 3.1 Actors in the Microenvironment

In creating value for customers, marketers must partner with other firms in the company's value delivery network. For example, Lexus can't create a high-quality ownership experience for its customers unless its suppliers provide quality parts and its dealers provide high sales and service quality.

Marketers must work in harmony with other company departments to create customer value and relationships. For example, Wal-Mart's marketers can't promise us low prices unless its operations department delivers low costs.

Customers are the most important actors in the company's microenvironment. The aim of the entire value delivery system is to serve target customers and create strong relationships with them.

building relationships with other company departments, suppliers, marketing intermediaries, customers, competitors, and various publics, which combine to make up the company's value delivery network.

The Company

In designing marketing plans, marketing management takes other company groups into account—groups such as top management, finance, research and development (R&D), purchasing, operations, and accounting. All of these interrelated groups form the internal environment. Top management sets the company's mission, objectives, broad strategies, and policies. Marketing managers make decisions within the strategies and plans made by top management. As we discussed in Chapter 2, marketing managers must work closely with other company departments. Other departments have an impact on the marketing department's plans and actions. And under the marketing concept, all of these functions must 'think consumer.' They should work in harmony to provide superior customer value and relationships.

Suppliers

Suppliers form an important link in the company's overall customer value delivery system. They provide the resources needed by the company to produce its goods and services. Supplier problems can seriously affect marketing. Marketing managers must watch supply availability and costs. Supply shortages or delays, labor strikes, and other events can cost sales in the short run and damage customer satisfaction in the long run. Rising supply costs may force price increases that can harm the company's sales volume.

Most marketers today treat their suppliers as partners in creating and delivering customer value.

Marketing Intermediaries

Marketing intermediaries
Firms that help the company to promote, sell, and distribute its goods to final buyers.

Marketing intermediaries help the company to promote, sell, and distribute its products to final buyers. They include resellers, physical distribution firms, distributors, agents, marketing services agencies, and financial intermediaries. *Resellers* are distribution channel firms that help the company find customers or make sales to them. These include wholesalers and retailers that buy and resell merchandise. Selecting and partnering with resellers is not easy. No longer do manufacturers have many small, independent resellers from which to choose. They now face large and growing reseller organizations such as Wal-Mart, Carrefour, Watani, Union Coop, IKEA, ACE, Lulu, and Sharaf DG. These organizations frequently have enough power to dictate terms or even shut smaller manufacturers out of large markets.

Physical distribution firms help the company to stock and move goods from their points of origin to their destinations. *Distributors* and *agents* are organizations based in the markets that generally have a contractual relationship with the principal company to buy their products and to distribute them in the local market. For example, Al-Futtaim Motors is the distributor for Toyota in the UAE. *Marketing services agencies* are the marketing research firms, advertising agencies, media firms, and marketing consultancy firms that help the company target and promote its products to the right markets. *Financial intermediaries* include banks, credit companies, insurance companies, and other businesses that help finance transactions or insure against the risks associated with the buying and selling of goods.

Like suppliers, marketing intermediaries form an important component of the company's overall value delivery system. In its search to create satisfying customer relationships, the company must do more than just improve its own performance. It must partner effectively with marketing intermediaries to improve the performance of the entire system.

Thus, today's marketers recognize the importance of working with their intermediaries as partners rather than simply as channels through which they sell their products. For example, when Pepsi signs on as the exclusive beverage provider for a fast-food chain, such as KFC, Pizza Hut or Hardee's, it provides much more than just soft drinks. It also pledges powerful marketing support.

Competitors

The marketing concept states that to be successful, a company must provide greater customer value and satisfaction than its competitors do. Thus, marketers must do more than simply adapt to the needs of target consumers. They must also gain strategic advantage by positioning their offerings strongly against competitors' offerings in the minds of consumers.

No single competitive marketing strategy is best for all companies. Each firm should consider its own size and industry position compared to those of its competitors. Large firms with dominant positions in an industry can use certain strategies that smaller firms cannot afford. But being large is not enough. There are winning strategies for large firms, but there are also losing ones. And small firms can develop strategies that give them better rates of return than large firms enjoy.

Publics

Public

Any group that has an actual or potential interest in or impact on an organization's ability to achieve its objectives.

The company's marketing environment also includes various publics. A **public** is any group that has an actual or potential interest in or impact on an organization's ability to achieve its objectives. We can identify seven types of publics:

- *Financial publics.* This group influences the company's ability to obtain funds. Banks, investment houses, and stockholders are the major financial publics.

- *Media publics.* This group carries news, features, and editorial opinion. It includes newspapers, magazines, and radio and television stations.

- *Government publics.* Management must take government developments into account. Marketers must often consult the company's lawyers on issues of product safety, truth in advertising, and other matters.

- *Citizen-action publics.* A company's marketing decisions may be questioned by consumer organizations, environmental groups, minority groups, and others. Its public relations department can help it stay in touch with consumer and citizen groups.

- *Local publics.* This group includes neighborhood residents and community organizations. Large companies usually appoint a community relations officer to deal with the community, attend meetings, answer questions, and contribute to worthwhile causes. As an example, consider the BurJuman Breast Cancer Awareness campaign in the UAE, which

The organizations supporting the BurJuman Breast Cancer Awareness campaign recognize the importance of local and community publics.

has run successfully for a number of years in partnership with Welcare Hospital. This campaign is supported by a number of major companies, including Kodak, ENOC/EPPCO, the Ministry of Social Affairs, TECOM Investments (Dubai Technology, Electronic Commerce, and Media Free Zone), Hertz, and GEMS (Global Education Management Systems).[8] These organizations recognize the importance of community publics through their involvement in raising community awareness of this important health issue.

- *General public.* A company needs to be concerned about the general public's attitude toward its products and activities. The public's image of the company affects its buying. In 2008 there were many public protests after Danish newspapers republished a controversial cartoon of the Prophet Muhammad (PBUH) with a bomb in his turban.[9] In response, the Union Cooperative Society in Dubai took all Danish products off its shelves.

- *Internal publics.* This group includes workers, managers, volunteers, and the board of directors. Large companies use newsletters and other means to inform and motivate their internal publics. When employees feel good about their company, this positive attitude spills over to external publics.

A company can prepare marketing plans for these major publics as well as for its customer markets. Suppose the company wants a specific response from a particular public, such as goodwill, favorable word of mouth, or donations of time or money. The company would have to design an offer to this public that is attractive enough to produce the desired response.

Customers

As we've emphasized throughout, customers are the most important actors in the company's microenvironment. The aim of the entire value delivery system is to serve target customers and create strong relationships with them. The company might target any or all of five types of customer markets. *Consumer markets* consist of individuals and households that buy goods and services for personal consumption. *Business markets* buy goods and services for further processing or for use in their production process, whereas *reseller markets* buy goods and services to resell at a profit. *Government markets* are made up of government agencies that buy goods and services to produce public services or transfer the goods and services to others who need them. Finally, *international markets* consist of these buyers in other countries, including consumers, producers, resellers, distributors, agents and governments. Each market type has special characteristics that call for careful study by the seller.

Author Comment | The macroenvironment consists of broader forces that affect the actors in the microenvironment.

The Company's Macroenvironment (pp 71–72)

The company and all of the other actors operate in a larger macroenvironment of forces that shape opportunities and pose threats to the company. **Figure 3.2** shows the six major forces in the company's macroenvironment. In the remaining sections of this chapter, we examine these forces and show how they affect marketing plans.

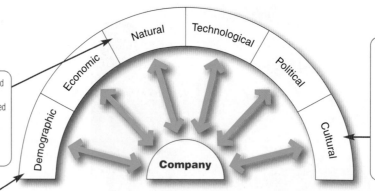

Concern for the natural environment has spawned a so-called green movement in industries ranging from PCs to diesel locomotives. In 2007, for example, HP recovered and recycled 113 million kilograms of electronics globally, equivalent to some 800 jumbo jets. The goal of many companies today is environmental sustainability—strategies and practices that the planet can support indefinitely.

Changing demographics mean changes in markets, which in turn require changes in marketing strategies. For example, Amerprise Financial now targets aging baby boomers with the promise that it will help them "envision what exactly you want to do in the next phase of your life."

Marketers also want to be socially responsible citizens in their markets and communities. For example, shoe brand TOMS was *founded* on a cause: "No complicated formulas It's simple," says the company's founder. "You buy a pair of TOMS and I give a pair to a child in need on your behalf."

FIGURE | **3.2** Major Forces in the Company's Macroenvironment

---

Author Comment | Changes in demographics—in the nature of human populations—mean changes in markets. So they are very important to marketers. We'll start by looking at one of the biggest demographic trends globally—the changing age structure of the population.

Demography
The study of human populations in terms of size, density, location, age, gender, race, occupation, and other statistics.

Demographic environment (pp 72–79)

Demography is the study of human populations in terms of size, density, location, age, gender, race, occupation, and other statistics. The demographic environment is of major interest to marketers because it involves people, and people make up markets. The world population is growing at a rapid rate. It now exceeds 6.6 billion people and will grow to 8.1 billion by the year 2030.[10] The world's large and highly diverse population poses both opportunities and challenges.

Changes in the world demographic environment have major implications for business. For example, consider China. More than a quarter of a century ago, to curb its rapidly increasing population, the Chinese government passed regulations limiting families to one child each. As a result, Chinese children—known as 'little emperors and empresses'—have been showered with attention and luxuries under what's known as the 'six-pocket syndrome.' As many as six adults—two parents and four doting grandparents—may be indulging the whims of each only child.

The little emperors, now ranging in age from newborns to mid-20s, are affecting markets for everything from children's products to financial services, restaurants, and luxury goods. Parents with only one child at home now spend about 40 percent of their income on their cherished child, creating huge market opportunities for children's educational products. For example, Time Warner targeted the lucrative Chinese children's market with an interactive language course called English Time, a 200-lesson, 40-CD set that takes as long as four years for a child to complete. The course sells for US$3,300, more than a year's salary for many Chinese parents.[11]

At the other end of the spectrum, Starbucks is targeting China's older 'little emperors', positioning itself as a new kind of informal but indulgent meeting place.[12]

China's one-child rule created a generation who have been pampered by parents and grandparents and have the means to make luxury purchases. Instead of believing in traditional Chinese collective goals, these young people embrace individuality. "Their view of this world is very different," says the president of Starbucks Greater China. "They have never gone through the hardships of our generation." Starbucks is in tune with that, he says, given its customized drinks, personalized service, and original music compilations.[13]

Thus, marketers keep close track of demographic trends and developments in their markets, both at home and abroad. They track changing age and family structures, geographic population shifts, educational characteristics, and population diversity. Here, we discuss some demographic trends in the Arab world.

Changing Age Structure of the Population

The population of the Arab world was estimated to be 274 million in 2008 and may reach about 350 million by 2020. Currently the youth population (up to 14 years of age) is a significant 32 percent of the total population, at around 44.6 million. The Arab world has one of the highest birth rates globally. From a marketer's perspective, this makes the region a strong potential market for baby, child, and teen products and brands. The population within the age group of 15–64 years is 64 percent or 91.2 million people. From an economic standpoint, this group represents the majority spending power of the overall US$1.8 trillion annual income.[14]

A significant demographic trend in the Arab world is the changing age structure of the population, with more younger and older people. Overall, the Arab world's population, similar to other populations in other geographic regions, contains several generational groups. These groups are sometimes given labels by marketers and researchers in order to identify and consider their collective characteristics and behaviors. Here, we discuss the three largest such groups—sometimes labeled 'the baby boomers,' 'Generation X,' and 'the Millennials'—and their impact on today's marketing strategies.

The Baby Boomers '**Baby boomers**' is a term sometimes used to refer to the generation that was born between 1946 and 1964. The term is most often used in North America and Western Europe, referring to a generation born after the Second World War which began to enjoy privileges that had not been available to their parents. Nevertheless, this same generation can also be identified in the Arab world, and it broadly shares some similar characteristics with Western counterparts. For example, over the years, this 1940s–60s generation has been one of the most powerful forces shaping today's marketing environment. This generation accounts for about 30 percent of the population in the Arab world.

The youngest boomers are aged in their mid-forties; the oldest are entering their sixties. The maturing boomers are rethinking the purpose and value of their work, responsibilities, and relationships. As they reach their peak earning and spending years, the boomers form a profitable market for financial services, luxury goods, home improvements, holidays, travel and entertainment, health and fitness products, and just about everything else.

It would be a mistake to think of the aging boomers as phasing out or slowing down. Today's boomers often 'think young' no matter how old they are. In fact, the boomers are spending large amounts of money on products and services. And unlike previous generations, boomers are retiring later and working more after retirement. Rather than viewing themselves as phasing out, they see themselves as entering new life phases. For example, some cosmetics brands such as Dove, L'Oréal, and Olay use 50- or 60-something models to appeal to boomer women globally. And they use sensible, aspirational appeals aimed at confident, older consumers who aren't trying to fight the aging process. "Boomers are saying 'I'm aging, but I'm going to do it in a way that's graceful and still about who I am,'" says a marketer for Unilever's Dove Pro.Age brand. Says another marketer, "I don't think boomers want to be young again—I don't think they feel old in the first place."[15]

Perhaps no one is targeting the baby boomers more energetically than the financial services industry. In coming years, the aging boomers will transfer some billions of dollars in retirement funds and other savings into new investments. They'll also be inheriting large amounts of money as their parents pass away. Emirates NBD bank targets the baby boomers with its 'Income Builder Plan.'

In designing and marketing its successful *'Income Builder Plan – Retirement'* product, Emirates NDB has carefully targeted the issues and requirements of the generation nearing, entering, or in early retirement. As the bank states on its website:

Demographics and business: Chinese regulations limiting families to one child have resulted in what's known as the 'six-pocket syndrome.' Chinese children and teens are being showered with attention and luxuries, creating opportunities for marketers.

Baby boomers

A term used in the West, and sometimes also globally, to refer to the generation of people born between 1946 (the end of World War II) and 1964.

Emirates NDB is one of many companies in the financial sector which are successfully targeting the generation of people nearing or entering retirement.

"Retirement should not be the helpless phase in life filled with struggle, dependence, and compromise on quality living. Today you have the choice of making your retirement exciting with quality life. It just requires a disciplined savings approach to make sure that you enjoy the retired life."

'*Income Builder Plan – Retirement*' provides a means for clients to plan their needs for retirement income in a straightforward manner. The bank aims to attract new customers through a combination of the simplicity of the plan along with the significant advantage of guaranteed returns. It enables investors to decide how much money they wish to save for retirement, and guarantees the annuity that they want to receive. The plan also aims to encourage clients to have a disciplined approach to saving, by offering the benefit of a steady retirement income without fluctuations if the savings agreements are maintained by clients.

Investors are also offered benefits to protect their plan in case of unfortunate events such as disability, and they are offered some protection against unpredictable financial market conditions. The strong appeal to potential clients is that they can plan to enjoy the same quality of life in retirement that they enjoy currently.[16]

Generation X. The baby boom was followed by a period of low birth rate, creating another generation of people, this time born between 1965 and 1976. Canadian author Douglas Coupland coined the term **Generation X**, because this generation is in the shadow of the boomers and lacks obvious distinguishing characteristics.

The Generation Xers are defined as much by their shared experiences as by their age. In North America and Western Europe, they experienced increasing parental divorce rates and higher employment for their mothers. Having grown up during times of recession and corporate downsizing, they developed a more cautious economic outlook. Although they seek success, they are less materialistic; they prize experience, not acquisition. For many of the Gen Xers that are parents, family comes first, career second. From a marketing viewpoint, the Gen Xers are a skeptical bunch. They tend to research products before they consider a purchase, and they tend to be less receptive to overt marketing pitches.

The Gen Xers are displacing the lifestyles, culture, and materialistic values of the baby boomers. Many companies are focusing on Gen Xers as a major target segment. For example, Dubai Islamic Bank targets its sharia-compliant Takaful product at this age group:

The Al Islami Takaful Program is a sharia-compliant alternative to conventional life insurance products. The appeal of Takaful programs is that they offer various plan options which combine savings and investments to suit particular customer needs, circumstances, and priorities. Dubai Islamic Bank promotes the plans by emphasizing the focus on offering investors peace of mind and taking care of the future of their loved ones. The Takaful programs include a provision for the payment of Takaful benefits to investors' beneficiaries or heirs in the event of their death. Overall, the programs have particular appeal to those with families to support, by giving the investor comfort in the knowledge that the future of their loved ones is provided for. As the bank's marketing literature puts it:

"As an individual you have many dreams…

A day when your child graduates from a prestigious university

Generation X

The generation of people born between 1965 and 1976 in the 'birth dearth' following the baby boom.

A day when your child gets married

A day when you relax in the comfort of your dream home

A day when you start leading a retired life with enough savings to take care of you and much more."[17]

Dubai Islamic Bank's message for its Takaful programs clearly targets a generation in mid-life, who are focused on family priorities and have aspirations for their children's futures, as well as for their own future and retirement.

Millennials (or Generation Y)
The generation of children of the baby boomers, born between 1977 and 2000.

Millennials. Both the baby boomers and Gen Xers will one day be passing the reins to the **Millennials** (also sometimes called Generation Y or the echo boomers). Born between 1977 and 2000, these children of the baby boomers outnumber the Gen Xers and even the baby boomer segment. This group includes several age cohorts: *tweens* (aged 8–12), *teens* (13–19), and *young adults* (the 20-somethings). The younger Millennials are just beginning to wield their buying power. The older ones have now graduated from universities and are moving up in their careers, significantly expanding both their earning and their spending. The Millennials are a diverse bunch.

One thing that all Millennials have in common is their utter fluency and comfort with computer, digital, and Internet technology. "Whereas Gen X spent a lot of time in front of the TV," says one expert, the Millennials "are always 'on.' They're consumers of every imaginable means of communication: TV, radio, cell phone, Internet, video games—often simultaneously."[18]

Each Millennial segment constitutes a huge and attractive market. However, reaching these message-saturated segments effectively requires creative marketing approaches. For example, marketers are increasingly exploiting the opportunities offered by media formats including Facebook, Twitter, Google ads, mobile phone marketing, and many other formats, most of which were not even imagined just a few years ago.

Generational Marketing. Do marketers need to create separate products and marketing programs for each generation? Some experts warn that marketers need to be careful about turning off one generation each time they craft a product or message that appeals effectively to another. Others caution that each generation spans decades of time and many socioeconomic levels. For example, marketers often split the baby boomers into three smaller groups—leading-edge boomers, core boomers, and trailing-edge boomers—each with its own beliefs and behaviors. Similarly, they split the Millennials into tweens, teens, and young adults.

Thus, marketers need to form more precise age-specific segments within each group. More importantly, defining people by their birth date may be less effective than segmenting them by their lifestyle, life stage, or the common values they seek in the products they buy. We will discuss many other ways to segment markets in Chapter 7. **Real Marketing 3.1** considers an example of how companies are responding to the changing habits and work patterns of customers and the cultural diversity of their markets.

The Changing Arab Family

The traditional household consists of a husband, wife, and children and often grandparents. In a traditional Arab family, gender and age are often the basis for defining roles and responsibilities. The father will

The changing Arab family: Although traditional roles are still taught in most Arab families, recent years have seen many changes including increased female education and employment.

Real Marketing 3.1

Niching:
'On the Run'
in Egypt

"On The Run" convenience stores at filling stations successfully meet the needs of a generation of commuters and busy professionals.

ExxonMobil, recognizing the importance of value-added services for customers visiting its numerous filling stations, opened a chain of convenience stores called On the Run. Located at key Esso and Mobil retail sites, the convenience stores have been successfully introduced to the Egyptian market. Globally, ExxonMobil has opened more than 1,000 On the Run stores and in so doing has accommodated the needs of different cultures, markets, and consumers, while sharing a common concept and worldwide expertise.

The aim of On the Run is to offer motorists and others fast-food, pastries, drinks, and convenience items. The key to the approach is the three terms fast, fresh and friendly. In Egypt, the On the Run concept is appealing to consumers who like to buy quality groceries on the go, particularly on their way to work, on their way home, and while traveling. In fact, the brand has become so strong that it attracts a large number of premium customers, who value freshness, speed, and quality of service. On the Run has also attracted La Poire, a premium dessert company, to sell its quality products inside the stores, thus further enriching the brand's image. On the Run has a large pool of loyal customers, who might select a Mobil filling station in order to pass by the store en-route. The brand's key success factor is the focus on the profitable niche market as well as the clear positioning strategy.

On the Run focuses primarily on a quality service, delivered by offering top-quality products, a variety of ready-made and fresh products that suit on-the-go customers, good customer service, and well-organized displays. A key challenge On the Run is facing is optimizing its operation to manage the increasing flow of customers, particularly during peak times.

Pricing is not a problem for On the Run. Its target market is not price sensitive and customers usually buy products in small quantities. Accordingly, a premium pricing strategy is deployed.

Another key success factor for On the Run is the excellent distribution network, which is channeled through a large number of Mobil filling stations across Egypt. On the Run does not need to advertise its services. Word of mouth has been found effective enough to attract a large number of customers. Further, the value propostition is highly dependent on the service offered and the availability of quality products. Customers seek a quick and enjoyable experience, and that's what On the Run focuses on.

Source: Mobil Egypt's website, www.mobilegypt.com/Egypt-English/LCW/Fuels.asp.

usually be the head of the household and be responsible for providing for the financial needs of the family, while the mother usually takes responsibility for raising children and running the house. Generally, inherited values and traditions are still taught to the next generation. Sons are taught to become protectors of their sisters and to assist their fathers with male responsibilities both at home and outside the household. Daughters are still encouraged to provide emotional support to family members as well as to assist their mothers in domestic duties.

However, the Arab family is not immune to change. Recent years have seen an increase in female employment, with the father and mother both providing for the family needs and household chores being done by maids and servants. Similarly, in the past most major decisions relating to the family would have been taken by the father, but more recently there is an increased involvement of the mother and more joint decision making. These changing structures and roles are largely due to the provision of free education to both males and females (as bound by law in many Arab countries), rather than due to economic necessity.[19]

The position of women is often the focus of discussions and research into changing roles. Although Arab culture and traditions and the Islamic religion emphasize the importance of women's roles in running the house and raising children, Arab women are often not universally confined to this role. Even before the emergence of Islam, women were successful businesswomen, and they still fulfill business roles throughout the region, though they may find it necessary to conduct business in an inconspicuous way for cultural reasons.

New families and households are forged when couples are joined together in marriage. A daughter will normally live in her family home until she is married. Once married, she will move to her husband's home. Sons, on the other hand, might move to their own house when they marry, though at least one son will usually live at the family home even if he is married, in order to take care of the parents.

A deep awareness of cultural trends and the composition of typical families and households is vital for marketers. This can be particularly challenging for companies expanding into new countries and cultures which differ significantly from the cultures in the countries in which they have previously operated.

Geographic Shifts in Population

We are currently experiencing a period of great migration between and within countries. More expatriates are coming to the Arab world lured by high income and a high standard of living, driven by the increasing global demand for oil and petroleum.

For example, in the Gulf Cooperation Council (GCC) countries, there have been some unique changes to population patterns. Unlike many other countries, the nationals of most Gulf countries are now a minority population within their own countries. Official data showed the UAE's total native population stood at 947,997 in mid 2010, nearly 11.4 percent of the country's total population of 8.264 million. In Saudi Arabia, Bahrain, and Oman nationals represent no more than 60 percent of the populations. The high level of immigration has resulted in enormous population growth: populations of the GCC countries have jumped from 7,766,000 in 1970 to 13,700,000 in 1980, and to 41,154,000 in 2008.[20] The highest annual growth rate took place during the period of 1975–1985, because the oil boom of the 1970s resulted in a large influx of foreign labor. More recently, the levels of growth have slowed. Between 2000 and 2005 population growth in the Gulf countries averaged 3.3 percent. Nevertheless, the growth of the construction sector in Dubai and Qatar has meant there has still been a continued arrival of foreign labor in these countries. In terms of overall demographics, the influx of foreign labor in GCC countries has shaped the sex and age structure of the populations—there are more immigrant men aged 20–40 years old. Moreover, the need for foreign labor in the GCC countries is likely to continue for some years to come.[21] There are signals that the migrant workforce employed in sectors such as construction will gain more of a voice in future. For example, the International Labour Organisation (ILO) has encouraged energy-rich Gulf countries to protect millions of migrant workers by reforming the sponsor system, introducing a minimum wage, and allowing foreign workers to form representative organizations to protect their rights.[22]

Education and Employment

Since the global recession, unemployment rates have been rising across the Arab world. This has prompted government reassessment of education policies and training schemes in some countries.

Staying with our example of demographic trends in the GCC, unemployment rates rose significantly to reach 8.8 percent in the GCC in 2009 and increased toward 10.5 percent in 2010, which had a particular impact on the nationals in the population (as we discussed, there is still a demand for foreign unskilled

Migrant laborers form a significant part of the population in the GCC.

labor).[23] A 'GCC Unemployment: Sustainable Economies' report in 2010 suggested that governments in the GCC should lead initiatives encouraging entrepreneurship. It also argued that governments should provide small-scale investment opportunities for the unemployed and for new graduates, and should encourage private educational institutions to implement training schemes for these groups. The report suggested that governments should encourage unemployed citizens to develop their entrepreneurial ambitions by offering them financial incentives. Finally, it stressed that governments should focus on key sectors, such as solar energy, education, and healthcare, where there are job opportunities.

The second annual Arab Youth Survey involved face-to-face interviews with 2,000 Arab youths in nine countries. The researchers found that 46 percent of young Arabs would prefer to get a job in the government sector. In the UAE, that figure increased to 61 percent. Sultan Sooud Al Qassemi, chairman of the Young Arab Leaders UAE Chapter, commented that this was "a disaster" and that the government could not employ that many Emiratis.[24]

Increasing Diversity

The ethnic and racial dimension of countries varies enormously. For example, at one end of the spectrum is Japan, which retains a largely Japanese ethnic population. At the other end of the spectrum, the United States is a relatively new population made up of a 'melting pot' of people from all over the world.

Even within the Arab world, different countries vary in their population makeup. In Egypt, for example, Egyptians form by far the largest ethnic group at around 91 percent of the population.[25] As we've already seen, countries in the GCC are much more diverse, with over 3 million foreigners. Asians, mainly from India, Pakistan, Bangladesh, Afghanistan, Sri Lanka, Indonesia, and the Philippines account for more than half the expatriate community in the GCC.[26]

Marketers now face increasingly diverse markets, both at home and abroad, as their operations become more international in scope. In the Arab world, because of the increasing number of expatriates, the population is getting more diverse. About 89 percent of the UAE population, for example, is expatriate. Of this, more than half is from the Indian subcontinent—which creates a huge market for Indian ethnic products.[27]

Companies in the Arab world are targeting ethnic groups with specific products, services, and promotions. For example, let's have a look at how Western Union refined ethnic marketing and brought mobile remittances to the region.

> Labor migration and the money-transfer market are both booming. This boom results from an increase in economic migration, as more people travel to seek work and a better quality of life. Immigrants send money to their families in their country of origin, through remittances. The remittance market totals about US$290 billion globally, with an annual growth rate of 8 percent. In 2006 Arab world remittances totalled US$59 billion.
>
> Western Union introduced the first electronic money-transfer service in 1871, but only expanded outside the American market about 20 years ago. It now deals with businesses and individuals in over 200 countries. Its customers are mostly economic migrants who want to use money-transfer services to send money back home—a market segment with a complex customer base. The key attributes that Western Union claims to offer are speed, reliability, convenience, and trust. Western Union formed a regional partnership in 2008 with the Injaz Money Exchange Company in Saudi Arabia. Injaz has branches throughout all of Saudi, having initially been formed to serve the 1.4 million Indian expatriates in the country. Money transfer had previously been done either through demand drafts or through hawala. Although remittance payments are more expensive than demand drafts, they have the benefit of being faster.
>
> Western Union has noticed that there are some differences between people of different nationalities. In general it finds that expatriates from South Asia or the Arab world are more price sensitive, while Europeans tend to look more for convenience, security, and speed.

A further issue when dealing with people from different ethnic groups is the question of language. Western Union aims to work in a wide range of languages to tailor its marketing to each group, ensuring that it offers the most suitable value proposition. The range of marketing approaches is very wide, perhaps including balloons and outdoor advertising which might be in Russian, Tagalog, or Hindi. The company also organizes many community events, for example flying in an Indian singer or supporting bowling events for Filipinos in Bahrain.[28]

As populations in different countries grow more diverse, successful marketers will continue to diversify their marketing programs to take advantage of opportunities in fast-growing segments.

<table>
<tr><td>

**Author | The economic environ-
Comment | ment can offer both
opportunities and threats. For example,
a recent economic downturn took a
big bite out of Apple's sales growth
and stock performance. Premium
products such as iPhones and iPods are
often hardest hit in troubled economic
times. Said then-CEO Steve Jobs, "Our
stock is being buffeted by factors
much larger than ourselves."**

</td></tr>
</table>

Economic environment

Factors that affect consumer buying power and spending patterns.

Economic Environment (pp 79–80)

Markets require buying power as well as people. The **economic environment** consists of factors that affect consumer purchasing power and spending patterns. Marketers must pay close attention to major trends and consumer spending patterns both across and within their world markets.

Nations vary greatly in their levels and distribution of income. Some countries have *industrial economies*, which constitute rich markets for many different kinds of goods. At the other extreme are *subsistence economies*—they consume most of their own agricultural and industrial output and offer few market opportunities. In between are *developing economies*, which can offer outstanding marketing opportunities for the right kinds of products.

Consider India with its population of 1.1 billion people. In the past, only India's elite could afford to buy a car. In fact, only one in seven Indians now owns one. But recent dramatic changes in India's economy have produced a growing middle class and rapidly rising incomes. Now, to meet the new demand, European, North American, and Asian automakers are introducing smaller, more-affordable vehicles into India. But they'll have to find a way to compete with India's Tata Motors, which has unveiled the least expensive car ever in this market, the Tata Nano. Dubbed 'the people's car,' the Nano sells for only 100,000 rupees (about US$2,500). It can seat four passengers, gets 50 miles per gallon, and travels at a top speed of 60 miles per hour. The car is designed to be India's Model T—the car that puts the developing nation on wheels. For starters, Tata hopes to sell one million of these vehicles a year.[29]

Following are some of the major economic trends in the Arab region and globally:

Economic environment: To capture India's growing middle class, Tata Motors introduced the small, affordable Tata Nano, designed to be India's Model T—the car that puts the developing nation on wheels.

Changes in Income

In recent years, consumers in rich developed countries (including Arab consumers from mostly oil and gas producing countries) fell into a consumption frenzy, fueled by income growth, a boom in the stock market, rapid increases in housing values, and other economic good fortune. They bought and bought, seemingly without caution, amassing record levels of debt. However, the free spending and high expectations of those days were dashed by the recent economic downturn. Today's 'tapped-out' consumers are now repaying debts acquired during earlier spending splurges, sweating out increased mortgage and household expenses, and saving ahead for children's university tuition payments and retirement.

These financially squeezed consumers are spending more carefully. *Value marketing* has become the watchword for many marketers. Rather than offering high quality at a high price, or lesser quality at very low prices, marketers are looking for ways to offer today's more financially cautious buyers greater value—just the right combination of product quality and good service at a fair price.

Changing economic conditions can have a big impact on even the most successful companies. For example, the recent economic downturn slowed Apple's sales growth and stock performance. Premium digital devices, such as the iPhone and iPod, account for more than 40 percent of Apple's sales. In a troubled economy, such products are often the hardest hit. When Apple issued lower-than-expected sales forecasts, its stock price went down drastically. "Apple sells premium products, and every [sign] we get on the economy is a negative one," said an analyst at the time. "[Not even] Apple's products are immune to that," said former Apple CEO Steve Jobs. "Our stock is being buffeted by factors a lot larger than ourselves."[30]

Marketers should pay attention to *income distribution* as well as income levels. Over the past several decades, the rich have grown richer, the middle class has shrunk, and the poor have remained poor. It is not unusual for the top 1 percent of a nation's earners to own over 20 percent of that nation's gross income, and the top 10 percent to own nearly half of that income. In contrast, the bottom 50 percent of a nation's earners often receive less than 15 percent of the gross income.[31]

This distribution of income has created a tiered market. Many companies in the Arab world—such as Debenhams and Neiman-Jashanmal department stores—aggressively target the affluent. Others—such as Dirham stores—target those with more modest means. Still other companies tailor their marketing offers across a range of markets, from the affluent to the less affluent.

Changing Consumer Spending Patterns

Food, housing, and transportation use up the most household income. However, consumers at different income levels have different spending patterns. Some of these differences were noted over a century ago by Ernst Engel, who studied how people shifted their spending as their income rose. He found that as family income rises, the percentage spent on food declines, the percentage spent on housing remains about constant (except for such utilities as gas, electricity, and public services, which decrease), and both the percentage spent on most other categories and that devoted to savings increase. **Engel's laws** generally have been supported by later studies.

Changes in major economic variables such as income, cost of living, interest rates, and savings and borrowing patterns have a large impact on the marketplace. Companies watch these variables by using economic forecasting. Businesses do not have to be wiped out by an economic downturn or caught short in a boom. With adequate warning, they can take advantage of changes in the economic environment.

Engel's laws

Differences noted over a century ago by Ernst Engel in how people shift their spending across food, housing, transportation, health care, and other goods and services categories as family income rises.

Author Comment | Today's enlightened companies are developing environmentally sustainable strategies in an effort to create a world economy that the planet can support indefinitely.

Natural Environment (pp 80–82)

The **natural environment** involves the natural resources that are needed as inputs by marketers or that are affected by marketing activities. Environmental concerns have grown steadily during the past three decades. In many cities around the world, air and water pollution have reached dangerous levels. World concern continues to mount about the possibilities of global warming, and many environmentalists fear that we soon will be buried in our own trash.

Marketers should be aware of several trends in the natural environment. The first involves growing *shortages of raw materials*. Air and water may seem to be infinite resources, but some groups see long-run dangers. Air pollution chokes many of the world's large cities, and water shortages are already a big problem in some parts of the world. By 2030, more than one in three of the world's human beings will not have enough water to drink.[32] Renewable resources, such as forests and food, also have to be used wisely. Nonrenewable

Natural environment

Natural resources that are needed as inputs by marketers or that are affected by marketing activities.

resources, such as oil, coal, and various minerals, pose a serious problem. Firms making products that require these scarce resources face large cost increases, even if the materials remain available.

A second environmental trend is *increased pollution.* Industry will almost always damage the quality of the natural environment. Consider the disposal of chemical and nuclear wastes; the dangerous mercury levels in the ocean; the quantity of chemical pollutants in the soil and food supply; and the littering of the environment with nonbiodegradable bottles, plastics, and other packaging materials.

A third trend is *increased government intervention* in natural resource management. The governments of different countries vary in their concern and efforts to promote a clean environment. One example of a country in the Arab region that has paid attention to environmental issues is Qatar. It has passed a number of laws and statutes to protect and maintain the environment. It has also set up the Supreme Council for the Environment and Natural Reserves (SCENR). This organization aims to achieve its policy objectives by ensuring that all governmental and non-governmental institutions join forces and use educational and media activities to spread environmental awareness.[33]

Other examples from the Arab world include the Environment Agency—Abu Dhabi (EAD)—a governmental agency that was established in 1996. EAD is "committed to protecting and managing biodiversity, providing a clean environment and promoting Sustainable Development in the Emirate of Abu Dhabi."[34] In a similar way, Saudi Arabia formed the Meteorological and Environmental Protection Administration (MEPA), which is responsible for environmental protection— a key role in a country undergoing rapid development of its infrastructure and industry.

Environmental sustainability

Developing strategies and practices that create a world economy that the planet can support indefinitely.

Some counties do little about pollution, largely because they lack the needed funds or political will. Even the richer nations lack the vast funds and political accord needed to mount a worldwide environmental effort. The general hope is that companies around the world will accept more social responsibility, and that less expensive devices can be found to control and reduce pollution.

Concern for the natural environment has developed the so-called green movement. Today, enlightened companies go beyond what government regulations dictate. They are developing strategies and practices that support **environmental sustainability**—an effort to create a world economy that the planet can support indefinitely. They are responding to consumer demands with more environmentally responsible products.

For example, General Electric is using its 'ecomagination' to create products for a better world—cleaner aircraft engines, cleaner locomotives, cleaner fuel technologies. And in 2005, GE launched its Evolution series locomotives—diesel engines that cut fuel consumption by 5 percent and emissions by 40 percent compared with locomotives built just a year earlier. Up next is a triumph of sheer coolness: a GE hybrid diesel–electric locomotive that, just like a Prius, captures energy from braking and will improve mileage by 10 percent.[35]

Other companies are developing recyclable or biodegradable packaging, recycled materials and components, better pollution controls, and more energy-efficient operations. For example, HP is pushing legislation to force recycling of old televisions, computers, and other electronic equipment:[36]

HP wants your old PCs back. For decades the computer maker has invested in recycling systems, giving it a head start against competitors. In 2007, HP recovered 113 million kilograms of electronics globally—equivalent to more than 800 jumbo jets. HP also reused 30 million kilograms of hardware to be refurbished

Ecomagination from GE uses advanced environmental technology to turn a plentiful resource like the sun into precious energy that could power homes and businesses all over the region. As the Middle East continues to grow, GE is at the forefront in providing energy solutions for a brighter tomorrow.

GE imagination at work   ecomagination

Supporting environmental sustainability: GE has responded to the consumer demand for increased environmental responsibility from corporations, by using "ecomagination" to create cleaner fuel technologies.

for resale or donation. Its goal was to reduce PC energy usage 25 percent by 2010. No other electronics maker at the time had a recycling, reuse, and resale program on this scale. HP's efforts have made it the darling of environmentalists, but its agenda isn't entirely altruistic. "We see legislation coming," says HP's vice president for corporate, social, and environmental responsibility. "A lot of companies haven't stepped up to the plate.... If we do this right, it becomes an advantage to us."

Thus, companies today are looking to do more than just good deeds. More and more, they are recognizing the link between a healthy ecology and a healthy economy. They are learning that environmentally responsible actions can also be good business.

> **Author Comment** | Technological advances are perhaps the most dramatic forces affecting today's marketing strategies. Just think about the tremendous impact of the web, which emerged only in the mid-1990s, on marketing. You'll see examples of the surging world of online marketing many times in every chapter and we'll discuss it in detail in Chapter 13.

Technological environment

Forces that create new technologies, creating new product and market opportunities.

Technological environment (pp 82–83)

The **technological environment** is perhaps the most dramatic force now shaping our destiny. Technology has released such wonders as antibiotics, robotic surgery, miniaturized electronics, laptop computers, and the Internet. It also has released such horrors as nuclear missiles, chemical weapons, and assault rifles. It has released such mixed blessings as the automobile, television, and credit cards.

Our attitude toward technology depends on whether we are more impressed with its wonders or its blunders. For example, what would you think about having tiny little transmitters implanted in all of the products you buy that would allow the tracking of products from their point of production through use and disposal? On the one hand, it would provide many advantages to both buyers and sellers. On the other hand, it could be a bit scary. Either way, it's already happening:[37]

Imagine a world in which every product contains a tiny transmitter, loaded with information. As you stroll through the supermarket aisles, shelf sensors detect your selections and beam ads to your shopping cart screen, offering special deals on related products. As your cart fills, scanners detect that you might be buying for a dinner party; the screen suggests a dessert to go with the meal you've planned. When you leave the store, exit scanners total up your purchases and automatically charge them to your credit card. At home, readers track what goes into and out of your pantry, updating your shopping list when stocks run low. For Friday dinner, you put the biryani mix into your 'smart oven,' which follows instructions from an embedded chip and cooks it to perfection.

Seem far-fetched? Not really. In fact, it might soon become a reality, thanks to tiny radio-frequency identification (RFID) transmitters—or 'smart chips'—that can be embedded in the products you buy. Beyond benefits to consumers, the RFID chips also give producers and retailers an amazing new way to track their products electronically—anywhere in the world, anytime, automatically—from factories, to warehouses, to retail shelves, to recycling centers. Many large firms are adding fuel to the RFID fire.

The technological environment changes rapidly. Think of all of today's common products that were not available 100 years ago, or even 30 years ago. Saladin did not know about automobiles, airplanes, radios, or the electric light. Ibn Sina did not know about television, aerosol cans, automatic

Technological environment: Technology is perhaps the most dramatic force shaping the marketing environment.

dishwashers, air conditioners, antibiotics, or computers. Franklin Delano Roosevelt did not know about xerography, synthetic detergents, tape recorders, birth control pills, jet engines, or earth satellites. President Nasser did not know about personal computers, cellphones, the Internet, or googling.

New technologies create new markets and opportunities. However, every new technology replaces an older technology. Transistors hurt the vacuum-tube industry; xerography hurts the carbon-paper business; CDs hurt phonograph records; and digital photography hurts the film business. When old industries fought or ignored new technologies, their businesses declined. Thus, marketers should watch the technological environment closely. Companies that do not keep up will soon find their products outdated. And they will miss new product and market opportunities.

Scientists today are researching a wide range of promising new products and services, ranging from practical solar energy, electric cars, paint-on computer and entertainment video displays, and powerful computers that you can wear or fold into your pocket, to go-anywhere concentrators that produce drinkable water from the air.

Today's research is usually carried out by research teams rather than by lone inventors such as Ibn Sina, Thomas Edison, Samuel Morse, or Alexander Graham Bell. Many companies are adding marketing people to R&D teams to try to obtain a stronger marketing orientation. Scientists also speculate on fantasy products, such as flying cars, three-dimensional televisions, and space colonies. The challenge in each case is not only technical but also commercial—to make *practical*, *affordable* versions of these products.

As products and technology become more complex, the public needs to know that these are safe. Thus, government agencies investigate and ban potentially unsafe products. For example, SASO (Saudi Arabian Standards Organization) in the Kingdom of Saudi Arabia is responsible for ensuring that the products imported into Saudi Arabia comply with all its standards and regulations. Marketers should be aware of regulations like these when applying new technologies and developing new products, and of the impact that higher research costs may have on pricing.

> **Author Comment** | Even the most liberal advocates of the free-market system agree that the system works best with at least some regulation. But beyond regulation, most companies want to be socially responsible. Check the website of almost any company and you'll find long lists of good deeds and environmentally responsible actions. For example, try the Nike Responsibility page (www.nikebiz.com/responsibility/) or Johnson & Johnson's Community page (www.jnj.com/community/index.htm). We'll focus directly on marketing and social responsibility in Chapter 17.

Political and Social Environment (pp 83–85)

Marketing decisions are strongly affected by developments in the political environment. The **political environment** consists of laws, government agencies, and pressure groups that influence or limit various organizations and individuals in a given society.

Legislation Regulating Business

Even the most liberal advocates of free-market economies agree that the system works best with at least some regulation. Well-conceived regulation can encourage competition and ensure fair markets for goods and services. Thus, governments develop *public policy* to guide commerce—sets of laws and regulations that limit business for the good of society as a whole. Almost every marketing activity is subject to a wide range of laws and regulations.

Increasing Legislation. Legislation affecting business around the world has increased steadily over the years. For example, in the UAE the Ministry of Economy declared in April 2010 that it is in the process of developing new laws as part of modernizing the legislative system and enhancing the business environment in line with the UAE strategic vision for 2021. The first aim of these new laws is to fill any gaps in commercial regulations. The second is to promote efficiency, transparency, and investor confidence throughout the business sector.[38]

Business legislation globally has been enacted for a number of reasons. The first is to *protect companies* from each other. Although business executives may praise competition, they sometimes try to neutralize it when it threatens them. So laws are passed to define and prevent unfair competition.

Political environment

Laws, government agencies, and pressure groups that influence and limit various organizations and individuals in a given society.

The second purpose of government regulation is to *protect consumers* from unfair business practices. Some firms, if left alone, would make low quality products, invade consumer privacy, tell lies in their advertising, and deceive consumers through their packaging and pricing. Unfair business practices have been defined and are enforced by various agencies.

The third purpose of government regulation is to *protect the interests of society* against unrestrained business behavior. Profitable business activity does not always create a better quality of life. Regulation arises to ensure that firms take responsibility for the social costs of their production or products.

Changing Government Agency Enforcement. International marketers will encounter dozens, or even hundreds, of agencies set up to enforce trade policies and regulations. In the UAE, for example, the Consumer Protection Department (CPD) oversees enforcement of regulations including law No: 6 of 2006, which tackles issues relating to the rights of consumer, responsibilities and liabilities and specifying penalties to be imposed on people for selling substandard goods. The CPD has a number of responsibilities, such as increasing consumers' awareness, monitoring and controling prices, working to prevent monopolies, and responding to consumers' complaints.[39]

Because such government agencies have some discretion in enforcing the laws, they can have a major impact on a company's marketing performance.

New laws and their enforcement will continue to increase. Business executives must watch these developments when planning their products and marketing programs. Marketers need to know about the major laws protecting competition, consumers, and society. They need to understand these laws at the local, state, national, and international levels.

Increased Emphasis on Ethics and Socially Responsible Actions

Written regulations cannot possibly cover all potential marketing abuses, and existing laws are often difficult to enforce. However, beyond written laws and regulations, business is also governed by social codes and rules of professional ethics.

Socially Responsible Behavior. Enlightened companies encourage their managers to look beyond what the regulatory system allows and simply 'do the right thing.' These socially responsible firms actively seek out ways to protect the long-run interests of their consumers and the environment.

The recent increased number of business scandals and increased concerns about the environment have created fresh interest in the issues of ethics and social responsibility. Almost every aspect of marketing involves such issues. Unfortunately, because these issues usually involve conflicting interests, well-meaning people can honestly disagree about the right course of action in a given situation. Thus, many industrial and professional trade associations have suggested codes of ethics. And more companies are now developing policies, guidelines, and other responses to complex social responsibility issues.

The boom in Internet marketing has created a new set of social and ethical issues. Critics worry most about online privacy issues. There has been an explosion in the amount of personal digital data available. Users, themselves, supply some of it. They voluntarily place highly private information on social networking sites such as MySpace or on genealogy sites, which are easily searched by anyone with a PC.

However, much of the information is systematically developed by businesses seeking to learn more about their customers, often without consumers realizing that they are under the microscope. Legitimate businesses plant cookies on consumers' PCs and collect, analyze, and share digital data from every mouse click consumers make at their websites. Critics are concerned that companies may now know *too* much, and that some companies might use digital data to take unfair advantage of consumers. Although most companies fully disclose their Internet privacy policies, and most work to use data to benefit their customers, abuses do occur. As a result, consumer advocates and policymakers are taking action to protect consumer privacy.

Princess Haya Bint Al Hussein, wife of HH Sheikh Mohammed Bin Rashid Al Maktoum, vice president and prime minister of the UAE, seen launching the "Breast Cancer Awareness" program at the Dubai Chamber of Commerce and Industry.

Throughout the text, we present 'Real Marketing' features that summarize the main public policy and social responsibility issues surrounding major marketing decisions. These features discuss the legal issues that marketers should understand and the common ethical and societal concerns that marketers face. In Chapter 17, we discuss a broad range of societal marketing issues in greater depth.

Cause-Related Marketing. To exercise their social responsibility and build more positive images, many companies are now linking themselves to worthwhile causes. These days, every product seems to be tied to some cause. IKEA UAE announced that it would donate one euro (approximately AED 5) for every soft toy sold between November 1 and December 31, 2010 in support of UNICEF's education program, an initiative which is one of the world's largest cause-related marketing campaigns.[40]

Cause-related marketing has become a primary form of corporate giving. It lets companies 'do well by doing good' by linking purchases of the company's products or services with fundraising for worthwhile causes or charitable organizations. Companies in the Arab world are slowly adopting cause-related marketing campaigns. As part of its social awareness initiative 'Making it Our Business,' Dubai Chamber of Commerce and Industry collaborates with Vital Voices Global Partnership and the US Middle East Partnership for Breast Cancer Awareness and Research, in the ongoing fight against breast cancer.[41]

Cause-related marketing has stirred some controversy. Critics worry that cause-related marketing is more a strategy for selling than a strategy for giving—that 'cause-related' marketing is really 'cause-exploitative' marketing. Thus, companies using cause-related marketing might find themselves walking a fine line between increased sales and an improved image, and facing charges of exploitation.

However, if handled well, cause-related marketing can greatly benefit both the company and the cause. The company gains an effective marketing tool while building a more positive public image. The charitable organization or cause gains greater visibility and important new sources of funding and support.

> **Author Comment** | Cultural factors strongly affect how people think and how they consume. So marketers are keenly interested in the cultural environment.

Cultural environment

Institutions and other forces that affect society's basic values, perceptions, preferences, and behaviors.

Cultural Environment (pp 85–88)

The **cultural environment** is made up of institutions and other forces that affect a society's basic values, perceptions, preferences, and behaviors. People grow up in a particular society that shapes their basic beliefs and values. They absorb a world view that defines their relationships with others. The following cultural characteristics can affect marketing decision making.

Persistence of Cultural Values

People in a given society hold many beliefs and values. Their core beliefs and values have a high degree of persistence. For example, Muslims believe in praying five times a day, in working, getting married, giving to charity, and being honest. These beliefs shape more specific attitudes and behaviors found in everyday life. *Core* beliefs and values are passed on from parents to children and are reinforced by schools, mosques, business, and government.

Secondary beliefs and values are more open to change. Believing in marriage is a core belief; believing that people should get married early in life is a secondary belief. Marketers have some chance of changing secondary values but little chance of changing core values. For example, family-planning marketers could argue more effectively that people should get married later than not get married at all.

Shifts in Secondary Cultural Values

Although core values are fairly persistent, cultural swings do take place. Consider the impact of popular sports personalities, movie personalities, and other celebrities on young people's hairstyling and clothing norms. Marketers want to predict cultural shifts in order to spot new opportunities or threats. Several firms offer 'futures' forecasts in this connection. For example, the Yankelovich Monitor has tracked consumer value trends for years. Its annual State of the Consumer report analyzes and interprets the forces that shape consumers' lifestyles and their marketplace interactions. The major cultural values of a society are expressed in people's views of themselves and others, as well as in their views of organizations, society, nature, and the universe.

People's Views of Themselves. People vary in their emphasis on serving themselves versus serving others. Some people seek personal pleasure, wanting fun, change, and escape. Others seek self-realization through religion, recreation, or the avid pursuit of careers or other life goals. People use products, brands, and services as a means of self-expression, and they buy products and services that match their views of themselves.

The Yankelovich Monitor identifies several consumer segments whose purchases are motivated by self-views. Here are two examples:[42]

Do-It-Yourselfers—Recent Movers. Embodying the whole do-it-yourself attitude, these active consumers not only tackle home improvement projects on their own, but they also view the experience as a form of self-expression. They view their homes as their havens, especially when it's time to kick back and relax. Undertaking decorating, remodeling, and auto maintenance projects to save money and have fun, Do-It-Yourselfers view their projects as personal victories over the high-priced marketplace. Mostly families with children at home, these consumers also enjoy playing board and card games and renting movies. As recent movers, they're actively spending to turn their new home into a castle.

Adventurers. These adventuresome individuals rarely follow a single path or do the same thing twice. These folks view the experience as far more exciting than the entertainment value. Although they may be appreciative of the arts (including movies, museums, photography, and music), they are more likely to engage in activities most think are too dangerous, and they like to view themselves as doing things others wouldn't dare to do.

Marketers can target their products and services based on such self-views. For example, MasterCard targets Adventurers who might want to use their credits cards to quickly set up the experience of a lifetime. It tells these consumers, "There are some things in life that money can't buy. For everything else, there's MasterCard."

People's Views of Others. In past decades, observers have noted several shifts in people's attitudes toward others. Recently, for example, many trend trackers have seen a new wave of 'cocooning,' in which people are going out less with others and are staying home more to enjoy the creature comforts of home and hearth—from the networked home office, to home entertainment centers, to

2 week vacation to Chile: $4,500

(deciding to miss your return flight: priceless)

There are 192 countries in the world and MasterCard® can help you see every single one. From Kathmandu to the Great Wall of China, no other card is more accepted worldwide. Go to priceless.com for fresh travel ideas and great escapes. there are some things money can't buy. for your next adventure, there's MasterCard.™

MasterCard

People's self-views: With its "priceless" campaign, MasterCard targets "Adventurers" who imagine themselves doing things others wouldn't dare do. MasterCard can help them quickly set up the experience of a lifetime—"deciding to miss your return flight: priceless."

just finding a quiet spot to plug into their iPods while they check into their favorite web hangouts. "Call it Cocooning in the Digital Age," says one observer. "With DVD players in most homes, broadband connections proliferating, scores of new video game titles being released each year, and nearly 400 cable channels, consumers can be endlessly entertained right in their own living room or home theater."[43]

This trend suggests less demand for theater-going and greater demand for home improvement, home office, and home entertainment products. And "as the … 'nesting' or 'cocooning' trend continues, with people choosing to stay home and entertain more often, the trend of upgrading outdoor living spaces has [grown rapidly]," says a home industry analyst. People are adding amenities that make the old house "home, sweet home" for family and friends.[44]

People's Views of Organizations.   People vary in their attitudes toward corporations, government agencies, trade unions, universities, and other organizations. By and large, people are willing to work for major organizations and expect them, in turn, to carry out society's work.

The past two decades have seen a sharp decrease in confidence in and loyalty toward business and political organizations and institutions. In the workplace, there has been an overall decline in organizational loyalty. Waves of company downsizings bred cynicism and distrust. In just the last decade, corporate scandals at Enron, WorldCom, and Tyco; record-breaking profits for big oil companies during a time of all-time high prices at the pump; and other questionable activities have resulted in a further loss of confidence in big business. In the Arab world, there has also been a number of scandals related to big business specially related to the real-estate boom. For example:

"Abid Al Boom, the owner of Abid Al Boom Management and Development Properties, was a struggling businessman in 2004, driving around in a car worth just dhs30,000. But three years later, prosecutors allege, he was living a jet-set lifestyle with 53 high-end cars, a yacht and two boats on which he would throw parties for his friends and hold business meetings. He also splashed out on personalized number plates and gave generous donations to football clubs to boost his profile. The details of his spending spree emerged at Dubai Misdemeanors Court, where he is on trial for the 'betrayal of trust' of 3,700 investors. It was alleged he took nearly dhs900 million from them."[45]

Many people today see work not as a source of satisfaction but as a required chore to earn money to enjoy their nonwork hours. This trend suggests that organizations need to find new ways to win consumer and employee confidence.

People's Views of Society.   People vary in their attitudes toward their society—patriots defend it, reformers want to change it, malcontents want to leave it. People's orientation to their society influences their consumption patterns and attitudes toward the marketplace.

People's Views of Nature.   People vary in their attitudes toward the natural world—some feel ruled by it, others feel in harmony with it, and still others seek to master it. A long-term trend has been people's growing mastery over nature through technology and the belief that nature is bountiful. More recently, however, people have recognized that nature is finite and fragile, that it can be destroyed or spoiled by human activities.

Food producers have also found fast-growing markets for natural and organic products. For example, UAE residents are generally becoming more health conscious and opting for a less-processed, more natural diet.

Currently, very few of the UAE's farms grow organic produce. However, a recent report indicated that the organic food market has been growing at a rate of 20–24 percent annually.[46] The government's Ministry of Environment and Water and Ministry of Health aim to promote the organic movement. The environmental ministry aims to create 3,000 hectares of agricultural land dedicated to organic farming, while the health ministry promotes organic food as part of a healthy diet. In the UAE, the most popular organic product is currently baby food, though fruit, vegetables, and breakfast cereals are also popular. The increasing popularity of health-conscious diets has been demonstrated in the Gulfood exhibition in

Reflecting people's increased interest in a natural diet, the profile of organic produce has increased year by year at the famous Gulfood exhibition, held annually in Dubai.

Dubai. At this exhibition—the region's largest trade exhibition for food, drink, food service, and hospitality equipment— there is clearly an increasing trend in the availability of organic produce.[47]

People's Views of the Universe.   Finally, people vary in their beliefs about the origin of the universe and their place in it. In the Arab world, Islam as a religion is followed by the majority of the population, and its influence is visible in most landscapes through the distinct minarets of the mosques and the lyrical call to prayers (Adhan). In people's daily lives, religion is a strong part of the rituals and culture, be it Islam, Christianity, or Judaism. Individual, family, community, and societal values to a large extent are based on religious values. Reflection of Islam's influence is apparent in foods and any other consumables that must be devoid of any *Haram* ingredients (pork, alcohol, etc). The month of Ramadan is another example of the influence of Islam in the Arab world, when Muslims fast from dawn to dusk during the whole month to gain spiritual strength. To a foreigner it would seem that the day begins after break of the fast in the evening— everything comes alive at night and people shop till early hours of the morning.

9/11, terrorism, and other global events have affected the way people in the Arab region think about religion and Islam in particular. These have polarized people's views and beliefs, which has fueled the growth of Islamic banking and Islamic products and brands in the region. On the other hand, some sections of the youth populations, aided by access to information via the Internet and mobile technology, are influenced by Western lifestyles. The Arab society is changing fast, embracing global brands like McDonalds, Nike, Gucci, and other lifestyle brands in search for their changing values and identity.

Author Comment | Rather than simply watching and reacting, companies should take proactive steps with respect to the marketing environment.

Responding to the Marketing Environment (pp 88-89)

Someone once observed, "There are three kinds of companies: those who make things happen, those who watch things happen, and those who wonder what's happened."[48] Many companies view the marketing environment as an uncontrollable element to which they must react and adapt. They passively accept the marketing environment and do not try to change it. They analyze the environmental forces and design strategies that will help the company avoid the threats and take advantage of the opportunities the environment provides.

Other companies take a *proactive* stance toward the marketing environment. Rather than simply watching and reacting, these firms take aggressive actions to affect the publics and forces in their marketing environment. By taking action, companies can often overcome seemingly uncontrollable environmental events. For example, whereas some companies view the seemingly ceaseless online rumor mill as something over which they have no control, others work proactively to prevent or counter negative word of mouth.

Marketing management cannot always control environmental forces. In many cases, it must settle for simply watching and reacting to the environment. For example, a company would have little success trying to influence geographic population shifts, the economic environment, or major cultural values. But whenever possible, smart marketing managers will take a *proactive* rather than *reactive* approach to the marketing environment (see **Real Marketing 3.2**).

Real Marketing 3.2

First National Bank:

Leading Through Innovation

For years Lebanon has been marketing beauty services, particularly cosmetic surgery. Speaking about the holiday season, Roger El Khoury, head surgeon at the Beirut Beauty Clinic, told CNN: "We are very busy at this time of year—we work like restaurants. When everyone is on vacation, we're working. Every holiday period is busy; people prefer to come here during their vacations, mainly for privacy or secrecy problems." People also come for the quality of service that Lebanon is reputed to deliver.

With an estimated 25 percent increase in the number of surgical procedures performed in 2010, cosmetic surgery in Lebanon has become a true attraction and a focal industry targeting the Arab world and Africa. The top three forms of surgery carried out are rhinoplasty, filling, and lifting.

A study conducted by Mr Maher Mezher, Head of Marketing at First National Bank (FNB) and a marketing professor at Saint-Joseph University, found that a lot of Lebanese people believe that beauty is a factor in achieving success, that it raises one's self-confidence, and can even help one to find a good job. But cosmetic surgery, especially good quality surgery, is not cheap.

Patients in Lebanon started asking doctors and hospitals to accept payment in instalments to make surgery more affordable and accessible. Some customers even started seeking out underground surgeons to provide them with the services at a lower cost. This resulted in multiple cases of unsatisfied customers, who became more self-conscious of their physical appearance rather than feeling more attractive or having a problem corrected.

In 2007, FNB in Lebanon started creating an unprecedented product—plastic surgery loan—to meet the needs of the Lebanese consumer. The product, launched on April 30, 2007, is a US$500 to US$5,000 loan to be used for plastic surgery. The loan is available to the whole market, but it is especially targeted to persons wounded by the Lebanese war (reconstructive surgery), persons born with a certain defection (reconstructive or esthetic surgery), persons who have experienced an accident or an illness (reconstructive surgery), and persons willing to pamper themselves, with a focus on appearance (esthetic surgery).

The product is very simple to apply for. Without any collateral and only proof of income, applicants can receive up to US$3,000. A loan of up to US$5,000 can be granted if applicants provide some form of guarantee. The minimum requirements make it easier to apply for a plastic surgery loan than a regular personal loan.

In the first month that the product became available, FNB received as many as 300 enquiries a day, whereas normally it would expect to receive about 40. Within the first two weeks, applicants were queuing in the bank.

The impact of the product was huge. FNB did more than 160 free interviews on international media channels such as CNN and BBC. Mr Maher Mezher delivered speeches on the FNB marketing innovation case study all over the world. Hundreds of students built their university projects around FNB's plastic surgery loan, and also its fertility loan.

The plastic surgery loan has been the subject of much controversy. Is the product promoting superficiality or is it a service that is serving market needs in a structured way? The availability of the loan was debated by major media outlets such as CNN, BBC, Reuters, Figaro, M6, Russia Today, and many other television and radio stations, newspapers, magazines, and websites.

The best spokespeople for the plastic surgery loans are the surgeons themselves. With the loans, the doctors have more clients who can afford their services. When the product was launched, doctors started familiarizing their patients with the plastic surgery loan options. The plastic surgery clinics started distributing brochures that explained about the loans and how to get them. Having doctors as spokespeople could not have been a better deal for FNB. In that regard, Mr Mezher said, "We will be giving our customers the privacy to go to their surgeons instead of visiting the branch for confidentiality and privacy." Accordingly, FNB managed to acquire most plastic surgery centers and plastic surgeons as customers.

The campaign hit the right target and delivered the right message. The beautiful girl portrayed on FNB's billboards and communication material was the perfect face to imply that, with the loan, customers could

FERTILITY LOAN

Targeting couples facing fertility difficulties: The ad is very simple, yet very expressive.

look as perfect and natural as the woman in the advertisement. The selection of the face for the campaign was right on target for the Lebanese market.

FNB continues to reshape the banking industry and raise the bar with new, innovative products based on defining customer needs and their entire surrounding environment. For example, FNB has launched a fertility loan, which has gained international exposure and positioned the bank as both innovative and humanitarian. The fertility loan covers fertility treatments, stem cell collection and preservation, delivery expenses, and baby accessories. It has led FNB to win three distinguished achievement awards for the most innovative retail banking product.

A market study conducted by Mr Maher Mezher showed that 18.7 percent of Lebanese couples could not have babies without medical assistance. With the average couple in Lebanon marrying between the ages of 30 and 32 years, and most newlyweds waiting for one to three years before attempting to have children, the age of conception is brought close to 35 years. Medical research indicates that overall individual fertility starts to decrease at 35 years. In 2008, there were 20 infertility centers in Lebanon. Some of them performed between 60 and 100 in vitro fertilizations per month. This meant that the market really had a need for the services. All the results mentioned in the study encouraged Mezher to develop and launch the fertility loan.

Mr Maher Mezher stated: "We believe that when innovation is built on science it can be repeated; that's why in 2008 we launched the Fertility Loan, again the first of its kind in the world." He added, "Needs are constantly changing therefore defining needs and trying to satisfy them is my job as a head of marketing."

Sources: "Plastic surgery loan," First National Bank website, http://fnb.com.lb; Barry Nield, CNN, November 19, 2010, http://articles.cnn.com/2010-11-19/world/Lebanon.plastic.surgery_1_cosmetic-surgery-surgery-industry-hajj?_s=PM:WORLD.

This case was provided by Mohamed Radwan, adjunct faculty member at the American University in Cairo and managing director for Platinum Partners.

REVIEWING Objectives AND KEY Terms

This chapter and the next two chapters examine the environments of marketing and how companies analyze these environments to better understand the marketplace and consumers. Companies must constantly watch and manage the *marketing environment* in order to seek opportunities and ward off threats. The marketing environment consists of all the actors and forces influencing the company's ability to transact business effectively with its target market.

OBJECTIVE 1   Describe the environmental forces that affect the company's ability to serve its customers. (pp 68–72)

The company's *microenvironment* consists of other actors close to the company that combine to form the company's value delivery network or that affect its ability to serve its customers. It includes the company's *internal environment*—its several departments and management levels—as it influences marketing decision making. *Marketing channel firms*—suppliers and marketing intermediaries, including resellers, distributors, agents, physical distribution firms, marketing services agencies, and financial intermediaries—co-operate to create customer value. Five types of customer *markets* include consumer, business, reseller, government, and international markets. *Competitors* vie with the company in an effort to serve customers better. Finally, various *publics* have an actual or potential interest in or impact on the company's ability to meet its objectives.

The *macroenvironment* consists of larger societal forces that affect the entire microenvironment. The six forces making up the company's macroenvironment include demographic, economic, natural, technological, political, and cultural forces. These forces shape opportunities and pose threats to the company.

OBJECTIVE 2   Explain how changes in the demographic and economic environments affect marketing decisions. (pp 72–80)

Demography is the study of the characteristics of human populations. Today's *demographic environment* shows a changing age structure, shifting family profiles, geographic population shifts, a better-educated and more white-collar population, and increasing diversity. The *economic environment* consists of factors that affect buying power and patterns. The economic environment is characterized by more consumer concern for value and shifting consumer spending patterns. Today's squeezed consumers are seeking greater value—just the right combination of good quality and service at a fair price. The distribution of income is also shifting. The rich have grown richer, the middle class has shrunk, and the poor have remained poor, leading to a two-tiered market. Many companies now tailor their marketing offers to two different markets—the affluent and the less affluent.

OBJECTIVE 3   Identify the major trends in the firm's natural and technological environments. (pp 80–83)

The *natural environment* shows three major trends: shortages of certain raw materials, higher pollution levels, and more government intervention in natural resource management. Environmental concerns create marketing opportunities for alert companies. The *technological environment* creates both opportunities and challenges. Companies that fail to keep up with technological change will miss out on new product and marketing opportunities.

OBJECTIVE 4   Explain the key changes in the political and cultural environments. (pp 83–88)

The *political environment* consists of laws, agencies, and groups that influence or limit marketing actions. The political environment has undergone three changes that affect marketing worldwide: increasing legislation regulating business, strong government agency enforcement, and greater emphasis on ethics and socially responsible actions. The *cultural environment* is made up of institutions and forces that affect a society's values, perceptions, preferences, and behaviors. The environment shows trends toward digital 'cocooning,' a lessening trust of institutions, increasing patriotism, greater appreciation for nature, a new spiritualism, and the search for more meaningful and enduring values.

OBJECTIVE 5   Discuss how companies can react to the marketing environment. (pp 88–89)

Companies can passively accept the marketing environment as an uncontrollable element to which they must adapt, avoiding threats and taking advantage of opportunities as they arise. Or they can take a *proactive* stance, working to change the environment rather than simply reacting to it. Whenever possible, companies should try to be proactive rather than reactive.

KEY Terms

OBJECTIVE 1

Marketing
environment (p 68)
Microenvironment (p 68)
Macroenvironment (p 68)
Marketing
intermediaries (p 69)
Public (p 70)

OBJECTIVE 2

Demography (p 72)
Baby boomers (p 73)
Generation X (p 74)
Millennials
(Generation Y) (p 75)
Economic environment (p 79)
Engel's laws (p 80)

OBJECTIVE 3

Natural environment (p 80)
Environmental sustainability (p 81)
Technological environment (p 82)

OBJECTIVE 4

Political environment (p 83)
Cultural environment (p 85)

DISCUSSING & APPLYING THE Concepts

Discussing the Concepts

1. Name and describe the elements of a company's microenvironment and give an example illustrating why each is important.

2. List some of the demographic trends of interest to marketers in the Arab world and discuss whether these trends pose opportunities or threats for marketers.

3. Discuss current trends in the economic environment of which marketers must be aware and provide examples of companies' responses to each trend.

4. Discuss the primary reasons why a company would hire someone to campaign on particular issues or to lobby government.

5. Compare and contrast core beliefs/values and secondary beliefs/values. Provide an example of each and discuss the potential impact marketers have on each.

6. How should marketers respond to the changing environment?

Applying the Concepts

1. In a small group, select a current television program and explain how it might affect the cultural environment.

2. Find out about an agency or organization that has regulatory authority over marketing practices. Investigate how the agency regulates business activities in general and marketing activities in particular. Describe the processes it uses if a complaint is made.

3. Cause-related marketing has grown considerably over the past 10 years. Visit www.causemarketingforum.com and learn about companies winning Halo Awards for outstanding cause-related marketing programs. Present two award-winning case studies to your class.

FOCUS ON Technology

Have you ever gone phishing? Probably not, but the Internet enables unscrupulous individuals to 'phish' for your personal information. This and other types of attacks aimed at stealing your identity or your money are called 'social engineering.' Social engineering is a remake of an old-fashioned con game that tricks people into giving information and then uses it to rob them. You might receive an email, supposedly from PayPal, Amazon.com, or your bank, asking you to update your personal information. To make it easier for you, says the message, just click on the link in the email to input your information. Don't do it! The click will take you to a site that looks legitimate but is really a skillfully designed fake, often located in another country. Even if you don't enter any personal information, just clicking on the link might put software on your computer that can track your keystrokes, revealing login and password information to the crooks.

1. Discuss two recommendations for how consumers might protect themselves from such Internet scams.

2. Phishing scams also victimize businesses. Investigate how businesses can deal with this problem and discuss recommendations for marketers who face this threat.

FOCUS ON Ethics

Since the mid-1990s, companies such as Northfield Laboratories and Biopure have been testing blood substitutes in the hope of attaining approval by the U.S. Food and Drug Administration (FDA). Blood substitutes are oxygen-carrying products designed to replace donated human blood. Unlike human donor blood, these products can be stored without refrigeration for long periods and don't have to be crossed-matched with a patient's blood type. These characteristics offer significant advantages in battlefield and trauma applications. However, clinical trials indicate that using blood substitutes results in a 30 percent increase in the risk of death and nearly as high a risk in having a heart attack, leading some to criticize the FDA for allowing continued clinical trials.

A recent study published in the *Journal of the American Medical Association* faulted the FDA for not conducting prompt analysis of previous studies and claimed that the risks of using blood substitutes were evident as early as 2000. The FDA claimed it was aware of these risks but deemed some products worthy of further research. Some critics are pushing for more stringent legislation governing product testing, particularly if there are potentially significant health risks.

1. Discuss the environmental forces acting on these companies. What are Northfield's and Biopure's responsibilities and possible reactions to these environmental forces?

2. Is it ethical for these companies to continue clinical trials in this case?

MARKETING BY THE Numbers

China and India are emerging markets that will have a significant impact on the world in coming years. With China's population at over 1.3 billion and India's at 1 billion, they are the two most populous countries, comprising almost 40 percent of the world's population. The economies of both countries are growing at phenomenal rates as well. The term 'Chindia' is used to describe the growing power of these two countries, and predictions are that these two will overtake the United States as the largest economies in the world within just a few decades.

1. Discuss a demographic and an economic trend related to Chindia's power and its impact on marketers in the United States. Support your discussion of these trends with statistics.

2. Using the chain ratio method described in Appendix 2: Marketing by the Numbers, discuss factors to consider when estimating total market demand for automobiles in China or India.

VIDEO Case

TOMS Shoes

"Get involved: Changing a life begins with a single step." This sounds like a mandate from a nonprofit volunteer organization. But in fact, this is the motto of a for-profit shoe company located in Santa Monica, California. In 2006, Tom Mycoskie founded TOMS Shoes because he wanted to do something different. He wanted to run a company that would make a profit while at the same time help the needy of the world.

Specifically, for every pair of shoes that TOMS sells, it gives a pair of shoes to a needy child somewhere in the world. So far, the company has given away tens of thousands of pairs of shoes and is on track to give away hundreds of thousands. Can TOMS succeed and thrive based on this idealistic concept? That all depends on how TOMS executes its strategy within the constantly changing marketing environment.

After viewing the video featuring TOMS Shoes, answer the following questions about the marketing environment:

1. What trends in the marketing environment have contributed to the success of TOMS Shoes?

2. Did TOMS Shoes first scan the marketing environment in creating its strategy, or did it create its strategy and fit the strategy to the environment? Does this matter?

3. Is TOMS's strategy more about serving needy children or about creating value for customers? Explain.

COMPANY Case

Al Jazirah: The Genius Inventor

THE HOT WEATHER

Air conditioning is one of the most crucial appliances in almost all homes and businesses in the Arab world. The Saudi Arabian climate can be characterized as a desert climate, with wide fluctuations in day and night temperatures. The climate is typified by high temperatures in the summer, often rising to 45 degrees Celsius or more, while in spring and autumn, the average temperature is around 29 degrees Celsius. Apart from the coastal areas, the climate is rather dry and leaves people with an uncomfortable breathing experience. The climate in the Kingdom of Saudi Arabia has resulted in the installation of air conditioning in most domestic and commercial buildings. Sales of air conditioners reach 2.1 million units per year. Air conditioners are installed in every new building.

COOLING CONCEPTS

Have you ever noticed how cool it feels on the beach on a hot summer day? The cooling of the air is the result of water evaporation—and that's how an evaporative cooler works. An evaporative cooler is essentially an enclosed box with vented sides, containing three elements: a centrifugal fan (or 'blower'), an electric motor with pulleys, and a water pump to wet the evaporative cooling pads. To cool, the centrifugal fan draws ambient air in through the unit's vents and the cooling pads; heat in the air then evaporates water from the pads, which are kept constantly damp to maintain the cooling process. An evaporative cooling unit is mounted on the roof or on the exterior wall of a building, and the cool air is delivered to the building through a vent.

THE MARKET

The culture in the Kingdom of Saudi Arabia is luxury-driven. The consumer generally has a large purchasing power and tends to buy expensive things. In recent years, the culture has grown to a more established structure, so that consumers look for the true value and advantage of the products they purchase.

Another new trend in the culture, which is still in development, is environmental and energy consciousness. With energy at a low cost, consumers tended to use it at high levels. Now, through government and corporate efforts, consumers are being made aware of the impact of high energy consumption on world prices and the environment.

Another characteristic of the culture is the eagerness to acquire new technologies and to become early adopters of the world's latest trends, hence consumers like to buy high-end products such as the latest mobile phones, laptops, and cars.

THE RIGHT PRODUCT FOR THE MACROENVIRONMENT

Al Jazirah was established in 1973, when it became the first factory of its kind in the Arab world to produce evaporative coolers under the Al Jazirah brand. Today, Al Jazirah evaporative coolers are number one in the world.

Al Jazirah manufactures the coolers at five factories (four in Saudi Arabia plus one in Sudan) and distributes them via 30 showrooms located across Saudi Arabia, wholesalers, and an agent network.

The company delivers a product that is perfect for the surrounding environment. The evaporative cooler represents a technological invention and overcomes all the aspects that made previous air conditioning solutions less desirable to the consumer. It is odor free—the first coolers to be invented had a moldy odor, so much so that they were called swamp coolers in the United States—and quieter than other models, thanks to a special engine. With the outer casing made of plastic or an anti-rust metal, the life of the product is extended. Durability is also ensured through the cooling pads, which are made of aspen or cellulose so that salt residuals generated from the evaporating water can be rinsed off. One of the biggest advantages of Al Jazirah evaporative coolers is their electricity-saving capabilities. Evaporative coolers, generally, are good at saving energy, but Al Jazirah has managed to escalate that energy saving to 80 percent. A further benefit is the purification of air from dust and other particles, which creates a cleaner environment for the user.

In 2010, Al Jazirah won the award for the best innovative Saudi firm for 'Products & Patents from Innovation to the Market,' presented by INNOVABIA. In 2011, Al Jazirah secured the 'Number one client and the best evaporative coolers portfolio' award by NIDEC Corporation—owner of the multinational brands Emerson & US Motors.

Al Jazirah's marketing focuses on matching the consumers' heritage and their culture. All marketing communication is centered on the customer's daily life, for example, highlighting their outdoor exercises, their atmosphere, and their overall life style. This puts the air conditioning product very close to the consumers' hearts.

SUCCESS

Al Jazirah's evaporative coolers are widely available to the market in a wide portfolio of brands that meet different needs. The company has a 60 percent market share of all evaporative coolers sold in the Kingdom of Saudi Arabia. Its operations have grown beyond its home town to 18 countries worldwide. Al Jazirah's focus now is on the manufacture of coolers in Sudan for the local market there.

Source: www.al-jazierah.com/en/Default.aspx.

This case was provided by Mohamed Radwan, adjunct faculty member at the American University in Cairo and managing director for Platinum Partners.

Questions

1. What are the factors in the macroenvironment that triggered the need for evaporative coolers in the Kingdom of Saudi Arabia?

2. How did Al Jazirah capitalize on these factors?

3. What would be the best company policy: to integrate with regular air conditioners or to compete with them?

4. Based on analysis of the region's macroenvironment, which countries do you think Al Jazirah should target? Why?

Chapter 4	Part 1	Defining Marketing and the Marketing Process (Chapters 1, 2)
	Part 2	Understanding the Marketplace and Consumers (Chapters 3, 4, 5, 6)
	Part 3	Designing a Customer-Driven Strategy and Mix (Chapters 7, 8, 9, 10, 11, 12, 13, 14)
	Part 4	Extending Marketing (Chapters 15, 16, 17)

Marketing Research

Chapter PREVIEW

In the previous chapter, you learned about the complex and changing marketing environment. In this chapter, we continue our exploration of how marketers gain insights into consumers and the marketplace. We look at how companies develop and manage information about important marketplace elements—customers, competitors, products, and marketing programs. To succeed in today's marketplace, companies must know how to turn mountains of marketing information into fresh customer insights that will help them deliver greater value to customers.

We'll start this chapter with a story about Maktoob Research, which unveiled Arab Eye, the Arab world's 'First Interactive Online Consumer Community.' The main purpose of Arab Eye is to offer consumers in the Arab world an opportunity to share their opinions.

Arab Eye targets the general public. It aims to form a dynamic community of consumers who participate in online surveys and polls on various topics that relate to specific areas of interest. Both English and Arabic interfaces are featured on the website, which contains a wide range of elements designed to ensure that the surveys reach the targeted consumers. These elements include a personal login and a profile page for members. Members can easily update and view their profile to make sure that they receive surveys that match their profile and interests.

Arab Eye allows its members to link with others in the community through chat rooms and discussion boards. It also offers exciting rewards to members by way of a points system. When members take part in polls, surveys and discussions, they collect points which can be redeemed against CashU credit. Members can spend the credit within the CashU network, which includes leading gift shops and online games, as well as Skype.[1]

"We believe at Maktoob Research that good research starts with good sampling, hence our sample is our active members, making it essential for us to ensure that the members are appropriately selected and are kept interested in taking surveys," said Marouane Sanhaji, Maktoob Research's panel manager. "One of the fundamental factors that differentiate credible and successful research firms from the rest of the pack is the amount of attention they give to the actual people who spend their valuable time answering online surveys. By introducing 'Arab Eye', we seek to provide our members with an exciting and rewarding community environment while offering

them a dynamic platform to express their thoughts, ideas and opinions."

One of the exclusive features of Arab Eye is that it allows members to turn into researchers by posting poll questions or by putting further questions on the discussion boards. Accordingly, members can view updated results of their poll questions on the website.

Maktoob Research has been growing steadily and has become the research partner for several leading companies from around the Arab world. For example, Maktoob Research conducted a survey of 800 mothers from the UAE, Saudi Arabia, and Kuwait for Kraft Foods' biscuit brand, Oreo. The survey investigated the milk-consumption habits amongst children and the creative ways in which mothers encourage their children to drink milk.

Maktoob Research's rapid expansion, reputation, and popularity across the Arab world have taken its activities global. For example, the company conducted an online survey on behalf of the White House, commissioned by InterMedia, a major international research and consulting organization. This survey assessed the impact of U.S. President Barack Obama's speech in Cairo, about America's relationship with Islam and

> Maktoob Research provides Arab Eye, the largest online consumer panel in the Arab world.

the Arab world. The researchers gathered reactions from a cross section of the public in Arab nations, including Egypt, Morocco, Saudi Arabia, and Syria, to establish how the Arab world viewed changing relationships between the United States and the Muslim world in general, and Arab nations in particular. Over 75 percent of the survey respondents claimed they viewed the speech

> **Maktoob Research has developed the website 'Arab Eye' to engage interactively with consumers and gain a better understanding of their opinions and habits.**

favorably, while more than 50 percent believed, based on the President's speech, that U.S. policies towards the Arab world and towards their individual countries would get better. The findings of the Maktoob Research survey on the impact of and reactions to President Obama's address to the Muslim world were highlighted prominently in the official White House press release.[2]

The Maktoob Research story demonstrates the value of good customer information and how it can be used to develop good products and marketing programs. Companies also need an abundance of information on competitors, resellers, and other actors and marketplace forces. But more than just gathering information, marketers must *use* the information to gain powerful *customer and market insights*.

> **Author Comment** | Marketing information by itself has little value. The value is in the *customer insights* gained from the information and how these insights are used to make better marketing decisions.

Marketing Information and Customer Insights (pp 95-97)

To create value for customers and to build meaningful relationships with them, marketers must first gain fresh, deep insights into what customers need and want. Companies use such customer insights to develop competitive advantage. "In today's hypercompetitive world," states a marketing expert, "the race for competitive advantage is really a race for customer and market insights." Such insights come from good marketing information.[3]

Consider Apple's phenomenally successful iPod. The iPod wasn't the first digital music player but Apple was the first to get it right. Apple's research uncovered a key insight about how people want to consume digital music—they want to take all their music with them but they want personal music players to be unremarkable. This insight led to two key design goals—make it as small as a deck of cards and build it to hold 1,000 songs. Add some of Apple's design and usability magic to this insight, and you have a recipe for a hit. Apple's expanded iPod line now captures more than 75 percent market share.

However, although customer and market insights are important for building customer value and relationships, these insights can be very difficult to obtain. Customer needs and buying motives are often anything but obvious—consumers themselves usually can't tell you exactly what they need and why they buy. To gain good customer insights, marketers must effectively manage marketing information from a wide range of sources.

Today's marketers have ready access to plenty of marketing information. With the recent explosion of information technologies, companies can now generate information in great quantities. In fact, most marketing managers are overloaded with data and are often overwhelmed by it. Still, despite this data surplus, marketers frequently complain that they lack enough information of the right kind. They don't need *more* information, they need *better* information. And they need to make better *use* of the information they already have. Says another marketing information expert, "transforming today's vast, ever-increasing volume of consumer information into actionable marketing insights…is the number-one challenge for digital-age marketers."[4]

Thus, a company's marketing research and information system must do more than simply generate lots of information. The real value of marketing

Key customer insights, plus a dash of Apple's design and usability magic, have made the iPod a blockbuster. It now captures more than 75 percent market share.

Objective Outline

Customer insights
Fresh understandings of customers and the marketplace derived from marketing information that become the basis for creating customer value and relationships.

Marketing Information System (MIS)
People and procedures for assessing information needs, developing the needed information, and helping decision makers to use the information to generate and check customer and market insights.

research and marketing information lies in how it is used—in the **customer insights** that it provides. "The value of the market research department is not determined by the number of studies that it does," says a marketing expert, "but by the business value of the *insights* that it produces and the decisions that it influences." Says another expert, "Companies that gather, disseminate, and apply deep customer insights obtain powerful, profitable, sustainable competitive advantages for their brands."[5]

Based on such thinking, many companies are now restructuring and renaming their marketing research and information functions. They are creating 'customer insights teams,' headed by a vice president of customer insights and made up of representatives from all of the firm's functional areas. For example, the head of marketing research at Kraft Foods is called the director of consumer insights and strategy.

Customer insights groups collect customer and market information from a wide variety of sources—ranging from traditional marketing research studies, through mixing with and observing consumers, to monitoring consumer online conversations about the company and its products. Then, they *use* the marketing information to develop important customer insights from which the company can create more value for its customers. For example, Unilever's customer insights group states its mission simply as "getting better at understanding our consumers and meeting their needs."[6]

In gathering and using customer insights, however, companies must be careful not to go too far and become *customer controlled*. The idea is not to give customers everything they request. Rather, it's to understand customers to the core and give them what they need—to create value for customers as a means of capturing value for the firm in return.[7]

So companies must design effective marketing information systems that give managers the right information, in the right form, at the right time, and help them to use this information to create customer value and stronger customer relationships. A **marketing information system (MIS)** consists of people and procedures for assessing informational needs, developing the needed information, and helping decision makers to use the information to generate and check customer and market insights that can be used in real marketing activities.

■ FIGURE | 4.1 The Marketing Information System

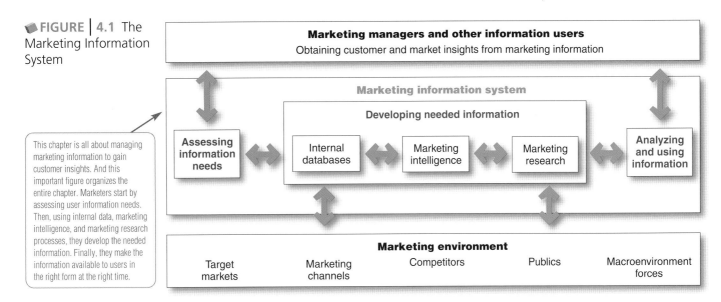

This chapter is all about managing marketing information to gain customer insights. And this important figure organizes the entire chapter. Marketers start by assessing user information needs. Then, using internal data, marketing intelligence, and marketing research processes, they develop the needed information. Finally, they make the information available to users in the right form at the right time.

■ **Figure 4.1** shows that the MIS begins and ends with information users—marketing managers, internal and external partners, and others who need marketing information. First, it interacts with these information users to *assess information needs*. Next, it interacts with the marketing environment to *develop needed information* through internal company databases, marketing intelligence activities, and marketing research. Finally, the MIS helps users to analyze and use the information to develop customer insights, make marketing decisions, and manage customer relationships.

Author | Comment The marketing information system begins and ends with users—with assessing their information needs and then delivering information that meets those needs.

Assessing Marketing Information Needs (pp 97–98)

The marketing information system primarily serves the company's marketing and other managers. However, it may also provide information to external partners, such as suppliers, resellers, or marketing services agencies. For example, Google Trends offers its customers data about the number of times a certain word is searched for, the number of times it appears on the news, and the geographical region of the people who have searched for it the most. This information is used by Google's advertisers to find the hottest words and to assess their online marketing expenditure with the company.

A good marketing information system balances the information users would *like* to have against what they really *need* and what is *feasible* to offer. The company begins by interviewing managers to find out what information they would like. Some managers will ask for whatever information they can get without thinking carefully about what they really need. Too much information can be as harmful as too little.

Other managers may forget about things they ought to know, or they may not know to ask for some types of information they should have. For example, managers might need to know about surges in favorable or unfavorable consumer 'word-of-web' discussions about their brands on blogs or online social networks. Because they do not know about these discussions, they do not think to ask about them. The MIS must monitor the marketing environment in order to provide decision makers with information they should have in order to better understand customers and make key marketing decisions.

Sometimes the company cannot provide the needed information, either because it is not available or because of MIS limitations. For example, a brand manager might want to know how competitors will change their advertising budgets next year and how these changes will affect industry market shares. The information on planned budgets probably is not available. Even if it is, the company's MIS might not be advanced enough to forecast resulting changes in market shares.

Finally, the costs of obtaining, analyzing, storing, and delivering information can mount quickly. The company must decide whether the value of insights gained from additional information is worth the costs of providing it, and both value and cost are often hard to assess. By itself, information has no worth; its value comes from its *use*. In many cases, additional information will do little to change or improve a manager's decision, or the costs of the information may exceed the returns from improved customer insights and decision making. Marketers should not assume that additional information will always be worth obtaining. Rather, they should weigh carefully the costs of getting more information against the benefits resulting from it.[8] While most multinational companies operating in the Arab world understand the importance of research to the success of their businesses, local businesses—particularly small- and medium-sized enterprises (SMEs)—consider research budgets a large or unjustified investment, which negatively affects their performance.

> **Author Comment** | The problem isn't *finding* information—the world is bursting with information from a glut of sources. The real challenge is to find the *right* information—from inside and outside sources—and to turn it into customer insights.

Developing Marketing Information (pp 98–100)

Marketers can obtain the needed information from *internal data, marketing intelligence,* and *marketing research.*

Internal Data

Internal databases

Electronic collections of consumer and market information obtained from data sources within the company network.

Many companies build extensive **internal databases**—electronic collections of consumer and market information obtained from data sources within the company network. Marketing managers can readily access and work with information in the database to identify marketing opportunities and problems, plan programs, and evaluate performance.

Information in the database can come from many sources. The marketing department provides information on customer transactions, demographics, psychographics, and buying behavior. The customer-service department keeps records of customer satisfaction or service problems. The accounting department prepares financial statements and keeps detailed records of sales, costs, and cash flows. Operations reports on production schedules, shipments, and inventories. The sales force reports on reseller reactions and competitor activities, and marketing channel partners provide data on point-of-sale transactions. Capturing such information can provide powerful customer insights and competitive advantage.

Here is an example of how companies use their internal databases to make better marketing decisions:

Internal databases can be a valuable tool for customer relationship management. For example, companies may use their internal databases to offer special rewards or loyalty schemes to particular customers.

Mobile service providers in the Arab world, such as Zain, Mobily, Etisalat, Mobinil and Vodafone, have comprehensive databases of their customers. The major challenge they face is using this wealth of information in an effective manner. Such databases can be used to develop customer relationship management (CRM) campaigns. They are useful for tracking customers' spending trends, and for segmenting the customers accordingly. They also have value in being able to identify the most valuable customers, who should be treated more favorably in order to drive their loyalty. Mobinil's loyalty program, called Mobinil Star, is designed to offer various rewards to its top customers in appreciation for their loyalty.[9] Vodafone's loyalty program, called Vodafone One, gives points to its customers for every one pound they spend on its network.[10]

Internal databases can usually be accessed more quickly and cheaply than other information sources, but they also present some problems. Because the internal information is likely to have been collected for other purposes, it may be incomplete or in the wrong form for making marketing decisions. For example, sales and cost data used by the accounting department for preparing financial statements must be adapted for use in evaluating the value of a specific customer segment, sales force, or channel performance. Data also age quickly; keeping the database current requires a major effort. In addition, a large company produces mountains of information, which must be well integrated and readily accessible so that managers can find it easily and use it effectively. Managing that much data requires highly sophisticated equipment and techniques.

Marketing Intelligence

Marketing intelligence

The systematic collection and analysis of publicly available information about consumers, competitors, and developments in the marketing environment.

Marketing intelligence is the systematic collection and analysis of publicly available information about consumers, competitors, and developments in the marketplace. The goal of marketing intelligence is to improve strategic decision making by understanding the consumer environment, assessing and tracking competitors' actions, and providing early warnings of opportunities and threats.

The gathering of marketing intelligence has grown dramatically as more and more companies are now busily searching for information on the marketplace and on their competitors. Techniques range from monitoring Internet buzz or observing consumers first-hand to quizzing the company's own employees, benchmarking competitors' products, researching the Internet, and participating in industry trade shows.

Good marketing intelligence can help marketers to gain insights into how consumers talk about and connect with their brands. Many companies send out teams of trained observers to mix with customers as they use and talk about the company's products. Other companies routinely monitor consumers' online chatter with the help of online monitoring services such as Nielsen Online or BrandIntel. For example, Ford Motor Company employs the marketing intelligence firm BrandIntel to monitor blogs and other Internet sites. Ford wants to know what people are saying about its products, their performance, and their looks. It also wants to know about any important issues—positive or negative—that might have consumers buzzing online about specific Ford models. For example, if BrandIntel discovers unanswered product questions or service complaints, it forwards them to Ford's customer-service staff. When appropriate, the service staff can respond online, identifying themselves and asking if they can join the online discussions.[11]

Companies also need to actively monitor competitors' activities. Firms use competitive intelligence to gain early warnings of competitor moves and strategies, new product launches, new or changing markets, and potential competitive strengths and weaknesses. A recent analysis by consulting firm PricewaterhouseCoopers found that companies employing competitive intelligence as a critical element in their strategic thinking grow 20 percent faster than those that do not.[12]

Much competitor intelligence can be collected from people inside the company—executives, engineers and scientists, purchasing agents, and the sales force. The company can also obtain important intelligence information from suppliers, resellers, and key customers. Or it can get good information by observing competitors and monitoring their published information. It can buy and analyze competitors' products, monitor their sales, check for new patents, and examine various types of physical evidence. For example, one company regularly checks out competitors' parking lots—full lots might indicate plenty of work and prosperity; half-full lots might suggest hard times.

Competitors often reveal intelligence information through their annual reports, business publications, trade

Many companies routinely monitor consumers' online chatter with the help of monitoring services such as Nielsen Online.

show exhibits, press releases, advertisements, and web pages. The web has become a valuable source of competitive intelligence. Using Internet search engines, marketers can search specific competitor names, events, or trends and see what turns up. Moreover, most companies now place volumes of information on their websites, providing details to attract customers, partners, suppliers, investors, or franchisees. This can provide a wealth of useful information about competitors' strategies, markets, new products, facilities, and other happenings.

The intelligence game goes both ways. Facing determined marketing intelligence efforts by competitors, most companies are now taking steps to protect their own information. For example, Unilever conducts widespread competitive intelligence training. Employees are taught not just how to collect intelligence information but also how to protect company information from competitors. According to a former Unilever employee, "We were even warned that spies from competitors could be posing as drivers at the minicab company we used." Unilever even performs random checks on internal security.

The growing use of marketing intelligence raises a number of ethical issues. Although most of the preceding techniques are legal, and some are considered to be sensibly competitive, some may involve questionable ethics. Clearly, companies should take advantage of publicly available information. However, with all the legitimate intelligence sources now available, a company does not need to break the law or accepted codes of ethics to get good intelligence.

> **Author** | Whereas marketing intel-
> **Comment** | ligence involves actively
> scanning the general marketing envi-
> ronment, marketing research involves
> more focused studies to gain customer
> insights relating to specific marketing
> decisions.

Marketing Research (pp 100–112)

In addition to marketing intelligence information about general consumer, competitor, and marketplace happenings, marketers often need formal studies that provide customer and market insights for specific marketing situations and decisions. For example, Google wants to know how web searchers will react to a proposed redesign of its site. Or Samsung wants to know how many and what kinds of people will buy its next-generation LCD televisions. In such situations, marketing intelligence will not provide the detailed information needed. Managers will need marketing research.

Marketing research is the systematic design, collection, analysis, and reporting of data relevant to a specific marketing situation facing an organization. Companies use marketing research in a wide variety of situations. For example, marketing research gives marketers insights into customer motivations, purchase behavior, and satisfaction. It can help them to assess market potential and market share or to measure the effectiveness of pricing, product, distribution, and promotion activities.

Some large companies have their own research departments that work with marketing managers on marketing research projects. This is how Procter & Gamble, Unilever, and many other corporate giants handle marketing research. In addition, these companies—like their smaller counterparts—frequently hire outside research specialists to consult with management on specific marketing problems and to conduct marketing research studies. Sometimes firms simply purchase data collected by outside firms to aid in their decision making.

The marketing research process has four steps (see ◀ **Figure 4.2**): defining the problem and research objectives, developing the research plan, implementing the research plan, and interpreting and reporting the findings.

Marketing research

The systematic design, collection, analysis, and reporting of data relevant to a specific marketing situation facing an organization.

Defining the Problem and Research Objectives

Marketing managers and researchers must work closely together to define the problem and agree on research objectives. The manager best understands the decision for which information is needed; the researcher best understands marketing research and how to obtain the information. Defining the problem and research objectives is often the hardest step in the research process. The manager may know that something is wrong, without knowing the specific causes.

After the problem has been defined carefully, the manager and researcher must set the research objectives. A marketing research project might have one of three types of objectives. The objective of **exploratory research** is to gather information that will help define

Exploratory research

Marketing research to gather preliminary information that will help define problems and suggest ways to respond.

The Marketing
Research Process

| Defining the problem and research objectives | Developing the research plan for collecting information | Implementing the research plan—collecting and analyzing the data | Interpreting and reporting the findings |

This first step in the marketing research process is probably the most difficult, but is also the most important one. It guides the entire research process. It's pretty frustrating to reach the end of a large and expensive research project only to learn that you were addressing the wrong problem!

Descriptive research
Marketing research to better describe marketing problems, situations, or markets, such as the market potential for a product or the demographics and attitudes of consumers.

Causal research
Marketing research to test hypothesis about cause-end-effect relationships.

the problem and suggest ways to respond. The objective of **descriptive research** is to describe things, such as the market potential for a product, or the demographics and attitudes of consumers who buy the product. The objective of **causal research** is to test ideas about cause-and-effect relationships. For example, would a 10 percent decrease in tuition at a private college result in an enrollment increase sufficient to offset the reduced tuition? Managers often start with exploratory research and later follow with descriptive or causal research.

The statement of the problem and research objectives guides the entire research process. The manager and researcher should put the statement in writing to be certain that they agree on the purpose and expected results of the research.

Developing the Research Plan

Once the research problems and objectives have been defined, researchers must determine the exact information needed, develop a plan for gathering it efficiently, and present the plan to management. The research plan outlines sources of existing data and spells out the specific research approaches, contact methods, sampling plans, and instruments that researchers will use to gather new data.

Research objectives must be translated into specific information needs. For example, suppose Danone was considering introducing its yogurt products in the Egyptian market. Danone's managers wondered how Egyptian consumers would react to their products, and what marketing tools would help to penetrate the market. The proposed research might call for the following specific information:

- The demographic, economic, and lifestyle characteristics of Egyptian yogurt users
- Consumption patterns among different Egyptian family members
- The status and strengths of key competitors
- Retailer reactions to the proposed new product line: Where would they display it?
- Initial forecasts of sales.

Danone's brand managers will need these and many other types of information to decide on how to effectively enter the Egyptian market.

The research plan should be presented in a *written proposal*. A written proposal is especially important when the research project is large and complex or when an outside firm carries it out. The proposal should cover the management problems addressed and the research objectives, the information to be obtained, and the way the results will help management decision making. The proposal also should include research costs.

Secondary data
Information that already exists somewhere, having been collected for another purpose.

Primary data
Information collected for the specific purpose at hand.

To meet the manager's information needs, the research plan can call for gathering secondary data, primary data, or both. **Secondary data** consist of information that already exists somewhere, having been collected for another purpose. **Primary data** consist of information collected for the specific purpose at hand.

Gathering Secondary Data

Researchers usually start by gathering secondary data. The company's internal database provides a good starting point. However, the company can also tap into a wide assortment of external information sources, including commercial data services and government sources (see ● **Table 4.1**).

● TABLE | 4.1   Selected External Information Sources

For Business Data:

Business Monitor Online's Middle East and Africa Country Risk Service (www.businessmonitor.com/bmo/MEA) provides market research, analysis, and industry trends in the region

International Marketing and Economic Services (IMES) (http://imesconsulting.com/cresearch.php) provides custom market research on Arab world markets

A Database of Marketing Research Companies in Saudi Arabia (www.the-saudi.net/directory/marketing.htm)

TNS Global (www.tnsglobal.com/global) is a global marketing research company, with regional market research hubs in Dubai, Jeddah, Riyadh, Beirut, Cairo, Casablanca, and Algeria

Synovate (www.synovate.com/) is a global marketing research company available in Saudi Arabia, United Arab Emirates, Algeria, Egypt, and Morocco

IPSOS (www.ipsos.com/) is a global marketing research company available in Bahrain, Egypt, Iraq, Jordan, Kuwait, Lebanon, Morocco, Saudi Arabia, Syria, and United Arab Emirates

Nielsen (http://nielsen.com) provides point-of-sale scanner data on sales, market share, and retail prices; data on household purchasing; and data on television audiences (a unit of VNU NV). It is available in Algeria, Egypt, Morocco, and Tunisia

Experian Consumer Research (Simmons) (http://smrb.com) provides detailed analysis of consumer patterns in 400 product categories in selected markets

SymphonyIRI Group (www.symphonyiri.com) provides supermarket scanner data for tracking grocery product movement and new product purchasing data

IMS Health (http://imshealth.com) tracks drug sales, monitors performance of pharmaceutical sales representatives, and offers pharmaceutical market forecasts

Arbitron (http://arbitron.com) provides local-market and Internet radio audience and advertising expenditure information, among other media and ad spending data

J.D. Power and Associates (http://jdpower.com) provides information from independent consumer surveys of product and service quality, customer satisfaction, and buyer behavior

Dun & Bradstreet (http://dnb.com) maintains a database containing information on more than 50 million individual companies around the globe

comScore (http://comscore.com) provides consumer behavior information and geodemographic analysis of Internet and digital media users around the world

Thomson Dialog (www.dialog.com) offers access to more than 900 databases containing publications, reports, newsletters, and directories covering dozens of industries

LexisNexis (http://lexisnexis.com) features articles from business, consumer, and marketing publications plus tracking of firms, industries, trends, and promotion techniques

Factiva (http://factiva.com) specializes in in-depth financial, historical, and operational information on public and private companies

Hoover's, Inc. (http://hoovers.com) provides business descriptions, financial overviews, and news about major companies around the world

BBC World News (http://bbcworldnews.com) reports global news and covers the markets and news-making companies in detail

For Government Data:

American Chamber of Commerce in the MENA Region (www.amchammena.org) provides information and reports on industries in the region in order to foster business relationships with the United States. Members include Egypt, Lebanon, Jordan, Morocco, Tunisia, Algeria, Bahrain, and Abu Dhabi

Central Agency for Public Mobilization and Statistics (CAPMAS) (www.capmas.gov.eg/) provides statistical information and reports on the Egyptian markets

For Internet Data:

ClickZ (http://clickz.com) brings together a wealth of information about the Internet and its users, from consumers to e-commerce

Interactive Advertising Bureau (http://iab.net) covers statistics about advertising on the Internet

Jupiter Research (http://jupiterresearch.com) monitors web traffic and ranks the most popular sites

Over **60,000** data variables collected from **30,000+** American consumers annually on **8,000+** brands and **450+** product categories

■ Simmons National Consumer Study (NCS)
• First syndicated national survey launched in the U.S.
• Market Research Council accredited

■ Simmons National Hispanic Consumer Study (NHCS)
• Surveys over 8,000 Hispanic adults living in the U.S. annually providing Hispanic-only information on acculturation, language usage and preference, nativity, and country of origin
• Market Research Council accredited

■ Multi-Media Engagement Study (MME)
• Provides ratings on the cognitive, behavioral and emotional involvement consumers have with media vehicles
• The only syndicated, cross-channel engagement measurement tool available

■ Experian Local Market Services (ELMS)
• Access to detailed information on consumers in each of the 209 Media Markets, detailing their purchasing habits, lifestyles, and psychographics

■ Simmons GreenAware®
• Green segmentation targeting system profiling American Consumers into four consumer segments based on buying behavior, attitudes, opinions, lifestyle and media usage

Understand ■
Communicate ■
Measure ■

600 Third Avenue | New York, NY 10016
212.471.2850 | www.ExperianConsumerResearch.com

Consumer database services such as Experian Consumer Research sell an incredible wealth of information on everything from the products consumers buy and the brands they prefer to their lifestyles, attitudes, and media preferences.

Commercial online databases
Computerized collections of information available from online commercial sources or via the Internet.

Companies can buy secondary data reports from outside suppliers. For example, Nielsen sells buyer data from a consumer panel of more than 260,000 households in 27 countries worldwide, with measures of trial and repeat purchasing, brand loyalty, and buyer demographics. Experian Consumer Research (Simmons) sells information on more than 8,000 brands in 450 product categories, including detailed consumer profiles that assess everything from the products consumers buy and the brands they prefer to their lifestyles, attitudes, and media preferences. The MONITOR service by Yankelovich sells information on important social and lifestyle trends. These and other firms supply high-quality data to suit a wide variety of marketing information needs.[13]

Using **commercial online databases**, marketing researchers can conduct their own searches of secondary data sources. General database services such as Dialog and ProQuest put an incredible wealth of information at the keyboards of marketing decision makers. Beyond commercial websites offering information for a fee, almost every industry association, government agency, business publication, and news medium offers free information to those persistent enough to find their websites. There are so many websites offering data that finding the right ones can become an almost overwhelming task.

Web search engines can also be a big help in locating relevant secondary information sources. However, they can also be very frustrating and inefficient.

Secondary data can usually be obtained more quickly and at a lower cost than primary data. Also, secondary sources can sometimes provide data an individual company cannot collect on its own—information that either is not directly available or would be too expensive to collect. For example, it would be too expensive for Danone's marketers to conduct a continuing retail store audit to find out about the market shares, prices, and displays of competitors' brands. But it can buy ready-made retail audit information from one of the available marketing research companies in the region.

Secondary data can also present problems. The needed information may not exist—researchers can rarely obtain all the data they need from secondary sources. For example, Danone will not find existing information about consumer reactions to its yogurt products that it has not yet placed on the market. Even when data can be found, the information might not be very usable. The researcher must evaluate secondary information carefully to make certain it is *relevant* (fits research project needs), *accurate* (reliably collected and reported), *current* (up-to-date enough for current decisions), and *impartial* (objectively collected and reported).

Primary Data Collection

Secondary data provide a good starting point for research and often help to define research problems and objectives. In most cases, however, the company must also collect primary data. Just as researchers must carefully evaluate the quality of secondary information, they also must take great care when collecting primary data. They need to make sure that it will be relevant, accurate, current, and unbiased. ● **Table 4.2** shows that designing a plan for primary data collection calls for a number of decisions on *research approaches*, *contact methods*, *sampling plan*, and *research instruments*.

Research Approaches

Research approaches for gathering primary data include observation, surveys, and experiments. Here, we discuss each one in turn.

Observational research
Gathering primary data by observing relevant people, actions, and situations.

Observational Research. **Observational research** involves gathering primary data by observing relevant people, actions, and situations. For example, a bank might evaluate

● TABLE | 4.2   Planning Primary Data Collection

Research Approaches	Contact Methods	Sampling Plan	Research Instruments
Observation	Mail	Sampling unit	Questionnaire
Survey	Telephone	Sample size	Mechanical instruments
Experiment	Personal	Sampling procedure	
	Online		

possible new branch locations by checking traffic patterns, neighborhood conditions, and the location of competing branches.

Researchers often observe consumer behavior to gather customer insights they can't obtain by simply asking customers questions. Others employ 'Mindcams,' which allow a company to observe through the consumer's eye in their natural environments.

Observational research can obtain information that people are unwilling or unable to provide. In some cases, observation may be the only way to obtain the needed information. In contrast, some things simply cannot be observed, such as feelings, attitudes and motives, or private behavior. Long-term or infrequent behavior is also difficult to observe. Finally, observations can be very difficult to interpret. Because of these limitations, researchers often use observation along with other data collection methods.

Ethnographic research
A form of observational research that involves sending trained observers to watch and interact with consumers in their 'natural habitat.'

A wide range of companies now use **ethnographic research**. Ethnographic research involves sending trained observers to watch and interact with consumers in their 'natural habitat.' Consider this example:[14]

Mobile phone maker Nokia wants to add two billion new customers by the end of the decade. To do so, it has invested heavily in ethnographic research, focusing especially on emerging economies. Nokia deploys teams of anthropologists to study deeply the behavior of mobile phone owners in vast markets such as China, Brazil, and India. By 'living with the locals,' Nokia gathers subtle insights into each local culture. For example, it knows first-hand that 50 percent of the world's women keep their phones in their handbags (and miss 20 percent of their calls).

One of the biggest discoveries came from researchers studying how people in poor rural areas overcome some of the barriers to communication they face in their daily lives. Surprisingly, although usually considered a one-owner item, mobile phones in these areas are often used by entire families or even villages because of the cost. Based on this finding, Nokia designed its 1200 and 1208 phones, which make shared use the top priority. The affordable phones offer many useful and durable features and are robust enough to accommodate many different people using them. For example, they contain a long-life battery and multiple phone books so each member of a family or village can keep his or her own contacts and numbers separately from others.

Ethnographic Research: Teams of Nokia anthropologists 'live with the locals' in emerging economies to glean subtle insights into each local culture. Such insights resulted in the robust Nokia 1200 phone, which makes shared use a top priority.

Observational and ethnographic research often yield the kinds of details that just don't emerge from traditional research questionnaires or focus groups. Whereas traditional quantitative research approaches seek to test known hypotheses and obtain answers to well-defined product or strategy questions, observational research can generate fresh customer and market insights. "The beauty of ethnography," says a research expert, is that it "allows companies to zero in on their customers' unarticulated desires."[15] Another researcher agrees, "Classic market research doesn't go far enough. It can't grasp what people can't imagine or articulate."[16] For example, Procter & Gamble relied on deep ethnographic research before introducing its Ariel Hand Wash brand in the Egyptian market. This research is discussed in detail in the Company Case at the end of the chapter.

Survey research

Gathering primary data by asking people questions about their knowledge, attitudes, preferences, and buying behavior.

Survey Research.   **Survey research**, the most widely used method for primary data collection, is the approach best suited for gathering *descriptive* information. A company that wants to know about people's knowledge, attitudes, preferences, or buying behavior can often find out by asking them directly.

The major advantage of survey research is its flexibility—it can be used to obtain many different kinds of information in many different situations. Surveys addressing almost any marketing question or decision can be conducted by phone or mail, in person, or on the web. However, survey research also presents some problems. Sometimes people are unable to answer survey questions because they cannot remember or have never thought about what they do and why. People may be unwilling to respond to unknown interviewers or about things they consider private. Respondents may answer survey questions even when they do not know the answer in order to appear smarter or more informed. Or they may try to help the interviewer by giving pleasing answers. According to Heba Kelada, senior research director at Ipsos Egypt, "Respondents tend to many times over-claim." Finally, busy people may not take the time to complete a survey, or they might resent the intrusion into their privacy.

Experimental research

Gathering primary data by selecting matched groups of subjects, giving them different treatments, controlling related factors, and checking for differences in group responses.

Experimental Research.   Whereas observation is best suited for exploratory research and surveys for descriptive research, **experimental research** is best suited for gathering *causal* information. Experiments involve selecting matched groups of subjects, giving them different treatments, controlling unrelated factors, and checking for differences in group responses. Thus, experimental research tries to explain cause-and-effect relationships.

For example, before adding a new sandwich to its menu, McDonald's might use experiments to test the effects on sales of two different prices it might charge. It could introduce the new sandwich at one price in one city and at another price in another city. If the cities are similar, and if all other marketing efforts for the sandwich are the same, then differences in sales in the two cities could be related to the price charged.

Contact Methods

Information can be collected by mail, telephone, personal interview, or online. ● **Table 4.3** shows the strengths and weaknesses of each of these contact methods.

Mail, Telephone, and Personal Interviewing.   *Mail questionnaires* can be used to collect large amounts of information at a low cost per respondent. Respondents may give more honest answers to more personal questions on a mail questionnaire than to an

● TABLE | 4.3   Strengths and Weaknesses of Contact Methods

	Mail	**Telephone**	**Personal**	**Online**
Flexibility	Poor	Good	Excellent	Good
Quantity of data that can be collected	Good	Fair	Excellent	Good
Control of interviewer effects	Excellent	Fair	Poor	Fair
Control of sample	Fair	Excellent	Good	Excellent
Speed of data collection	Poor	Excellent	Good	Excellent
Response rate	Poor	Poor	Good	Good
Cost	Good	Fair	Poor	Excellent

Source: Adapted with permission of the authors from *Marketing Research: Measurement and Method*, 7th ed., by Donald S. Tull and Del I. Hawkins. Copyright 1993 by Macmillan Publishing Company.

unknown interviewer in person or over the phone. Also, no interviewer is involved to bias the respondent's answers.

However, mail questionnaires are not very flexible—all respondents answer the same questions in a fixed order. Mail surveys usually take longer to complete, and the response rate—the number of people returning completed questionnaires—is often very low. Finally, the researcher often has little control over the mail questionnaire sample. Even with a good mailing list, it is hard to control who at the mailing address fills out the questionnaire.

Telephone interviewing is one of the best methods for gathering information quickly, and it provides greater flexibility than mail questionnaires. Interviewers can explain difficult questions and, depending on the answers they receive, skip some questions or probe on others. Response rates tend to be higher than with mail questionnaires, and interviewers can ask to speak to respondents with the desired characteristics or even by name.

However, with telephone interviewing, the cost per respondent is higher than with mail questionnaires. Also, people may not want to discuss personal questions with an interviewer. The method introduces interviewer bias—the way interviewers talk, how they ask questions, and other differences may affect respondents' answers. Different interviewers may interpret and record responses differently, and under time pressures some interviewers might even cheat by recording answers without asking questions.

Personal interviewing takes two forms—individual and group interviewing. *Individual interviewing* involves talking with people in their homes or offices, on the street, or in shopping malls. Such interviewing is flexible. Trained interviewers can guide interviews, explain difficult questions, and explore issues as the situation requires. They can show subjects actual products, advertisements, or packages and observe reactions and behavior. However, individual personal interviews may cost three to four times as much as telephone interviews.

Group interviewing consists of inviting six to ten people to meet with a trained moderator to talk about a product, service, or organization. Participants normally are paid a small sum for attending. The moderator encourages free and easy discussion, hoping that group interactions will bring out actual feelings and thoughts. At the same time, the moderator 'focuses' the discussion—hence the name: **focus group interviewing**.

Researchers and marketers watch the focus group discussions from behind one-way glass and comments are recorded in writing or on video for later study. Today, focus group researchers can even use videoconferencing and Internet technology to connect marketers in distant locations with live focus group action. Using cameras and two-way sound systems, marketing executives in a far-off boardroom can look in and listen, using remote controls to zoom in on faces and scan the focus group at will.

Along with observational research, focus group interviewing has become one of the major qualitative marketing research tools for gaining fresh insights into consumer thoughts and feelings. However, focus group studies present some challenges. They usually employ small samples to keep time and costs down, and it may be hard to generalize from the results. Moreover, consumers in focus groups are not always open and honest about their real feelings, behavior, and intentions in front of other people.

Thus, although focus groups are still widely used, many researchers are changing their approach to focus group design. For example, Cammie Dunaway, chief marketing officer at the search-engine company Yahoo!, prefers "immersion groups"—four or five people with whom Yahoo!'s product designers talk informally, without a focus group moderator present. That way, rather than just seeing videos of consumers reacting to a moderator, Yahoo! employees can work directly with select customers to design new products and programs. "The outcome is richer if [consumers] feel included in our process, not just observed," says Dunaway.[17]

Focus group interviewing
Personal interviewing that involves inviting six to ten people to gather for a few hours with a trained interviewer to talk about a product, service, or organization. The interviewer 'focuses' the group discussion on important issues.

Online marketing research
Collecting primary data online through Internet surveys, online focus groups, web-based experiments, or tracking consumers' online behavior.

Online Marketing Research. The growth of the Internet has had a dramatic impact on the conduct of marketing research. Increasingly, researchers are collecting primary data through **online marketing research**—*Internet surveys, online panels, experiments,* and *online focus groups*. By one estimate, global online research spending reached an estimated

US$4.4 billion in 2008, triple the amount spent in 2005. An estimated one-quarter to one-third of all research will be conducted online by 2010.[18]

Online research can take many forms. A company can use the web as a survey medium. It can include a questionnaire on its website and offer incentives for completing it. It can use email, web links, or web pop-ups to invite people to answer questions and possibly win a prize. It can create online panels that provide regular feedback or conduct live discussions or online focus groups. Beyond surveys, researchers can conduct experiments on the web. They can experiment with different prices, use different headlines, or offer different product features on different websites or at different times to learn the relative effectiveness of their offers. Or they can set up virtual shopping environments and use them to test new products and marketing programs. Finally, a company can learn about the behavior of online customers by following their click streams as they visit the website and move to other sites.

The Internet is especially well suited to *quantitative* research—conducting marketing surveys and collecting data. Internet penetration in the Arab world grew quickly from 2000 to 2011. ● **Table 4.4** lists the Internet penetration in Arab world countries as a percentage. While the average penetration is 27.2 percent across the 22 countries (compared with 30.2 percent world average), it is clear that this penetration varies from country to country, ranging from 69 percent in the UAE to less than 1 percent in Iraq and Somalia.

● **TABLE | 4.4** Internet Penetration in Arab Countries

Country	Population (2011) in millions	Internet Users (2011) in millions	Penetration %
United Arab Emirates	5.1	3.6	69
Bahrain	1.2	0.6	66.5
Qatar	0.8	0.6	53.7
Kuwait	2.6	1.1	53.3
Morocco	32	13.2	48.4
Saudi Arabia	26.1	11.4	43.6
Tunisia	6	3.6	42.4
Jordan	5	1.7	41.3
Lebanon	4.1	1.2	33.9
Syria	2.5	4.5	29
Egypt	82.1	20.1	26.8
Oman	3	1.5	24.5
Algeria	35	4.7	19.8
Sudan	45	4.2	12
Palestine	2.6	1.4	9.3
Libya	6.6	0.3	7.8
Comoros	0.8	0.02	5.4
Mauritania	3.3	0.08	3.2
Djibouti	0.8	0.06	3.1
Yemen	24.1	2.3	2.8
Iraq	30.4	0.9	2.3
Somalia	9.9	0.1	1.1
Total	**355.1**	**77.2**	**Average = 27.2**

As response rates for traditional survey approaches decline and costs increase, the web is quickly replacing mail and the telephone as the dominant data collection methodology. One industry analyst estimates that consumer packaged-goods firms may now invest as much as two-thirds of their total quantitative survey budgets online. And Internet surveys now command nearly 80 percent of all online research spending.[19]

Web-based survey research offers some real advantages over traditional telephone and mail approaches. The most obvious advantages are speed and low costs. "Faster. Cheaper. It boils down to that," concludes a marketing research executive.[20] By going online, researchers can quickly and easily distribute Internet surveys to thousands of respondents simultaneously via email or by posting them on selected websites. Responses can be almost immediate, and because respondents themselves enter the information, researchers can tabulate, review, and share research data as they arrive.

Online research usually costs much less than research conducted through mail, telephone, or personal interviews. Using the Internet gets rid of most of the postage, telephone, interviewer, and data-handling costs associated with the other approaches. As a result, Internet surveys typically cost 15 to 20 percent less than mail surveys and 30 percent less than telephone surveys. Moreover, sample size has little impact on costs. Once the questionnaire is set up, there's little difference in cost between 10 and 10,000 respondents on the web.

Beyond their speed and cost advantages, web-based surveys also tend to be more interactive and engaging, easier to complete, and less intrusive than traditional telephone or mail surveys. As a result, they usually garner higher response rates. The Internet is an excellent medium for reaching the hard-to-reach—the often-elusive teen, single, affluent, and well-educated audiences. It's also good for reaching working mothers and other people who lead busy lives. Such people are well represented online, and they can respond in their own space and at their own convenience.

Real Marketing 4.1 discusses a strategic alliance that was formed between Nielsen and Facebook.com in order to generate effective online research analysis.

Whereas marketing researchers have rushed to use the Internet for quantitative surveys and data collection, they are now also adopting *qualitative* web-based research approaches—such as online focus groups or in-depth interviews. Many marketers have learned that the Internet can provide a fast, low-cost way to gain qualitative customer insights.

Online focus groups

Gathering a small group of people online with a trained moderator to chat about a product, service, or organization and gain qualitative insights about consumer attitudes and behavior.

The primary qualitative web-based research approach is **online focus groups**. Such focus groups offer many advantages over traditional focus groups. Participants can log in from anywhere—all they need is a laptop and an Internet connection. Thus, the Internet works well for bringing together people from different parts of the country or world, especially those in higher-income groups who can't spare the time to travel to a central site. Also, researchers can conduct and monitor online focus groups from just about anywhere, avoiding travel, lodging, and facility costs. Finally, although online focus groups require some advance scheduling, results are almost immediate.

Online focus groups can take any of several formats. Most occur in real time, in the form of online chat room discussions in which participants and a moderator sit around a virtual table exchanging comments. Alternatively, researchers might set up an online message board on which respondents interact over the course of several days or a few weeks. Participants log in daily and comment on focus group topics. The focus group moderator monitors the online interactions and redirects the discussion as required to keep the group on track. This ongoing message board format gives participants a chance to reflect on their responses, to talk to others, and to check out products in the real world as the group progresses. It also gives researchers the opportunity to make ongoing adjustments as the discussion unfolds. As a result, this online approach can produce much more data and deeper insights than single-session, in-person focus groups.

Although low in cost and easy to administer, online focus groups can lack the real-world dynamics of more personal approaches. The online world is devoid of the eye contact, body language, and direct personal interactions found in traditional focus group

Real Marketing 4.1

Collecting Brand Information in the Arab World

The Nielsen Company and Facebook have formed a strategic alliance to help marketers make better use of the Internet to develop and market new products. The long-term strategy is to combine Facebook's global consumer reach with Nielsen's market research expertise to provide global marketers with better insight and information. As an example, the first product of the collaboration, Nielsen BrandLift, enables marketers around the world to measure the effectiveness of their Facebook advertising, using polls on Facebook to evaluate consumer attitudes and purchase intentions with regard to display advertising on the site. After an initial launch in the United States, BrandLift is now available to all Facebook advertisers. [21]

Facebook's partnership with Nielsen, the most dominant research company in television advertising, provides Facebook with a golden opportunity to steal expensive ads, particularly from Fortune 500 companies. Google has failed for years to offer good value that would attract Nielsen to such a partnership due to the less effective ability of search ads to create demand for new products and brands. Facebook's key strength lies in the immediate feedback capability; something that even television lacks.

Nielson claims that the alliance is good news for Arab world brands and businesses. The most recent Nielsen Online Marketing Intelligence report indicates that the most visited websites in the Arab world are entertainment or social websites at 48 percent, and search engines at 34 percent, while 28 percent of consumers surveyed bought products or services online.

Online advertising in the Arab world has grown significantly over the past few years. For example, in 2006, Sarmady Communications was finding it difficult to attract website advertisers. It realized that its existing business involved creating content in selling advertising, so decided that it could increase its cash flow by offering to create websites. Four years later, Sarmady has three offices and its websites (sports and entertainment) have attracted companies such as Toyota, BMW, Adidas, and Telecom Egypt. Further, the company's revenues have more than tripled, reaching US$2 million in 2009, with projections to more than double this in 2010.

Several experts confirm that online advertising in the Arab world has great potential for growth. According to Ahmed Nassef, managing director for Yahoo! in the Middle East: "The numbers are there and we have a vibrant advertising market of as much as $9 Billion in the Gulf Arab countries and elsewhere in the region."

Piyush Mathur, Nielsen's regional managing director, Middle East, North Africa and Pakistan, said: "This alliance marks an exciting step in developing contemporary research capabilities to provide a wide range of media and consumer insights. Facebook is a clear leader in a very important and fast growing social network industry and together we hope to provide a better understanding of consumer interactions with the three screens of television, mobile and personal computers."

It is clear that BrandLift has great potential in the Arab world. It allows new and fast-growing local and regional brands to research and reach their customers effectively; and thus build their brands and explore potential regional and international expansion.

Nielsen with Facebook together support companies to collect information about their brands.

Sources: "The Nielsen Company and Facebook Form Strategic Alliance," *AMEInfo*, September 24, 2009, www.ameinfo.com/210160.html; Alaa Shahine and Massoud A. Derhally, "Online Advertising Spending Surges in the Middle East," *BusinessWeek*, June 3, 2010, www.businessweek.com/magazine/content/10_24/b4182021808328.htm.

research. And the Internet format—running, typed commentary and online 'emoticons' (punctuation marks that express emotion, such as :-) to signify happiness)—greatly restricts respondent expressiveness. The impersonal nature of the Internet can prevent people from interacting with each other in a normal way and getting excited about a concept. To overcome these shortcomings, some researchers are now adding real-time audio and video to their online focus groups.

Although the use of online marketing research is growing rapidly, both quantitative and qualitative web-based research does have drawbacks. For one, restricted Internet access can make it difficult to get a broad cross section of respondents—because many people still lack web access.[22] However, with Internet penetration growing, this is less of a problem. Another major problem is controlling who's in the online sample. Without seeing respondents, it's difficult to know who they really are. Finally, online surveys can be dry and lacking in dynamics compared with other, more personal approaches. To overcome such sample and context problems, many online research firms use opt-in communities and respondent panels.

Perhaps the most explosive issue facing online researchers concerns consumer privacy. Some fear that unethical researchers will use the email addresses and confidential responses gathered through surveys to sell products after the research is completed. They are concerned about the use of technologies that collect personal information online without the respondents' consent. Failure to address such privacy issues could result in angry, less co-operative consumers, and increased government intervention. Despite these concerns, most industry insiders predict healthy growth for online marketing research.[23]

Sampling Plan

Sample

A segment of the population selected for marketing research to represent the population as a whole.

Marketing researchers usually draw conclusions about large groups of consumers by studying a small sample of the total consumer population. A **sample** is a segment of the population selected for marketing research to represent the population as a whole. Ideally, the sample should be representative so that the researcher can make accurate estimates of the thoughts and behaviors of the larger population.

Designing the sample requires three decisions. First, *who* is to be surveyed (what *sampling unit*)? The answer to this question is not always obvious. For example, to study the decision-making process for a family automobile purchase, should the researcher interview the husband, wife, other family members, dealership salespeople, or all of these? The researcher must determine what information is needed and who is most likely to have it.

Secondly, *how many* people should be surveyed (what *sample size*)? Large samples give more reliable results than small samples. However, larger samples usually cost more, and it is not necessary to sample the entire target market or even a large portion to get reliable results. If well chosen, samples of less than 1 percent of a population can often give good reliability.

Thirdly, *how* should the people in the sample be *chosen* (what *sampling procedure*)? ● **Table 4.5** describes different kinds of samples. Using *probability samples*, each population member has a known chance of being included in the sample, and researchers can calculate confidence limits for sampling error. But when probability sampling costs too much or takes too much time, marketing researchers often take *nonprobability samples*, even though their sampling error cannot be measured. These varied ways of drawing samples have different costs and time limitations as well as different accuracy and statistical properties. Which method is best depends on the needs of the research project.

Research Instruments

In collecting primary data, marketing researchers have a choice of two main research instruments—the *questionnaire* and *mechanical devices*.

Questionnaires.   The *questionnaire* is by far the most common instrument, whether administered in person, by telephone, or online. Questionnaires are very flexible—there are many ways to ask questions. *Closed-end questions* include all the possible answers, and

●**TABLE | 4.5**   Types of Samples

Probability Sample	
Simple random sample	Every member of the population has a known and equal chance of selection.
Stratified random sample	The population is divided into mutually exclusive groups (such as age groups), and random samples are drawn from each group.
Cluster (area) sample	The population is divided into mutually exclusive groups (such as blocks), and the researcher draws a sample of the groups to interview.
Nonprobability Sample	
Convenience sample	The researcher selects the easiest population members from which to obtain information.
Judgment sample	The researcher uses his or her judgment to select population members who are good prospects for accurate information.
Quota sample	The researcher finds and interviews a prescribed number of people in each of several categories.

subjects make choices among them. Examples include multiple-choice questions and scale questions. *Open-end questions* allow respondents to answer in their own words. In a survey of airline users, Singapore Airlines might simply ask, "What is your opinion of Singapore Airlines?" Or it might ask people to complete a sentence: "When I choose an airline, the most important consideration is...." These and other kinds of open-end questions often reveal more than closed-end questions because they do not limit respondents' answers.

Open-end questions are especially useful in exploratory research, when the researcher is trying to find out *what* people think but not measuring *how many* people think in a certain way. Closed-end questions, on the other hand, provide answers that are easier to interpret and tabulate.

Researchers should also use care in the *wording* and *ordering* of questions. They should use simple, direct, unbiased wording. Questions should be arranged in a logical order. The first question should create interest if possible, and difficult or personal questions should be asked last so that respondents do not become defensive. A carelessly prepared questionnaire usually contains many errors (see ● **Table 4.6**).

Implementing the Research Plan

The researcher next puts the marketing research plan into action. This involves collecting, processing, and analyzing the information. Data collection can be carried out by the company's marketing research staff or by outside firms. The data collection phase of the marketing research process is generally the most expensive and the most subject to error. Researchers should watch closely to make sure that the plan is implemented correctly. They must guard against problems with contacting respondents, with respondents who refuse to co-operate or who give biased answers, and with interviewers who make mistakes or take shortcuts.

Researchers must also process and analyze the collected data to isolate important information and findings. They need to check data for accuracy and completeness and code it for analysis. The researchers then tabulate the results and compute statistical measures.

Interpreting and Reporting the Findings

The market researcher must now interpret the findings, draw conclusions, and report them to management. The researcher should not try to overwhelm managers with numbers and fancy statistical techniques. Rather, the researcher should present important findings and insights that are useful in the major decisions faced by management.

However, interpretation should not be left only to the researchers. They are often experts in research design and statistics, but the marketing manager knows more about the

● **TABLE** | 4.6 A 'Questionable Questionnaire'

Suppose that a school director has prepared the following questionnaire to use in interviewing the parents of prospective students. How would you assess each question?

1. What is your exact income? *People don't usually know their exact income, nor do they want to reveal their income that closely. Moreover, a researcher should never open a questionnaire with such a personal question.*

2. Are you a strong or weak supporter of student activities for your child? *What do 'strong' and 'weak' mean?*

3. Does your child behave themselves well at school? Yes ( ) No ( ) *'Behave' is a relative term. Furthermore, are yes and no the best response options for this question? Besides, will people answer this honestly and objectively? Why ask the question in the first place?*

4. In how many activities has your child been involved in the last year? This year? *Who can remember this?*

5. What are the most salient and determinant attributes in your evaluation of schools? *What are salient and determinant attributes? Don't use big words on me!*

6. Do you think it is right to deprive your child of the opportunity to grow into a mature person through the experience of student activities? *A loaded question. Given the bias, how can any parent answer yes?*

problem and the decisions that must be made. The best research means little if the manager accepts faulty interpretations from the researcher without question. Similarly, managers may be biased—they might tend to accept research results that show what they expected and to reject those that they did not expect or hope for. In many cases, findings can be interpreted in different ways, and discussions between researchers and managers will help point to the best interpretations. So managers and researchers must work together closely when interpreting research results, and both must share responsibility for the research process and resulting decisions.

> **Author Comment** | We've talked generally about managing customer relationships throughout the book. But here, 'customer relationship management' (CRM) has a much narrower data-management meaning. It refers to capturing and using customer data from all sources to manage customer interactions and build customer relationships.

Analyzing and Using Marketing Information (pp 112-114)

Information gathered in internal databases and through marketing intelligence and marketing research usually requires additional analysis. And managers may need help applying the information to gain customer and market insights that will improve their marketing decisions. This help may include advanced statistical analysis to learn more about the relationships within a set of data. Information analysis might also involve the application of analytical models that will help marketers make better decisions.

Once the information has been processed and analyzed, it must be made available to the right decision makers at the right time. In the following sections, we look deeper into analyzing and using marketing information.

Customer Relationship Management (CRM)

The question of how best to analyze and use individual customer data presents special problems. Most companies are saturated with information about their customers. In fact, smart companies capture information at every possible customer *touch point*. These touch points include customer purchases, sales force contacts, service and support calls, website visits, satisfaction surveys, credit and payment interactions, market research studies—every contact between the customer and the company.

Customer relationship management (CRM)

Managing detailed information about individual customers and carefully managing customer 'touch points' in order to maximize customer loyalty.

The trouble is that this information is usually scattered widely across the organization. It is buried deep in the separate databases and records of different company departments. To overcome such problems, many companies are now turning to **customer relationship management (CRM)** to manage detailed information about individual customers and carefully manage customer touch points in order to maximize customer loyalty.

CRM first emerged in the early 2000s. Many companies rushed in, implementing overly ambitious CRM programs that produced disappointing results and many failures. More recently, however, companies are moving ahead more cautiously and implementing CRM systems that really work.

CRM consists of sophisticated software and analytical tools that integrate customer information from all sources, analyze it in depth, and apply the results to build stronger customer relationships. CRM integrates everything that a company's sales, service, and marketing teams know about individual customers to provide a 360-degree view of the customer relationship.

CRM analysts develop *data warehouses* and use sophisticated *data mining* techniques to analyze the rich information hidden in customer data. A data

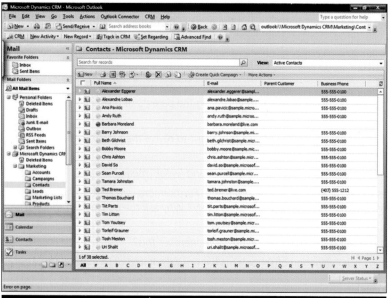

CRM systems are used widely by companies to gather and analyze customer and sales information, applying the results to build stronger customer relationships.

warehouse is a companywide electronic database of finely detailed customer information that needs to be filtered to come up with useful analysis. The purpose of a data warehouse is not just to gather information, but to pull it together into a central, accessible location. Then, once the data warehouse brings the data together, the company uses high-powered data mining techniques to analyze the loads of data and dig out interesting findings about customers.

These findings often lead to marketing opportunities. By using CRM to understand customers better, companies can provide higher levels of customer service and develop deeper customer relationships. They can use CRM to pinpoint high-value customers, target them more effectively, cross-sell the company's products, and create offers tailored to specific customer requirements.

For example, mobile operators in the region, such as Zain, Etisalat, Mobinil, and Vodafone use CRM in order to track customers. This allows them to segment them based on the revenues they generate. As a result, premium customers identified are treated as 'VIPs' and are provided with exceptional services and special offers to ensure their loyalty to the company.

CRM benefits don't come without cost or risk, either in collecting the original customer data or in maintaining and mining it. The most common CRM mistake is to view CRM only as a technology and software solution. But technology alone cannot build profitable customer relationships. "CRM is not a technology solution—you can't achieve...improved customer relationships by simply slapping in some software," says a CRM expert. Instead, CRM is just one part of an effective overall *customer relationship management strategy*. "Focus on the *R*," advises the expert. "Remember, a relationship is what CRM is all about."[24]

Distributing and Using Marketing Information

Marketing information has no value until it is used to gain customer insights and make better marketing decisions. Thus, the marketing information system must make the information readily available to the managers and others who make marketing decisions or deal with customers. In some cases, this means providing managers with regular performance reports, intelligence updates, and reports on the results of research studies.

But marketing managers may also need nonroutine information for special situations and on-the-spot decisions. For example, a sales manager having trouble with a large customer may want a summary of the account's sales and profitability over the past year. Or a retail store manager who has run out of a best-selling product may want to know the current inventory levels in the chain's other stores. Increasingly, therefore, information distribution involves entering information into databases and making it available in a timely, user-friendly way.

Many firms use a company *intranet* to facilitate this process. The intranet provides ready access to research information, reports, shared work documents, contact information for employees and other stakeholders, and more.

In addition, companies are increasingly allowing key customers and value-network members to access account, product, and other data on demand through *extranets*. Suppliers, customers, resellers, and select other network members may access a company's extranet to update their accounts, arrange purchases, and check orders against inventories to improve customer service. For example, Wal-Mart's RetailLink extranet system provides suppliers with a two-year history of every product's daily sales in every Wal-Mart store worldwide, letting them track when and where their products are selling and current inventory levels. And retailer Target's PartnersOnline extranet lets its suppliers/partners review current sales, inventory, delivery, and forecasting data. Such information sharing helps Target, its suppliers, and its customers by elevating the performance of the supply chain.[25]

Thanks to modern technology, today's marketing managers can gain direct access to the information system at any time and from virtually any location. They can tap into the system while working at a home office, from a hotel room, or from the local Starbucks through a wireless network—anyplace where they can turn on a laptop and link up. Such systems allow managers to get the information they need directly and quickly and to tailor it to their own needs. From just about anywhere, they can obtain information from company or outside databases, analyze it using statistical software, prepare reports and presentations, and communicate directly with others in the network.

Other Marketing Information Considerations (pp 114–118)

This section discusses marketing information in two special contexts: marketing research in small businesses and nonprofit organizations, and international marketing research. Finally, we look at public policy and ethics issues in marketing research.

Marketing Research in Small Businesses and Nonprofit Organizations

Just like larger firms, small organizations need market information and the customer and market insights that it can provide. Start-up businesses need information about their potential customers, industries, competitors, unfilled needs, and reactions to new market offers. Existing small businesses must track changes in customer needs and wants, reactions to new products, and changes in the competitive environment.

Managers of small businesses and nonprofit organizations often think that marketing research can be done only by experts in large companies with big research budgets. True, large-scale research studies are beyond the budgets of most small businesses. However, many of the marketing research techniques discussed in this chapter also can be used by smaller organizations in a less formal manner and at little or no expense.

For small and medium businesses, marketing research is vital but costly. Funding is often available through organisations such as the Industrial Modernisation Centre (IMC) in Egypt.

"Too [few] small-business owners have a…marketing mind-set," says a small-business consultant. "You have to think like Procter & Gamble. What would they do before launching a new product? They would find out who their customer is and who their competition is."[26]

Managers of small businesses and nonprofit organizations can obtain good marketing insights simply by *observing* things around them and talking with their customers. They can conduct informal *surveys* using small convenience samples. Small organizations can also obtain most of the secondary data available to large businesses. And many associations, local media, chambers of commerce, and government agencies provide special help to small organizations. For example, the Industrial Modernisation Centre (IMC) in Egypt provides businesses, particularly small and medium enterprises, with financial and technical support. Part of the funding is directed for professional research studies that are considered expensive for these companies.[27]

Finally, small businesses can collect a considerable amount of information at very little cost on the Internet. They can scour competitor and customer websites and use Internet search engines to research specific companies and issues.

In summary, secondary data collection, observation, surveys, and experiments can all be used effectively by small organizations with small budgets. However, although these informal research methods are less complex and less costly, they still must be conducted with care. Managers must think carefully about the objectives of the research, formulate questions in advance, recognize the biases introduced by smaller samples and less skilled researchers, and conduct the research systematically.[28]

International Marketing Research

International marketing research has grown tremendously over the past decade. In 1995, the top 25 global marketing research organizations had total combined revenues of US$5.7 billion, with 45 percent of these revenues coming from outside companies' home countries. By 2007, total revenues for the top 200 organizations had grown to US$18.5 billion.[29] However, the Global Market Research report for 2010 reported a 4.6 percent decline in global turnover in 2009. This is the first decline since the report began measuring the global market in 1988.[30]

International marketing researchers follow the same steps as domestic researchers, from defining the research problem and developing a research plan to interpreting and reporting the results. However, these researchers often face more and different problems. Whereas domestic researchers deal with fairly homogeneous markets within a single country, international researchers deal with diverse markets in many different countries. These markets often vary greatly in their levels of economic development, cultures and customs, and buying patterns.

In many foreign markets, the international researcher may have a difficult time finding good secondary data. Some countries have almost no research services at all. Some of the largest international research services do operate in many countries. For example, Nielsen Corporation (owned by The Nielsen Company, the world's largest marketing research company) has offices in more than 100 countries, including Hong Kong, Cyprus, Algeria, Egypt, Morocco, and Tunisia.[31] However, most research firms operate in only a relative handful of countries. Thus, even when secondary information is available, it usually must be obtained from many different sources on a country-by-country basis, making the information difficult to combine or compare.

Because of the scarcity of good secondary data, international researchers often must collect their own primary data. For example, they may find it difficult simply to develop good samples. Researchers in developed countries can use current telephone directories, email lists, census tract data, and any of several sources of socioeconomic data to construct samples. However, such information is largely lacking in many countries in the Arab world.

Cultural differences from country to country cause additional problems for international researchers. Language is the most obvious obstacle. For example, questionnaires must be prepared in one language and then translated into the languages of each country researched. Responses then must be translated back into the original language for analysis and interpretation. This adds to research costs and increases the risks of error.

Some research services firms are large international organizations. Nielsen has offices in more than 100 countries—here, the website for Germany is shown.

Translating a questionnaire from one language to another is anything but easy. Many expressions, phrases, and statements mean different things in different cultures.

Consumers in different countries also vary in their attitudes toward marketing research. People in one country may be very willing to respond; in other countries, non-response can be a major problem. Customs in some countries may prevent people from talking with strangers. In certain cultures within the Arab world, research questions often are considered too personal.

Despite these problems, as global marketing grows, global companies have little choice but to conduct such international marketing research. Although the costs and problems associated with international research may be high, the costs of not doing it—in terms of missed opportunities and mistakes—might be even higher. Once recognized, many of the problems associated with international marketing research can be overcome or avoided.

Public Policy and Ethics in Marketing Research

Most marketing research benefits both the sponsoring company and its consumers. Through marketing research, companies learn more about consumers' needs, resulting in more satisfying products and services and stronger customer relationships. However, the misuse of marketing research can also harm or annoy consumers. Two major public policy and ethics issues in marketing research are intrusions on consumer privacy and the misuse of research findings.

Intrusions on Consumer Privacy

Many consumers feel positive about marketing research and believe that it serves a useful purpose. Some actually enjoy being interviewed and giving their opinions. However, others strongly resent or even mistrust marketing research. They worry that marketers are building huge databases full of personal information about customers. Or they fear that researchers might use sophisticated techniques to examine our deepest feelings, and then use this knowledge to manipulate our buying.

There are no easy answers when it comes to marketing research and privacy. For example, is it a good or bad thing that marketers track and analyze consumers' web clicks and target ads to individuals based on their browsing behavior?

Consumers may also have been taken in by previous 'research surveys' that actually turned out to be attempts to sell them something. Still other consumers confuse legitimate marketing research studies with promotional efforts and say "no" before the interviewer can even begin. Most, however, simply resent the intrusion. They dislike mail, telephone, or web surveys that are too long or too personal or that interrupt them at inconvenient times.

Increasing consumer resentment has become a major problem for the marketing research industry, leading to lower survey response rates in recent years. Just as companies face the challenge of researching valuable but potentially sensitive consumer data while also maintaining consumer trust, consumers struggle with the trade-offs between personalization and privacy. Although many consumers willingly exchange personal information for free services, easy credit, discounts, upgrades, points, and all sorts of rewards, they also worry about the growth in online identity theft. One study found that 62 percent of consumers express concern over personal privacy when buying online, an increase of 47 percent over a year earlier. So it's no surprise that they are now less than willing to reveal personal information on websites.[32]

The marketing research industry is considering several options for responding to this problem.

Many major companies have now appointed a chief privacy officer (CPO), whose job is to safeguard the privacy of consumers who do business with the company. IBM's CPO claims that her job requires "multidisciplinary thinking and attitude." She needs to get all

Real Marketing 4.2

Luxury Brands in the UAE

Synovate, a market intelligence firm, carried out a global study on luxury brands, looking at over-spending and indulgence as reported by over 8,100 people across 11 very different markets. It found that two in three people in the UAE occasionally treat themselves to a luxury purchase. Only 25 percent of UAE respondents admitted feeling any regret over luxury purchases, compared with 33 percent of respondents across the world.

First, it was crucial to specifically define what is meant by luxury. The Synovate survey showed that luxury means different things depending on where you live. The top three results across all 11 markets revealed that 35 percent considered luxury as everything over and above what they need; 17 percent described luxury as a lifestyle (26 percent in the UAE, the highest response in the survey); and 16 percent thought of luxury as time to do exactly what you want. Per-Henrik Karlsson, Synovate's business development director in Dubai, stated that media and advertising there are geared towards luxury brands, which is consistent with the above finding. "This creates aspirational behavior among expats, tourists and locals alike. It starts even before you arrive, as the Emirates Airlines pre-landing video about Dubai is all about shopping, luxury cars and hotels. And once on the ground, it's everywhere: the main highway is full of billboards advertising luxury brands. Even eating out in Dubai is part of this lifestyle, with some luxury brands operating their own food and beverage outlets in malls." According to these results, branded products are attracted to this market, which allows them to grow and expand, given the importance of brand image to UAE consumers.

The researchers compared these findings with findings from a number of other countries. For example, they found that 49 percent of respondents in the Netherlands considered luxury to be everything beyond what is needed. 18 percent of respondents in both the United Kingdom (UK) and France chose the answer: "Luxury appeals to my senses...it is beautiful fabric, delicious food and so on." In contrast, the most popular response in India, at 28 percent, was that,

A global market research study into luxury brands showed that "luxury" means different things in different countries. In the UAE, over 65% of respondents occasionally treat themselves to luxury purchases.

"Luxury is more about quality than it is about price."

For many people, luxury is apparent even without a logo. For others, the logo is essential. Overall, 47 percent of consumers in the 11 markets said they prefer to buy items with logos, while 34 percent preferred items without. When analyzed according to nationality, the results show a division in attitudes: the strongest preferences for logoed items were in India (79 percent), Hong Kong (68 percent) and the UAE (58 percent). In relation to the UAE, Karlsson pointed out that: "Showing off logos is not seen as bad taste. In fact, another newly popular trend here is buying brands that show oversized logos, like certain shirts—the showier, the better."

In the Netherlands, Synovate researcher Karen Oerlemans said: "The Dutch dislike people with tons of attitude. People who do flash their wealth with big designer logos are frowned upon. This attitude translates to the way the Dutch look at luxury goods. They buy luxury because it makes them feel good. It is not about the reputation of the brand or to flaunt it to others. Luxury is not a way of life."

Another interesting finding about UAE consumers was that 14 percent of them most value the feeling "that I have something my friends and colleagues do not have." As Karlsson explained, "People here like to show off their wealth and their ability to buy the latest 'in' products, so they tend to change high-tech items and fashion brands frequently irrespective of needs. The flip side of this was illustrated in a recent Synovate survey about automobiles, with a enormous 63 percent of

people in the UAE admitting they're jealous of friends who have a better car."

Once you have decided to buy luxury, how long does it take you to research before making a decision? The Synovate survey assessed decisiveness, asking shoppers to comment on the statement "As soon as I decide I want it, I buy it." Shoppers in the UAE were among the most decisive, with 23 percent agreeing with the statement, a figure exceeded only by India, with 28 percent. As Karlsson points out: "Impulse buying is quite normal in Dubai, again linked to one-upmanship. If something new is released onto the market, people buy it immediately so they can have something no one else has." Hence, it is recommended that companies' marketing communication focuses on the share of voice in their plans in order to make use of this trend.

Synovate asked people what one luxury brand item they would most enjoy purchasing, assuming the cost was not a factor. Not surprisingly, people responded with expensive items; cars being the most popular (at 31 percent), followed by fine jewelry, designer clothing, and a great gadget (11 percent each). The UAE (28 percent) was first in selecting fine jewelry. "Gold and jewelry are culturally seen as an asset and a sign of wealth and affluence in the UAE," commented Karlsson. "These items are also seen as an investment; if times get difficult people can always sell their gold and jewelry." Luxury watches were topped by 15 percent in the UAE as well. Karlsson noted: "People in the UAE, particularly Dubai, often

Continued on next page ▼

Real Marketing 4.2 Continued ▼

own several luxury watches. Again, one reason is that it's acceptable—in fact, desirable—to display wealth. And luxury watches are usually decorated with jewels, so they're also seen as an investment." In the UAE, 49 percent of respondents said that the resale value of a luxury brand item is important to them.

The survey also asked about 'little' luxuries, finding that food and beverage luxuries topped the list (19 percent), followed by sporting equipment or clothing (18 percent). In the UAE, leather accessories was the top

answer (16 percent), second to Hong Kong (19 percent).

In what Synovate called 'Practical luxury,' 49 percent of people in the UAE would buy secondhand luxuries, topped only by the U.S. (59 percent) and the U.K. (51 percent). Interestingly, the UAE has the highest rate of window shoppers looking for luxury brands, (69 percent) and the highest proportion of

people who look at or read about luxury brands via celebrity endorsed adverts in magazines or on television (64 percent).

It is worth mentioning that such trends are expected to hold in other Arab countries. The collectivist nature of the Arab world's culture might be a reason for these results. It would be interesting to replicate this research in other Arab countries and compare the results.

Source: "Global Survey Shows Luxury is a Lifestyle in UAE," *AMEInfo*, December 22, 2009, www.ameinfo.com/219479.html.

company departments, from technology, legal, and accounting to marketing and communications working together to safeguard customer privacy.[33]

The credit card company American Express, which deals with a considerable volume of consumer information, has long taken privacy issues seriously. The company developed a set of formal privacy principles in 1991, and in 1998 it became one of the first companies to post privacy policies on its website. Its online Internet privacy statement tells customers in clear terms what information American Express collects and how it uses it, how it safeguards the information, and how it uses the information to market to its customers (with instructions on how to opt out).[34]

In the end, if researchers provide value in exchange for information, customers will gladly provide it. For example, Amazon.com's customers do not mind if the firm builds a database of products they buy in order to provide future product recommendations. This saves time and provides value. The best approach is for researchers to ask only for the information they need, to use it responsibly to provide customer value, and to avoid sharing information without the customer's permission.

Misuse of Research Findings

Research studies can be powerful persuasion tools; companies often use study results as claims in their advertising and promotion. Today, however, many research studies appear to be little more than vehicles for pitching the sponsor's products. In fact, in some cases, the research surveys appear to have been designed just to produce the intended effect. Few advertisers openly fix their research designs or deliberately misrepresent the findings; most abuses tend to be subtle 'stretches.'

For example, the choice of wording in a survey can greatly affect the conclusions reached. In the end, however, unethical or inappropriate actions cannot simply be regulated away. Each company must accept responsibility for policing the conduct and reporting of its own marketing research to protect consumers' best interests and its own.

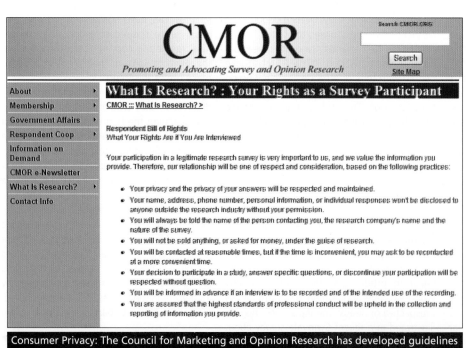

Consumer Privacy: The Council for Marketing and Opinion Research has developed guidelines to help promote responsible marketing research.

REVIEWING Objectives AND KEY Terms

To create value for customers and to build meaningful relationships with them, marketers must first gain fresh, deep insights into what customers need and want. Such insights come from good marketing information. As a result of the recent explosion of marketing technology, companies can now obtain great quantities of information, sometimes even too much. The challenge is to transform today's vast volume of consumer information into actionable customer and market insights. A company's marketing research and information system must do more than simply generate lots of information. The real value of marketing research and marketing information lies in how it is used—in the customer insights that it provides.

OBJECTIVE 1 **Explain the importance of information in gaining insights about the marketplace and customers. (pp 95-97)**

The marketing process starts with a complete understanding of the marketplace and consumer needs and wants. Thus, the company needs solid/good information in order to produce superior value and satisfaction for customers. The company also requires information on competitors, resellers, and other actors and forces in the marketplace. Increasingly, marketers are viewing information not only as an input for making better decisions but also as an important strategic asset and marketing tool.

OBJECTIVE 2 **Define the marketing information system and discuss its parts. (pp 97-100)**

The *marketing information system (MIS)* consists of people and procedures for assessing information needs, developing the needed information, and helping decision makers to use the information to generate and validate actionable customer and market insights. A well-designed information system begins and ends with users.

The MIS first *assesses information needs*. The marketing information system primarily serves the company's marketing and other managers, but it may also provide information to external partners. Then, the MIS *develops information* from internal databases, marketing intelligence activities, and marketing research. *Internal databases* provide information on the company's own operations and departments. Such data can be obtained quickly and cheaply but often needs to be adapted for marketing decisions. *Marketing intelligence* activities supply everyday information about developments in the external marketing environment. *Market research* consists of collecting information relevant to a specific marketing problem faced by the company. Lastly, the MIS helps users to analyze and use the information to develop customer insights, make marketing decisions, and manage customer relationships.

OBJECTIVE 3 **Outline the steps in the marketing research process. (pp 100-112)**

The first step in the marketing research process involves *defining the problem and setting the research objectives,* which may be exploratory, descriptive, or causal research. The second step consists of *developing a research plan* for collecting data from primary and secondary sources. The third step calls for *implementing the marketing research plan* by gathering, processing, and analyzing the information. The fourth step consists of *interpreting and reporting the findings.* Additional information analysis helps marketing managers apply the information and provides them with sophisticated statistical procedures and models from which to develop more rigorous findings.

Both *internal* and *external* secondary data sources often provide information more quickly and at a lower cost than primary data sources, and they can sometimes yield information that a company cannot collect by itself. However, needed information might not exist in secondary sources. Researchers must also evaluate secondary information to ensure that it is *relevant, accurate, current,* and *impartial.* Primary research must also be evaluated for these features. Each primary data collection method—*observational, survey,* and *experimental*—has its own advantages and disadvantages. Similarly, each of the various research contact methods—mail, telephone, personal interview, and online—also has its own advantages and drawbacks.

OBJECTIVE 4 **Explain how companies analyze and use marketing information. (pp 112-114)**

Information gathered in internal databases and through marketing intelligence and marketing research usually requires more analysis. This may include advanced statistical analysis or the application of analytical models that will help marketers make better decisions. To analyze individual customer data, many companies have now acquired or developed special software and analysis techniques—called *customer relationship management (CRM)*—that integrate, analyze, and apply the mountains of individual customer data contained in their databases.

Marketing information has no value until it is used to make better marketing decisions. Thus, the marketing information system must make the information available to the managers and others who make marketing decisions or deal with customers. In some cases, this means providing regular reports and updates; in other cases it means making nonroutine information available for special situations and on-the-spot decisions. Many firms use company intranets and extranets to facilitate this process. Thanks to modern technology, today's marketing managers can gain direct access to the information system at any time and from virtually any location.

OBJECTIVE 5 Discuss the special issues some marketing researchers face, including public policy and ethics issues. (pp 114–118)

Some marketers face special marketing research situations, such as those conducting research in small business, nonprofit, or international situations. Marketing research can be conducted effectively by small businesses and nonprofit organizations with limited budgets. International marketing researchers follow the same steps as domestic researchers but often face more and different problems. All organizations need to act responsibly to major public policy and ethical issues surrounding marketing research, including issues of intrusions on consumer privacy and misuse of research findings.

KEY Terms

OBJECTIVE 1

Customer insights (p 96)

OBJECTIVE 2

Marketing Information System (MIS) (p 96)
Internal databases (p 98)
Marketing intelligence (p 99)

OBJECTIVE 3

Marketing research (p 100)
Exploratory research (p 100)

Descriptive research (p 101)
Causal research (p 101)
Secondary data (p 101)
Primary data (p 101)
Commercial online databases (p 103)
Observational research (p 103)
Ethnographic research (p 104)
Survey research (p 105)
Experimental research (p 105)

Focus group interviewing (p 106)
Online marketing research (p 106)
Online focus groups (p 108)
Sample (p 110)

OBJECTIVE 4

Customer relationship management (CRM) (p 112)

DISCUSSING & APPLYING THE Concepts

Discussing the Concepts

1. Discuss the real value of marketing research and marketing information and how that value is attained.

2. Which information is more valuable to marketing managers—information from internal databases, from marketing intelligence, or from marketing research? How do these information sources differ?

3. Explain the differences between primary and secondary data. When is each appropriate and how are they collected?

4. What are the advantages of web-based survey research over traditional survey research?

5. How does customer relationship management (CRM) help companies develop customer insights and deliver superior customer value?

6. What are the similarities and differences when conducting research in another country versus the domestic market?

Applying the Concepts

1. Visit www.zoomerang.com or another free online web survey site. Using the tools at the site, design a five-question survey on the entertainment opportunities in your area. Send the survey to six friends and look at the results. What did you think of the online survey method?

2. Assume you are interested in opening a children's retail clothing store specializing in upscale children's fashions for newborns through to 10-year-olds. You are unsure whether there is enough demand in your area to be profitable. In a small group, discuss what information you need before making this decision and decide on which secondary sources can provide that information. Furthermore, assume you plan to conduct a survey to better estimate demand for this product and describe the best primary data collection method for your needs.

3. One source of competitive marketing intelligence is a company's website. Visit Apple's website (www.apple.com) to search for information that might be useful to competitors. Write a brief report of what you found.

FOCUS ON Technology

If you've ever complained to friends about a bad product or service experience, the marketer probably never heard you. That is, until now. If you complain on a social networking site, you just might get a response. Infegy, Inc. is just one of many businesses that offer the opportunity for other businesses to monitor their web presence through the eyes of the average web user. Infegy offers its clients a product called Social Radar. It measures public opinion, pinpoints key influences, and monitors trends. Social Radar can not only alert the business that its products and services are being discussed on a forum or featured in a blog, it can also pinpoint where these comments are coming from, how many people are reading them, and whether they are complimentary or not. The system can also pick up on competitors' products and services and provide feedback on comments made on those too. Infegy, like other social-site monitoring companies, can help its clients to make the best use of the data.

1. Search 'social media monitoring' on a search engine to find companies specializing in monitoring social media. Many of these sites discuss examples of how businesses use their service. Discuss two examples in which businesses used social media monitoring successfully.

2. Monitoring 'tagging' is hailed as the way to keep tabs on the Internet. Explain what is meant by a 'tag' and explain why monitoring such tags is beneficial for marketers.

FOCUS ON Ethics

In 2008, the Egyptian Cabinet Information and Decision Support Center ran an empirical study on the determinants of happiness and life satisfaction in Egypt.[35] The results showed that unhappiness is most apparent among old people, the unemployed, and males. On the other hand, a positive relation appears between happiness and income level, health state, and life satisfaction. Moreover higher education has no significant effect on the happiness level in comparison with high school education. One of the other observations was the significant effect of most of those variables on life satisfaction.

The sample results show that 73.5 percent are happy, and 9.7 percent are extremely happy. Accordingly, 14.8 percent are not happy and only 2.03 percent are extremely unhappy. Hence, the results were published by newspapers reporting that Egyptians are one of the happiest nations worldwide.

1. View the study at *www.idsc.gov.eg*. Does the Egyptian Cabinet Information and Decision Support Center explain its methodology and how the data is collected? Describe how the data is collected and critique the information for its usefulness.

2. Does the sampling procedure represent all segments in the society? Were the terms used in the survey clear and self-descriptive to the target sample?

MARKETING BY THE Numbers

Marketers will frequently use statistics to try and justify claims and to make their products and services appear to be more universally preferred than other brands. The truth is that statistics can appear to mean anything. Rarely do marketers reveal just how many respondents were asked to comment and under what kind of conditions. It is impossible to know whether a claim of 70 percent approval was the result of canvassing several hundred people or the first 10 likely candidates. Even a 70 percent approval rate could infer that 30 percent of respondents gave a negative answer. Customer approval based on average ratings can also be inaccurate; for example, approval based on a scale of 1–3, with 1 being dissatisfied and 3 being very satisfied, is weighted toward the center value. Market share claims are particularly problematic to independently measure and assess. How is the market share being calculated? What is the definition of a market? Traditionally market share is calculated in two different ways. It can be calculated as a percentage of the total market, so if a business sells 46 of the 100 units sold, then it has a 46 percent market share. It may also be based on revenue, so if the value of the products sold is US$4,600 in a market worth US$10,000, then the market share is also 46 percent. For more discussion of the financial and quantitative implications of marketing decisions, see Appendix 2: Marketing by the Numbers.

1. Using census data on health insurance coverage in your country develop statistics, such as percentages, to support the argument that the government should insist on private health insurance. Use any portion of the data you deem important to support your argument.

2. Use the same data to develop different statistics to support the counterargument to the previous question. That is, interpret the data and present it in a way that supports the need for sweeping health care reforms to switch to government-provided health care for all. Again, use any portion of the data you deem important to support your argument.

VIDEO Case

ZIBA

How do companies design new products? Quite often, they get someone else to do it for them. That's where design firms such as ZIBA come in. ZIBA is one of a new breed of consultancies whose sole purpose is to help corporations better understand customer needs and turn that understanding into groundbreaking new products.

The foundation for ZIBA's product development process is market research. That research seeks to understand the brand itself, the competition, and market trends. But most important,

ZIBA's research efforts center on getting to know the customer. It has taken a novel approach to market research by utilizing the likes of social anthropologists and cultural ethnographers to get to the heart of what makes consumers tick. Their efforts often include actually following customers around, observing them in their natural environment, and understanding their experiences.

The unique focus that ZIBA takes has earned it contracts with major corporations including P&G, KitchenAid, Logitech, Microsoft, and Intel, as well as with various small start-up companies.

After viewing the video featuring ZIBA, answer the following questions about new-product development:

1. Illustrate some ways in which ZIBA engages in each phase of the marketing research process.

2. Discuss the various ways in which ZIBA's research efforts are focused on customer relationships.

3. Identify evidence of how ZIBA uses the information that it acquires to make marketing decisions.

COMPANY Case

ARIEL IN EGYPT: THE VALUE OF CONSUMER INSIGHT

P&G Egypt began its operations in 1986, producing Camay soap and Crest toothpaste at a built facility plant located at the 6th of October city, right outside Cairo. For the remainder of the decade, P&G continued expanding its manufacturing operations, including a synthetic detergent tower in 1990 to produce the Ariel brand. Ariel was introduced in Egypt in 1986 as a washing machine detergent (Ariel Low Suds). The brand is positioned as "a detergent with excellent cleaning performance, tough stain removal, and superior whiteness."

It is very important to distinguish between a detergent for automatic washing machines (Low Suds) and a detergent for hand wash (High Suds). In developing countries, a very high percentage of the population cannot afford to buy an automatic washing machine. By 1989, the laundry bar was dominating the hand wash and non-automatic washing machine market in Egypt, while the automatic washing machine market was still premature. In 1990, P&G decided to introduce Ariel High Suds for hand wash and non-automatic washing machines to strengthen its operation and benefit from the potential target market. The challenge was to educate consumers to shift from using bar soap to a premium detergent like Ariel.

MARKETING RESEARCH

One of Procter & Gamble's secrets of success is its heavy reliance on marketing research. Despite criticisms of being relatively slow to enter potential markets, P&G would rather study the market extensively and invest in valuable research that helps it not only introduce successful products, but also sustain this success for a long period of time. P&G conducted extensive research in the Egyptian market through various qualitative research methods. The company realized the importance of deeply understanding the details of consumers' cleaning behavior, so it decided to utilize an ethnographic research method, whereby managers and researchers spent full days at consumers' houses observing their behavior and informally talking to them. It was discovered that the cleaning process was very long and Ariel would provide them with a solution that both saves time and ensures superior cleaning.

Prior to Ariel's introduction, consumers used to have a washing day, where several activities were performed. Soaking was the first step conducted by most consumers, with the objective of getting garments cleaner and removing stains. This process required more than 8 hours, so many consumers used to do it overnight. Most consumers used detergents in soaking, while few used bleach. Boiling was the second step in the washing process. The objective of boiling was to remove stains, better clean, ensure whiteness, and prevent infection. This process used to last for about 30–40 minutes. Rubbing was the last step in the washing process, mainly to ensure cleaning and stain removal, especially for whites. In this long process, housewives were mainly using bar soaps, then started step by step to use powder detergents.

EDUCATING CONSUMERS: CHANGING THE RULES OF THE GAME

The idea of superior performance using the power of built-in additives was totally new to the market and consumers needed extensive efforts and education to first believe in this new technology, and second to decide to use it. One of the major challenges that faced Ariel was changing consumers' habits. As a matter of fact, the first trial activities showed that consumers were resistant to the idea. It was thought that they would appreciate time saved, but surprisingly, they did not. They used to have a whole day of washing. This washing day was a gathering event for rural women to see each other and chat. They were also competing for the best cleaning recipes! Asking them to use one detergent that substitutes all their effort faced a strong social resistance. Cleaning for these women was like cooking; it was used to show how competent they were. The marketing team had to find a way to convince these consumers of the value offered and change their social habits. And that was quite a challenge!

TRIAL ACTIVITIES

P&G started educating consumers through trial activities to skim through the market and reach consumers personally. Obviously advertising was not the tool to use at this stage of market development. There was a need to show consumers what the product is capable of. In 1991, P&G launched one of the biggest door-to-door (DTD) activities in the region, covering 5.5 million homes in 6 months (almost 95 percent of the total urban population), and consumers were offered the product at 20 percent of its price. A year later, another DTD activity was executed, covering 3.8 million homes. In parallel, the product was pushed to consumers through in-store promotions, and to customers through sales forces to reinforce distribution and ensure product availability in the areas covered by trial activities.

However, the marketing team was not satisfied with the results achieved. Consumers had not been convinced yet, and most of them used the product occasionally, while maintaining their washing habits. People needed to be convinced face-to-face. Also, they needed to relate to the brand emotionally and link it to their daily lives. It looked like a tough challenge, but the P&G team was determined to overcome it. The question was: How?

THE 'ROAD SHOW' CONCEPT: THE BREAKTHROUGH

Again, P&G decided to rely on its strongest competency: Research. The objective was to find a creative way to talk to consumers and convince them about the product. From there, came the idea of meeting consumers where they gathered. Research indicated two possible gathering events: 1) The 'Utensils Washing Day,' where women used to gather next to the lake in the morning to talk and wash their utensils; 2) The Marketplace 'El Souk,' where people gathered to buy stuff and see each other. From an execution standpoint, the first option was not possible, and option 2 seemed more realistic. Extensive research was conducted on these Souks, mapping the whole 26 governorates in Egypt at that time. 824 Souks were identified all over the country and through them P&G expected to target at least 90 percent of women (as well as men if they are the decision makers, especially in conservative areas like Upper Egypt).

The 'Ariel Road Show' was the first broad-scale innovative sampling program in Egypt, and since then, it has become a famous marketing tool worldwide, replicated in several countries. Road shows were one of the pillars for Ariel's success. The idea was to have a van or a big truck with branding all over, bringing joy to people. At first, the road show was used as an entertainment vehicle to attract consumers and create awareness. A clown was used to play with children, while raffles were introduced and prizes were distributed. Meanwhile, Ariel packs were first sold at a very low price, then at a discounted price, then at full price. At the beginning, people were on the top of the small trucks, playing music to attract consumers. Then, bigger trucks were used, well-equipped with huge television screens, videos, and advertisements, along with a big sound system and microphones, playing the most popular songs at that time. It was a full day of entertainment for thousands of people. Also, Ariel attracted consumers by painting villages with Ariel logos to increase awareness and popularity. Afterwards, the P&G team started to do some demonstrations, i.e. take a piece of clothing, ask one of the women to put some mud or dirt on it, and ask her to wash it in front of everybody. Field challenges were also introduced to convince system users that Ariel does it all.

Nowadays, Ariel is still the leading hand wash detergent in Egypt. There is no doubt that the quality marketing research conducted before introducing the product in the market was effective in reaching consumers and building a bond between them and the brand.

Questions for Discussion

1. Evaluate the research techniques used by Ariel in the case.

2. Do you think the company should have used a quantitative research technique instead? Justify your answer.

3. The Ariel brand manager wonders whether the size of the Ariel packages was appropriate. Design a research plan to answer this question.

4. Imagine Persil decides to enter the market a year later. What would you recommend Ariel do to protect its market share?

Source: A case study authored by Ahmed Tolba and published at El-Khazindar Business Research and Case Center (KCC) at the American University in Cairo.

Chapter 5

Part 1	Defining Marketing and the Marketing Process (Chapters 1, 2)
Part 2	Understanding the Marketplace and Consumers (Chapters 3, 4, 5, 6)
Part 3	Designing a Customer-Driven Strategy and Mix (Chapters 7, 8, 9, 10, 11, 12, 13, 14)
Part 4	Extending Marketing (Chapters 15, 16, 17)

Consumer Behavior

Chapter PREVIEW

In the previous chapter, you studied how marketers obtain, analyze, and use information to understand the marketplace and to assess marketing programs. In this and the next chapter, we'll continue with a closer look at the most important element of the marketplace—customers. The aim of marketing is to affect how customers think and act. To affect the *whats, whens,* and *hows* of buying behavior, marketers must first understand the *whys*. In this chapter, we look at *final consumer* buying influences and processes. In the next chapter, we'll study the buyer behavior of *business customers*. You'll see that understanding buyer behavior is an essential but very difficult task.

To get a better sense of the importance of understanding consumer behavior, let's look at the impact of football on consumers in the Arab world; specifically in Egypt and Saudi Arabia.

Al-Ahly and Zamalek are Egypt—and Africa's—strongest local football clubs, founded in 1907 and 1911 respectively. Al-Ahly was ranked as the top African club of the twentieth century by the Confederation of African Football, while Zamalek was ranked second. Matches between Al-Ahly and Zamalek have "always been Egyptian football's premier showdown."[1] Most Egyptians can't resist watching the two teams play against each other as part of the annual league championship. Egypt comes to a standstill when the two giants meet. For 90 per cent of the nation, the Al-Ahly–Zamalek game is their number one priority. People cancel appointments and postpone trips in order to watch it. Rivalry between the fans is great and splits the nation into two. *Ahlawis* (Al-Ahly fans) are considered to be in a different social category from *Zamalkawys* (Zamalek fans).

When the two teams meet, the stadium gates open hours before kick-off and the road to the stadium is usually blocked with cars and buses of supporters, who blow horns and wave flags—red for Al-Ahly and white for Zamalek. Inside the stadium the two sets of fans sit at opposite ends and the sounds of the clubs' anthems fill the air. Al-Ahly and Zamalek are the topic of conversation in coffee shops, Internet cafés, office corridors, and taxis. Throughout Egypt, the presence of Al-Ahly and Zamalek is felt in some form or another.

At a national level, Egypt has always been a leading football team in Africa. In 2010, Egypt became the first African nation to win three consecutive cups in the continent. Egyptians have a strong attachment to the national side, as was evident during the qualifying matches of the World Cup in 2009. The qualifying game between Egypt and Algeria was of great importance to the Egyptians, and the tension between the two countries ran high. The Egyptian supporters inside and outside the stadium prayed every five minutes for God to bestow victory upon the Egyptian team. In the lead up to the game, advertisements cor-responded to the Egyptian dream and carried the slogans: "Pray for Egypt," and "God support Egypt." Moreover, patriotic songs and motivational television talk show hosts dominated Egyptian media. Advertisements too were based on the nation's hopes for footballing success. It would have been difficult for listeners not to hear the frequently aired radio advertisements inspiring 80 million Egyptians to pray for victory in the game. It would have been even more difficult for people to ignore the many billboards, plastered with the Egyptian flag, again asking the public to pray. "Flags, indeed, seemed everywhere, hanging from buildings, draped over cars, waving in the hands of passers-by. Car horns, fireworks, even live ammunition, formed the soundtrack to what was becoming an aggressively emotional occasion."[2]

Before, during, and after the broadcasting of the match, the Egyptian audience was bombarded with all kinds of ads from leading multinational companies such as Pepsi and Coca-Cola. While Pepsi was the official sponsor of the 2008 African Cup of Nations in Ghana, Coca-Cola launched a campaign carrying the slogan "Sponsor of the Egyptian Supporters." In this campaign, Coca-Cola profiled different types of Egyptian supporters in a very humorous manner. It iden-tified groups of support-ers it named Optimists, Pessimists, Experts, Ignorants, New Comers, Emotionals, and Fanatics, among others. At the end of each ad broadcast, it was mentioned how a spe-cific group supported the Egyptian team and how

> **Al-Ahly and Zamalek were formed in 1907 and 1911 respectively. They represent the strongest African clubs in the past decade.**

Coca-Cola was with them—"Coca-Cola: the Sponsor of the Egyptian Supporter." This was a creative strategy to appeal to Egyptian consumers without paying any sponsorship fees.

In Egypt, everyone is expected to like football. Everyone tries to show their support and enjoyment for the sport ahead of crucial matches, if only to be part of a social group that they aspire to belong to.

Football stars in Egypt are considered celebrities. According to the International Federation of Football History and Statistics (IFFHS), Egyptian footballer Mohamed Aboutrika was the world's most popular footballer in 2007, followed by Saudi's Yasser Al Qahtany. More than one million people voted for Aboutrika in that poll. Tapping into Egyptian players' popularity, Vodafone signed the entire Al-Ahly team as celebrities to be used in its ads. The team members were considered powerful representatives of the message in Vodafone's campaign: "I am Vodafone." Etisalat, the UAE telecoms giant, on entering the Egyptian market, realized the significance of the football culture in Egypt and decided to sponsor the Egyptian national football league.

The popularity of football is not limited to Egypt. The sport is popular in several other Arab countries, too, including Saudi Arabia—a leading football power in Asia, which has qualified several times for the World Cup. The Saudis' love of football is less apparent than the Egyptians', but football is Saudi Arabia's most popular sport. As in Egypt, Saudi's local league is dominated by two rival teams: Al-Hilal and Al-Ittihad. Choosing to support one team over another does not say a lot about your social identity, but football in general represents a great interest for Saudis—as is evident by the number of football fans who cram into restaurants and cafés at times of key matches. Customers who wish to book a restaurant on the day of a high-profile football match must do so at least two days in advance. Men, women, and families show their support for the national Saudi team by painting their faces and hair, by wearing clothes in green and white—to represent the Saudi flag—and by singing the national anthem.

Realizing the importance of football to Saudi society, the Saudi telecommunication giant Zain decided to sponsor the Saudi Arabia Professional Football League, now commonly known as the Zain league. HRH Hussam bin Saud bin Abdulaziz Al Saud, chairman of Zain Saudi Arabia, said the decision to sponsor the

Al-Ahly vs. Zamalek matches represent the oldest derby in Africa and the Arab world, and are considered one of the oldest derbies worldwide.

league was "borne out of a belief in the vital importance of sport in Saudi society."[3] HRH Prince Nawaf Bin Faisal Bin Fahd Bin Abdul Aziz, vice president of Youth Welfare, vice president of the Saudi Football Association, and head of the Saudi Professional Football League Commission, said the sponsorship would help finance the new Saudi football environment, encourage investment, aid profession growth, and ameliorate the standard of football as whole in Saudi Arabia. Mobily, another telecommunication company in Saudi, has links with the football team Al-Hilal. Footballers such as Yasser Al-Qahtani, Wilhelmsson, and Mirel Radoi feature in Mobily ads, and at the end of the ad the message "Official Partner" of Al-Hilal appears. Mobily has signed a contract to associate itself with Al-Hilal for five years, ending in 2012. Such an agreement is common in the Saudi league, but what sets this contract apart from others is the amount paid by Mobily to Al-Hilal Football Club—SR 200 million (US$54.79million).

There is no question that marketing cannot be effective without understanding consumers' behavior; and football has a significant effect on consumers' behavior in the Arab world.[4]

> Football has a strong influence on consumer behavior in Egypt, Saudi Arabia, and many other countries. When rival Egyptian football teams Al-Ahly and Zamalek meet, the country comes to a standstill and the match dominates public attention. Multinational companies such as Coca-Cola and Pepsi jump at the chance to reach such a large captive audience, and queue up for advertising opportunities.

Consumer buyer behavior

The buying behavior of final consumers—individuals and households that buy goods and services for personal consumption.

Consumer market

All the individuals and households that buy goods and services for personal consumption.

The football example shows that many different factors affect consumer buying behavior. Buying behavior is never simple, yet understanding it is the essential task of marketing management. **Consumer buyer behavior** refers to the buying behavior of final consumers—individuals and households that buy goods and services for personal consumption. All of these final consumers combine to make up the **consumer market**. The world consumer market consists of more than 6.6 *billion* people who annually consume an estimated US$65 trillion worth of goods and services. The Arab world's 22 countries comprise about 5 percent of the world's population and 3 percent of the world's GDP.[5]

Consumers around the world vary tremendously in age, income, education level, and tastes. They also buy an incredible variety of goods and services. How these diverse

Objective Outline

consumers relate with each other and with other elements of the world around them impacts on their choices among various products, services, and companies. Here we examine the fascinating array of factors that affect consumer behavior, with an emphasis on Arab world consumers.

| **Author Comment** | Despite the simple-looking model in Figure 5.1, understanding the whys of buying behavior is very difficult. Says one expert, "the mind is a whirling, swirling, jumbled mass of neurons bouncing around." |

Model of Consumer Behavior (pp 126–127)

Consumers make many buying decisions every day, and the buying decision is the focal point of the marketer's effort. Most large companies research consumer buying decisions in great detail to answer questions about what consumers buy, where they buy, how and how much they buy, when they buy, and why they buy. Marketers can study actual consumer purchases to find out what they buy, where, and how much. But learning about the *whys* of consumer buying behavior is not so easy—the answers are often locked deep within the consumer's mind.

Often, consumers themselves don't know exactly what influences their purchases. Their behavior is not a result of organized reasoning; it is rather driven by continuously changing thoughts in their minds. The central question for marketers is: How do consumers respond to various marketing efforts the company might use? The starting point is the stimulus-response model of buyer behavior shown in 🐚 **Figure 5.1**. A stimulus is something that causes something else to happen, develop, or become more active. This figure shows that marketing and other stimuli enter the consumer's 'black box' and produce certain responses. Marketers must figure out what is in the buyer's black box.

Marketing stimuli consist of the four Ps: product, price, place, and promotion. Other stimuli include major forces and events in the buyer's environment: economic, technological, political, and cultural. All these inputs enter the buyer's black box, where they are turned into a set of observable buyer responses: the buyer's brand and company relationship behavior and what he or she buys, when, where, and how often.

The marketer wants to understand how the stimuli are changed into responses inside the consumer's black box, which has two parts. First, the buyer's characteristics influence how he or she perceives and reacts to the stimuli. Secondly, the buyer's decision process itself affects the buyer's behavior. We look first at buyer characteristics as they affect buyer behavior and then discuss the buyer decision process.

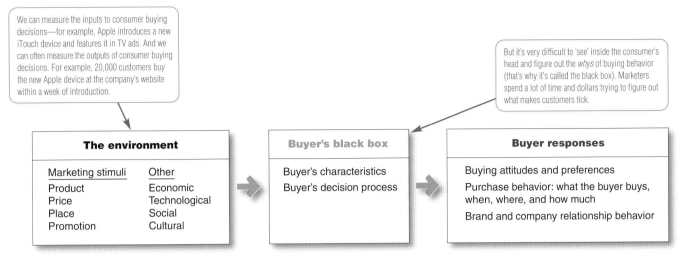

We can measure the inputs to consumer buying decisions—for example, Apple introduces a new iTouch device and features it in TV ads. And we can often measure the outputs of consumer buying decisions. For example, 20,000 customers buy the new Apple device at the company's website within a week of introduction.

But it's very difficult to 'see' inside the consumer's head and figure out the *whys* of buying behavior (that's why it's called the black box). Marketers spend a lot of time and dollars trying to figure out what makes customers tick.

The environment

Marketing stimuli	Other
Product	Economic
Price	Technological
Place	Social
Promotion	Cultural

Buyer's black box

Buyer's characteristics
Buyer's decision process

Buyer responses

Buying attitudes and preferences
Purchase behavior: what the buyer buys, when, where, and how much
Brand and company relationship behavior

FIGURE | 5.1 Model of Buyer Behavior

Author Comment | Many, many levels of factors affect our buying behavior—from broad cultural and social influences to motivations, beliefs, and attitudes lying deep within us. For example, why did you buy that specific mobile phone?

Characteristics Affecting Consumer Behavior (pp 127–139)

Consumer purchases are influenced strongly by cultural, social, personal, and psychological characteristics, shown in **Figure 5.2**. For the most part, marketers cannot control such factors, but they must take them into account.

Cultural Factors

Cultural factors exert a broad and deep influence on consumer behavior. The marketer needs to understand the role played by the buyer's *culture*, *subculture*, and *social class*.

Culture

Culture
The set of basic values, perceptions, wants, and behaviors learned by a member of society from family and other important institutions.

Culture is the most basic cause of a person's wants and behavior. Human behavior is largely learned. Growing up in a society, a child learns basic values, perceptions, wants, and behaviors from the family and other important institutions. Every group or society has a culture, and cultural influences on buying behavior may vary greatly from country to country. Failure to adjust to these differences can result in ineffective marketing or embarrassing mistakes.

Prof. Geert Hofstede defined five dimensions to analyze and compare cultures across the world: Power Distance Index, Uncertainty Avoidance Index, Individualism, Masculinity, and Long-Term Orientation. Using research conducted in Egypt, Iraq, Kuwait, Lebanon, Libya, Saudi Arabia, and the UAE, Hofstede developed a measure of the Arab world. Of

FIGURE | 5.2
Factors Influencing Consumer Behavior

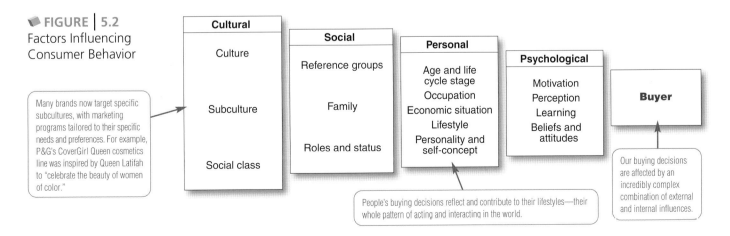

Many brands now target specific subcultures, with marketing programs tailored to their specific needs and preferences. For example, P&G's CoverGirl Queen cosmetics line was inspired by Queen Latifah to "celebrate the beauty of women of color."

Cultural	Social	Personal	Psychological	Buyer
Culture	Reference groups	Age and life cycle stage	Motivation	
Subculture	Family	Occupation	Perception	
		Economic situation	Learning	
Social class	Roles and status	Lifestyle	Beliefs and attitudes	
		Personality and self-concept		

People's buying decisions reflect and contribute to their lifestyles—their whole pattern of acting and interacting in the world.

Our buying decisions are affected by an incredibly complex combination of external and internal influences.

course, it is not accurate to consider the seven countries representative of all Arab countries; nor is it logical to assume that all countries have similar cultures. However, it is interesting to analyze Hofstede's findings and come up with reasonable conclusions on the Arab world's culture.

Hofstede identified a high Power Distance Index (PDI) ranking in the Arab world. This indicates high levels of inequality of power and wealth. People expect and accept that leaders will separate themselves from the majority. This condition has historically been accepted as part of each country's cultural heritage.

Hofstede also identified a high Uncertainty Avoidance Index (UAI). This indicates that people are uncomfortable with uncertainty. Strict rules, laws, policies, and regulations are put in place to minimize or reduce this level of uncertainty. The ultimate goal is to control everything and so eliminate or avoid the unexpected. However, this means that people do not readily accept change and are risk averse.

Large PDI and UAI scores, 80 and 68 respectively, suggest that people in Arab world societies are likely to follow a hierarchical system in which there is little social mobility. According to Hofstede, the combination of these two dimensions produces a situation in which leaders have ultimate power and authority, and allows them to set laws and regulations that reinforce their leadership and control.

The Masculinity Index (MAS) is the Arab world's third highest dimension, though at 52 it is only slightly higher than the 50.2 world average. This score suggests that women in the Arab world have limited rights.

The lowest Hofstede dimension for the Arab world is for Individualism (IDV). With a score of 38, it is significantly below the world average of 64. This shows the existence of a Collectivist society rather than an Individualist culture. In a Collectivist culture, there is a close long-term commitment to the member 'group,' in other words to the family, extended family, or extended relationships. In this culture, loyalty is vital and overrides most other societal rules.

Hofstede notes that the Muslim faith is the predominant religion for these countries and it is not always easy to establish its effects and influences.[6]

Marketers are always trying to spot *cultural shifts* in order to discover new products that might be wanted. For example, the increasing numbers of fast-food chains, multinational corporations, shopping malls, and hypermarkets in the Arab world have created a significant cultural shift toward 'Western' behaviors. There are various fast-food chains operating in the region. McDonald's is currently operating in 14 Arab countries. **Real Marketing 5.1** discusses McDonald's challenges in the Arab world.

A recent study analyzed Saudi managers' evaluations of the role of MNCs. The research focused on the contribution of MNCs in four areas: political, cultural, economic, and technological. Perhaps not surprisingly, the researchers found that the managers considered that MNCs have both positive and negative effects. Positive effects include the crucial role of MNCs in establishing export capacity, improving productivity, managerial skills, and job creation. The most obvious negative impacts are on political independence, and on values and consumption patterns.[7]

The number of shopping malls has increased significantly in the region. In fact, there are about 40 shopping malls in the UAE alone. According to global research conducted by AC Nielsen in 2006, the UAE is ranked second on global recreational shopping after Hong Kong. The study indicated that 30 percent of UAE consumers shop at least once a week. This represents an excellent opportunity for retailers operating in the Arab countries.[8]

Another trend in the Arab world is the growth of hypermarkets and large supermarkets which have significantly affected shopping behavior in the region. While there are multinational chains, such as Carrefour, that are successfully operating in several Arab countries, there are also local and regional chains, such as Spinney's and Lulu (a chain operated by the Emke Group).

The Emke Group, an Abu Dhabi-based retail giant, has supermarkets, hypermarkets, and malls spread all over the UAE, Oman, Qatar, Bahrain, Kuwait, and Saudi Arabia. It is one of the biggest Indian-owned conglomerates in the Gulf with varied businesses

Real Marketing 5.1

How McDonald's Markets to the Arab Consumers

McDonald's is one of the largest networks of fast-food restaurants in the world. The company continuously attempts to strengthen its position in the world market. With the growing trend toward Westernization, the Arab world is considered a potentially growing market. McDonald's operates franchise stores in 14 Arab countries. A key element in McDonald's strategy is to adapt its traditional American approach to local culture, food habits, and lifestyles. For example, in some countries of the Arab world, McDonald's outlets are divided along male and female lines in accordance with local custom.

As well as adapting the restaurants themselves, McDonald's tailors its menu to meet the food culture or preferences of different countries. The McDonald's menu varies widely in different parts of the world. In the Arab world, for example, the company launched 'McArabia,' a product that McDonald's intended to match regional tastes and preferences.

The challenge was to find the product that would combine McDonald's traditional global principles and standards with the local cuisine and habits of Arabs. Intensive research was conducted to come up with the right product that would satisfy both dimensions. More precisely, the selection of the product considered the fact that pork products are forbidden in Islam. The company tried to use elements of traditional local cuisine, while corresponding to McDonald's brand image. Eventually, the company introduced McArabia as a sandwich containing some local ingredients, such as Arab bread, grilled chicken, lettuce, tomatoes, and Arab sauce.

Before introducing McArabia to the market, McDonald's analyzed to what extent the product would be successful. First, it was necessary to ensure that the product matched local tastes. For McDonald's the potential success of McArabia in various markets in

McArabia—A sandwich from McDonald's targets the Arab market by providing a grilled burger in pita bread.

the Arab world would mean an increase in sales as well as a growth in the popularity of McDonald's at large.

To forecast the potential of McArabia, McDonald's conducted intensive research to predict consumers' reactions toward the introduction of the new product. Moreover, specialists analyzed the local cuisine and local food markets. All ingredients that might be unacceptable to the local people were removed and substituted with local alternatives. The results of the research were promising and showed that McArabia was expected to succeed in most Arab countries as well as Muslim countries with similar food habits. Therefore, the potential market of McArabia was quite large. Further, McDonald's relied on dietitians in the development of the product, and accordingly, managed to determine what ingredients would be most applicable to the new product and yield the best reactions from consumers.

A financial analysis of the new product revealed that McArabia was not more expensive to produce than traditional McDonald's products. Therefore, the next step was to

find the appropriate suppliers and design efficient promotion and distribution strategies. Although McArabia was a local/regional product, the company decided to import the Arab bread from Britain and the chicken from Malaysia. Only the Arab sauce was supplied locally. Interestingly, depending on international suppliers did not affect the price of the product dramatically and allowed the company to charge a price that was considered acceptable for the local markets. Also, McDonald's succeeded in distributing the new McArabia product effectively in the Arab world, capitalizing on the large network of stores in 14 Arab countries. It also realized that effective distribution was not enough, and marketed the product through a carefully planned advertising campaign, using billboards and printed media.

The McArabia initiative indicates how McDonald's values its business in the Arab world. While the popularity of McDonald's in the Arab world was decreasing, McArabia was a means of getting closer to Arab consumers and changing its public image in the region.

Sources: Mohammed Alkhereiji, "McDonald's Launches McArabia," *Arab News Staff*, March 5, 2003; A. di. Benedetto, *New Product Management*, New York: Random House, 2004; R. C. Benfari, *Understanding and Changing Your Management Style*, San Francisco: Jossey-Bass, 1999; H. S. Gitlow, *The Deming Guide to Quality and Competitive Position*, Englewood Cliffs, N.J.: Prentice-Hall, 1997; Richard Leiby, "You Want Falafel With That?" *Washington Post*, March 17, 2003.

operating in 15 countries spread over three continents. It employs more than 22,000 people from over 29 countries. It operates popular brands of retail chain stores that include the Lulu chain of supermarkets, department stores, hypermarkets, and now shopping malls. The group's retail chains cater to over 350,000 customers everyday. It enjoys over 32 percent of the total retail market share in the Gulf, including 75 Lulu hypermarkets all around the region. In 2009, the group registered an annual sales turnover of US$2.57 billion, a 30% increase on the previous year.[9]

Subculture

Subculture
A group of people with shared value systems based on common life experiences and situations.

Each culture contains smaller **subcultures**, or groups of people with shared value systems based on common life experiences and situations. Subcultures include nationalities, religions, racial groups, and geographic regions. Many subcultures make up important market segments, and marketers often design products and marketing programs tailored to their needs.

There are several commonalities among Arab countries, including language (Arabic) and religion (Islam). However, there are some minority groups that live in the region who speak different languages and/or exercise different religions. In fact, foreigners constitute a very high percentage of the population in countries such as the UAE and Qatar. Moreover, there are differences among Arabs in the different countries. Arabs in the Gulf countries are different from those in North African countries, where the French and Berber languages are widely spoken.

Social Class

Social class
Relatively permanent and ordered divisions in a society whose members share similar values, interests, and behaviors.

Almost every society has some form of social class structure. **Social classes** are society's relatively permanent and ordered divisions whose members share similar values, interests, and behaviors. For example, in the USA, social scientists have identified seven typical social classes, as shown in 🍃 **Figure 5.3**.

🍃 **FIGURE** | 5.3
The Major American Social Classes

America's social classes show distinct brand preferences. Social class is not determined by a single factor, but by a combination of all of these factors.

Wealth · Education · Occupation · Income

Upper Class
Upper Uppers (1 percent): The social elite who live on inherited wealth. They give large sums to charity, own more than one home, and send their children to the finest schools.

Lower Uppers (2 percent): Americans who have earned high income or wealth through exceptional ability. They are active in social and civic affairs and buy expensive homes, educations, and cars.

Middle Class
Upper Middles (12 percent): Professionals, independent businesspersons, and corporate managers who possess neither family status nor unusual wealth. They believe in education, are joiners and highly civic minded, and want the 'better things in life.'

Middle Class (32 percent): Average-pay white- and blue-collar workers who live on 'the better side of town.' They buy popular products to keep up with trends. Better living means owning a nice home in a nice neighborhood with good schools.

Working Class
Working Class (38 percent): Those who lead a 'working-class lifestyle,' whatever their income, school background, or job. They depend heavily on relatives for economic and emotional support, for advice on purchases, and for assistance in times of trouble.

Lower Class
Upper Lowers (9 percent): The working poor. Although their living standard is just above poverty, they strive toward a higher class. However, they often lack education and are poorly paid for unskilled work.

Lower Lowers (7 percent): Visibly poor, often poorly educated unskilled laborers. They are often out of work and some depend on public assistance. They tend to live a day-to-day existence.

Social class is not determined by a single factor, such as income, but is measured as a combination of occupation, income, education, wealth, and other variables. In some social systems, members of different classes are reared for certain roles and cannot change their social positions. In other countries, however, the lines between social classes are not fixed and rigid; people can move to a higher social class or drop into a lower one.

An Arab Example: Social Classes in the UAE

A study by Advamac Inc. notes that the Emirati society is divided into two social categories: nationals (*Al-Muwateneen*) and foreign immigrants, or 'incomers' (*Al-Wafedeen*).[10]

The nationals group, in turn, is made up of four main classes: (1) the ruling Sheikhly families, who are immensely wealthy and hold the highest political positions and power; (2) the merchant class, (the al-tujjar) who were traditionally pearl merchants but now sell international consumer goods; (3) the new middle class, an increasing number of professionals who have benefitted from free state education, and (4) low-income groups, including newly settled Bedouin nomads, former pearl divers, and oasis farmers.

The immigrants are also made up of a hierarchy of groups that receive different economic and social rewards: (1) top professionals and international contractors; (2) middle-range professionals, including school teachers, skilled technicians, and company salesmen; and (3) low-paid, semi-skilled and unskilled workers. In general, the nationals benefit from state laws and business regulations and thus make up a privileged minority.[11]

The UAE model applies to the whole Gulf region, with minor variance here and there. The rest of the Arab world, comprising larger populations, looks different. The social classes are divided in standard A, B, C, and D classes of locals, based on income or lifestyle—A being the highest. The marketers divide the categories in close proximity, but with variance based on the products they sell. Most fast-moving consumer goods (FMCGs) address A and B together.

Within the classes, consumers are subcategorized to, for example, B+, B, and B− to further segment the consumer. One of the ongoing issues faced is the growth of the gap between the income groups, resulting in slimming down in the target segments on top of the pyramid and increasing the size of the segments at the bottom of the pyramid.

Group
Two or more people who interact to accomplish individual or mutual goals.

Marketers are interested in social class because people within a given social class tend to exhibit similar buying behavior. Social classes show distinct product and brand preferences in areas such as clothing, home furnishings, leisure activity, and automobiles.

Social Factors

A consumer's behavior also is influenced by social factors, such as the consumer's *small groups*, *family*, and *social roles* and *status*.

Groups and Social Networks

Many small **groups** influence a person's behavior. Groups that have a direct influence and to which a person belongs are called membership groups. In contrast, reference groups serve as direct (face-to-face) or indirect points of comparison or reference in forming a person's attitudes or behavior. People often are influenced by reference groups to which they do not belong. For example, an aspirational group is one to which the individual wishes to belong, as when a young football player hopes to someday emulate football stars, and play professional football. In fact, Egyptian football fans created a Facebook group called 'Abo Treka Fans' to share their appreciation of

This advertisement is written in Arabic as well as English to communicate the message to different nationalities living in the UAE.

the Egyptian football player Mohamed Abo Treka, who has become Egypt's newest idol according to the website FIFA.com.

Marketers try to identify the reference groups of their target markets. Reference groups expose a person to new behaviors and lifestyles, influence the person's attitudes and self-concept, and create pressures to conform that may affect the person's product and brand choices. The importance of group influence varies across products and brands. It tends to be strongest when the product is visible to others whom the buyer respects.

Word-of-Mouth Influence and Buzz Marketing.   Marketers of brands subjected to strong group influence must figure out how to reach **opinion leaders**—people within a reference group who, because of special skills, knowledge, personality, or other characteristics, exert social influence on others. Some experts call this segment *the influentials* or *leading adopters*. One recent study found that these influencers are "four times more likely than average consumers to belong to five or more organizations, four times more likely to be considered experts, and twice as likely to recommend a product they like." And when influential friends talk, consumers listen. Another survey found that nearly 78 percent of respondents trusted "recommendations from consumers," 15 percentage points higher than the second most-credible source, newspapers.[12]

Marketers often try to identify opinion leaders for their products and direct marketing efforts toward them. They use *buzz marketing* by enlisting or even creating opinion leaders to serve as 'brand ambassadors' who spread the word about their products. Many companies are now creating brand ambassador programs in an attempt to turn influential but everyday customers into brand evangelists.

Consumer-goods maker Procter & Gamble (P&G) has created a huge word-of-mouth marketing arm—Vocalpoint—consisting of 350,000 mothers. This army of natural-born buzzers leverages the power of peer-to-peer communication to spread the word about brands. Vocalpoint recruits 'connectors'—people with vast networks of friends and a gift for chat. They create buzz not just for P&G brands but for those of other client companies as well.[13]

Except for educating Vocalpointers about products, the company doesn't coach the mothers. The connectors themselves choose whether or not to pitch the product to friends and what to say. What's more, they do the work without pay. What's in it for them? For one thing, they receive a steady flow of coupons and samples. But more important, it makes them insiders, seeing cool new ideas before their friends have them. Secondly, it gives them a voice. "They're filled with great ideas, and they don't think anybody listens to them," says Steve Knox, chief executive of P&G's Tremor.com, which aims to connect with youths' huge social networks.[14]

Online Social Networks.   Over the past few years, a new type of social interaction has exploded onto the scene—online social networking. **Online social networks** are online communities where people socialize or exchange information and opinions. Social networking media range from blogs to social networking websites, such as MySpace.com, and YouTube, to entire virtual worlds, such as Second Life. This new form of high-tech buzz has big implications for marketers.

Marketers are working to harness the power of these new social networks to promote their products and build closer customer relationships. Instead of throwing more one-way commercial messages at ad-weary consumers, they hope to use social networks to *interact* with consumers and become a part of their conversations and lives.

The use of social networks in the Arab world has been growing at a fast pace. ●**Table 5.1** indicates that the Middle East and Africa regions enjoyed a 66 percent growth in the number of social network visitors in 2008 (compared with an average growth of 25 percent across the world). Facebook.com in particular grew by 153 percent, and the number of Facebook.com users in the Middle East and Africa region increased by five times during the same period.

Companies can even create their own social networks. For example, P&G set up Capessa (www.capessa.com), "a gathering place for real women to share their stories, offer their personal wisdom and practical advice, improve their lives, and be inspired. The only

Opinion leader
Person within a reference group who, because of special skills, knowledge, personality, or other characteristics, exerts social influence on others.

Online social networks
Online social communities—blogs, social networking websites, or even virtual worlds—where people socialize or exchange information and opinions.

● TABLE | 5.1 Growth in Social Networking and Use of Facebook.com 2007–8

Social Networking Growth by Worldwide Region, June 2008 vs. June 2007
Total Worldwide Audience, Age 15+, Home and Work Locations

	Unique Visitors (000)		
	Jun-07	**Jun-08**	**% Change**
Worldwide	**464,437**	**580,510**	**25%**
Asia Pacific	162,738	200,555	23%
Europe	122,527	165,256	35%
North America	120,848	131,255	9%
Latin America	40,098	53,248	33%
Middle East - Africa	**18,226**	**30,197**	**66%**

Source: "Social Networking Explodes Worldwide as Sites Increase their Focus on Cultural Relevance," press release, August 12, 2008, www.comscore.com/Press_Events/Press_Releases/2008/08/Social_Networking_World_Wide.

Worldwide Growth for Facebook.com, **June 2008 vs. June 2007**
Total Worldwide Audience, Age 15+, Home and Work Locations

	Total Unique Visitors (000)		
	Jun-2007	**Jun-2008**	**% Change**
FACEBOOK.COM	**52,167**	**132,105**	**153%**
North America	35,698	49,248	38%
Europe	8,751	35,263	303%
Asia Pacific	3,712	20,712	458%
Middle East - Africa	**2,974**	**14,951**	**403%**
Latin America	1,033	11,931	1055%

Source: "Social Networking Explodes Worldwide as Sites Increase their Focus on Cultural Relevance," press release, August 12, 2008, www.comscore.com/Press_Events/Press_Releases/2008/08/Social_Networking_World_Wide.

thing that's missing is the kitchen table." The site gives women a place to express themselves and P&G an opportunity to observe and learn more about their needs and feelings.[15]

But marketers must be careful when tapping into online social networks. Results are difficult to measure and control. Ultimately, the users control the content, so online network marketing attempts can easily backfire. We will dig deeper into online social networks as a marketing tool in Chapter 13.

Family

Family members can strongly influence buyer behavior. The family is the most important consumer buying organization in society, and it has been researched extensively. Marketers are interested in the roles and influence of the husband, wife, and children on the purchase of different products and services.

Husband-wife involvement varies widely by product category and by stage in the buying process, and buying roles change with evolving consumer lifestyles. According to a recent survey, men in the Arab world have three and a half times the purchasing power of women.[16]

Family buying: Family buying roles are changing. For example, in the United States, men now account for about 40 percent of all food-shopping dollars, while women influence 50 percent of all new technology purchases.

Galal Amin, the famous Egyptian economist, authored a book entitled *Whatever Happened to the Egyptians?*, which discusses the changes that have taken place in the Egyptian society from the 1950s to the start of the twenty-first century. He states that older generation women spent most of their time at home, particularly cooking. The role of women, he infers, was restricted merely to housework. He mentions that the whole past generation of women was deprived by all means from earning their independent living away from their husbands. Men at the time were regarded as their source of economic security. Today's women have witnessed a greater economic independence, as they seek work and education outside their homes. According to Amin, in many aspects, women are now men's equals in companies and universities in Egypt. While this applies to many Arab countries, there are some exceptions, as in Saudi Arabia, for instance. Saudi women have more limited job opportunities. Nonetheless, even Saudi Arabia has started lately to grant women more freedom to join the workforce. According to a study published in *The Guardian* in 2006, "the world of work is opening up to [Saudi] women and economic freedom is beginning to empower them. Gradually, Saudis are beginning to realise that the exclusion of women from meaningful activity outside the home just to preserve old desert traditions is a waste of talent and resources. More than half the kingdom's university graduates are female and yet women account for only about 5% of the workforce."[17]

Amin also highlights that the spread of the *hijab* (head scarf worn by Muslim women) has allowed women who were housebound to go outside for work and education. In fact, the hijab, and other Islamic clothes, should be considered by marketers when targeting Arab women.

Children may also have a strong influence on family buying decisions, having a direct impact for a large number of products. Some advertisers have positioned their common household products, such as soap, as directly targeting children's influence in the buying decision. The nature of family life in the Arab world brings children into a lot of the buying decisions, especially at supermarkets, malls, or restaurants. With some marketing efforts directed at children, families are influenced to eat at certain restaurants, buy certain cheeses or cereals, or shop at a certain store.

Roles and Status

A person belongs to many groups—family, clubs, organizations. The person's position in each group can be defined in terms of both role and status. A role consists of the activities people are expected to perform according to the persons around them. Each role carries a status reflecting the general esteem given to it by society.

People usually choose products appropriate to their roles and status. Consider the various roles of a 30-year-old man from the Arab world. He is a brand manager at work, a husband and father at home, as well as a football fan. This consumer requires different kinds of clothes depending on his role and status.

Personal Factors

A buyer's decisions also are influenced by personal characteristics such as the buyer's *age* and *life-cycle stage, occupation, economic situation, lifestyle,* and *personality and self-concept.*

Age and Life-Cycle Stage

People change the goods and services they buy over their lifetimes. Tastes in food, clothes, furniture, and recreation are often age related. Buying is also shaped by the stage of the family life-cycle—the stages through which families might pass as they mature over time. Marketers often define their target markets in terms of life-cycle stage and develop appropriate products and marketing plans for each stage.

Traditional family life-cycle stages include young singles and married couples with children. Today, however, marketers are increasingly catering to a growing number of alternative, nontraditional stages such as singles marrying later in life, childless couples, extended parents (those with young adult children returning home), and others.

A typical sporting and social club would like to target members of all ages. A kindergarten would serve babies below 4 years old; sports teams would serve children from 4 to 20 years old; sports and games would serve teenagers; social activities target young adults (up to 40 years old); and lounges would serve parents and older people. The club should satisfy the needs of all segments in order to maximize their use of the club's services.

Occupation

A person's occupation affects the goods and services bought. Workers tend to buy more rugged work clothes, whereas executives buy more business suits. Marketers try to identify the occupational groups that have an above-average interest in their products and services. A company can even specialize in making products needed by a given occupational group.

Economic Situation

A person's economic situation will affect product choice. Marketers of income-sensitive goods watch trends in personal income, savings, and interest rates. If economic indicators point to a recession, marketers can take steps to redesign, reposition, and reprice their products accordingly. Some marketers target consumers who have lots of money and resources, charging prices to match. For example, Orascom Hotels and Development (OHD) developed and sold luxurious and expensive properties targeting high-end owners in Egypt. At the same time, OHD contributed to the establishment of Orascom Housing Communities (OHC), which initiated Orascom's 'Low-Income Housing Project,' which satisfies the need of price-sensitive owners.

Lifestyle

Lifestyle
A person's pattern of living as expressed in his or her activities, interests, and opinions.

People coming from the same subculture, social class, and occupation may have quite different lifestyles. **Lifestyle** is a person's pattern of living as expressed in his or her psychographics. It involves measuring consumers' major AIO dimensions—activities (work, hobbies, shopping, sports, social events), interests (food, fashion, family, recreation), and opinions (about themselves, social issues, business, products). Lifestyle captures something more than the person's social class or personality. It profiles a person's whole pattern of acting and interacting in the world.

When used carefully, the lifestyle concept can help marketers understand changing consumer values and how they affect buying behavior. Consumers don't just buy products, they buy the values and lifestyles those products represent. Recently, BlackBerry has introduced its newest mobile phone in several Arab countries. It has achieved initial success by attracting consumers who seek a cool lifestyle through using the phones' new features, including the chatting system (BBM).

Personality
The unique psychological characteristics that lead to relatively consistent and lasting responses to one's own environment.

Personality and Self-Concept

Each person's distinct personality influences his or her buying behavior. **Personality** refers to the unique psychological characteristics that lead to relatively consistent and lasting responses to one's own environment. Personality is usually described in terms of traits such as self-confidence, dominance, sociability, autonomy, defensiveness, adaptability, and aggressiveness. Personality can be useful in analyzing consumer behavior for certain product or brand choices.

Brand personality
The specific mix of human traits that may be attributed to a particular brand.

The idea is that brands also have personalities, and that consumers are likely to choose brands with personalities that match their own. A **brand personality** is the specific mix of human traits that may be attributed to a particular brand. Researcher and academic Jennifer Aaker identified five brand personality traits:[18]

Lifestyle: BlackBerry has achieved initial success by attracting consumers with an interest in a cool lifestyle and social networking.

1. Sincerity (down-to-earth, honest, wholesome, and cheerful)
2. Excitement (daring, spirited, imaginative, and up-to-date)
3. Competence (reliable, intelligent, and successful)
4. Sophistication (upper class and charming)
5. Ruggedness (outdoorsy and tough).

Most well-known brands are strongly associated with one particular trait: the automaker Jeep with 'ruggedness,' Apple with 'excitement,' the BBC with 'competence,' and the Dove brand of soap with 'sincerity.' Hence, these brands will attract persons who are high on the same personality traits.

Many marketers use a concept related to personality—a person's *self-concept* (also called *self-image*). The basic self-concept premise is that people's possessions contribute to and reflect their identities—that is, 'we are what we have.' Thus, in order to understand consumer behavior, the marketer must first understand the relationship between consumer self-concept and possessions.

Galaxy advertised for its 'Galaxy Rendezvous' events through the 'Me-Time' campaign. It calls working women to take a moment to connect and enjoy their true self by enjoying their time while indulging their senses.

Psychological Factors

A person's buying choices are further influenced by four major psychological factors: *motivation*, *perception*, *learning*, and *beliefs and attitudes*.

Motivation

Motive (drive)

A need that is sufficiently pressing to direct the person to seek satisfaction of the need.

A person has many needs at any given time. Some are biological, arising from states of tension such as hunger, thirst, or discomfort. Others are psychological, arising from the need for recognition, esteem, or belonging. A need becomes a motive when it is aroused to a sufficient level of intensity. A **motive** (or drive) is a need that is sufficiently pressing to direct the person to seek satisfaction. Psychologists have developed theories of human motivation. Two of the most popular—the theories of psychologists Sigmund Freud and Abraham Maslow—have quite different meanings for consumer analysis and marketing.

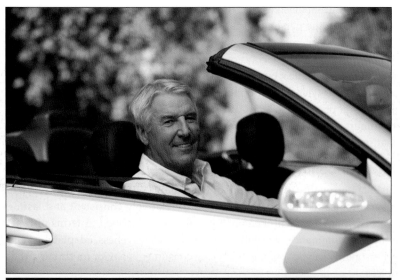

Motivation: An aging consumer who buys a sporty convertible might explain that he or she simply likes the feel of the wind in his or her thinning hair. At a deeper level, the person may be buying the car to feel young and independent again.

Sigmund Freud assumed that people are largely unconscious about the real psychological forces shaping their behavior. Freud's theory suggests that a person's buying decisions are affected by subconscious motives that even the buyer may not fully understand. Thus, an aging consumer who buys a sporty BMW 330Ci convertible might explain that he simply likes the feel of the wind in his thinning hair. At a deeper level, he may be trying to impress others with his success. At a still deeper level, he may be buying the car to feel young and independent again.

The term *motivation research* refers to qualitative research designed to probe consumers' hidden, subconscious motivations. Consumers often don't know or can't describe just why they act as they do. Thus, motivation researchers use a variety of probing techniques to uncover underlying emotions and attitudes toward brands and buying situations.

Many companies employ teams of psychologists, anthropologists, and other social scientists to carry out motivation research. One ad agency routinely conducts one-on-one, therapy-like interviews to delve into the inner workings of consumers. Another company asks consumers to describe their favorite brands as animals or cars (say, Cadillacs versus Chevrolets) in order to assess the prestige associated with various brands. Still others rely on dream therapy, or soft lights and mood music to better understand depths of consumer thinking.

Such projective techniques seem ridiculous, and some marketers dismiss such motivation research as ineffective. But many marketers use such approaches, now sometimes

◖FIGURE | 5.4

Maslow's Hierarchy of Needs

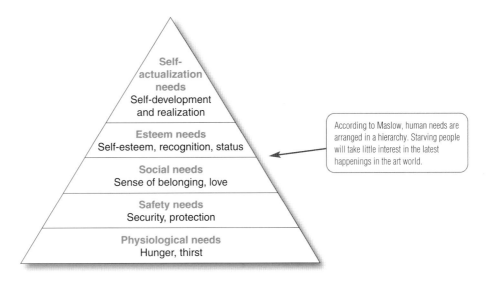

Self-
actualization
needs
Self-development
and realization

Esteem needs
Self-esteem, recognition, status

Social needs
Sense of belonging, love

Safety needs
Security, protection

Physiological needs
Hunger, thirst

According to Maslow, human needs are arranged in a hierarchy. Starving people will take little interest in the latest happenings in the art world.

called *interpretive consumer research,* to delve into consumers' mindsets and develop better marketing strategies.[19]

Abraham Maslow sought to explain why people are driven by particular needs at particular times. Why does one person spend much time and energy on personal safety and another on gaining the esteem of others? Maslow's answer is that human needs are arranged in a hierarchy, as shown in ◖ **Figure 5.4**, from the most pressing at the bottom to the least pressing at the top.[20] They include *physiological* needs, *safety* needs, *social* needs, *esteem* needs, and *self-actualization* needs.

A person tries to satisfy the most important need first. When that need is satisfied, it will stop being a motivator and the person will then try to satisfy the next most important need. For example, starving people (physiological need) will not take an interest in the latest happenings in the art world (self-actualization needs), nor in how they are seen or esteemed by others (social or esteem needs), nor even in whether they are breathing clean air (safety needs). But as each important need is satisfied, the next most important need will come into play.

Perception

The process by which people select, organize, and interpret information to form a meaningful picture of the world.

Selective perception: It's impossible for people to pay attention to the thousands of ads they're exposed to every day, so they screen most of them out.

Perception

A motivated person is ready to act. How the person acts is influenced by his or her own perception of the situation. All of us learn by the flow of information through our five senses: sight, hearing, smell, touch, and taste. However, each of us receives, organizes, and interprets this sensory information in an individual way. **Perception** is the process by which people select, organize, and interpret information to form a meaningful picture of the world.

People can form different perceptions of the same stimulus because of three perceptual processes: selective attention, selective distortion, and selective retention. People are exposed to a great amount of stimuli every day. For example, people are exposed to an estimated 3,000 to 5,000 ad messages every day.[21] It is impossible for a person to pay attention to all these stimuli. *Selective attention*—the tendency for people to screen out most of the information to which they are exposed—means that marketers must work especially hard to attract the consumer's attention.

Even noticed stimuli do not always come across in the intended way. Each person fits incoming information into an existing mindset. *Selective distortion* describes the tendency of people to interpret information in a way that will support what they already believe. For example, if you distrust a company, you might perceive even honest ads from the company as questionable. Selective distortion means that marketers must try to understand the mindsets of consumers and how these will affect interpretations of advertising and sales information.

People also will forget much of what they learn. They tend to retain information that supports their attitudes and beliefs. Because of *selective retention*, consumers are likely to remember good points made about a brand they favor and to forget good points made about competing brands. Because of selective attention, distortion, and retention, marketers must work hard to get their messages through. This fact explains why marketers use so much drama and repetition in sending messages to their market.

Interestingly, although most marketers worry about whether their offers will be perceived at all, some consumers worry that they will be affected by marketing messages without even knowing it—through *subliminal advertising*. Numerous studies by psychologists and consumer researchers have found little or no link between subliminal messages and consumer behavior. Recent brainwave studies have found that in certain circumstances, our brains may register subliminal messages. However, it appears that subliminal advertising simply doesn't have the power attributed to it by its critics. Most advertisers make fun of the notion of an industry conspiracy to manipulate consumers through 'invisible' messages. Says one industry insider, "[Some consumers believe we are] wizards who can manipulate them at will, which is not true. As we know, just between us, most of [us] have difficulty getting a 2 percent increase in sales with the help of $50 million in media."[22]

Learning

Learning

Changes in an individual's behavior arising from experience.

When people act, they learn. **Learning** describes changes in an individual's behavior arising from experience. Learning theorists say that most human behavior is learned. Learning occurs through the interplay of drives, stimuli, cues, responses, and reinforcement.

A *drive* is a strong internal stimulus that calls for action. A drive becomes a motive when it is directed toward a particular *stimulus object*. For example, a person's drive for self-actualization might motivate him or her to look into buying a camera. The consumer's response to the idea of buying a camera is conditioned by the surrounding cues. *Cues* are minor stimuli that determine when, where, and how the person responds. For example, the person might spot several camera brands in a shop window, hear of a special sale price, or discuss cameras with a friend. These are all cues that might influence a consumer's *response* to his or her interest in buying the product.

Suppose the consumer buys a Nikon camera. If the experience is rewarding, the consumer will probably use the camera more and more, and his or her response will be *reinforced*. Then, the next time the consumer shops for a camera, or some similar product, the probability is greater that he or she will buy a Nikon product. The practical significance of learning theory for marketers is that they can build up demand for a product by associating it with strong drives, using motivating cues, and providing positive reinforcement.

Beliefs and Attitudes

Belief

A descriptive thought that a person holds about something.

Through doing and learning, people acquire beliefs and attitudes. These, in turn, influence their buying behavior. A **belief** is a descriptive thought that a person has about something. Beliefs may be based on real knowledge, opinion, or faith and may or may not carry an emotional charge. Marketers are interested in the beliefs that people formulate about specific products and services, because these beliefs make up product and brand images that affect buying behavior. If some of the beliefs are wrong and prevent purchase, the marketer will want to launch a campaign to correct them.

Attitude

A person's consistently favorable or unfavorable evaluations, feelings, and tendencies toward an object or idea.

People have attitudes regarding religion, politics, clothes, music, food, and almost everything else. **Attitude** describes a person's relatively consistent evaluations, feelings, and tendencies toward an object or idea. Attitudes put people into a frame of mind of liking or disliking things, of moving toward or away from them. Our camera buyer may hold attitudes such as 'Buy the best,' 'The Japanese make the best electronics products in the world,'

Nestlé's bottled water campaign appeals to consumer attitudes about health and well-being by emphasizing the importance of drinking enough water.

and 'Creativity and self-expression are among the most important things in life.' If so, the Nikon camera would fit well into the consumer's existing attitudes.

Attitudes are difficult to change. A person's attitudes fit into a pattern, and to change one attitude may require difficult adjustments in many others. Thus, a company should usually try to fit its products into existing attitudes rather than attempt to change attitudes. For example, today's beverage marketers now cater to people's new attitudes about health and well-being with drinks that do a lot more than just taste good or quench your thirst. Nestlé launched a campaign aiming to increase consumers' consumption of bottled water. The campaign emphasized the healthy importance of water, capitalizing on new trends in the Egyptian market.

We can now appreciate the many forces acting on consumer behavior. The consumer's choice results from the complex interplay of cultural, social, personal, and psychological factors.

> **Author Comment** | Some purchases are simple and routine, even habitual. Others are far more complex—involving extensive information gathering and evaluation—and are subject to sometimes subtle influences. For example, think of all that goes into a new car buying decision.

Types of Buying Decision Behavior (pp 139–141)

Buying behavior differs greatly for a tube of toothpaste, an iPod, financial services, and a new car. More complex decisions usually involve more buying participants and more buyer effort. 🖙 **Figure 5.5** shows types of consumer buying behavior based on the degree of buyer involvement and the degree of differences among brands.

Complex Buying Behavior

Complex buying behavior
Consumer buying behavior in situations characterized by high consumer involvement in a purchase and significant perceived differences among brands.

Consumers undertake **complex buying behavior** when they are highly involved in a purchase and perceive significant differences among brands. Consumers may be highly involved when the product is expensive, risky, purchased infrequently, and highly self-expressive. Typically, the consumer has much to learn about the product category. For example, a PC buyer may not know what attributes to consider. Many product features carry no real meaning: a '3.4GHz Pentium processor,' 'WUXGA active matrix screen,' or '4GB dual-channel DDR2 DRAM memory.'

This buyer will pass through a learning process, first developing beliefs about the product, then attitudes, and then making a thoughtful purchase choice. Marketers of

Buying behavior varies greatly for different types of products. For example, someone buying an expensive new PC might undertake a full information-gathering and brand evaluation process.

	High involvement	Low involvement
Significant differences between brands	Complex buying behavior	Variety-seeking buying behavior
Few differences between brands	Dissonance-reducing buying behavior	Habitual buying behavior

At the other extreme, for low-involvement products, consumers may simply select a familiar brand out of habit. For example, what brand of salt do you buy and why?

🖙 **FIGURE | 5.5** Four Types of Buying Behavior

Source: Adapted from Henry Assael, *Consumer Behavior and Marketing Action* (Boston: Kent Publishing Company, 1987), p. 87. Copyright © 1987 by Wadsworth, Inc. Printed by permission of Kent Publishing Company, a division of Wadsworth, Inc.

high-involvement products must understand the information-gathering and evaluation behavior of high-involvement consumers. They need to help buyers learn about product-class attributes and their relative importance. They need to differentiate their brand's features, perhaps by describing the brand's benefits using print media with long copy. They must motivate store salespeople and the buyer's acquaintances to influence the final brand choice.

Dissonance-Reducing Buying Behavior

Dissonance-reducing buying behavior

Consumer buying behavior in situations characterized by high involvement but few perceived differences among brands.

Dissonance-reducing buying behavior occurs when consumers are highly involved with an expensive, infrequent, or risky purchase, but see little difference among brands. For example, consumers buying carpeting may face a high-involvement decision because carpeting is expensive and self-expressive. Yet buyers may consider most carpet brands in a given price range to be the same. In this case, because perceived brand differences are not large, buyers may shop around to learn what is available, but buy relatively quickly. They may respond primarily to a good price or to purchase convenience.

After the purchase, consumers might experience *postpurchase dissonance* (after-sale discomfort) when they notice certain disadvantages of the purchased carpet brand or hear favorable things about brands not purchased. To counter such dissonance, the marketer's after-sale communications should provide evidence and support to help consumers feel good about their brand choices.

Habitual Buying Behavior

Habitual buying behavior

Consumer buying behavior in situations characterized by low consumer involvement and few significantly perceived brand differences.

Habitual buying behavior occurs under conditions of low consumer involvement and little significant brand difference. For example, take salt. Consumers have little involvement in this product category—they simply go to the store and reach for a brand. If they keep reaching for the same brand, it is out of habit rather than strong brand loyalty. Consumers appear to have low involvement with most low-cost, frequently purchased products.

In such cases, consumer behavior does not pass through the usual belief-attitude-behavior sequence. Consumers do not search extensively for information about the brands, evaluate brand characteristics, and make weighty decisions about which brands to buy. Instead, they passively receive information as they watch television or read magazines. Ad repetition creates *brand familiarity* rather than *brand conviction*. Consumers do not form strong attitudes toward a brand; they select the brand because it is familiar. Because they are not highly involved with the product, consumers may not evaluate the choice even after purchase. Thus, the buying process involves brand beliefs formed by passive learning, followed by purchase behavior, which may or may not be followed by evaluation.

Because buyers are not highly committed to any brands, marketers of low-involvement products with few brand differences often use price and sales promotions to stimulate product trial. In advertising for a low-involvement product, ad copy should stress only a few key points. Visual symbols and imagery are important because they can be remembered easily and associated with the brand. Ad campaigns should include high repetition of short-duration messages. Television is usually more effective than print media because it is a low-involvement medium suitable for passive learning. Advertising planning should be based on classical conditioning theory, in which buyers learn to identify a certain product by a symbol repeatedly attached to it.

Variety-Seeking Buying Behavior

Variety-seeking buying behavior

Consumer buying behavior in situations characterized by low consumer involvement but significant perceived brand differences.

Consumers undertake **variety-seeking buying behavior** in situations characterized by low consumer involvement but significant perceived brand differences. In such cases, consumers often do a lot of brand switching. For example, when buying cookies, a consumer may hold some beliefs, choose a cookie brand without much evaluation, and then evaluate that brand during consumption. But the next time, the consumer might pick another brand out of boredom or simply to try something different. Brand switching occurs for the sake of variety rather than because of dissatisfaction.

In such product categories, the marketing strategy may differ for the market leader and minor brands. The market leader will try to encourage habitual buying behavior by dominating shelf space, keeping shelves fully stocked, and running frequent reminder advertising. Challenger firms will encourage variety seeking by offering lower prices, special deals, coupons, free samples, and advertising that presents reasons for trying something new.

Need recognition
The first stage of the buyer decision process, in which the consumer recognizes a problem or need.

Author Comment | The actual purchase decision is just part of a much larger buying process—starting with need recognition through how you feel after making the purchase. Marketers want to be involved throughout the buyer decision process.

The Buyer Decision Process (pp 141–143)

Now that we have looked at the influences that affect buyers, we are ready to look at how consumers make buying decisions. ✦ **Figure 5.6** shows that the buyer decision process consists of five stages: *need recognition, information search, evaluation of alternatives, purchase decision*, and *postpurchase behavior*. Clearly, the buying process starts long before the actual purchase and continues long after. Marketers need to focus on the entire buying process rather than on just the purchase decision.

The figure suggests that consumers pass through all five stages with every purchase. But in more routine purchases, consumers often skip or reverse some of these stages. A woman buying her regular brand of toothpaste would recognize the need and go right to the purchase decision, skipping information search and evaluation. However, we use the model in **Figure 5.6** because it shows all the considerations that arise when a consumer faces a new and complex purchase situation.

Need Recognition

The buying process starts with **need recognition**—the buyer recognizes a problem or need. The need can be triggered by *internal stimuli* when one of the person's normal needs—hunger, thirst—rises to a level high enough to become a drive. A need can also be triggered by *external stimuli*. For example, an advertisement or a discussion with a friend might get you thinking about buying a new car. At this stage, the marketer should research consumers to find out what kinds of needs or problems arise, what brought them about, and how they led the consumer to this particular product.

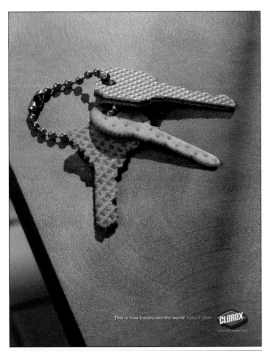

Need recognition can be triggered by advertising. This innovative ad from Clorox clothing detergent reminds parents that "This is how babies see the world. Keep it clean."

Information Search

An interested consumer may or may not search for more information. If the consumer's drive is strong and a satisfying product is near at hand, the consumer is likely to buy it then. If not, the consumer may store the need in memory or undertake an **information search** related to the need. For example, once you've decided you need a new car, at the least, you will probably pay more attention to car ads, cars owned by friends, and car conversations. Or you may actively search the web, talk with friends, and gather information in other ways. The amount of searching you do will depend on the strength of your drive, the amount of information you start with, the ease of obtaining more information, the value you place on additional information, and the satisfaction you get from searching.

Consumers can obtain information from any of several sources. These include *personal sources* (family, friends, neighbors, acquaintances), *commercial sources* (advertising, salespeople, dealer websites, packaging, displays), *public sources* (mass media, consumer rating

The buying process starts long before the actual purchase and continues long after. In fact, it might result in a decision *not* to buy. Therefore, marketers must focus on the entire buying process, not just the purchase decision.

◆ FIGURE | **5.6** Buyer Decision Process

Information search

The stage of the buyer decision process in which the consumer is roused to search for more information; the consumer may simply have heightened attention or may go into an active information search.

organizations, Internet searches), and *experiential sources* (handling, examining, using the product). The relative influence of these information sources varies with the product and the buyer.

Generally, the consumer receives the most information about a product from commercial sources—those controlled by the marketer. The most effective sources, however, tend to be personal. Commercial sources normally *inform* the buyer, but personal sources *assure* or *evaluate* products for the buyer. A recent survey found that 78 percent of consumers found recommendations from others to be the most-credible form of endorsement. As one marketer states, "It's rare that an advertising campaign can be as effective as a neighbor leaning over the fence and saying, 'This is a wonderful product.'" Increasingly, that 'fence' is a virtual one, as more and more customers pour through the online ratings and reviews of other buyers on sites such as Amazon.com before making a purchase.[23]

As more information is obtained, the consumer's awareness and knowledge of the available brands and features increase. In your car information search, you may learn about the several brands available. The information might also help you to drop certain brands from consideration. A company must design its marketing mix to make prospects aware of and knowledgeable about its brand. It should carefully identify consumers' sources of information and the importance of each source.

Evaluation of Alternatives

We have seen how the consumer uses information to arrive at a set of final brand choices. How does the consumer choose among the alternative brands? The marketer needs to know about **alternative evaluation**—that is, how the consumer processes information to arrive at brand choices. Unfortunately, consumers do not use a simple and single evaluation process in all buying situations. Instead, several evaluation processes are at work.

Alternative evaluation

The stage of the buyer decision process in which the consumer uses information to evaluate alternative brands in the choice set.

The consumer arrives at attitudes toward different brands through some evaluation procedure. How consumers go about evaluating purchase alternatives depends on the individual consumer and the specific buying situation. In some cases, consumers use careful calculations and logical thinking. At other times, the same consumers do little or no evaluating; instead they buy on impulse and rely on intuition. Sometimes consumers make buying decisions on their own; sometimes they turn to friends, consumer guides, or salespeople for buying advice.

Suppose you've narrowed your car choices to three brands. And suppose that you are primarily interested in four attributes—styling, operating economy, warranty, and price. By this time, you've probably formed beliefs about how each brand rates on each attribute. Clearly, if one car rated best on all the attributes, we could predict that you would choose it. However, the brands will no doubt vary in appeal. You might base your buying decision on only one attribute, and your choice would be easy to predict. If you wanted styling above everything else, you would buy the car that you think has the best styling. But most buyers consider several attributes, each with different importance. If we knew the importance that you assigned to each of the four attributes, we could predict your car choice more reliably.

Marketers should study buyers to find out how they actually evaluate brand alternatives. If they know what evaluative processes go on, marketers can take steps to influence the buyer's decision.

Purchase Decision

Purchase decision

The buyer's decision about which brand to purchase.

In the evaluation stage, the consumer ranks brands and forms purchase intentions. Generally, the consumer's **purchase decision** will be to buy the most preferred brand, but two factors can come between the purchase *intention* and the purchase *decision*. The first factor is the *attitudes of others*. If someone important to you thinks that you should buy the lowest-priced car, then the chances of you buying a more expensive car are reduced.

The second factor is *unexpected situational factors*. The consumer may form a purchase intention based on factors such as expected income, expected price, and expected product benefits. However, unexpected events may change the purchase intention. For example, the economy might take a turn for the worse, a close competitor might drop its price, or a friend might report being disappointed in your preferred car. Thus, preferences and even purchase intentions do not always result in actual purchase choice.

Postpurchase Behavior

Postpurchase behavior

The stage of the buyer decision process in which the consumers take further action after purchase, based on their satisfaction or dissatisfaction.

The marketer's job does not end when the product is bought. After purchasing the product, the consumer will be satisfied or dissatisfied and will engage in **postpurchase behavior** of interest to the marketer. What determines whether the buyer is satisfied or dissatisfied with a purchase? The answer lies in the relationship between the *consumer's expectations* and the product's *perceived performance*. If the product falls short of expectations, the consumer is disappointed; if it meets expectations, the consumer is satisfied; if it exceeds expectations, the consumer is delighted. The larger the gap between expectations and performance, the greater the consumer's dissatisfaction. This suggests that sellers should promise only what their brands can deliver so that buyers are satisfied.

Cognitive dissonance

Buyer discomfort caused by postpurchase conflict.

Almost all major purchases, however, result in **cognitive dissonance**, or discomfort caused by postpurchase conflict. After the purchase, consumers are satisfied with the benefits of the chosen brand and are glad to avoid the drawbacks of the brands not bought. However, every purchase involves compromise. So consumers feel uneasy about acquiring the drawbacks of the chosen brand and about losing the benefits of the brands not purchased. Thus, consumers feel at least some postpurchase dissonance for every purchase.[24]

Why is it so important to satisfy the customer? Customer satisfaction is a key to building profitable relationships with consumers—to keeping and growing consumers and reaping their customer lifetime value. Satisfied customers buy a product again, talk favorably to others about the product, pay less attention to competing brands and advertising, and buy other products from the company. Many marketers go beyond merely *meeting* the expectations of customers—they aim to *delight* the customer (see **Real Marketing 5.2**).

A dissatisfied consumer responds differently. Bad word of mouth often travels farther and faster than good word of mouth. It can quickly damage consumer attitudes about a company and its products. But companies cannot simply rely on dissatisfied customers to volunteer their complaints when they are dissatisfied. Most unhappy customers never tell the company about their problem. Therefore, a company should measure customer satisfaction regularly. It should set up systems that *encourage* customers to complain. In this way, the company can learn how well it is doing and how it can improve.

By studying the overall buyer decision, marketers may be able to find ways to help consumers move through it. For example, if consumers are not buying a new product because they do not perceive a need for it, marketing might launch advertising messages that trigger the need and show how the product solves customers' problems. If customers know about the product but are not buying because they hold unfavorable attitudes toward it, the marketer must find ways either to change the product or change consumer perceptions.

Author Comment | Here, we look at some special considerations in new-product buying decisions.

The Buyer Decision Process for New Products (pp 143–146)

We have looked at the stages buyers go through in trying to satisfy a need. Buyers may pass quickly or slowly through these stages, and some of the stages may even be reversed. Much depends on the nature of the buyer, the product, and the buying situation.

New product

A good, service, or idea that is perceived by some potential customers as new.

We now look at how buyers approach the purchase of new products. A **new product** is a good, service, or idea that is perceived by some potential customers as new. It may have been around for a while, but our interest is in how consumers learn about products for the

Real Marketing 5.2

Lexus:
Delighting Customers After the Sale to Keep Them Coming Back

To delight customers and keep them coming back, the Lexus Covenant promises that its dealers will "treat each customer as we would a guest in our home" and "go to any lengths to serve them better."

Close your eyes for a minute and picture a typical car dealership. Not impressed? Talk to a friend who owns a Lexus, and you'll no doubt get a very different picture. The typical Lexus dealership is...well, anything but typical. And some Lexus dealers will go to almost any extreme to take care of customers and keep them coming back. Consider the following examples: "We care and it shows" is the motto of Lexus dealer in Dubai—Al-Futtaim Motors. 'Guests' at Lexus service center are greeted by friendly customer service staff and after handing over the vehicle for the service, they are invited to the sumptuous lounge with comfortable armchairs and sofas where they are served with different types of coffee and juice with croissants and other snacks. While relaxing in the lounge with a cappuccino, croissants, and their favorite magazine guests can watch their cars being serviced through a wall-to-wall glass window. Guests can also catch up with their favorite news or television program with the 37-inch flat screen television in the lounge. "We would like to provide a very pleasant experience to our guests while their car is being serviced," mentions Customer Service Manager Mr Hossain. In addition to the lounge, complimentary coffee, and snacks, customer perks include free car washes.

For many people, a trip to the auto-dealer means a mind-numbing hour or two in a plastic chair with some tattered magazines and stale coffee. But Lexus in Dubai turns this into a positive experience for the potential customer through its guest lounge, refreshments and most importantly its well-trained customer service officers.

Lexus knows that good marketing doesn't stop with making the sale. Keeping customers happy *after* the sale is the key to building lasting relationships. Dealers have

a common goal: to delight customers and keep them coming back. Lexus believes that if you "delight the customer, and continue to delight the customer, you will have a customer for life." And Lexus understands just how valuable a customer can be—it estimates that the average lifetime value of a Lexus customer is AED 2,000,000 (approximately US$500,000).

Despite the amenities, few Lexus customers spend much time hanging around the dealership. Lexus knows that the best dealership visit is the one that you don't have to make at all. So it builds customer-pleasing cars to start with—high-quality cars that need little servicing. In its 'Lexus Covenant,' the company vows that it will make "the finest cars ever built." And in industry surveys, Lexus rates at or near the top in quality.

Still, when a car does need to be serviced, Lexus goes out of its way to make it easy and painless. And a service can be booked by telephone or online, helping the guests to save time. The car comes back spotless, thanks to a complimentary cleaning to remove bugs and road grime from the exterior and smudges from the leather interior.

And when a customer does bring a car in, Lexus repairs it right the first time, on

time. Dealers know that their well-heeled customers have money, "but what they don't have is time." So dealers like Al-Futtaim in the UAE are always testing systems that will cut a customer's wait. "I'm not in the car business," says one dealer. "I'm in the service business."

According to its website, from the very start Lexus set out to "[revolutionize] the luxury motoring experience through its passionate commitment to the finest products and the most satisfying automobile ownership experience. We vow to value the customer as an important individual; to do things right the first time; and to always exceed expectations." The Lexus Covenant also proclaims that, "Lexus will treat each customer as we would a guest in our own home." Al-Futtaim Lexus fully embraces this philosophy.

By all accounts, Lexus has lived up to its ambitious customer-satisfaction promise. It has created what appear to be the world's most satisfied car owners. Lexus regularly tops customer-satisfaction ratings worldwide. Customer satisfaction translates into sales and customer loyalty. Once a Lexus customer, always a Lexus customer—Lexus retains 84 percent of customers who've gone to the dealership for service.

Sources: Lexus UAE, 2011, www.lexus.ae; Jean Halliday, "Car Dealers Court Existing Buyers," *Advertising Age*, March 1, 2004, http://adage.com/article/news/car-dealers-court-existing-buyers/97852; Denny Hatch, "Delight Your Customers," *Target Marketing Mag*, April 2002, www.targetmarketingmag.com/article/delight-your-customers-28933/1; "Lexus Covenant," Lexus website, accessed at www.lexus.com/lexusvisionusa/about_covenant.html#, May 2011.

Great performance
even on sensitive skin.

85% of 68 men agree

Influencing the adoption process: This Gillette Fusion ad raises consumer awareness, provides information, and uses statistics to help consumers evaluate the product. Gillette also uses adverts with money-saving coupons to encourage consumers to try out the razors.

Adoption process
The mental process through which an individual passes from first hearing about an innovation to final adoption.

first time and make decisions on whether to adopt them. We define the **adoption process** as "the mental process through which an individual passes from first learning about an innovation to final adoption," and *adoption* as the decision by an individual to become a regular user of the product.[25]

Stages in the Adoption Process

Consumers go through five stages in the process of adopting a new product:

- *Awareness:* The consumer becomes aware of the new product, but lacks information about it.

- *Interest:* The consumer seeks information about the new product.

- *Evaluation:* The consumer considers whether trying the new product makes sense.

- *Trial:* The consumer tries the new product on a small scale to improve his or her estimate of its value.

- *Adoption:* The consumer decides to make full and regular use of the new product.

This model suggests that the new-product marketer should think about how to help consumers move through these stages. For example, to encourage consumers to try its new Gillette Fusion razor, its manufacturer, P&G, featured coupons offering substantial savings. HP has a rebate program for large format printers, offering their existing Arab world customers money back on their old printers when they upgrade to a new model. Similarly, a luxury car producer might find that many potential customers know about and are interested in its new model but aren't buying because of uncertainty about the model's benefits and the high price. The producer could launch a 'take one home for the weekend' promotion to high-value prospects to move them into the trial process and lead them to purchase.

Individual Differences in Innovativeness

People differ greatly in their readiness to try new products. In each product area, there are 'consumption pioneers' and early adopters. Other individuals adopt new products much later. People can be classified into the adopter categories shown in ● **Figure 5.7**. After a slow start, an increasing number of people adopt the new product. The number of adopters reaches a peak and then drops off as fewer nonadopters remain. Innovators are defined as the first 2.5 percent of the buyers to adopt a new idea (those beyond two standard deviations

● **FIGURE | 5.7**

Adopter Categorization on the Basis of Relative Time of Adoption of Innovations

Source: Reprinted with permission of the Free Press, a Division of Simon & Schuster, from *Diffusion of Innovations*, Fifth Edition, by Everett M. Rogers. Copyright © 2003 by the Free Press

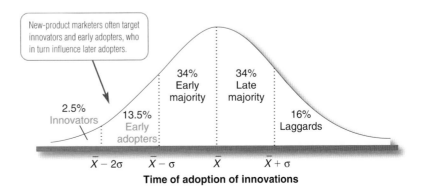

New-product marketers often target innovators and early adopters, who in turn influence later adopters.

2.5%
Innovators

13.5%
Early adopters

34%
Early majority

34%
Late majority

16%
Laggards

$\bar{X} - 2\sigma$ $\bar{X} - \sigma$ $\bar{X}$ $\bar{X} + \sigma$

Time of adoption of innovations

from mean adoption time); the early adopters are the next 13.5 percent (between one and two standard deviations); and so forth.

The five adopter groups have differing values. *Innovators* are venturesome—they try new ideas at some risk. *Early adopters* are guided by respect—they are opinion leaders in their communities and adopt new ideas early but carefully. The *early majority* are deliberate—although they rarely are leaders, they adopt new ideas before the average person. The *late majority* are skeptical—they adopt an innovation only after a majority of people have tried it. Finally, *laggards* are tradition bound—they are suspicious of changes and adopt the innovation only when it has become something of a tradition itself.

This adopter classification suggests that an innovating firm should research the characteristics of innovators and early adopters and should direct marketing efforts toward them. In general, innovators tend to be relatively younger, better educated, and higher in income than later adopters and nonadopters. They are more receptive to unfamiliar things, rely more on their own values and judgment, and are more willing to take risks. They are less brand loyal and more likely to take advantage of special promotions such as discounts, coupons, and samples.

Influence of Product Characteristics on Rate of Adoption

The characteristics of the new product affect its rate of adoption. Some products catch on almost overnight—for example, the iPod and BlackBerry, which flew off retailers' shelves at an astounding rate from the day they were introduced. Others take a longer time to gain acceptance. For example, since the first high-definition (HD) televisions were introduced in the Arab world a few years ago the retail off take has been slow. MENA satellite TV is currently the only big player; less than one percent of regional TV households watch digital broadcasts from domestic providers such as Etisalat and QTel. But this is beginning to change: aggressive fiber and DTT initiatives mean HDTV will be available in most domestic markets in two to five years.[26]

Five characteristics are especially important in influencing an innovation's rate of adoption. For example, consider the characteristics of HDTV in relation to the rate of adoption:

- *Relative advantage*: the degree to which the innovation appears superior to existing products. HDTV offers substantially improved picture quality. This will speed its rate of adoption.

- *Compatibility*: the degree to which the innovation fits the values and experiences of potential consumers. HDTV, for example, is highly compatible with the lifestyles of the TV-watching public. However, many programs and channels are still not yet available in HD, and this has slowed HDTV adoption.

- *Complexity*: the degree to which the innovation is difficult to understand or use. HDTVs are not very complex and, therefore, once more programming is available and prices come down, they will take less time to penetrate homes than more complex innovations.

- *Divisibility*: the degree to which the innovation may be tried on a limited basis. Early HDTVs and HD cable and satellite systems were very expensive, slowing the rate of adoption. As prices fall, adoption rates will increase.

- *Communicability*: the degree to which the results of using the innovation can be observed or described to others. Because HDTV lends itself to demonstration and description, its use will spread faster among consumers.

Other characteristics influence the rate of adoption, such as initial and ongoing costs, risk and uncertainty, and social approval. The new-product marketer must research all these factors when developing the new product and its marketing program.

REVIEWING Objectives AND KEY Terms

The world consumer market consists of more than 6.6 billion people. Consumers around the world vary greatly in age, income, education level, and tastes. Understanding how these differences affect *consumer buying behavior* is one of the biggest challenges marketers face.

OBJECTIVE 1 Define the consumer market and construct a simple model of consumer buyer behavior (pp 126-127).

The *consumer market* consists of all the individuals and households who buy or acquire goods and services for personal consumption. The simplest model of consumer buyer behavior is the stimulus-response model. According to this model, marketing stimuli (the four Ps) and other major forces (economic, technological, political, cultural) enter the consumer's 'black box' and produce certain responses. Once in the black box, these inputs produce observable buyer responses, such as product choice, brand choice, purchase timing, and purchase amount.

OBJECTIVE 2 Name the four major factors that influence consumer buyer behavior (pp 127-139).

Consumer buyer behavior is influenced by four key sets of buyer characteristics: cultural, social, personal, and psychological. Although many of these factors cannot be influenced by the marketer, they can be useful in identifying interested buyers and in shaping products and appeals to serve consumer needs better. *Culture* is the most basic determinant of a person's wants and behavior. It includes the basic values, perceptions, preferences, and behaviors that a person learns from family and other important institutions. *Subcultures* are 'cultures within cultures' that have distinct values and lifestyles and can be based on anything from age to ethnicity. People with different cultural and subcultural characteristics have different product and brand preferences. As a result, marketers may want to focus their marketing programs on the special needs of certain groups.

Social factors also influence a buyer's behavior. A person's *reference groups*—family, friends, social networks, professional associations—strongly affect product and brand choices. The buyer's age, life-cycle stage, occupation, economic circumstances, lifestyle, personality, and other *personal characteristics* influence his or her buying decisions. Consumer *lifestyles*—the whole pattern of acting and interacting in the world—are also an important influence on purchase decisions. Finally, consumer buying behavior is influenced by four major *psychological factors*—motivation, perception, learning, and beliefs and attitudes. Each of these factors provides a different perspective for understanding the workings of the buyer's black box.

OBJECTIVE 3 List and define the major types of buying decision behavior and the stages in the buyer decision process (pp 139-143).

Buying behavior may vary greatly across different types of products and buying decisions. Consumers undertake *complex buying*

behavior when they are highly involved in a purchase and perceive significant differences among brands. *Dissonance-reducing behavior* occurs when consumers are highly involved but see little difference among brands. *Habitual buying behavior* occurs under conditions of low involvement and little significant brand difference. In situations characterized by low involvement but significant perceived brand differences, consumers engage in *variety-seeking buying behavior.*

When making a purchase, the buyer goes through a decision process consisting of *need recognition, information search, evaluation of alternatives, purchase decision*, and *postpurchase behavior*. The marketer's job is to understand the buyer's behavior at each stage and the influences that are operating. During *need recognition*, the consumer recognizes a problem or need that could be satisfied by a product or service in the market. Once the need is recognized, the consumer is interested to seek more information and moves into the *information search* stage. With information in hand, the consumer proceeds to *alternative evaluation,* during which the information is used to evaluate brands in the choice set. From there, the consumer makes a *purchase decision* and actually buys the product. In the final stage of the buyer decision process, *postpurchase behavior,* the consumer takes action based on satisfaction or dissatisfaction.

OBJECTIVE 4 Describe the adoption and diffusion process for new products (pp 143-146).

The product adoption process is comprised of five stages: awareness, interest, evaluation, trial, and adoption. Initially, the consumer must become aware of the new product. *Awareness* leads to *interest*, and the consumer seeks information about the new product. Once information has been gathered, the consumer enters the *evaluation* stage and considers buying the new product. Next, in the *trial* stage, the consumer tries the product on a small scale to improve his or her estimate of its value. If the consumer is satisfied with the product, he or she enters the *adoption* stage, deciding to use the new product fully and regularly.

With regard to diffusion of new products, consumers respond at different rates, depending on the consumer's characteristics and the product's characteristics. Consumers may be innovators, early adopters, early majority, late majority, or laggards. *Innovators* are willing to try risky new ideas; *early adopters*—often community opinion leaders—accept new ideas early but carefully; the *early majority*—rarely leaders—decide deliberately to try new ideas, doing so before the average person does; the *late majority* try an innovation only after a majority of people have adopted it; whereas *laggards* adopt an innovation only after it has become a tradition itself. Manufacturers try to bring their new products to the attention of potential early adopters, especially those who are opinion leaders.

KEY Terms

OBJECTIVE 1

Consumer buyer behavior (p 125)
Consumer market (p 125)

OBJECTIVE 2

Culture (p 127)
Subculture (p 130)
Social class (p 130)
Group (p 131)
Opinion leader (p 132)
Online social networks (p 132)
Lifestyle (p 135)

Personality (p 135)
Brand personality (p 135)
Motive (drive) (p 136)
Perception (p 137)
Learning (p 138)
Belief (p 138)
Attitude (p 138)

OBJECTIVE 3

Complex buying behavior (p 139)
Dissonance-reducing buying
behavior (p 140)

Habitual buying behavior (p 140)
Variety-seeking buying behavior (p 140)
Need recognition (p 141)
Information search (p 142)
Alternative evaluation (p 142)
Purchase decision (p 142)
Postpurchase behavior (p 143)
Cognitive dissonance (p 143)

OBJECTIVE 4

New product (p 143)
Adoption process (p 145)

DISCUSSING & APPLYING THE Concepts

Discussing the Concepts

1. How do consumers respond to various marketing efforts the company might use? List the buyer characteristics that affect buyer behavior and discuss which one(s) influence you most when making a new car purchase decision.

2. Name and describe the types of consumer buying behavior. Which one would you most likely use if deciding on a laptop computer purchase and which for picking a restaurant for dinner?

3. Explain the stages of the consumer buyer decision process and describe how you or your family went through this process to make a recent purchase.

4. How might a marketer influence a consumer's information search through each of the four information sources discussed in the chapter?

5. What is a 'new' product and how do consumers go about deciding whether to adopt a new product?

6. What product characteristics influence an innovation's rate of adoption? Discuss the characteristics of mobile navigation systems in relation to the rate of adoption.

Applying the Concepts

1. Marketers often target consumers before, during, or after a trigger event, an event in one's life that triggers change. For example, after having a child, new parents have an increased need for baby furniture, clothes, diapers, car seats, and lots of other baby-related goods. Consumers who never paid attention to marketing efforts for certain products may now be focused on ones related to their life change. In a small group, discuss other trigger events that may provide opportunities to target the right buyer at the right time.

2. You are the vice president of marketing for a small software company that has developed new and novel spam-blocking software. You are charged with selecting the target market for the product launch. Discuss the adopter groups shown in Figure 5.7 and explain how this knowledge can help you with your targeting decision.

3. How did you decide on the college or university you are currently attending? Describe the factors that influenced your decision and the decision-making process you followed.

FOCUS ON Technology

With so many choices available, the decision process for consumers can be daunting, especially for high-risk purchases. Looking for a new digital camera, computer, sunscreen, or coffee maker? Product reviews abound that provide information on products in just about every category. In Australia, ProductReview.com.au pays visitors for reviewing everyday products from cars to televisions. Reviewers select products that they have bought and then review them and receive reward points. The reviewers also get paid for referring buyers to a website.

Without doubt, ProductReview.com.au is popular and successful. The site has over 20,000 unique visitors every day (75 percent of whom are Australians) and over 1 million page views a month. As of September 2008, the site had 30,000 registered users and some 40,000 consumer reviews and ratings on thousands of products.

1. Go to the U.S. ConsumerSearch.com (www.consumersearch. com), select a product category that interests you, and learn about the best products/brands in that category. Which review is rated the best? Which brand is rated best by the reviewers? Based on this analysis, which product brand would you select as a purchaser? How useful is this website? Write a brief report explaining your answers to these questions.

2. Many websites provide consumer reviews. The sites usually feature a rating system and actual written reviews. How influential are these types of reviews to you when you're deciding on a purchase?

FOCUS ON Ethics

Apple's iPod revolutionized music listening, with over 100 million iPods sold worldwide. However, iPod and other brands of MP3 players have revolutionized the music industry as well, causing sales of pre-recorded CDs to plummet and music file downloading from the Internet—both legal and illegal—to skyrocket. Pay-per-song sites, such as Apple's iTunes, let consumers purchase songs legally and inexpensively. While purchases of songs from these types of sites continue to increase, illegal music file sharing is increasing as well,

with hundreds of millions of files downloaded illegally each year. Research also indicates half of 14- to 24-year-olds were happy to share all of the music on their hard drives with other people.

1. Discuss how marketers can combat this problem.

2. What is the situation regarding illegal downloads in your own country, and what steps are being taken by the government and the music industry to stop it?

MARKETING BY THE Numbers

Consumers may often evaluate products and services by making comparisons between the attributes of competing brands. Added to this is a weighting for each of the attributes, which aim to reflect the relative importance of them. For a particular brand, the key attributes and their weighting was as follows:

Style (0.4)

Cost (0.3)

Delivery time (0.2)

Warranty (0.1)

The consumers were asked to rate each of the brands on a sliding scale of 1–7 with 1 rating the product low and 7 extremely high. For brand A the scores were respectively 6, 6, 7, and 2. For brand B they were 5, 3, 4, and 4. For brand C the results were 6, 5, 5, and 5 and for brand D, they were 4, 7, 6, and 3.

The score for each brand can be calculated by multiplying the importance weight for each attribute by the brand's score on that attribute. These weighted scores are then summed to determine the score for that brand. The scores given are meant to suggest, as far as the consumer is concerned, that the particular brand performs better in this aspect than the other competing brands. A tied score simply suggests that there is no discernible difference in performance between two or more of the brands in that category.

For more discussion of the financial and quantitative implications of marketing decisions, see Appendix 2: Marketing by the Numbers.

1. Determine the scores for brands A, B, C, and D. Which brand would a consumer likely choose?

2. Why might the results be somewhat misleading?

VIDEO Case

Wild Planet
Of the many factors that affect consumer buyer behavior, social responsibility is playing an increasing role. While there have always been companies that have integrated 'doing good' with corporate strategy, a new generation of activist entrepreneurs has now taken up the reins. The ones most likely to succeed are those who recognize that beyond just doing good, social responsibility can provide a powerful means for connecting with consumers.

For example, Wild Planet markets high-quality, nonviolent toys that encourage kids to be imaginative and creative and to explore the world around them. Wild Planet sells more than just toys. It sells positive play experiences. To better understand those experiences, the company conducts a tremendous amount of consumer research through state-of-the-art methods to better understand

consumer buyer behavior. Wild Planet even created a Toy Opinion Panel to evaluate current products and develop new product ideas.

After viewing the video featuring Wild Planet, answer the following questions about consumer buyer behavior:

1. Explain how each of the four sets of factors affecting consumer behavior affects the consumer purchase process as it relates to toys from Wild Planet.

2. What demographic segment of consumers is Wild Planet targeting?

3. Visit the Wild Planet website at www.wildplanet.com to learn more about the company. How does the website help consumers through the buyer decision process?

COMPANY Case

Arabic BlackBerry:
Adapting to the Language of the Market

In October 2007, the launch of the first Arabic BlackBerry was announced in the UAE. The device had Arabic language input and an Arabic interface. Up until this point, the BlackBerry was restricted to U.S. and European use. The new initiative to bring the BlackBerry to the Arab world and Africa had begun.

The UAE's mobile phone provider telco Etisalat collaborated with the creators of the BlackBerry, RIM (Research InMotion), to create the Arabic version of the email smart phone. The device allows Arabic customers to compose Arabic emails, browse Arabic websites, and input Arabic text into the PIM (personal information management) software applications. The device is fully integrated with IBM Lotus Domino, Microsoft Exchange, and Novell GroupWise servers.

The BlackBerry has brought about the buzz word 'push email' into the business world. The concept is actually very simple. It works on the principle that rather than pulling emails at intervals on a mobile handset, the technology actually allows the emails to be pushed. In other words, each and every email is delivered instantaneously and individually to handsets.

In the Arab world, the move toward a mobile workforce is gathering pace. Many businesses in the region want and need the flexibility of having their employees out in the field with the capacity of receiving emails and the ability to send them. Nokia's Head of Enterprise Solutions in the Near and Middle East, Joe Devassy, explained: "Do [the businesses] have a mobility strategy? No. A lot is happening accidentally. It's not as if the IT managers in most companies in the Middle East actually have a plan like they do for installing networks or firewalls. It's happening more randomly, but there's definitely a lot of interest there from governments, banks, and the hospitality industry across all the verticals really."

Rather than the handset manufacturers or service providers trying to create a demand for the product, it has been the enterprises themselves that have been driving the conversion to push emails. In fact, some employees have been buying their own handsets to make their jobs easier, to match their mobile roles, and to ensure they are instantly contactable wherever they are based. This is confirmed by Harout Bedrossian, Motorola's regional sales manager for the Middle East: "The funny thing is that we've also seen individuals within the enterprises who have shown demand and started adopting devices even though their own companies and management didn't show any interest in the device. They know about the brands and about the technology and when it enters the region, they don't wait for their companies. They just go out and buy the handsets."

At present, the one thing holding the widespread adoption of the technology back is other businesses in the supply chain and those who are either unwilling or unable to adopt the technology. Some simply do not understand its value, while others are unaware of the emerging technological benefits of the system. In order for any new technology to reach its potential, all of those in a supply chain need to be using the same technology. That way, the needs of the customer can be paramount and can drive the day-to-day use of the technology. Husni El Assi, general manager of Sony Ericsson Middle East, explained the difficulties: "One of the main challenges is the lack of awareness in the technology itself and its benefits. We have an ongoing educational program for our distributors and retailers,

and that is how we update our business partners on the latest innovations and the latest technologies available in the mobile communications industry. In addition to that, we have our merchandising team which is in regular contact with the trade and helps to educate and inform the retailers on a regular basis."

One of the major drivers in the adoption of push email in the Arab world has been the fact that the handset vendors, the network providers, and the businesses that have already invested in them are all supporting the same system. Harout Bedrossian, with Motorola's regional mobile-device unit, confirmed that this was the case: "We have operators in the region as well as mobile device manufacturers pushing push email in the region. Etisalat, Du—companies from Oman to Saudi—everybody has started actively marketing push email, be it Blackberry or Microsoft Exchange. Demand has therefore picked up considerably."

The long-term adoption of the system is entirely reliant on the resellers of the products that can make use of push email. The retailers dealing with customers on a daily basis need to feel that they are stakeholders in the technology and that they have a vested interest in pushing the system in the Arab world. It would be their role to help to raise the awareness customers have of the product to the end users. In this way, the end users that had adopted the system early on can then be used to explain it to others and to highlight its virtues in the business.

Nasir Aijaz, a senior manager at EmitacMobile Solutions (EMS), was a key player in the distribution of the BlackBerry in the Arab world. It was EMS that extolled the benefits of the BlackBerry and the push email system. Aijaz explained: "The phenomena is that everyone wants to be connected all of the time. It's the convenience that is attached to it—users don't want to carry around laptops—the biggest thing that a device like a Blackberry offers is the freedom to move. Information is available anytime, anywhere, and the workforce is always connected. It offers better customer service and retention, a more productive workforce, and a more efficient use of limited resources."

Certainly, the adoption of push email is the first step in improving the mobility and communications between and within businesses in the Arab world. Ultimately, it is hoped that this will open the door to other services and applications that will allow users to experience the advantages of an office environment no matter where they may be. Devassy explained the potential behind the adoption of push email and what it could bring in the future: "When we're offering a solution, we're offering a platform for mobilizing everything. So when we go to the business—we say you can mobilize push email, but push email alone is very basic, and it will be pervasive. In 24 months, it'll be just like SMS. Everyone with a phone will have push email. What we're saying is if you first start with push email and you find that your staff are comfortable with push email, then on the same platform we can also mobilize your ERP, and your CRM, and your field force and sales force. We can pretty much mobilize your whole organization, but it has to happen step by step, and push email is just the first step."

Aijaz was firmly of the opinion that the BlackBerry would only get better and this would accelerate the mobility and freedom of the users: "The Blackberry add-ons can connect to CRM systems or even GPRS systems. Recently I saw an airline booking and confirmation system on a Blackberry. You can book your tickets, cancel, or amend them, and it will tell you about cancellations and delays to your flights. These add-on functions are becoming very important."

Resellers of the products that can deliver push email are vital in making sure that the products not only retain their popularity, but also new users are drawn to them as solutions to their communication problems. The profusion of additional features and applications is the key to this, to keeping the product fresh and up to date. Not only this, the resellers have a vested interest in ensuring that the push email system remains a product in great demand, as it is lucrative to them. Bedrossian explained: "Firstly, resellers need to understand how to get the device to work in the user's corporate e-mail. When they take it out of the box, end users expect it to work so resellers need to be able to facilitate that."

Clearly, there is great competition between the handset sellers to become the leading device that achieves the dominant market share in the Arab world. Each handset manufacturer is working hard with developers to ensure that they offer applications that can be resold at the point of purchase by the resellers, not only to lock the user into a particular handset, but also to provide the reseller with a valuable, ongoing income stream. Devassy explained the skills that resellers would need in order to take full advantage of the commercial opportunities: "In terms of skills, they need basic networking, networking integration, messaging, and some element of expertise in security. If the channel wants to take advantage of everything from ERP to push email, then it would be great if they're already into doing developments in Java for devices, or if they are partners of Oracle, SAP or Siebel. These kinds of resellers would potentially see the benefits of partnering with Nokia."

Some of the other handset manufacturers see things rather differently and are at pains to point out that their competitors are trying to make the technology appear too complicated in order to ensure that the resellers are part of the supply chain. In other words, they believe that push email is very straightforward and can be easily understood by the end user, so there is no need to involve resellers and make the application seem more complex than it is. They feel that this will only inhibit the adoption of the system. One such critic is Vishnu Vardhan, who is the executive director of the mobile handset vendors HTC: "Push email is very simple to implement. Only a few parameters need to be changed. People like to complicate things. They like to make out that push email is some complicated technology, but it's very simple." HTC's handsets have been made simpler by the involvement of Microsoft. All of the handsets are Windows Mobile handsets. They are easy to set up and use, either by the end user or the software vendor.

Marketing the handsets and the push email in the Arab world has not been as effective as it could be. Although it is popular, it has not achieved the market penetration of the U.S. or Europe yet. There are other issues, too, which have impeded the adoption of the push email system. The devices are very expensive. In itself, this is not the issue, but replacement costs would be prohibitive if the devices were lost or stolen. This has certainly held back many businesses from making the investment. The other key issue is security and the fact that sensitive data could be lost or stolen by a company's competitors. The vendors and resellers have a tough job on their hands to convince the end users that the data is safe and that it can be managed and removed from the handset remotely. Bedrossian explained the concerns: "We see a lot of IT managers asking for protection and data security, as company-sensitive data is in a small handheld device that you can easily leave in a taxi or a restaurant without noticing. So, the next level of contribution that a reseller can add is providing advice on how to protect data on the device through password protected applications or antivirus applications."

HTC is facing a similar task in trying to allay the fears of users. However, the company has the backing of Microsoft, which is seen as an advantage. As Vardhan explained: "This is a Microsoft product. They have addressed the security issue. They make sure it is fully secure from the moment you buy it."

Nokia's long-term plan is to provide a product and a service that can effectively replace the laptop as the mobile business gadget of choice. This will require a change in people's attitudes because the mobile phone is still seen as an ancillary business tool. Devassy explained the conundrum facing Nokia: "The PC came from the business to the home. The mobile phone is going from the home to the business. When the PC was in businesses, they had already thought about compatibility, manageability, security and so on, so getting it into the home was easier. Our challenge is that the phone is a consumer tool, and we're putting a consumer tool into the business."

All of the push email handsets are still premium priced at this stage of their introduction into the Arab world. It is understandable and the norm for high-technology products. Resellers earn a considerable margin from the sale of each, and the retention of the margin is vital in order for the resellers to continue to promote the push email. Bedrossian explained why this arrangement with the resellers was so vital to the introduction of the technology: "Currently push email devices retail at $300-plus, and the profit margins are really worth the effort and time. But the prices will drop soon. Moore's law still stands: Within 18 months, the price of new technology tends to halve. It's still true today and will be for push email."

For Nokia, push email is just the beginning; it is just the first stage in the development of a truly mobile office service, as Devassy hoped: "We tell resellers to not consider push email as the area where you will make all your money. Your money will come when you mobilize other applications. Push email is just a foot in the door. Your whole strategy cannot be based purely on push email."

So where is the market in the Arab world for push email, BlackBerry handsets, and the competing devices? The UAE is a key battleground for vendors because there are huge numbers of corporations sited there. Saudi Arabia is, of course, a major market, as are Kuwait, Bahrain, Qatar, and Oman. The BlackBerry is doing exceptionally well in Jordan, but as far as Aijaz is concerned, the main market has to be Saudi Arabia: "Saudi really has the highest potential, and it's gradually picking up. We're launching the Arabic Blackberry in the GCC soon. The current versions display Arabic, but the new one will allow you to write in Arabic as well, and with the Arabic device we expect demand in Saudi to really pick up."

So who has been buying into push email as early adopters of the technology? Banks and the hospitality and the financial sectors have been the main purchasers. Most small-to-medium-sized businesses are waiting it out until the price drops and the technology is fully proven. Once these two factors fall into place, the demand for the new technology will be enormous.

Questions for Discussion

1. Analyze the decision process that buyers of a typical push email device go through before purchasing the device.

2. Apply the concept of aspirational groups to the BlackBerry brand. Should marketers have boundaries with regard to this concept?

3. Explain how both positive and negative consumer attitudes toward a brand like BlackBerry might develop. How might someone's attitude toward BlackBerry change?

4. What role does the BlackBerry appear to be playing in the development of the mobile handset market in the Arab world?

Sources: Dawinderpal Sahota, "You've Got Mail," *Arabian Business*, July 1, 2007, www.arabianbusiness.com/you-ve-got-mail-58428.html; additional information from ITP, www.itp.net; Nokia, www.nokia.ae; Digital Media Asia, www.digitalmediaasia.com; and BlackBerry, www.blackberry.com.

Chapter 6

Part 1   Defining Marketing and the Marketing Process (Chapters 1, 2)
Part 2   Understanding the Marketplace and Consumers (Chapters 3, 4, 5, 6)
Part 3   Designing a Customer-Driven Strategy and Mix (Chapters 7, 8, 9, 10, 11, 12, 13, 14)
Part 4   Extending Marketing (Chapters 15, 16, 17)

Business Markets and Business Buyer Behavior

Chapter
PREVIEW

In the previous chapter, you studied *final consumer* buying behavior and factors that influence it. In this chapter, we'll do the same for *business customers*— those that buy goods and services for use in producing their own products and services or for resale to others. As when selling to final buyers, firms marketing to business customers must build profitable relationships with them by creating superior customer value.

Let us take a look at an Arab company which is growing business rapidly regionally and internationally by applying the principles of business-to-business marketing.

Advanced Electronics Company (AEC) is a Saudi company, established in 1988. It was created to focus on strategic areas such as advanced manufacturing technologies, communication systems, and product support. Since the 1980s it has grown rapidly and is now a leading high-technology engineering and manufacturing company in the Kingdom.[1]

Its impressive international customer list includes Boeing, Lockheed Martin, Rockwell International, Thales, U.S. Army CECOM, Lucent Technologies, Ericsson, Siemens, Alcatel, and Nokia. Its Arab world customer list is equally impressive, including Saudi Armed Forces, Saudi Ministry of Water and Electricity, Saudi Aramco, Saudi Telecom Company, and Mobily.

Advanced Electronics Company's business is to manage "design, development, manufacturing, upgrade, support and integration of electronic products and systems for military, civil and industrial customers."[2] The company has gained considerable technological knowledge through two approaches. First, it has formed partnerships with international companies such as Cisco, HP, Acer, and Statron. Secondly, it has developed its own research and development (R&D) capabilities. Through these two approaches, AEC has developed sophisticated design and manufacturing capabilities. The company continually invests in expanding its R&D activities, manufacturing, test processes, and manpower development.[3]

In its business approach AEC focuses on a small number of large organizational customers, rather than selling and marketing its products to a large number of small buyers. These large organizational customers each provide a large revenue stream to AEC. Some of these relationships are long term and strategic in nature, which means that AEC and its customers become partners in developing new or customized products. This in turn assures AEC a continued business relationship with its customers.

AEC has a diverse portfolio of commercial and industrial products sold to large business customers. Its product and solutions list is grouped into a number of broad categories including:

Energy Systems, Industrial Systems, and Telecom Systems. To succeed in its business-to-business markets, AEC must design good products as well as make them available to customers to suit their unique requirements: in other words, to customize each product. It must work closely and deeply with its business customers to become a strategic, problem-solving partner. To market its products and services successfully AEC has to understand deeply the needs and requirements of its customers and identify how to provide superior value, which often requires a very intensive approach. The partnership approach adopted is reflected in its mission statement: "To provide our valued customers quality, competitive and advanced solutions to their satisfaction while serving local community. Our employees and business partners will share our success, and our shareholders will receive a sustained, superior return on their investment."[4]

AEC is involved in a number of projects in the fields of defense, telecommunication, civil, and industrial projects; it also provides products and service for major international companies. For example, AEC successfully won a contract from the Saudi Electricity Company— Eastern Region to upgrade the GAS turbine control system for the city of Dammam and northern area power plants. These kinds of contracts are not one-off purchase decisions by the organizational buyers. They are actually the result of a number of smaller decisions made by the buying organization at various levels over a significant timeframe. Most of the time the selling organization

> Advanced Electronics Company produces wide-ranging products for the business market.

has to develop a very good understanding of the buyer organization's requirements, limitations, and most importantly its decision-making process. The selling organization also has to clearly understand the criteria on which the buyer organization will base its decision to award the contract.

Another way in which AEC has successfully grown its business is by entering into strategic partnerships with other businesses in order to win contracts or target new opportunities. As an example of forming strategic partnerships in the business market, Acer, the Taiwan-based PC giant, finalized an agreement with AEC in 2006 to produce PCs jointly in the Kingdom with the intention to secure major government contracts in Saudi Arabia. This partnership is managed under directives from the Saudi government, which launched its 'PCs for homes' initiative, aiming to make PCs more affordable. Mohammad Ebrahim Al Swaiyel, governor of the Communication and Information Commission (CITC), had earlier indicated that PC makers who set up operations in the Kingdom would be favored over other suppliers—hence the AEC and Acer project. Through this project AEC wants to focus on the huge small- and medium-sized business (SMB) market in Saudi Arabia. Establishing a local production site would enable it to provide better delivery times. "The announcement can be viewed as a major expansion of Acer's Saudi activity," said Philip Ashkar, sales and marketing director of Acer Middle East. "The Riyadh plant will open up massive inroads into the corporate segment, add a timely boost to efforts in the lucrative SMB space, as well as allowing Acer to further consolidate its position in the retail sector," he went on to add.[5]

Hardware rivals HP have already established an assembly plant in Saudi Arabia, and Fujitsu Siemens Computers (FSC) plans to set up a PC assembly or final configuration facility in the Arab world.

AEC has finalised an agreement with Acer to produce PCs in Saudi Arabia.

To succeed in the large-scale contracts which characterize its business-to-business markets, AEC must design good products as well as customize them to suit the unique requirements of each customer. It must work closely and deeply with its business customers to become a strategic, problem-solving partner. To market its products and services successfully AEC has to understand deeply the needs and requirements of its customers and identify how to provide superior value.

Acer and AEC will establish the first PC production plant in the Kingdom, and will thus be in a good position to target key customers and government organizations. It is this type of focus which is driving AEC's business rapidly in the Arab world.

Like AEC, in one way or another, most large companies sell to other organizations. Companies such as Masafi, DuPont, Airbus, IBM, and countless other firms sell *most* of their products to other businesses. Even large consumer-products companies, which make products used by final consumers, must first sell their products to other businesses. For example, Unilever makes many familiar consumer brands—food brands such as Lipton, Knorr, and Brooke Bond; beauty products such as Sunsilk, Fair and Lovely, Dove, Close-up, Lux, and Lifebuoy; and detergents such as Surf and Omo. But to sell these products to consumers, Unilever must first sell them to its local distributors, wholesalers, and retailer customers, who in turn serve the consumer market.

Business buyer behavior refers to the buying behavior of the organizations that buy goods and services for use in the production of other products and services that are sold, rented, or supplied to others. It also includes the behavior of retailing and wholesaling firms that acquire goods to resell or rent them to others at a profit. In the **business buying process**, business buyers determine which products and services their organizations need to purchase and then find, evaluate, and choose among alternative suppliers and brands. *Business-to-business marketers* must do their best to understand business markets and business buyer behavior. Then, like businesses that sell to final buyers, they must build profitable relationships with business customers by creating superior customer value.

Business buyer behavior
The buying behavior of the organizations that buy goods and services for use in the production of other products and services or to resell or rent them to others at a profit.

Business buying process
The decision process by which business buyers determine which products and services their organizations need to purchase, and then find, evaluate, and choose among alternative suppliers and brands.

Objective Outline

OBJECTIVE 1 **Define the business market and explain how business markets differ from consumer markets.**

OBJECTIVE 2 **Identify the major factors that influence business buyer behavior.**

OBJECTIVE 3 **List and define the steps in the business buying decision process.**

OBJECTIVE 4 **Compare the institutional and government markets and explain how institutional and government buyers make their buying decisions.**

Author Comment Business markets operate 'behind the scenes' to most consumers. Most of the things you buy involve many sets of business purchases before you ever see them.

Business Markets (pp 154–158)

The business market is *huge*. In fact, business markets involve far more dollars and items than do consumer markets. For example, think about the large number of business transactions involved in the production and sale of a single set of Dunlop tires. Various suppliers sell Dunlop the rubber, steel, equipment, and other goods that it needs to produce tires. Dunlop then sells the finished tires to local distributors, who in turn sell these to the retailers. The consumers finally buy the tires from the retailers. Thus, many sets of *business* purchases were made for only one set of *consumer* purchases. In addition, Dunlop sells tires as original equipment to manufacturers that fit them on new vehicles, and as replacement tires to companies that maintain their own fleets of company cars, trucks, buses, or other vehicles.

In some ways, business markets are similar to consumer markets. Both involve people who assume buying roles and make purchase decisions to satisfy needs. However, business markets differ in many ways from consumer markets. The main differences, shown in ● **Table 6.1**, are in *market structure and demand*, the *nature of the buying unit*, and the *types of decisions and the decision process* involved.

Market Structure and Demand

The business marketer normally deals with *far fewer but far larger buyers* than the consumer marketer does. Even in large business markets, a few buyers often account for most of the purchasing. For example, when Dunlop sells replacement tires to final consumers, its potential market includes the owners of the millions of cars currently in use in the Arab region and around the world. But Dunlop's fate in the business market depends on getting orders from one of only a handful of large automakers. Similarly, Black & Decker sells its power tools and outdoor equipment to tens of millions of consumers worldwide. However, it must sell these products through huge retail customers such as ACE and Carrefour.

Derived demand
Business demand that ultimately comes from (derives from) the demand for consumer goods.

Further, business demand is **derived demand**—it ultimately derives from the demand for consumer goods. Hewlett-Packard and Dell buy Intel microprocessor chips because consumers buy personal computers. If consumer demand for diamond jewelry

● TABLE | 6.1   Characteristics of Business Markets

Market Structure and Demand

Business markets contain *fewer but larger buyers.*

Business buyer demand is *derived* from final consumer demand.

Demand in many business markets is *more inelastic*—not affected as much in the short run by price changes.

Demand in business markets *fluctuates more*, and more quickly.

Nature of the Buying Unit

Business purchases involve *more buyers.*

Business buying involves a *more professional purchasing effort.*

Types of Decisions and the Decision Process

Business buyers usually face *more complex buying decisions.*

The business buying process is *more formalized.*

In business buying, buyers and sellers work more closely together and build close long-term *relationships.*

drops, so will the demand for diamonds. Therefore, business-to-business marketers sometimes promote their products directly to final consumers to increase business demand. For example, Intel advertises heavily to personal computer buyers, selling computers on the virtues of Intel microprocessors. "Multiply your mobility," it tells consumers—"great computing starts with Intel inside." The increased demand for Intel chips boosts demand for the PCs containing them, and both Intel and its business partners win.

Many business markets have *inelastic demand*; that is, total demand for many business products is not affected much by price changes, especially in the short run. A drop in the price of leather will not cause shoe manufacturers to buy much more leather unless it results in lower shoe prices that, in turn, will increase consumer demand for shoes.

Finally, business markets have more *fluctuating demand*. The demand for many business goods and services tends to change more and more quickly than the demand for consumer goods and services does. A small percentage increase in consumer demand can cause large increases in business demand. Sometimes a rise of only 10 percent in consumer demand can cause as much as a 200 percent rise in business demand during the next period.

Nature of the Buying Unit

Compared with consumer purchases, a business purchase usually involves *more decision participants* and a *more professional purchasing effort.* Often, business buying is done by trained purchasing agents who spend their working lives learning how to buy better. The more complex the purchase, the more likely it is that several people will participate in the decision-making process. Buying committees made up of technical experts and top management are common in the buying of major goods. Beyond this, business-to-business marketers now face a new breed of higher-level, better-trained supply managers. Therefore, companies must have well-trained marketers and salespeople to deal with these well-trained buyers.

Derived demand: Intel advertises heavily to personal computer buyers, advising them on the virtues of Intel microprocessors—both Intel and its business partners benefit.

Types of Decisions and the Decision Process

Business buyers usually face *more complex* buying decisions than do consumer buyers. Business purchases often involve large sums of money, complex technical and economic considerations, and interactions among many people at many levels of the buyer's organization. Because the purchases are more complex, business buyers may take longer to make their decisions. The business buying process also tends to be *more formalized* than the consumer buying process. Large business purchases usually call for detailed product specifications, written purchase orders, careful supplier searches, and formal approval.

Finally, in the business buying process, the buyer and seller are often much *more dependent* on each other. Business-to-business marketers may roll up their sleeves and work closely with their customers during all stages of the buying process—from helping customers define problems, to finding solutions, to supporting after-sale operation. They often customize their offerings to individual customer needs. In the short run, sales go to suppliers who meet buyers' immediate product and service needs. In the long run, however, business-to-business marketers keep a customer's sales and create customer value by meeting current needs *and* by partnering with customers to help them solve their problems. For example, when Aramex supplies a broad range of logistics services and resources to its business customers, it asks them "How can we develop tailor-made solutions for you?" (See **Real Marketing 6.1**.)

In recent years, relationships between customers and suppliers have been changing from downright adversarial to close and chummy. In fact, many customer companies are now practicing **supplier development**, systematically developing networks of supplier-partners to ensure an appropriate and dependable supply of products and materials that they will use in making their own products or resell to others. For example, the machinery maker Caterpillar no longer calls its buyers 'purchasing agents'—they are managers of 'purchasing and supplier development.' Wal-Mart doesn't have a 'Purchasing Department,' it has a 'Supplier Development Department.' And giant Swedish furniture retailer IKEA doesn't just buy from its suppliers, it involves them deeply in the process of delivering a stylish and affordable lifestyle to IKEA's customers.

Supplier development
Systematic development of networks of supplier-partners to ensure an appropriate and dependable supply of products and materials for use in making products or reselling them to others.

IKEA, the world's largest furniture retailer, is the quintessential global cult brand. Customers from Beijing to Moscow to Riyadh, flock to the US$27 billion Scandinavian retailer's more than 276 huge stores in 36 countries, drawn by IKEA's trendy but simple and practical furniture at affordable prices. But IKEA's biggest obstacle to growth isn't opening new stores and attracting customers. Rather, it's finding enough of the right kinds of *suppliers* to help design and produce the billions of dollars of affordable goods that those customers will carry out of its stores. IKEA currently relies on about 1,800 suppliers in more than 50 countries to stock its shelves. If the giant retailer continues at its current growth rate, it will need to double its supply network...IKEA doesn't just rely on spot suppliers who might be available when needed. Instead, it has systematically developed a robust network of supplier-partners that reliably provide the more than 10,000 items it stocks. IKEA's designers start with a basic customer value proposition. Then, they find and work closely with key suppliers to bring that proposition to market. And IKEA does more than just buy from suppliers; it also involves them deeply in the process of designing and making stylish but affordable products to keep IKEA's customers coming back.[6]

Giant Scandinavian furniture retailer IKEA doesn't just buy from its suppliers. It involves them deeply in the process of designing and making stylish but affordable furniture that keeps customers coming back.

Real Marketing 6.1

Aramex Partners with Business Customers

The familiar sight of an Aramex delivery van might make most people think of a driver arriving at their door with a parcel. Perhaps a gift sent from a relative or friend in another country. Indeed, Aramex's success has been largely based on its ability to deliver to your door with speed and efficiency. Its international and domestic express services provide pick-up and delivery of small packages from city to city and across the globe, to ordinary people at home and to office addresses. Yet, perhaps surprisingly, Aramex's business-to-business partnerships make up a much larger part of its revenues than the consumer/ retail part. In other words, the most profitable customers for Aramex are not the residential customers who receive the packages, but the business customers who send them. This is because business customers have a complex logistics process to organize, including purchase orders, inventory, order status checks, invoices, payments, returned merchandise, and fleets of delivery vehicles. Aramex has invested in understanding these complex needs and developing customized solutions to business customers in an effort to help its clients reduce inventory costs, increase transaction speed, and improve sales by implementing customer requirements more efficiently.

Aramex has become a very successful logistics partner. Its client base exceeds 50,000 companies, based mainly in the Arab world, Europe, India, and America, and includes trading companies, banks, service and information companies, manufacturing, regional distribution companies, and express companies. To achieve this, Aramex has used and developed its strengths effectively, combining local knowledge, state-of-the-art technology, and international standards. It has also understood that clients are looking for comprehensive solutions to their complex logistics and supply chain requirements, and has invested in developing such solutions. It now has one of the largest logistics and transportation networks in the world, enabling it to take care of all the complex challenges business customers face with their logistics and to reduce their costs in the process. It is usually much more expensive for each individual company to establish

The sequence of events leading to a parcel being delivered at your door is much more complex than you might imagine. By positioning itself as a strategic logistics partner for its business clients, Aramex helps to handle those complex distribution problems effectively.

its own end-to-end logistics and supply chain process than to make use of an existing supply chain, which in effect spreads the enormous cost of overheads over a large client base. Furthermore, Aramex has identified that business clients want to be treated individually, and feel that their company's unique needs are being met exactly as they need them to be. To achieve this, Aramex provides tailor-made solutions and establishes close partner relationships with its clients. The company prefers close one-on-one relationships with business customers, so that an Aramex team can build experience with them in order to customize solutions to fit their business models and needs. For example, it will install inventory software and train customers' staff on how to use logistics and supply chain management software.

The company also provides its logistics services based on industry type, so that different teams can understand each industry or organization-type, and thus offer better services. Aramex has also employed a strategy that targets the small and medium enterprise segment, with the client base distributed across all major industries.

Let's look at a couple of examples of Aramex's close partnership relationships with clients. In 2009 Aramex teamed up with the Saudi Professional League (SPL)—the most popular football competition held annually in Saudi Arabia—and became the sole global distributor for SPL merchandise. Fans who order their team's branded merchandise, such as caps and jerseys, on the SPL online store, receive them at their door through Aramex's global network. This service is offered to fans anywhere in the world.

"In the Middle East and across the globe, fans of the SPL can join the game in spirit, wearing their favourite team's gear or collecting them as memorabilia. Aramex is happy to make this process easier and unite fans of the league in supporting their team. As well, we are pleased to support the League in taking this popular game to fans across the world," said Hussein Hachem, Aramex's CEO for the Gulf region. "We have already started delivery of the online orders in the region and beyond, from the streets of Jeddah to the suburbs of London, New York and even down under in Australia. The SPL has a major following worldwide, and Aramex is happy to connect them to the game through this simple, and reliable service."

In another example of business-to-business marketing, Aramex agreed a contract with Wataniya Mobile, one of the region's new mobile telecommunications operators. Aramex was to manage Wataniya's logistics and distribution requirements in Palestine. Under the contract, it will provide "a range of integrated logistics services for Wataniya Mobile, including network logistics, retail distribution and logistics management and support of various marketing initiatives."

The agreement with Wataniya expands Aramex's portfolio of partnerships with telecommunications companies and also enhances its servicing capabilities for the sector. As part of the contract, Aramex will provide a range of services including processing of inbound orders, inventory management, and SIM packaging. It will also handle the distribution of

Continued on next page ▼

retail items (e.g. SIM cards, scratch cards and handsets) to franchisees, distributors, and customer service centers across Palestine.

"Being awarded this contract by one of the region's leading telecommunications companies illustrates the high level of service and solutions customisation Aramex is able to deliver to clients," said Iyad Kamal, Aramex chief logistics officer. "This partnership is a mark of recognition of the quality of our previous performance and our established presence in serving key sectors, such as telecoms, both in the region and worldwide.

"We have all the components in place to put the full range of our international express and logistics expertise at the service of Wataniya Mobile. Wataniya Mobile is a welcomed addition to Aramex's portfolio of regional telecommunications operators."

As these examples show, Aramex has successfully developed deep working relationships with business clients in order to meet their requirements as closely as possible and to inspire long-term loyalty. As a result, its residential consumers (you and me) also benefit.

Sources: "Aramex Introduces Global Distribution of SPL Merchandise," *AME Info*, November 1, 2009, www.ameinfo.com/214425.html; "Aramex Signs Key Contract with Wataniya Mobile to Provide Integrated Logistics Services," *AME Info*, April 22, 2009, www.ameinfo.com/193655.html; Aramex website, accessed 2011, www.aramex.com; with additional information from Hassan Awan, "Aramex One of a Kind," *The National Investor*, January 22, 2008; "Aramex PJSC Equity Report," JordanInvest, May 2007, www.jordinvest.com.jo/Portals/0/Equity%20Report%20-%20ARAMEX.pdf; Kareem Z. Murad and Rasha Hamdan, "Aramex: A Regional Brand on a Global Mission," Shuaa Capital, May 27, 2008.

Author Comment │ Business buying decisions can range from routine to incredibly complex, involving only a few or very many decision makers and buying influences.

Business Buyer Behavior (pp 158–162)

At the most basic level, marketers want to know how business buyers will respond to various marketing stimuli. ◖ **Figure 6.1** shows a model of business buyer behavior. In this model, marketing and other stimuli affect the buying organization and produce certain buyer responses. These stimuli enter the organization and are turned into buyer responses. In order to design good marketing strategies, the marketer must understand what happens within the organization to turn stimuli into purchase responses.

Within the organization, buying activity consists of two major parts: the buying center, made up of all the people involved in the buying decision, and the buying decision process. The model shows that the buying center and the buying decision process are influenced by internal organizational, interpersonal, and individual factors as well as by external environmental factors.

The model in **Figure 6.1** suggests four questions about business buyer behavior: What buying decisions do business buyers make? Who participates in the buying process? What are the major influences on buyers? How do business buyers make their buying decisions?

Major Types of Buying Situations

There are three major types of buying situations.[7] At one extreme is the *straight rebuy*, which is a fairly routine decision. At the other extreme is the *new task*, which may call for thorough research. In the middle is the *modified rebuy*, which requires some research.

Straight rebuy

A business buying situation in which the buyer routinely reorders something without any modifications.

In a **straight rebuy**, the buyer reorders something without any changes. It is usually handled on a routine basis by the purchasing department. Based on past buying satisfaction, the buyer simply chooses from the various suppliers on its list. 'In' suppliers try to

---

◖ **FIGURE** │ **6.1**

The Model of Business Buyer Behavior

In some ways, business markets are similar to consumer markets—this model looks a lot like the model of consumer buyer behavior presented in Figure 5.1. But there are some major differences, especially in the nature of the buying unit, the types of decisions made, and the decision process.

The environment	
Marketing stimuli	**Other stimuli**
Product	Economic
Price	Technological
Place	Political
Promotion	Cultural
	Competitive

The buying organization

The buying center

Buying decision process

(Interpersonal and individual influences)

(Organizational influences)

Buyer responses
Product or service choice
Supplier choice
Order quantities
Delivery terms and times
Service terms
Payment

maintain product and service quality. They often propose automatic reordering systems so that the purchasing agent will save reordering time. 'Out' suppliers try to find new ways to add value or exploit dissatisfaction so that the buyer will consider them.

Modified rebuy

A business buying situation in which the buyer wants to modify product specifications, prices, terms, or suppliers.

In a **modified rebuy**, the buyer wants to change product specifications, prices, terms, or suppliers. The modified rebuy usually involves more decision participants than does the straight rebuy. The in suppliers may become nervous and feel pressured to put their best foot forward to protect an account. Out suppliers may see the modified rebuy situation as an opportunity to make a better offer and gain new business.

New task

A business buying situation in which the buyer purchases a product or service for the first time.

A company buying a product or service for the first time faces a **new-task** situation. In such cases, the greater the cost or risk, the larger the number of decision participants and the greater their efforts to collect information. The new-task situation is the marketer's greatest opportunity and challenge. The marketer not only tries to reach as many key buying influences as possible but also provides help and information.

The buyer makes the fewest decisions in the straight rebuy and the most in the new-task decision. In the new-task situation, the buyer must decide on product specifications, suppliers, price limits, payment terms, order quantities, delivery times, and service terms. The order of these decisions varies with each situation, and different decision participants influence each choice.

Many business buyers prefer to buy a complete solution to a problem from a single seller instead of buying separate products and services from several suppliers and putting them together. The sale often goes to the firm that provides the most complete *system* for meeting the customer's needs and solving its problems. Such **systems selling** (or **solutions selling**) is often a key business marketing strategy for winning and holding accounts.

Systems selling (or solutions selling)

Buying a packaged solution to a problem from a single seller, thus avoiding all the separate decisions involved in a complex buying situation.

Thus, as we discovered in **Real Marketing 6.1**, transportation and logistics giant Aramex does more than just ship packages for its business customers. It develops entire solutions to customers' transportation and logistics problems. For example, when Nuqul Group launched ABC4Office in 2009, Jordan's first full-service provider in the market for office supplies, it contracted Aramex to develop a comprehensive supply chain that would provide full business support.

The ABC4Office service is claimed to offer "complete business solutions under one roof." It is said to increase the productivity and effectiveness of small projects and thus help businesses to achieve their goals, through the use of office product brands that satisfy international Service Excellence Standards. Aramex's key role in this venture was to provide comprehensive supply chain solutions. The agreement enables business owners to furnish their offices with the latest products, offering a quality service, credibility, and professionalism. All products are delivered within 24 hours of order placement. Customer service personnel are available for clients, offering a personalized service customized to the needs of each client, following up on their orders and giving them detailed information on their stock reports.

Commenting on the agreement, Mr Nidal Eses, CEO of Nuqul Group, said: "We are very proud of the inauguration of our latest venture and the implementation of this unique concept in collaboration with Aramex, the leading express and logistics specialist with extensive expertise in this field. This project was built on in-depth market research to effectively identify and answer the needs of the Jordanian market and offer the latest office supply solutions to maximize work efficiency and increase productivity and sales. We have also been careful to offer these services at suitable prices in line with our dedication to playing a positive role in supporting businesses, particularly in the face of the current economic challenges, our agreement with Aramex has been formulated to complement the success of our business model."[8]

Participants in the Business Buying Process

Buying center

All the individuals and units that play a role in the purchase decision-making process.

Who does the buying of the trillions of dollars' worth of goods and services needed by business organizations? The decision-making unit of a buying organization is called its **buying center**—all the individuals and units that play a role in the business purchase decision-making process. This group includes the actual users of the product or service, those who make the buying decision, those who influence the buying decision, those who do the actual buying, and those who control buying information.

The buying center includes all members of the organization who play any of five roles in the purchase decision process.[9]

Users
Members of the buying organization who will actually use the purchased product or service.

Influencers
People in an organization's buying center who affect the buying decision; they often help define specifications and also provide information for evaluating alternatives.

Buyers
The people in the organization's buying center who make an actual purchase.

Deciders
People in the organization's buying center who have formal or informal power to select or approve the final suppliers.

Gatekeepers
People in the organization's buying center who control the flow of information to others.

- **Users** are members of the organization who will use the product or service. In many cases, users initiate the buying proposal and help define product specifications.
- **Influencers** often help define specifications and also provide information for evaluating alternatives. Technical personnel are particularly important influencers.
- **Buyers** have formal authority to select the supplier and arrange terms of purchase. Buyers may help shape product specifications, but their major role is in selecting vendors and negotiating. In more complex purchases, buyers might include high-level officers participating in the negotiations.
- **Deciders** have formal or informal power to select or approve the final suppliers. In routine buying, the buyers are often the deciders, or at least the approvers.
- **Gatekeepers** control the flow of information to others. For example, purchasing agents often have authority to prevent salespersons from seeing users or deciders. Other gatekeepers include technical personnel and even personal secretaries.

The buying center is not a fixed and formally identified unit within the buying organization. It is a set of buying roles assumed by different people for different purchases. Within the organization, the size and makeup of the buying center will vary for different products and for different buying situations. For some routine purchases, one person—say, a purchasing agent—may assume all the buying center roles and serve as the only person involved in the buying decision. For more complex purchases, the buying center may include 20 or 30 people from different levels and departments in the organization.

The buying center concept presents a major marketing challenge. The business marketer must learn who participates in the decision, each participant's relative influence, and what evaluation criteria each decision participant uses. This can be difficult. Says one supplier of health care information technology solutions to large hospitals:

The buying center can vary in size depending on the complexity of the purchase.

You have to understand what [doors] to knock on. A lot of salespeople give up on working with hospitals because they don't understand how big the business is, and you have a lot of people you have to deal with. You also have to understand that you're selling to committees, which means 10 or 20 people have to make a decision. For them to make a decision they have to have lots of meetings, and sales can [take] anywhere from six months to two years.[10]

The buying center usually includes some obvious participants who are involved formally in the buying decision. For example, the decision to buy a corporate jet will probably involve the company's CEO, chief pilot, a purchasing agent, some legal staff, a member of top management, and others formally charged with the buying decision. It may also involve less obvious, informal participants, some of whom may actually make or strongly affect the buying decision. Sometimes, even the people in the buying center are not aware of all the buying participants. For example, the decision about which corporate jet to buy may actually be made by a corporate board member who has an interest in flying and who knows a lot about aircraft. This board member may work behind the scenes to sway the decision. Many business buying decisions result from the complex interactions of ever-changing buying center participants.

Major Influences on Business Buyers

Business buyers are subject to many influences when they make their buying decisions. Some marketers assume that the major influences are economic. They think buyers will favor the supplier who offers the lowest price or the best product or the most service. They concentrate on offering strong economic benefits to buyers. However, business buyers actually respond to both economic and personal factors. Far from being cold, calculating, and impersonal, business buyers are human and social as well. They react to both reason and emotion.

Today, most business-to-business marketers recognize that emotion plays an important role in business buying decisions. When suppliers' offers are very similar, business buyers have little basis for strictly rational choice. Because they can meet organizational goals with any supplier, buyers can allow personal factors to play a larger role in their decisions. However, when competing products differ greatly, business buyers are more accountable for their choices and tend to pay more attention to economic factors. 🔳 **Figure 6.2** lists various groups of influences on business buyers—environmental, organizational, interpersonal, and individual.[11]

Environmental Factors

Business buyers are heavily influenced by factors in the current and expected *economic environment*, such as the level of primary demand, the economic outlook, and the cost of money. Another environmental factor is *shortages* in key materials. Many companies now are more willing to buy and hold larger inventories of scarce materials to ensure adequate supply. Business buyers also are affected by technological, political, and competitive developments in the environment. Finally, *culture and customs* can strongly influence business buyer reactions to the marketer's behavior and strategies, especially in the international marketing environment (see **Real Marketing 6.2**). The business buyer must watch these factors, determine how they will affect the buyer, and try to turn these challenges into opportunities.

Organizational Factors

Each buying organization has its own objectives, policies, procedures, structure, and systems, and the business marketer must understand these factors well. Questions such as these arise: How many people are involved in the buying decision? Who are they? What are their evaluative criteria? What are the company's policies and limits on its buyers?

🔳 **FIGURE | 6.2**

Major Influences on Business Buyer Behavior

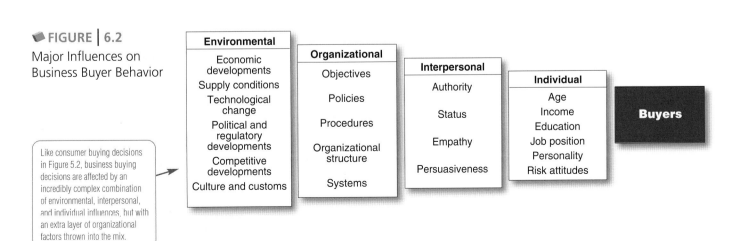

Like consumer buying decisions in Figure 5.2, business buying decisions are affected by an incredibly complex combination of environmental, interpersonal, and individual influences, but with an extra layer of organizational factors thrown into the mix.

Environmental	Organizational	Interpersonal	Individual	
Economic developments	Objectives	Authority	Age	**Buyers**
Supply conditions	Policies	Status	Income	
Technological change	Procedures	Empathy	Education	
Political and regulatory developments	Organizational structure	Persuasiveness	Job position	
Competitive developments	Systems		Personality	
Culture and customs			Risk attitudes	

Interpersonal Factors

The buying center usually includes many participants who influence each other, so *interpersonal factors* also influence the business buying process. However, it is often difficult to assess such interpersonal factors and group dynamics. Buying center participants do not wear tags that label them as 'key decision maker' or 'not influential.' Nor do buying center participants with the highest rank always have the most influence. Participants may influence the buying decision because they control rewards and punishments, are well liked, have special expertise, or have a special relationship with other important participants. Interpersonal factors are often very subtle. Whenever possible, business marketers must try to understand these factors and design strategies that take them into account.

Individual Factors

Each participant in the business buying decision process brings in personal motives, perceptions, and preferences. These individual factors are affected by personal characteristics such as age, income, education, professional identification, personality, and attitudes toward risk. Also, buyers have different buying styles. Some may be technical types who make in-depth analyses of competitive proposals before choosing a supplier. Other buyers may be intuitive negotiators who are good at pitting the sellers against one another for the best deal.

> **Author Comment** | A business organisation can go through all the eight stages of the buying process, or skip some satges, based on the nature of the procurement.

The Business Buying Process (pp 158–162)

Figure 6.3 lists the eight stages of the business buying process.[12] Buyers who face a new-task buying situation usually go through all stages of the buying process. Buyers making modified or straight rebuys may skip some of the stages. We will examine these steps for the typical new-task buying situation.

Problem Recognition

Problem recognition
The first stage of the business buying process in which someone in the company recognizes a problem or need that can be met by acquiring a good or a service.

The buying process begins when someone in the company recognizes a problem or need that can be met by acquiring a specific product or service. **Problem recognition** can result from internal or external stimuli. Internally, the company may decide to launch a new product that requires new production equipment and materials. Or a machine may break down and need new parts. Perhaps a purchasing manager is unhappy with a current supplier's product quality, service, or prices. Externally, the buyer may get some new ideas at a trade show, see an ad, or receive a call from a salesperson who offers a better product or a lower price.

In fact, in their advertising, business marketers often alert customers to potential problems and then show how their products provide solutions. For example, a Sharp ad notes that a multifunction printer can present data security problems and asks "Is your MFP a portal for identity theft?" The solution? Sharp's data security kits "help prevent sensitive information from falling into the wrong hands."

> Buyers facing new, complex buying decisions usually go through all of these stages. Those making rebuys often skip some of the stages. Either way, the business buying process is usually much more complicated than this simple flow diagram suggests.

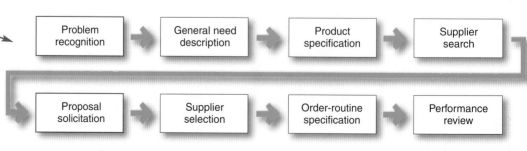

FIGURE | 6.3 Stages of the Business Buying Process

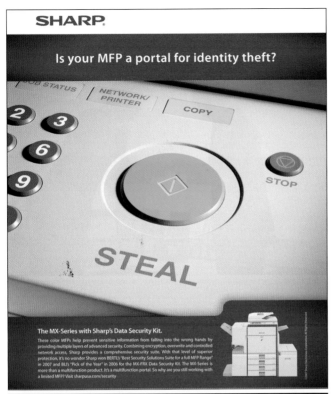

Problem recognition: Sharp uses ads like this one to alert customers to potential problems and then provide solutions.

General Need Description

Having recognized a need, the buyer next prepares a **general need description** that describes the characteristics and quantity of the needed item. For standard items, this process presents few problems. For complex items, however, the buyer may need to work with others—engineers, users, consultants—to define the item. The team may want to rank the importance of reliability, durability, price, and other attributes desired in the item. In this phase, the alert business marketer can help the buyers define their needs and provide information about the value of different product characteristics.

Product Specification

The buying organization next develops the item's technical **product specifications**, often with the help of a value analysis engineering team. *Product value analysis* is an approach to cost reduction in which components are studied carefully to determine if they can be redesigned, standardized, or made by less costly methods of production. The team decides on the best product characteristics and specifies them accordingly. Sellers, too, can use value analysis as a tool to help secure a new account. By showing buyers a better way to make an object, outside sellers can turn straight rebuy situations into new-task situations that give them a chance to obtain new business.

Supplier Search

The buyer now conducts a **supplier search** to find the best vendors. The buyer can compile a small list of qualified suppliers by reviewing trade directories, doing computer searches, or phoning other companies for recommendations. Today, more and more companies are turning to the Internet to find suppliers. For marketers, this has leveled the playing field—the Internet gives smaller suppliers many of the same advantages as larger competitors.

The newer the buying task, and the more complex and costly the item, the greater the amount of time the buyer will spend searching for suppliers. The supplier's task is to get listed in major directories and build a good reputation in the marketplace. Salespeople should watch for companies in the process of searching for suppliers and make certain that their firm is considered.

Proposal Solicitation

In the **proposal solicitation** stage of the business buying process, the buyer invites qualified suppliers to submit proposals. In response, some suppliers will send only a catalog or a salesperson. However, when the item is complex or expensive, the buyer will usually require detailed written proposals or formal presentations from each potential supplier.

Business marketers must be skilled in researching, writing, and presenting proposals in response to buyer proposal solicitations. Proposals should be marketing documents, not just technical documents. Presentations should inspire confidence and should make the marketer's company stand out from the competition.

Supplier Selection

The members of the buying center now review the proposals and select a supplier or suppliers. During **supplier selection**, the buying center often will draw up a list of the desired supplier attributes and their relative importance. Such attributes include product and service quality, reputation, on-time delivery, ethical corporate behavior,

General need description
The stage in the business buying process in which the company describes the general characteristics and quantity of a needed item.

Product specification
The stage of the business buying process in which the buying organization decides on and specifies the best technical product characteristics for a needed item.

Supplier search
The stage of the business buying process in which the buyer tries to find the best vendors.

Proposal solicitation
The stage of the business buying process in which the buyer invites qualified suppliers to submit proposals.

Supplier selection
The stage of the business buying process in which the buyer reviews proposals and selects a supplier or suppliers.

Real Marketing 6.2

International

Marketing Manners:

When in Rome, Do as the Romans Do

Picture this: Consolidated Amalgamation, Inc. thinks it's time that the rest of the world enjoyed the same fine products it has offered American consumers for two generations. It dispatches Vice President Harry E. Slicksmile to Europe, the Arab world, Africa, and Asia to explore the territory. Mr Slicksmile stops first in London, where he makes short work of some bankers—he rings them up on the phone. He handles Parisians with similar ease: After securing a table at La Tour d'Argent, he greets his luncheon guest, the director of an industrial engineering firm, with the words, "Just call me Harry, Jacques."

In Germany, Mr Slicksmile is busy. Whisking through a lavish, state-of-the-art multimedia marketing presentation on his Toshiba tablet laptop, he shows that he *knows* how to make a buck. Heading on to Milan, Harry strikes up a conversation with the Japanese businessman sitting next to him

Companies must help their managers understand international customers and customs. For example, Japanese people revere the business card as an extension of self—they do not hand it out to people, they present it.

on the plane. He flips his card onto the guy's tray and, when the two say goodbye, shakes hands warmly and clasps the man's right arm. Later, for his appointment with the owner of an Italian packaging design firm, our hero wears his comfy corduroy sports coat, khaki pants, and Topsiders. Everybody knows Italians are zany and laid back.

Mr Slicksmile next swings through Saudi Arabia, where he coolly presents a potential client with a multimillion-dollar proposal in a classy pigskin binder. At his next stop in Beijing, China, he talks business over lunch

with a group of Chinese executives. After completing the meal, he drops his chopsticks into his bowl of rice and presents each guest with an elegant Tiffany clock as a reminder of his visit. Then, at his final junket in Phuket, Thailand, Mr Slicksmile wastes no time diving into his business proposal before treating his Thai clients to a first-class lunch.

A great tour, sure to generate a pile of orders, right? Wrong. Six months later, Consolidated Amalgamation has nothing to show for the trip but a stack of bills. Abroad, they weren't wild about Harry.

honest communication, and competitive prices. The members of the buying center will rate suppliers against these attributes and identify the best suppliers.

Buyers may attempt to negotiate with preferred suppliers for better prices and terms before making the final selections. In the end, they may select a single supplier or a few suppliers. Many buyers prefer multiple sources of supplies to avoid being totally dependent on one supplier and to allow comparisons of prices and performance of several suppliers over time. Today's supplier development managers want to develop a full network of supplier-partners that can help the company bring more value to its customers.

Order-Routine Specification

Order-routine specification
The stage of the business buying process in which the buyer writes the final order with the chosen supplier(s), listing the technical specifications, quantity needed, expected time of delivery, return policies, and warranties.

The buyer now prepares an **order-routine specification**. It includes the final order with the chosen supplier or suppliers and lists items such as technical specifications, quantity needed, expected time of delivery, return policies, and warranties. In the case of maintenance, repair, and operating items, buyers may use blanket contracts rather than periodic purchase orders. A blanket contract creates a long-term relationship in which the supplier promises to resupply the buyer as needed at agreed prices for a set time period.

Many large buyers now practice *vendor-managed inventory*, in which they turn over ordering and inventory responsibilities to their suppliers. Under such systems, buyers share sales and inventory information directly with key suppliers. The suppliers then monitor inventories and replenish stock automatically as needed. For example, most major

This hypothetical case has been exaggerated for emphasis. But experts say success in international business has a lot to do with knowing the territory and its people. By learning English and extending themselves in other ways, the world's business leaders have met Americans more than halfway. In contrast, Americans too often do little except assume that others will march to their music. "We want things to be 'American' when we travel. Fast. Convenient. Easy. So we become 'ugly Americans' by demanding that others change," says one American world trade expert. "I think more business would be done if we tried harder."

Poor Harry tried, all right, but in all the wrong ways. The British do not, as a rule, make deals over the phone as much as Americans do. It's not so much a 'cultural' difference as a difference in approach. A proper Frenchman neither likes instant familiarity—questions about family, church, or alma mater—nor refers to strangers by their first names. "That poor fellow, Jacques, probably wouldn't show anything, but he'd recoil. He'd *not* be pleased," explains an expert on French business practices. "It's considered poor taste," he continues. "Even after months of business dealings, I'd wait for him or her to make the invitation [to use first names].... You are always right, in Europe, to say 'Mister.'"

Harry's flashy presentation would likely have been a flop with the Germans, who dislike overstatement and showiness. And when Harry grabbed his new Japanese acquaintance by the arm, the executive probably considered him disrespectful and presumptuous. Japan, like many Asian countries, has a 'no-contact culture' in which even shaking hands is a strange experience. Harry made matters worse by tossing his business card. Japanese people revere the business card as an extension of self and as an indicator of rank. They do not *hand* it to people, they *present* it—with both hands. In addition, the Japanese are sticklers about rank. Unlike Americans, they don't heap praise on subordinates in a room; they will praise only the highest-ranking official present.

Hapless Harry also goofed when he assumed that Italians are like Hollywood's stereotypes of them. The flair for design and style that has characterized Italian culture for centuries is embodied in the businesspeople of Milan and Rome. They dress beautifully and admire flair, but they dislike garishness or impropriety in others' attire.

To the Saudi Arabians, the pigskin binder would have been considered vile. An American salesman who really did present such a binder was unceremoniously tossed out and his company was blacklisted from working with Saudi businesses. In China, Harry's casually dropping his chopsticks could have been misinterpreted as an act of aggression. Stabbing chopsticks into a bowl of rice and leaving them signifies death to the Chinese. The clocks Harry offered as gifts might have confirmed such dark intentions. To 'give a clock' in Chinese sounds the same as 'seeing someone off to his end.' Finally, not surprisingly, Harry failed in his Phuket junket—in Thailand, it's off limits to speak about business matters until after the meal is served and eaten.

Thus, to compete successfully in global markets, or even to deal effectively with international firms in their home markets, companies must help their managers to understand the needs, customs, and cultures of international business buyers. "When doing business in a foreign country and a foreign culture—particularly a non-Western culture—assume nothing," advises an international business specialist. "Take nothing for granted. Turn every stone. Ask every question. Dig into every detail. Because cultures really are different, and those differences can have a major impact." So the old advice is still good advice: When in Rome, do as the Romans do.

Sources: Portions adapted from Susan Harte, "When in Rome, You Should Learn to Do What the Romans Do," *Atlanta Journal-Constitution*, January 22, 1990, pp. D1, D6. Additional information and examples from James K. Sebenius, "The Hidden Challenge of Cross-Border Negotiatons," *Harvard Business Review*, March 2002, pp. 76–85; Gary Stroller, "Doing Business Abroad? Simple Faux Pas Can Sink You," *USA Today*, August 24, 2007, p. 1B; and Janette S. Martin and Lillian H. Chaney, *Global Business Etiquette: A Guide to International Communication and Customs* (Westport, CT: Greenwood Press, 2008); and information accessed at www.executiveplanet.com, December 2008.

suppliers to large retailers such as Wal-Mart, Worsleys—the only intermerchant paper trader in the UK—Baxter International, and YCH—a supply-chains solutions company in Singapore—assume vendor-managed inventory responsibilities.

Performance Review

In this stage, the buyer reviews supplier performance. The buyer may contact users and ask them to rate their satisfaction. The **performance review** may lead the buyer to continue, modify, or drop the arrangement. The seller's job is to monitor the same factors used by the buyer to make sure that the seller is giving the expected satisfaction.

Performance review
The stage of the business buying process in which the buyer assesses the performance of the supplier and decides to continue, modify, or drop the arrangement.

The eight-stage buying-process model provides a simple view of the business buying as it might occur in a new-task buying situation. The actual process is usually much more complex. In the modified rebuy or straight rebuy situation, some of these stages would be compressed or bypassed. Each organization buys in its own way, and each buying situation has unique requirements.

Different buying center participants may be involved at different stages of the process. Although certain buying-process steps usually do occur, buyers do not always follow them in the same order, and they may add other steps. Often, buyers will repeat certain stages of the process. Finally, a customer relationship might involve many different types of purchases ongoing at a given time, all in different stages of the buying process. The seller must manage the total customer relationship, not just individual purchases.

Author Comment | More and more business buyers are adopting e-procurement due to higher efficiency.

E-Procurement: Buying on The Internet (pp 166–167)

E-procurement

Purchasing through electronic connections between buyers and sellers—usually online.

Advances in information technology have changed the face of the business-to-business marketing process. Electronic purchasing, often called **e-procurement**, has grown rapidly in recent years. Virtually unknown less than a decade ago, online purchasing is standard procedure for most companies today. E-procurement gives buyers access to new suppliers, lowers purchasing costs, and hastens order processing and delivery. In turn, business marketers can connect with customers online to share marketing information, sell products and services, provide customer support services, and maintain ongoing customer relationships.

Companies can do e-procurement in any of several ways. They can conduct *reverse auctions*, in which they put their purchasing requests online and invite suppliers to bid for the business. Or they can engage in online *trading exchanges,* through which companies work collectively to facilitate the trading process. For example, Exostar is an online trading exchange that connects buyers and sellers in the aerospace and defense industry. Its goal is to improve trading efficiency and reduce costs among industry trading partners. Initially a collaboration between five leading aerospace and defense companies—BAE Systems, Rolls-Royce, Boeing, Lockheed Martin, and Raytheon—Exostar has now connected more than 300 procurement systems and 40,000 trading partners in 20 countries around the world.

Companies also can conduct e-procurement by setting up their own *company buying sites.* For example, General Electric operates a company trading site on which it posts its buying needs and invites bids, negotiates terms, and places orders. Or companies can create *extranet links* with key suppliers. For instance, they can create direct procurement accounts with suppliers such as Worsleys, through which company buyers can purchase equipment, materials, and supplies directly.

Business-to-business marketers can help customers who wish to purchase online by creating well-designed, easy-to-use websites. For example, *BtoB* magazine rated the site of Sun Microsystems—a market leader in network computing hardware, software, and services—as one of its "10 great B-to-B websites."[13]

A few years ago, Sun Microsystems completely redesigned its website. It was most interested in finding a better way to present deep information on its thousands of complex server, storage, and software products and services while also giving the site a more humanistic view. Sun came up with a tab-driven menu design that puts an enormous amount of information within only a few clicks of customers' computers. Action-oriented menu labels—such as Evaluate, Get, Use, and Maintain—leave nothing to the imagination and make navigation a snap. Beyond product pictures and specifications, the site provides video walk-throughs of products, along with success stories of how other customers have benefited from doing business with Sun.

Customers can even create personalized MySun portals. "We provide you with a customized experience," says Sun's VP-Sun Web Experience. "Maybe you've downloaded software. Based on that download, you'll see a filtered blog, training classes that are available, and a link to unreleased code you can try out. It's integrated support tailored to the type of Sun products

Online buying: This Sun Microsystems site helps customers who want to purchase online by providing deep information on its thousands of complex products and services. Users who still need help can take advantage of the site's interactive features to request an immediate phone call, an email, or a live online chat with a Sun representative.

you use." Users who still need help can take advantage of the site's interactive features to request an immediate phone call, an email, or a live online chat in French, German, English, or Spanish with a Sun representative.

Business-to-business e-procurement yields many benefits. First, it shaves transaction costs and results in more efficient purchasing for both buyers and suppliers. A web-powered purchasing program eliminates the paperwork associated with traditional requisition and ordering procedures and helps an organization keep better track of all purchases.

E-procurement reduces the time between order and delivery. Time savings are particularly dramatic for companies with many overseas suppliers. Adaptec, a leading supplier of computer storage, used an extranet to tie all of its Taiwanese chip suppliers together in a kind of virtual family. Now messages from Adaptec flow in seconds from its headquarters to its Asian partners, and Adaptec has reduced the time between the order and delivery of its chips from as long as 16 weeks to just 55 days—the same turnaround time for companies that build their own chips.

Finally, beyond the cost and time savings, e-procurement frees purchasing people to focus on more strategic issues. For many purchasing professionals, going online means reducing drudgery and paperwork and spending more time managing inventory and working creatively with suppliers. "That is the key," says an HP purchasing executive. "You can now focus people on value-added activities. Procurement professionals can now find different sources and work with suppliers to reduce costs and to develop new products."[14]

The rapidly expanding use of e-procurement, however, also presents some problems. For example, at the same time that the web makes it possible for suppliers and customers to share business data and even collaborate on product design, it can also erode decades-old customer–supplier relationships. Many buyers now use the power of the web to pit suppliers against one another and to search out better deals, products, and turnaround times on a purchase-by-purchase basis.

E-procurement can also create potential security disasters. Although email and home-banking transactions can be protected through basic encryption, the secure environment that businesses need to carry out confidential interactions is sometimes still lacking. Companies are spending millions for research on defensive strategies to keep hackers at bay. Cisco Systems, for example, specifies the types of routers, firewalls, and security procedures that its partners must use to safeguard extranet connections. In fact, the company goes even further—it sends its own security engineers to examine a partner's defenses and holds the partner liable for any security breach that originates from its computers.

> **Author Comment** | These two nonbusiness organizational markets provide attractive opportunities for many companies. Because of their unique nature, we give them special attention here.

Institutional and Government Markets (pp 167–170)

So far, our discussion of organizational buying has focused largely on the buying behavior of business buyers. Much of this discussion also applies to the buying practices of institutional and government organizations. However, these two nonbusiness markets have additional characteristics and needs. In this final section, we address the special features of institutional and government markets.

Institutional Markets

Institutional market

Schools, hospitals, nursing homes, prisons, and other institutions that provide goods and services to people in their care.

The **institutional market** consists of schools, hospitals, nursing homes, prisons, and other institutions that provide goods and services to people in their care. Institutions differ from one another in their sponsors and in their objectives. For example, there are general hospitals that cater to all types of people. By contrast, there are hospitals that provide free specialized health care for children, whereas government-run military veterans' hospitals located around the world provide special services to veterans.[15] Each institution has different buying needs and resources.

Institutional markets can be huge. As an example, consider the massive and expanding Saudi health insurance market:

Although the price of oil, which contributes significantly to the country's GDP, has been fluctuating between high and low, the Saudi government is continuing to invest heavily in health infrastructure development, which in 2009, was behind only education and manpower in terms of budget allocation for capital expenditure.

In 2007, the Saudi government established the National Company for Unified Purchase of Medicines and Medical Appliances, to act as the sole supplier of medicines and medical appliances to government health institutions. The company was set up to bring down the prices of medical devices and pharmaceuticals by preventing overcharging.

The Saudi Food and Drug Authority (SFDA) was given the task of developing and enforcing a regulatory system for medical devices. This included establishing licensing procedures for manufacturers and suppliers. In what is a first step in developing a regulatory framework for medical devices, the SFDA in 2007 started the Medical Devices National Registry (MDNR), which is a voluntary web-based project involving the registration of manufacturers, agents, and suppliers in the country.

The government is working on expanding the health insurance sector, which in 2009 was valued at around SR5 billion (US$1.3 billion). This is expected to increase by a further SR2 billion (US$533 million) in the short term with new regulations introduced in January 2009 that will further expand the insurance scheme to Saudi nationals working in small and medium enterprises in the private sector. The large private sector companies already provide health insurance for their employees.[16]

Many institutional markets are characterized by low budgets and 'customers' with restricted choices. For example, hospital patients have little choice but to eat whatever food the hospital supplies. A hospital purchasing agent has to decide on the quality of food to buy for patients. Because the food is provided as a part of a total service package, the buying objective is not profit. Nor is strict cost minimization the goal—patients receiving poor-quality food will complain to others and damage the hospital's reputation. Thus, the hospital purchasing agent must search for institutional food vendors whose quality meets or exceeds a certain minimum standard and whose prices are low.

Many marketers set up separate divisions to meet the special characteristics and needs of institutional buyers. For example, Kellogg's Food Away from Home business unit produces, packages, prices, and markets its broad assortment of cereals, cookies, snacks, and other products to better serve the specific food service requirements of hospitals, colleges, the military, and other institutional markets.[17]

Government Markets

Government market
Governmental units—national, regional, and local—that purchase or rent goods and services for carrying out the main functions of government.

The **government market** offers large opportunities for many companies, both big and small. In most countries, government organizations are major buyers of goods and services. Government buying and business buying are similar in many ways. But there are also differences that must be understood by companies that wish to sell products and services to governments. To succeed in the government market, sellers must locate key decision makers, identify the factors that affect buyer behavior, and understand the buying decision process.

Government organizations typically require suppliers to submit bids, and normally they award the contract to the lowest bidder. In some cases, the government unit will make allowances for the supplier's superior quality or reputation for completing contracts on time. Governments will also buy on a negotiated contract basis, primarily in the case of complex projects involving major R&D costs and risks, and in cases where there is little competition.

Government organizations tend to favor domestic suppliers over foreign suppliers. Saudi Arabia published its revised government procurement procedures in August 2006, and a number of royal decrees apply to government procurement. A 1983 decree states that contractors must subcontract 30 percent of the value of any government contract, including support services, to companies that are majority-owned by Saudi nationals. The tender regulations give preference to products of Saudi origin, provided they satisfy the procurement requirements. Saudi Arabia also gives priority to GCC products, through giving them a 10 percent price preference over products from foreign suppliers.

Howerer, most saudi contracts are negotiated outside these regulations on a case-by-case basis. Foreign suppliers that are successful in gaining government contracts must establish a training program for Saudi nationals. The government may favor joint venture companies which include a Saudi partner, and encourage all suppliers to use Saudi goods and services. Large military projects may also be based on a further requirement to offset particular costs.

In addition, the Saudi Council of Ministers in 2003 moved to create increased transparency in government procurement. It stated that information must be made public on matters including the parties involved, dates, financial values, a brief description, the duration and place of execution, and point of contact information.[18]

Like consumer and business buyers, government buyers are affected by environmental, organizational, interpersonal, and individual factors. One unique thing about government buying is that it is carefully watched by outside publics interested in how the government spends taxpayers' money. Because their spending decisions are subject to public review, government organizations require considerable paperwork from suppliers, who often complain about excessive paperwork, bureaucracy, regulations, decision-making delays, and frequent shifts in procurement personnel.

Given all the red tape, why would any firm want to do business with the government? The reasons are quite simple: Purchases by governments are huge. For example, the Saudi government's spending on e-transactions is currently around Dh 3.6 billion (US$1 billion). That country's Knowledge Economy City (KEC) in Medina is an SR 30 billion (US$8 billion) development by the Saudi General Investment Authority. It covers 4.8 million square meters and is expected to create 20,000 new jobs in knowledge-based industries. The government sector is by far the largest purchaser of IT products and services in the country. With an annual market of US$5.5 billion the sector is one of the largest and fastest growing in the region.[19]

Gradually governments are providing would-be suppliers with detailed guides describing how to sell to the government in Arab countries. For example, the Jordanian Ministry of Finance has the following website through which suppliers can submit tenders and bids for government contracts: www.gsd.gov.jo.

Still, suppliers have to master the system and find ways to cut through the red tape, especially for large government purchases. Consider Envisage Technologies in the United States, a small software development company that specializes in Internet-based training applications and human resource management platforms. All of its contracts fall in the government sector; 65 percent are with the government. Envisage uses a website to gain access to smaller procurements, often receiving responses within 14 days. However, it puts the most work into seeking large, highly coveted contracts. A comprehensive bid proposal for one of these contracts can easily run from 600 to 700 pages because of paperwork requirements. And the company's president estimates that to prepare a single bid proposal the firm has spent as many as 5,000 man-hours over the course of a few years.[20]

Noneconomic criteria also play a growing role in government buying. Government buyers are asked to favor depressed business firms and areas; small business firms; minority-owned firms; and business firms that avoid race, gender, or age discrimination. Sellers need to keep these factors in mind when deciding to seek government business.

Many companies that sell to the government have not been very marketing oriented for a number of reasons. Total government spending is determined by elected officials rather than by any marketing effort to develop this market. Government buying has emphasized price, making suppliers invest their effort in technology to bring costs down. When the product's characteristics are specified carefully, product differentiation is not a marketing factor. Nor do advertising or personal selling matter much in winning bids on an open-bid basis.

Some companies, however, have established separate government marketing departments. These companies anticipate government needs and projects, participate in the product specification phase, gather competitive intelligence, prepare bids carefully, and produce stronger communications to describe and enhance their companies' reputations.

Other companies have set up customized marketing programs for government buyers. For example, Dell has specific business units tailored to meet the needs of national, regional, and local government buyers. Dell offers its customers tailor-made Premier Dell. com web pages that include special pricing, online purchasing, and service and support for each government entity.

During the past decade, governments are gradually moving their purchases online. For example, Dubai Municipality in 2009 was awarded the Best Middle East e-Government Portal award during the 10th Middle East Information and Communication Technology Excellence Awards. The award recognized its combined e-services, provided by various government organizations, which allow businesses and citizens to gain access to all government services in one place (www.dm.gov.ae). It recognized Dubai Municipality's e-Government portal as offering an example of best practice for regional e-Government organizations. The e-Government initiative was started in 1999, and has been a pioneer in providing e-services in both Dubai and the surrounding region. A customer satisfaction survey, in 2004, reported that 78 percent of the customers considered the Municipality's e-services to be 'excellent.'[21]

Such sites allow authorized agencies to buy everything from office supplies, food, and information technology equipment to construction services through online purchasing. Online, governments not only sell stocked merchandise through their websites but also create direct links between buyers and contract suppliers. Internet systems promise to eliminate much of the hassle sometimes found in dealing with government purchasing.[22]

REVIEWING Objectives AND KEY Terms

Business markets and consumer markets are alike in some key ways. For example, both include people in buying roles who make purchase decisions to satisfy needs. But business markets also differ in many ways from consumer markets. For one thing, the business market is very large, far larger than the consumer market. Within Saudi Arabia alone, the business market includes organizations that annually purchase billions of dollars' worth of goods and services.

OBJECTIVE 1 Define the business market and explain how business markets differ from consumer markets.
(pp 154–158)

The *business market* comprises all organizations that buy goods and services for use in the production of other products and services or for the purpose of reselling or renting them to others at a profit. Compared with consumer markets, business markets usually have fewer, larger buyers who are more geographically concentrated. Business demand is derived demand, and the business buying decision usually involves more, and more, professional buyers.

OBJECTIVE 2 Identify the major factors that influence business buyer behavior. (pp 158–162)

Business buyers make decisions that vary with the three types of *buying situations:* straight rebuys, modified rebuys, and new tasks. The decision-making unit of a buying organization—the *buying center*—can consist of many different persons playing many different roles. The business marketer needs to know the following: Who are the major buying center participants? In what decisions do they exercise influence and to what degree? What evaluation criteria does each decision participant use? The business marketer also needs to understand the major environmental, organizational, interpersonal, and individual influences on the buying process.

OBJECTIVE 3 List and define the steps in the business buying decision process. (pp 162–167)

The *business buying decision process* itself can be quite involved, with eight basic stages: problem recognition, general need description, product specification, supplier search, proposal solicitation, supplier selection, order-routine specification, and performance review. Buyers who face a new-task buying situation usually go through all stages of the buying process. Buyers making modified or straight rebuys may skip some of the stages. Companies must manage the overall customer relationship, which often includes many different buying decisions in various stages of the buying decision process.

Recent advances in information technology have given birth to e-procurement, by which business buyers are purchasing all kinds of products and services online. The Internet gives business buyers access to new suppliers, lowers purchasing costs, and hastens order processing and delivery. However, e-procurement can also erode customer–supplier relationships and create potential security problems. Still, business marketers are increasingly connecting with customers online to share marketing information, sell products and services, provide customer support services, and maintain ongoing customer relationships.

OBJECTIVE 4 Compare the institutional and government markets and explain how institutional and government buyers make their buying decisions. (pp 167–170)

The *institutional market* comprises schools, hospitals, prisons, and other institutions that provide goods and services to people in their care. These markets are characterized by low budgets and captive patrons. The *government market,* which is vast, consists of government units—national, regional, and local—that purchase or rent goods and services for carrying out the main functions of government.

Government buyers purchase products and services for defense, education, public welfare, and other public needs. Government buying practices are highly specialized and specified, with open bidding or negotiated contracts characterizing most of the buying.

Government buyers operate under the watchful eye of government auditors, parliament, Shura councils, and private watchdog groups. Hence, they tend to require more forms and signatures, and to respond more slowly and deliberately when placing orders.

KEY Terms

OBJECTIVE 1

Business buyer behavior (p 153)
Business buying process (p 153)
Derived demand (p 154)
Supplier development (p 156)

OBJECTIVE 2

Straight rebuy (p 158)
Modified rebuy (p 159)
New task (p 159)
Systems selling (solutions selling) (p 159)

Buying center (p 159)
Users (p 160)
Influencers (p 160)
Buyers (p 160)
Deciders (p 160)
Gatekeepers (p 160)

OBJECTIVE 3

Problem recognition (p 162)
General need description (p 163)
Product specification (p 163)

Supplier search (p 163)
Proposal solicitation (p 163)
Supplier selection (p 163)
Order-routine specification (p 164)
Performance review (p 165)
E-procurement (p 166)

OBJECTIVE 4

Institutional market (p 167)
Government market (p 168)

DISCUSSING & APPLYING THE Concepts

Discussing the Concepts

1. Compare and contrast business and consumer markets.

2. Discuss several ways in which a straight rebuy differs from a new-task situation.

3. In a buying center purchasing process, which buying center participant is most likely to make each of the following statements?
   - "This bonding agent better be good, because I have to put this product together."
   - "I specified this bonding agent on another job, and it worked for them."
   - "Without an appointment, no sales rep gets in to see Ms Johnson."
   - "Okay, it's a deal—we'll buy it."
   - "I'll place the order first thing tomorrow."

4. List the major influences on business buyer behavior. Why is it important for the business-to-business marketer to understand these major influences?

5. Name and briefly describe the stages of the business buying process.

6. How do the institutional and government markets differ from business markets?

Applying the Concepts

1. Business buying occurs worldwide, so marketers need to be aware of cultural factors influencing business customers. In a small group, select a country and develop a multimedia presentation on proper business etiquette and manners, including appropriate appearance, behavior, and communication. Include a map showing the location of the country as well as a description of the country in terms of demographics, culture, and its economic history.

2. Interview a business person to learn how purchases are made in his or her organization. Ask this person to describe a straight rebuy, a modified rebuy, and a new-task buying situation that took place recently or of which he or she is aware (define them if necessary). Did the buying process differ based on the type of product or purchase situation? Ask the business person to explain the role he or she played in a recent purchase and to discuss the factors that influenced the decision. Write a brief report of your interview by applying the concepts you learned in this chapter regarding business buyer behavior.

3. Government procurement (buying goods and services for the government) is big business. It is a massive part of international trade, given the considerable size of the procurement market (often 10–15 percent of the GDP of countries), and the process benefits domestic and foreign stakeholders in terms of increased competition. The process is also prone to corruption, however. The effort of the World Trade Organization (WTO) to create transparent and non-discriminatory procurement procedures is generally considered to be the best tool to achieve 'value for money' because it optimizes competition among suppliers. Go to the WTO's website (www.wto.org) and read about government procurement. Then write a brief report on three major areas of the WTO's work on this issue.

FOCUS ON Technology

In today's competitive marketplace, many businesses strive to cut costs. One solution is for business buyers to drive down supplier prices. Online reverse auctions allow businesses to do this more efficiently and effectively. Reverse auctions, often called e-auctions, are conducted online with the buyer and seller roles reversed. Buyers announce auctions months in advance and vendors qualify to participate. During the live online auction, suppliers have a short time in which to bid down their prices anonymously. Such auctions started in the aerospace and automotive industries to reduce costs on commodity parts but have now spread to other industries. Buyers don't always go with the lowest bidder, but the process puts pressure on suppliers to reduce prices and in turn reduce their own costs to maintain profitability. Although heralded as a best practices tool by some, reverse auctions are loathed by others. Some

suppliers, bitten by the reverse auctions bug of their customers, turn around and reduce costs by requiring such auctions for their own suppliers.

1. Discuss at least three pros and cons of reverse auctions for buyers. Do the same for suppliers. Are reverse auctions used by businesses in your country?

2. How can a supplier succeed in reverse auctions? How can it avoid them altogether?

FOCUS ON Ethics

China is an emerging economic giant with almost endless potential for business opportunities. *Guan xi*—meaning 'connections' or 'relationships'—is a Chinese way of doing business and is practically considered an art form there. It involves exchanging 'favors' when you need something done. Many Chinese businesspeople see it as a way to solidify relationships, get things done, and cultivate well-being. To Westerners, however, it often looks more like graft in the form of bribery, nepotism, gift giving, and kickbacks. Transparency International, a German-based corruption watchdog, ranks China along with India, Russia, Taiwan, Turkey, Malaysia, and South Africa as the countries with the

most rampant corruption. However, China is cracking down by enacting stricter anticorruption laws and prosecuting violators. In 2007, China's former director of the State Food and Drug Administration was executed for taking bribes.

1. Is it right for countries to impose their ethical views and behavior on other cultures, such as China?

2. What are the consequences for overseas companies that refuse to engage in less-than-ethical practices that foreign businesses or governments expect or that competitors use in foreign markets?

MARKETING BY THE Numbers

A number of different industry classification systems are used around the world. The systems are designed to help organize the statistical data that's available on different industrial and economic activities so that they can be compared on a year-to-year basis. The International Standard Industrial Classification (ISIC), the development of which was heavily influenced by the British SIC system, was first issued by the United Nations in 1948. The latest ISIC version was designed in 2006. In the late 1990s, Canada, Mexico, and the United States collaborated on the North

American Industry Classification System (NAICS). The United States and Canada adopted the NAICS in 1997. Mexico did so a year later.

1. Look up 'SIC code' on the Internet. What do the four digits of the SIC code represent? What industry is represented by the SIC code 3674?

2. How can marketers use SIC codes to better deliver customer satisfaction and value?

VIDEO Case

Eaton

With nearly 60,000 employees doing business in 125 countries and sales last year of more than US$11 billion, Eaton is one of the world's largest suppliers of diversified industrial goods. Eaton's products make cars more peppy, semi-trucks safer to drive, and airliners more fuel efficient. So why haven't you heard of the company? Because Eaton sells its products not to end consumers but to other businesses.

At Eaton, business-to-business marketing means working closely with customers to develop a better product. So the company partners with its sophisticated, knowledgeable clients to create total solutions that meet their needs. Along the way, Eaton maps the decision-making process to better understand the concerns and interests of decision makers. In the end, Eaton's suc-

cess depends on its ability to provide high-quality, dependable customer service and product support. Through service and support, Eaton develops a clear understanding of consumer needs and builds stronger relationships with clients.

After viewing the video featuring Eaton, answer the following questions about business markets and business buyer behavior:

1. What is Eaton's value proposition?

2. Who are Eaton's customers? Describe Eaton's customer relationships.

3. Discuss the different ways that Eaton provides value beyond that which companies can provide for themselves.

COMPANY Case

Boeing: Selling a Dream(liner)

Think about the biggest purchase that you've ever made. Was it a car? A computer? A piece of furniture or an appliance? Think about the time you put in to researching that decision, all the factors that you considered in making your choice, and how much the purchase ultimately cost.

Now imagine that you are part of a buying team for a major airline considering the purchase of multiple commercial jets, each costing over US$100 million. A slightly different situation? Such are the customers that Boeing deals with every day. Selling commercial and military aircraft involves some of the most complicated transactions in the world. At those prices, a single sale can add up to billions of dollars. And beyond initial prices, Boeing's clients must consider numerous factors that affect longer-term operating and maintenance costs. As a result, the airplane purchase process is nerve-rackingly slow, often taking years from the first sales presentation to the day Boeing actually delivers an airplane.

For such purchases, Boeing knows that it takes more than fast talk and a firm handshake to sell expensive aircraft—it takes a lot of relationship building. So Boeing invests heavily in managing customer relationships. Individual salespeople head up an extensive team of company specialists—sales and service technicians, financial analysts, planners, engineers—all dedicated to finding ways to understand and satisfy airline customer needs. These teams work closely with clients through the lengthy buying process. Even after receiving an order, salespeople stay in almost constant contact to keep ensuring the customer stays satisfied. The success of customer relationships depends on performance and trust. "When you buy an airplane, it is like getting married," quips Alan Mallaly, the head of Boeing's commercial airplane division. "It is a long-term relationship."

But even with this care in managing customer relationships, Boeing has experienced more than its share of challenges over the past decade. For starters, its only major rival, France-based Airbus, began to overtake Boeing in product innovation during the 1990s. In the wake of September 11, 2001, Boeing lost its industry lead in commercial airplane sales to Airbus. To make matters worse, Boeing soon found itself in the midst of a series of ethical scandals. In the early 2000s, the company faced two separate cases of cheating to win defense contracts with the U.S. Air Force. The scandals resulted in a Department of Justice investigation, the ousting of Boeing's CEO, prison terms for two other executives, and the loss of billions of dollars in business. To make matters even worse, in the face of a scandalous extramarital affair, the next CEO stepped down as well.

AN AIRLINE'S DREAM

With its reputation sullied and its financial situation suffering, Boeing got back to the business of serving its corporate clients. In April 2004, the giant airplane maker announced the program launch of its 787 Dreamliner, Boeing's first all-new aircraft since the 777, launched a decade earlier. The Dreamliner is not the world's biggest passenger jet—Airbus's A380 and even Boeing's own 747 are bigger. But with the 787, Boeing saw more potential in the midsized wide-body market. From the beginning, it set out to create a jet with groundbreaking innovations that would

translate into true benefits for its customers, the type of benefits that really stand out to buyers and executives at major airlines.

Some 50 percent of the Dreamliner's fuselage is made from lightweight carbon-fiber materials. The plane is also made in one single piece, eliminating 40,000 to 50,000 fasteners and 1,500 aluminum sheets and putting it in a design class with the B-2 stealth bomber. Combined with other weight-saving design features and advanced engine technologies, the 787 is the world's lightest and most fuel efficient passenger jet, using 20 percent less fuel than comparably sized planes.

Another major benefit that the Boeing 787 Dreamliner brings to its category is flexibility. The 787 line is designed for multiple configurations that carry between 210 and 330 passengers. The plane also offers increased cargo capacity, a fuel range of up to 13,700 nautical kilometers, and a maximum speed of Mach .85. Thus, the 787 brings big-jet speed, range, and capacity to the midsize market, rivaling the jumbo jets.

The cockpit of the 787 is also loaded with tech toys that will enhance safety and cut departure delays. The advances include a system that self-monitors the plane's vital functions and reports maintenance requirements to ground-based computer systems.

Whereas the airlines will certainly notice all of these improvements, airline passengers will also approve of many new 787 design features. The interior of the Dreamliner is designed to reduce long-haul flying misery and to better imitate life on the ground. The Dreamliner is 60 percent quieter than other planes in its class. It features more legroom, lighting that automatically adjusts to time zone shifts, and higher cabin pressure and humidity, making the flying experience more comfortable and reducing common flying symptoms such as headaches, dry mouth, and fatigue. The Dreamliner also boasts the largest-ever overhead storage bins, 19-inch self-dimming windows, and a wireless Internet and entertainment system.

"We looked at every aspect of the flying experience," says Tom Cogan, chief project engineer for the 787. "It's not just an evolutionary step. From my perspective it almost borders on revolutionary." Opinions of industry insiders support Cogan's statement. Many analysts strongly believe that the 787 Dreamliner will one day be regarded as the plane that charted the next age of commercial aviation.

Boeing officially launched the 787 program in April 2004. Even with the stratospheric list price of US$162 million and the fact that Boeing was not promising delivery for at least four years, companies scrambled to place orders. Japan's All Nippon Airways jumped in first with a record order for 50 Dreamliners. To date, 56 companies from six continents have lined up with orders for 892 of Boeing's newest aeronautic darling. That makes the Dreamliner the most successful new aircraft launch and the fastest-selling plane in the history of the industry.

Combined with record sales for its 737 and freighter lines, Boeing's annual sales soared. In 2005, Boeing shattered its records with orders for 1,002 commercial airplanes, edging within inches of Airbus's lead. That number is even more striking considering that Boeing and Airbus combined for a total of 622 orders in 2004. The sales spike was so dramatic that no one in the industry expected the numbers to repeat. But in 2006, Boeing reclaimed its title as the industry sales leader by surpassing Airbus with orders for 1,044 more jets. Even more stunning, 2007 brought the third straight record-breaking year for Boeing with 1,413 orders.

DREAM, OR NIGHTMARE?

As if massive revenue success weren't enough, Boeing was riding high for other reasons as well. In 2005, when Jim McNerney took over as CEO for Boeing, he instituted a massive cost-cutting program that resulted in an 84 percent increase in company earnings on an 8 percent increase in revenue for 2007. Combined with the soaring orders, Boeing's stock price peaked at a record US$107 in July of 2007. With over US$60 billion in revenue, Boeing once again reigned as the world's biggest aerospace company and the USA's largest exporter. But Mr McNerney knew better than to revel in the glory of the then-current successes. Across the Atlantic, Airbus had committed severe production blunders resulting in its first jumbo A380s being delivered 22 months late, leading to a major shakeup in management at the French firm. Boeing had projected that it would deliver its first 787 to All Nippon in May of 2008. With that date still more than a year away, McNerney knew that his biggest challenge would be to keep the Dreamliner on track.

McNerney had good reason for concern. The Dreamliner was not only an innovative design, it was being built by an innovative process that outsourced 70 percent of the work to dozens of partnering firms. Boeing's promises with respect to deadlines and delivery dates could only be met if all the pieces of the puzzle came together as planned. Even though it had so many orders secured, customers were counting on Boeing to make good. The last thing that it needed was for customer relationships to be rocked by delays or other problems.

But by mid-2007, the 787 production process was plagued with problems. Parts shortages and other bottlenecks led suppliers to ship incomplete sections of the first few planes to Boeing's final assembly line in Everett, Washington. By mid-2008, the date of the first 787 delivery had been pushed back three times. All Nippon would not take possession of its first plane until at least 15 months past the original deadline. To make matters worse, Boeing announced that it would only deliver 25 Dreamliners in the first year, rather than the previous estimate of 109.

Months later, Boeing Commercial Airplanes President Scott Carson announced that Boeing had made solid progress in overcoming start-up issues. He apologized and promised that the company would work closely with each customer to minimize the impact of the delays. Boeing also suggested that it would offer incentives and penalty payments as part of that process (some analysts estimate that Boeing could be liable for as much as US$4 billion in concessions and penalties). Still, understandably, Boeing's commercial customers quickly grew impatient. The delays began raising havoc with customer relationships. Boeing's biggest customer, All Nippon, stated, "We are extremely disappointed: This is the third delay in the delivery of the first aircraft and we still have no details about the full delivery schedule. We would urge Boeing to provide us with a 120 percent definitive schedule as soon as possible."

As Boeing's customers consider what is happening in the purchase process, it is easy to see how each might become seriously conflicted. On the one hand, they see the promise of a Dreamliner that they believe strongly will provide tremendous benefits, perhaps unlike any previous aircraft. On the other hand, every delay costs them dearly. The delays upset plans to begin new routes and retire old aircraft, events that translate directly into revenue and profits. Customer options are limited—there's only one competitor, and its product in this class is substantially inferior to the Dreamliner. And even if customers switch, Airbus does not have planes sitting on the shelves waiting to be purchased. However, Boeing's customers still have the option of canceling 787 orders and making do with what they have.

RIDING OUT THE STORM

Regardless of what its customers do, the way Boeing handles the 787 crisis will most certainly affect customer relations and *future* orders. Boeing has a lot on its side. The innovativeness of the current product line, expertise in supply chain management, and the strength of its sales teams in managing customer relationships will all help to resolve the problems with the Dreamliner program. But Boeing had these things going for it before the crisis began. The question is, what will Boeing do differently in the future?

In a 2008 memo to employees, CEO McNerney said, "The simple reality is that it's time to get it done—and done right." McNerney has made it very clear that he expects more from everyone involved in the 787 Dreamliner program, from the top down. He has reached deeply into the company's executive roster, plucking a team from Boeing's defense unit to straighten out the Dreamliner process. He is pushing executives to act more aggressively. This includes sticking their noses into suppliers' operations, even stationing Boeing employees on the factory floors of every major supplier.

McNerney himself is more directly involved with the 787 program. He gets daily briefings on the plane's progress. He frequently makes his presence known on factory floors and even visits with assembly line workers. "We've got 240 programs in the company, and there's one that's got more of my attention right now than any one, and that's the 787," Mr McNerney said. "I hope we are [eventually] defined by the 787. Just not right this instant."

Mr McNerney took over as CEO well after the Dreamliner program was under way, so the current problems are not being attributed to him. But customers and others throughout the industry are watching him closely to see how he handles the situation. Says Charlie Smith, chief investment officer with Fort Pitt Capital Group, "No matter what other successes Jim McNerney has at Boeing, he will be judged on how he handles the 787. He's either going to win big or lose big," he said. And McNerney's outcome will be directly shared by the Boeing Corporation, including the teams that must deal day in and day out with anxious and frustrated customers.

Questions for Discussion

1. Discuss the nature of the market structure and demand for the Dreamliner. What are the implications of this for Boeing and its customers?

2. What examples of the major types of buying situations do you see in the case? Discuss the implications of each in terms of marketing strategy.

3. List the specific features of the Dreamliner. What customer benefits result from each?

4. Discuss the customer buying process for a Boeing airplane. In what major ways does this process differ from the buying process a passenger might go through in choosing an airline?

5. What marketing recommendations would you make to McNerney as he continues to try to resolve the problems with the 787 Dreamliner program?

Sources: Josh Dean, "Fast 50 2008: Boeing," *Fast Company*, February, 2008, p. 106; Laurence Zuckerman, "Selling Airplanes with a Smile," *New York Times*, February 17, 2002, p. 3.2; J. Lynn Lunsford, "Boeing CEO Fights Headwind," *Wall Street Journal*, April 25, 2008, p. B1; Michael V. Copeland, "Boeing's Big Dream," *Fortune*, April 24, 2008, accessed online at www.money.cnn.com; Marilyn Adams, "Boeing Bounces Back Against Odds," *USA Today*, January 11, 2007, p. 1B; David Greising, "Boeing 787 Delayed Again," *Chicago Tribune*, April 10, 2008, http://articles.chicagotribune.com.

PART 3

Designing a Customer-Driven Strategy and Mix

Chapter 7

Part 1   Defining Marketing and the Marketing Process (Chapters 1, 2)
Part 2   Understanding the Marketplace and Consumers (Chapters 3, 4, 5, 6)
Part 3   Designing a Customer-Driven Strategy and Mix (Chapters 7, 8, 9, 10, 11, 12, 13, 14)
Part 4   Extending Marketing (Chapters 15, 16, 17)

Customer-Driven Marketing
Strategy Segmentation, Targeting, and Positioning

Chapter PREVIEW

So far, you've learned what marketing is and about the importance of understanding consumers and the marketplace environment. With that as background, you're now ready to delve deeper into marketing strategy and tactics. This chapter looks further into key customer-driven marketing strategy decisions—how to divide up markets into meaningful customer groups (*segmentation*), choose which customer groups to serve (*targeting*), create market offerings that best serve targeted customers (*differentiation*), and position the offerings in the minds of consumers (*positioning*). Then, the chapters that follow explore the tactical marketing tools—the Four Ps—by which marketers bring these strategies to life. A good example of segmentation in the Arab world is Damas, as discussed in the example here.

Damas Group is a jewelry and watch retailer that has expanded into 18 countries around the world with about 450 stores. The group is the most widespread jewelry and watch retailer in the Arab world, in terms of number of stores. The group has subsidiaries mainly in the Arab world, India, and Italy. It also has jointly controlled entities and associates in the Arab world, Europe, North Africa, and other locations. Damas sells its own brands, and it also sells other top international and Arab world brands.

It might be perceived that Damas focuses merely on the high-end consumer, yet this is not absolutely correct. Essentially, Damas targets three types of consumers through selling its brands in three types of stores: Les Exclusives stores, Semi-Exclusive stores, and Damas 22K stores. The Les Exclusives stores mainly serve "high net worth consumers," and offer highly extravagant worldwide brands in addition to Damas' own products. Semi-Exclusive stores target "upper-middle income consumers" with products that are relatively less unique, but appeal to a broader spectrum of consumers, such as tourists and expatriates, professionals, and office workers. These stores sell international brands, along with Damas' products. Thirdly, Damas 22K stores target "middle income and working class immigrant populations," and sell Damas' products along with some regional brands. While the above are the main stores, Damas targets other segments by selling in other stores, such as Damas Kids for youngsters and families, and Mono-stores specializing in certain global brands, including Tiffany & Co, Paspaley, Graff, Parmigiani, Stefan Hafner, Links of London, Roberto Coin, Roberta Porrati and Folli Follie.[1]

Let's take a closer look at Damas' A-segment in its Les Exclusives Boutiques. In Dubai, Damas holds the Luxury Week event, which displays the extravagant and up-to-date jewelry and watch collections at the city's renowned shopping site. Shoppers at that event are treated with gifts with every purchase they make. The occasion, which is attended by journalists and VIPs, gives A-class buyers the chance to purchase the latest fashionable brands in the jewelry and watch markets brought from all over the world. The list ranges from standard brands to modish celebrated worldwide brand names, such as Carrera y Carrera and Mikimoto; world-renowned Italian jewelry brands such as Roberto Coin, Marco Bicego, Fope, Luca Carati, and Leo Pizzo; famous Spanish brand Magerit; in addition to a wide collection of watches crafted by legendary watch brands, including Chronoswiss, Parmigiani, Perrelet, Roger Dubuis, and Sarcar.

Tamjid Abdullah, deputy managing director, Damas, says: "In keeping with the growing international profile of Dubai, Damas has always sought to bring customers a versatile array of brands acknowledged for their style definition and creative exuberance. And I am happy to say that it is their enthusiastic appreciation and support of our efforts that has provided us the incentive to forge ahead as true pioneers. During the Damas Luxury Week, shoppers will be treated to a thrilling selection of the most exclusive diamond, gold and pearl jewelry collections, by the world's leading jewelry and watch brands. Such events also provide brilliant testimony to the tremendous trust Damas enjoys with its international partners."[2]

> **Damas has its own designs, targeting different segments from different age ranges and different income levels.**

Recently, Les Exclusives Boutiques in the UAE have added a new collection of the leading Italian design house, Roberto Coin. Roberto Coin is featured by its best-selling Cento Collection, which is based on the artistic designs of the luxurious 100-facet Cento diamonds. In Les Exclusives shops, Roberto Coin offers the latest of its collections. Tawhid Abdullah, managing director of Damas, added: "The extensive Roberto Coin collection has been launched to create [a] distinct modern look for contemporary woman and set a different trend this festive season. Thus on one side it captures the hearts of discerning followers of fashion and on the other complement[s] the personality of the wearer. Roberto Coin's vibrant creations blend color and an eye for detail that has helped the brand carve a niche in the highly competitive Middle East market and Mr Coin's recent visit to Dubai is proof of his close affinity to jewelry lovers in this part of the globe."[3]

Roberto Coin, CEO of the brand, commented: "You must understand that Roberto Coin is a niche jewelry brand which unwaveringly upholds and perfects its standards to stay at the top by constant innovation and creativity. We use some of the world's finest jewels and our treatment of the most precious metals and stones have given new meaning to the words 'top-class.' Thus I create jewelry for a woman who has her own personal style, is intelligent, witty and has grace. So it is natural that my inspiration comes from the elegance of femininity."[4]

Around the world, Roberto Coin's name appeals to the A-segment; this includes famous Hollywood stars and VIPs in all fields in Europe. Roberto Coin now is positioned among the most famous jewelry brands in the United States, and is the leading Italian jewelry brand. Roberto Coin finds his target niche in the Arab world as well. Coin said, "The Middle East is a very important market for us and the growth potential for Italian jewelry is enormous. I am extremely happy to know that Roberto Coin has found a loyal following driven by a huge demand from the style conscious of the region."[5]

The Arab world has become a promising region for the most luxurious brands, local and global. In fact, the region displays a wide array of demographic segmentation from highly rich to low-income buyers. This makes it easy for marketers to find their target; however, it is a tougher job to convey sound product positioning.

Damas Les Exclusives in Dubai holds the Luxury Week event, which displays the extravagant and up-to-date jewelry and watch collections at the city's renowned shopping site.

> When Damas decided to target and position itself in the market, it created a variety of store brands targeting the different segments not only by income but also according to age and ethnicity.

Market segmentation
Dividing a market into smaller groups with distinct needs, characteristics, or behavior that might require separate marketing strategies or mixes.

Market targeting (targeting)
The process of evaluating each market segment's attractiveness and selecting one or more segments to enter.

Differentiation
Actually differentiating the market offering to create superior customer value.

Positioning
Arranging for a market offering to occupy a clear, distinctive, and desirable place relative to competing products in the minds of target consumers.

Companies today recognize that they cannot appeal to all buyers in the marketplace, or at least not to all buyers in the same way. Buyers are too numerous, too widely scattered, and too varied in their needs and buying practices. Moreover, the companies themselves vary widely in their abilities to serve different segments of the market. Instead, a company must identify the parts of the market that it can serve best and most profitably. It must design customer-driven marketing strategies that build the *right* relationships with the *right* customers.

Thus, most companies have moved away from mass marketing and toward *target marketing*—identifying market segments, selecting one or more of them, and developing products and marketing programs tailored to each. Instead of scattering their marketing efforts, firms are focusing on the buyers who have greater interest in the values they create best.

Figure 7.1 shows the four major steps in designing a customer-driven marketing strategy. In the first two steps, the company selects the customers that it will serve. **Market segmentation** involves dividing a market into smaller groups of buyers with distinct needs, characteristics, or behaviors that might require separate marketing strategies or mixes. The company identifies different ways to segment the market and develops profiles of the resulting market segments. **Market targeting** (or **targeting**) consists of evaluating each market segment's attractiveness and selecting one or more market segments to enter.

In the final two steps, the company decides on a value proposition—on how it will create value for target customers. **Differentiation** involves actually differentiating the firm's market offering to create superior customer value. **Positioning** consists of arranging for a market offering to occupy a clear, distinctive, and desirable place relative to competing products in the minds of target consumers. We discuss each of these steps in turn.

Objective Outline

Author Comment | Market segmentation addresses the first simple-sounding marketing question: What customers will we serve? The answer will be different for each company. For example, The Four Seasons targets the top 5 percent of corporate and leisure travelers. Holiday Inn targets middle-class people traveling on a budget.

Market Segmentation (pp 178–186)

Buyers in any market differ in their wants, resources, locations, buying attitudes, and buying practices. Through market segmentation, companies divide large, heterogeneous markets into smaller segments that can be reached more efficiently and effectively with products and services that match their unique needs. In this section, we discuss four important segmentation topics: segmenting consumer markets, segmenting business markets, segmenting international markets, and requirements for effective segmentation.

Segmenting Consumer Markets

There is no single way to segment a market. A marketer has to try different segmentation variables, alone and in combination, to find the best way to view the market structure. ● **Table 7.1** outlines the major variables that might be used in segmenting consumer markets. Here we look at the major *geographic, demographic, psychographic,* and *behavioral* variables.

Geographic Segmentation

Geographic segmentation calls for dividing the market into different geographical units such as nations, regions, provinces, parishes, cities, or even neighborhoods. A company

Geographic segmentation
Dividing a market into different geographical units such as nations, provinces, regions, cities, or neighborhoods.

●FIGURE | 7.1
Designing a Customer-Driven Marketing Strategy

In concept, marketing boils down to two questions: (1) Which customers will we serve? and (2) How will we serve them? Of course, the tough part is coming up with good answers to these simple-sounding but difficult questions. The goal is to create more value for the customers we serve than competitors do.

Select customers to serve

Segmentation
Divide the total market into smaller segments

Targeting
Select the segment or segments to enter

Create value for targeted customers

Decide on a value proposition

Differentiation
Differentiate the market offering to create superior customer value

Positioning
Position the market offering in the minds of target customers

178

● **TABLE | 7.1**   Major Segmentation Variables for Consumer Markets

Geographic	Examples
World region or country	Western Europe, Arab world, Pacific Rim, China, India, Canada, Mexico, North America
Country region	North Africa, The Gulf, Near East
City or metro size	Under 5,000; 5,000–20,000; 20,000–50,000; 50,000–100,000; 100,000–250,000; 250,000–500,000; 500,000–1,000,000; 1,000,000–4,000,000; over 4,000,000
Density	Urban, suburban, ex-urban, rural
Climate	Northern, southern

Demographic	Examples
Age	Under 6, 6–11, 12–19, 20–34, 35–49, 50–64, 65+
Gender	Male, female
Family size	1–2, 3–4, 5+
Family life cycle	Young, single; married, no children; married with children; widowed; older, married, no children under 18; older, single; other
Income	Under US$20,000; $20,000–$30,000; $30,000–$50,000; $50,000–$100,000; $100,000–$250,000; $250,000 and over
Occupation	Professional and technical; managers, officials, and proprietors; clerical; sales; craftspeople; supervisors; farmers; retired; students; homemakers; unemployed
Education	Primary school or less; some secondary school; secondary school graduate; some college; college graduate
Religion	Muslim, Christian, Jewish, other
Nationality	Egyptian, Saudi, Syrian, Lebanese, American, British, French, Indian

Psychographic	Examples
Social class	Lower lowers, upper lowers, working class, middle class, upper middles, lower uppers, upper uppers
Lifestyle	Achievers, strivers, survivors
Personality	Compulsive, gregarious, authoritarian, ambitious

Behavioral	Examples
Occasions	Regular occasion; special occasion; holiday; seasonal
Benefits	Quality, service, economy, convenience, speed
User status	Nonuser, ex-user, potential user, first-time user, regular user
User rates	Light user, medium user, heavy user
Loyalty status	None, medium, strong, absolute
Readiness stage	Unaware, aware, informed, interested, desirous, intending to buy
Attitude toward product	Enthusiastic, positive, indifferent, negative, hostile

may decide to operate in one or a few geographical areas, or to operate in all areas but pay attention to geographical differences in needs and wants.

Many companies today are localizing their products, advertising, promotion, and sales efforts to fit the needs of individual regions, cities, and even neighborhoods. For example, one consumer-products company ships additional cases of its 'power bar' (protein bars) to stores in neighborhoods near Gold's Gym centers. Citibank offers different mixes of branch banking services depending on neighborhood demographics. And the ice-cream maker Baskin Robbins practices what it calls 'three-mile marketing,' emphasizing local events and promotions close to its local store locations. On a global scale, video game companies create different versions of their games depending on the world region in which the game is sold.

For example, Protrac Online is an Egyptian company that specializes in providing the latest technologies in geo-marketing research and services by employing researchers, data analysts, and geo-professionals, and a large scale of data maps and tools. Protrac refers to geo-marketing as a sophisticated marketing science that uses geographical information for analyzing distribution channels of products. Protrac provides insight into the competition and target segments surrounding a specific distribution point. Hence, this allows companies to understand the specific changes needed in terms of distributing products so as to better serve the targeted consumers. This is based on the assumption that people buy products or use services based on the product's or the service's proximity. Geo-marketing allows Protrac's clients to see the map of their outlets and their competitors' outlets as well. This also allows clients to understand where to go to pursue their target. Accordingly, geo-marketing can be of highly effective benefit to all kinds of marketing applications.

Protrac offers three types of products: Geographical Digital Maps, Socio-Demographic Data, and Trade Channels Census and Survey Data. Hossam Ragheb, CEO of Protrac, said that using digital maps for marketing purposes is crucial, especially for Fast-Moving Consumer Goods companies (FMCGs), such as Coca-Cola, Proctor & Gamble, and Unilever. Ragheb added that "[for suppliers] to know where to sell the products ... and where this outlet is, not only in terms of address, but the [demographics] of the area—[for example] how many people above 15 years [of age] are living in this area—gives them a sort of direction to know which products should go where."[6]

Geographic information systems are used for marketing purposes, in defining the location of the target market, distribution channels, and socio-demographic data.

Some companies are seeking to cultivate as-yet-untapped geographic territory. For example, some large companies are fleeing the fiercely competitive major cities and suburbs to set up shops in small towns. Meanwhile others are developing new store concepts that will give them access to higher-density urban areas. Metro Group has done a mix of both. It opened a chain of wholesale retail shops, Makro, which run using a subscription-only access. Not only is Makro different from any other wholesale retail model but also the shops are located outside of the main cities but in low-income areas close to them.

Demographic Segmentation

Demographic segmentation
Dividing the market into groups based on variables such as age, gender, family size, family life cycle, income, occupation, education, religion, race, generation, and nationality.

Demographic segmentation divides the market into groups based on variables such as age, gender, family size, family life cycle, income, occupation, education, religion, race, generation, and nationality. Demographic factors are the most popular bases for segmenting customer groups. One reason is that consumer needs, wants, and usage rates often vary closely with demographic variables. Another is that demographic variables are easier to measure than most other types of variables. Even when marketers first define segments using other bases, such as benefits sought or behavior, they must know segment demographic characteristics in order to assess the size of the target market and to reach it efficiently.

Age and life-cycle segmentation
Dividing a market into different age and life-cycle groups.

Age and Life-Cycle Stage.   Consumer needs and wants change with age. Some companies use **age and life-cycle segmentation**, offering different products or using different marketing approaches for different age and life-cycle groups. For example, whereas

HP targets adult buyers with its "The Computer Is Personal Again" campaign, along with ads featuring price and value, it developed a special "Society for Parental Mind Control" campaign targeting teenagers. Research shows that although parents are the predominant buyers of computers, teens are key recommenders. "It's such an old story, but kids are the arbiters of cool," says one analyst.[7]

Marketers must be careful to guard against stereotypes when using age and life-cycle segmentation. Although some 80-year-olds fit the weary stereotypes, others play tennis. Similarly, whereas some 40-year-old couples are sending their children off to college, others are just beginning new families. Thus, age is often a poor predictor of a person's life cycle, health, work or family status, needs, and buying power. Companies marketing to mature consumers usually employ positive images and appeals.

Gender segmentation

Dividing a market into different groups based on gender.

Gender. **Gender segmentation** has long been used in clothing, cosmetics, toiletries, and magazines. For example, Heineken decided to target men for its non-alcoholic beer Birell, and developed a campaign called "Be a Man". On the other hand, Galaxy targeted women with its chocolate and emphasized that in its advertising campaigns.

Income segmentation

Dividing a market into different income groups.

Income. The marketers of products and services such as automobiles, clothing, cosmetics, financial services, and travel have long used **income segmentation**. Many companies target affluent consumers with luxury goods and convenience services.

Luxury yachts can easily cost over US$1 million, and are targeted at the most affluent section of society.

However, not all companies that use income segmentation target the affluent. For example, many retailers—such as pound and dollar stores—successfully target low- and middle-income groups. The core market for such stores is families with incomes under US$30,000. When real-estate experts scout locations for new pound and dollar stores, they look for lower-middle-class neighborhoods where people wear less-expensive shoes and drive old cars that drip a lot of oil.

With their low-income strategies, stores such as these have become fast-growing retailers. They have been so successful that giant discounters are taking notice. An example of income segmentation in the Arab world is mobile phone service providers targeting low-income populations. Companies such as Zain, Qtel, STC, and Etisalat earn most of their revenues from countries where the populations are large with low income, as in Sub-Saharan Africa and South Asia. The main challenge for those companies is the low generated revenues per mobile phone user, which comes as a result of competitive and price-cutting measures taken by companies in the field.[8]

Psychographic Segmentation

Psychographic segmentation

Dividing a market into different groups based on social class, lifestyle, or personality characteristics.

Psychographic segmentation divides buyers into different groups based on social class, lifestyle, or personality characteristics. People in the same demographic group can have very different psychographic characteristics.

In Chapter 5, we discussed how the products people buy reflect their *lifestyles*. As a result, marketers often segment their markets by consumer lifestyles and base their marketing strategies on lifestyle appeals. Marketers also use *personality* variables to segment markets. For example, Sprite launched a new campaign called "This is who I am…," targeting teenagers who are rebellious and independent. This is considered a very unique and emerging segment in the Arab world.

Behavioral Segmentation

Behavioral segmentation

Dividing a market into groups based on consumer knowledge, attitudes, uses, or responses to a product.

Behavioral segmentation divides buyers into groups based on their knowledge, attitudes, uses, or responses to a product. Many marketers believe that behavior variables are the best starting point for building market segments.

Occasion segmentation

Dividing the market into groups according to occasions when buyers get the idea to buy, actually make their purchase, or use the purchased item.

Occasions. Buyers can be grouped according to occasions when they get the idea to buy, actually make their purchase, or use the purchased item. **Occasion segmentation** can help firms build up product usage. For example, many marketers prepare special offers and ads for holiday occasions. Ramadan and the two Islamic Feasts are the most critical times in the Arab world, where offers and advertisements intensify as a result of increased viewership driven from family and group gatherings. **Real Marketing 7.1** discusses how consumers behave during the holy month of Ramadan.

Benefits Sought. A powerful form of segmentation is to group buyers according to the different *benefits* that they seek from the product. **Benefit segmentation** requires finding the major benefits people look for in the product class, the kinds of people who look for each benefit, and the major brands that deliver each benefit.

Champion athletic wear segments its markets according to benefits that different consumers seek from its activewear. For example, 'Fit and Polish' consumers seek a balance between function and style—they exercise for results but want to look good doing it. 'Serious Sports Competitors' exercise heavily and live in and love their activewear—they seek performance and function. By contrast, 'Value-Seeking Parents' have low sports interest and low activewear involvement—they buy for the family and seek durability and value. Thus, each segment seeks a different mix of benefits. Champion must target the benefit segment or segments that it can serve best and most profitably, using appeals that match each segment's benefit preferences.

Benefit segmentation

Dividing the market into groups according to the different benefits that consumers seek from the product.

User Status. Markets can be segmented into nonusers, ex-users, potential users, first-time users, and regular users of a product. Marketers want to reinforce and retain regular users, attract targeted nonusers, and revive relationships with ex-users.

Included in the potential users group are consumers facing life-stage changes—such as newlyweds and new parents—who can be turned into heavy users.

Usage Rate. Markets can also be segmented into light, medium, and heavy product users. Heavy users are often a small percentage of the market but account for a high percentage of total consumption. For example, Burger King targets what it calls 'Super Fans,' young (age 18 to 34), burger-eating males who make up 18 percent of the chain's customers but account for almost half of all customer visits. They eat at Burger King an average of 16 times a month.[9] Burger King targets these Super Fans openly with ads that exalt huge burgers containing meat, cheese, and more meat and cheese.

Loyalty Status. A market can also be segmented by consumer loyalty. Consumers can be loyal to brands (Apple), stores (Carrefour), and companies (Toyota). Buyers can be divided into groups according to their degree of loyalty. Some consumers are completely loyal—they buy one brand all the time. For example, Apple Computer has an almost cultlike following of loyal users:[10]

There are Mac folks who happen to own a Mac and use it for emailing, blogging, browsing, buying, and social networking. Then there are the Apple diehards—the Mac fanatics who buy Apple products and accessories that maximize their Mac lives. Some of these fans buy two iPhones—one for themselves and the other just to take apart, to see what it looks like on the inside, and maybe, just to marvel at Apple's ingenious ability to cram so much into a tight little elegant package. These Mac fanatics (also called MacHeads or Macolytes) see Apple founder and CEO Steve Jobs as a wizard of technology. Say the word 'Apple'

Consumer loyalty: 'Mac fanatics'—fanatically loyal Apple Computer users—helped keep Apple afloat during the lean years, and they are now at the forefront of Apple's burgeoning empire.

Real Marketing 7.1

Ramadan Spirit in the Arab World

An example of occasional targeting in the Arab world is the holy month of Ramadan. According to a study conducted by Maktoob Research regarding Ramadan in the region, 71 percent of respondents believe that the month enables them to experience a feeling of "solidarity and brotherhood with fellow Muslims." The study has found out that 67 percent perceive Ramadan to be a commercial occasion for many companies. The study gathered the opinions of 6,128 Muslims from around the Arab world, just ahead of the holy month in 2008.

Discussing the results, Tamara Deprez, director of Maktoob Research, added: "The survey's findings show that despite the pace of modern life and the changes in people's lifestyle, the Arab world retains its spiritual essence and remains largely tradition-bound where matters of faith are concerned—more so during the Holy Month of Ramadan." It was discovered that most of the respondents enjoyed having *Iftar* (breaking their fast) with their families at home compared with the significant portion, but not a majority, who said that they liked to have Iftar in restaurants.

Ramadan is also characterized by the sense of charity. During Ramadan, in many countries in the Arab world, just before the dusk prayer (the time for fast breaking), people hurry to one another in streets to give little snacks, saying, "Ramadan Kareem, Iftar Shahy" ("Hearty Iftar"). People are there always to provide each other with dates and drinks, ensuring that people have their Iftar on time. Also, rich Muslim people rush to make *Mawa'ed Rahaman* (free public eateries), where poor people are offered free food at Iftar time. Accordingly, it is a good chance for businesses to show their support in corporate social responsibility (CSR) and to promote the Ramadan spirit. For instance, in 2008, Saudi Telecom (STC) set up a food tent to cater for more than 7,000 people daily in Ramadan in more than 80 different locations all around Jeddah. McDonald's provided Iftar, incorporating entertainment activities for orphans in one of the malls. There is also the Food Bank, sponsored by Olympic Group and Elsewedy Cables, which delivered food to low-income people during

the month. Further, some food and beverage companies offer free products on streets at Iftar time, primarily aiming to promote those products. In addition, Ramadan is considered an optimal time to reach the consumer through television advertisements. In Egypt, both the finance and transport ministries broadcast their advertisements throughout the month.

In countries such as the UAE, companies market their products in line with the Ramadan theme of family gathering. For example, du, the mobile services provider, made special Ramadan offers in 2009 to enable families to keep in touch with each other even if they are in distant locations. The Ramadan promotional offer entailed 1 fils credit (0.3 US cents) for each second of night-time worldwide calls, and users can double their call time using the Pay as You Go services. "du's desire to help its valued customers strengthen their social bonds and communicate more easily with loved ones during the Holy Month is the foundation of all our Ramadan offers," said Farid Faraidooni, executive vice president, Commercial, du. "As a telecom provider with strong local roots, we know the high value all residents place on staying in touch. Our unique offers give customers the peace of mind that comes with affordability, plus the flexibility and convenience of exceptional calling benefits during a very special time of year." du's main offer during the night time aims to serve customers who have been fasting during the day, through exclusive price cuts during the month of Ramadan. Customers get 1 fils free credit for every international call made during the night time. No matter how far away family members are, du provides the same price deductions on calls.

Another interesting consumer behavior during the holy month of Ramadan is the special types of foods that are demanded during that time. For example, stores selling Eastern desserts, such as *Konafa*, *Basbousa*,

Often charity work and social activities increase during the holy month of Ramadan, which affects the demand and supply of nutrition products.

and the like experience a substantial increase in demand during Ramadan, and they face the challenge of satisfying the large number of customers queuing in lines, particularly right before Iftar time. Of course, the price of television ads skyrockets during the month as a result of family gatherings in front of the television after Iftar, to watch programs and soap operas. As a result, companies intensify their advertising campaigns during the month, in anticipation of increased demand and viewership.

Sources: "Ramadan Continues to Inspire the Faithful Throughout the Arab World," Maktoob Research, 2008, www.maktoob-research.com/PR-Maktoob%20 Research-Ramadan-English-FINAL.pdf; "Special Ramadan Offers from du," *BI-ME*, August 18, 2009, www.bi-me.com/main.php?id=39691&t=1; Safaa Abdoun, "The Spirit of Giving During Ramadan," *The Daily News Egypt*, September 19, 2008, www. thedailynewsegypt.com; Amira Howeidy, "Made to Measure," *Al Ahram Weekly*, September 10–16, 2009, Issue No. 964, http://weekly.ahram.org. eg/2009/964/eg5.htm.

in front of Mac fans and they'll go into ecstasy about the superiority of the brand. Put two MacHeads together and you'll never shut them up. "The Mac [comes] not just as a machine in a box, it [comes] with a whole community," notes one observer. Such fanatically loyal users helped keep Apple afloat during the lean years, and they are now at the forefront of Apple's rapidly growing empire.[11]

Other consumers are somewhat loyal—they are loyal to two or three brands of a given product or favor one brand while sometimes buying others. Still other buyers show no loyalty to any brand. They either want something different each time they buy or they buy whatever's on sale.

A company can learn a lot by analyzing loyalty patterns in its market. It should start by studying its own loyal customers. For example, by studying Mac fanatics, Apple can better pinpoint its target market and develop marketing appeals. By studying its less-loyal buyers, the company can detect which brands are most competitive with its own. By looking at customers who are shifting away from its brand, the company can learn about its marketing weaknesses.

Using Multiple Segmentation Bases

Marketers rarely limit their segmentation analysis to only one or a few variables. Rather, they often use multiple segmentation bases in an effort to identify smaller, better-defined target groups. Thus, a bank may not only identify a group of wealthy retired adults but also, within that group, distinguish several segments based on their current income, assets, savings and risk preferences, housing, and lifestyles.

Such segmentation provides a powerful tool for marketers of all kinds. It can help companies to identify and better understand key customer segments, target them more efficiently, and tailor market offerings and messages to their specific needs.

Segmenting Business Markets

Consumer and business marketers use many of the same variables to segment their markets. Business buyers can be segmented geographically, demographically (industry, company size), or by benefits sought, user status, usage rate, and loyalty status. Yet, business marketers also use some additional variables, such as customer *operating characteristics, purchasing approaches, situational factors,* and *personal characteristics*. By going after segments instead of the whole market, companies can deliver just the right value proposition to each segment served and capture more value in return.

Almost every company serves at least some business markets. For example, Visa targets businesses in one of the four merchant levels based on Visa transaction volumes over a 12-month period. Level one are merchants processing over six million Visa transactions annually, level two are merchants channel-processing one to six million Visa transactions per year, level three are merchants processing 20,000 to one million Visa e-commerce transactions per year, and so on, for every level of merchant. The overall business offering is variable: the higher the level, the more privileges are offered, and the lower rates the merchant pays.[12]

Many companies set up separate systems for dealing with larger or multiple-location customers. For example, IBM first segments customers into main industries, including banking, and aviation. Next, company salespeople work with independent partners to handle smaller, local, or regional customers in each segment. But many national, multiple-location customers have special needs that may reach beyond the scope of individual partners. So IBM uses national account managers to help its dealer networks handle its national accounts.

Within a given target industry and customer size, the company can segment by purchase approaches and criteria. As in consumer segmentation, many marketers believe that *buying behavior* and *benefits* provide the best basis for segmenting business markets.[13]

Segmenting International Markets

Few companies have either the resources or the will to operate in all, or even most, of the countries that dot the globe. Although some large companies, such as Coca-Cola or Sony, sell products in more than 200 countries, most international firms focus on a smaller set.

Operating in many countries presents new challenges. Different countries, even those that are close together, can vary greatly in their economic, cultural, and political makeup. Thus, just as they do within their domestic markets, international firms need to group their world markets into segments with distinct buying needs and behaviors.

Companies can segment international markets using one or a combination of several variables. They can segment by *geographic location*, grouping countries by regions such as Western Europe, the Pacific Rim, the Arab world, or Africa. Geographic segmentation assumes that nations close to one another will have many common traits and behaviors. Although this is often the case, there are many exceptions. For example, companies in the Arab world face the challenge of classifying customers across the region, and they need to effectively segment the market in a way that allows them to satisfy varied customers' needs. It does not make sense to group countries such as Qatar (with small population and high income) with a country such as Sudan (with large population and low income). Also, it would be strange to group countries in North Africa (Tunisia, Algeria, and Morocco) with Gulf countries given the differences in language and culture.

World markets can also be segmented on the basis of *economic factors*. For example, countries might be grouped by population income levels or by their overall level of economic development. A country's economic structure shapes its population's product and service needs and, therefore, the marketing opportunities it offers. Countries can be segmented by *political and legal factors* such as the type and stability of government, receptivity to foreign firms, monetary regulations, and amount of bureaucracy. *Cultural factors* can also be used, grouping markets according to common languages, religions, values and attitudes, customs, and behavioral patterns.

An important aspect in the Arab world is the availability of media channels that are being watched by consumers through satellite broadcasting. Companies targeting consumers of different countries in the region benefit from that; yet they face the challenge of sending consistent messages to all countries. As a result, they attempt to find attractive regional intermarket segments.

Segmenting international markets based on geographic, economic, political, cultural, and other factors assumes that segments should consist of clusters of countries. However, as new communications technologies, such as satellite television and the Internet, connect consumers around the world, marketers can define and reach segments of like-minded consumers no matter where in the world they are. Using **intermarket segmentation** (also called *cross-market segmentation*), they form segments of consumers who have similar needs and buying behaviors even though they are located in different countries. For example, Coca-Cola creates special programs to target teens, core consumers of its soft drinks the world over.

> Coca-Cola wants to relate to the world's teens. To accomplish that, the global soft drinks marketer needed to figure out what the majority of teens finds appealing. The answer: music. So, throughout the world, Coca-Cola links itself with the local pop music scene. For example, in the United States, Coke is the official sponsor of *American Idol*, the country's number-one television show and a teen magnet. In the Arab world, Coca-Cola commercials feature Arab pop stars, such as Nancy Ajram—Coca-Cola even sponsors her world tour. In Europe, Coke has created the Coca-Cola Music Network, which features signed and unsigned musicians online at CokeMusic.com, on stage, and in podcasts. And in Uganda, Coca-Cola sponsored the search for a new MTV VJ. The winner, Carol Mugasha, became host of the weekly music chart show *MTV Coca-Cola Chart Express*.[14]

Intermarket segmentation

Forming segments of consumers who have similar needs and buying behavior even though they are located in different countries.

Requirements for Effective Segmentation

Clearly, there are many ways to segment a market, but not all segmentations are effective. For example, buyers of table salt could be divided into blond and brunette customers. But hair color obviously does not affect the purchase of salt. Furthermore, if all salt buyers bought the same amount of salt each month, believed that all salt is the same, and wanted to pay the same price, the company would not benefit from segmenting this market.

The 'Leftie' segment can be hard to identify and measure. As a result, few companies tailor their offers to left-handers. However, some nichers such as Anything Left-Handed in the United Kingdom target this segment.

To be useful, market segments must be:

- *Measurable:* The size, purchasing power, and profiles of the segments can be measured. Certain segmentation variables are difficult to measure. For example, there are many left-handed people in the world. Yet few products are targeted toward this left-handed segment. The major problem may be that the segment is hard to identify and measure. There is little data on the demographics of 'lefties.' Private data companies keep reams of statistics on other demographic segments but not on left-handers.

- *Accessible:* The market segments can be effectively reached and served. Suppose a fragrance company finds that heavy users of its brand are single men and women who stay out late and socialize a lot. Unless this group lives or shops at certain places and is exposed to certain media, its members will be difficult to reach.

- *Substantial:* The market segments are large or profitable enough to serve. A segment should be the largest possible homogeneous group worth pursuing with a tailored marketing program. It would not pay, for example, for an automobile manufacturer to develop cars especially for people whose height is greater than two meters.

- *Differentiable:* The segments are conceptually distinguishable and respond differently to different marketing mix elements and programs. If married and unmarried women respond similarly to a sale on perfume, they do not constitute separate segments.

- *Actionable:* Effective programs can be designed for attracting and serving the segments. For example, although one small airline identified seven market segments, its staff was too small to develop separate marketing programs for each segment.

Author Comment | Now that we've divided the market into segments, it's time to answer that first seemingly simple marketing strategy question we raised in Figure 7.1: Which customers will the company serve?

Market Targeting (pp 186–192)

Market segmentation reveals the firm's market segment opportunities. The firm now has to evaluate the various segments and decide how many and which segments it can serve best. We now look at how companies evaluate and select target segments.

Evaluating Market Segments

In evaluating different market segments, a firm must look at three factors: segment size and growth, segment structural attractiveness, and company objectives and resources. The company must first collect and analyze data on current segment sales, growth rates, and expected profitability for various segments. It will be interested in segments that have the right size and growth characteristics.

But 'right size and growth' is a relative matter. The largest, fastest-growing segments are not always the most attractive ones for every company. Smaller companies may lack the skills and resources needed to serve the larger segments. Or they may find these segments too competitive. Such companies may target segments that are smaller and less attractive, in an absolute sense, but that are potentially more profitable for them.

The company also needs to examine major structural factors that affect long-run segment attractiveness.[15] For example, a segment is less attractive if it already contains many strong and aggressive *competitors*. The existence of many actual or potential *substitute products* may limit prices and the profits that can be earned in a segment. The relative *power of buyers* also affects segment attractiveness. Buyers with strong bargaining power relative to sellers will try to force prices down, demand more services, and set competitors against one another—all at the expense of seller profitability. Finally, a segment may be less attractive

This figure covers a pretty broad range of targeting strategies, from mass marketing (virtually no targeting) to individual marketing (customizing products and programs to individual customers). An example of individual marketing: At myMMs.com you can order a batch of M&Ms with your face and personal message printed on each little candy.

| Undifferentiated (mass) marketing | Differentiated (segmented) marketing | Concentrated (niche) marketing | Micromarketing (local or individual marketing) |

Targeting broadly   **Targeting narrowly**

if it contains *powerful suppliers* who can control prices or reduce the quality or quantity of ordered goods and services.

Even if a segment has the right size and growth and is structurally attractive, the company must consider its own objectives and resources. Some attractive segments can be dismissed quickly because they do not mesh with the company's long-run objectives. Or the company may lack the skills and resources needed to succeed in an attractive segment. For example, given current economic conditions, the economy segment of the automobile market is large and growing. But given its objectives and resources, it would make little sense for luxury-performance carmaker BMW to enter this segment. A company should enter only segments in which it can create superior customer value and gain advantages over competitors.

Selecting Target Market Segments

After evaluating different segments, the company must decide which and how many segments it will target. A **target market** consists of a set of buyers who share common needs or characteristics that the company decides to serve. Market targeting can be carried out at several different levels. ◆ **Figure 7.2** shows that companies can target very broadly (undifferentiated marketing), very narrowly (micromarketing), or somewhere in between (differentiated or concentrated marketing).

Undifferentiated Marketing

Using an **undifferentiated marketing** (or **mass-marketing**) strategy, a firm might decide to ignore market segment differences and target the whole market with one offer. This mass-marketing strategy focuses on what is *common* in the needs of consumers rather than on what is *different*. The company designs a product and a marketing program that will appeal to the largest number of buyers.

As noted earlier in the chapter, most modern marketers have strong doubts about this strategy. Difficulties arise in developing a product or brand that will satisfy all consumers. Moreover, mass marketers often have trouble competing with more focused firms that do a better job of satisfying the needs of specific segments and niches.

Differentiated Marketing

Using a **differentiated marketing** (or **segmented marketing**) strategy, a firm decides to target several market segments and designs separate offers for each. General Motors tries to produce a car for every "purse, purpose, and personality." Procter & Gamble markets six different laundry detergent brands, which compete with each other on supermarket shelves.

By offering product and marketing variations to segments, companies hope for higher sales and a stronger position within each market segment. Developing a stronger position within several segments creates more total sales than undifferentiated marketing across all segments.

But differentiated marketing also increases the costs of doing business. A firm usually finds it more

Target market
A set of buyers sharing common needs or characteristics that the company decides to serve.

Undifferentiated (mass) marketing
A market-coverage strategy in which a firm decides to ignore market segment differences and go after the whole market with one offer.

Differentiated (segmented) marketing
A market-coverage strategy in which a firm decides to target several market segments and designs separate offers for each.

Differentiated marketing: Procter & Gamble markets six different laundry detergents, including Tide—each with multiple forms and formulations—that compete with each other on store shelves.

expensive to develop and produce, say, 10 units of 10 different products than 100 units of one product. Developing separate marketing plans for the separate segments requires extra marketing research, forecasting, sales analysis, promotion planning, and channel management. And trying to reach different market segments with different advertising campaigns increases promotion costs. Thus, the company must weigh increased sales against increased costs when deciding on a differentiated marketing strategy.

Concentrated Marketing

Concentrated (niche) marketing
A market-coverage strategy in which a firm goes after a large share of one or a few segments or niches.

Using a **concentrated marketing** (or **niche marketing**) strategy, instead of going after a small share of a large market, the firm goes after a large share of one or a few smaller segments or niches. For example, Bindawood, a local supermarket chain in the Kingdom of Saudi Arabia, has many stores in different areas in Mecca and Madinah that target mainly the visitors of the holy sites.

Through concentrated marketing, the firm achieves a strong market position because of its greater knowledge of consumer needs in the niches it serves and the special reputation it acquires. It can market more *effectively* by fine-tuning its products, prices, and programs to the needs of carefully defined segments. It can also market more *efficiently*, targeting its products or services, channels, and communications programs toward only consumers that it can serve best and most profitably.

Whereas segments are fairly large and normally attract several competitors, niches are smaller and may attract only one or a few competitors. Niching lets smaller companies focus their limited resources on serving niches that may be unimportant to or overlooked by larger competitors. Many companies start as nichers to get a foothold against larger, more resourceful competitors and then grow into broader competitors. Aramex offers new services such as "Shop and Ship" for the customers in the Arab world willing to buy products from online shops in the United States and Europe, in order to differentiate itself from large competitors such as DHL, UPS, and FedEx.

In contrast, as markets change, some megamarketers develop niche markets to create sales growth. For example, in recent years, Pepsi has introduced several niche products, such as Seven-Up with Lemon, Pepsi Twist, and Miranda Tangerine. Today, the low cost of setting up shop on the Internet makes it even more profitable to serve seemingly miniscule niches. Small businesses, in particular, are realizing riches from serving small niches on the web.

Concentrated marketing can be highly profitable. At the same time, it involves higher-than-normal risks. Companies that rely on one or a few segments for all of their business will suffer greatly if the segment turns sour. Or larger competitors may decide to enter the same segment with greater resources. For these reasons, many companies prefer to diversify in several market segments. In the Arab world, there is a clear need for Islamic banking services. As a result, a variety of banks, led by HSBC, introduced Islamic banking initiatives in the region. **Real Marketing 7.2** highlights the concept of Islamic banking and its application in the Arab world.

Micromarketing

Micromarketing
The practice of tailoring products and marketing programs to the needs and wants of specific individuals and local customer groups—includes local marketing and individual marketing.

Differentiated and concentrated marketers tailor their offers and marketing programs to meet the needs of various market segments and niches. At the same time, however, they do not customize their offers to each individual customer. **Micromarketing** is the practice of tailoring products and marketing programs to suit the tastes of specific individuals and locations. Rather than seeing a customer in every individual, micromarketers see the individual in every customer. Micromarketing includes *local marketing* and *individual marketing*.

Local marketing
Tailoring brands and promotions to the needs and wants of local customer groups—cities, neighborhoods, and even specific stores.

Local Marketing. **Local marketing** involves tailoring brands and promotions to the needs and wants of local customer groups—cities, neighborhoods, and even specific stores. For example, McDonald's introduced a new sandwich, McArabia, which suited the local culture in the Arab world.

Advances in communications technology have given rise to a new high-tech version of location-based marketing. By coupling mobile phone services with GPS devices, many marketers are now targeting customers wherever they are with what they want.[16]

Real Marketing 7.2

Islamic Banking

A significant type of behavioral targeting taking place in the Arab world is Islamic banking. A recent report by Morgan Stanley analyzing Dubai Islamic Bank and Kuwait Finance House has concluded that Islamic assets will have increased to 18 percent of total assets in the GCC'S banking system by 2012. Currently, there are 22 Islamic banks that possess more than US$300 billion of sharia-compliant assets. An analyst at Morgan Stanley says: "There are a number of reasons why the sector is growing, and will continue to grow, strongly. A buoyant macro-economic backdrop and increased infrastructure spending, and continued diversification from oil economies are driving the banking sector generally... In terms of factors behind the growth in Islamic finance, a greater focus on Islamic identity, government backing for the development and promotion of Islamic banking, low penetration, and competition among conventional banks makes Islamic banking more attractive, and more favorable industry dynamics are all likely to fuel the growth."

Despite the expected growth in that behavioral segment, which fosters the Islamic identity, there are some obstacles to the concept. The main difficulty remains that the product is not a regular one that can easily be identified. As such, Islamic banks are subject to more than one regulatory body, such as the local Central Banks as well as the Shari'a Supervisory Board (SSB), which must be established by the banks to advise them and ensure that all their activities are compliant with *Shari'a* Islamic rules principles, in order to formulate Islamic services. Another issue is the fact that people tend to be less familiar with how the system works compared with the regular banking systems. There are also some aspects in Islamic banking that are not welcomed by other financial institutions and customers, such as not allowing hedging (fixing currency value for long periods in the currency exchange market). A 2008 Morgan Stanley report, however, suggests an exponential growth for the sector.

Islamic banking mainly targets 'devout Muslims' in Muslim communities and Muslim minorities in non-Muslim countries. In addition, it attracts non-Muslim individuals and societies that demand ethical financial solutions. Islamic financial institutions were established in the 1960s and 1970s. Since that time Islamic bank-

Islamic banking has gained a strong reputation in the past few years, especially after the financial crisis in 2008 which revealed many of the defects in international banking systems.

ing has sprawled in several Islamic countries primarily in the Arab world, South and Southeast Asia, and in the West where Muslim minorities live. Now Bahrain is the most flourishing country in the Islamic finance field; other non-Arab cities enjoyed growth in the field, including Kuala Lumpur and London. Islamic banks are available in different formats, including "commercial banks, investment banks, investment and finance companies, insurance (Takaful) companies, and financial service companies." However, they pursue distinct banking models: private organizations in a traditional economy (in the GCC and the West), national banking institutions (such as those in Sudan, Iran, and Pakistan), and dual banking systems (such as in Malaysia and the UAE). Moreover, they are present in different models: fully Islamic institutions, Islamic subsidiaries of traditional banking groups, and Islamic banking 'windows' inside traditional banks.

Islamic banking services range from commercial banking to syndicated transactions and equities, and have recently moved into debt issuance and structured products. The growth in the segment is attributed to the growing economy of oil-producing countries. Thus, this made the Islamic financial services highly demanded by a large number of people.

Let's take a look at an example of an international bank that has adapted to the needs of the Islamic segment. HSBC Amanah—Islamic Financial Solutions was "established to serve the particular financial needs of Muslim communities." According

to HSBC's mission, "Amanah is committed to improving the lives of our customers worldwide by providing them with the highest quality Islamic banking solutions." Accordingly, there is commitment to Shari'a to the greatest extent. HSBC Islamic banking services are present in several GCC countries, including Bahrain, UAE, Saudi Arabia, Qatar, and other non-Arab Muslim countries, including Bangladesh, Brunei, Indonesia, Malaysia, and other countries as well.

HSBC Amanah is supervised by the Global Shari'a Advisory Board (GSAB) and Regional Shari'a Committees (RSC). Moreover, HBSC has a team of professionals who are there to guarantee that Shari'a are applied in 'letter' and 'spirit.' GSAB pursues continuous updating of the Islamic financial services. The board consists of delegate scholars from all RSC of HSBC Amanah and other Shari'a scholars from all around the world. HSBC depends on known scholars from different origins to ensure the convention of all scholars on its Islamic financial matters.

Amanah has different Islamic services all using the same principles, yet they are based on the needs of the various types of customers. There are three common Islamic financial instruments, which are:

- *Mudaraba*: An investment partnership, whereby an agreement takes place between an investor (or financer) and an entrepreneur or investment manager, called the *Mudarib*. They both divide risks

Continued on next page ▼

Real Marketing 7.2 Continued ▼

and profits. When there are profits, they earn their agreed-upon shares. When there are losses, the investor incurs a loss of capital, whereas the Mudarib loses time and effort.

- *Ijara*, which means an Islamic lease. The financial institution buys an asset and leases it to a customer in return for a set monthly fee. The

lessee has the choice to purchase the asset at the end of the lease.

- *Murabaha*, which is a sale at an agreed-upon profit. In this transaction, the bank buys something

from a third party and sells it to a client at a set profit on a deferred payment system. Murabaha ensures that the client buys something without taking interest on a loan.

Sources: Justin Smith, "Morgan Stanley Initiates Coverage on Islamic Banking Stocks," *BI-ME*, February 19, 2008, www.bi-me.com/main.php?id=17576&t=1&c=34&cg=; "Our Vision," "The Industry," "Shariah Supervision," and "Financial Instruments," HSBC Amanah, www.hsbcamanah.com/amanah/about-amanah/islamic-banking.

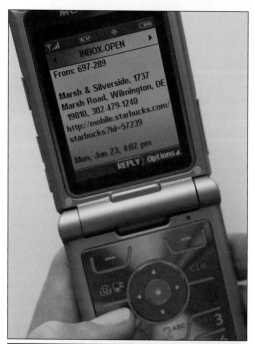

Local marketing: By coupling mobile phone services with GPS devices, marketers such as Starbucks are now targeting customers wherever they are with what they want.

Location. Location. Location. This is the mantra of the real-estate business. But it may not be long before marketers quote it, too. "Location-based technology allows [marketers] to reach people when they're mobile, near their stores, looking to make a decision," says one marketing expert. "When customers get information—even advertising information—linked to their location, research shows that's often perceived as value-added information, not as an advertisement." For example, Starbucks recently launched a store locator service for mobile devices, which allows people to use their phones and in-car GPS systems to search for the nearest Starbucks shop. A consumer sends a text message to "MYSBUX" (697289) including his or her postal code. Within 10 seconds, Starbucks replies with up to three nearby store locations. Starbucks plans to expand the service to include a wider range of text-messaging conversations with local customers that will "showcase Starbucks as a brand that truly listens." Such location-based marketing will grow astronomically as the sales of GPS devices skyrocket.

Local marketing has some drawbacks. It can drive up manufacturing and marketing costs by reducing economies of scale. It can also create logistics problems as companies try to meet the varied requirements of different regional and local markets. Further, a brand's overall image might be diluted if the product and message vary too much in different localities.

Still, as companies face increasingly fragmented markets, and as new supporting technologies develop, the advantages of local marketing often outweigh the drawbacks. Local marketing helps a company to market more effectively in the face of pronounced regional and local differences in demographics and lifestyles. It also meets the needs of the company's first-line customers—retailers—who prefer more finely tuned product assortments for their neighborhoods.

Individual marketing
Tailoring products and marketing programs to the needs and preferences of individual customers—also labeled 'one-to-one marketing,' 'customized marketing,' and 'markets-of-one marketing.'

Individual Marketing. In the extreme, micromarketing becomes **individual marketing**— tailoring products and marketing programs to the needs and preferences of individual customers. Individual marketing has also been labeled *one-to-one marketing, mass customization,* and *markets-of-one marketing.*

The widespread use of mass marketing has obscured the fact that for centuries consumers were served as individuals: The tailor custom-made the suit, the cobbler designed shoes for the individual, the cabinetmaker made furniture to order. Today, however, new technologies are permitting many companies to return to customized marketing. More powerful computers, detailed databases, robotic production and flexible manufacturing, and interactive communication media such as cellphones and the Internet—all have combined to foster 'mass customization.' *Mass customization* is the process through which firms interact one-to-one with masses of customers to design products and services tailor-made to individual needs.

Dell creates custom-configured computers. Visitors to Nike's NikeID website can personalize their sneakers by choosing from hundreds of colors.

Marketers are also finding new ways to personalize promotional messages. Service providers such as Vodafone have been sending customers personalized office stationery,

John Deere manufactures a wide range of seeding equipment and other planting equipment that matches the various needs of customers' specifications.

calendars, and giveaways showing their names and titles. Newsletters from different providers have mapped customer interests to make their material more relevant and personal.

Business-to-business marketers are also finding new ways to customize their offerings. For example, John Deere manufactures seeding equipment that can be configured in more than two million versions to individual customer specifications. The seeders are produced one at a time, in any sequence, on a single production line. Mass customization provides a way to stand out against competitors.

Unlike mass production, which eliminates the need for human interaction, one-to-one marketing has made relationships with customers more important than ever. Just as mass production was the marketing principle of the past century, interactive marketing is becoming a marketing principle for the twenty-first century. The world appears to be coming full circle—from the good old days when customers were treated as individuals, to mass marketing when nobody knew your name, and back again.

The move toward individual marketing mirrors the trend in consumer *self-marketing*. Increasingly, individual customers are taking more responsibility for shaping both the products they buy and the buying experience. Consider two business buyers with two different purchasing styles. The first sees several salespeople, each trying to persuade him to buy his or her product. The second sees no salespeople but rather logs on to the web. She searches for information on available products; interacts online with various suppliers, users, and product analysts; and then decides which offer is best. The second purchasing agent has taken more responsibility for the buying process, and the marketer has had less influence over the buying decision.

As the trend toward more interactive dialogue and less marketing monologue continues, marketers will need to influence the buying process in new ways. They will need to involve customers more in all phases of the product development and buying processes, increasing opportunities for buyers to practice self-marketing.

Choosing a Targeting Strategy

Companies need to consider many factors when choosing a market-targeting strategy. Which strategy is best depends on *company resources*. When the firm's resources are limited, concentrated marketing makes the most sense. The best strategy also depends on the degree of *product variability*. Undifferentiated marketing is more suited for uniform products such as grapefruit or steel. Products that can vary in design, such as cameras and automobiles, are more suited to differentiation or concentration. The *product's life-cycle stage* also must be considered. When a firm introduces a new product, it may be practical to launch only one version, and undifferentiated marketing or concentrated marketing may make the most sense. In the mature stage of the product life cycle, however, differentiated marketing begins to make more sense.

Another factor is *market variability*. If most buyers have the same tastes, buy the same amounts, and react the same way to marketing efforts, undifferentiated marketing is appropriate. Finally, *competitors' marketing strategies* are important. When competitors use differentiated or concentrated marketing, undifferentiated marketing can be suicidal. Conversely, when competitors use undifferentiated marketing, a firm can gain an advantage by using differentiated or concentrated marketing, focusing on the needs of buyers in specific segments.

Socially Responsible Target Marketing

Smart targeting helps companies to be more efficient and effective by focusing on the segments that they can satisfy best and most profitably. Targeting also benefits consumers—companies serve specific groups of consumers with offers carefully tailored to their needs. However, target marketing sometimes generates controversy and concern. The biggest issues usually involve the targeting of vulnerable or disadvantaged consumers with controversial or potentially harmful products.

Not only does Colgate offer a wide selection of products targeting children, but also it holds many campaigns for children in the Arab world to increase awareness about the importance of brushing their teeth.

For example, over the years, marketers in a wide range of industries—from cereal and toys to fast food and fashion—have been heavily criticized for their marketing efforts directed toward children. Critics worry that premium offers and high-powered advertising appeals presented through the mouths of lovable animated characters will overwhelm children's defenses. Other problems arise when the marketing of adult products spills over into the child segment—intentionally or unintentionally. Some critics have even called for a complete ban on advertising to children.

The growth of the Internet and other carefully targeted direct media has raised fresh concerns about potential targeting abuses. The Internet allows increasing refinement of audiences and, in turn, more precise targeting. This might help makers of questionable products or deceptive advertisers to more readily victimize the most vulnerable audiences. Unprincipled marketers can now send tailor-made deceptive messages directly to the computers of millions of unsuspecting consumers.[17]

Not all attempts to target children, minorities, or other special segments draw such criticism. In fact, most provide benefits to targeted consumers. For example, Pantene markets Relaxed and Natural hair products to women of color. Samsung markets the Jitterbug phone directly to seniors who need a simpler cellphone that is bigger and has a louder speaker. And Colgate makes a large selection of toothbrush shapes and toothpaste flavors for children. Such products help make tooth brushing more fun and get children to brush longer and more often.

Thus, in target marketing, the issue is not really *who* is targeted but rather *how* and for *what*. Controversies arise when marketers attempt to profit at the expense of targeted segments—when they unfairly target vulnerable segments or target them with questionable products or tactics. Socially responsible marketing calls for segmentation and targeting that serve not just the interests of the company but also the interests of those targeted.

Author Comment | At the same time that it's answering the first simple-sounding question (Which customers will we serve?), the company must be asking the second question (How will we serve them?). For example, Ritz-Carlton serves the top 5 percent of corporate and leisure travelers. Its value proposition is 'The Ritz-Carlton Experience'—one that "enlivens the senses, instills a sense of well-being, and fulfills even the unexpressed wishes and needs of our guests."

Product position

The way the product is defined by consumers on important attributes—the place the product occupies in consumers' minds relative to competing products.

Differentiation and Positioning (pp 192–198)

Beyond deciding which segments of the market it will target, the company must decide on a *value proposition*—on how it will create differentiated value for targeted segments and what positions it wants to occupy in those segments. A **product's position** is the way the product is *defined by consumers* on important attributes—the place the product occupies in consumers' minds relative to competing products. "Products are created in the factory, but brands are created in the mind," says a positioning expert.[18]

Tide is positioned as a powerful, all-purpose family detergent. At Subway restaurants, you "Eat Fresh." In the automobile market, Mercedes and Cadillac are positioned on luxury, and Porsche and BMW on performance. Volvo positions powerfully on safety. And Toyota positions its fuel-efficient, hybrid Prius as a high-tech solution to the energy shortage. "How far will you go to save the planet?" it asks.

Consumers are overloaded with information about products and services. They cannot reevaluate products every time they make a buying decision. To simplify the buying process, consumers organize products, services, and companies into categories and 'position' them in their minds. A product's position is the complex set of perceptions, impressions, and feelings that consumers have for the product compared with competing products.

Consumers position products with or without the help of marketers. But marketers do not want to leave their products' positions to chance. They must *plan* positions that will give their products the greatest advantage in selected target markets, and they must design marketing mixes to create these planned positions.

FIGURE | 7.3
Positioning Map:
Large Luxury Sport
Utility Vehicles

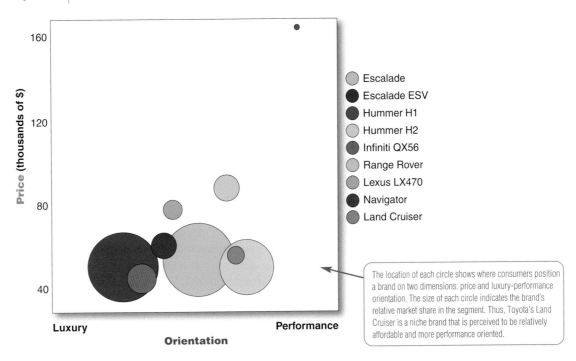

FIGURE | 7.3
Positioning Map:
Large Luxury Sport
Utility Vehicles

The location of each circle shows where consumers position a brand on two dimensions: price and luxury-performance orientation. The size of each circle indicates the brand's relative market share in the segment. Thus, Toyota's Land Cruiser is a niche brand that is perceived to be relatively affordable and more performance oriented.

Positioning Maps

In planning their differentiation and positioning strategies, marketers often prepare *perceptual positioning maps*, which show consumer perceptions of their brands versus competing products on important buying dimensions. **Figure 7.3** shows a positioning map for the U.S. large luxury sport utility vehicle market.[19]

Choosing a Differentiation and Positioning Strategy

Some firms find it easy to choose a differentiation and positioning strategy. For example, a firm well known for quality in certain segments will go for this position in a new segment if there are enough buyers seeking quality. But in many cases, two or more firms will go after the same position. Then, each will have to find other ways to set itself apart. Each firm must differentiate its offer by building a unique bundle of benefits that appeals to a substantial group within the segment.

Above all else, a brand's positioning must serve the needs and preferences of well-defined target markets. For example, Mobinil is positioning itself in the Egyptian market as the competent local service provider, and builds its communication campaigns on the concept of patriotism. On the other hand, Vodafone is positioning itself as an international and professional brand.

The differentiation and positioning task consists of three steps: identifying a set of differentiating competitive advantages upon which to build a position, choosing the right competitive advantages, and selecting an overall positioning strategy. The company must then effectively communicate and deliver the chosen position to the market.

Identifying Possible Value Differences and Competitive Advantages

To build profitable relationships with target customers, marketers must understand customer needs better than competitors do and deliver more customer value. To the extent that a company can differentiate and position itself as providing superior customer value, it gains **competitive advantage**.

But solid positions cannot be built on empty promises. If a company positions its product as *offering* the best quality and service, it must actually differentiate the product so

Competitive advantage
An advantage over competitors gained by offering greater customer value, either through lower prices or by providing more benefits that justify higher prices.

Toughbook is positioned as the durable, reliable, wireless notebook that can protect the customer's work even in the toughest environments.

that it *delivers* the promised quality and service. Companies must do much more than simply shout out their positions in ad slogans and taglines. They must first *live* the slogan.

To find points of differentiation, marketers must think through the customer's entire experience with the company's product or service. An alert company can find ways to differentiate itself at every customer-contact point. In what specific ways can a company differentiate itself or its market offer? It can differentiate along the lines of *product, services, channels, people,* or *image.*

Through *product differentiation* brands can be differentiated on features, performance, or style and design. Thus, Panasonic positions its Toughbook PCs, designed to stand up to rugged use on the road or in the field. The Toughbook website offers "Tough Stories," complete with pictures of battered and abused Toughbooks still functioning well.

Beyond differentiating its physical product, a firm can also differentiate the services that accompany the product. Some companies gain *services differentiation* through speedy, convenient, or careful delivery. For example, Al-Baraka Bank has positioned itself as "the commercial Islamic Bank"—it offers retail, corporate and investment banking, and treasury services which should abide by the principles of Islamic Shari'a.[20] Others differentiate their service based on high-quality customer care. Lexus makes fine cars but is perhaps even better known for the quality service that creates outstanding ownership experiences for Lexus owners.

Firms that practice *channel differentiation* gain competitive advantage through the way they design their channel's coverage, expertise, and performance. Amazon.com and GEICO set themselves apart with their smooth-functioning direct channels. Companies can also gain a strong competitive advantage through *people differentiation*—hiring and training better people than their competitors do. And Singapore Airlines enjoys an excellent reputation, largely because of the grace of its flight attendants. People differentiation requires that a company select its customer-contact people carefully and train them well. For example, the entertainment company Disney trains its theme park people thoroughly to ensure that they are competent, polite, and friendly—from the hotel check-in agents, to the monorail drivers, to the ride attendants, to the people who sweep its parks. Each employee is carefully trained to understand customers and to "make people happy."

Even when competing offers look the same, buyers may perceive a difference based on company or brand *image differentiation.* A company or brand image should convey the product's distinctive benefits and positioning. Developing a strong and distinctive image calls for creativity and hard work. A company cannot develop an image in the public's mind overnight using only a few advertisements. If Ritz-Carlton means quality, this image must be supported by everything the company says and does.

Symbols—such as the McDonald's golden arches, the Nike swoosh, or Google's colorful logo—can provide strong company or brand recognition and image differentiation. The company might build a brand around a famous person, as Nike did with its Air Jordan basketball shoes and Tiger Woods golfing products. Some companies even become associated with colors, such as IBM (blue), UPS (brown), or Coca-Cola (red). The chosen symbols, characters, and other image elements must be communicated through advertising that conveys the company's or brand's personality.

Choosing the Right Competitive Advantages

Suppose a company is fortunate enough to discover several potential differentiations that provide competitive advantages. It now must choose the ones on which it will build its positioning strategy. It must decide *how many* differences to promote and *which ones.*

How Many Differences to Promote. Many marketers think that companies should aggressively promote only one benefit to the target market. Ad man Rosser Reeves, for example, said a company should develop a *unique selling proposition* (USP) for each brand and stick to it. Each brand should pick an attribute and tout itself as 'number one' on that attribute. Buyers tend to remember number one better, especially in this overcommunicated society. Thus, Wal-Mart promotes its always low prices and Burger King promotes personal choice—"have it your way."

Other marketers think that companies should position themselves on more than one differentiator. This may be necessary if two or more firms are claiming to be best on the same attribute. Today, in a time when the mass market is fragmenting into many small segments, companies are trying to broaden their positioning strategies to appeal to more segments.

For example, S.C. Johnson recently introduced a new Pledge multi-surface cleaner. Known mainly as a brand for cleaning and dusting wood furniture, the new Pledge is positioned as a cleaner that works on wood, electronics, glass, marble, stainless steel, and other surfaces. Says its website, "No need to keep switching products—this multi-surface cleaner is perfect for a quick and easy cleanup of the whole room!" Clearly, many buyers want these multiple benefits. The challenge was to convince them that one brand can do it all. However, as companies increase the number of claims for their brands, they risk disbelief and a loss of clear positioning.

Which Differences to Promote.   Not all brand differences are meaningful or worthwhile; not every difference makes a good differentiator. Each difference has the potential to create company costs as well as customer benefits. A difference is worth establishing to the extent that it satisfies the following criteria:

- *Important:* The difference delivers a highly valued benefit to target buyers.
- *Distinctive:* Competitors do not offer the difference, or the company can offer it in a more distinctive way.
- *Superior:* The difference is superior to other ways that customers might obtain the same benefit.
- *Communicable:* The difference is communicable and visible to buyers.
- *Preemptive:* Competitors cannot easily copy the difference.
- *Affordable:* Buyers can afford to pay for the difference.
- *Profitable:* The company can introduce the difference profitably.

Many companies have introduced differentiations that failed one or more of these tests. When the Westin Stamford Hotel in Singapore once advertised that it is the world's tallest hotel, it was a distinction that was not important to most tourists—in fact, it turned many off. Thus, choosing competitive advantages upon which to position a product or service can be difficult, yet such choices may be crucial to success.

Selecting an Overall Positioning Strategy

Value proposition
The full positioning of a brand—the full mix of benefits upon which it is positioned.

The full positioning of a brand is called the brand's **value proposition**—the full mix of benefits upon which the brand is differentiated and positioned. It is the answer to the customer's question "Why should I buy your brand?" Volvo's value proposition hinges on safety but also includes reliability, roominess, and styling, all for a price that is higher than average but seems fair for this mix of benefits.

Figure 7.4 shows possible value propositions upon which a company might position its products. In the figure, the five green cells represent winning value propositions—differentiation and positioning that gives the company competitive advantage. The red cells, however, represent losing value propositions. The center yellow cell represents at best a marginal proposition. In the following sections, we discuss the five winning value propositions upon which companies can position their products: more for more, more for the same, the same for less, less for much less, and more for less.

More for More.   'More-for-more' positioning involves providing the most upscale product or service and charging a higher price to cover the higher costs. Ritz-Carlton Hotels, Mont Blanc writing instruments, Mercedes automobiles—each claims superior quality, craftsmanship, durability, performance, or style and charges a price to match. Not only is the market offering high in quality, it also gives prestige to the buyer. It symbolizes status and a loftier lifestyle. Often, the price difference exceeds the actual increment in quality.

FIGURE | 7.4

Possible Value Propositions

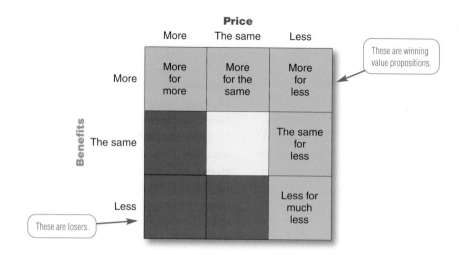

Sellers offering 'only the best' can be found in every product and service category, from hotels, restaurants, food, and fashion to cars and household appliances. Consumers are sometimes surprised, even delighted, when a new competitor enters a category with an unusually high-priced brand. Starbucks coffee entered as a very expensive brand in a largely commodity category. When Apple premiered its iPhone, it offered higher-quality features than a traditional cellphone, with a hefty price tag to match.

In general, companies should be on the lookout for opportunities to introduce a 'more-for-more' brand in any underdeveloped product or service category. Yet 'more-for-more' brands can be vulnerable. They often invite imitators who claim the same quality but at a lower price. Luxury goods that sell well during good times may be at risk during economic downturns when buyers become more cautious in their spending.

More for the Same.   Companies can attack a competitor's more-for-more positioning by introducing a brand offering comparable quality but at a lower price. For example, Toyota introduced its Lexus line with a 'more-for-the-same' value proposition versus Mercedes and BMW. Its first ad headline read: "Perhaps the first time in history that trading a $72,000 car for a $36,000 car could be considered trading up." It communicated the high quality of its new Lexus through rave reviews in car magazines and through a widely distributed video-tape showing side-by-side comparisons of Lexus and Mercedes automobiles. It published surveys showing that Lexus dealers were providing customers with better sales and service experiences than were Mercedes dealerships. Many Mercedes owners switched to Lexus, and the Lexus repurchase rate has been 60 percent, twice the industry average.

The Same for Less.   Offering 'the same for less' can be a powerful value proposition—everyone likes a good deal. Hypermarkets, such as Carrefour, also use this positioning. They don't claim to offer different or better products. Instead, they offer many of the same brands as department stores and specialty stores but at deep discounts based on superior purchasing power and lower-cost operations. Other companies develop imitative but lower-priced brands in an effort to lure customers away from the market leader. For example, AMD makes less-expensive versions of Intel's market-leading microprocessor chips.

Less for Much Less.   A market almost always exists for products that offer less and therefore cost less. Few people need, want, or can afford 'the very best' in everything they buy. In many cases, consumers will gladly settle for less than optimal performance or give up some of the extra features in exchange for a lower price. For example, Nokia has a series of mobile phones with limited features for lower prices targeting consumers who are not willing to pay for features they will not use.

'Less-for-much-less' positioning involves meeting consumers' lower performance or quality requirements at a much lower price. For example, Chinese products have invaded the Arab world markets with relatively low quality products, but at very low prices, which have attracted a large number of consumers.

Home Centre in Egypt was one of the first movers in the direction of 'more for less' offers after the revolution in January 2011.

Positioning statement

A statement that summarizes company or brand positioning—it takes this form: To (target segment and need) our (brand) is (concept) that (point-of-difference).

More for Less.   Of course, the winning value proposition would be to offer 'more for less.' Many companies claim to do this. And, in the short run, some companies can actually achieve it. Several mobile operators have built consumption segments where the more minutes a user consumes talking on the phone, the cheaper each minute becomes. For example, Zain, a mobile operator in Kuwait, offers unlimited communication at a fixed price based on the duration of users' subscription. For a one-day unlimited usage, the user pays US$5.4 per day; if the user subscribes for a week, they pay US$3.6 per day, and if the user subscribes for 30 days, they pay US$2.8 per day.[21]

Yet in the long run, companies will find it very difficult to sustain such best-of-both positioning. Offering more usually costs more, making it difficult to deliver on the 'for-less' promise. Companies that try to deliver both may lose out to more focused competitors.

All said, each brand must adopt a positioning strategy designed to serve the needs and wants of its target markets. 'More for more' will draw one target market, 'less for much less' will draw another, and so on. Thus, in any market, there is usually room for many different companies, each successfully occupying different positions. The important thing is that each company must develop its own winning positioning strategy, one that makes it special to its target consumers.

Developing a Positioning Statement

Company and brand positioning should be summed up in a **positioning statement**. The statement should follow the form: *To (target segment and need) our (brand) is (concept) that (point-of-difference).*[22] For example: "To busy, mobile professionals who need to always be in the loop, BlackBerry is a wireless connectivity solution that gives you an easier, more reliable way to stay connected to data, people, and resources while on the go."[23]

Note that the positioning first states the product's membership in a category (wireless connectivity solution) and then shows its point-of-difference from other members of the category (easier, more reliable connections to data, people, and resources). Placing a brand in a specific category suggests similarities that it might share with other products in the category. But the case for the brand's superiority is made on its points of difference.

Sometimes marketers put a brand in a surprisingly different category before indicating the points of difference. Nestlé's Nescafé brand has several products in the instant coffee market, including Nescafé Gold, positioned as better instant coffee, and Nescafé Espresso, positioned as the Italian instant coffee (instant coffee that looks better and tastes like espresso). The positioning of Nescafé Espresso as gourmet coffee puts it in a completely different category versus the other instant coffee products in the market.

Communicating and Delivering the Chosen Position

Once it has chosen a position, the company must take strong steps to deliver and communicate the desired position to target consumers. All the company's marketing mix efforts must support the positioning strategy.

Positioning the company calls for concrete action, not just talk. If the company decides to build a position on better quality and service, it must first *deliver* that position. Designing the marketing mix—product, price, place, and promotion—involves working out the tactical details of the positioning strategy. Thus, a firm that seizes on a more-for-more position knows that it must produce high-quality products, charge a high price, distribute through high-quality dealers, and advertise in high-quality media. It must hire and train more service people, find retailers who have a good reputation for service, and develop sales and advertising messages that broadcast its superior service. This is the only way to build a consistent and believable more-for-more position.

Companies often find it easier to come up with a good positioning strategy than to implement it. Establishing a position or changing one usually takes a long time. In contrast, positions that have taken years to build can quickly be lost. Once a company has built the desired position, it must take care to maintain the position through consistent performance and communication. It must closely monitor and adapt the position over time to match changes in consumer needs and competitors' strategies. However, the company should avoid abrupt changes that might confuse consumers. Instead, a product's position should evolve gradually as it adapts to the ever-changing marketing environment.

REVIEWING Objectives AND KEY Terms

In this chapter, you've learned about the major elements of a customer-driven marketing strategy: segmentation, targeting, differentiation, and positioning. Marketers know that they cannot appeal to all buyers in their markets, or at least not to all buyers in the same way. Buyers are too numerous, too widely scattered, and too varied in their needs and buying practices. Therefore, most companies today practice *target marketing*—identifying market segments, selecting one or more of them, and developing products and marketing mixes tailored to each.

OBJECTIVE 1 Define the major steps in designing a customer-driven marketing strategy: market segmentation, targeting, differentiation, and positioning. (p 177)

Customer-driven marketing strategy begins with selecting which customers to serve and deciding on a value proposition that best serves them. It consists of four steps. *Market segmentation* is the act of dividing a market into distinct groups of buyers with different needs, characteristics, or behaviors who might require separate products or marketing mixes. Once the groups have been identified, *market targeting* evaluates each market segment's attractiveness and selects one or more segments to serve. Market targeting consists of designing strategies to build the *right relationships* with the *right customers*. *Differentiation* involves actually differentiating the market offering to create superior customer value. *Positioning* consists of positioning the market offering in the minds of target customers.

OBJECTIVE 2 List and discuss the major bases for segmenting consumer and business markets. (pp 178–186)

There is no single way to segment a market. Therefore, the marketer tries different variables to see which give the best segmentation opportunities. For consumer marketing, the major segmentation variables are geographic, demographic, psychographic, and behavioral. In *geographic segmentation*, the market is divided into different geographical units such as nations, regions, provinces, parishes, cities, or neighborhoods. In *demographic segmentation*, the market is divided into groups based on demographic variables, including age, gender, family size, family life cycle, income, occupation, education, religion, race, generation, and nationality. In *psychographic segmentation*, the market is divided into different groups based on social class, lifestyle, or personality characteristics. In *behavioral segmentation*, the market is divided into groups based on consumers' knowledge, attitudes, uses, or responses to a product.

Business marketers use many of the same variables to segment their markets. But business markets also can be segmented

by business consumer *demographics* (industry, company size), *operating characteristics, purchasing approaches, situational factors,* and *personal characteristics*. The effectiveness of segmentation analysis depends on finding segments that are *measurable, accessible, substantial, differentiable,* and *actionable*.

OBJECTIVE 3 Explain how companies identify attractive market segments and choose a market-targeting strategy. (pp 186–192)

To target the best market segments, the company first evaluates each segment's size and growth characteristics, structural attractiveness, and compatibility with company objectives and resources. It then chooses one of four market-targeting strategies—ranging from very broad to very narrow targeting. The seller can ignore segment differences and target broadly using *undifferentiated (or mass) marketing*. This involves mass producing, mass distributing, and mass promoting about the same product in about the same way to all consumers. Or the seller can adopt *differentiated marketing*—developing different market offers for several segments. *Concentrated marketing* (or *niche marketing*) involves focusing on only one or a few market segments. Finally, *micromarketing* is the practice of tailoring products and marketing programs to suit the tastes of specific individuals and locations. Micromarketing includes *local marketing* and *individual marketing*. Which targeting strategy is best depends on company resources, product variability, product life-cycle stage, market variability, and competitive marketing strategies.

OBJECTIVE 4 Discuss how companies differentiate and position their products for maximum competitive advantage in the marketplace. (pp 192–198)

Once a company has decided which segments to enter, it must decide on its *differentiation and positioning strategy*. The differentiation and positioning task consists of three steps: identifying a set of possible differentiations that create competitive advantage, choosing advantages upon which to build a position, and selecting an overall positioning strategy. The brand's full positioning is called its *value proposition*—the full mix of benefits upon which the brand is positioned. In general, companies can choose from one of five winning value propositions upon which to position their products: more for more, more for the same, the same for less, less for much less, or more for less. Company and brand positioning are summarized in positioning statements that state the target segment and need, positioning concept, and specific points of difference. The company must then effectively communicate and deliver the chosen position to the market.

KEY Terms

OBJECTIVE 1

Market segmentation (p 177)
Market targeting (targeting) (p 177)
Differentiation (p 177)
Positioning (p 177)

OBJECTIVE 2

Geographic segmentation (p 178)
Demographic segmentation (p 180)
Age and life-cycle segmentation (p 180)
Gender segmentation (p 181)
Income segmentation (p 181)

Psychographic segmentation (p 181)
Behavioral segmentation (p 181)
Occasion segmentation (p 181)
Benefit segmentation (p 182)
Intermarket segmentation (p 185)

OBJECTIVE 3

Target market (p 187)
Undifferentiated (mass) marketing (p 187)
Differentiated (segmented) marketing (p 187)

Concentrated (niche) marketing (p 188)
Micromarketing (p 188)
Local marketing (p 188)
Individual marketing (p 190)

OBJECTIVE 4

Product position (p 192)
Competitive advantage (p 193)
Value proposition (p 195)
Positioning statement (p 197)

DISCUSSING & APPLYING THE Concepts

Discussing the Concepts

1. Briefly describe the four major steps in designing a customer-driven marketing strategy.

2. Name and describe the four major sets of variables that might be used in segmenting consumer markets. Which segmenting variable(s) do you think Starbucks is using?

3. Explain how marketers can segment international markets.

4. Compare and contrast undifferentiated, differentiated, concentrated, and micromarketing targeting strategies. Which strategy is best?

5. What is a product's 'position' and how do marketers know what it is?

6. Name and define the five winning value propositions described in the chapter. Which value proposition describes Wal-Mart? Explain your answer.

Applying the Concepts

1. The chapter described psychographics as one major variable used by marketers when segmenting consumer markets. SRI Consulting has developed a typology of consumers based on their values and lifestyles; specifically it places U.S. adult consumers into one of eight segments. Go to the website (www.sric-bi.com), and click on the VALS survey in the right side of the page. Take the test. How accurately do the VALS types describe you? What amendments to the survey would you need to make in order for it to be more appropriate to your country's adult consumers. How would the survey results be affected if your changes were made?

2. Assume you work at a regional university in your country. The traditional market for the university is post-secondary school students in your region who have attained sufficiently high qualifications. However, the university's target market is shrinking. In addition, it will decrease by around 5 percent over the course of the next 10 years. Recommend other potential market segments the university could pursue, and discuss the criteria it should consider to ensure that the segments you identified are effectively targeted.

3. Form a small group and create an idea for a new reality television show. Using the format provided in the chapter, develop a positioning statement for this television show. What competitive advantage does the show have over existing shows? How many and which differences would you promote?

FOCUS ON Technology

Have you noticed that ads on websites seem to reflect your interests? Do you ever wonder if someone is watching your Internet behavior? Well, someone (that is, a computer) probably is watching and tracking you. Marketers use such tracking information to send targeted ads to consumers—it's called behavioral targeting. You've no doubt heard of 'cookies,' the files deposited on your computer when you visit a website. If you've ever given personally identifying information at a site, it remembers you when you return—it's all stored in the cookie file. But even if you don't give personally identifying information on a website, Internet protocol addresses (IP addresses) can be tracked to follow where you go and where you've been on the Internet. This tracking lets marketers tailor web pages, information, offers, and prices to individuals based on their behavioral characteristics. Behavioral targeting is coveted because it allows marketers to implement micromarketing strategies.

1. TACODA is a behavioral targeting ad network. Visit www.tacoda.com to learn more about this company. Explore this website to learn how it lets marketers send Internet ads to targeted consumers. Then, write a brief report explaining behavioral targeting and how marketers are using it.

2. Many individuals are concerned that Internet behavioral tracking violates their privacy. Most websites have access to users' IP addresses. Do IP addresses alone qualify as 'user identifiable' information? Learn more about this issue and write a brief report about it.

FOCUS ON Ethics

The increasing number of infomercials and advertisements in the Arab world for weight control pills has started to trigger reactions in society. People have been bombarded with advertisements featuring beautiful bodies in revealing clothing, sitting lazily and ingesting multiple food supplements, and ending up looking like movie stars. The vast majority of these supplements are not approved by any formal authority or regulated by any government. There is no authority that places standards on what should or could be shown to the masses and what message it should communicate.

Many of these products turn out to be a scam, with no actual value. The organizations offering these products are able to advertise them on television to the majority of the Arab world because of the lack of regulatory authority. Critics argue that the ads are misleading the customers about what could be a health-damaging product, and also that the resulting aspiration for achieving the perfect body through instant, non-effective, and non-healthy means requires some supervision and management.

The channels showing these ads have also been criticized for their role in promoting them. Some channels have taken the initiative of managing the material being advertised. That has resulted in new satellite channels which use a business model of plugging in the infomercials into entertainment programs to overcome the limitations of the television channels and also to save the cost of their advertisement.

1. Do you think the channels that show the infomercials have any form of liability?

2. Give an example of an organization or a governmental authority that has taken the responsibility of managing the honesty of a television advertisement.

MARKETING BY THE Numbers

China's fast-paced economic growth and the Chinese's increasing levels of disposable income have had a major impact on the pet industry. The latest research suggests that pet ownership is on the rise in China. The demand for pet food products in the country is also growing. Although the pet food market in China is still small by Western standards, it offers high growth potential.

1. Refer to Appendix 2: Marketing by the Numbers. Carry out research to estimate what the potential market for dog food in China might be.

2. What big, overseas pet food companies are already doing business in China?

3. How does the Mexican market for pet food compare with China's pet food market?

VIDEO Case

Meredith

The Meredith Corporation has developed an expertise in building customer relationships through segmentation, targeting, and positioning. Amazingly, however, it has done this by focusing on only half of the population—the female half. Meredith has developed the largest database of any U.S. media company and uses that database to meet the specific needs and desires of women.

Meredith is known for leading titles such as *Better Homes and Gardens*, *Family Circle*, and *Ladies' Home Journal*. But that list has grown to a portfolio of 14 magazines and more than 200 special interest publications. Through these magazines alone, Meredith regularly reaches about 30 million readers. By focusing on core categories of home, family, and personal development, Meredith has developed a product mix designed to meet various needs of women. This creates multiple touch points as individual women engage with more than one magazine, as well as with specialty books and websites.

After viewing the video featuring Meredith, answer the following questions about segmenting, targeting, and positioning:

1. On what main variables has Meredith focused in segmenting its markets?

2. Which target marketing strategy best describes Meredith's efforts? Support your choice.

3. How does Meredith use its variety of products to build relationships with the right customers?

COMPANY Case

The Arab Online World— Microsoft Maren

The Arab world has become more and more lucrative for the international market over the years. It is one of the largest growing regions in the world and provides many organizations with huge growth potential. The Arab world alone has 63,240,946 Internet users as of 2010, out of a total population of 212,336,924. That means that more than 29 percent of the population are Internet users. The North Africa region has 40,356,400 Internet users as of 2010, out of a total population of 205,716,142, equivalent to 19 percent of the population. Over the last 10 years, Internet usage in the Arab world has shown growth of around 1,825 percent compared with 432 percent for the rest of the world.

The Arabic language is the seventh most spoken language worldwide. It is estimated that 18 percent of Arabic speakers are Internet users. Between 2000 and 2010 the amount of online content in the Arabic language grew by 2,501 percent, far outstripping the rest of the world and making the potential for marketing in the region huge.

The Internet has become the life blood of many organizations. Companies such as Microsoft, Google, Yahoo!, Amazon, and Facebook make their living when more people are online, and it is not a modest living by any means. As a result of the nature and the culture of the region, the product offering to the Arab world has to be customized to meet their lifestyle and expectations.

BARRIERS
One of the barriers to increasing Internet usage in the Arab world is language. The rich culture of the Arab world is not yet matched by the content and usage online. Many companies have started building Arabic versions of their products, which are strictly targeted at the lucrative, growing region.

With all these companies being in the interactive business, they faced problems communicating with the users in their language. Even where the products were in Arabic, the user had several challenges in using them.

Microsoft launched its Arabic language support in the early 1990s, allowing users to type in their native language within the Microsoft products and online. The language plug-in was highly appreciated, but left the customer with much to desire. Keyboards did not have Arabic support, and the users were unaccustomed to the letter layout.

The users were so familiar with the QWERTY keyboard that learning a new keyboard layout was very challenging for many of them. The first attempt to break that barrier was with typing teachers. Many were published, downloaded, and used. But typing teachers were insufficient and required a great deal of effort on the part of the user. Another approach was the virtual keyboard, in the Arabic alphabet, but this required continuous switching between applications to produce the Arabic text the user desired.

THE MOVEMENT OF THE PEOPLE
Independently, the users resorted to transliteration: this involves using Roman characters to spell out Arabic words phonetically. This approach creates what is known as Arabish (also known as 'Aralish,' 'Franco-Arabic, or Arabizi'). This character encoding of Arabic to the Roman alphabet and the Hindu-Arabic numerals is also known as Arabic Chat Alphabet because it is most commonly used to communicate on online chat services. Some users have also developed special notations to use in place of letters that don't exist in the Roman alphabet. For example:

The user types: ana raye7 el gam3a el sa3a 3 el 3asr.

Meaning: "انا رايح الجامعه الساعه 3 العصر"

English translation: "I'm going to college at 3pm."

The user types: kif sa7tak, chou 3am ta3mil?.

Saying: "كيف صحتك, شو عمتعمل؟"

English translation: "How is your health, what are you doing?"

As soon as organizations became aware of the massive trend of Arabish, wanting to tap into this market, they started advertising and communicating in this language form. Ads using the Arabish language began to appear online, on television, on products and even in movie posters.

ARABISH IS NOT ENOUGH
After capitalizing on the Arabish language, and as Internet usage grew tremendously, controversy started. There was a backlash against Arabish, with some believing it was changing the heritage of the Arab world. Reacting to this controversy, by knowing their customers well, companies such as Microsoft began to offer actual Arabic text in order to assure the maximum reach, acceptance, and adoption of their products by all sectors of society.

A team at Microsoft's Innovation Lab, led by Mostafa Ashour, started to build a product that translated Arabish into Arabic. Microsoft Maren, though not the first of its kind, was the most impressive. Microsoft Maren seamlessly integrated into Windows and allowed users to capitalize on their familiarity with the QWERTY keyboard, and still produce Arabic text. For example, if a user typed "saba7 el kheir" meaning "good morning", صباح الخير would appear on the screen.

The advantage Maren had over rival products was that it was built into the users' system, and logging in to websites, typing, copying, and pasting were no longer required.

The product was welcomed by online users. Now the users' chat, blogs, posts, and comments were perfectly accessible to all their target audience. There were more than 250,000 downloads of Maren from Microsoft pages alone, in addition to those downloaded from other sources. Mostafa Ashour, program manager at Microsoft, says, "This is a real life scenario where communicating in your own language makes all the difference. Expressing your intense feelings of joy or sorrow is better served using your native tongue. Maren helps you communicate efficiently in Arabic if you lack access to an Arabic keyboard or you are not familiar with one."

The evolution of products for the Arab world is very interesting to observe, by knowing the market, not least because companies can trap into the huge potential for sales in the region.

Questions for Discussion

1. Using www.internetworldstats.com select one country in the Arab world and analyze the market demographics, then select a lucrative market segment and explain your choice.

2. For that segment propose a product offering based on Internet usage that delivers value to the customer.

3. Define the positioning that you will offer to your customers based on what you know about the behavior of the selected segment.

4. How does the launch of Maren affect the business of Microsoft in the Arab world?

Sources: "Internet World Stats: Usage and Population Statistics," 2011, www.internetworldstats.com; "Your Maren Story," Miscrosoft Maren (MSDN Blogs), July 22, 2009, http://blogs.msdn.com/b/maren/archive/2009/07/22/your-maren-story.aspx; "Arabic chat albhabet," wikipedia, http://en.wikipedia.org/wiki/Arabic_chat_alphabet.

This case was provided by Mohamed Radwan, adjunct faculty member at the American University in Cairo and managing director for Platinum Partners.

Chapter 8

Part 1   Defining Marketing and the Marketing Process (Chapters 1, 2)
Part 2   Understanding the Marketplace and Consumers (Chapters 3, 4, 5, 6)
Part 3   Designing a Customer-Driven Strategy and Mix (Chapters 7, 8, 9, 10, 11, 12, 13, 14)
Part 4   Extending Marketing (Chapters 15, 16, 17)

Products, Services, and Brands Building Customer Value

Chapter PREVIEW

Now that you've had a good look at customer-driven marketing strategy, we'll take a deeper look at the marketing mix—the tactical tools that marketers use to implement their strategies and deliver superior customer value. In this and the next chapter, we'll study how companies develop and manage products and brands. Then, in the chapters that follow, we'll look at pricing, distribution, and marketing communication tools.

The product is usually the first and most basic marketing consideration. We'll start with a question that seems simple: What *is* a product? As it turns out, however, the answer is not so simple.

First, let's look at an interesting example of Bahrain Islamic Bank, and how it has developed its product portfolio to create customer value and foster long-term relationships. At the same time, it has focused on delivering service which exceeds expectations, and on building a brand that will connect deeply with customers. How has the bank achieved this?

Bahrain Islamic Bank (BisB) was the first Islamic commercial bank in the Kingdom of Bahrain, established in 1979. Since then, the bank has recorded steady growth. At the end of 2010, shareholders' funds reached nearly 100 million Bahraini dinars (US$265 million), with assets in excess of BD 936 million (US$2.4 billion). These levels are considered significant given the population of Bahrain, and the fact that BisB is a financial institution focused on Islamic banking and finance products, which is somewhat more specialized than traditional banking and finance.

In 2009 BisB launched its new corporate identity, aiming to communicate with its fresh new mandate of exceeding customer expectations, both from an aspirational and a functional perspective. BisB chose to feature its new corporate identity and brand logo on numerous billboard advertisements, including signage on roadways, and by using large LCD video screens at major intersections in Bahrain.

BisB has developed and created its leading position in the Islamic banking sector by adopting innovative Islamic investment and financing products, supported by superior retail and corporate banking services that position the bank ahead of its key competitors. The bank is listed on the Bahrain Stock Exchange, and local and regional financial institutions are major shareholders. The bank operates under the supervision and regulatory framework of the Central Bank of Bahrain.

With 13 branches in Bahrain, BisB has established the largest network among Islamic banks in Bahrain, where the bank can actively market its products. These branches offer quality banking products and services such as financing and investment opportunities, which are compliant with sharia'a requirements for individual and corporate customers.

BisB created its new brand with three core values in mind: partnership, being fair, and being transparent. In terms of 'partnership,' the bank earns the trust and respect of its customers and business partners by providing them with the reassurance of a strong and indispensible partnership. The bank takes the position of being confident with its customers and offering assurance. The idea is actually to engage customers with the possibilities of the future and what it means for them. The customer as a partner should also benefit from the bank and its specific products, which the customer is encouraged to use or to purchase. Furthermore, the bank presents each product and service in the simplest and most direct way. The bank makes an upfront effort to communicate clearly and to avoid the use of unnecessary banking jargon. The bank always attempts to demystify the banking process by being open and transparent.

> **BisB developed its new brand identity with three core values in mind: partnership, being fair, and being transparent.**

BisB major branded products include:

- **Iqra** is an investment product which translates into English as 'read.' The product is geared for saving for endeavors such as higher education, buying a house, marriage, or any other personal aspiration. Iqra guides you to fulfill your dreams by investing today and pursuing your ambitions tomorrow. The Iqra investment product offers a low entry deposit level, a life insurance component, and a 3 percent expected profit rate. Investors in Iqra must make regular deposits into the account for a minimum of 18 months.

- **Vevo** is a product created for the youth and young adult segment from ages 15 to 25. The product is a savings account with an ATM card. Essentially the account and ATM card are designed to help you plan, save, and spend wisely for the future. Vevo comes from the word 'Vivo,' which is Latin for 'Within the living.' BisB created Vevo to fit into the young account holder's life and includes value for purchasing on such items as mobile phone contracts and charges, and regular discounts at over 100 stores across Bahrain. BisB offers this unique product with a fun brand name in order to attract and inspire younger clients and to establish a long-term account holder for the bank.

- **Tas'heel** is a personal finance product with a reasonable financing rate, which makes it attractive as a method for financing any large endeavor, such as tuition. The personal finance product acts much like a personal line of credit that can be accessed for a variety of financing needs. The product can also be used for business purposes. The product allows holders to buy equipment for a prospective business or for the purchase of goods from outside of Bahrain for the purposes of resale. The product can even allow the holder to use its financing capabilities as a down payment to purchase real estate in Bahrain.

- **BisB e-card,** which is a Visa Virtuon product, allows the holder to purchase goods from leading and major retailers in the U.S. online, have a registered U.S. post office box, and pay for purchases using the BisB e-card. Purchases are shipped using TNT, one of the world's leading delivery service providers.

- **Tejoori Al Islami** is a savings account that allows the customer to win substantial cash prizes as a reward on their savings. The Tejoori Al Islami account is a normal Mudaraba-based investment account, and all prizes are paid from the shareholders' promotional prize account. Tejoori Al Islami is widely promoted across Bahrain and winners' names are published regularly to reinforce the idea of actually winning.

> BisB has developed a strong portfolio of products and services both for business and for retail, based on the Islamic banking model.

The bank has built a banking franchise based on solid retail branches, strategically located across Bahrain, with a strong parent brand 'BisB,' and by creating and developing its own portfolio of differentiated banking product offerings. BisB regularly promotes itself using both radio advertising and outdoor advertising. The bank is staffed primarily by Bahrainis, demonstrating the bank's strong understanding of the domestic banking market, and especially the Islamic banking segment it serves. The bank also offers a very strong portfolio of corporate-grade investment products and services, again based on the Islamic banking model.[1]

> BisB's portfolio of products is based on its deep understanding of customer requirements and its intention to foster long-term relationships with retail and business customers. It understands the importance of delivering outstanding service to retain customer loyalty, and integrates Islamic values into the foundation of its business. Its new brand identity was created to communicate these values to customers.

Source: *This case was provided by Mike Lewicki, University College of Bahrain.*

As the opening example shows, in their search to create customer relationships, marketers must build and manage products and brands that connect with customers. This chapter begins with a question that is not as simple as it seems: *What is a product*? After addressing this question, we look at ways to classify products in consumer and business markets. Then we discuss the important decisions that marketers make regarding individual products, product lines, and product mixes. Next, we look into the critically important issue of how marketers build and manage brands. Finally, we examine the characteristics and marketing requirements of a special form of product —services.

Objective Outline

Author Comment | As you'll see, this is a deceptively simple question with a very complex answer.

Product
Anything that can be offered to a market for attention, acquisition, use, or consumption that might satisfy a want or need.

Service
Any activity or benefit that one party can offer to another that is essentially intangible and does not result in the ownership of anything.

What Is a Product? (pp 204–209)

We define a **product** as anything that can be offered to a market for attention, acquisition, use, or consumption that might satisfy a want or need. Products are more than just tangible goods (i.e. physical things that can be touched). Broadly defined, products include physical objects, services, events, persons, places, organizations, ideas, or a mix of all of these entities. Throughout this book we will use the term product broadly to include all of these entities. Thus, a BMW X6, an Apple iPod, a Nokia mobile phone, a caffe mocha at Starbucks, and a bottle of Masafi are all products. A product can also be a vacation in Europe, a sharia-compliant investment in Dubai Islamic Bank, and advice from your doctor.

We also give special attention to **services** because of their importance in the local and global economy. Services are a form of product that consists of activities, benefits, or satisfaction offered for sale that are essentially intangible (in other words, can't be physically touched) and do not result in the ownership of anything. Examples include having a haircut, flying in an aircraft, operating a savings account in your bank, or going to the cinema. We will look at services more closely later in this chapter.

Products, Services, and Experiences

Product is a key element in the overall *market offering*. Marketing-mix planning begins with building an offering that brings value to target customers. This offering becomes the basis upon which the company builds profitable customer relationships.

A company's market offering often includes both tangible goods and services. At one extreme, the offer may consist of a *pure tangible good*, such as soap, toothpaste, or salt—no services accompany the product. At the other extreme are *pure services*, for which the offer consists primarily of a service. Examples include a doctor's appointment, physiotherapy, or legal services from your lawyer. Between these two extremes, however, many goods-and-services combinations are possible.

Today, as products and services become more commoditized, many companies are moving to a new level in creating value for their customers. To differentiate their offers, beyond simply making products and delivering services they are creating and managing customer *experiences* with their brands or company.

Core, actual, and augmented product: People who buy a BlackBerry are buying more than a mobile phone, email device, or organizer. They are buying freedom and on-the-go connectivity to people and resources.

Experiences have always been an important part of marketing for some companies. The entertainment company Disney has long manufactured dreams and memories through its movies and theme parks. And Nike has long declared, "It's not so much the shoes but where they take you." In the Arab world Nike's slogan "Just do it" is just as well recognized due to the popularity of the brand.

Companies that market experiences realize that customers are really buying much more than just products and services. They are buying what those offers will *do* for them.

Levels of Product and Services

Product planners need to think about products and services on three levels (see **Figure 8.1**). Each level adds more customer value. The most basic level is the *core customer value*, which addresses the question *What is the buyer really buying?* When designing products, marketers must first define the core, problem-solving benefits or services that consumers seek. People who buy a BlackBerry smartphone are buying more than a cellphone, email device, or personal organizer. They are buying freedom and on-the-go connectivity to people and resources.

At the second level, product planners must turn the core benefit into an *actual product*. They need to develop product and service features, design, a quality level, a brand name, and packaging. For example, the BlackBerry is an actual product. Its name, parts, styling, features, packaging, and other attributes have all been combined carefully to deliver the core customer value of staying connected.

Finally, product planners must build an *augmented product* around the core benefit and actual product by offering additional consumer services and benefits. The BlackBerry solution offers more than just a communications device. It provides consumers with a complete solution to mobile connectivity problems. Thus, when consumers buy a BlackBerry, the company and its dealers also might give buyers a warranty on parts and workmanship, instructions on how to use the device, quick repair services when needed, and a toll-free telephone number and website to use if they have problems or questions.

FIGURE | 8.1
Three Levels of Product

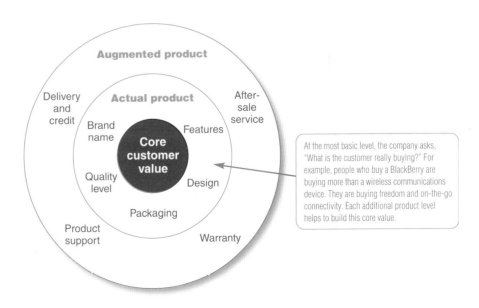

At the most basic level, the company asks, "What is the customer really buying?" For example, people who buy a BlackBerry are buying more than a wireless communications device. They are buying freedom and on-the-go connectivity. Each additional product level helps to build this core value.

Consumers see products as bundles of benefits that satisfy their needs. When developing products, marketers first must identify the *core customer value* that consumers seek from the product. They must then design the *actual* product and find ways to *augment* it in order to create this customer value and the most satisfying customer experience.

Product and Service Classifications

Products and services fall into two broad classes based on the types of consumers that use them—*consumer products* and *industrial products*. Broadly defined, products also include other marketable entities such as experiences (e.g., desert safari), organizations (e.g., Emirates Airline), persons (e.g., Nancy Ajram), places (e.g., Dubai), and ideas (e.g., social welfare).

Consumer Products

Consumer product

A product bought by final consumers for personal consumption.

Consumer products are products and services bought by final consumers for personal consumption. Marketers usually classify these products and services further based on how consumers go about buying them. Consumer products include *convenience products, shopping products, specialty products*, and *unsought products*. These products differ in the ways consumers buy them and, therefore, in how they are marketed (see ● **Table 8.1**).

Convenience product

A consumer product that customers usually buy frequently, immediately, and with a minimum of comparison and buying effort.

Convenience products are consumer products and services that customers usually buy frequently, immediately, and with a minimum of comparison and buying effort. Examples include soap, newspapers, chewing gum, bread, milk, cereal, magazines, and fast food. Convenience products are usually low priced, and marketers place them in many locations (especially the corner shops or *Bagalas*) to make them readily available when customers need them.

Shopping product

A consumer product that the customer, in the process of selection and purchase, usually compares on such bases as suitability, quality, price, and style.

Shopping products are less frequently purchased consumer products and services that customers compare carefully on suitability, quality, price, and style. When buying shopping products and services, consumers spend much time and effort in gathering information and making comparisons. Examples include furniture, clothing, cars, major appliances, and hotel and airline services. Shopping products marketers usually distribute their products through fewer outlets but provide more sales support to help customers in their comparison efforts.

● **TABLE | 8.1**   Marketing Considerations for Consumer Products

Marketing Considerations	Type of Consumer Product			
	Convenience	**Shopping**	**Specialty**	**Unsought**
Customer buying behavior	Frequent purchase, little planning, little comparison or shopping effort, low customer involvement	Less frequent purchase, much planning and shopping effort, comparison of brands on price, quality, style	Strong brand preference and loyalty, special purchase effort, little comparison of brands, low price sensitivity	Little product awareness, knowledge (or, if aware, little or even negative interest)
Price	Low price	Higher price	High price	Varies
Distribution	Widespread distribution, convenient locations	Selective distribution in fewer outlets	Exclusive distribution in only one or a few outlets per market area	Varies
Promotion	Mass promotion by the producer	Advertising and personal selling by both producer and resellers	More carefully targeted promotion by both producer and resellers	Aggressive advertising and personal selling by producer and resellers
Examples	Toothpaste, magazines, laundry detergent	Major appliances, televisions, furniture, clothing	Luxury goods, such as Rolex watches or fine crystal	Life insurance, Red Crescent blood donations

Specialty product

A consumer product with unique characteristics or brand identification for which a significant group of buyers is willing to make a special purchase effort.

Specialty products are consumer products and services with unique characteristics or brand identification for which a significant group of buyers is willing to make a special purchase effort. Examples include specific brands of cars, high-priced photographic equipment, designer clothes, and the services of medical or legal specialists. A house in Palm Jumeirah, for example, is a specialty product because buyers are usually willing to travel great distances to buy one. Buyers normally do not compare specialty products. They invest only the time needed to reach the seller carrying the wanted products.

Unsought product

A consumer product that the consumer either does not know about or knows about but does not normally think of buying.

Unsought products are consumer products that the consumer either does not know about or knows about but does not normally think of buying. Most major new innovations are unsought until the consumer becomes aware of them through advertising. Classic examples of known but unsought products and services are life insurance, blood donations to the Red Crescent, and medical check-ups. By their very nature, unsought products require a lot of advertising, personal selling, and other marketing efforts.

Industrial Products

Industrial product

A product bought by individuals and organizations for further processing or for use in conducting a business.

Industrial products are those purchased for further processing or for use in conducting a business. Thus, the distinction between a consumer product and an industrial product is based on the *purpose* for which the product is bought. If a consumer buys a printer for personal use at home, the printer is a consumer product. If the same consumer buys the same printer for use in a business, the printer is an industrial product.

The three groups of industrial products and services include materials and parts, capital items, and supplies and services. *Materials and parts* include raw materials and manufactured materials and parts. Raw materials consist of farm products (wheat, cotton, livestock, fruits, vegetables) and natural products (fish, lumber, crude petroleum, iron ore). Manufactured materials and parts consist of component materials (iron, yarn, cement, wires) and component parts (small motors, tires, castings). Most manufactured materials and parts are sold directly to industrial users. Price and service are the major marketing factors; branding and advertising tend to be less important.

Capital items are industrial products that aid in the buyer's production or operations, including installations and accessory equipment. Installations consist of major purchases such as buildings (factories, offices) and fixed equipment (generators, drill presses, large computer systems, elevators). Accessory equipment includes portable factory equipment and tools (hand tools, lift trucks) and office equipment (computers, fax machines, desks). They have a shorter life than installations and simply aid in the production process.

The final group of industrial products is *supplies and services*. Supplies include operating supplies (lubricants, coal, paper, pencils) and repair and maintenance items (paint, nails, brooms). Supplies are the convenience products of the industrial field because they are usually purchased with a minimum of effort or comparison. Business services include maintenance and repair services (window cleaning, computer repair) and business advisory services (legal, management consulting, advertising). Such services are usually supplied under contract.

Organizations, Persons, Places, and Ideas

In addition to tangible products and services, in recent years marketers have broadened the concept of a product to include other market offerings—organizations, persons, places, and ideas.

Organizations often carry out activities to 'sell' the organization itself. Organization marketing consists of activities undertaken to create, maintain, or change the attitude and behavior of target consumers toward an organization. Both profit and not-for-profit organizations practice organization marketing. Organizations use public relations or corporate image advertising to create a positive image and market themselves to their target markets. For example, Al Rostamani Group's '50 Years of Excellence' campaign was launched to create awareness about the group of companies' strong heritage in the region and to reinforce the values of 'commitment and care' with the brand. Following the campaign, Al Rostamani International Exchange was awarded the status of Super Brand in 2010 by the Superbrands Council UAE.[2]

Similarly not-for-profit organizations such as charities, museums, and performing arts groups market their organizations in order to raise funds and attract members; for example, Noor Dubai, a charity organization, raised Dhs 400 million (around US$109 million) through a strong marketing campaign.

People can also be thought of as products. *Person marketing* consists of activities undertaken to create, maintain, or change attitudes or behavior toward particular people. People ranging from presidents, entertainers, and sports figures to professionals such as doctors, lawyers, and architects use person marketing to build their reputations. The skillful use of marketing can turn a person's name into a powerhouse brand. Carefully managed and well-known names such as television star Oprah Winfrey, designer Yves Saint Laurent, and U.S.-based businessman Donald Trump now adorn everything from sports apparel, housewares, and magazines to book clubs and casinos. Such well-known, well-marketed names hold substantial branding power. And businesses, charities, and other organizations use well-known personalities to help sell their products or causes. For example, big-name companies—such as Coca-Cola and Damas—have recently featured Nancy Ajram, the award-winning Arab pop star, in their advertisements and promotions to promote their business in the Arab youth market.

Person marketing: Arab pop star Nancy Ajram has been successfully marketed as a high-profile personality. Due to this success she has also been courted and featured by several large companies, including Damas, Coca-Cola and Sony, to promote their products.

In 2009 Sony Ericsson also signed up Nancy Ajram as the new face of its Walkman® Phones range. For Sony, "the young artist … is an ideal personification of everything the Walkman® Phones stand for—fun and music." Sony Ericsson held a launch event for Walkman® Phones, at which it also released a 'Nancy Special Edition' phone—a pink, pretty version with Nancy Ajram's signature on it.[3]

Another company featuring Nancy in its recent advertising is jewelry retailer Damas. Damas' management commented on its decision to use Nancy to promote its Farfasha products: "The celebrity must embody and exude the same image as the product being endorsed. They must be a perfect role model for the brand's target market. Nancy is one of the most popular young superstars in the Arab world. With millions of followers cutting across socio-economic and geographic boundaries, her status as a young cultural icon has made her one of the most sought-after endorsers of several well-known products and services. Damas' own brand Farfasha is synonymous to what Nancy Ajram represents—beautiful, vibrant, modern, and high-energy of the young generation."[4]

Place marketing involves activities undertaken to create, maintain, or change attitudes or behavior toward particular places. Cities, states, regions, and even entire nations compete to attract tourists, new residents, conventions, and company offices and factories. Bahrain has launched a campaign, "Business Friendly Bahrain," to attract more business to the Kingdom. "Malaysia Truly Asia" is the tourist campaign for Malaysia. In March 2009, Dubai launched a huge global tourism campaign to promote the Emirate internationally, themed "Keep Discovering Dubai." The campaign involved Emirates Group, the Dubai Department of Tourism and Commerce Marketing (DTCM), Dubai hoteliers, and Destination Management Companies (DMCs). The campaign was a significant investment for these partners, with an estimated cost of around AED 50 million (US$13.6 million).[5]

Ideas can also be marketed. In one sense, all marketing is the marketing of an idea, whether it is the general idea of brushing your teeth or the specific idea that Crest toothpastes create "healthy, beautiful smiles for life." Here, however, we narrow our focus to the marketing of *social ideas*. This area has been called **social marketing**, defined by the Social Marketing Institute as the use of commercial marketing concepts and tools in programs designed to influence individuals' behavior to improve their well-being and that of society.[6]

Social marketing
The use of commercial marketing concepts and tools in programs designed to influence individuals' behavior to improve their well-being and that of society.

Social marketing programs include public health campaigns, for example to reduce smoking. Other social marketing efforts include environmental campaigns to promote wilderness protection, clean air, and conservation. Still others address issues such as family planning, human rights, and racial equality. The power of social marketing is evident in the following example from Egypt.

> As in many other countries throughout the world, diarrhea is the most common cause of death for children under two years of age in Egypt. But the introduction of oral rehydration solution (ORS)—a solution of salts, sugar, and water—saved an estimated 130,000 infants in the country over 2 years. Deaths associated with diarrhea have reduced by nearly two-thirds since 1980.
>
> The key to saving lives is to inform mothers, pharmacists, doctors, and nurses about ORS and to ensure that they use the solution in the proper way at the proper time. In Egypt this process of educating people about ORS was accelerated by using commercial marketing methods for socially useful purposes. The National Control of Diarrheal Diseases Project spread the message through a carefully planned communications strategy, co-ordinating mass media, market research, and evaluation; it also communicated through a number of channels, including via the Ministry of Health, medical professionals, the private sector, and foreign technical assistants.[7]

But social marketing involves much more than just advertising—the Social Marketing Institute (SMI) encourages the use of a broad range of marketing tools. "Social marketing goes well beyond the promotional '*P*' of the marketing mix to include every other element to achieve its social change objectives," says SMI's executive director.[8]

> **Author Comment** | Now that we've answered the "What is a product?" question, let's dig into the specific decisions that companies must make when designing and marketing products and services.

Product and Service Decisions (pp 209-215)

Marketers make product and service decisions at three levels: individual product and service decisions, product line decisions, and product mix decisions. We discuss each in turn.

Individual Product and Service Decisions

Figure 8.2 shows the important decisions in the development and marketing of individual products and services. We will focus on decisions about *product attributes*, *branding*, *packaging*, *labeling*, and *product support services*.

Product and Service Attributes

Developing a product or service involves defining the benefits that it will offer. These benefits are communicated and delivered by product attributes such as *quality*, *features*, and *style and design*.

Product quality
The characteristics of a product or service that bear on its ability to satisfy stated or implied customer needs.

Product Quality. **Product quality** is one of the marketer's major positioning tools. Quality has a direct impact on product or service performance; thus, it is closely linked to customer value and satisfaction. In the narrowest sense, quality can be defined as 'freedom from defects.' But most customer-centered companies go beyond this narrow definition. Instead, they define quality in terms of creating customer value and satisfaction. For example, Siemens defines quality this way: "Quality is when our customers come back and our products don't."[9]

Total quality management (TQM) is an approach in which all the company's people are involved in constantly improving the quality of products, services, and business processes. For most top companies, customer-driven quality has become a way of doing business.

> Don't forget Figure 8.1! The focus of all of these decisions is to create core customer value.

FIGURE | 8.2
Individual Product Decisions

Today, companies are taking a 'return on quality' approach, viewing quality as an investment and holding quality efforts accountable for bottom-line results.

Product quality has two dimensions—level and consistency. In developing a product, the marketer must first choose a *quality level* that will support the product's positioning. Here, product quality means *performance quality*—the ability of a product to perform its functions. For example, a Rolls-Royce provides higher performance quality than a Chevrolet automobile: it has a smoother ride, is more comfortable, and lasts longer. Companies rarely try to offer the highest possible performance quality level—few customers want or can afford the high levels of quality offered in products such as a Rolls-Royce automobile, or a Rolex watch. Instead, companies choose a quality level that matches target market needs and the quality levels of competing products.

Beyond quality level, high quality also can mean high levels of quality consistency. Here, product quality means *conformance quality*—freedom from defects and *consistency* in delivering a targeted level of performance. All companies should strive for high levels of conformance quality. In this sense, a Chevrolet can have just as much quality as a Rolls-Royce. Although a Chevy doesn't perform at the same level as a Rolls-Royce, it can deliver as consistently the quality that customers pay for and expect.

Product Features. A product can be offered with varying features. A basic model, one without any extras, is the starting point. The company can create higher-level models by adding more features. Features are a competitive tool for differentiating the company's product from competitors' products. Being the first producer to introduce a valued new feature is one of the most effective ways to compete.

How can a company identify new features and decide which ones to add to its product? The company should periodically survey buyers who have used the product and ask these questions: How do you like the product? Which specific features of the product do you like most? Which features could we add to improve the product? The answers provide the company with a rich list of feature ideas. The company can then assess each feature's *value* to customers versus its *cost* to the company. Features that customers value highly in relation to costs should be added.

Product Style and Design. Another way to add customer value is through distinctive *product style and design*. Design is a larger concept than style. *Style* simply describes the appearance of a product. Styles can be very appealing or boring. An exciting style may grab attention and produce a pleasing look, but it does not necessarily make the product *perform* better.

Unlike style, *design* is more than skin deep—it goes to the very heart of a product. Good design contributes to a product's usefulness as well as to its looks.

Design begins with a deep understanding of customer needs. More than simply creating product or service attributes, it involves shaping the customer's product-use experience.

Consider the example of Dyson's 'Airblade' product.

The problem with conventional hand dryers is that they don't work! Either they don't dry your hands at all, or they take so long to work that you get impatient and just wipe your damp hands on your clothes, or have warm, wet hands which act as a breeding ground for germs. This was the challenge taken on by the design team at Dyson: come up with a new type of hand dryer that works quickly and hygienically. And it had to be energy-efficient and better for the environment, too.

Product design: Dyson has become known for taking an innovative approach to redesigning conventional products to improve the user experience. The Dyson Airblade is one such example, revolutionizing hand dryers.

The result was Dyson Airblade™. The idea behind this innovative product is that it creates a high-speed 'sheet' of air. Speed is the key. People place their hands inside the gap, and the high-speed air (a steam flowing at over 600 kilometers per hour) dries their hands completely within 10 seconds. The sheet of air acts like an invisible windscreen wiper to wipe moisture from hands, leaving them completely dry.

Once the idea had been developed, it underwent extensive biological and scientific testing by Dyson's in-house microbiologists, as well as research conducted by Leeds University and Bradford University in the UK.

Energy-efficiency has been achieved through the development of a long-life, low-energy 'digital motor' to power the Airblade, which uses up to 83 percent less energy compared with conventional hand dryers. It costs less to use and it's better for the environment too.

In the UK, the Airblade is in use in many airports, museums, restaurants, offices, and public places. Its success is set to spread: it is currently being installed in several locations and malls in the Arab world.[10]

Thus, product designers should think less about product attributes and technical specifications and more about how customers will use and benefit from the product.

Branding

Perhaps the most distinctive skill of professional marketers is their ability to build and manage brands. A **brand** is a name, term, sign, symbol, or design, or a combination of these, that identifies the maker or seller of a product or service. Consumers view a brand as an important part of a product, and branding can add value to a product. Customers attach meanings to brands and develop brand relationships. For example, most consumers would perceive a bottle of Chanel perfume as a high-quality, expensive product. But the same perfume in an unmarked bottle would likely be viewed as lower in quality, even if the fragrance was identical.

Branding has become so strong that today hardly anything goes unbranded. Salt is packaged in branded containers, common nuts and bolts are packaged with a distributor's label, and automobile parts—spark plugs, tires, filters—bear brand names that differ from those of the automakers. Even fruits, vegetables, dairy products, and poultry are branded—Sunkist oranges, Al Ain fresh milk, Mazaa mango juice, and Masafi mineral water.

Branding helps buyers in many ways. Brand names help consumers identify products that might benefit them. Brands also say something about product quality and consistency—buyers who always buy the same brand know that they will get the same features, benefits, and quality each time they buy. Branding also gives the seller several advantages. The brand name becomes the basis on which a whole story can be built about a product's special qualities. The seller's brand name and trademark provide legal protection for unique product features that otherwise might be copied by competitors. And branding helps the seller to segment markets. For example, Toyota Motor Corporation can offer the major Lexus and Toyota brands, each with numerous sub-brands—such as Corolla, Camry, Prius, Yaris, Land Cruiser, Prodo, Rav4, and others—not just one general product for all consumers.

Building and managing brands are perhaps the marketer's most important tasks. We will discuss branding strategy in more detail later in the chapter.

Packaging

Packaging involves designing and producing the container or wrapper for a product. Traditionally, the primary function of the package was to hold and protect the product. In recent times, however, numerous factors have made packaging an important marketing tool as well. Increased competition and clutter on retail store shelves means that packages must now perform many sales tasks—from attracting attention, to describing the product, to making the sale.

Brand
A name, term, sign, symbol, design, or a combination of these, that identifies the products or services of one seller or a group of sellers and differentiates them from those of competitors.

Packaging
The activities of designing and producing the container or wrapper for a product.

Innovative packaging can give a company an advantage over competitors and boost sales. With Heinz's 'refrigerator-door-fit' bottle, Heinz ketchup sales jumped 12 percent in the four months following its introduction.

Companies are realizing the power of good packaging to create immediate consumer recognition of a brand. For example, an average supermarket such as Spinneys or Union Coop stocks 45,000 items; the average hypermarket (e.g., Carrefour, Watania) can carry as many as 150,000 items. The typical shopper may pass by some 300 items per minute, and more than 70 percent of all purchase decisions are likely to be made in stores. In this highly competitive environment, the package may be the seller's last and best chance to influence buyers. Thus, for many companies, the package itself has become an important promotional medium.[11]

Poorly designed packages can cause headaches for consumers and lost sales for the company. By contrast, innovative packaging can give a company an advantage over competitors and boost sales. Sometimes even seemingly small packaging improvements can make a big difference. For example, Heinz revolutionized the 170-year-old condiments industry by turning the ketchup bottle upside down, letting customers quickly squeeze out even the last bit of ketchup. At the same time, it adopted a 'refrigerator-door-fit' shape that not only slots into shelves more easily but also has a cap that is simpler for children to open. In the four months following the introduction of the new package, sales jumped 12 percent. What's more, the new package also works as a promotional tool. Says a packaging analyst, "When consumers see the Heinz logo on the fridge door every time they open it, it's taking marketing inside homes."[12]

In recent years, product safety has also become a major packaging concern. We have all learned to deal with hard-to-open 'childproof' packaging. And after a series of product tampering scares during the 1980s (involving products being opened and deliberately poisoned or interfered with before sale), most drug producers and food makers now put their products in tamper-resistant packages. In making packaging decisions, the company also must heed growing environmental concerns. Fortunately, many companies have gone 'green' by reducing their packaging and using environmentally responsible packaging materials.

Labeling

Labels range from simple tags attached to products to complex graphics that are part of the package. They perform several functions. At the very least, the label *identifies* the product or brand, such as the name 'Chiquita' stamped on bananas. The label might also *describe* several things about the product—who made it, where it was made, when it was made, its contents, how it is to be used, and how to use it safely. Finally, the label might help to *promote* the brand, support its positioning, and connect with customers. For many companies, labels have become an important element in broader marketing campaigns.

Along with the positives, labeling also raises concerns. There has been a long history of legal concerns about packaging and labels. Numerous government laws have held that false, misleading, or deceptive labels or packages constitute unfair competition. Labels can mislead customers, fail to describe important ingredients, or fail to include needed safety warnings. As a result, many nations regulate labeling. GCC (Gulf Cooperation Council) countries are trying to standardize labeling by ensuring Arabic language is used on the label for key information. For example, since 2008, all pre-packaged food products in the UAE have to be labeled with an Arabic label. This development followed from the recently approved GCC standard and subsequent UAE consumer protection law, both of which require Arabic labeling on certain food products.[13]

Labeling has been affected in recent times by *unit pricing* (stating the price per unit of standard measure), *open dating* (stating the expected shelf life of the product), and *nutritional labeling* (stating the nutritional values in the product). In many countries, such as the United States and countries in the European Union, nutritional labeling laws require sellers to provide detailed nutritional information on food products. Sellers must ensure that their labels contain all the required information in the countries in which they sell their products.

Product support services: Hewlett-Packard (HP) promises "HP Total Care—expert help for every stage of your computer's life. From choosing it, to configuring it, to protecting it, to tuning it up—all the way to recycling it."

Product line

A group of products that are closely related because they function in a similar manner, are sold to the same customer groups, are marketed through the same types of outlets, or fall within given price ranges.

Product Support Services

Customer service is another element of product strategy. A company's offer usually includes some support services, which can be a minor or a major part of the total offering. Later in the chapter, we will discuss services as products in themselves. Here, we discuss services that augment actual products.

The first step is to survey customers periodically to assess the value of current services and to obtain ideas for new ones. Once the company has assessed the quality of various support services to customers, it can take steps to fix problems and add new services that will both delight customers and yield profits to the company.

Many companies are now using a sophisticated mix of phone, email, fax, Internet, and interactive voice and data technologies to provide support services that were not possible before. For example, Hewlett-Packard (HP) offers a complete set of sales and after-sale services. It promises "HP Total Care—expert help for every stage of your computer's life. From choosing it, to configuring it, to protecting it, to tuning it up—all the way to recycling it." Customers can click onto the HP Total Care service portal that offers online resources for HP products and 24/7 tech support, which can be accessed via email, instant online chat, and telephone.[14]

Product Line Decisions

Beyond decisions about individual products and services, product strategy also calls for building a product line. A **product line** is a group of products that are closely related because they function in a similar manner, are sold to the same customer groups, are marketed through the same types of outlets, or fall within given price ranges. For example, Unilever produces several lines of toothpastes, including Signal, Close-up, and Pepsodent. Johnson & Johnson produces several lines of skin creams, including Johnson's Baby, Neutrogena, Ph5.5, and Roc.

The major product line decision involves *product line length*— the number of items in the product line. The line is too short if the manager can increase profits by adding items; the line is too long if the manager can increase profits by dropping items. Managers need to analyze their product lines regularly to assess each product item's sales and profits and to understand how each item contributes to the line's overall performance.

Product line length is influenced by company objectives and resources. For example, one objective might be to allow for 'upselling,' a strategy by which customers move up to the next higher level/premium product. For example, BMW wants to move customers up from its 3-series models to 5- and 7-series models. Another objective might be to allow cross-selling: Hewlett-Packard sells printers as well as cartridges. Still another objective might be to protect against economic swings: Inditex runs several clothing-store chains (including Zara, Bershka, and Oysho) covering different price points.

A company can expand its product line in two ways: by *line filling* or by *line stretching*. *Product line filling* involves adding more items within the present range of the line. There are several reasons for product line filling: reaching for extra profits, satisfying dealers, using excess capacity, being the leading full-line company, and plugging holes to keep out competitors. However, line filling is overdone if it results in cannibalization (i.e. one product takes sales away from another product within the same company) and customer confusion. The company should ensure that new items are noticeably different from existing ones.

Product line stretching occurs when a company lengthens its product line beyond its current range. The company can stretch its line downward, upward, or both ways. Companies located at the upper end of the market can stretch their lines *downward*. A company may stretch downward to fulfill a market opportunity that otherwise would attract a new competitor or to respond to a competitor's attack on the upper end. Or it may add low-end products because it finds faster growth taking place in the low-end segments. Mercedes stretched its line downwards for all these reasons. Facing a slow growth luxury market and attacks by Japanese automakers on its high-end positioning, it successfully introduced its Mercedes C-Class cars. These models sells in the range of US$30,000 without harming the firm's ability to sell other Mercedes at much higher prices.

Companies can also stretch their product lines *upward*. Sometimes, companies stretch upward in order to add prestige to their current products. Or they may be attracted by a faster growth rate or higher margins at the higher end. For example, some years ago, each of the leading Japanese auto companies introduced an upmarket automobile: Honda launched Acura; Toyota launched Lexus; and Nissan launched Infiniti. They used entirely new names rather than their own names.

Companies in the middle range of the market may decide to stretch their lines in *both directions*. Marriott did this with its hotel product line. Along with regular Marriott hotels, it added eight new branded hotel lines to serve both the upper and lower ends of the market. For example, Renaissance Hotels & Resorts aims to attract and please top executives; Fairfield Inn by Marriott, vacationers and business travelers on a tight travel budget; and Courtyard by Marriott, salespeople and other "road warriors."[15] The major risk with this strategy is that some travelers will trade down after finding that the lower-price hotels in the Marriott chain give them pretty much everything they want. However, Marriott would rather capture its customers who move downward than lose them to competitors.

Product Mix Decisions

Product mix (or product portfolio)
The set of all product lines and items that a particular seller offers for sale.

A company with several product lines has a product mix. A **product mix** (or product portfolio) consists of all the products and items that a particular seller offers for sale. Unilever's product mix consists of four major product lines: food, household cleaning, cosmetics, and personal care products. Each product line has several sub-lines. For example, in personal care Unilever has the following product lines: oral-care, skin-care, and hair-care.

A company's product mix has four important dimensions: width, length, depth, and consistency. Product mix *width* refers to the number of different product lines the company carries. For example, Colgate markets a fairly contained product mix, consisting of personal care and home care products; by comparison 3M markets more than 60,000 products. A large supermarket may stock around 100,000 to 120,000 items.

Product mix *length* refers to the number of items the company carries within its product lines. Unilever usually carries a number of brands within each line. For example, its personal care line includes Lux liquid soaps and body washes, Dove body wash, Pears liquid soap and bars, Lifebuoy liquid soap and bars, Rexona deodorant spray and roll-on, etc.

Product mix *depth* refers to the number of versions offered of each product in the line. Colgate toothpaste comes in 13 varieties: Colgate Total, Colgate Tartar Control, Colgate 2-in-1, Colgate Cavity Protection, Colgate Sensitive, Colgate Fresh Confidence, Colgate Max Fresh, Colgate Simply White, Colgate Sparkling White, Colgate Kids Toothpaste, Colgate Luminous, Colgate Baking Soda & Peroxide, and Ultrabrite. Then each variety comes in its own special forms and formulation. For example, you

Colgate offers product mix depth with toothpaste in 13 varieties.

can buy Colgate Total in regular, mint fresh stripe, whitening paste and gel, advanced fresh gel, or 2-in-1 liquid gel versions.

Finally, the *consistency* of the product mix refers to how closely related the various product lines are in end use, production requirement, distribution channels, or some other way. Colgate's product lines are consistent as they are consumer products that go through the same distribution channels. The lines are less consistent as they perform different functions for the consumers.

These product mix dimensions provide the handles for defining the company's product strategy. The company can increase its business in four ways.

1. It can add new product lines—widen its product mix. In this way its new lines are built on the company's reputation of its other lines.

2. The company can lengthen its existing product lines to become a more full-line company.

3. It can add more versions of each product and thus deepen its product mix.

4. The company can pursue more product line consistency, or less, depending on whether it wants to have a strong reputation in a single field or in several fields.

Branding Strategy: Building Strong Brands (pp 215-224)

Author Comment | A brand represents everything that a product or service means to consumers. As such, brands are valuable assets to a company. For example, when you hear someone say "Coca-Cola," what do you think, feel, or remember? What about "Ferrari"? Or "Google"?

Some analysts see brands as *the* major enduring asset of a company, outlasting the company's specific products and facilities. John Stewart, former CEO of Quaker Oats, once said, "If this business were split up, I would give you the land and bricks and mortar, and I would keep the brands and trademarks, and I would fare better than you." A former CEO of McDonald's declared, "If every asset we own, every building, and every piece of equipment were destroyed in a terrible natural disaster, we would be able to borrow all the money to replace it very quickly because of the value of our brand ... The brand is more valuable than the totality of all these assets."[16]

Thus, brands are powerful assets that must be carefully developed and managed. In this section, we examine the key strategies for building and managing brands.

Brand Equity

Brands are more than just names and symbols. They are a key element in the company's relationships with consumers. Brands represent consumers' perceptions and feelings about a product and its performance—everything that the product or service *means* to consumers. In the final analysis, brands exist in the heads of consumers. As one well-respected marketer once said, "Products are created in the factory, but brands are created in the mind."[17]

Brand equity
The differential effect that knowing the brand name has on customer response to the product or its marketing.

A powerful brand has high *brand equity.* **Brand equity** is the differential effect that knowing the brand name has on customer response to the product and its marketing. It's a measure of the brand's ability to capture consumer preference and loyalty. A brand has positive brand equity when consumers react more favorably to it than to a generic or unbranded version of the same product. It has negative brand equity if consumers react less favorably than to an unbranded version.

Brands vary in the amount of power and value they hold in the marketplace. Some brands—such as Coca-Cola, Nike, Vivendi Universal, GE, McDonald's, Yamaha, and others—become larger-than-life icons that maintain their power in the market for years, even generations. Other brands create fresh consumer excitement and loyalty, brands such as Google, YouTube, Apple, eBay, and Wikipedia. These brands win in the marketplace not simply because they deliver unique benefits or reliable service. Rather, they succeed because they forge deep connections with customers. Consider consumers' reactions in the United States following Coca-Cola's decision to change the formulation of its

Coca-Cola's brand equity is so strong that the company's experiments with changing the formulation of Coke received a massive negative backlash from consumers.

Coke and introduce a new formulation that—according to blind taste tests—received more favorable feedback from consumers:

> Consumer reaction was swift but, unfortunately for Coca-Cola, negative. In Seattle, retired real-estate investor Gay Mullins founded the 'Old Cola Drinkers of America' and set up a hotline for angry consumers. A Beverly Hills wine merchant bought 500 cases of 'vintage Coke' and sold them at a premium. Meanwhile, back at Coca-Cola headquarters, roughly 1,500 calls a day and literally truck-loads of mail poured in, virtually all condemning the company's actions. Finally, after several months of slumping sales, Coca-Cola announced that the old formulation would return as 'Coca-Cola Classic' and join 'new' Coke in the marketplace. Coca-Cola learned the lesson: it is not about the formulation, but about the strong bond between the brand and its loyal customers.[18]

Ad agency Young & Rubicam's Brand Asset Valuator measures brand strength along four consumer perception dimensions: *differentiation* (what makes the brand stand out), *relevance* (how consumers feel it meets their needs), *knowledge* (how much consumers know about the brand), and *esteem* (how highly consumers regard and respect the brand). Brands with strong brand equity rate high on all of these dimensions. A brand must be distinct, or consumers will have no reason to choose it over other brands. But the fact that a brand is highly differentiated doesn't necessarily mean that consumers will buy it. The brand must stand out in ways that are relevant to consumers' needs. But even a differentiated, relevant brand is far from a shoe-in. Before consumers will respond to the brand, they must first know about and understand it. And that familiarity must lead to a strong, positive consumer-brand connection (see **Real Marketing 8.1**).[19]

Thus, positive brand equity derives from consumer feelings about and connections with a brand. Consumers sometimes bond *very* closely with specific brands. For example, one Michigan couple had such a passion for Black & Decker's DeWalt power tool brand that they designed their entire wedding around it. They wore trademark DeWalt black-and-yellow T-shirts, made their way to a wooden chapel that they'd built with their DeWalt gear, exchanged vows and power tools, and even cut cake with a power saw. Joked the wife about her husband (a carpenter by trade), "He loves DeWalt nearly as much as he loves me."[20]

A brand with high brand equity is a very valuable asset. *Brand valuation* is the process of estimating the total financial value of a brand. Measuring such value is difficult. However, according to one estimate, the brand value of Google is a whopping US$86 billion, with GE and Microsoft close behind at US$71 billion and Coca-Cola at US$58 billion. Other brands rating among the world's most valuable include China Mobile, Nokia, IBM, Apple, McDonald's, and Toyota.[21]

High brand equity provides a company with many competitive advantages. A powerful brand enjoys a high level of consumer brand awareness and loyalty. Because consumers expect stores to carry the brand, the company has more leverage in bargaining with resellers. Because the brand name carries high credibility, the company can more easily launch line and brand extensions. A powerful brand offers the company some defense against fierce price competition.

Above all, however, a powerful brand forms the basis for building strong and profitable customer relationships. The fundamental asset underlying brand equity is *customer equity*—the value of the customer relationships that the brand creates. A powerful brand is important, but what it really represents is a profitable set of loyal customers. The proper focus of marketing is building customer equity, with brand management serving as a major marketing tool. Companies need to think of themselves not as portfolios of products, but as portfolios of customers.

Real Marketing 8.1

Breakaway Brands: Connecting with Customers

"Big blue-chip companies like General Electric and Microsoft do many things well," notes a brand analyst, "but showing up on lists of the hottest brands is typically not one of them. Yet these two lumbering giants both made their way onto brand consultancy Landor Associates' annual Breakaway Brands ranking—a comprehensive survey that measures consumer sizzle."

Each year, brand consultancy Landor Associates, an arm of ad agency Young & Rubicam, conducts a Top Ten Breakaway Brands survey in which it identifies the 10 brands with the greatest percentage gains in brand health and business value as a result of superb brand strategy and execution over a three-year period. The survey taps Young & Rubicam's Brand Asset Valuator, a database of responses from 9,000 consumers evaluating 2,500 brands measured across 56 metrics. Landor looks at brand factors such as differentiation, relevance, esteem, and knowledge. At the same time, another consultancy, BrandEconomics, assesses the financial performance of the brand ('Economic Value Added'). Combined, the Brand Asset Valuator and Economic Value Added models provide a brand valuation based on both consumer and financial measures.

Ideas about achieving brand strength, that elusive blend of awareness and trust, have changed in the past decade. "It's no longer, What can we blast out there about ourselves?" says another branding expert. "Brand theory now asks, How can we connect with the community in a really meaningful way?" It's a big question. Armed with information about price and quality, today's consumer is a tough challenge. But, says the expert, "if you're willing to talk directly and deeply to your audience, you can become a strong brand without a lot of fanfare."

The most recent Breakaway Brands list includes a strange agglomeration, from hot technology brands such as iPod and BlackBerry, to blue chips such as GE and Microsoft, to down-and-dirty discount retailers such as the retail discount chains TJ Maxx and Costco.

Breakaway brand BlackBerry has perfected a truly unique community-building tool. Today, it is becoming increasingly difficult within the business community to imagine life before BlackBerry.

Top Ten Breakaway Brands

1. TJ Maxx
2. iPod
3. BlackBerry
4. Stonyfield Farm
5. Samsung
6. Costco
7. Propel
8. Barnes & Noble
9. GE
10. Microsoft

Missing are some brand titans such as Coca-Cola (big but not growing very fast) and fresh-faced young brands like MySpace (the consumer panel consists of adults 18 years and older, so the youth-centric sensation doesn't show up yet). But Landor found that each brand that did make the list embraced one or more of three themes. "Today it's all about *trust*, *community*, and creating a *dialogue* with your customer that shares real knowledge," says Landor's chief marketing officer. That is, all of the brands really connect with customers.

So, how are older brands such as Microsoft and GE connecting with consumers? Microsoft's resurrection from its corporate-bad-guy status of past years results from several factors. More consumer-connecting products such as its Xbox game console now give Microsoft a cachet that even dominant Office-related brands such as PowerPoint and Word never could. And the good works of the Bill & Melinda Gates Foundation have also helped to boost consumer trust and community, helping to foster perceptions of a kinder, gentler Microsoft. Finally, as new corporate bogeymen like Google and MySpace owner News Corp. begin throwing their weight around, Microsoft now "comes off as

an underdog even though it is a behemoth," says the brand expert.

GE's appearance on the Breakaway Brands List derives almost entirely from its 'ecomagination' environmental efforts. Between 2005 and 2010, the company aimed to more than double its annual research budget for cleaner technologies—like energy-efficient refrigerators and wind turbines. In 2006, GE's increasing connections with customer and community concerns about the environment generated US$12 billion in revenues from 45 ecomagination products and services. "They are trying to turn that entire ship into the ecovessel of the future," says Landor's chief marketing executive.

iPod and BlackBerry—that's more like it! These are brands that you'd expect to see on a Breakaway Brands list. Among brands that foster customer community, the iPod is an obvious winner by virtue of its ability to create an online music ecosystem virtually overnight. With each new product introduction, iPod and Apple advance the causes of democratizing technology and approachable innovation. Similarly, BlackBerry maker Research In Motion perfected a truly unique community-building tool: a user-friendly device that lets business people stay connected to their jobs and to each other. "Today, virtually the world over," says a Landor analyst, "it is becoming increasingly difficult among the business community to imagine life 'BB' (Before BlackBerry)."

If iPod and BlackBerry seem like naturals for a Breakaway Brands list, an unlikely pair of retailers—TJ Maxx and Costco—just

Continued on next page

Real Marketing 8.1 Continued ▼

don't seem to fit. Yet in these difficult days of rising costs and spiraling economics, the two fast-growing discounters are creating treasure-hunt experiences that build strong emotional bonds with customers. TJ Maxx—at number-one, no less—fulfills the fantasy of luxury for less. At TJ Maxx, saving is no longer a priority reserved for the lower- and middle-income consumers. Now, even the most affluent shopper can experience the "thrill of the save" and the euphoria of a great "Maxx Moment." Similarly, Costco helps customers to save on everyday purchases while also experiencing great deals on high-end products. Says the Landor analyst,

Costco has "perfected the art of understanding not only what customers need, but also what they fantasize about, and putting both at their fingertips."

As proves true each year, Landor's Breakaway Brands List includes some old standbys and a number of pleasant surprises. As the analyst concludes: "In today's uncertain world it is no wonder that organizations have to work harder and harder to gain the

trust of their [customers] in order to be successful. What's more, [with brands], as in life, trust must be earned, not bought, and it must be constantly validated. The…marketers at the helm of this year's Top Ten Breakaway Brands understand not only the need to connect with their customers and instill trust, they also understand that brand is one of the most powerful tools available for making those coveted relationships a reality."

Sources: Based on information from Matthew Boyle, "Microsoft and GE: Not Old and in the Way," *Fortune*, November 12, 2007, p. 28; Ellen McGirt, "Breakaway Brands," *Fortune*, September 18, 2006, p. 27; and Chelsea Greene, "Using Brands to Drive Business Results," Landor Brands, November 2008, accessed at www.wpp.com/WPP/Marketing/ReportsStudies/Usingbrandstodrivebusinessresults.htm.

Building Strong Brands

> Brands are powerful assets that must be carefully developed and managed. As this figure suggests, building strong brands involves many challenging decisions.

Branding poses challenging decisions to the marketer. 🔖 **Figure 8.3** shows that the major brand strategy decisions involve brand positioning, brand name selection, brand sponsorship, and brand development.

FIGURE | 8.3 Major Brand Strategy Decisions

Brand Positioning

Marketers need to position their brands clearly in target customers' minds. They can position brands at any of three levels.[22] At the lowest level, they can position the brand on *product attributes*. For example, Procter & Gamble invented the disposable diaper category with its Pampers brand. Early Pampers marketing focused on attributes such as fluid absorption, fit, and disposability. In general, however, attributes are the least desirable level for brand positioning. Competitors can easily copy attributes. More importantly, customers are not interested in attributes as such; they are interested in what the attributes will do for them.

A brand can be better positioned by associating its name with a desirable *benefit*. Thus, Pampers can go beyond technical product attributes and talk about the resulting containment and skin-health benefits from dryness. "There are fewer wet bottoms in the world because of us," says Jim Stengel, P&G's global marketing officer. Some successful brands positioned on benefits are Volvo (safety), FedEx (guaranteed on-time delivery), Nike (performance), and Lexus (quality).

The strongest brands go beyond attribute or benefit positioning. They are positioned on strong *beliefs and values*. These brands pack an emotional wallop. Brands such as Godiva, Starbucks, Apple, and Victoria's Secret rely less on a product's tangible attributes and more on creating surprise, passion, and excitement surrounding a brand. Successful brands engage customers on a deep, emotional level. Thus, P&G knows that, to parents, Pampers mean much more than just containment and dryness. According to P&G's Stengel:[23]

If you go back, we often thought of our brands in terms of functional benefits. But when we began listening very closely to customers, they told us Pampers meant much more to them—Pampers are more about parent–child relationships and total baby care. So we started to say, "We want to be a brand experience; we want to be there to help support parents and babies as they grow and develop." In the initial days people thought we were nuts. How can a diaper help a baby's development? But babies wear diapers 24/7 for almost three years. It actually reorients R&D to ask a question like "How can we help babies sleep better?" Why are we concerned about babies sleeping better? Because sleep is important to brain development. It helps relationship skills. Thinking like that, we're able to help improve life for our consumers. The equity of great brands has to be something that a consumer finds inspirational and the organization finds inspirational. You know, our baby care business didn't start growing aggressively until we changed Pampers from being about dryness to being about helping mom with her baby's development.

When positioning a brand, the marketer should establish a mission for the brand and a vision of what the brand must be and do. A brand is the company's promise to deliver a specific set of features, benefits, services, and experiences consistently to the buyers. The brand promise must be simple and honest. Tulip Inn, for example, offers clean rooms, low prices, and good service but does not promise expensive furniture or large bathrooms. In contrast, Bilderberg hotels offers luxurious rooms and a truly memorable experience but does not promise low prices. Chery, the leading Chinese car brand, promises low prices, minimum defects, and good customer service, but does not promise superior luxuries. On the other hand, BMW stresses on "elegance and sheer driving pleasure," but does not promise low prices.

Brand Name Selection

A good name can add greatly to a product's success. However, finding the best brand name is a difficult task. It begins with a careful review of the product and its benefits, the target market, and proposed marketing strategies. After that, naming a brand becomes part science, part art, and a measure of instinct.

Desirable qualities for a brand name include the following: (1) It should suggest something about the product's benefits and qualities. Examples: Beautyrest (mattresses), Die Hard (batteries), Intensive Care (lotion), Curves (women's fitness centers). (2) It should be easy to pronounce, recognize, and remember: iPod Touch, and easyJet. (3) The brand name should be distinctive: Lexus, Virgin. (4) It should be extendable: Amazon.com began as an online bookseller but chose a name that would allow expansion into other categories. (5) The name should translate easily into foreign languages. Before changing its name to Exxon, Standard Oil rejected the name Enco, which it learned meant a stalled engine when pronounced in Japanese. (6) It should be capable of registration and legal protection. A brand name cannot be registered if it infringes on existing brand names.

Choosing a new brand name is hard work. After a decade of choosing quirky names (Yahoo!, Google) or trademark-proof made-up names (Novartis, Aventis, Lycos), today's style is to build brands around names that have real meaning. For example, names like Silk (soy milk), Method (home products), Smartwater (beverages), and Blackboard (school software) are simple and make intuitive sense. But with trademark applications soaring, *available* new names can be hard to find. Try it yourself. Pick a product and see if you can come up with a better name for it. How about Moonshot? Tickle? Vanilla? Treehugger? Simplicity? Google them and you'll find that they're already taken.

Once chosen, the brand name must be protected. Many firms try to build a brand name that will eventually become identified with the product category. Brand names such as Kleenex, Levi's, JELL-O, BAND-AID, Scotch Tape, Formica, and Ziploc have succeeded in this way. However, their very success may threaten the company's rights to the name. Many originally protected brand names—such as cellophane, aspirin, nylon, kerosene, linoleum, yo-yo, trampoline, escalator, thermos, and shredded wheat (cereal)—are now generic names that any seller can use. To protect their brands, marketers present them carefully using the word 'brand' and the registered trademark symbol, as in "BAND-AID® Brand Adhesive Bandages." Even the long-standing "I am stuck on BAND-AID and BAND-AID's stuck on me" commercial jingle (song) has now become "I am stuck on BAND-AID *brand* and BAND-AID's stuck on me."

Brand Sponsorship

A manufacturer has four sponsorship options. The product may be launched as a *national brand* (or *manufacturer's brand*), as when Sony and Kellogg's sell their output under their own brand names (Sony Bravia HDTV or Weetabix Crunchy Bran Frosted Flakes cereal). Or the manufacturer may sell to resellers who give the product a *private brand* (also called a *store brand* or *distributor brand*). Although most manufacturers create their own brand names, others market *licensed brands*. Finally, two companies can join forces and *co-brand* a product. Carrefour Hypermarket introduced a portfolio of over 600 products under the names of Carrefour and No.1.

National Brands Versus Store Brands. National brands (or manufacturers' brands) have long dominated the retail scene. In recent times, however, an increasing number of retailers and wholesalers have created their own **store brands** (or *private brands*). Store brand sales are soaring. In fact, they are growing much faster than national brands. In all, private brands now capture a significant amount of supermarket sales. Private-label apparel brands capture a 45 percent share of all U.S. apparel sales.[24]

Once known as 'generic' or 'no-name' brands, today's store brands are a far cry from the early no-frills generics. Store brands now offer much greater selection and higher quality. Rather than simply creating low-end generic brands that offer a low-price alternative to national brands, retailers are now moving toward higher-end private brands that boost both the store's revenues and its image. As store brand selection and quality have improved, so have consumer confidence and acceptance. Many consumers now identify themselves as frequent buyers of store brands.[25]

It seems that almost every retailer now carries its own store brands. Wal-Mart's private brands account for a whopping 40 percent of its sales: brands such as Sam's Choice beverages and food products; Equate pharmacy, health, and beauty products; and White Cloud brand toilet tissue, diapers, detergent, and fabric softener. Its private label brands alone generate nearly twice the sales of all P&G brands.[26] Grocery giant Kroger markets some 8,000 items under a variety of private brands, such as Private Selection, Kroger Brand, F.M.V. (For Maximum Value), Naturally Preferred, and Everyday Living. And Costco, the world's largest warehouse club, offers a staggering array of goods and services under its Kirkland Signature brand. Costco customers can buy anything from Kirkland Signature rotisserie chickens to a US$3,439-per-person Kirkland Signature Tahitian cruise package. At the other end of the spectrum, upscale retailer Saks Fifth Avenue carries its own clothing line, which features US$98 men's ties, US$200 halter-tops, and US$250 cotton dress shirts.

In the so-called *battle of the brands* between national and private brands, retailers have many advantages. They control what products they stock, where they go on the shelf, what prices they charge, and which ones they will feature in local circulars. Retailers often price their store brands lower than comparable national brands, thereby appealing to the budget-conscious shopper in all of us. Although store brands can be hard to establish and costly to stock and promote, they also yield higher profit margins for the reseller. And they give resellers exclusive products that cannot be bought from competitors, resulting in greater store traffic and loyalty. Fast-growing U.S. retailer Trader Joe's, which carries 80 percent store brands, began creating its own brands so that "we could put our destiny in our own hands," says the company's president.[27]

To compete with store brands, leading brand marketers must invest in R&D to bring out new brands, new features, and continuous quality improvements. They must design strong advertising programs to maintain high awareness and preference. And they must

Store brand (or private brand)
A brand created and owned by a reseller of a product or service.

BIGGER. BETTER. MORE ABSORBENT.

ONLY IN THEATRES NOVEMBER 2004
SpongeBobMovie.com

Licensing: The cable TV channel Nickelodeon has developed a stable full of hugely popular characters—such as SpongeBob SquarePants—that generate billions of dollars of retail sales each year.

find ways to 'partner' with major distributors in a search for distribution economies and improved joint performance.

Licensing. Most manufacturers take years and spend millions to create their own brand names. However, some companies license names or symbols previously created by other manufacturers, names of well-known celebrities, or characters from popular movies and books. For a fee, any of these can provide an instant and proven brand name.

Apparel and accessories sellers pay large royalties to adorn their products—from blouses to ties, and linens to luggage—with the names or initials of well-known fashion innovators such as Calvin Klein, Tommy Hilfiger, Gucci, or Armani. Sellers of children's products attach an almost endless list of character names to clothing, toys, school supplies, linens, dolls, lunch boxes, cereals, and other items. Licensed character names range from classics such as Sesame Street, Disney, Asterix, Winnie the Pooh, the Muppets, Scooby Doo, and Dr. Seuss characters to the more recent Dora the Explorer, Powerpuff Girls, Rugrats, Blue's Clues, and Harry Potter characters. And currently a number of top-selling retail toys are products based on television shows and movies, such as the Spiderman Deluxe Spinning Web Blaster and the Talking Friendship Adventures Dora.

Name and character licensing has grown rapidly in recent years. Licensing can be a highly profitable business for many companies. For example, Nickelodeon has developed a stable full of hugely popular characters, such as Dora the Explorer, Go, Diego, Go!, and SpongeBob SquarePants. Dora alone has generated more than US$5.3 billion in retail sales in under five years. "When it comes to licensing its brands for consumer products, Nickelodeon has proved that it has the Midas touch," states a brand licensing expert.[28]

Co-branding

The practice of using the established brand names of two different companies on the same product.

Co-branding. Although companies have been **co-branding** products for many years, there has been a recent resurgence in co-branding. Co-branding occurs when two established brand names of different companies are used on the same product. For example, Sony Corporation and Telefonaktiebolaget LM Ericsson combined forces and established a joint venture, Sony Ericsson, in 2001. The objective was to offer "the most attractive and innovative global brand in the mobile handset industry." They benefited from Sony's expertise in telecommunication and entertainment industries along with Ericsson's expertise in the mobile industry. For example, financial services firms often partner with other companies to create co-branded credit cards, such as when Chase and United Airlines joined forces to create the Chase United Travel Card. Similarly, Costco teamed with mattress maker Stearns & Foster to market a line of Kirkland Signature by Stearns & Foster mattress sets. And Nike and Apple co-branded the Nike+iPod Sport Kit, which lets runners link their Nike shoes with their iPod Nanos to track and enhance running performance in real time.[29]

In most co-branding situations, one company licenses another company's well-known brand to use in combination with its own. Co-branding offers many advantages. Because each brand dominates in a different category, the combined brands create broader consumer appeal and greater brand equity. Co-branding also allows a company to expand its existing brand into a category it might otherwise have difficulty entering alone. For example, Nickelodeon Family Suites by Holiday Inn gives the cable channel Nickelodeon yet another opportunity to become a deeper part of viewers' lives. And it provides Holiday Inn with a shot at a new, younger travel market made up of young parents who grew up watching Nick. Similarly, the Nike+iPod arrangement gives Apple a presence in the sports and fitness market. At the same time, it helps Nike to bring new value to its customers.[30]

Co-branding also has limitations. Such relationships usually involve complex legal contracts and licenses. Co-branding partners must carefully co-ordinate their advertising, sales promotion, and other marketing efforts. Finally, when co-branding, each partner must trust that the other will take good care of its brand. For example, consider the marriage between the retailer Kmart and the Martha Stewart Everyday housewares brand. When Kmart declared bankruptcy before being acquired by Sears, it cast a shadow on the Martha Stewart brand. In turn, when Martha Stewart, the brand's founder, was convicted and jailed for illegal financial dealings, it created negative associations for Kmart. Finally, Kmart was further embarrassed when Martha Stewart Living Omnimedia recently struck major licensing agreements with Macy's and Lowe's, two other retailers, announcing that it would separate from Kmart when the current contract ends in 2009. Thus, as one manager puts it, "Giving away your brand is a lot like giving away your child—you want to make sure everything is perfect."[31]

Brand Development

A company has four choices when it comes to developing brands (see 🛒 **Figure 8.4**). It can introduce *line extensions*, *brand extensions*, *multibrands*, or *new brands*.

Line extension

Extending an existing brand name to new forms, colors, sizes, ingredients, or flavors of an existing product category.

Line Extensions. **Line extensions** occur when a company extends existing brand names to new forms, colors, sizes, ingredients, or flavors of an existing product category. Thus, Morton Salt has expanded its line to include regular iodized salt plus Morton Coarse Kosher Salt, Morton Sea Salt, Morton Lite Salt (low in sodium), Morton Popcorn Salt, Morton Salt Substitute, and several others. The vast majority of all new-product activity consists of line extensions.

A company might introduce line extensions as a low-cost, low-risk way to introduce new products. Or it might want to meet consumer desires for variety, to use excess capacity, or simply to command more shelf space from resellers. However, line extensions involve some risks. An overextended brand name might lose its specific meaning. For example, you can now pick from an array of seven different Jeep SUV models—Commander, Grand Cherokee, Compass, Patriot, Liberty, Wrangler, and Wrangler Unlimited. It's unlikely that many customers will fully appreciate the differences across the many similar models, and such 'Jeep creep' can cause consumer confusion or even frustration.

Another risk is that sales of an extension may come at the expense of other items in the line. For example, Toyota has introduced a variety of sedan cars to cater to the needs of different consumer segments. The portfolio includes the Avalon, Camry, Camry Solara, Corolla, Matrix, Prius, Venza, and Yaris. The original Doritos Tortilla Chips have now morphed into a full line of 20 different types and flavors of chips, including such high-decibel flavors as Blazin' Buffalo Ranch, Black Pepper Jack, and Fiery Habanero. Although the line seems to be doing well, the original Doritos chips seem like just another flavor. A line extension works best when it takes sales away from competing brands, not when it 'cannibalizes' the company's other items.

Brand extension

Extending an existing brand name to new product categories.

Brand Extensions. A **brand extension** extends a current brand name to new or modified products in a new category. For example, Kimberly-Clark extended its market-leading Huggies brand from disposable diapers to a full line of toiletries for tots, from shampoos,

🛒 **FIGURE** | **8.4**

Brand Development Strategies

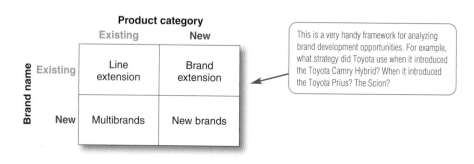

lotions, and diaper-rash ointments to baby wash, disposable washcloths, and disposable changing pads. Nestlé capitalized on its strength in the dairy market, and extended its brand in various industries, including the bottled water market. Victorinox extended its venerable Swiss Army brand from multitool knives to products ranging from cutlery and ballpoint pens to watches, luggage, and apparel. And P&G has leveraged the strength of its Mr Clean household cleaner brand to launch several new lines: cleaning pads (Magic Eraser), bathroom cleaning tools (Magic Reach), and home auto-cleaning kits (Mr Clean AutoDry). It's even launching Mr Clean-branded car washes.

A brand extension gives a new product instant recognition and faster acceptance. It also saves the high advertising costs usually required to build a new brand name. At the same time, a brand extension strategy involves some risk. Brand extensions such as Bic pantyhose, Heinz pet food, Life Savers gum, and Clorox laundry detergent met early deaths. The extension may confuse the image of the main brand. And if a brand extension fails, it may harm consumer attitudes toward the other products carrying the same brand name.

Furthermore, a brand name may not be appropriate to a particular new product, even if it is well made and satisfying—would you consider flying on Hooters Air or drinking Hooters energy drink? How about an Evian water-filled padded bra? All of these products failed. Companies that are tempted to transfer a brand name must research how well the brand's associations fit the new product.[32]

Multibrands. Companies often introduce additional brands in the same category. Thus, Procter & Gamble markets many different brands in each of its product categories. *Multibranding* offers a way to establish different features and appeal to different buying motives. It also allows a company to lock up more reseller shelf space.

A major drawback of multibranding is that each brand might obtain only a small market share, and none may be very profitable. The company may end up spreading its resources over many brands instead of building a few brands to a highly profitable level. These companies should reduce the number of brands they sell in a given category and set up tighter screening procedures for new brands.

New Brands. A company might believe that the power of its existing brand name is waning and a new brand name is needed. Or it may create a new brand name when it enters a new product category for which none of the company's current brand names are appropriate. For example, Toyota created the separate Scion brand, targeted toward younger consumers.

As with multibranding, offering too many new brands can result in a company spreading its resources too thin. And in some industries, such as consumer packaged goods, consumers and retailers have become concerned that there are already too many brands, with too few differences between them. Thus, Unilever, Frito-Lay, Nestlé, and other large consumer-product marketers are now pursuing *megabrand* strategies—weeding out weaker or slower-growing brands and focusing their marketing dollars only on brands that can achieve the number-one or number-two market share positions with good growth prospects in their categories.

Managing Brands

Companies must manage their brands carefully. First, the brand's positioning must be continuously communicated to consumers. Major brand marketers often spend huge amounts on advertising to create brand awareness and to build preference and loyalty. For example, Vodafone spends more than US$400 million annually to promote its brand. McDonald's spends more than US$1.7 billion.[33]

Such advertising campaigns can help to create name recognition, brand knowledge, and maybe even some brand preference. However, the fact is that brands are not maintained by advertising but by the *brand experience*. Today, customers come to know a brand through a wide range of contacts and touch points. These include advertising, but also personal experience with the brand, word of mouth, company web pages, and many others. The company must put as much care into managing these touch points as it does into producing its ads. "Managing each customer's experience is perhaps the most important ingredient in building [brand] loyalty," states one branding expert. "Every memorable interaction...must be completed with excellence and...must reinforce your brand essence." A former Disney executive agrees: "A brand is a living entity, and it is enriched or undermined cumulatively over time, the product of a thousand small gestures."[34]

The brand's positioning will not take hold fully unless everyone in the company lives the brand. Therefore, the company needs to train its people to be customer centered. Even better, the company should carry on internal brand building to help employees understand and be enthusiastic about the brand promise. Many companies go even further by training and encouraging their distributors and dealers to serve their customers well.

Finally, companies need to periodically audit their brands' strengths and weaknesses. They should ask: Does our brand excel at delivering benefits that consumers truly value? Is the brand properly positioned? Do all of our consumer touch points support the brand's positioning? Do the brand's managers understand what the brand means to consumers? Does the brand receive proper, sustained support? The brand audit may turn up brands that need more support, brands that need to be dropped, or brands that must be rebranded or repositioned because of changing customer preferences or new competitors.

International and Regional Branding Decisions

Local companies in the Arab world face fierce competition from global companies that capitalize on their expertise and size. The question is: How can local brands compete and succeed against global brands? One solution is to rely on a differentiation strategy and target a niche market. However, many local brands in the Arab world have succeeded in dominating their markets by benefiting from their local knowledge of consumer needs and preferences. Many of them have even extended their operations internationally as well as regionally.

One advantage of being in the Arab world is the cultural similarity—at least through language—that renders regional growth relatively easy. Broadcasting channels such as ART, Al-Jazeera, Rotana, and Melody have expanded into most of the countries in the region. They also have created an attractive regional advertising medium. Moreover, Gulf-based companies such as Savola and Arma have found regional markets attractive for their fast-moving consumer products. Also, a variety of local banks have grown within the region. The Lebanon-based Bank Audi has branches in Egypt, Saudi Arabia, Qatar, Jordan, Syria, Sudan, and the UAE, and the has now started to further expand in Europe and Africa. Orascom Telecom, an Egyptian mobile telecommunications company, established operations in Iraq, Algeria and Tunisia, along with Pakistan, Bangladesh, and Zimbabwe. These success stories should encourage local players to build strong brands and aspire to grow regionally and internationally. **Real Marketing 8.2** looks at how one brand has grown both regionally and internationally.

Author Comment | As noted at the start of the chapter, services are 'products,' too—just intangible ones. So all of the product topics we've discussed so far apply to services as well as to physical products. However, in this final section, we'll focus on the special characteristics and marketing needs that set services apart.

Services Marketing (pp 224–232)

Services have grown dramatically in recent years. Services are growing even faster in the world economy, making up 64 percent of gross world product.[36]

Service industries vary greatly. *Governments* offer services through courts, employment services, hospitals, military services, police and fire departments, the postal service, and schools. *Private not-for-profit organizations* offer services through museums, charities, mosques, colleges, foundations, and hospitals. A large number of *business organizations* offer services—airlines, banks, hotels, insurance companies, consulting firms, medical and legal practices, entertainment companies, real-estate firms, retailers, and others.

Real Marketing 8.2

Fayrouz:
An International Brand Built in the Region

Fayrouz is a fruit-flavored non-alcoholic malt-based soft drink. It was established in Egypt in 1997 by Al-Ahram Beverages Company (ABC), the only manufacturer of beer, wine, premium spirits, and malt beverages in the country. The brand was successful despite fierce competition from Coca-Cola and Pepsi, who dominated the market. Fayrouz enjoyed a growth of 800 percent in five years, growing to sales of around 11.8 million gallons per year in Egypt. Fayrouz's production process avoids fermentation, and thus no alcohol is produced. As a result, Al-Azhar University in Cairo has certified the product *halal*, (permissible in Islam).[35]

In the biggest financial deal in Egypt's history, Heineken (one of the world's largest brewers), paid US$280 million in 2010 to buy the owner of the Fayrouz brand, ABC. Heineken found in ABC's brands Fayrouz and Birell a large and attractive market in the Arab world. Later, Heineken founded Fayrouz International Company in Switzerland in 2003. The aim was to grow Fayrouz sales worldwide. According to Albert Holtzappel, Heineken's spokesman in Amsterdam, "malt drinks have found a gap in the spectrum of beverages. They form their own category. You cannot compare them to soft drinks that are too sweet and don't have body, and you cannot compare them to beer, either." Steven Keefer, ABC's head of marketing division at that time, confirmed this statement by saying that, "Fayrouz drinkers are going for the taste. They're going for the health benefits of malt, to a secondary degree. They're going for the fact that it is a religiously acceptable brand, it represents values that connect with the consumer."

Fayrouz was positioned as a premium malt-based drink targeting out-going high-class young men and women. It utilized effective communication campaigns and built a good image in the minds of its target market. The primary communication campaign focused on the slogan: "The Natural Evolution of Soft Drinks." Despite the relatively high price compared with Coca-Cola and Pepsi, Fayrouz succeeded in gaining acceptance among target consumers because of its focused image and unique message.

The product has been offered in two types of packages: a can and a small glass bottle. Recently, Fayrouz introduced a large-size bottle as well. In addition, there are various flavors offered: apple, pineapple, mango, raspberry, pear, and peach. To launch the peach flavor drink in Saudi Arabia in 2007, the company organized a Kingdom-wide road show, during which more than 500,000 free cans were sampled. It used an innovative technology called Segway, an automated riding rolling wheel, by which it offered product samples to consumers with a range of genders, ages, and nationalities, followed by fun quizzes and competitions. In this way it hoped to boost the Fayrouz brand's position further across the region. According to Osama Abdul Rahman, country manager, Fayrouz, Kingdom of Saudi Arabia, "it embodies Fayrouz brand uniqueness being a new refreshing premium adult soft drink that provides natural change from daily routines and traditional soft drinks, not only because it is the first flavor of its kind ever used in a car-

Fayrouz was developed as a brand to meet local market needs in Egypt, but the product's appeal has accelerated its growth into international markets too.

bonated soft drink, but also because it has no rivals, and no look-alike in terms of quality, packaging and presentation."

Nowadays, Fayrouz International attempts to keep growing and expanding in international markets. Its unique ingredients and its exotic positioning allowed it to generate remarkable success in a short period of time. It will be interesting to monitor the brand's performance in the coming years in the Arab world as well as internationally.

Sources: "Heinken Eyes Islamic Beer Market," *CNN Money,* January 13, 2003; Stephen Khan, "Brewers go Head to Head in Battle for Muslim Markets," *The Observer,* August 10, 2003, www.guardian.co.uk/world/2003/aug/10/stephenkhan.theobserver; "International Brewers Buy into Mideast Malternatives," *Modern Brewery Age,* March 3, 2003; "Near Beer a Hit in Middle East," *Taipei Times,* February 12, 2003; "Fayrouz Peach Flavor Drink 'Hits the Ground Running,'" *Arab News,* August 24, 2007; and Fayrouz International website, http://fayrouzinternational.com/?page_id=62.

Nature and Characteristics of a Service

A company must consider four special service characteristics when designing marketing programs: *intangibility, inseparability, variability,* and *perishability* (see ▼ **Figure 8.5**).

Service intangibility means that services cannot be seen, tasted, felt, heard, or smelled before they are bought. For example, people undergoing cosmetic surgery cannot see the result before the purchase. Airline passengers have nothing but a ticket and the promise that

Service intangibility
A major characteristic of services—they cannot be seen, tasted, felt, heard, or smelled before they are bought.

FIGURE | 8.5
Four Service Characteristics

Although services are 'products' in a general sense, they have special characteristics and marketing needs. The biggest differences come from the fact that services are essentially intangible and that they are created through direct interactions with customers. Think about your experiences with an airline versus Nike or Apple.

Intangibility

Services cannot be seen, tasted, felt, heard, or smelled before purchase

Inseparability

Services cannot be separated from their providers

Services

Variability

Quality of services depends on who provides them and when, where, and how

Perishability

Services cannot be stored for later sale or use

they and their luggage will arrive safely at the intended destination, hopefully at the same time. To reduce uncertainty, buyers look for 'signals' of service quality. They draw conclusions about quality from the place, people, price, equipment, and communications that they can see.

Therefore, the service provider's task is to make the service tangible in one or more ways and to send the right signals about quality. One analyst calls this *evidence management,* in which the service organization presents its customers with organized, honest evidence of its capabilities. Consider the following example:

In 2009, Emaar Healthcare Group (the healthcare subsidiary of Emaar Properties PJSC) opened the largest outpatient facility in the region, The Dubai Mall Medical Centre.[37]

The Dubai Mall Medical Centre strongly emphasizes its standards of customer service and "patient-centric experience" alongside its commitments to international best practices in medicine. It offers a range of treatments by specialists from many medical fields. The Centre's healthcare management company, EHL, states: "At each EHL facility, patients will find a group of dedicated and compassionate professionals, who use cutting-edge technology and combine it with their unparalleled know-how, and a commitment to personal attention. This is what separates EHL from the rest, and is the factor that contributes most to the group's continued growth."[38]

The Centre focuses on providing exceptional customer service standards in every communication with each patient or visitor. This includes a sequence of interactions:

- As soon as patients enter the parking garage, a friendly attendant is available to greet and direct them.

- Once inside, the concierge welcomes them and makes any personal arrangements such as flights and accommodation.

- A 'patient relations co-ordinator' then escorts the patient to a registration desk and provides them with a drink while they sign in.

- A designated nurse greets the patient and escorts them to the area for the nursing assessment, and alerts the doctor when they are ready to be seen.

Such level of detailed care in interactions continues throughout the medical treatment and afterwards, with an effort to consider and address the patient's every need.

Physical goods are produced, then stored, later sold, and still later consumed. In contrast, services are first sold, then produced and consumed at the same time. In services marketing, the service provider is the

The Dubai Mall Medical Centre aims to deliver excellent customer service through a "patient-centric experience." It considers every interaction that a patient has in the Centre, from arrival to departure.

Service inseparability
A major characteristic of services—they are produced and consumed at the same time and cannot be separated from their providers.

Service variability
A major characteristic of services—their quality may vary greatly, depending on who provides them and when, where, and how.

Service perishability
A major characteristic of services—they cannot be stored for later sale or use.

product. **Service inseparability** means that services cannot be separated from their providers, whether the providers are people or machines. If a service employee provides the service, then the employee becomes a part of the service. Because the customer is also present as the service is produced, *provider–customer interaction* is a special feature of services marketing. Both the provider and the customer affect the service outcome.

Service variability means that the quality of services depends on who provides them as well as when, where, and how they are provided. For example, some hotels—say, Jumeirah Group hotels in Dubai—have reputations for providing better service than others. Still, within a given Jumeirah Group hotel, one registration-counter employee may be cheerful and efficient, whereas another standing just a few feet away may be unpleasant and slow. Even the quality of a single Jumeirah Group hotel employee's service varies according to his or her energy and frame of mind at the time of each customer encounter.

Service perishability means that services cannot be stored for later sale or use. Some doctors charge patients for missed appointments because the service value existed only at that point and disappeared when the patient did not show up. The perishability of services is not a problem when demand is steady. However, when demand fluctuates, service firms often have difficulties. For example, because of rush-hour demand, public transportation companies have to own much more equipment than they would if demand were even throughout the day. Thus, service firms often design strategies for producing a better match between demand and supply. Hotels and resorts charge lower prices in the off-season to attract more guests. And restaurants hire part-time employees to serve during peak periods.

Jumeirah's core essence to Stay Different™ embodies its promise to guests to deliver "passionate service, delivered by our multinational team of warm and friendly colleagues."

Service-profit chain
The chain that links service firm profits with employee and customer satisfaction.

Marketing Strategies for Service Firms

Just like manufacturing businesses, good service businesses use marketing to position themselves strongly in chosen target markets. BMW promises "The ultimate driving machine"; Jaguar says "The art of performance." Jumeirah's core message, to Stay Different™, promises guests unique experiences, focusing on the specific needs of luxury travelers and emphasizing the importance of personal experiences.

These and other service firms establish their positions through traditional marketing mix activities. However, because services differ from tangible products, they often require additional marketing approaches.

The Service-Profit Chain

In a service business, the customer and front-line service employee *interact* to create the service. Effective interaction, in turn, depends on the skills of front-line service employees and on the support processes backing these employees. Thus, successful service companies focus their attention on *both* their customers and their employees. They understand the **service-profit chain**, which links service firm profits with employee and customer satisfaction. This chain consists of five links:[39]

- *Internal service quality:* superior employee selection and training, a quality work environment, and strong support for those dealing with customers, which results in…
- *Satisfied and productive service employees:* more satisfied, loyal, and hardworking employees, which results in…
- *Greater service value:* more effective and efficient customer value creation and service delivery, which results in…
- *Satisfied and loyal customers:* satisfied customers who remain loyal, repeat purchase, and refer other customers, which results in…
- *Healthy service profits and growth:* superior service firm performance.

Therefore, reaching service profits and growth goals begins with taking care of those who take care of customers. In fact, founder and former CEO of Southwest Airlines, Herb Kelleher, always put employees first, not customers. His reasons? "If they're happy, satisfied, dedicated, and energetic, they'll take good care of customers," he says. "When the customers are happy, they come back, and that makes shareholders happy."[40] Consider Four Seasons Hotels and Resorts, a chain legendary for outstanding service:[41]

At Four Seasons, every guest is a somebody. Other exclusive resorts pamper their guests, but Four Seasons offers a subtler brand of doting: helpful rather than subservient; instinctive rather than programmed. So it's easy to understand why Four Seasons has a cult-like clientele. As one Four Seasons Maui guest recently told a manager, "If there's a heaven, I hope it's run by Four Seasons." What makes the Four Seasons so special? It's the staff. The chain knows that happy, satisfied employees make for happy, satisfied customers. "Personal service is not something you can dictate as a policy," says the company's founder and CEO. "It comes from the culture. How you treat your employees is how you expect them to treat the customer."

And Four Seasons treats its employees well. Compared with the competition, Four Seasons salaries are in the 75th to 90th percentile, with generous retirement and profit-sharing plans. All employees—seamstresses, valets, the ski concierge, the general manager—eat together regularly, free, in the hotel cafeteria. Another great perk: free rooms. After six months, any staffer can stay three nights free per year at any Four Seasons hotel or resort. That number increases to six nights after a year and steadily thereafter. The room stays make employees feel as important and pampered as the guests. Says a Four Seasons Maui pool attendant about his free stays, "You walk in and you say, 'Yeah, I'm somebody.'" Says another Maui employee, "You come back from those trips on fire. You want to do so much for the guest." As a result, the Four Seasons staff love the hotel just as much as customers do. Although guests can check out anytime they like, employees never want to leave. The yearly turnover for full-time employees is around 18 percent, half the industry average. And that's the biggest secret to Four Seasons' success.

Internal marketing
Orienting and motivating customer-contact employees and supporting service people to work as a team to provide customer satisfaction.

Thus, service marketing requires more than just traditional external marketing using the Four Ps. **Figure 8.6** shows that service marketing also requires *internal marketing* and *interactive marketing*. **Internal marketing** means that the service firm must orient and motivate its customer-contact employees and support service people to work as a *team* to provide customer satisfaction. Marketers must get everyone in the organization to be customer centered. In fact, internal marketing must *precede* external marketing.

For example, Four Seasons hires the right people, orients them carefully, instills in them a sense of pride, and motivates them by recognizing and rewarding outstanding service deeds. Says one analyst, "Every job applicant, whether hoping to fold laundry or teach yoga, goes through at least four interviews." "We look for people who say 'I'd be proud to be a doorman,'" says the CEO. Once hired, the training never stops. The most important

FIGURE | 8.6
Three Types of Service Marketing

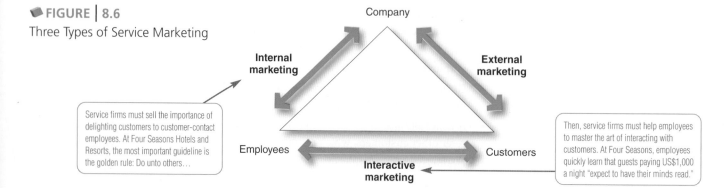

Service firms must sell the importance of delighting customers to customer-contact employees. At Four Seasons Hotels and Resorts, the most important guideline is the golden rule: Do unto others…

Then, service firms must help employees to master the art of interacting with customers. At Four Seasons, employees quickly learn that guests paying US$1,000 a night "expect to have their minds read."

guideline, contends the CEO, is "the golden rule: Do unto others [as you would have them do unto you]… That's not a gimmick," he says. "In the hiring process, we're looking for people who are very comfortable with this idea."[42] As a result, Four Seasons employees know what good service is and are highly motivated to give it.

Interactive marketing
Training service employees in the fine art of interacting with customers to satisfy their needs.

Interactive marketing means that service quality depends heavily on the quality of the buyer–seller interaction during the service encounter. In product marketing, product quality often depends little on how the product is obtained. But in services marketing, service quality depends on both the service deliverer and the quality of the delivery. Service marketers, therefore, have to master interactive marketing skills. Thus, Four Seasons selects only people with an innate 'passion to serve' and instructs them carefully in the fine art of interacting with customers to satisfy their every need. Employees learn quickly that guests paying US$1,000 a night "expect to have their [minds] read." All new hires complete a three-month training regimen that includes improvisation exercises to help them anticipate guest behavior.

In today's marketplace, companies must know how to deliver interactions that are not only 'high-touch' but also 'high-tech.' For example, customers can log onto the Dubai Islamic Bank website and access financial account information and make after-hours transactions. Customers seeking more personal interactions can contact service representatives by telephone or visit a local Dubai Islamic Bank branch to "talk with Ahmed." Thus, Dubai Islamic Bank has mastered interactive marketing at all three levels—calls, clicks, *and* personal visits.

Today, as competition and costs increase, and as productivity and quality decrease, more service marketing sophistication is needed. Service companies face three major marketing tasks: They want to increase their *service differentiation*, *service quality*, and *service productivity*.

Managing Service Differentiation

In these days of intense price competition, service marketers often complain about the difficulty of differentiating their services from those of competitors. To the extent that customers view the services of different providers as similar, they care less about the provider than the price.

The solution to price competition is to develop a differentiated offer, delivery, and image. The *offer* can include innovative features that set one company's offer apart from competitors' offers. Jumeirah Group offers car-rental, banking, and business-center services in its hotel lobbies and free high-speed Internet connections in its hotel rooms. Emirates Airline differentiates its offers through Skywards frequent-flyer award programs and special services, and offers limousine pick-up and drop-off for all business- and first-class passengers in major destinations around the world. Service companies can differentiate their service *delivery* by having more able and reliable customer-contact people, by developing a superior physical environment in which the service product is delivered, or by designing a superior delivery process. For example, many grocery chains now offer online shopping and home delivery as a better way to shop than having to drive, park, wait in line, and carry groceries home.

Finally, service companies also can work on differentiating their *images* through symbols and branding. Well-known service symbols include the red and green logo of Dubai shopping festival, entertainment company MGM's lion, and the McDonald's 'golden arches.'

Managing Service Quality

A service firm can differentiate itself by delivering consistently higher quality than its competitors provide. Like manufacturers before them, most service industries have now joined the customer-driven quality movement (see **Real Marketing 8.3**). And like product marketers, service providers need to identify what target customers expect with regard to service quality.

Unfortunately, service quality is harder to define and judge than product quality. For instance, it is harder to agree on the quality of a haircut than on the quality of a hair dryer. Customer retention is perhaps the best measure of quality—a service firm's ability to keep its customers depends on how consistently it delivers value to them.

Real Marketing 8.3

Service Marketing

What are the characteristics of a service? The characteristics differ from business to business and service to service. But are there any commonalities? Service, of course, extends into the sale of products because customers need service before, during, and after the sale is made.

A restaurant is a prime example—service oriented, but it sells food and drink, which are products. Not only does the customer expect that the food and drink is of an excellent standard, but he also wants to have a quick and courteous service and polite and helpful waiting staff. It does not matter if the food is Michelin Three Star or a burger; the expectations are the same.

The problem with a service, in its strictest sense, is that it is intangible. A customer cannot own a service; neither can the business that sells it to the person. It lasts for the duration of the use of that service, such as an aircraft flight lasting five hours. The attention to the service needs to focus on that time that the customer is using the service. Because the customer also knows the duration of that service, their expectations are focused on that period too. According to a survey carried out on airlines, cost does not have any real bearing on customers' expectations. The low-cost airline easyJet, which operates across Europe, scores consistently

Top-flight customer service: Singapore Airlines' customer-satisfaction success is based on employee training, development, communication, investment, and professionalism.

highly for employee helpfulness and efficiency. easyJet, however, is beaten on service by two other continental budget airlines, Germanwings and Wizz Air of Hungary.

Higher cost airlines such as British Airways, according to some 30,000 customers that were surveyed on customer service, ranked mediocre on most counts and fared particularly badly on short-haul flights. Singapore Airlines came out top among the long-haul carriers, with a customer-satisfaction score of 85 percent. Narrowly behind them were India's Jet Airways (with 84 percent) and Air New Zealand with 80 percent.

Intangibility of service is a constant problem; the experience a customer gets from the service is therefore bound to have a major impact on how the customer perceives that service. As real-estate agents will confirm, their service is both intangible and consequential. Customer confidence and loyalty is based on the real-estate agent being able to provide an unbeatable service that is said to incorporate "reliability, pleasant surprise, recovery and fairness."

Services are also perishable. The classic example is that of an airline seat or a seat at an event. Once the aircraft has closed

Top service companies set high service-quality standards. They watch service performance closely, both their own and that of competitors. They do not settle for merely good service; they aim for 100 percent defect-free service.

Unlike product manufacturers who can adjust their machinery and inputs until everything is perfect, service quality will always vary, depending on the interactions between employees and customers. As hard as they try, even the best companies will have an occasional late delivery, burned steak, or grumpy employee. However, good *service recovery* can turn angry customers into loyal ones. In fact, good recovery can win more customer purchasing and loyalty than if things had gone well in the first place. Therefore, companies should take steps not only to provide good service every time but also to recover from service mistakes when they do occur.

The first step is to *empower* front-line service employees—to give them the authority, responsibility, and incentives they need to recognize, care about, and tend to customer needs. For example, consider Customer Affairs and Service Audits (CASAs) in Emirates Airline. These audits involve three specific areas: customer relations (Arab community), customer relations (worldwide), and service audit. CASAs focus on people who have expressed dissatisfaction in the past. Their main objective is to win each customer's loyalty back, and dissuade them from using competitor products. They have developed a number of ways of checking quality regularly and auditing services in various ways, for example

for passengers or the event has started, any unsold seat is lost; it cannot be stored and sold later. In other words, services tend to be developed and used at the same time.

The tickets for the Beijing Olympics went on sale in December 2007. By the end of January 2008, 75 percent of those tickets were still unsold. Across all of the events throughout August 8–24, 2008, several million tickets were made available. Some of the key events, particularly those where the Chinese had major medal hopes, were massively oversubscribed from the moment the tickets went on sale. By June 2008, the sales had reached 6 million, with the Chinese having purchased 3.43 million, including 800,000 that had been reserved for the primary and middle-school students. The balance went to National Olympic Committees, the International Federations, the International Olympic Committee, and sponsors. This was in stark contrast to the Sydney Olympics in 2000, where some 40 percent of the tickets remained unsold.

Heterogeneity is another feature of services; it is the notion of making each service experience identical. Ideally, a business would want the customer to experience the same level of customer service in all of the outlets, aircraft, or other customer service environments. The problem with heterogeneity is that it is very difficult to exactly replicate the experience of each and every customer. On an airline flight, the steward may be new and not used to the demands of the customers.

Customer service training is therefore key to ensuring that service expectations are met and that employees are aware of the requirements of both the organization and the customers. A prime example is the training on customer service that Dubai Taxi Agency at the Roads and Transport Authority (RTA) provides to its taxi drivers. The courses, which are modeled on world-class modules, aim to improve the performance of taxi drivers and the level of service they provide to passengers spanning a wide spectrum of community members.

"The Agency is adopting these modules to provide its drivers an exposure to various skills needed to upgrade the level of service rendered to customers in keeping with the tourist profile of the emirate of Dubai and its standing as a premier business and commercial hub in the region," said Ammar bin Tamim, director of fleet drivers affairs department at Dubai Taxi Agency. "Customer service ranks high in the priority of Dubai Taxi Agency, which is keen on sending drivers to training courses which provide them with demonstrable improvement in their skills, broaden their knowledge base and empower them to deliver quality services in a professional manner."

The RTA training syllabus aims to provide taxi drivers with the key ingredients to lead to success. The successful driver is defined as one who will provide a safe, comfortable, and highly satisfying service to passengers of all types, including the elderly, women, children, and people with special needs.

Training also includes several other areas such as 'advanced customer service' (including communication, attitude, basic knowledge of the English language); 'the taxi' (including vehicle cleaning, inspection, air-conditioning, and dealing with the onboard systems), and 'the driver' (including health, morals, and courteous attitude toward road users).

In 2008, Bill Price, a former vice president of global customer services at Amazon, penned a book entitled *The Best Service Is No Service: How to Liberate your Customers from Customer Service, Keep them Happy, and Control Costs*. A snappy title to be sure, but Price maintained that customers usually seek service from a business when something has not gone according to plan. Something is wrong, the product is faulty, it has not been delivered, or the charge made was incorrect. Price believes that if the business gets it all correct, then customers do not need customer service at all. He believes that 'no service' is a major advantage to both the customer and the business. The customer does not have to spend her time and effort trying to make the business sort a problem out, and the business itself does not have to divert resources to sorting out the problem. Costs are cut, some of the savings can be passed on to the customer, and the rest retained as profit for the business.

Sources: Quotes and other information from *The Telegraph*, www.telegraph.co.uk; Air Transport Users Council, www.auc.org.uk; Travel Mole, www.travelmole.com; Birmingham City Council, www.birmingham.gov.uk; "Dubai Taxi Continues Intensive Training of Cabdrivers," *AME Info*, April 2, 2009, www.ameinfo.com/191208.html; and Institute of Customer Service, www.instituteofcustomerservice.com.

using ground inspection, in-flight inspection, mystery shoppers, and customer feedback. There are CASA teams operating in relation to all of Emirates primary markets.[43]

Managing Service Productivity

With their costs rising rapidly, service firms are under great pressure to increase service productivity. They can do so in several ways. They can train current employees better or hire new ones who will work harder or more skillfully. Or they can increase the quantity of their service by giving up some quality. The provider can 'industrialize the service' by adding equipment and standardizing production, as in McDonald's assembly-line approach to fast-food retailing. Finally, the service provider can harness the power of technology. Although we often think of technology's power to save time and costs in manufacturing companies, it also has great—and often untapped—potential to make service workers more productive.

However, companies must avoid pushing productivity so hard that doing so reduces quality. Attempts to industrialize a service or to cut costs can make a service company more efficient in the short run. But they can also reduce its longer-run ability to innovate, maintain service quality, or respond to consumer needs and desires. Many airlines are learning this lesson the hard way as they attempt to streamline and economize in the face of rising costs.

The no-frills budget airline or low-cost carrier Air Arabia flies from Sharjah airport. Traveling on budget airlines is less comfortable than traveling on the other UAE-based airlines, Emirates Airline or Etihad Airways. Seats are locked in the upright position, so people have less space. Customers have to pay for drinks and food on board. However, booking more than a few weeks in advance will ensure that passengers can make their journeys for a relatively low cost.

Thus, in attempting to improve service productivity, companies must be mindful of how they create and deliver customer value. In short, they should be careful not to take the 'service' out of service.

REVIEWING Objectives AND KEY Terms

A product is more than a simple set of tangible features. Each product or service offered to customers can be viewed on three levels. The *core customer value* consists of the core problem-solving benefits that consumers seek when they buy a product. The *actual product* exists around the core and includes the quality level, features, design, brand name, and packaging. The *augmented product* is the actual product plus the various services and benefits offered with it, such as a warranty, free delivery, installation, and maintenance.

OBJECTIVE 1 Define *product* and the major classifications of products and services. (pp 204–209)

Broadly defined, a *product* is anything that can be offered to a market for attention, acquisition, use, or consumption that might satisfy a want or need. Products include physical objects but also services, events, persons, places, organizations, ideas, or mixes of these entities. *Services* are products that consist of activities, benefits, or satisfactions offered for sale that are essentially intangible, such as banking, hotel, tax preparation, and home-repair services.

Products and services fall into two broad classes based on the types of consumers that use them. *Consumer products*—those bought by final consumers—are usually classified according to consumer shopping habits (convenience products, shopping products, specialty products, and unsought products). *Industrial products*—purchased for further processing or for use in conducting a business—include materials and parts, capital items, and supplies and services. Other marketable entities—such as organizations, persons, places, and ideas—can also be thought of as products.

OBJECTIVE 2 Describe the decisions companies make regarding their individual products and services, product lines, and product mixes. (pp 209–215)

Individual product decisions involve product attributes, branding, packaging, labeling, and product support services. *Product attribute* decisions involve product quality, features, and style and design. *Branding* decisions include selecting a brand name and developing a brand strategy. *Packaging* provides many key benefits, such as protection, economy, convenience, and promotion. Package decisions often include designing *labels*, which identify, describe, and possibly promote the product. Companies also develop *product support services* that enhance customer service and satisfaction and safeguard against competitors.

Most companies produce a product line rather than a single product. A *product line* is a group of products that are related in function, customer-purchase needs, or distribution channels. *Line stretching* involves extending a line downward, upward, or in both directions to occupy a gap that might otherwise be filled by a competitor. In contrast, *line filling* involves adding items within the present range of the line. All product lines and items offered to customers by a particular seller make up the *product mix*. The mix can be described by four dimensions: width, length, depth, and consistency. These dimensions are the tools for developing the company's product strategy.

OBJECTIVE 3 Discuss branding strategy—the decisions companies make in building and managing their brands. (pp 215–224)

Some analysts see brands as *the* major enduring asset of a company. Brands are more than just names and symbols—they embody everything that the product or service *means* to consumers. *Brand equity* is the positive differential effect that knowing the brand name has on customer response to the product or service. A brand with strong brand equity is a very valuable asset.

In building brands, companies need to make decisions about brand positioning, brand name selection, brand sponsorship, and brand development. The most powerful *brand positioning* builds around strong consumer beliefs and values. *Brand name selection* involves finding the best brand name based on a careful review of product benefits, the target market, and proposed marketing strategies. A manufacturer has four *brand sponsorship* options: it can launch a *manufacturer's brand* (or national brand), sell to resellers who use a *private brand*, market *licensed brands*, or join forces with another company to *co-brand* a product. A company also has four choices when it comes to developing brands. It can introduce *line extensions*, *brand extensions*, *multibrands*, or *new brands*.

Companies must build and manage their brands carefully. The brand's positioning must be continuously communicated to consumers. Advertising can help. However, brands are not maintained by advertising but by the *brand experience*. Customers come to know a brand through a wide range of contacts and interactions. The company must put as much care into managing these touch points as it does into producing its ads. Thus, managing a company's brand assets can no longer be left only to brand managers. Some companies are now setting up brand asset management teams to manage their major brands. Finally, companies must periodically audit their brands' strengths and weaknesses. In some cases, brands may need to be repositioned because of changing customer preferences or new competitors.

OBJECTIVE 4 **Identify the four characteristics that affect the marketing of a service and the additional marketing considerations that services require.** (pp 224–232)

Services are characterized by four key characteristics: they are *intangible, inseparable, variable,* and *perishable.* Each characteristic poses problems and marketing requirements. Marketers work to find ways to make the service more tangible, to increase the productivity of providers who are inseparable from their products, to standardize the quality in the face of variability, and to improve demand movements and supply capacities in the face of service perishability.

Good service companies focus attention on *both* customers and employees. They understand the *service-profit chain,* which links service firm profits with employee and customer satisfaction. Services marketing strategy calls not only for external marketing but also for *internal marketing* to motivate employees and *interactive marketing* to create service delivery skills among service providers. To succeed, service marketers must create *competitive differentiation,* offer high *service quality,* and find ways to increase *service productivity.*

KEY Terms

OBJECTIVE 1

Product (p 204)
Service (p 204)
Consumer product (p 206)
Convenience
product (p 206)
Shopping product (p 206)
Specialty product (p 207)
Unsought product (p 207)
Industrial product (p 207)
Social marketing (p 208)

OBJECTIVE 2

Product quality (p 209)
Brand (p 211)
Packaging (p 211)
Product line (p 213)
Product mix (product portfolio) (p 214)

OBJECTIVE 3

Brand equity (p 215)
Store brand (private brand) (p 220)
Co-branding (p 221)

Line extension (p 222)
Brand extension (p 222)

OBJECTIVE 4

Service intangibility (p 225)
Service inseparability (p 227)
Service variability (p 227)
Service perishability (p 227)
Service-profit chain (p 227)
Internal marketing (p 228)
Interactive marketing (p 229)

DISCUSSING & APPLYING THE Concepts

Discussing the Concepts

1. What is a product and how can product planners build customer value?

2. How does an industrial product differ from a consumer product? Discuss the types of industrial products and provide an example of each.

3. Discuss the product attributes through which benefits are communicated and delivered to customers.

4. Define brand equity. What competitive advantages does high brand equity provide a company?

5. Discuss the brand development strategies marketers use to develop brands. Provide an example of each strategy.

6. Describe the four characteristics of services that marketers must consider when designing marketing programs. How do the services offered by a dentist differ from those offered by a drug store regarding these characteristics?

Application Questions

1. The Coca-Cola Company produces concentrate, which is then sold to various licensed Coca-Cola bottlers throughout the world. The bottlers, who hold territorially exclusive contracts with the company, produce the finished product in cans and bottles from the concentrate in combination with filtered water and sweeteners. Visit your national Coca-Cola website and examine the list of brands. Name and define the four dimensions of a company's product mix and describe Coca-Cola's product mix on these dimensions.

2. Using the six qualities that a good brand name should possess, create a brand name for a personal care product that has the following positioning statement: "Intended for X-Games sports participants and enthusiasts, is a deodorant that combines effective odor protection with an enduring and seductive fragrance that will enhance your romantic fortunes."

3. Many retailers have their own private-label brands. What does this mean, and are the brands too powerful a force in marketing?

FOCUS ON Technology

UFLY Online (www.uflyonline.com) is considered the first Arab world travel agency with ambitious plans to ride high on the increasing demand for e-ticketing in the Middle East and North Africa (MENA) region. UFLY Online introduces to the public a one-stop-shopping facility, offering a wider and better choice at very competitive rates, in addition to 24-hour-a-day convenience. The company has offices in Dubai, Abu Dhabi, Muscat, and Beirut.

UFLY Online provides access to flights, hotels, and car hire throughout the world. The flights are from Arab origins, currently the UAE, Lebanon, Jordan, Kuwait, Egypt, Bahrain, Qatar, and Saudi Arabia. The website offers booking services for over 47,000 hotels worldwide. After only one year of operation in the MENA area, online traffic to the UFLY Online website was heavy, reaching more than 2,000 visitors daily. The main features attracting customers to UFLY Online are the flexibility of being able to pay by cash or credit card, and the fact that it also provides instant access to the most competitive negotiated fares in each country.

Before its launch, there were some concerns that cultural preferences for this region might not match the way the service is represented. In other words, it was foreseen that it might not be easy to draw Arab customers away from the face-to-face purchasing they were used to. But on the other hand, there was a level of confidence that enough people were used to air ticket Internet bookings for the system to work.

Based on these insights, UFLY Online has formulated its operational and promotional strategy based on online affiliations, strategic alliances, and co-branding agreements, to promote the online booking concept and e-commerce in the Arab world.

Going the extra mile, UFLY Online has established promotional deals with American Express Middle East and KLM, and among other leading Internet service providers in the Middle East, such as Arabia.com, thisiscyberia.com, Terranet.com, and Ajeeb.com. UFLY Online has proven that e-commerce for travel is now a reality in the region.

1. How does a service such as UFLY Online benefit both passengers and airline companies?

2. Is there a similar service in your country? To what source do travelers in your country and elsewhere turn for airline booking?

FOCUS ON Ethics

Digital Terrestrial Television (DTTV or DTT) is a digital technology that aims to provide a wider range of channels (also better sound and vision) using aerial broadcasts to conventional antenna. Effectively, it replaces analog television and is in varying stages of being rolled out across the world. The problem is that consumers of the new technology must buy new equipment such as set-top boxes and antennae in order to view digital broadcasts.

Britain, Sweden, and Spain launched digital services in their countries in 1998, 1999, and 2000, respectively. Still other countries launched digital services in 2006 and 2007. And while take-up in the Arab world is moving more slowly, Tunisia began the switch from analog to digital terrestrial broadcasting on March 15, 2010, and Saudi Arabia has grown the largest digital terrestrial television network in the region.

Despite a major publicity campaign in Britain to warn viewers about the digital switchover, almost half of the televisions sold in the country in the first seven months of 2007 were analog sets, even though the sets would be unable to receive broadcast signals after the switchover without their owners paying for extra

equipment. Consumers are generally confused about the reasons for the switch over to digital, believing that the effort is related to any one of the following factors:

- The updating of their countries' broadcasting networks
- So their governments can make money
- To give viewers more choices
- So retailers can make money
- To free up airwaves.

1. Why are countries switching to digital programming? Research the switchover taking place in your country, and write a brief report about what you have learned about the transition and how it is going.

2. Television stations and many consumers have already incurred costs related to the switchover. Is it right for governments to mandate actions that will require businesses and consumers to pay money for new equipment or services to continue receiving free television over the airways?

MARKETING BY THE Numbers

A business has introduced a new confectionery brand that comes in flavors such as mint chocolate, mocha, chocolate-almond, and raspberry-almond with white chocolate. The confections are wrapped in iridescent colors and sold in re-closable cartons. The business also intends to do this with its other, already established brands. The new products carry a higher wholesale price for the company (US$0.48 per ounce versus US$0.30 per ounce for the original product). They also come with higher variable costs (US$0.35 per ounce versus US$0.15 per ounce for the original product).

1. What brand development strategy is this business undertaking?

2. Assume the company expects to sell 300 million ounces of the new product within the first year following its introduction. However, half of those sales are expected to come from buyers who would normally purchase the company's original brand. In other words, the new product will cannibalize some of the old product's sales. Assume the company normally sells 1 billion ounces per year of its original product, and it will incur an increase in fixed costs of US$5 million during the first year it produces the new brand. Will the new product be profitable for the company?

VIDEO Case

Swiss Army Brands

It seems appropriate that Swiss Army Brands, maker of multifunction knives, has become a multiproduct brand. Victorinox Swiss Army Inc. has made its famous knives for more than 100 years. Former product line extensions included different variations of the standard Swiss Army knife for applications such as fishing, golf, and an accessory for women's purses.

But the popularity of the Swiss Army knife has enabled the company to expand into all manner of consumer goods, including watches, luggage, apparel, and other lines. These brand extensions have been based on consumer research to ensure that each fits within the concept that consumers hold for the brand. The success that Swiss Army Brands has achieved through expansion has even allowed it to open its own retail stores.

After viewing the video featuring Swiss Army Brands, answer the following questions about product and branding strategies:

1. How might brand extensions affect Swiss Army Brands, in both positive and negative ways?
2. Why did Swiss Army Brands open retail stores? How do these stores help the company build its brand?
3. Do you think Swiss Army Brands could extend its brand to any type of product? What additional products and lines might Swiss Army Brands consider?

COMPANY Case

Alshaya: The House of Brands

Alshaya was founded in 1890 as a trading company between India and the GCC countries. The scale and variety of products were not very wide, but very suitable for the market. Four generations later, in just less than 100 years, particularly in 1983, Alshaya realized the growth potential in the market. People all around the Arab world were traveling to shop for its fashion products in the U.S. and Europe. The trend became very wide, and people started searching for their preferred brands in their local market.

Accordingly, Alshaya acquired its first international franchise, Mothercare. Mothercare is a British retailer, specializing in products for expectant mothers and young children. The first operation of Mothercare started in Kuwait, the home town of Alshaya group. The brand was a huge success; it invited the minds behind the business to seek more of that success.

Realizing that people seek more than fashion items, Alshaya expanded its portfolio quickly to 55 retail brands, including many of the world's most recognized names in fashion and footwear, food service, health and beauty, pharmacy, optics, home furnishings, and office supplies brands. Today, Alshaya operates in more than 2,000 stores in 15 countries. Alshaya positions its basket of brands as "carefully chosen to bring the highest quality products to the region's premier retail locations."

Looking at Alshaya's portfolio, one can see that the organization has grown to become a tycoon in retailing international brands in the Arab world and beyond. Alshaya operations span the Kingdom of Saudi Arabia, Kuwait, United Arab Emirates, Bahrain, Qatar, Oman, Lebanon, Turkey, Jordan, and Egypt. It has recently expanded its operations to Russia, Cyprus, Poland, the Czech Republic, and Slovakia.

Apart from its other business portfolio, which serves hotels, real-estate, and automotive sectors, Alshaya focuses on brands that sell convenience products, shopping products, and specialty products to assure that they have the best coverage of the shopping customer base. The launching of the brands that Alshaya retails is fast paced and vibrant.

In 2008, Alshaya opened the first H&M store in the Arab world in Oman. The H&M stores have quickly swept the Middle East and North Africa making them one of the group's biggest hits. That was based on capitalizing on the brand equity and the value for money that H&M offers in its products.

In January 2009, Alshaya signed an agreement with Office Depot, where it will be granted the franchise rights for all channels in the Kingdom of Saudi Arabia, the United Arab Emirates, Kuwait, the Kingdom of Bahrain, Qatar, and Oman. "We are very pleased to have Office Depot as our partner," said Mohammed Alshaya, executive chairman of M.H. Alshaya Co. "We believe there is a significant market for these products and services throughout the Middle East. We look forward to using our experience and regional knowledge to firmly establish Office Depot as the natural choice for businesses and individuals for all of their office supply needs."

"Office Depot understands the importance of developing a retail business in the Middle East and is partnering with a very experienced company such as Alshaya," said Ernst Wessel, vice president international franchise development.

Alshaya first launched Payless into the Arab world market in March 2009 and operates 22 stores in four markets; Kuwait, the Kingdom of Saudi Arabia, Bahrain, and the UAE. In 2010, Alshaya expanded its Payless operation to reach as far as Russia. Like Alshaya, Payless stores deliver a 'House of Brands' strategy offering well-recognized brands, and featuring the latest on-trend styles at a great price. Through licensing arrangements or acquisitions, the brand portfolio offered in Payless stores includes Airwalk®, Dexter®, Predictions, Smartfit, Disney characters, Marvel characters (Iron Man, Star Wars), SpongeBob, and Hannah Montana.

In March 2010, M.H. Alshaya Co. officially opened the first Pottery Barn Kids retail store in Dubai. Also in March 2010, American Eagle Outfitters Inc., a leading lifestyle apparel brand, opened its first flagship store outside of North America and its first stores in the Middle East in Dubai through Alshaya. A further store in Kuwait opened in the same month. In March 2011, Dorothy Perkins, a popular British fashion brand, opened its first store in Poland, operated by Alshaya.

Throughout the last few years, many more brands have been launched by Alshaya in many destinations around the Arab world and beyond. Alshaya told the *Financial Times*: "Whenever there is something that makes sense and we understand how we can turn it around or encourage it to take on more aggressive expansion…we will look into it."

More Value to its Customers

From one point of view, Alshaya's huge success can be credited to the choice of brands it delivers to the market. Another point of view would argue that the locations where it positions its brands are very strategic and, with the brand names, are guaranteed to build a success story.

Nevertheless one cannot credit the success story to one factor. The work done in building the strategy and the marketing execution has to be recognized.

One of the campaigns for due recognition was run in 2007: MasterCard and Alshaya joined marketing efforts and launched the MasterCard and Alshaya 10% Discount Promotion in Kuwait. They offered MasterCard cardholders the chance to benefit from a 10 percent discount when making purchases with their MasterCard debit or credit cards at any of Alshaya Group's retail and restaurant outlets throughout Kuwait.

Ihab Zaghloul, vice president, acceptance and business development, Middle East and Levant, MasterCard Worldwide,

said: "MasterCard is very pleased to launch the MasterCard & Alshaya 10% Discount Promotion in Kuwait, cooperating closely with the Alshaya Group representing many international retail & restaurant brands and with participating customer banks." Along the same lines, Camille Hajji, corporate marketing manager, Alshaya retail division, said, "The Alshaya Group is thrilled with the MasterCard & Alshaya 10% Discount Promotion, one of the most exciting campaigns ever run in Kuwait."

Through continuous efforts to understand the market needs and follow world trends, Alshaya continues to be the house of brands for the region.

Questions for Discussion

1. Choose one of Alshaya brands. What are the core, actual and augmented product benefits of the brand?

2. What are the sources of equity for any given Alshaya brand?

3. Select one of Alshaya category of brands, how would you better integrate and position the category and its brands?

Sources: "Our Brands," Alshaya company website, www.alshaya.com/Brands.jsp; Andrew England, "Alshaya Group Spreads Web of Familiar Brands Through Eastern Europe," June 12, 2008, www.ft.com; "Office Depot, M.H. Alshaya sign franchise agreement," *AME Info*, January 11, 2009, www.ameinfo.com/180713.html; "MasterCard Joins with the Alshaya Group to Offer MasterCard Cardholders in Kuwait a 10% Discount," press release, February 28, 2007.

This case was provided by Mohamed Radwan, adjunct faculty member at the American University in Cairo and managing director for Platinum Partners.

Chapter 9

Part 1   Defining Marketing and the Marketing Process (Chapters 1, 2)
Part 2   Understanding the Marketplace and Consumers (Chapters 3, 4, 5, 6)
Part 3   Designing a Customer-Driven Strategy and Mix (Chapters 7, 8, 9, 10, 11, 12, 13, 14)
Part 4   Extending Marketing (Chapters 15, 16, 17)

New-Product Development and Product Life-Cycle Strategies

Chapter PREVIEW

In the previous chapter, you learned how marketers manage and develop products and brands. In this chapter, we'll look into two additional product topics: developing new products and managing products through their life cycles. New products are the lifeblood of an organization. However, new-product development is risky, and many new products fail. So, the first part of this chapter lays out a process for finding and growing successful new products. Once introduced, marketers want their products to enjoy long and happy lives. In the second part of the chapter, you'll see that every product passes through several life-cycle stages and that each stage poses new challenges requiring different marketing strategies and tactics. Finally, we'll wrap up our product discussion by looking at two additional considerations: social responsibility in product decisions, and international product and services marketing.

To begin, consider Apple. More than two decades ago, as an early new-product innovator, Apple got off to a fast and impressive start. But only a decade later, as its creative initiatives slowed down, Apple found itself on the brink of extinction. That set the stage for one of the most remarkable turnarounds in corporate history. Read on to see how Apple's cofounder, Steve Jobs, used lots of innovation and creative new products to first start the company and then revive it again 20 years later.

From the very start, the tale of Apple is a tale of incredible creativity and customer-driven innovation. Under the leadership of its cofounder and creative genius, Steve Jobs, Apple's very first personal computers, introduced in the late 1970s, stood apart because of their user-friendly look and feel. The company's Macintosh computer, launched in 1984, and its LaserWriter printers blazed new trails in desktop computing and publishing, making Apple an early industry leader in both innovation and market share.

But then things took an ugly turn for Apple. In 1985, after tumultuous struggles with the new president he'd hired only a year earlier, Steve Jobs left Apple. With Jobs gone, Apple's creative initiatives slowed down. By the late 1980s, the company's fortunes declined as a new wave of PC machines, sporting Intel chips and Microsoft software, swept the market. By the mid- to late-1990s, Apple's sales had dropped to US$5 billion, 50 percent off previous highs. And its once-commanding share of the personal computer market had dropped to a tiny 2 percent. Even the most passionate Apple fans—the 'MacHeads'—wavered, and the company's days seemed numbered.

Yet Apple has engineered a remarkable turnaround. In the second quarter of 2011, sales soared to a record US$24 billion, almost triple the sales of the same quarter three years earlier. Profits rose 13-fold in that same three-year period. "To say Apple Computer is hot just doesn't do the company justice," said one analyst. "Apple is smoking, searing, blisteringly hot, not to mention hip, with a side order of funky.... Gadget geeks around the world have crowned Apple the keeper of all things cool."[1]

What caused this breathtaking turnaround? Apple rediscovered the magic that had made the company so successful in the first place: customer-driven creativity and new-product innovation. The remarkable makeover began with the return of Steve Jobs in 1997. Since leaving Apple, Jobs had started a new computer company, NeXT. He'd then bought out Pixar Animation Studios, turning it into an entertainment-industry powerhouse. Jobs returned to Apple determined to breathe new creative life and customer focus into the company he'd cofounded 20 years earlier.

Jobs' first task was to revitalize Apple's computer business. For starters, in 1998 Apple launched the iMac personal computer, which featured a sleek, egg-shaped monitor and hard drive, all in one unit, in a futuristic translucent turquoise casing. With its one-button Internet access, this machine was designed specifically for surfing the Internet (hence the 'i' in 'iMac'). The dramatic iMac was hailed for its design and attracted a large number of buyers. Within a year, it had sold more than a million units.

Jobs next unleashed Mac OS X, a groundbreaking new Apple operating system that

> "Apple is smoking, searing, blisteringly hot, not to mention hip, with a side order of funky—it's the keeper of all things cool."

served as the launch pad for a new generation of Apple computers and software products. Consider iLife, a bundle of lifestyle applications that comes with every new Mac. It includes applications such as iMovie (for video editing), iDVD (for recording movies, digital-photo slide shows, and music onto TV-playable DVDs), iPhoto (for managing and touching up digital pictures), GarageBand (for making and mixing your own music), iWeb (for creating websites and blogs and getting them online), and iWork (for making presentations and newsletters).

The iMac and Mac OS X put Apple back on the map in personal computing. But Jobs knew that Apple, still a nicher claiming just a 6 percent share of the U.S. market, for example, would never catch up in computers with dominant competitors such as Dell and HP. Real growth and stardom would require even more creative thinking. And it just doesn't get much more creative than the iPod and iTunes—innovations that would completely change the way people acquire and listen to music.

A music fan himself, Jobs noticed that kids by the millions were using computers and CD writers to download digital songs from then-illegal online services such as Napster, and then burning their own music CDs. He moved quickly to make CD burners standard equipment on all Macs. Then, to help users download music and manage their music databases, Apple's programmers created state-of-the-art jukebox software called iTunes.

Even before iTunes hit the streets, according to Apple watcher Brent Schendler, Jobs "recognized that although storing and playing music on your computer was pretty cool, wouldn't it be even cooler if there was a portable, Walkman-type player that could hold all your digital music so that you could listen to it anywhere?" Less than nine months later, Apple introduced the sleek and sexy iPod. In another 18 months, the Apple iTunes Music Store opened on the web, enabling consumers to legally download CDs and individual songs.[2]

The results, of course, have been astonishing. The iPod now ranks as one of the greatest consumer electronics hits of all time. By March 2008, Apple had sold more than 119 million iPods, and more than four billion songs had been downloaded from the iTunes Store. "We had hoped to sell a million songs in the first six months, but we did that in the first six days," notes an Apple spokesman.[3] The iPod captures more than 70 percent of the music-player market; and Apple's iTunes Store is currently the number-two music store—online or offline—in the world (Wal-Mart is number one). iTunes is aware of people's music tastes in the Arab world and includes a section for Middle Eastern music. Within this section there are different types of music associated with countries in the region, such as Egypt, Lebanon, Saudi Arabia, and the UAE. iTunes is one of the most significant music stores in the region.

Apple's success is attracting a group of large, resourceful competitors. To stay ahead, the company must keep its eye on the consumer and continue to innovate. So, Apple isn't standing still. Following the debut of its incredibly popular iPhone, Apple has introduced movie rentals via iTunes, which can be watched on an iPod, iPhone, PC, iPad, or via Apple TV; MacBook Air, the world's thinnest notebook computer; and Time Capsule, an appliance that

Apple's cofounder, Steve Jobs, used lots of innovation and creative new products to first start the company and then to revive it 20 years later.

automatically and wirelessly backs up everything on your Mac. Apple has also opened more than 200 chic and gleaming Apple Stores, making it the world's fastest-growing retail chain. And observers see a host of new products just on or just over the horizon, such as iHome (a magical device that powers all your digital home entertainment devices) and an iPod on wheels (a digital hub that integrates your iPod with your car's entertainment system). In the Arab world, the iPad enjoys great success. According to a worldwide survey, the majority of consumers interested in the iPad are from Arab countries. Moreover, Alshop, a popular online shopping portal, described the response to the launch of the iPad in Dubai as "crazy demand."[4]

For the fifth straight year, Apple was named the world's most innovative company in Boston Consulting Group's 'Most Innovative Company' survey of 2,500 senior executives worldwide. Apple received an amazing 25 percent of the votes, twice the number of runner-up 3M and three times that of third-place Microsoft. The innovative company also topped the most recent *Fortune* magazine list of America's most admired companies.

Thus, almost overnight, it seems, Steve Jobs has transformed Apple from a failing niche computer maker to a major force in consumer electronics, digital music, and video, and who knows what else in the future. And he's done it through innovation—by helping those around him to "Think Different" (Apple's motto) in their quest to bring value to customers. *Fortune* sums it up this way: "Apple has demonstrated how to create real, breathtaking growth by dreaming up products so new and ingenious that they have upended one industry after another. Jobs' utter dedication to discovery and excellence has created a culture that has made Apple a symbol of innovation. There, innovation is a way of life."[5]

Through dazzling creativity and customer-driven new-product innovation, Apple has engineered a remarkable turnaround in recent years. At Apple, innovation is a way of life.

In August 2011, the surprise resignation of Steve Jobs as Apple's CEO was announced. But despite the departure of its iconic founder, Apple is in a strong position to continue building on its success.

Objective Outline

As the Apple story suggests, companies that excel at developing and managing new products reap big rewards. Every product seems to go through a life cycle—it is born, goes through several phases, and eventually dies as newer products come along that create greater value for customers. This product life cycle presents two major challenges: First, because all products eventually decline, a firm must be good at developing new products to replace aging ones (the challenge of new-product development). Secondly, the firm must be good at adapting its marketing strategies in the face of changing tastes, technologies, and competition as products pass through life-cycle stages (the challenge of product life-cycle strategies). We first look at the problem of finding and developing new products and then at the problem of managing them successfully over their life cycles.

New-Product Development Strategy (pp 240–241)

Author Comment | New products are the life-blood of a company. As old products mature and fade away, companies must develop new ones to take their place. For example, only 10 years after it unveiled its first iPod, half of Apple's revenues came from other new products such as iPhones and iPads. By the end of 2010, iPad sales represented 75 percent of all sales of tablet PCs worldwide.

New-product development
The development of original products, product improvements, product modifications, and new brands through the firm's own product-development efforts.

A firm can obtain new products in two ways. One is through acquisition—by buying a whole company, a patent, or a license to produce someone else's product. The other is through the firm's own **new-product development** efforts. By new products we mean original products, product improvements, product modifications, and new brands that the firm develops through its own research-and-development efforts. In this chapter, we concentrate on new-product development.

New products are important—both to customers and to the marketers who serve them. For companies, new products are a key source of growth. For customers, they bring new solutions and variety to their lives. Yet innovation can be very expensive and very risky. New products face low success rates. According to one estimate, 90 percent of all new products fail. Each year, companies lose an estimated US$20 billion to US$30 billion on failed food products alone.[6]

Why do so many new products fail? There are several reasons. Although an idea may be good, the company may overestimate market size. The actual product may be poorly designed. Or it might be incorrectly positioned, launched at the wrong time, priced too high, or poorly advertised. A high-level executive might push a favorite idea despite poor marketing research findings. Sometimes the costs of product development are higher than expected, and sometimes competitors fight back harder than expected.

Keda Tea: A story of a successful marketing communication plan that was out of sync with its operations cycle. This type of problem can be deeply harmful, especially in the introductory phase of a product.

Mansour Group introduced Keda Tea in the Egyptian market. Keda Tea is a high-quality blend Kenyan tea that satisfies the tastes of Egyptian tea-drinkers. The tea is clarified and filtered locally at Seclam factory, where it is also packaged using the most advanced packing technology.[7]

Keda Tea launched with a successful advertising campaign in order to raise awareness of the product, but consumers couldn't find it on the shelves. There was a production problem, which affected Keda Tea's performance in the market.

Arma Food Industries, established in Cairo in 1992, is one of the leading edible oil and ghee manufacturers in Egypt. Arma aims to provide high-quality products for the Egyptian and export markets. It has many successful brands in Egypt including Crystal cooking oil, the leading brand in the Egyptian market. In 2006, Arma decided to introduce Oxi, a mid-tier automatic detergent—and a totally new market for the company. The detergents market in Egypt is very competitive. Procter & Gamble and Henkel have been leading the market for many years and both companies have strong and credible brand names. While Arma's management understood the edible oil and ghee markets well, it was not fully aware of the detergent market. Then, Arma faced a crisis concerning pricing and production. First, it set a relatively high price for Oxi given the competitive market. Secondly, the formula itself was not correct and it caused damage to consumers' washing machines. As a result, Arma stopped production and recalled the product from the market. Arma decided to deal with the crisis and re-entered the market again in 2008. However, the problems that had occurred in the introductory phase had damaged the image and credibility of the brand.

Companies should always be cautious, especially in the introductory period because consumers' perceptions, at this stage, are highly vulnerable.[8]

Author Comment | Companies can't just hope that they'll stumble across good new products. Instead, they must develop a systematic new-product development process.

The New-Product Development Process (pp 241–250)

Companies face a problem—they must develop new products, but the odds weigh heavily against success. In all, to create successful new products, a company must understand its consumers, markets, and competitors and develop products that deliver superior value to customers. It must carry out strong new-product planning and set up a systematic, customer-driven new-product development process for finding and growing new products. **Figure 9.1** shows the eight major steps in this process.

New-product development starts with good new-product ideas—*lots* of them. For example, a recent IBM online "Innovation Jam" generated 46,000 ideas, of which IBM planned to develop only 10.

Whereas the first step of this process generates a large number of new-product ideas, the remaining steps reduce that number and develop the best ideas into profitable products.

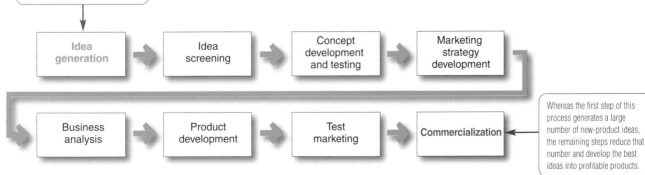

FIGURE | 9.1 Major Stages in New-Product Development

Idea Generation

Idea generation

The systematic search for new-product ideas.

New-product development starts with **idea generation**—the systematic search for new-product ideas. A company typically generates hundreds of ideas, even thousands, in order to find a few good ones. For example, IBM recently held an "Innovation Jam"—a kind of online suggestion box—in which it invited IBM and customer employees worldwide to submit ideas for new products and services. The massive brainstorming session generated some 46,000 ideas from 150,000 people in more than 160 countries over 3 days. Since the jam fest, however, IBM has cut down this surge of ideas to only 10 products, businesses, and services that it plans to develop.[9]

Major sources of new-product ideas include internal sources and external sources such as customers, competitors, distributors and suppliers, and others.

Internal Idea Sources

Using internal sources, the company can find new ideas through formal research and development. However, in one recent survey, 750 global CEOs reported that only 14 percent of their innovation ideas came from traditional R&D. Instead, 41 percent said employees and 36 percent said customers.[10]

Internal new-product idea sources: Samsung built a special Value Innovation Program Center in which company researchers, engineers, and designers comingle to come up with creative new-product ideas.

Thus, companies can pick the brains of employees—from executives to scientists, engineers, and manufacturing staff to salespeople. Using today's new Web 2.0 technology, many companies are making it everybody's business to come up with great ideas. For example, Cisco has set up an internal wiki called Idea Zone or I-Zone, through which any Cisco employee can propose an idea for a new product or comment on or modify someone else's proposed idea. Since its inception, I-Zone has generated more than 400 business ideas, and another 10,000 people have added to those ideas. Cisco selects ideas that draw the most activity for further development. So far 12 I-Zone ideas have reached the project stage and four new Cisco business units have been formed.[11]

Some companies have developed successful 'intrapreneurial' programs that encourage employees to think up and develop new-product ideas. For example, Samsung built a special Value Innovation Program (VIP) Center in Suwon, South Korea, to encourage and support internal new-product innovation.

External Idea Sources

Companies can also obtain good new-product ideas from any of a number of external sources. For example, distributors and suppliers can contribute ideas. Distributors are close to the market and can pass on information to the company about consumer problems and new-product possibilities. Suppliers can tell the company about new concepts, techniques, and materials that can be used to develop new products. Competitors are another important source. Companies watch competitors' ads to get clues about their new products. They buy competing new products, take them apart to see how they work, analyze their sales, and decide whether they should bring out a new product of their own. Other idea sources include trade magazines, shows, and seminars; government agencies; advertising agencies; marketing research firms; university and commercial laboratories; and inventors. Some companies seek the help of outside new-product consultancies and design firms. Many companies are also turning to online collaborative communities to help solve new-product problems.

Says P&G's CEO, "Someone outside your organization today knows how to answer your specific question, solve your specific problem, or take advantage of your current opportunity

Product ideas from customers: Advice from 250 train-set enthusiasts resulted in the LEGO Santa Fe Super Chief train-set, a blockbuster new product that sold out in less than two weeks.

better than you do. You need to find them and find a way to work collaboratively and productively with them." It is estimated that 35 percent of P&G's new products today have elements that originated outside the company, up from 15 percent in 2000.[12]

Perhaps the most important source of new-product ideas is customers themselves. The company can analyze customer questions and complaints to find new products that better solve consumer problems. Company engineers or salespeople can meet with and work alongside customers to get suggestions and ideas. The toymaker LEGO did just that when it invited 250 LEGO train-set enthusiasts to visit one of its offices to assess new designs. The group gave LEGO lots of new ideas, and the company put them to good use. The result was the Santa Fe Super Chief train-set. Thanks to word-of-mouth endorsements from the 250 enthusiasts, LEGO sold the first 10,000 units in less than two weeks with no additional marketing.[13]

Other companies actively solicit ideas from customers and turn customers into joint creators. For example, Dell set up an interactive website forum called IdeaStorm that asks consumers for insights on how to improve its product offering. Users post suggestions, the community votes, and the most popular ideas rise to the top. Only two months after launching, the site had received some 3,850 ideas and 236,000 votes. Michael Dell sees such customer-driven innovation as a key to reenergizing Dell. "We are at our best when we are hearing directly from customers," says Dell. "We listen, learn, and then improve and innovate based on what our customers want."[14]

Finally, customers often create new products and uses on their own, and companies can benefit by putting them on the market. For example, for years customers were spreading the word that Avon Skin-So-Soft bath oil and moisturizer was also a terrific bug repellent. Whereas some consumers were content simply to bathe in water scented with the fragrant oil, others carried it in their backpacks to mosquito-infested campsites or kept a bottle on the decks of their beach houses. Avon turned the idea into a complete line of Skin-So-Soft Bug Guard products, including Bug Guard Mosquito Repellant Moisturizing Towelettes and Bug Guard Plus, a combination moisturizer, insect repellent, and sunscreen.[15]

Although customer input on new products yields many benefits, companies must be careful not to rely too heavily on what customers say. For some products, especially highly technical ones, customers may not know what they need. "You can't ask people what they want if it's around the next corner," says former Apple CEO Steve Jobs. And even when they think they know what they want, adds an innovation management consultant, "Merely giving people what they want isn't always enough. People want to be surprised; they want something that's better than they imagined, something that stretches them in what they like."[16]

Idea Screening

Idea screening

Screening new-product ideas in order to spot good ideas and drop poor ones as soon as possible.

The purpose of idea generation is to create a large number of ideas. The purpose of the succeeding stages is to reduce that number. The first idea-reducing stage is **idea screening**, which helps spot good ideas and drop poor ones as soon as possible. Product-development costs rise greatly in later stages, so the company wants to go ahead only with the product ideas that will turn into profitable products.

Many companies require their executives to write up new-product ideas in a standard format that can be reviewed by a new-product committee. The write-up describes the product or service, the proposed customer value proposition, the target market, and the competition. It makes some rough estimates of market size, product price, development time and costs, manufacturing costs, and rate of return. The committee then evaluates the idea against a set of general criteria.

One marketing expert proposes an R-W-W ("real, win, worth it") new-product screening framework that asks three questions. First, Is it real? Is there a real need and desire for the product and will customers buy it? Is there a clear product concept and will the product satisfy the market? Secondly, Can we win? Does the product offer a sustainable competitive advantage? Does the company have the resources to make the product a success? Finally, Is it worth doing? Does the product set the company's overall growth strategy? Does it offer sufficient profit potential? The company should be able to answer yes to all three R-W-W questions before developing the new-product idea further.[17]

Concept Development and Testing

Product concept

A detailed version of the new-product idea stated in meaningful consumer terms.

An attractive idea must be developed into a **product concept**. It is important to distinguish between a product idea, a product concept, and a product image. A product idea is an idea for a possible product that the company can see itself offering to the market. A product concept is a detailed version of the idea stated in meaningful consumer terms. A product image is the way consumers perceive an actual or potential product.

Concept Development

Suppose that a car manufacturer has developed a practical battery-powered all-electric car. Its initial prototype is a sleek, sporty convertible that sells for about US$100,000.[18] However, it plans to introduce more-affordable, mass-market models that will compete with today's hybrid-powered cars. This 100 percent electric car will accelerate from 0 to 60 in 4 seconds, travel more than 400 kilometers on a single charge, recharge from a normal 120-volt electrical outlet, and cost about one penny a mile to power.

Looking ahead, the marketer's task is to develop this new product into alternative product concepts, find out how attractive each concept is to customers, and choose the best one. It might create the following product concepts for the electric car:

Concept development: The initial Tesla electric car will go from 0 to 60mph in 4 seconds, travel more than 400 kilometers on a single charge, and cost about a penny a mile to power.

- Concept 1 An affordable midsize car designed as a second family car to be used around town for running errands and visiting friends.
- Concept 2 A midpriced sporty compact appealing to young singles and couples.
- Concept 3 A 'green' car appealing to environmentally conscious people who want practical, low-polluting transportation.
- Concept 4 A high-end midsize utility vehicle appealing to those who love the space SUVs provide but do not like the poor gas mileage.

Concept Testing

Concept testing

Testing new-product concepts with a group of target consumers to find out if the concepts have strong consumer appeal.

Concept testing calls for testing new-product concepts with groups of target consumers. The concepts may be presented to consumers symbolically or physically. Here, in words, is concept 3:

An efficient, fun-to-drive, battery-powered compact car that seats four. This 100 percent electric wonder provides practical and reliable transportation with no pollution. It goes more than 250 miles on a single charge and costs pennies per mile to operate.

It's a sensible, responsible alternative to today's pollution-producing gas-guzzlers. It's priced, fully equipped, at US$25,000.

Many firms routinely test new-product concepts with consumers before attempting to turn them into actual new products. For some concept tests, a word or picture description might be sufficient. However, a more concrete and physical presentation of the concept will increase the reliability of the concept test. After being exposed to the concept, consumers then may be asked to react to it by answering questions such as those in ● **Table 9.1**.

● **TABLE | 9.1** Questions for Battery-Powered Electric Car Concept Test

1. Do you understand the concept of a battery-powered electric car?
2. Do you believe the claims about the car's performance?
3. What are the major benefits of the battery-powered electric car compared with a conventional car?
4. What are its advantages compared with a gas-electric hybrid car?
5. What improvements in the car's features would you suggest?
6. For what uses would you prefer a battery-powered electric car to a conventional car?
7. What would be a reasonable price to charge for the car?
8. Who would be involved in your decision to buy such a car? Who would drive it?
9. Would you buy such a car (definitely, probably, probably not, definitely not)?

The answers to such questions will help the company decide which concept has the strongest appeal. For example, the last question asks about the consumer's intention to buy. Suppose 2 percent of consumers say they "definitely" would buy, and another 5 percent say "probably." The company could project these figures to the full population in this target group to estimate sales volume. Even then, the estimate is uncertain because people do not always carry out their stated intentions.

Marketing Strategy Development

Suppose the car maker finds that concept 3 for the fuel-cell-powered electric car tests best. The next step is **marketing strategy development**, designing an initial marketing strategy for introducing this car to the market.

Marketing strategy development
Designing an initial marketing strategy for a new product based on the product concept.

The marketing strategy statement consists of three parts. The first part describes the target market; the planned value proposition; and the sales, market share, and profit goals for the first few years. Thus:

> The target market is younger, well-educated, moderate- to high-income individuals, couples, or small families seeking practical, environmentally responsible transportation. The car will be positioned as more fun to drive and less polluting than today's internal combustion engine or hybrid cars. The company will aim to sell 100,000 cars in the first year, at a loss of not more than US$15 million. In the second year, the company will aim for sales of 120,000 cars and a profit of US$25 million.

The second part of the marketing strategy statement outlines the product's planned price, distribution, and marketing budget for the first year:

> The battery-powered electric car will be offered in three colors—red, green, and blue—and will have a full set of accessories as standard features. It will sell at a retail price of US$25,000—with 15 percent off the list price to dealers. Dealers who sell more than 10 cars per month will get an additional discount of 5 percent on each car sold that month. A marketing budget of US$50 million will be split 50–50 between a national media campaign and local event marketing. Advertising and website will emphasize the car's fun spirit and low emissions. During the first year, US$100,000 will be spent on marketing research to find out who is buying the car and their satisfaction levels.

The third part of the marketing strategy statement describes the planned long-run sales, profit goals, and marketing-mix strategy:

> We intend to capture a 3 percent long-run share of the total auto market and realize an after-tax return on investment of 15 percent. To achieve this, product quality will start high and be improved over time. Price will be raised in the second and third years if competition permits. The total marketing budget will be raised each year by about 10 percent. Marketing research will be reduced to US$60,000 per year after the first year.

Business Analysis

Business analysis

A review of the sales, costs, and profit projections for a new product to find out whether these factors satisfy the company's objectives.

Once management has decided on its product concept and marketing strategy, it can evaluate the business attractiveness of the proposal. **Business analysis**. involves a review of the sales, costs, and profit projections for a new product to find out whether they satisfy the company's objectives. If they do, the product can move to the product-development stage.

To estimate sales, the company might look at the sales history of similar products and conduct market surveys. It can then estimate minimum and maximum sales to assess the range of risk. After preparing the sales forecast, management can estimate the expected costs and profits for the product, including marketing, R&D, operations, accounting, and finance costs. The company then uses the sales and costs figures to analyze the new product's financial attractiveness.

Product Development

Product development

Developing the product concept into a physical product in order to ensure that the product idea can be turned into a workable market offering.

So far, for many new-product concepts, the product may have existed only as a word description, a drawing, or perhaps a crude mock-up. If the product concept passes the business test, it moves into **product development.** Here, R&D or engineering develops the product concept into a physical product. The product-development step, however, now calls for a large jump in investment. It will show whether the product idea can be turned into a workable product.

The R&D department will develop and test one or more physical versions of the product concept. R&D hopes to design a prototype that will satisfy and excite consumers and that can be produced quickly and at budgeted costs. Developing a successful prototype can take days, weeks, months, or even years depending on the product and prototype methods.

Often, products undergo rigorous tests to make sure that they perform safely and effectively, or that consumers will find value in them. Companies can do their own product testing or outsource testing to other firms that specialize in testing.

Marrakech Light and Cool brands entered the Moroccan fruit drinks and vegetable drinks market in 2009. Their introduction to the market was the manufacturer's answer to a call for 'lite' and low-calorie versions of drinks for people concerned about their health. Product testing proved there was a market for the drinks. The drinks' eventual launch into the soft drinks market fuelled growth and stimulated demand.

How best to package our drink Fanta World Pina Colada, wondered Coca-Cola. Would customers buy it if it were sold in a bottle shaped like a football? Extensive product testing showed that they would. As a result, Coca-Cola launched the Fanta drink in its innovative packaging to the Moroccan market in 2010, to coincide with the FIFA World Cup.[19]

At Gillette, almost everyone gets involved in new-product testing. Every working day at Gillette, 200 volunteers from various departments come to work unshaven, troop to the

Product testing: Gillette uses employee-volunteers to test new shaving products—"We bleed so you'll get a good shave at home," says a Gillette employee.

second floor of the company's gritty South Boston plant, and enter small booths with a sink and mirror. There they take instructions from technicians on the other side of a small window as to which razor, shaving cream, or aftershave to use. The volunteers evaluate razors for sharpness of blade, smoothness of glide, and ease of handling. "We bleed so you'll get a good shave at home," says one Gillette employee.

A new product must have the required functional features and also convey the intended psychological characteristics. The battery-powered electric car, for example, should strike consumers as being well built, comfortable, and safe. Management must learn what makes consumers decide that a car is well built. To some consumers, this means that the car has 'solid-sounding' doors. To others, it means that the car is able to withstand heavy impact in crash tests. Consumer tests are conducted in which consumers test-drive the car and rate its attributes.

Test Marketing

Test marketing

The stage of new-product development in which the product and marketing program are tested in realistic market settings.

If the product passes concept and product tests, the next step is **test marketing**, the stage at which the product and marketing program are introduced into realistic market settings. Test marketing gives the marketer experience with marketing the product before going to the great expense of full introduction. It lets the company test the product and its entire marketing program—targeting and positioning strategy, advertising, distribution, pricing, branding and packaging, and budget levels.

The amount of test marketing needed varies with each new product. Test-marketing costs can be high, and it takes time that may allow competitors to gain advantages. When the costs of developing and introducing the product are low, or when management is already confident about the new product, the company may do little or no test marketing. In fact, test marketing by consumer-goods firms has been declining in recent years. Companies often do not test-market simple line extensions or copies of successful competitor products.

However, when introducing a new product requires a big investment, when the risks are high, or when management is not sure of the product or marketing program, a company may do a lot of test marketing. For instance, KFC has recently launched a major new product— Kentucky Grilled Chicken. Although the fast-food chain built its legacy on serving crispy, seasoned fried chicken, it hopes that the new product will lure back health-conscious consumers who dropped fried chicken from their diets. "This is transformational for our brand," says KFC's chief food innovation officer. Given the importance of the decision, KFC will have conducted more than three years of product and market testing before rolling Kentucky Grilled Chicken out widely. "You might say, 'what took you so long,'" says the chain's president. "I've asked that question a couple of times myself. The answer is we had to get it right."[20]

Although test-marketing costs can be high, they are often small when compared with the costs of making a major mistake. Still, test marketing doesn't guaranty success. For example, Procter & Gamble tested its Fit Wash produce rinse heavily for five years. Although market tests suggested the product would be successful, P&G pulled the plug on it shortly after its introduction.[21]

When using test marketing, consumer-products companies usually choose one of three approaches— standard test markets, controlled test markets, or simulated test markets.

Test marketing: KFC test marketed its new Kentucky Grilled Chicken product for three years before rolling it out widely. Says the chain's president, "We had to get it right."

Standard Test Markets

Using standard test markets, the company finds a small number of representative test cities, conducts a full marketing campaign in these cities, and uses store audits, consumer and distributor surveys, and other measures to gage product performance. The results are used to forecast national sales and profits, discover potential product problems, and fine-tune the marketing program. KFC used standard test markets for its new Kentucky Grilled Chicken in a number of cities. At these sites, KFC tested both the new product and its full marketing program, including new store signage and a series of ads.

Standard test markets have some drawbacks. They can be very costly and they may take a long time. Moreover, competitors can monitor test market results or interfere with them by cutting their prices in test cities, increasing their promotion, or even buying up the product being tested. Finally, test markets give competitors a look at the company's new product well before it is introduced nationally. Thus, competitors may have time to develop defensive strategies, and may even beat the company's product to the market.

Despite these disadvantages, standard test markets are still the most widely used approach for major in-market testing. However, many companies today are shifting toward quicker and cheaper controlled and simulated test-marketing methods.

Controlled Test Markets

Several research firms keep controlled panels of stores that have agreed to carry new products for a fee. Controlled test-marketing systems such as ACNielsen's Scantrack and Information Resources, Inc.'s BehaviorScan track individual consumer behavior for new products from the television set to the checkout counter.

Controlled test markets, such as BehaviorScan, usually cost less than standard test markets. Also, because retail distribution is 'forced' in the first week of the test, controlled test markets can be completed much more quickly than standard test markets. As in standard test markets, controlled test markets allow competitors to get a look at the company's new product. And some companies are concerned that the limited number of controlled test markets used by the research services may not be representative of their products' markets or target consumers. However, the research firms are experienced in projecting test market results to broader markets and can usually account for biases in the test markets used.

Simulated Test Markets

Companies can also test new products in a simulated shopping environment. The company or research firm shows ads and promotions for a variety of products, including the new product being tested, to a sample of consumers. It gives consumers a small amount of money and invites them to a real or laboratory store where they may keep the money or use it to buy items. The researchers note how many consumers buy the new product and competing brands.

This simulation provides a measure of trial and the commercial's effectiveness against competing commercials. The researchers then ask consumers the reasons for their purchase or nonpurchase. Some weeks later, they interview the consumers by phone to determine product attitudes, usage, satisfaction, and repurchase intentions. Using sophisticated computer models, the researchers then project national sales from results of the simulated test market. Recently, some marketers have begun to use interesting new high-tech approaches, such as virtual reality and the Internet, to simulated test market research.

Simulated test markets overcome some of the disadvantages of standard and controlled test markets. They usually cost much less, can be run in eight weeks, and keep the new product out of competitors' view. Yet, because of their small samples and simulated shopping environments, many marketers do not think that simulated test markets are as accurate or reliable as larger, real-world tests. Still, simulated test markets are used widely, often as 'pretest' markets. Because they are fast and inexpensive, they can be run to quickly assess a new product or its marketing program.

Many marketers are now using new simulated marketing technologies to reduce the costs of test marketing and to speed up the process. For example, snack maker Frito-Lay

New test-marketing technologies: Frito-Lay worked with research firm Decision Insight to create an online virtual convenience store in which to test new snack products and marketing ideas.

worked with research firm Decision Insight to create an online virtual convenience store in which to test new products and marketing ideas.[22]

Commercialization

Commercialization
Introducing a new product into the market.

Test marketing gives management the information needed to make a final decision about whether to launch the new product. If the company goes ahead with **commercialization**—introducing the new product into the market—it will face high costs. The company may need to build or rent a manufacturing facility. And, in the case of a major new consumer packaged good, it may spend hundreds of millions of dollars for advertising, sales promotion, and other marketing efforts in the first year. For example, when Unilever introduced its Sunsilk hair care line, it spent US$200 million in one country alone, including US$30 million for nontraditional media such as MySpace ads and profiles, mall displays that used audio to catch passersby, 3-D ads in tavern bathrooms, and cinema ads.[23]

The company launching a new product must first decide on introduction timing. If the car maker's new battery-powered electric car will eat into the sales of the company's other cars, its introduction may be delayed. If the car can be improved further, or if the economy is down, the company may wait until the following year to launch it. However, if competitors are ready to introduce their own battery-powered models, the company may push to introduce its car sooner.

Next, the company must decide where to launch the new product—in a single location, a region, the national market, or the international market. Few companies have the confidence, capital, and capacity to launch new products into full national or international distribution right away. Instead, they develop a planned market rollout over time. For example, Danone introduced Activia first in Spain in 1986, and when it showed success and fast market growth there, it was launched in 49 countries around the world. Activia increased its activities across countries using the '360 degrees campaign,' which means that it is utilizing all the communications tools in order to reach more consumers.

马上找到，无处不"Wow"! "Wow"，保护无处不在!

WindowsVista.com/China

Commercialization: Microsoft launched its new Windows Vista operating system in a swift global rollout. Its immense "Wow!" advertising blitz hit more than 30 markets worldwide simultaneously, creating some 6.6 billion global impressions in just its first two months.

Some companies, however, may quickly introduce new models into the full national market. Companies with international distribution systems may introduce new products through swift global rollouts. Microsoft did this with its Windows Vista operating system, using an immense advertising blitz to launch Vista simultaneously in more than 30 markets worldwide. The campaign targeted 6.6 billion global impressions in just its first two months.[24]

Author Comment │ Above all else, new-product development must focus on creating customer value. Apple's cofounder Steve Jobs is obsessed with the Apple user's experience. For every new product that Apple introduces, it's clear that someone actually asked, "how can we make life better for our customers?"

Managing New-Product Development (pp 250–253)

The new-product development process shown in **Figure 9.1** highlights the important activities needed to find, develop, and introduce new products. However, new-product development involves more than just going through a set of steps. Companies must take a holistic approach to managing this process. Successful new-product development requires a customer-centered, team-based, and systematic effort. In many cases, product development may consist of introducing an adapted version of an existing product for a different market (see **Real Marketing 9.1** for a great example).

Customer-Centered New-Product Development

Above all else, new-product development must be customer-centered. When looking for and developing new products, companies often rely too heavily on technical research in their R&D labs. But like everything else in marketing, successful new-product development begins with a thorough understanding of what consumers need and value. **Customer-centered new-product development** focuses on finding new ways to solve customer problems and create more customer-satisfying experiences.

One recent study found that the most successful new products are ones that are differentiated, solve major customer problems, and offer a compelling customer value proposition. Another study showed that companies that directly engage their customers in the new-product innovation process had twice the return on assets and triple the growth in operating income of firms that don't.[25]

Customer-centered new-product development

New-product development that focuses on finding new ways to solve customer problems and create more customer-satisfying experiences.

Juhayna Food Industries has been working for years on changing the dairy market in Egypt, by changing consumer awareness, and hence behavior. The low-income market segment was against the idea of packed and stored milk; a large percentage of consumers perceived that milk bought from farmers was fresher, healthier, and creamier. Most consumers' common practice was to buy their milk fresh, boil it, cool it down, and observe the cream layer on the surface to make sure that the milk was healthy and rich. The milk was poured out of a bucket and sold to consumers in plastic bags. Since the majority of consumers were living on a day-by-day source of income, this buying pattern gave them more flexibility in buying their actual daily consumption of milk, so they didn't have to store excess amounts. It also gave them a wider window in which they were able to buy milk more than once a day (usually twice a day), depending on the fresh milk delivery schedule of the farmers.

Juhayna Food Industries realized that, in order to penetrate this segment and at the same time guarantee a safer source of milk in the market, it should develop a product that could cope with dominant perceptions. Building on that conclusion, the company launched newly-branded milk, offered in pouches to target the medium- to low-income market segments. The pouches were printed irregularly and made loose, to look like the plastic bags to which the consumer was accustomed. The new milk was at first offered in the market in 200 ml and 500 ml pouches, with a relatively low price, to overcome price and perception barriers in medium- and low-income segments. The milk was branded Bekhiro, an Arabic word indicating richness and freshness at the same time. The milk branding and packaging succeeded in grabbing the attention of the desired segments, and gave an indirect impression that the product was freshly packed and offered to the market on a daily basis. Bekhiro milk sales continue to grow and currently contribute 50 percent of Juhayna's milk sales volume.[26]

Thus, customer-centered new-product development begins and ends with solving customer problems. As one expert asks: "What is innovation after all, if not products and services that offer fresh thinking in a way that meets the needs of customers?"[27] Says another expert, "Getting consumer insights at the beginning of the process, using those insights consistently and respectfully throughout the process, and communicating them in a compelling form when you go to market is critical to a product's success in the market these days."[28]

Team-Based New-Product Development

Good new-product development also requires a total-company, cross-functional effort. Some companies organize their new-product development process into the orderly sequence of steps shown in **Figure 9.1**, starting with idea generation and ending with commercialization. Under this *sequential product-development* approach, one company department works individually to complete its stage of the process before passing the new product along to the next department and stage. This orderly, step-by-step process can help bring control to complex and risky projects. But it also can be dangerously slow. In fast-changing, highly competitive markets, such slow-but-sure product development can result in product failures, lost sales and profits, and crumbling market positions.

In order to get their new products to market more quickly, many companies use a **team-based new-product development** approach. Under this approach, company departments work closely together in cross-functional teams, overlapping the steps in the product-development process to save time and increase effectiveness. Instead of passing the new product from department to department, the company assembles a team of people from various departments that stay with the new product from start to finish. Such teams usually include people from the marketing, finance, design, manufacturing, and legal departments, and even supplier and customer companies. In the sequential process, a bottleneck at one phase can seriously slow the entire project. In the team-based approach, if one area hits snags, it works to resolve them while the team moves on.

The team-based approach does have some limitations. For example, it sometimes creates more organizational tension and confusion than the more orderly sequential approach. However, in rapidly changing industries facing increasingly shorter product life cycles, the rewards of fast and flexible product development far exceed the risks. Companies that combine a customer-centered approach with team-based new-product development gain a big competitive edge by getting the right new products to market faster.

Systematic New-Product Development

Finally, the new-product development process should be holistic and systematic rather than compartmentalized and haphazard. Otherwise, few new ideas will surface, and many good ideas will sputter and die. To avoid these problems, a company can install an innovation management system to collect, review, evaluate, and manage new-product ideas.

The company can appoint a respected senior person to be the company's innovation manager. It can set up web-based idea management software and encourage all company stakeholders—employees, suppliers, distributors, dealers—to become involved in finding and developing new products. It can assign a cross-functional innovation management committee to evaluate proposed new-product ideas and help bring good ideas to market. It can create recognition programs to reward those who contribute the best ideas.

The innovation management system approach yields two favorable outcomes. First, it helps create an innovation-oriented company culture. It shows that top management supports, encourages, and rewards innovation. Secondly, it will yield a larger number

Team-based new-product development

An approach to developing new products in which various company departments work closely together, overlapping the steps in the product-development process to save time and increase effectiveness.

Real Marketing 9.1

Nasamat Al Riyadh: TMG's New Product in the Kingdom of Saudi Arabia

Nasamat Al-Riyadh is the outcome of the accumulated experience of Talaat Moustafa Group (TMG) and Al Oula real-estate companies. With over 37 years' experience in the real-estate development and housing industry, TMG Holding is the leading real-estate developer in Egypt, with a land bank of 50 million square meters and having developed over 8.5 million square meters. The group has adopted a vision of 'community development,' aimed at upper- and middle-class customers who want to live in self-sustained residential cities and community complexes. The company's most prominent developments are Al-Rehab City and Madinaty, with a total of 43.5 million square meters of land and around 800,000 target residents.

TMG also operates in the hotels and resorts market. For example, it has developed three luxury hotels: the Nile Plaza in Cairo, San Stefano in Alexandria, and the Four Seasons in Sharm El Sheikh, and it is developing other hotel and resort projects.

TMG identified the opportunity of developing new compounds in the Arab world, specifically in the Kingdom of Saudi Arabia (KSA). Accordingly, TMG, in partnership with Al Oula, has established a new entity called Thabat, which will own the Nasamat Al-Riyadh project in eastern KSA. Thabat specializes in developing residential and commercial communities throughout the KSA. It aims to consider the country's Islamic foundations, its customs and traditions, and merge those with the residents' requirements relating to comfort, technology, and investment opportunities.

Nasamat Al-Riyadh is planned to be a state-of-the art project in the region. The

Talaat Moustafa Group and Al Oula work on property development and construction projects in the Arab world.

project is intended for a more affluent market than Madinaty and Al-Rehab, which target middle- and upper-class customers in Egypt. Nasamat Al-Riyadh is planned to match the needs of the Saudi market, which is a wealthy society for the region, so the expectations of customers tend to surpass the needs of many other markets in the Arab world. This sophisticated project provides a golden opportunity for TMG to prove itself away from the Egyptian market and to make use of all its experience in similar projects in conjunction with another successful entity such as Al Oula.

TMG owns a construction company—Alexandria Construction Company—which is the leading construction company for almost all of TMG's projects, including Al-Rehab and Madinaty. At the time of writing, it had not yet been decided whether Thabat would contract Alexandria Construction Company for Nasamat Al-Riyadh or not, and to date TMG

is not pursuing this contract for many reasons. For example, Alexandria Construction Company's experience and success has mainly been in Egypt. Furthermore, TMG considers this project a testing step for regional expansion. Finally, TMG believes that contracting such a project to an experienced local construction company may simplify things; the contractor must be familiar with the KSA market needs.

Construction of Nasamat Al-Riyadh began in 2010 and completion is planned for 2016. The project will cover an area of three million square meters, with 4,145 residential buildings and villas. In addition to sports facilities, shopping malls, schools, mosques, and medical services, the amenities will include security and maintenance services, as well as public services such as a police station, a civil defense facility, social and cultural centers, and post offices.

Sources: "Nasamat Al Riyadh," TMG Holding website, 2009, http://new.talaatmoustafa.com/inside. aspx?id=85&menuid=22; "Launch of Sales on Nasamat Al Riyadh," TMG Holding Facebook profile, November 21, 2009, www.facebook.com; "About TMG," TMG Holding website, 2009, http://new.talaatmoustafa.com/ inside.aspx?id=2&menuid=0.

of new-product ideas, among which will be found some especially good ones. The good new ideas will be more systematically developed, producing more new-product successes. No longer will good ideas wither for the lack of a sounding board or a senior product advocate.

Thus, new-product success requires more than simply thinking up a few good ideas, turning them into products, and finding customers for them. It requires a holistic approach for finding new ways to create valued customer experiences, from generating and screening

Google is both spectacularly successful and wildly innovative. At Google, innovation is more than just a process. It's in the air, in the spirit of the place.

new-product ideas to creating and rolling out want-satisfying products to customers.

More than this, successful new-product development requires a whole-company commitment. At companies known for their successful new-product track-record—such as Google, Sony, Skype, Apple, IDEO, and Virgin Atlantic—the entire culture encourages, supports, and rewards innovation. Consider Google, which recently topped *Fast Company* magazine's list of the world's most innovative companies, and which regularly ranks among everyone else's top two or three innovators. Google is spectacularly successful. Despite formidable competition from giants such as Baidu and Yahoo!, Google's share in its core business—online search—has climbed to a decisive 56 percent. Google is also wildly innovative. But at Google, innovation is more than a process—it's part of the company's DNA.[29]

Google's famously chaotic innovation process has unleashed a flurry of diverse products, ranging from a blog search engine (Google Blog Search), an email service (Gmail), an online payment service (Google Checkout), and a news portal (Google News) to a universal platform for mobile-phone applications (Google Android) and projects for mapping and exploring the world (Google Maps and Google Earth). And in 2011, the company launched Field Trials for a new social networking platform, Google +. "Talk to Googlers at various levels and departments, and one powerful theme emerges: Whether they're designing search engines for the blind or preparing meals for their colleagues, these people feel that their work can change the world…The marvel of Google is its ability to continue to instill a sense of creative fearlessness and ambition in its employees. Prospective hires are often asked, 'If you could change the world using Google's resources, what would you build?' But here, this isn't a goofy or even theoretical question: Google wants to know, because thinking—and building—on that scale is what Google does. This, after all, is the company that wants to make available online every page of every book ever published. Smaller-gauge ideas die of disinterest." When it comes to innovation, "Google is different…But the difference isn't tangible. It's in the air, in the spirit of the place."

Author Comment | A company's products are born, they then grow, mature, and decline, just as living things do. To remain vital, the firm must continually develop new products and manage them effectively through their life cycles.

Product Life-Cycle Strategies (pp 253–258)

After launching the new product, management wants the product to enjoy a long and happy life. Although it does not expect the product to sell forever, the company wants to earn a decent profit to cover all the effort and risk that went into launching it. Management is aware that each product will have a life cycle, although its exact shape and length is not known in advance.

Figure 9.2 shows a typical **product life cycle** (PLC), the course that a product's sales and profits take over its lifetime. The product life cycle has five distinct stages:

Product life cycle
The course of a product's sales and profits over its lifetime. It involves five distinct stages: product development, introduction, growth, maturity, and decline.

1. *Product development* begins when the company finds and develops a new-product idea. During product development, sales are zero and the company's investment costs mount.

2. *Introduction* is a period of slow sales growth as the product is introduced in the market. Profits are nonexistent in this stage because of the heavy expenses of product introduction.

3. *Growth* is a period of rapid market acceptance and increasing profits.

4. *Maturity* is a period of slowdown in sales growth because the product has achieved acceptance by most potential buyers. Profits level off or decline because of increased marketing outlays to defend the product against competition.

5. *Decline* is the period when sales fall off and profits drop.

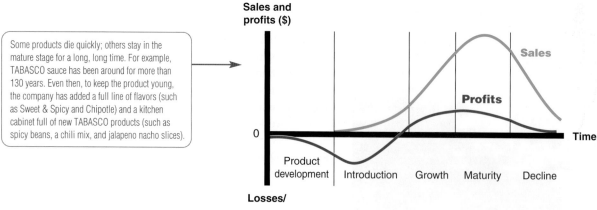

Some products die quickly; others stay in the mature stage for a long, long time. For example, TABASCO sauce has been around for more than 130 years. Even then, to keep the product young, the company has added a full line of flavors (such as Sweet & Spicy and Chipotle) and a kitchen cabinet full of new TABASCO products (such as spicy beans, a chili mix, and jalapeno nacho slices).

FIGURE | 9.2 Sales and Profits over the Product's Life from Inception to Decline

Not all products follow this product life cycle. Some products are introduced and die quickly; others stay in the mature stage for a long, long time. Some enter the decline stage and are then cycled back into the growth stage through strong promotion or repositioning. It seems that a well-managed brand could live forever. Such venerable brands as Coca-Cola, Reuters, Schering, HSBC, Siemens, and TABASCO, for instance, are still going strong after more than 100 years.

The PLC concept can describe a product class (gasoline-powered automobiles), a product form (SUVs), or a brand (the Ford Escape). The PLC concept applies differently in each case. Product classes have the longest life cycles—the sales of many product classes stay in the mature stage for a long time. Product forms, in contrast, tend to have the standard PLC shape. Product forms such as dial telephones and cassette tapes passed through a regular history of introduction, rapid growth, maturity, and decline.

A specific brand's life cycle can change quickly because of changing competitive attacks and responses. For example, although laundry soaps (product class) and powdered detergents (product form) have enjoyed fairly long life cycles, the life cycles of specific brands have tended to be much shorter. Today's leading brands of powdered laundry soap are Ariel and Persil; the leading brands 75 years ago were Rabso and Savo.

The PLC concept also can be applied to what are known as styles, fashions, and fads. Their special life cycles are shown in **Figure 9.3**. A **style** is a basic and distinctive mode of expression. For example, styles appear in homes (Islamic, Ottoman, modern), clothing (formal, casual), and art (realist, surrealist, abstract). Once a style is invented, it may last for generations, passing in and out of vogue. A style has a cycle showing several periods of renewed interest. A **fashion** is a currently accepted or popular style in a given field. For example, in some countries, the more formal 'business attire' look of corporate dress of the 1980s and 1990s gave way to the 'business casual' look of today. Fashions tend to grow slowly, remain popular for a while, and then decline slowly.

Fads are temporary periods of unusually high sales driven by consumer enthusiasm and immediate product or brand popularity.[30]

Style
A basic and distinctive mode of expression.

Fashion
A currently accepted or popular style in a given field.

Fad
A temporary period of unusually high sales driven by consumer enthusiasm and immediate product or brand popularity.

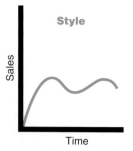

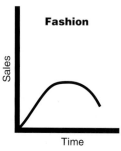

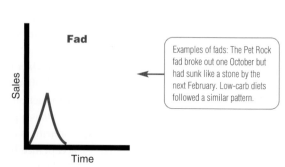

Examples of fads: The Pet Rock fad broke out one October but had sunk like a stone by the next February. Low-carb diets followed a similar pattern.

FIGURE | 9.3 Styles, Fashions, and Fads

The PLC concept can be applied by marketers as a useful framework for describing how products and markets work. And when used carefully, the PLC concept can help in developing good marketing strategies for different stages of the product life cycle. But using the PLC concept for forecasting product performance or for developing marketing strategies presents some practical problems. For example, in practice, it is difficult to forecast the sales level at each PLC stage, the length of each stage, and the shape of the PLC curve. Using the PLC concept to develop marketing strategy also can be difficult because strategy is both a cause and a result of the product's life cycle. The product's current PLC position suggests the best marketing strategies, and the resulting marketing strategies affect product performance in later life-cycle stages.

Moreover, marketers should not blindly push products through the traditional stages of the product life cycle. "As marketers instinctively embrace the old life-cycle paradigm, they needlessly consign their products to following the curve into maturity and decline," notes one marketing professor. Instead, marketers often defy the 'rules' of the life cycle and position their products in unexpected ways. By doing this, "companies can rescue products foundering in the maturity phase of their life cycles and return them to the growth phase. And they can catapult new products forward into the growth phase, passing over obstacles that could slow consumers' acceptance."[31]

The moral of the product life cycle is that companies must continually innovate or they risk extinction. No matter how successful its current product lineup, for future success, a company must skillfully manage the life cycles of existing products. And to grow, it must develop a steady stream of new products that bring new value to customers.

We looked at the product-development stage of the product life cycle in the first part of the chapter. We now look at strategies for each of the other life-cycle stages.

Introduction Stage

Introduction stage
The product life-cycle stage in which the new product is first distributed and made available for purchase.

The **introduction stage** starts when the new product is first launched. Introduction takes time, and sales growth is apt to be slow. Well-known products such as instant coffee, frozen foods, and HDTVs lingered for many years before they entered a stage of more rapid growth.

In this stage, compared with other stages, profits are negative or low because of the low sales and high distribution and promotion expenses. Much money is needed to attract distributors and build their inventories. Promotion spending is relatively high to inform consumers of the new product and get them to try it. Because the market is not generally ready for product refinements at this stage, the company and its few competitors produce basic versions of the product. These firms focus their selling on those buyers who are the most ready to buy.

A company, especially the market pioneer, must choose a launch strategy that is consistent with the intended product positioning. It should realize that the initial strategy is just the first step in a grander marketing plan for the product's entire life cycle. If the pioneer chooses its launch strategy to make a fortune, it may be sacrificing long-run revenue for the sake of short-run gain. As the pioneer moves through later stages of the life cycle, it must continuously formulate new pricing, promotion, and other marketing strategies. It has the best chance of building and retaining market leadership if it plays its cards correctly from the start.

Growth Stage

Growth stage
The product life-cycle stage in which a product's sales start climbing quickly.

If the new product satisfies the market, it will enter a **growth stage**, in which sales will start climbing quickly. The early adopters will continue to buy, and later buyers will start following their lead, especially if they hear favorable word of mouth. Attracted by the opportunities for profit, new competitors will enter the market. They will introduce new-product features, and the market will expand. The increase in competitors leads to an increase in the number of distribution outlets, and sales jump just to build reseller inventories. Prices remain where they are or fall only slightly. Companies keep their promotion spending at the same or a slightly higher level. Educating the market remains a goal, but now the company must also meet the competition.

Profits increase during the growth stage as promotion costs are spread over a large volume and as unit manufacturing costs fall. The firm uses several strategies to sustain rapid market growth as long as possible. It improves product quality and adds new-product features and models. It enters new market segments and new distribution channels. It shifts some advertising from building product awareness to building product conviction and purchase, and it lowers prices at the right time to attract more buyers.

In the growth stage, the firm faces a trade-off between high market share and high current profit. By spending a lot of money on product improvement, promotion, and distribution, the company can capture a dominant position. In doing so, however, it gives up maximum current profit, which it hopes to make up in the next stage (see **Real Marketing 9.2**).

Maturity Stage

Maturity stage
The product life-cycle stage in which sales growth slows or levels off.

At some point, a product's sales growth will slow down and the product will enter a **maturity stage**. This maturity stage normally lasts longer than the previous stages, and it poses strong challenges to marketing management. Most products are in the maturity stage of the life cycle, and therefore most of marketing management deals with the mature product.

The slowdown in sales growth results in many producers with many products to sell. In turn, this overcapacity leads to greater competition. Competitors begin marking down prices, increasing their advertising and sales promotions, and upping their product-development budgets to find better versions of the product. These steps lead to a drop in profit. Some of the weaker competitors start dropping out, and the industry eventually contains only well-established competitors.

Although many products in the mature stage appear to remain unchanged for long periods, most successful ones are actually evolving to meet changing consumer needs. Product managers should do more than simply ride along with or defend their mature products—a good offense is the best defense. They should consider modifying the market, product, and marketing mix.

In modifying the market, the company tries to increase the consumption of the current product. It may look for new users and new market segments, as when Birrell, Premium Non-Alcoholic Beer, started to target men only, assuming that the taste of Birrell would appeal only to male consumers. The company decided to change Birrell's positioning in order to better target an attractive and large segment.

The manager may also look for ways to increase usage among present customers. For example, Nestlé was aiming to increase KitKat's sales, so in its advertising it associated KitKat with spare time and encouraged consumers to eat it as a snack during breaks. The new slogan "Have a break, have a KitKat" conveyed this new positioning.

The company might also try modifying the product—changing characteristics such as quality, features, style, or packaging to attract new users and to inspire more usage. It can improve the product's styling and attractiveness. It might improve the product's quality and performance—its durability, reliability, speed, and taste. Thus, makers of consumer food and household products introduce new flavors, colors, scents, ingredients, or packages to enhance performance and revitalize consumer buying. For example, TABASCO hot pepper sauce may have been around for more than 130 years, but to keep the brand young, the company has added a full line of flavors (such as Garlic, Sweet & Spicy, and Chipotle) and a kitchen cabinet full of new products under the TABASCO name (such as steak sauces, spicy beans, a chili mix, jalapeno nacho slices, and even a TABASCO lollipop).

Finally, the company can try modifying the marketing mix—improving sales by changing one or more marketing-mix elements. The company can offer new or improved services to buyers. It can cut prices to attract new users and competitors' customers. It can launch a better advertising campaign or use aggressive sales promotions—trade deals, money-off,

Real Marketing 9.2

Etisalat Challenges Different Stages of the Product Life Cycle

Etisalat Telecom is a growing company that has attracted millions of subscribers in many countries across the world, including the UAE, Saudi Arabia, Sudan, Pakistan, Tanzania, Benin, Burkina Faso, Gabon, Niger, Togo, Central African Republic, Ivory Coast, and Afghanistan. With a market value of approximately 84 billion Dhs (US$23 billion), Etisalat is today on the verge of being ranked amongst the top 10 operators in the world.

In 2010, Etisalat reported annual net revenues of 31.3 billion Dhs (US$8.5 billion) and net profits of 7.6 billion Dhs (US$2 billion), making it one of the most profitable telecom groups in the world.

The UAE was the birthplace of this major corporation. Etisalat enjoyed the benefits from entering the Emirati telecommunication market at an early stage. It differentiated itself from competitors by offering a one-stop shop for mobile and fixed-line voice and data services to individuals, enterprises and international telecommunication companies, Internet service providers (ISPs), content providers, and mobile operators. In the UAE, Etisalat is seen as an innovative pacesetter in the telecommunication market, and thanks to the company the UAE is one of the top 10 nations in the world in terms of the availability of new technologies. Etisalat's success in the UAE market at an early stage was not only financial. The company built a strong brand image and the sense of belonging to a fast-growing market.

Mobily is the official brand name of Etihad Etisalat, the second mobile service provider in the Kingdom of Saudi Arabia. In 2005, Mobily paid SAR12.21 billion (US$3.26 billion) for its GSM license and a subsequent SAR753.75 million (US$201 million) for its 3G license. Mobily entered the Saudi market as the second mobile operator after Al-Jawal, which is mainly state-owned. In 2005, mobile telecommunication in Saudi Arabia was at an early growth stage, and Etisalat decided to capitalize on that.

In the summer of 2004, when Mobily won the license to operate in Saudi Arabia, the company managed to raise SAR8.8125 billion (US$2.35 billion) in capital, the largest syndicated Islamic loan at the time. At the dawn of 2007, Mobily set a new record when the company raised a subsequent SAR10.781 billion (US$2.875 billion) in Islamic financing. In 2007, Etisalat set a record by attracting the first million subscribers in less than 90 days after launching in 32 cities. Mobily brought coverage to 79.2 percent of the population and launched high-volume mobile data bundles in May 2007.

Mobily has differentiated itself in the Saudi market by building the largest High Speed Pack Access (HSPA) network in the region, covering around 92 percent of the populated areas in the Kingdom and over 16 cities with WiMAX service. Moreover, Mobily was the first Saudi operator to launch the BlackBerry platform to businesses at the end of 2006. It brought BlackBerry Internet services to the masses in mid-2007 and launched Apple iPhone 3G in February 2009.

Etisalat entered the Egyptian market in 2006, after the National Telecommunication Regulatory Authority (NTRA) declared that the company had won the bid to become the third mobile operator in Egypt. Etisalat paid US$2.83 billion, which is the highest fee paid to obtain a license of a third network in the Middle East. Ownership was divided among Etisalat (66 percent), Egypt Post (20 percent), National Bank of Egypt (10 percent), and Commercial International Bank (4 percent).

In Egypt, Etisalat had a key competitive advantage: It was the first company to offer 3G technology. While this technology seemed attractive, the company was aware that it was not enough to compete with the two strong operators (Mobinil and Vodafone) that shared the market almost equally. Moreover, Mobinil and Vodafone were both planning to purchase the 3G license (estimated to cost around US$566 million).

At that time, the telecommunication mobile industry in Egypt was at the end of the growth stage, where meeting competition is essential. Both Mobinil and Vodafone were offering good prices, advertising heavily, penetrating lower segments, and designing creative promotions. Etisalat identified three key opportunities for growth. First, domestic roaming, which allows Etisalat to use Mobinil

Etisalat faced different challenges in each of the countries it entered. Such challenges were strongly linked to the product life cycle in each country.

and Vodafone's networks inside Egypt in locations it does not cover; secondly, the sharing of equipment with current operators; thirdly, allowing customers to change operators without changing their phone number. Etisalat believed that with these three opportunities it would be able to offer lower prices than competitors, while cutting many operational costs.

Etisalat succeeded, by way of all the opportunities offered in such a growing market, to meet its end-of-year target in 2007. It reached three million customers at the end of September. Mohammad Hassan Omran, Etisalat chairman, expected that Etisalat would reach 10 million customers by the end of 2010. Etisalat exceeded expectations, announcing in June 2010 that it had reached a customer base of 14 million within three years of its launch.

As shown, Etisalat joined different markets at different stages of their product life cycle and faced fierce competition in each of these markets. It had to adapt to different competitive situations, adopt different strategies, and employ different tactics to cope with the various dynamics in each of these markets.

Sources: "Company Profile," Etisalat website, www.etisalat.com/html/company-profile.html; "Etisalat Misr Signs up 3 Million Customers Ahead of Target," *MEED*, November 24, 2007, www.meed.com/sectors/telecoms-and-it/etisalat-misr-signs-up-3-million-customers-ahead-of-target/293423.article; "Etisalat Misr's Customer Base Reaches 14 Million," *Gulf Telenews*, June 12, 2010, http://gulftelenews.com; "Etisalat Scoops Third GSM Licence," *MEED*, July 7, 2006, www.meed.com/sectors/telecoms-and-it/etisalat-scoops-third-gsm-licence/248629.article.

premiums, and contests. In addition to pricing and promotion, the company can also move into new marketing channels to help serve new users.

Decline Stage

The sales of most product forms and brands eventually dip. The decline may be slow, as in the case of oatmeal cereal, or rapid, as in the cases of cassette and VHS tapes. Sales may plunge to zero, or they may drop to a low level where they continue for many years. This is the **decline stage**.

Decline stage

The product life-cycle stage in which a product's sales decline.

Sales decline for many reasons, including technological advances, shifts in consumer tastes, and increased competition. As sales and profits decline, some firms withdraw from the market. Those remaining may prune their product offerings. They may drop smaller market segments and marginal trade channels, or they may cut the promotion budget and reduce their prices further.

Carrying a weak product can be very costly to a firm, and not just in profit terms. There are many hidden costs. A weak product may take up too much of management's time. It often requires frequent price and inventory adjustments. It requires advertising and sales-force attention that might be better used to make 'healthy' products more profitable. A product's failing reputation can cause customer concerns about the company and its other products. The biggest cost may well lie in the future. Keeping weak products delays the search for replacements, creates a lopsided product mix, hurts current profits, and weakens the company's foothold on the future.

For these reasons, companies need to pay more attention to their aging products. A firm's first task is to identify those products in the decline stage by regularly reviewing sales, market shares, costs, and profit trends. Then, management must decide whether to maintain, harvest, or drop each of these declining products.

Management may decide to maintain its brand without change in the hope that competitors will leave the industry. For example, Procter & Gamble made good profits by remaining in the declining liquid soap business as others withdrew. Or management may decide to reposition or reinvigorate the brand in the hope of moving it back into the growth stage of the product life cycle. P&G has done this with several brands, including Mr Clean and Old Spice. Also, Sofitel in the UAE has repositioned its brand image after the opening of Dubai Jumeirah Beach—the French hotel brand moved into the luxury segment in the UAE.

Management may decide to harvest the product, which means reducing various costs (plant and equipment, maintenance, R&D, advertising, sales force) and hoping that sales hold up. If successful, harvesting will increase the company's profits in the short run. Or management may decide to drop the product from the line. It can sell it to another firm or simply liquidate it at loss value.

● **Table 9.2** summarizes the key characteristics of each stage of the product life cycle. The table also lists the marketing objectives and strategies for each stage.[32]

Author Comment | Let's look at just a few more product topics, including regulatory and social responsibility issues and the special challenges of marketing products internationally.

Additional Product and Service Considerations (pp 258–261)

Here, we'll wrap up our discussion of products and services with two additional considerations: social responsibility in product decisions and issues of international product and service marketing.

Product Decisions and Social Responsibility

Product decisions have attracted much public attention. Marketers should carefully consider public policy issues and regulations regarding acquiring or dropping products, patent protection, product quality and safety, and product warranties.

● **TABLE | 9.2** Summary of Product Life-Cycle Characteristics, Objectives, and Strategies

Characteristics	Introduction	Growth	Maturity	Decline
Sales	Low sales	Rapidly rising sales	Peak sales	Declining sales
Costs	High cost per customer	Average cost per customer	Low cost per customer	Low cost per customer
Profits	Negative	Rising profits	High profits	Declining profits
Customers	Innovators	Early adopters	Middle majority	Laggards
Competitors	Few	Growing number	Stable number beginning to decline	Declining number
Marketing objectives				
	Create product awareness and trial	Maximize market share	Maximize profit while defending market share	Reduce expenditure and milk the brand
Strategies				
Product	Offer a basic product	Offer product extensions, service, warranty	Diversify brand and models	Phase out weak items
Price	Use cost-plus	Price to penetrate market	Price to match or beat competitors	Cut price
Distribution	Build selective distribution	Build intensive distribution	Build more intensive distribution	Go selective: phase out unprofitable outlets
Advertising	Build product awareness among early adopters and dealers	Build awareness and interest in the mass market	Stress brand differences and benefits	Reduce to level needed to retain hard-core loyals
Sales promotion	Use heavy sales promotion to entice trial	Reduce to take advantage of heavy consumer demand	Increase to encourage brand switching	Reduce to minimal level

Source: Philip Kotler and Kevin Lane Keller, *Marketing Management*, 13th ed. (Upper Saddle River, NJ: Prentice Hall, 2009), p. 288.

Regarding new products, governments may prevent companies from adding products through acquisitions if the effect threatens to lessen competition. Companies dropping products must be aware that they have legal obligations, written or implied, to their suppliers, dealers, and customers who have a stake in the dropped product. Companies must also obey patent laws when developing new products. A company cannot make its product illegally similar to another company's established product.

Manufacturers must comply with specific laws regarding product quality and safety. Different countries around the world have different laws to protect consumers from unsafe and adulterated food, drugs, and cosmetics. Various acts provide for the inspection of sanitary conditions in the meat- and poultry-processing industries. Safety legislation has been passed to regulate fabrics, chemical substances, automobiles, toys, and drugs and poisons. Numerous countries ban or seize potentially harmful products and set severe penalties for violation of their laws. If consumers have been injured by a product that has a defective design, they can sue manufacturers or dealers.

International Product and Services Marketing

International product and service marketers face special challenges. First, they must figure out what products and services to introduce and in which countries. Then, they must decide how much to standardize or adapt their products and services for world markets.

おばあちゃんの字みると、
なんだか、ほっとするよ。

キットカラトよ。
サクサク、

吉里みたいや、ぬみたいか、潮みたい。
ネットメール、発売中
郵便局と Kit Kat は、受験生を応援します。

Nestlé Kit Kat chocolate bar in Japan benefits from the co-incidental similarity between the bar's name and the Japanese phrase *kitto katsu*, which roughly translates to "You will surely win!" The brand's innovative "May cherries blossom" campaign has turned the Kit Kat bar and logo into national good luck charms.

On the one hand, companies would like to standardize their offerings. Standardization helps a company to develop a consistent worldwide image. It also lowers the product design, manufacturing, and marketing costs of offering a large variety of products. On the other hand, markets and consumers around the world differ widely. Companies must usually respond to these differences by adapting their product offerings. For example, Nestlé sells a variety of very popular Kit Kat flavors in Japan that might make the average Western chocolate-lover's stomach turn, such as green tea, red bean and soy sauce. Beyond taste, Kit Kat's strong following in Japan may also be the result of some unintended cultural factors.

In recent years, Kit Kat—the world's number-two chocolate bar behind Snickers—has become very popular in Japan. Some of this popularity, no doubt, derives from the fact that the notoriously sweet-toothed Japanese love the bar's taste. But part of the bar's appeal may also be attributed to the coincidental similarity between its name and the Japanese phrase *kitto katsu*, which roughly translates in Japanese as "You will surely win!" Spotting this opportunity, marketers for Nestlé Japan developed an innovative Juken (college entrance exam) Kit Kat campaign. The multimedia campaign positions the Kit Kat bar and logo as good luck charms during the highly stressful university entrance exam season. Nestlé even developed a cherry-flavored Kit Kat bar in packaging containing the message "May cherries blossom," wishing students luck in achieving their dreams. The campaign has been such a hit in Japan that it has led to a nationwide social move-ment to cheer up students for Juken. Kit Kat has also become an even broader national good luck charm. For example, a large flag featuring the Kit Kat logo and the phrase "kitto katsu!" has been used by fans of professional football team Jubilo IWATA, which is sponsored by Nestlé Japan.[33]

Packaging also presents new challenges for international marketers. Packaging issues can be subtle. For example, names, labels, and colors may not translate easily from one country to another. A firm using yellow flowers in its logo might fare well in Canada but meet with disaster in Mexico, where a yellow flower symbolizes death or disrespect. Similarly, although Nature's Gift might be an appealing name for gourmet mushrooms in America, it would be deadly in Germany, where *Gift* means poison. Packaging may also need to be tailored to meet the physical characteristics of consumers in various parts of the world. For instance, soft drinks are sold in smaller cans in Japan to fit the smaller Japanese hand better. Thus, although product and package standardization can produce benefits, companies must usually adapt their offerings to the unique needs of specific international markets.

Service marketers also face special challenges when going global. Some service industries have a long history of international operations. For example, the commercial banking industry was one of the first to grow internationally. Banks had to provide global services in order to meet the foreign exchange and credit needs of their home country clients wanting to sell overseas. In recent years, many banks have become truly global. HSBC, for example, assists over 3.2 million businesses across the globe to start up, develop, and grow through a comprehensive range of commercially specific products and services. HSBC's international network comprises around 8,000 offices in

88 countries and territories in Europe, the Asia-Pacific region, the Americas, the Arab world, and Africa. HSBC has positioned itself as the "World's Local Bank," indicating its dedication to localizing its services. In the Arab world, HSBC has introduced Islamic banking services to satisfy a very important regional need.[34]

Professional and business services industries such as accounting, management consulting, and advertising have also globalized. The international growth of these firms followed the globalization of the client companies they serve. For example, as more clients employ worldwide marketing, research, and advertising strategies, marketing research agencies have responded by globalizing their own operations. Neilsen employs advanced data-collection methodologies and measurement science to help businesses turn new and traditional sources of data into customer intelligence to better manage their brands, launch and grow product portfolios, optimize their media mix, and establish meaningful customer relationships. Neilsen is operating in more than 100 countries and serves international clients such as Nestlé and Danone.

Retailers are among the latest service businesses to go global. As their home markets become saturated, retailers such as Wal-Mart, Office Depot, and Saks Fifth Avenue are expanding into faster-growing markets abroad. For example, since 1995, Wal-Mart has entered 13 countries; its international division's sales grew nearly 18 percent last year, skyrocketing to more than US$90.6 billion. Foreign retailers are making similar moves. Arab world shoppers can now buy products in French-owned Carrefour stores. Carrefour, the world's second-largest retailer behind Wal-Mart, now operates more than 12,500 stores in more than 30 countries. It is the leading retailer in Europe, Brazil, and Argentina and the largest foreign retailer in China.[35]

The trend toward growth of global service companies will continue, especially in banking, airlines, telecommunications, and professional services. Today, service firms are no longer simply following their manufacturing customers. Instead, they are taking the lead in international expansion.

REVIEWING Objectives AND KEY Terms

A company's current products face a limited lifespan and must be replaced by newer products. But new products can fail—the risks of innovation are as great as the rewards. The key to successful innovation lies in a total-company effort, strong planning, and a systematic new-product development process.

OBJECTIVE 1 | Explain how companies find and develop new-product ideas. (pp 240–241)

Companies find and develop new-product ideas from a variety of sources. Many new-product ideas stem from internal sources. Companies conduct formal research and development, pick the brains of their employees, and brainstorm at executive meetings. Other ideas come from external sources. By conducting surveys and focus groups and analyzing customer questions and complaints, companies can generate new-product ideas that will meet specific consumer needs. Companies track competitors' offerings and inspect new products, dismantling them, analyzing their performance, and deciding whether to introduce a similar or improved product. Distributors and suppliers are close to the market and can pass along information about consumer problems and new-product possibilities.

OBJECTIVE 2 | List and define the steps in the new-product development process and the major considerations in managing this process. (pp 241–253)

The new-product development process consists of eight sequential stages. The process starts with idea generation. Next comes idea screening, which reduces the number of ideas based on the company's own criteria. Ideas that pass the screening stage continue through product concept development, in which a detailed version of the new-product idea is stated in meaningful consumer terms. In the next stage, concept testing, new-product concepts are tested with a group of target consumers to determine whether the concepts have strong consumer appeal. Strong concepts proceed to marketing strategy development, in which an initial marketing strategy for the new product is developed from the product concept. In the business-analysis stage, a review of the sales, costs, and profit projections for a new product is conducted to determine whether the new product is likely to satisfy the company's objectives. With positive results here, the ideas become more concrete through product development and test marketing and finally are launched during commercialization.

New-product development involves more than just going through a set of steps. Companies must take a systematic, holistic approach to managing this process. Successful new-product development requires a customer-centered, team-based, systematic effort.

OBJECTIVE 3 **Describe the stages of the product life cycle and how marketing strategies change during the product life cycle. (pp 253–258)**

Each product has a life cycle marked by a changing set of problems and opportunities. The sales of the typical product follow an S-shaped curve made up of five stages. The cycle begins with the product-development stage in which the company finds and develops a new-product idea. The introduction stage is marked by slow growth and low profits as the product is distributed to the market. If successful, the product enters a growth stage, which offers rapid sales growth and increasing profits. Next comes a maturity stage in which sales growth slows down and profits stabilize. Finally, the product enters a decline stage in which sales and profits dwindle. The company's task during this stage is to recognize the decline and to decide whether it should maintain, harvest, or drop the product.

In the introduction stage, the company must choose a launch strategy consistent with its intended product positioning. Much money is needed to attract distributors and build their inventories and to inform consumers of the new product and achieve trial. In the growth stage, companies continue to educate potential consumers and distributors. In addition, the company works to stay ahead of the competition and sustain rapid market growth by improving product quality, adding new-product features and models, entering new market segments and distribution channels, shifting advertising from building product awareness to building product conviction and purchase, and lowering prices at the right time to attract new buyers.

In the maturity stage, companies continue to invest in maturing products and consider modifying the market, the product, and the marketing mix. When modifying the market, the company attempts to increase the consumption of the current product. When modifying the product, the company changes some of the product's characteristics—such as quality, features, or style—to attract new users or inspire more usage. When modifying the marketing mix, the company works to improve sales by changing one or more of the marketing-mix elements. Once the company recognizes that a product has entered the decline stage, management must decide whether to maintain the brand without change, hoping that competitors will drop out of the market; harvest the product, reducing costs and trying to maintain sales; or drop the product, selling it to another firm or liquidating it at salvage value.

OBJECTIVE 4 **Discuss two additional product issues: socially responsible product decisions and international product and services marketing. (pp 258–261)**

Marketers must consider two additional product issues. The first is social responsibility. This includes public policy issues and regulations involving acquiring or dropping products, patent protection, product quality and safety, and product warranties. The second involves the special challenges facing international product and service marketers. International marketers must decide how much to standardize or adapt their offerings for world markets.

KEY Terms

OBJECTIVE 1
New-product development (p 240)

OBJECTIVE 2
Idea generation (p 242)
Idea screening (p 243)
Product concept (p 244)
Concept testing (p 244)
Marketing strategy development (p 245)

Business analysis (p 246)
Product development (p 246)
Test marketing (p 247)
Commercialization (p 249)
Customer-centered new-product development (p 250)
Team-based new-product development (p 251)

OBJECTIVE 3
Product life cycle (p 253)
Style (p 254)
Fashion (p 254)
Fad (p 254)
Introduction stage (p 255)
Growth stage (p 255)
Maturity stage (p 256)
Decline stage (p 258)

DISCUSSING & APPLYING THE Concepts

Discussing the Concepts

1. Name and describe the major steps in the new-product development process.

2. Discuss the benefits and drawbacks of test marketing and explain why some companies do or do not use test marketing for new products. Name and describe the three approaches to test marketing.

3. Explain why successful new-product development requires a customer-centered, team-based, and systematic effort.

4. Name and describe the five stages of the product life cycle. Identify a product class, product form, or brand that is in each stage.

5. Explain the differences among styles, fashions, and fads and give an example of each.

6. Discuss the special challenges facing international product and service marketers.

Applying the Concepts

1. Think of a problem that really bugs you or a need you have that is not satisfied by current market offerings. In a small group, brainstorm ideas for a new product or service that solves this problem or satisfies this need.

2. Coca-Cola has sustained success in the maturity stage of the product life cycle for many years. Visit Coca-Cola's website (www.thecoca-colacompany.com/heritage/ourheritage. html) and discuss how Coca-Cola has evolved over the years. Identify ways that Coca-Cola can continue to evolve to meet changing consumer needs and wants.

3. Write a marketing strategy statement for a new, fully functioning, folding bicycle.

FOCUS ON Technology

The music industry is an area of business that is facing tremendous challenges. Not only are many of its products (singers, bands, and acts) suffering from increasingly short product life cycles, but there are also other concerns. The market is moving very quickly, tastes are constantly changing, and an act's fan base may never be big enough or loyal enough to warrant long-term commitment by a label to the act. The financial support and investment necessary to sustain an act that is not performing in terms of sales can no longer be justified.

Add to this the question of technology and the industry faces great difficulties. The Internet can allow consumers to acquire their music at little or no cost to them, which translates to little or no income for the industry. File sharing and swapping are rife. There has been a decline in sales of traditional formats such as CDs, and this has meant that income is down and profits have taken a hit.

Those that support file sharing and swapping blame the industry directly, pointing to its greed in artificially keeping the price of CDs too high and not responding to obvious consumer reluctance to continue to pay inflated prices.

1. Currently, in what stage of the product life cycle are CDs?

2. How can the music industry turn this around to its advantage? Is it too late?

FOCUS ON Ethics

Does your computer have a floppy disk drive or use the DOS operating system? Do you listen to music on a cassette deck? How about recording movies on a VCR tape? You probably answered no. In fact, you may not even be aware of these products. All are examples of obsolete products. But did marketers plan it that way? Many companies have been accused of using planned obsolescence as a strategy to make more money. However, new products often provide greater value for customers, especially in fast-changing industries such as computers and electronics. But what happens to the old products? This creates a growing concern over electronic waste, called e-waste. Although e-waste represents only 2 percent of the trash in our landfills, some analysts estimate that it accounts for 70 percent of overall toxic waste. Although recycling programs are increasing and are required by law in some countries, the waste is often shipped for recycling or disposal to landfills in China, Ghana, Kenya, India, and other developing countries, where concerns over worker and environmental welfare are more lax.

1. Who should be responsible for the proper disposal of electronic products no longer needed—consumers or manufacturers? Is it appropriate to ship e-waste to developing countries? Discuss alternative solutions.

2. Visit several electronics manufacturers' websites to learn if they offer electronic recycling programs. Are manufacturers doing enough? Write a brief report on what you learned. Focus on the experience in your own country.

MARKETING BY THE Numbers

A manufacturer of ready-made meals sells to the trade at US$1 per unit. The manufacturer has fixed overheads of US$104,000 and generates a profit of US$124,000. Its four product ranges are Indian, Chinese, Thai, and Greek. Calculations have been made in respect of the revenue generated for each range, cost of ingredients, other variable costs, and contribution made to profits. For the Indian range the figures are US$90,000, $15,000, $15,000, and $60,000. For the Chinese range they are US$120,000, $25,000, $25,000, and $70,000. For the Thai range they are US$70,000, $10,000, $10,000, and $48,000. And finally for the Greek range they are US$70,000, $10,000, $10,000, and $50,000.

1. What is the contribution per unit for each of the four product lines?

2. What is the average contribution per unit across the four product lines?

3. Which product line produces the best and worst contribution per unit?

VIDEO **Case**

Electrolux

Since the 1920s, Swedish company Electrolux has been making and selling home appliances worldwide. Decade after decade, the company, originally known for its vacuum cleaners, has been turning out innovative products in a way that seems to magically predict what will work for consumers. The success of Electrolux's new-product development process results from more than just technological and design expertise. More importantly, it is rooted in what the company calls "consumer insight."

The concept of consumer insight is integrated into the Electrolux marketing strategy. It involves starting with the customer and working backward to design the product. Electrolux employs various methods to get deep into the consumer's mind and to understand consumer needs. It then boils down that information to form concepts and, from concepts, it designs prod-

ucts. Because of its customer-centric approach, Electrolux refers to itself as the "thoughtful" design innovator and has for years stood behind the slogan "Thinking of you."

After viewing the video featuring Electrolux, answer the following questions about the company's new-product development process:

1. What is consumer insight? What are some ways in which Electrolux develops consumer insight?
2. Describe how Electrolux might go about developing products if it were focused solely on engineering and technology. What might be the result of this product-development process?
3. With household appliances in mind, identify some consumer trends from the video, as well as any others that you can think of. Explain how new products could take advantage of each trend.

COMPANY **Case**

Activia in Egypt

DANONE AROUND THE WORLD

Groupe Danone is a French company established in 1925. Initially, the company produced dairy products; it then gradually introduced several new brands in different product categories. It sells about six million cups of yogurt a day in almost 100 flavors, styles, and sizes. Activia is the company's top-selling brand of yogurt worldwide. Dannon® is the name of the US subsidiary company and is associated with one of its brands over there. It is sold under the names Dannon or Danone, depending on the country it is sold in. Its official name in Egypt is Danone. The company prides itself on consistently delivering high-quality, wholesome products and responding to consumers' needs with nutritious, innovative new products and flavors.

DANONE EGYPT

Danone was introduced in Egypt during 2005, after its acquisition of Olait along with its headquarters and factories. It first launched Danone core (the regular yogurt) in 110 g and 80 g plain, Danone sugar yogurt, Danone lite, Danone fruits with various flavors (berry, strawberry, pineapple, and apricot), and Danone Mixy for children. In June 2008, the company introduced Activia.

ACTIVIA ENTERS THE MARKET

Danone launched Activia for the first time in 1986 in Spain and it soon became available all over Europe. A group of researchers discovered the importance of bacteria in the digestion process and went on to develop a technique with which they could culture the 'good' bacteria and insert it into the yogurt. The bacterium Actiregularis was custom-made for Danone. Activia is now prevalent in 68 countries around the globe. It is one of the fastest-growing products innovated by Danone. Its sales are estimated at US$14 billion annually.

Activia was introduced to the Egyptian market in June 2008, then with just one product: plain 110 g. The probiotics market in

Egypt was still at the introduction stage, and Danone's aim was to grow the market. On July 16, 2009, Danone Egypt introduced two flavors of Activia yogurt, vanilla and honey.

THE PROBIOTICS MARKET IN EGYPT BEFORE ACTIVIA

Prior to Activia's launch, probiotics comprised just 0.2 percent of the total yogurt market in Egypt. There were two key players in the market: Nestlé, which introduced Nesvita as a pro-digestion fat-free powdered milk with Actifibras; and Juhayna, which introduced Juhayna Digestive, the oldest player in the yogurt market. Lactel then introduced Lactel B Active after Activia's launch.

ACTIVIA'S PERFORMANCE

By June 2009, a year after the introduction of Activia, the probiotics market had witnessed fast growth, increasing from 0.2 percent to 5.7 percent, of which Activia captured more than 76 percent (4.3 percent of the total yogurt market). Activia maintained its leadership in the probiotics market, reaching 84 percent in early 2010 (5.7 percent out of 6.8 percent of the total yogurt market). Also, consumer research revealed the taste of Activia to be the best liked among all the yogurt brands in Egypt (including other Danone brands).

CHALLENGES IN THE MARKET

It was not easy for Danone to grow and lead the probiotics market in Egypt because of the low awareness of probiotic yogurts in general. But Danone nevertheless considered probiotic yogurt a good business opportunity and began working to tackle those challenges.

Danone attempted to raise awareness of the vitality of probiotic yogurts, to show how they positively affect the digestive system, and help those who have digestion problems. To achieve these goals, Danone developed advertising campaigns and PR activities, including a '360° Campaign,' whereby the company used all available communication tools to reach its target market.

Accordingly, Danone designed television, radio, and print ads; held press conferences; issued press releases; printed point of purchase materials, flyers, and brochures; and organized sampling in large supermarkets, universities, and hypermarkets. All these communication tools carried a consistent message to the consumer stressing that the product is 100 percent natural and guarantees to improve the digestion process. The campaign was successful and very quickly Danone increased awareness of the Activia brand in the Egyptian market and consumers began to view the product as credible and relevant to them.

To tackle the issue of credibility, Danone continually relayed the message that Activia is 100 percent natural and really improves digestion. Danone repeated its message consistently through different advertising campaigns and PR activities. It published articles in leading women's magazines by well-known physicians discussing the effectiveness of Activia yogurt to improve digestion. It also contacted physicians and explained to them the benefits of Activia. Many well-known physicians were convinced and decided to advise their patients to eat Activia regularly. Such support for the product increased the credibility of Activia and probiotics yogurts in Egypt. In addition, Activia launched a campaign called the "Activia Challenge," which aimed to further raise Activia's credibility and encourage immediate purchase. The company's challenge to consumers was this: eat Activia regularly for 15 days and it will help improve digestion. If no improvement is felt, you will get your money back. This cam-paign was very effective in increasing the product's credibility as well as encouraging consumers to try the product. However, its impact on consumers' trust and belief is yet to be proven.

In November 2008, the company faced a different challenge—an increase in the prices of raw materials and packaging. The company decided to increase the price of Activia by about 17 percent. Several promotions were launched in order to reduce the effect of the price increase on sales. Moreover, the introduction of additional flavors assisted in increasing Activia's sales in the market.

Because Activia has raised awareness and increased the size of the probiotics market in less than two years, Activia's example is considered one of the success stories new-product introduction. Smart consumer-centered strategies allowed Activia to become a leader in the Egyptian market very quickly.

Questions for Discussion

1. Evaluate the timing at which Activia entered the market.

2. In which stage of the product life cycle is Activia? Based on that stage, is Danone employing good marketing strategies?

3. Propose a strategy for Activia's next product life-cycle phase.

4. Discuss the potential threats to Activia's future success. What will help Danone avoid a premature decline for Activia?

Source: Based on author's interview with Mohammed Ali, Brand Manager at Danone.

Chapter 10

Part 1	Defining Marketing and the Marketing Process (Chapters 1, 2)
Part 2	Understanding the Marketplace and Consumers (Chapters 3, 4, 5, 6)
Part 3	Designing a Customer-Driven Strategy and Mix (Chapters 7, 8, 9, 10, 11, 12, 13, 14)
Part 4	Extending Marketing (Chapters 15, 16, 17)

Pricing

Chapter PREVIEW

Next, we look at a second major marketing mix tool—pricing. If effective product development, promotion, and distribution sow the seeds of business success, effective pricing is the harvest. Firms successful at creating customer value with the other marketing mix activities must still capture some of this value in the prices they earn. Yet, despite its importance, many firms do not handle pricing well. In this chapter, we'll look at internal and external considerations that affect pricing decisions and examine general pricing approaches. We will then dig into pricing strategies. Let's start by looking at the approach to pricing made by one of the largest retailers operating in the Arab world, Carrefour.

The French retail chain Carrefour was established in 1959. Since then, it has enjoyed great success, particularly in Europe, Latin America, and Asia. Over the past 40 years, Carrefour has grown to become the second largest retailer in the world and the largest in Europe. It has 15,500 grocery stores that exist in one of four formats: as a hypermarket, a supermarket, a hard discount, or a convenience store.

Carrefour recently entered the Arab world and it has enjoyed high growth rates in very short periods of time. According to Planet Retail, a U.K. researcher specializing in global retail trends, Carrefour is ranked the top hypermarket in the Middle East.[1] It has stores in Syria, Jordan, Egypt, Saudi Arabia, Kuwait, Qatar, the UAE, and Oman. The number of stores in each country is steadily increasing; the company aimed to open 25 hypermarkets and 100 supermarkets in Saudi Arabia by 2010.

Carrefour Saudi was established in 2004 with a vision of offering the widest choice of world-class brands at the most reasonable prices. It opened 11 branches in Riyadh, Khobar, Jeddah, Dammam, and Madinah. Keen to open an additional 20 stores in Saudi within the next seven years, and in order to adhere to government regulations, Carrefour has formed a joint venture between Al Olayan Group and the Majid Al-Futtaim Group.

There is a wide customer base for Carrefour in Saudi Arabia. Mr Abdullah Ahmed Al-Ahmed, Carrefour vice president, reported in an interview that "a single Carrefour store in Saudi Arabia receives 20,000 customers daily, who perform about 5,000 transactions on our sales counters...About 40 percent of the customers are expatriates, mainly because we have stocked the best products of their own countries, while we always care to cater to the diverse ethnic tastes and food habits of different nationalities." Moreover, Carrefour's Saudi customers are very satisfied with its pricing strategy as well as its promotional programs. As Mr Abdullah said, "Carrefour's customers are utterly satisfied with the level of prices, the quantity and quality of perishable items and above all services."[2] The future looks bright for Carrefour Saudi.

Carrefour Saudi relies heavily on price in order to attract a wide range of customers, particularly in Ramadan, the holy month in which the consumption rate increases tremendously. Since its entry in the market, Carrefour has competed fiercely by offering low prices as well as designing attractive promotional campaigns. For example, Carrefour Saudi launched its first

> Carrefour has become an integral part of the Saudi society and provides special offers to coincide with the different occasions in the Kingdom of Saudi Arabia.

campaign with the slogan, "lowest prices and so much more." This campaign featured aggressive discounts and valuable prizes, such as diamonds, gold, and Japanese and American cars. A week before Ramadan, Carrefour announces in full and half-page advertisements its bumper sales and the special promotions on offer.

Carrefour aims to increase its net profit and market share by expanding its presence in Saudi Arabia. According to Mr Abdullah, "Our feasibility study has shown that the Kingdom needs 40 more hypermarkets and 100 more supermarkets between now and 2015."[3]

Pricing played an important role in Carrefour's growth in Saudi Arabia. It was the key to success and expansion in a dynamic and competitive retail market. For this reason, it was quite important to exceed consumers' expectations through understanding their needs and priorities. The key question is: How can Carrefour maintain its low prices and sustain its leadership in a competitive environment?

Carrefour has opened a fifth market in Saudia Arabia. It is one of a series of new stores opening in the Kingdom, with opportunities for even more hypermarkets available.

A joint venture between Al Olayan Group and the Majid Al-Futtaim Group has been established with the aim of launching more than 20 Carrefour stores all over the Kingdom of Saudi Arabia. Carrefour uses pricing strategies and price promotions to increase its customer base and to succeed in a competitive environment.

Pricing: The challenge is to harvest the customer value the company creates. Says Panera Bread Company's CEO, Ronald Shaich, pictured here, "Give people something of value, and they'll happily pay for it."

Companies today face a fierce and fast-changing pricing environment. Value-seeking customers have put increased pricing pressure on many companies. "Thank the Wal-Mart phenomenon," says one analyst. "These days, we're all cheapskates in search of a spend-less strategy." In response, it seems that almost every company is looking for ways to slash prices.[4]

Yet, cutting prices is often not the best answer. Reducing prices unnecessarily can lead to lost profits and damaging price wars. It can signal to customers that the price is more important than the customer value a brand delivers. Instead, companies should sell value, not price. They should persuade customers that paying a higher price for the company's brand is justified by the greater value they gain. The challenge is to find the price that will let the company make a fair profit by getting paid for the customer value it creates. "Give people something of value," says Ronald Shaich, CEO of Panera Bread Company, "and they'll happily pay for it."[5]

Author Comment | Setting the right price is one of the marketer's most difficult tasks. A host of factors come into play. But finding and implementing the right pricing strategy is critical to success.

What Is a Price? (pp 267–269)

In the narrowest sense, **price** is the amount of money charged for a product or service. More broadly, price is the sum of all the values that customers give up in order to gain the benefits of having or using a product or service. Historically, price has been the major factor affecting buyer choice. In recent decades, nonprice factors have gained increasing

Objective Outline

Price
The amount of money charged for a product or service, or the sum of the values that customers exchange for the benefits of having or using the product or service.

importance. However, price still remains one of the most important elements determining a firm's market share and profitability.

Price is the only element in the marketing mix that produces revenue; all other elements represent costs. Price is also one of the most flexible marketing mix elements. Unlike product features and channel commitments, prices can be changed quickly. At the same time, pricing is the number-one problem facing many marketing executives, and many companies do not handle pricing well. One frequent problem is that companies are too quick to reduce prices in order to get a sale rather than convincing buyers that their product's greater value is worth a higher price. Other common mistakes include pricing that is too cost-oriented rather than customer-value oriented, and pricing that does not take the rest of the marketing mix into account.

Some managers view pricing as a big headache, preferring instead to focus on the other marketing mix elements. However, smart managers treat pricing as a key strategic tool for creating and capturing customer value. Prices have a direct impact on a firm's bottom line. A small percentage improvement in price can generate a large percentage in profitability. More importantly, as a part of a company's overall value proposition, price plays a key role in creating customer value and building customer relationships.

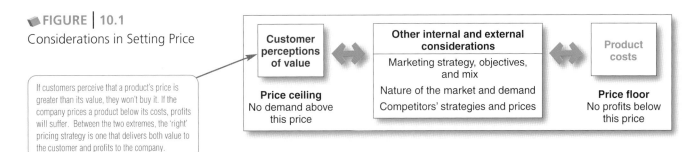

■ FIGURE | 10.1
Considerations in Setting Price

If customers perceive that a product's price is greater than its value, they won't buy it. If the company prices a product below its costs, profits will suffer. Between the two extremes, the 'right' pricing strategy is one that delivers both value to the customer and profits to the company.

Factors to Consider When Setting Prices

The price the company charges will fall somewhere between one that is too high to produce any demand and one that is too low to produce a profit. ■ **Figure 10.1** summarizes the major considerations in setting price. Customer perceptions of the product's value set the ceiling for prices. If customers perceive that the price is greater than the product's value, they will not buy the product. Product costs set the floor for prices. If the company prices the product below its costs, company profits will suffer. In setting its price between these two extremes, the company must consider a number of other internal and external factors, including its overall marketing strategy and mix, the nature of the market and demand, and competitors' strategies and prices.

Author Comment | Pricing decisions are primarily customer-oriented. Delivering value to customers is the basis to pricing decisions.

Customer Perceptions of Value (pp 269–271)

In the end, the customer will decide whether a product's price is right. Pricing decisions, like other marketing mix decisions, must start with customer value. When customers buy a product, they exchange something of value (the price) in order to get something of value (the benefits of having or using the product). Effective, customer-oriented pricing involves understanding how much value consumers place on the benefits they receive from the product and setting a price that captures this value.

Value-Based Pricing

Good pricing begins with a complete understanding of the value that a product or service creates for customers. **Value-based pricing** uses buyers' perceptions of value, not the seller's cost, as the key to pricing. Value-based pricing means that the marketer cannot design a product and marketing program and then set the price. Price is considered along with the other marketing-mix variables *before* the marketing program is set.

Value-based pricing

Setting price based on buyers' perceptions of value rather than on the seller's cost.

■ **Figure 10.2** compares value-based pricing with cost-based pricing. Cost-based pricing is product driven. The company designs what it considers to be a good product, adds up the costs of making the product, and sets a price that covers costs and gives a target profit. Marketing must then convince buyers that the product's value at that price justifies

■ FIGURE | 10.2
Value-Based Pricing
Versus Cost-Based
Pricing

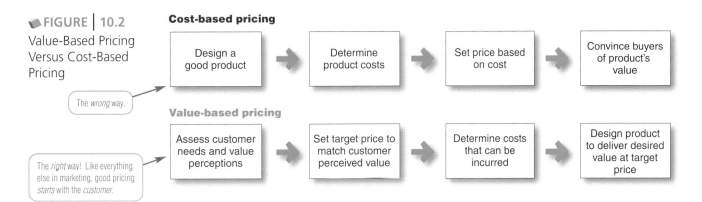

The *wrong* way.

The *right* way! Like everything else in marketing, good pricing *starts* with the *customer*.

its purchase. If the price turns out to be too high, the company must settle for lower mark-ups or lower sales, both resulting in disappointing profits.

Value-based pricing reverses this process. The company first assesses customer needs and value perceptions. It then sets its target price based on customer perceptions of value. The targeted value and price then drive decisions about what costs can be incurred and the resulting product design. As a result, pricing begins with analyzing consumer needs and value perceptions, and price is set to match consumers' perceived value.

It's important to remember that 'good value' is not the same as 'low price.' For example, some car buyers consider the luxurious Bentley Continental GT automobile to be good value, even at an eye-popping price of US$175,000:[6]

> Stay with me here, because I'm about to [tell you why] a certain automobile costing US$175,000 is not actually expensive, but is in fact a tremendous value. Every Bentley GT is built by hand, an Old World bit of automaking requiring 160 hours per vehicle. Craftsmen spend 18 hours simply stitching the perfectly joined leather of the GT's steering wheel, almost as long as it takes to assemble an entire VW Golf. The results are impressive: Dash and doors are mirrored with walnut veneer, floor pedals are carved from aluminum, window and seat toggles are cut from actual metal rather than plastic, and every air vent is perfectly chromed…The sum of all this is a fitted cabin that approximates that of a US$300,000 vehicle, matched to an engine the equal of a US$200,000 automobile, within a car that has brilliantly incorporated…technological sophistication. As I said, the GT is a bargain. [Just ask anyone on the lengthy waiting list.] The waiting time to bring home your very own GT is currently half a year.

A company using value-based pricing must find out what value buyers assign to different competitive offers. However, companies often find it hard to measure the value customers will attach to its product. For example, calculating the cost of ingredients in a meal at a fancy restaurant is relatively easy. But assigning a value to other satisfactions such as taste, environment, relaxation, conversation, and status is very hard. And these values will vary both for different consumers and different situations.

Still, consumers will use these perceived values to evaluate a product's price, so the company must work to measure them. Sometimes, companies ask consumers how much they would pay for a basic product and for each benefit added to the offer. Or a company might conduct experiments to test the perceived value of different product offers. According to an old Russian proverb, there are two fools in every market—one who asks too much and one who asks too little. If the seller charges more than the buyers' perceived value, the company's sales will suffer. If the seller charges less, its products sell very well. But they produce less revenue than they would if they were priced at the level of perceived value.

We now examine two types of value-based pricing: *good-value pricing* and *value-added pricing*.

Good-Value Pricing

During the past decade, marketers have noted a fundamental shift in consumer attitudes toward price and quality. Many companies have changed their pricing approaches to bring them into line with changing economic conditions and consumer price perceptions. More and more, marketers have adopted **good-value pricing** strategies—offering just the right combination of quality and good service at a fair price.

In many cases, this has involved introducing less-expensive versions of established, brand-name products. To meet the tougher economic times and more frugal consumer spending habits, some fast-food restaurants offer 'value menus.' Armani offers the less-expensive, more-casual Armani Exchange fashion line. And Volkswagen recently reintroduced the Rabbit, an economical car with a base price under US$16,000, because "The people want an entry-level price and top-level features."[7]

In other cases, good-value pricing has involved redesigning existing brands to offer more quality for a given price or the same quality for less. Some companies even succeed

Good-value pricing
Offering just the right combination of quality and good service at a fair price.

by offering less value but at rock-bottom prices. Chinese products are also invading the Arab world, and they are relying on low prices to attract consumers. There are many Arab importers who are purchasing Chinese products and rebranding them in order to offer acceptable quality with low prices (see **Real Marketing 10.1**).

An important type of good-value pricing at the retail level is *everyday low pricing (EDLP)*. EDLP involves charging a constant, everyday low price with few or no temporary price discounts. In contrast, *high-low pricing* involves charging higher prices on an everyday basis but running frequent promotions to lower prices temporarily on selected items. In recent years, high-low pricing has given way to EDLP in retail settings. The king of EDLP is Wal-Mart, which practically defined the concept. Except for a few sale items every month, Wal-Mart promises everyday low prices on everything it sells.

Value-Added Pricing

Value-added pricing
Attaching value-added features and services to differentiate a company's offers and charge higher prices.

Value-based pricing doesn't mean simply charging what customers want to pay or setting low prices to meet the competition. In many marketing situations, the challenge is to build the company's *pricing power*—its power to escape price competition and to justify higher prices and margins. To increase pricing power, a firm must retain or build the value of its market offering. This is especially true for suppliers of commodity products, which are characterized by little differentiation and intense price competition.

To increase their pricing power, many companies adopt **value-added pricing** strategies. Rather than cutting prices to match competitors', they attach value-added features and services to differentiate their offers and thus support higher prices. Consider Hacienda White, one of the resorts in Egypt's Palm Hills. Developments. It is a new summer destination featuring luxurious and modern homes for those who are seeking a splendid resort. Palm Hills Developments has set high prices for villas and chalets because they come with many extra services and benefits, such as the clubhouse, mall, luxurious services, and the social image. Thus, the higher prices demanded by Hacienda have not negatively affected demand for the properties due to the high perceived value-added services.

Author Comment | Costs set the floor for price but the goal isn't always to minimize costs. In fact, many firms invest in higher costs so that they can claim higher prices and margins (think about Bentley automobiles). The key is to manage the spread between costs and prices—how much the company makes for the customer value it delivers.

Company and Product Costs (pp 271–276)

Whereas customer-value perceptions set the price ceiling, costs set the floor for the price that the company can charge. **Cost-based pricing** involves setting prices based on the costs for producing, distributing, and selling the product plus a fair rate of return for its effort and risk. A company's costs may be an important element in its pricing strategy.

Some companies, such as Wal-Mart and Acer, work to become the 'low-cost producers' in their industries. Companies with lower costs can set lower prices that result in smaller margins but greater sales and profits. Other companies, however, intentionally pay higher costs so that they can claim higher prices and margins. For example, it costs more to make a 'built by hand' Bentley than a Toyota Camry. But the higher costs result in higher quality, justifying that eye-popping US$175,000 price. The key is to manage the spread between costs and prices—how much the company makes for the customer value it delivers.

Cost-based pricing
Setting prices based on the costs for producing, distributing, and selling the product plus a fair rate of return for effort and risk.

Types of Costs

A company's costs take two forms, fixed and variable. **Fixed costs** (also known as **overheads**) are costs that do not vary with production or sales level. For example, a company must pay each month's bills for rent, heat, interest, and executive salaries, whatever the company's output. **Variable costs** vary directly with the level of production. Each PC produced by Sony involves a cost of computer chips, wires, plastic, packaging, and other inputs. These costs tend to be the same for each unit produced. They are called variable costs because their total varies with the number of units produced. **Total costs** are the sum of the fixed and variable costs for any given level of production. Management wants to charge a price that will at least cover the total production costs at a given level of production.

Fixed costs (overheads)
Costs that do not vary with production or sales level.

Variable costs
Costs that vary directly with the level of production.

Total costs
The sum of the fixed and variable costs for any given level of production.

Real Marketing 10.1

Cheap Chinese Products Flood Arab Markets

Chinese products are flooding into the Arab world, winning customers with low prices while still providing acceptable quality. Chinese companies' understanding of the culture, religion, and habits of the Arab world has allowed them to grow and expand quickly in the region.

The Egyptian market has been lucrative for Chinese manufacturers. According to the Ministry of Commerce of the People's Republic of China, bilateral trade between China and Egypt reached about US$6.24 billion by the end of 2008, almost a 50 percent increase compared with 2006. Moreover, there are currently 352 Chinese enterprises in Egypt, with investment of about US$430 million. *The Times* also reported that Chinese exports to Egypt have increased by 50 percent since 2006. This huge amount of investment reveals how the Egyptian market welcomes Chinese products.

In 2010, the chairman of China's sovereign wealth fund, which manages US$300 billion, considered the Arab world to be one of the very attractive regions for Chinese products because of its growing economy, even during financial crises. The Egyptian economy has been growing by 5 percent over the past two years despite the global crisis. For this reason, the chairman of China's sovereign wealth fund decided to push foreign direct investment back to around US$10 billion a year.

It was very important for the Chinese investors to know what would enable them to enter the Egyptian market quickly and successfully. In general, Egyptians found Chinese products very attractive because they offered satisfactory quality at low prices. According to a popular Chinese newspaper, Egyptians prefer buying Chinese products in their daily life as they find them "cheap and the quality is OK."

Chinese mobile phones are a typical example of the widespread penetration of Chinese products, and an example of the conflict between regulations and the need for cheap products.

All kinds of different Chinese products are available in Egypt, items as diverse as the Egyptian flag, Ramadan products, stationery, motorbikes, cars, house equipment, electronic machines, and so on. For 'low involvement' products, a reduction in quality does not seem to be considered important by most consumers if they benefit from a lower price. For example, during the African Cup, many Egyptians bought flags made in China, because they were cheaper and more durable than the flags made in Egypt.

Other Chinese products such as electronics, cars, motorbikes, and house equipment penetrate the Egyptian market. From 2004 to 2006, the largest Egyptian agent company for Chinese motorcycles sold 100,000 units and the rate grew year after year. Users of the Chinese Car Forum, in 2007, stated that "We need to produce at least 10,000 motorbikes every month to meet our market demand [in Egypt]." The motorbikes are cheap compared with other motorbikes; they cost LE2,500 ($US420), which is relatively cheap compared with the competition.

In Egypt, Chinese products that offer satisfactory quality at relatively low prices are successful, particularly because a large number of consumers are looking for good value. The pricing strategy deployed by Chinese companies meets the demands of different market segments and creates new markets. Chinese companies identified a gap in the market and grabbed the business opportunity.

Sources: "China, Egypt Eye Closer Economic Ties," *China Daily*, September 27, 2010, www.chinadaily.com.cn/bizchina/2010-09/27/content_11352522.htm; "Chinese Goods Popular in Egypt," *Xinhua News Agency*, December 21, 2007, www.china.org.cn/english/business/236533.htm; China Car Forums, www.chinacarforums.com/forum/showthread.php?t=2928.; Dena Rashed, "China Comes to Town," *Al-Ahram Weekly Online*, February 21–27, 2008, http://weekly.ahram.org.eg/2008/885/feature.htm; "Egyptians Favor Chinese Products in Everyday Life," Ministry of Commerce of the People's Republic of China, Department of Information Technology, November 20, 2007, http://xxhs2.mofcom.gov.cn/aarticle/commonnews/200711/20071105234900.html.

The company must watch its costs carefully. If it costs the company more than competitors to produce and sell its product, the company will need to charge a higher price or make less profit, putting it at a competitive disadvantage.

Costs at Different Levels of Production

To price wisely, management needs to know how its costs vary with different levels of production. For example, suppose a company has built a plant to produce 1,000 calculators a day. ▶ **Figure 10.3A** shows the typical short-run average cost curve (SRAC). It shows

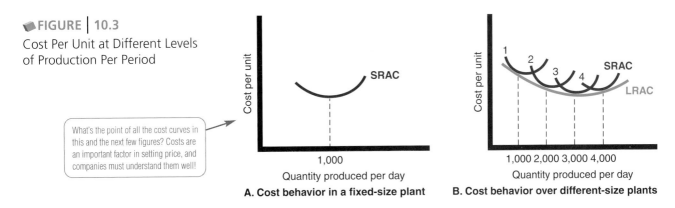

FIGURE | 10.3

Cost Per Unit at Different Levels
of Production Per Period

> What's the point of all the cost curves in
> this and the next few figures? Costs are
> an important factor in setting price, and
> companies must understand them well!

A. Cost behavior in a fixed-size plant

B. Cost behavior over different-size plants

that the cost per calculator is high if the company's factory produces only a few a day. But as production moves up to 1,000 calculators a day, average cost falls. This is because fixed costs are spread over more units, with each one bearing a smaller share of the fixed cost. The company can try to produce more than 1,000 calculators a day, but average costs will increase because the plant becomes inefficient. Workers have to wait for machines, the machines break down more often, and workers get in each other's way.

If the company believed it could sell 2,000 calculators a day, it should consider building a larger plant. The plant would use more efficient machinery and work arrangements. Also, the unit cost of producing 2,000 calculators a day would be lower than the unit cost of producing 1,000 units a day, as shown in the long-run average cost (LRAC) curve (**Figure 10.3B**). In fact, a 3,000-capacity plant would even be more efficient, according to **Figure 10.3B**. But a 4,000-daily production plant would be less efficient because of increasing diseconomies of scale—too many workers to manage, paperwork slowing things down, and so on. **Figure 10.3B** shows that a 3,000-daily production plant is the best size to build if demand is strong enough to support this level of production.

Costs as a Function of Production Experience

Suppose the company runs a plant that produces 3,000 calculators a day. As it gains experience in producing calculators, it learns how to do it better. Workers learn shortcuts and become more familiar with their equipment. With practice, the work becomes better organized, and the company finds better equipment and production processes. With higher volume, the company becomes more efficient and gains economies of scale. As a result, average cost tends to fall with accumulated production experience. This is shown in **Figure 10.4**.[8] Thus, the average cost of producing the first 100,000 calculators is US$10 per calculator. When the company has produced the first 200,000 calculators, the average cost falls to US$9. After its accumulated production experience doubles again to 400,000, the average cost is US$7. This drop in the average cost with accumulated production experience is called the **experience curve** (or the **learning curve**).

If a downward-sloping experience curve exists, this is highly significant for the company. Not only will the company's unit production cost fall, but it will fall faster if the

Experience curve (learning curve)
The drop in the average per-unit production cost that comes with accumulated production experience.

FIGURE | 10.4

Cost Per Unit as a Function of
Accumulated Production: The
Experience Curve

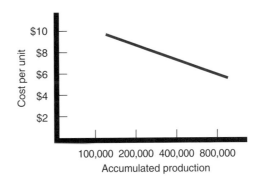

company makes and sells more during a given time period. But the market has to stand ready to buy the higher output. And to take advantage of the experience curve, the company must get a large market share early in the product's life cycle. This suggests the following pricing strategy: it should price its calculators low; its sales will then increase, and its costs will decrease through gaining more experience, and then it can lower its prices further.

However, a single-minded focus on reducing costs and exploiting the experience curve will not always work. Experience-curve pricing carries some major risks. The aggressive pricing might give the product a cheap image. The strategy also assumes that competitors are weak and not willing to fight it out by meeting the company's price cuts. Finally, while the company is building volume under one technology, a competitor may find a lower-cost technology that lets it start at prices lower than those of the market leader, who still operates on the old experience curve.

Cost-Plus Pricing

Cost-plus pricing
Adding a standard markup to the cost of the product.

The simplest pricing method is **cost-plus pricing**—adding a standard markup to the cost of the product. Construction companies, for example, submit job bids by estimating the total project cost and adding a standard markup for profit. Lawyers, accountants, and other professionals typically price by adding a standard markup to their costs. Some sellers tell their customers they will charge cost plus a specified markup; for example, aerospace companies price this way to the government.

To illustrate markup pricing, suppose a toaster manufacturer had the following costs and expected sales:

Variable costs	US$10
Fixed costs	US$300,000
Expected unit sales	US50,000

Then the manufacturer's cost per toaster is given by the following:

$$\text{Unit Cost} = \text{Variable Cost} + \frac{\text{Fixed Costs}}{\text{Unit Sales}} = \text{US\$10} + \frac{\text{US\$300,000}}{50,000} = \text{US\$16}$$

Now suppose the manufacturer wants to earn a 20 percent markup on sales. The manufacturer's markup price is given by the following:[9]

$$\text{Markup Price} = \frac{\text{Unit Cost}}{(1 - \text{Desired Return on Sales})} = \frac{\text{US\$16}}{1 - .2} = \text{US\$20}$$

The manufacturer would charge dealers US$20 per toaster and make a profit of US$4 per unit. The dealers, in turn, will mark up the toaster. If dealers want to earn 50 percent on the sales price, they will mark up the toaster to US$40 (US$20 + 50% of US$40). This number is equivalent to a *markup on cost* of 100 percent (US$20/US$20).

Does using standard markups to set prices make sense? Generally, no. Any pricing method that ignores demand and competitor prices is not likely to lead to the best price. Still, markup pricing remains popular for many reasons. First, sellers are more certain about costs than about demand. By tying the price to cost, sellers simplify pricing—they do not need to make frequent adjustments as demand changes. Secondly, when all firms in the industry use this pricing method, prices tend to be similar and price competition is thus minimized. Thirdly, many people feel that cost-plus pricing is fairer to both buyers and sellers. Sellers earn a fair return on their investment but do not take advantage of buyers when buyers' demand becomes great.

Break-even pricing (target profit pricing)
Setting price to break even on the costs of making and marketing a product, or setting price to make a target profit.

Break-Even Analysis and Target Profit Pricing

Another cost-oriented pricing approach is **break-even pricing** (or a variation called **target profit pricing**). The firm tries to determine the price at which it will break even

FIGURE | 10.5
Break-Even Chart for
Determining Target Price

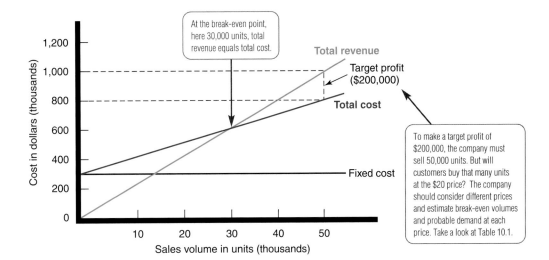

or make the target profit it is seeking. Such pricing is used by General Motors, which prices its automobiles to achieve a 15 to 20 percent profit on its investment. This pricing method is also used by public utilities, which are constrained to make a fair return on their investment.

Target pricing uses the concept of a *break-even chart*, which shows the total cost and total revenue expected at different sales volume levels. **Figure 10.5** shows a break-even chart for the toaster manufacturer discussed here. Fixed costs are US$300,000 regardless of sales volume. Variable costs are added to fixed costs to form total costs, which rise with volume. The total revenue curve starts at zero and rises with each unit sold. The slope of the total revenue curve reflects the price of US$20 per unit.

The total revenue and total cost curves cross at 30,000 units. This is the *break-even volume*. At US$20, the company must sell at least 30,000 units to break even, that is, for total revenue to cover total cost. Break-even volume can be calculated using the following formula:

$$\text{Break-Even Volume} = \frac{\text{Fixed Cost}}{\text{Price} - \text{Variable Cost}} = \frac{\text{US\$300,000}}{\text{US\$20} - \text{US\$10}} = 30,000$$

If the company wants to make a target profit, it must sell more than 30,000 units at US$20 each. Suppose the toaster manufacturer has invested US$1,000,000 in the business and wants to set price to earn a 20 percent return, or US$200,000. In that case, it must sell at least 50,000 units at US$20 each. If the company charges a higher price, it will not need to sell as many toasters to achieve its target return. But the market may not buy even this lower volume at the higher price. Much depends on the price elasticity and competitors' prices.

The manufacturer should consider different prices and estimate break-even volumes, probable demand, and profits for each. This is done in ● **Table 10.1**. The table shows that as price increases, break-even volume drops (column 2). But as price increases, demand for the toasters also falls off (column 3). At the US$14 price, because the manufacturer clears only US$4 per toaster (US$14 less US$10 in variable costs), it must sell a very high volume to break even. Even though the low price attracts many buyers, demand still falls below the high break-even point, and the manufacturer loses money. At the other extreme, with a US$22 price the manufacturer clears US$12 per toaster and must sell only 25,000 units to break even. But at this high price, consumers buy too few toasters, and profits are negative. The table shows that a price of US$18 yields the highest profits. Note that none of the prices produce the manufacturer's target profit of US$200,000. To achieve this target return, the manufacturer will have to search for ways to lower fixed or variable costs, thus lowering the break-even volume.

● TABLE | 10.1   Break-Even Volume and Profits at Different Prices

(1) Price (US$)	(2) Unit demand needed to break even	(3) Expected unit demand at given price	(4) Total revenue (US$) (1) × (3)	(5) Total costs* (US$)	(6) Profit (US$) (4) – (5)
$14	75,000	71,000	$994,000	$1,010,000	–$16,000
16	50,000	67,000	1,072,000	970,000	102,000
18	37,500	60,000	1,080,000	900,000	180,000
20	30,000	42,000	840,000	720,000	120,000
22	25,000	23,000	506,000	530,000	–24,000

*Assumes fixed costs of US$300,000 and constant unit variable costs of US$10.

> **Author Comment** Setting prices is not only based on value and costs. There are various internal and external factors that must be analyzed before making critical pricing decisions.

Other Internal and External Considerations Affecting Price Decisions (pp 276–283)

Customer perceptions of value set the upper limit for prices and costs set the lower limit. However, in setting prices within these limits, the company must consider a number of other internal and external factors. Internal factors affecting pricing include the company's overall marketing strategy, objectives, and marketing mix, as well as other organizational considerations. External factors include the nature of the market and demand, competitors' strategies and prices, and other environmental factors.

Overall Marketing Strategy, Objectives, and Mix

Price is only one element of the company's broader marketing strategy. Thus, before setting price, the company must decide on its overall marketing strategy for the product or service. If the company has selected its target market and positioning carefully, then its marketing mix strategy, including price, will be fairly straightforward. For example, when Honda developed its Acura brand to compete with European luxury-performance cars in the higher-income segment, this required charging a high price. In contrast, when it introduced the Honda Fit model its positioning required charging a low price. Thus, pricing strategy is largely determined by decisions on market positioning.

Pricing may play an important role in helping to accomplish company objectives at many levels. A firm can set prices to attract new customers or to profitably retain existing ones. It can set prices low to prevent competition from entering the market or set prices at competitors' levels to stabilize the market. It can price to keep the loyalty and support of resellers or to avoid government intervention. Prices can be reduced temporarily to create excitement for a brand. Or one product may be priced to help the sales of other products in the company's line.

Price is only one of the marketing mix tools that a company uses to achieve its marketing objectives. Price decisions must be co-ordinated with product design, distribution, and promotion decisions to form a consistent and effective integrated marketing program. Decisions made for other marketing mix variables may affect pricing decisions. For example, a decision to position the product on high-performance quality will mean that the seller must charge a higher price to cover higher costs. And producers whose resellers are expected to support and promote their products may have to build larger reseller margins into their prices.

Companies often position their products on price and then tailor other marketing mix decisions to the prices they want to charge. Here, price is a crucial product-positioning

Target costing

Pricing that starts with an ideal selling price, then targets costs that will ensure that the price is met.

factor that defines the product's market, competition, and design. Many firms support such price-positioning strategies with a technique called **target costing**, a potent strategic weapon. Target costing reverses the usual process of first designing a new product, determining its cost, and then asking, "Can we sell it for that?" Instead, it starts with an ideal selling price based on customer-value considerations and then targets costs that will ensure that the price is met. For example, when Honda set out to design the Fit, it began with a US$13,950 starting price point and 34-mpg operating efficiency firmly in mind. It then designed a stylish little car with costs that allowed it to give target customers those values.

Other companies deemphasize price and use other marketing mix tools to create *nonprice* positions. Often, the best strategy is not to charge the lowest price but rather to differentiate the marketing offer to make it worth a higher price. For example, Silkor, a laser medical center in Lebanon, charges the highest price in the market, yet succeeds in capturing 40 percent of the market share and US$52 million annual sales. This great success results from the company's understanding of its customers, who demand a unique atmosphere and special treatment. The company focuses on quality, safety, and atmosphere rather than price.

Some marketers even position their products on *high* prices, featuring high prices as part of their product's appeal (see **Real Marketing 10.2**).

Thus, marketers must consider the total marketing strategy and mix when setting prices. If the product is positioned on nonprice factors, then decisions about quality, promotion, and distribution will strongly affect price. If price is a crucial positioning factor, then price will strongly affect decisions made about the other marketing mix elements. But even when featuring price, marketers need to remember that customers rarely buy on price alone. Instead, they seek products that give them the best value in terms of benefits received for the prices paid.

Organizational Considerations

Management must decide who within the organization should set prices. Companies handle pricing in a variety of ways. In small companies, prices are often set by top management rather than by the marketing or sales departments. In large companies, pricing is typically handled by divisional or product line managers. In industrial markets, salespeople may be allowed to negotiate with customers within certain price ranges. Even so, top management sets the pricing objectives and policies, and it often approves the prices proposed by lower-level management or salespeople.

In industries in which pricing is a key factor (airlines, aerospace, steel, railroads, oil), companies often have pricing departments to set the best prices or to help others in setting them. These departments report to the marketing department or top management. Others who have an influence on pricing include sales managers, production managers, finance managers, and accountants.

The Market and Demand

As noted earlier, good pricing starts with an understanding of how customers' perceptions of value affect the prices they are willing to pay. Both consumer and industrial buyers balance the price of a product or service against the benefits of owning it. Thus, before setting prices, the marketer must understand the relationship between price and demand for the company's product. In this section, we take a deeper look at the price-demand relationship and how it varies for different types of markets. We then discuss methods for analyzing the price-demand relationship.

Pricing in Different Types of Markets

The seller's pricing freedom varies with different types of markets. Economists recognize four types of markets, each presenting a different pricing challenge.

Under *pure competition*, the market consists of many buyers and sellers trading in a uniform commodity such as wheat, copper, or financial securities. No single buyer or seller has

Real Marketing 10.2

The World Wonder, Dubai

For an example of pure luxury in the Arab world, look no further than the real-estate industry in the UAE, particularly in Dubai. Dubai has witnessed some of the most wondrous real-estate projects the world has ever seen. Many ultra-luxurious projects have been designed to attract the elites of the world to the city of Dubai, where celebrities have become property owners. The luxury collection of Dubai's real estate includes Palm Jumeirah, Jebel Ali, World Island, and Burj Khalifa. Each of these real-estate projects is a world wonder.

Palm Jumeirah is an island developed by the Emirati real-estate developer, Nakheel. The island is designed to look like a palm tree from above and consists of a collection of the most luxurious villas and apartments in the world. Jebel Ali is a project established by the same company and designed in the same palm-tree style but in a different location. Nakheel also designed the World Island, 300 islands in the shape of the world map. In 2010, Emaar, the well-established Emirati-based real-estate developer, built the tallest building in the world at 828 meters high, named the Burj Khalifa. Each of these projects represents one of the most lavish living spots in the world. To promote them, Dubai has encouraged celebrities to purchase properties and allowed them to establish their own buildings and facilities, such as golf courses.

Dubai's real-estate industry has marketed its products under the names of Formula One champions Michael Schumacher and Nikki Lauder, and golf stars Tiger Woods, Ernie Els, and Gary Player. To put its real-estate business on the world-elite level, Nakheel invited celebrities such as Brad Pitt and Angelina Jolie, the famous Hollywood couple, to the island. Moreover, world football stars, including David Beckham and 12 members of the England World Cup team are now owners of villas in Palm Jumeriah, driving attention in the UK media and attracting elite British buyers.

Dubai real-estate projects have often caught the attention of the most famous actors and sports champions. Not only that, Burj Khalifa has also attracted Giorgio Armani,

the well-known luxury fashion designer, to jointly develop with Emaar the first Armani Hotel in the tower. Armani introduced its first Armani Residence on levels 9 to 16 at Burj Khalifa. There are 144 private apartments at the Armani Residence, personally designed by Giorgio Armani himself. "Reflecting the essence of Burj Khalifa, all the homes have been designed to the highest standards and offer an unparalleled lifestyle choice for residents," the managing director of UAE, Emaar Properties, Mr Ahmad Al Matrooshi, said. The apartments are one- and two-bedroom suites that range from 100 to 200 square meters. Their prices are jaw-dropping, ranging from US$3.5 to US$9 million.

The developments in Dubai and celebrities' associations with them have had the effect of raising the status of Dubai and the price of real estate compared with other cities around the world. As of February 2009, Dubai headed the list of 59 cities in 34 "emerging countries" based on the "highest average residential property prices," setting a record price per square meter of US$7,000 as reported by Market Data, a report released by REIDIN.com, the top online information services provider. Dubai is followed by Singapore, with average price per square meter of US$6,600, then Moscow, Hong Kong, and Beijing. In addition, rental prices have soared. In February 2009, the average residential rental price in the Central Business District, downtown Dubai, was between US$17.54 and US$56.41 per square meter per month, with apartment prices in that area varying from US$3444.16 to US$9861.17. Further, the property prices had quadrupled in the five years prior to 2008 as a result of new laws entitling foreigners to own real estate and the increasing numbers of expatriate workers.

Despite that, Dubai house prices plunged by 70 percent in the year to 2009, affected by the world economic crisis, due to a lower demand for real estate and the failure of banks to continue mortgage lending. Real-estate analysts claimed that the decline in real-estate

The iconic Palm Jumeirah: A project that exemplifies the fast development of Dubai in the real-estate market.

prices was expected to continue for a considerable period of time. The decreasing prices led real-estate developers to resort to increasing their already high debt levels, reaching AED172.74 billion (US$47 billion) in 2008. Industry analysts believed that real-estate developers would seek to reduce their property stocks in order to survive the crisis.

By the end of 2009, the negative effect of the world crisis on real-estate prices in Dubai had relented. In 2009, the mean selling price in Dubai reached AED950 per square foot for apartments and AED1,000 per square foot for villas—a decline of 16 percent and 9 percent respectively year on year.

Prestigious locations such as Palm Jumeirah, an iconic development, saw their prices unaffected by the world crisis. However, other projects were adversely affected, such as Business Bay and International City, which witnessed the steepest falls (23 percent) since quarter one of 2009. Villas such as those in Jumeirah Park were subject to steep declines in selling prices (34 percent) in the first quarter of 2009, followed by Arabian Ranches, which dropped by 29 percent. Likewise, apartments experienced dramatic price declines within the same period (49 percent). Rentals, too, were negatively affected, with a decrease of 24 percent for apartments and 18 percent for villas throughout 2009.

While real-estate prices are expected to be volatile in the coming years, Dubai's luxurious real estate will continue to be recognized for its high quality.

Sources: "Celebrities Bring Stardom to Dubai Towers," *AME Info*, February 12, 2008, www.ameinfo.com/149766.html; "Burj Khalifa Readies to Welcome First Residents," *BI-ME*, February 23, 2010, www.bi-me.com; "Armani Residences, Burj Dubai—World's Tallest Tower," Verzun Property Collection, www.verzun.com; "Dubai Ranks First Among Cities With Highest Average Residential Property Prices at US$7,000 Per Square Metre," *BI-ME*, April 28, 2009, www.bi-me.com; "Dubai Home Prices May Fall 70%, Prompting Major Industry Restructure," *BI-ME*, April 22, 2009, www.bi-me.com; "Dubai Apartment and Villa Prices Stable at Year End," *BI-ME*, January 13, 2010, www.bi-me.com/main.php?id=43400&t=1&c=34&cg=4&mset=.

much effect on the going market price. A seller cannot charge more than the going price, because buyers can obtain as much as they need at that price. Nor would sellers charge less than the market price, because they can sell all they want at this price. If price and profits rise, new sellers can easily enter the market. In a purely competitive market, marketing research, product development, pricing, advertising, and sales promotion play little or no role. Thus, sellers in these markets do not spend much time on marketing strategy.

Under *monopolistic competition*, the market consists of many buyers and sellers who trade over a range of prices rather than a single market price. A range of prices occurs because sellers can differentiate their offers to buyers. Either the physical product can be varied in quality, features, or style, or the accompanying services can be varied. Buyers see differences in sellers' products and will pay different prices for them. Sellers try to develop differentiated offers for different customer segments and, in addition to price, freely use branding, advertising, and personal selling to set their offers apart. Thus, Kohler differentiates itself from dozens of other kitchen and bath fixture brands through strong branding and advertising. Its ad campaign—"The Bold Look of Kohler"—emphasizes the brand's passion for design and craftsmanship, reducing the impact of price. Because there are many competitors in such markets, each firm is less affected by competitors' pricing strategies than in oligopolistic markets.

Under *oligopolistic competition*, the market consists of a few sellers who are highly sensitive to each other's pricing and marketing strategies. The product can be uniform (steel, aluminum) or nonuniform (cars, computers). There are few sellers because it is difficult for new sellers to enter the market. Each seller is alert to competitors' strategies and moves. If a steel company slashes its price by 10 percent, buyers will quickly switch to this supplier. The other steelmakers must respond by lowering their prices or increasing their services.

In a *pure monopoly,* the market consists of one seller. The seller may be a government monopoly (e.g. the Bahrain government's postal service), a private regulated monopoly (e.g. a power company) or a private nonregulated monopoly (e.g. DuPont when it introduced nylon). Pricing is handled differently in each case. In a regulated monopoly, the government permits the company to set rates that will yield a 'fair return.' Nonregulated monopolies are free to price at what the market will bear. However, they do not always charge the full price for a number of reasons: a desire not to attract competition, a desire to penetrate the market faster with a low price, or a fear of government regulation.

Analyzing the Price-Demand Relationship

Demand curve
A curve that shows the number of units the market will buy in a given time period, at different prices that might be charged.

Each price the company might charge will lead to a different level of demand. The relationship between the price charged and the resulting demand level is shown in the **demand curve** in ◆ **Figure 10.6**. The demand curve shows the number of units the market will buy in a given time period at different prices that might be charged. In the normal case, demand and price are inversely related; that is, the higher the price, the lower the demand. Thus, the company would sell less if it raised its price from P_1 to P_2. In short, consumers with limited budgets probably will buy less of something if its price is too high.

◆FIGURE | 10.6
Demand Curves

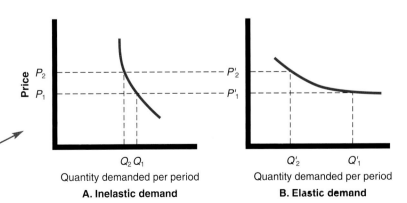

Price and demand are related—no big surprise there. Usually, higher prices result in lower demand. But in the case of some prestige goods, the relationship might be reversed. A higher price signals higher quality and status, resulting in more demand, not less.

A. Inelastic demand

B. Elastic demand

The demand curve sometimes slopes upward: Gibson was surprised to learn that its high-quality instruments didn't sell as well at lower prices.

In the case of prestige goods, the demand curve sometimes slopes upward. Consumers think that higher prices mean more quality. For example, Gibson Guitar Corporation once toyed with the idea of lowering its prices to compete more effectively with rivals such as Yamaha and Ibanez, which make cheaper guitars. To its surprise, Gibson found that its instruments didn't sell as well at lower prices. "We had an inverse [price-demand relationship]," noted Gibson's chief executive. "The more we charged, the more product we sold." At a time when other guitar manufacturers have chosen to build their instruments more quickly, cheaply, and in greater numbers, Gibson still promises guitars that "are made one-at-a-time, by hand. No shortcuts. No substitutions." It turns out that low prices simply aren't consistent with "Gibson's century-old tradition of creating investment-quality instruments that represent the highest standards of imaginative design and masterful craftsmanship."[10]

Most companies try to measure their demand curves by estimating demand at different prices. The type of market makes a difference. In a monopoly, the demand curve shows the total market demand resulting from different prices. If the company faces competition, its demand at different prices will depend on whether competitors' prices stay constant or change with the company's own prices.

Price Elasticity of Demand

Price elasticity

A measure of the sensitivity of demand to changes in price.

Marketers also need to know **price elasticity**—how responsive demand will be to a change in price. Consider the two demand curves in **Figure 10.6**. In **Figure 10.6A**, a price increase from P_1 to P_2 leads to a relatively small drop in demand from Q_1 to Q_2. In **Figure 10.6B**, however, the same price increase leads to a large drop in demand from Q'_1 to Q'_2. If demand hardly changes with a small change in price, we say the demand is *inelastic*. If demand changes greatly, we say the demand is *elastic*. The price elasticity of demand is given by the following formula:

$$\text{Price Elasticity of Demand} = \frac{\% \text{ Change in Quantity Demanded}}{\% \text{ Change in Price}}$$

Suppose demand falls by 10 percent when a seller raises its price by 2 percent. Price elasticity of demand is therefore –5 (the minus sign confirms the inverse relation between price and demand) and demand is elastic. If demand falls by 2 percent with a 2 percent increase in price, then elasticity is –1. In this case, the seller's total revenue stays the same: The seller sells fewer items but at a higher price that preserves the same total revenue. If demand falls by 1 percent when price is increased by 2 percent, then elasticity is –1/2 and demand is inelastic. The less elastic the demand, the more it pays for the seller to raise the price.

What determines the price elasticity of demand? Buyers are less price sensitive when the product they are buying is unique or when it is high in quality, prestige, or exclusiveness. They are also less price sensitive when substitute products are hard to find or when they cannot easily compare the quality of substitutes. Finally, buyers are less price sensitive when the total expenditure for a product is low relative to their income or when the cost is shared by another party.[11]

If demand is elastic rather than inelastic, sellers will consider lowering their prices. A lower price will produce more total revenue. This practice makes sense as long as the extra costs of producing and selling more do not exceed the extra revenue. At the same time, most firms want to avoid pricing that turns their products into commodities. In recent years, forces such as deregulation, dips in the economy, and the instant price comparisons afforded by the Internet and other technologies have increased consumer price sensitivity, turning products ranging from telephones and computers to new automobiles into commodities in some consumers' eyes.

Marketers need to work harder than ever to differentiate their offerings when a dozen competitors are selling virtually the same product at a comparable or lower price. More than ever, companies need to understand the price sensitivity of their customers and the trade-offs people are willing to make between price and product characteristics. In the words of marketing consultant Kevin Clancy, those who target only the price sensitive are "leaving money on the table."

Competitors' Strategies and Prices

In setting its prices, the company must also consider competitors' costs, prices, and market offerings. Consumers will base their judgments of a product's value on the prices that competitors charge for similar products. A consumer who is thinking about buying a Canon digital camera will evaluate Canon's customer value and price against the value and prices of comparable products made by Kodak, Nikon, Sony, and others.

In addition, the company's pricing strategy may affect the nature of the competition it faces. If Canon follows a high-price, high-margin strategy, it may attract competition. A low-price, low-margin strategy, however, may stop competitors or drive them out of the market. Canon needs to benchmark its costs and value against competitors' costs and value. It can then use these benchmarks as a starting point for its own pricing.

In assessing competitors' pricing strategies, the company should ask several questions. First, how does the company's market offering compare with competitors' offerings in terms of customer value? If consumers perceive that the company's product or service provides greater value, the company can charge a higher price. If consumers perceive less value relative to competing products, the company must either charge a lower price or change customer perceptions to justify a higher price.

Next, how strong are current competitors and what are their current pricing strategies? If the company faces a host of smaller competitors charging high prices relative to the value they deliver, it might charge lower prices to drive weaker competitors out of the market. If the market is dominated by larger, low-price competitors, the company may decide to target un-served market niches with value-added products at higher prices.

For example, Annie Bloom's Books, a small independent bookseller in the United States, isn't likely to win a price war against giant sellers such as Amazon.com or Barnes & Noble—it doesn't even try. Instead, the shop relies on its personal approach, cozy atmosphere, and friendly and knowledgeable staff to turn local book lovers into loyal patrons, even if they have to pay a little more. Customers writing on a consumer review website recently gave Annie Bloom's straight five-star ratings, supported by the kinds of comments you likely wouldn't see for Barnes & Noble:[12]

Pricing against larger, low-price competitors: Independent bookstore Annie Bloom's Books isn't likely to win a price war against Amazon.com or Barnes & Noble. Instead, it relies on outstanding customer service and a cozy atmosphere to turn book lovers into loyal customers.

A good bookstore can feel like a sacred place to me. Annie Bloom's is one of those places. This place radiates love. Their fine selection of books is arranged in a way that lets you know the people who work here are very interested in books, too. The air is cool and has a certain literary smell. I can't explain it. This is a bookstore where you could spend all afternoon just browsing, getting swept up into different stories and ways of thinking.

Annie Bloom's is not the biggest bookstore, nor the most convenient to park at, nor are the prices incredibly discounted, nor is the bathroom easy to find.... However, it is one of the friendliest bookstores in town. It is just big enough for a solid hour of browsing. And it has a talented, smart, and long-term staff with incredible taste. You'll find common bestsellers here, but you'll also find all those cool books that you never see featured at Barnes & Noble. [It's a] bookstore for the book crowd. Good customer service here! PS: [It] has a kid's play area in the back.

Finally, the company should ask: How does the competitive landscape influence customer price sensitivity?[13] For example, customers will be more price sensitive if they see few differences between competing products. They will buy whichever product costs the least. The more information customers have about competing products and prices before buying, the more price sensitive they will be. Easy product comparisons help customers to assess the value of different options and to decide what prices they are willing to pay. Finally, customers will be more price sensitive if they can switch easily from one product alternative to another.

What principle should guide decisions about what price to charge relative to those of competitors? The answer is simple in concept but often difficult in practice: No matter what price you charge—high, low, or in between—be certain to give customers superior value for that price.

Other External Factors

When setting prices, the company also must consider a number of other factors in its external environment. *Economic conditions* can have a strong impact on the firm's pricing strategies. Economic factors such as boom or recession, inflation, and interest rates affect pricing decisions because they affect both consumer perceptions of the product's price and value and the costs of producing a product.

The company must also consider what impact its prices will have on other parties in its environment. How will *resellers* react to various prices? The company should set prices that give resellers a fair profit, encourage their support, and help them to sell the product effectively. The *government* is another important external influence on pricing decisions. Finally, *social concerns* may need to be taken into account. For example, in the Arab world, Ramadan has a special significance for all retailers, who organize promotional campaigns and discounts to encourage high consumption.

Ramadan is a holy month, whereby all Muslims around the world fast, and accordingly, consumers' behavior changes significantly. People consume more products and buy in large quantities during this month. For this reason, companies and all types of retailers, especially groceries, supermarkets, and hypermarkets, increase stocks of all products and offer appealing promotions to encourage consumers to buy more. Governments in the region ensure that prices are low during Ramadan, because the high demand could push up inflation. This indicates that retailers and companies are not fully in control of pricing during the month.

According to Dr Hashim Al Nuaimi, director of the Consumer Protection Department in the UAE, retailers are urged by the ministry to reduce prices and provide bargain offers. Moreover, the government organizes a committee during Ramadan that is responsible for price monitoring as well as inspection visits. This committee also collects feedback from customers in order to ensure that price regulations are implemented consistently across the country.[14] This system exists in many countries in the region, including Bahrain, where Prime Minister Shaikh Khalifa Bin Salman has ordered inspection teams to take action against stores that raise food prices during Ramadan.[15]

In Egypt, some retailers and food and beverage companies use Ramadan to market their products through aggressive discounts and attractive promotions because they rely on bulk purchasing. Meanwhile, other retailers increase their prices. In 2009, the Consumer Protection Association stated that there was a clear decline in the average prices of most food commodities during Ramadan. Thirteen food products recorded a significant decline in price in retail outlets, including edible oils (38 percent), flour (25 percent), natural and manufactured butter and packaged beans (17 percent), eggs (24 percent), and meat (12 percent), among others. On the other hand, some products recorded an increase in price, led by sauces (18 percent). As for retailers in Egypt, there was a huge gap between the requirements of consumer associations and the implementation at various supermarket chains, which continued to raise their prices during Ramadan in spite of the government's restrictions.[16] Similarly, in Saudi Arabia, prices of fruit and vegetables doubled in some retail stores.[17]

Generally, in the Arab world, it is advisable to offer low prices during Ramadan in order to attract consumers and keep good relations with governments. Despite some special cases of price increases, there is a trend in the Arab world to maintain lower prices during Ramadan to show generosity and to emphasize the spirit of the holy month.

In setting prices, a company's short-term sales, market share, and profit goals may need to be tempered by broader societal considerations. We will examine public policy issues in pricing later in this chapter.

So far in this chapter, you have learned that price is an important marketing mix tool for both creating and capturing customer value. You have explored the many internal and external factors that affect a firm's pricing decisions and examined three general approaches to setting prices. In this section, we'll look at pricing strategies available to marketers—new-product pricing strategies, product mix pricing strategies, price adjustment strategies, and price reaction strategies.

> **Author Comment** | Pricing new products can be especially challenging. Just think about all the things you'd have to consider in pricing a new cellphone, say the first Apple iPhone. What's more, you'd have to start thinking about the price—along with many other marketing considerations—at the very beginning of the design process.

New-Product Pricing Strategies (pp 283–284)

Pricing strategies usually change as the product passes through its life cycle. The introductory stage is especially challenging. Companies bringing out a new product face the challenge of setting prices for the first time. They can choose between two broad strategies: *market-skimming pricing* and *market-penetration pricing*.

Market-Skimming Pricing

Market-skimming pricing
Setting a high price for a new product to skim maximum revenues layer by layer from the segments willing to pay the high price; the company makes fewer but more profitable sales.

Many companies that invent new products set high initial prices to 'skim' revenues layer by layer from the market. Sony frequently uses this strategy, called **market-skimming pricing** (or **price skimming**). When Sony introduced the world's first high-definition television (HDTV) to the Japanese market in 1990, the high-tech sets cost US$43,000. These televisions were purchased only by customers who really wanted the new technology and could afford to pay a high price for it. Sony rapidly reduced the price over the next several years to attract new buyers. By 1993 a 28-inch HDTV cost a Japanese buyer just over US$6,000. In 2001, a Japanese consumer could buy a 40-inch HDTV for about US$2,000, a price that many more customers could afford. An entry-level HDTV set now sells for less than US$500 in many countries, and prices continue to fall. In this way, Sony skimmed the maximum amount of revenue from the various segments of the market.[18]

Market skimming makes sense only under certain conditions. First, the product's quality and image must support its higher price and enough buyers must want the product at that price. Secondly, the costs of producing a smaller volume cannot be so high that they cancel the advantage of charging more. Finally, competitors should not be able to enter the market easily and undercut the high price.

Market-Penetration Pricing

Market-penetration pricing
Setting a low price for a new product in order to attract a large number of buyers and a large market share.

Rather than setting a high initial price to skim off small but profitable market segments, some companies use **market-penetration pricing**. They set a low initial price in order to *penetrate* the market quickly and deeply—to attract a large number of buyers quickly and win a large market share. The high sales volume results in falling costs, allowing the companies to cut their prices even further. For example, Dell used penetration pricing to enter the personal computer market, selling high-quality computer products through lower-cost direct channels. Its sales increased fast when HP, Apple, and other competitors selling through retail stores could not match its prices. And giant electronics retailer Sharaf DG used penetration pricing to boost its success in the GCC market:

The bigger, the better. That has been the mantra at Sharaf DG: It may be a hard-headed world of electronics, but even if you are looking for a functional laptop or a business-brained BlackBerry, you automatically get drawn into the pleasurable world of a 'feel-good' shopping experience. Sharaf DG's brand proposition is: Go big on range, value, and service. And, of course, space.

Electronics retailer Sharaf DG used penetration pricing to boost its success in the GCC market.

An offshoot of the Sharaf Group set up in 1976 by Ibrahim Sharaf and Sharafuddin Sharaf (the group had interests in shipping, logistics, fashion retail, and the travel trade), Sharaf DG came into its own in 2004 when it was decided that the group's high-street retail chain of electronics goods, Sharaf Enterprises, needed a leg-up. "After studying various international formats from Europe, the U.S., the Far East and Japan, we decided on the big-box store—or the destination store format," recalls CEO Nilesh Khalkho.

Along with space, there was the trio of range, value, and service factored in. "When we say range, we mean width and depth," Llewellyn Couto, manager, marketing and communications, explains. "In the LCD TV segment alone, for instance, we have 147 options—not just brands, but the entire array of each brand."

To keep up with the value clause, a dedicated team does price surveys all across the marketplace, so that Sharaf DG's prices can be kept the lowest. The idea is to bust the perception that hypermarkets have the best deals going. "If hypermarkets have to sell stuff cheaper than we do, they would have to change their business model—which they can't," adds Khalkho.

Sharaf DG has been known to offer discounts of between 25 and 50 percent on leading electronics brands during the Dubai Shopping Festival. Not surprisingly, Sharaf DG's main consumer attractions are its pricing strategies, summarized in the slogans: "If you don't find it at Sharaf DG, you get it free" and "Lowest price guaranteed."[19]

Several conditions must be met for this low-price strategy to work. First, the market must be highly price sensitive so that a low price produces more market growth. Secondly, production and distribution costs must fall as sales volume increases. Finally, the low price must help keep out the competition, and the penetration pricer must maintain its low-price position—otherwise, the price advantage may be only temporary.

> **Author Comment** | Most individual products are part of a broader product mix and must be priced accordingly. For example, Gillette prices its Fusion razors low. But once you buy the razor, you're a captive customer for its higher-margin replacement cartridges.

Product Mix Pricing Strategies (pp 284–286)

The strategy for setting a product's price often has to be changed when the product is part of a product mix. In this case, the firm looks for a set of prices that maximizes the profits on the total product mix. Pricing is difficult because the various products have related demand and costs and face different degrees of competition. We now take a closer look at the five product mix pricing situations summarized in ● **Table 10.2**: *product line pricing, optional-product pricing, captive-product pricing, by-product pricing,* and *product bundle pricing.*

Product Line Pricing

Companies usually develop product lines rather than single products. For example, Masafi Juice offers some 15 different juice drinks in three sizes at prices ranging from under

● TABLE | 10.2 Product Mix Pricing Strategies

Strategy	Description
Product line pricing	Setting prices across an entire product line
Optional-product pricing	Pricing optional or accessory products sold with the main product
Captive-product pricing	Pricing products that must be used with the main product
By-product pricing	Pricing low-value by-products to get rid of them
Product bundle pricing	Pricing bundles of products sold together

Product line pricing
Setting the price steps between various products in a product line based on cost differences between the products, customer evaluations of different features, and competitors' prices.

US$0.50 to US$2.50. In **product line pricing**, management must decide on the price steps to set between the various products in a line.

The price steps should take into account cost differences between the products in the line. More importantly, they should account for differences in customer perceptions of the value of different features. For example, Masafi sells its 1 liter PET juice pack at US$1.37 and its 1 liter TETRA juice pack for US$2.20. Although the cost of the juice in both pack types is the same, the price difference is due to the added value of the TETRA packs. Masafi's task is to establish perceptions of value of the two types of pack that support the price difference.

Optional-Product Pricing

Optional-product pricing
The pricing of optional or accessory products along with a main product.

Many companies use **optional-product pricing**—offering to sell optional or accessory products along with their main product. Refrigerators come with optional ice makers. And when you order a new PC, you can select from a huge choice of hard drives, docking systems, software options, service plans, and carrying cases.

Optional-product pricing is evident in the way automobile prices are quoted. Automobile dealers almost always advertise the basic model of the vehicle. However, when a consumer visits the showroom, most of the space is dedicated to vehicles with full options and higher prices. The basic model is stripped of so many conveniences and optional extras that most buyers choose at least some of those optional extras and hence end up paying a higher price than anticipated.

Captive-Product Pricing

Captive-product pricing
Setting a price for products that must be used along with a main product, such as blades for a razor and film for a camera.

Companies that make products that must be used along with a main product are using **captive-product pricing**. Examples of captive products are razor blade cartridges, video games, and printer cartridges. Producers of the main products (razors, video game consoles, and printers) often price them low and set high markups on the supplies. For example, Gillette sells low-priced razors but makes money on the replacement cartridges. You can buy a Gillette Fusion razor with a replacement cartridge and storage case for under US$8.50. But once you've bought the razor, you're committed to buying replacement cartridges at US$24.95 an eight-pack. Companies that use captive-product pricing must be careful—consumers trapped into buying expensive supplies may come to resent the brand that trapped them.

In the case of services, this captive-product pricing is called *two-part pricing*. The price of the service is broken into a *fixed fee* plus a *variable usage rate*. Many mobile phone companies charge a flat rate for a basic calling plan, then charge for minutes over what the plan allows. The service firm must decide how much to charge for the basic service and how much for the variable usage. The fixed amount should be low enough to persuade customers to buy into the service; profit can be made on the variable fees.

By-Product Pricing

Producing products and services often generates by-products. If the by-products have no value and if getting rid of them is costly, this will affect the pricing of the main product.

By-product pricing
Setting a price for by-products in order to make the main product's price more competitive.

Using **by-product pricing**, the company seeks a market for these by-products to help offset the costs of disposing of them and to help make the price of the main product more competitive. The by-products themselves can even turn out to be profitable.

For example, Shell is developing innovative ways to use sulphur, a by-product of natural gas production. Shell in Qatar is using sulphur to replace cement in concrete and also to replace some of the bitumen used in asphalt, an important material used in road construction. The profits that Shell makes from its uses of sulphur will help it to keep a competitive price on the natural gas it sells.

Product Bundle Pricing

Product bundle pricing
Combining several products and offering the bundle at a reduced price.

Using **product bundle pricing**, sellers often combine several of their products and offer the bundle at a reduced price. For example, fast-food restaurants like McDonald's bundle burger, fries, and a cold drink at a 'combo' price. Resorts sell specially priced vacation packages that include airfare, accommodations, meals, and entertainment. And Zain, Etisalat, and other cable companies bundle cable service, phone service, and high-speed Internet connections at a low combined price. Price bundling can promote the sales of products consumers might not otherwise buy, but the combined price must be low enough to get them to buy the bundle.[20]

> **Author Comment** | Setting the base price for a product is only the start. The company must then adjust the price to adjust for customer and situational differences. When was the last time you paid the full suggested retail price for something?

Price-Adjustment Strategies (pp 286–292)

Companies usually adjust their basic prices to account for various customer differences and changing situations. Here we examine the seven price adjustment strategies summarized in ● **Table 10.3**: *discount and allowance pricing, segmented pricing, psychological pricing, promotional pricing, geographical pricing, dynamic pricing,* and *international pricing.*

Discount and Allowance Pricing

Most companies adjust their basic price to reward customers for certain responses, such as early payment of bills, volume purchases, and off-season buying. These price adjustments—called *discounts* and *allowances*—can take many forms.

Discount
A straight reduction in price on purchases during a stated period of time.

The many forms of **discounts** include a *cash discount*, a price reduction to buyers who pay their bills promptly. A *quantity discount* is a price reduction to buyers who buy large volumes. Such discounts provide an incentive to the customer to buy more from one given seller, rather than from many different sources.

A *functional discount* (also called a *trade discount*) is offered by the seller to trade-channel members who perform certain functions, such as selling, storing, and record keeping. A *seasonal discount* is a price reduction to buyers who buy merchandise or services out of season. For example, many hotels and airlines will offer reduced prices outside of peak tourist season. Seasonal discounts may help the seller to keep production steady during an entire year.

● **TABLE | 10.3** Price Adjustment Strategies

Strategy	Description
Discount and allowance pricing	Reducing prices to reward customer responses such as paying early or promoting the product
Segmented pricing	Adjusting prices to allow for differences in customers, products, or locations
Psychological pricing	Adjusting prices for psychological effect
Promotional pricing	Temporarily reducing prices to increase short-run sales
Geographical pricing	Adjusting prices to account for the geographic location of customers
Dynamic pricing	Adjusting prices continually to meet the characteristics and needs of individual customers and situations
International pricing	Adjusting prices for international markets

Segmented Pricing

Segmented pricing
Selling a product or service at two or more prices, where the difference in prices is not based on differences in costs.

Companies will often adjust their basic prices to allow for differences in customers, products, and locations. In **segmented pricing**, the company sells a product or service at two or more prices, even though the difference in prices is not based on differences in costs.

Segmented pricing takes several forms. Under *customer-segment* pricing, different customers pay different prices for the same product or service. Museums, for example, may charge a lower admission for students and senior citizens. Under *product-form pricing*, different versions of the product are priced differently but not according to differences in their costs. For instance, a 1 liter bottle (about 34 ounces) of Evian mineral water may cost US$1.59 at your local supermarket. But a 5-ounce aerosol can of Evian Brumisateur Mineral Water Spray sells for a suggested retail price of US$11.39 at beauty boutiques and spas. The water is all from the same source in the French Alps and the aerosol packaging costs little more than the plastic bottles. Yet you pay about 5 cents an ounce for one form and US$2.28 an ounce for the other.

Using *location pricing*, a company charges different prices for different locations, even though the cost of offering each location is the same. For instance, cinema halls vary their seat prices because of audience preferences for certain locations. Finally, using *time pricing*, a firm varies its price by the season, the month, the day, and even the hour. Some public utilities vary their prices to commercial users by time of day and weekend versus weekday. Segmented pricing goes by many names. Robert Cross, a longtime consultant to the airlines, calls it *revenue management*. According to Cross, the practice ensures that "companies will sell the right product to the right consumer at the right time for the right price."[21] Airlines, hotels, and restaurants call it *yield management* and practice it religiously.

Product-form pricing: Evian water in a 1 liter bottle might cost you 5 cents an ounce at your local supermarket, whereas the same water might cost US$2.28 an ounce when sold in 5 ounce aerosol cans as Evian Brumisateur Mineral Water Spray moisturizer.

The airlines, for example, routinely set prices hour-by-hour—even minute-by-minute—depending on seat availability, demand, and competitor price changes. Thus, the price you pay for a given seat on a given flight might vary greatly depending not just on class of service, but also on when and where you buy the ticket. Furthermore, the person sitting next to you might have paid half that price or twice as much.

For segmented pricing to be an effective strategy, certain conditions must exist. The market must be segmentable, and the segments must show different degrees of demand. The costs of segmenting and watching the market cannot exceed the extra revenue obtained from the price difference. Of course, the segmented pricing must also be legal.

Most importantly, segmented prices should reflect real differences in customers' perceived value. Consumers in higher price tiers must feel that they're getting their extra money's worth for the higher prices paid. By the same token, companies must be careful not to treat customers in lower price tiers as second-class citizens. Otherwise, in the long run, the practice will lead to customer resentment and ill will. For example, in recent years, the airlines have angered customers at both ends of the airplane. Passengers paying full fare for business- or first-class seats often feel that they are being overcharged. At the same time, passengers in lower-priced economy-class seats feel that they're being ignored or abused. In all, the airlines today face many very difficult pricing issues.

Psychological Pricing

Psychological pricing
A pricing approach that considers the psychology of prices and not simply the economics; the price is used to say something about the product.

Price says something about the product. For example, many consumers use price to judge quality. A US$100 bottle of perfume may contain only US$5 worth of scent, but some people are willing to pay the US$100 because this price indicates something special.

In using **psychological pricing**, sellers consider the psychology of prices and not simply the economics. For example, consumers usually perceive higher-priced products as having higher quality. When they can judge the quality of a product by examining it or by calling on past experience with it, they use price less to judge quality. But when they cannot judge quality because they lack the information or skill, price becomes an important quality signal.

Reference prices
Prices that buyers carry in their minds and refer to when they look at a given product.

Another aspect of psychological pricing is **reference prices**—prices that buyers carry in their minds and refer to when looking at a given product. The reference price might be formed by noting current prices, remembering past prices, or assessing the buying situation. Sellers can influence or use these consumers' reference prices when setting price. For example, a company could display its product next to more expensive ones in order to imply that it belongs in the same class. Department stores often sell women's clothing in separate departments differentiated by price: Clothing found in the more expensive department is assumed to be of better quality.

For most purchases, consumers don't have all the skill or information they need to figure out whether they are paying a good price. They don't have the time, ability, or inclination to research different brands or stores, compare prices, and get the best deals. Instead, they may rely on certain cues that signal whether a price is high or low. Interestingly, such pricing cues are often provided by sellers:[22]

It's Saturday morning and you stop by your local supermarket to pick up a few items for tonight's party. Walking through the aisles, you're bombarded with prices. But are they good prices? If you're like most shoppers, you don't really know. So to help you out, retailers themselves give you a host of subtle and not-so-subtle signals telling you whether a given price is relatively high or low. For example, *sales signs* shout out "Sale!", "Reduced", or "Now 2 for only…!" *Prices ending in 9* let you know that the product has to be a bargain. You probably know a good price on a 12-pack of Coke when you see one, so a low price there suggests that the store's other prices must be low as well. A *price-matching guarantee* also suggests that one store's prices are lower than another's—how else could they make such a promise?

Are such pricing signals really helpful hints, or are they just retailer ploys? These tactics certainly work for the retailer. For example, research shows that the word *sale* beside a price (even without actually varying the price) can increase demand by more than 50 percent. But do these signals really help customers? The answer, often, is yes—careful buyers really can take advantage of such cues to find good buys. And if used properly, retailers can use such tactics to provide useful price information to their customers, building more solid customer relationships. Used improperly, however, they can mislead consumers, tarnishing a brand and damaging customer relationships.

Even small differences in price can signal product differences. Consider a mobile phone priced at US$300 compared with one priced at US$299.99. The actual price difference is only US$0.01, but the psychological difference can be much greater. For example, some consumers will see the US$299.99 as a price in the US$200 range rather than the US$300 range. The US$299.99 will more likely be seen as a bargain price, whereas the US$300 price suggests more quality.

Promotional Pricing

Promotional pricing
Temporarily pricing products below the list price, and sometimes even below cost, to increase short-run sales.

With **promotional pricing**, companies will temporarily price their products below list price and sometimes even below cost to create buying excitement and urgency. Promotional pricing takes several forms. A seller may simply offer *discounts* from normal prices to increase sales and reduce inventories. Sellers also use *special-event pricing* in certain seasons to draw more customers. Manufacturers sometimes offer *cash rebates* to consumers.

Retailers in Dubai have transformed their approach in keeping with the spirit of Ramadan. For example, most malls, hypermarkets, and grocery stores now offer late-night opening hours up to 1.00 am. They may launch promotions to encourage sales during the holiest period on the Islamic calendar. For some retailers and food manufacturers, Ramadan creates 12 to 20 per cent of their annual sales, with consumers focusing on foodstuffs, garments, and household and gift items. For example, LuLu Hypermarkets has created a special Ramadan kit of 20 products, including essentials such as rice, sugar, tea, milk powder, and oil, sold at a price 15 percent cheaper than normal.[23] Retailers also encourage charity initiatives during the month-long religious observance.

Some manufacturers offer *low-interest financing*, *longer warranties*, or *free maintenance* to reduce the consumer's 'price.' This practice has become another favorite of the car industry. Rebates have been popular with car makers and producers of durable goods and small appliances, but they are also used with consumer packaged goods. For example, Al Rostamani Trading Co. in Ramadan 2009 offered to beat any offers or promotions for Japanese car brands on its Suzuki cars over the Ramadan period. This promotion offered to beat any offers in maintenance, insurance, payments, or accessories, provided there was a match with other Japanese cars of the same specification.[24]

Promotional pricing, however, can have adverse effects. Used too frequently and copied by competitors, price promotions can create customers who wait until brands go on sale before buying them. Or, constantly reduced prices can damage a brand's value in the eyes of customers. Marketers sometimes become addicted to promotional pricing, using price promotions as a quick fix instead of working through the difficult process of developing effective longer-term strategies for building their brands. The use of promotional pricing can also lead to industry price wars. Such price wars usually play into the hands of only one or a few competitors—those with the most efficient operations. For example, in the face of intense competition with Intel, computer chip maker Advanced Micro Devices (AMD) began to aggressively reduce its prices. Intel retaliated with even lower prices. In the resulting price war, AMD has seen its margins and profits drop significantly against those of its larger rival.[25]

Promotional pricing: Companies offer promotional prices to create buying excitement and urgency.

The point is that promotional pricing can be an effective means of generating sales for some companies in certain circumstances. But it can be damaging for other companies or if done regularly and frequently.

Geographical Pricing

A company also must decide how to price its products for customers located in different parts of the country or world. Should the company risk losing the business of more-distant customers by charging them higher prices to cover the higher shipping costs? Or should the company charge all customers the same prices regardless of location? We will look at five **geographical pricing** strategies for the following hypothetical situation:

Geographical pricing

Setting prices for customers located in different parts of the country or world.

The Afdal Paper Company is located in Jeddah, Saudi Arabia, and sells paper products to customers all over the Gulf Cooperation Council (GCC) countries. The cost of freight is high and affects the companies from whom customers buy their paper. Afdal wants to establish a geographical pricing policy. It is trying to determine how to price a US$15,000 order for 10 tons of facial tissue to three specific customers: Customer A (Abu Dhabi), Customer B (Manama, Bahrain), and Customer C (Amman, Jordan).

One option is for Afdal to ask each customer to pay the shipping cost from the Jeddah factory to the customer's location. All three customers would pay the same factory price of US$1,500 per ton of facial tissue, but with Customer A paying, say, US$100 per ton for shipping, Customer B US$150 per ton, and Customer C US$250 per ton.

FOB-origin pricing
A geographical pricing strategy in which goods are placed free on board a carrier; the customer pays the freight from the factory to the destination.

Uniform-delivered pricing
A geographical pricing strategy in which the company charges the same price plus freight to all customers, regardless of their location.

Zone pricing
A geographical pricing strategy in which the company sets up two or more zones. All customers within a zone pay the same total price; the more distant the zone, the higher the price.

Basing-point pricing
A geographical pricing strategy in which the seller designates some city as a basing point and charges all customers the freight cost from that city to the customer.

Freight-absorption pricing
A geographical pricing strategy in which the seller absorbs all or part of the freight charges in order to get the desired business.

Called **FOB-origin pricing,** this practice means that the goods are placed *free on board* (hence, *FOB*) a carrier. At that point the title and responsibility pass to the customer, who pays the freight from the factory to the destination. Because each customer picks up its own cost, supporters of FOB pricing feel that this is the fairest way to manage freight charges. The disadvantage, however, is that Afdal will be a high-cost firm to distant customers.

Uniform-delivered pricing is the opposite of FOB pricing. Here, the company charges the same price plus freight to all customers, regardless of their location. The freight charge is set at the average freight cost. Suppose this is US$150. Uniform-delivered pricing therefore results in a higher charge to the Abu Dhabi customer (who pays US$150 freight instead of US$100) and a lower charge to the Amman customer (who pays US$150 instead of US$250). Although the Abu Dhabi customer would prefer to buy paper from another local paper company that uses FOB-origin pricing, Afdal has a better chance of winning over the Amman customer. Other advantages of uniform-delivered pricing are that it is fairly easy to administer and it lets the firm advertise its price nationally.

Zone pricing falls between FOB-origin pricing and uniform-delivered pricing. The company sets up two or more zones. All customers within a given zone pay a single total price; the more distant the zone, the higher the price. For example, Afdal might set up a GCC Zone and charge US$100 freight to all customers in this zone; a Levant Zone in which it charges US$250; and a Saudi Zone in which it charges US$75. In this way, the customers within a given price zone receive no price advantage from the company. Using **basing-point pricing**, the seller selects a given city as a "basing point" and charges all customers the freight cost from that city to the customer location, regardless of the city to which the goods are actually shipped.

Finally, the seller who is anxious to do business with a certain customer or geographical area might use **freight-absorption pricing**. Using this strategy, the seller absorbs all or part of the actual freight charges in order to get the desired business. The seller might reason that if it can get more business, its average costs will fall and more than compensate for its extra freight cost. Freight-absorption pricing is used for market penetration and to hold on to increasingly competitive markets.

Dynamic Pricing

The Arab world has been a trading route for thousands of years. Silk from China and spices from India were traded in these markets for frankincense. Throughout most of history, prices were set by negotiation between buyers and sellers. Even now, prices are negotiated in the Souq or traditional markets in most countries in the Middle East. In these Souqs one can negotiate the price of products ranging from the latest high-tech electronic items to traditional spices.

Fixed price policies—setting one price for all buyers—are a relatively modern idea that arose with the development of large-scale retailing at the end of the nineteenth century in the Western world. In the Arab world, fixed price pricing has come into practice in the last 50 years. Today, most prices are set this way. However, some companies are now reversing the fixed pricing trend. They are using **dynamic pricing**—adjusting prices continually to meet the characteristics and needs of individual customers and situations.

Dynamic pricing
Adjusting prices continually to meet the characteristics and needs of individual customers and situations.

For example, think about how the Internet has affected pricing. From the mostly fixed pricing practices of the past century, the web seems now to be taking us back—into a new age of fluid pricing. The flexibility of the Internet allows web sellers to instantly and constantly adjust prices on a wide range of goods based on demand dynamics. In many cases, this involves regular changes in the prices that web sellers set for their goods. In others, such as eBay, Priceline, and Souq.com, consumers negotiate the final prices they pay.

"The fundamental principle behind Souq.com's success over the past 5 years has been its complete, end-to-end service offering for both buyers and sellers," said Ronaldo Mouchawar, CEO of Souq.com. "It offers marketing, buying, selling, electronic payment and product pickup/delivery from one easy to use, completely secure location,

Internet-based companies such as eBay and Souq.com are able to offer dynamic pricing to attract customers.

enabling both individuals and businesses to sell their goods and services to millions of online users easily. For example, one of the many hurdles to broader e-commerce adoption regionally has been the lack of availability of alternative payment methods to credit cards. At Souq.com, we integrated a prepaid card payment method (cashU) which is an Internet payment service that allows users to purchase CashU credit and pay for items online safely and without the use of credit cards. We also developed Souq SafePay, which is the only service of its kind to secure and verify all transactions between buyer and seller, providing 100% guaranteed transactional security for that extra peace of mind. For users who don't want to part with their cash until they receive their goods, we also offer a 'Cash on Delivery' service where cash payment is made to the courier upon delivery of goods."[26]

Dynamic pricing offers many advantages for marketers. For example, Internet sellers such as Amazon.com can use their databases to predict a specific shopper's desires, measure his or her spending habits, instantly tailor products to fit that shopper's behavior, and price products accordingly. Catalog retailers doing business on the web can change prices instantly according to changes in demand or costs, changing prices for specific items on a day-by-day or even hour-by-hour basis.

Buyers also benefit from the web and dynamic pricing. A wealth of price comparison sites—such as Ostamyy.com and docstoc.com in the Arab world, as well as Yahoo! Shopping, Bizrate.com, NexTag.com, Epinions.com, PriceGrabber.com, mySimon.com, and PriceScan.com—offer instant product and price comparisons from thousands of vendors.

Buyers can also negotiate prices at online auction sites and exchanges. Suddenly the centuries-old art of haggling is back in fashion. Want to sell that antique carpet that's been collecting dust for generations? Post it on eBay, the world's biggest online flea market. Want to name your own price for a hotel room or rental car? Visit Priceline.com or another reverse auction site.

Dynamic pricing can also be controversial. Most customers would find it annoying to learn that the person in the next seat on that flight paid 10 percent less just because he or she happened to call at the right time or buy through the right sales channel. Amazon.com learned this some years ago when it experimented with lowering prices to new customers in order to win their business. When regular customers learned through Internet chatter that they were paying generally higher prices than first-timers, they protested loudly. An embarrassed Amazon.com halted the experiments.

Dynamic pricing makes sense in many contexts—it adjusts prices according to market forces, and it often works to the benefit of the customer. But marketers need to be careful not to use dynamic pricing to take advantage of certain customer groups, damaging important customer relationships.

International Pricing

Companies that market their products internationally must decide what prices to charge in the different countries in which they operate. In some cases, a company can set a uniform worldwide price. For example, Boeing sells its jetliners at about the same price everywhere, whether in the United States, Europe, the Arab world, or elsewhere. However, most companies adjust their prices to reflect local market conditions and cost considerations.

The price that a company should charge in a specific country depends on many factors, including economic conditions, competitive situations, laws and regulations, and development of the wholesaling and retailing system. Consumer perceptions and preferences also may vary from country to country, calling for different prices. Or the company may have different marketing objectives in various world markets, which require changes in pricing strategy. For example, Samsung might introduce a new product into mature markets in highly developed countries with the goal of quickly gaining mass-market share—this would call for a penetration-pricing strategy. In contrast, it might enter a less-developed market by targeting smaller, less price-sensitive segments; in this case, market-skimming pricing makes sense.

Cost plays an important role in setting international prices. People traveling abroad are often surprised to find that goods that are inexpensive at home may be expensive in other countries. A pair of Levi's jeans selling for US$50 in Saudi Arabia might go for US$63 in Tokyo and US$88 in Paris. A McDonald's Big Mac selling for US$4.25 in Kuwait might cost US$7.50 in Reykjavik, Iceland; and an Oral-B toothbrush selling for US$3 in Abu Dhabi might cost US$10 in China. Conversely, a Gucci handbag costing only US$140 in Milan, Italy, might fetch US$300 in Jeddah. In some cases, such price increases may result from differences in selling strategies or market conditions. In most cases, however, it is simply due to the higher cost of selling in another country—including wages, rents, import duties, cost of product modifications, shipping and insurance, exchange rate fluctuations, and distribution costs. Thus, international pricing presents some special problems and complexities.

Author Comment | When and how should a company change its price? What if costs rise, putting the squeeze on profits? What if the economy sags and customers become more price-sensitive? Or what if a major competitor raises or drops its prices? As Figure 10.7 suggests, companies face many price-changing options.

Price Changes (pp 292–294)

After developing their pricing structures and strategies, companies often face situations in which they must initiate price changes or respond to price changes by competitors.

Initiating Price Changes

In some cases, the company may find it desirable to initiate either a price cut or a price increase. In both cases, it must anticipate possible buyer and competitor reactions.

Initiating Price Cuts

Several situations may lead a firm to consider cutting its price. One such circumstance is excess capacity. Another is falling demand in the face of strong price competition. In such cases, the firm may aggressively cut prices to boost sales and share. But as the airline, fast-food, automobile, and other industries have learned in recent years, cutting prices in an industry loaded with excess capacity may lead to price wars as competitors try to hold on to market share.

A company may also cut prices in a drive to dominate the market through lower costs. Either the company starts with lower costs than its competitors, or it cuts prices in the hope of gaining market share that will further cut costs through larger volume. Carrefour used this strategy to become the Gulf's largest retailer.

Initiating Price Increases

A successful price increase can greatly improve profits. For example, if the company's profit margin is 3 percent of sales, a 1 percent price increase will boost profits by 33 percent if sales volume is unaffected. A major factor in price increases is cost inflation. Rising

Initiating price increases: Rising crude oil prices and overdemand have led to rapidly rising gasoline prices, resulting in charges that the major oil companies are enriching themselves by exploiting customers.

costs squeeze profit margins and lead companies to pass cost increases along to customers. Another factor leading to price increases is overdemand: When a company cannot supply all that its customers need, it may raise its prices, ration products to customers, or both. Consider the worldwide oil price, which started from mid US$40 in 2007 and went up to over US$130 per barrel in 2008, mainly due to high global demand for oil.

When raising prices, the company must avoid being perceived as an opportunistic profiteer. For example, facing rapidly rising gasoline prices, angry customers are accusing the major oil companies of enriching themselves at the expense of consumers. Customers have long memories, and they will eventually turn away from companies or even whole industries that they perceive as charging excessive prices. In the extreme, claims of price for profiteering may even bring about increased government regulation.

There are some techniques for avoiding these problems. One is to maintain a sense of fairness surrounding any price increase. Price increases should be supported by company communications telling customers why prices are being raised. Making low-visibility price moves first is also a good technique: Some examples include dropping discounts, increasing minimum order sizes, and curtailing production of low-margin products. The company sales force should help business customers find ways to economize.

Wherever possible, the company should consider ways to meet higher costs or demand without raising prices. For example, it can consider more cost-effective ways to produce or distribute its products. It can shrink the product or substitute less-expensive ingredients instead of raising the price. Or it can 'unbundle' its market offering, removing features, packaging, or services and separately pricing elements that were formerly part of the offer.

Buyer Reactions to Price Changes

Customers do not always interpret price changes in a straightforward way. A price *increase*, which would normally lower sales, may have some positive meanings for buyers. For example, what would you think if Rolex *raised* the price of its latest watch model? On the one hand, you might think that the watch is even more exclusive or better made. On the other hand, you might think that Rolex is simply being greedy by charging what the customers will pay.

Similarly, consumers may view a price *cut* in several ways. For example, what would you think if Rolex were to suddenly cut its prices? You might think that you are getting a better deal on an exclusive product. More likely, however, you'd think that quality had been reduced, and the brand's luxury image might be tarnished.

Competitor Reactions to Price Changes

A firm considering a price change must worry about the reactions of its competitors as well as those of its customers. Competitors are most likely to react when the number of firms involved is small, when the product is uniform, and when the buyers are well informed about products and prices.

How can the firm anticipate the likely reactions of its competitors? The problem is complex because, like the customer, the competitor can interpret a company price cut in many ways. It might think the company is trying to grab a larger market share, or that it's doing badly and trying to boost its sales. Or it might think that the company wants the whole industry to cut prices to increase total demand.

The company must guess each competitor's likely reaction. If all competitors behave alike, this amounts to analyzing only a typical competitor. In contrast, if the competitors do not behave alike—perhaps because of differences in size, market shares, or policies—then separate analyzes are necessary. However, if some competitors will match the price change, there is good reason to expect that the rest will also match it.

Responding to Price Changes

Here we reverse the question and ask how a firm should respond to a price change by a competitor. The firm needs to consider several issues: Why did the competitor change the

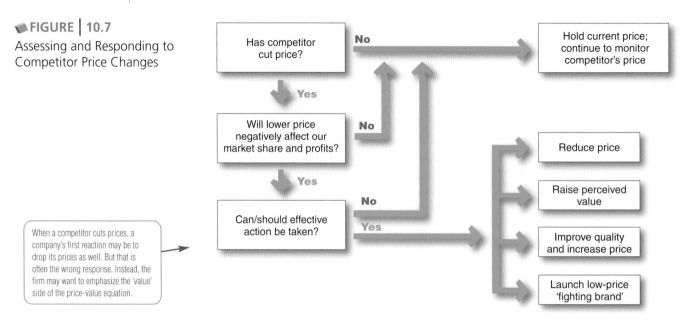

Assessing and Responding to
Competitor Price Changes

When a competitor cuts prices, a company's first reaction may be to drop its prices as well. But that is often the wrong response. Instead, the firm may want to emphasize the 'value' side of the price-value equation.

price? Is the price change temporary or permanent? What will happen to the company's market share and profits if it does not respond? Are other competitors going to respond? Besides these issues, the company must also consider its own situation and strategy and possible customer reactions to price changes.

◣**Figure 10.7** shows the ways a company might assess and respond to a competitor's price cut. Suppose the company learns that a competitor has cut its price and decides that this price cut is likely to harm company sales and profits. It might simply decide to hold its current price and profit margin. The company might believe that it will not lose too much market share, or that it would lose too much profit if it reduced its own price. Or it might decide that it should wait and respond when it has more information on the effects of the competitor's price change. However, waiting too long to act might let the competitor get stronger and more confident as its sales increase.

If the company decides that effective action can and should be taken, it might make any of four responses. First, it could *reduce its price* to match the competitor's price. It may decide that the market is price sensitive and that it would lose too much market share to the lower-priced competitor. Cutting the price will reduce the company's profits in the short run. Some companies might also reduce their product quality, services, and marketing communications to retain profit margins, but this will ultimately hurt long-run market share. The company should try to maintain its quality as it cuts prices.

Alternatively, the company might maintain its price but *raise the perceived value* of its offer. It could improve its communications, stressing the relative value of its product over that of the lower-price competitor. The firm may find it cheaper to maintain price and spend money to improve its perceived value than to cut price and operate at a lower margin. Or, the company might *improve quality and increase price*, moving its brand into a higher price-value position. The higher quality creates greater customer value, which justifies the higher price. In turn, the higher price preserves the company's higher margins.

Finally, the company might *launch a low-price 'fighting brand'*—adding a lower-price item to the line or creating a separate lower-price brand. This is necessary if the particular market segment being lost is price sensitive and will not respond to arguments of higher quality. Thus, to counter store brands and other low-price entrants in the tea market and to protect its market leadership position for the Lipton tea brand, Unilever sells different pack sizes of Brooke Bond tea which are priced competitively to others.

REVIEWING Objectives AND KEY Terms

Companies today face a fierce and fast-changing pricing environment. Firms successful at creating customer value with the other marketing mix activities must still capture some of this value in the prices they earn. The first part of this chapter looks at internal and external considerations that affect pricing decisions and examines general pricing approaches. In the second part of the chapter, we see that pricing decisions are subject to an incredibly complex array of environmental and competitive forces. A company sets not a single price, but rather a *pricing structure* that covers different items in its line. This pricing structure changes over time as products move through their life cycles. The company adjusts product prices to reflect changes in costs and demand and to account for variations in buyers and situations. As the competitive environment changes, the company considers when to initiate price changes and when to respond to them.

OBJECTIVE 1 | Answer the question "What is a price?" and discuss the importance of understanding customer value perceptions when setting prices. (pp 267–271)

Price can be defined narrowly as the amount of money charged for a product or service. Or it can be defined more broadly as the sum of the values that consumers exchange for the benefits of having and using the product or service. The pricing challenge is to find the price that will let the company make a fair profit by getting paid for the customer value it creates.

Despite the increased role of nonprice factors in the modern marketing process, price remains an important element in the marketing mix. It is the only marketing mix element that produces revenue; all other elements represent costs. Price is also one of the most flexible elements of the marketing mix. Unlike product features and channel commitments, price can be raised or lowered quickly. Even so, many companies are not good at handling pricing—pricing decisions and price competition are major problems for many marketing executives. Pricing problems often arise because managers are too quick to reduce prices, prices are too cost oriented rather than customer-value oriented, or prices are not consistent with the rest of the marketing mix.

Good pricing begins with a complete understanding of the value that a product or service creates for customers and setting a price that captures that value. Customer perceptions of the product's value set the ceiling for prices. If customers perceive that the price is greater than the product's value, they will not buy the product. *Value-based pricing* uses buyers' perceptions of value, not the seller's cost, as the key to pricing.

Companies can pursue either of two types of value-based pricing. *Good-value pricing* involves offering just the right combination of quality and good service at a fair price. Everyday low pricing (EDLP) is an example of this strategy. *Value-added pricing* involves attaching value-added features and services to differentiate the company's offers and support charging higher prices.

OBJECTIVE 2 | Discuss the importance of company and product costs in setting prices, as well as other internal and external factors affecting pricing decisions. (pp 271–283)

The price the company charges will fall somewhere between one that is too high to produce any demand and one that is too low to produce a profit. Whereas customer perceptions of value set the ceiling for prices, company and product costs set the floor. If the company prices the product below its costs, its profits will suffer. *Cost-based pricing* involves setting prices based on the costs for producing, distributing, and selling the product plus a fair rate of return for effort and risk.

Costs are an important consideration in setting prices. However, cost-based pricing is product-driven rather than customer-driven. The company designs what it considers to be a good product and sets a price that covers costs plus a target profit. If the price turns out to be too high, the company must settle for lower markups or lower sales, both resulting in disappointing profits. The company must watch its costs carefully. If it costs the company more than it costs competitors to produce and sell its product, the company must charge a higher price or make less profit, putting it at a competitive disadvantage.

Total costs are the sum of the fixed and variable costs for any given level of production. Management wants to charge a price that will at least cover the total costs at a given level of production. To price wisely, management also needs to know how its costs vary with different levels of production and accumulated production experience. Cost-based pricing approaches include *cost-plus pricing* and *break-even pricing* (or target profit pricing).

Other *internal* factors that influence pricing decisions include the company's overall marketing strategy, objectives, mix, and organization for pricing. Common pricing objectives might include survival, current profit maximization, market share leadership, or customer retention and relationship building. Price decisions must be co-ordinated with product design, distribution, and promotion decisions to form a consistent and effective marketing program.

Other *external* pricing considerations include the nature of the market and demand, competitors' strategies and prices, and environmental factors such as the economy, reseller needs, and government actions. Ultimately, the customer decides whether the company has set the right price. The customer weighs the price against the perceived values of using the product—if the price exceeds the sum of the values, consumers will not buy. So the company must understand concepts like demand curves (the price-demand relationship) and price elasticity (consumer sensitivity to prices). Consumers also compare a product's price to the prices of competitors' products. A company therefore must learn the customer value and prices of competitors' offers.

OBJECTIVE 3 | Describe the major strategies for pricing imitative and new products. (pp 283–284)

Pricing is a dynamic process. Companies design a *pricing structure* that covers all their products. They change this structure over time and adjust it to account for different customers and situations. Pricing strategies usually change as a product passes through its life cycle. The company can decide on one of several price-quality strategies for introducing a product that is similar to a competitor's, including premium pricing, economy pricing, good value, or overcharging. In pricing innovative new products, it can use *market-skimming pricing* by initially setting high prices to 'skim' the maximum amount of revenue from various segments of the market. Or it can use *market-penetrating pricing* by setting a low initial price to penetrate the market deeply and win a large market share.

OBJECTIVE 4 **Explain how companies find a set of prices that maximizes the profits from the total product mix.** (pp 284–286)

When the product is part of a product mix, the firm searches for a set of prices that will maximize the profits from the total mix. In *product line pricing*, the company decides on price steps for the entire set of products it offers. In addition, the company must set prices for *optional products* (optional or accessory products included with the main product), *captive products* (products that are required for use of the main product), *by-products* (waste or residual products produced when making the main product), and *product bundles* (combinations of products at a reduced price).

OBJECTIVE 5 **Discuss how companies adjust their prices to take into account different types of customers and situations.** (pp 286–292)

Companies apply a variety of *price adjustment strategies* to account for differences in consumer segments and situations. One is *discount and allowance pricing*, whereby the company establishes cash, quantity, functional, or seasonal discounts, or varying types of allowances. A second strategy is *segmented pricing*, where the company sells a product at two or more prices to accommodate different customers, product forms, locations, or times. Sometimes companies consider more than economics in their pricing decisions, using *psychological pricing* to better communicate a product's intended position. In *promotional pricing*, a company offers discounts or temporarily sells a product below list price as a special event, sometimes even selling below cost as a loss leader.

Another approach is *geographical pricing*, whereby the company decides how to price to distant customers, choosing from such alternatives as FOB-origin pricing, uniform-delivered pricing, zone pricing, basing-point pricing, and freight-absorption pricing. Finally, *international pricing* means that the company adjusts its price to meet different conditions and expectations in different world markets.

OBJECTIVE 6 **Discuss the key issues related to initiating and responding to price changes.** (pp 292–294)

When a firm considers initiating a *price change*, it must consider customers' and competitors' reactions. There are different implications to *initiating price cuts* and *initiating price increases*. Buyer reactions to price changes are influenced by the meaning customers see in the price change. Competitors' reactions flow from a set reaction policy or a fresh analysis of each situation.

There are also many factors to consider in responding to a competitor's price changes. The company that faces a price change initiated by a competitor must try to understand the competitor's intent as well as the likely duration and impact of the change. If a swift reaction is desirable, the firm should preplan its reactions to different possible price actions by competitors. When facing a competitor's price change, the company might sit tight, reduce its own price, raise perceived quality, improve quality and raise price, or launch a fighting brand.

KEY Terms

OBJECTIVE 1	Target costing (p 277)	**OBJECTIVE 5**
Price (p 268)	Demand curve (p 279)	Discount (p 286)
Value-based pricing (p 269)	Price elasticity (p 280)	Segmented pricing (p 287)
Good-value pricing (p 270)		Psychological pricing (p 287)
Value-added pricing (p 271)	**OBJECTIVE 3**	Reference prices (p 288)
	Market-skimming pricing (p 283)	Promotional pricing (p 288)
OBJECTIVE 2	Market-penetration	Geographic pricing (p 289)
Cost-based pricing (p 271)	pricing (p 283)	FOB-origin pricing (p 290)
Fixed costs (overheads) (p 271)		Uniform-delivered pricing (p 290)
Variable costs (p 271)	**OBJECTIVE 4**	Zone pricing (p 290)
Total costs (p 271)	Product line pricing (p 285)	Basing-point pricing (p 290)
Experience curve (learning curve) (p 273)	Optional-product pricing (p 285)	Freight-absorption
Cost-plus pricing (p 274)	Captive-product pricing (p 285)	pricing (p 290)
Break-even pricing (target profit pricing) (p 274)	By-product pricing (p 286)	Dynamic pricing (p 290)
	Product bundle pricing (p 286)	

DISCUSSING & APPLYING THE Concepts

Discussing the Concepts

1. What is price? List five other words that mean the same thing as price (for example, value).

2. Explain the differences between value-based pricing and cost-based pricing.

3. Compare and contrast fixed and variable costs and give an example of each.

4. Discuss other internal and external considerations besides cost and customer perceptions of value that affect pricing decisions.

5. Name and describe the four types of markets recognized by economists and discuss the pricing challenges posed by each.

6. Explain market-skimming and market-penetration pricing strategies. Why would a marketer of innovative high-tech products choose market-skimming pricing rather than market-penetration pricing when launching a new product?

7. Name and briefly describe the five product mix pricing decisions.

8. Compare and contrast the geographic pricing strategies companies use for customers located in different parts of the country or world. Which strategy is best?

9. What factors influence the price a company charges in different countries?

10. Why would a company consider cutting its price?

Applying the Concepts

1. In a small group, discuss your perceptions of value and how much you are willing to pay for the following products: automobiles, frozen dinners, jeans, and athletic shoes. Are there differences among members of your group? Explain why those differences exist. Discuss some examples of brands of these products that are positioned to deliver different value to consumers.

2. Find estimates of price elasticity for a variety of consumer goods and services. Explain what a price elasticity of 0.5 and of 2.4 mean. (Note: these are absolute values, as price elasticity is usually negative.)

3. What does the following positioning statement suggest about the firm's marketing objectives, marketing-mix strategy, and costs? "No one beats our prices. We crush the competition."

4. Identify three price-comparison shopping websites and shop for an MP3 player of your choice. Compare the price ranges given at these three websites.

5. Convert US$1.00 to the currencies of five other countries (you can do this at www.xe.com/ucc/). What implications do currency exchange rates hold for setting prices in other countries?

6. You are an owner of a small independent chain of coffeehouses competing head-to-head with Starbucks. The retail price your customers pay for coffee is exactly the same as at Starbucks. The wholesale price you pay for roasted coffee beans has increased by 25 percent. You know that you cannot absorb this increase and that you must pass it on to your customers. However, you are concerned about the consequences of an open price increase. Discuss three alternative price-increase strategies that address these concerns.

FOCUS ON Technology

Apple has had good success in Japan in the past. However, the company knew that its new iPhone was behind local technology in Japan and that it was designed to work on communications networks that were older and slower than the ones that the Japanese used. To compensate for the shortcomings of the standard iPhone, Apple released the 3G version in July 2008 with the capacity to work twice as fast as the first generation iPhone. It had built-in GPS for expanded location-based mobile phone services and software support for Microsoft Exchange ActiveSync and other third-party applications. The still faster iPhone 4 was released in 2010.

1. The prices of the iPhone 3G in Japan were 23,040 yen (US$277) and 34,560 yen (US$415) for the 8 and 16GB versions, respectively. Why might Apple have different pricing structures across the world?

2. Give examples of recent high-tech products that have come down in price over a relatively short period of time.

3. How has the iPhone been received in the Arab world markets?

FOCUS ON Ethics

You've heard of a monopoly, but have you ever heard of a *monopsony*? A monopsony involves one powerful buyer and many sellers. The buyer is so powerful that it can drive prices down. An example of pure monopsony is a business that is the only buyer of labor in an isolated region. A business like this is able to pay lower wages than it would under competition. Cases of pure monopsony are rare, although monopsonistic elements are found wherever there are many sellers and few purchasers.

1. Is there an example of a monopsony in your own country? Explain why this might be the case.

2. Is it fair that a buyer can exert so much power over a supplier? Are there any benefits to consumers?

MARKETING BY THE Numbers

A business sells fashionable and up-to-date covers for mobile phones. The phone covers are handmade and sold to retailers at US$12 per unit. The mobile phone covers cost the business US$4 to manufacture. The business does not pay its sales teams a fixed salary; instead they are paid a flat rate of US$0.50 commission per unit sold to retailers. The distribution costs are also US$0.50 and the factory's fixed costs are US$4,000 per month. The business needs to make a series of key calculations to ascertain how it is performing. Refer to Appendix 2: Marketing by the Numbers for guidance on how to make these calculations.

1. What is the variable cost of producing 1,000 mobile phone covers?

2. What is the contribution earned from each mobile phone cover?

3. A business increases its price per unit from US$5 to US$6. At US$5 the sales were 6,000 units; they are now 5,500. Explain how the price change has affected demand.

4. If there is a 40 percent rise in the rent paid by a business for its factory unit, what will happen to the fixed cost line on a break-even chart?

VIDEO Case

IKEA

Lots of companies have idealistic missions. But IKEA's vision, "To create a better everyday life for the many people," seems somewhat implausible. How can a company that makes furniture improve everyday life for the masses? Interestingly, the most important part of that strategy is price. For every product that it designs, from sofas to plastic mugs, IKEA starts with a target price. The target price is one that's deemed affordable, making the product accessible to the masses.

Only then does IKEA begin the grueling process of creating a high-quality, stylish, and innovative product that can be delivered to the customer for that target price. As IKEA points out, anyone can make high-quality goods for a high price or poor-quality

goods for a low price. The real challenge is making high-quality products at a low price. To do so requires a relentless focus on costs combined with a thirst for innovation. That has been IKEA's quest for more than 65 years.

After viewing the video featuring IKEA, answer the following questions about the company's pricing strategy:

1. What is IKEA's promise of value?

2. Referring to the Klippan sofa, illustrate how IKEA delivers its promise of value to consumers.

3. Based on the concepts from the text, does IKEA employ a value-based pricing approach or a cost-based pricing approach? Support your answer.

COMPANY Case

Flydubai Pricing Strategy

FLYDUBAI ENTERS THE AIRLINE MARKET

Flydubai entered the airline market in 2009 with a new strategy that differentiated it from the competition: a new and unique pricing strategy for the UAE market. It positioned itself from the start as a low-cost carrier, offering passengers low-cost tickets in order to satisfy the demand in the market. The company believed that the regional market was ready for a low-cost carrier, with a wide range of customers searching for low-cost flights.

In order to be able to offer cheap flights, flydubai had to eliminate as many travel complexities as possible and reduce its operating costs. Consequently, flydubai prices include taxes and each passenger is allowed to carry one piece of hand baggage, weighing up to 10 kg.

Flydubai's main purpose is to bring more people to and from Dubai. It strives for "excellence, reliability and an international, pro-business approach," according to an airline official. Moreover, it is attempting to promote Dubai's commercial and tourism sectors by offering travelers a new and inexpensive service.

FLYDUBAI'S EXPANSION

At first, flydubai concentrated on establishing itself in the Gulf Cooperation Council (GCC) area and neighboring countries. In 2009, it expanded its operation to cover 16 destinations and began services to Colombo in Sri Lanka. In 2010, flydubai

launched operations in India with a direct flight between Dubai and Lucknow. In March 2010, the CEO, Ghaith Al Ghaith, announced that flydubai was flying to 21 destinations and carrying 600,000 customers.

The airline has had an outstanding performance compared with the rest of the industry. According to the International Air Transport Association (IATA), airlines lost an estimated US$9.4 billion (34.52 billion Dh) in 2010. Airlines in the Arab world, however, enjoyed growth of 23.6 percent in revenue passenger kilometers (RPKs), a key industry metric.

GROWTH TARGETS

Flydubai expected to double its business in 2010, increasing the number of employees from 500 to 800, and serving a million customers from around the world. Moreover, according to Mr Al-Ghaith, the company aims to become the second largest airline operating out of Dubai International Airport after Emirates, surpassing Indian carriers operating several flights each day to the UAE. Flydubai plans to reach 25 destinations during 2011, and in addition, it has confirmed that it intends to launch ancillary services, including holiday packages and travel insurance, by the end of the year.

Flydubai is not considered a direct competitor to Emirates, as they operate in different sectors. However, it is believed that the success of flydubai has had a negative effect on Emirates' income. According to Mr Al-Ghaith, the company is bringing a new business model to the market that will stimulate demand and enhance airline services in the region. The airline, through its differentiated pricing strategy, has created a new demand and has enjoyed unprecedented growth in its first year. As Mr Al-Gaith has said, "We have big plans for the future and we hope to continue to be as successful as we have been in our first year."

COMPETITION BETWEEN AIRLINES DURING RAMADAN

The holy month of Ramadan is known as the month of generosity; it's a time to give and spend time with family and friends. Airline companies have become adept at offering special discounts to suit customers' needs in this special month. For example, in 2009, Emirates developed the "Fly For Less" concept, whereby all passengers traveling to or via Dubai during Ramadan were offered accommodation packages. In addition, it announced discounts on 17 destinations, including Cairo, Delhi, and Istanbul.

Etihad Airways has also announced "world deals," offering discounts during August and September, to destinations in several countries including Germany, the United States, and China.

Not only do regional airlines offer special deals during Ramadan, but European airlines such as British Airways, Lufthansa, and Turkish Airlines have also joined the price-cutting war. Lufthansa, the German airline, has offered discounts on flights from the Arab world to Europe during Ramadan and the feast holiday as well as round trips of Europe. British Airways also plans to reduce economy airfares to popular destinations in Europe and North America during Ramadan.

Airlines have tailored their services to ensure that passengers who are fasting receive the highest standards of service. Iftar is offered on board Emirates flights in order to ensure relaxing trips with high-quality food.

FLYDUBAI DURING RAMADAN

Flydubai has attempted to grasp this opportunity by tailoring special offers to its passengers, while facing fierce regional and international competition. The company announced that it would be "giving all passengers a 100% reimbursement of their fare if they travel between 15th August and 6th September 2010 during the holy month of Ramadan." It was the only airline offering passengers the full fare refund within these dates. Passengers paid only the taxes on their flights, with the fares refunded by email in the form of a voucher for use with flydubai by December 2010. The airline hoped that this strategy would allow it to grow its business during Ramadan, while at the same time building a loyal customer base to sustain its future growthing.

Questions for Discussion

1. Describe flydubai's pricing strategy. How do you evaluate it?

2. Is this business model sustainable?

3. Describe flydubai's target markets. How price-sensitive are they?

4. How do you evaluate flydubai's offering in Ramadan? Do you think it is going to be successful given the fierce competition?

5. What challenges do you expect flydubai to face in the near future?

Sources: "Dubai's Low Cost Airline Named 'flydubai,'" flydubai website, June 25, 2008, http://flydubai.com/english/news-and-updates/news/news/dubai's-low-cost-airline-named-flydubai.aspx.; "Flydubai Marks Successful First 12 Months," June 8, 2010, *Trade Arabia,* www.tradearabia.com/news/TTN_181136.html; "Flydubai Launches New Offer for Ramadan," *AME Info,* July 20, 2010, www.ameinfo.com/238303.html; additional information from Nadia Saleem, "Flydubai Celebrate First Anniversary with New Routes," *Gulf News,* June 1, 2010, http://gulfnews.com/business/aviation/flydubai-celebrates-first-anniversary-with-new-routes-1.635188; Robeel Haq, "Flydubai Offers Full Refund to Ramadan Passengers," *Arabian Supply Chain,* July 18, 2010, www.arabiansupplychain.com/article-4557-flydubai-offers-full-refund-to-ramadan-passengers/; "Flydubai to Double Route Network by 2011," *Take Off Africa,* June 2010, Vol. 6, http://takeoffafrica.com/issue/june-2010-vol-6/article/flydubai-to-double-route-network-by-2011.

Chapter 11

Part 1   Defining Marketing and the Marketing Process (Chapters 1, 2)
Part 2   Understanding the Marketplace and Consumers (Chapters 3, 4, 5, 6)
Part 3   Designing a Customer-Driven Strategy and Mix (Chapters 7, 8, 9, 10, 11, 12, 13, 14)
Part 4   Extending Marketing (Chapters 15, 16, 17)

Communicating

Customer Value

Integrated Marketing Communications Strategy

Chapter PREVIEW

In this and the next two chapters, we'll examine the last of the marketing mix tools—promotion. Companies must do more than just create customer value. They must also use promotion to clearly and persuasively communicate that value. Promotion is not a single tool but, rather, a mix of several tools. Under the concept of *integrated marketing communications*, the company must carefully co-ordinate these promotion elements to deliver a clear, consistent, and compelling message about the organization and its brands. We'll begin by introducing you to the various promotion mix tools. Next, we'll examine the rapidly changing communications environment and the need for integrated marketing communications. Finally, we'll discuss the steps in developing marketing communications and the promotion budgeting process. In the next two chapters, we'll visit the specific marketing communications tools.

To start this chapter let's look at one of the world's biggest marketers, Unilever, and at one of today's biggest challenges, which is how to integrate communications for launching a new product in the market.

Unilever Arabia launched their Pond's range of skin creams, with Pond's Age Miracle as the flagship product, in the Gulf Cooperation Council (GCC) states in March 2009. During the launch Unilever carefully integrated and co-ordinated its many communications channels to deliver a clear, consistent, and compelling message about the new Pond's range—in other words, Unilever used an integrated marketing communications strategy.

With total revenue of US$62 billion in 2010, Unilever is one of the largest fast-moving consumer goods companies in the world. It operates in more than 100 countries worldwide. Unilever's portfolio includes some of the best-known global brands, including Dove, Vaseline, Sunsilk, Clear, Knorr, Omo, Lux, Lifebuoy, Closeup, Signal, Fair & Lovely, and Lipton. In many categories these brands are global leaders. Unilever's global mission is to help people feel good, look good and get more out of life with brands and services that are good for them and for others. With local offices and partnerships in 20 countries across North Africa and the Middle East, Unilever is one of the single largest television advertisers in the region.

Unilever's Pond's brand is worth over US$982 million worldwide and is the biggest retail face care brand in the world as measured by independent market research. Within Unilever, Pond's is known as a 'masstige' face care brand (a range that falls between prestige and the mass face care segment).

Launching Pond's into the Arab world presented a major new opportunity for Unilever Arabia, with a potential regional face care market worth about US$70 million. Unilever undertook extensive market research which showed the following trends among potential customers in the region:

- Only 38 percent use a face care product and 41 percent still use a body lotion on their face.
- 37 percent want young-looking skin but only 4 percent use an anti-aging product.
- 50 percent want lighter, spotless skin but only 17 percent use a skin-lightening product.
- 60 percent still use toilet soap on their face and 20 percent use only water!

Unilever launched Pond's Age Miracle to exploit this market opportunity in 2009. Age Miracle is an anti-aging beauty product, which Unilever claims will result in younger-looking skin in just seven days (which the company backs with a money-back guarantee).

It took the Pond's brand team over a year to launch the Age Miracle range in the Arab world. The launch was supported by an impressive array of marketing tactics including in-store installations, off-shelf displays, 'brand ambassadors' in stores, a public relations plan, unbranded pre-launch editorials, a trip to the Pond's Institute in New York for influential magazine editors, branded post-launch editorials, television commercials, outdoor and in-mall advertising, print campaigns, an introduction through a launch conference, and branding in retail outlets.

Pond's Age Miracle product, pictured here, generated significant press coverage in the Arab world.

With so many competing brands in the market, the Pond's brand team mainly relied on public relations (PR) to build consumer brand awareness and credibility. Public relations was chosen owing to the fact that the target audience greatly rely on word of mouth and expert opinion before making their choice. Unilever had developed separate roles for each medium; the role of advertising was to generate awareness, PR to gain credibility, in-store promotion to engage the target audience on a one-to-one with the in-store activations and also to translate awareness of the brand into a purchase.

One of the main PR strategies was the trip for the top 10 most influential beauty editors in the GCC to the Pond's Institute in New York. The Pond's team aimed to turn every detail of the trip into a touch point, and brand representation was vital. The team's objective was to give the beauty editors a genuine feeling of the benefits of using Pond's through the experience of using the product. Additional objectives were to familiarize them with the full range of Pond's products and to demonstrate the product's claims, in the hope of encouraging the beauty editors to write positively about Pond's.

Immediately following the trip to the Pond's Institute, the brands team focused on the post-trip objectives: CDs were sent by the brands team to the magazines to document the coverage of their trip.This was planned to sustain coverage of Pond's after the launch, giving extra publicity for the brand. The trip was also covered on various beauty programs. As a result, Pond's Age Miracle range was able to generate a strong PR campaign valued at about US$347,000.

The brands team also created the Pond's Brand Council, consisting of three influential figures from the skin and beauty industries in the Arab world to represent Pond's in the media. Leila Obeid, one of the council members, has 30 years' experience as a professional beautician, beauty consultant, and owner/manager of an esthetical beauty center, Centre Obeid in Baabdat, and has created, produced, and presented beauty-related shows such asthe beauty segment on the morning show "Morning World" (Aalam al Sabah) and "Natural is More Beautiful" (Tabi3e Ajmal), presented during Ramadan.

Pond's brands team used an array of different advertising and PR media, including outdoor campaigns.

Another council member, Joelle Mardinian, a television personality and make-up artist to the stars, worked with MBC as a professional stylist and make-up artist in her own show. Dr Ali Al Tukmatchy, the third member of the council, has more than 30 years of practice in Dubai.

Pond's Arabia Brand Council was officially introduced to the press on March 4, 2009. About 500 people were invited for the occasion including local and regional media and key consumer opinion leaders. The brand council members spoke about their involvement and experience with Pond's. Audiences were also shown footage of the editors' trip to the Pond's Institute.

Finally, Pond's Age Miracle was launched to the trade with below the line (BTL) campaigns across the region and to the consumer with a strong above the line (ATL) campaign.

As a result of the integrated marketing communications campaign, Pond's in the Gulf achieved nearly 5 percent of the market within two months of launching.[1]

> **The brands team at Unilever Arabia implemented an ambitious integrated marketing campaign to launch Pond's Age Miracle skin creams into the regional market. The brand gained a 5 percent market share only two months after launching.**

Promotion mix (or marketing communications mix)
The specific blend of promotion tools that the company uses to persuasively communicate customer value and build customer relationships.

Author Comment | The promotion mix is the marketer's bag of tools for communicating with customers and other stakeholders. All of these many tools must be carefully co-ordinated under the concept of integrated marketing communications in order to deliver a clear and compelling message.

Building good customer relationships calls for more than just developing a good product, pricing it attractively, and making it available to target customers. Companies must also *communicate* their value propositions to customers, and what they communicate should not be left to chance. All of their communications must be planned and blended into carefully integrated marketing communications programs. Just as good communication is important in building and maintaining any kind of relationship, it is a crucial element in a company's efforts to build profitable customer relationships.

The Promotion Mix (pp 301–302)

A company's total **promotion mix**—also called its **marketing communications mix**—consists of the specific blend of advertising, public relations, personal selling, sales promotion, and direct-marketing tools that the company uses to persuasively communicate

Objective Outline

Advertising

Any paid form of nonpersonal presentation and promotion of ideas, goods, or services by an identified sponsor.

Sales promotion

Short-term incentives to encourage the purchase or sale of a product or service.

Personal selling

Personal presentation by the firm's sales force for the purpose of making sales and building customer relationships.

Public relations

Building good relations with the company's various publics by obtaining favorable publicity, building up a good corporate image, and handling or heading off unfavorable rumors, stories, and events.

Direct marketing

Direct connections with carefully targeted individual consumers to both obtain an immediate response and cultivate lasting customer relationships.

customer value and build customer relationships. Definitions of the five major promotion tools follow:[2]

- **Advertising:** Any paid form of nonpersonal presentation and promotion of ideas, goods, or services by an identified sponsor.
- **Sales promotion:** Short-term incentives to encourage the purchase or sale of a product or service.
- **Personal selling:** Personal presentation by the firm's sales force for the purpose of making sales and building customer relationships.
- **Public relations:** Building good relations with the company's various publics by obtaining favorable publicity, building up a good corporate image, and handling or heading off unfavorable rumors, stories, and events.
- **Direct marketing:** Direct connections with carefully targeted individual consumers to both obtain an immediate response and cultivate lasting customer relationships—the use of direct mail, the telephone, direct-response television, email, the Internet, and other tools to communicate directly with specific consumers.

Each category involves specific promotional tools used to communicate with consumers. For example, advertising includes television and radio broadcast, print, Internet, outdoor, and other forms. Sales promotion includes discounts, coupons, displays, and demonstrations. Personal selling includes sales presentations, trade shows, and incentive programs. Public relations includes press releases, sponsorships, special events, and web pages. And direct marketing includes catalogs, telephone marketing, kiosks, the Internet, mobile, and more.

At the same time, marketing communication goes beyond these specific promotion tools. The product's design, its price, the shape and color of its package, and the stores that sell it *all* communicate something to buyers. Thus, although the promotion mix is the company's primary communication activity, the entire marketing mix—promotion *and* product, price, and place—must be co-ordinated for greatest communication impact.

Integrated Marketing Communications (pp 303–306)

In past decades, marketers perfected the art of mass marketing—selling highly standardized products to masses of customers. In the process, they developed effective mass-media communications techniques to support these strategies. Large companies now routinely invest millions or even billions of dollars in television, magazine, or other mass-media advertising, reaching tens of millions of customers with a single ad. Today, however, marketing managers face some new marketing communications realities. Perhaps no other area of marketing is changing so profoundly as marketing communications, creating both exciting and scary times for marketing communicators.

The New Marketing Communications Landscape

Several major factors are changing the face of today's marketing communications. First, consumers are changing. In this digital, wireless age, they are better informed and more communications empowered. Rather than relying on marketer-supplied information, they can use the Internet and other technologies to seek out information on their own. More than that, they can more easily connect with other consumers to exchange brand-related information or even to create their own marketing messages.

Secondly, marketing strategies are changing. As mass markets have fragmented, marketers are shifting away from mass marketing. More and more, they are developing focused marketing programs designed to build closer relationships with customers in more narrowly defined micromarkets. Vast improvements in information technology are speeding the movement toward segmented marketing. Today's marketers can amass detailed customer information, keep closer track of customer needs, and tailor their offerings to narrowly defined target groups.

Finally, sweeping changes in communications technology are causing remarkable changes in the ways in which companies and customers communicate with each other. The digital age has spawned a host of new information and communication tools—from mobile phones and iPods, to satellite and cable television systems, to the many faces of the Internet (email, social networks, brand websites, and so much more). The new communications technologies give companies exciting new media for interacting with targeted consumers. At the same time, they give consumers more control over the nature and timing of messages they choose to send and receive.

The new marketing communications landscape: The digital age has spawned a host of new information and communication tools—from mobile phones and iPods to the Internet and satellite and cable television systems.

The Shifting Marketing Communications Model

The explosive developments in communications technology and changes in marketer and customer communication strategies have had a dramatic impact on marketing communications. Just as mass marketing once gave rise to a new generation of mass-media communications, the new digital media have given birth to a new marketing communications model.

Although television, magazines, and other mass media remain very important, their dominance is declining. Advertisers are now adding a broad selection of more-specialized and highly targeted media to reach smaller customer segments with more-personalized, interactive messages. The new media range from specialty magazines, cable television channels, and video on demand (VOD) to Internet catalogs, email, podcasts, cellphones, and online social networks. In all, companies are doing less *broadcasting* and more *narrowcasting*.

Some advertising industry experts even predict a doom-and-gloom 'chaos scenario,' in which the old mass-media communications model will collapse entirely. They believe that marketers will increasingly abandon traditional mass media in favor of new digital technologies. These new technologies will let marketers "reach—and have a conversation with—small clusters of consumers who are consuming not what is force-fed to them, but exactly what they want."[3]

For example, just think about what's happening to television viewing these days. "Adjust your set," says one reporter, "television is changing as quickly as the channels. It's on cell phones. It's on digital music players. It's on almost anything with a screen. Shows can be seen at their regular times or when you want [with or without the commercials]. Some 'TV' programs aren't even on cable or network or satellite; they're being created just for Internet viewing."[4]

Many large advertisers are shifting their advertising budgets away from network television in favor of more targeted, cost-effective, interactive, and engaging media. "The ad industry's plotline used to be a lot simpler: Audiences are splintering off in dozens of new directions, watching TV shows on iPods, watching movies on video game players, and listening to radio on the Internet," observes one analyst. So marketers must "start planning how to reach consumers in new and unexpected ways." Says the CEO and creative director of one large ad agency, "There's no medium we don't perform in."[5]

Rather than a 'chaos scenario,' however, other industry insiders see a more gradual shift to the new marketing communications model. They note that broadcast television and other mass media still capture a lion's share of the promotion budgets of most major marketing firms, a fact that isn't likely to change quickly. Although some may question the future of the 30-second spot, it's still very much in use today. Last year, more than 43 percent of advertising dollars in the United States were spent on national and local television commercials versus 7.6 percent on Internet advertising. "So if you think that TV is an aging dinosaur," says one media expert, "maybe you should think again." Another expert agrees: "Does TV work? Of course it does. It's just not the only game in town anymore."[6]

Thus, it seems likely that the new marketing communications model will consist of a shifting mix of both traditional mass media and a wide array of exciting, new, more-targeted, more-personalized media. The challenge for traditional advertisers is to bridge the 'media divide' that too often separates traditional creative and media approaches from new interactive and digital ones. Many established advertising agencies are struggling with this transition especially in the back drop of the economic slowdown post-2008 (see **Real Marketing 11.1**).

The Need for *Integrated* Marketing Communications

The shift toward a richer mix of media and communication approaches poses a problem for marketers. Consumers today are bombarded by commercial messages from a broad range of sources. But consumers don't distinguish between message sources the way marketers do. In the consumer's mind, messages from different media and promotional approaches all become part of a single message about the company. Conflicting messages from these different sources can result in confused company images, brand positions, and customer relationships.

All too often, companies fail to integrate their various communications channels. The result is confused communications to consumers. Mass-media advertisements say one thing, while a price promotion sends a different signal, and a product label creates still another message. Company sales literature says something altogether different and the company's website seems out of sync with everything else.

Real Marketing 11.1

Economic Slowdown and the Digital Advertising Boom in the Arab World

In January 2010, Ramzi Raad, chairman and CEO of TBWA\RAAD Middle East, was presented with the prestigious Dubai Lynx Advertising Person of the Year Award. A key figure in Middle Eastern and North African advertising for almost 40 years, Ramzi had previously been ranked amongst the World's Most Influential Arabs on Arabian Business's 100 Most Powerful List.

In a statement, organizers of the third-Dubai International Advertising Festival, said: "The Advertising Person of the Year honors someone who, by their efforts, energy, and dedication has lifted the presence and pro-file of the region within the international advertising, marketing, and communications community, be it at a national or regional level. . . . Ramzi has been, and continues to be, an instrumental figure in the development and growth of the advertising and commu-nication industry throughout the Middle East and North Africa. We are delighted to pay tribute to his dedication and success."

Below are excerpts from an interview of Ramzi Raad by Kippreport.com, where he considers the Arab world's advertising indus-try since the 2008 economic slowdown and why he expects digital advertising to boom:

Kipp: What's going on with the advertising industry?

Raad: Everybody is interested in what's happening to the advertising market, and there are a lot of reports that there is a dramatic drop and the situation is very depressing. And regretfully the people who are supposed to give a better story and a clearer picture are not doing that. The reality is the advertising market has not been hit as badly as people think. And the facts show a different situation that people are failing to see because they keep looking at it from a very insular angle.

Kipp: Ok. What's the other angle?

Raad: For the past six or seven years [before the economic slowdown, from 2001 and 2002 onwards], the industry in the MENA region has grown 20 to 25 percent year on year, which was not in line with the rest of the world where growth was following a much slower pace. So we've been follow-ing a different pattern because the world was not growing with these percentages. If we look at the UAE alone in the past two years it has been growing by over 40 per-cent. So even if the markets, suffer we will still be seeing positive growth.

Kipp: How about the effect of the crisis on the advertising industry; do you think it will change the way that everyone does business?

Raad: In periods of crisis, advertisers are very picky on results. They want to spend money where they can see results. So there is a sort of shift from brand image advertising, into advertising that helps products sell. This is resulting in a switch toward digital media. I don't mean traditional digital advertising, like banners that intrude on your internet surfing, but dynamic campaigns, which advertisers can use to interact with their brand, product, consumers, users and so on. More and more advertisers are using it to generate a dialogue with the consumer.

And when I say digital media it's not a switch from the major medium, which is television.When you're talking about mov-ing consumer goods, television remains to be the major medium. Globally, tele-vision still commands like 38 percent of the advertising spend. In our part of the world, television has a share of 43 percent of the total ad spend in the MENA region.

But online advertising in this region represents only 1 percent; this will change. Globally, Internet advertising is command-ing 10.2 percent. It's estimated that by the year 2020 the internet will take 80 percent of the total advertising spend globally.

Kipp: That's a huge shift.

Raad: Definitely, and to be able to catch up with the world shift it's going to take a lot of effort.We have to gear ourselves up, hire the talent or train people on how to plan and execute dynamic digital campaigns.

Kipp: How do you think that sort of a shift will be perceived in this part of the world? Do you think it's too new?

Raad: Definitely, it's new. We're all stamped-ing to develop the expertise. This is a new media and you need to develop the knowl-edge and the expertise, noting the many challenges of language and the perception of governments towards certain social sites.

Ramzi Raad remains positive about the outlook for the advertising industry in the post-recession environment, and the opportunities presented to advertisers by the Internet.

At the beginning everybody thought 'I'll do a web banner or something and everyone will be happy.' But that's not enough anymore.

Kipp: Do you think that a lot of people are shifting toward digital media because they know exactly how many hits that they get?

Raad: It's partly that. And that is the first step in making the decision to use digi-tal advertising. But the more you learn about the medium, the more you realize it's beyond the hits: it's how the consumer, the reader and the internet surfer will engage with your message.

For instance, recently we discovered that many Saudi ladies spend a good part of the day on the internet. This creates a new opportunity for us because you can reach these ladies, you can engage in a two-way dialogue with them. It's a good way to interact with Saudi society.

Kipp: But how long do you think it will take before the changes will actually happen?

Raad: It's happening, although we're defi-nitely lagging behind the more advanced world. We won't get to 80 percent spend levels by 2020, but I'm sure we'll be mov-ing forward quickly. The fact is that many of our markets are very restrictive, and the use of new media is still perceived with caution. But the internet has captured the imagination of the youth. That's very important for us.

Sources: Interview extracted from Dana El Baltaji, "Conversations with an Advertising Don," *Kipp Report,* May 21, 2009, www.kippreport.com/2009/05/conversations-with-an-advertising-don/; additional information and quotes from "Dubai Lynx Honours Ramzi Raad, Chairman & CEO of TBWA\RAAD Middle East, With Advertising Person of The Year Award," Shoot Online, January 20, 2010, www.shootonline.com.

FIGURE | 11.1
Integrated Marketing
Communications

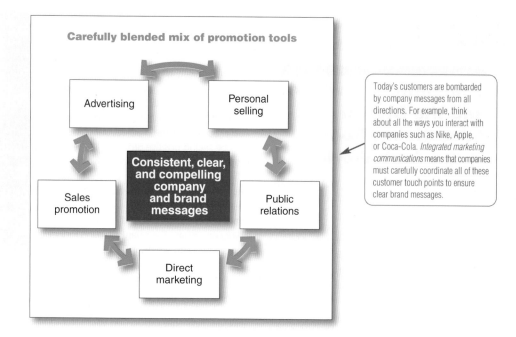

Carefully blended mix of promotion tools

Advertising

Personal selling

Consistent, clear, and compelling company and brand messages

Sales promotion

Public relations

Direct marketing

Today's customers are bombarded by company messages from all directions. For example, think about all the ways you interact with companies such as Nike, Apple, or Coca-Cola. *Integrated marketing communications* means that companies must carefully coordinate all of these customer touch points to ensure clear brand messages.

Integrated marketing communications (IMC)

Carefully integrating and co-ordinating the company's many communications channels to deliver a clear, consistent, and compelling message about the organization and its brands.

The problem is that these communications often come from different parts of the company as well as different agencies. Advertising messages are planned and implemented by the advertising department or an advertising agency. Personal selling communications are developed by sales management. Other company specialists are responsible for public relations, sales promotion events, Internet marketing, and other forms of marketing communications. However, whereas these companies have separated their communications tools, customers won't. Mixed communications from these sources will result in blurred consumer brand perceptions.

Today, more companies are adopting the concept of **integrated marketing communications (IMC)**. Under this concept, as illustrated in **Figure 11.1**, the company carefully integrates its many communications channels to deliver a clear, consistent, and compelling message about the organization and its brands.

IMC calls for recognizing all touch points where the customer may encounter the company and its brands. Each *brand contact* will deliver a message, whether good, bad, or indifferent. Says one advertising executive, "the world has evolved to a place where brands that need to speak to their audience have to understand that everything they do is media."[7] The company wants to deliver a consistent and positive message with each contact. IMC leads to a total marketing communications strategy aimed at building strong customer relationships by showing how the company and its products can help customers solve their problems.

IMC ties together all of the company's messages and images. The company's television and print advertisements have the same message, look, and feel as its email and personal selling communications. And its public relations materials project the same image as its website or social network presence. Often, different media play unique roles in attracting, informing, and persuading consumers, and these roles must be carefully co-ordinated under the overall marketing communications plan.

In the past, no one person or department was responsible for thinking through the communication roles of the various promotion tools and co-ordinating the promotion mix. To help implement integrated marketing communications, some companies appoint a marketing communications director who has overall responsibility for the company's communications efforts. This helps to produce better communications consistency and greater sales impact. It places the responsibility in someone's hands—where none existed before—to unify the company's image as it is shaped by thousands of company activities.

Author Comment | To develop effective marketing communications, you must first understand the general communications process.

A View of the Communications Process (pp 307–308)

Integrated marketing communications involve identifying the target audience and shaping a co-ordinated promotional program to obtain the desired audience response. Too often, marketing communications focus on immediate awareness, image, or preference goals in the target market. But this approach to communication is too shortsighted. Today, marketers are moving toward viewing communications as *managing the customer relationship over time*.

Because customers differ, communications programs need to be developed for specific segments, niches, and even individuals. And, given the new interactive communications technologies, companies must ask not only, "How can we reach our customers?" but also, "How can we find ways to let our customers reach us?"

Thus, the communications process should start with an audit of all the potential touch points that target customers may have with the company and its brands. For example, someone purchasing a new kitchen appliance may talk to others, see television ads, read articles and ads in newspapers and magazines, visit various websites for prices and reviews, and check out appliances in one or more stores. The marketer needs to assess what influence each of these communications experiences will have at different stages of the buying process. This understanding will help marketers allocate their communication budget more efficiently and effectively.

To communicate effectively, marketers need to understand how communication works. Communication involves the nine elements shown in ◗ **Figure 11.2**. Two of these elements are the major parties in a communication—the *sender* and the *receiver*. Another two are the major communication tools—the *message* and the *media*. Four more are major communication functions—*encoding*, *decoding*, *response*, and *feedback*. The last element is *noise* in the system. Definitions of these elements follow and are applied to a McDonald's "I'm lovin' it" television commercial for fast food.

- *Sender:* The *party sending the message* to another party—here, McDonald's.
- *Encoding:* The process of *putting thought into symbolic form*—McDonald's advertising agency assembles words, sounds, and illustrations into an advertisement that will convey the intended message.

◗ **FIGURE | 11.2**
Elements in the Communications Process

There is a lot going on in this figure! For example, apply this model to McDonald's. To create great adertising—such as its long-running "I'm lovin' it" campaign—McDonald's must thoroughly understand its customers and how communication works.

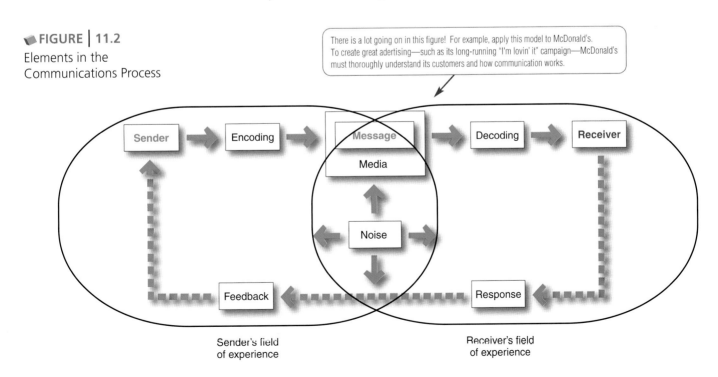

Sender's field of experience

Receiver's field of experience

- *Message:* The *set of symbols* that the sender transmits—the actual McDonald's ad.
- *Media:* The *communication channels* through which the message moves from sender to receiver—in this case, television and the specific television programs that McDonald's selects.
- *Decoding:* The process by which the receiver *assigns meaning to the symbols* encoded by the sender—a consumer watches the McDonald's ad and interprets the words and images it contains.
- *Receiver:* The *party receiving the message* sent by another party—the customer who watches the McDonald's ad.
- *Response:* The *reactions of the receiver* after being exposed to the message—any of hundreds of possible responses, such as the consumer likes McDonald's better, is more likely to eat at McDonald's next time, hums the "I'm lovin' it" jingle, or does nothing.
- *Feedback:* The part of the *receiver's response communicated back to the sender*—McDonald's research shows that consumers remember the ad, or consumers write or call McDonald's praising or criticizing the ad or products.
- *Noise:* The *unplanned static or distortion* during the communications process, which results in the receivers getting a different message than the one the sender sent—the consumer is distracted while watching the commercial and misses its key points.

For a message to be effective, the sender's encoding process must mesh with the receiver's decoding process. The best messages consist of words and other symbols that are familiar to the receiver. The more the sender's field of experience overlaps with that of the receiver, the more effective the message is likely to be. Marketing communicators may not always *share* their consumer's field of experience. For example, an advertising copywriter from one socioeconomic stratum might create ads for consumers from another stratum—say, wealthy business owners. However, to communicate effectively, the marketing communicator must *understand* the consumer's field of experience.

This model points out several key factors in good communication. Senders need to know what audiences they wish to reach and what responses they want. They must be good at encoding messages that take into account how the target audience decodes them. They must send messages through media that reach target audiences, and they must develop feedback channels so that they can assess the audience's response to the message.

> **Author Comment** | Now that we understand how communication works, it's time to turn all of those promotion mix elements into an actual marketing communications program.

Steps in Developing Effective Marketing Communications (pp 308–313)

We now examine the steps in developing an effective integrated communications and promotion program. Marketers must do the following: Identify the target audience, determine the communication objectives, design a message, choose the media through which to send the message, select the message source, and collect feedback.

Identifying the Target Audience

A marketing communicator starts with a clear target audience in mind. The audience may be current users or potential buyers, those who make the buying decision or those who influence it. The audience may be individuals, groups, special publics, or the general public. The target audience will heavily affect the communicator's decisions on *what* will be said, *how* it will be said, *when* it will be said, *where* it will be said, and *who* will say it.

Determining the Communication Objectives

Once the target audience has been defined, the marketers must decide what response they seek. Of course, in many cases, they will seek a *purchase* response. But purchase may be only the result of a long consumer decision-making process. The marketing

Buyer-readiness stages
The stages consumers normally pass through on their way to making a purchase; they are awareness, knowledge, liking, preference, conviction, and purchase.

communicator needs to know where the target audience now stands and to what stage it needs to be moved. The target audience may be in any of six **buyer-readiness stages**, the stages consumers normally pass through on their way to making a purchase. These stages are *awareness*, *knowledge*, *liking*, *preference*, *conviction*, and *purchase* (see 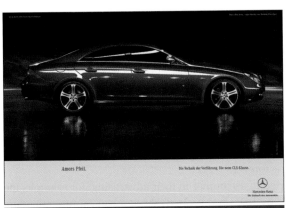 **Figure 11.3**).

The marketing communicator's target market may be totally unaware of the product, know only its name, or know only a few things about it. The communicator must first build *awareness* and *knowledge*. For example, when Mercedes launched the CLS model in 2004, it started to build awareness through a 'teaser' campaign. The CLS model's offline creative had already adopted the line, "The technology of seduction." The teaser banners followed that lead, inviting people to send in email addresses and personal information in return for a chance to be at the official launch of the CLS in Lebanon.

The teasers were followed by a 'reveal' campaign, which typically used many aspects of online marketing, such as online TV advertising, and grassroots and viral marketing through video email shots. The campaign aimed, in this way, to reach the maximum audience and make them aware of the new addition to the Mercedes fleet.[8]

Assuming that target consumers *know* about the product, how do they *feel* about it? Once potential buyers knew about the CLS, Mercedes' marketers wanted to move them through successively stronger stages of feelings toward the new model. These stages included *liking* (feeling favorable about the car), *preference* (preferring CLS to other luxury cars), and *conviction* (believing that CLS is the best luxury car for them). Mercedes' marketers used a combination of the promotion mix tools to create positive feelings and conviction. Advertising built an emotional brand connection and illustrated the CLS' design and features. Press releases and other public relations activities helped build up anticipation for the release of the CLS model. And a packed website informed potential buyers about technical specs, answered FAQs, and so on.

Finally, some members of the target market might be convinced about the product, but not quite get around to making the *purchase*. Potential CLS buyers might have decided to wait for more information or for the price to drop. The communicator must lead these consumers to take the final step. Actions might include offering special promotional prices, add-ons, rebates, or premiums. Mercedes might send out emails to customers of other Mercedes products, urging them to buy the eye-catching CLS as their next car.

Of course, marketing communications alone could not create positive feelings and purchases for the CLS model. The model itself must provide superior value for the customer. In fact, outstanding marketing communications can actually speed the demise of a poor product. The more quickly potential buyers learn about the poor product, the more quickly they become aware of its faults. Thus, good marketing communication calls for "good deeds followed by good words."

Designing a Message

Having defined the desired audience response, the communicator turns to developing an effective message. Ideally, the message should get *Attention*, hold *Interest*, arouse *Desire*, and obtain *Action* (a framework known as the *AIDA model*). In practice, few messages take the consumer all the way from awareness to purchase, but the AIDA framework suggests the desirable qualities of a good message.

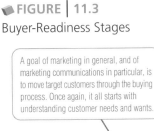
Mercedes launched the new CLS model in 2004 via a teaser campaign to get potential customers interested and encourage them to find out more.

FIGURE | 11.3

Buyer-Readiness Stages

A goal of marketing in general, and of marketing communications in particular, is to move target customers through the buying process. Once again, it all starts with understanding customer needs and wants.

| Awareness | Knowledge | Liking | Preference | Conviction | **Purchase** |

When putting the message together, the marketing communicator must decide what to say (*message content*) and how to say it (*message structure* and *format*).

Message Content

The marketer has to figure out an appeal or theme that will produce the desired response. There are three types of appeals: rational, emotional, and moral. *Rational appeals* relate to the audience's self-interest. They show that the product will produce the desired benefits. Examples are messages showing a product's quality, economy, value, or performance. Thus, in one ad, Lifebuoy soap claims strong disinfectant qualities that will kill most germs and keep the consumer healthy.

Emotional appeals attempt to stir up either negative or positive emotions that can motivate purchase. Communicators may use emotional appeals ranging from love, joy, and humor to fear and guilt. Advocates of emotional messages claim that they attract more attention and create more belief in the sponsor and brand. "Brain science has proved [that] consumers feel before they think, and feelings happen fast," says one expert. "Real persuasion is emotional in nature."[9] Thus, Michelin sells tires using mild fear appeals, showing families riding in cars and telling parents "Michelin: Because so much is riding on your tires." And the Diamond Trading Company runs emotional ads showing men surprising the women they love with diamond jewelry. Concludes one commercial, "With every waking moment love grows. A diamond is forever."

These days, companies have started to use humor in their advertising; for example, the introduction advertisement of 3D TV by LD. Used properly, humor can capture attention, make people feel good, and give a brand personality. However, advertisers must be careful when using humor. Used poorly, it can detract from comprehension, wear out its welcome fast, overshadow the product, or even irritate consumers.

Dubai Cares uses moral appeal to encourage participation in its many activities.

Moral appeals are directed to the audience's sense of what is 'right' and 'proper.' They are often used to urge people to support social causes such as a cleaner environment or aid to the disadvantaged. For example, the UAE-based philanthropic establishment Dubai Cares invited audiences to participate in a walk that symbolized the daily endurance of millions of children in order to attend school. Participants raised money to support school children in developing countries.

Message Structure

Marketers must also decide how to handle three message structure issues. The first is whether to draw a conclusion or leave it to the audience. Research suggests that in many cases, rather than drawing a conclusion, the advertiser is better off asking questions and letting buyers come to their own conclusions. The second message structure issue is whether to present the strongest arguments first or last. Presenting them first gets strong attention but may lead to an anticlimactic ending.

The third message structure issue is whether to present a one-sided argument (mentioning only the product's strengths) or a two-sided argument (touting the product's strengths while also admitting its shortcomings). Usually, a one-sided argument is more effective in sales presentations—except when audiences are highly educated or likely to hear opposing claims, or when the communicator has a negative association to overcome. In this spirit, Heinz ran the message "Heinz Ketchup is slow good" and Listerine mouthwash ran the message "Listerine tastes bad twice a day." In such cases, two-sided messages can enhance the advertiser's credibility and make buyers more resistant to competitor attacks.

Message Format

The marketing communicator also needs a strong *format* for the message. In a print ad, the communicator has to decide on the headline, copy, illustration, and color. To attract

Galaxy used eye-catching forms and pictures in order to attract attention.

attention, advertisers can use novelty and contrast; eye-catching pictures and headlines; distinctive formats; message size and position; and color, shape, and movement. If the message is to be carried over the radio, the communicator has to choose words, sounds, and voices. The 'sound' of an ad promoting banking services should be different from one promoting an iPod.

If the message is to be carried on television or in person, then all these elements plus body language have to be planned. Presenters plan every detail—their facial expressions, gestures, dress, posture, and hairstyles. If the message is carried on the product or its package, the communicator has to watch texture, scent, color, size, and shape. For example, one study revealed that people make subconscious judgments about an item within 90 seconds of initial viewing and that up to 90 percent of that assessment is based on color. Another study suggests that color increases brand recognition by up to 80 percent. Thus, in designing effective marketing communications, marketers must consider color and other seemingly unimportant details carefully.[10] For example, consider the Galaxy New Shape print ad aimed at enticing consumers to fall in love with the new beautifully shaped and softly melting Galaxy tablet. Galaxy used eye-catching forms and pictures in order to attract attention.

Choosing Media

The communicator must now select *channels of communication*. There are two broad types of communication channels—*personal* and *nonpersonal*.

Personal Communication Channels

Personal communication channels
Channels through which two or more people communicate directly with each other, including face to face, on the phone, through mail or email, or even through an Internet chat.

In **personal communication channels**, two or more people communicate directly with each other. They might communicate face to face, on the telephone, through mail or email, or even through an Internet 'chat.' Personal communication channels are effective because they allow for personal addressing and feedback.

Some personal communication channels are controlled directly by the company. For example, company salespeople contact target buyers. But other personal communications about the product may reach buyers through channels not directly controlled by the company. These channels might include independent experts—consumer advocates, online buying guides, and others—making statements to buyers. Or they might be neighbors, friends, family members, and associates talking to target buyers. This last channel, **word-of-mouth influence**, has considerable effect in many product areas.

Word-of-mouth influence
Personal communication about a product between target buyers and neighbors, friends, family members, and associates.

When Nielsen Global carried out an online consumer survey in the UAE, it found that 95 percent of Internet consumers trust recommendations from people they know; word of mouth is the most trusted medium. From a similar survey of over 25,000 Internet consumers from 50 countries, researchers found that recommendations from personal acquaintances and opinions posted by consumers online were the most trusted forms of advertising globally. Nielsen discovered that 90 percent of Internet consumers worldwide trust recommendations from people they know, and 70 percent trust consumer opinions posted online.[11]

Personal influence carries great weight for products that are expensive, risky, or highly visible. Consider the power of simple customer reviews on Amazon.com:

It doesn't matter how loud or often you tell consumers your "truth," few today are buying a big-ticket item before they know what existing users have to say about the product. This is a low-trust world. That's why "recommendation by a relative or friend" comes out on top in just about every survey of purchasing influences. A recent study found that more than 90 percent of customers trust "recommendations from consumers," whereas trust in ads runs from a high of about 40 percent to less than 10 percent. It's also a major reason for Amazon's success in growing sales per customer. Who hasn't made an Amazon purchase based on another customer's review or the "Customers who bought this also bought…" section? And it explains what a recent Shop.org survey found—that 96 percent of retailers find ratings and reviews to be an effective tactic in lifting online sales.[12]

Companies can take steps to put personal communication channels to work for them. For example, they can create *opinion leaders* for their brands—people whose opinions are sought by others—by supplying influencers with the product on attractive terms or by educating them so that they can inform others. **Buzz marketing** involves cultivating opinion leaders and getting them to spread information about a product or service to others in their communities.

Buzz marketing

Cultivating opinion leaders and getting them to spread information about a product or service to others in their communities.

In 2008, Catch, a digital agency based in Dubai, teamed up with international agency Vanksen, a global leader in buzz marketing. The aim was to bring the latest online marketing tools to the Arab world, tailoring Vanksen's word-of-mouth marketing platforms and strategies to the needs of regional markets. Word-of-mouth platforms of this type are designed to encourage bloggers to generate online recommendations.

Consumers in the Arab world are increasingly looking online for information about products and services, and the Internet plays a large role in shaping opinions. Brands can thus gain competitive advantage by using word-of-mouth marketing techniques including buzz, blogs, viral and social media marketing. "There is nothing like culture-buzz, as a platform, in existence in the region, nor are there any other agencies focusing on this aspect of digital marketing," said Anthony Rischard, CEO at Catch.

An additional reason for forming the partnership was to create buzz on- and offline. Information that starts online travels far in the offline realm. This may occur through print, with more and more journalists following blogs themselves, or by phone and face-to-face conversation.

One of Vanksen's key strengths is in fostering relationships with bloggers through its BuzzParadise website. The company briefs bloggers on its clients and its clients' products, lets them experience the products, and then allows them to write their own comments. Catch's contribution was to bring its knowledge of local markets and local bloggers.

Emmanuel Vivier, CEO and cofounder of Vanksen, said, "Given the cluttered and fractured nature of media in the Middle East, 'traditional' web advertising is no longer enough to break through—cutting edge viral, digital word of mouth, and buzz marketing techniques must be a central part of the mix."

A number of studies have demonstrated the benefits of online engagement with consumers. A Bayt.com and YouGovSiraj study, which focused on consumers in the Arab world, suggested that the Internet came second behind only word of mouth as a source of information for purchase decisions, and was particularly important for those who had a higher household income.

A Maktoob study considered younger consumers and found that 70 percent of people under 25 in Jordan, Egypt, Saudi Arabia, and the UAE considered the Internet to be the best source of information. Maktoob also found that there were more than 40 million Internet users in the Arab world, not counting mobile digital users.[13]

Nonpersonal Communication Channels

Nonpersonal communication channels

Media that carry messages without personal contact or feedback, including major media, atmospheres, and events.

Nonpersonal communication channels are media that carry messages without personal contact or feedback. They include major media, atmospheres, and events. Major *media* include print media (newspapers, magazines, directmail), broadcast media (radio, television), display media (billboards, signs, posters), and online media (email, company websites, online social and sharing networks). *Atmospheres* are designed environments that create or reinforce the buyer's leanings toward buying a product. Thus, lawyers' offices and banks are designed to communicate confidence and other qualities that might be valued by clients. *Events* are staged occurrences that communicate messages to target audiences. For example, public relations departments arrange press conferences, grand openings, shows and exhibits, public tours, and other events.

Nonpersonal communication affects buyers directly. In addition, using mass media often affects buyers indirectly by causing more personal communication. Communications first flow from television, magazines, and other mass media to opinion leaders and then from these opinion leaders to others. Thus, opinion leaders step between the mass media and their audiences and carry messages to people who are less exposed to media. This suggests that mass communicators should aim their messages directly at opinion leaders, letting them carry the messages to others. Interestingly, marketers often use nonpersonal communication channels to replace or stimulate personal communication by embedding consumer endorsements or word-of-mouth testimonials in their ads and other promotions.

Selecting the Message Source

In either personal or nonpersonal communication, the message's impact on the target audience is also affected by how the audience views the communicator. Messages delivered by highly credible sources are more persuasive. Thus, many companies promote to doctors, dentists, and other health care providers to motivate these professionals to recommend their products to patients. And marketers hire celebrity endorsers—well-known athletes, actors, musicians, and even cartoon characters—to deliver their messages. For example, Sensodyne toothpaste and Oral-B use dentists to promote these brands, Lifebuoy and Dettol have used doctor or doctor-like personalities, while Pantene has worked with Mona Zaki in commercials to deliver its message, appealing to women wanting healthy, shiny hair like hers.

But companies must be careful when selecting celebrities to represent their brands. Picking the wrong spokesperson can result in embarrassment and a tarnished image.

Mona Zaki provided celebrity endorsement for Pantene in hair care commercials.

Collecting Feedback

After sending the message, the communicator must research its effect on the target audience. This involves asking the target audience members whether they remember the message, how many times they saw it, what points they recall, how they felt about the message, and their past and present attitudes toward the product and company. The communicator would also like to measure behavior resulting from the message—how many people bought a product, talked to others about it, or visited the store.

Feedback on marketing communications may suggest changes in the promotion program or in the product offer itself. For example, Gulf Air uses television and newspaper advertising to inform consumers in certain areas about the airline, its routes, and its fares. Suppose feedback research shows that 80 percent of all fliers in an area recall seeing the airline's ads and are aware of its flights and prices. Now imagine that 60 percent of those fliers have flown Gulf Air but only 20 percent were satisfied. These results suggest that although promotion is creating *awareness*, the airline isn't giving consumers the *satisfaction* they expect. Therefore, Gulf Air needs to improve its service while staying with the successful communication program. In contrast, suppose the research shows that only 40 percent of consumers in a particular area are aware of Gulf Air. Of those consumers who are aware, 30 percent have flown with the airline, but 80 percent return as customers. In this case, Gulf Air needs to strengthen its promotion program to take advantage of its power to create customer satisfaction.

Author Comment | In this section, we'll look at the promotion budget-setting process and at how marketers blend the various marketing communication tools into a smooth-functioning integrated promotion mix.

Setting the Total Promotion Budget and Mix (pp 314–319)

We have looked at the steps in planning and sending communications to a target audience. But how does the company decide on the total *promotion budget* and its division among the major promotional tools to create the *promotion mix*? By what process does it blend the tools to create integrated marketing communications? We now look at these questions.

Setting the Total Promotion Budget

One of the hardest marketing decisions facing a company is how much to spend on promotion. It is not surprising that industries and companies vary widely in how much they spend on promotion. Promotion spending may be 10 to 12 percent of sales for consumer packaged goods, 14 percent for cosmetics, and only 1 percent for industrial machinery products. Within a given industry, both low and high spenders can be found.[14] **Real Marketing 11.2** considers Qatar Airways' approach to marketing spending.

How does a company decide on its promotion budget? Here, we look at four common methods used to set the total budget for advertising: the *affordable method*, the *percentage-of-sales method*, the *competitive-parity method*, and the *objective-and-task method*.[15]

Affordable Method

Affordable method
Setting the promotion budget at the level management thinks the company can afford.

Some companies use the **affordable method**: They set the promotion budget at the level they think the company can afford. Small businesses often use this method, reasoning that the company cannot spend more on advertising than it has. They start with total revenues, deduct operating expenses and capital outlays, and then devote some portion of the remaining funds to advertising.

Unfortunately, this method of setting budgets completely ignores the effects of promotion on sales. It tends to place promotion last among spending priorities, even in situations in which advertising is critical to the firm's success. It leads to an uncertain annual promotion budget, which makes long-range market planning difficult. Although the affordable method can result in overspending on advertising, it more often results in underspending.

Percentage-of-Sales Method

Percentage-of-sales method
Setting the promotion budget at a certain percentage of current or forecasted sales or as a percentage of the unit sales price.

Other companies use the **percentage-of-sales method**, setting their promotion budget at a certain percentage of current or forecasted sales. Or they budget a percentage of the unit sales price. The percentage-of-sales method has advantages. It is simple to use and helps management think about the relationships between promotion spending, selling price, and profit per unit.

Despite these claimed advantages, however, the percentage-of-sales method has little to justify it. It wrongly views sales as the *cause* of promotion rather than as the *result*. Although studies have found a positive correlation between promotional spending and brand strength, this relationship often turns out to be effect and cause, not cause and effect. Stronger brands with higher sales can afford the biggest ad budgets.

Thus, the percentage-of-sales budget is based on availability of funds rather than on opportunities. It may prevent the increased spending sometimes needed to turn around falling sales. Because the budget varies with year-to-year sales, long-range planning is difficult. Finally, the method does not provide any basis for choosing a *specific* percentage, except what has been done in the past or what competitors are doing.

Competitive-Parity Method

Competitive-parity method
Setting the promotion budget to match competitors' outlays.

Still other companies use the **competitive-parity method**, setting their promotion budgets to match competitors' outlays. They monitor competitors' advertising or get industry promotion spending estimates from publications or trade associations, and then set their budgets based on the industry average.

Real Marketing 11.2

Qatar Airways

Qatar Airways makes enormous efforts in its marketing activities.

Qatar Airways was established on November 22, 1993 and began operating on January 20, 1994. It was originally privately owned by members of the Qatari royal family, but was re-launched in 1997 under a new management team. Currently, the government of Qatar holds a 50 percent stake in Qatar Airways, with the remainder held by private investors. Over the years, Qatar Airways has grown into one of the most competitive airlines in the world.

Qatar Airways launched flights to its hundredth destination, the Syrian city of Aleppo, during the first half of 2011. Its routes span Europe, the Middle East, Africa, South Asia, North and South America, and the Asia Pacific region. In 2011, the airline operated over 90 aircraft, and by 2013, the fleet size is expected to rise to over 120 aircraft. The airline also has one of the youngest fleets in the industry, with an average aircraft age of under four years. Qatar Airways currently has 200 new aircraft on order, for delivery over the next few years, worth over US$40 billion.

Qatar Airways was ranked as the third-best airline in the world in the annual 2010 Skytrax passenger survey, and was named Best Business Class In The World at the 2010 World Airline Awards. At the 2011 World Travel Awards, Qatar Airways' business class was voted best in the region for the sixth year running, while in 2009, its business class was voted best in the world.

During 2003 Qatar Airways carried 3.3 million passengers, with this rising to 4.6 million in 2004. This increase has continued over recent years, with passenger numbers exceeding 14 million in 2009/2010. The airline was expected to carry more than 16 million passengers in 2010/11.

These accomplishments were possible as a result of huge marketing efforts, including the following:

- In April 2011, for its 100th destination celebration, it offered customers two tickets for the price of one.
- In March 2011, a new advertising campaign highlighted the unique characteristics of each region within the airline's expanding global network. For example, specific advertisements featured India, Europe, Australia, and so on.
- In March 2011, it sponsored a career fair in London and took part in ITB Berlin—the world's largest travel show.
- In early 2011, the airline sponsored the 10th Annual Tour of Qatar cycling event in Doha and was the Official Carrier for the Qatar ExxonMobil Open 2011 Tennis Tournament.
- In December 2010, Qatar Airways sponsored the International Film Festival of India, and flew three U.S.astronauts between the United States and the Gulf.
- In October 2010, the airline was named the Official Airline of the Doha Tribeca Film Festival, hosted the opening night gala after-party, and offered VIP access to the WTA Championships.
- In January 2010, Qatar Airways continued its support of the Qatar Orphan Foundation following a fundraising car rally.

As shown above, the list of marketing activities is long; the airline clearly makes a considerable effort to communicate effectively around the globe. Based on analysis of Google searches for the top four GCC airlines, it can be seen that the marketing efforts of Qatar Airways are paying off.

Several people have argued that Qatar Airways' marketing spend is too high. Ulrich Schulte-Strathaus, Secretary General of the Association of European Airlines, suggested in one speech that the huge growth realized by GCC airlines was not based on their aspiration to grow and make money, but was part of the complete country economical plan to enhance their overall economy, saying, "These airlines are owned by their respective governments and operated as an instrument of national strategy." He also said, referring to Emirates, Qatar Airways, and Etihad Airways: "And evidently, the Emirates of the Gulf region are satisfied with the value-added created by their investments or believe that in the long-run these investments will generate macro-economic, vertically integrated returns of the magnitude sufficient to warrant the investment." The question he raised that is relevant here is, "But does it make sense for airlines and travelers worldwide if three carriers—two of which have never made a profit—collectively commit 100 billion dollars to transforming the aviation map of the world?"

In response to his speech, Qatar Airways CEO, Akbar Al Baker, said: "I would like to pose a question to Mr Schulte-Strathaus: Can he tell me of any country of the world which does not consider its air transport industry, be that an individual airline or a multitude of them, as part of national interests? Was it not the case that the U.S. government provided its airlines with cash outlays and tax breaks, as well as war insurance subsidies after September 11 in order to ensure the continuity of the U.S. air transport industry? Is it not the case even further that the position

Continued on next page ▼

of the U.S. has consistently been to preserve the national identity and ownership of the U.S. airlines? And on the other side of the Atlantic, doesn't Mr. Schulte-Strathaus consider the billions of euros that are allowed under the EU laws to pump into airlines for 'restructuring purposes' as a manifestation of the strategic national interest in supporting national airlines and what they represent economically and socially?" He later added, "The European airlines were pioneers in a large number of areas. We in

the Gulf airlines community have learnt a lot from them. They should accept competition and that the customer being in the driver's seat."

From a marketing perspective, this raises a key question: How can Qatar Airways optimize its efforts and so produce the maximum impact at the right cost?

Sources: Remarks by Ulrich Schulte-Strathaus, Secretary General, Association of European Airlines, "2011: A Year of Many Crossroads and a Year to Act, Not Delay," International Aviation Club of Washington, January 18, 2011, transcript available at www.iacwashington.org/speeches/2011-01-18-IACSpeech.pdf; "Qatar Airways CEO Hits Back At Comments Made By Association of European Airlines Secretary General Over Dramatic Rise Of Gulf Carriers," press release, Qatar Airways website, February 10, 2011, www.qatarairways.com/global/en/newsroom/archive/PressRelease1_10Feb11.html.

This case was provided by Mohamed Radwan, adjunct faculty member at the American University in Cairo and managing director for Platinum Partners.

Two arguments support this method. First, competitors' budgets represent the collective wisdom of the industry. Secondly, spending what competitors spend helps prevent promotion wars. Unfortunately, neither argument is valid. There are no grounds for believing that the competition has a better idea of what a company should be spending on promotion than does the company itself. Companies differ greatly, and each has its own special promotion needs. Finally, there is no evidence that budgets based on competitive parity prevent promotion wars.

Objective-and-Task Method

Objective-and-task method
Developing the promotion budget by (1) defining specific objectives, (2) determining the tasks that must be performed to achieve these objectives, and (3) estimating the costs of performing these tasks. The sum of these costs is the proposed promotion budget.

The most logical budget-setting method is the **objective-and-task method**, whereby the company sets its promotion budget based on what it wants to accomplish with promotion. This budgeting method entails (1) defining specific promotion objectives, (2) determining the tasks needed to achieve these objectives, and (3) estimating the costs of performing these tasks. The sum of these costs is the proposed promotion budget.

The advantage of the objective-and-task method is that it forces management to spell out its assumptions about the relationship between dollars spent and promotion results. But it is also the most difficult method to use. Often, it is hard to figure out which specific tasks will achieve stated objectives. For example, suppose Sony wants 95 percent awareness for its latest camcorder model during the six-month introductory period. What specific advertising messages and media schedules should Sony use to attain this objective? How much would these messages and media schedules cost? Sony management must consider such questions, even though they are hard to answer.

Shaping the Overall Promotion Mix

The concept of integrated marketing communications suggests that the company must blend the promotion tools carefully into a co-ordinated *promotion mix*. But how does the company determine what mix of promotion tools it will use? Companies within the same industry differ greatly in the design of their promotion mixes. Al Hathboor International, Avon's cosmetic products distributor in the UAE , mainly promotes the products through door-to door selling and direct marketing, while Unilever promotes its cosmetics range through strong TV, print and other indirect forms of promotions. We now look at factors that influence the marketer's choice of promotion tools.

The Nature of Each Promotion Tool

Each promotion tool has unique characteristics and costs. Marketers must understand these characteristics in shaping the promotion mix.

Advertising. Advertising can reach masses of geographically spread out buyers at a low cost per exposure, and it enables the seller to repeat a message many times. For example, television advertising can reach huge audiences.

Beyond its reach, large-scale advertising says something positive about the seller's size, popularity, and success. Because of advertising's public nature, consumers tend to view advertised products as more legitimate. Advertising is also very expressive—it allows the company to dramatize its products through the artful use of visuals, print, sound, and color. On the one hand, advertising can be used to build up a long-term image for a product (such as Coca-Cola ads). On the other hand, advertising can trigger quick sales (as when a department store such as Carrefour advertises weekend specials).

Advertising also has some shortcomings. Although it reaches many people quickly, advertising is impersonal and cannot be as directly persuasive as can company salespeople. For the most part, advertising can carry on only a one-way communication with the audience, and the audience does not feel that it has to pay attention or respond. In addition, advertising can be very costly. Although some advertising forms, such as newspaper and radio advertising, can be done on smaller budgets, other forms, such as network television advertising, require very large budgets.

With personal selling, the customer feels a greater need to listen and respond, even if the response is a polite "no thank you."

Personal Selling. Personal selling is the most effective tool at certain stages of the buying process, particularly in building up buyers' preferences, convictions, and actions. It involves personal interaction between two or more people, so each person can observe the other's needs and characteristics and make quick adjustments. Personal selling also allows all kinds of customer relationships to spring up, ranging from matter-of-fact selling relationships to personal friendships. An effective salesperson keeps the customer's interests at heart in order to build a long-term relationship by solving customer problems. Finally, with personal selling, the buyer usually feels a greater need to listen and respond, even if the response is a polite "No thank you."

These unique qualities come at a cost, however. A sales force requires a longer-term commitment than does advertising—advertising can be turned on and off, but sales force size is harder to change. Personal selling is also the company's most expensive promotion tool. Firms often spend up to three times as much on personal selling as they do on advertising.

Sales Promotion. Sales promotion includes a wide assortment of tools—coupons, contests, money-off deals, premiums, and others—all of which have many unique qualities. They attract consumer attention, offer strong incentives to purchase, and can be used to dramatize product offers and to boost sagging sales. Sales promotions invite and reward quick response—whereas advertising says, "Buy our product," sales promotion says, "Buy it now." Sales promotion effects are often short-lived, however, and often are not as effective as advertising or personal selling in building long-run brand preference and customer relationships.

Public Relations. Public relations is very believable—news stories, features, sponsorships, and events seem more real and believable to readers than ads do. Public relations can also reach many prospects who avoid salespeople and advertisements—the message gets to the buyers as 'news' rather than as a sales-directed communication. And, as with advertising, public relations can dramatize a company or product. Marketers tend to underuse public relations or to use it as an afterthought. Yet a well-thought-out public relations campaign used with other promotion mix elements can be very effective and economical.

Direct Marketing. Although there are many forms of direct marketing—direct mail and catalogs, telephone marketing, online marketing, and others—they all share four distinctive characteristics. Direct marketing is *less public*: The message is normally directed to a specific person. Direct marketing is *immediate* and *customized*: Messages can be prepared very quickly and can be tailored to appeal to specific consumers. Finally, direct marketing is *interactive*: It allows a dialogue between the marketing team and the consumer, and messages can be altered depending on the consumer's response. Thus, direct marketing is well suited to highly targeted marketing efforts and to building one-to-one customer relationships.

Promotion Mix Strategies

Marketers can choose from two basic promotion mix strategies—*push* promotion or *pull* promotion. ◗ Figure 11.4 contrasts the two strategies. The relative emphasis on the specific promotion tools differs for push and pull strategies. A **push strategy** involves 'pushing' the product through marketing channels to final consumers. The producer directs its marketing activities (primarily personal selling and trade promotion) toward channel members to induce them to carry the product and to promote it to final consumers.

Using a **pull strategy**, the producer directs its marketing activities (primarily advertising and consumer promotion) toward final consumers to induce them to buy the product. If the pull strategy is effective, consumers will then demand the product from channel members, who will in turn demand it from producers. Thus, under a pull strategy, consumer demand 'pulls' the product through the channels.

Some industrial-goods companies use only push strategies; some direct-marketing companies use only pull. However, most large companies use some combination of both. For example, Unilever and P&G use mass-media advertising and consumer promotions to pull their products, and a large sales force and trade promotions to push their products through the channels. In recent years, consumer goods companies have been decreasing the pull portions of their mixes in favor of more push. This has caused concern that they may be driving short-run sales at the expense of long-term brand equity.

Companies consider many factors when designing their promotion mix strategies, including *type of product/market* and the *product life-cycle stage*. For example, the importance of different promotion tools varies between consumer and business markets. Business-to-consumer companies usually 'pull' more, putting more of their funds into advertising, followed by sales promotion, personal selling, and then public relations. In contrast, business-to-business marketers tend to 'push' more, putting more of their funds into personal selling, followed by sales promotion, advertising, and public relations. In general, personal selling is used more heavily with expensive and risky goods and in markets with fewer and larger sellers.

The effects of different promotion tools also vary with stages of the product life cycle. In the introduction stage, advertising and public relations are good for producing high

Push strategy
A promotion strategy that calls for using the sales force and trade promotion to push the product through channels. The producer promotes the product to channel members who in turn promote it to final consumers.

Pull strategy
A promotion strategy that calls for spending a lot on advertising and consumer promotion to induce final consumers to buy the product, creating a demand vacuum that 'pulls' the product through the channels.

◗ FIGURE | 11.4
Push versus Pull Promotion Strategy

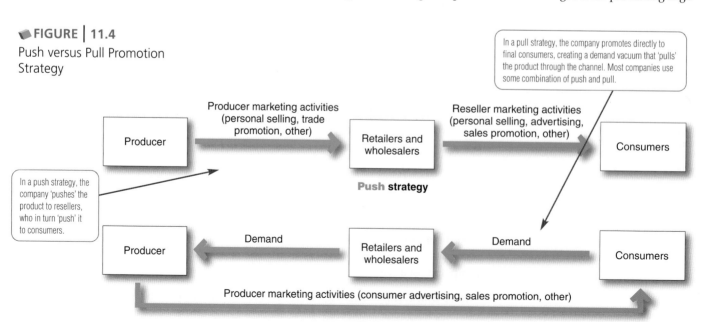

awareness, and sales promotion is useful in promoting early trial. Personal selling must be used to get the trade to carry the product. In the growth stage, advertising and public relations continue to be powerful influences, whereas sales promotion can be reduced because fewer incentives are needed. In the mature stage, sales promotion again becomes important relative to advertising. Buyers know the brands, and advertising is needed only to remind them of the product. In the decline stage, advertising is kept at a reminder level, public relations is dropped, and salespeople give the product only a little attention. Sales promotion, however, might continue to be strong.

Integrating the Promotion Mix

Having set the promotion budget and mix, the company must now take steps to see that all of the promotion mix elements are smoothly integrated. Here is a checklist for integrating the firm's marketing communications.[16]

- *Start with customers.* Identify all customer touch points for the company and its brands. Work to ensure that communications at each touch point are consistent with the overall communications strategy and that communications efforts are occurring when, where, and how *customers* want them.

- *Analyze trends—internal and external—that can affect the company's ability to do business.* Look for areas where communications can help the most. Determine the strengths and weaknesses of each communications function. Develop a combination of promotional tactics based on these strengths and weaknesses.

- *Audit the areas of communications spending throughout the organization.* Itemize the communications budgets and tasks and consolidate these into a single budgeting process. Reassess all communications expenditures by product, promotional tool, stage of the life cycle, and observed effect.

- *Team up in communications planning.* Engage all communications functions in joint planning. Include customers, suppliers, and other stakeholders at every stage of communications planning.

- *Create compatible themes, tones, and quality across all communications media.* Make sure each element carries the company's unique primary messages and selling points. This consistency achieves greater impact and prevents the unnecessary duplication of work across functions.

- *Create performance measures that are shared by all communications elements.* Develop systems to evaluate the combined impact of all communications activities.

- *Appoint a director responsible for the company's persuasive communications efforts.* This move encourages efficiency by centralizing planning and creating shared performance measures.

Author Comment | Marketers should think beyond what's legal and communicate openly and responsibly with customers. Good customer relationships are built on honesty and trust.

Socially Responsible Marketing Communication (pp 319–320)

In shaping its promotion mix, a company must be aware of the large body of legal and ethical issues surrounding marketing communications. Most marketers work hard to communicate openly and honestly with consumers and resellers. Still, abuses may occur, and public policy makers have developed a substantial body of laws and regulations to govern advertising, sales promotion, personal selling, and direct-marketing activities. In this section, we discuss issues regarding advertising, sales promotion, and personal selling. We discuss issues regarding direct marketing in Chapter 13.

Advertising and Sales Promotion

By law, companies must avoid false or deceptive advertising. Advertisers must not make false claims, such as suggesting that a product cures something when it does not.

Al Baik Food Systems in Saudi Arabia helped to organize the 'Nazeeh and Wartan' anti-littering campaign as part of its corporate social responsibility.

They must avoid ads that have the capacity to deceive, even though no one actually may be deceived. An automobile cannot be advertised as getting 50 kilometers per liter unless it does so under typical conditions, and a diet bread cannot be advertised as having fewer calories simply because its slices are thinner.

Sellers must avoid bait-and-switch advertising that attracts buyers under false pretenses. For example, a large retailer advertised a sewing machine at US$179. However, when consumers tried to buy the advertised machine, the seller downplayed its features, placed faulty machines on showroom floors, understated the machine's performance, and took other actions in an attempt to switch buyers to a more expensive machine. Such actions are both unethical and illegal.

A company's trade promotion activities also are closely regulated. For example, under the laws of some nations, sellers cannot favor certain customers through their use of trade promotions. They must make promotional allowances and services available to all resellers on proportionately equal terms.

Beyond simply avoiding legal pitfalls, such as deceptive or bait-and-switch advertising, companies can use advertising and other forms of promotion to encourage and promote socially responsible programs and actions. For example, Al Baik Food Systems in Saudi Arabia organized the 'Nazeeh and Wartan' anti-littering campaign as part of its corporate social responsibility initiative aimed at encouraging the society to protect and care for the environment. The campaign encouraged children to follow the example of Nazeeh, a cartoon character, who is depicted as being clean and tidy.

Personal Selling

A company's salespeople must follow the rules of 'fair competition.' Some countries have enacted deceptive sales acts that spell out what is not allowed. For example, salespeople may not lie to consumers or mislead them about the advantages of buying a product. To avoid bait-and-switch practices, salespeople's statements must match advertising claims.

Much personal selling involves business-to-business trade. In selling to businesses, salespeople may not offer bribes to purchasing agents or to others who can influence a sale. They may not obtain or use technical or trade secrets of competitors through bribery or industrial espionage. Finally, salespeople must not disparage competitors or competing products by suggesting things that are not true.[17]

REVIEWING Objectives AND KEY Terms

In this chapter, you've learned how companies use integrated marketing communications (IMC) to communicate customer value. Modern marketing calls for more than just creating customer value by developing a good product, pricing it attractively, and making it available to target customers. Companies also must clearly and persuasively *communicate* that value to current and prospective customers. To do this, they must blend five promotion mix tools, guided by a well-designed and implemented integrated marketing communications strategy.

OBJECTIVE 1 Define the five promotion mix tools for communicating customer value. (pp 301–302)

A company's total *promotion mix*—also called its *marketing communications mix*—consists of the specific blend of *advertising, personal selling, sales promotion, public relations*, and *direct-marketing* tools that the company uses to persuasively communicate customer value and build customer relationships. Advertising includes any paid form of nonpersonal presentation and promotion of ideas, goods, or services by an identified sponsor. In contrast, public relations focuses on building good relations with the company's various publics by obtaining favorable unpaid publicity. Personal selling is any form of personal presentation by the firm's sales force for the purpose of making sales and building customer relationships. Firms use sales promotion to provide short-term incentives to encourage the purchase or sale of a product or service. Finally, firms seeking immediate response from targeted individual customers use nonpersonal direct-marketing tools to communicate with customers.

OBJECTIVE 2 Discuss the changing communications landscape and the need for integrated marketing communications. (pp 303–306)

Recent shifts toward targeted or one-to-one marketing, coupled with advances in information and communication technology, have had a dramatic impact on marketing communications. As marketing communicators adopt richer but more fragmented media and promotion mixes to reach their diverse markets, they risk creating a communications hodgepodge for consumers. To prevent this, more companies are adopting the concept of *integrated marketing communications (IMC)*. Guided by an overall IMC strategy, the company works out the roles that the various promotional tools will play and the extent to which each will be used. It carefully co-ordinates the promotional activities and the timing of when major campaigns take place. Finally, to help implement its integrated marketing strategy, the company appoints a marketing communications director, who has overall responsibility for the company's communications efforts.

OBJECTIVE 3 Outline the communications process and the steps in developing effective marketing communications. (pp 307–313)

The communications process involves nine elements—two major parties (sender, receiver), two communication tools (message, media), four communication functions (encoding, decoding, response, and feedback), and noise. To communicate effectively, marketers must understand how these elements combine to communicate value to target customers.

In preparing marketing communications, the communicator's first task is to *identify the target audience* and its characteristics. Next, the communicator has to determine the *communication objectives* and define the response sought, whether it be *awareness, knowledge, liking, preference, conviction,* or *purchase.* Then a *message* should be constructed with an effective content and structure. *Media* must be selected, both for personal and nonpersonal communication. The communicator must find highly credible sources to deliver messages. Finally, the communicator must collect *feedback* by watching how much of the market becomes aware, tries the product, and is satisfied in the process.

OBJECTIVE 4 Explain the methods for setting the promotion budget and factors that affect the design of the promotion mix. (pp 314–320)

The company has to decide how much to spend on promotion. The most popular approaches are to spend what the company can afford, to use a percentage of sales, to base promotion on competitors' spending, or to base it on an analysis and costing of the communication objectives and tasks. The company has to divide the *promotion budget* among the major tools to create the *promotion mix.* Companies can pursue a *push* or a *pull* promotional strategy, or a combination of the two. The best specific blend of promotion tools depends on the type of product/market, the buyer's readiness stage, and the product life-cycle stage. People at all levels of the organization must be aware of the many legal and ethical issues surrounding marketing communications. Companies must work hard and proactively at communicating openly, honestly, and agreeably with their customers and resellers.

KEY Terms

OBJECTIVE 1

Promotion mix (marketing communications mix) (p 301)
Advertising (p 302)
Sales promotion (p 302)
Personal selling (p 302)
Public relations (p 302)
Direct marketing (p 302)

OBJECTIVE 2

Integrated marketing communications (IMC) (p 306)

OBJECTIVE 3

Buyer-readiness stages (p 309)
Personal communication channels (p 311)
Word-of-mouth influence (p 311)
Buzz marketing (p 312)
Nonpersonal communication channels (p 312)

OBJECTIVE 4

Affordable method (p 314)
Percentage-of-sales method (p 314)
Competitive-parity method (p 314)
Objective-and-task method (p 316)
Push strategy (p 318)
Pull strategy (p 318)

DISCUSSING & APPLYING THE Concepts

Discussing the Concepts

1. List and briefly describe the five major promotion mix tools.

2. Discuss the three major factors changing the face of today's marketing communications.

3. Name and briefly describe the nine elements of the communications process. Why do marketers need to understand these elements?

4. List the steps in developing effective marketing communications.

5. Name and describe the common methods for setting promotion budgets.

6. Compare and contrast push and pull promotion strategies. Which promotion tools are most effective in each?

Applying the Concepts

1. Describe the three types of appeals used in marketing communications messages and develop three different advertisements for the same brand of a product of your choice, each using a different appeal.

2. Energizer is introducing a new line of batteries that provide a longer life than its existing models. The brand manager for the new line believes most of the promotion budget should be spent on consumer and trade promotions, but the assistant brand manager thinks that the promotion mix should emphasize television advertising. Partner with another student. Play the roles of the brand manager and assistant brand manager and debate their opposing views on advertising versus promotion.

FOCUS ON Technology

Worldwide global advertising expenditures grew 2 percent in 2009, despite the recession, down from 7 percent in 2008. Developing markets are now becoming an important part of that growth, compensating for slower growth in more developed markets. It is estimated that by the end of 2011, China will have become the second largest advertising market, and Russia will have grown to sixth. It is also estimated that in 2011, global expenditure for advertising on the Internet will reach US$106.6 billion, and its overall market share will have grown from 15 to 20 percent. In 2010, the Internet overtook newspapers as the second largest advertising medium. Since 2008, global advertising expenditures have increased from US$450,110 million to a record of about US$457,192 million in 2010.

Marketers need to be accountable for these expenditures, so audience measurement is crucial. Technological solutions abound to help marketers assess how many people might see, read,

or hear their marketing messages. For example, Nielsen Media Research, the goliath of television audience measurement, uses written diary and People Meter technology. But new upstarts are now entering the ring with other measurement tools that reflect the changing landscape of television viewing—live viewing, time-shift viewing, video-on-demand, online viewing, and mobile viewing. Even the once low-tech magazine audience measurement is getting a high-tech upgrade through radio frequency identification (RFID) tags embedded in individual magazines to measure each time they are opened or closed.

1. Research media audience measurement methods for electronic and print media and discuss how technology is changing the way media audiences are measured.

2. Are these audience measurement techniques adequate when accounting for the return on promotional expenditures? Explain.

FOCUS ON Ethics

In October 2007, the Jeddah Municipality in Saudi Arabia announced a new rule that would fine and cut phone connections of small businesses that paste illegal advertisements on houses and at public places. The municipality was responding to a massive number of complaints from members of the public about advertisements defacing people's homes, doorways, and public property.

In the UAE in September 2007, the Sharjah Municipality launched a crackdown on illegally sited advertisements. The municipality began removing advertisements that obstructed "any archaeological, cultural, or religious buildings." Other advertisements that affected traffic flow or hindered drivers' vision were

also removed. The municipality also began fining those placing advertisements in illegal locations. The crackdown was part of a drive to avoid "chaos on the streets."

Back in 2002, a similar three-month campaign was launched in Dubai; it was backed by Emirates Neon, a signage and outdoor advertising agency in the UAE.

1. Fly posting is an integral part of advertising; therefore, it is acceptable. Discuss.

2. Fly posting can be seen as a form of guerrilla marketing. What do you understand to be the meaning of this term?

MARKETING BY THE Numbers

If the objective of marketing and advertising is to increase sales it makes sense to measure up the costs against the returns. But is that really reasonable? Can an advertising expense of US$1 generate sales of US$5? Surely if it was that straightforward and the

relationship between spending and income were that predictable, no business would ever fail.

For more discussion of the financial and quantitative implications of marketing decisions, see Appendix 2: Marketing by the Numbers.

1. Using information regarding industry and leading advertisers' advertising-to-sales ratios (see, http://company.news-record.com/advertising/advertising/ratio.html), recommend percentages of sales that advertisers in the following industries should use to set next year's advertising budget:

department stores, educational services, carpets and rugs, and hotels and motels.

2. How do these figures relate to your own country? Are there comparable sets of data available?

VIDEO Case

Crispin Porter + Bogusky

Crispin Porter + Bogusky (Crispin) may not be the oldest advertising agency in the world. It isn't the biggest either. But it has been working over time to prove that it is the most innovative firm at integrating marketing promotions. In fact, Crispin relies very little on the king of all advertising channels, broadcast television. Instead, Crispin has worked miracles for companies such as Virgin Atlantic Airways, BMW's MINI Cooper, and Burger King by employing nontraditional campaigns on limited budgets.

Crispin attributes its success to the fact that it redefined what an advertisement is. Customer appropriate messages, Crispin discovered, could be delivered in many different ways. So its realm of 'ad space' includes things as obscure as the side of a mailbox or an oversized phone booth in an airport. By communicating a message in many different ways, Crispin has developed a reputation for truly integrating marketing communications.

After viewing the video featuring Crispin, answer the following questions about advertising and promotions:

1. Alex Bogusky once said, "Anything and everything is an ad." What does this mean? How is Crispin demonstrating this mantra?

2. In what ways has Crispin differentiated itself from other advertising agencies?

3. Give some examples as to how Crispin balances strategy with creativity.

COMPANY Case

Burger King: Promoting a Food Fight

In early 2004, as Burger King's CEO Brad Blum reviewed the company's 2003 outcomes, he decided once again that he had to do something to spice up BK's bland performance. Industry leader McDonald's had just reported a 9 percent sales jump in 2003 to a total of US$22.1 billion while number-two BK's U.S. sales had *slipped* about 5 percent to US$7.9 billion. Further, number-three Wendy's sales had spiked 11 percent to US$7.4 billion, putting it in a position to overtake BK.

Blum surprised the fast-food industry by abruptly firing the firm's advertising agency, Young & Rubicam (Y&R), and awarding its global creative account to a small, Miami-based, upstart firm, Crispin Porter + Bogusky (Crispin). The switch marked the fifth time in four years that BK had moved its account! Ad agency Y&R had gotten the US$350 million BK account only 10 months earlier. To help revive BK's sales, it had developed a campaign with the theme "The Fire's Ready," which focused on BK's flame-broiled cooking method versus frying. However, observers found the message to be flat and uninspiring, and the declining sales sealed Y&R's fate.

With the move to Crispin, there was no shortage of speculation that the fickle Burger King would soon move again. Many saw BK as a bad client, impossible to work for. Others predicted that the awarding of this account would ruin Crispin's quirky culture. But in announcing the Crispin selection, Blum indicated he had challenged the firm to develop "groundbreaking, next-level, results-oriented, and innovative advertising that strongly connects

with our core customers." BK automatically became the small firm's largest client, but Crispin was not without an impressive track record. The creative shop was known for its offbeat, unorthodox, and even irreverent promotions. Because its clients often had little money for advertising, Crispin found inexpensive ways to gain attention, veering away from the traditional mass media.

Crispin had produced award-winning, low-budget campaigns for BMW's MINI Cooper, IKEA furniture, Sunglass Hut, and Virgin Atlantic Airways, forging a reputation as an out-of-the-box, results-oriented agency. Along the way, Crispin developed some loose 'rules.' Among them were the following:

- Zero in on the product.
- Kick the TV commercial habit.
- Find the sweet spot (the overlap between product characteristics and customer needs).
- Surprise = buzz = exposure.
- Don't be timid.
- Think of advertising as a product rather than a service.

HIT AFTER HIT FOR THE KING

It was these rules that guided Crispin's work for BK. Within a month of getting the burger giant's account, Crispin recommended going back to the firm's "Have It Your Way" tagline, developed by BK's second advertising agency, BBDO, way back in 1974. Crispin argued that it could take that old phrase and make it relevant to today's customers. Although Crispin's pitch may have initially seemed 'same-old,' it was anything but. Uncharacteristic of its past campaigns, Crispin kicked off the new BK campaign with TV commercials. In a series of offbeat ads that were a takeoff on the comedy series *The Office*, office workers competed and compared their 'made my way' BK burgers, reinforcing the message that each customer could have a custom-made burger—no matter how unusual it might be. Crispin planned an entire package of promotions around the new-old theme, including everything from in-store signage to messages on cups.

Although *The Office* ads were unusual and catchy, they were also mainstream media. However, the TV campaign created an environment for the real Crispin approach to emerge. To promote BK's TenderCrisp chicken, Crispin launched a microsite, www.subservientchicken.com. Among other things, the site featured a man dressed in a chicken suit who would respond by performing any commands that visitors typed in to a text box. The only indication that the site was sponsored by Burger King was a small icon marked, "BK Tendercrisp." When Crispin launched the site, it told only 20 people—all of whom were friends of people who worked at the agency. Within the first 10 days, 20 million people visited the site, with the average visitor spending more than 7 minutes.

As a follow-up to the Subservient Chicken promotion, Crispin created a campaign to launch a new BK product, chicken fries. The promotion was based on a faux heavy metal band called Coq Roq (the lead singer's name was Fowl Mouth). The whole idea was to create the charade of a real band, complete with songs, videos, cellphone ring tones, and promotional merchandise. Crispin targeted this campaign squarely at what it perceived to be the main BK target market—young men. Whatever those young men thought of Coq Roq, it led them to buy more than 100 million orders of chicken fries in the first four weeks of the new product launch.

Crispin clearly demonstrated with both the Subservient Chicken and CoqRoq campaigns that it was a master at viral marketing—using unusual methods to get attention and to generate buzz and word of mouth. Despite the success of these campaigns in producing lots of website hits, many analysts wondered if they would turn around BK's sliding market share. There was also speculation as to whether or not Crispin could continue to produce ideas that would keep BK strong in the fast-food fights.

A VIRAL TURNAROUND

Largely because of years of poor performance, tension had been mounting between Burger King's franchisees and the corporation. Initially, the new direction of its ad campaigns didn't help. Franchisees hated the viral web campaigns, as they did an earlier Crispin campaign featuring an eerie bobblehead-looking King with a huge ceramic head.

But at Burger King's 2006 annual franchisee convention, the feeling in the air was "long live the king." CEO Blum debuted a new Crispin ad entitled, "Manthem." A parody of performer Helen Reddy's song, "I Am Woman," the spot was yet another example of BK's strategy to unapologetically embrace the young, male, fast-food "super fan." Manthem's lyrics spurned "chick food" and gleefully exalted the meat, cheese, and more meat and cheese combos that turn "innies into outies," all the while showing guys burning their briefs and pushing a minivan off a bridge.

After openly revolting at the convention the year before, BK's restaurant operators rose to their feet in a thunderous ova-

tion, demanding an encore. They now embraced the kind of uncomfortably edgy advertising that they had rejected not so long before. Why this sudden change of heart?

Perhaps it was because Burger King was on the verge of a public offering. Or maybe it was because sales and profits go a long way in healing wounds. "I feel much better this year than I have in the last three, four, or five years," said Mahendra Nath, owner/operator of 90 stores. With sales up multiple years in a row, another franchisee, Alex Salgueiro, said, "I think our competitors are scared of the King … they should be. They say, 'What's with the King?' and my answer is 'It's better than clowns.'"

With BK's fortunes apparently changing, franchisees were much less likely to question the irreverent Crispin promotional tactics, whether they liked them or not. And why would they? With the young male demographic providing nearly half of all Burger King visits, Mr Salgueiro said it best: "All opinions boil down to traffic and sales. Once that happens, everybody has to shut up with their opinion. We have a very old franchisee base at this point and some of us don't understand our customers. We have a lot of gray hair."

NO END IN SIGHT

The creative ads have continued to flow, including the humorous series to promote the Western Whopper. The spots, based on the tagline, "Bring out your inner cowboy," featured people from all walks of life developing huge handlebar moustaches after eating Burger King fare. The ads were accompanied by a link to www.petmoustache.com, where people could register, upload a photo, and design a custom moustache. The moustache would then take on a life of its own. "It sends you e-mails that say, 'Hey, I miss you and why haven't you waxed me?' If you neglect it, it grows willy-nilly and wild," explained Rob Reilly, a creative director for Crispin.

But the most recent BK/Crispin promotional tactic took things to a whole new level. For the 50th anniversary of the Whopper, Crispin created the "Whopper Freakout" campaign. In doing so, Crispin did something it had never done before. Mr Reilly explained the reasoning behind what can only be described as Whopper deprivation:

> If you really want to prove [that the Whopper is still America's favorite burger] put your money where your mouth is and let's take it off the menu and film natural reactions from people. We knew technically we could pull it off, but this is really a social experiment, that's the new ground we're breaking, using a social experiment as marketing. There's no fake dialogue, no fake customers. We were really testing this: If you deprive people of a thing they love, even down to a hamburger, will they react with a thing that's visceral?

Visceral is truly what they got. The eight-minute film is taken from the perspective of hidden cameras in a real Burger King restaurant. After being told by employees that the Whopper had been discontinued, customers revolt in a way that only truly distraught brand-loyal fans could. In the movie, customers scoff, twitch, roll their heads, demand to speak to managers, and even yell. Some of the more wistful subjects give folksy anecdotes about family bonding and passage into manhood, all based on the Whopper.

Crispin plugged the film's website with 30-second spot ads and then let the viral marketing forces take over. The results were nothing short of astounding. The microsite received more than one million visits at an average logged time of 8:33. But what really stood out was that visitors watched the video in its entirety four million times, meaning that most visitors watched several times. Multiple parodies of the ad emerged on the web. The campaign won a 2008 *Creativity* magazine award and IAG research found recall of the campaign to be the highest of any it had seen in its six-year history.

But all these measures amount to very little if the overall objective is not achieved. On that score, Crispin has delivered in spades for the flame-broiler. Burger King is in its fourth consecutive year of same-store sales growth. Not only is it growing, but BK is currently delivering a solid thrashing to McDonald's and Wendy's, who are blaming the recession, housing crisis, and fuel prices for sluggish growth. BK 2007 system-wide revenue reached US$13.2 billion, up nearly 60 percent since Crispin assumed the account. Burger King is also showing healthy profits, rising stock prices, and strong international growth.

Many analysts are giving Crispin's promotional efforts the bulk of the credit for Burger King's success. "They're doing a super job on the advertising front," said UBS analyst David Palmer. "They're clearly connecting with the super fan that is the young, hungry male." Despite the previous speculation that Crispin would fail, the firm is now into its fifth year as Burger King's promotional agency, with no sign of being shown the door. As long as Crispin continues to hit home runs with its creative promotions, its franchisees, shareholders, and customers alike will continue to shout, "Long live the King!"

Questions for Discussion

1. What are Burger King's communication objectives for its target audience?

2. With its focus on the "super fan," does BK risk alienating other customers? What are the implications of this?

3. Why is viral or buzz marketing effective? Analyze the design of the Subservient Chicken website's message, including content, structure, and format. What can you conclude from this analysis?

4. Do the TV and viral elements of BK's campaigns work well together? What additional elements and media might Crispin add to the integrated marketing communications campaign?

5. What other recommendations would you make to BK and Crispin to help them improve the integration of Burger King's promotion mix?

Sources: Emily Bryson York, "Economy, Rivals, No Match for BK's Marketing," *Advertising Age*, May 1, 2008, p.4; "2008 Creativity Award Winner: Burger King: Whopper Freakout," *Creativity*, May 14, 2008, accessed http://creativity-online.com/news/2008-creativity-award-winner-burger-king-whopper-freakout/127035; Kevin, Kingsbury, "Burger King Swings to Net Profit," *Wall Street Journal*, August 24, 2007, accessed online at www.wsj.com; Barbara Lippert, "King of All Media," *Adweek*, November 20, 2006, accessed online at www.adweek.com; Kamau High, "BK Intros 'Inner Cowboy,'" *Adweek*, June 5, 2007, accessed online at www.adweek.com; Kate Macarthur, "BK Rebels Fall in Love with King," *Advertising Age*, May 1, 2006, p. 1; Elaine Walker, "Franchisees, Burger King Work to Mend Rift," *Miami Herald*, March 27, 2006.

Chapter 12

Part 1   Defining Marketing and the Marketing Process (Chapters 1, 2)
Part 2   Understanding the Marketplace and Consumers (Chapters 3, 4, 5, 6)
Part 3   Designing a Customer-Driven Strategy and Mix (Chapters 7, 8, 9, 10, 11, 12, 13, 14)
Part 4   Extending Marketing (Chapters 15, 16, 17)

Promotion

Mix Strategies
Advertising, Public Relations and Sales

Chapter
PREVIEW

Now that we've looked at overall integrated marketing communications planning, let's look more deeply into the specific marketing communications tools. In this chapter, we'll explore advertising, public relations, personal selling, and sales promotion. Advertising involves communicating the company's or brand's value proposition by using paid media to inform, persuade, and remind consumers. Public relations involves building good relations with various company publics—from consumers and the general public to the media, investor, donor, and government publics. As with all of the promotion mix tools, advertising and public relations must be blended into the overall integrated marketing communications (IMC) program. In the latter part of this chapter we'll also discuss two more elements of IMC—personal selling and sales promotion.

Let's start by looking at an advertising agency and a series of its advertising campaigns. TBWA\RAAD Dubai was runner-up in the category Agency of the Year 2010, in the Dubai Lynx Awards.[1] This award is made on the basis of scores of entries in the fields of television and cinema, print, outdoor and radio, direct and sales promotion, interactive, integrated, and craft sections.

In its short 10-year history, TBWA\RAAD has upset the status quo of the advertising industry by climbing into the top five agency networks in the region. It has won several awards, including the MENA Advertising Personality for 2010, a Cannes Lion, and the only Grand Prix at the GEMAS Advertising Effectiveness Awards 2010.

TBWA\RAAD was established in Dubai in February 2000. The founder, Ramzi Raad, was repeatedly asked if he really believed that there was a place left for a new agency in the crowded arena of the Middle East, and his response was very clear; TBWA\RAAD was launched with the philosophy to 'change the rules' of communication across the region, a thought that was inspired from advertisers' insight.

Today, TBWA\RAAD operates a network of 13 full service agencies across the Arab world and North Africa, employing more than 600 people. It also operates a PR consultancy network, Ketchum-Raad Middle East, and a shopper marketing operation, Integer Middle East.

For each campaign, TBWA\RAAD always starts with a situation analysis in order to understand the client's business and market, identify problems or opportunities, and help determine the right strategy to address them and achieve the client's objectives. Armed with the right strategy and relevant consumer insights, the team develops a 'Big Idea.' This idea is then presented as the central thrust of the campaign, which is designed to capture a larger share of the future for the brand by 'disrupting' the standard rules of advertising in a given market, thus attracting maximum exposure and attention. Here are some examples of the campaigns produced by TBWA\RAAD:

TBWA\RAAD was appointed in 2008 to launch the Qatar Foundation. This independent, private, nonprofit chartered organization, located in Doha, Qatar, was founded in 1995 by decree of His Highness Sheikh Hamad Bin Khalifa Al-Thani, Emir of the State of Qatar. The Qatar Foundation is dedicated to turning Qatar into a knowledge-based economy. Its activities are focused on education, scientific research, and community development, building on the organization's diverse range of administrative skills and human development programs. Overall, the organization's dual mission is, first, to prepare people to meet the challenges of an ever-changing world, and, second, to make Qatar a leader in innovative education and research.

TBWA\RAAD's objective was to establish a distinct visual identity for the brand and unify the Foundation's various branches under one voice. The campaign was developed to engage, inspire curiosity, and inform the world of the Qatar Foundation's unique and visionary position as the Middle East's centre of excellence for education and research.

In its situation analysis, TBWA\RAAD identified that, although the Qatar Foundation has three distinct pillars (Education, Science and Research, and Community Development), there has been a common misconception amongst the Foundation's target audience that it focuses primarily on education. In fact, the Qatar

> **TBWA\Raad designed a campaign for the launch of the first ever Abu Dhabi Grand Prix in 2009.**

Foundation includes 87 separate entities under the three pillars, each with its separate purpose and target audience.

In order to address people's misconception, TBWA\RAAD developed the 'Big Idea' for the campaign inspired by the brand's vision of 'Unlocking People's Potential.' The idea was to focus on the key mission of innovative education and research. This campaign was executed through a combination of print, outdoor, and television advertising in Qatar and around the MENA region, as well as in major European, American, and Asian capitals. A launch event was also organized, focusing on the key concept of 'THINK.' This campaign produced extremely positive results in the following months:

- Website visitors increased by 213 percent.

- Unique visitors were up 140 percent.

- Monthly page views were up by 162 percent.

Finally, and most importantly, following this campaign, the Qatar Foundation has become an umbrella brand in the eye of the consumer for all of the 87 separate entities.

In 2009, the global recession left car dealers competing fiercely to clear stock through big discounts and immediate customer benefits. Meanwhile, customers were playing a waiting game, worried by the prospect of unemployment and potential economic downfall. The Nissan dealer Arabian Automobiles Company created a truly compelling package of five offers— unbeatable in value when placed side by side with competitors'. TBWA\RAAD's challenge was to communicate this new deal to customers in an exciting way that was all about the offer, ignoring standard convention.

TBWA\RAAD's insight was that customers were looking for a good deal which was not only clearly communicated, but also sympathetic to their uncertain situation. The offer had to be unbeatable, communicate with the customer on both functional and emotional levels, and at the same time be entertaining.

The 'Big Idea' was to create five distinct superhero characters for the five distinct offers in a campaign, which became famously known as 'The Unbeatable Five.' As it turned out there was no better time to buy a Nissan.

And the results of this campaign?

- Each day from when the promotion started, call enquiries doubled their normal level (they increased from 80 to over 150 calls on average per day).

- This creative route was considered an example of best practice when it came to effective tactical campaigns. It even received good PR coverage with an AVE (advertising value equivalent) of US$19,000. The value to Nissan of this press coverage would have been about US$19,000.

The 1st Abu Dhabi Formula 1 Grand Prix was held in the UAE capital on November 1, 2009. This was a momentous event for the country. The requirement was to create a local, regional, and international communication program that would produce a heightened buzz and momentum around the event. It would need to engage local audiences who generally didn't have any interest in Formula 1 racing, and help ensure

TBWA\Raad designed a campaign for the launch of the first ever Abu Dhabi Grand Prix in 2009.

all tickets were sold out within the first month of activity.

In its situation analysis, TBWA\RAAD found that tickets rarely sold out in the UAE, even when hosting significant international events, and the proportion of local attendees venturing out to anything other than locally focused events was usually very low. TBWA\RAAD's insight was to make the event relevant to all audiences by making it a part of the national conversation, thus creating a buzz and a desire in local people to attend and be part of the event.

Its 'Big Idea' for the campaign was to make the race date famous. Conversations around the country would start with the question, "Where will you be on November, 1?" Everyone should be talking about the event and the date—and everyone has to want to be there!

TBWA\RAAD delivered this message across all channels and languages to build a strong call to action, which everyone could identify with. It also approached these challenges in several unconventional ways, such as the heavy use of well-designed and brightly covered outdoor spaces all around the UAE, which were instantly noticeable and memorable. The campaign also used radio and even downloadable ringtones. The idea aimed to create momentum and excitement, thus passing the rush and excitement of Formula 1 to the general public.

As a result of this campaign:

- All tickets for the event were sold out, thus making the first major race of the UAE a huge success.

- It successfully positioned Abu Dhabi as a viable host venue and put the capital on the world map.

TBWA\RAAD handles a long list of other accounts, including Nissan, Infiniti, Etihad, Visa, Dubai Shopping Festival, Henkel, Axiom, Energizer, Pepsi's AMP energy drink, Standard Chartered Bank, DU's Anayou, Adidas, GSK, Ferrari World Abu Dhabi, Almarai, TwoFour 54, Mars, Michelin, Omantel, and Oman Tourism. It "creates and manages brand behaviours in the modern world through 'Disruptive Ideas' brought to life using Media Arts."[2]

> For each campaign, TBWA/RAAD's strategy is to undertake a situation analysis to understand its client's business and market, from which it develops an 'Insight' about how to achieve its client's objectives most effectively. It then creates a 'Big Idea' as the central thrust of its campaign, through which it can make an impact on the target audience by 'disrupting' the standard rules of advertising in a given market, thus attracting maximum attention.

Objective Outline

As we discussed in the previous chapter, companies must do more than simply create customer value. They must also clearly and persuasively communicate that value to target consumers. In this chapter, we'll take a closer look at some marketing communications tools, advertising, public relations, personal selling and sales promotion.

Author Comment | You already know a lot about advertising—you are exposed to it every day. But here we'll look behind the scenes at how companies make advertising decisions.

Advertising (pp 328–341)

Advertising can be traced back to the very beginnings of recorded history. Archaeologists working in the countries around the Mediterranean Sea have dug up signs announcing various events and offers. The Romans painted walls to announce gladiator fights, and the Phoenicians painted pictures promoting their wares on large rocks along parade routes. During the golden age in Greece, town criers announced the sale of cattle, crafted items, and even cosmetics. An early 'singing commercial' went as follows: "For eyes that are shining, for cheeks like the dawn / For beauty that lasts after girlhood is gone / For prices in reason, the woman who knows / Will buy her cosmetics from Aesclyptos."

Modern advertising, however, is a far cry from these early efforts. Worldwide advertising spending exceeds an estimated US$604 billion. MENA (Middle East and North Africa) advertising spend is about US$13.7 billion. Procter & Gamble, the world's largest advertiser, in 2008 spent US$8.5 billion on different advertising campaigns around the world.[3]

Although advertising is used mostly by business firms, a wide range of not-for-profit organizations, professionals, and social agencies also use advertising to promote

Advertising
Any paid form of nonpersonal presentation and promotion of ideas, goods, or services by an identified sponsor.

328

FIGURE | 12.1
Major Advertising Decisions

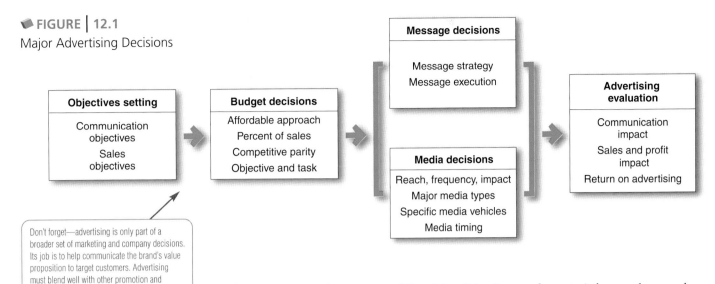

FIGURE | 12.1
Major Advertising Decisions

Don't forget—advertising is only part of a broader set of marketing and company decisions. Its job is to help communicate the brand's value proposition to target customers. Advertising must blend well with other promotion and marketing mix decisions.

their causes to various target publics. Advertising is a good way to inform and persuade, whether the purpose is to sell Coca-Cola worldwide or to encourage people in a developing nation to use birth control.

Marketing management must make four important decisions when developing an advertising program (see **Figure 12.1**): *setting advertising objectives, setting the advertising budget, developing advertising strategy* (*message decisions* and *media decisions*), and *evaluating advertising campaigns*.

Setting Advertising Objectives

The first step is to set *advertising objectives*. These objectives should be based on past decisions about the target market, positioning, and the marketing mix, which define the job that advertising must do in the total marketing program. The overall advertising objective is to help build customer relationships by communicating customer value. Here, we discuss specific advertising objectives.

Advertising objective

A specific communication task to be accomplished with a specific target audience during a specific period of time.

An **advertising objective** is a specific communication *task* to be accomplished with a specific *target* audience during a specific period of *time*. Advertising objectives can be classified by primary purpose—whether the aim is to *inform, persuade,* or *remind*. **Table 12.1** lists examples of each of these specific objectives.

Informative advertising is used heavily when introducing a new product category. In this case, the objective is to build primary demand. Thus, early producers of DVD players first had to inform consumers of the image quality and convenience benefits of the new product. *Persuasive advertising* becomes more important as competition increases. Here, the company's objective is to build selective demand. For example, once DVD players became established, Sony began trying to persuade consumers that *its* brand offered the best quality for their money.

Some persuasive advertising has become *comparative advertising,* in which a company directly or indirectly compares its brand with one or more other brands. Comparative advertising has been used for products ranging from soft drinks and pain relievers to computers, batteries, car rentals, and credit cards. For example, in its comparative campaign, the auto-rental company Avis positioned itself against market-leading Hertz by claiming, "We try harder." And Apple's "I'm a Mac; I'm a PC" ads take jabs at rival Windows-based computers.

Reminder advertising is important for mature products—it helps to maintain customer relationships and keep consumers thinking about the product. Expensive Coca-Cola television ads primarily build and maintain the Coca-Cola brand relationship rather than inform or persuade customers to buy in the short run.

● **TABLE | 12.1** Possible Advertising Objectives ← The overall advertising goal is to help build customer relationships by communicating customer value.

Informative advertising	
Communicating customer value	Suggesting new uses for a product
Building a brand and company image	Informing the market of a price change
Telling the market about a new product	Describing available services and support
Explaining how the product works	Correcting false impressions

Persuasive advertising	
Building brand preference	Persuading customers to purchase now
Encouraging switching to your brand	Persuading customers to receive a sales call
Changing customer's perception of product value	Convincing customers to tell others about the brand

Reminder advertising	
Maintaining customer relationships	Reminding consumers where to buy the product
Reminding consumers that the product may be needed in the near future	Keeping the brand in the customer's mind during off-seasons

Advertising's goal is to help move consumers through the buying process. Some advertising is designed to move people to immediate action. For example, a Carrefour newspaper advert for a weekend sale encourages immediate store visits. However, many of the other ads focus on building or strengthening long-term customer relationships. For example, a Nike television ad, in which well-known athletes work through extreme challenges in their Nike gear, never directly asks for a sale. Instead, the goal is to somehow change the way the customers think or feel about the brand.

Setting the Advertising Budget

Advertising budget

The money and other resources allocated to a product or company advertising program.

After determining its advertising objectives, the company next sets its **advertising budget** for each product. Four commonly used methods for setting promotion budgets are discussed in Chapter 11. Here we discuss some specific factors that should be considered when setting the advertising budget.

A brand's advertising budget often depends on its *stage in the product life cycle*. For example, new products typically need large advertising budgets to build awareness and to gain consumer trial. In contrast, mature brands usually require lower budgets as a ratio to sales. *Market share* also impacts on the amount of advertising needed: because building the market or taking market share from competitors requires larger advertising spending than does simply maintaining current share, low-share brands usually need more advertising spending as a percentage of sales. Also, brands in a market with many competitors and high advertising clutter must be advertised more heavily to be noticed above the noise in the market. Undifferentiated brands—those that closely resemble other brands in their product class (soft drinks, laundry detergents)—may require heavy advertising to set them apart. When the product differs greatly from competitors' products, advertising can be used to point out the differences to consumers.

No matter what method is used, setting the advertising budget is no easy task. Companies such as Coca-Cola and Unilever have built sophisticated statistical models to determine the relationship between promotional spending and brand sales, and to help determine the 'optimal investment' across various media. Still, because so many factors affect advertising effectiveness, some controllable and others not, measuring the results of advertising spending remains an inexact science. In most cases, managers must rely on large doses of judgment along with more quantitative analysis when setting advertising budgets.[4]

Developing Advertising Strategy

Advertising strategy

The strategy by which the company accomplishes its advertising objectives. It consists of two major elements: creating advertising messages and selecting advertising media.

Advertising strategy consists of two major elements: creating advertising *messages* and selecting advertising *media*. In the past, companies often viewed media planning as secondary to the message-creation process. The creative department first created good advertisements, and then the media department selected and purchased the best media for carrying these advertisements to desired target audiences. This often caused friction between creatives and media planners.

Today, however, soaring media costs, more-focused target marketing strategies, and the increase of new media have promoted the importance of the media-planning function. The decision about which media to use for an ad campaign—television, magazines, cell-phones, a website, or email—is now sometimes more critical than the creative elements of the campaign. As a result, more and more, advertisers are orchestrating a closer harmony between their messages and the media that deliver them.[5]

In fact, in a really good ad campaign, you often have to ask "Is that a media idea or a creative idea?" For example, BMW created a huge buzz for its quirky, anything-but-ordinary little British-made MINI car with an anything-but-ordinary Let's Motor campaign.

> The Let's Motor campaign employed a rich mix of unconventional media, care-fully integrated to create personality for the car and a tremendous buzz of excite-ment among consumers. To create buzz, the company put MINIs in all kinds of imaginative places. In the United States, it mounted them atop Ford Excursion SUVs and drove them around 22 major cities, highlighting the car's sensible size. It set up 'MINI Ride' displays outside department stores, featuring an actual MINI that looked like a children's ride. "Rides $16,850. Quarters only," the sign said. Displays in airport terminals featured oversized newspaper vending machines and pay phones next to billboards showing the undersized MINI and proclaiming, "Makes everything else seem a little too big." The car was also promoted on the Internet, in ads painted on city buildings, and on cards handed out at auto shows. In addition, BMW created MINI games, MINI booklets, MINI suitcases, and MINI placements in movies. It worked closely with selected maga-zines to create memorable print ads. For example, ads in *Wired* magazine contained a cardboard fold-out of a MINI, suggest-ing that readers assemble it and drive it around their desks making "putt-putt" noises. The Let's Motor campaign has been a smashing success, creating an almost cult-like follow-ing for the personable little car. Were these clever media ideas or clever creative ideas? They were both, the product of a tight media–creative partnership.

Close media-creative partnerships: The MINI Let's Motor cam-paign used a rich mix of conventional and unconventional media, carefully integrated to create personality for the car and a tremendous buzz of excitement among consumers.

Creating the Advertising Message

No matter how big the budget, advertising can succeed only if advertisements gain attention and communicate well. Good adver-tising messages are especially important in today's costly and clut-tered advertising environment. For example, the MENA region has seen a large increase in the number of television channels. In 1993 there were only 18 free-to-air channels; by 2010 this had increased to 487 channels.[6] Add the countless magazine titles, radio stations, and a continuous barrage of catalogs, direct mail, email and online ads, and out-of-home media, and it is possible to see that consumers are being bombarded with ads at home, at work, and at all points in between. As a result, consumers are exposed to thousands of commercial messages every day.[7]

Breaking through the Clutter. Until recently, television viewers were pretty much a captive audience for advertisers. But today's digital wizardry has given consumers a rich new set of information and entertainment choices. With the growth in cable and satellite television, the Internet, video on demand (VOD), video downloads, and DVD rentals, today's viewers have many more options. Digital technology has also given consumers a wide range of tools for choosing what they watch or don't watch. Increasingly, consumers are choosing *not* to watch ads. They 'zap' commercials by fast-forwarding through recorded programs. With the remote control, they mute the sound during a commercial or 'zip' around the channels to see what else is on. A recent study found that 40 percent of all television viewers now switch channels when the commercial break starts.[8]

Adding to the problem is the rapid growth of DVR (digital video recorder) systems. Although DVRs increase total television watching, research shows that 86 percent of DVR owners fast-forward through all or most commercials. As a result, according to one study, about 20 percent of brands experienced lower sales in ad-skipping households.

Thus, advertisers can no longer force-feed the same old type of ad messages to captive consumers through traditional media. Just to gain and hold attention, today's advertising messages must be better planned, more imaginative, more entertaining, and more rewarding to consumers. "Interruption or disruption as the fundamental premise of marketing" no longer works, says one advertising executive. Instead, "you have to create content that is interesting, useful, or entertaining enough to invite [consumers]." According to another, "Everything is about control. If an ad is interesting to you, you'll have a conversation with the brand. If it's not, it's a waste of time."[9]

In fact, many marketers are now subscribing to a new merging of advertising and entertainment, dubbed "Madison & Vine." You've probably heard of Madison Avenue. It's the New York City street that houses the headquarters of many of the United States'

Advertising clutter: Today's consumers, armed with a variety of tools, can choose what they watch and don't watch. Advertising messages must be better planned, more imaginative, more entertaining, and more rewarding to consumers.

largest advertising agencies. You may also have heard of Hollywood & Vine, the intersection of Hollywood Avenue and Vine Street in Hollywood, California, long the symbolic heart of the U.S. entertainment industry. Now, Madison Avenue and Hollywood & Vine are coming together to form a new intersection—*Madison & Vine*—that represents the merging of advertising and entertainment in an effort to break through the clutter and create new avenues for reaching consumers with more engaging messages.

Message Strategy. The first step in creating effective advertising messages is to plan a *message strategy*—to decide what general message will be communicated to consumers. The purpose of advertising is to get consumers to think about or react to the product or company in a certain way. People will react only if they believe that they will benefit from doing so. Thus, developing an effective message strategy begins with identifying customer *benefits* that can be used as advertising appeals. Ideally, advertising message strategy will follow directly from the company's broader positioning and customer value strategies.

Message strategy statements tend to be plain, straightforward outlines of benefits and positioning points that the advertiser wants to stress. The advertiser must next develop a compelling **creative concept**—or '*big idea*'—that will bring the message strategy to life in a distinctive and memorable way. At this stage, simple message ideas become great ad campaigns. Usually, a copywriter and art director will team up to generate many creative concepts, hoping that one of these concepts will turn out to be the big idea. The creative concept may emerge as a visualization, a phrase, or a combination of the two.

The creative concept will guide the choice of specific appeals to be used in an advertising campaign. *Advertising appeals* should have three characteristics. First, they should be *meaningful*, pointing out benefits that make the product more desirable or interesting to consumers. Secondly, appeals must be *believable*—consumers must believe that the product or service will deliver the promised benefits. However, the most meaningful and believable benefits may not be the best ones to feature. Appeals should also be *distinctive*—they should tell how the product is better than the competing brands. For example, the most meaningful benefit of owning a wristwatch is that it keeps accurate time, yet few watch ads feature this benefit. Instead, based on the distinctive benefits they offer, watch advertisers might select any of a number of advertising themes. For years, Timex has promoted its watches with the slogan "Takes a lickin' and keeps on tickin'," using ad campaigns showing its watches being subjected to various kinds of harsh treatment, which all helped to showcase their durability. In contrast, Fossil has featured style and fashion, whereas Rolex stresses luxury and status.

Message Execution.   The advertiser now has to turn the big idea into an actual ad execution that will capture the target market's attention and interest. The creative team must find the best approach, style, tone, words, and format for executing the message. Any message can be presented in different **execution styles**, such as the following:

- *Slice of life:* This style shows one or more 'typical' people using the product in a normal setting. For example, Lifebuoy soap shows amongst primary school students how Lifebuoy cleans germs and keeps them healthy.

- *Lifestyle:* This style shows how a product fits in with a particular lifestyle. Damas showed Nancy Ajram to promote its products in different glamorous settings.

- *Fantasy:* This style creates a fantasy around the product or its use. For example, the Lipton forest fruit tea commercial shows women of all ages running into pools of giant red fruits while the Willy Wonka song, "Pure Imagination," plays. Women in the commercial are taking bites of these fruits and having fun. The ad closes with, "It's your relaxation time."

- *Mood or image:* This style builds a mood or image around the product or service, such as beauty, love, or serenity. Few claims are made about the product except through suggestion. Nivea Happy Time Body Lotion moves the focus away from skin care and instead concentrates on happiness. It encourages you to feel happy in your skin so you can enjoy your day!

- *Musical:* This style shows people or cartoon characters singing about the product. For example, in Egypt, Chipseco potato chips' television commercials are built around a song that explains the line texture on the chips, the crunchy sound, and great flavors.

- *Personality symbol:* This style creates a character that represents the product. The character might be *animated* (La Vache Qui Rit cheese animated cow character, Comfort fabric softener characters, which resemble softness) or *real* (Nancy Ajram for Coca-Cola and Damas).

- *Technical expertise:* This style shows the company's expertise in making the product. Thus, Lays chips of Saudi Arabia communicates through its ads how Lays is made of natural potatoes that are cultivated from green fields (in one television ad, a grandchild

Creative concept
The compelling 'big idea' that will bring the advertising message strategy to life in a distinctive and memorable way.

Execution style
The approach, style, tone, words, and format used for executing an advertising message.

La Vache Qui Rit is an example of an animated character used as a personality symbol to represent a product.

is asking his grandfather where Lays chips come from, and the grandfather explains how they take care of the field in order to get the fresh potato Lays chips).

- *Scientific evidence:* This style presents survey or scientific evidence that the brand is better or better liked than one or more other brands. Wrigley's Extra chewing gum uses scientific evidence to convince buyers that Extra is better than other brands in washing away food particles and thus helping in fighting cavities.

- *Testimonial evidence or endorsement:* This style features a highly believable or likable source endorsing the product. It could be an ordinary person saying how much they like a given product. For example, Garnier partners with famous Arab actress Hend Sabry, who appears in the television commercials and print ads for Garnier Color Naturals and Garnier skin care products.

The advertiser also must choose a *tone* for the ad. Unilever always uses a positive tone: Its ads say something very positive about its products. Other advertisers now use edgy humor to break through the commercial clutter. For example, Fanta commercials are famous for humor.

The advertiser must use memorable and attention-grabbing *words* in the ad. For example, Barbican, a flavored malt beverage, is the drink of choice for the younger generation. Barbican uses the sentence "It's My Life" in its communication instead of saying "The Young Generation Drink," in order to link the drink to its primary market in a creative manner.

Finally, *format* elements make a difference to an ad's impact as well as its cost. A small change in ad design can make a big difference to its effect. In a print ad, the *illustration* is the first thing the reader notices—it must be strong enough to draw attention. Next, the *headline* must effectively entice the right people to read the copy. Finally, the *copy*—the main block of text in the ad—must be simple but strong and convincing. Moreover, these three elements must effectively work *together* to persuasively present customer value.

Consumer-Generated Messages. Taking advantage of today's interactive technologies, many companies are now tapping consumers for message ideas or actual ads. They are searching existing video sites, setting up their own sites, and sponsoring ad-creation contests and other promotions.

Sometimes, marketers capitalize on consumer videos that are already posted on sites hosted by YouTube, MySpace, Google, and Yahoo! For example, one of the most viewed amateur videos on the web last year showed Diet Coke mixed with Mentos candies to produce shooting fountains of soda. The video produced a windfall of free buzz for Coca-Cola. To gain even more mileage, Coca-Cola hired the amateur videographers—a professional juggler and a lawyer—to create another video and to star in a 30-second Coke ad.[10]

In another case, when Chevrolet ran a promotion for its Tahoe SUV allowing consumers to write their own text for video clips of the vehicle, it got some unexpected negative results. Many of the user-created ads contained critical gibes about the big SUV's poor gas mileage, high operating costs, and harmful environmental impact. Thus, marketers should be cautious when inviting consumer creative inputs.[11]

If used carefully, however, consumer-generated advertising efforts can produce big benefits. First, for relatively little expense, companies can collect new creative ideas, as well as fresh perspectives on the brand and what it actually means to consumers. "Companies have [their own] vision of what they want their brand to be," says the founder of Adcandy.

com, a website that solicits consumer ideas for product and company taglines. "But if everyone is saying your brand is something else, it may be a battle. Powerful things come from the street, from the people who use the product."[12]

Secondly, consumer-paigns can boost consumer involvement and get consumers talking and thinking about a brand and its value to them. Not only do marketers get "a peek into the public's consciousness and what they are thinking…[but] by participating and interacting, [consumers] develop a vested interest in your brand," says the Adcandy.com founder. Adds another marketer, "Engage a satisfied customer in a dialogue about a product—and give them a forum to express their creative aspirations for that product—and you will have a brand advocate who speaks from the heart."[13]

Selecting Advertising Media

Advertising media

The vehicles through which advertising messages are delivered to their intended audiences.

The major steps in **advertising media** selection are (1) deciding on *reach, frequency, and impact*; (2) choosing among major *media types*; (3) selecting specific *media vehicles*; and (4) deciding on *media timing*.

Deciding on Reach, Frequency, and Impact. To select media, the advertiser must decide on the reach and frequency needed to achieve advertising objectives. *Reach* is a measure of the *percentage* of people in the target market who are exposed to the ad campaign during a given period of time. For example, the advertiser might try to reach 70 percent of the target market during the first three months of the campaign. *Frequency* is a measure of how many *times* the average person in the target market is exposed to the message. For example, the advertiser might want an average exposure frequency of three.

But advertisers want to do more than just reach a given number of consumers a specific number of times. The advertiser also must decide on the desired *media impact*—the *qualitative value* of a message exposure through a given medium. For example, the same message in one magazine (say, a news magazine) may be more believable than in another (say, a tabloid). For products that need to be demonstrated, messages on television may have more impact than messages on radio because television uses sight *and* sound. Products for which consumers provide input on design or features might be better promoted at an interactive website than in a direct mailing.

More generally, the advertiser wants to choose media that will *engage* consumers rather than simply reach them. For example, for television advertising, "how relevant a program is for its audience and where the ads are inserted are likely to be much more important than whether the program was a [ratings] winner" numbers-wise, says one expert. "This is about 'lean to' TV rather than 'lean back.'"

Although the TV ratings company Nielsen is beginning to measure levels of television *media engagement*, such measures are hard to come by for most media. "All the measurements we have now are media metrics: ratings, readership, listenership, click-through rates," says an executive of the Advertising Research Foundation, but engagement, "happens inside the consumer, not inside the medium. What we need is a way to determine how the targeted prospect connected with, got engaged with, the brand idea. With engagement, you're on your way to a relationship.…"[14]

Choosing Among Major Media Types. The media planner has to know the reach, frequency, and impact of each of the major media types. As summarized in ● **Table 12.2**, the major media types are television, the Internet, newspapers, direct mail, magazines, radio, and outdoor. Advertisers can also choose from a wide array of new digital media, such as cellphones and other digital devices, which reach consumers directly. Each medium has advantages and limitations. Media planners consider many factors when making their media choices. They want to choose media that will effectively and efficiently present the advertising message to target customers. Thus, they must consider each medium's impact, message effectiveness, and cost.

● **TABLE | 12.2**   Profiles of Major Media Types

Medium	Advantages	Limitations
Television	Good mass-marketing coverage; low cost per exposure; combines sight, sound, and motion; appealing to the senses	High absolute costs; high clutter; fleeting exposure; less audience selectivity
Internet	High selectivity; low cost; immediacy; interactive capabilities	Relatively low impact; the audience controls exposure
Newspapers	Flexibility; timeliness; good local market coverage; broad acceptability; high believability	Short life; poor reproduction quality; small pass-along audience
Direct mail	High audience selectivity; flexibility; no ad competition within the same medium; allows personalization	Relatively high cost per exposure, 'junk mail' image
Magazines	High geographic and demographic selectivity; credibility and prestige; high-quality reproduction; long life and good pass-along readership	Long ad purchase lead time; high cost; no guarantee of position
Radio	Good local acceptance; high geographic and demographic selectivity; low cost	Audio only, fleeting exposure; low attention ('the half-heard' medium); fragmented audiences
Outdoor	Flexibility; high repeat exposure; low cost; low message competition; good positional selectivity	Little audience selectivity; creative limitations

> Typically, it's not a question of which one medium to use. Rather, the advertiser selects a mix of media and blends them into a fully integrated marketing communications campaign. Each medium plays a specific role.

The mix of media must be reexamined regularly. For a long time, television and magazines dominated in the media mixes of national advertisers, with other media often neglected. However, as discussed previously, the media mix appears to be shifting. As mass-media costs rise, audiences shrink, and exciting new digital media emerge, many advertisers are finding new ways to reach consumers. They are supplementing the traditional mass media with more-specialized and highly targeted media that cost less, target more effectively, and engage consumers more fully.

For example, cable television and satellite television systems are booming. Such systems allow narrow programming formats such as all sports, all news, nutrition, arts, home improvement and gardening, cooking, travel, history, finance, and others that target select groups.

Advertisers can take advantage of such 'narrowcasting' to focus in on special market segments rather than use the broader approach offered by network broadcasting. Cable and satellite television media seem to make good sense. But, increasingly, ads are popping up in far-less-likely places. In their efforts to find less-costly and more-highly targeted ways to reach consumers, advertisers have discovered a dazzling collection of 'alternative media.' These days, no matter where you go or what you do, you will probably run into some new form of advertising.[15]

Tiny billboards attached to shopping carts, ads on shopping bags, and advertising on supermarket floors urge you to buy JELL-O Pudding Pops or Pampers, while ads roll by on the store's checkout conveyor touting your local Toyota dealer. Step outside and there goes a public bus sporting an ad for Dubai Metro. You escape to the park, only to find billboard-size video screens running Mitsubishi Pajero ads.

These days, you're likely to find ads—well, anywhere. Ad space is being sold on DVD cases, parking-lot tickets, delivery trucks, pizza boxes, and ATMs.

Such alternative media seem a bit far-fetched, and they sometimes irritate consumers. But for many marketers, these media can save money and provide a way to hit selected consumers where they live, shop, work, and play. Of course, all this may leave you wondering if there are any commercial-free havens remaining for ad-weary consumers. Public elevators, perhaps, or stalls in a public restroom? Forget it! Each has already been invaded by innovative marketers.

Another important trend affecting media selection is the rapid growth in the number of 'media multitaskers,' people who absorb more than one medium at a time:[16]

It looks like people who aren't satisfied with 'just watching TV' are in good company. According to a recent survey, three-quarters of U.S. TV viewers read the newspaper while they watch TV, and two-thirds of them go online during their TV time. Another study indicates that the tasks now carried out in a typical day would have taken 31 hours to do 10 years ago with more primitive systems. What's more, if today's kids are any indication, media multitasking is on the rise. 73 percent of multitasking kids are engaged in 'active multitasking,' with the content in one medium influencing concurrent behavior in another. It's not uncommon to find a teenager simultaneously on Facebook, listening to a mix of music on iTunes, and talking on the cellphone to a friend—all while, in the midst of the multimedia chaos, trying to complete an essay he's got open in a Word file a few layers down on his desktop.

Media planners need to take such media interactions into account when selecting the types of media they will use.

Selecting Specific Media Vehicles. The media planner now must choose the best *media vehicles*—specific media within each general media type. For example, television vehicles include sitcoms and news programs. Magazine vehicles include news, fashion, and sports publications.

Media planners must compute the cost per thousand persons reached by a vehicle. For example, if a full-page, four-color advertisement in a national edition of *Gulf News* costs US$215,800 and *Gulf News'* readership is 100,000 people, the cost of reaching each group of 1,000 persons is about US$2,158. The same advertisement in *Khaleej Times* may cost only U$108,000 but reach only 60,000 persons—at a cost per thousand of about US$1,800. The media planner ranks each magazine by cost per thousand and favors those magazines with the lower cost per thousand for reaching target consumers.[17]

The media planner must also consider the costs of producing ads for different media. Whereas newspaper ads may cost very little to produce, flashy television ads can be very costly. For example, a typical television commercial might cost anything from US$70,000 to US$400,000 or more to produce.

In selecting specific media vehicles, the media planner must balance media costs against several media effectiveness factors. First, the planner should evaluate the media vehicle's *audience quality*. For a Pampers disposable diapers advertisement, for example, *Parenting* magazine would have a high exposure value; *Weekend* would have a low exposure value. Secondly, the media planner should consider *audience engagement*. Readers of the fashion magazine *Ahlan*, for example, typically pay more attention to ads than do *Arabian Business* readers. Thirdly, the planner should assess the vehicle's *editorial quality*—*Time* and the *Financial Times* are more believable and prestigious than magazines such as *7Days*.

Deciding on Media Timing. The advertiser must also decide how to schedule the advertising over the course of a year. Suppose sales of a product peak in December and drop in March. The firm can vary its advertising to follow the seasonal pattern, to oppose the seasonal pattern, or to be the same all year. Most firms do some seasonal advertising. For example, major airlines advertise more heavily before major holidays.

Finally, the advertiser has to choose the pattern of the ads. *Continuity* means scheduling ads evenly within a given period. *Pulsing* means scheduling ads unevenly over a given time period. Thus, 52 ads could either be scheduled at one per week during the year or pulsed in several bursts. The idea behind pulsing is to advertise heavily for a short period to build awareness that carries over to the next advertising period. Those who favor pulsing feel that it can be used to achieve the same impact as a steady schedule but at a much lower cost. However, some media planners believe that although pulsing achieves minimal awareness, it sacrifices depth of advertising communications.

Evaluating Advertising Effectiveness and Return on Advertising Investment

Return on advertising investment
The net return on advertising investment divided by the costs of the advertising investment.

Advertising accountability and **return on advertising investment** have become hot issues for most companies. Two separate recent studies show that advertising effectiveness has fallen 40 percent over the past decade and that 37.3 percent of advertising budgets are wasted. This leaves top management and many companies asking their marketing managers, "How do we know that we're spending the right amount on advertising?" and "What return are we getting on our advertising investment?" According to a recent survey, measuring advertising's efficiency and effectiveness is the number-one issue in the minds of today's advertisers.[18]

Advertisers should regularly evaluate two types of advertising results: the communication effects and the sales and profit effects. Measuring the *communication effects* of an ad or ad campaign tells whether the ads and media are communicating the ad message well. Individual ads can be tested before or after they are run. Before an ad is placed, the advertiser can show it to consumers, ask how they like it, and measure message recall or attitude changes resulting from it. After an ad is run, the advertiser can measure how the ad affected consumer recall or product awareness, knowledge, and preference. Pre- and post-evaluations of communication effects can be made for entire advertising campaigns as well.

Advertisers have got pretty good at measuring the communication effects of their ads and ad campaigns. However, *sales and profit* effects of advertising are often much harder to measure. For example, what sales and profits are produced by an ad campaign that increases brand awareness by 20 percent and brand preference by 10 percent? Sales and profits are affected by many factors other than advertising—such as product features, price, and availability.

One way to measure the sales and profit effects of advertising is to compare past sales and profits with past advertising expenditures. Another way is through experiments. For example, to test the effects of different advertising spending levels, Coca-Cola could vary the amount it spends on advertising in different market areas and measure the differences in the resulting sales and profit levels. More complex experiments could be designed to include other variables, such as differences in the ads or media used.

However, because so many factors affect advertising effectiveness, some controllable and others not, measuring the results of advertising spending remains an inexact science. For example, dozens of advertisers spend lavishly on high-profile sports-game ads each year. Although they sense that the returns are worth the sizable investment, few could actually measure or prove it. A recent survey of marketing and advertising agency executives concluded that over 80 percent of marketers don't measure return on investment because it's just too difficult to measure.[19] The study cited earlier asked advertising managers if they would be able to "forecast the impact on sales" of a 10 percent cut in advertising spending—63 percent said no.

"Marketers are tracking all kinds of data and they still can't answer basic questions [about advertising accountability]," says a marketing analyst, "because they don't have real models and metrics by which to make sense of it." Advertisers are measuring "everything they can, and that ranges from how many people respond to an ad to how many sales are closed and then trying to hook up those two end pieces," says another analyst. "The tough part is, my goodness, we've got so much data. How do we sift through it?"[20] Thus, although the situation is improving as marketers seek more answers, managers often must rely on large doses of judgment along with quantitative analysis when assessing advertising performance.

Other Advertising Considerations

In developing advertising strategies and programs, the company must address two additional questions. First, how will the company organize its advertising function—who will perform which advertising tasks? Secondly, how will the company adapt its advertising strategies and programs to the complexities of international markets?

Organizing for Advertising

Different companies organize in different ways to handle advertising. In small companies, advertising might be handled by someone in the sales department. Large companies set up advertising departments whose job it is to set the advertising budget, work with the ad agency, and handle other advertising not done by the agency. Most large companies use outside advertising agencies because they offer several advantages.

Advertising agency

A marketing services firm that assists companies in planning, preparing, implementing, and evaluating all or portions of their advertising programs.

How does an **advertising agency** work? Advertising agencies were started in the mid- to late-1800s by salespeople and brokers who worked for the media and received a commission for selling advertising space to companies. As time passed, the salespeople began to help customers prepare their ads. Eventually, they formed agencies and grew closer to the advertisers than to the media.

Today's agencies employ specialists who can often perform advertising tasks better than the company's own staff can. Agencies also bring an outside point of view to solving the company's problems, along with lots of experience from working with different clients and situations. So, today, even companies with strong advertising departments of their own use advertising agencies.

Some ad agencies are huge—the largest U.S. agency, BBDO Worldwide, has world-wide annual gross revenue of more than US$1.9 billion. In recent years, many agencies have grown by gobbling up other agencies, thus creating huge agency holding companies. The largest of these agency 'megagroups,' Omnicom Group, includes several large advertising, public relations, and promotion agencies with combined worldwide revenues of almost US$12.7 billion.[21] Most large advertising agencies have the staff and resources to handle all phases of an advertising campaign for their clients, from creating a marketing plan to developing ad campaigns and preparing, placing, and evaluating ads.

International Advertising Decisions

International advertisers face many complexities not encountered by domestic advertisers. The most basic issue concerns the degree to which global advertising should be adapted to the unique characteristics of various country markets. Some large advertisers have attempted to support their global brands with highly standardized worldwide advertising, with campaigns that work as well in Bangkok as they do in Riyadh. For example, McDonald's now unifies its creative elements and brand presentation under the familiar "I'm lovin' it" theme in all of its 100-plus markets worldwide. Coca-Cola co-ordinates worldwide advertising for its flagship brand under the theme, "The Coke Side of Life." Unilever's Dove for real beauty campaign launched globally essentially had the same elements across the different markets, but nonetheless these elements were also customized to the needs of local markets to appeal to the consumers. Let's take a look at the Arab version in **Real Marketing 12.1**.

In recent years, the increased popularity of online social networks and video sharing has boosted the need for advertising standardization for global brands. Most big marketing and advertising campaigns include a large online presence. Connected consumers can now move easily across borders via the Internet, making it difficult for advertisers to roll out adapted campaigns in a controlled, orderly fashion. As a result, at the very least, most global consumer brands co-ordinate their websites internationally.

Standardization produces many benefits—lower advertising costs, greater global advertising co-ordination, and a more consistent worldwide image. But it also has drawbacks. Most importantly, it ignores the fact that country markets differ greatly in their cultures, demographics, and economic conditions. Thus, most international advertisers 'think globally but act locally.' They develop global advertising *strategies* that make their worldwide advertising efforts more efficient and consistent. Then they adapt their advertising *programs* to make them more responsive to consumer needs and expectations within local markets.

For example, Apple uses "I'm a Mac; I'm a PC" commercials in many countries. In some markets, such as Spain, France, Germany, and Italy, it uses U.S. versions of the ads dubbed in the local language. However, it rescripts and reshoots the ads to fit the Japanese culture.

Real Marketing 12.1

Dove: Championing Real Beauty in the Arab World

In 2006, Unilever Arabia launched Dove's 'Campaign for Real Beauty' in the Arab world. This successful campaign had already been adopted in Europe, the United States, and parts of Asia, with the aim of encouraging people to question concepts of personal appearance and beauty.

In the United States and Europe, the campaign signified a change in the way health and beauty products were advertised: instead of using images of models or actresses recognized for their beauty, it used everyday women. Unilever adapted this concept for its Arab world campaign. It developed images which were then used across various media, including billboard advertising, a website, and discussion panels.

"Dove is all about being honest, being natural," said Peter Dekkers, the general manager of Unilever at the time. "The essence of the campaign is basically to debunk the stereotypes of beauty and redefine the meaning of beauty. This campaign has been developed globally but of course the Middle East is a region where there are some limitations, especially when it comes to using women in advertising campaigns."

For this reason, the campaign was tailored to suit the different conditions in the GCC, though the company retained the focus on encouraging people to question pre-conceived ideas about personal appearance. The campaign used images of everyday women, drawing attention to the perception of beauty in terms of shape, size, and hair type, and challenging the standard supermodel imagery based on fantasy and illusion. The advertising campaign was complemented by in-store promotions, various activities in shopping malls, a website (www. campaignforrealbeauty.ae), and a regional SMS text campaign.

Rola Tassabehji, regional brand manager for Dove, said: "Following the launch of the regional ads, there has been an emotional outpour from women across the region who genuinely identified with the campaign. The general consensus has been: at last, images of women who look like us."

The Campaign for Real Beauty was conceived following a worldwide study of 3,300 women. This found that only 2 percent of women were comfortable describing themselves as beautiful. The study also found that 37 percent of Arab girls between the ages of 15 and 17 were considering having cosmetic surgery, and 27 percent of women between the ages of 18 and 64 thought such procedures were an option for themselves.

Studies focused on Saudi Arabia showed that nine in 10 women were unhappy with their physical features. A further 63 percent of Arab women said that they felt threatened by the ideals of beauty presented by the media and entertainment industries—of Arab women being tall, thin, 20 years old, well manicured, and with straight, black hair.

Commenting on the research, Rabee Abu Kishek, marketing manager at Unilever Arabia at the time, said: "The Saudi-based study has shown that Arab women are ready to break the beauty stereotypes that have for long prevented many of them from feeling attractive. Dove's message is simple: Be beautiful in your own unique style—take care of yourself and reach your own beauty potential."

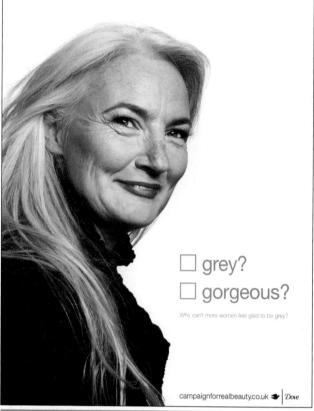

☐ grey?
☐ gorgeous?

Why can't more women feel glad to be grey?

campaignforrealbeauty.co.uk ➤ *Dove*

Dove's "Campaign for Real Beauty" has been a spectacular advertising hit by challenging the standard supermodel-type body images used in most adverts and instead showing images of real, everyday women.

Sources: Roger Field, "Dover Unveils New Media Campaign," *Arabian Business*, February 1, 2006, www.arabianbusiness.com/dove-unveils-new-media-campaign-209284.html; and "Dove's Campaign for Real Beauty Hailed a Success," press release, May 31, 2006, accessed at www.zawya.com.

What's funny in one culture can seem ill-mannered in another. In the American ads, a nerdy PC guy keeps getting outclassed by his hip Mac counterpart, who uses pointed banter that demonstrates how Macs are better. But in Japanese culture, where direct-comparison ads have long been frowned upon, it's rude to brag about one's strengths. So Japanese versions of the ads include subtle changes to emphasize that Macs and PCs are not that different. Instead of clothes that cast PC clearly as a nerd and Mac as a hipster, PC wears plain office attire and Mac weekend fashion, highlighting the work/home divide between the devices more than personality differences. In the first ad of the series, Mac even gives PC a nickname: *waaku*—a playful Japanese version of the word 'work.' PC's body language is a big source of the humor in Japan: Mac looks embarrassed when PC touches his shoulder or hides behind Mac's legs to avoid viruses. "PC constantly makes friendship-level approaches that Mac rejects in a friendly-irritated way," says a Tokyo brand consultant. "The Western Mac ads would backfire in Japan, because the Mac would appear to lack class." In fact, the jury is still out on whether even the toned-down comparative ads will work there.[22]

Global advertisers face several special problems. For instance, advertising media costs and availability differ vastly from country to country. Countries also differ in the extent to which they regulate advertising practices. Many countries have extensive systems of laws restricting how much a company can spend on advertising, the media used, the nature of advertising claims, and other aspects of the advertising program. Such restrictions often require advertisers to adapt their campaigns from country to country.

For example, alcoholic products cannot be advertised in Muslim countries. In many countries, Sweden and Canada, for example, snack food ads are banned from kids' television. To play it safe, McDonald's advertises itself as a family restaurant in Sweden. Comparative ads, although acceptable and even common in the United States and Canada, are less commonly used in the United Kingdom and are illegal in India and Brazil. China bans sending email for advertising purposes to people without their permission and all advertising email that is sent must be titled "advertisement."

China also has restrictive censorship rules for TV and radio advertising; for example, the words *the best* are banned, as are ads that "violate social customs" or present women in "improper ways." McDonald's once avoided government sanctions there by publicly apologizing for an ad that crossed cultural norms by showing a customer begging for a discount. Similarly, Coca-Cola's Indian subsidiary was forced to end a promotion that offered prizes, such as a trip to Hollywood, because it violated India's established trade practices by encouraging customers to buy in order to 'gamble.'[23]

Thus, although advertisers may develop global strategies to guide their overall advertising efforts, specific advertising programs must usually be adapted to meet local cultures and customs, media characteristics, and advertising regulations.

Author Comment | Not long ago, public relations was considered a marketing stepchild because of its limited marketing use. That situation is changing fast, however, as more marketers recognize PR's brand-building power.

Public relations
Building good relations with the company's various publics by obtaining favorable publicity, building up a good corporate image, and handling or heading off unfavorable rumors, stories, and events.

Public Relations (pp 341–345)

Another major mass-promotion tool is **public relations**—building good relations with the company's various publics by obtaining favorable publicity, building up a good corporate image, and handling or heading off unfavorable rumors, stories, and events.

Public relations departments may perform any or all of the following functions:[24]

- *Press relations or press agency:* Creating and placing newsworthy information in the news media to attract attention to a person, product, or service.
- *Product publicity:* Publicizing specific products.
- *Public affairs:* Building and maintaining national or local community relations.
- *Lobbying:* Building and maintaining relations with legislators and government officials to influence legislation and regulation.
- *Investor relations:* Maintaining relationships with shareholders and others in the financial community.
- *Development:* Public relations with donors or members of nonprofit organizations to gain financial or volunteer support.

Public relations is used to promote products, people, places, ideas, activities, organizations, and even nations. Companies use public relations to build good relations with consumers, investors, the media, and their communities. 'Dubai the City That Cares' charity campaign chose the image of Dubai as a city with a heart. Trade associations have used public relations to rebuild interest in declining commodities such as eggs, apples, potatoes, and milk. For example, the U.S. milk industry's popular 'Got Milk?' PR campaign featuring celebrities with milk mustaches reversed a long-standing decline in milk consumption.[25]

By 1994, milk consumption had been in decline for 20 years. The general perception was that milk was unhealthy, outdated, just for kids, or good only with cookies and cake. To counter these notions, the National Fluid Milk Processors Education Program (MilkPEP) began a PR campaign featuring milk be-mustached celebrities and the tag-line "Got Milk?" The campaign has not only been wildly popular, it has been successful as well—not only did it stop the decline, milk consumption actually increased. The campaign is still running.

Although initially targeted at women in their twenties, the campaign has been expanded to other target markets and has gained cult status with teens, much to their parents' delight. Starting with basic print ads featuring a musician, actor, or sports idol, the campaign has naturally spread to the Internet. One website (www.whymilk.com) appeals to mothers in search for America's first "Chief Health Officer." Another (www.bodybymilk.com) targets young people, who can bid on gear using saved milk UPCs, go behind the scenes of the latest "Got Milk?" photo shoot, or get facts about "everything you ever need to know about milk." There are milk mustache MySpace pages of celebrities such as David Beckham. The milk marketers even created the world's first branded emoticon—the milk mustache.

The Role and Impact of Public Relations

Public relations can have a strong impact on public awareness at a much lower cost than advertising can. The company does not pay for the space or time in the media. Rather, it pays for staff to develop and circulate information and to manage events. If the company develops an interesting story or event, it could be picked up by several different media, having the same effect as advertising that would cost millions of dollars. And it would have more credibility than advertising.

Public relations results can sometimes be spectacular. Consider the repositioning of Philadelphia cream cheese in the Arab world.[26] At the Middle East Public Relations Association (Mepra) Awards 2010, Dubai-based PR consultancy GolinHarris won the Best Practice in Consumer Relations award for an entry titled 'How Cheese Inspired a Region of Women.' The entry was part of the company's campaign for Philadelphia cream cheese, produced by Kraft Foods.

Philadelphia had previously been used largely in desserts, but the producers decided to reposition it in the spreadable cheese category. GolinHarris developed a communications strategy to work alongside a thematic campaign designed to increase market penetration. The producers aimed to encourage consumers to trial Philadelphia as a "spreadable cheese with a unique taste advantage."

GolinHarris Dubai developed a new style of campaign for the Arab world, called 'Spread Some Inspiration.' This celebrated the achievements of previously unknown female heroes in the Gulf and emphasized the lighter, fun brand attributes of Philadelphia. 'Spread Some Inspiration' was about ordinary women who had risen to an occasion and achieved something extraordinary, or women who had had a positive impact through education, social work, business, sports or the arts.

The campaign was introduced on International Women's Day 2010. Women in the GCC were invited to share their unique stories of success on the campaign website (www.spreadphiladelphia.com). The website became an open forum where women could describe

You're invited to spread some **inspiration** *with Philadelphia Cream Cheese*

Philadelphia cream cheese's award-winning PR campaign for 'Spread some inspiration' became one of the most widely talked about PR campaigns targeting women in the Arab world, resulting in a return of 25 times the investment.

their own stories or stories of other women who in some way had had a positive impact on their community. A panel of judges was made up of three exceptional women from the GCC. They shortlisted three of the most compelling stories, and the most inspirational story was chosen by public vote.

GolinHarris' campaign became one of the most discussed PR campaigns targeting women in the Arab world. It created a return of 25 times the investment and, more importantly, played a key role in meeting the client's marketing goals.

Despite its potential strengths, public relations is sometimes described as a marketing stepchild because of its often limited and scattered use. The PR department is often located at corporate headquarters or with a third-party agency. Its staff is so busy dealing with various publics—stockholders, employees, legislators, the press—that PR programs to support product marketing objectives may be ignored. Moreover, marketing managers and PR practitioners do not always speak the same language. Whereas many PR practitioners see their jobs as simply communicating, marketing managers tend to be much more interested in how advertising and public relations affect brand building, sales and profits, and customer relationships.

This situation is changing, however. Although public relations still captures only a small portion of the overall marketing budgets of most firms, it can be a powerful brand-building tool. Two well-known marketing consultants even go so far as to conclude that advertising doesn't build brands, public relations does. In their book *The Fall of Advertising & the Rise of PR*, the consultants proclaim that the dominance of advertising is over, and that public relations is quietly becoming the most powerful marketing communications tool.

> The birth of a brand is usually accomplished with [public relations], not advertising. Our general rule is [PR] first, advertising second. [Public relations] is the nail, advertising the hammer. [PR] creates the credentials that provide the credibility for advertising.... Anita Roddick built The Body Shop into a major brand with no advertising at all. Instead, she traveled the world on a relentless quest for publicity.... Until recently Starbucks Coffee didn't spend a hill of beans on advertising, either. In 10 years, the company spent less than US$10 million on advertising, a trivial amount for a brand that delivers annual sales [in the billions]. Wal-Mart stores became the world's largest retailer...with very little advertising.... On the Internet, Amazon. com became a powerhouse brand with virtually no advertising.[27]

Although the book created much controversy, and most advertisers wouldn't agree about the "fall of advertising" part of the title, the point is a good one. Advertising and public relations should work hand in hand within an integrated marketing communications program to build brands and customer relationships.

Major Public Relations Tools

Public relations uses several tools. One of the major tools is *news*. PR professionals find or create favorable news about the company and its products or people. Sometimes news stories occur naturally, and sometimes the PR person can suggest events or activities that would create news. *Speeches* can also create product and company publicity. Increasingly, company executives must field questions from the media or give talks at trade associations or sales meetings, and these events can either build or hurt the company's image. Another common PR tool is *special events*, ranging from news conferences, press tours, grand openings, and fireworks displays to laser shows, hot air balloon releases, multimedia presentations, or educational programs designed to reach and interest target publics.

Public relations people also prepare *written materials* to reach and influence their target markets. These materials include annual reports, brochures, articles, and company newsletters and magazines. *Audiovisual materials*, such as slide-and-sound programs, DVDs, and online videos are being used increasingly as communication tools. *Corporate identity materials* can also help create a corporate identity that the public immediately recognizes. Logos, stationery, brochures, signs, business forms, business cards, buildings, uniforms, and company cars and trucks—all become marketing tools when they are attractive, distinctive, and memorable. Finally, companies can improve public goodwill by contributing money and time to *public service activities*.

As we discussed in Chapter 5, many marketers are now also designing *buzz marketing* campaigns to generate excitement and favorable word of mouth for their brands. Buzz marketing takes advantage of *social networking* processes by getting consumers themselves to spread information about a product or service to others in their communities. For example, consumer-products maker Johnson & Johnson used buzz marketing to launch its Aveeno Positively Ageless product line:

> To build buzz for its new line, Johnson & Johnson employed talented street artist Julian Beever—the "Pavement Picasso"—to create a 3D "Fountain of Youth" chalk drawing on a sidewalk in the heart of New York City. Although the drawing captivated thousands of passersby, Aveeno turned "Fountain of Youth" into an online event via a four-minute, time-lapse video of the artist at work posted on YouTube (www.youtube.com/watch?v=hfn8Dz_13Ms). In addition the brand distributed the video to more than 50 blogs, with 21 responding by promoting the YouTube posting. With a soft "Aveeno Presents" slate at the beginning of the video and a closeup of the Fountain of Youth artwork showing the Aveeno logo at the end, the spot was well branded but without appearing to be commercial. The video reverberated through video sites and the blogosphere via strong word of mouth. Within two weeks, on YouTube alone, the video was viewed more than 65,000 times and grew to reach 121,346 viewings within one month. As of May 2011, the YouTube video had been viewed almost 2 million times.[28]

A company's website is another important PR vehicle. Consumers and members of other publics often visit websites for information or entertainment. Such sites can be extremely popular. For example, Maktoob is one of the top five most-visited websites in the Arab world.

Buzz marketing: Aveeno used social networking processes to get consumers to spread the word about its new product line. It worked with the famous 'Pavement Picasso' street artist to grab attention.

Maktoob Inc. is an Internet services company based in Jordan, and known for being the first Arabic/English email service provider. In 1998, its founders, Samih Toukan and Hussam Khoury, introduced a free email service with Arabic support for emails when no other free email service was available. They also helped users without Arabic keyboards or browsers to send and receive emails by using a virtual keyboard, using Java applets that had better Arabic support. Its large user base has led the company to create several channels for Arab users, and it has introduced many new sites and services not found previously in an Arabic format, though the content of these sponsored channels can be patchy. Over the years, it has also acquired a number of regional sites that showed potential for growth.[29]

Websites can also be ideal for handling crisis situations. For example, when several bottles of Odwalla apple juice were found to contain E. coli bacteria, Odwalla initiated a massive product recall. Within only three hours, it set up a website laden with information about the crisis and Odwalla's response. Company staffers also combed the Internet looking for newsgroups discussing Odwalla and posted links to the site. In this age where "it's easier to disseminate information through e-mail marketing, blogs, and online chat," notes an analyst, "public relations is becoming a valuable part of doing business in a digital world."[30]

As with the other promotion tools, in considering when and how to use product public relations, management should set PR objectives, choose the PR messages and vehicles, implement the PR plan, and evaluate the results. The firm's public relations should be blended smoothly with other promotion activities within the company's overall integrated marketing communications effort.

Author Comment | Personal selling is the interpersonal arm of the promotion mix. A company's salespeople create and communicate customer value through personal interactions with customers.

Personal Selling (pp 245–247)

Author Robert Louis Stevenson once noted that "everyone lives by selling something." Companies all around the world use sales forces to sell products and services to business customers and final consumers. But sales forces are also found in many other kinds of organizations. For example, colleges use recruiters to attract new students, and museums and fine arts organizations use fund-raisers to contact donors and raise money. In the coming section, we examine personal selling's role in the organization, sales force management decisions, and the personal selling process.

Personal selling

Personal presentation by the firm's sales force for the purpose of making sales and building customer relationships.

Personal selling is one of the oldest professions in the world. The people who do the selling go by many names: salespeople, sales representatives, district managers, account executives, sales consultants, sales engineers, agents, and account development reps to name just a few.

People hold many stereotypes of salespeople—including some unfavorable ones. Salesmen are often perceived as attempting to deceive consumers and convince buyers to purchase unneeded products.

However, modern salespeople are very different from these unfortunate stereotypes. Today, most salespeople are well-educated, well-trained professionals who add value for customers and maintain long-term customer relationships. They listen to their customers, assess customer needs, and organize the company's efforts to solve customer problems.[31]

In today's hypercompetitive markets, "buying is not about transactions anymore," says one sales expert. "Salespeople must know their customers' businesses better than customers do and align themselves with customers' strategies." That creates an entirely new role for salespeople. These days, "salespeople must have a deep business knowledge, combined with the credibility to sell to [empowered, well-informed buying] executives," says another expert. Today, sales is about building customer relationships through a "focus on differentiation and linking those differences to the customer's realization of value."

Consider Boeing, the aerospace giant competing in the tough worldwide commercial aircraft market. It takes more than fast talk and a warm smile to sell expensive high-tech aircraft. A single big sale can easily run into billions of dollars. Boeing salespeople head up an extensive team of company specialists—sales and service technicians, financial analysts, planners,

Professional selling: It takes more than fast talk and a warm smile to sell high-tech aircraft, a single big sale can easily run into billions of dollars. Success depends on building solid, long-term relationships with customers.

engineers—all dedicated to finding ways to satisfy airline customer needs. The selling process is extremely slow—it can take two or three years from the first sales presentation to the day the sale is announced. After getting the order, salespeople then must stay in almost constant touch to make certain the customer stays satisfied. Success depends on building solid, long-term relationships with customers, based on performance and trust.

Salesperson
An individual representing a company to customers by performing one or more of the following activities: prospecting, communicating, selling, servicing, information gathering, and relationship building.

The term **salesperson** covers a wide range of positions. At one extreme, a salesperson might be largely an *order taker*, such as the department store salesperson standing behind the counter. At the other extreme are *order getters*, whose positions demand *creative selling* and *relationship building* for products and services ranging from appliances, industrial equipment, and airplanes to insurance and information technology services. Here, we focus on the more creative types of selling and on the process of building and managing an effective sales force.

The Role of the Sales Force

Personal selling is the interpersonal arm of the promotion mix. Advertising consists largely of nonpersonal communication with target consumer groups. In contrast, personal selling involves interpersonal interactions between salespeople and individual customers—whether face-to-face, by telephone, via email, through video or web conferences, or by other means. Personal selling can be more effective than advertising in more complex selling situations. Salespeople can probe customers to learn more about their problems and then adjust the marketing offer and presentation to fit the special needs of each customer.

The role of personal selling varies from company to company. Some firms have no salespeople at all—for example, companies that sell only online or through catalogs, or companies that sell through manufacturer's reps, sales agents, or brokers. In most firms, however, the sales force plays a major role. In companies that sell business products and services, such as IBM or DuPont, the company's salespeople work directly with customers. In consumer product companies, such as Unilever and Adidas, the sales force plays an important behind-the-scenes role. It works with wholesalers and retailers to gain their support and to help them be more effective in selling the company's products.

Linking the Company with Its Customers

The sales force serves as a critical link between a company and its customers. In many cases, salespeople serve both masters—the seller and the buyer. First, they *represent the company to customers*. They find and develop new customers and communicate information about the company's products and services. They sell products by approaching customers, presenting their products, answering objections, negotiating prices and terms, and closing sales. In addition, salespeople provide customer service and carry out market research and intelligence work.

At the same time, salespeople *represent customers to the company*, acting inside the firm as 'champions' of customers' interests and managing the buyer–seller relationship. Salespeople relay customer concerns about company products and actions back inside to those who can handle them. They learn about customer needs and work with other marketing and nonmarketing people in the company to develop greater customer value.

In fact, to many customers, the salesperson *is* the company—the only tangible manifestation of the company that they see. Hence, customers may become loyal to salespeople as well as to the companies and products they represent. This concept of 'salesperson-owned loyalty' lends even more importance to the

Salespeople link the company with its customers. To many customers, the salesperson is the company.

salesperson's customer relationship building abilities. Strong relationships with the salesperson will result in strong relationships with the company and its products. Conversely, poor salesperson relationships will probably result in poor company and product relationships.[32]

Co-ordinating Marketing and Sales

Ideally, the sales force and the firm's other marketing functions should work together closely to create value jointly for both customers and the company. Unfortunately, however, some companies still treat marketing and sales as separate functions. When this happens, the separated marketing and sales functions often don't get along well. When things go wrong, the marketers (marketing planners, brand managers, and researchers) blame the sales force for its poor execution of an otherwise splendid strategy. In turn, the sales team blames the marketers for being out of touch with what's really going on with customers. The marketers sometimes feel that salespeople have their 'feet stuck in the mud' whereas salespeople feel that the marketers have their 'heads stuck in the clouds.' Neither group fully values the other's contributions. If not repaired, such disconnects between marketing and sales can damage customer relationships and company performance.

A company can take several actions to help bring its marketing and sales functions closer together. At the most basic level, it can *increase communications* between the two groups by arranging joint meetings and by spelling out when and with whom each group should communicate. The company can create *joint assignments*.[33]

It's important to create opportunities for marketers and salespeople to work together. This will make them more familiar with each other's ways of thinking and acting. It's useful for marketers, particularly brand managers and researchers, to occasionally go along on sales calls. They should also sit in on important account-planning sessions. Salespeople, in turn, should help to develop marketing plans. They should sit in on product-planning reviews and share their deep knowledge about customers' purchasing habits. They should preview ad and sales-promotion campaigns. Jointly, marketers and salespeople should generate a playbook for expanding business with the top 10 accounts in each market segment. They should also plan events and conferences together.

A company can also create *joint objectives and reward systems* for sales and marketing or appoint *marketing-sales liaisons*—people from marketing who 'live with the sales force' and help to co-ordinate marketing and sales force programs and efforts. Finally, the firm can appoint a *chief revenue officer* (or *chief customer officer*)—a high-level marketing executive who oversees both marketing and sales. Such a person can help infuse marketing and sales with the common goal of creating value for customers in order to capture value in return.

Sales force management
The analysis, planning, implementation, and control of sales force activities. It includes designing sales force strategy and structure and recruiting, selecting, training, supervising, compensating, and evaluating the firm's salespeople.

Author Comment | Here's another definition of sales force management: Planning, organizing, leading, and controlling personal contact programs designed to achieve profitable customer relationships. Here again, the goal of every marketing activity is to create customer value and build customer relationships.

Managing the Sales Force (pp 347–355)

We define **sales force management** as the analysis, planning, implementation, and control of sales force activities. It includes designing sales force strategy and structure and recruiting, selecting, training, compensating, supervising, and evaluating the firm's salespeople. These major sales force management decisions are shown in ◤ **Figure 12.2** and are discussed in the following sections.

◤ FIGURE | 12.2
Major Steps in Sales Force Management

The goal? You guessed it! The company wants to build a skilled and motivated sales team that will help to create customer value and build strong customer relationships.

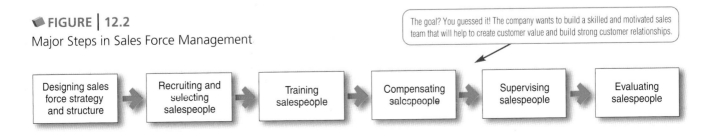

Designing Sales Force Strategy and Structure

Marketing managers face several sales force strategy and design questions. How should salespeople and their tasks be structured? How big should the sales force be? Should salespeople sell alone or work in teams with other people in the company? Should they sell in the field or by telephone or on the web? We address these issues next.

Sales Force Structure

A company can divide sales responsibilities along any of several lines. The decision is simple if the company sells only one product line to one industry with customers in many locations. In that case the company would use a *territorial sales force structure*. However, if the company sells many products to many types of customers, it might need a *product sales force structure*, a *customer sales force structure*, or a combination of the two.

Territorial sales force structure
A sales force organization that assigns each salesperson to an exclusive geographic territory in which that salesperson sells the company's full line.

Territorial Sales Force Structure. In the **territorial sales force structure**, each salesperson is assigned to an exclusive geographic area and sells the company's full line of products or services to all customers in that territory. This organization clearly defines each salesperson's job and fixes accountability. It also increases the salesperson's desire to build local customer relationships that, in turn, improve selling effectiveness. Finally, because each salesperson travels within a limited geographic area, travel expenses are relatively small.

A territorial sales organization is often supported by many levels of sales management positions. For example, Cisco Systems uses a territorial structure in the MENA region, in which each salesperson is responsible for selling all Cisco products in a specific geographical area. The main focus of the salesperson at Cisco is to satisfy the different needs of the customers in the assigned territory by maintaining strong and close relations with the different partners in that territory.

Product sales force structure
A sales force organization under which salespeople specialize in selling only a portion of the company's products or lines.

Product Sales Force Structure. Salespeople must know their products—especially when the products are numerous and complex. This need, together with the growth of product management, has led many companies to adopt a **product sales force structure**, in which the sales force sells along product lines. For example, GE employs different sales forces within different product and service divisions of its major businesses. Within GE Infrastructure, for instance, the company has separate sales forces for aviation, energy, transportation, and water-processing products and technologies. Within GE Healthcare, it employs different sales forces for diagnostic imaging, life sciences, and integrated IT solutions products and services. In all, a company as large and complex as GE might have dozens of separate sales forces serving its diverse product and service portfolio.

The product structure can lead to problems, however, if a single large customer buys many different company products. For example, pharmaceutical and medical appliances, whether local or multinational, have several product divisions, each with a separate sales force. Using a product sales force structure might mean that several salespeople end up calling on the same hospital on the same day. This means that they travel over the same routes and wait to see the same customer's purchasing agents. These extra costs must be compared with the benefits of better product knowledge and attention to individual products.

Customer sales force structure
A sales force organization under which salespeople specialize in selling only to certain customers or industries.

Customer Sales Force Structure. More and more companies are now using a **customer sales force structure**, in which they organize the sales force along customer or industry lines. Separate sales forces may be set up for different industries, for serving current customers versus finding new ones, and for major accounts versus regular accounts. Many companies even have special sales forces set up to handle the needs of individual large customers.

Organizing the sales force around customers can help a company to build closer relationships with important customers. Consider HSBC Bank, which categorizes its corporate customers; accordingly it provides special services, special loan rates, and special discounts depending on the size of transactions and the importance of the customers.

Complex Sales Force Structures. When a company sells a wide variety of products to many types of customers over a broad geographic area, it often combines several types of sales force structures. Salespeople can be specialized by customer and territory, by product and territory, by product and customer, or by territory, product, and customer. No single structure is best for all companies and situations. Each company should select a sales force structure that best serves the needs of its customers and fits its overall marketing strategy.

A good sales structure can mean the difference between success and failure. Companies should periodically review their sales force organizations to be certain that they serve the needs of the company and its customers. Over time, sales force structures can grow complex, inefficient, and unresponsive to customers' needs.

Sales Force Size

Once the company has set its structure, it is ready to consider *sales force size*. Sales forces may range in size from only a few salespeople to tens of thousands. Some sales forces are huge—for example, Xerox employs 16,000 salespeople; American Express, 23,400; PepsiCo, 36,000; and Aflac, 56,000.[34] Salespeople constitute one of the company's most productive—and most expensive—assets. Therefore, increasing their number will increase both sales and costs. Various global consulting companies recognized companies' needs to optimize the use of their sales forces, and offered them effective software solutions. Aphidas is an excellent example of a company that offers such services in the Arab world. With headquarters in Dubai, and Indian offices in Delhi and Hyderabad, the company is helping its customers in the Middle East realize the power of Software as a Service (SaaS). This primarily offers benefits relating to the adoption of complex enterprise software projects. Aphidas has also formed a strategic partnership with Salesforce.com, a major world supplier of customer relationship management (CRM) systems.[35]

Many companies use some form of *workload approach* to set sales force size. Using this approach, first a company groups accounts into different classes according to size, account status, or other factors related to the amount of effort required to maintain them. It then determines the number of salespeople needed to call on each class of accounts the desired number of times.

The company might think as follows: suppose we have 1,000 Type-A accounts and 2,000 Type-B accounts; Type-A accounts require 36 calls a year and Type-B accounts require 12 calls a year. In this case, the sales force's *workload*—the number of calls it must make per year—is 60,000 calls [(1,000 × 36) + (2,000 × 12) = 36,000 + 24,000 = 60,000]. Suppose our average salesperson can make 1,000 calls a year. Thus, we need 60 salespeople (60,000 ÷ 1,000).[36]

Other Sales Force Strategy and Structure Issues

Sales management must also decide who will be involved in the selling effort and how various sales and sales support people will work together.

Outside and Inside Sales Forces. The company may have an **outside sales force** (or *field sales force*), an **inside sales force**, or both. Outside salespeople travel to call on customers in the field. Inside salespeople conduct business from their offices via telephone, the Internet, or visits from buyers.

Some inside salespeople provide support for the outside sales force, freeing them to spend more time selling to major accounts and finding new prospects. For example, *technical sales support people* provide technical information and answers to customers' questions. *Sales assistants* provide administrative backup for outside salespeople. They call ahead and confirm appointments, follow up on deliveries, and answer customers' questions when outside salespeople cannot be reached. Using such combinations of inside and outside salespeople can help to serve important customers better. As one sales manager notes, "You have the support and easy access to the inside rep and the face-to-face relationship building of the outside rep."[37]

Outside sales force (or field sales force)
Outside salespeople who travel to call on customers in the field.

Inside sales force
Inside salespeople who conduct business from their offices via telephone, the Internet, or visits from prospective buyers.

Other inside salespeople do more than just provide support. *Telemarketers* and *web sellers* use the phone and Internet to find new leads and qualify prospects or to sell and service accounts directly. Telemarketing and web selling can be very effective, less costly ways to sell to smaller, harder-to-reach customers. Depending on the complexity of the product and customer, for example, a telemarketer can make from 20 to 33 decision-maker contacts a day, compared with the average of 4 that an outside salesperson can make.

For many types of products and selling situations, phone or web selling can be as effective as a personal sales call. Notes a DuPont telemarketer: "I'm more effective on the phone. [When you're in the field], if some guy's not in his office, you lose an hour. On the phone, you lose 15 seconds.... Through my phone calls, I'm in the field as much as the rep is."

What's more, although they may seem impersonal, the phone and Internet can be surprisingly personal when it comes to building customer relationships.

Team Selling. As products become more complex, and as customers grow larger and more demanding, a single salesperson simply can't handle all of a large customer's needs. Instead, most companies now use **team selling** to service large, complex accounts. Sales teams can unearth problems, solutions, and sales opportunities that no individual salesperson could. Such teams might include experts from any area or level of the selling firm—sales, marketing, technical and support services, R&D, engineering, operations, finance, and others.

In many cases, the move to team selling mirrors similar changes in customers' buying organizations. "Buyers implementing team-based purchasing decisions have necessitated the equal and opposite creation of team-based selling—a completely new way of doing business for many independent, self-motivated salespeople," says a sales force analyst. "Today, we're calling on teams of buying people, and that requires more firepower on our side," agrees one sales vice president. "One salesperson just can't do it all—can't be an expert in everything we're bringing to the customer. We have strategic account teams, led by customer business managers."[38]

Some companies, such as IBM, Xerox, and Procter & Gamble, have used teams for a long time. P&G sales reps are organized into "customer business development (CBD) teams." Each CBD team is assigned to a major P&G customer, such as Wal-Mart, Tesco, or Boots pharmacy. Teams consist of a customer business development manager, several account executives (each responsible for a specific category of P&G products), and specialists in marketing strategy, operations, information systems, logistics, and finance. This organization places the focus on serving the complete needs of each important customer. It lets P&G "grow business by working as a 'strategic partner' with our accounts, not just as a supplier. Our goal: to grow their business, which also results in growing ours."[39]

Team selling does have some pitfalls. For example, salespeople are by nature competitive and have often been trained and rewarded for outstanding individual performance. Salespeople who are used to having customers all to themselves may have trouble learning to work with and trust others on a team. In addition, selling teams can confuse or overwhelm customers who are used to working with only one salesperson. Finally, difficulties in evaluating individual contributions to the team selling effort can create some sticky compensation issues.

Recruiting and Selecting Salespeople

At the heart of any successful sales force operation is the recruitment and selection of good salespeople. The performance difference between an average salesperson and a top salesperson can be substantial. In a typical sales force, the top 30 percent of the salespeople might bring in 60 percent of the sales. Thus, careful salesperson selection can greatly increase overall sales force performance. Beyond the differences in sales performance, poor selection results in costly turnover. When a salesperson quits, the costs of finding and training a new salesperson—plus the costs of lost sales—can be very high. Also, a sales

Renkus-Heinz, U.S.-based manufacturer of audio operations networks and electronics, appointed Mr Norbert Bau in March 2010 as its sales representative for the Middle East, based in Dubai. Bau was a high-caliber candidate for the position, with extensive global sales experience and a background as a professional sound engineer.[40]

force with many new people is less productive, and turnover disrupts important customer relationships.

What sets great salespeople apart from all the rest? In an effort to profile top sales performers, Gallup Management Consulting Group, a division of the Gallup polling organization, has interviewed hundreds of thousands of salespeople. Its research suggests that the best salespeople possess four key talents: intrinsic motivation, disciplined work style, the ability to close a sale, and perhaps most important, the ability to build relationships with customers.[41]

Super salespeople are motivated from within—they have an unrelenting drive to excel. Some salespeople are driven by money, a desire for recognition, or the satisfaction of competing and winning. Others are driven by the desire to provide service and to build relationships. The best salespeople possess some of each of these motivations. They also have a disciplined work style. They lay out detailed, organized plans and then follow through in a timely way.

But motivation and discipline mean little unless they result in closing more sales and building better customer relationships. Super salespeople build the skills and knowledge they need to get the job done. Perhaps most important, top salespeople are excellent customer problem solvers and relationship builders. They understand their customers' needs. Talk to sales executives and they'll describe top performers in these terms: Empathetic. Patient. Caring. Responsive. Good listeners. Top performers can put themselves on the buyer's side of the desk and see the world through their customers' eyes. They don't want just to be liked, they want to add value for their customers.

When recruiting, a company should analyze the sales job itself and the characteristics of its most successful salespeople to identify the traits needed by a successful salesperson in its industry. Then, it must recruit the right salespeople. The human resources department looks for applicants by getting names from current salespeople, using employment agencies, placing classified ads, searching the web, and working through college placement services. Another source is to attract top salespeople from other companies. Proven salespeople need less training and can be productive immediately.

Recruiting will attract many applicants from whom the company must select the best. The selection procedure can vary from a single informal interview to lengthy testing and interviewing. Many companies give formal tests to sales applicants. Tests typically measure sales aptitude, analytical and organizational skills, personality traits, and other characteristics. But test scores provide only one piece of information in a set that includes personal characteristics, references, past employment history, and interviewer reactions.

Training Salespeople

New salespeople may spend anywhere from a few weeks or months to a year or more in training. Then, most companies provide continuing sales training via seminars, sales meetings, and web e-learning throughout the salesperson's career. Although training can be expensive, it can also yield dramatic returns. For example, one recent study showed that sales training conducted by a major telecommunications firm paid for itself in 16 days and resulted in a six-month return on investment of 812 percent.[42]

Training programs have several goals. First, salespeople need to know about customers and how to build relationships with them. So the training program must teach them about different types of customers and their needs, buying motives, and buying habits. And it must teach them how to sell effectively and train them in the basics of the selling process. Salespeople also need to know and identify with the company, its products, and its competitors. So an effective training program teaches them about the company's objectives, organization, and chief products and markets, and about the strategies of major competitors.

Today, many companies are adding e-learning to their sales training programs. Most e-learning is web-based but many companies now offer on-demand training for personal digital assistants, cellphones, and even video iPods. Online and other e-learning approaches cut training costs and make training more efficient. One recent study estimates that companies spend 40 cent of every sales training dollar on travel and lodging. Such costs can be greatly reduced through web-based training. As a result, last year, companies did 33 percent of their corporate training online, up from 24 percent two years earlier.[43]

Online training may range from simple text-based product information, to Internet-based sales exercises that build sales skills, to sophisticated simulations that re-create the dynamics of real-life sales calls. Unfortunately, the value of online training is not well perceived in the region except in minor cases; however, corporations organize regular sales training sessions. Such sessions can be products/services related or sales and sales management skills related. In all cases, at least yearly there is a round meeting for the sales force to refresh and acquire new information and skills.

Compensating Salespeople

To attract good salespeople, a company must have an appealing compensation plan. Compensation is made up of several elements—a fixed amount, a variable amount, expenses, and fringe benefits. The fixed amount, usually a salary, gives the salesperson some stable income. The variable amount, which might be commissions or bonuses based on sales performance, rewards the salesperson for greater effort and success.

Management must decide what *mix* of these compensation elements makes the most sense for each sales job. Different combinations of fixed and variable compensation give rise to four basic types of compensation plans—straight salary, straight commission, salary plus bonus, and salary plus commission. The sales force compensation plan can both motivate salespeople and direct their activities. Compensation should direct salespeople toward activities that are consistent with overall sales force and marketing objectives.

Supervising and Motivating Salespeople

New salespeople need more than a territory, compensation, and training—they need supervision and motivation. The goal of *supervision* is to help salespeople 'work smart' by doing the right things in the right ways. The goal of *motivation* is to encourage salespeople to work hard and energetically toward sales force goals. If salespeople work smart and work hard, they will realize their full potential, to their own and the company's benefit.

Supervising Salespeople

Companies vary in how closely they supervise their salespeople. Many help their salespeople to identify target customers and set call norms.

Figure 12.3 shows how salespeople spend their time. On average, active selling time accounts for only 10 percent of total working time! If selling time could be raised from 10 percent to 30 percent, this would triple the time spent selling.[44] Consider the changes GE made to increase its sales force's face-to-face selling time.[45]

When Jeff Immelt became General Electric's new chairman, he was disappointed to find that members of the sales team were spending far more time on deskbound administrative chores than in face-to-face meetings with customers and prospects. "He said we needed to turn that around," recalls Venki Rao, an IT leader in global sales and marketing at GE Power Systems, a division focused on energy systems and products. "[We need] to spend four days a week in front of the customer and one day for all the admin stuff." GE Power's salespeople spent much of their time at

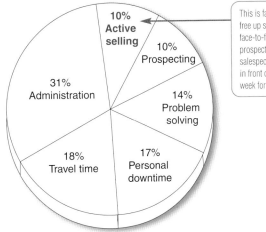

FIGURE | 12.3

How Salespeople Spend Their Time

Source: Proudfoot Consulting. Data used with permission.

10%
Active selling

10%
Prospecting

14%
Problem solving

17%
Personal downtime

18%
Travel time

31%
Administration

This is far too little. Companies need to free up salespeople to spend much more face-to-face time with customers and prospects. For example, GE wants its salespeople to "spend four days a week in front of the customer and one day a week for all the admin stuff."

their desks because they had to go to many sources for the information needed to sell multimillion-dollar turbines, turbine parts, and services to energy companies worldwide. To fix the problem, GE created a new sales portal, a kind of "one-stop shop" for just about everything the salespeople need. The sales portal connects the vast array of existing GE databases, providing everything from sales tracking and customer data to parts pricing and information on planned outages. GE also added external data, such as news feeds. "Before, you were randomly searching for things," says Bill Snook, a GE sales manager. Now, he says, "I have the sales portal as my home page, and I use it as the gateway to all the applications that I have." The sales portal has freed Snook and 2,500 other users around the globe from once time-consuming administrative tasks, greatly increasing their face time with customers.

Many firms have adopted *sales force automation systems*—computerized, digitized sales force operations that let salespeople work more effectively anytime, anywhere. Companies now routinely equip their salespeople with technologies such as laptops, smart phones, wireless web connections, webcams for video conferencing, and customer-contact and relationship management software.

Selling and the Internet. Perhaps the fastest-growing technology tool is the Internet. The Internet offers explosive potential for conducting sales operations and for interacting with and serving customers. More and more companies are now using the Internet to support their personal selling efforts—not just for selling but for everything from training salespeople to conducting sales meetings and servicing accounts.

Sales organizations around the world are now saving money and time by using a host of web approaches to train reps, hold sales meetings, and even conduct live sales

Sales force automation: Many sales forces have gone high tech, equipping salespeople with everything from smart phones, wireless web connections, and videoconferencing tools to customer-contact and relationship management software that helps them to be more effective and efficient.

presentations. The web can be a good tool for selling to hard-to-reach customers. For example, consider the pharmaceuticals industry:[46]

> The big pharmaceutical companies currently employ some 87,000 sales reps (often called 'detailers') to reach roughly 600,000 practicing physicians. However, these reps are finding it harder than ever to get through to the busy doctors. "Doctors need immense amounts of medical information, but their patient loads limit their ability to see pharmaceutical reps or attend outside conferences," says an industry researcher. As a result, the average call lasts only for a few minutes and only a minimum percentage of sales calls on doctors result in quality, two-way discussions. The answer: Increasingly, it's the web. The pharmaceutical companies now regularly use product websites, printed brochures, and video conferencing to help reps deliver useful information to physicians on their home or office PCs. One study in the United States found that last year more than 200,000 physicians participated in 'e-detailing'—the process of receiving drug marketing information via the web—a 400 percent jump in only three years. More than 20 percent have now substituted e-detailing for face-to-face meetings with reps entirely. Using direct-to-doctor web conferences, pharmaceuticals reps can make live, interactive medical sales presentations to any physician with a PC and web access, saving both the customer's and the rep's time.

Web-based technologies can produce big organizational benefits for sales forces. They help conserve salespeople's valuable time, save travel costs, and give salespeople a new vehicle for selling and servicing accounts. But the technologies also have some drawbacks. For starters, they're not cheap. And such systems can intimidate low-tech salespeople or clients. What's more, web tools are susceptible to server crashes and other network difficulties—not a happy event when you're in the midst of an important sales meeting or presentation. Finally, there are some things you just can't do or teach via the web, things that require personal interactions.

For these reasons, some high-tech experts recommend that sales executives use web technologies to supplement training, sales meetings, and preliminary client sales presentations, but resort to old-fashioned, face-to-face meetings when the time draws near to close the deal.

Motivating Salespeople

Beyond directing salespeople, sales managers must also motivate them. Some salespeople will do their best without any special urging from management. To them, selling may be the most fascinating job in the world. But selling can also be frustrating. Salespeople often work alone and they must sometimes travel away from home. They may face aggressive competing salespeople and difficult customers. Therefore, salespeople often need special encouragement to do their best.

Management can boost sales force morale and performance through its organizational climate, sales quotas, and positive incentives. *Organizational climate* describes the feeling that salespeople have about their opportunities, value, and rewards for a good performance. Some companies treat salespeople as if they are not very important and performance suffers accordingly. Other companies treat their salespeople as valued contributors and allow virtually unlimited opportunity for income and promotion. Not surprisingly, these companies enjoy higher sales force performance and less turnover.

Many companies motivate their salespeople by setting **sales quotas**—standards stating the amount they should sell and how sales should be divided among the company's products. Compensation is often related to how well salespeople meet their quotas. Companies also use various *positive incentives* to increase sales force effort. *Sales meetings* provide social occasions, breaks from routine, chances to meet and talk with 'company brass,' and opportunities to air feelings and to identify with a larger group. Companies also sponsor *sales contests* to spur the sales force to make a selling effort above what would normally be expected. Other incentives include honors, merchandise and cash awards, trips, and profit-sharing plans.

Sales quota

A standard that states the amount a salesperson should sell and how sales should be divided among the company's products.

Evaluating Salespeople and Sales-Force Performance

We have thus far described how management communicates what salespeople should be doing and how it motivates them to do it. This process requires good feedback. And good feedback means getting regular information about salespeople to evaluate their performance.

Management gets information about its salespeople in several ways. The most important source is *sales reports,* including weekly or monthly work plans and longer-term territory marketing plans. Salespeople also write up their completed activities on *call reports* and turn in *expense reports* for which they are partly or wholly repaid. The company can also monitor the sales and profit performance data in the salesperson's territory. Additional information comes from personal observation, customer surveys, and talks with other salespeople.

Using various sales force reports and other information, sales management evaluates members of the sales force. It evaluates salespeople on their ability to 'plan their work and work their plan.' Formal evaluation forces management to develop and communicate clear standards for judging performance. It also provides salespeople with constructive feedback and motivates them to perform well.

> **Author Comment** | So far, we've examined how sales management develops and implements overall sales force strategies and programs. In this section, we'll look at how individual salespeople and sales teams sell to customers and build relationships with them.

The Personal Selling Process (pp 355–358)

We now turn from designing and managing a sales force to the actual personal selling process. The **selling process** consists of several steps that the salesperson must master. These steps focus on the goal of getting new customers and obtaining orders from them. However, most salespeople spend much of their time maintaining existing accounts and building long-term customer *relationships*. We discuss the relationship aspect of the personal selling process in a later section.

Selling process
The steps that the salesperson follows when selling, which include prospecting and qualifying, preapproach, approach, presentation and demonstration, handling objections, closing, and follow-up.

Steps in the Selling Process

As shown in 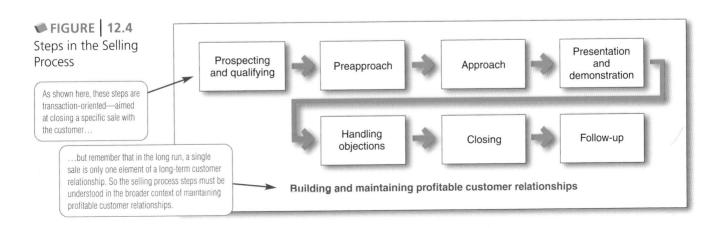 Figure 12.4, the selling process consists of seven steps: prospecting and qualifying, preapproach, approach, presentation and demonstration, handling objections, closing, and follow-up.

Prospecting and Qualifying

Prospecting
The step in the selling process in which the salesperson or company identifies qualified potential customers.

The first step in the selling process is **prospecting**—identifying qualified potential customers. Approaching the right potential customers is crucial to selling success. As one sales expert puts it, "If the sales force starts chasing anyone who is breathing and seems to have a budget, you risk accumulating a roster of expensive-to-serve, hard-to-satisfy customers who never respond to whatever value proposition you have." He continues, "The solution to this isn't rocket science. [You must] train salespeople to actively scout the right prospects." Another expert concludes, "Increasing your prospecting effectiveness is the fastest single way to boost your sales."[47]

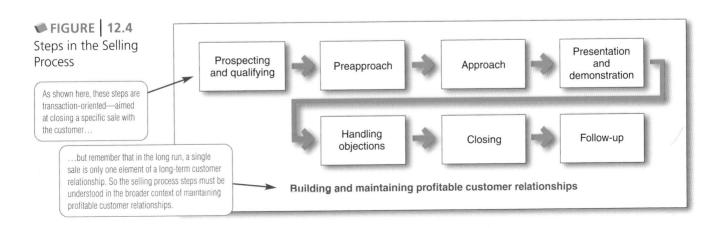

FIGURE | 12.4
Steps in the Selling Process

As shown here, these steps are transaction-oriented—aimed at closing a specific sale with the customer…

…but remember that in the long run, a single sale is only one element of a long-term customer relationship. So the selling process steps must be understood in the broader context of maintaining profitable customer relationships.

Prospecting and qualifying → Preapproach → Approach → Presentation and demonstration → Handling objections → Closing → Follow-up

Building and maintaining profitable customer relationships

The salesperson must often approach many prospects to get just a few sales. Although the company supplies some leads, salespeople need skill in finding their own. The best source is referrals. Salespeople can ask current customers for referrals and cultivate other referral sources, such as suppliers, dealers, noncompeting salespeople, and bankers. They can also search for prospects in directories or on the web and track down leads using the telephone and direct mail. Or they can drop in unannounced on various offices (a practice known as 'cold calling').

Salespeople also need to know how to *qualify* leads—that is, how to identify the good ones and screen out the poor ones. Prospects can be qualified by looking at their financial ability, volume of business, special needs, location, and possibilities for growth.

Preapproach

Before calling on a prospect, the salesperson should learn as much as possible about the organization (what it needs, who is involved in the buying) and its buyers (their characteristics and buying styles). This step is known as the **preapproach.** "Revving up your sales starts with your preparation," says one sales consultant. "A successful sale begins long before you set foot in the prospect's office." Preapproach begins with good research. The salesperson can consult standard industry and online sources, acquaintances, and others to learn about the company. Then, the salesperson must apply the research to develop a customer strategy. "Being able to recite the prospect's product line in your sleep isn't enough," says the consultant. "You need to translate the data into something useful for your client."[48]

The salesperson should set *call objectives*, which may be to qualify the prospect, to gather information, or to make an immediate sale. Another task is to decide on the best approach, which might be a personal visit, a phone call, or a letter or email. The best timing should be considered carefully because many prospects are busiest at certain times. Finally, the salesperson should give thought to an overall sales strategy for the account.

Approach

During the **approach** step, the salesperson should know how to meet and greet the buyer and get the relationship off to a good start. This step involves the salesperson's appearance, opening lines, and the follow-up remarks. The opening lines should be positive to build goodwill from the beginning of the relationship. This opening might be followed by some key questions to learn more about the customer's needs or by showing a display or sample to attract the buyer's attention and curiosity. As in all stages of the selling process, listening to the customer is crucial.

Presentation and Demonstration

During the **presentation** step of the selling process, the salesperson tells the 'value story' to the buyer, showing how the company's offer solves the customer's problems. The *customer-solution approach* fits better with today's relationship marketing focus than does a hard-sell or glad-handing approach. Buyers today want answers, not smiles; results, not razzle-dazzle. Moreover, they don't want just products—they want to know how those products will add value to their businesses. They want salespeople who listen to their concerns, understand their needs, and respond with the right products and services.

But before salespeople can *present* customer solutions, they must *develop* solutions to present. Many companies now train their salespeople to go beyond product thinking. ESRI Northeast Africa, originally a distributor of ESRI Inc, a GIS software leader, in the northeast Africa region, has branched out to provide geographic information system professional services using the ESRI Inc. technology in the Gulf region. Moreover, the company has started to introduce such services in its original territory. In order to do this, ESRI Northeast Africa has had to train and develop the sales force's skills to present solutions rather than products.[49]

The qualities that buyers *dislike most* in salespeople include being pushy, late, deceitful, and unprepared or disorganized. The qualities they *value most* include good listening, empathy, honesty, dependability, thoroughness, and follow-through. Great salespeople know how to sell, but more importantly they know how to listen and to build strong customer relationships. Says one professional, "Salespeople must have the right answers, certainly, but they also have to learn how to ask those questions and listen."[50]

Preapproach

The step in the selling process in which the salesperson learns as much as possible about a prospective customer before making a sales call.

Approach

The step in the selling process in which the salesperson meets the customer for the first time.

Presentation

The step in the selling process in which the salesperson tells the 'value story' to the buyer, showing how the company's offer solves the customer's problems.

Presentation technology: Today's salespeople are employing advanced presentation technologies that allow for full multimedia presentations—in person, online, or both.

Handling objections

The step in the selling process in which the salesperson seeks out, clarifies, and overcomes customer objections to buying.

Closing

The step in the selling process in which the salesperson asks the customer for an order.

Follow-up

The last step in the selling process in which the salesperson follows up after the sale to ensure customer satisfaction and repeat business.

Finally, salespeople must also plan their presentation methods. Good interpersonal communication skills count when it comes to making effective sales presentations. However, today's media-rich and cluttered communications environment presents many new challenges for sales presenters.[51]

Thus, today's salespeople are employing advanced presentation technologies that allow for full multimedia presentations to only one or a few people. The venerable old flip chart has been replaced by CDs and DVDs, online presentation technologies, interactive white boards, and handheld and laptop computers with sophisticated presentation software.

Handling Objections

Customers almost always have objections during the presentation or when asked to place an order. The problem can be either logical or psychological, and objections are often unspoken. In **handling objections**, the salesperson should use a positive approach, seek out hidden objections, ask the buyer to clarify any objections, take objections as opportunities to provide more information, and turn the objections into reasons for buying. Every salesperson needs training in the skills of handling objections.

Closing

After handling the prospect's objections, the salesperson now tries to close the sale. Some salespeople do not get around to **closing** or do not handle it well. They may lack confidence, feel guilty about asking for the order, or fail to recognize the right moment to close the sale. Salespeople should know how to recognize closing signals from the buyer, including physical actions, comments, and questions. For example, the customer might sit forward and nod approvingly or ask about prices and credit terms.

Salespeople can use one of several closing techniques. They can ask for the order, review points of agreement, offer to help write up the order, ask whether the buyer wants this model or that one, or note that the buyer will lose out if the order is not placed now. The salesperson may offer the buyer special reasons to close, such as a lower price or an extra quantity at no charge. Moreover in the Arab market, it is normal that the salesperson offers a special discount at closure of the deal in order to maximize the buyer's level of satisfaction.

Follow-Up

The last step in the selling process—**follow-up**—is necessary if the salesperson wants to ensure customer satisfaction and repeat business. Right after closing, the salesperson should complete any details on delivery time, purchase terms, and other matters. The salesperson then should schedule a follow-up call when the initial order is received to make sure there is proper installation, instruction, and servicing. This visit would reveal any problems, assure the buyer of the salesperson's interest, and reduce any buyer concerns that might have arisen since the sale.

Personal Selling and Managing Customer Relationships

The steps in the selling process as just described are *transaction oriented*—their aim is to help salespeople close a specific sale with a customer. But in most cases, the company is not simply seeking a sale: it has targeted a major customer that it would like to win and keep. The company would like to show that it has the capabilities to serve the customer over the long haul in a mutually profitable *relationship*. The sales force usually plays an important role in building and managing profitable customer relationships. Thus, as shown in **Figure 12.4**, the selling process must be understood in the context of building and maintaining profitable customer relationships.

Today's large customers favor suppliers who can sell and deliver a co-ordinated set of products and services to many locations, and who can work closely with customer teams to improve products and processes. For these customers, the first sale is only the beginning of the relationship. Unfortunately, some companies ignore these relationship realities. They sell their products through separate sales forces, each working independently to close sales.

Other companies, however, recognize that winning and keeping accounts requires more than making good products and directing the sales force to close lots of sales. Most companies want their salespeople to practice value selling—demonstrating and delivering superior customer value and capturing a return on that value that's fair for both the customer and the company. Value selling requires listening to customers, understanding their needs, and carefully co-ordinating the whole company's efforts to create lasting relationships based on customer value.

> **Author Comment** | Sales promotion is the most short-term of the promotion mix tools. Whereas advertising or personal selling says "buy," sales promotion says "buy now."

Sales Promotion (pp 358–363)

Personal selling and advertising often work closely with another promotion tool, sales promotion. **Sales promotion** consists of short-term incentives to encourage purchase or sales of a product or service. Whereas advertising offers reasons to buy a product or service, sales promotion offers reasons to buy *now*.

Sales promotion
Short-term incentives to encourage the purchase or sale of a product or service.

Examples of sales promotions are found everywhere. A freestanding insert in the Sunday newspaper contains a coupon offering US$1 off Nescafé. An email from Amazon.com offers free shipping on your next purchase over US$100. The end-of-the-aisle display in the local supermarket tempts impulse buyers with a wall of Coke cases. An executive buys a new Sony laptop and gets a free carrying case, or a family buys a new Ford Escape and receives a factory rebate of US$1,000. A hardware store chain receives a 10 percent discount on selected Black & Decker portable power tools if it agrees to advertise them in local newspapers. Sales promotion includes a wide variety of promotion tools designed to stimulate earlier or stronger market response.

Rapid Growth of Sales Promotion

Sales promotion tools are used by most organizations, including manufacturers, distributors, retailers, and not-for-profit institutions. See **Real Marketing 12.2** for an example from the Arab world. They are targeted toward final buyers (*consumer promotions*), retailers and wholesalers (*trade promotions*), business customers (*business promotions*), and members of the sales force (*sales force promotions*). Today, in the average consumer packaged-goods company, sales promotion accounts for the largest percentage of all marketing expenditures.

Several factors have contributed to the rapid growth of sales promotion, particularly in consumer markets. First, inside the company, product managers face greater pressures to increase their current sales, and promotion is viewed as an effective short-run sales tool. Secondly, externally, the company faces more competition, and competing brands are less differentiated. Increasingly, competitors are using sales promotion to help differentiate their offers. Thirdly, advertising efficiency has declined because of rising costs and media clutter. Finally, consumers have become more likely to look around for a good deal, and ever-larger retailers are demanding more deals from manufacturers.

The growing use of sales promotion has resulted in *promotion clutter*, similar to advertising clutter. Consumers are increasingly tuning out promotions, weakening the ability of promotions to trigger immediate purchase. Manufacturers are now searching for ways to rise above the clutter, such as offering larger coupon values, creating more dramatic point-of-purchase displays, or delivering promotions through new interactive media, such as the Internet or mobile phones.

In developing a sales promotion program, a company must first set sales promotion objectives and then select the best tools for accomplishing these objectives.

Sales promotions are found everywhere. For example, many newspapers are loaded with freestanding inserts that promote strong and immediate market response.

Real Marketing 12.2

Qatar Automobiles Company

A successful example of sales promotion in the Arab world is supplied by Qatar Automobiles Company (QAC), one of the top dealers of Mitsubishi motors and Fuso trucks in the region. QAC employs a wide array of sales promotion tools to retain its customers' loyalty, including price discounts and appealing financial solutions. It often launches special promotions to coincide with particular occasions. For instance, one joint campaign with Doha Bank offered attractive financial solutions (such as a low interest rate for repaying a loan, and no down payment) on Mitsubishi vehicles in the holy month of Ramadan.

Khalid Abu Shaa'ban, a former general manager of QAC, said "[our] promotion is a value addition for customers, who are looking at competitive rates for automotive purchases." The car dealership does not depend merely on pre-sales promotion tools, but also on after-sales promotion tools embodied in its Mitsubishi-geared service center. The service center offers various kinds of vehicle servicing, in addition to providing original spare parts. It services up to 100 cars daily.

Ignoring the lure of QAC's sales promotions is not easy. QAC offers lifetime warranty on the different models of Mitsubishi vehicles and advises customers on their optimal financial solution in buying a vehicle. In 2009, QAC earned its ninth award as the year's 'best Fuso sales achiever.'

In 2010, QAC initiated another powerful sales promotion campaign, which included providing all potential Mitsubishi consumers with "the benefits of free registration, free comprehensive insurance and lifetime warranty." The campaign set QAC as the lowest-priced Mitsubishi dealer in Qatar in 2009.

Yann Lassade, General Manager of QAC, said, "The name of QAC and the Mitsubishi brand go hand in hand with the best sales

Qatar Automobiles Company is one of the top dealers of Mitsubishi motors, like this ASX model, in the region.

promotions on the market. As with any automotive business, we are looking to capture the largest market share and seal our leading position with first-class products and services.... However, we, at QAC, understand the significance behind a loyal customer base and this can only be achieved by planning a strategy that is geared towards our target segment's needs, lifestyles and expectations."

Extending the effect of its sales promotion campaigns, QAC also launched event-marketing tools. For instance, in 2010, it united with NBK Automobiles, a Mercedes Benz dealer, to endorse consumer safety at the Consumer Protection Exhibition that took place in Doha. Consumers were made aware of the difference between original Mitsubishi spare parts and accessories versus cheaper substitutes through a practical demonstration.

QAC believes Qatari consumers are more concerned about their safety than ever before when choosing which car to buy. One of QAC's main objectives is to build long-lasting loyalty with its customers. Khalid Shaa'ban, a former general manager of QAC, said, "[today], more than ever, safety standards are a top priority and as an automobile dealer, we are committed to offering service initiatives that add to the convenience of our customers." He added, "The new Mitsubishi service centre will be a state-of-the-art facility that employs modern equipment and manned by experienced professionals. Our goal is to be the first-stop destination for all Mitsubishi owners for their service support needs." The service center provides original car parts and professional maintenance services delivered by the experienced QAC crew.

Sources: "Qatar Automobiles Company Extends Value Promotion on Mitsubishi Vehicles," BI-ME, October 25, 2009, www.bi-me.com; "Qatar Automobiles Company Beats Expectations," BI-ME, February 21, 2010, www.bi-me.com; "QAC Offers Lowest Prices on Mitsubishi Models," *AME Info*, February 21, 2010, www.ameinfo.com/224597.html; "Qatar Autombiles Strengthens Customer Support," BI-ME, October 6, 2009, www.bi-me.com.

Sales Promotion Objectives

Sales promotion objectives vary widely. Sellers may use *consumer promotions* to urge short-term customer buying or to enhance customer brand involvement. Objectives for *trade promotions* include getting retailers to carry new items and more inventory, buy ahead, or promote the company's products and give them more shelf space. For the *sales force*, objectives include getting more sales force support for current or new products or getting salespeople to sign up new accounts.

Sales promotions are usually used together with advertising, personal selling, direct marketing, or other promotion mix tools. Consumer promotions must usually be advertised and can add excitement and pulling power to ads. Trade and sales force promotions support the firm's personal selling process.

In general, rather than creating only short-term sales or temporary brand switching, sales promotions should help to reinforce the product's position and build long-term *customer relationships*. If properly designed, every sales promotion tool has the potential to build both short-term excitement and long-term consumer relationships. Increasingly, marketers are avoiding quick fix, price-only promotions in favor of promotions designed to build brand equity.

Examples include all of the loyalty cards and loyalty offers that have sprung up in recent years. Most hotels, supermarkets, and airlines offer frequent-guest/buyer/flyer programs giving rewards to regular customers. For example, Kuwait Airways offers its members different types of membership cards: Oasis Blue, Oasis Silver, and Oasis Gold. The Oasis Blue is just an entry membership that offers double the mileage for traveling business class, and triple the mileage for traveling first class; accordingly the member can be eligible for Oasis Silver or Gold. Oasis Silver offers extra services, including priority reservations wait listing, extra luggage, lounge access, and fast-track immigration at London Heathrow and Kuwait airports. Oasis Gold adds further services, such as a free limousine in Kuwait and extra weight for the extra luggage.

Major Sales Promotion Tools

Many tools can be used to accomplish sales promotion objectives. Descriptions of the main consumer, trade, and business promotion tools follow.

Consumer Promotions

Consumer promotions

Sales promotion tools used to boost short-term customer buying and involvement or to enhance long-term customer relationships.

The **consumer promotions** include a wide range of tools—from samples, coupons, refunds, premiums, and point-of-purchase displays to contests, sweepstakes, and event sponsorships.

Samples are offers of a trial amount of a product. Sampling is the most effective—but most expensive—way to introduce a new product or to create new excitement for an existing one. Some samples are free; for others, the company charges a small amount to offset its cost. The sample might be delivered door-to-door, sent by mail, handed out in a store or kiosk, attached to another product, or featured in an ad. Sometimes, samples are combined into sample packs, which can then be used to promote other products and services. Sampling can be a powerful promotional tool.

Coupons are certificates that give buyers a saving when they purchase specified products. Consumers often love coupons.[52] Coupons can promote early trial of a new brand or stimulate sales of a mature brand. However, because there are so many different coupon offers around, the level of actual use of coupons by consumers has been declining in recent years. Thus, most major consumer-goods companies are issuing fewer coupons and targeting them more carefully.

Marketers are also developing new outlets for distributing coupons, such as supermarket shelf dispensers, electronic point-of-sale coupon printers, email and online media, or even mobile text-messaging systems. Mobile couponing is very popular in Europe, India, and Japan, and it's now gaining popularity in the United States.

Cash refunds (or *rebates*) are like coupons except that the price reduction occurs after the purchase rather than at the retail outlet. The consumer sends a proof of purchase to the manufacturer, who then refunds part of the purchase price by mail. Rebate is not yet a common practice in the Arab world; however it is more familiar in the United States.

Price packs offer consumers savings off the regular price of a product. The producer marks the reduced prices directly on the label or package. Price packs can be single packages sold at a reduced price (such as two for the price of one), or two related products banded together (such as a toothbrush and toothpaste). Price packs are very effective—even more so than coupons—in stimulating short-term sales.

Premiums are goods offered either free or at low cost as an incentive to buy a product, ranging from toys included with kids' products to phone cards and DVDs. A premium may come inside the package (in-pack), outside the package (on-pack), or through the mail. For example, over the years, McDonald's has offered a variety of premiums in its Happy Meals—from Teeny Beanie Babies to Speed Racers. For the past two years, in the United States, the fast-food chain has featured *American Idol* [reality TV]-inspired musical toy characters in its Happy Meals, each representing a favorite music genre. Even though similar programs, such as *Star Academy* and *Arab's Got Talent*, exist in the Arab world, no similar premiums are offered. Premiums, however, do tend to be based on famous animated movies and global TV shows.

Advertising specialties, also called *promotional products,* are useful articles imprinted with an advertiser's name, logo, or message that are given as gifts to consumers. Typical items include T-shirts and other apparel, pens, coffee mugs, calendars, key rings, mouse pads, matches, tote bags, coolers, golf balls, and caps. Such items can be very effective. The "best of them stick around for months, subtly burning a brand name into a user's brain," notes a promotional products expert.[53]

Point-of-purchase (POP) promotions include displays and demonstrations that take place at the point of sale. Think of your last visit to the local specialty store you frequent. Chances are good that you were tripping over aisle displays, promotional signs, 'shelf talkers,' or demonstrators offering free tastes of featured food products. Unfortunately, many retailers do not like to handle the hundreds of displays, signs, and posters they receive from manufacturers each year. Manufacturers have responded by offering better POP materials, offering to set them up, and tying them in with television, print, or online messages.

Contests, sweepstakes, and games give consumers the chance to win something, such as cash, trips, or goods, by luck or through extra effort. A *contest* calls for consumers to submit an entry—a jingle, guess, suggestion—to be judged by a panel that will select the best entries. A *sweepstake* calls for consumers to submit their names for a draw. A *game* presents consumers with something—bingo numbers, missing letters—every time they buy, which may or may not help them win a prize. Such promotions can create considerable brand attention and consumer involvement.[54] Radio channels, such as Nogoom FM, Rotana FM, and Panorama FM, encourage people to send text messages related to specific topics or brands. Customers offer suggestions for new campaigns or jingles for football games, and so on. The best recommendations win prizes, whether monetary or gifts such as game tickets.

> Doritos [snack food] recently ran a "Get It. Taste It. Name It" sweepstake asking consumers to taste its newest flavor, initially labeled X-13D, and then suggest a name and write an ad for it. Those who submitted a name or ad were entered into the sweepstake to become one of 100 Doritos Flavor Masters. Winners were selected through a random draw. As Flavor Masters, the 100 grand-prize winners got the chance to take part in Doritos research and development, giving feedback on future flavor ideas. Each also got a year's supply of Doritos, 52 coupons good for one bag per week. The X-13D chips, packaged in a black bag with a label that looked like it was lifted from a science lab, built a lot of buzz. The promotion pulled in more than 100,000 entries within only a month of launch. And the promotion sparked considerable online chatter as bloggers wrote about stumbling upon the distinctive bag in convenience stores and tackled the question of what the flavor really was.

Event marketing
Creating a brand-marketing event or serving as a sole or participating sponsor of events created by others.

Finally, marketers can promote their brands through **event marketing** (or *event sponsorships*). They can create their own brand-marketing events or serve as sole or participating sponsors of events created by others. The events might include anything from mobile brand tours to festivals, reunions, marathons, concerts, or other sponsored gatherings. Event marketing is huge, and it may be the fastest-growing area of promotion.[55]

Most companies sponsor brand events. Motorcycle maker Harley-Davidson holds 'HOG Rallies' and Harley biker reunions that draw hundreds of thousands of bikers each year. Procter & Gamble creates numerous events for its major brands. Consider this example:

> Pampers Egypt recently sponsored events related to mother–child relationships. The events attracted celebrities as well as child physicians, along with invited mothers and children. Pampers also sponsored a radio show discussing challenges and problems that mothers face with their babies. Such activities proved successful in growing the size of the market and associating the Pampers brand with emotional traits such as caring.

Trade promotions

Sales promotion tools used to persuade resellers to carry a brand, give it shelf space, promote it in advertising, and push it to consumers.

Trade Promotions

Manufacturers direct more sales promotion dollars toward retailers and wholesalers (81 percent) than to final consumers (19 percent).[56] **Trade promotions** can persuade resellers to carry a brand, give it shelf space, promote it in advertising, and push it to consumers. Shelf space is so scarce these days that manufacturers often have to offer price-offs, allowances, buy-back guarantees, or free goods to retailers and wholesalers to get products on the shelf and, once there, to keep them on it.

Manufacturers use several trade promotion tools. Many of the tools used for consumer promotions—contests, premiums, displays—can also be used as trade promotions. Or the manufacturer may offer a straight *discount* off the list price on each case purchased during a stated period of time (also called a *price-off, off-invoice,* or *off-list*). Manufacturers also may offer an *allowance* (usually so much off per case) in return for the retailer's agreement to feature the manufacturer's products in some way. An advertising allowance compensates retailers for advertising the product. A display allowance compensates them for using special displays.

Manufacturers may offer *free goods,* which are extra cases of merchandise, to resellers who buy a certain quantity or who feature a certain flavor or size. They may offer *push money*—cash or gifts to dealers or their sales forces to 'push' the manufacturer's goods. Manufacturers may give retailers free *specialty advertising items* that carry the company's name, such as pens, pencils, calendars, paperweights, matchbooks, memo pads, and yardsticks.

Business Promotions

Business promotions

Sales promotion tools used to generate business leads, stimulate purchases, reward customers, and motivate salespeople.

Companies spend billions of dollars each year on promotion to industrial customers. **Business promotions** are used to generate business leads, stimulate purchases, reward customers, and motivate salespeople. Business promotions include many of the same tools used for consumer or trade promotions. Here, we focus on two additional major business promotion tools—conventions and trade shows, and sales contests.

Many companies and trade associations organize *conventions and trade shows* to promote their products. Firms selling to the industry show their products at the trade show. Vendors receive many benefits, such as opportunities to find new sales leads, contact customers, introduce new products, meet new customers, sell more to present customers, and educate customers with publications and audiovisual materials. Trade shows also help companies reach many prospects not reached through their sales forces.

Some trade shows are huge. For example, at 2010 Dubai International Pharmaceuticals and Technologies conference and exhibition (DUPHAT), 300 exhibitors attracted more than 7,000 visitors from 72 countries.

A *sales contest* is a contest for salespeople or dealers to motivate them to increase their sales performance over a given period. Sales contests motivate and recognize good company performers, who may receive trips, cash prizes, or other gifts. Some companies award points for performance, which the receiver can turn in for any of a variety of prizes. Sales contests work best when they are tied to measurable and achievable sales objectives (such as finding new accounts, reviving old accounts, or increasing account profitability).

Some trade shows are huge: At the International Consumer Electronics Show, 2,700 exhibitors attracted more than 141,000 professional visitors in 2008.

Developing the Sales Promotion Program

Beyond selecting the types of promotions to use, marketers must make several other decisions in designing the full sales promotion program. First, they must decide on the *size of the incentive.* A certain minimum incentive is necessary if the promotion is to succeed; a larger incentive will produce more sales response. The marketer also must set *conditions for partici-pation*. Incentives might be offered to everyone or only to select groups.

Marketers must decide how to *promote and distribute the promotion* program itself. A US$2-off coupon could be given out in a package, at the store, via the Internet, or in an advertisement. Each distribution method involves a different level of reach and cost. Increasingly, marketers are blending several media into a total campaign concept. The *length of the promotion* is also important. If the sales promotion period is too short, many prospects (who may not be buying during that time) will miss it. If the promotion runs too long, the deal will lose some of its 'act now' force.

Evaluation is also very important. Many companies fail to evaluate their sales promotion programs, and others evaluate them only superficially. Yet marketers should work to mea-sure the returns on their sales promotion investments, just as they should seek to assess the returns on other marketing activities. The most common evaluation method is to compare sales before, during, and after a promotion. Marketers should ask: Did the promotion attract new customers or more purchasing from current customers? Can we hold onto these new customers and purchases? Will the long-run customer relationship and sales gains from the promotion justify its costs?

Clearly, sales promotion plays an important role in the total promotion mix. To use it well, the marketer must define the sales promotion objectives, select the best tools, design the sales promotion program, implement the program, and evaluate the results. Moreover, sales promotion must be co-ordinated carefully with other promotion mix elements within the overall integrated marketing communications program.

REVIEWING Objectives AND KEY Terms

This chapter is the second chapter covering the third mar-keting mix element—promotion. The previous chapter dealt with overall integrated marketing communications. This one investigates each promotion mix element (advertising, pub-lic relations, personal selling, and sales promotion) in detail. Companies must do more than make good products—they have to inform consumers about product benefits and carefully position products in consumers' minds. To do this, they must master *advertising* and *public relations*. *Personal selling* is the interpersonal arm of the communications mix. Sales promotion consists of short-term incentives to encourage the purchase or sale of a product or service.

OBJECTIVE 1 Define the role of advertising and the major decisions involved in developing an advertising program. (pp 328–341)

Advertising—the use of paid media by a seller to inform, per-suade, and remind buyers about its products or organization—is an important promotion tool for communicating the value that marketers create for their customers. Worldwide ad spending exceeds US$600 billion. Advertising takes many forms and has many uses. Although advertising is used mostly by business firms, a wide range of not-for-profit organizations, professionals, and social agencies also use advertising to promote their causes to various target publics. *Public relations*—gaining favorable publicity and creating a favorable company image—is the least used of the major promotion tools, although it has great potential for building consumer awareness and preference.

Advertising decision making involves decisions about the advertising objectives, the budget, the message, the media, and, finally, the evaluation of results. Advertisers should set clear tar-get, task, and timing *objectives*, whether the aim is to inform, persuade, or remind buyers. Advertising's goal is to move consum-ers through the buyer-readiness stages discussed in the previous chapter. Some advertising is designed to move people to imme-diate action. However, many of the ads you see today focus on building or strengthening long-term customer relationships. The advertising *budget* can be based on sales, on competitors' spend-ing, or on the objectives and tasks of the advertising program. The size and allocation of the budget depends on many factors.

Advertising strategy consists of two major elements: creating advertising *messages* and selecting advertising *media*. The *mes-sage decision* calls for planning a message strategy and executing it effectively. Good advertising messages are especially important in today's costly and cluttered advertising environment. Just to gain and hold attention, today's advertising messages must be better planned, more imaginative, more entertaining, and more reward-ing to consumers. In fact, many marketers are now subscribing to a new merging of advertising and entertainment, dubbed 'Madison & Vine.' The *media decision* involves defining reach, frequency, and impact goals; choosing major media types; selecting media vehicles; and deciding on media timing. Message and media decisions must be closely co-ordinated for maximum campaign effectiveness.

Finally, *evaluation* calls for evaluating the communication and sales effects of advertising before, during, and after the advertis-ing is placed. Advertising accountability has become a hot issue for most companies. Increasingly, top management is asking: "What return are we getting on our advertising investment?" and "How do we know that we're spending the right amount?" Other important advertising issues involve *organizing* for advertising and dealing with the complexities of international advertising.

OBJECTIVE 2 Define the role of public relations in the promotion mix and explain its usage by companies. (pp 341–345)

Public relations—gaining favorable publicity and creating a favorable company image—is the least used of the major promotion tools, although it has great potential for building consumer awareness and preference. Public relations is used to promote products, people, places, ideas, activities, organizations, and even nations. Companies use public relations to build good relations with consumers, investors, the media, and their communities. Public relations can have a strong impact on public awareness at a much lower cost than advertising can, and public relations results can sometimes be spectacular. Although public relations still captures only a small portion of the overall marketing budgets of most firms, it is playing an increasingly important brand-building role.

Companies use public relations to communicate with their publics by setting PR objectives, choosing PR messages and vehicles, implementing the PR plan, and evaluating PR results. To accomplish these goals, PR professionals use several tools such as *news, speeches,* and *special events.* They also prepare *written, audiovisual,* and *corporate identity materials* and contribute money and time to *public service activities. Buzz marketing* is a form of public relations that gets consumers themselves to spread word-of-mouth information about the company and its brands. The Internet has also become a major PR tool.

OBJECTIVE 3 Discuss the role of a company's salespeople in creating value for customers and building customer relationships, and the six major sales force management steps. (pp 345–355)

Most companies use salespeople and many companies assign them an important role in the marketing mix. For companies selling business products, the firm's salespeople work directly with customers. Often, the sales force is the customer's only direct contact with the company and therefore may be viewed by customers as representing the company itself. In contrast, for consumer-product companies that sell through intermediaries, consumers usually do not meet salespeople or even know about them. The sales force works behind the scenes, dealing with wholesalers and retailers to obtain their support and helping them become effective in selling the firm's products.

As an element of the promotion mix, the sales force is very effective in achieving certain marketing objectives and carrying out such activities as prospecting, communicating, selling and servicing, and information gathering. But with companies becoming more market oriented, a customer-focused sales force also works to produce both *customer satisfaction* and *company profit.* The sales force plays a key role in developing and managing profitable *customer relationships.*

High sales force costs necessitate an effective sales management process consisting of six steps: designing sales force strategy and structure, recruiting and selecting, training, compensating, supervising, and evaluating salespeople and sales force performance.

In designing a sales force, sales management must address strategy issues such as what type of sales force structure will work best (territorial, product, customer, or complex structure); how large the sales force should be; who will be involved in the selling effort; and how its various salespeople and sales-support people will work together (inside or outside sales forces and team selling).

To hold down the high costs of hiring the wrong people, salespeople must be recruited and selected carefully. In recruiting salespeople, a company may look to job duties and the characteristics of its most successful salespeople to suggest the traits it wants in new recruits. It must then look for applicants through recommendations of current salespeople, employment agencies, classified ads, the Internet, and contacting college students. In the selection process, the procedure can vary from a single informal interview to lengthy testing and interviewing. After the selection process is complete, training programs familiarize new salespeople not only with the art of selling but also with the company's history, its products and policies, and the characteristics of its market and competitors.

The sales force compensation system helps to reward, motivate, and direct salespeople. In compensating salespeople, companies try to have an appealing plan, usually close to the going rate for the type of sales job and needed skills. In addition to compensation, all salespeople need supervision, and many need continuous encouragement because they must make many decisions and face many frustrations. Periodically, the company must evaluate their performance to help them do a better job. In evaluating salespeople, the company relies on getting regular information gathered through sales reports, personal observations, customers' letters and complaints, customer surveys, and conversations with other salespeople.

OBJECTIVE 4 Discuss the personal selling process, distinguishing between transaction-oriented marketing and relationship marketing, and explain the process of developing and implementing a sales campaign. (pp 355–363)

The art of selling involves a seven-step *selling process: prospecting and qualifying, preapproach, approach, presentation and demonstration, handling objections, closing,* and *follow-up.* These steps help marketers close a specific sale and as such are *transaction oriented.* However, a seller's dealings with customers should be guided by the larger concept of *relationship marketing.* The company's sales force should help to orchestrate a whole-company effort to develop profitable long-term relationships with key customers based on superior customer value and satisfaction.

Sales promotion campaigns call for setting sales promotions objectives (in general, sales promotions should be *consumer relationship building*); selecting tools; and developing and implementing the sales promotion program by using *consumer promotion tools* (from coupons, refunds, premiums, and point-of-purchase promotions to contests, sweepstakes, and events), *trade promotion tools* (discounts, allowances, free goods, push money), and *business promotion tools* (conventions, trade shows, sales contests), as well as deciding on such things as the size of the incentive, the conditions for participation, how to promote and distribute the promotion package, and the length of the promotion. After this process is completed, the company evaluates its sales promotion results.

KEY Terms

OBJECTIVE 1

Advertising (p 328)
Advertising objective (p 329)
Advertising budget (p 330)
Advertising strategy (p 331)
Creative concept (p 333)
Execution style (p 333)
Advertising media (p 335)
Return on advertising
investment (p 338)
Advertising agency (p 339)

OBJECTIVE 2

Public relations (p 341)

OBJECTIVE 3

Personal selling (p 345)
Salesperson (p 346)
Sales force management (p 347)
Territorial sales force structure (p 348)
Product sales force structure (p 348)
Customer sales force
structure (p 348)
Outside sales force (*field sales
force*) (p 349)
Inside sales force (p 349)
Team selling (p 350)
Sales quota (p 354)
Selling process (p 355)

Prospecting (p 355)
Preapproach (p 356)
Approach (p 356)
Presentation (p 356)
Handling objections (p 357)
Closing (p 357)
Follow-up (p 357)

OBJECTIVE 4

Sales promotion (p 358)
Consumer promotions (p 360)
Event marketing (p 361)
Trade promotions (p 362)
Business promotions (p 362)

DISCUSSING & APPLYING THE Concepts

Discussing the Concepts

1. List and briefly describe the four important decisions marketing managers must make when developing an advertising program.
2. Define the terms *reach, frequency*, and *impact*.
3. Discuss the tools used by public relations professionals.
4. Define *sales promotion* and discuss its objectives.
5. Name and describe the types of trade sales promotions.

Applying the Concepts

1. Any message can be presented using different execution styles. Select a brand and target audience and design two advertisements, each using a different execution style to deliver the same message to the target audience but in a different way. Identify the types of execution styles you are using and present your advertisements.

2. Recommend three advertising media for a campaign to introduce a new line of men's personal care products under a LeBron James label.

3. In a small group, discuss the major public relations tools and develop three public relations items for each of the following: a hospital, a restaurant, and any brand of your choice.

FOCUS ON Technology

Have you ever watched your favorite television program and wished you could immediately buy the clothes your favorite character was wearing or learn more about the car he or she was driving? Or how about ordering a pizza while watching an ad? Well, now you can—with interactive television. Marketers are increasingly using this vehicle to interact with consumers. For example, Unilever, one of the largest consumer packaged-goods companies, is banking on consumers wanting more information and interactivity from their televisions and is planning several interactive TV-ad deals with DIRECTV and Comcast cable. Interactive TV works by providing links, known as triggers, that when clicked take viewers into a longer advertisement. These longer ads, called long-form or long-tail advertising, provide opportunities for deeper interaction.

1. Will interactive television catch on with consumers? What might be slowing the adoption of this innovative advertising technique?

2. Discuss the types of products or services that would benefit most from interactive television advertising.

FOCUS ON Ethics

Free samples, gifts, expensive trips, dinners, and entertainment—these tools have been, and in some cases still are, widely used by pharmaceutical companies to influence doctors' prescribing behavior. Physicians control the majority of health care expenditures through their prescription-writing authority. Although direct-to-consumer advertising expenditures have grown exponentially over the past decade, an estimated 90 percent of pharmaceutical marketing dollars are directed at physicians. Research has shown that pharmaceutical companies' marketing tactics do influence physicians, causing them to prescribe more expensive drugs over less expensive alternatives. Critics proclaim that these tactics are unethical. However, the pharmaceutical companies claim that their sales representatives help keep health care professionals well informed in this rapidly changing industry.

1. Is it ethical for pharmaceutical sales representatives to influence physicians' prescribing behavior using free samples and promotional gifts?

2. National and international trade associations in the pharmaceuticals industry have codes of conduct regarding interactions with health care professionals. Visit the website of the International Federation of Pharmaceutical Manufacturers and Associations (IFPMA) (http://ifpma.org/) and examine its code of ethics regarding sales activities. Write a brief report about what you learn.

MARKETING BY THE Numbers

Donya is the first newspaper from Saudi Arabia aimed at Arabian women, including housewives, professionals, students, and others.

1. Using the International Advertising L.L.C. (www.iamediaservice.com) website, determine the cost of placing a full-page advertisement in two Egyptian newspapers, one magazine for Oman and the UAE, and one for *Donya*. What is the total circulation of the newspapers?

2. Calculate the costs of running these advertisements for six issues, taking into account any discounts that may be offered.

VIDEO Case

The Principal Financial Group

The Principal Financial Group delivered strong growth in its first six years as a public company. Operating earnings grew from US$577 million in 2001 to US$1.06 billion in 2007 alone. In that same year, total assets under management soared from US$98 billion to US$311 billion. The Principal also achieved a 16.4 percent return on equity for 2007, compared with 8.9 percent for 2001. As a result, its stock price increased 236 percent from its opening price at the October 2001 initial public offering (IPO) through its closing price at year-end 2007.

One of the biggest reasons for this success is The Principal Financial Group's strongly customer-centered sales force. The company's varied and complex product line (from retirement products to insurance) demands the one-on-one attention of a salesperson who understands how to build customer relationships. The company's sales force has helped make The Principal a global player in the financial services industry.

After viewing the video featuring The Principal Financial Group, answer the following questions:

1. How is the sales force at The Principal Financial Group structured?

2. Identify the selling process of the company. Give evidence of each step.

3. How does The Principal build long-term customer relationships through its sales force?

COMPANY Case

Coca-Cola: Advertising Hits

When you think of Coca-Cola, what comes to mind? It wouldn't be surprising if you thought first of Coke ads. In the history of advertising, perhaps no other company has had such a strong and continuous impact on society through advertising. Not only have Coke's ads been successful at selling its soft drinks, but decade after decade Coca-Cola's ads and campaigns have influenced people by making their way into the hearts and minds of consumers.

A BRIEF HISTORY

In the 1920s in the United States, Coca-Cola shifted its advertising strategy, focusing for the first time on creating brand loyalty. It began advertising the soft drink as fun and refreshing. Coke's 1929 campaign slogan was, "The Pause that Refreshes." To this day, that slogan remains number two on *Advertising Age*'s top 100 slogans of all time.

In the Arab world, however, Coca-Cola has had a few challenges; Coca-Cola was banned from Arab world countries during the 1967 Arab and Israel war for its dealings with Israel. It was able to resume business in the region after about 20 years, when it sponsored a youth soccer tournament in Saudi Arabia in 1989. During this absence Pepsi became the dominant market leader in the carbonated soft drink market. Since its return, Coca-Cola has found itself facing an uphill struggle battling with Pepsi over market share by using all forms of promotions, pricing, and brand strategies.

The carbonated soft drinks (CSD) manufacturers regard most of the Arab world markets as 'young' markets; growth in this region's business is driven by the youth population. The Saudi CSD market saw double-digit growth (10–15 percent) after Coca-Cola entered the market driven by strong investments in advertising and promotions by both Pepsi and Coca-Cola. According to Middle East *Grocer* magazine, the carbonated drinks sales in the region doubled between 1993 and 2003 to US$850 million. It is estimated that the market is currently well over a billion dollars.

Coca-Cola adopts a wide range of approaches to secure main-aisle or other prime positions in the supermarket. For example, it may put free items (such as glasses, barbecue spatulas, or iceboxes) into drinks packs. It also adopts philanthropic approaches, for example supporting youth centers, garbage pick-up drives, and a children's cancer hospital in Egypt. The company handed out school supplies in Palestine and gave computers to schools in Jordan; in Lebanon, it planted cedar trees. In the Gulf states, Coca-Cola supported the Disabled Children Association in Saudi Arabia and the Red Crescent Society in the UAE.

CELEBRITY INPUT

Coca-Cola has also broadcast advertising films with plots about Ramadan, with local personalities enjoying the starring roles. The Omani ace rally driver Hamed Al-Wahaibi endorsed Coca-Cola, as did Saudi pop singer Abdul Majeed Abdullah.

Coca-Cola seemed to gain advertising superiority from 2005 onwards when it nominated Nancy Ajram as the Coca-Cola star and official celebrity sponsor and spokesperson for the region. Commenting on Nancy Ajram's fit with Coca-Cola brand values, the company's PR director said, "Nancy Ajram fits perfectly well with the image and values of Coca-Cola, and we believe in local rising talents and we like to accompany them on their journey and contribute to their recognition and success. Nancy is one of the youngest Arab WMA winners and is an important icon of this generation's Arabic music. She has been a rising star year on year and is loved by millions of people across the Arab world. Nancy is appreciated by a large fan base and she represents fresh, young, optimistic, happy and successful messages all of them Coca-Cola values."

Coca-Cola launched the campaign "The Coca-Cola Side of Life" in 2006. It was a simple idea that drinking Coca-Cola makes people happy; it tastes good; and it's an invitation to live on a brighter, more positive side of life. "We live in a world where we make choices every day and The Coca-Cola Side of Life encourages people to make those choices positive ones," said the public affairs and communications manager of Coca-Cola Middle East at the time. "This new campaign is different. It is fresh, vibrant, and modern. It invites people to create their own positive reality, to be spontaneous, listen to their hearts and live life in full color." The fully integrated campaign consisting of television, outdoor, print executions, viral marketing, and public relations activities was simultaneously implemented across the Middle East.

Later in 2007, Nancy released her Coca-Cola Side of Life commercial featuring a new single, *El Donya Helwa* (*Life is Beautiful*). This, Nancy's seventh commercial, was considered one of her most successful, representing her style and Coca-Cola's with colors, happiness, and music; it led her to release a live album featuring the single. In February and March 2008, Nancy released three Coca-Cola commercials that featured a brand new hit from her long-awaited album.

Coca-Cola also launched the "Open Happiness" campaign in the Arab world in 2009. Building on the award-winning "Coke Side of Life" campaign, "Open Happiness" was the new platform for all integrated marketing for brand Coca-Cola. Including new points of sale (POS), promotions, outdoor and print advertising, digital and music components, the campaign invited people to welcome small moments of joy and happiness into their lives. This was a global campaign but translated locally and adapted to fit with local values. Music played a central role in the new campaign, with a new track, 'Eftah Tefrah,' by Nancy Ajram gaining large popularity among the youth population.

In 2010, Coca-Cola sponsored the 2010 FIFA World Cup™. Coca-Cola Middle East created a suitable soundtrack for the global marketing campaign by recording a collaboration between African hip-hop artist K'naan and superstar Nancy Ajram. The song 'Wavin' Flag—Coca-Cola Celebration Mix,' was released in many countries and formed a centerpiece for the campaign. It was used on all TV commercials during the FIFA World Cup™ Trophy Tour, and on the online digital platform.

Murat Ozgel, marketing director, Coca-Cola Middle East, said: "The Coca-Cola football campaign is one of the biggest that has ever been put together, and the theme song is a major tool that will bring out the celebration in the hearts of all the fans. We are proud to have Nancy Ajram on board, she is unique not only in her music but also as a person, and we are confident that her representation of the song will capture everyone's hearts."

"It is a privilege to be involved in the Coca-Cola World Cup Anthem, a song that is sure to bring happiness to so many people," commented Nancy Ajram. "There is no other time during the year when the entire world will celebrate the same thing at the same time. This song is full of happiness and feelings of unity and celebration, and we hope it will touch the hearts of every person experiencing the 2010 World Cup." A global television audience of more than 700 million was estimated to have watched the FIFA World Cup final.

As a further feature of the campaign, Coca-Cola launched its 2010 FIFA World Cup promotion using beverage cans with laser-etched tabs. The promotion was used on Coke and Fanta brands in countries including Yemen, Iraq, Jordan, the UAE, and Saudi Arabia. Once the can was opened, certain consumers had a chance to win a range of football-related prizes. The promotion started a month before the World Cup and ran throughout the event.

Despite Coca-Cola's all-out effort to dislodge Pepsi from the number one position in the CSD market, Pepsi is defending its market leadership position in the Arab world, fighting to retain, rather than gain, market share. Coca-Cola in the Arab world, on the other hand, is the underdog with momentum who seems to be enjoying the fight.

Questions for Discussion

1. Consider Coca-Cola's advertising throughout its history in the Arab world. Identify as many commonalities as possible for its various ads and campaigns.

2. Analyze the 2010 FIFA World Cup™ 'Wavin' Flag—Coca-Cola Celebration Mix' ad, based on the process of creating an advertising message as outlined in the text.

3. Discuss issues of selecting advertising media for the 'Wavin' Flag—Coca-Cola Celebration Mix' ad. How might this process differ from that of other Coca-Cola campaigns? From other campaigns for other companies?

4. Based on the information in this case, how might Coca-Cola measure the effectiveness of the 'Wavin' Flag—Coca-Cola Celebration Mix' ad? What else might Coca-Cola want to measure?

Sources: "Q & A: Antoine Tayyar, Public Affairs and Communication Director for Coca Cola Middle East," *Iloubnan.info,* June 29, 2009, www.iloubnan.info/business/actualite/id/35976; "Happiness in a Bottle: The Coca-Cola Side of Life Campaign Channels Optimism to the Middle East," *AME Info*, December 17, 2006, www.ameinfo.com/105607.html; "Coca-Cola Middle East to Release K'naan and Nancy Ajram Track and Music Video in 50 Countries in Support of Its sponsorship of the 2010 FIFA World Cup™," *Al Bawaba,* May 23, 2005, www1.albawaba.com; additional information from "Arab League Ends Its Ban of Coca-Cola," *Inquirer Wire Services*, May 7, 1991, accessed at http://articles.philly.com/1991-05-07/business/25795845_1_coca-cola-coca-cola-arab-league; Sarah Diston, "Cola Giants Continue Battle for Middle East Market," *Just-Drinks.com,* April 6, 2001, www.just-drinks.com; "Coke and Pepsi Battle it Out," *AME Info*, April 8, 2004, www.ameinfo.com/37492-more1.html; "Coca-Cola's Global Campaign Launched in Middle East," *Trade Arabia,* May 28, 2009, www.tradearabia.com/news/MEDIA_162129.html; "FIFA Expects Global TV Audience of 700 Million for World Cup Final," *Cape Breton Post*, July 11, 2010, www.capebretonpost.com; "Coca-Cola Kicked Off World Cup Promotion in Middle East," *Packaging Essentials,* January 29, 2011, www.packagingessentials.com; Lucinda Watrous, "The History of Coca-Cola's Advertising," *Associated Content*, January 14, 2008, accessed online at www.associatedcontent.com</ulink.

Chapter 13

Part 1	Defining Marketing and the Marketing Process (Chapters 1, 2)
Part 2	Understanding the Marketplace and Consumers (Chapters 3, 4, 5, 6)
Part 3	Designing a Customer-Driven Strategy and Mix (Chapters 7, 8, 9, 10, 11, 12, 13, 14)
Part 4	Extending Marketing (Chapters 15, 16, 17)

Direct and Online Marketing Building Direct Customer Relationships

Chapter PREVIEW

In the previous two chapters, you learned about communicating customer value through integrated marketing communication (IMC) and about four specific elements of the marketing communications mix—advertising, publicity, personal selling, and sales promotion. In this chapter, we'll look at the final IMC element, direct marketing, and at its fastest-growing form, online marketing. Actually, direct marketing can be viewed as more than just a communications tool. In many ways it constitutes an overall marketing approach—a blend of communication and distribution channels all rolled into one. As you read on, remember that although this chapter examines direct marketing as a separate tool, it must be carefully integrated with other elements of the promotion mix.

For starters, let's first look at Amazon.com. In less than 15 years, Amazon.com has blossomed from an obscure dot-com upstart into one of the best-known names on the Internet. According to one estimate, 52 percent of people who shopped the Internet last year started at Amazon.com. How has Amazon.com become such an incredibly successful direct and online marketer in such a short time? It's all about creating direct, personal, satisfying customer experience. Few direct marketers do that as well as Amazon.com.

When you think of shopping on the web, chances are good that you think first of Amazon.com. Amazon.com first opened its virtual doors in 1995, selling books out of founder Jeff Bezos's garage in suburban Seattle. The online pioneer still sells books—*lots and lots* of books. But it now sells just about everything else as well, from music, videos, electronics, tools, housewares, apparel, groceries, and kids' products to loose diamonds and lobsters. "We have the Earth's Biggest Selection," declares the company's website.

In little more than a decade, Amazon.com has become one of the best-known names on the web. In perfecting the art of online selling, it has also rewritten the rules of marketing. Many analysts view Amazon.com as *the* model for businesses in the digital age. They predict that it will one day become the Wal-Mart of the Internet.

Amazon.com has grown explosively. Its annual sales have rocketed from a modest US$15 million in 1996 to more than US$15 *billion* today. In only the past five years, its sales have nearly quadrupled. Although it took Amazon.com eight years to turn its first full-year profit in 2003, profits have since surged more than 13-fold. More than 72 million active customers now spend an average of US$184 a year at Amazon.com. One study estimates that 52 percent of all consumers who went to the Internet to shop last year started at Amazon.com. Fifty percent of Amazon.com's sales come from overseas.

What has made Amazon.com one of the world's premier direct marketers? To its core, the company is relentlessly customer driven. "The thing that drives everything is creating genuine value for customers," says founder Jeff Bezos. "If you focus on what customers want and build a relationship, they will allow you to make money." In one promotion in Japan, for example, Bezos donned a delivery driver's uniform and went house to house with packages.

His point: everything at Amazon—from top to bottom—begins and ends with the customer.

Anyone at Amazon.com will tell you that the company wants to do much more than just sell books or DVDs or digital cameras. It wants to deliver a special *experience* to every customer. "The customer experience really matters," says Bezos. "We've focused on just having a better store, where it's easier to shop, where you can learn more about the products, where you have a bigger selection, and where you have the lowest prices. You combine all of that stuff together and people say, 'Hey, these guys really get it.'"

And customers do get it. Most Amazon.com regulars feel a surprisingly strong relationship with the company, especially given the almost complete lack of actual human interaction. Amazon.com obsesses over making each customer's experience uniquely personal. For example, the Amazon.com website greets customers with their very own personalized home page, and the site's 'Recommended for you' feature prepares personalized product recommendations. Amazon.com was first to use 'collaborative filtering' technology, which sifts through each customer's past purchases and the purchasing patterns of customers with similar profiles to come up with personalized site content. "We

Says Amazon founder Jeff Bezos: "We are not great advertisers. So we start with customers, figure out what they want, and figure out how to get it to them."

want Amazon.com to be the right store for you as an individual," says Bezos. "If we have 72 million customers, we should have 72 million stores."

Visitors to Amazon.com's website receive a unique blend of benefits: huge selection, good value, convenience, and what the company calls "discovery." In books alone, for example, Amazon.com offers an easily searchable virtual selection of more than 3 million titles, 15 times more than in any physical bookstore. Good value comes in the form of reasonable prices, plus free delivery on orders over US$25. And at Amazon.com, it's irresistibly convenient to buy. You can log on, find anything and everything you want, and order with a single mouse click, all in less time than it takes to find a parking space at the local mall.

But it's the "discovery" factor that makes the Amazon.com marketing experience really special. Once on the website, you're compelled to stay for a while—looking, learning, and discovering. Amazon.com has become a kind of online community, in which customers can browse for products, research purchase alternatives, share opinions and reviews with other visitors, and chat online with authors and experts. In this way, Amazon.com does much more than just sell goods on the web. It creates direct, personalized customer relationships and satisfying online experiences. Year after year, Amazon.com comes in number one or number two on the American Customer Satisfaction Index, regardless of industry.

In fact, Amazon.com has become so good at managing online relationships that many traditional 'bricks-and-mortar' retailers are turning to Amazon for help in adding more 'clicks' to their 'bricks.' For example, Amazon.com now partners with well-known retailers such as Target and Bebe to help them run their web interfaces. And to create even greater selection and convenience for customers, Amazon.com allows competing retailers—from mom-and-pop operations to Marks & Spencer—to offer their products on its website, creating a virtual shopping mall of incredible proportions. It even encourages customers to sell used items on the site.

Amazon.com is constantly on the lookout for innovative new ways to use the power of the web and direct marketing to create more shopping selection, value, convenience, and discovery for customers. For example, it started Amazon Prime, a program by which members pay US$79 per year and get free two-day shipping on all orders and next-day shipping for US$3.99 on any order. Amazon.com now offers music downloading, with the music files not restricted by digital rights management software (DRM), which means that (unlike iTunes) you can freely and conveniently copy the songs. All four major music labels promptly signed on. The web merchant also launched Amazon Giver and Amazon Grapevine, applications for social-networking website Facebook. These features allow Facebook users to see and purchase what their friends want via wish lists and to view recent public activity on the retail site.

And recently, Amazon.com took another bold customer-convenience and personalization step. It introduced the Kindle, a US$399 wireless reading device for downloading books, blogs, magazines, newspapers, and other matter. Lighter and thinner than a typical paperback book, the Kindle wireless reader connects like a cell-phone, letting customers buy and download content of personal interest—from the *Wall Street Journal* or *Time* magazine to the latest *New York Times* bestsellers—from home or on the go in less than 60 seconds. The Kindle has a paper-like electronic-ink display that's easy to read even in bright daylight. In all, Amazon.com is betting that the Kindle will prove to be an ultimate direct-marketing device.

So, what do you think? Will Amazon.com become the Wal-Mart of the web? That remains to be seen. But whatever its fate, the direct and online pioneer has forever changed the face of marketing. Most importantly, Amazon.com has set a very high bar for the online customer experience. "The reason I'm so obsessed with…the customer experience is that I believe [that our success] has been driven exclusively by that experience," says Jeff Bezos. "We are not great advertisers. So we start with customers, figure out what they want, and figure out how to get it to them."[1]

Finally, it is important to highlight that Amazon.com has not yet taken advantage of the opportunities that exist in the Arab world to extend its operations fully into this market. Being an online store, its global presence should not be a challenge. Nevertheless, in different parts of the world, different experiences need to be offered to customers. The product mix sold on the website could be more matched to the needs and buying patterns of the Arab world. The language barrier could also have a large impact on Amazon.com's potential business in the region. If the user interface was provided in Arabic, sales from customers in the Arab world would likely increase dramatically. Another impacting factor is the price of shipping to the region compared with the shipping prices for the other countries Amazon.com operates in. It remains to be seen whether Amazon.com will consider the Arab world market an opportunity not to be missed.

> Amazon.com obsesses over making each customer's experience uniquely personal. "If we have 72 million customers, we should have 72 million stores."

> In perfecting the art of online selling, Amazon.com has rewritten the rules of marketing. The web pioneer excels at creating personal, satisfying direct marketing customer experiences. However, Amazon.com has a big opportunity to expand into the Arab world and target the needs of customers in this large market.

Objective Outline

Many of the marketing and promotion tools that we've examined in previous chapters were developed in the context of *mass marketing*: targeting broad markets with standardized messages and offers distributed through intermediaries. Today, however, with the trend toward more narrowly targeted marketing, many companies are adopting *direct marketing*, either as a primary marketing approach, as in Amazon.com's case, or as a supplement to other approaches. In this section, we explore the exploding world of direct marketing.

Direct marketing
Connecting directly with carefully targeted individual consumers to both obtain an immediate response and cultivate lasting customer relationships.

Direct marketing consists of connecting directly with carefully targeted individual consumers to both obtain an immediate response and cultivate lasting customer relationships. Direct marketers communicate directly with customers, often on a one-to-one, interactive basis. Using detailed databases, they tailor their marketing offers and communications to the needs of narrowly defined segments or even individual buyers.

Beyond brand and relationship building, direct marketers usually seek a direct, immediate, and measurable consumer response. For example, as we learned in the chapter-opening story, Amazon.com interacts directly with customers on its website to help them discover and buy almost anything and everything on the Internet, with only a few clicks of the mouse button. Similarly, Dell interacts directly with customers, by telephone or through its website, to design built-to-order systems that meet customers' individual needs. Buyers can order directly from Dell, and Dell quickly and efficiently delivers the new computers to their homes or offices.

Author Comment | For most companies, direct marketing is a supplemental channel or medium. But for many other companies today—such as Amazon.com, eBay, or Otlob—direct marketing is a complete way of doing business.

The New Direct Marketing Model (pp 370–371)

Early direct marketers—catalog companies, direct mailers, and telemarketers—gathered customer names and sold goods mainly by mail and telephone. Today, however, driven by rapid advances in database technologies and new marketing media—especially the Internet—direct marketing has undergone a dramatic change.

In previous chapters, we've discussed direct marketing as direct distribution—as marketing channels that contain no intermediaries. We also include direct marketing as one element of the promotion mix—as an approach for communicating directly with consumers. In reality, direct marketing is both these things and more.

Most companies still use direct marketing as a supplementary channel or medium. Thus, Lexus markets its cars mostly through mass-media advertising and its high-quality dealer network but also supplements these channels with direct marketing. Its direct marketing includes promotional DVDs and other materials mailed directly to prospective buyers and a web page (www.lexus.com) that provides consumers with information about various models, competitive comparisons, financing, and dealer locations. Similarly, most department stores such as Harrods or Macy's sell the majority of their merchandise off their store shelves but also sell through direct mail and online catalogs. In the Arab world, direct and online marketing have started to develop. For example, Souq.com provides an online marketplace for selling directly to consumers, and the website is used by companies in countries such as Kuwait, Jordan, Egypt, the UAE and the Kingdom of Saudi Arabia.

However, for many companies today, direct marketing is more than just a supplementary channel or advertising medium. For these companies, direct marketing—especially in its most recent transformation, online marketing—constitutes a complete model for doing business. Rather than using direct marketing and the Internet only as supplemental approaches, firms employing this new *direct model* use it as the *only* approach. Companies such as Amazon.com, eBay, and Otlob have built their entire approach to the marketplace around direct marketing. The direct model is rapidly changing the way that companies think about building relationships with customers.

<table>
<tr><td>**Author** | Direct marketing—
Comment | especially online
marketing—is growing explosively.
It's at the heart of the trend toward
building closer, more interactive
customer relationships.</td></tr>
</table>

Growth and Benefits of Direct Marketing (pp 371–373)

Direct marketing has become one of the fastest-growing forms of marketing. Accordingly, the Arab Direct Marketing Association (ADMA) was launched in 2009 by Makkah Governor, Prince Khaled El-Faisal. The main objective of this forum is to develop direct marketing in the pan-Arab community. "In launching the ADMA today, we take an important step toward building a world marketing community, a community that shares common challenges and opportunities, and can work together for the benefit of all," said New York-based Direct Marketing Association (DMA) President and CEO John A. Greco, Jr. (ADMA is a new affiliate to DMA). "DMA is proud to be part of building what for most companies here will be a totally new approach to marketing," said Greco.[2]

Direct marketing continues to become more web-oriented, and Internet marketing is claiming a fast-growing share of direct marketing spending and sales. Today, the Internet accounts for only about 20 percent of direct marketing-driven sales. However, the DMA predicts that over the next five years Internet marketing expenditures will grow at a blistering 16 percent a year, more than three times faster than expenditures in other direct marketing media. Internet-driven sales will grow by almost 15 percent.

Whether employed as a complete business model or as a supplement to a broader integrated marketing mix, direct marketing brings many benefits to both buyers and sellers.

Benefits to Buyers

For buyers, direct marketing is convenient, easy, and private. Direct marketers never close their doors, and customers don't have to battle traffic, find parking spaces, and walk long distances through stores to find products. From the comfort of their homes or offices, they can browse catalogs or company websites at any time of the day or night. Business buyers can learn about products and services without tying up time with salespeople.

Direct marketing gives buyers ready access to a wealth of products. For example, unrestrained by physical boundaries, direct marketers can offer an almost unlimited selection

Otlob has introduced a new concept of online shopping which helped the penetration of online shopping in the Arab region for both consumers and companies.

to consumers almost anywhere in the world. Just compare the huge selections offered by many web merchants with the small ranges of their offline counterparts. For instance, log onto Bulbs.com, "the web's number-one light bulb superstore," and you'll have instant access to every imaginable kind of light bulb or lamp—incandescent bulbs, fluorescent bulbs, projection bulbs, surgical bulbs, automotive bulbs—you name it. Similarly, Otlob.com carries the menus of 118 restaurants and fast-food chains, which cover 28 diverse food categories in Egypt. Customers can easily access the menus of any of these food services and order their favorite meals. There is no place other than the web that can include all these types of food and menus. In addition, the order arrives to customers at the time they choose.

Direct marketing channels also give buyers access to a wealth of comparative information about companies, products, and competitors. Good catalogs or websites often provide more information in more useful forms than even the most helpful retail salesperson can. For example, the Amazon.com site offers more information than most of us can digest, ranging from top-10 product lists, extensive product descriptions, and expert and user product reviews to recommendations based on customers' previous purchases.

Finally, direct marketing is interactive and immediate—buyers can interact with sellers by telephone or on the seller's website to create exactly the configuration of information, products, or services they desire, and then order them on the spot. Moreover, direct marketing gives consumers a greater measure of control. Consumers decide which catalogs they will browse and which websites they will visit.

Benefits to Sellers

For sellers, direct marketing is a powerful tool for building customer relationships. Using database marketing, today's marketers can target small groups or individual consumers and promote their offers through personalized communications. Because of the one-to-one nature of direct marketing, companies can interact with customers by telephone or online, learn more about their needs, and tailor products and services to specific customer tastes. In turn, customers can ask questions and volunteer feedback.

Direct marketing also offers sellers a low-cost, efficient, speedy alternative for reaching their markets. Direct marketing has grown rapidly in business-to-business marketing, partly in response to the ever-increasing costs of marketing through the sales force. When personal sales calls cost an average of more than US$320 per contact, they should be made only when necessary and to high-potential customers and prospects.[3] Lower-cost-per-contact media—such as telemarketing, direct mail, and company websites—often prove more cost effective.

Similarly, online direct marketing results in lower costs, improved efficiencies, and speedier handling of channel and logistics functions, such as order processing, inventory handling, and delivery. Direct marketers such as Amazon.com or Waffar.com also avoid the expense of maintaining a store and the related costs of rent, insurance, and utilities, passing the savings along to customers.

Direct marketing can also offer greater flexibility. It allows marketers to make ongoing adjustments to their prices and programs, or to make immediate, timely, and personal announcements and offers.

Finally, direct marketing gives sellers access to buyers that they could not reach through other channels. Smaller firms can mail catalogs to customers outside their local markets and post toll-free telephone numbers to handle orders and inquiries. Internet marketing is a truly global medium that allows buyers and sellers to click from one country to another in seconds. A web user from Amman or Beirut can access an online Gucci catalog as easily as someone living in the United States, the direct retailer's home country. Even small marketers find that they have ready access to global markets.

Customer database
An organized collection of comprehensive data about individual customers or prospects, including geographic, demographic, psychographic, and behavioral data.

Customer Databases and Direct Marketing (p 373)

Effective direct marketing begins with a good customer database. A **customer database** is an organized collection of comprehensive data about individual customers or prospects, including geographic, demographic, psychographic, and behavioral data. A good customer database can be a potent relationship-building tool. The database gives companies a 360-degree view of their customers and how they behave. A company is no better than what it knows about its customers.

In consumer marketing, the customer database might contain a customer's demographics (age, income, family members, and birthdays), psychographics (activities, interests, and opinions), and buying behavior (buying preferences and the recency, frequency, and monetary value—RFM—of past purchases). In business-to-business marketing, the customer profile might contain the products and services the customer has bought, past volumes and prices, key contacts (and their ages, birthdays, hobbies, and favorite foods), competing suppliers, status of current contracts, estimated customer spending for the next few years, and assessments of competitive strengths and weaknesses in selling and servicing the account.

Some of these databases are huge. For example, Internet portal Yahoo! records every click made by every visitor, adding some 400 billion bytes of data per day to its database—the equivalent of 800,000 books. And Wal-Mart captures data on every item, for every customer, for every store, every day. Its database contains more than 1 petabyte of data—that's a quadrillion bytes, far greater than the storage capacity of 250,000 4-gigabyte flash drives.[4]

Yahoo! keeps a record of every click made by every visitor, forming a massive customer database.

Companies use their databases in many ways. They use databases to locate good potential customers and to generate sales leads. They can mine their databases to learn about customers in detail, and then fine-tune their market offerings and communications to the special preferences and behaviors of target segments or individuals. In all, a company's database can be an important tool for building stronger long-term customer relationships.

Like many other marketing tools, database marketing requires a special investment. Companies must invest in computer hardware, database software, analytical programs, communication links, and skilled personnel. The database system must be user-friendly and available to various marketing groups, including those in product and brand management, new-product development, advertising and promotion, direct mail, telemarketing, web marketing, field sales, order fulfillment, and customer service. However, a well-managed database should lead to sales and customer-relationship gains that will more than cover its costs.

Forms of Direct Marketing (pp 373–379)

The major forms of direct marketing—as shown in Figure 13.1—include personal selling, direct-mail marketing, catalog marketing, telephone marketing, direct-response television marketing, kiosk marketing, new digital direct-marketing technologies, and online marketing. We examined personal selling in depth in Chapter 12. Here, we examine the other direct-marketing forms.

FIGURE | 13.1

Forms of Direct Marketing

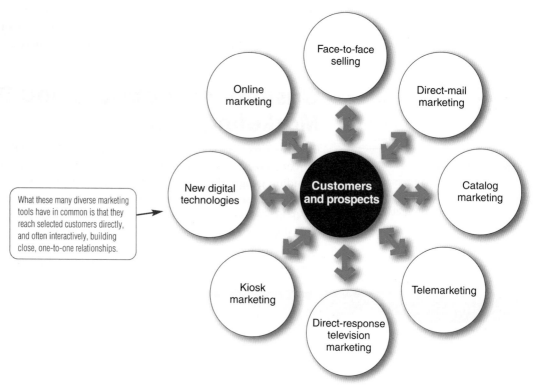

What these many diverse marketing tools have in common is that they reach selected customers directly, and often interactively, building close, one-to-one relationships.

Direct-Mail Marketing

Direct-mail marketing

Direct marketing by sending an offer, announcement, reminder, or other item to a person at a particular physical or virtual address.

Direct-mail marketing involves sending an offer, announcement, reminder, or other item to a person at a particular physical or virtual address. Using highly selective mailing lists, direct marketers send out millions of mail pieces each year—letters, catalogs, ads, brochures, samples, CDs and DVDs, and other 'salespeople with wings.' In the United States, direct mail is by far the largest direct-marketing medium: the DMA reports that direct mail (including both catalog and non-catalog mail) drives more than a third of all U.S. direct marketing sales.[5]

Direct mail is well suited to direct, one-to-one communication. It permits high target-market selectivity, can be personalized, is flexible, and allows easy measurement of results. Although direct mail costs more per thousand people reached than mass media such as television or magazines, the people it reaches are much better prospects. Direct mail has proved successful in promoting all kinds of products, from books, music, DVDs, and magazine subscriptions to insurance, gift items, clothing, gourmet foods, and industrial products. Charities also use direct mail heavily to raise billions of dollars each year.

The direct mail industry constantly seeks new methods and approaches. For example, CDs and DVDs are now among the fastest-growing direct mail media. One study showed that including a CD or DVD in a marketing offer generates responses between 50 to 1,000 percent greater than traditional direct mail.[6] New forms of delivery have also become popular, such as *voice mail, text messaging,* and *email.* However, permission-based mobile marketing (via cellphones) is growing rapidly and email is booming as a direct marketing tool. Today's email messages have moved far beyond the drab text-only messages of old. The new breed of email ad uses animation, interactive links, streaming video, and personalized audio messages to reach out and grab attention.

Email, mobile, and other new forms deliver direct mail at incredible speeds compared with the post office's slow pace. Yet, much like mail delivered through traditional channels, they may be resented as 'junk mail' or spam if sent to people who have no interest in them. For this reason, smart marketers are targeting their direct mail carefully so as not to waste their money and recipients' time. They are designing permission-based programs, sending email and mobile ads only to those who want to receive them. We will discuss email and mobile marketing in more detail later in the chapter.

Although the new digital direct-mail forms are gaining popularity, the traditional form is still by far the most widely used. Despite the clutter, traditional direct mail can be highly effective, especially for reaching certain segments that don't get as much direct mail as the general population. Companies such as Aramex still offer a direct-mail delivery service to companies, which implies there is a continuous demand for such services in the Arab world. Also, it is common in some countries in the Arab world for companies to use direct mail to reach their target audiences, attached to, for example, gas, power, and water bills. Bank and credit card statements mail with information from sponsors about joint offers between the bank and merchants. Hotels also send direct mail, often on a quarterly basis, to their health club members, golf club members, and regular guests, with details of promotions and hotel events. For example, the JW Marriott in Cairo sends its publication, *JW Dimensions*, on a quarterly basis to its regular guests and golf club members, with information about the events that have happened and promotions for the coming period.

Telephone Marketing

Telephone marketing
Using the telephone to sell directly to customers.

Telephone marketing involves using the telephone to sell directly to consumers and business customers. Telephone marketing now accounts for nearly 20 percent of all direct marketing-driven sales. We're all familiar with telephone marketing directed toward consumers, but business-to-business marketers also use telephone marketing extensively, accounting for more than 55 percent of all telephone marketing sales.[7] Telephone marketing is also a major fund-raising tool for nonprofit groups. In the Arab world, telephone marketing is mainly used for credit card offers, discount cards, and travel offers.

Marketers use *outbound* telephone marketing to sell directly to consumers and businesses. They use *inbound* toll-free numbers to receive orders from television and print ads, direct mail, or catalogs. The use of toll-free numbers has taken off in recent years as more and more companies have begun using them, and as current users have added new features such as toll-free fax numbers. To accommodate this rapid growth, new toll-free area codes have been added.

Properly designed and targeted telephone marketing provides many benefits, including purchasing convenience and increased product and service information. However, the explosion in unsolicited outbound telephone marketing over the years annoyed many consumers, who objected to the almost daily 'junk phone calls' that pulled them away from the dinner table or filled the answering machine.

Many marketers are shifting their call-center activity from making cold calls to often resentful customers to managing existing customer relationships. They are developing 'opt-in' calling systems, in which they provide useful information and offers to customers who have invited the company to contact them by phone or email. These "sales tactics have [produced] results as good—or even better—than telemarketing," declares one analyst. "The opt-in model is proving [more] valuable for marketers [than] the old invasive one."[8]

Direct-Response Television Marketing

Direct-response television marketing
Direct marketing via television, including direct-response television advertising (or infomercials) and home shopping channels.

Direct-response television marketing takes one of two major forms. The first is *direct-response television advertising* (DRTV). Direct marketers air television spots, often 60 or 120 seconds long, which persuasively describe a product and give customers a toll-free number or website for ordering. Television viewers also often encounter full 30-minute or longer advertising programs, or *infomercials*, for a single product.

For years, infomercials have been associated with somewhat questionable pitches for juicers and other kitchen gadgets, get-rich-quick schemes, and nifty ways to stay in shape without working very hard at it.

Direct-response television commercials are usually cheaper to make and the media purchase is less costly. Moreover, unlike most media campaigns, direct-response ads always include a toll-free number or web address, making it easier for marketers to track the impact of their pitches. For these reasons, DRTV is growing more quickly than traditional broadcast and cable advertising. Some DRTV experts even predict that in 5 or 10 years, as marketers

Automated self-service kiosks provide companies with a powerful marketing tool. They help customers with their purchases and give companies valuable information at the same time.

seek greater returns on their advertising investments, all television advertising will be some form of direct-response advertising. "In a business environment where marketers are obsessed with return on investment," notes one such expert, "direct response is tailor-made—[marketers can] track phone calls and Web-site hits generated by the ads. [They can] use DRTV to build brand awareness while simultaneously generating leads and sales."[9]

Kiosk Marketing

As consumers become more and more comfortable with computer and digital technologies, many companies are placing information and ordering machines—called *kiosks* (in contrast to vending machines, which dispense actual products)—in stores, airports, and other locations. Kiosks are popping up everywhere these days, from self-service hotel and airline check-in devices to in-store ordering kiosks that let you order merchandise not carried in the store.

In-store Kodak, Fuji, and HP kiosks let customers transfer pictures from memory sticks, mobile phones, and other digital storage devices, edit them, and make high-quality color prints. Kiosks in Hilton hotel lobbies let guests view their reservations, get room keys, view pre-arrival messages, check in and out, and even change seat assignments and print boarding passes for flights on any of 18 airlines.

Business marketers also use kiosks. For example, Dow Plastics places kiosks at trade shows to collect sales leads and to provide information on its 700 products. The kiosk system reads customer data from encoded registration badges and produces technical data sheets that can be printed at the kiosk or faxed or mailed to the customer. The system has resulted in a 400 percent increase in qualified sales leads.[10]

Automated self-service kiosks are emerging in the Arab world, providing companies with a powerful marketing tool. Retail Kiosk Solutions in Kuwait supplies kiosks to companies that wish to reach their customers this way.

The automated self-service kiosk (ASK) is a new and growing retail tool for companies in the Arab world. ASKs are popular in Kuwait and Dubai, and are expected to emerge in other countries. ASKs improve retail functions in ways that suit consumers' preferences and needs. They are fully automated and user-friendly.

There are many features that give ASKs an edge over other retail options. For example, as well as serving as instant access points, they encourage constant usage because of the many related services that they offer. For maximum customer reach, a kiosk should be positioned strategically, in a way that encourages the consumer to use it constantly, not just on the spot. Kiosks can be easily used by any customer, because their touch-screen application is designed to facilitate the self-service process. The system is supported by multi-lingual interfaces, running both Arabic and English operations, and is customized to consumers' requirements.

Diverse services offered by ASKs include:

- The purchase of prepaid vouchers for multi-vendor services
- The purchase and renewal of services
- Bill inquiry and payment
- SMS/MMS
- E-ticketing
- The dispensing and refilling of smart, privilege, and SIM cards
- Customer satisfaction surveys, promotions, and general customer comments.

The kiosks are equiped with broadband connectivity for remote monitoring, offer a diverse range of payment methods to suit all types of customers, and feature a barcode reader, which assists in making payments. The hardware and software are of a modular design, meaning that more products or services can be easily added to the system.

This smart kiosk is currently found in 26 locations in Kuwait, with a view to further expansion.[11]

New Digital Direct Marketing Technologies

Today, thanks to a wealth of new digital technologies, direct marketers can reach and interact with consumers just about anywhere, at anytime, about almost anything. Here, we look into several exciting new digital direct marketing technologies: mobile phone marketing, podcasts and vodcasts, and interactive TV (ITV).

Mobile Phone Marketing

With more than 260 million Americans alone now subscribing to wireless services, many marketers view mobile phones as the next big direct marketing medium. About 80 percent of consumers in the United States use cellphones and about 60 percent of those people also text message. In Egypt, mobile service providers claimed that by 2010 they would sell more than 60 million lines in a country of 80 million people.

Within five years, an estimated 40 percent of mobile phone subscribers will use their phones to access the web. Some 23 percent of mobile phone users have seen advertising on their phones in the last 30 days and about half of them responded to the ads.[12]

A growing number of consumers—especially younger ones—are using their mobile phones as a 'third screen' for text messaging, surfing the wireless web, watching downloaded videos and shows, and checking email. According to one expert, "the [mobile] phone, which makes on-the-go conversing so convenient, is morphing into a content device, a kind of digital Swiss Army knife with the capability of filling its owner's every spare minute with games, music, live and on-demand TV, web browsing, and, oh yes, advertising." Mobile phones allow "marketers to reach consumers anytime, anywhere, on a device they love."[13] A recent study estimated that spending on mobile marketing would grow from US$1.8 billion in 2007 to as much as US$24 billion worldwide by 2013.[14]

Marketers of all kinds—from Lipton tea and Carrefour, to Red Tags, Apple, Vodafone, and Radisson Hotels—are now integrating mobile phones into their direct marketing. Mobile phone promotions include everything from ring-tone giveaways, mobile games, text-in contests, and ad-supported content to retailer announcements of discounts, specials sales, and gift suggestions. For example, McDonald's recently put a promotion code on 20 million Big Mac packages in a joint sweepstakes contest with a concert promoter, urging participants to enter to win prizes and to text in from concerts. Some 40 percent of contest entries came via text messaging, resulting in a 3 percent sales gain for McDonald's. More importantly, 24 percent of those entering via mobile phones opted in to receive future promotions and messages.[15]

As with other forms of direct marketing, however, companies must use mobile marketing responsibly or risk angering already ad-weary consumers. Most people are initially skeptical about receiving mobile phone ad messages. But they often change their minds if the ads deliver value in the form of lower mobile phone bills, useful information, entertaining content, or discounted prices and coupons for their favorite products and services. A recent study in the U.S. found that 42 percent of mobile phone users are open to mobile advertising if it's relevant.[16] When used properly, mobile marketing can greatly enrich the buyer's experience.

Mobile marketing: Mobile phones and wireless devices have quietly become the newest, hottest frontier for big brand messages.

With podcasting, consumers can download files via the Internet to an iPod or other handheld device and listen to or view them whenever and wherever they wish.

Podcasts and Vodcasts

Podcasting and vodcasting are the latest on-the-go, on-demand technologies. The name *podcast* derives from Apple's now-everywhere iPod. With podcasting, consumers can download audio files (podcasts) or video files (vodcasts) via the Internet to an iPod or other handheld device and then listen to or view them whenever and wherever they wish. They can search for podcast topics through sites such as iTunes or through podcast networks such as PodTrac, Podbridge, or PodShow. These days, you can download podcasts or vodcasts on an exploding array of topics, everything from your favorite radio show, a recent television program, or current sports features to the latest music video or commercial.

One recent study predicts that the U.S. podcast audience will reach 65 million by 2012, up from 6 million in 2005.[17] Even though podcasting is becoming very popular in the U.S. and Europe, this form of technology has not yet penetrated the Arab world; however, the increasing demand for iPods and iPhones in the region is noticeable. As a result, this new medium is drawing much attention from marketers. Many are now integrating podcasts and vodcasts into their direct marketing programs in the form of ad-supported podcasts, downloadable ads and informational features, and other promotions.

For example, Volvo sponsors podcasts on Autoblog. Also, Hot Topic sponsors its own new music podcast featuring underground bands. The Walt Disney World Resort offers weekly podcasts on a mix of topics, including behind-the-scenes tours, interviews, upcoming events, and news about new attractions. New podcasts automatically download to subscribers' computers, where they can transfer them to portable media players to enjoy and share them.

Interactive TV (ITV)

Interactive TV (ITV) lets viewers interact with television programming and advertising using their remote controls. In the past, ITV has been slow to catch on. However, the technology now appears poised to take off as a direct marketing medium. A recent poll in the U.S. indicated that 66 percent of viewers would be "very interested" in interacting with commercials that piqued their interest.[18] And satellite broadcasting systems such as DIRECTV, EchoStar, and Time Warner are now offering ITV capabilities. Interestingly, such systems did not enter the Arab world, but similar concepts have started to penetrate the market, including Internet Protocol Television (IPTV). For example, STC in the Kingdom of Saudi Arabia introduced IPTV for its customers in 2010.

Interactive TV gives marketers an opportunity to reach targeted audiences in an interactive, more involving way. For example, shopping channel HSN recently developed a 'Shop by Remote' interactive TV service that allows viewers to immediately purchase any item on HSN using their remote. Procter & Gamble ran interactive ads for its Tide to Go detergent brand. The 30-second TV spots contained remote control links, giving interested consumers instant access to more information about the product, as well as coupons and the opportunity to enter a sweepstake to win a trip to an amusement park. Similarly, Nike's "Quick Is Deadly" campaign for its Zoom training-shoe line included more than 20 minutes of interactive content accessible to Dish Network subscribers with digital video recorders.[19]

Nike made interactive content available in ads featuring several Nike endorsers, including basketball's Steve Nash, runner Lauren Fleshman, Olympic sprinters Asafa Powell and Sanya Richards, and tennis player Rafael Nadal. Using zip-code information in each Dish unit, users were able to find stores carrying the shoe at the click of a button. The campaign stopped short of actually letting viewers buy the shoes directly from their sets, although the technology enables that function. Research shows that the level of viewer engagement with interactive TV is much higher than with 30-second spots. "We've gotten to the point where all media needs to be interactive," says a creative director at Nike's advertising agency.

Mobile phone marketing, podcasts and vodcasts, and interactive TV offer exciting direct marketing opportunities. But marketers must be careful to use these new direct marketing approaches wisely. As with other direct marketing forms, marketers who use them risk a negative response from consumers who may resent such marketing as an invasion of their privacy. Marketers must target their direct marketing offers carefully, bringing real value to customers rather than making unwanted intrusions into their lives.

Online Marketing (pp 379–384)

> **Author Comment** | Online direct marketing spending is growing at a blistering pace—about 16 percent a year. The web now accounts for about 20 percent of direct marketing-driven sales.

As noted earlier, **online marketing** is the fastest-growing form of direct marketing. Recent technological advances have created a digital age. Widespread use of the Internet is having a dramatic impact on both buyers and the marketers who serve them. In this section, we examine how marketing strategy and practice are changing to take advantage of today's Internet technologies.

Marketing and the Internet

Online marketing
Company efforts to market products and services and build customer relationships over the Internet.

Much of the world's business today is carried out over digital networks that connect people and companies. The Internet, a vast public web of computer networks, connects users of all types all around the world to each other and to an amazingly large information repository. The web has fundamentally changed customers' notions of convenience, speed, price, product information, and service. As a result, it has given marketers a whole new way to create value for customers and build relationships with them.

Internet usage and impact continue to grow steadily around the world. Between 2000 and 2009, the average penetration was 19.1 percent across 22 countries. However, the level of penetration varies widely among countries, ranging from 60.9 percent in the UAE to just 1 percent in Iraq and Somalia.[20]

Click-only companies
The so-called dot-coms, which operate only online without any brick-and-mortar market presence.

All kinds of companies now market online. **Click-only companies** operate only on the Internet. They include a wide array of firms, from *e-tailers* such as Souq.com that sell products and services directly to final buyers via the Internet to *search engines and portals* (such as Yahoo!, Google, and Baidu), *transaction sites* (Waffar.com), and *content sites* (*The Financial Times* on the web, ESPN.com, Encyclopaedia Britannica Online, and Al Jazeera). After a frenzied and rocky start in the 1990s, many click-only dot-coms are now prospering in today's online marketspace.

As the Internet grew, the success of the dot-coms caused existing *brick-and-mortar* manufacturers and retailers to reexamine how they served their markets. Now, almost all of these traditional companies have set up their own online sales and communications channels, becoming **click-and-mortar companies**. It's hard to find a company today that doesn't have a substantial Web presence.

Click-and-mortar companies
Traditional brick-and-mortar companies that have added online marketing to their operations.

In fact, many click-and-mortar companies are now having more online success than their click-only competitors. In a recent ranking of the top 10 online retail sites, only two were click-only retailers. All of the others were multichannel retailers.[21] For example, the retailer Office Depot's more than 1,000 office-supply superstores rack up annual sales of US$15.5 billion in more than 42 countries. But you might be surprised to learn that Office Depot's fastest recent growth has come not from its traditional 'brick-and-mortar' channels, but from the Internet.[22]

Office Depot's online sales have soared in recent years, now accounting for 31 percent of total sales. Selling on the web lets Office Depot build deeper, more personalized relationships with customers, large and small. For example, a large customer such as Siemens or P&G can create lists of approved office products at discount prices and then let company departments or even individuals do their own online purchasing. This reduces ordering costs, cuts through the red tape, and speeds up the ordering process

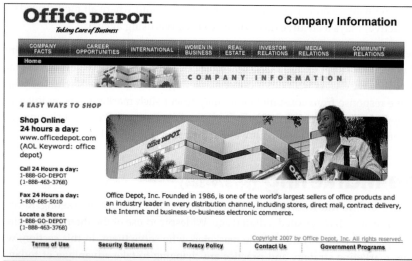

Click-and-mortar marketing: No click-only or brick-only seller can match the call, click, or visit convenience and support afforded by retailer Office Depot's '4 easy ways to shop.'

for customers. At the same time, it encourages companies to use Office Depot as a sole source for office supplies. Even the smallest companies find 24-hour-a-day online ordering easier and more efficient. Importantly, Office Depot's web operations don't steal from store sales. Instead, the OfficeDepot.com site actually builds store traffic by helping customers find a local store and check stock. In return, the local store promotes the website through in-store kiosks. If customers don't find what they need on the shelves, they can quickly order it via the web from the kiosk. Thus, Office Depot now offers a full range of contact points and delivery modes—online, by phone or fax, and in the store. No click-only or brick-only seller can match the call, click, or visit convenience and support afforded by Office Depot's click-and-mortar model.

In the Arab world, online and direct marketing are still growing, yet they are significantly affecting several spheres of business, religious, and political activity. This in turn creates further opportunities for e-business in the region. **Real Marketing 13.1** demonstrates several examples of successful online businesses in the Arab world.

Online Marketing Domains

The four major online marketing domains are shown in ➤**Figure 13.2**. They include B2C (business-to-consumer), B2B (business-to-business), C2C (consumer-to-consumer), and C2B (consumer-to-business).

Business-to-Consumer (B2C)

Business-to-consumer (B2C) online marketing

Businesses selling goods and services online to final consumers.

The popular press has paid the most attention to **business-to-consumer (B2C) online marketing**—businesses selling goods and services online to final consumers. Today's consumers can buy almost anything online—from clothing, kitchen gadgets, and airline tickets to computers and cars. Online consumer buying continues to grow at a healthy rate.[24]

Perhaps more importantly, in the U.S., the Internet now influences 35 percent of total retail sales—sales transacted online plus those carried out offline but encouraged by online research. By 2010, the Internet will influence a staggering 50 percent of total retail sales.[25] Although there are no statistics for the Arab world, there is an increasing demand for online shopping in the region. Thus, smart marketers are employing integrated multichannel strategies that use the web to drive sales to other marketing channels.

As more and more people find their way onto the web, the population of online consumers is becoming more mainstream and diverse. The web now offers marketers

➤**FIGURE** | **13.2**

Online Marketing Domains

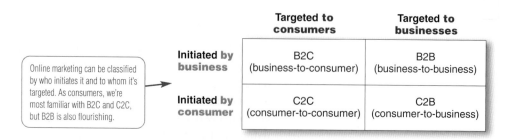

Online marketing can be classified by who initiates it and to whom it's targeted. As consumers, we're most familiar with B2C and C2C, but B2B is also flourishing.

	Targeted to consumers	Targeted to businesses
Initiated by business	B2C (business-to-consumer)	B2B (business-to-business)
Initiated by consumer	C2C (consumer-to-consumer)	C2B (consumer-to-business)

Real Marketing 13.1

Online Business in the Arab World

Across the Arab world, the use of e-commerce and online marketing has grown enormously in the last few years. Although it is still at the early stages, the online market is expanding rapidly as the number of Internet users increases dramatically.

Several online businesses have emerged in the Arab world over the past decade, offering different services and products; such as nefsak.com, cobone.com, elsou2.com, and souq.com. Although the businesses still have a limited product and services offering, they are seeing increased numbers of customers, which indicates a high potential for future growth.

Nefsak.com is one of the growing online marketplaces in Egypt, selling a diverse range of products including books, computer software and hardware, electronics games and toys, beauty and care products, home appliances, mobile phones, music, movies, and stationery. Different payment methods exist to suit customers' preferences, including credit card, cash on delivery, gift certificates, and bank deposit/transfer. This flexibility has allowed nefsak.com to build customers' confidence in terms of making secure payments.

Launched in July 2010 in Dubai, cobone.com features a daily market-focused deal on the best things to do, see, eat, and buy in cities across the Arab world. Cobone.com sends its registered clients extreme promotions on a wide variety of objects. The deals are only available for 24 hours and are constantly updated. The company operates in Abu Dhabi, Amman, Bahrain, Beirut, Cairo, Damman, Doha, Dubai, Jeddah, Kuwait, Riyadh, and Sharjah. The service seems to be addictive; users regularly come back to check for new offers.

Souq.com is an online marketplace that operates in Jordan, Saudi Arabia, and the UAE. It offers a wide range of products such as books, stationery, clothes, computers, motors, electronics, and furniture, as well as

real-estate projects. The website is verified by Visa and MasterCard, which increases the credibility of the company (this is an essential factor in the company's success, due to security issues in the region).

Not only is the business sector benefiting from online marketing opportunities, but there are also religious, cultural, and political areas that are highly affected by online marketing in the region. For example, in Egypt, the opposition movement against the previous government in early 2010 had a significant online presence through websites and social networks. Online marketing tools assisted the opposition movement to spread and broadcast its ideas and ideologies rapidly. Some organizations have their own websites. For example, ikhwanweb.com is the official website for the Muslim Brotherhood in the region, where it publishes its news, communicates its opinions, and recruits new members. Copts.com is an American-based website that represents the U.S. Copts Association, founded by Michael Mounir in 1996. This association claims to represent the Christian minority in Egypt, and uses online marketing to seek equal opportunities and treatment with Muslims. A final example exists in Tunisia, where people have created WikiProject—Tunisia, which aims to foster fair and accurate writing of more and better articles about the country.

In addition to the use of the Internet by large organizations, random movements and political groups use social networks, such as Facebook and Twitter, to get their voices heard. Similarly, many opposition move-

Even though online shopping is facing many barriers and obstacles in the Arab world, this industry is growing in the region.

ments in countries such as Tunisia, Libya, and Bahrain are using online tools to spread their ideologies and beliefs, and to increase the pace of changes in the region. The main benefit of social networks is their widespread, massive, and intrusive nature—they can even reach a non-politically savvy audience. Also noteworthy are the different types of message vehicles that can be used within the same media, such as videos, articles, and personal comments.

A similar example, but in the context of entrepreneurship, is Wamda. Wamda was created by Abraaj Capital and its subsidiary Riyada Enterprise Development (RED), with the aim of maximizing the entrepreneurial potential of the MENASA region. Abraaj believes that entrepreneurship is built on investment in knowledge, capacity-building programs, and long-term partnerships. It has created a fan page on Facebook to gather and share creative and innovative ideas.

The above examples indicate that online marketing has started to change the way businesses and politics are developing in the Arab world. There is no doubt that it will have a significant impact in the future.

Sources: Based on information at www.nefsak.com, http://otlob.com, http://egypt.stores.souq.com, http://wamda.com, www.ikhwanweb.com, and www.copts.com.

---

a palette of different kinds of consumers seeking different kinds of online experiences. However, Internet consumers still differ from traditional offline consumers in their approaches to buying and in their responses to marketing. In the Internet exchange process, customers initiate and control the contact. Traditional marketing targets a somewhat passive audience. In contrast, online marketing targets people who actively select which websites they will visit and what marketing information they will receive about which products and under what conditions. Thus, the new world of online marketing requires new marketing approaches.

People now go online to order a wide range of goods—clothing from Gap, books, electronics, or about just about anything else from Otlob.com or Waffar.com.

Business-to-Business (B2B)

Business-to-business (B2B) online marketing

Businesses using B2B websites, email, online catalogs, online trading networks, and other online resources to reach new business customers, serve current customers more effectively, and obtain buying efficiencies and better prices.

Although the popular press has given the most attention to B2C websites, **business-to-business (B2B) online marketing** is also flourishing. B2B marketers use B2B websites, email, online product catalogs, online trading networks, and other online resources to reach new business customers, serve current customers more effectively, and obtain buying efficiencies and better prices.

Most major business-to-business marketers now offer product information, customer purchasing, and customer-support services online. For example, corporate buyers can visit Sun Microsystems' website (www.sun.com), select detailed descriptions of Sun's products and solutions, request sales and service information, and interact with staff members. Some major companies conduct almost all of their business on the web. Networking equipment and software maker Cisco Systems takes more than 80 percent of its orders over the Internet.

Beyond simply selling their products and services online, companies can use the Internet to build stronger relationships with important business customers. For example, Dell has set up customized websites for more than 113,000 business and institutional customers worldwide. These individualized Premier/Dell.com sites help business customers to more efficiently manage all phases of their Dell computer buying and ownership. Each customer's Premier.Dell.com website can include a customized online computer store, purchasing and asset management reports and tools, system-specific technical information, links to useful information throughout Dell's extensive website, and more. The site makes all the information a customer needs in order to do business with Dell available in one place, 24 hours a day, 7 days a week.[26]

Consumer-to-Consumer (C2C)

Consumer-to-consumer (C2C) online marketing

Online exchanges of goods and information between final consumers.

Much **consumer-to-consumer (C2C) online marketing** and communication occurs on the web between interested parties over a wide range of products and subjects. In some cases, the Internet provides an excellent means by which consumers can buy or exchange goods or information directly with one another. For example, Souq.com, Amazon.com Auctions, Elmazad.com, eBay, and other auction sites offer popular market spaces for displaying and selling almost anything, from art and antiques, coins and stamps, and jewelry to computers and consumer electronics.

eBay's C2C online trading community of more than 275 million registered users worldwide (greater than the combined populations of France, Germany, Italy, and Britain!) transacted some US$60 billion in trades last year. At any given time, the company's website lists more than 115 million items up for auction in more than 50,000 categories. Such C2C sites give people access to much larger audiences than the local market or newspaper classifieds. Interestingly, based on its huge success in the C2C market, eBay has now attracted more than 500,000 B2C sellers, ranging from small businesses peddling their regular wares to large businesses liquidating excess inventory at auction.[27]

In the Arab world, Facebook groups have become a great medium for people to sell products online. The website allows people to post pictures, chat online, and write blogs and reviews. For security purposes, most payments are conducted through cash on delivery.

In other cases, C2C involves interchanges of information through Internet forums that appeal to specific special-interest groups. Such activities may be organized for commercial or noncommercial purposes. An example is web logs, or *blogs*, online journals where people post their thoughts, usually on a narrowly defined topic. Blogs can be about anything, from politics or baseball to haiku, car repair, or the latest television series. There are currently about 15 million active blogs read by 57 million people. Such numbers give blogs—especially those with large and devoted followings—substantial influence.[28]

Social networks, such as Facebook and Twitter, have an impact not only on business life in the Arab region, but also on the whole social, political life of the region's youth.

Many marketers are now tapping into blogs as a medium for reaching carefully targeted consumers. One way is to advertise on an existing blog or to influence content there. Consider this example:

When Nescafé launched its Dolce Gusto coffee maker in France last year, it turned to bloggers. It placed an ad on French website BlogBang.com, which has a community of more than 2,000 bloggers. The site sent a message to its members telling them about the ad campaign, which came in the form of an interactive game. The bloggers were asked to put a link to the game on their sites. In return, Dolce Gusto's home page posted links to the blogs that joined up. "The advantage of using blogs is that the message gets around very quickly," says the Dolce Gusto brand manager, "and it focuses on our target audience" of 25- to 35-year-olds. "It really created a marketing buzz." Within three weeks of its launch, Dolce Gusto's ad was displayed on 500 blogs, and 320,000 people had played the online game.[29]

Other companies set up their own blogs. For example, GM maintains a blog called FastLane that helps it connect with its core consumers in a virtual grassroots kind of way. The blog is penned by GM executives, including Vice Chairman Bob Lutz, who some claim is the big reason for its popularity. The company says it wants all kinds of feedback—so the blog includes both positive and negative comments from readers. Says Lutz, "I'd say the biggest surprise is the passion in which people respond and comment on the blogs. You're getting the real deal there. There is so much passion that even the negative comments are palatable, and indeed, often helpful." The FastLane blog receives about 3,000 visitors a day, helping GM build or rebuild relationships with customers. "If there is a gap between GM's excellence and people's perception of it, we believe blogs are a great opportunity to change those perceptions," says GM's digital marketing chief.[30]

As a marketing tool, blogs offer some advantages. They can offer a fresh, original, personal, and cheap way to reach today's fragmented audiences. However, the blogosphere is cluttered and difficult to control. "Blogs may help companies bond with consumers in exciting new ways, but they won't help them control the relationship," says a blog expert. Such web journals remain largely a C2C medium. "That isn't to suggest companies can't influence the relationship or leverage blogs to engage in a meaningful relationship," says the expert, "but the consumer will remain in control."[31]

Whether or not they actively participate in the blogosphere, companies should show up, monitor, and listen to them. For example, Starbucks sponsors its own blog (www.MyStarbucksIdea.com) but also closely follows consumer dialog on the 30 or more other third-party online sites devoted to the brand. It then uses the customer insights it gains from all of these proprietary and third-party blogs to adjust its marketing programs. For instance, it recently altered the remaining installments of a four-part podcast based on the negative blog feedback it gleaned on the first one.[32]

In all, C2C means that online buyers don't just consume product information—increasingly, they create it. As a result, 'word of web' is joining 'word of mouth' as an important buying influence.

Consumer-to-business (C2B) online marketing
Online exchanges in which consumers search out sellers, learn about their offers, and initiate purchases, sometimes even driving transaction terms.

Consumer to Business (C2B)

The final online marketing domain is **consumer-to-business (C2B) online marketing**. Thanks to the Internet, today's consumers are finding it easier to communicate with companies. Most companies now invite prospects and customers to send in suggestions and questions via company websites. Beyond this, rather than waiting for an invitation, consumers can search out sellers on the web, learn about their offers, initiate purchases, and give feedback. Using the web, consumers can even drive transactions with businesses, rather than the other way around. For example, using ewaseet.com, would-be buyers can bid for airline tickets, hotel rooms, rental cars, cruises, and vacation packages, leaving the sellers to decide whether to accept their offers.

Consumers can also use websites such as GetSatisfaction.com, Complaints.com, and PlanetFeedback.com to ask questions, offer suggestions, lodge complaints, or deliver compliments to companies. GetSatisfaction.com provides "people-powered customer service" by creating a user-driven customer-service community. The site provides forums where customers discuss problems they're having with the products and services of 2,500 companies—from Apple to Zappos.com—whether the company participates or not. GetSatisfaction.com also provides tools by which companies can adopt GetSatisfaction.com as an official customer service resource. Since launching in 2007, the site has drawn more than a million unique visitors.[33] C2B online marketing has not been yet developed in the Arab world. Websites such as Priceline.com, GetSatisfaction.com, and others might have potential in the coming years if, once introduced, they start to promote the power of business driven by the consumer rather than by corporations.

Setting up an Online Marketing Presence (pp 384–390)

Clearly, all companies need to consider moving online. Companies can conduct online marketing in any of the four ways shown in ◗ **Figure 13.3**: by creating a website, placing ads and promotions online, setting up or participating in online social networks, or using email.

Creating a Website

For most companies, the first step in conducting online marketing is to create a website. However, beyond simply creating a website, marketers must design an attractive site and find ways to get consumers to visit the site, stay around, and come back often.

Types of Websites

Corporate (or brand) website
A website designed to build customer goodwill, collect customer feedback, and supplement other sales channels, rather than to sell the company's products directly.

Websites vary greatly in purpose and content. The most basic type is a **corporate (or brand) website**. These sites are designed to build customer goodwill, collect customer feedback, and supplement other sales channels, rather than to sell the company's products directly. They typically offer a rich variety of information and other features in an effort to answer customer questions, build closer customer relationships, and generate excitement about the company or brand.

For example, Unilever's campaignforrealbeauty.com site doesn't sell Dove soaps and lotions. But it does provide a place for people interested in the cause of women and girls' self-esteem to share their thoughts, view ads and viral videos such as "Dove Evolution" or

◗**FIGURE | 13.3**
Setting Up for Online Marketing

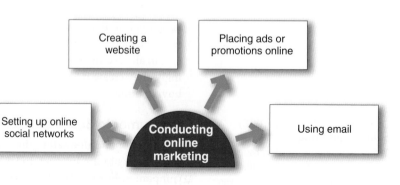

It's hard to find a company today that doesn't have a substantial web presence. The first step is one or more websites. But most large companies use all of these approaches. Don't forget, they all need to be integrated—with each other and with the rest of the promotion mix.

"Onslaught," and download self-esteem assessment tools and workbooks. They can even register for a free training guide to become a Dove Real Beauty Workshop for Girls facilitator. Such websites, once brushed aside as digital 'brochureware,' are now attracting consumers in numbers that vie with flashier consumer sites and even traditional mass media.[34]

Marketing website

A website that engages consumers in interactions that will move them closer to a direct purchase or other marketing outcome.

Other companies create a **marketing website**. These sites engage consumers in an interaction that will move them closer to a direct purchase or other marketing outcome. For example, visitors to SonyStyle.com can search through dozens of categories of Sony products, learn more about specific items, and read expert product reviews. They can check out the latest hot deals, place orders online, and pay by credit card, all with a few mouse clicks.

Pepsi Arabia operates a marketing website where customers can see various ads, listen to music, play games, and connect with Pepsi brands. Moreover, customers can design a can of Pepsi, telephone covers, and T-shirts. A similar example is MBC's website, where customers can vote for shows, play games, or even upload videos as part of competitions or to be used in MBC campaigns.

Designing Effective Websites

Creating a website is one thing; getting people to *visit* the site is another. To attract visitors, companies aggressively promote their websites in offline print and broadcast advertising, and through ads and links on other sites. But today's web users are quick to abandon any website that doesn't measure up. The key is to create enough value and excitement to get consumers who come to the site to stick around and come back again. This means that companies must constantly update their sites to keep them current, fresh, and useful.

For some types of products, attracting visitors is easy. Consumers buying new cars, computers, or financial services will be open to information and marketing initiatives from sellers. Marketers of lower-involvement products, however, may face a difficult challenge in attracting website visitors. If you're in the market for a computer and you see a banner ad that says, "The top 10 PCs under US$800," you'll likely click on the banner. But what kind of ad would get you to visit a site like dentalfloss.com?

A key challenge is designing a website that is attractive on first view and interesting enough to encourage repeat visits. Many marketers create colorful, graphically sophisticated websites that combine text, sound, and animation to capture and hold attention (for examples, see www.looneytunes.com or www.nike.com). To attract new visitors and to encourage revisits, suggests one expert, online marketers should pay close attention to the seven Cs of effective website design:[35]

- *Context:* the site's layout and design
- *Content:* the text, pictures, sound, and video that the website contains
- *Community:* the ways that the site enables user-to-user communication
- *Customization:* the site's ability to tailor itself to different users or to allow users to personalize the site
- *Communication:* the ways the site enables site-to-user, user-to-site, or two-way communication
- *Connection:* the degree that the site is linked to other sites
- *Commerce:* the site's capabilities to enable commercial transactions.

And to keep customers coming back to the site, companies need to embrace yet another 'C'—constant change.

At the very least, a website should be easy to use, look professional, and be physically attractive. Ultimately, however, websites must also be *useful*. When it comes to web surfing and shopping, most people prefer substance over style and function over flash. Thus, effective websites contain deep and useful information, interactive tools that help buyers find and evaluate products of interest, links to other related sites, changing promotional offers, and entertaining features that lend relevant excitement.

Effective websites: Check out the above Glidden website at www.glidden.com. The Web Marketing Association judged this as one of 2010's best websites. Applying the seven Cs of effective website design, do you agree that this is a good website?

Maintaining a top website is a complex and ongoing task. For example, The Walt Disney Company recently overhauled its Disney.com site for the second time in only two years:[36]

The changes to Disney.com will introduce more free videos (including full-length movies like *Finding Nemo*) as well as more games and things for visitors to do with their mobile phones. For instance, little girls (or bigger ones) who create fairy avatars in a virtual world called Pixie Hollow will be able to use their mobile phones to create pet butterflies for their fairies. "I'm going to want to use my phone to feed and love my butterfly all the time," said Disney's executive vice president for mobile content. "That kind of emotional vesting is what we're after." With the changes, Disney is trying to position its website more as a place that entertains and less of one that exists to promote Disney wares. No longer will the site ask youngsters to navigate through categories like "Movies," "TV," and "Live Events." New options will include "Games," "Videos," and "Characters" and will emphasize how to find immediate entertainment. "It's a repositioning of our digital front door," says another Disney Online executive. The constant changes reflect the fast pace at which online is evolving. The previous site overhaul increased unique visitors to Disney.com by about 40 percent to nearly 30 million a month, making it the number-one web destination for children and family-oriented websites. The average user spends 45 minutes per visit. But refreshing the site is an ongoing process. "Our initial instincts [have been] right," says the executive. "We just need to take it much further."

Placing Ads and Promotions Online

Online advertising
Advertising that appears while consumers are surfing the web, including display ads, search-related ads, online classifieds, and other forms.

As consumers spend more and more time on the Internet, many companies are shifting more of their marketing dollars to **online advertising** to build their brands or to attract visitors to their websites. Online advertising is becoming a major medium. Last year, U.S. companies alone spent more than US$21 billion on online advertising, up an incredible 26 percent over the previous year, and more than they spent on newspaper, outdoor, or radio advertising. Online ad spending will jump to more than US$42 billion by 2011, rivaling or surpassing the amount spent on magazines and even television.[37] Here, we discuss forms of online advertising and promotion and their future.

Forms of Online Advertising

The major forms of online advertising include display ads, search-related ads, and online classifieds. Online display ads might appear anywhere on an Internet user's screen. The most common form is *banners*, banner-shaped ads found at the top, bottom, left, right, or center of a web page. For instance, a web surfer looking up airline schedules or fares might encounter a flashing banner that screams, "Rent a car from Alamo and get up to two days free!" Clicking on the ad takes consumers to the Alamo website, where they can redeem the promotion.

Interstitials are online display ads that appear between screen changes on a website, especially while a new screen is loading. For example, visit www.marketwatch.com and you'll probably see a 10-second ad for Visa, Verizon, Dell, or another sponsor before the home page loads. *Pop-ups* are online ads that appear suddenly in a new window in front of the window being viewed. Such ads can multiply out of control, creating a major annoyance. As a result, Internet services and web browser providers have developed applications that let users block most pop-ups. But not to worry. Many advertisers have now developed pop-*unders*, new windows that evade pop-up blockers by appearing behind the page you're viewing.

With the increase in broadband Internet access in homes, many companies are developing exciting new *rich media* display ads, which incorporate animation, video, sound, and interactivity. Rich media ads attract and hold consumer attention better than traditional banner ads. They employ techniques such as float, fly, and snapback—animations that jump out and sail over the web page before retreating to their original space.

But many rich media ads do more than create a little bit of jumping animation—they also create interactivity. Many of today's rich media ads provide consumers with product information, a brand experience, and even local or online buying options without taking them away from the site they are viewing.

Another growth area for online advertising is *search-related ads* (or *contextual advertising*), in which text-based ads and links appear alongside search engine results on sites such as Google and Yahoo! For example, search Google for "HDTV." At the top and side of the resulting search list, you'll see inconspicuous ads for 10 or more advertisers, ranging from Circuit City, Best Buy, and Amazon.com to Dish Network, Nextag.com, and TigerDirect.com. Nearly all of Google's US$16.59 billion in revenues come from ad sales. An advertiser buys search terms from the search site and pays only if consumers click through to its site. Search-related ads account for some 41 percent of all online advertising expenditures, more than any other category of online advertising.[38]

Other Forms of Online Promotion

Other forms of online promotion include content sponsorships, alliances and affiliate programs, and viral advertising.

Using *content sponsorships,* companies gain name exposure on the Internet by sponsoring special content on various websites, such as news or financial information or special-interest topics. For example, Scotts, the lawn-and-garden products company, sponsors the Local Forecast section on WeatherChannel.com. Sponsorships are best placed in carefully targeted sites where they can offer relevant information or service to the audience. Internet companies can also develop *alliances and affiliate programs,* in which they work with other companies, online and offline, to 'promote each other.' For example, through its Amazon Associates Program, Amazon.com has more than 900,000 affiliates who post Amazon.com banners on their websites.

Finally, online marketers use **viral marketing**, the Internet version of word-of-mouth marketing. Viral marketing involves creating a website, video, email message, or other marketing event that is so infectious that customers will want to pass it along to their friends. One observer describes viral marketing as "addictive, self-propagating advertisment that lives on websites, blogs, cellphones, message boards, and even in real-world stunts."[39] Because customers pass the message or promotion along to others, viral marketing can be very inexpensive. And when the information comes from a friend, the recipient is much more likely to open and read it.

Although marketers usually have little control over where their viral messages end up, a well-concocted viral campaign can gain vast exposure.

Viral marketing
The Internet version of word-of-mouth marketing—websites, videos, email messages, or other marketing events that are so infectious that customers will want to pass them along to friends.

Online social networks
Online social communities—blogs, social networking websites, or even virtual worlds—where people socialize or exchange information and opinions.

Creating or Participating in Online Social Networks

As we discussed in Chapter 5, the popularity of the Internet has resulted in a rash of **online social networks** or *web communities.* Countless independent and commercial websites have

Real Marketing 13.2

Social Networks in the Arab World

Social networks are growing in popularity in the Arab world. Businesses are increasingly using Facebook, LinkedIn, and Twitter to capitalize on a new opportunity to reach their target markets effectively.

The introduction of Arabic on Facebook encouraged Arab users to join and extensively use the service. **Figure 13.4** shows the growth in Facebook usage that occurred from May 2010 to June 2010, and from September 2009 to October 2010. The number of Egyptian Facebook users increased by 76.3 percent from September 2009 to June 2010.

The advertising features in Facebook allow companies to choose which network to target (for example, universities, schools, regions). Moreover, companies can focus on the appropriate demographics (gender, age) and customize their offers and messages accordingly to suit the targeted segments. Online marketing is appealing to companies because they find it cost-effective, and because it provides valuable information on consumers' responses and reactions.

There are many examples of companies in the Arab world that are using social networks to advertise and promote their products. Moreover, there are businesses that are primarily established on Facebook and fully depend on their social network presence to expand and grow.

Large companies have recognized the growth of social networks in the region

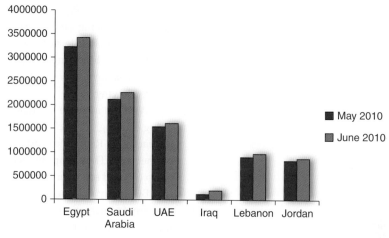

FIGURE | 13.4

Facebook Usage Growth in the Arab World

Source: InsideFacebook.com.

and have started to include online advertisements, fan pages, groups, and events in their communication plans. Examples of companies with fan pages in the Arab world include Coca-Cola Egypt (207,000 members); Pepsi Arabia (335,000 members); Zain (190,000 members); and Vodafone Egypt (662,000 members). These large numbers, correct as of May 2011, indicate how close loyal consumers have become to companies' news, promotional activities, and offers.

Similarly, small businesses have expanded on Facebook. In the Arab world, particularly in Egypt, many photographers market their services through social networks. Their fan pages indicate their popularity and the quality of their work. Examples of new Egyptian photographers who are benefiting from social networks and have large fan pages include Ahmed Hayman (10,900 members); Fadi Gwanni (10,100 members); and Timothy E. Kaldas (8,000 members). For photographers, it is very important that customers can see samples of their artwork, and more importantly, provide them with immediate feedback and reviews. For this reason, photography is one of several professions that have been significantly stimulated by the growth of social networks in the region.

Sources: Data from Inside Facebook, www.insidefacebook.com; Facebook profiles of various Arab countries, accessed at www.facebook.com; Kermit Pattison, "How to Market Your Business with Facebook," *The New York Times*, November 11, 2009, www.nytimes.com.

arisen that give consumers online places to meet, socialize, and exchange views and information. These days, it seems, almost everyone is buddying up on MySpace or Facebook, tuning into the day's hottest videos at YouTube, or even living a surprisingly real fantasy life as an avatar on Second Life. And, of course, wherever consumers meet, marketers will surely follow. More and more marketers are now starting to ride the huge social networking wave.

Marketers can engage in online communities in two ways: They can participate in existing web communities or they can set up their own. Joining existing networks seems easiest. Thus, many major brands—from Burger King and Coca-Cola, to Nokia, Toyota, and Mango—have set up Facebook pages and profiles. Cook Door, for instance, has amassed more than 60,000 Facebook 'friends,' fellow users who have chosen to associate themselves with this profile. Similarly, the Apple Students group on Facebook, which offers information and deals on Apple products, has more than 500,000 members. **Real Marketing 13.2** showcases a variety of social networks in the Arab world.

Many companies are now launching their own targeted web communities, such as the Nike Plus website, where thousands of runners upload, track, and compare their performances.

Although the large online social networks such as MySpace and Facebook have grabbed most of the headlines, a new breed of more focused niche networks has recently emerged. These more focused networks cater to the needs of smaller communities of like-minded people, making them ideal vehicles for marketers who want to target special interest groups.

But participating successfully in existing online social networks presents challenges. First, online social networks are new and results are hard to measure. Most companies are still experimenting with how to use them effectively. Secondly, such web communities are largely user controlled. The company's goal is to make the brand a part of consumers' conversations and their lives. However, marketers can't simply muscle their way into consumers' online interactions—they need to earn the right to be there. "You're talking about conversations between groups of friends," says one analyst. "And in those conversations a brand has no right to be there, unless the conversation is already about that brand." Says another expert, "Being force-fed irrelevant content, or feeling tricked into taking in a brand, is a major turn-off." Rather than intruding, marketers must learn to become a valued part of the online experience.[40]

When it comes to online networks, it's not enough just to be there. For example, when Toyota's Scion first opened a Second Life showroom last year, it quickly became a top destination. But only a few months later, Second Life residents had largely deserted the showroom. Toyota's mistake? It failed to understand that driving adds little value in a virtual world where Second Life avatars can walk underwater, fly, and 'beam' themselves around. Instead, as in any other marketing endeavor, companies participating in web communities must learn how to add value for consumers in order to capture value in return.

To avoid the mysteries and challenges of building a presence on existing online social networks, many companies are now launching their own targeted web communities. For example, Coca-Cola has developed a Sprite Yard mobile phone network—available to web-ready phones—where members can set up profiles, post pictures, and meet new friends. On Nike's Nike Plus website, some 200,000 runners upload, track, and compare their performances. More than half visit the site at least four times a week, and Nike plans eventually to have 15 percent or more of the world's 100 million runners actively participating in the Nike Plus online community.

Using Email

Email is an important online marketing tool. A recent study of ad, brand, and marketing managers found that nearly half of all the companies surveyed use email marketing to reach customers.[41]

To compete effectively in this ever-more-cluttered email environment, marketers are designing 'enriched' email messages—animated, interactive, and personalized messages full of streaming audio and video. Then, they are targeting these attention-grabbers more carefully to those who want them and will act upon them.

Spam
Unsolicited, unwanted commercial email messages.

But there's a dark side to the growing use of email marketing. The explosion of **spam**—unsolicited, unwanted commercial email messages that clog up our email boxes—has produced consumer irritation and frustration. In 2009 for the first time, the total number of spam emails sent worldwide surpassed the number of person-to-person emails. According to one research company, spam now accounts for between 80 to 95 percent of all email sent.[42] Email marketers walk a fine line between adding value for consumers and being intrusive.

To address these concerns, most legitimate marketers now practice *permission-based email marketing,* sending email pitches only to customers who 'opt in.' Financial services firms such as Charles Schwab use configurable email systems that let customers choose what they want to get. Others, such as Yahoo! or Amazon.com, include long lists of opt-in boxes for different categories of marketing material. Amazon.com targets opt-in customers with a limited number of helpful "we thought you'd like to know" messages based on their expressed preferences and previous purchases. Few customers object and many actually welcome such promotional messages.

When used properly, email can be the ultimate direct marketing medium. Blue-chip marketers such as Coca-Cola, Marriott, Thomas Cook, and others use it regularly, and with great success. Email lets these marketers send highly targeted, tightly personalized, relationship-building messages to consumers who actually *want* to receive them.

Given its targeting effectiveness and low costs, email can be an outstanding marketing investment. In the U.S., according to the Direct Marketing Association, email marketing produces a return on investment 40 to 50 percent higher than other forms of direct-marketing media.[43]

The Promise and Challenges of Online Marketing

Online marketing continues to offer both great promise and many challenges for the future. Its most ardent apostles still envision a time when the Internet and online marketing will replace magazines, newspapers, and even stores as sources for information and buying. Most marketers, however, hold a more realistic view. To be sure, online marketing will become a successful business model for some companies—Internet firms such as Amazon.com, eBay, and Google; and direct marketing companies such as Dell. However, for most companies, online marketing will remain just one important approach to the marketplace that works alongside other approaches in a fully integrated marketing mix.

Despite the many challenges, companies large and small are quickly integrating online marketing into their marketing strategies and mixes. As it continues to grow, online marketing will prove to be a powerful direct marketing tool for improving sales, communicating company and product information, delivering products and services, and building deeper customer relationships.

Author Comment | Although we mostly benefit from direct marketing, like most other things in life, it has its dark side as well. Marketers and customers alike must guard against irritating or harmful direct marketing practices.

Public Policy Issues in Direct Marketing (pp 390–392)

Direct marketers and their customers usually enjoy mutually rewarding relationships. Occasionally, however, a darker side emerges. The aggressive and sometimes dishonest tactics of a few direct marketers can bother or harm consumers, giving the entire industry a bad reputation. Abuses range from simple excesses that irritate consumers to instances of unfair practices or even outright deception and fraud. The direct marketing industry has also faced growing invasion-of-privacy concerns, and online marketers must deal with Internet security issues.

Irritation, Unfairness, Deception, and Fraud

Direct marketing excesses sometimes annoy or offend consumers. Most of us dislike direct-response television commercials that are too loud, too long, and too insistent. Our mailboxes fill up with unwanted junk mail, our email boxes bulge with unwanted spam, and our computer screens flash with unwanted banner or pop-under ads.

Beyond irritating consumers, some direct marketers have been accused of taking unfair advantage of impulsive or less-sophisticated buyers. Television shopping channels and program-long 'infomercials' targeting television-addicted shoppers seem to be the worst culprits. They feature smooth-talking hosts, elaborately staged demonstrations, claims of drastic price reductions, 'while they last' time limitations, and unequaled ease of purchase to inflame buyers who have low sales resistance.

Phishing is a common form of Internet fraud, involving identity theft.

Worse yet, so-called 'heat merchants' design mailers and write copy intended to mislead buyers. Even well-known direct mailers have been accused of deceiving consumers. A few years back, sweepstakes promoter Publishers Clearing House paid US$52 million to settle accusations that its high-pressure mailings confused or misled consumers, especially the elderly, into believing that they had won prizes or would win if they bought the company's magazines.[44]

Fraudulent schemes, such as investment scams or phony collections for charity, have also multiplied in recent years. *Internet fraud*, including identity theft and financial scams, has become a serious problem. Last year alone, the U.S. Federal Internet Crime Complaint Center (IC3) received more than 90,000 complaints related to Internet fraud involving monetary loss, with a total dollar loss of US$239 million.[45]

One common form of Internet fraud is *phishing*, a type of identity theft that uses deceptive emails and fraudulent websites to fool users into divulging their personal data. According to email security firm MessageLabs, 1 in 87 emails is now tagged as a phishing scam, compared with 1 in 500 a year ago. Although many consumers are now aware of such schemes, phishing can be extremely costly to those caught in the net. It also damages the brand identities of legitimate online marketers who have worked to build user confidence in web and email transactions.[46]

Many consumers also worry about *online security*. They fear that unscrupulous snoopers will eavesdrop on their online transactions, picking up personal information or intercepting credit and debit card numbers. In a recent survey, 68 percent of participants said they were concerned that their credit or debit card information will be stolen if they use their cards for online purchases. More than one-third also see the Internet as the medium most likely to result in identity theft. [47] Internet shoppers are also concerned about contracting annoying or harmful viruses, spyware, and other malware (malicious software). A recent Google study of 4.5 million websites found that 10 percent of them were downloading malware:[48]

> Spyware programs track where you go on the Internet and clutter your screen with annoying pop-up advertisements for everything from pornography to wireless phone plans. Spyware can get stuck in your computer's hard drive as you shop, chat, or download a song. It might arrive attached to that clever video you just nabbed at no charge. Web security company McAfee estimates that nearly three-quarters of all sites listed in response to Internet searches for popular phrases like "free screen savers" or "digital music" attempt to install some form of advertising software in visitors' computers. Once lodged there, spyware can sap a PC's processing power, slow its functioning, and even cause it to crash.

Another Internet marketing concern is that of *access by vulnerable or unauthorized groups*. For example, marketers of adult-oriented materials have found it difficult to restrict access by minors. For example, 13 percent of the respondents in a recent *Consumer Reports* magazine survey had children in their household registered as MySpace users who were under the online community's official minimum age of 14. The survey also indicated that many parents haven't prepared their children for potential online risks.[49]

Invasion of Privacy

Invasion of privacy is perhaps the toughest public policy issue now confronting the direct marketing industry. Consumers often benefit from database marketing—they receive more offers that are closely matched to their interests. However, many critics worry that marketers may know *too* much about consumers' lives and that they may use this knowledge to take unfair advantage of consumers. At some point, they claim, the extensive use of databases intrudes on consumer privacy.

These days, it seems that almost every time consumers enter a sweepstake, apply for a credit card, visit a website, or order products by mail, telephone, or the Internet, their names enter some company's already huge database. Using sophisticated computer technologies, direct marketers can use these databases to 'microtarget' their selling efforts. *Online privacy* causes special concerns. Most online marketers have become skilled at collecting and analyzing detailed consumer information. For example, behavioral tracking systems use data about consumers' web travels to deliver relevant ads to them. As web tracking technology grows in sophistication, digital privacy experts worry that unscrupulous marketers will use such information to take unfair advantage of unknowing customers.

Some consumers and policy makers worry that the ready availability of information may leave consumers open to abuse if companies make unauthorized use of the information in marketing their products or exchanging databases with other companies. For example, they ask, should phone companies be allowed to sell marketers the names of customers who frequently call the toll-free numbers of catalog companies? Should credit card companies be allowed to make data on their millions of cardholders worldwide available to merchants who accept their cards? Is it right for credit bureaus to compile and sell lists of people who have recently applied for credit cards—people who are considered prime direct marketing targets because of their spending behavior? Or is it right for governments to sell the names and addresses of driver's license holders, along with height, weight, and gender information, allowing apparel retailers to target tall or overweight people with special clothing offers?

In their drives to build databases, companies sometimes get carried away. For example, Microsoft caused substantial privacy concerns when one version of its Windows software used a Registration Wizard that sneaked into users' computers. When users went online to register, without their knowledge, Microsoft 'read' the configurations of their PCs to learn about the major software products they were running. Users protested loudly and Microsoft abandoned the practice.

REVIEWING Objectives AND KEY Terms

Let's revisit this chapter's key concepts. This chapter is the last of three chapters covering the final marketing mix element—promotion. The previous chapters dealt with advertising, publicity, personal selling, and sales promotion. This one investigates the fast-growing field of direct and online marketing.

OBJECTIVE 1 Define direct marketing and discuss its benefits to customers and companies. (pp 370–373)

Direct marketing consists of direct connections with carefully targeted individual consumers to both obtain an immediate response and cultivate lasting customer relationships. Using detailed databases, direct marketers tailor their offers and communications to the needs of narrowly defined segments or even individual buyers.

For buyers, direct marketing is convenient, easy to use, and private. It gives buyers ready access to a wealth of products and information, at home and around the globe. Direct marketing is also immediate and interactive, allowing buyers to create exactly

the configuration of information, products, or services they desire, then order them on the spot. For sellers, direct marketing is a powerful tool for building customer relationships. Using database marketing, today's marketers can target small groups or individual consumers, tailor offers to individual needs, and promote these offers through personalized communications. It also offers them a low-cost, efficient alternative for reaching their markets. As a result of these advantages to both buyers and sellers, direct marketing has become the fastest-growing form of marketing.

OBJECTIVE 2 Identify and discuss the major forms of direct marketing. (pp 373–379)

The main forms of direct marketing include personal selling, direct-mail marketing, catalog marketing, telephone marketing, direct-response television marketing, kiosk marketing, and online marketing. We discussed personal selling in the previous chapter.

Direct-mail marketing, the largest form of direct marketing, consists of the company sending an offer, announcement, reminder, or other item to a person at a specific address. Recently, new forms of mail delivery have become popular, such as email and text message marketing. Some marketers rely on catalog marketing—selling through catalogs mailed to a select list of customers, made available in stores, or accessed on the web. Telephone marketing consists of using the telephone to sell directly to consumers. Direct-response television marketing has two forms: direct-response advertising (or infomercials) and home shopping channels. Kiosks are information and ordering machines that direct marketers place in stores, airports, and other locations. In recent years, a number of new digital direct marketing technologies have emerged, including mobile marketing, podcasts and vodcasts, and interactive television. Online marketing involves online channels that digitally link sellers with consumers.

OBJECTIVE 3 **Explain how companies have responded to the Internet and other powerful new technologies with online marketing strategies. (pp 379–384)**

Online marketing is the fastest-growing form of direct marketing. The Internet enables consumers and companies to access and share huge amounts of information with just a few mouse clicks. In turn, the Internet has given marketers a whole new way to create value for customers and build customer relationships. It's hard to find a company today that doesn't have a substantial web marketing presence.

Online consumer buying continues to grow at a healthy rate. Many Arab online users now also use the Internet to shop. Perhaps more importantly, the Internet influences offline shopping. Thus, smart marketers are employing integrated multichannel strategies that use the web to drive sales to other marketing channels.

OBJECTIVE 4 **Discuss how companies go about conducting online marketing to profitably deliver more value to customers. (pp 384–390)**

Companies of all types are now engaged in online marketing. The Internet gave birth to the *click-only* dot-coms, which operate only online. In addition, many traditional brick-and-mortar companies have now added online marketing operations, transforming themselves into *click-and-mortar* competitors. Many click-and-mortar companies are now having more online success than their click-only competitors.

Companies can conduct online marketing in any of four ways: by creating a website, placing ads and promotions online, setting up or participating in web communities and online social networks, or using email. The first step typically is to set up a website. Beyond simply setting up a site, however, companies must make their sites engaging, easy to use, and useful in order to attract visitors, hold them, and bring them back again.

Online marketers can use various forms of online advertising and promotion to build their Internet brands or to attract visitors to their websites. Forms of online promotion include online display advertising, search-related advertising, content sponsorships, alliances and affiliate programs, and viral marketing—the Internet version of word-of-mouth marketing. Online marketers can also participate in online social networks and other web communities, which take advantage of the C2C properties of the web. Finally, email marketing has become a fast-growing tool for both B2C and B2B marketers. Whatever direct marketing tools they use, marketers must work hard to integrate them into a cohesive marketing effort.

OBJECTIVE 5 **Overview the public policy and ethical issues presented by direct marketing. (pp 390–392)**

Direct marketers and their customers usually enjoy mutually rewarding relationships. Sometimes, however, direct marketing presents a darker side. The aggressive and sometimes dishonest tactics of a few direct marketers can bother or harm consumers, giving the entire industry a bad reputation. Abuses range from simple excesses that irritate consumers to instances of unfair practices or even outright deception and fraud. The direct marketing industry has also faced growing concerns about invasion-of-privacy and Internet security issues. Such concerns call for strong action by marketers and public policymakers to curb direct marketing abuses. In the end, most direct marketers want the same things that consumers want: honest and well-designed marketing offers targeted only toward consumers who will appreciate and respond to them.

KEY Terms

OBJECTIVE 1

Direct marketing (p 370)
Customer database (p 373)

OBJECTIVE 2

Direct-mail marketing (p 374)
Telephone marketing (p 375)
Direct-response television marketing (p 375)

OBJECTIVE 3

Online marketing (p 379)
Click-only companies (p 379)
Click-and-mortar companies (p 379)
Business-to-consumer (B2C) online marketing (p 380)
Business-to business (B2B) online marketing (p 382)
Consumer-to-consumer (C2C) online marketing (p 382)

Consumer-to-business (C2B) online marketing (p 383)

OBJECTIVE 4

Corporate (brand) website (p 384)
Marketing website (p 385)
Online advertising (p 386)
Viral marketing (p 387)
Online social networks (p 387)
Spam (p 389)

DISCUSSING & APPLYING THE Concepts

Discussing the Concepts

1. Discuss the benefits of direct marketing to both buyers and sellers.

2. A local oriental rug cleaning company has contacted you for advice on setting up its customer database. It needs this database for customer-relationship management and for direct marketing of new products and services. Describe the qualities and features it must consider for an effective database and how it might go about creating one.

3. Name and describe the major forms of direct marketing.

4. Explain the ways in which companies can conduct online marketing.

5. Compare and contrast the different forms of online advertising. What factors should a company consider in deciding among these different forms?

6. Why is privacy a tough public policy issue confronting the direct marketing industry and what is being done to address this issue?

Applying the Concepts

1. Visit your favorite retail website and evaluate the site according to the seven Cs of effective website design.

2. Visit Nike's website at http://nikeid.nike.com and design your own shoe. Print out your shoe design and bring it to class. Do you think the price is appropriate for the value received from being able to customize your shoe? Identify and describe two other websites that allow buyers to customize products.

3. Consumers in some countries can register with do-not-call registries to avoid unwanted phone solicitations from marketers. But what can consumers do to reduce unsolicited mail and email? Find out how consumers can do this and report your findings.

FOCUS ON Technology

A 2008 survey of the Arab world's major banks across the UAE, Saudi Arabia, Lebanon, Kuwait, and Bahrain looked at transactional security and risk mitigation: online identity theft, third-party online attacks, and online financial frauds. Over 20 percent of banks reported they had been the victims of phishing during 2007. Over 70 percent of banks did not have a dedicated budget for online security. Recently there have been major increases in identity theft and online financial frauds, including external and internal frauds. In response to the findings of the survey, the banks have begun looking at identity management, fraud prevention, and risk management. Actual awareness of the problem within the banks is very low, with only 75 percent of the banks being aware that there are major problems facing them.

1. Find articles about two data security breaches in your country. How did the breaches occur, and who is potentially affected by them?

2. What can organizations and businesses do to ensure adequate data security for their members and customers? What can consumers do to protect themselves if their personal information has been compromised?

FOCUS ON Ethics

Technoethics, a field of study that examines ethical issues related to technology, has recently been applied to many areas in Internet marketing. Blogs are an example of a growing Internet marketing technology that presents many ethical issues. For instance, is it ethical for a company to ask consumers to blog favorably about a product? Is it ethical for companies to pay these consumers to blog? Should a company fire an employee who blogs negatively about the company? Other technologies created by leading Internet marketers to improve customer satisfaction on the Internet are also raising issues. Amazon.com, one of the most reputable Internet marketers, has been criticized for its wish list, which lets customers list books and other products they would like to receive from friends and family. It seems harmless, even helpful. But what many consumers don't know is that the wish list can be viewed by anyone, and that such information can be used to create databases of everyone from apparent liberals to gun owners and teenage girls.

Companies on the cutting edge of technology, like Amazon.com, are constantly criticized for having their updated technology fail on them. Likewise, the immensely popular online social network MySpace is currently suffering with a problem by which some users' sites have been re-routed to adult content sites.

1. Is it ethical for an advertiser to pay a consumer to blog favorably about a product? What about to fire an employee for presenting negative issues on his or her blog?

2. What can companies do to reduce the negative public relations effects of such technoethical issues?

MARKETING BY THE Numbers

Telemarketing is the new sales force. The practice can cost as little as 10 percent of the costs of dispatching a salesperson, keeping the person on the road, and paying all of his or her incidental costs. What is more, a telemarketer can speak to more decision makers each day, arguably nine or ten times as many as a conventional salesperson. Of course, businesses are interested in switching over to telemarketers. But are they right to do so in the long run?

1. Use the ROI calculator at this website www.marketingtoday. com/tools/roi_calculator.htm and insert the following telemarketing numbers in the "Input Data" section:

   Number of customers being called (use "number of pieces you are mailing or emailing"): 1,000

Total program costs: US$30,000

There will be a 20 percent response rate, and a 5 percent purchase rate

Average profit per sale: US$10,000

What ROI would a company with these numbers achieve by using telemarketers versus regular salespeople?

2. Research the use of call centers and telemarketing in your country. What key trends do you see?

VIDEO Case

Google

It's mind-boggling to think that only 15 years ago, a company like Google was not within the realm of possibility. Yet when the World Wide Web went online, the foundation was set for Google's mission: to organize the world's information and make it universally accessible and useful.

Google was not the first search engine. But it has become the most successful. Its primary reason for success has been its customer-focused strategy. For Google, there are two basic types of customers. For the Internet search services customer, Google has been relentless in developing products that are both innovative and user-friendly. Google now offers dozens of services, including foreign language translation, stock quotes, maps, phone book listings, images, video, and news headlines. And the most amazing thing about these services? They are all free.

Google can offer all of its services free of charge because of its second customer, advertisers. Google has turned Internet advertising upside down. Today, products such as AdWords (keyword search advertising) and AdSense (a method that generates only the most relevant ads for client websites) are breaking new ground because they result in ads that are actually useful and helpful to consumers.

After viewing the Google video, answer the following online marketing questions:

1. Brainstorm the many benefits that Google provides for consumers.

2. Brainstorm the many benefits that Google provides for online marketers.

3. Visit www.google.com. For each of the four major e-marketing domains, discuss Google's presence.

COMPANY Case

ELSOU2.COM: THE FIRST ONLINE SUPERMARKET IN THE ARAB WORLD

The idea of the online grocery was not introduced to the Arab world before Ms Perihan Abou Zeid, cofounder of Elsou2.com, brought it to Egypt in January 2010. Within nine months Elsou2.com, the only online grocery in the market, was able to cover a large part of Cairo. This demonstrated that Elsou2.com was not only able to increase its market share rapidly, but was also, in the process, creating a new market demand.

THE BUSINESS IDEA

After graduating from the American University in Cairo, Abou Zeid traveled to Canada. Here, she realized how important online grocery stores were to Canadians; they had grown rapidly in popularity due to the long distances between stores and homes. She began to think about introducing the concept to Egypt, comparing the situations in Egypt and Canada by analyzing the need of the target market. The business model had succeeded in Canada because it stressed convenience and solved the problem of consumers having to drive long distances to get their groceries. Similarly, in Egypt, traveling to supermarkets and grocery stores is often problematic because of busy traffic and the lack of parking areas, so convenience would be a significant benefit to Egyptian consumers too.

After some basic analysis, she started to talk to experts from different disciplines in order to assess the feasibility of the idea. She asked for input from marketing, computer science, and e-commerce experts in order to build a comprehensive picture for the new business.

THE PARTNERSHIP

Abou Zeid contacted her friend Sherif Saleh, a computer science major and expert in this field. She presented the idea to him and after detailed discussions both were excited to turn the idea into a reality, although they were aware of the operations problems that would arise. They decided to move to the research phase to identify market gaps and opportunities, analyzing consumers' perceptions of the idea and willingness to try an online service. Research findings were fascinating and encouraged the partners to establish the new business. They found that the number of Internet users in Egypt was increasing at a high rate (see figure below) presenting an opportunity for more players in the retail market.

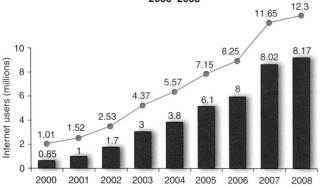

Internet Penetration and Number of Users in Egypt, 2000–2008

Source: Ministry of Communication and Information Technology (MCIT) in Egypt, "The Future of the Internet Economy in Egypt," March 2009, www.egyptictindicators.gov.eg.

MARKET OPPORTUNITY

The figures below indicate a significant increase in Internet penetration in Egypt as well as a high level of usage (50 percent of users access the Internet daily and spend 1–8 hours online). These findings motivated Abou Zeid and Saleh to launch the project as soon as they could. Another finding regarding the retail market in Egypt also encouraged them to proceed; as shown below, the expansion of the retail industry was booming in the country and projected to grow to 3.5 times that of the UAE.

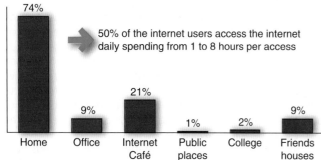

Internet Usage in Egypt

50% of the internet users access the internet daily spending from 1 to 8 hours per access

Source: "Internet Usage in Egypt," 2009, Central Agency for Public Mobilisation and Statistics (CAPMAS), National Bank of Egypt.

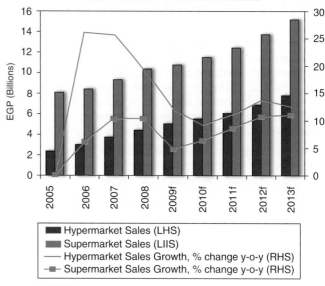

Egypt Hypermarket and Supermarket Sales—Historical Data and Forecasts

- Hypermarket Sales (LHS)
- Supermarket Sales (LIIS)
- Hypermarket Sales Growth, % change y-o-y (RHS)
- Supermarket Sales Growth, % change y-o-y (RHS)

f = BMI forecast.

Source: "Egypt Food and Drink Report Q4 2008," *Business Monitor International*, October 2008, www.researchandmarkets.com. "Expansion of the Egyptian Retail Industry," 2009, Central Agency for Public Mobilisation and Statistics (CAPMAS), National Bank of Egypt.

LAUNCHING THE BUSINESS

After they had completed the initial research phase, they moved toward turning the business opportunity into reality. They chose the name 'ElSou2.com' based on research, and started working on ElSou2.com's vision, mission, and business model. The company's vision included penetrating the Egyptian market and then expanding in the Arab world. Its primary aim was "becoming the market leader of online grocery in the region." The company's unique selling proposition focused on convenience.

TARGET MARKET AND PAYMENT METHOD

ElSou2.com targets young Egyptian women aged 25 to 45 years old. The payment method is cash on delivery, which suits the target market in the region, because paying online via Visa or MasterCard is perceived as a highly risky method, with consumers fearful of scams. ElSou2.com plans to introduce the credit card payment method in 2011, once customers trust the service, in order to facilitate the purchasing process as well as increase options to customers.

PRODUCT OFFERING

ElSou2.com offers a wide range of products to encourage customers to conduct all their purchases online. Product offerings include beverages; fruits and vegetables; spices, seasoning and herbs; condiments, sauces and salad dressings; oil and vinegar; dairy, eggs and seafood; personal and house care; infant and childcare; bakery and bread; cereal and breakfast foods; grains, pasta and sides; and more.

COMPETITION

At the end of 2010 there was still no direct competition to ElSou2.com in Egypt. However, it certainly faced indirect competition from traditional retailers, such as supermarkets, hypermarkets, and groceries. Moreover, several supermarkets and hypermarkets offer a delivery service when customers order over the phone. It is also anticipated that other companies will join ElSou2.com in the online market once demand grows. Other online businesses will probably consider expanding their services and entering the online grocery market.

THE OPERATION

Operations are the most challenging component in Elsou2.com's business process because the company promises its customers a high level of convenience and a fast delivery service. For this reason, they modified the workflow 20 times until they reached the maximum efficiency and effectiveness.

The diagram below illustrates Elsou2.com's online orders supply chain. The company developed a process that guarantees

Elsou2.com Online Orders Supply Chain

convenience and fast deliveries to all customers. The operation for the user is very simple. But once the user completes his or her order, the back office works to deliver the order in the least possible time. As shown in the figure, the technology team prints out the reports: one for the accounting department and one for the warehouse operator. The accountant issues a receipt and the warehouse prepares the order. Then, the order with the payment collection summary is given to the delivery staff, and within one to three hours, the order is delivered to the consumer. Although the operations part is challenging, it is the heart of the business, ensuring that the value proposition promised to consumers is met.

THE FUTURE

ElSou2.com is trying to build a strong brand and establish leadership in the market in order to expand into different geographic areas in Egypt and across the Arab world. The forecasted income statement below assumes growth rates of 15–30 percent in the coming three years, as well as significant growth in advertising revenues. Also, the pricing strategy is aggressive at the beginning, and it is assumed that significant gross profit margins will be realized in future years. In a challenging and unpredictable market, the company should be very careful in deploying its marketing strategies and capitalizing on the growing online market, while protecting its business against anticipated competitive moves.

ElSou2.com has great potential to grow; yet the market in Egypt is still developing, and the potential expansion into other areas of the Arab world will be challenging.

Forecasted Income Statement

		7%	15%	20%	30%
Yearly Growth Rate (Orders)		7%	15%	20%	30%
Yearly Growth Rate (Ads)		30%	50%	70%	40%
Sales	**Year 1**	**Year 2**	**Year 3**	**Year 4**	**Year 5**
Orders	3,363,000.00	3,598,410.00	4,138,171.50	4,965,805.80	6,455,547.54
Advertising	10,000.00	13,000.00	19,500.00	33,150.00	46,410.00
Total Revenues	3,373,000.00	3,611,410.00	4,157,671.50	4,998,955.80	6,501,957.54
Expenses					
Cost of Goods Sold	3,295,750.00	3,238,582.00	3,517,465.28	3,972,677.79	5,164,484.44
Marketing	33,730.00	36,114.10	41,576.72	49,989.56	65,019.58
Electricity & Gas	3600	3780	3969	4167.45	4375.82
Salaries	27000	28350	39767.5	31255.875	32818.66875
Rental	12000	13200	14520	15972	17569.2
Total Expenses	3,372,080.00	3,320,023.10	3,607,298.49	4,074,062.67	5,284,267.71
Total Expenses as a % of Sales	100%	92%	87%	81%	81%
Gross Profit	920.00	291,383.90	550,373.01	924,893.13	1,217,689.83
Profit Margin	0%	8%	13%	19%	19%
Net Profit (Loss) After Tax (20%)	736.00	233,107.12	440,298.41	739,914.50	974,151.87

Amount in EGP		Year 1	Year 2	Year 3	Year 4	Year 5
Initial Investment	(245,150.00)					
Project Annual Income		736.00	233,107.12	440,298.41	739,914.50	974,151.87
Accumulated Income		(244,414.00)	(11,306.88)	428,991.53	1,168,906.03	2,143,057.89
Total Expenses		3,372,080.00	3,320,026.10	3,607,298.49	4,074,062.67	5,284,267.71
Break-even Month		12				

Initial Investment	Year 1		Year 2	Year 3	Year 4	Year 5
-245150	736.00		233,107.12	440,298.41	739,914.50	974,151.87
IRR		85%				
ROIC		974%				

Elsou2.com's Forecasted Income Statement

Questions for Discussion

Conduct a brief analysis of the marketing environment and the forces shaping the development of ElSou2.com.

1. Discuss ElSou2.com's business model. Which benefits are most important in terms of creating value for consumers in the short and long term?

2. Which e-marketing tools would you recommend the company use to grow its business? Why?

3. What are the major challenges that the company is expected to face?

4. What recommendations can you make for ElSou2.com to realize future growth?

Sources: This case is authored by Laila Yassin and Ahmed Tolba, based on an interview with Perihan Abou Zeid, ElSou2.com cofounder. Copyright El-Khazindar Business Research and Case Center (KCC), the American University in Cairo.

Chapter 14

Part 1   Defining Marketing and the Marketing Process (Chapters 1, 2)
Part 2   Understanding the Marketplace and Consumers (Chapters 3, 4, 5, 6)
Part 3   Designing a Customer-Driven Strategy and Mix (Chapters 7, 8, 9, 10, 11, 12, 13, 14)
Part 4   Extending Marketing (Chapters 15, 16, 17)

Managing Marketing Channels

Chapter PREVIEW

We now arrive at the third marketing mix tool—distribution. Firms rarely work alone in creating value for customers and building profitable customer relationships. Instead, most are only a single link in a larger supply chain and marketing channel. As such, an individual firm's success depends not only on how well *it* performs but also on how well its *entire marketing channel* competes with competitors' channels. To be good at customer relationship management, a company must also be good at partner relationship management. The first part of this chapter explores the nature of marketing channels and the marketer's channel design and management decisions. We then examine physical distribution—or logistics—an area that is growing dramatically in importance and sophistication. In the latter part of this chapter we'll look more closely at the major channel intermediaries—retailers, wholesalers, agents, and distributors.

We'll start with a look at a company that faces tremendous challenges, not because of its product but because of the location of the producers.

Al Zaytoun is a nonprofit community interest organization-founded in 2004 to create and develop a UK market for artisan Palestinian produce. The company is a co-operative and a member of the International Fair Trade Association. As a member, its objectives lie with the welfare of the producing communities. It works closely with olive oil co-operatives, producers, and associated businesses, representing 14 co-operatives (6 of which are organic) and a total of 1,700 olive oil producers. Al Zaytoun is one of the organizations which supply olive oil to Zaytoun in the United Kingdom.

Zaytoun's goal is to enable Palestinian farmers to receive a fair price for the olive oil they harvest. Its key objectives are as follows:

- To establish co-operatives that enable farmers to improve the quality of their oil.
- To increase sales internationally that generate a valuable source of income through growing distribution and wholesale networks.
- To continue the campaign that highlights the impact of the Occupation and the Wall on poverty for farmers in Palestine.

Olive oil is a major crop for the Palestinians and provides work for around 65 percent of the population. It has become far more difficult to grow and harvest the crop due to the continued problems in the region. Due to a lack of access to international markets, around half of the olive oil crop is wasted. Ultimately, the goal is for the olive oil producers to gain access to the international market by creating a marketing channel and new supply chain. There have been key advances:

- Supported co-operatives have eradicated the olive fly.
- Oil production increased 40 percent between 2005 and 2008.

- Local committees train farmers in harvest, storage, and production techniques.
- Equipment such as stainless steel tanks have been improved to maintain the oil's quality.

In 2007, Zaytoun managed to sell 70,000 liters of Palestinian olive oil. This compares favorably with the 15,000 liters sold in the first year (2004). Because the business has to be sustainable, volunteers have worked for the business for two years without pay, yet support is there for the burgeoning operation. The Manchester-based Olive Co-op, which runs responsible tourism study tours to the West Bank, and the fair trade co-op Equal Exchange have been instrumental in helping the business create a transparent supply chain. Cafédirect's chairman, Martin Meteyard, was among the supporters to underwrite a nearly US$40,000 loan taken out by the business to help Palestinian farmers make the necessary investments that come with increasing production to deal with larger orders.

The supply chain is fragile. A container of oil that was meant to arrive in the United Kingdom for Christmas 2004 was held up in Italy and did not arrive until February 2005. The business also finds it difficult to explain to Palestinian farmers that British customers

> **Al Zaytoun is a nonprofit organization working to ensure Palestinian farmers receive a fair price for the olive oil they have harvested.**

(and others) are prepared to pay premium prices for the olive oil when there are cheaper alternatives. The business has also discovered that it is not always wise to use the political situation in the region as a marketing tool. Gardener recalled a situation when a retailer was presented with the first versions of the bottle labels: "We had our labels all printed up with 'Palestinian Olive Oil—Resisting The Occupation.' They liked the oil and wanted to take it, but said very nicely that just 'Produce of Palestine' would do fine for their clientele."

Palestinian olive oil producers face almost insurmountable odds in their production as well as in the transportation of their olives. Israeli authorities have often confiscated or denied access to land, dug up trees, or diverted the water supply.

The olive oil is now officially registered as an organic product. Effectively, this means that it can be exported to the European Union. The oil is bottled by the co-operatives and then transported to the United Kingdom. The majority of the oil is sold in advance through Zaytoun's network of outlets and customers. There are continued delays by customs and checkpoints, which end up reducing the shelf life of the product. The business knows that this is an obstacle that must be overcome if the product is to have a fighting chance of developing a stronger overseas market.

As Zaytoun admits in its marketing materials, "Distribution is the biggest hurdle facing a grassroots initiative like Zaytoun. We owe our success to the many (extra)ordinary individuals from all walks of life, who have come forward and offered to distribute Palestinian olive oil from their homes, their workplaces, churches, mosques, synagogues, and at community events; plus those who have encouraged their food stores to sell our products. We are keen to maintain our 'grassroots' contacts, and will continue to supply solidarity and fair trade distributors."[1]

The project continues to adapt to the environment and the challenges facing it. Step by step problems in the supply chain and the marketing channels are being ironed out. The process may take time to fully develop; however, their own supply chain, as far as local partners are concerned, is now in place: "We source olive oil through all of these suppliers and are developing markets in the U.K. for their other products including: olive oil soap from Nablus, couscous from Gaza, almonds and za'atar from Jenin, and dates from a cooperative near Jericho. Also, Zaytoun's policy is that as far as possible all value-added activities for these products are kept within the Palestinian economy. To this end both the bottling, printing and labeling is done in Palestine. We're also actively working to source all our packaging materials through Palestinian suppliers."[2]

In 2010, Zaytoun was focusing on market access for products from women's co-operatives in Palestine, specifically za'atar, maftoul, and sun-dried tomatoes. Funds from the former Fairtrade Café at St Mary's Church, Islington, London, supported this work.

Al Zaytoun must overcome the issue of a fragile supply chain if it is to successfully conquer overseas markets.

> Olive oil is a major crop for Palestinian farmers, providing much-needed work. However, due to difficulties farmers have in getting their products to the international market, half of the olive oil crop is wasted. There is a fragile supply chain and, as a spokesperson for Al Zaytoun, a nonprofit organization, admits: "Distribution is the biggest hurdle facing a grassroots initiative." There are enormous continuing hurdles in establishing the supply chain.

As the Al Zaytoun story shows, good distribution strategies can contribute strongly to customer value and create competitive advantage for both a firm and its channel partners. It demonstrates that firms cannot bring value to customers by themselves. Instead, they must work closely with other firms in a larger value delivery network.

Author Comment | These are pretty hefty terms for what's really a simple concept: A company can't go it alone in creating customer value. It must work within an entire network of partners to accomplish this task. Individual companies and brands don't compete, their entire value delivery networks do.

Supply Chains and the Value Delivery Network (pp 401–403)

Producing a product or service and making it available to buyers requires building relationships not just with customers, but also with key suppliers and resellers in the company's *supply chain*. This supply chain consists of 'upstream' and 'downstream' partners. Upstream from the company is the set of firms that supply the raw materials, components, parts, information, finances, and expertise needed to create a product or service. Marketers, however, have traditionally focused on the 'downstream' side of the supply chain—on the *marketing channels*

Objective Outline

Value delivery network: In making and marketing iPod Touch products, Apple manages an entire network of people within Apple plus suppliers and resellers outside the company who work effectively together to give final customers "So much to touch."

(or *distribution channels*) that look toward the customer. Downstream marketing channel partners, such as wholesalers and retailers, form a vital connection between the firm and its customers.

The term *supply chain* may be too limited—it takes a *make-and-sell* view of the business. It suggests that raw materials, productive inputs, and factory capacity should serve as the starting point for market planning. A better term would be *demand chain* because it suggests a *sense-and-respond* view of the market. Under this view, planning starts with the needs of target customers, to which the company responds by organizing a chain of resources and activities with the goal of creating customer value.

As defined in Chapter 2, a **value delivery network** is made up of the company, suppliers, distributors, and ultimately customers who 'partner' with each other to improve the performance of the entire system. For example, in making and marketing its iPod Touch products, Apple manages an entire network of people within Apple plus suppliers and resellers outside the company who work together effectively to give final customers "So much to touch."

Value delivery network
The network made up of the company, suppliers, distributors, and ultimately customers who 'partner' with each other to improve the performance of the entire system in delivering customer value.

This chapter focuses on marketing channels—on the downstream side of the value delivery network. We examine four major questions concerning marketing channels: What is the nature of marketing channels and why are they important? How do channel firms interact and organize to do the work of the channel? What problems do companies face in designing and managing their channels? What role do physical distribution and supply chain management play in attracting and satisfying customers? We will also look at marketing channel issues from the viewpoint of retailers and wholesalers.

Author Comment | In this section, we look at the 'downstream' side of the value delivery network—the marketing channel organizations that connect the company and its customers. To understand their value, imagine life without retailers—say, grocery stores or department stores.

The Nature and Importance of Marketing Channels (pp 403–405)

Few producers sell their goods directly to the final users. Instead, most use intermediaries to bring their products to market. They try to forge a **marketing channel** (or **distribution channel**)—a set of interdependent organizations that help make a product or service available for use or consumption by the consumer or business user.

Marketing channel (or distribution channel)
A set of interdependent organizations that help make a product or service available for use or consumption by the consumer or business user.

A company's channel decisions directly affect every other marketing decision. Pricing depends on whether the company works with international chains such as Carrefour or national discount chains such as Union Coop, uses high-quality specialty stores such as Sharaf DG, or sells directly to consumers via the web. The firm's sales force and communications decisions depend on how much persuasion, training, motivation, and support its channel partners need. Whether a company develops or acquires certain new products may depend on how well those products fit the capabilities of its channel members.

Companies often pay too little attention to their distribution channels, sometimes with damaging results. In contrast, many companies have used imaginative distribution systems to *gain* a competitive advantage. FedEx's creative and imposing distribution system made it a leader in express delivery.

Distribution channel decisions often involve long-term commitments to other firms. For example, companies such as Toyota, Nestlé, or Sony can easily change their advertising, pricing, or promotion programs. They can scrap old products and introduce new ones as market tastes demand. But when they set up distribution channels through contracts with franchisees, independent dealers, or large retailers, they cannot readily replace these channels with company-owned stores or websites if conditions change. Therefore, management must design its channels carefully, with an eye on tomorrow's likely selling environment as well as today's.

How Channel Members Add Value

Why do producers give some of the selling job to channel partners? After all, doing so means giving up some control over how and to whom they sell their products. Producers use intermediaries because they create greater efficiency in making goods available to target markets. Through their contacts, experience, specialization, and scale of operation, intermediaries usually offer the firm more than it can achieve on its own.

🔖 **Figure 14.1** shows how using intermediaries can provide economies. **Figure 14.1A** shows three manufacturers, each using direct marketing to reach three customers. This system requires nine different contacts. **Figure 14.1B** shows the three manufacturers working through one distributor, which contacts the three customers. This system requires only six contacts. In this way, intermediaries reduce the amount of work that must be done by both producers and consumers.

From the economic system's point of view, the role of marketing intermediaries is to transform the assortments of products made by producers into the assortments wanted by consumers. Producers make narrow assortments of products in large quantities, but consumers want broad assortments of products in small quantities. Marketing channel members buy large quantities from many producers and break them down into the smaller quantities and broader assortments wanted by consumers.

◥ FIGURE │ 14.1

How Adding a Distributor
Reduces the Number of
Channel Transactions

Marketing channel intermediaries
make buying a lot easier for
consumers. Again, think about
life without grocery retailers. How
would you go about buying that
12-pack of Coke or any of the
hundreds of other items that you
now routinely drop into your
shopping cart?

A. Number of contacts without a distributor
$M \times C = 3 \times 3 = 9$

B. Number of contacts with a distributor
$M + C = 3 + 3 = 6$

For example, Unilever makes millions of bars of Lux soap each day, but you want to
buy only a few bars at a time. So hypermarkets such as Carrefour buy Lux soap by the
truckload and stock it on their stores' shelves. In turn, you can buy a single bar of Lux
soap, along with a shopping cart full of small quantities of toothpaste, shampoo, and other
related products as you need them. Thus, intermediaries play an important role in matching supply and demand.

In making products and services available to consumers, channel members add value
by bridging the major time, place, and possession gaps that separate goods and services
from those who would use them. Members of the marketing channel perform many key
functions. Some help to complete transactions:

- *Information:* Gathering and distributing marketing research and intelligence informa-
  tion about the marketing environment needed for planning and helping the exchange.
- *Promotion:* Developing and spreading persuasive communications about an offer.
- *Contact:* Finding and communicating with prospective buyers.
- *Matching:* Shaping and fitting the offer to the buyer's needs, including activities such
  as manufacturing, grading, assembling, and packaging.
- *Negotiation:* Reaching an agreement on price and other terms of the offer so that owner-
  ship or possession can be transferred.

Others help to fulfill the completed transactions:

- *Physical distribution:* Transporting and storing goods.
- *Financing:* Acquiring and using funds to cover the costs of the channel work.
- *Risk taking:* Assuming the risks of carrying out the channel work.

The question is not *whether* these functions need to be performed—they must be—
but rather *who* will perform them. To the extent that the manufacturer performs these
functions, its costs go up and its prices must be higher. When some of these functions
are shifted to intermediaries, the producer's costs and prices may be lower, but the intermediaries must charge more to cover the costs of their work. In dividing the work of the
channel, the various functions should be given to the channel members who can add the
most value for the cost.

Number of Channel Levels

Channel level

A layer of intermediaries that performs
some work in bringing the product and
its ownership closer to the final buyer.

Companies can design their distribution channels to make products and services available to
customers in different ways. Each layer of marketing intermediaries that performs some work
in bringing the product and its ownership closer to the final buyer is a **channel level**. Because
the producer and the final consumer both perform some work, they are part of every channel.

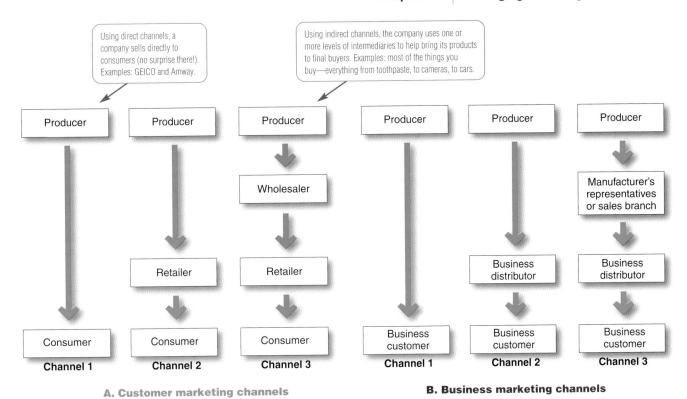

Using direct channels, a company sells directly to consumers (no surprise there!). Examples: GEICO and Amway.

Using indirect channels, the company uses one or more levels of intermediaries to help bring its products to final buyers. Examples: most of the things you buy—everything from toothpaste, to cameras, to cars.

A. Customer marketing channels

B. Business marketing channels

 FIGURE | **14.2** Consumer and Business Marketing Channels

Direct marketing channel
A marketing channel that has no intermediary levels.

Indirect marketing channel
A marketing channel containing one or more intermediary levels.

The *number of intermediary levels* indicates the *length* of a channel. **Figure 14.2A** shows several consumer distribution channels of different lengths. Channel 1, called a **direct marketing channel,** has no intermediary levels; the company sells directly to consumers. In the Arab world, there has been less direct-to-consumer selling than in other global regions, but companies such as VIE in Lebanon and Tianshi in the UAE, Lebanon, and Kuwait are starting to grow. The remaining channels in **Figure 14.2A** are **indirect marketing channels,** containing one or more intermediaries.

 Figure 14.2B shows some common business distribution channels. The business marketer can use its own sales force to sell directly to business customers. Or it can sell to various types of intermediaries, who in turn sell to these customers. Consumer and business marketing channels with even more levels can sometimes be found. From the producer's point of view, a greater number of levels means less control and greater channel complexity. Moreover, all of the institutions in the channel are connected by several types of *flows*. These include the *physical flow* of products, the *flow of ownership*, the *payment flow*, the *information flow*, and the *promotion flow*. These flows can make even channels with only one or a few levels very complex.

Author Comment | Channels are made up of more than just boxes and arrows on paper. They are behavioral systems made up of real companies and people who interact to accomplish their individual and collective goals. Like groups of people, sometimes they work well together and sometimes they don't.

Channel Behavior and Organization (pp 405–411)

Distribution channels are more than simple collections of firms tied together by various flows. They are complex behavioral systems in which people and companies interact to accomplish individual, company, and channel goals. Some channel systems consist only of informal interactions among loosely organized firms. Others consist of formal interactions guided by strong organizational structures. Moreover, channel systems do not stand still— new types of intermediaries emerge and whole new channel systems evolve. Here we look at channel behavior and at how members organize to do the work of the channel.

Channel Behavior

A marketing channel consists of firms that have partnered for their common good. Each channel member depends on the others. For example, a Nokia dealer depends on Nokia to design mobile phones that meet consumer needs. In turn, Nokia depends on the dealer to attract consumers, to persuade them to buy Nokia mobiles, and to service mobiles after the sale. Each Nokia dealer also depends on other dealers to provide good sales and service that will uphold the brand's reputation. In fact, the success of individual Nokia dealers depends on how well the entire Nokia marketing channel competes with the channels of other mobile manufacturers.

Each channel member plays a specialized role in the channel. For example, consumer electronics maker Samsung's role is to produce electronics products that consumers will like and to create demand through advertising. Sharaf DG's role is to display these Samsung products in convenient locations, to answer buyers' questions, and to complete sales. The channel will be most effective when each member assumes the tasks it can do best.

Ideally, because the success of individual channel members depends on overall channel success, all channel firms should work together smoothly. They should understand and accept their roles, co-ordinate their activities, and co-operate to attain overall channel goals. However, individual channel members rarely take such a broad view. Co-operating to achieve overall channel goals sometimes means giving up individual company goals. Although channel members depend on one another, they often act alone in their own short-run best interests. They often disagree on who should do what and for what rewards. Such disagreements over goals, roles, and rewards generate **channel conflict**.

Horizontal conflict occurs among firms at the same level of the channel. For instance, some Nokia dealers in Riyadh might complain that the other dealers in the city steal sales from them by pricing too low or by advertising outside their assigned territories.

Vertical conflict, conflict between different levels of the same channel, is even more common. For example, Goodyear, the tire company, created hard feelings and conflict in its U.S. market with its premier independent-dealer channel when it began selling through mass-merchant retailers:[3]

Channel conflict

Disagreement among marketing channel members on goals and roles—who should do what and for what rewards.

For more than 60 years, Goodyear sold replacement tires in the U.S. exclusively through its premier network of independent Goodyear dealers. Then, in the 1990s, Goodyear shattered tradition and jolted its dealers by agreeing to sell its tires through mass-merchants such as Sears and Wal-Mart, placing dealers in direct competition with the most potent retailers. It even opened its own no-frills, quick-serve Just Tires discount stores, designed to fend off low-priced competitors. Goodyear claimed that value-minded tire buyers were increasingly buying from cheaper, multibrand discount outlets and department stores, and that it simply had to put its tires where many consumers were going to buy them.

Not surprisingly, Goodyear's aggressive moves into new channels set off a surge of channel conflict, and dealer relations deteriorated rapidly. Some of Goodyear's best dealers defected to competitors. Other angry dealers struck back by taking on competing brands of cheaper private-label tires. Such dealer actions weakened the Goodyear name, and the company's replacement tire sales—which make up 71 percent of its U.S. revenues—went flat, dropping the company into a more than decade-long profit slump. Although Goodyear has since actively set about repairing fractured dealer relations, it still has not fully recovered. "We lost sight of the fact that it's in our interest that our dealers succeed," admits a Goodyear executive.

Channel conflict: In the U.S., Goodyear created conflict with its premiere independent-dealer channel when it began selling through mass-merchant retailers. Fractured dealer relations weakened the Goodyear name and dropped the company into a more than a decade-long profit slump.

Some conflict in the channel takes the form of healthy competition. Such competition can be good for the channel—without it, the channel could become passive and noninnovative. But severe or prolonged conflict, as in the case of Goodyear, can disrupt channel effectiveness and cause lasting harm to channel relationships. Companies should manage channel conflict to prevent it from getting out of hand.

Vertical Marketing Systems

For the channel as a whole to perform well, each channel member's role must be specified and channel conflict must be managed. The channel will perform better if it includes a firm, agency, or mechanism that provides leadership and has the power to assign roles and manage conflict.

Historically, *conventional distribution channels* have lacked such leadership and power, often resulting in damaging conflict and poor performance. One of the biggest channel developments over the years has been the emergence of *vertical marketing systems* that provide channel leadership. 🢂 **Figure 14.3** contrasts the two types of channel arrangements.

A **conventional distribution channel** consists of one or more independent producers, wholesalers, and retailers. Each is a separate business seeking to maximize its own profits, perhaps even at the expense of the system as a whole. No channel member has much control over the other members, and no formal means exists for assigning roles and resolving channel conflict.

In contrast, a **vertical marketing system (VMS)** consists of producers, wholesalers, and retailers acting as a unified system. One channel member owns the others, has contracts with them, or wields so much power that they must all co-operate. The VMS can be dominated by the producer, wholesaler, or retailer.

We look now at three major types of VMSs: *corporate, contractual,* and *administered.* Each uses a different means for setting up leadership and power in the channel.

Corporate VMS

A **corporate VMS** integrates successive stages of production and distribution under single ownership. Co-ordination and conflict management are attained through regular organizational channels. Some examples of companies using corporate VMS follow.

Abu Dhabi National Oil Company (ADNOC) is a major UAE group owning a diverse range of energy and petrochemical companies and producing over 2.7 million barrels of oil a day. ADNOC integrates a range of upstream and downstream activities, each carried out by one of the group's 14 specialist subsidiary and joint venture companies. ADNOC's upstream

---

Conventional distribution channel
A channel consisting of one or more independent producers, wholesalers, and retailers, each a separate business seeking to maximize its own profits, even at the expense of profits for the system as a whole.

Vertical marketing system (VMS)
A distribution channel structure in which producers, wholesalers, and retailers act as a unified system. One channel member owns the others, has contracts with them, or has so much power that they all co-operate.

Corporate VMS
A vertical marketing system that combines successive stages of production and distribution under single ownership—channel leadership is established through common ownership.

🢂 **FIGURE** | 14.3

Comparison of Conventional Distribution Channel with Vertical Marketing System

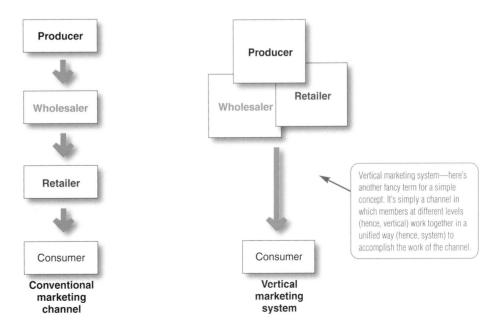

Vertical marketing system—here's another fancy term for a simple concept. It's simply a channel in which members at different levels (hence, vertical) work together in a unified way (hence, system) to accomplish the work of the channel.

operation includes exploration, development, and production of the oil and gas; its down-stream operation includes the distribution, marketing, and shipping of the products.

ADNOC Distribution operates a vast network of service stations and convenience stores. Its service stations are equipped with the most advanced technology for automated car wash and vacuuming, lube services, and tire repair, with Autocare services available in Abu Dhabi, Al Ain, the Western Region and the Northern Emirates.[4]

Al Maya Group is an example of an organization with a solid supply chain and a well-controlled distribution channel. Al Maya Group started operations as a stand-alone supermarket in Ajman, UAE, in the latter part of 1979. The group's flexibility and well-established distribution chain has enabled it to maintain sustainable growth since its establishment. During the group's middle phases of recognition, a vertical integration model was implemented, leading to the establishment of the Al Maya central warehouse distribution depot. The establishment of that facility was considered a turning point in the performance and future of the group. The central warehouse distribution depot handles a variety of established global brands and is considered the largest distribution center in the UAE. The warehouse portfolio involves Pocari Sweat, Ornamin C, Vochelle chocolates, Diamond aluminum foil, American Garden, and Daily Fresh, among host of other products. The creation of this facility gave Al Maya greater control and flexibility to deliver products to several supermarket chains within the GCC. In other words, establishing the warehouse provided the group with the necessary tools to dominate the supermarket field and support further growth.

Al Maya Group has also launched the Al Manal Food Packing Division, based in the Al Quoz area of Dubai. The Al Manal division has been supplying the food and beverage industries in the UAE for over 20 years. The roots of the company can be traced back to the very successful British-based Natco Pvt. Ltd., which was established by Al Maya owner and chairman, Mr L.K. Pagarani. Al Manal Packing has more than 1,000 products in its portfolio and is continuously working on the development of new ranges based on market requirements. Within this broad base of products, the brands Daily Fresh and Real Value have become renowned household names. Al Manal packs for and continuously supplies an extensive portfolio of leading retailers in the Arab world.

Moving along the vertical integration model, Al Maya Group is planning to commission a mayonnaise and ketchup manufacturing facility. This step is expected to further enhance the group's ability to deliver greater customer satisfaction and loyalty by supplying quality products at exceptional value.

Contractual VMS

Contractual VMS
A vertical marketing system in which independent firms at different levels of production and distribution join together through contracts to obtain more economies or sales impact than they could achieve alone.

A **contractual VMS** consists of independent firms at different levels of production and distribution, who join together through contracts to obtain more economies or sales impact than each could achieve alone. Channel members co-ordinate their activities and manage conflict through contractual agreements.

Franchise organization
A contractual vertical marketing system in which a channel member, called a franchisor, links several stages in the production-distribution process.

The **franchise organization** is the most common type of contractual relationship—a channel member called a *franchisor* links several stages in the production-distribution process. Franchising is an important business model for small to medium enterprises (SMEs). The Arab world is seeing prolific growth in franchising as international and local brands try to increase market penetration. The franchise market in the Arab world is estimated to be worth US$30 billion, with average annual growth of 25 percent.[5]

A key factor in encouraging this growth is the very rapid increase in retail activity occuring across the region, with the opening of more and more shopping malls and entertainment centers. For example, a number of international and regional brands have moved to sell their products in locations such as Dubai's Mall of the Emirates. "The Middle East franchise market will continue on its current growth pattern and, together with the development of the retail industry, we predict a very bright future for the sector, which is growing at 20–25 percent per annum," says Sary Hamway, CEO of international franchise consultants, Franchise Excellence.[6]

There are three types of franchises. The first type is the *manufacturer-sponsored retailer franchise system*—for example, Toyota and its network of franchised dealers. The second type is the *manufacturer-sponsored wholesaler franchise system*—Coca-Cola licenses bottlers (wholesalers) in various markets who buy Coca-Cola syrup concentrate and then bottle and sell the finished product to retailers in local markets (Dubai Refreshments is the sole franchisee and distributor for the UAE).The third type is the *service-firm-sponsored retailer franchise system*—examples are found in the auto-rental business (Hertz, Avis), the fast-food service business (McDonald's, Burger King), and the motel business (Holiday Inn, Ramada Inn).

The fact that most consumers cannot tell the difference between contractual and corporate VMSs shows how successfully the contractual organizations compete with corporate chains.

Administered VMS

Administered VMS

A vertical marketing system that co-ordinates successive stages of production and distribution, not through common ownership or contractual ties, but through the size and power of one of the parties.

In an **administered VMS**, leadership is assumed not through common ownership or contractual ties but through the size and power of one or a few dominant channel members. Manufacturers of a top brand can obtain strong trade co-operation and support from resellers. For example, Sony, Procter & Gamble, and the food company Kraft can command unusual co-operation from resellers regarding displays, shelf space, promotions, and price policies. Large retailers such as Carrefour, Azizia Panda, and Lulu can exert strong influence on the manufacturers that supply the products they sell.

Horizontal Marketing Systems

Horizontal marketing system

A channel arrangement in which two or more companies at one level join together to follow a new marketing opportunity.

Another channel development is the **horizontal marketing system**, in which two or more companies at one level join together to follow a new marketing opportunity. By working together, companies can combine their financial, production, or marketing resources to accomplish more than any one company could alone.

Companies might join forces with competitors or noncompetitors. They might work with each other on a temporary or permanent basis, or they may create a separate company. For example, McDonald's and Subway have opened their restaurants in petrol stations in Dubai. McDonald's and Subway benefit from the petrol stations' heavy traffic, and the petrol stations' pull in hungry motorists.

McDonald's operates their restaurants in or alongside petrol stations in Dubai. They benefit from stations' heavy store traffic, while petrol stations pull in hungry motorists.

As another example, Coca-Cola and Nestlé formed a joint distribution venture, Beverage Partners Worldwide, to market ready-to-drink coffees, teas, and flavored milks in more than 40 countries worldwide. Coke provides worldwide experience in marketing and distributing beverages, and Nestlé contributes two established brand names—Nescafé and Nestea.[7]

Multichannel Distribution Systems

Multichannel distribution system

A distribution system in which a single firm sets up two or more marketing channels to reach one or more customer segments.

In the past, many companies used a single channel to sell to a single market or market segment. Today, with the proliferation of customer segments and channel possibilities, more and more companies have adopted **multichannel distribution systems**—often called *hybrid marketing channels*. Such multichannel marketing occurs when a single firm sets up two or more marketing channels to reach one or more customer segments. The use of multichannel systems has increased greatly in recent years.

Most large companies distribute through multiple channels. For example, you could buy a familiar green and yellow John Deere lawn tractor from a neighborhood John Deere dealer or from Lowe's. A large farm or forestry business would buy larger John Deere equipment from a premium full-service dealer and its sales force.

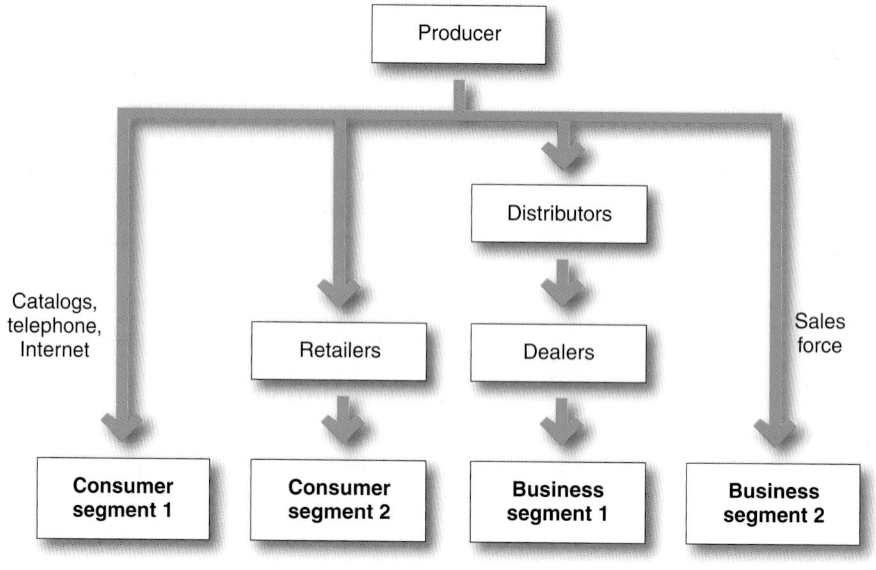

📖 **Figure 14.4** shows a multichannel marketing system. In the figure, the producer sells directly to consumer segment 1 using direct-mail catalogs, telemarketing, and the Internet, and reaches consumer segment 2 through retailers. It sells indirectly to business segment 1 through distributors and dealers, and to business segment 2 through its own sales force.

These days, almost every large company and many small ones distribute through multiple channels. For example, Aftron Electronics, part of the Al-Futtaim Group, based in the UAE, sells electronics products from televisions to freezers and air conditioners to consumers and commercial users through several channels. It has its own showrooms in Dubai, but mainly sells through a large network of retailers and supermarkets including EMKE Group, Al Falah Hyper Market, Lulu, Plug-Ins, Hyper Panda, Géant, E Max, Sharaf DG, Sharaf Digital, Safeer Group, and KM Trading. It exports to other countries in the Arab world through distributors including Omasco for Oman and Domasco for Qatar. It also offers institutional sales to corporate clients, which in the past have included Emarat, Dubai Drydocks, and Onyx Electrochemical Services.[8]

Multichannel distribution systems offer many advantages to companies facing large and complex markets. With each new channel, the company expands its sales and market coverage and gains opportunities to tailor its products and services to the specific needs of diverse customer segments. But such multichannel systems are harder to control, and they generate conflict as more channels compete for customers and sales.

Changing Channel Organization

Changes in technology and the explosive growth of direct and online marketing are having a profound impact on the nature and design of marketing channels. One major trend is toward **disintermediation**—a big term with a clear message and important consequences. Disintermediation occurs when product or service producers cut out intermediaries and go directly to final buyers, or when radically new types of channel intermediaries displace traditional ones.

Thus, in many industries, traditional intermediaries are dropping by the wayside. For example, companies such as Air Arabia and other airlines sell directly to final buyers, cutting travel agents from their marketing channels altogether. In other cases, new forms of resellers are displacing traditional intermediaries. For example, online marketing is growing rapidly, taking business from traditional brick-and-mortar

Disintermediation
The cutting out of marketing channel intermediaries by product or service producers, or the displacement of traditional resellers by radical new types of intermediaries.

Airarabia.com sells air tickets directly to final buyers, cutting out travel agents as marketing channel intermediaries.

retailers. Consumers can buy airline tickets and hotel rooms from Expedia.com; electronics from Sharaf DG.com; clothes and accessories from Desertstore.com; and books, videos, toys, jewelry, sports, consumer electronics, home and garden items, and almost anything else from Amazon.com; all without ever stepping into a traditional retail store. Online music download services such as iTunes and Yahoo! Music are threatening the very existence of traditional music-store retailers.

Similarly, to remain competitive, product and service producers must develop new channel opportunities, such as the Internet and other direct channels. However, developing these new channels often brings them into direct competition with their established channels, resulting in conflict.

To ease this problem, companies often look for ways to make going direct a plus for the entire channel. For example, Panasonic knows that many customers would prefer to buy its electronics goods online. But selling directly through its website would create conflicts with retail partners and its own subsidiary stores. So, although Panasonic's Middle East website provides detailed information about the company's products, you can't buy a new Panasonic television, camcorder, or vacuum cleaner there. Instead, the Panasonic website refers you to resellers' websites and stores across the Arab world and North Africa. Thus, Panasonic's direct marketing helps both the company and its channel partners.

<table>
<tr><td>**Author Comment** | Like everything else in marketing, good channel design begins with analyzing customer needs. Remember, marketing channels are really *customer-value delivery networks*.</td></tr>
</table>

Channel Design Decisions (pp 411–415)

We now look at several channel decisions manufacturers face. In designing marketing channels, manufacturers struggle between what is ideal and what is practical. A new firm with limited capital usually starts by selling in a limited market area. Deciding on the best channels might not be a problem: the problem might simply be how to convince one or a few good intermediaries to handle the line.

If successful, the new firm can branch out to new markets through the existing intermediaries. In smaller markets, the firm might sell directly to retailers; in larger markets, it might sell through distributors. In one part of the region, it might grant exclusive franchises; in another, it might sell through all available outlets. Then, it might add a web store that sells directly to hard-to-reach customers. In this way, channel systems often evolve to meet market opportunities and conditions.

For maximum effectiveness, however, channel analysis and decision making should be more purposeful. **Marketing channel design** calls for analyzing consumer needs, setting channel objectives, identifying major channel alternatives, and evaluating them.

Marketing channel design

Designing effective marketing channels by analyzing consumer needs, setting channel objectives, identifying major channel alternatives, and evaluating them.

Analyzing Consumer Needs

As noted previously, marketing channels are part of the overall *customer-value delivery network*. Each channel member and level adds value for the customer. Thus, designing the marketing channel starts with finding out what target consumers want from the channel. Do consumers want to buy from nearby locations or are they willing to travel to more distant centralized locations? Would they rather buy in person, by phone, or online? Do they value breadth of assortment or do they prefer specialization? Do consumers want many add-on services (delivery, repairs, installation), or will they obtain these elsewhere? The faster the delivery, the greater the assortment provided, and the more add-on services supplied, the greater the channel's service level.

Providing the fastest delivery, greatest assortment, and most services may not be possible or practical. The company and its channel members may not have the resources or skills needed to provide all the desired services. Also, providing higher levels of service results in higher costs for the channel and higher prices for consumers. The company must balance consumer needs not only against the feasibility and costs of meeting these needs but also against customer price preferences. The success of discount retailing shows that consumers will often accept lower service levels in exchange for lower prices.

Setting Channel Objectives

Companies should state their marketing channel objectives in terms of targeted levels of customer service. Usually, a company can identify several segments wanting different levels of service. The company should decide which segments to serve and the best channels to use in each case. In each segment, the company wants to minimize the total channel cost of meeting customer-service requirements.

The company's channel objectives are also influenced by the nature of the company, its products, its marketing intermediaries, its competitors, and the environment. For example, the company's size and financial situation determine which marketing functions it can handle itself and which it must give to intermediaries. Companies selling perishable products may require more direct marketing to avoid delays and too much handling.

In some cases, a company may want to compete in or near the same outlets that carry competitors' products. In other cases, companies may avoid the channels used by competitors. For example, nefsak.com, the Egyptian retailer of books and consumer goods, has gained an advantage over its traditional store-based competitors by reaching customers online.

Finally, environmental factors such as economic conditions and legal constraints may affect channel objectives and design. For example, in a depressed economy, producers want to distribute their goods in the most economical way, using shorter channels and dropping unneeded services that add to the final price of the goods.

Identifying Major Alternatives

When the company has defined its channel objectives, it should next identify its major channel alternatives in terms of *types* of intermediaries, the *number* of intermediaries, and the *responsibilities* of each channel member.

Types of Intermediaries

A firm should identify the types of channel members available to carry out its channel work. Most companies face many channel member choices. For example, in some countries, Dell sells directly to final consumers and business buyers only through its sophisticated phone and Internet marketing channel. It also sells directly to large corporate, institutional, and government buyers using its direct sales force. However, in some countries it has now begun to sell indirectly through retailers in order to reach more consumers and to match competitors. To establish its business in the Arab world, Dell has partnered with retailers such as Quest, Metra, and Absis. It also sells indirectly through 'value-added resellers,' independent distributors and dealers who develop computer systems and applications tailored to the special needs of small- and medium-sized business customers.

Using many types of resellers in a channel provides both benefits and drawbacks. For example, by selling through retailers and value-added resellers in addition to its own direct channels, Dell can reach more and different kinds of buyers. However, some of these channels will be more difficult to manage and control than selling directly to customers. And the direct and indirect channels will compete with each other for many of the same customers, causing potential conflict. In fact, in the United States, Dell is already finding itself 'stuck in the middle,' with its direct sales reps complaining about new competition from retail stores, while at the same time value-added resellers complain that the direct sales reps are undercutting their business.[9]

Number of Marketing Intermediaries

Companies must also determine the number of channel members to use at each level. Three strategies are available: intensive distribution, exclusive distribution, and selective distribution. Producers of convenience products and common raw materials typically seek **intensive distribution**—a strategy in which they stock their products in as many outlets as possible. These products must be available where and when consumers want them. For example, toothpaste, chocolate, and other similar items are sold in thousands of outlets to provide maximum brand exposure and consumer convenience. Kraft, Coca-Cola, Unilever, and other consumer-goods companies distribute their products in this way.

By contrast, some producers purposely limit the number of intermediaries handling their products. The extreme form of this practice is **exclusive distribution**, in which the producer gives only a limited number of dealers the exclusive right to distribute its products in their territories. Exclusive distribution is often found in the distribution of luxury automobiles and prestige women's clothing. For example, exclusive Rolex watches are typically sold by only a handful of authorized dealers in any given market area. In Dubai, Rolex watches are sold only through Ahmed Seddiqi and Sons. By granting exclusive distribution, Rolex gains stronger dealer selling support and more control over dealer prices, promotion, and services. Exclusive distribution also enhances the brand's image and allows for higher markups.

Between intensive and exclusive distribution lies **selective distribution**—the use of more than one, but fewer than all, of the intermediaries who are willing to carry a company's products. Most television, furniture, and home appliance brands are distributed in this manner. For example, LG and General Electric sell their major appliances through dealer networks and selected large retailers. By using selective distribution, they can develop good working relationships with selected channel members and expect a better-than-average selling effort. Selective distribution gives producers good market coverage with more control and less cost than does intensive distribution.

Intensive distribution
Stocking the product in as many outlets as possible.

Exclusive distribution
Giving a limited number of dealers the exclusive right to distribute the company's products in their territories.

Exclusive distribution: Rolex sells its watches exclusively through only a handful of authorized dealers in any given market. Such limited distribution enhances the brand's image and generates stronger retailer support.

Selective distribution
The use of more than one, but fewer than all, of the intermediaries who are willing to carry the company's products.

Responsibilities of Channel Members

The producer and intermediaries need to agree on the terms and responsibilities of each channel member. They should agree on price policies, conditions of sale, territorial rights, and specific services to be performed by each party. The producer should establish a list price and a fair set of discounts for intermediaries. It must define each channel member's territory, and it should be careful about where it places new resellers.

Mutual services and duties need to be spelled out carefully, especially in franchise and exclusive distribution channels. For example, McDonald's provides franchisees with promotional support, a record-keeping system, training at Hamburger University, and general management assistance. In turn, franchisees must meet company standards for physical facilities and food quality, co-operate with new promotion programs, provide requested information, and buy specified food products.

Evaluating the Major Alternatives

Suppose a company has identified several channel alternatives and wants to select the one that will best satisfy its long-run objectives. Each alternative should be evaluated against economic, control, and adaptive criteria.

Using *economic criteria*, a company compares the likely sales, costs, and profitability of different channel alternatives. What will be the investment required by each channel alternative, and what returns will result? The company must also consider *control issues*. Using intermediaries usually means giving them some control over the marketing of the product, and some intermediaries take more control than others. Other things being equal, the company prefers to keep as much control as possible. Finally, the company must apply *adaptive criteria*. Channels often involve long-term commitments, yet the company wants to keep the channel flexible so that it can adapt to environmental changes. Thus, to be considered, a channel involving long-term commitments should be greatly superior on economic and control grounds.

Designing International Distribution Channels

International marketers face many additional complexities in designing their channels. Each country has its own unique distribution system that has evolved over time and changes very slowly. These channel systems can vary widely from country to country. Thus, global marketers must usually adapt their channel strategies to the existing structures within each country.

In some markets, the distribution system is complex and hard to penetrate, consisting of many layers and large numbers of intermediaries. At the other extreme, distribution systems in developing countries may be scattered, inefficient, or altogether lacking. For example, China and India are huge markets, each with populations well over one billion people. However, because of inadequate distribution systems, most companies can profitably access only a small portion of the population located in each country's most affluent cities. "China is a very decentralized market," notes a China trade expert. "[It's] made up of two dozen distinct markets sprawling across 2,000 cities. Each has its own culture.... It's like operating in an asteroid belt." China's distribution system is so fragmented that logistics costs amount to 15 percent of the nation's GDP, far higher than in most other countries. After years of effort, even Wal-Mart executives admit that they have been unable to assemble an efficient supply chain in China.[10]

Sometimes customs or government regulation can greatly restrict how a company distributes products in global markets. For example, it wasn't an inefficient distribution structure that caused problems for Avon in China—it was restrictive government regulations. Fearing the growth of multilevel marketing schemes, the Chinese government banned door-to-door selling altogether in 1998, forcing Avon to abandon its traditional direct

International channel complexities: When the Chinese government banned door-to-door selling, Avon had to abandon its traditional direct-marketing approach and sell through retail shops.

marketing approach and sell through retail shops. The Chinese government recently gave Avon and other direct sellers permission to sell door-to-door again, but that permission is tangled in a web of restrictions. Fortunately for Avon, its earlier focus on store sales is helping it weather the restrictions better than most other direct sellers.[11]

International marketers face a wide range of channel alternatives. Designing efficient and effective channel systems between and within various country markets poses a difficult challenge.

<table>
<tr><td>**Author Comment** | Now it's time to implement the chosen channel design and to work with selected channel members to manage and motivate them.</td></tr>
</table>

Marketing channel management
Selecting, managing, and motivating individual channel members and evaluating their performance over time.

Channel Management Decisions (pp 415–417)

Once the company has reviewed its channel alternatives and decided on the best channel design, it must implement and manage the chosen channel. **Marketing channel management** calls for selecting, managing, and motivating individual channel members and evaluating their performance over time.

Selecting Channel Members

Producers vary in their ability to attract qualified marketing intermediaries. Some producers have no trouble signing up channel members. For example, when Toyota first introduced its Lexus line in the United States, it had no trouble attracting new dealers. In fact, it had to turn down many would-be resellers.

At the other extreme are producers who have to work hard to line up enough qualified intermediaries. For example, when Timex first tried to sell its inexpensive watches through regular jewelry stores, most jewelry stores refused to carry them. The company then managed to get its watches into mass-merchandise outlets. This turned out to be a wise decision because of the rapid growth of mass-merchandising.

When selecting intermediaries, the company should determine what characteristics distinguish the better ones. It will want to evaluate each channel member's years in business, other lines carried, growth and profit record, co-operativeness, and reputation. If the intermediary is a sales agent, the company will want to evaluate the number and character of other lines carried and the size and quality of the sales force. If the intermediary is a retail store that wants exclusive or selective distribution, the company will want to evaluate the store's customers, location, and future growth potential.

Managing and Motivating Channel Members

Once selected, channel members must be continuously managed and motivated to do their best. The company must sell not only *through* the intermediaries but also *to* and *with* them. Most companies see their intermediaries as first-line customers and partners. They practice strong *partner relationship management (PRM)* to forge long-term partnerships with channel members. This creates a value delivery system that meets the needs of both the company *and* its marketing partners. For example, heavy-equipment manufacturer Caterpillar and its worldwide network of independent dealers work in close harmony to find better ways to bring value to customers. Dealers play a vital role in almost every aspect of Caterpillar's operations. For Toys "R" Us, successful expansion into the Arab world was dependent on building the right relationships with the right channel partners (see **Real Marketing 14.1**).

In managing its channels, a company must convince distributors that they can succeed better by working together as part of a cohesive value delivery system. Thus, Procter & Gamble works closely with Carrefour to create superior value for final consumers. The two jointly plan merchandising goals and strategies, inventory levels, and advertising and promotion programs.

Real Marketing 14.1

Toys "R" Us

The Arab world is a tempting market for global retailer Toys "R" Us, comprising some of the top toy-importing countries in the world. The question is how the company would handle its supply chain.

The toy market in the Arab world is valued at US$1.5 billion per year and experiences annual growth of 11.8 per cent. This has not gone unnoticed by Toys "R" Us, which, since 1995, has operated as part of the Al-Futtaim Group. Al-Futtaim Group is one of the leading trading companies in the UAE, representing well-known global brands including Toyota, Panasonic, Marks & Spencer, IBM, and IKEA. As a result, the corporationis bound to know a thing or two about efficient logistics operations in the region. Combined with Toys "R" Us' reputation for managing smooth supply chains in the United States and Europe, the implementation of a market-leading model for storage and distribution should be a relatively simple task.

"We buy merchandise from all over the world and deal with more than 300 manufacturers to get the best possible prices for our customers," explains Devrim Anadol, buying and logistics manager at Toys "R" Us. "We plan our ranges according to worldwide trends, movie releases, seasonality and consumer behaviour in the GCC. And of course we take into account our sales targets and financial objectives."

Toys "R" Us operates in the UAE, Bahrain, Qatar, Oman, Kuwait, and Egypt, and its products mainly arrive from China, Europe, and the United States. Subsequently, it relies on comprehensive support from its third-party logistics partners to ensure an efficient supply chain. "Considering the number of countries and the number of vendors that we deal with, our operation requires a flawless process and great teamwork," Anadol emphasizes. "To ensure the smooth flow of the supply chain, it is imperative that the logistics 'parts' work in perfect unison."Toys "R" Us relies on major third-party logistics businesses to help it deliver its successful operations, including Agility, UPS, DHL, and Aramex. Devrim Anadol explains how the system works in practice.

"The first step in getting the merchandise is, of course, processing the purchase orders and we get support from UPS worldwide consolidation services on this," he says. "UPS operates in 224 countries and supports us by origin coordination, which means

Toys "R" Us buys its merchandise from more than 300 manufacturers all over the world, then distributes these to its outlets in the UAE, Bahrain, Qatar, Oman, Kuwait, and Egypt. In order to ensure smooth and efficient warehousing and distribution, it has to rely on comprehensive support from its third-party logistics partners.

timely shipments, assisting on consolidation and follow up with the suppliers on ship windows and documentation. Basically, UPS gets the containers to our central warehouse in Jebel Ali Free Zone, Dubai."

Once containers have arrived at the distribution centre, the Toys "R" Us team must plan how they will transfer the stock."Our inventory control team pushes the stock to stores and they plan how much to send and when to send. They work according to our marketing calendar, seasonality and consumer demand," Anadol continues.When you consider that this involves 15,000 different stock-keeping units, it becomes clear that this no easy task. "We use IBM AS400 to help us on this complicated replenishment activity, and our inventory control team replenishes all UAE stores daily and twice a week out of the UAE," he adds.

The next stage in the supply chain involves working with the Toys "R" Us partner company Agility, the retailer's warehouse operator in Jebel Ali. "After the inventory control team writes the transfers, this information goes to Agility, which is mainly responsible for clearing the containers at Dubai ports and item picking in the distribution centre," says Anadol. Agility carries out tasks such as loading the trucks, re-packing promotional products, applying Arabic labels, as well as carrying out a yearly stock count and planning work

for the peak sales period. The Jebel Ali facility is around 8,000 cubic meters (CBM). Anadol continues: "We have a team of 15 colleagues, two dedicated customer support representatives and one account manager based there. They move around 2,000 CBM to 3,000 CBM per month during the peak period."

After leaving the Agility facility, transportation is carried out by DHL and Aramex. "We use DHL for road networks in GCC and sea freight. We also have two trucks from Aramex and they replenish our stores in the UAE," Anadol explains.

The logistics of the Toys "R" Us supply chain clearly needs careful planning. "It looks complicated, but when you put everything together, it works fine… However, it's imperative that everyone does their job 100% correctly. It's all about teamwork."

Overall, Toys "R" Us aims to make the most of each service provider's unique strengths, whether those be extensive global networks, reliable fleets, or warehouse expertise."Each of our logistics partners is focusing on something particular. We are happy with the services each one is providing," concludes Anadol. "It's a complicated chain and so appreciation is very important. Everyone did a great job [last year] and we want this to continue in the current year. It's really important for motivating ourselves and our partners."

Source: "Toy Story," *Arabian Business*, April 9, 2010, www.arabianbusiness.com/toy-story-155168.html.

Many companies are now installing integrated high-tech partner relationship management systems to co-ordinate their whole-channel marketing efforts. Just as they use customer relationship management (CRM) software systems to help manage relationships with important customers, companies can now use supply chain management (SCM) software to help recruit, train, organize, manage, motivate, and evaluate relationships with channel partners.

Public Policy and Distribution Decisions

For the most part, companies are legally free to develop whatever channel arrangements suit them. Many producers and wholesalers like to develop exclusive channels for their products. When the seller allows only certain outlets to carry its products, this strategy is called *exclusive distribution*. When the seller requires that these dealers not handle competitors' products, its strategy is called *exclusive dealing*. Both parties can benefit from exclusive arrangements: The seller obtains more loyal and dependable outlets, and the dealers obtain a steady source of supply and stronger seller support. But exclusive arrangements also exclude other producers from selling to these dealers. In certain countries, they are legal as long as they do not substantially lessen competition or tend to create a monopoly, and as long as both parties enter into the agreement voluntarily.

Exclusive dealing often includes *exclusive territorial agreements*. In the Arab world, exclusive agents and exclusive distributors are commonly used by foreign companies to distribute and sell their products in the local markets. The producer may agree not to sell to other dealers in a given area, or the buyer may agree to sell only in its own territory. For example, Al-Futtaim Motors is the exclusive distributor of Toyota motors in Dubai. This means that Toyota will only sell to Al-Futtaim Motors in Dubai and not to any other company. The first practice is normal under franchise systems as a way to increase dealer enthusiasm and commitment. It is also perfectly legal—a seller has no legal obligation to sell through more outlets than it wishes. The second practice, whereby the producer tries to keep a dealer from selling outside its territory, has become a major legal issue.

Producers of a strong brand sometimes sell it to dealers only if the dealers will take some or all of the rest of the line. This is called full-line forcing. Such *tying agreements* sometimes violate laws if they tend to lessen competition substantially. The practice may prevent consumers from freely choosing among competing suppliers of these other brands.

Nevertheless, exclusive dealerships are a very common practice in the Arab world. There are some limitations and laws that regulate it. One of these laws, in the Gulf States, mandates that exclusive dealerships should not be given to expatriates. In May 2011, the Qatar state cabinet put forward a proposal to the advisory council which argued that in exceptional cases non-citizens should be allowed to own exclusive dealerships of foreign goods and services. The council unanimously rejected the proposal, saying that allowing non-citizens to own agencies would cause immense damage to the national economy.[12]

Author Comment | Marketers used to simply call this 'physical distribution.' But as these titles suggest, the topic has grown in importance, complexity, and sophistication.

Marketing Logistics and Supply Chain Management (pp 417–423)

In today's global marketplace, selling a product is sometimes easier than getting it to customers. Companies must decide on the best way to store, handle, and move their products and services so that they are available to customers in the right assortments, at the right time, and in the right place. Logistics effectiveness has a major impact on both customer satisfaction and company costs. Here we consider the nature and importance of logistics management in the supply chain, goals of the logistics system, major logistics functions, and the need for integrated logistics management.

Nature and Importance of Marketing Logistics

To some managers, marketing logistics means only trucks and warehouses. But modern logistics is much more than this. **Marketing logistics**—also called **physical distribution**—involves

Marketing logistics (or physical distribution)
Planning, implementing, and controlling the physical flow of materials, final goods, and related information from points of origin to points of consumption to meet customer requirements at a profit.

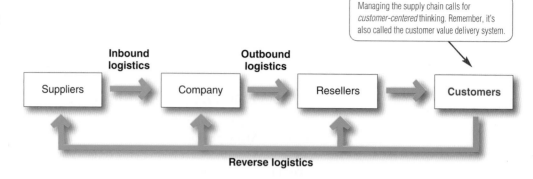

FIGURE | **14.5**
Supply Chain Management

> Managing the supply chain calls for *customer-centered* thinking. Remember, it's also called the customer value delivery system.

Inbound logistics **Outbound logistics**

Suppliers → Company → Resellers → Customers

Reverse logistics

planning, implementing, and controlling the physical flow of goods, services, and related information from points of origin to points of consumption to meet customer requirements at a profit. In short, it involves getting the right product to the right customer in the right place at the right time.

In the past, physical distribution planners typically started with products at the plant and then tried to find low-cost solutions to get them to customers. However, today's marketers prefer *customer-centered* logistics thinking, which starts with the marketplace and works backward to the factory, or even to sources of supply. Marketing logistics involves not only *outbound distribution* (moving products from the factory to resellers and ultimately to customers) but also *inbound distribution* (moving products and materials from suppliers to the factory) and *reverse distribution* (moving broken, unwanted, or excess products returned by consumers or resellers). That is, it involves entire **supply chain management**—managing upstream and downstream value-added flows of materials, final goods, and related information among suppliers, the company, resellers, and final consumers, as shown in **Figure 14.5**.

Supply chain management
Managing upstream and downstream value-added flows of materials, final goods, and related information among suppliers, the company, resellers, and final consumers.

The logistics manager's task is to co-ordinate activities of suppliers, purchasing agents, marketers, channel members, and customers. These activities include forecasting, information systems, purchasing, production planning, order processing, inventory, warehousing, and transportation planning.

Companies today are placing greater emphasis on logistics for several reasons. First, companies can gain a powerful competitive advantage by using improved logistics to give customers better service or lower prices. Secondly, improved logistics can yield tremendous cost savings to both the company and its customers. As much as 20 percent of an average product's price is accounted for by shipping and transport alone. This far exceeds the cost of advertising and many other marketing costs. What's more, transportation costs have risen more than 50 percent over the past decade. By itself, Ford has more than 500 million tons of finished vehicles, production parts, and aftermarket parts in transit at any given time, running up an annual logistics bill of around US$4 billion.[13] Reducing even a small fraction of these costs can mean substantial savings.

Thirdly, the explosion in product variety has created a need for improved logistics management. For example, 30 years ago the average grocery in the Gulf would stock about 250 items, now it carries about 15,000 items, while hypermarkets such as Carrefour, Géant, and Lulu may carry more than 100,000 items. Ordering, shipping, stocking, and controlling such a variety of products presents a sizable logistics challenge.

The importance of logistics: At any given time, Ford has more than 500 million tons of finished vehicles, production parts, and aftermarket parts in transit, running up an annual logistics bill of around US$4 billion.

Improvements in information technology have also created opportunities for major gains in distribution efficiency. Today's companies are using sophisticated supply chain management software, web-based logistics systems, point-of-sale scanners, uniform product codes, satellite tracking, and electronic transfer of order and payment data. Such technology lets them quickly and efficiently manage the flow of goods, information, and finances through the supply chain.

Finally, more than almost any other marketing function, logistics affects the environment and a firm's environmental sustainability efforts. Transportation, warehousing, packaging, and other logistics functions are typically the biggest supply chain contributors to the company's environmental footprint. At the same time, they also provide one of the most fertile areas for cost savings.

Goals of the Logistics System

Some companies state their logistics objective as providing maximum customer service at the least cost. Unfortunately, no logistics system can *both* maximize customer service *and* minimize distribution costs. Maximum customer service implies rapid delivery, large inventories, flexible assortments, liberal returns policies, and other services—all of which raise distribution costs. In contrast, minimum distribution costs imply slower delivery, smaller inventories, and larger shipping lots—which represent a lower level of overall customer service.

The goal of marketing logistics should be to provide a *targeted* level of customer service at the least cost. A company must first research the importance of various distribution services to customers and then set desired service levels for each segment. The objective is to maximize *profits*, not sales. Therefore, the company must weigh the benefits of providing higher levels of service against the costs. Some companies offer less service than their competitors and charge a lower price. Other companies offer more service and charge higher prices to cover higher costs.

Major Logistics Functions

Given a set of logistics objectives, the company is ready to design a logistics system that will minimize the cost of attaining these objectives. The major logistics functions include *warehousing, inventory management, transportation*, and *logistics information management*.

Warehousing

Production and consumption cycles rarely match, so most companies must store their goods while they are waiting to be sold. For example, LG, Panasonic, and other air conditioner manufacturers may run their factories all year long and store up products for the heavy spring and summer buying seasons. The storage function can be used to overcome differences in needed quantities and timing, ensuring that products are available when customers are ready to buy them.

A company must decide on *how many* and *what types* of warehouses it needs and *where* they will be located. The company might use either *storage warehouses* or *distribution centers*. Storage warehouses store goods for moderate to long periods. **Distribution centers** are designed to move goods rather than just store them. They are large and highly automated warehouses designed to receive goods from various plants and suppliers, take orders, fill them efficiently, and deliver goods to customers as quickly as possible.

Distribution center

A large, highly automated warehouse designed to receive goods from various plants and suppliers, take orders, fill them efficiently, and deliver goods to customers as quickly as possible.

For example, Wal-Mart operates a network of 169 huge distribution centers around the globe. A single center, serving the daily needs of 75 to 100 Wal-Mart stores, typically contains some 1 million square feet of space (about 92,000 square meters) under a single roof. At a typical center, laser scanners route as many as 190,000 cases of goods per day along more than 8 kilometers of conveyer belts, and the center's 1,000 workers load or unload some 500 trucks daily.[14]

Like almost everything else these days, warehousing has seen dramatic changes in technology in recent years. Outdated materials-handling methods are steadily being replaced by newer, computer-controlled systems requiring few employees. Computers and scanners read orders and direct lift trucks, electric hoists, or robots to gather goods, move them to loading docks, and issue invoices.

Inventory Management

Inventory management also affects customer satisfaction. Here, managers must maintain the delicate balance between carrying too little inventory and carrying too much. With too little stock, the firm risks not having products when customers want to buy. To remedy this, the firm may need costly emergency shipments or production. Carrying too much inventory results in higher-than-necessary inventory-carrying costs and stock obsolescence. Thus, in managing inventory, firms must balance the costs of carrying larger inventories against resulting sales and profits.

Many companies have greatly reduced their inventories and related costs through *just-in-time* logistics systems. With such systems, producers and retailers carry only small inventories of parts or merchandise, often only enough for a few days of operations. New stock arrives exactly when needed, rather than being stored in inventory until being used. Just-in-time systems require accurate forecasting along with fast, frequent, and flexible delivery so that new supplies will be available when needed. However, these systems result in substantial savings in inventory-carrying and handling costs.

Marketers are always looking for new ways to make inventory management more efficient. In the not-too-distant future, handling inventory might even become fully automated. For example, in Chapter 3 we discussed RFID or 'smart tag' technology, by which small transmitter chips are embedded in or placed on products and packaging—on everything from flowers and razors to tires. 'Smart' products could make the entire supply chain—which accounts for nearly 75 percent of a product's cost—intelligent and automated.

RFID could make the entire supply chain—which accounts for nearly 75 percent of a product's cost—intelligent and automated.

Companies using RFID would know, at any time, exactly where a product is located physically within the supply chain. 'Smart shelves' would not only tell them when it's time to reorder, but would also place the order automatically with their suppliers. Such exciting new information technology applications will revolutionize distribution as we know it. Many large and resourceful marketing companies, such as Wal-Mart, Procter & Gamble, Kraft, IBM, and HP, are investing heavily to make the full use of RFID technology a reality.[15]

Transportation

The choice of transportation carriers affects the pricing of products, delivery performance, and condition of the goods when they arrive—all of which will affect customer satisfaction. In shipping goods to its warehouses, dealers, and customers, the company can choose among five main transportation modes: truck, rail, water, pipeline, and air, along with an alternative mode for digital products—the Internet.

Trucks have increased their share of transportation steadily and now account for nearly 35 percent of total cargo ton-kilometers (more than 60 percent of actual tonnage).[16] Trucks are highly flexible in their routing and time schedules, and they can usually offer faster service than railroads. They are efficient for short hauls of high-value merchandise. Trucking firms have evolved in recent years to become full-service providers of global transportation services.

Railroads are one of the most cost-effective modes for shipping large amounts of bulk products—coal, sand, minerals, and farm and forest products—over long distances. In recent years, railroads have increased their customer services by designing new equipment to handle special categories of goods, providing flatcars for carrying truck trailers by rail (piggyback), and providing in-transit services such as the diversion of shipped goods to other destinations en route and the processing of goods en route.

Water carriers transport large amounts of goods by ships and barges on coastal and inland waterways. Although the cost of water transportation is very low for shipping bulky, low-value, nonperishable products such as sand, coal, grain, oil, and metallic ores, water transportation is the slowest mode and may be affected by the weather.

Pipelines are a specialized means of shipping petroleum, natural gas, and chemicals from sources to markets. Most pipelines are used by their owners to ship their own products.

Although *air* carriers transport only a small percentage of goods, they are an important transportation mode. Airfreight rates are much higher than rail or truck rates, but airfreight is ideal when speed is needed or distant markets have to be reached. Among the most frequently airfreighted products are perishables (fresh fish, cut flowers) and high-value, low-bulk items (technical instruments, jewelry). Companies find that airfreight also reduces inventory levels, packaging costs, and the number of warehouses needed.

The *Internet* carries digital products from producer to customer via satellite, cable, or phone wire. Software firms, the media, music companies, and education all make use of the Internet to transport digital products. Although these firms primarily use traditional transportation to distribute DVDs, newspapers, and more, the Internet holds the potential for lower product distribution costs. Whereas planes, trucks, and trains move freight and packages, digital technology moves information bits.

Intermodal transportation
Combining two or more modes of transportation.

Shippers also use **intermodal transportation**—combining two or more modes of transportation. For example, combining airfreight and trucking, or sea freight and trucking. Combining modes provides advantages that no single mode can deliver. Each combination offers advantages to the shipper. For example, not only is the combination of train and truck cheaper than trucking alone but it also provides flexibility and convenience.

In choosing a transportation mode for a product, shippers must balance many considerations: speed, dependability, availability, cost, and others. Thus, if a shipper needs speed, air and truck are the prime choices. If the goal is low cost, then water or pipeline might be best.

Logistics Information Management

Companies manage their supply chains through information. Channel partners often link up to share information and to make better joint logistics decisions. From a logistics perspective, information flows such as customer transactions, billing, shipment and inventory levels, and even customer data are closely linked to channel performance. The company wants to design a simple, accessible, fast, and accurate process for capturing, processing, and sharing channel information.

Information can be shared and managed in many ways but most sharing takes place through traditional or Internet-based *electronic data interchange (EDI)*, the computerized exchange of data between organizations. Wal-Mart, for example, maintains EDI links with almost all of its 91,000 suppliers. And where it once took eight weeks, using EDI, Krispy Kreme, the doughnut maker, can now turn around 1,000 supplier invoices and process the checks in only a single week.[17]

In some cases, suppliers might actually be asked to generate orders and arrange deliveries for their customers. Many large retailers—such as Carrefour and LuLu hypermarket—work closely with major suppliers such as Unilever and Procter & Gamble to set up *vendor-managed inventory* (VMI) systems or *continuous inventory replenishment* systems. Using VMI, the customer shares real-time data on sales and current inventory levels with the supplier. The supplier then takes full responsibility for managing inventories and deliveries. Some retailers even go so far as to shift inventory and delivery costs to the supplier. Such systems require close co-operation between the buyer and seller.

Integrated logistics management
The logistics concept that emphasizes teamwork, both inside the company and among all the marketing channel organizations, to maximize the performance of the entire distribution system.

Integrated Logistics Management

Today, more and more companies are adopting the concept of **integrated logistics management**. This concept recognizes that providing better customer service and trimming distribution costs require *teamwork*, both inside the company and among all the marketing channel organizations. Inside, the company's various departments must work closely together to maximize the company's own logistics performance. Outside, the company must integrate its logistics system with those of its suppliers and customers to maximize the performance of the entire distribution network.

Cross-Functional Teamwork Inside the Company

Most companies assign responsibility for various logistics activities to many different departments—marketing, sales, finance, operations, and purchasing. Too often, each function tries to optimize its own logistics performance without regard for the activities of the other functions. However, transportation, inventory, warehousing, and information management activities interact, often in an inverse way. Lower inventory levels reduce inventory-carrying costs. But they may also reduce customer service and increase costs from stockouts, back orders, special production runs, and costly fast-freight shipments. Because distribution activities involve strong trade-offs, decisions by different functions must be co-ordinated to achieve better overall logistics performance.

The goal of integrated supply chain management is to harmonize all of the company's logistics decisions. Close working relationships among departments can be achieved in several ways. Some companies have created permanent logistics committees made up of managers responsible for different physical distribution activities. Companies can also create supply chain manager positions that link the logistics activities of functional areas. For example, Procter & Gamble has created supply managers, who manage all of the supply chain activities for each of its product categories.

Finally, companies can employ sophisticated, system-wide supply chain management software, now available from a wide range of software enterprises large and small, from SAP and Oracle to Infor and Logility. The worldwide market for supply chain management software topped an estimated US\$6.5 billion last year and will reach an estimated US\$11.6 billion by 2013.[18] The important thing is that the company must co-ordinate its logistics and marketing activities to create high market satisfaction at a reasonable cost.

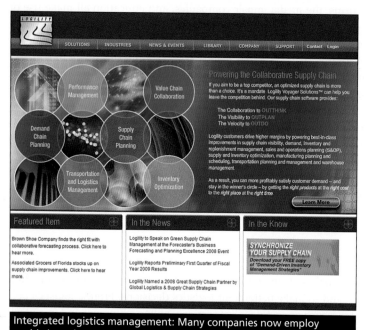

Integrated logistics management: Many companies now employ sophisticated, systemwide supply chain management software, available from companies such as Logility.

Building Logistics Partnerships

Companies must do more than improve their own logistics. They must also work with other channel partners to improve whole-channel distribution. The members of a marketing channel are linked closely in creating customer value and building customer relationships. One company's distribution system is another company's supply system. The success of each channel member depends on the performance of the entire supply chain. For example, IKEA can create its stylish but affordable furniture and deliver the IKEA lifestyle only if its entire supply chain—consisting of thousands of merchandise designers and suppliers, transport companies, warehouses, and service providers—operates at maximum efficiency and with customer-focused effectiveness.

Third-Party Logistics

Most big companies love to make and sell their products. But many hate the associated hard work in logistics. They hate the bundling, loading, unloading, sorting, storing, reloading, transporting, customs clearing, and tracking required to supply their factories and get products out to customers. They hate it so much that a growing number of firms now outsource some or all of their logistics to **third-party logistics (3PL) providers**. Here's an example:[19]

Pharma World Holdings, based in Dubai, is one of the few 3PL providers operating in the pharmaceutical and healthcare sectors in the Arab world. Key to its success is

Third-party logistics (3PL) provider
An independent logistics provider that performs any or all of the functions required to get its client's product to market.

the company's distribution and warehousing hub, based in the Jebel Ali Free Zone (JAFZA) in Dubai, a global trade and shipment center. Pharma World's one-stop 3PLs are available to international and local manufacturers. Pharma World claims that its operation is unique in the region.

At present, the distribution of pharmaceutical products in the UAE requires foreign manufacturers to supply products through distributors. Those distributors place and receive orders directly from the original manufacturers. Business development group director of Pharma World Holdings, Maher Kheder, argues that the existing model "lacks flexibility and means that principals need to find a distributor with excellent regional knowledge to optimise the process."

To offset these challenges Pharma World Holdings first accepts orders directly from the customers of the pharmaceutical products' manufacturers. It then transports the products from their warehousing facility and invoices customers. In addition, it advises manufacturers about stock levels and can also process reports on returns and provide other support services. Pharma World aims to link principals with distributors effectively and efficiently, and improves the quality of service.[20]

These third-party logistics providers—companies such as UPS Supply Chain Solutions, DHL Logistics, Momentum Logistics, and Aramex—help clients to tighten up sluggish, overstuffed supply chains, slash inventories, and get products to customers more quickly and reliably. For example, as we saw in Chapter 6, Aramex's supply chain management solutions provide clients with a wide range of logistics services, from inventory control, warehousing, and transportation management to customer service and fulfillment. According to a survey of chief logistics executives at Fortune 500 companies, 82 percent of these companies use third-party logistics (also called *3PL, outsourced logistics,* or *contract logistics*) services. In just the past 10 years, the revenues for third-party logistics companies have increased dramatically.[21]

Companies use third-party logistics providers for several reasons. First, because getting the product to market is their main focus, these providers can often do it more efficiently and at lower cost. Outsourcing typically results in cost savings of between 15 and 30 percent. Secondly, outsourcing logistics frees a company to focus more intensely on its core business. Finally, integrated logistics companies understand increasingly complex logistics environments.

Third-party logistics partners can be especially helpful to companies attempting to expand their global market coverage. For example, companies distributing their products across Europe face a bewildering array of environmental restrictions that affect logistics, including packaging standards, truck size and weight limits, and noise and emissions pollution controls. By outsourcing its logistics, a company can gain a complete pan-European distribution system without incurring the costs, delays, and risks associated with setting up its own system.

Author Comment | You already know a lot about retailers. You deal with them every day—store retailers, service retailers, online retailers, and others.

Retailing (pp 423–427)

What is retailing? We all know that Carrefour, Lulu, Spinneys, Union Coop, ACE, and IKEA are retailers, but so are Avon representatives, Amazon.com, and a doctor seeing patients. **Retailing** includes all the activities involved in selling products or services directly to final consumers for their personal, nonbusiness use. Many institutions—manufacturers, wholesalers, and retailers—do retailing. But most retailing is done by **retailers**: businesses whose sales come *primarily* from retailing.

Retailing
All activities involved in selling goods or services directly to final consumers for their personal, nonbusiness use.

Retailer
A business whose sales come primarily from retailing.

Retailing plays a very important role in most marketing channels. Each year, retailers account for more than US$100 billion of sales to final consumers in the GCC. They connect brands to consumers in what marketing agency OgilvyAction calls "the last mile"—the final stop in the consumer's path to purchase. It's the "distance a consumer travels between an attitude and an action," explains OgilvyAction's CEO. "Nearly 70 percent of purchase decisions are made near or in the store." Thus, retailers "reach consumers at key moments of truth, ultimately [influencing] their actions at the point of purchase."[22]

In fact, many marketers are now embracing the concept of *shopper marketing*, the idea that the retail store itself is an important marketing medium. Shopper marketing involves focusing the entire marketing process—from product and brand development to logistics, promotion, and merchandising—toward turning shoppers into buyers at the point of sale. Of course, every well-designed marketing effort focuses on customer buying behavior. But the concept of shopper marketing suggests that these efforts should be co-ordinated around the shopping process itself. Shopper marketing emphasizes the importance of the retail environment on customer buying.[23]

Although most retailing is done in retail stores, in recent years *nonstore retailing* has been growing much faster than has store retailing. Nonstore retailing includes selling to final consumers through the Internet, direct mail, catalogs, the telephone, and other direct-selling approaches. We discussed such direct-marketing approaches in detail in Chapter 13. In this chapter, we focus on store retailing.

Types of Retailers

Retail stores come in all shapes and sizes—from your local hairstyling salon or family-owned restaurant, through large hypermarkets such as Carrefour, to discounters such as the Dirham or Riyal stores. The most important types of retail stores are described in ● **Table 14.1** and discussed in the following sections. They can be classified in terms of several characteristics, including the *amount of service* they offer, the breadth and depth of their *product lines*, the *relative prices* they charge, and how they are *organized*.

Amount of Service

Different types of customers and products require different amounts of service. To meet these varying service needs, retailers may offer one of three service levels—self-service, limited service, and full service.

Self-service retailers serve customers who are willing to perform their own locate-compare-select process to save time or money. Self-service is the basis of all discount operations and is

● TABLE | 14.1   Major Store Retailer Types

Type	Description	Examples
Specialty stores	Carry a narrow product line with a deep assortment, such as apparel stores, sporting-goods stores, furniture stores, florists, and bookstores. A clothing store would be a *single-line* store, a men's clothing store would be a *limited-line store,* and a men's custom-shirt store would be a *superspecialty* store.	Sharaf DG, Radio, Shack, Magrudy, Splash
Department stores	Carry several product lines—typically clothing, home furnishings, and household goods—with each line operated as a separate department managed by specialist buyers or merchandisers.	Jashanmal, Debenhams
Supermarkets	A relatively large, low-cost, low-margin, high-volume, self-service operation designed to serve the consumer's total needs for grocery and household products.	Union Coop, Choithram, Spinneys
Convenience stores	Relatively small stores located near residential areas, open long hours seven days a week, and carrying a limited line of high-turnover convenience products at slightly higher prices.	EPPCO, ADNOC, Stop and Shop, and local corner grocery store (*Bakala*)
Discount stores	Carry standard merchandise sold at lower prices with lower margins and higher volumes.	Riyal and Dirham stores
Hypermarkets	Very large stores traditionally aimed at meeting consumers' total needs for routinely purchased food and nonfood items. Includes combined supermarket and discount stores, and *category killers*, which carry a deep assortment in a particular category and have a knowledgeable staff.	Carrefour, Lulu, Géant, Sharaf DG (category killer)

typically used by retailers selling convenience goods (such as supermarkets) and branded, fast-moving shopping goods (such as Géant or Carrefour). *Limited-service retailers*, such as Splash, Shoe Mart, or Sun and Sand, provide more sales assistance because they carry more shopping goods about which customers need information. Their increased operating costs result in higher prices.

In *full-service retailers*, such as high-end specialty stores (for example, Paris Gallery) and first-class department stores (such as Jashanmal) salespeople assist customers in every phase of the shopping process. Full-service stores usually carry more specialty goods for which customers need or want assistance or advice. They provide more services resulting in much higher operating costs, which are passed along to customers as higher prices.

Product Line

Specialty store
A retail store that carries a narrow product line with a deep assortment within that line.

Department store
A retail organization that carries a wide variety of product lines—each line is operated as a separate department managed by specialist buyers or merchandisers.

Supermarket
A large, low-cost, low-margin, high-volume, self-service store that carries a wide variety of grocery and household products.

Convenience store
A small store, located near a residential area, that is open long hours seven days a week and carries a limited line of high-turnover convenience goods.

Hypermarket
A store much larger than a regular supermarket that offers a large assortment of routinely purchased food products, nonfood items, and services.

Service retailer
A retailer whose product line is actually a service, including hotels, airlines, banks, colleges, and many others.

Retailers can also be classified by the length and breadth of their product assortments. Some retailers, such as **specialty stores**, carry narrow product lines with deep assortments within those lines. Today, specialty stores are flourishing. The increasing use of market segmentation, market targeting, and product specialization has resulted in a greater need for stores that focus on specific products and segments.

In contrast, **department stores** carry a wide variety of product lines. In recent years, department stores have been squeezed between more focused and flexible specialty stores on the one hand, and more efficient, lower-priced discounters on the other. In response, many have added promotional pricing to meet the discount threat. Others have stepped up the use of store brands and single-brand designer shops to compete with specialty stores. Still others are trying catalog, telephone, and web selling. Service remains the key differentiating factor. Retailers such as Paris Gallery, Saks, Debenhams, and other high-end department stores are doing well by emphasizing exclusive merchandise and high-quality service.

Supermarkets are the most frequently shopped type of retail store. Today, however, they are facing slow sales growth because of slower population growth and an increase in competition from discount supercenters on the one hand and upscale specialty food stores on the other.

In the battle for 'share of stomachs,' some supermarkets are cutting costs, establishing more-efficient operations, lowering prices, and attempting to compete more effectively with food discounters. However, they are finding it difficult to profitably match the low prices of super low-cost operators such as Carrefour. In contrast, many other large supermarkets have moved upscale, providing improved store environments and higher-quality food offerings, such as from-scratch bakeries, gourmet deli counters, natural foods, and fresh seafood departments. For example, Spinneys has clearly positioned itself as the upscale retailer of fresh food, bread products, and gourmet deli items through its extended assortment of these products. This is also reflected in the premium price at which these items are sold to consumers.

Convenience stores are small stores that carry a limited line of high-turnover convenience goods. Much of convenience store revenues come from sales of petrol; a majority of in-store sales are from snack food and beverages.[24] Convenience stores in the Arab world also take the form of small corner stores or *bakkala*, which service residents living or working close to the shop. They generally offer a higher level of service than the average supermarket, such as home delivery of orders taken by phone, which is reflected by their higher prices.

Hypermarkets are much larger than regular supermarkets and offer a large assortment of routinely purchased food products, nonfood items, and services. Carrefour, Lulu and other discount retailers offer very large combination food and discount stores. Whereas an average supermarket brings in about US$270,000 a week in sales, a hypermarket brings in about US$1.5 million a week.

Finally, for many retailers, the product line is actually a service. **Service retailers** include hotels and motels, banks, airlines, colleges, hospitals, cinema halls, tennis clubs, bowling alleys, restaurants, repair services, hair salons, and dry cleaners.

Relative Prices

Retailers can also be classified according to the prices they charge (see **Table 14.1**). Most retailers charge regular prices and offer normal-quality goods and customer service. Others offer higher-quality goods and service at higher prices. The retailers that feature low prices are discount stores and off-price retailers.

Discount store

A retail operation that sells standard merchandise at lower prices by accepting lower margins and selling at higher volume.

A **discount store** sells standard merchandise at lower prices by accepting lower margins and selling higher volume. The early discount stores cut expenses by offering few services and operating in warehouse-like facilities in low-rent, heavily traveled districts. Today's discounters have improved their store environments and increased their services, while at the same time keeping prices low through lean, efficient operations. Leading discounters now dominate the retail scene, and world-leading retailer Wal-Mart—what one financial guru calls "the retailing machine of all time"—dominates the discounters.[25]

Independent off-price retailer

An off-price retailer that is either independently owned and run or is a division of a larger retail corporation.

The three main types of off-price retailers are *independents, factory outlets,* and *warehouse clubs.* **Independent off-price retailers** are either independently owned and run or are divisions of larger retail corporations. **Factory outlets**—manufacturer-owned and operated stores by firms such as Nike and others—sometimes group together in *factory outlet malls* and *value-retail centers,* where dozens of outlet stores offer prices as low as 50 percent below retail on a wide range of mostly surplus, discounted, or irregular goods.

Factory outlet

An off-price retailing operation that is owned and operated by a manufacturer and that normally carries the manufacturer's surplus, discontinued, or irregular goods.

Organizational Approach

Although many retail stores are independently owned, others band together under some form of corporate or contractual organization. The major types of retail organizations—*corporate chains, voluntary chains, retailer co-operatives, franchise organizations,* and *merchandising conglomerates*—are described in ● Table 14.2.

Chain stores

Two or more outlets that are commonly owned and controlled.

Chain stores are two or more outlets that are commonly owned and controlled. They have many advantages over independents. Their size allows them to buy in large quantities at lower prices and gain promotional economies. They can hire specialists to deal with areas such as pricing, promotion, merchandising, inventory control, and sales forecasting.

Franchise

A contractual association between a manufacturer, wholesaler, or service organization (a franchisor) and independent businesspeople (franchisees) who buy the right to own and operate one or more units in the franchise system.

Another form of contractual retail organization is a **franchise**. The main difference between franchise organizations and other contractual systems (voluntary chains and retail co-operatives) is that franchise systems are normally based on some unique product or service; on a method of doing business; or on the trade name, goodwill, or patent that the franchisor

● TABLE | 14.2   Major Types of Retail Organizations

Type	Description	Examples
Corporate chain store	Two or more outlets that are commonly owned and controlled. Corporate chains appear in all types of retailing, but they are strongest in department stores, food stores, drug stores, shoe stores, and women's clothing stores.	Carrefour, Lulu, Union Coop in the Arab world. Examples from the United States and other regions include: Sears, Kroger (grocery stores), CVS (drug stores), Williams-Sonoma (cookware and housewares)
Voluntary chain	Wholesaler-sponsored group of independent retailers engaged in group buying and merchandising.	Examples from the United States and other regions include: Independent Grocers Alliance (IGA), Dolt Best hardware, Western Auto, True Value hardware
Retailer co-operative	Group of independent retailers who set up a central buying organization and conduct joint promotion efforts.	Examples from the United States and other regions include: Associated Grocers (groceries), Ace (hardware)
Franchise organization	Contractual association between a franchisor (a manufacturer, wholesaler, or service organization) and franchisees (independent businesspeople who buy the right to own and operate one or more units in the franchise system). Franchise organizations are normally based on some unique product or service, on a method of doing business, or on a trade name, goodwill, or patent that the franchisor has developed.	McDonald's, Subway, Pizza Hut, Starbucks, Gloria Jeans, Dunkin' Donuts

Franchising: These days, it's almost impossible to stroll down a city block or drive on a street without seeing a McDonald's.

has developed. Franchising has been prominent in fast food and restaurants, motels, and health and fitness centers.

Once considered upstarts among independent businesses, franchises now command a large part of all retail sales around the world. In many parts of the world, it's nearly impossible to stroll down a city block or drive on a city street without seeing a McDonald's. One of the best-known and most successful franchisers, McDonald's now has more then 32,000 stores in 117 countries. It serves nearly 52 million customers a day and racks up nearly US$47 billion in annual systemwide sales. More than 78 percent of McDonald's restaurants worldwide are owned and operated by franchisees. They have recently been overtaken by Subway, one of the fastest-growing franchises, with more than 34,000 shops in 98 countries.[26]

Finally, *merchandising conglomerates* are corporations that combine several different retailing forms under central ownership. An example is Centrepoint from Landmark Group, which aims to benefit from synergies between its core retail concepts—Babyshop, Shoe Mart, Splash, and Lifestyle. By placing all of these outlets under a single identity it hopes to offer a single destination shopping experience. Centrepoint has 53 stores across the GCC and Jordan and plans to have over 100 stores across the region by 2011, which would make it the largest retail brand in the Arab world. For consumers, the most visible change has been in shop design, which Landmark claims will produce a more stimulating shopping experience for the whole family, while offering the same value for money. The aim for this operator in the mid-market retail sector is to shape consumer perceptions, increase brand worth, and fuel future growth.[27]

Retailer Marketing Decisions (pp 427–431)

Retailers are always searching for new marketing strategies to attract and hold customers. In the past, retailers attracted customers with unique product assortments and more or better services. Today, retail assortments and services are looking more and more alike. Many brand manufacturers, in their drive for volume, have placed their brands almost everywhere. You can find most consumer brands not only in department stores but also in mass-merchandise discount stores, off-price discount stores, and on the web. Thus, it's now more difficult for any one retailer to offer exclusive merchandise.

Service differentiation among retailers has also decreased. Many department stores have trimmed their services, whereas discounters have increased theirs. Customers have become smarter and more price sensitive. They see no reason to pay more for identical brands, especially when service differences are shrinking. For all these reasons, many retailers today are rethinking their marketing strategies.

As shown in ✎ **Figure 14.6**, retailers face major marketing decisions about *segmentation and targeting, store differentiation and positioning*, and the *retail marketing mix*.

Segmentation, Targeting, Differentiation, and Positioning Decisions

Retailers must first segment and define their target markets and then decide how they will differentiate and position themselves in these markets. Should the store focus on upscale, midscale, or downscale shoppers? Do target shoppers want variety, depth of assortment, convenience, or low prices? Until they define and profile their markets, retailers cannot make consistent decisions about product assortment, services, pricing, advertising, store decor, or any of the other decisions that must support their positions.

Too many retailers, even big ones, fail to define their target markets and positions clearly. They tried to have something for everyone and end up satisfying no market well. In contrast, successful retailers define their target markets well and position themselves strongly. For example, Lulu positions itself strongly on low prices.

Product Assortment and Services Division

Retailers must decide on three major product variables: *product assortment*, *services mix*, and *store atmosphere*.

The retailer's *product assortment* should differentiate the retailer while matching target shoppers' expectations. One strategy is to offer merchandise that no other competitor carries, such as store brands or national brands on which it holds exclusives. For example, Saks gets exclusive rights to carry a well-known designer's labels. It also offers its own private-label lines—the Saks Fifth Avenue Signature, Classic, and Sport collections.

Another strategy is to feature blockbuster merchandising events—Lulu hypermarket is known for running spectacular shows featuring goods from a certain country, such as India or China. Finally, the retailer can differentiate itself by offering a highly targeted product assortment—for example, Curry House Dubai specializes in Indian cuisine.

The *store's atmosphere* is another important element in the reseller's product arsenal. The retailer wants to create a unique store experience, one that suits the target market and moves customers to buy. For example, consider the partnership in Saudi Arabia between Givori, the luxury accessorizer specializing in mobile phone art, and Harvey Nichols, the one-stop retailer specializing in luxury items. The partnership's expansion into the Kingdom followed Givori's operation in Harvey Nichols, Dubai. The two partners were encouraged by Saudi customers' demand for fashionable mobile phones and accessories, and the use of quality materials and craftsmanship. Launched in 2007, the Givori brand uses luxury materials, including exotic skins, mother of pearl, Swarovski crystals, and rare European vintage trinkets to create high-quality handsets. "Givori's presence in Harvey Nichols is an asset to the store, and we are confident that our valued clientele will be inspired by the luxury pieces," stated Betina Qubbaj, events and personal shopping manager, Harvey Nichols, Riyadh. "Saudi consumers are fashion savvy, with a taste for the decadence and the exclusivity that the Givori brand is known for, and which it has certainly brought to the table."

The design of the Givori store aims to reflect the company's products, with sleek design and functional display areas. Handling and using the mobile phones is encouraged, and staff areavailable to give advice and answer any questions.[28]

Today's successful retailers carefully orchestrate virtually every aspect of the consumer store experience, down to the music, lighting, and even the smells (see **Real Marketing 14.2**).

Real Marketing 14.2

Orchestrating the Retail Experience

The next time that you step into a retail store—whether it sells consumer electronics, hardware, or high fashion—stop and carefully consider your surroundings. Think about the store's layout and displays. Listen to the background sounds. Smell the smells. Chances are good that everything in the store, from the layout and lighting to the music and even the smells, has been carefully orchestrated to help shape your shopping experience—and to open your wallet. In most cases, you're probably being affected in ways so subtle that you don't even realize what's happening to you.

It all starts at the store entrance. According to one reporter, "what's in the entrance is the spring on the trap"—it pulls you in and puts you in the mood to buy. "The entrance is important because it hints at what's inside that you must have."

In City Stars' mall, Stars Center, as soon as the visitors leave their cars in the parking area and enter the mall, they find a massage service. Even though it's a paid service, the visitors feel that the luxury factor in the mall will be high. Another service offered is a few hours' babysitting for their children at the Baby Academy. The value preposition is, "Let your kids have fun with us while we free your hands to enjoy your mall experience." Even though this is another paid service, it still sets the visitors in the state of mind of relaxing and enjoying their mall experience.

At an ACE store, the entranceway lures shoppers in with an open floor plan so they get a better 'vista' of the store. Floor-to-ceiling racks of goods, long the signature of the warehouse store, are now further back. Further-down displays of expensive goods—riding lawn mowers, upscale porch furniture, and a home design center for redecorating kitchen, bathroom, and flooring—are clustered so they are visible from the front door. All are ways to engage you in the store and draw you in.

In a department store, you're funneled from the entrance past the store's most expensive goods through a maze of aisles and into departments that are set up as stores-within-a-store. Then you find yourself on 'the race-track,' an oval aisle that carries you around the entire store to get a look at everything. Mini-displays called trend stations are parked in the middle of aisles to stop shoppers' progress and entice them to look and buy.

Meanwhile, everything in a well-designed store is carefully constructed to create just the right moods and actions. At a Sony Style store, for instance, it's all designed to encourage touch, from the silk wallpaper to the smooth maple wood cabinets, to the etched-glass countertops. Products are displayed like museum pieces and set up for you to touch and try. Once you touch something, Sony figures, you'll buy it. Sony Style even has mini-living rooms set up to showcase what its 40-inch flat-panel television would look like over a fireplace. "We've had customers bring in their architect and say, 'Re-create this in my house. I want the whole setup,'" says a Sony retail executive.

A store's lighting can affect anything from your moods to the pace at which you move and shop. Bright lighting can create excitement, whereas softer lighting can create a mellow mood. Many retailers adjust lighting to regulate shoppers' 'blink rates'—the slower you blink, they reason, the more likely you are to browse, pause, and eventually buy.

Sound is another important element of the retail experience. "Music has been used by retailers for decades as a way to identify their stores and affect a shopper's mood, to make you feel happy, nostalgic, or relaxed so that you linger," notes the reporter. They now hire 'audio architects' to develop music and sounds that fit their unique positioning.

Perhaps the hottest store environment frontier these days is scent—that's right, the way the store smells. Anyone who's walked into a mall has been enticed by the smell of cinnamon buns or chocolate chip cookies. Now, most large retailers are developing signature scents that you smell only in their stores. Eastern incense makers are very famous for their signature odors. Walking past them in the mall,

Next time you shop, stop, look, and listen. Successful retailers like Sony Style orchestrate every aspect of the shopper store experience, down to the music, lighting, and even the smells (a subtle fragrance of vanilla and mandarin orange).

one cannot help but be overwhelmed with a scent associated with deep Arab world tradition. This is the same scent that you are greeted with when you walk into an elegant *deshdasha* shop. The scents are associated with the history, the culture, and the clothes they represent.

At a Sony Style store, the subtle fragrance of vanilla and mandarin orange—designed exclusively for Sony—wafts down on shoppers, relaxing them and helping them believe that this is a very nice place to be. Sony decided to create its own store scent as one way to make the consumer electronics it sells less intimidating, particularly to women. At Sony's Madison Avenue store in New York, the scent is even pumped onto the street. "From research, we found that scent is closest to the brain and will evoke the most emotion, even faster than the eye," says the Sony retail executive. "Our scent helps us create an environment like no other." A scents expert agrees: "Scent is so closely aligned with your emotions, it's so primitive."

Thus, in their quest to orchestrate the optimal shopper experience, today's successful retailers leave no store environment stone unturned. The next time you visit a store, stop, look, and listen. See if you can spot the subtle and not-so-subtle things that retailers do to affect what you feel, think, and buy in their stores. "Most people know they are being influenced subliminally when they shop," says a retail consumer behavior expert. "They just may not realize how much."

Sources: Extracts, quotes, and other information are from or adapted from Mindy Fetterman and Jayne O'Donnall, "Just Browsing at the Mall? That's What You Think," *USA Today*, September 1, 2006, accessed at www.usatoday.com; Ylan Q. Mui, "Dollars and Scents," *Washington Post*, December 19, 2006, p. D01, and Denise Power, "Something Is in the Air: Panel Says Scent Sells," *WWD*, March 25, 2008, p. 14.

Such 'experiential retailing' confirms that retail stores are much more than simply assortments of goods. They are environments to be experienced by the people who shop in them. Store atmospheres offer a powerful tool by which retailers can differentiate their stores from those of competitors.

Price Decision

A retailer's price policy must fit its target market and positioning, product and service assortment, and competition. All retailers would like to charge high markups and achieve high volume, but the two seldom go together. Most retailers seek *either* high markups on lower volume (most specialty stores) *or* low markups on higher volume (mass merchandisers and discount stores).

Ahmed Siddiqi and Sons is a chain that sells premium and exclusive Swiss watches. It carries brands such as Rolex, Baume & Mercier, A. Lange & Söhne, Audemars Piguet, and Bovet. A purchase there can easily set one back US$30,000 or more. Every item is exclusive and the patrons are pampered by attention from the management. Ahmed Siddiqi and Sons sells at a low volume but reaps a healthy margin on each sale. Hour Choice, on the other hand, carries medium- to low-price watches such as Timex, Citizen, Seiko, Swiss, and Tissot. Its business model depends on selling high volumes with a low margin.

Retailers must also decide on the extent to which they will use sales and other price promotions. Some retailers use no price promotions at all, competing instead on product and service quality rather than on price. Other retailers practice *high-low pricing*—charging higher prices on an everyday basis, coupled with frequent sales and other price promotions to increase store traffic, create a low-price image, or attract customers who will buy other goods at full prices. Still others—such as Carrefour, Lulu, Dirham and Riyal, among other mass retailers—practice *everyday low pricing (EDLP)*, charging constant, everyday low prices with few sales or discounts. Which strategy is best depends on the retailer's marketing strategy and the pricing approaches of competitors.

Promotion Decision

Retailers use any or all of the promotion tools—advertising, personal selling, sales promotion, public relations, and direct marketing—to reach consumers. They advertise in newspapers, magazines, radio, television, and on the Internet. Advertising may be supported by newspaper inserts, catalogs, and direct mail. Personal selling requires careful training of salespeople in how to greet customers, meet their needs, and handle their complaints. Sales promotions may include in-store demonstrations, displays, contests, and visiting celebrities. Public relations activities, such as press conferences and speeches, store openings, special events, newsletters, magazines, and public service activities, are always available to retailers. Most retailers have also set up websites, offering customers information and other features and often selling merchandise directly.

Place Decision

Retailers often point to three critical factors in retailing success: *location*, *location*, and *location*! It's very important that retailers select locations that are accessible to the target market in areas that are consistent with the retailer's positioning. For example, Apple locates its stores in high-end malls and trendy shopping districts—not low-rent strip malls on the edge of town. Small retailers may have to settle for whatever locations they can find or afford. Large retailers, however, usually employ specialists who select locations using advanced methods.

Most stores today cluster together to increase their customer pulling power and to give consumers the convenience of one-stop shopping.

Shopping center

A group of retail businesses planned, developed, owned, and managed as a unit.

A **shopping center** is a group of retail businesses planned, developed, owned, and managed as a unit. A *regional shopping center*, or *regional shopping mall*, the largest and most dramatic shopping center, contains from 40 to over 200 stores, including 2 or more full-line department stores. It is like a covered mini-downtown and attracts customers from a wide area. A *community shopping center* contains between 15 and 40 retail stores. It normally contains a branch of a department store or variety store, a supermarket, specialty stores, professional offices, and sometimes a bank. Most shopping centers are *neighborhood shopping centers* that generally contain between 5 and 15 stores. They are close and convenient for consumers. They usually contain a supermarket, perhaps a discount store, and several service stores—dry cleaner, drugstore, video-rental store, barber or beauty shop, hardware store, local restaurant, or other stores.[29]

Author Comment | Whereas retailers primarily sell goods and services directly to final consumers for personal use, wholesalers sell primarily to those buying for resale or business use. Because wholesalers operate behind the scenes, they are largely unknown to final consumers. But they are very important to their business customers.

Wholesaling (pp 431)

Wholesaling includes all activities involved in selling goods and services to those buying for resale or business use. We call **wholesalers** those firms engaged *primarily* in wholesaling activities.

Wholesaling

All activities involved in selling goods and services to those buying for resale or business use.

> Wholesalers buy mostly from producers and sell mostly to retailers, industrial consumers, and other wholesalers. As a result, many of the largest and most important wholesalers are largely unknown to final consumers.

Wholesaler

A firm engaged primarily in wholesaling activities.

Why are wholesalers important to sellers? For example, why would a producer use wholesalers rather than selling directly to retailers or consumers? Simply put, wholesalers add value by performing one or more of the following channel functions:

- *Selling and promoting:* Wholesalers' sales forces help manufacturers reach many small customers at a low cost. The wholesaler has more contacts and is often more trusted by the buyer than the distant manufacturer.

- *Buying and assortment building:* Wholesalers can select items and build assortments needed by their customers, thereby saving the consumers much work.

- *Bulk breaking:* Wholesalers save their customers money by buying in carload lots and breaking bulk (breaking large lots into small quantities).

- *Warehousing:* Wholesalers hold inventories, thereby reducing the inventory costs and risks of suppliers and customers.

- *Transportation:* Wholesalers can provide quicker delivery to buyers because they are closer than the producers.

- *Financing:* Wholesalers finance their customers by giving credit, and they finance their suppliers by ordering early and paying bills on time.

- *Risk bearing:* Wholesalers absorb risk by taking title and bearing the cost of theft, damage, spoilage, and obsolescence.

- *Market information:* Wholesalers give information to suppliers and customers about competitors, new products, and price developments.

- *Management services and advice:* Wholesalers often help retailers train their sales clerks, improve store layouts and displays, and set up accounting and inventory control systems.

Agents And Distributors (pp 431–432)

In the Arab world, agents and distributors are also vital links in the marketing channel. They represent specific product lines within certain geographic areas.

Local agents usually do not take possession or ownership of the goods; rather they act as brokers between alocal buyer and a foreign company. The agents will keep a percentage of the total deal as their transaction fee.

Local agent

An agent who acts as a broker between a local buyer and a foreign company.

MADI International, based in the UAE, is an exclusive distributor for internationally reputed brands in haircare, skincare, nailcare, makeup, salon equipment and furniture.

Exclusive distributors are much more involved in the marketing channel. They will regularly buy specified products from the foreign company, stock them in warehouses, and sell them to a retailer and wholesaler in a specified geographic area. They will also provide credit to the retailer and wholesaler. In the UAE, MADI International specializes in international brands of haircare, skincare, and nailcare products, makeup, salon equipment, and furniture. It formed a partnership with Procter & Gamble (P&G), becoming the exclusive distributor in the UAE and Qatar of Wella Professionals, a leading product in the professional haircare market.

Chairman Mohamad Madi commented: "P&G and MADI International have a long history of partnership starting in 1995, when we were appointed to be the distributor of the KADUS brand. The new agreement to distribute products under the Wella Professionals brand reaffirms the quality of our services and the success of our marketing strategy. MADI International has a comprehensive network of partners and contacts across the region, which will be crucial in boosting the market share of Wella Professionals, especially with the launch of the 'Wella Trends Collection 2010' in the region. We are confident that we can build up this new collection of superior haircare products as a leading choice among professional salons in the region.

"The appointment of MADI International is an important strategic decision that we believe will enable us to effectively penetrate and maintain a strong presence in key growth markets in the region. MADI International's reputation as a leading distributor in the beauty industry will also complement our own marketing initiatives and reinforce our brand value."[30]

Exclusive distributor

A representative who buys, stocks, and sells the products of a foreign company to a retailer and wholesaler in his or her territory.

MADI International's distribution network covers the UAE, Kuwait, Lebanon, and Qatar, and it is aiming to expand into Saudi Arabia. Regional distributors like MADI are generally preferred by the principal organization due to the simplified process of dealing with one distributor for the region instead of one for each country. The regional distributor also gains through economies of scale. By leveraging its overheads, such as admininistrative and ordering costs, it brings the overall cost down. Sometimes these distributors are required to work closely with the reseller or final customers to develop the market, and their skill in serving the market becomes an important selection criterion.

Al-Jammaz in Saudi Arabia, SouthComp Polaris in North Africa, and Marsons in Pakistan are authorized distributors of Cisco products. They are responsible for managing relationships with IT resellers as well as "providing distribution operational excellence, reseller development, and sufficient coverage in developing the small-to-medium businesses in these territories." They are also expected to increase their market coverage and provide support to resellers, with the aim of increasing customer satisfaction. Cisco selects its distributors based on their ability to provide support to resellers and to be able to extend credit to the market. It also considers potential distributors' core competencies in new technologies, geographical reach, and the ability to integrate with Cisco's systems and processes.[31] Exclusive distributors will generally earn a margin of about 20 percent for their role in this link, but after all expenses have been deducted (e.g. employees' salaries, warehousing, logistics), their net profit sometimes can be as low as 4 percent. The relationship between the agent and the distributor is governed by the agency law of the relevant country.

REVIEWING Objectives AND KEY Terms

Marketing channel decisions are among the most important decisions that management faces. A company's channel decisions directly affect every other marketing decision. Management must make channel decisions carefully, incorporating today's needs with tomorrow's likely selling environment. Some companies pay too little attention to their distribution channels, but others have used imaginative distribution systems to gain competitive advantage.

In this chapter we also looked at retailing and wholesaling, which consist of many organizations bringing goods and services from the point of production to the point of use. We considered the nature and importance of retailing, major types of retailers, and the decisions retailers make. We then examined wholesalers as well as distributors and agents.

OBJECTIVE 1 **Explain why companies use marketing channels and discuss the functions these channels perform.** (pp 401–405)

Most producers use intermediaries to bring their products to market. They try to forge a *marketing channel* (or *distribution channel*)—a set of interdependent organizations involved in the process of making a product or service available for use or consumption by the consumer or business user. Through their contacts, experience, specialization, and scale of operation, intermediaries usually offer the firm more than it can achieve on its own.

Marketing channels perform many key functions. Some help *complete* transactions by gathering and distributing *information* needed for planning and aiding exchange, by developing and spreading persuasive *communications* about an offer, by performing *contact* work—finding and communicating with prospective buyers, by *matching*—shaping and fitting the offer to the buyer's needs, and by entering into *negotiation* to reach an agreement on price and other terms of the offer so that ownership can be transferred. Other functions help to *fulfill* the completed transactions by offering *physical distribution*—transporting and storing goods, *financing*—acquiring and using funds to cover the costs of the channel work, and *risk taking*—assuming the risks of carrying out the channel work.

OBJECTIVE 2 **Discuss how channel members interact and how they organize to perform the work of the channel.** (pp 405–411)

The channel will be most effective when each member is assigned the tasks it can do best. Ideally, because the success of individual channel members depends on overall channel success, all channel firms should work together smoothly. They should understand and accept their roles, co-ordinate their goals and activities, and co-operate to attain overall channel goals. By co-operating, they can more effectively sense, serve, and satisfy the target market.

In a large company, the formal organization structure assigns roles and provides needed leadership. But in a distribution channel made up of independent firms, leadership and power are not formally set. Traditionally, distribution channels have lacked the leadership needed to assign roles and manage conflict. In recent years, however, new types of channel organizations have appeared that provide stronger leadership and improved performance.

OBJECTIVE 3 **Identify the major channel alternatives open to a company.** (pp 411–417)

Each firm identifies alternative ways to reach its market. Available means vary from direct selling to using one, two, three, or more intermediary *channel levels*. Marketing channels face continuous and sometimes dramatic change. Three of the most important trends are the growth of *vertical*, *horizontal*, and *multichannel marketing systems*. These trends affect channel co-operation, conflict, and competition.

Channel design begins with assessing customer channel service needs and company channel objectives and constraints. The company then identifies the major channel alternatives in terms of the *types* of intermediaries, the *number* of intermediaries, and the *channel responsibilities* of each. Each channel alternative must be evaluated according to economic, control, and adaptive criteria. *Channel management* calls for selecting qualified intermediaries and motivating them. Individual channel members must be evaluated regularly.

OBJECTIVE 4 **Discuss the nature and importance of marketing logistics and integrated supply chain management.** (pp 417–423)

Just as firms are giving the marketing concept increased recognition, more business firms are paying attention to *marketing logistics* (or *physical distribution*). Logistics is an area of potentially high cost savings and improved customer satisfaction. Marketing logistics addresses not only *outbound distribution* but also *inbound distribution* and *reverse distribution*. That is, it involves entire *supply chain management*—managing value-added flows between suppliers, the company, resellers, and final users. No logistics system can both maximize customer service and minimize distribution costs. Instead, the goal of logistics management is to provide a *targeted* level of service at the least cost. The major logistics functions include *warehousing, inventory management, transportation*, and *logistics information management*.

The *integrated supply chain management* concept recognizes that improved logistics requires teamwork in the form of close working relationships across functional areas inside the company and across various organizations in the supply chain. Companies can achieve logistics harmony among functions by creating cross-functional logistics teams, integrative supply manager positions, and senior-level logistics executives with cross-functional authority. Channel partnerships can take the form of cross-company teams, shared projects, and information-sharing systems. Today, some companies are outsourcing their logistics functions to third-party logistics (3PL) providers to save costs, increase efficiency, and gain faster and more effective access to global markets.

OBJECTIVE 5 Explain the role of retailers in the distribution channel. Describe the major types of retailers and the decisions they make. (pp 423–431)

Retailing includes all activities involved in selling goods or services directly to final consumers for their personal, nonbusiness use. Retail stores come in all shapes and sizes, and new retail types keep emerging. Store retailers can be classified by the *amount of service* they provide (self-service, limited service, or full service), *product line sold* (specialty stores, department stores, supermarkets, convenience stores, superstores, and service businesses), and *relative prices* (discount stores and off-price retailers). Today, many retailers are banding together in corporate and contractual *retail organizations* (corporate chains, voluntary chains, retailer co-operatives, franchise organizations, and merchandising conglomerates).

Retailers are always searching for new marketing strategies to attract and hold customers. They face major marketing decisions about segmentation and targeting, store differentiation and positioning, and the retail marketing mix.

Retailers must first segment and define their target markets and then decide how they will differentiate and position themselves in these markets. Those that try to offer something for everyone end up satisfying no market well. In contrast, successful retailers define their target markets well and position themselves strongly.

Guided by strong targeting and positioning, retailers must decide on a retail marketing mix—product and services assortment, price, promotion, and place. Retail stores are much more than simply an assortment of goods—beyond the products and services they offer, today's successful retailers carefully orchestrate virtually every aspect of the consumer store experience. A retailer's price policy must fit its target market and positioning, products and services assortment, and competition. Retailers use any or all of the promotion tools—advertising, personal selling, sales promotion, public relations, and direct marketing—to reach consumers. Finally, it's very important that retailers select locations that are accessible to the target market in areas that are consistent with the retailer's positioning.

Retailers operate in a harsh and fast-changing environment, which offers threats as well as opportunities. New retail forms continue to emerge to meet new situations and consumer needs, but the life cycle of new retail forms is getting shorter—retailers must pay attention to the wheel-of-retailing concept. Other trends in retailing include the rapid growth of nonstore retailing, retail convergence (the merging of consumers, products, prices, and retailers), the rise of megaretailers, the growing importance of retail technology, the global expansion of major retailers, and the resurgence of retail stores as consumer communities or hangouts.

OBJECTIVE 6 Explain the major types of wholesalers and their marketing decisions. (pp 431–432)

Wholesaling includes all the activities involved in selling goods or services to those who are buying for the purpose of resale or for business use. Wholesalers fall into three groups. First, *merchant wholesalers* take possession of the goods. They include *full-service wholesalers* (wholesale merchants, industrial distributors) and *limited-service wholesalers* (cash-and-carry wholesalers, truck wholesalers, drop shippers, rack jobbers, producers' co-operatives, and mail-order wholesalers). Secondly, *brokers* and *agents* do not take possession of the goods but are paid a commission for aiding buying and selling. Finally, *manufacturers' sales branches and offices* are wholesaling operations conducted by nonwholesalers to bypass the wholesalers.

Like retailers, wholesalers must target carefully and position themselves strongly. And, like retailers, wholesalers must decide on product and service assortments, prices, promotion, and place. Progressive wholesalers constantly watch for better ways to meet the changing needs of their suppliers and target customers. They recognize that, in the long run, their only reason for existence comes from adding value by increasing the efficiency and effectiveness of the entire marketing channel. As with other types of marketers, the goal is to build value-adding customer relationships.

KEY Terms

OBJECTIVE 1

Value delivery network (p 403)
Marketing channel (distribution channel) (p 403)
Channel level (p 404)
Direct marketing channel (p 405)
Indirect marketing channel (p 405)

OBJECTIVE 2

Channel conflict (p 406)
Conventional distribution channel (p 407)
Vertical marketing system (VMS) (p 407)
Corporate VMS (p 407)
Contractual VMS (p 408)
Franchise organization (p 408)
Administered VMS (p 409)
Horizontal marketing system (p 409)
Multichannel distribution system (p 409)
Disintermediation (p 410)

OBJECTIVE 3

Marketing channel design (p 411)
Intensive distribution (p 413)
Exclusive distribution (p 413)
Selective distribution (p 413)
Marketing channel management (p 415)

OBJECTIVE 4

Marketing logistics (physical distribution) (p 417)
Supply chain management (p 418)
Distribution center (p 419)
Intermodal transportation (p 421)
Integrated logistics management (p 421)
Third-party logistics (3PL) provider (p 422)

OBJECTIVE 5

Retailing (p 423)
Retailer (p 423)

Specialty store (p 425)
Department store (p 425)
Supermarket (p 425)
Convenience store (p 425)
Hypermarket (p 425)
Service retailer (p 425)
Discount store (p 426)
Independent off-price retailer (p 426)
Factory outlet (p 426)
Chain stores (p 426)
Franchise (p 426)
Shopping center (p 431)

OBJECTIVE 6

Wholesaling (p 431)
Wholesaler (p 431)
Local agent (p 431)
Exclusive distributor (p 432)

DISCUSSING & APPLYING THE Concepts

Discussing the Concepts

1. Explain how channel members add value for manufacturers and consumers.
2. Discuss the various types of conflict that may arise in the channel of distribution. Is all channel conflict bad?
3. What factors does a cosmetics company need to consider when designing its marketing channel for a new low-priced line of cosmetics?
4. Describe the major types of vertical marketing systems and provide an example of each.
5. Discuss the complexities international marketers face when designing channels in other countries.
6. List and briefly describe the major logistics functions. Provide an example of a decision a logistics manager would make for each major function.
7. Discuss how retailers and wholesalers add value to the marketing system. Explain why marketers are embracing the concept of *shopper marketing*.
8. Different types of customers and products require different amounts of service. Discuss the different levels of retailer service and give one example of each.
9. Discuss the different organizational approaches for retailers and provide an example of each.
10. Explain how wholesalers add value in the channel of distribution.

Applying the Concepts

1. Ward's Berry Farm specializes in fresh strawberries, which it sells to a variety of retailers through a produce wholesale distributor. Form a small group and have each member assume one of the following roles: berry farmer, wholesaler, and grocery retailer. In your role, discuss three things that might have recently angered you about the other channel members. Take turns voicing your gripes and attempting to resolve the conflict.
2. Visit http://electronics.howstuffworks.com/rfid.htm# and watch the video 'How UPS Smart Labels Work.' You can also learn more about RFID technology from this site. What impact will RFID tags have on each of the major logistical functions? What are the biggest current obstacles to adopting this technology?
3. Choose three retailers that you buy from often. Classify these retailers in terms of the characteristics presented in the chapter. Next, use **Table 14.1** on page 424 to categorize each retailer.
4. Deciding on a target market and positioning for a retail store are very important marketing decisions. In a small group, develop the concept for a new retail store. Who is the target market for your store? How is your store positioned? What retail atmospherics will enhance this positioning effectively to attract and satisfy your target market?

FOCUS ON Technology

No vacation in Dubai would be complete without a trip to one of its shopping malls for some designer goods. In just the last 5 years, over 15 malls have been built across the city. The massive Emirates Mall is home to famous British department store Harvey Nichols. However, traders selling copycat designer goods were subjected to widespread police raids in 2007; during these raids the police and trading standards agents seized hundreds of fake handbags, watches, and items of clothing.

Shop owners resorted to dumping their stock or hiding it away before they could be caught with the counterfeit goods.

One trader said, "The police were very thorough and wanted to look at all the shops' stock rooms. There was a lot of panic and people had to throw stock away or have it taken away in a van to be put in storage."[32]

1. The global market in counterfeit goods is enormous. What can designer businesses do about the trade?
2. Online auction houses such as eBay have clear policies about counterfeit designer goods, but what can they practically do about it?

FOCUS ON Ethics

Parallel imports, *gray products*, and *price diversion* all represent the same activity—diverting imported products meant for one market at lower prices and reselling them at higher profits in other markets. This happens in many industries, including apparel, high-tech electronics, auto parts, luxury goods, and cosmetics. The textbook you're using now might be a gray product if it was intended for an international market but you purchased it from Amazon.com for much less than what you'd pay at your bookstore or the publisher's website. As another example, gray traders purchase mobile phones in poorer countries, such as Pakistan or India, and resell them in the UAE or Saudi Arabia, where higher prices garner profits for the

traders. In fact, parallel importing of most products is legal, and some experts claim that it's just the free market working. In some cases, though, counterfeit goods are mixed in with the legitimate brands. Parallel imported mobile phones are 100 percent identical to the original ones. Parallel imports are possible because the manufacturers of original mobile phones sell their products at different prices within the region in order to maximize their profits.

1. Learn more about this phenomenon. Who receives value in such transactions? Who loses value?
2. How are manufacturers dealing with this problem?

MARKETING BY THE Numbers

A small business prepares and delivers snacks to local businesses. It has four product lines and has worked out the selling price, variable labor costs, variable material costs, and the number of units sold. For its standard sandwich range, the figures are respectively US$2, $0.40, $0.20, and 9,000 units. For the deluxe sandwich, the figures are $3, $0.45, $0.55, and 12,000 units. For the business's standard wrap, the figures are US$2.50, $0.40, $0.30, and 6,000 units, and finally for the deluxe wrap, the figures are US$3.50, $0.40, $0.50, and 4,000 units. Assume that fixed costs are US$22,000. Refer to Appendix 2: Marketing by the Numbers to answer the following questions.

1. What is the sales revenue for each of the product lines?

2. What is the total sales revenue?

3. What is the contribution per product line?

4. What is the total contribution of the product lines?

5. What is the level of profit or loss for the business?

By breaking down a business into cost and profit centers, budget holders will be expected to effectively bid and argue the case for any capital expenditure that they wish to be allocated to their center. The business will always have a limited amount of funds available to purchase these types of assets and it needs to be assured that any investment in these assets will provide the greatest possible benefits and financial returns to the business. Some capital expenditure costs are unavoidable, perhaps when a fleet of vehicles needs to be replaced, or when an adjacent property needs to be purchased in order to expand.

Each expenditure item is analyzed within the context of the overall activities of the organization. They are assessed to see if they are central to the smooth running of the operation. Not only will the costs and benefits be measured, but also the potential consequences if the capital expenditure is not approved.

1. Why might it be unfair to allocate the full costs of overheads to particular cost and profit centers, purely based on the amount of space that they occupy or the number of employees in that center?

VIDEO Case

Progressive

Progressive has attained top-tier status in the insurance industry by focusing on innovation. Progressive was the first company to offer drive-in claims services, installment payment of premiums, and 24/7 customer service. But some of Progressive's most innovative moves involve its channels of distribution. Whereas most insurance companies distribute their products to consumers via intermediary agents or direct-to-consumer methods, Progressive was one of the first companies to recognize the value in doing both. In the late 1980s, it augmented its agency distribution with a direct toll-free-number channel.

In 1995, Progressive moved into the future by becoming the first major insurer in the world to launch a website. In 1997, customers could buy auto insurance policies online in real time. Today, at Progressive's website, customers can do everything from managing their own account information to reporting claims directly. Progressive even offers a one-stop concierge claim service.

After viewing the Progressive video, answer the following questions about marketing channels:

1. Apply the concept of the supply chain to Progressive.

2. Using the model of consumer and business channels found in the chapter, sketch out as many channels for Progressive as you can. How does each of these channels meet distinct customer needs?

3. Discuss the various ways that Progressive has had an impact on the insurance industry.

COMPANY Case

Zara: The Technology Giant of the Fashion World

One global retailer is expanding at a dizzying pace. It's on track for what appears to be world domination of its industry. Having built its own state-of-the art distribution network, the company is leaving the competition in the dust in terms of sales and profits, not to mention speed of inventory management and turnover. Wal-Mart you might think? Dell possibly? Although these two retail giants definitely fit the description, we're talking here about Zara, the flagship specialty chain of Spain-based clothing conglomerate, Inditex.

This dynamic retailer is known for selling stylish designs that resemble those of big-name fashion houses, but at moderate prices. "We sell the latest trends at low prices, but our clients value our design, quality, and constant innovation," a company spokesman said. "That gives us the advantage even in highly competitive, developed markets, including Britain." More interesting is the way that Zara achieves its mission.

FAST-FASHION—THE NEWEST WAVE

A handful of European specialty clothing retailers are taking the fashion world by storm with a business model that has come to be known as 'fast-fashion.' In short, these companies can recognize and respond to fashion trends very quickly, create products that mirror the trends, and get those products onto shelves much faster and more frequently than the industry norm. Fast-fashion retailers include Sweden's Hennes&Mauritz (H&M), Britain's Top Shop, Spain's Mango, and the Netherland's Mexx. Although all of these companies are successfully employing the fast-fashion concept, Zara leads the pack on virtually every level.

For example, 'fast' at Zara means that it can take a product from concept through design, manufacturing, and store-shelf placement in as little as two weeks, much quicker than any of its fast-fashion competitors. For more mainstream clothing chains, the process takes months.

This gives Zara the advantage of virtually copying fashions from the pages of *Vogue* and having them on the streets in dozens of countries before the next issue of the magazine even hits the newsstands! When Spain's Crown Prince Felipe and Letizia Ortiz Rocasolano announced their engagement, the bride-to-be wore a stylish white trouser suit. This raised some eyebrows, given that it violated royal protocol. But European women loved it and within a few weeks, hundreds of them were wearing a nearly identical outfit they had purchased from Zara.

But Zara is more than just fast. It's also prolific. In a typical year, Zara launches about 11,000 new items. Compare that with the 2,000 to 4,000 items introduced by both H&M and Gap. In the fashion world, this difference is huge. Zara stores receive new merchandise two to three times each week, whereas most clothing retailers get large shipments on a seasonal basis, four to six times per year.

As part of its strategy to introduce more new items with greater frequency, Zara also produces items in smaller batches. Thus, it assumes less risk if an item doesn't sell well. But smaller batches also means exclusivity, a unique benefit from a mass-market retailer that draws fashion-conscious young people through Zara's doors like a magnet. When items sell out, they are not restocked with another shipment. Instead, the next Zara shipment contains something new, something different. Popular items can appear and disappear within a week. Consumers know that if they like something, they have to buy it or miss out. Customers are enticed to check out store stock more often, leading to very high levels of repeat patronage. But it also means that Zara doesn't have to follow the industry pattern of marking products down as the season progresses. Thus, Zara reaps the benefit of prices that average much closer to the list price.

THE VERTICAL SECRET TO ZARA'S SUCCESS

Just how does Zara achieve such mind-blowing responsiveness? The answer lies in its distribution system. In 1975, Amancio Ortega opened the first Zara store in Spain's remote northwest town of La Coruña, home to Zara's headquarters. Having already worked in the textile industry for two decades, his experience led him to design a system in which he could control every aspect of the supply chain, from design and production to distribution and retailing. He knew, for example, that in the textile business, the biggest markups were made by wholesalers and retailers. He was determined to maintain control over these activities.

Ortega's original philosophy forms the heart of Zara's unique, rapid-fire supply chain today. But it's Zara's high-tech information system that has taken vertical integration in the company to an unprecedented level. According to CEO Pablo Isla, "Our information system is absolutely avant-garde. It's what links the shop to our designers and our distribution system."

Zara's vertically integrated system makes the starting point of a product concept hard to nail down. At Zara's headquarters,

creative teams of more than 300 professionals carry out the design process. But they act on information fed to them from the stores. This goes far beyond typical point-of-sales data. Store managers act as trend spotters. Every day they report hot fads to headquarters, enabling popular lines to be tweaked and slow movers to be whisked away within hours. If customers are asking for a rounded neck on a vest rather than a V neck, such an item can be in stores in seven to ten days. This process would take traditional retailers months.

Managers also consult a personal digital assistant every evening to check what new designs are available and place their orders according to what they think will sell best to their customers. Thus, store managers help shape designs by ensuring that the creative teams have real-time information based on the observed tastes of actual consumers. Mr Ortega refers to this as the democratization of fashion.

When it comes to sourcing, Zara's supply chain is unique as well. Current conventional wisdom calls for manufacturers in all industries to outsource their goods globally to the cheapest provider. Thus, most of Zara's competitors contract manufacturing out to low-wage countries, notably Asia. But Zara makes 40 percent of its own fabrics and produces more than half of its own clothes, rather than relying on a hodgepodge of slow-moving suppliers. Even things that are farmed out are done locally in order to maximize time efficiency. Nearly all Zara clothes for its stores worldwide are produced in its remote northeast corner of Spain.

As it completes designs, Zara cuts fabric in-house. It then sends the designs to one of several hundred local co-operatives for sewing, minimizing the time for raw material distribution. When items return to Zara's facilities, they are ironed by an assembly line of workers who specialize in a specific task (lapels, shoulders, and so on). Clothing items are wrapped in plastic and transported on conveyor belts to a group of giant warehouses.

Zara's warehouses are a vision of modern automation as swift and efficient as any automotive or consumer electronics plant. Human labor is a rare sight in these cavernous buildings. Customized machines patterned after the equipment used by overnight parcel services process up to 80,000 items an hour. The computerized system sorts, packs, labels, and allocates clothing items to every one of Zara's 1,495 stores. For stores within a 24-hour drive, Zara delivers goods by truck, whereas it ships merchandise via cargo jet to stores farther away.

DOMESTIC MANUFACTURING PAYS OFF

The same philosophy that has produced such good results for Zara has led parent company Inditex to diversify. Its other chains now include underwear retailer Oysho, teen-oriented Bershka and Stradivarius, children's Kiddy's Class, menswear Massimo Duti, and casual and sportswear chain Pull & Bear. Recently, Inditex opened its first nonclothing chain, Zara Home. Each chain operates under the same style of vertical integration perfected at Zara.

Making speed the main goal of its supply chain has really paid off for Inditex. In only three years, its sales and profits more than doubled. Last year, revenues increased over 15 percent over the previous year to US$14.5 billion. Not bad considering retail revenue growth worldwide averages single digits, and many major retailers were feeling the effects of slowing economies worldwide. Perhaps more importantly, Inditex's total profits grew by 25 percent last year to US$1.8 billion. Most of this performance was driven by Zara, now ranked number 64 on Interbrand's list of top 100 most valuable worldwide brands.

Although Inditex has grown rapidly, it wants more. Last year it opened 560 new stores worldwide (most of those were Zara stores) and plans to do the same this year. That's even considering an entry into the fast-growing Indian market. Global retailers are pushing into India in droves in response to India's thirst for premium brands. Zara can really capitalize on this trend. With more than one ribbon-cutting ceremony per day, Inditex could increase its number of stores from the current 3,890 to more than 5,000 stores in more than 70 countries by the end of this decade.

European fast-fashion retailers have thus far expanded cautiously in the United States (Zara has only 32 stores stateside). But the threat has U.S. clothing retailers rethinking the models they have relied on for years. According to one analyst, the industry may soon experience a reversal from outsourcing to China to "Made in the USA."

U.S. retailers are finally looking at lost sales as lost revenue. They know that in order to capture maximum sales they need to turn their inventory much quicker. The disadvantage of importing from China is that it requires a longer lead time of between three to six months from the time an order is placed to when the inventory is stocked in stores. By then the trends may have changed and you're stuck with all the unsold inventory. If retailers want to refresh their merchandise quicker, they will have to consider sourcing at least some of the merchandise locally.

So being the fastest of the fast-fashion retailers has not only paid off for Zara, the model has reconfigured the fashion landscape everywhere. Zara has blazed a trail for cheaper and cheaper fashion-led mass-retailers, has put the squeeze on mid-priced fashion, and has forced luxury brands to scramble to find ways to set themselves apart from Zara's look-alike designs. Leadership certainly has its perks.

Questions for Discussion

1. As completely as possible, sketch the supply chain for Zara from raw materials to consumer purchase.

2. Discuss the concepts of horizontal and vertical conflict as they relate to Zara.

3. Which type of vertical marketing system does Zara employ? List all the benefits that Zara receives by having adopted this system.

4. Does Zara experience disadvantages from its 'fast-fashion' distribution system? Are these disadvantages offset by the advantages?

5. How does Zara add value for the customer through major logistics functions?

Sources: James Hall, "Zara Helps Fashion Profit for Inditex," *Daily Telegraph*, April 1, 2008, p. 12; Christopher Bjork, "New Stores Boost Inditex's Results," *Wall Street Journal*, June 12, 2008, p. B4; "The Future of Fast-Fashion," *The Economist*, June 18, 2005, accessed online at www.economist.com; John Tagliabue, "A Rival to Gap that Operates Like Dell," *New York Times*, May 30, 2003, p. W1; Elizabeth Nash, "Dressed For Success," *Independent*, March 31, 2006, p. 22; Sarah Mower, "The Zara Phenomenon," *Evening Standard*, January 13, 2006, p. 30; also see www.inditex.com, accessed November 2008; Parija Bhatnagar, "Is 'Made in U.S.A' Back in Vogue?" CNN Money, March 1, 2006, http://money.cnn.com.

PART 4

Extending Marketing

Chapter 15

Part 1 Defining Marketing and the Marketing Process (Chapters 1, 2)
Part 2 Understanding the Marketplace and Consumers (Chapters 3, 4, 5, 6)
Part 3 Designing a Customer-Driven Strategy and Mix (Chapters 7, 8, 9, 10, 11, 12, 13, 14)
Part 4 Extending Marketing (Chapters 15, 16, 17)

Creating Competitive Advantage

Chapter PREVIEW

In previous chapters, you explored the basics of marketing. You've learned that the aim of marketing is to create value *for* customers in order to capture value *from* consumers in return. Good marketing companies win, keep, and grow customers by understanding customer needs, designing customer-driven marketing strategies, constructing value-delivering marketing programs, and building customer and marketing partner relationships. In the final three chapters, we'll extend this concept to three special areas—creating competitive advantage, global marketing, and marketing ethics and social responsibility.

In this chapter, we pull all of the marketing basics together. Understanding customers is an important first step in developing profitable customer relationships, but it's not enough. To gain competitive advantage, companies must use this understanding to design market offers that deliver more value than the offers of *competitors* seeking to win the same customers. In this chapter, we look first at competitor analysis, the process companies use to identify and analyze competitors. Then, we examine competitive marketing strategies by which companies position themselves against competitors to gain the greatest possible competitive advantage.

Bahrain Polytechnic is an exciting educational venture that is full of potential. It opened in 2008 with a promise to deliver work-ready graduates to the Bahraini market. In the past, many employment opportunities have been given to expatriate workers rather than to citizens of Bahrain. Bahrain Polytechnic, however, aims to change that by producing young graduates who will have the range of skills needed for the work place as the economy in the Gulf region expands and diversifies.

Bahrain Polytechnic was established by the Bahraini government to address the need for a skilled labor force. This post-secondary institution's approach is to develop and deliver programs, qualifications, and courses in conjunction with businesses, industries, professions, and international education and training institutions. This strategy, set by the board of trustees, will ensure that Bahrain Polytechnic students graduate with skills that meet the needs of the local labor market.

The polytechnic developed its brand and corporate slogan to communicate the message that Bahrain Polytechnic is a 'star.' This invokes ideas such as the possibilities of tomorrow and an inspiration for Bahrain Polytechnic students—that they too can become stars and have an impact on Bahrain's efforts in the Gulf region and globally.

Bahrain Polytechnic will, within a few short years, complete its state-of-the-art campus, making this government initiative a template for other institutions in the region to follow.

Bahrain Polytechnic, from its introductory stages, has intentionally created a number of clear competitive advantages that position it at the forefront of educational initiatives in Bahrain, in the six Gulf states, and even internationally when considering

recent post-secondary educational start-ups. There are six principle competitive advantages that Bahrain Polytechnic has identified as key to its long-term performance, its overall brand equity, and its overall sustainability.

First, Bahrain Polytechnic offers relevant curriculum and degree programs for the region, including business streams in management, marketing, banking and finance, accounting and sales, and additional degree programs in subjects such as engineering technology, information and communications technology, and international logistics management, among others. Secondly, it believes in 'work integrated learning,' a method which ensures that educational activities have relevance and can be applied to the workplace. Bahrain Polytechnic places an emphasis on work integration as a key element in preparing its students for the

> **Bahrain Polytechnic believes in "work-integrated learning" by combining academic and practical activities that would render graduates ready for work upon graduation.**

world of work, and recognizes the importance of student-centered learning as a focus for its course delivery. Students learn through a combination of academic and work-related activities, which assists them to become work-ready graduates.

Work integrated learning includes work placements based on agreed learning contracts, industry projects, co-operative education, internship programs, work simulations, and mentoring. Thirdly, Bahrain Polytechnic's teaching faculty numbers close to 200 highly qualified individuals from nations such as New Zealand, Australia, Ireland, the United States, Canada, and Bahrain. The fact that teaching staff are experts in their field enables them to deliver learning outcomes to the student population.

Fourthly, the polytechnic decided from the outset that it would have a general commitment to quality education on a self-regulating basis. The self-driven Bahrain Polytechnic initiative is to be a quality organization with strong organizational hierarchy, faculty, and faculty support staff, and aims to regularly review the curriculum so that it remains relevant to the polytechnic's mission.

Fifthly, in the community, Bahrain Polytechnic students are active in numerous sporting events, and the organization regularly attends education trade shows and participates at various conferences, which all help students togain more real-world experiences. The polytechnic's slogan, 'Connecting Generations, Inspiring Innovations,' communicates the organization's intergenerational approach. Students will learn and develop themselves through mentors, who will guide them through the educational process in school and outside in the community. Students upon graduation will be regarded as the new stars of Bahrain.

Finally, Bahrain Polytechnic has a competitive advantage because it is the first state-of-the-art higher education campus in Bahrain, can accommodate a large student population (5,000 to 7,000 students), will be the foundation for educational and learning

transformation in Bahrain, and will be a model for other Gulf States.

Bahrain Polytechnic has, from the outset, differentiated itself from the competition by creating and developing its own competitive advantages over its competitors in Bahrain.[1]

Bahrain Polytechnic aims to generate quality graduates with a range of skills that would allow them to positively affect the Gulf economies.

Bahrain Polytechnic aims to produce graduates who will have the skills needed for jobs in the Gulf over the next few years, as the region builds on and diversifies its resource economy.

Source: *This case was provided by Mike Lewicki, University College of Bahrain.*

Today's companies face their toughest competition ever. In previous chapters, we argued that to succeed in today's fiercely competitive marketplace, companies will have to move from a product-and-selling philosophy to a customer-and-marketing philosophy. Guerrino De Luca, president and CEO of Logitech, puts it well: "It is now more critical than ever to keep the people who buy and use our products at the center of our focus—for all our customers to be delighted by their experience with our products."[2]

This chapter spells out in more detail how companies can go about outperforming competitors in order to win, keep, and grow customers. To win in today's marketplace, companies must become adept not just in *managing products*, but in *managing customer relationships* in the face of determined competition. Understanding customers is crucial, but it's not enough. Building profitable customer relationships and gaining **competitive advantage** requires delivering *more* value and satisfaction to target consumers than *competitors* do. Customers will see competitive advantages as *customer advantages*, giving the company an edge over its competitors.

In this chapter, we examine *competitive marketing strategies*—how companies analyze their competitors and develop successful, value-based strategies for building and maintaining profitable customer relationships. The first step is **competitor analysis**, the

Competitive advantage
An advantage over competitors gained by offering consumers greater value than competitors do.

Competitor analysis
The process of identifying key competitors; assessing their objectives, strategies, strengths and weaknesses, and reaction patterns; and selecting which competitors to attack or avoid.

Objective Outline

Competitive marketing strategies
Strategies that strongly position the company against competitors and that give the company the strongest possible strategic advantage.

Author Comment | Creating competitive advantage begins with a thorough understanding of competitors' strategies. But before a company can analyze its competitors, it must first identify them—a task that's not as simple as it seems.

process of identifying, assessing, and selecting key competitors. The second step is developing **competitive marketing strategies** that strongly position the company against competitors and give it the greatest possible competitive advantage.

Competitor Analysis (pp 442–449)

To plan effective marketing strategies, the company needs to find out all it can about its competitors. It must constantly compare its marketing strategies, products, prices, channels, and promotions with those of close competitors. In this way the company can find areas of potential competitive advantage and disadvantage. As shown in ◗ **Figure 15.1**, competitor analysis involves first identifying and assessing competitors and then selecting which competitors to attack or avoid.

Identifying Competitors

Normally, identifying competitors would seem a simple task. At the narrowest level, a company can define its competitors as other companies offering similar products and services to the same customers at similar prices. Thus, Zara might see Mango as a major competitor, but not Chanel or Christian Dior. Ritz-Carlton might see Four Seasons hotels as a major competitor, but not Movenpick Hotels, the Holiday Inn, or any of the thousands of bed-and-breakfasts.

But companies actually face a much wider range of competitors. The company might define competitors as all firms making the same product or class of products. Thus, Ritz-Carlton would see itself as competing against all other hotels. Even more broadly, competitors might include all companies making products that supply the same service. Here Ritz-Carlton would see itself competing not only against other hotels but also against anyone who supplies rooms for weary travelers. Finally, and still more broadly, competitors might include all companies that compete for the same consumer dollars. Here Ritz-Carlton would see itself competing with travel and leisure services, from cruises and summer homes to vacations abroad.

Companies must avoid 'competitor myopia.' A company is more likely to be 'buried' by its hidden competitors than its current ones. For example, it wasn't direct competitors that put an end to Western Union's telegram businesses after 161 years; it was cellphones and the Internet. And Kodak's film business didn't suffer at the hands of direct competitor Fujifilm; it lost out to competitors that Kodak didn't see coming—Sony, Canon, and other digital camera makers, along with a host of digital image developers

◆ FIGURE | 15.1
Steps in Analyzing Competitors

Identifying competitors isn't as easy as it seems. For example, when film cameras dominated, Kodak saw Fujifilm as its only major competitor. But its real competitor turned out to be digital imaging, including other digital camera makers and a host of digital image developers and online image-sharing services.

| Identifying the company's competitors | → | Assessing competitors' objectives, strategies, strengths and weaknesses, and reaction patterns | → | Selecting which competitors to attack or avoid |

and online image-sharing services. Perhaps the classic example of competitor myopia is Encyclopaedia Britannica:[3]

> For more than 200 years, Encyclopaedia Britannica saw itself as competing with other publishers of printed reference books and encyclopedia sets selling for as much as US$2,200 per set. However, it learned a hard lesson when the world went digital in the 1990s. Microsoft introduced *Encarta*, a CD-ROM encyclopedia that sold for only US$50. *Encarta* and other digital encyclopedias took the market by storm, followed quickly by web-based encyclopedias and reference sources. As a result, Britannica's sales dropped 50 percent during the next seven years. As it turns out, Britannica's real competitors weren't other print publishers; they were the computer, the Internet, and digital content. Britannica still publishes its flagship 32-volume *Encyclopaedia Britannica* and several other printed reference sets. However, it also offers popular DVD and web versions of its information services. Britannica recognizes competitors ranging from World Book to Microsoft to free web upstarts such as Wikipedia, the bottom-up, dynamic, nonprofit, Internet-based encyclopedia "that anyone can edit."

Companies can identify their competitors from the *industry* point of view. They might see themselves as being in the oil industry, the pharmaceutical industry, or the beverage industry. A company must understand the competitive patterns in its industry if it hopes to be an effective player in that industry. Companies can also identify competitors from a *market* point of view. Here they define competitors as companies that are trying to satisfy the same customer need or build relationships with the same customer group.

From an industry point of view, Pepsi might see its competition as Coca-Cola and the makers of other soft drink brands. From a market point of view, however, the customer really wants 'thirst quenching.' This need can be satisfied by bottled water, energy drinks, fruit juice, iced tea, or many other fluids. Similarly, Hallmark's Binney & Smith, maker of Crayola crayons, might define its competitors as other makers of crayons and children's drawing supplies. But from a market point of view, it would include all firms making recreational and educational products for children. In general, the market concept of competition opens the company's eyes to a broader set of actual and potential competitors.

Assessing Competitors

Having identified the main competitors, marketing management now asks: What are competitors' objectives—what does each seek in the marketplace? What is each competitor's strategy? What are various competitor's strengths and weaknesses, and how will each react to actions the company might take?

Determining Competitors' Objectives

Each competitor has a mix of objectives. The company wants to know the relative importance that a competitor places on current profitability, market share growth, cash flow, technological leadership, service leadership, and other goals. Knowing a competitor's mix of objectives reveals whether the competitor is satisfied with its current situation and how it might react to different competitive actions. For example, a company that pursues low-cost leadership will react much more strongly to a competitor's cost-reducing manufacturing breakthrough than to the same competitor's advertising increase.

A company also must monitor its competitors' objectives for various segments. If the company finds that a competitor has discovered a new segment, this might be an opportunity.

Strategic groups: Bugatti belongs to the automobile industry strategic group, offering a narrow line of higher-quality automobiles supported by good service.

Strategic group

A group of firms in an industry following the same or a similar strategy.

Benchmarking

The process of comparing the company's products and processes to those of competitors or leading firms in other industries to identify best practices and find ways to improve quality and performance.

If it finds that competitors plan new moves into segments now served by the company, it will be alerted and, hopefully, deal with the threat successfully.

Identifying Competitors' Strategies

The more that one firm's strategy resembles another firm's strategy, the more the two firms compete. In most industries, the competitors can be sorted into groups that pursue different strategies. A **strategic group** is a group of firms in an industry following the same or a similar strategy in a given target market. For example, in the automobile industry, Toyota and Honda belong to the same strategic group. Each produces a full line of medium-price automobiles supported by good service. In contrast, Porsche and Bugatti belong to a different strategic group. They produce a narrower line of higher-quality automobiles, offer a higher level of service, and charge a premium price.

Some important insights emerge from identifying strategic groups. For example, if a company enters one of the groups, the members of that group become its key competitors. Thus, if the company enters the first group, against Toyota and Honda, it can succeed only if it develops strategic advantages over these competitors.

Although competition is most intense within a strategic group, there is also rivalry among groups. First, some of the strategic groups may appeal to overlapping customer segments. For example, no matter what their strategy, all major automobile manufacturers will go after the employees and families segment. Secondly, the customers may not see much difference in the offers of different groups—they may see little difference in quality between Toyota and Honda. Finally, members of one strategic group might expand into new strategy segments. Thus, Toyota's Lexus competes in the premium-quality, premium-price line with Bugatti and Porsche.

The company needs to look at all of the dimensions that identify strategic groups within the industry. It must understand how each competitor delivers value to its customers. It needs to know each competitor's product quality, features, and mix; customer services; pricing policy; distribution coverage; sales force strategy; and advertising and sales promotion programs. And it must study the details of each competitor's R&D, manufacturing, purchasing, financial, and other strategies.

Assessing Competitors' Strengths and Weaknesses

Marketers need to assess each competitor's strengths and weaknesses carefully in order to answer a critical question: What *can* our competitors do? As a first step, companies can gather data on each competitor's goals, strategies, and performance over the past few years. Admittedly, some of this information will be hard to obtain. For example, business-to-business marketers find it hard to estimate competitors' market shares because they do not have the same syndicated data services that are available to consumer packaged-goods companies.

Companies normally learn about their competitors' strengths and weaknesses through secondary data, personal experience, and word of mouth. They can also conduct primary marketing research with customers, suppliers, and dealers. Or they can **benchmark** themselves against other firms, comparing the company's products and processes to those of competitors or leading firms in other industries to identify best practices and find ways to improve quality and performance. Benchmarking has become a powerful tool for increasing a company's competitiveness.

Estimating Competitors' Reactions

Next, the company wants to know: What *will* our competitors do? A competitor's objectives, strategies, and strengths and weaknesses go a long way toward explaining its likely actions. They also suggest its likely reactions to company moves such as price cuts, promotion increases, or new-product introductions. In addition, each competitor has a certain philosophy of doing business, a certain internal culture and guiding beliefs. Marketing managers need a deep understanding of a given competitor's ways of thinking if they want to anticipate how the competitor will act or react.

Each competitor reacts differently. Some do not react quickly or strongly to a competitor's move. They may feel their customers are loyal, they may be slow in noticing the move, or they may lack the funds to react. Some competitors react only to certain types of moves and not to others. Other competitors react swiftly and strongly to any action. Thus, Procter & Gamble does not let a new detergent come easily into the market. Many firms avoid direct competition with P&G and look for easier prey, knowing that P&G will react fiercely if challenged.

In some industries, competitors live in relative harmony; in others, they fight constantly. Knowing how major competitors react gives the company clues on how best to attack competitors or how best to defend the company's current positions.

Selecting Competitors to Attack and Avoid

A company has already largely selected its major competitors through prior decisions on customer targets, distribution channels, and marketing-mix strategy. Management now must decide which competitors to compete against most vigorously.

Strong or Weak Competitors

The company can focus on one of several classes of competitors. Most companies prefer to compete against *weak competitors*. This requires fewer resources and less time. But in the process, the firm may gain little. You could argue that the firm also should compete with *strong competitors* in order to sharpen its abilities. Moreover, even strong competitors have some weaknesses, and succeeding against them often provides greater returns.

Customer value analysis
Analysis conducted to determine what benefits target customers value and how they rate the relative value of various competitors' offers.

A useful tool for assessing competitor strengths and weaknesses is **customer value analysis**. The aim of customer value analysis is to determine the benefits that target customer value and how customers rate the relative value of various competitors' offers. In conducting a customer value analysis, the company first identifies the major attributes that customers value and the importance customers place on these attributes. Next, it assesses the company's and competitors' performance on the valued attributes.

The key to gaining competitive advantage is to take each customer segment and examine how the company's offer compares to that of its major competitors. As shown in ⬛ **Figure 15.2**, the company wants to find the 'strategic sweet spot'—the place where it meets customers' needs in a way that rivals can't. If the company's offer delivers greater

⬛ FIGURE | 15.2

Strategic Sweet Spot versus Competitors

Source: Adapted from David J. Collins and Michael G. Rukstad, "Can You Say What Your Strategy Is?" Harvard Business Review, April 2008, p. 89. Copyright © 2008 by the President and Fellows of Harvard College; all rights reserved.

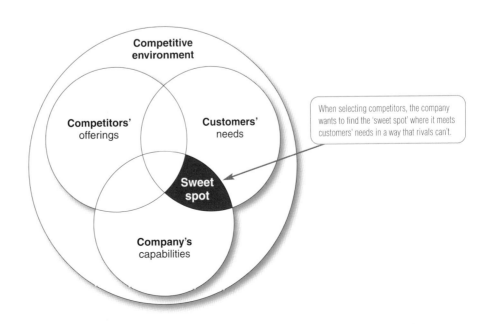

When selecting competitors, the company wants to find the 'sweet spot' where it meets customers' needs in a way that rivals can't.

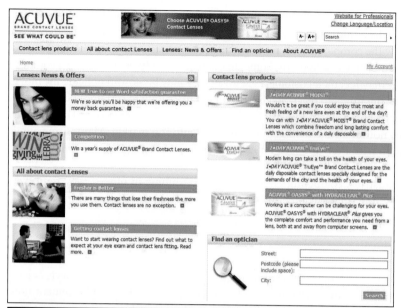

After driving smaller competitors from the market, Bausch & Lomb faced larger, more resourceful ones, such as Johnson & Johnson's Vistakon division, which developed the innovative Acuvue contact lens.

value by exceeding the competitor's offer on important attributes, the company can charge a higher price and earn higher profits, or it can charge the same price and gain more market share. But if the company is seen as performing at a lower level than its major competitor on some important attributes, it must invest in strengthening those attributes or finding other important attributes where it can build a lead on the competitor.

Close or Distant Competitors

Most companies will compete with *close competitors*— those that resemble them most—rather than *distant competitors*. Thus, Nike competes more against Adidas than against Timberland or Ralph Loren Polo. And Carrefour competes against Spinneys rather than Bloomingdale's or Galeries Lafayette.

At the same time, the company may want to avoid trying to 'destroy' a close competitor. For example, in the late 1970s, Bausch & Lomb, founder of the brand Ray-Ban, which was sold to Italian Luxottica Group in 1999, moved aggressively against other soft lens manufacturers with great success. However, this forced weak competitors to sell out to larger firms such as Johnson & Johnson. As a result, Bausch & Lomb then faced much larger competitors—and it suffered the consequences. Johnson & Johnson acquired Vistakon, a small nicher with only US$20 million in annual sales. Backed by Johnson & Johnson's deep pockets, the small but nimble Vistakon developed and introduced its innovative Acuvue disposable lenses. With Vistakon leading the way, Johnson & Johnson is now a top contact lens maker, while Bausch & Lomb lags in fourth place. In this case, success in hurting a close rival brought in tougher competitors.

'Good' or 'Bad' Competitors

A company really needs and benefits from competitors. The existence of competitors results in several strategic benefits. Competitors may share the costs of market and product development and help to legitimize new technologies. They may serve less-attractive segments or lead to more product differentiation. Finally, competitors may help increase total demand. For example, you might think that an independent coffeehouse surrounded by Starbucks stores might have trouble staying in business. But that's often not the case:[4]

> Coffee-shop owners around the United States have discovered that the corporate steamroller known as Starbucks is actually good for their business. It turns out that when a Starbucks comes to the neighborhood, the result is new converts to the latte-drinking fold. When all those converts overrun the local Starbucks, the independents are there to catch the spillover. In fact, some independent storeowners now actually try to open their stores near a Starbucks if they can. That's certainly not how the coffee giant planned it. "Starbucks is actually *trying* to be ruthless," says the owner of a small coffeehouse chain in Los Angeles. But "in its predatory store-placement strategy, Starbucks has been about as lethal a killer as a fluffy bunny rabbit."

However, a company may not view all of its competitors as beneficial. An industry often contains 'good' competitors and 'bad' competitors.[5] Good competitors play by the rules of the industry. Bad competitors, in contrast, break the rules. They try to buy share rather than earn it, take large risks, and play by their own rules.

For example, Yahoo! Music Unlimited sees Napster, Rhapsody, AOL Music, Amazon. com, and most other digital music download services as good competitors. They share a common platform, so that music bought from any of these competitors can be played on almost any playback device. However, it sees Apple's iTunes Music Store as a bad competitor, one that plays by its own rules at the expense of the industry as a whole.[6]

> With the iPod, Apple initially created a closed system with mass-appeal. In 2003, when the iPod was the only game in town, Apple cut deals with the four major music labels that locked up its device. The music companies wanted to sell songs on iTunes, but they were afraid of Internet piracy. So Apple promised to wrap their songs in its FairPlay digital rights management (DRM) technology—the only copy-protection encryption that is compatible with iPods and iPhones. Other digital music services such as Yahoo! Music Unlimited and Napster reached similar deals with the big music labels. When Apple refused to license FairPlay to them, those companies turned to Microsoft for DRM technology. But that meant that none of the songs sold by those services could be played on the wildly popular iPod and vice versa. The situation has been a disaster for Apple's competitors. Although some recording labels, notably EMI and Universal Music Group, are now foregoing DMR technology in an effort to weaken the bargaining power they gave to Apple by first insisting on it, iTunes still holds a commanding 80 percent of the digital music market.

The implication is that 'good' companies would like to shape an industry that consists of only well-behaved competitors. A company might be smart to support good competitors, aiming its attacks at bad competitors. Thus, Yahoo! Music Unlimited, Napster, and other digital music competitors will no doubt support one another in trying to break Apple's stranglehold on the market.

Finding Uncontested Market Spaces

Rather than competing head to head with established competitors, many companies seek out unoccupied positions in uncontested market spaces. They try to create products and services for which there are *no* direct competitors. Called a 'blue ocean strategy,' the goal is to make competition irrelevant:[7]

> Companies have long engaged in head-to-head competition in search of profitable growth. They have flocked for competitive advantage, battled over market share, and struggled for differentiation. Yet in today's overcrowded industries, competing head-on results in nothing but a bloody "red ocean" of rivals fighting over a shrinking profit pool. In their book *Blue Ocean Strategy*, two marketing professors contend that although most companies compete within such red oceans, the strategy isn't likely to create profitable growth in the future. Tomorrow's leading companies will succeed not by battling competitors but by creating "blue oceans" of uncontested market space. Such strategic moves—termed "value innovation"—create powerful leaps in value for both the firm and its buyers, creating all new demand and rendering rivals obsolete. By creating and capturing blue oceans, companies can largely take rivals out of the picture.

An example of a company exhibiting blue-ocean thinking is Cirque du Soleil, which reinvented the circus as a higher form of modern entertainment. At a time when the circus industry was declining, Cirque du Soleil innovated by eliminating high cost and controversial elements such as animal acts and instead focused on the theatrical experience. Cirque du Soleil did not compete with then market leader Ringling Bros. and Barnum & Bailey—it was altogether different from anything that preceded it. Instead, it created an uncontested new market space that made existing competitors irrelevant. The results have been spectacular. Thanks to its blue-ocean strategy, in only its first 20 years, Cirque du Soleil achieved more revenues than Ringling Bros. and Barnum & Bailey achieved in its first 100 years. **Real Marketing 15.1** illustrates an example of a blue-ocean strategy in the Arab world.

Real Marketing 15.1

Middle Eastern Airlines Filling the Market Gaps

Let's take a look at how airlines based in the Arab world managed to compete with other carriers around the world at the advent of the global economic crisis in 2009.

Airlines in the region embraced the 'blue ocean competitive strategy,' attacking unsaturated market gaps, which enabled them to pass through the period unharmed, and eventually reap a benefit. These carriers' main focus became long-haul travel, which was under-served at the time by airlines based in the Arab world. This came at a time when European airlines decided to downsize their capacity, so Arab airlines had a golden opportunity to capture that portion of the market.

In January 2009, airlines in the Arab world featured on the list of top performers in the airline industry, according to the International Air Transport Association (IATA). Compared with the same month in 2008, the regional companies had seen passenger demand increase by 23 percent. Asian-Pacific carriers had experienced an increase of 6.5 percent, while Latin American carriers had a boost of 11 percent. "Arab airlines were able to increase their market share tremendously, and that's why they concluded the year with double digit growth," said Abdul Wahab Teffaha, secretary general of the Arab Air Carriers Organisation.

When talking about Arab carriers, it is worth noting 'The Big Three.' Etihad, Emirates, and Qatar Airways are the major players in the region, competing aggressively with European and Asian airlines in the profitable long-haul market. The Big Three monitored the market gaps and responded accordingly, opting for expansion. Emirates, for instance, paved the way its non-stop services to Tokyo, Amsterdam, Prague, and Madrid. Etihad, as well, started

Airlines in the Arab world deployed a 'blue ocean competitive strategy' to fill untapped market gaps.

its flights to Japan, with its Nagoya-to-Abu Dhabi and Abu Dhabi-to-Tokyo services. Also, Etihad launched routes to Sydney, Brisbane, and Melbourne in Australia.

Qatar Airways serves many of the world's most popular cities, linking them with its center in Doha. Most of Qatar Airways' fleet, as of 2010, consisted of Boeing 777s—ideal for long-haul flights. In 2010, the airline bought more Boeing 777s to meet increasing demand. Having such a large fleet represents a competitive advantage for Qatar Airways.

Akbar Al Baker, CEO of Qatar Airways, said:

The Boeing 777 has become the cornerstone of our fleet. It is a tool for profitability, but also a platform for delivering the highest customer satisfaction. Its service reliability and cabin architecture, coupled with our innovative interiors and world-class in-flight service have made the 777 the airplane of choice for our passengers...

Boeing 777-200 LRs will help us open up new ultra long-haul markets as we expand and identify new opportunities further.

Moreover, Qatar Airways is a good example of the use of differentiated competitive strategy based on service excellence. Qatar Airways claims to offer superior in-flight service, which is backed up by various awards and customer surveys that have recognized its quality of service; for example, it has been voted the third-best airline worldwide, based on an annual Skytrax survey of 18 million global respondents. In this survey, the carrier was also voted as providing the Best Business Class Catering internationally, as well as being voted Best Airline in the Middle East for five consecutive years. As further evidence, Qatar Airways emphasizes that it was the first carrier to obtain the Staff Service Excellence Award in the Middle East in the Skytrax study, and also won the Best Cabin Staff Award for seven years running.

Sources: "Middle East Airlines Increase Global Market Share," *AME Info*, March 8, 2010, www.ameinfo.com/226085.html; "Qatar Airways Expands Boeing 777 Fleet with Additional Aircraft Orders," *AME Info*, July 22, 2010, www.ameinfo.com/238475.html; "Qatar Airways' New Tokyo Route Sets Off Expansion Drive in Asia," *BI-ME*, July 2, 2010, www.bi-me.com.

Designing a Competitive Intelligence System

We have described the main types of information that companies need about their competitors. This information must be collected, interpreted, distributed, and used. The cost in money and time of gathering competitive intelligence is high, and the company must design its competitive intelligence system in a cost-effective way.

The competitive intelligence system first identifies the vital types of competitive information needed and the best sources of this information. Then, the system continuously collects information from the field (sales force, channels, suppliers, market research firms, trade associations, websites) and from published data (government publications, speeches, articles). Next the system checks the information for validity and reliability, interprets it, and organizes it in an appropriate way. Finally, it sends key information to relevant decision makers and responds to inquiries from managers about competitors.

With this system, company managers will receive timely intelligence information about competitors in the form of phone calls, emails, bulletins, newsletters, and reports. In addition, managers can connect with the system when they need an interpretation of a competitor's sudden move, or when they want to know a competitor's weaknesses and strengths, or when they need to know how a competitor will respond to a planned company move.

Smaller companies that cannot afford to set up formal competitive intelligence offices can assign specific executives to watch specific competitors. Thus, a manager who used to work for a competitor might follow that competitor closely; he or she would be the 'in-house expert' on that competitor. Any manager needing to know the thinking of a given competitor could contact the assigned in-house expert.

> **Author Comment** | Now that we've identified competitors and know all about them, it's time to design a strategy for gaining competitive advantage.

Competitive Strategies (pp 449–459)

Having identified and evaluated its major competitors, the company now must design broad competitive marketing strategies by which it can gain competitive advantage through superior customer value. But what broad marketing strategies might the company use? Which ones are best for a particular company, or for the company's different divisions and products?

Approaches to Marketing Strategy

No one strategy is best for all companies. Each company must determine what makes the most sense given its position in the industry and its objectives, opportunities, and resources. Even within a company, different strategies may be required for different businesses or products. Johnson & Johnson uses one marketing strategy for its leading brands in stable consumer markets—such as Band-Aid, Listerine, or Johnson's baby products—and a different marketing strategy for its other healthcare businesses and products—such as Johnson & Johnson Vision Care and Lifescan, which market contact lenses and glucometers and strips respectively.

Companies also differ in how they approach the strategy-planning process. Many large firms develop formal competitive marketing strategies and implement them thoroughly. However, other companies develop strategy in a less formal and orderly fashion. Some companies, such as Harley-Davidson, Virgin Atlantic Airways, and BMW's MINI Cooper business, succeed by breaking many of the rules of marketing strategy. Such companies don't operate large marketing departments, conduct expensive marketing research, spell out elaborate competitive strategies, and spend huge sums on advertising. Instead, they sketch out strategies informally, stretch their limited resources, live close to their customers, and create more satisfying solutions to customer needs. They form buyer's clubs, use buzz marketing, and focus on winning customer loyalty. It seems that not all marketing must follow in the footsteps of marketing giants such as IBM and Unilever.

In fact, approaches to marketing strategy and practice often pass through three stages: entrepreneurial marketing, formulated marketing, and intrepreneurial marketing.

Wild Peeta engages its customers by continuously communicating with them, seeking their input from the color of its chairs to the new products it wants to introduce.

twitter.com/wildpeeta
facebook.com/peetapower

Entrepreneurial marketing

Most companies are started by individuals who live by their wits. They visualize an opportunity, construct flexible strategies on the backs of envelopes, and knock on every door to gain attention. For example, Wild Peeta®, a quick-service restaurant in Dubai, started in this way. It was the vision of two Emirati brothers, and it took them seven years to develop and finally launch the business, with the help of the Sheikh Mohammed Establishment for Young Business Leaders.

Wild Peeta has two primary product ranges: Wild Peeta Sandwiches (fusion shawarmas) and Wild Paradise Salads. All products are prepared daily, many of them on the premises, using the freshest regional ingredients. The company believes that consumers who are pressed for time do not need to compromise on the nutritional value of their meals: They call it "Good food, served fast." It has vegetarian versions of dishes, which are also suitable for vegans.

Wild Peeta's booming young business focuses its menu on identified customer needs, whether the meal is breakfast, lunch, dinner, or just a snack. The aim of the highly personalized order process is to ensure that customers are actively involved in their food choices. This Emirati brand portrays a young, exciting, modern, and dynamic image. Its primary communication goal is to raise awareness both of the brand and of its socially conscious menu. 'Participative' communication is largely carried out through Twitter and Facebook, where the company involves its 8,000 regular followers in, for example, selecting the store furniture, naming menu items, and even choosing the music they play in-store. As a result, their community, who have developed a sense of ownership and responsibility towards their brand, regularly hold social events (Tweetups) at their restaurants.

Formulated marketing

As small companies achieve success, they inevitably move toward more formulated marketing. They develop formal marketing strategies and adhere to them closely. With 85 percent of the company now owned by Groupe Danone, Stonyfield Farm has developed a formal marketing department that carries out market research and plans strategy. Although Stonyfield may remain less formal in its strategy than the Unilevers of the marketing world, it employs many of the tools used in these more developed marketing companies.

Intrepreneurial marketing

Many large and mature companies get stuck in formulated marketing. They pore over the latest advertising numbers, scan market research reports, and try to fine-tune their competitive strategies and programs. These companies sometimes lose the marketing creativity and passion that they had at the start. They now need to reestablish within their companies the entrepreneurial spirit and actions that made them successful in the first place. They need to encourage more initiative and 'intrepreneurship' at the local level. They need to refresh their marketing strategies and try new approaches. Their brand and product managers need to get out of the office, start living with their customers, and visualize new and creative ways to add value to their customers' lives.

The bottom line is that there are many approaches to developing effective competitive marketing strategy. There will be a constant tension between the formulated side of marketing and the creative side. It is easier to learn the formulated side of marketing, which has occupied most of our attention in this book. But we have also seen how marketing creativity and passion in the strategies of many of the companies we've studied—whether small or large, new or mature—have helped to build and maintain success in the marketplace. With this in mind, we now look at broad competitive marketing strategies companies can use.

Basic Competitive Strategies

Almost three decades ago, Michael Porter suggested four basic competitive positioning strategies that companies can follow—three winning strategies and one losing one.[8] The three winning strategies include:

- *Overall cost leadership:* Here the company works hard to achieve the lowest production and distribution costs. Low costs let it price lower than its competitors and win a large market share. Air Arabia, Dell, and Lulu hypermarket are leading practitioners of this strategy.

- *Differentiation:* Here the company concentrates on creating a highly differentiated product line and marketing program so that it comes across as the class leader in the industry. Most customers would prefer to own this brand if its price is not too high. IBM and the equipment-maker Caterpillar follow this strategy in information technology and services and heavy construction equipment, respectively.

- *Focus:* Here the company focuses its effort on serving a few market segments well rather than going after the whole market. For example, the hotel chain the Ritz-Carlton focuses on the top 5 percent of corporate and leisure travelers, and Thuraya, a satellite mobile provider, offers its niche services to people with extreme working conditions.

Companies that pursue a clear strategy—one of the above—will likely perform well. The firm that carries out that strategy best will make the most profits. But firms that do not pursue a clear strategy—middle-of-the-roaders—do the worst. Retailer Choithram and Sons and Gulf Air encountered difficult times because they did not stand out as the lowest in cost, highest in perceived value, or best in serving some market segment. Middle-of-the-roaders try to be good on all strategic counts, but end up being not very good at anything.

Two marketing consultants, Michael Treacy and Fred Wiersema, offer a more customer-centered classification of competitive marketing strategies.[9] They suggest that companies gain leadership positions by delivering superior value to their customers. Companies can pursue any of three strategies—called *value disciplines*—for delivering superior customer value. These are:

- *Operational excellence:* The company provides superior value by leading its industry in price and convenience. It works to reduce costs and to create a lean and efficient value-delivery system. It serves customers who want reliable, good-quality products or services, but who want them cheaply and easily. Examples include Carrefour and Air Arabia.

- *Customer intimacy:* The company provides superior value by precisely segmenting its markets and tailoring its products or services to match exactly the needs of targeted customers. It specializes in satisfying unique customer needs through a close relationship with and intimate knowledge of the customer. It builds detailed customer databases for segmenting and targeting, and empowers its marketing people to respond quickly to customer needs. Customer-intimate companies serve customers who are willing to pay a premium to get precisely what they want. They will do almost anything to build long-term customer loyalty and to capture customer lifetime value. Examples include Emirates Airline, Lexus, and Ritz-Carlton hotels.

- *Product leadership:* The company provides superior value by offering a continuous stream of leading-edge products or services. It aims to make its own and competing products obsolete. Product leaders are open to new ideas, relentlessly pursue new solutions, and work to get new products to market quickly. They serve customers who want state-of-the-art products and services, regardless of the costs in terms of price or inconvenience. Examples include Nokia and Apple.

Some companies successfully pursue more than one value discipline at the same time. For example, Aramex excels at both operational excellence and customer intimacy. However, such companies are rare—few firms can be the best at more than one of these disciplines. By trying to be *good at all* of the value disciplines, a company usually ends up being *best at none.*

FIGURE | 15.3

Competitive Market Positions and Roles

> Each market position calls for a different competitive strategy. For example, the market leader wants to expand total demand and protect or expand its share. Market nichers seek market segments that are big enough to be profitable but small enough to be of little interest to major competitors.

Market leader	Market challengers	Market followers	Market nichers
40%	30%	20%	10%

Treacy and Wiersema found that leading companies focus on and excel at a single value discipline, while meeting industry standards on the other two. Such companies design their entire value delivery network to single-mindedly support the chosen discipline. For example, Lulu knows that customer intimacy and product leadership are important. Compared with other discounters, it offers very good customer service and an excellent product assortment. Still, it purposely offers less customer service and less product depth than does Spinneys, which pursues customer intimacy. Instead, Lulu focuses obsessively on operational excellence—on reducing costs and streamlining its order-to-delivery process in order to make it convenient for customers to buy just the right products at the lowest prices.

By the same token, Ritz-Carlton wants to be efficient and to employ the latest technologies. But what really sets the luxury hotel chain apart is its customer intimacy. Ritz-Carlton creates custom-designed experiences to coddle its customers (see **Real Marketing 15.2**).

Classifying competitive strategies as value disciplines is appealing. It defines marketing strategy in terms of the single-minded pursuit of delivering superior value to customers. Each value discipline defines a specific way to build lasting customer relationships.

Competitive Positions

Market leader

The firm in an industry with the largest market share.

Market challenger

A runner-up firm that is fighting hard to increase its market share in an industry.

Market follower

A runner-up firm that wants to hold its share in an industry without changing things.

Market nicher

A firm that serves small segments that the other firms in an industry overlook or ignore.

Firms competing in a given target market, at any point in time, differ in their objectives and resources. Some firms are large, others small. Some have many resources, others are strapped for funds. Some are mature and established, others new and fresh. Some strive for rapid market share growth, others for long-term profits. And the firms occupy different competitive positions in the target market.

We now examine competitive strategies based on the roles firms play in the target market—leader, challenger, follower, or nicher. Suppose that an industry contains the firms shown in **Figure 15.3**. Forty percent of the market is in the hands of the **market leader**, the firm with the largest market share. Another 30 percent is in the hands of **market challengers**, runner-up firms that are fighting hard to increase their market share. Another 20 percent is in the hands of **market followers**, other runner-up firms that want to hold their share without changing things. The remaining 10 percent is in the hands of **market nichers**, firms that serve small segments not being pursued by other firms.

Table 15.1 shows specific marketing strategies that are available to market leaders, challengers, followers, and nichers.[10] Remember, however, that these classifications

TABLE | 15.1 Strategies for Market Leaders, Challengers, Followers, and Nichers

Market leader strategies	Market challenger strategies	Market follower strategies	Market nicher strategies
Expand total market	Full frontal attack	Follow closely	By customer, market, quality-price, service
Protect market share	Indirect attack	Follow at a distance	Multiple niching
Expand market share			

Real Marketing 15.2

Ritz-Carlton:
Creating Customer Intimacy

Ritz-Carlton, a chain of luxury hotels renowned for outstanding service, serves the top 5 percent of corporate and leisure travelers. The company's credo sets lofty customer-service goals: "The Ritz-Carlton is a place where the genuine care and comfort of our guests is our highest mission.... The Ritz-Carlton experience enlivens the senses, instills well-being, and fulfills even the unexpressed wishes and needs of our guests."

The credo is more than just words on paper—Ritz-Carlton delivers on its promises. In surveys of departing guests, some 95 percent report that they've had a truly memorable experience. In fact, at Ritz-Carlton, exceptional service encounters have become almost commonplace. Take the experiences of Nancy and Harvey Heffner of Manhattan, who stayed at The Ritz-Carlton Naples, in Naples, Florida (rated the best hotel in the United States and fourth best in the world, by *Travel + Leisure* magazine).

"The hotel is elegant and beautiful," Mrs Heffner said, "but more important is the beauty expressed by the staff. They can't do enough to please you." When the couple's son became sick last year in Naples, the hotel staff brought him hot tea with honey at all hours of the night, she said. When Mr Heffner had to fly home on business for a day and his return flight was delayed, a driver for the hotel waited in the lobby most of the night.

Such personal, high-quality service has also made The Ritz-Carlton a favorite among conventioneers. For seven of the last nine years, the luxury hotel came out on top in *Business Travel News*'s Top U.S. Hotel Chain Survey of business travel buyers. "They not only treat us like kings when we hold our top-level meetings in their hotels, but we just never get any complaints," comments one convention planner. Says another, who had recently held a meeting at The Ritz-Carlton Half Moon Bay, California, "The first-rate catering and convention services staff [and] The Ritz-Carlton's ambience and beauty—the elegant, Grand Dame-style

lodge, nestled on a bluff between two championship golf courses overlooking the Pacific Ocean—makes a day's work there seem anything but."

Since its incorporation in 1983, Ritz-Carlton has received virtually every major award that the hospitality industry bestows. In addition, it's the only hotel company ever to win the prestigious Malcolm Baldrige National Quality Award and one of only two companies from any industry to win the award twice. A recent *Consumer Reports* hotels issue ranked Ritz-Carlton the number-one luxury hotel company in all areas, including value, service, upkeep, and problem resolution. More than 90 percent of Ritz-Carlton customers return. And despite its hefty room rates, the chain enjoys a 70 percent occupancy rate, almost nine points above the industry average.

Most of the responsibility for keeping guests satisfied falls to Ritz-Carlton's customer-contact employees. Thus, the hotel chain takes great care in finding just the right personnel—'people who care about people.' Then, Ritz-Carlton goes to great lengths to rigorously—even fanatically—train employees in the art of coddling customers. New employees attend a two-day orientation, in which top management drums into them the '12 Ritz-Carlton Service Values.' Service Value number one: "I build strong relationships and create Ritz-Carlton guests for life." Ritz-Carlton trains every single employee worldwide every day, using a start-of-shift 15-minute meeting called 'the lineup' to remind them of its service values.

Employees are taught to do everything they can to avoid never losing a guest. "There's no negotiating at Ritz-Carlton when it comes to solving customer problems," says a quality executive. Staff learn that *anyone* who receives a customer complaint *owns* that complaint until it's resolved (Ritz-Carlton Service Value number six). They are trained to drop whatever they're doing to help a customer—no matter what they're doing or what their department. Ritz-Carlton employees are empowered to handle problems on the spot. Each employee can spend up to US$2,000 to redress a guest grievance without consulting higher-ups.

Beyond just fixing problems, Ritz-Carlton staff at all levels are "empowered to create unique, memorable, and personal experiences for our guests" (Ritz-Carlton Service

Value number three). The company expects employees to use their own good judgment rather than telling them what to do. "We are managing to outcomes, and the outcome is a happy guest," says Ritz-Carlton's vice president of global learning. "We don't care how you get there—as long as it's moral, legal, and ethical—but we want you to use your genuine talent, we want you to do what we call 'radar on, antenna up,' which means staying in the moment so you can read what a guest wants."

As a result, almost everyone who frequents The Ritz-Carlton has a 'you won't believe this' story to tell about their experiences there. Employee heroics seem almost commonplace. For example, an administrative assistant at The Ritz-Carlton Philadelphia once overheard a guest lamenting that he'd forgotten to pack a pair of formal shoes and would have to wear hiking boots to an important meeting. Early the next morning, she delivered to the awestruck man a new pair in his size and favorite color.

In another case, a business traveler arrived at The Ritz-Carlton Atlanta late on a cold, rainy December night, tired to the bone and suffering from a bad head cold. To her surprise and relief, hotel staff met her at the door, greeted her by name, and, seeing her condition, escorted her directly to her room. When she arrived at her room, to her amazement, she found fresh flowers, two boxes of cough drops, and a personally addressed get-well card awaiting her. Such 'Wow!' stories of service are read aloud every Monday to give Ritz-Carlton employees an understanding that they work among extraordinary people who do extraordinary things when the opportunity presents itself.

Ritz-Carlton instills a sense of pride in its employees. "You serve," they are told, "but you are not servants." The company motto states, "We are ladies and gentlemen serving ladies and gentlemen." "When you invite guests to your house," it tells them, "you want everything to be perfect." As a result, Ritz-Carlton's employees appear to be just as satisfied as its customers. Employee turnover is less than 25 percent a year, compared with an 85 percent industry average.

Thus, when it comes to creating customer intimacy, Ritz-Carlton sets the gold standard.

Continued on next page ▼

Real Marketing 15.2 Continued ▼

The key is ensuring that guests don't feel like just another nameless face walking through the door. "It's all about personalization," says the Ritz-Carlton executive. "It's about providing a unique, personal, memorable experience, and what each person can do within your own environment to make that happen."

Sources: Quotes and other information from Julio Barker, "Power to the People," *Incentive*, February 2008, p. 34; "The World's Best Hotels 2007—Where Luxury Lives," *Institutional Investor*, November 2007, p. 1; Edwin McDowell, "Ritz-Carlton's Keys to Good Service," *New York Times*, March 31, 1993, p. D1; "The Ritz-Carlton, Half Moon Bay," *Successful Meetings*, November 2001, p. 40; Bruce Serlen, "Ritz-Carlton Retains Hold on Corporate Deluxe Buyers," *Business Travel News,* February 7, 2005, pp. 15–17; Michael B. Baker, Four Seasons, Ritz-Carlton Tie as Deluxe Tier Leads Rate Growth," March 24, 2008, pp. 12–14; Margery Weinstein, "Service with a Smile," *Training*, March–April 2008, p. 40; and www.ritzcarlton.com, accessed October 2011.

often do not apply to a whole company, but only to its position in a specific industry. Large companies such as GE, Microsoft, Procter & Gamble, or Disney might be leaders in some markets and nichers in others. For example, Procter & Gamble leads in many segments, such as laundry detergents and shampoo. But it challenges Unilever in hand soaps and Kimberly-Clark in facial tissues. Such companies often use different strategies for different business units or products, depending on the competitive situations of each.

Market Leader Strategies

Most industries contain an acknowledged market leader. The leader has the largest market share and usually leads the other firms in price changes, new-product introductions, distribution coverage, and promotion spending. The leader may or may not be admired or respected, but other firms concede its dominance. Competitors focus on the leader as a company to challenge, imitate, or avoid. Some of the best-known market leaders are Wal-Mart (retailing), Microsoft (computer software), Caterpillar (earth-moving equipment), McDonald's (fast food), Nike (athletic footwear and apparel), and Google (Internet search services).

A leader's life is not easy. It must maintain a constant watch. Other firms keep challenging its strengths or trying to take advantage of its weaknesses. The market leader can easily miss a turn in the market and plunge into second or third place. A product innovation may come along and hurt the leader (as when Apple developed the iPod and took the market lead from Sony's Walkman portable audio devices). The leader might grow arrogant or complacent and misjudge the competition (as when Sears lost its lead to Wal-Mart). Or the leader might look old-fashioned against new and peppier rivals (as when Levi's lost serious ground to more current or stylish brands like Gap, Tommy Hilfiger, DKNY, or GUESS).

To remain number one, leading firms can take any of three actions. First, they can find ways to expand total demand. Secondly, they can protect their current market share through good defensive and offensive actions. Thirdly, they can try to expand their market share further, even if market size remains constant.

Expanding the Total Demand

The leading firm normally gains the most when the total market expands. If Americans, for example, eat more fast food, McDonald's stands to gain the most because it holds more than three times the fast-food market share of nearest competitor Burger King. If McDonald's can convince more Americans that fast food is the best eating-out choice in these economic times, it will benefit more than its competitors.

Market leaders can expand the market by developing new users, new uses, and more usage of its products. They usually can find *new users* or untapped market segments in many places. For example, McDonald's in 2003 introduced McArabia in the Arab market to meet a need for Arabic cuisine in fast food; it targeted the local consumer who wanted Arabic food in a fast-food format. McArabia is made of Arab bread, grilled chicken/grilled kofta, lettuce, tomatoes, and Arab sauce. Since its launch, it has remained a popular Arabic-themed sandwich available at all McDonald's outlets

McDonald's expanded by developing a new market: In 2003 it introduced McArabia in the Arab market to cater to the need for Arabic cuisine in fast food.

throughout the Arab world, and is especially popular in Morocco but also the United Arab Emirates and Saudi Arabia.

Marketers can expand markets by discovering and promoting *new uses* for the product. For example, Vaseline from Unilever is a skincare product originally launched to moisturize skin. However, since its launch Vaseline has come up with many uses of the product, one of which is called Vaseline Lip Therapy. Produced in small round tubes, this Vaseline product helps to protect lips from the drying effects of wind and cold weather. Another use of Vaseline has been in the prevention of nappy rash in babies. Unilever has promoted these new uses over time to gain more market share and sales from new uses of Vaseline.

Arm & Hammer baking soda, whose sales had flattened after 125 years, discovered that consumers were using baking soda as a refrigerator deodorizer. It launched a heavy advertising and publicity campaign focusing on this use and persuaded consumers to place an open box of baking soda in their refrigerators and to replace it every few months. Today, its website (www.armandhammer.com) features new uses—"Solutions for my home, my family, my body"—ranging from removing residue left behind by hairstyling products and sweetening garbage disposals, laundry hampers, refrigerators, and trash cans to creating a home spa in your bathroom.

Finally, market leaders can encourage *more usage* by convincing people to use the product more often or to use more per occasion. For example, Emirates' Skywards loyalty program encourages passengers to fly with Emirates more often by awarding them air-miles for every flight. If a new Skywards member can collect 25,000 or more skywards within a consecutive 12–13-month period, the member is moved from the basic blue to silver card membership, and as a result will enjoy free lounge entrance and priority check-in. Emirates encourages more uses by promoting package tours to attractive destinations. It also partners with numerous hotels and car-rental agencies who also share in awarding Skywards air-miles to customers, which in turn the customer can use to purchase more Emirates flights.

Protecting Market Share

While trying to expand total market size, the leading firm also must protect its current business against competitors' attacks. Wal-Mart must also constantly guard against Carrefour; Caterpillar against Komatsu; and McDonald's against Burger King.

What can the market leader do to protect its position? First, it must prevent or fix weaknesses that provide opportunities for competitors. It must always fulfill its value promise. Its prices must remain consistent with the value that customers see in the brand. It must work tirelessly to keep strong relationships with valued customers. The leader should 'plug holes' so that competitors do not jump in.

But the best defense is a good offense, and the best response is *continuous innovation*. The leader refuses to be content with the way things are and leads the industry in new products, customer services, distribution effectiveness, promotion, and cost cutting. It keeps increasing its competitive effectiveness and value to customers. And when attacked by challengers, the market leader reacts decisively. For example, in the tea drinks market, Lipton from Unilever has been relentless in the offense against challengers Twinings, Tetley, Typhoo, and Al Kozay.

The Lipton brand has roots in the GCC's tea culture, having been sold there since the 1930s. In the GCC, Lipton has 70 percent market share in the tea category and so is the undisputed market leader. In spite of aggressive behavior from competitors, a range of recent tea innovations has been launched in the region to cater to changing and adventurous tastes. These include green teas and a range of specialty teas with exotic fruit flavor varieties. Lipton also continues to outspend its competitors in advertising and promotions. In retail, Lipton absolutely dominates the tea market, with overwhelming presence on the shelf. Leaf tea remains a local favorite in Arabian society, and Lipton is constantly aiming

Lipton protects its market share through constant innovation to produce tea products which are tastier and easier to make, such as the pyramid tea bags.

to make it tastier and easier to make with innovations including Lipton Pyramid tea bags that give the leaves more room to move.

Expanding Market Share

Market leaders also can grow by increasing their market shares further. In many markets, small market share increases mean very large sales increases. For example, in the U.S. digital camera market, a 1 percent increase in market share is worth US$90 million; in carbonated soft drinks, US$720 million![11]

Studies have shown that, on average, profitability rises with increasing market share. Because of these findings, many companies have sought expanded market shares to improve profitability. GE, for example, declared that it wants to be at least number one or two in each of its markets or else get out. GE shed its computer, air-conditioning, small appliances, and television businesses because it could not achieve top position in these industries.

However, some studies have found that many industries contain one or a few highly profitable large firms, several profitable and more focused firms, and a large number of medium-sized firms with poorer profit performance. It appears that profitability increases as a business gains share relative to competitors in its *served market*. For example, Lexus holds only a small share of the total car market, but it earns a high profit because it is the leading brand in the luxury-performance car segment. And it has achieved this high share in its served market because it does other things right, such as producing high-quality products, creating good service experiences, and building close customer relationships.

Companies must not think, however, that gaining increased market share will automatically improve profitability. Much depends on their strategy for gaining increased share. There are many high-share companies with low profitability and many low-share companies with high profitability. The cost of buying higher market share may far exceed the returns. Higher shares tend to produce higher profits only when unit costs fall with increased market share, or when the company offers a superior-quality product and charges a premium price that more than covers the cost of offering higher quality.

Market Challenger Strategies

Firms that are second, third, or lower in an industry are sometimes quite large, such as Colgate, Ford, Spinneys, Avis, and Etihad Airways. These runner-up firms can adopt one of two competitive strategies: They can challenge the leader and other competitors in an aggressive bid for more market share (market challengers); or they can play along with competitors and not try to outdo them (market followers).

A market challenger must first define which competitors to challenge and its strategic objective. The challenger can attack the market leader, a high-risk but potentially high-gain strategy. Its goal might be to take over market leadership. Or the challenger's objective may simply be to take more market share.

Although it might seem that the market leader has the most going for it, challengers often have what some strategists call a 'second-mover advantage.' The challenger observes what has made the leader successful and improves upon it. For example, Carrefour brought the hypermarket concept to the Arab world, but after observing Carrefour's success, Hyper One in Egypt has managed to emulate the model. The Hyper One brand is similar to Carrefour's No. 1; the stores are located in the outskirts of the city; and they build on a one-story plan. Subsequently, Hyper One has managed to win over a substantially large customer base.[12]

Alternatively, the challenger can avoid the leader and instead challenge firms its own size, or smaller local and regional firms. These smaller firms may be underfinanced and not serving their customers well. It can be argued that Spinneys has pursued this strategy by taking away business from Choithram and the Union Coops.

How can the market challenger best attack the chosen competitor and achieve its strategic objectives? It may launch a full *frontal attack*, matching the competitor's product, advertising, price, and distribution efforts. It attacks the competitor's strengths rather than its weaknesses. The outcome depends on who has the greater strength and endurance.

If the market challenger has fewer resources than the competitor, however, a frontal attack makes little sense. Thus, many new market entrants avoid frontal attacks, knowing that the market leaders can head them off with expensive advertising campaigns, price wars, and other retaliations. Rather than challenging head-on, the challenger can make an *indirect attack* on the competitor's weaknesses or on gaps in the competitor's market coverage. It can find ways to establish itself using tactics that the existing leaders have trouble responding to or choose to ignore. For example, compare the vastly different strategies of two different European challengers—Virgin Drinks and Red Bull—when they entered the U.S. soft drink market in the late 1990s against market leaders Coca-Cola and PepsiCo.[13]

Virgin Drinks took on the leaders head-on, launching its own cola, advertising heavily, and trying to get into all the same retail outlets that stocked the leading brands. At Virgin Cola's launch, Virgin CEO Richard Branson even drove a tank through a wall of rivals' cans in New York's Times Square to symbolize the war he wished to wage on the big, established rivals. However, Coke's and Pepsi's viselike grip on U.S. shelf space proved impossible for Virgin Drinks to break. Although Virgin Drinks is still around, it has never gained more than a 1 percent share of the U.S. cola market.

Red Bull, by contrast, tackled the leaders indirectly. It entered the U.S. soft drink market with a niche product: a carbonated energy drink retailing at about twice what you would pay for a Coke or Pepsi. It started by selling Red Bull through unconventional outlets not dominated by the market leaders, such as bars and nightclubs, where twenty-somethings gulped down the caffeine-rich drink so they could dance all night. After gaining a loyal following,

Market challenger strategies: Virgin Drinks mounted a full frontal attack on Coca-Cola and PepsiCo but couldn't break the leaders' viselike grip on U.S. shelf space.

Red Bull used the pull of high margins to elbow its way into the corner store, where it now sits in refrigerated bins within arm's length of Coke and Pepsi. In the United States, where Red Bull enjoys a 65 percent share of the energy drink market, its sales are growing at about 35 percent a year.

Market Follower Strategies

Not all runner-up companies want to challenge the market leader. Challenges are never taken lightly by the leader. If the challenger's lure is lower prices, improved service, or additional product features, the leader can quickly match these to defuse the attack. The leader probably has more staying power in an all-out battle for customers.

A follower can gain many advantages. The market leader often bears the huge expenses of developing new products and markets, expanding distribution, and educating the market. By contrast, as with challengers, the market follower can learn from the leader's experience. It can copy or improve on the leader's products and programs, usually with much less investment. Although the follower will probably not overtake the leader, it often can be as profitable.

Following is not the same as being passive or a carbon copy of the leader. A market follower must know how to hold current customers and win a fair share of new ones. It must find the right balance between following closely enough to win customers from the market leader but following at enough of a distance to avoid retaliation. Each follower tries to bring distinctive advantages to its target market—location, services, financing. The follower is often a major target of attack by challengers. Therefore, the market follower must keep its manufacturing costs and prices low or its product quality and services high. It must also enter new markets as they open up.

Market Nicher Strategies

Almost every industry includes firms that specialize in serving market niches. Instead of pursuing the whole market, or even large segments, these firms target subsegments. Nichers are often smaller firms with limited resources. But smaller divisions of larger firms also may pursue niching strategies. Firms with low shares of the total market can be highly successful and profitable through smart niching.

Why is niching profitable? The main reason is that the market nicher ends up knowing the target customer group so well that it meets their needs better than other firms that casually sell to that niche. As a result, the nicher can charge a substantial markup over costs because of the added value. Whereas the mass-marketer achieves high volume, the nicher achieves high margins.

Nichers try to find one or more market niches that are safe and profitable. An ideal market niche is big enough to be profitable and has growth potential. It is one that the firm can serve effectively. Perhaps most importantly, the niche is of little interest to major competitors. And the firm can build the skills and customer goodwill to defend itself against a major competitor as the niche grows and becomes more attractive. For example, computer mouse and interface device maker Logitech is only a fraction the size of giant Microsoft. Yet, through skillful niching, it dominates the PC mouse market, with Microsoft as its runner-up. Here's another example of a profitable nicher in the Arab world.

> Arabian Adventure is a leader in the tours and safaris segment of the larger tourism and hospitality market. It is part of the Destination and Leisure Management division of Emirates, with offices in Dubai, Abu Dhabi, and Fujairah, and associates throughout the Gulf. The company specializes in providing high-quality destination management services. The 300 staff are fluent in many European and Asian languages, and aim to provide tailor-made services, such as in-resort assistance and transfers. African Adventure also offers specific experiences, such as city tours, desert driving, sand boarding, and camel riding—for individual holiday-makers and corporations seeking team-building activities.[14]

Arabian Adventures is an example of a company successfully targeting its offering at a market niche.

The key idea in niching is specialization. A market nicher can specialize along any of several market, customer, product, or marketing mix lines. For example, it can specialize in serving one type of *end user*, as when a law firm specializes in the criminal, civil, or business law markets. The nicher can specialize in serving a given *customer-size* group. Many nichers specialize in serving small and midsize customer groups who are neglected by the majors.

Some nichers focus on one or a few *specific customers*, selling their entire output to a single company, such as Carrefour or Toyota. Still other nichers specialize by *geographic market*, selling only in a certain locality, region, or area of the world. *Quality-price* nichers operate at the low or high end of the market. For example, HP specializes in the high-quality, high-price end of the hand-calculator market.

Niching carries some major risks. For example, the market niche may dry up, or it might grow to the point that it attracts larger competitors. For example, Alberto Culver a US$1.5 billion company has used a multiple niching strategy to grow profitably, and was acquired by Unilever in 2011. Alberto Culver has been known mainly for its Alberto VO5 hair products, so focused its marketing muscle on acquiring a stable of smaller niche brands. It has niched in hair, skin, and personal care products (Alberto VO5, St. Ives, Motions, Just for Me, Pro-Line, TRESemmé, and Consort men's hair products), seasonings and sweeteners (Molly McButter, Mrs. Dash, SugarTwin, Baker's Joy), and home products (static-cling fighter Static Guard). Most of its brands are number one in their niches.

Balancing Customer and Competitor Orientations (pp 459–460)

Whether a company is a market leader, challenger, follower, or nicher, it must watch its competitors closely and find the competitive marketing strategy that positions it most effectively. And it must continually adapt its strategies to the fast-changing competitive environment. This question now arises: Can the company spend *too* much time and energy tracking competitors, damaging its customer orientation? The answer is yes! A company can become so competitor centered that it loses its even more important focus on maintaining profitable customer relationships.

Competitor-centered company
A company whose moves are mainly based on competitors' actions and reactions.

A **competitor-centered company** is one that spends most of its time tracking competitors' moves and market shares and trying to find strategies to counter them. This approach has some pluses and minuses. On the positive side, the company develops a fighter orientation, watches for weaknesses in its own position, and searches out competitors' weaknesses. On the negative side, the company becomes too reactive. Rather than carrying out its own customer relationship strategy, it bases its own moves on competitors' moves. As a result, it may end up simply matching or extending industry practices rather than seeking innovative new ways to create more value for customers.

Customer-centered company
A company that focuses on customer developments in designing its marketing strategies and on delivering superior value to its target customers.

A **customer-centered company**, by contrast, focuses more on customer developments in designing its strategies. Clearly, the customer-centered company is in a better

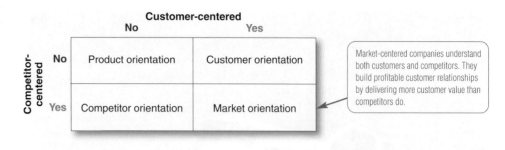

● FIGURE | 15.4

Evolving Company Orientations

position to identify new opportunities and set long-run strategies that make sense. By watching customer needs evolve, it can decide what customer groups and what emerging needs are the most important to serve. Then it can concentrate its resources on delivering superior value to target customers. In practice, today's companies must be **market-centered companies**, watching both their customers and their competitors. But they must not let competitor watching blind them to customer focusing.

● **Figure 15.4** shows that companies have moved through four orientations over the years. In the first stage, they were product oriented, paying little attention to either customers or competitors. In the second stage, they became customer oriented and started to pay attention to customers. In the third stage, when they started to pay attention to competitors, they became competitor oriented. Today, companies need to be market oriented, paying balanced attention to both customers and competitors. Rather than simply watching competitors and trying to beat them on current ways of doing business, they need to watch customers and find innovative ways to build profitable customer relationships by delivering more customer value than competitors do. As noted previously, marketing begins with a good understanding of consumers and the marketplace.

Market-centered company

A company that pays balanced attention to both customers and competitors in designing its marketing strategies.

REVIEWING Objectives AND KEY Terms

Today's companies face their toughest competition ever. Understanding customers is an important first step in developing strong customer relationships, but it's not enough. To gain competitive advantage, companies must use this understanding to design market offers that deliver more value than the offers of *competitors* seeking to win over the same customers. This chapter examines how firms analyze their competitors and design effective competitive marketing strategies.

OBJECTIVE 1 Discuss the need to understand competitors as well as customers through competitor analysis. **(pp 442–449)**

In order to prepare an effective marketing strategy, a company must consider its competitors as well as its customers. Building profitable customer relationships requires satisfying target consumer needs *better than competitors do*. A company must continuously analyze competitors and develop *competitive marketing strategies* that position it effectively against competitors and give it the strongest possible *competitive advantage*.

Competitor analysis first involves identifying the company's major competitors, using both an industry-based and a market-based analysis. The company then gathers information on competitors' objectives, strategies, strengths and weaknesses, and reaction patterns. With this information in hand, it can select competitors to attack or avoid. Competitive intelligence must be collected, interpreted, and distributed continuously. Company marketing managers should be able to obtain full and reliable information about any competitor affecting their decisions.

OBJECTIVE 2 Explain the fundamentals of competitive marketing strategies based on creating value for customers. **(pp 449–459)**

Which *competitive marketing strategy* makes the most sense depends on the company's industry, and on whether it is a market leader, challenger, follower, or nicher. A *market leader* has to mount strategies to expand the total market, protect market share, and expand market share. A *market challenger* is a firm that tries aggressively to expand its market share by attacking the leader, other runner-up companies, or smaller firms in the industry. The challenger can select from a variety of direct or indirect attack strategies.

A *market follower* is a runner-up firm that chooses not to change things too much, usually from fear that it stands to lose more than it might gain. But the follower is not without a strategy and seeks to use its particular skills to gain market growth. Some followers enjoy a higher rate of return than the leaders in their industry. A *market nicher* is a smaller firm that is unlikely to attract the attention of larger firms. Market nichers often become specialists in some end use, customer size, specific customer, geographic area, or service.

OBJECTIVE 3 **Illustrate the need for balancing customer and competitor orientations in becoming a truly market-centered organization.** (pp 459–460)

A competitive orientation is important in today's markets, but companies should not overdo their focus on competitors. Companies are more likely to be hurt by emerging consumer needs and new competitors than by existing competitors. *Market-centered companies* that balance consumer and competitor considerations are practicing a true market orientation.

KEY Terms

OBJECTIVE 1

Competitive advantage (p 441)
Competitor analysis (p 441)
Competitive marketing strategies (p 442)
Strategic group (p 444)

Benchmarking (p 444)
Customer value analysis (p 445)

OBJECTIVE 2

Market leader (p 452)
Market challenger (p 452)

Market follower (p 452)
Market nicher (p 452)

OBJECTIVE 3

Competitor-centered company (p 459)
Customer-centered company (p 459)
Market-centered company (p 460)

DISCUSSING & APPLYING THE Concepts

Discussing the Concepts

1. Which point of view is best for identifying competitors—industry or market?

2. Explain how having strong competitors can benefit a company.

3. What is the difference between entrepreneurial, intrepreneurial, and formulated marketing? What are the advantages and disadvantages of each?

4. Describe the three value disciplines for delivering superior customer value and explain why classifying competitive strategies in this way is appealing.

5. Discuss the strategies available to market leaders.

6. What are the advantages and disadvantages of a market-nicher competitive strategy?

Applying the Concepts

1. Form a small group and conduct a customer value analysis for five local restaurants. Who are the strong and weak competitors? For the strong competitors, what are their vulnerabilities?

2. Research 'blue ocean strategy' and discuss examples of companies that have succeeded in pursuing this strategy. Do companies succeeding in developing uncontested marketspaces necessarily have to be innovative upstarts?

3. Identify a company following a market niche strategy in each of the following industries: automobiles, restaurants, and airlines.

FOCUS ON Technology

Apple is the leader in MP3 players and wants to lead in the mobile smart phone segment, too. In May 2008, Orange announced a new agreement with Apple to bring the iPhone to Orange customers in Austria, Belgium, the Dominican Republic, Egypt, Jordan, Poland, Portugal, Romania, Slovakia, Switzerland, and Orange's African markets later in the year.

Apple had sold 5.4 million iPhones in March 2008. The new international deals will help it reach its 10 million per month unit goal; however, the big sales will come when it signs a deal with China Mobile and has access to some 369 million subscribers.

Apple is taking a smaller cut of the revenue from applications to encourage developers to focus on the iPhone. When the iPhone 3G was released there were upwards of 500 applications available within the first month. More than 10,000 applications could be downloaded by the end of 2008, rising to 95,000 in 2009 and more than 300,000 in 2010. Developers keep 70 percent of the money that they take in from paid-for consumer applications. This is a higher percentage than developers get from other applications markets in the cellphone industry. As a result, iPhone applications can be priced cheaper than similar applications for rivals BlackBerry and Windows Mobile smart phones. Additionally, the competitors offer fewer applications on their websites than does Apple.

1. What position does Apple hold in the smart phone industry? What competitive strategy is Apple using?

2. Why is Apple virtually giving away this platform to third-party applications developers? Wouldn't it be more profitable for Apple to generate more revenue from its Apple Store?

FOCUS ON Ethics

In Pakistan, the government's Monopoly Control Authority is charged with ensuring that mergers, cartels, and anticompetitive behavior by businesses are prevented. Cartels, however, are widespread and damaging. A cartel is effectively an arrangement between competing businesses to act in collusion with the target of raising prices and collective profits. The cartel attempts to create monopoly-like conditions in the marketplace in order to restrict supply and thereby increase the prices charged to customers. The major business areas in which cartels are openly active are in cement products, fertilizers, and cars and other vehicles. Due to this, cartels must be seen as manipulating and distorting the marketplace.

1. Research one of these product areas and discover which businesses are part of the cartel.

2. How might a government handle the existence of cartels and restrict any damaging effects they may have on the economy?

MARKETING BY THE Numbers

More than 750 million olive trees are cultivated worldwide, the greatest number (around 95 percent) being in the regions around the Mediterranean. The world production of olive oil is about 2,602 thousand tons, and 70 percent of the global olive oil production comes from the European Union. Spain, Italy, and Greece contribute 97 percent of European production. The Spanish produce around one million tons (44 percent of the world's production), and Italian production is nearly 520 thousand tons (20 percent of the world's production). At present, Greece produces about 340 thousand tons (13 percent of the world's production), making it the third largest olive oil producer in the world.

1. Research the Greek olive oil business and find out how many tons of olive oil the country exports. What percentage of Greek olive oil is exported, and which country is the main market?

2. Research Greece as a food producer and prepare a SWOT analysis that could be used by the Greek government to help it market the country's produce worldwide.

VIDEO Case

Umpqua Bank

The retail banking industry has become very competitive. And with a few powerhouses dominating the market, how is a small bank to thrive? By differentiating itself through a competitive advantage that the big guys can't touch.

That's exactly what Umpqua has done. Step inside a branch of this community bank and you'll see immediately that this is not your typical holiday club savings account/free household appliance bank. Umpqua's business model has transformed banking from retail drudgery into a holistic experience. Umpqua has created an environment in which people just love to hang out. It not only has its own music download service featuring local artists, it even has its own blend of coffee.

But beneath all these bells and whistles lies the core of what makes Umpqua so different—a rigorous service culture where every branch and employee gets measured on how well they serve customers. That's why every customer feels like they get the help and attention they need from employees.

After viewing the video featuring Umpqua Bank, answer the following questions about creating competitive advantage:

1. With what companies does Umpqua compete?

2. What is Umpqua's competitive advantage?

3. Will Umpqua be able to maintain this advantage in the long run? Why or why not?

COMPANY Case

Bose: Competing by Being Truly Different

In 2006, Forrester Research announced the results of its semi-annual survey ranking consumer electronics and personal computer companies on consumer trust. Based on a poll of more than 4,700 customers as to their opinions of 22 of the best-known consumer technology brands, the company drew the conclusion that people's trust in consumer technology companies was eroding.

Why is consumer trust important? It can be argued that high consumer trust is an indicator of high brand value. If a company's brand value is high, it is able to charge premium prices for its products. Similarly, when consumer trust decreases, so does brand value, which can have a negative affect on a company's profits and growth.

But despite the decline in trust for most technology companies, Forrester made another surprising finding. Consumer trust in the consumer electronics company the Bose Corporation is riding high. In fact, Bose far outscored all other companies in Forrester's survey. That's not bad, considering that it was the first time the company had been included in the survey. Forrester points out that these results are no fluke, noting that Bose has 10 million regular users but more than 17 million consumers who aspire to use the brand (compared with 7 million for next highest, Apple).

These high levels of consumer trust result from philosophies that have guided Bose for nearly 50 years. Most companies today focus heavily on building revenue, profits, and stock price. They try to outdo the competition by differentiating product lines with features and attributes that other companies do not have. While Bose doesn't exactly ignore such factors, its true competitive advantage is rooted in the company's unique corporate philosophy. Bose President Bob Maresca provides insights on that philosophy: "We are not in it strictly to make money," he says. Pointing to the company's focus on research and product innovation, he continues, "The business is almost a secondary consideration."

THE BOSE PHILOSOPHY

You can't understand Bose the company without taking a look at Bose the man. Amar Bose, the company's founder and still its CEO, has been in charge from the start. In the 1950s, Mr Bose was working on his third degree at the Massachusetts Institute of Technology. He had a keen interest in research and studied various areas of electrical engineering. He also had a strong interest in music. When he purchased his first hi-fi system—a model that he believed had the best specifications—he was very disappointed in the system's ability to reproduce realistic sound. So he set out to find his own solution. Thus began a stream of research that would ultimately lead to the founding of the Bose Corporation in 1964.

From those early days, Amar Bose worked around certain core principles that have guided the philosophy of the company. In conducting his first research on speakers and sound, he did something that has since been repeated time and time again at Bose. He ignored existing technologies and started entirely from scratch, something not very common in product development strategies.

In another departure from typical corporate strategies, Amar Bose plows all of the privately held company's profits back into research. This practice reflects his avid love of research and his belief that it will produce the highest quality products. But he also does this because he can. Bose has been quoted many times saying, "if I worked for another company, I would have been fired a long time ago," pointing to the fact that publicly held companies have long lists of constraints that don't apply to his privately held company. For this reason, Bose has always vowed that he will never take the company public. "Going public for me would have been the equivalent of losing the company. My real interest is research—that's the excitement—and I wouldn't have been able to do long-term projects with Wall Street breathing down my neck."

This commitment to research and development has led to the high level of trust that Bose customers have for the company. It also explains their almost cult-like loyalty. Customers know that the company cares more about their best interests—about making the best product—than about maximizing profits. But for a company not driven by the bottom line, Bose does just fine. According to market information firm NPD Group, Bose leads the market in home speakers with a 12.6 percent share. And that market share translates into financial performance. Although figures are tightly held by the private corporation, a recent known estimate of company revenue was US$1.8 billion for 2006. While that number doesn't come close to the US$88 billion Sony reported last year, it does represent a 38 percent gain in just two years.

GROUNDBREAKING PRODUCTS

The company that started so humbly now has a breadth of product lines beyond its core home audio line. Additional lines target a variety of applications that have captured Amar Bose's creative attention over the years, including military, automotive, home-building/remodeling, aviation, and professional and commercial sound systems. It even has a division that markets testing equipment to research institutions, universities, medical device companies, and engineering companies worldwide. The following are just a few of the products that illustrate the innovative breakthroughs produced by the company.

Speakers. Bose's first product, introduced in 1965, was a speaker. Expecting to sell US$1 million worth of speakers that first year, Bose made 60 but sold only 40. The original Bose speaker evolved into the 901 Direct/Reflecting speaker system launched in 1968. The speaker was so technologically advanced that the company still sells it today.

The system was designed around the concept that live sound reaches the human ear via direct as well as reflected channels (off walls, ceilings, and other objects). The configuration of the speakers was completely unorthodox. They were shaped like an eighth of a sphere and mounted facing into a room's corner. The speakers had no woofers or tweeters and were very small compared with the high-end speakers of the day. The design came much closer to the essence and emotional impact of live music than anything else on the market and won immediate industry acclaim.

However, Bose had a hard time convincing customers of the merits of these innovative speakers. At a time when woofers, tweeters, and size were everything, the 901 series initially flopped. In 1968, a retail salesman explained to Amar Bose why the speakers weren't selling:

Look, I love your speaker but I cannot sell it because it makes me lose all my credibility as a salesman. I can't explain to anyone why the 901 doesn't have any woofers or tweeters. A man came in and saw the small size, and he started looking in the drawers for the speaker cabinets. I walked over to him, and he said, "Where are you hiding the woofer?" I said to him, "There is no woofer." So he said, "You're a liar," and he walked out.

Bose eventually worked through the challenges of communicating the virtues of the 901 series to customers through innovative display and demonstration tactics. The product became so successful that Amar Bose now credits the 901 series for building the company.

The list of major speaker innovations at Bose is a long one. In 1975, the company introduced concert-like sound in the bookshelf-size 301 Direct/Reflecting speaker system. Fourteen years of research led to the 1984 development of acoustic waveguide speaker technology, a technology today found in the award-winning Wave radio, Wave music system, and Acoustic Wave music system. In 1986, the company again changed conventional thinking about the relationship between speaker size and sound. The Acoustimass system enabled palm-size speakers to produce audio quality equivalent to that of high-end systems many times their size. And most recently, Bose has again introduced the state-of-the-art with the MusicMonitor, a pair of compact computer speakers that rival the sound of three-piece subwoofer systems. It may sound simple, but at US$399, it's anything but.

Headphones. Bob Maresca recalls that, "Bose invested tens of million of dollars over 19 years developing headset technology before making a profit. Now, headsets are a major part of the business." Initially, Bose focused on noise reduction technologies to make headphones for pilots that would block out the high

level of noise interference from planes. Bose headphones didn't just muffle noise, they electronically canceled ambient noise so that pilots wearing them heard nothing but the sound coming through the phones. Bose quickly discovered that airline passengers could benefit as much as pilots from its headphone technology. Today, the Bose QuietComfort series, used in a variety of consumer applications, is the benchmark in noise canceling headphones. One journalist considers this product to be so significant that it made his list of "101 gadgets that changed the world" (some of the other inventions on the list included aspirin, paper, and the light bulb).

Automotive suspensions. Another major innovation from Bose has yet to be introduced. The company has been conducting research since 1980 on a product outside of its known areas of expertise: automotive suspensions. Amar Bose's interest in suspensions dates back to the 1950s when he bought both a Citroën DS-19 C and a Pontiac Bonneville, each riding on unconventional air suspension systems. Since that time, he has been obsessed with the engineering challenge of achieving good cornering capabilities without sacrificing a smooth ride. "In cars today, there's always a compromise between softness over bumps and roll and pitch during maneuvering," Bose said in a recent interview. The Bose Corporation is now on the verge of introducing a suspension that it believes eliminates that compromise.

The basics of the system include an electromagnetic motor installed at each wheel. Based on inputs from road sensing monitors, the motor can retract and extend almost instantaneously. If there is a bump in the road, the suspension reacts by 'jumping' over it. If there is a pothole, the suspension allows the wheel to extend downward, but then retracts it quickly enough that the pothole is not felt. In addition to these comfort producing capabilities, the wheel motors are strong enough to keep a car completely level during an aggressive maneuver such as cornering or stopping. In a recent interview about this system, Dr Bose said, "This system provides absolutely better handling than any sports car, and the most comfortable ride imaginable."

Thus far, Bose has invested more than US$100 million and 27 years in its groundbreaking suspension. And while it is ready to take the product to market, it is staying true to its philosophy by not rushing things. Bose plans first to partner with one automotive manufacturer in the near future. The cost of the system will put it in the class of higher-end luxury automobiles. But eventually, Bose anticipates that wider adoption and higher volume will bring the price down to the point where the suspension could be found in all but the least expensive cars.

At an age when most people have long since retired, 78-year-old Amar Bose still works every day, either at the company's headquarters or in his home. "He's got more energy than an 18-year-old," says Maresca. "Every one of the naysayers only strengthens his resolve." This work ethic illustrates the passion of the man who has shaped one of today's most innovative and yet most trusted companies. His philosophies have produced Bose's long list of groundbreaking innovations. Even now, as the company prepares to enter the world of automotive suspensions, it continues to achieve success by following another one of Dr Bose's basic philosophies: "The potential size of the market? We really have no idea. We just know that we have a technology that's so different and so much better that many people will want it."

Questions for Discussion

1. Based on the business philosophies of Amar Bose, how do you think the Bose Corporation goes about analyzing its competition?

2. Which of the text's three approaches to marketing strategy best describes Bose's approach?

3. Using the Michael Porter and Treacy and Wiersema frameworks presented in the text, which basic competitive marketing strategies does Bose pursue?

4. What is Bose's competitive position in its industry? Do its marketing strategies match this position?

5. In your opinion, is Bose a customer-centric company?

6. What will happen when Amar Bose leaves the company?

Sources: Jeffrey Krasner, "Shocks and Awe," *Boston Globe*, December 3, 2007, p. E1; Simon Usborne, "101 Gadgets That Changed the World," *Belfast Telegraph*, November 5, 2007, accessed online at www.belfasttelegraph.co.uk; Brian Dumaine, "Amar Bose," *Fortune Small Business*, September 1, 2004, accessed online at www.money.cnn.com/magazines/fsb/; Olga Kharif, "Selling Sound: Bose Knows," *BusinessWeek Online*, May 15, 2006, accessed online at www.businessweek.com; Mark Jewell, "Bose Tries to Shake Up Auto Industry," *Associated Press*, November 27, 2005; "Bose Introduces New QuietComfort 3 Acoustic Noise Cancelling Headphones," *Business Wire*, June 8, 2006; "Forrester Research Reveals The Most Trusted Consumer Technology Brands," press release accessed online at www.forrester.com; also see, "About Bose," accessed online at www.bose.com, June 2008.

Chapter 16

Part 1   Defining Marketing and the Marketing Process (Chapters 1, 2)
Part 2   Understanding the Marketplace and Consumers (Chapters 3, 4, 5, 6)
Part 3   Designing a Customer-Driven Strategy and Mix (Chapters 7, 8, 9, 10, 11, 12, 13, 14)
Part 4   Extending Marketing (Chapters 15, 16, 17)

The Global Marketplace

Chapter PREVIEW

You've now learned the fundamentals of how companies develop competitive marketing strategies to create customer value and build lasting customer relationships. In this chapter, we extend these fundamentals to global marketing. We've visited global topics in each previous chapter—it's difficult to find an area of marketing that doesn't contain at least some international issues. Here, however, we'll focus on special considerations that companies face when they market their brands globally. Advances in communication, transportation, and other technologies have made the world a much smaller place. Today, almost every firm, large or small, faces international marketing issues. In this chapter, we will examine six major decisions marketers make in going global.

To start things off, let's look at good old McDonald's. Despite its American roots, McDonald's is a truly global enterprise. Over the years, the company has learned many important lessons about adapting locally in global markets. Here, we'll examine McDonald's journey into Russia, now one of the crown jewels in its global empire.

Many Americans still think of McDonald's as their very own. The first McDonald's stand popped up in the U.S. state of California in 1954, and what could be more American than burger-and-fries fast food? But as it turns out, the characteristically all-American company now sells more burgers and fries outside the country than within. Nearly 65 percent of McDonald's US$22.8 billion of sales last year came from outside the United States, and its international sales grew at close to twice the rate of domestic sales growth.

McDonald's today is a truly global enterprise. Its 30,000 restaurants serve more than 52 million people in more than 100 countries each day. Few firms have more international marketing experience than McDonald's. But going global hasn't always been easy, and McDonald's has learned many important lessons in its journeys overseas. To see how far McDonald's has come, consider its experiences in Russia, a market that's very different culturally, economically, and politically from McDonald's American home nation.

McDonald's first set its sights on Russia (then a part of the Soviet Union) in 1976, when George Cohon, head of McDonald's in Canada, took a group of Soviet Olympics officials to a McDonald's while they visited the Montreal Olympic Games. Cohon was struck by how much the Soviets liked McDonald's hamburgers, fries, and other fare. Over the next 14 years, Cohon flew to Russia more than 100 times, first to get Soviet permission for McDonald's to provide food for the 1980 Moscow Olympics, and later to be allowed to open McDonald's restaurants in the country. He quickly learned that no one in Russia had any idea what a McDonald's was. The Soviets turned Cohon down flat on both requests.

Finally in 1988, as Premier Mikhail Gorbachev began to open the Russian economy, Cohon forged a deal with the city of Moscow to launch the first Russian McDonald's in Moscow's Pushkin Square. But obtaining permission was only the first step. Actually opening the restaurant brought a fresh set of challenges. Thanks to Russia's large and bureaucratic government structure, McDonald's had to obtain some 200 separate signatures just to open the single location. It had difficulty finding reliable suppliers for even such basics as hamburgers and buns. So McDonald's forked out over US$45 million to build a facility to produce these things itself. It even brought in technical experts from Canada with special strains of disease-resistant seed to teach Russian farmers how to grow Russet Burbank potatoes for French fries, and it built its own pasteurizing plant to ensure a plentiful supply of fresh milk.

When the Moscow McDonald's at Pushkin Square finally opened its doors in January 1990, it quickly won the hearts of

The Pushkin Square McDonald's is huge—26 cash registers and 900 seats.

Russian consumers. However, the company faced still more hurdles. The Pushkin Square restaurant is huge—26 cash registers and 900 seats (compared with 40–50 seats in a typical U.S. McDonald's). The logistics of serving customers on such a scale was daunting, made even more difficult by the fact that few employees or customers understood the fast-food concept.

Although American consumers were well acquainted with McDonald's, the Russian's were clueless. So, in order to meet its high standards for customer satisfaction in this new market, the U.S. restaurant chain had to educate employees about the time-tested McDonald's way of doing things. It trained Russian managers at Hamburger University and subjected each of 630 new employees (most of whom didn't know a Chicken McNugget from an Egg McMuffin) to 16 to 20 hours of training on such essentials as cooking meat patties, assembling Fillet-O-Fish sandwiches, and giving service with a smile. Back in those days, McDonald's even had to train consumers—most Muscovites had never seen a fast-food restaurant. Customers waiting in line were shown videos telling them everything from how to order and pay at the counter, to how to put their coats over the backs of their seats, to how to handle a Big Mac.

However, the new Moscow McDonald's got off to a spectacular start. An incredible 50,000 customers swarmed the restaurant during its first day of business. And in its usual way, McDonald's began immediately to build community involvement. On opening day, it held a kickoff party for 700 Muscovite orphans and then donated all opening-day proceeds to the Moscow children's fund.

Today, 20 years after opening its first restaurant there, McDonald's is thriving in Russia. The Pushkin Square location is now the busiest McDonald's in the world, and Russia is the crown jewel in McDonald's global empire. The company's 180 restaurants in 40 Russian cities each serve an average of 850,000 diners a year—twice the per-store traffic of any of the other 117 countries in which McDonald's operates.

Despite the long lines of customers, McDonald's has been careful about how rapidly it expands in Russia. In recent years, it has restrained its rapid growth strategy and focused instead on improving profitability and product and service quality. The goal is to squeeze more business out of existing restaurants and to grow slowly but profitably. One way to do that is to add new menu items to draw in consumers at different times of the day. So, as it did many years ago in the United States, McDonald's in Russia is now adding breakfast items.

Although only about 5 percent of Russians eat breakfast outside the home, more commuters in the big cities are leaving home earlier to avoid heavy traffic. The company hopes that the new breakfast menu will encourage commuters to stop off at McDonald's on their way to work. However, when the fast-food chain added breakfast items, it stopped offering its traditional hamburger fare

Moscow's Pushkin Square location is the busiest McDonald's in the world, and Russia is the crown jewel in McDonald's global empire.

during the morning hours. When many customers complained of 'hamburger withdrawal,' McDonald's introduced the Fresh McMuffin, an English muffin with a sausage patty topped with cheese, lettuce, tomato, and special sauce. The new sandwich became an instant hit.

To reduce the lines inside restaurants and to attract motorists, McDonald's is also introducing Russian consumers to drive-thru windows. At first, many Russians just didn't get the concept. Instead, they treated the drive-thru window as just another line, purchasing their food there, parking, and going inside to eat. Also, Russian cars often don't have cupholders, so drive-thru customers bought fewer drinks. However, as more customers get used to the concept, McDonald's is putting drive-thru and walk-up windows in about half of its new stores.

So, that's a look at McDonald's in Russia. But just as McDonald's has tweaked its formula in Russia, it also adjusts its marketing and operations to meet the special needs of local consumers in other major global markets. To be sure, McDonald's is a global brand. Its restaurants around the world employ a common global strategy—convenient food at affordable prices. And no matter where you go in the world—from Moscow to Montréal or Shanghai to Dubai City—you'll find those golden arches and a menu full of Quarter Pounders, Big Macs, fries, milkshakes, and other familiar items. But within that general strategic framework, McDonald's adapts to the subtleties of each local market. Says a McDonald's Europe executive, "Across Europe with 40 different markets, there are 40 sets of tastes. There are also differences within each market. We are a local market but a global brand."[1]

> McDonald's is a truly global enterprise. The company now sells more burgers and fries outside the United States than within.

In the past, companies paid little attention to international trade. Businesses focused their efforts on their local markets, where they produced and marketed to the local customers. If they could pick up some extra sales through exporting, that was fine. But the main market was usually at home. The home market was also much safer. Managers did not need to learn other languages, deal with strange and changing currencies, face political and legal uncertainties, or adapt their products to different customer needs and

Objective Outline

expectations. Today, however, the situation is much different. Organizations of all kinds, from Emirates, Etisalat, Al Islami Foods, and Coca-Cola to Nestlé and Jumeirah Group of hotels, have gone global.

Author Comment | The rapidly changing global environment provides both opportunities and threats. It's difficult to find a marketer today that isn't affected in some way by global developments.

Global Marketing Today (pp 468–469)

The world is shrinking rapidly with the advent of faster communication, transportation, and financial flows. Products developed in one country—Gucci purses, Sony electronics, McDonald's hamburgers, Japanese sushi, German BMWs—have found enthusiastic acceptance in other countries. We would not be surprised to hear about a Saudi businessman who is wearing Italian shoes, driving a German car, meeting an English friend at a Japanese restaurant, or who later returns home to watch the BBC on television.

International trade is booming. Since 1990, the number of multinational corporations in the world has grown from 30,000 to more than 60,000. Some of these multinationals are true giants. In fact, of the largest 150 'economies' in the world, only 76 are countries. The remaining 74 are multinational corporations. Wal-Mart, the world's largest company, has annual revenues greater than the gross domestic product (GDP) of all but the world's 24 largest-GDP countries.[2]

Even after the sharpest decline in more than 70 years, world trade rebounded with a record-breaking 14.5 percent surge in the volume of exports in 2010. World trade grew at a healthy rate from 2003 till 2008 from 4.5 to 11 percent annually, until 2009 when the global economic crisis sparked a 12.2 percent contraction in the volume of global trade—the largest such decline since World War II. In contrast global GDP grew at only 2.5 to 5 percent annually between 2003 and 2008, then contracted by 2.1 percent in 2009. World trade of products and services was valued at over US$15.5 trillion in 2009, which accounted for about 26 percent of worldwide GDP that year.[3]

Many companies have long been successful at international marketing: Coca-Cola, GE, IBM, Emirates, Jumeirah Group of hotels, Toyota, BP, IKEA, Nestlé, Nokia, and dozens

Many companies have made the world their market.

of other firms have made the world their market. Michelin, the tire manufacturer universally recognized as French, now does 32 percent of its business in North America; Johnson & Johnson, the maker of characteristically all-American products such as Band-Aids and Johnson's Baby Shampoo, does 45 percent of its business outside North America. And America's equipment-maker Caterpillar belongs more to the wider world, with 63 percent of its sales coming from outside the United States.[4]

But while global trade is growing, global competition is intensifying. Foreign firms are expanding aggressively into new international markets, and home markets are no longer as rich in opportunity. Few industries are now safe from foreign competition. If companies delay taking steps toward internationalizing, they risk being shut out of growing markets in western and eastern Europe, the Middle East, China and the Pacific Rim, Russia, and elsewhere. Firms that stay at home to play it safe might not only lose their chances to enter other markets but also risk losing their home markets. Domestic companies that never thought about foreign competitors suddenly find these competitors in their own areas.

Ironically, although the need for companies to go abroad is greater today than in the past, so are the risks. Companies that go global may face highly unstable governments and currencies, restrictive government policies and regulations, and high trade barriers. Corruption is also an increasing problem—officials in several countries often award business not to the best bidder but to the highest briber.

Global firm

A firm that, by operating in more than one country, gains R&D, production, marketing, and financial advantages in its costs and reputation that are not available to purely domestic competitors.

A **global firm** is one that, by operating in more than one country, gains marketing, production, R&D, and financial advantages that are not available to purely domestic competitors. The global company sees the world as one market. It minimizes the importance of national boundaries and develops 'transnational' brands. It raises capital, obtains materials and components, and manufactures and markets its goods wherever it can do the best job. For example, Otis Elevator, the world's largest elevator maker, has a customer base spread around the world, and works with global partners too. It gets its elevators' door systems from France, small geared parts from Spain, electronics from Germany, and special motor drives from Japan. It is based in the United States, but uses the U.S. only for systems integration. "Borders are so 20th century," says one global marketing expert. "Transnationals take 'stateless' to the next level."[5]

This does not mean that small and medium-size firms must operate in a dozen countries to succeed. These firms can practice global niching. But the world is becoming smaller, and every company operating in a global industry—whether large or small—must assess and establish its place in world markets.

The rapid move toward globalization means that all companies will have to answer some basic questions: What market position should we try to establish in our country, in our economic region, and globally? Who will our global competitors be and what are their strategies and resources? Where should we produce or source our products? What strategic alliances should we form with other firms around the world?

As shown in ◀ **Figure 16.1,** a company faces six major decisions in international marketing. We will discuss each decision in detail in this chapter.

> It's a big and beautiful but threatening world out there for marketers! Most large American firms have made the world their market. For example, once all-American McDonald's now captures 65 percent of its sales from outside the United States.

| Looking at the global marketing environment | ➡ | Deciding whether to go global | ➡ | Deciding which markets to enter | ➡ | Deciding how to enter the market | ➡ | Deciding on the global marketing program | ➡ | Deciding on the global marketing organization |

◀ **FIGURE** | **16.1** Major International Marketing Decisions

Author Comment | As if operating within a company's own borders wasn't difficult enough, going global adds many layers of complexities. For example, Coca-Cola markets its products in hundreds of countries around the globe. It must understand the varying trade, economic, cultural, and political environments in each market.

Looking at the Global Marketing Environment (pp 470–477)

Before deciding whether to operate internationally, a company must understand the international marketing environment. That environment has changed a great deal in the past two decades, creating both new opportunities and new problems.

The International Trade System

Companies looking abroad must start by understanding the international *trade system.* When selling to another country, a firm may face restrictions on trade between nations. Foreign governments may charge *tariffs,* taxes on certain imported products designed to raise revenue or to protect domestic firms. For example, China puts a 25 percent tariff on imported cars. Or they may set *quotas,* limits on the amount of foreign imports that they will accept in certain product categories. The purpose of a quota is to conserve on foreign exchange and to protect local industry and employment. Firms may also face *exchange controls,* which limit the amount of foreign exchange and the exchange rate against other currencies.

The company also may face *nontariff trade barriers,* such as biases against its bids, restrictive product standards, or excessive regulations. For example, foreign policymakers have criticized China for protectionist regulations and other actions that restrict access to several Chinese markets, including banking services.

> For years U.S. financial houses have dreamed of the day when they'll be allowed to offer banking services to individual Chinese savers. But critics complain that, despite China's promises to the World Trade Organization, Western banks are effectively fenced out by investment caps and regulations that make going solo frightfully expensive. In theory, foreign banks can open branches from Hainan to Harbin. But in reality, they can open only one branch a year, and each branch must have operating capital of US$50 million, a burden local banks don't face. Committing US$500 million to open 10 branches in a decade doesn't make a lot of sense, so foreign banks instead have bought stakes in local banks. But Beijing limits total foreign ownership in any Chinese bank to just 25 percent, leaving the foreign investors little say in strategy. Last year, for instance, Bank of America spent US$3 billion for 9 percent of China Construction Bank Corp. But the Americans have only one seat on the board and had to abandon their own mainland retail effort as part of the deal. Beijing denies any effort to block access to its market. True, foreigners control just 2 percent of assets in the banking system, notes a Chinese trade expert. "The problem is, the U.S. banking sector is not patient."[6]

At the same time, certain forces *help* trade between nations. Examples include the General Agreement on Tariffs and Trade (GATT) and various regional free trade agreements.

The World Trade Organization and GATT

The General Agreement on Tariffs and Trade (GATT) is a 64-year-old treaty designed to promote world trade by reducing tariffs and other international trade barriers. Since the treaty's inception in 1947, member nations (currently numbering 153) have met in eight rounds of GATT negotiations to reassess trade barriers and set new rules for international trade. The first seven rounds of negotiations reduced the average worldwide tariffs on manufactured goods from 45 percent to just 5 percent.[7]

Trade barriers: U.S. and other Western banks have been effectively fenced out of China's huge retail banking market by protectionist regulations.

The most recently completed GATT negotiations, dubbed the Uruguay Round, dragged on for seven long years before concluding in 1994. The benefits of the Uruguay Round will be felt for many years as the accord promotes long-term global trade growth. It reduced the world's remaining merchandise tariffs by 30 percent. The agreement also extended GATT to cover trade in agriculture and a wide range of services, and it toughened international protection of copyrights, patents, trademarks, and other intellectual property. Although the financial impact of such an agreement is difficult to measure, research suggests that cutting agriculture, manufacturing, and services trade barriers by one-third would boost the world economy by US$613 billion, the equivalent of adding another Turkey to the world economy.[8]

Beyond reducing trade barriers and setting global standards for trade, the Uruguay Round set up the World Trade Organization (WTO) to enforce GATT rules. In general, the WTO acts as an umbrella organization, overseeing GATT, mediating global disputes, and imposing trade sanctions. The previous GATT organization never possessed such authorities. A new round of GATT negotiations, the Doha Round, began in Doha, Qatar, in late 2001 and was set to conclude in 2005, but the discussions continue.[9]

Regional Free Trade Zones

Economic community

A group of nations organized to work toward common goals in the regulation of international trade.

Certain countries have formed *free trade zones* or **economic communities**. These are groups of nations organized to work toward common goals in the regulation of international trade.

The Gulf Cooperation Council. The Gulf Cooperation Council (GCC) was established in an agreement signed on May 25, 1981 in Riyadh, Saudi Arabia. The countries involved are Bahrain, Kuwait, Oman, Qatar, Saudi Arabia, and the UAE. These countries established the Council because of their geographic proximity, the special relations between them, and the similarities in their political systems based on "Islamic beliefs, joint destiny and common objectives." A key aim was to adopt free trade economic policies and set up a regional common market. According to the United Nations the population of the GCC gained more than 1.7 million in two years to reach 38.5 million by the end of 2008, and is likely to hit 53 million by 2020.[10]

The GCC is in the process of creating a common currency for the region. Nominal GDP for the GCC was recorded at about US$877 billion in 2010, and was forecast to rise to US$1,010 billion in 2011, according to a report by the Institute of International Finance.[11]

The European Union. Formed in 1957, the European Union (EU) set out to create a single European market by reducing barriers to the free flow of products, services, finances, and labor among member countries and developing policies on trade with nonmember nations. Today, the EU represents one of the world's single largest markets. Currently, it has 27 member countries containing close to half a billion consumers and accounts for more than 20 percent of the world's exports.[12]

European unification offers tremendous trade opportunities for non-European firms. However, it also poses threats. As a result of increased unification, European companies have grown bigger and more competitive. Perhaps an even greater concern, however, is that lower barriers *inside* Europe will create only thicker *outside* walls. Some observers envision a 'Fortress Europe' that heaps favors on firms from EU countries but hinders outsiders by imposing obstacles.

Progress toward European unification has been slow—many doubt that complete unification will ever be achieved. So far, 23 member nations have taken a significant step toward unification by adopting the euro as a common currency. The recession of 2009 and the resulting financial crises in Greece, Ireland, and Portugal have however caused controversy about its economic model and long-term sustainability.

However, even with the adoption of the euro, it is unlikely that the EU will ever go against 2,000 years of tradition and become the

The GCC is a regional common market.

'United States of Europe.' A community with two dozen different languages and cultures will always have difficulty coming together and acting as a single entity. Nevertheless, Europeans voted to adopt the Lisbon Treaty, which was signed by the EU member states on 13 December 2007 and entered into force on 1 December 2009. Among other significant changes, the Lisbon Treaty includes a more powerful European Parliament and the creation of a President of the European Council. Still, although only partly successful so far, unification has made Europe a global force with which to reckon, with a combined annual GDP of more than US$16.2 trillion in 2010.[13]

North American Free Trade Agreement. In 1994, the North American Free Trade Agreement (NAFTA) established a free trade zone among the United States, Mexico, and Canada. The agreement created a single market of 447 million people who produce and consume over US$16 trillion worth of goods and services annually. As it is implemented over a 15-year period, NAFTA will eliminate all trade barriers and investment restrictions among the three countries. Thus far, the agreement has allowed trade between the countries to flourish. In the dozen years following its establishment, trade among the NAFTA nations has risen 198 percent. U.S. merchandise exports to NAFTA partners grew 157 percent, compared with exports to the rest of the world at 108 percent. Canada and Mexico are now the first and second-largest trading partners of the United States.[14]

Other Free Trade Zones. Following the apparent success of NAFTA, in 2005 the Central American Free Trade Agreement (CAFTA) established a free trade zone between the United States and Costa Rica, the Dominican Republic, El Salvador, Guatemala, Honduras, and Nicaragua. And talks have been underway since 1994 to investigate establishing a Free Trade Area of the Americas (FTAA). This mammoth free trade zone would include 34 countries stretching from the Bering Strait to Cape Horn, with a population of more than 800 million and a combined GDP of about US$18.5 trillion.[15]

Other free trade areas have formed in Latin America and South America. For example, Mercosur links 11 Latin American and South American countries, and the Andean Community (CAN, for its Spanish initials) links 4 more. In late 2004, Mercosur and CAN agreed to unite, creating the Union of South American Nations (UNASUR), which is modeled after the EU. The UNASUR Constitutive Treaty was signed in May 2008 and the group became a legal entity in March 2011. With a population of more than 396 million, UNASUR makes up the largest trading bloc after NAFTA and the EU.[16]

Each nation has unique features that must be understood. A nation's readiness for different products and services and its attractiveness as a market to foreign firms depend on its economic, political-legal, and cultural environments.

Economic Environment

The international marketer must study each country's economy. Two economic factors reflect the country's attractiveness as a market: the country's industrial structure and its income distribution.

The country's *industrial structure* shapes its product and service needs, income levels, and employment levels. The four types of industrial structures are as follows:

- *Subsistence economies:* In a subsistence economy, the vast majority of people engage in simple agriculture. They consume most of their output and barter the rest for simple goods and services. They offer few market opportunities.

- *Raw material exporting economies:* These economies are rich in one or more natural resources but poor in other ways. Much of their revenue comes from exporting these resources. For example the GCC states are rich in petroleum and gas and a major part of their GDP is through exporting these resources. Other examples are Chile (tin and copper), and the Democratic Republic of the Congo (copper, cobalt, and coffee). These countries are good markets for large equipment, tools and supplies, and trucks. If there are many foreign residents and a wealthy upper class, they are also a market for luxury goods.

- *Industrializing economies:* In an industrializing economy, manufacturing accounts for 10 to 20 percent of the country's economy. Examples include Egypt, India, and Brazil. As manufacturing increases, the country needs more imports of raw textile materials, steel, and heavy machinery, and fewer imports of finished textiles, paper products, and automobiles. Industrialization typically creates a new rich class and a small but growing middle class, both demanding new types of imported goods.

- *Industrial economies:* Industrial economies are major exporters of manufactured goods, services, and investment funds. They trade goods among themselves and also export them to other types of economies for raw materials and semifinished goods. The varied manufacturing activities of these industrial nations and their large middle class make them rich markets for all sorts of goods.

The second economic factor is the country's *income distribution.* Industrialized nations may have low-, medium-, and high-income households. In contrast, countries with subsistence economies may consist mostly of households with very low family incomes. Still other countries may have households with only either very low or very high incomes. However, even poor or developing economies may be attractive markets for all kinds of goods, including luxuries. For example, many luxury-brand marketers are rushing to take advantage of China's rapidly developing consumer markets:[17]

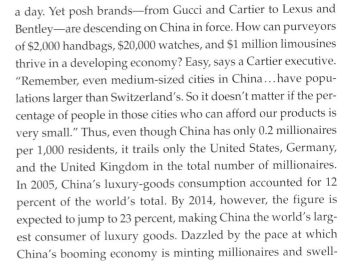

Economic environment: Many luxury brand marketers are rushing to take advantage of China's rapidly developing consumer markets.

More than half of China's 1.3 billion consumers can barely afford rice, let alone luxuries. According to the World Bank, more than 400 million Chinese live on less than US$2 a day. Yet posh brands—from Gucci and Cartier to Lexus and Bentley—are descending on China in force. How can purveyors of $2,000 handbags, $20,000 watches, and $1 million limousines thrive in a developing economy? Easy, says a Cartier executive. "Remember, even medium-sized cities in China…have populations larger than Switzerland's. So it doesn't matter if the percentage of people in those cities who can afford our products is very small." Thus, even though China has only 0.2 millionaires per 1,000 residents, it trails only the United States, Germany, and the United Kingdom in the total number of millionaires. In 2005, China's luxury-goods consumption accounted for 12 percent of the world's total. By 2014, however, the figure is expected to jump to 23 percent, making China the world's largest consumer of luxury goods. Dazzled by the pace at which China's booming economy is minting millionaires and swelling the ranks of the middle class, luxury brands are rushing to stake out shop space and tout their wares. "The Chinese are a natural audience for luxury goods," notes one analyst. After decades of socialism and poverty, China's elite are suddenly "keen to show off their newfound wealth."

Thus, country and regional economic environments will affect an international marketer's decisions about which global markets to enter and how.

Political-Legal Environment

Nations differ greatly in their political-legal environments. In considering whether to do business in a given country, a company should consider factors such as the country's attitudes toward international buying, government bureaucracy, political stability, and monetary regulations.

Some nations are very receptive to foreign firms; others are less accommodating. For example, India has tended to bother foreign businesses with import quotas, currency restrictions, and other limitations that make operating there a challenge. In contrast, neighboring Asian countries such as Singapore and Thailand court foreign investors and shower them with incentives and favorable operating conditions. Political and regulatory stability is another issue. For example, Venezuela's government is notoriously volatile—due to economic factors such as inflation and steep public spending—increasing the risk of doing business there. Although most international marketers still find the Venezuelan market attractive, the unstable political and regulatory situation will affect how they handle business and financial matters. In recent times the January 25th Revolution in Egypt caused a 9.93 percent decline in the stock market. Recent uprisings in other Arab countries could have unpredictable effects on the stock markets and on the opportunities for companies in those countries. Global businesses will probably monitor development in these markets closely before committing to invest further. In the long run democratically elected transparent government could foster greater confidence from global business.[18]

Companies must also consider a country's monetary regulations. Sellers want to take their profits in a currency of value to them. Ideally, the buyer can pay in the seller's currency or in other world currencies. Short of this, sellers might accept a blocked currency—one whose removal from the country is restricted by the buyer's government—if they can buy other goods in that country that they need themselves or can sell elsewhere for a needed currency. In addition to currency limits, a changing exchange rate also creates high risks for the seller.

Most international trade involves cash transactions. Yet many nations have too little hard currency to pay for their purchases from other countries. They may want to pay with other items instead of cash, which has led to a growing practice called **countertrade**. Countertrade takes several forms: *barter* involves the direct exchange of goods or services, as when Azerbaijan imported wheat from Romania in exchange for crude oil and Vietnam exchanged rice for Philippine fertilizer and coconuts. Another form is *compensation* (or *buyback*), whereby the seller sells a plant, equipment, or technology to another country and agrees to take payment in the resulting products. Thus, Japan's Fukusuke Corporation sold knitting machines and raw textile materials to Shanghai clothing manufacturer Chinatex in exchange for finished textiles produced on the machines. The most common form of countertrade is *counterpurchase*, in which the seller receives full payment in cash but agrees to spend some of the money in the other country. For example, Boeing sells aircraft to India and agrees to buy Indian coffee, rice, castor oil, and other goods and sell them elsewhere.[19]

Countertrade deals can be very complex. For example, a few years back, DaimlerChrysler agreed to sell 30 trucks to Romania in exchange for 150 Romanian jeeps, which it then sold to Ecuador for bananas, which were in turn sold to a German supermarket chain for German currency. Through this roundabout process, DaimlerChrysler finally obtained payment in German money.

Cultural Environment

Each country has its own folkways, norms, and taboos. When designing global marketing strategies, companies must understand how culture affects consumer reactions in each of its world markets. In turn, they must also understand how their strategies affect local cultures.

The Impact of Culture on Marketing Strategy

The seller must understand the ways that consumers in different countries think about and use certain products before planning a marketing program. There are often surprises. For example, the GCC market for fragrances is estimated at Dh11 billion (US$2.99 billion) per annum accounting for approximately 20 per cent of the world market, according to a recent international study. On top of this, the region's per capita spending in cosmetics and perfumes is said to be one of the highest in the world.[20] The average French man uses almost twice as many cosmetics and grooming aids as his wife. The Germans and the French eat more packaged, branded spaghetti than do Italians. Some 49 percent of Chinese eat on the way to work. Most American women let down their hair and take *off* make-up at bedtime, whereas 15 percent of Chinese women style their hair at bedtime and 11 percent put *on* make-up.[21]

Countertrade
International trade involving the direct or indirect exchange of goods for other goods instead of cash.

Overlooking cultural differences can result in embarrassing mistakes. China imposed a nationwide ban on a "blasphemous" kung fu–themed TV spot featuring professional basketball player LeBron James crushing a number of culturally revered Chinese figures.

Companies that ignore cultural norms and differences can make some very expensive and embarrassing mistakes.

Nike inadvertently offended Chinese officials when it ran an advertisement featuring [professional basketball player] LeBron James crushing a number of culturally revered Chinese figures in a kung-fu-themed TV spot. The Chinese government found that the ad violated regulations to uphold national dignity and respect of the "motherland's culture" and banned the multimillion-dollar campaign. Embarrassed, Nike released a formal apology.

Business norms and behavior also vary from country to country. For example, Western executives like to get right down to business and engage in fast and tough face-to-face bargaining. However, Japanese and other Asian businesspeople often find this behavior offensive. They prefer to start with polite conversation, and they rarely say no in face-to-face conversations. As another example, South Americans like to sit or stand very close to each other when they talk business—in fact, almost nose-to-nose. The North American business executive tends to keep backing away as the South American moves closer. Both may end up being offended. In the Arab world, rather than "hello" or "good morning," one should greet the Arab partner by saying "Assalamo Alaikum," which translates to "May peace be upon you and may God's blessings be with you." This is the traditional Islamic greeting exchanged in Arab countries.[22]

By the same token, companies that understand cultural nuances can use them to their advantage when positioning products and preparing campaigns internationally. Consider LG Electronics, the US$60 billion South Korean electronics, telecommunications, and appliance powerhouse. LG now operates in more than 39 countries and captures 86 percent of its sales from markets outside its home country. LG's global success rests on understanding and catering to the unique characteristics of each local market through in-country research, manufacturing, and marketing.[23] For example, in 2004 LG Electronics launched an innovative mobile (the F7100 Qibla), which was equipped with a Mecca indicator. The mobile phone has an embedded compass, direction indicator, and a prayer time (Azan time) alarm, and can be used in 500 cities worldwide. The company launched the product in a range of Arab world and North African nations.

Awareness of religious requirements was essential when the company developed the phone. The developers needed to be aware that Muslims perform their obligatory Salat prayers five times a day (sunrise, noon, afternoon, sunset, and midnight) and have to face Qibla while praying.

Thus, understanding cultural traditions, preferences, and behaviors can help companies not only to avoid embarrassing mistakes but also to take advantage of cross-cultural opportunities.

The Impact of Marketing Strategy on Cultures

Whereas marketers worry about the impact of culture on their global marketing strategies, others may worry about the impact of marketing strategies on global cultures. For example, social critics contend that large American multinationals such as McDonald's, Coca-Cola, Starbucks, Nike, Microsoft, Disney, and MTV aren't just 'globalizing' their brands, they are 'Americanizing' the world's cultures.

Down in the mall, between the fast-food joint and the bagel shop, a group of young people huddle in a flurry of baggy combat pants, skateboards, and slang. They size up a woman teetering past wearing DKNY, carrying *Time* magazine in one hand and a latte in the other. She brushes past a guy in a Yankees baseball cap who is talking on his Motorola cellphone about the Martin Scorsese film he saw last night.

It's a standard American scene—only this isn't America, it's Britain. U.S. culture is so pervasive, the scene could be played out in any one of dozens of cities. Budapest or Berlin, if not Bogota or Bordeaux. Even Manila or Moscow. As the unrivaled global superpower, America exports its culture on an unprecedented scale.... Sometimes, U.S. ideals get transmitted—such as individual rights, freedom of speech, and respect for women—and local cultures are enriched. At other times, materialism or worse becomes the message and local traditions get crushed.[24]

"Today, globalization often wears Mickey Mouse ears, eats Big Macs, drinks Coke or Pepsi, and does its computing [with Microsoft] Windows [software]," says Thomas Friedman, in his book *The Lexus and the Olive Tree*.[25] Critics worry that, under such 'McDomination,' countries around the globe are losing their individual cultural identities. Teens in India watch MTV and ask their parents for more Westernized clothes and other symbols of American pop culture and values. Grandmothers in small European villas no longer spend each morning visiting local meat, bread, and produce markets to gather the ingredients for dinner. Instead, they now shop at Wal-Mart Supercenters. Women in Saudi Arabia see American films and question their societal roles. In China, most people never drank coffee before Starbucks entered the market. Now Chinese consumers rush to Starbucks stores "because it's a symbol of a new kind of lifestyle."[26] Similarly, in China, where McDonald's operates over 80 restaurants in Beijing alone, nearly half of all children identify the chain as a domestic brand.

Such concerns have sometimes led to a backlash against American globalization. Well-known U.S. brands have become the targets of boycotts and protests in some international markets. As symbols of American capitalism, companies such as Coca-Cola, McDonald's, Nike, and KFC have been singled out by antiglobalization protestors in hot spots all around the world, especially when anti-American sentiment peaks.

Despite such problems, defenders of globalization argue that concerns of 'Americanization' and the potential damage to American brands are overblown. U.S. brands are doing very well internationally. In the most recent Millward Brown Optimor survey of global consumer brands, 11 of the top 15 brands were American-owned.[27] And based on a recent study of 3,300 consumers in 41 countries, researchers concluded that consumers did not appear to translate anti-American sentiment into antibrand sentiment. Many iconic American brands are prospering globally, even in some of the most unlikely places:[28]

Many iconic American brands are prospering globally, even in some of the most unlikely places. At this Tehran restaurant, American colas are the drink of choice. Coke and Pepsi have grabbed about half the national soft drink sales in Iran.

It's lunchtime in Tehran's tony northern suburbs, and around the crowded tables at Nayeb restaurant, elegant Iranian women in Jackie O sunglasses and designer jeans let their table chatter glide effortlessly between French, English, and their native Farsi. The only visual clues that these lunching ladies aren't dining at some smart New York City eatery but in the heart of Washington's Axis of Evil are the expensive Hermès scarves covering their blonde-tipped hair in deference to the mullahs. And the drink of choice? This being revolutionary Iran, where alcohol is banned, the women are making do with Coca-Cola. Yes, Coca-Cola. It's a hard fact for some of Iran's theocrats to swallow. They want Iranians to shun 'Great Satan' brands like Coke and Pepsi. Yet, the two American brands have grabbed about half the national soft drink sales in Iran, one of the Middle East's biggest drink markets. "I joke with customers not to buy this stuff because it's American," says a Tehran storekeeper, "but they don't care. That only makes them want to buy it more."

More fundamentally, most studies reveal that the cultural exchange goes both ways—America gets as well as gives cultural influence:[29]

> Hollywood dominates the global movie market—capturing 90 percent of audiences in some European markets. However, British television is giving as much as it gets in serving up competition to U.S. shows, spawning such hits as *The Office*, *American Idol*, and *Dancing with the Stars*. And although West Indian sports fans are now watching more basketball than cricket, and some Chinese young people are daubing the names of U.S. National Basketball Association superstars on their jerseys, the increasing popularity of American soccer has deep international roots. Even American childhood has increasingly been influenced by Asian and European cultural imports. Most kids know all about the Power Rangers, Tamagotchi and Pokémon, Sega and Nintendo. And J. K. Rowling's so-very-British Harry Potter books are shaping the thinking of a generation of American youngsters, not to mention the millions of American oldsters who've fallen under their spell as well. For the moment, English remains cyberspace's dominant language, and having web access often means that third-world youth have greater exposure to American popular culture. Yet these same technologies enable Balkan students studying in the United States to hear web-cast news and music from Serbia or Bosnia.

American companies have also learned that to succeed abroad they must adapt to local cultural values and traditions rather than trying to force their own. Disneyland Paris flopped at first because it failed to take local cultural values and behaviors into account. According to a Euro Disney executive, "When we first launched, there was the belief that it was enough to be Disney. Now we realize that our guests need to be welcomed on the basis of their own culture and travel habits."[30] That realization has made Disneyland Paris the number-one tourist attraction in Europe—with twice as many visitors each year as the Eiffel Tower. The movie-themed Walt Disney Studios Park now blends Disney entertainment and attractions with the history and culture of European film. A show celebrating the history of animation features Disney characters speaking six different languages. Rides are narrated by foreign-born stars speaking in their native tongues.

Thus, globalization is a two-way street. If globalization has Mickey Mouse ears, it is also wearing a French beret, talking on a Nokia cellphone, buying furniture at IKEA, driving a Toyota Camry, and watching a Sony big-screen plasma television.

Deciding Whether to Go Global (pp 477–478)

Not all companies need to venture into international markets to survive. For example, most local businesses need to market well only in the local marketplace. Operating domestically is easier and safer. Managers don't need to learn another country's language and laws. They don't have to deal with unstable currencies, face political and legal uncertainties, or redesign their products to suit different customer expectations. However, companies that operate in global industries, where their strategic positions in specific markets are affected strongly by their overall global positions, must compete on a regional or worldwide basis to succeed.

Any of several factors might draw a company into the international arena. Global competitors might attack the company's home market by offering better products or lower prices. The company might want to counterattack these competitors in their home markets to tie up their resources. The company's customers might be expanding abroad and require international servicing. Or the company's home market might be stagnant or shrinking, and foreign markets may present additional sales and profit opportunities. For example, to offset declines in the U.S. soft drinks market, Coca-Cola and Pepsi are rapidly expanding their presence in emerging markets such as Russia and China. And whereas Whirlpool's North American sales slipped by 1 percent last year, its European sales jumped 12 percent.[31]

Before going abroad, the company must weigh several risks and answer many questions about its ability to operate globally. Can the company learn to understand the preferences and buyer behavior of consumers in other countries? Can it offer competitively attractive products? Will it be able to adapt to other countries' business cultures and deal effectively with foreign nationals? Do the company's managers have the necessary international experience? Has management considered the impact of regulations and the political environments of other countries?

Because of the difficulties of entering international markets, most companies do not act until some situation or event thrusts them into the global arena. Someone—a domestic exporter, a foreign importer, a foreign government—may ask the company to sell abroad. Or the company may have a problem with overcapacity and need to find additional markets for its goods.

Deciding Which Markets to Enter (pp 478–479)

Before going abroad, the company should try to define its international *marketing objectives and policies*. It should decide what *volume* of foreign sales it wants. Most companies start small when they go abroad. Some plan to stay small, seeing international sales as a small part of their business. Other companies have bigger plans, seeing international business as equal to or even more important than their domestic business.

The company also needs to choose in *how many* countries it wants to market. Companies must be careful not to spread themselves too thin or to expand beyond their capabilities by operating in too many countries too soon. Next, the company needs to decide on the *types* of countries to enter. A country's attractiveness depends on the product, geographical factors, income and population, political climate, and other factors. The seller may prefer certain country groups or parts of the world. In recent years, many major new markets have emerged, offering both substantial opportunities and daunting challenges.

After listing possible international markets, the company must carefully evaluate each one. It must consider many factors. For example, P&G's decision to enter the Chinese toothpaste market with its Crest brand was an obvious one: China's huge population makes it the world's largest toothpaste market. And given that only 20 percent of China's rural dwellers now brush daily, this already huge market can grow even larger. Yet P&G must still question whether market size *alone* is reason enough for investing heavily in China.

P&G should ask some important questions: Can Crest compete effectively with dozens of local competitors, Colgate brand, and a state-owned brand managed by Unilever? Will the Chinese government remain stable and supportive? Does China provide for the needed production and distribution technologies? Can the company master China's vastly different cultural and buying differences? Crest's current success in China suggests that it could answer yes to all of these questions.[32]

P&G's decision to enter the Chinese toothpaste market with Crest is a no-brainer: China is the world's largest toothpaste market. But P&G must still question whether market size alone is reason enough for investing heavily in China.

"Just 10 years ago, Procter & Gamble's Crest brand was unknown to China's population, most of whom seldom—if ever—brushed their teeth," says one analyst. "Now P&G sells more tubes of toothpaste there than it does in America, where Crest has been on store shelves for 52 years." P&G achieved this by sending researchers to get a feel for what urban and rural Chinese were willing to spend and what flavors they preferred. It discovered that urban Chinese are happy to pay more than US$1 for tubes of Crest with exotic flavors such as Icy Mountain Spring and Morning Lotus Fragrance. But Chinese living in the countryside prefer the 50-cent Crest Salt White, since many rural Chinese believe that salt whitens the teeth. Armed with such insights, Crest now leads all competitors in China with a 25 percent market share.

● TABLE | 16.1 Indicators of Market Potential

Demographic characteristics	Sociocultural factors
Education	Consumer lifestyles, beliefs, and values
Population size and growth	Business norms and approaches
Population age composition	Cultural and social norms
	Languages

Geographic characteristics	Political and legal factors
Climate	National priorities
Country size	Political stability
Population density—urban, rural	Government attitudes toward global trade
Transportation structure and market accessibility	Government bureaucracy
	Monetary and trade regulations

Economic factors
GDP size and growth
Income distribution
Industrial infrastructure
Natural resources
Financial and human resources

Possible global markets should be ranked on several factors, including market size, market growth, cost of doing business, competitive advantage, and risk level. The goal is to determine the potential of each market, using indicators such as those shown in ● **Table 16.1**. Then the marketer must decide which markets offer the greatest long-run return on investment.

> **Author Comment** | A company has many options for entering an international market, from simply exporting its products to working jointly with foreign companies to holding its own foreign-based operations.

Deciding How to Enter the Market (pp 479–482)

Once a company has decided to sell in a foreign country, it must determine the best mode of entry. Its choices are *exporting, joint venturing,* and *direct investment.* ◥ **Figure 16.2** shows three market entry strategies, along with the options each one offers. As the figure shows, each succeeding strategy involves more commitment and risk, but also more control and potential profits.

> Direct investment—owning your own foreign-based operation—affords greater control and profit potential, but it's often riskier.

◥ FIGURE | 16.2
Market Entry Strategies

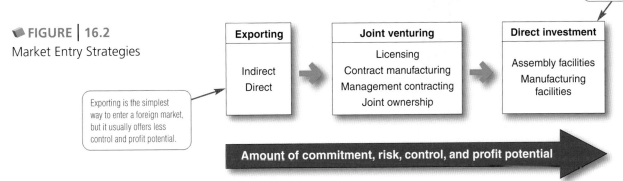

> Exporting is the simplest way to enter a foreign market, but it usually offers less control and profit potential.

Exporting	Joint venturing	Direct investment
Indirect Direct	Licensing Contract manufacturing Management contracting Joint ownership	Assembly facilities Manufacturing facilities

Amount of commitment, risk, control, and profit potential

Exporting

Entering a foreign market by selling goods produced in the company's home country, often with little modification.

Exporting

The simplest way to enter a foreign market is through **exporting**. The company may passively export its surpluses from time to time, or it may make an active commitment to expand exports to a particular market. In either case, the company produces all its goods in its home country. It may or may not modify them for the export market. Exporting involves the least change in the company's product lines, organization, investments, or mission.

Companies typically start with *indirect exporting*, working through independent international marketing intermediaries. Indirect exporting involves less investment because the firm does not require an overseas marketing organization or network. It also involves less risk. International marketing intermediaries bring know-how and services to the relationship, so the seller normally makes fewer mistakes.

Sellers may eventually move into *direct exporting*, whereby they handle their own exports. The investment and risk are somewhat greater in this strategy, but so is the potential return. A company can conduct direct exporting in several ways. It can set up a domestic export department that carries out export activities. It can set up an overseas sales branch that handles sales, distribution, and perhaps promotion. The sales branch gives the seller more presence and program control in the foreign market and often serves as a display center and customer-service center. The company can also send home-based salespeople abroad at certain times in order to find business. Finally, the company can do its exporting either through foreign-based distributors who buy and own the goods or through foreign-based agents who sell the goods on behalf of the company. It is common that several local firms in the Arab world start their international business operations by exporting to nearby countries in the region due to geographic proximity and common culture.

Joint venturing

Entering foreign markets by joining with foreign companies to produce or market a product or service.

Joint Venturing

A second method of entering a foreign market is **joint venturing**—joining with foreign companies to produce or market products or services. Joint venturing differs from exporting in that the company joins with a host country partner to sell or market abroad. It differs from direct investment in that an association is formed with someone in the foreign country. There are four types of joint ventures: licensing, contract manufacturing, management contracting, and joint ownership.

Licensing

A method of entering a foreign market in which the company enters into an agreement with a licensee in the foreign market.

Licensing

Licensing is a simple way for a manufacturer to enter international marketing. The company enters into an agreement with a licensee in the foreign market. For a fee or royalty, the licensee buys the right to use the company's manufacturing process, trademark, patent, trade secret, or other item of value. The company thus gains entry into the market at little risk; the licensee gains production expertise or a well-known product or name without having to start from scratch.

Coca-Cola markets internationally by licensing bottlers around the world and supplying them with the syrup needed to produce the product. Tokyo Disneyland Resort is owned and operated by Oriental Land Company under license from The Walt Disney Company. In the Arab world, many local companies rely on licensing international brands and operations to expand their businesses locally and regionally.

Licensing has potential disadvantages, however. The firm has less control over the licensee than it would over its own operations. Furthermore, if

Coca-Cola successfully reaches international markets by licensing bottling companies in different countries around the world.

the licensee is very successful, the firm has given up these profits, and if and when the contract ends, it may find it has created a competitor. Recently, several companies in the Arab world have decided to grow internationally through licensing and franchising their products. For example, Cilantro, the leading coffee shop chain, has attracted franchisees in the United Kingdom as well as various countries in the Gulf. Similarly, Egyptian food chains, such as Mo'men and Cook Door, have relied on franchising locally, regionally, and internationally to grow their presence. Mo'men is now available in the Gulf, as well as Asian countries such as Malaysia.

Contract Manufacturing

Contract manufacturing

A joint venture in which a company contracts with manufacturers in a foreign market to produce the product or provide its service.

Another option is **contract manufacturing**—the company contracts with manufacturers in the foreign market to produce its product or provide its service. Sears used this method in opening up department stores in Mexico and Spain, where it found qualified local manufacturers to produce many of the products it sells. The drawbacks of contract manufacturing are decreased control over the manufacturing process and loss of potential profits on manufacturing. The benefits are the chance to start faster, with less risk, and the later opportunity either to form a partnership with or to buy out the local manufacturer.

Management Contracting

Management contracting

A joint venture in which the domestic firm supplies the management know-how to a foreign company that supplies the capital; the domestic firm exports management services rather than products.

Under **management contracting**, the domestic firm supplies management know-how to a foreign company that supplies the capital. The domestic firm exports management services rather than products. Hilton uses this arrangement in managing hotels around the world.

Management contracting is a low-risk method of getting into a foreign market, and it yields income from the beginning. The arrangement is even more attractive if the contracting firm has an option to buy some share in the managed company later on. The arrangement is not sensible, however, if the company can put its scarce management talent to better uses or if it can make greater profits by undertaking the whole venture. Management contracting also prevents the company from setting up its own operations for a period of time.

Joint Ownership

Joint ownership

A joint venture in which a company joins investors in a foreign market to create a local business in which the company shares joint ownership and control.

Joint ownership ventures consist of one company joining forces with foreign investors to create a local business in which they share joint ownership and control. A company may buy an interest in a local firm, or the two parties may form a new business venture. Joint ownership may be needed for economic or political reasons. The firm may lack the financial, physical, or managerial resources to undertake the venture alone. Or a foreign government may require joint ownership as a condition for entry. Many international businesses targeting Gulf countries might be forced to establish a joint ownership to overcome restrictive laws and regulations.

Gulf countries have historically deployed a sponsorship system called 'Kafeel' or 'Kafala.' Under this system a worker may not enter the country without having a sponsor, and then the worker is not allowed to leave the country without the sponsor's permission. In addition, the sponsor can ban the employee from re-entering the country within up to five years of his departure. In 2009 Bahrain took the liberalizing step of abandoning this law, and was followed in 2010 by Kuwait.[33]

Joint ownership has certain drawbacks. The partners may disagree over investment, marketing, or other policies. Whereas many domestic firms might like to reinvest earnings for growth, some foreign firms might prefer to take out these earnings; and whereas domestic firms might emphasize the role of marketing, foreign companies might rely on personal selling.

Direct Investment

Direct investment

Entering a foreign market by developing foreign-based assembly or manufacturing facilities.

The biggest involvement in a foreign market comes through **direct investment**—the development of foreign-based assembly or manufacturing facilities. For example, HP has made direct investments in a number of major markets around the world, including India. It recently opened a second factory near Delhi to make PCs for the local market. Thanks to such commitments, HP has overtaken the favorite local brand, HCL, and now controls more than 21 percent of the market in India.[34]

If a company has gained experience in exporting and if the foreign market is large enough, foreign production facilities offer many advantages. The firm may have lower costs in the form of cheaper labor or raw materials, foreign government investment incentives, and freight savings. The firm may improve its image in the host country because it creates jobs. Generally, a firm develops a deeper relationship with government, customers, local suppliers, and distributors, allowing it to adapt its products to the local market better. Finally, the firm keeps full control over the investment and therefore can develop manufacturing and marketing policies that serve its long-term international objectives.

The main disadvantage of direct investment is that the firm faces many risks, such as restricted or devalued currencies, falling markets, or government changes. In some cases, a firm has no choice but to accept these risks if it wants to operate in the host country.

> **Author Comment** │ The major global marketing decision usually boils down to this: How much, if at all, should we adapt our marketing strategy and programs to local markets? How would the answer differ for Emirates or for Aramex?

Deciding on the Global Marketing Program (pp 482–488)

Companies that operate in one or more foreign markets must decide how much, if at all, to adapt their marketing strategies and programs to local conditions. At one extreme are global companies that use **standardized global marketing**, using largely the same marketing strategy approaches and marketing mix worldwide. At the other extreme is an **adapted global marketing**. In this case, the producer adjusts the marketing strategy and mix elements to each target market, bearing more costs but hoping for a larger market share and return.

Standardized global marketing
An international marketing strategy for using basically the same marketing strategy and mix in all the company's international markets.

Adapted global marketing
An international marketing strategy for adjusting the marketing strategy and mix elements to each international target market, bearing more costs but hoping for a larger market share and return.

The question of whether to adapt or standardize the marketing strategy and program has been much debated in recent years. On the one hand, some global marketers believe that technology is making the world a smaller place and that consumer needs around the world are becoming more similar. This paves the way for 'global brands' and standardized global marketing. Global branding and standardization, in turn, result in greater brand power and reduced costs from economies of scale.

On the other hand, the marketing concept holds that marketing programs will be more effective if tailored to the unique needs of each targeted customer group. If this concept applies within a country, it should apply even more across international markets. Despite global convergence, consumers in different countries still have widely varied cultural backgrounds. They still differ significantly in their needs and wants, spending power, product preferences, and shopping patterns. Because these differences are hard to change, most marketers adapt their products, prices, channels, and promotions to fit consumer desires in each country.

However, global standardization is not an all-or-nothing proposition. It's a matter of degree. Most international marketers suggest that companies should 'think globally but act locally'—that they should seek a balance between standardization and adaptation. The corporate level gives global strategic direction; regional or local units focus on individual consumer differences across global markets. Simon Clift, head of marketing for global consumer-goods giant Unilever, puts it this way: "We're trying to strike a balance between being mindlessly global and hopelessly local."[35]

McDonald's operates this way. It uses the same basic fast-food look, layout, and operating model in its restaurants around the world but adapts its menu to local tastes. In Japan, it offers up Ebi Filet-O-Shrimp burgers and fancy Salad Macs salad plates. In Korea it sells the Bulgogi Burger, a grilled pork patty on a bun with a garlicky soy sauce. In India, where cows are considered sacred, McDonald's serves McChicken, Filet-O-Fish, McVeggie (a vegetable burger), Pizza McPuffs, McAloo Tikki (a spiced-potato burger), and the Maharaja Mac—two all-chicken patties, special sauce, lettuce, cheese, pickles, onions on a sesame-seed bun. In the Arab world, it has introduced localized products, such as McArabia and McFalafel.

Similarly, to boost sales of Oreo cookies in China, Kraft Foods has tweaked its recipes and marketing programs to meet the tastes of Chinese consumers. It even developed a brand new Chinese version of the all-American classic (see **Real Marketing 16.1**).

Real Marketing 16.1

Oreos and Milk, Chinese-Style

Unlike its iconic American counterpart, the most popular Oreo cookie in China is long, thin, four-layered, and coated in chocolate. Still, the two kinds of Oreos, sold half a world apart, have one important thing in common: both are now best-sellers. But taking the dark chocolate American treasure to China has been no easy journey for Kraft Foods. Although the Oreo has long been the top-selling cookie in the United States, to make Oreos sell well in the world's most populous nation, Kraft has had to completely reinvent the popular cookie.

Oreos were first introduced in the United States in 1912, but it wasn't until 1996 that Kraft introduced Oreos to Chinese consumers. It began by selling the same Oreos in China that it markets in the United States—the ones that Americans love to twist apart to lick the creamy centers or dunk in milk until they're soggy. However, after nine years of trying mostly U.S. marketing themes and programs on Chinese consumers, Oreo sales remained flat. Physicist Albert Einstein's definition of insanity—doing the same thing repeatedly and expecting different results—"characterized what we were doing," says Kraft Foods International's vice president of marketing. To make things happen, he concluded, it was time for a major Oreo makeover.

First up: Kraft changed the Oreo management team. Whereas previous decisions about Oreo marketing in China had been made at arm's length by people in Kraft's headquarters, the company now handed the task of remaking the brand to an entrepreneurial team of local Chinese managers. The team began with in-depth research on Chinese consumers that yielded some interesting findings. First, the team learned, the Chinese weren't big cookie eaters. Despite China's immense population, the Chinese biscuit and cookie market was one-third the size of the U.S. market. Secondly, Chinese consumers weren't much enamored with the Oreos that Americans have come to crave. Traditional Oreos were too sweet for Chinese tastes. Also, standard packages of 14 Oreos, priced at 72 cents, were too expensive for most Chinese food budgets.

So for starters, the company developed 20 prototypes of reduced-sugar Oreos and tested them with Chinese consumers before arriving at a formula that tasted right. Kraft also introduced packages containing fewer Oreos for just 29 cents. However, some Chinese consumers still found even the reformulated Oreos too sweet. Said one 30-year-old consumer in the eastern part of Beijing, he liked the cookie but "many of my friends think I am a bit weird to stick to Oreo cookies—most think them too sweet to be accepted."

Kraft's research also revealed that Chinese consumers have a growing thirst for milk, which Kraft wasn't fully exploiting. So Kraft began a grassroots marketing campaign to educate Chinese consumers about the American tradition of pairing milk with cookies. The company created Oreo apprentice programs at 30 Chinese universities that drew 6,000 student applications. Three hundred of the applicants were trained to become Oreo brand ambassadors. Some of the students rode around Beijing on bicycles, outfitted with wheel covers resembling Oreos, and handed out cookies to more than 300,000 consumers.

Other ambassadors held Oreo-themed basketball games to reinforce the idea of dunking cookies in milk. Television commercials showed kids twisting apart Oreo cookies, licking the cream center, and dipping the chocolate cookie halves into glasses of milk. Kraft CEO Irene Rosenfeld calls the bicycle campaign "a stroke of genius that only could have come from local managers. [Letting] our local managers deal with local conditions will be a source of competitive advantage for us."

The product and marketing changes made a difference and Oreo sales in China improved. However, Kraft knew that if it was really serious about capturing a bigger share of the Chinese biscuit market, it needed to do more than just tweak its U.S. Oreo recipe and marketing. It needed to remake the Oreo itself.

So in 2006, Kraft introduced a second Oreo in China, one that looked almost nothing like the original. The new Chinese Oreo consisted of four layers of crispy wafer filled with vanilla and chocolate cream, coated in chocolate. The new Oreo was designed not only to satisfy the cravings of China's consumers, but also stand up to the challenges of selling and

To make Oreo cookies sell well in China, Kraft completely reinvented the popular all-American classic. Kraft has now begun selling the popular Chinese wafers elsewhere in Asia, as well as in Australia and Canada.

distributing across China's vast landscape. Kraft even developed a proprietary handling process to ensure that the chocolate product could withstand the cold climate in the north and the hot, humid weather in the south, yet still be ready to melt in the customer's mouth.

Kraft's efforts to reshape the Oreo brand and its marketing have paid off. Within a year of introduction, Oreo WaferSticks became the best-selling biscuit in China, outpacing HaoChiDian, a biscuit brand made by Chinese company Dali. The new Oreos are also outselling traditional round Oreos in China, and Kraft has begun selling the wafers elsewhere in Asia, as well as in Australia and Canada. Over the past two years, Kraft has doubled its Oreo revenues in China.

What's more, Kraft has learned, its 'think globally, act locally' approach applies not just to Oreos and not just in China but to all of its products worldwide. For example, to take advantage of the European preference for dark chocolate, Kraft is introducing dark chocolate in Germany under its Milka brand. Research in Russia showed that consumers there like premium instant coffee, so Kraft is positioning its Carte Noire freeze-dried coffee as upscale by placing it at film festivals, fashion shows, and operas. And in the Philippines, where iced tea is popular, Kraft last year launched iced-tea-flavored Tang. As a result of such moves, international business now represents 40 percent of Kraft's total sales. Kraft's profit in the European Union last year rose 48 percent, and profits in developing countries rose 57 percent, far outpacing U.S. profit growth.

Sources: Adapted from Julie Jargon, "Kraft Reformulated Oreo, Scores in China," *Wall Street Journal,* May 1, 2008, p. B1. Also see www.kraft.com, accessed October 2008.

Product

Five strategies allow for adapting product and marketing communication strategies to a global market (see ● **Figure 16.3**).[36] We first discuss the three product strategies and then turn to the two communication strategies.

Straight product extension

Marketing a product in a foreign market without any change.

Straight product extension means marketing a product in a foreign market without any change. Top management tells its marketing people, "Take the product as is and find customers for it." The first step, however, should be to find out whether foreign consumers use that product and what form they prefer.

Straight extension has been successful in some cases and disastrous in others. Kellogg's cereals, Gillette razors, and Black & Decker tools are all sold successfully in about the same form around the world. But General Foods introduced its standard powdered JELL-O in the British market only to find that British consumers prefer a solid wafer or cake form. Likewise, electronics-maker Philips began to make a profit in Japan only after it reduced the size of its coffeemakers to fit into smaller Japanese kitchens and its shavers to fit smaller Japanese hands. Straight extension is tempting because it involves no additional product development costs, manufacturing changes, or new promotion. But it can be costly in the long run if products fail to satisfy foreign consumers.

Product adaptation

Adapting a product to meet local conditions or wants in foreign markets.

Product adaptation involves changing the product to meet local conditions or wants. For example, Finnish cellphone maker Nokia customizes its cellphones for every major market. Developers build in basic voice recognition for Asia where keyboards are a problem and raise the ring volume so phones can be heard on crowded Asian streets. Nokia is also making a major push to create full-featured but tough and low-cost phones that meet the needs of less-affluent consumers in large developing countries such as India, China, and Kenya.[37]

> Looking for ways to make cellphones practical for people living in developing countries, Nokia has trekked to far corners of the globe, from the narrow alleys of Mumbai to the vast slums of Nairobi. The result is a wide range of new features especially designed for places with harsh weather and harsher living conditions. One example: The company created dustproof keypads—crucial in dry, hot countries with many unpaved roads, as Nokia executives learned from visits to customers' homes in India. Low price is also important. On a recent visit to slums outside Nairobi, members of the emerging markets team discovered that many people form buying clubs, pooling their money to buy handsets one at a time until every member has one. Now Nokia is looking for ways to encourage this form of self-financing. Communal finance is a far cry from manufacturing mobile phones, but Nokia knows it has to try all sorts of product and service ideas if it wants to capture its share of the industry's next 1 billion customers.

Product invention

Creating new products or services for foreign markets.

Product invention consists of creating something new for a specific country market. This strategy can take two forms. It might mean maintaining or reintroducing earlier product forms that happen to be well adapted to the needs of a given country. Or a company might create a new product to meet a need in a given country. For example, Sony added the 'U' model to its VAIO personal computer line to meet the unique needs of Japanese consumers. It found that Japanese commuters had difficulty using standard laptops on crowded rush-hour trains—standing commuters have no laps. So it created the U as a

> The real question buried in this figure is this: How much should a company standardize or adapt its products and marketing across global markets?

● **FIGURE | 16.3**

Five Global Product and Communications Strategies

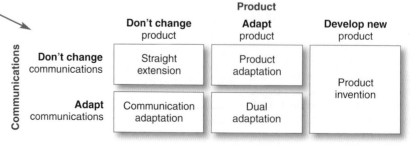

Real Marketing 16.2

Desserts in Ramadan

In the Arab world, Ramadan, the holy month, is very important and entails special eating habits. People tend to eat out more. They also gather at home during *Iftar* and *Shour* times, which further increases their food consumption. Most multinational companies in the region develop massive campaigns during Ramadan to engage consumers and shoppers in food-related activities. They participate in aggressive advertising, sales promotions, PR events, or new-product introductions.

However, traditional eating habits in Ramadan promote the consumption of some foods more than others. For example, in Ramadan sales of yogurt increase because it is perceived as enhancing digestion and helping fasting Muslims to avoid thirst. On the other hand, consumption of coffee drops significantly as consumers reduce their intake from three or four cups a day to about one or two. In Ramadan, many consumers switch to tea.

Desserts are very traditional in Ramadan; it is very important for an Arab family to eat oriental desserts such as konafa and baklawa after Iftar. That's why all oriental dessert shops consider Ramadan and the Feast their highest sales period and plan ahead to satisfy the huge demand. Sometimes Ramadan falls during the summer, and some companies have been quick to grasp the opportunity to promote cold desserts for the Arab world. One example is Nestlé Ice Cream in Egypt, which has encourged con-

sumers to deviate from traditional oriental desserts toward other options such as ice cream.

The idea Nestlé conceived was to convince consumers that they have other dessert options during the summer, including ice cream. Nestlé designed a two-phase campaign. In 2008 it introduced phase one, aiming simply to pursuade consumers to consider ice cream as an alternative option after Iftar. The television advertising portrayed a woman who purchased Carnavitleta, a Nestlé ice-cream brand, in the supermarket and the salesperson asking her in surprise, "Ice cream in Ramadan?" Then she replies that ice cream as a dessert will be better in Ramadan during summer than the other options. To support this advertising campaign, Nestlé Ice Cream launched a joint sales promotion with Nescafé to push ice cream on to people's shopping lists.

Phase two saw Nestlé Egypt launch Pops, a new brand of ice cream, to the Egyptian market in 2009. Its introduction was described in the market as 'Pops Mania.' The campaign was very strong and aggressive, and created a strong desire among consumers to try the product. The message behind the advertising campaign urged consumers to replace oriental desserts with Pops ice cream, and used humor to get its message across in a memorable way.

In 2010, Nestlé Egypt stopped using this message and changed to more conventional ice-cream advertisements. By then, ice cream had established itself as a serious consideration

Nestlé developed a new strategy for marketing its ice-cream products in the Arab world during Ramadan.

for shoppers during Ramadan, so Nestlé's primary objective instead became to encourage consumers to buy more.

Nestlé made a brilliant move to adapt to the environment and successfully penetrate the desserts market in Egypt during Ramadan. Nestlé is proof that by adapting to different cultures, companies can grasp opportunities and penetrate new markets.

Source: "Ice Cream in Egypt," *Euromonitor International*, December 2010, www.euromonitor.com/ice-cream-in-egypt/report.

'standing computer.' The U is lightweight and small: only seven inches wide with a five-inch diagonal screen. And it includes a touch screen and small keyboard that can be used while standing or on the move.[38]

Promotion

Companies can either adopt the same communication strategy they use in the home market or change it for each local market. Consider advertising messages. Some global companies use a standardized advertising theme around the world. Of course, even in highly standardized communications campaigns, some adjustments might be required for language and cultural differences. For example, Guy Laroche uses virtually the same ads for its Drakkar Noir fragrances in Europe as in Arab countries. However, it subtly tones down the Arab versions to meet cultural differences in attitudes toward sensuality. And although McDonald's uses its standardized "I'm lovin' it" theme worldwide, it varies its interpretations of the theme in different countries. **Real Marketing 16.2** describes how Nestlé carefully planned a promotional campaign in the Arab region.

Colors also are changed sometimes to avoid taboos in other countries. Purple is associated with death in most Latin American countries, white is a mourning color in Japan, and green is associated with jungle sickness in Malaysia. Even names must sometimes be adjusted. The global name for Microsoft's operating system, Vista, turned out to be a disparaging term for a frumpy old woman in Latvia.

Other companies follow a strategy of **communication adaptation**, fully adapting their advertising messages to local markets. Kellogg's ads in the United States promote the taste and nutrition of Kellogg's cereals versus competitors' brands. In France, where consumers drink little milk and eat little for breakfast, Kellogg's ads must convince consumers that cereals are a tasty and healthy option for breakfast. In India, where many consumers eat heavy, fried breakfasts, Kellogg's advertising convinces buyers to switch to a lighter, more nutritious breakfast diet.

Similarly, Coca-Cola sells its low-calorie beverage as Diet Coke in North America, the United Kingdom, and the Middle and Far East but as Coke Light elsewhere. According to Diet Coke's global brand manager, in Spanish-speaking countries Coke Light ads "position the soft drink as an object of desire, rather than as a way to feel good about yourself, as Diet Coke is positioned in the United States." This "desire positioning" plays off research showing that "Coca-Cola Light is seen in other parts of the world as a vibrant brand that exudes confidence."[39]

Globally, McDonald's rarely offers a delivery service in its outlets. However, in Egypt, due to traffic jams, the company decided to focus on the need to save time and effort as well as the fact that Egyptians enjoy home gatherings. Research indicated that the speed of delivery—while critical to consumers—was not satisfactory. Accordingly, McDonald's deployed a localized strategy to satisfy consumer needs in Egypt, and developed a strong transportation and operation network, which ultimately allowed the company to use the slogan "The Fastest Delivery in Egypt" in its advertisements.

Media also need to be adapted internationally because media availability and regulations vary from country to country. Television advertising time is very limited in Europe, for instance, ranging from four hours a day in France to none in Scandinavian countries. Advertisers must buy time months in advance, and they have little control over airtimes. However, mobile phone ads are much more widely accepted in Europe and Asia than in the United States. Magazines also vary in effectiveness. For example, magazines are a major medium in Italy but a minor one in Austria. Newspapers are national in the United Kingdom but are only local in Spain.[40]

Price

Companies also face many considerations in setting their international prices. For example, how might Black & Decker price its power tools globally? It could set a uniform price all around the world, but this amount would be too high a price in poor countries and not high enough in rich ones. It could charge what consumers in each country would bear, but this strategy ignores differences in the actual costs from country to country. Finally, the company could use a standard markup of its costs everywhere, but this approach might price Black & Decker out of the market in some countries where costs are high.

Regardless of how companies go about pricing their products, their foreign prices probably will be higher than their domestic prices for comparable products. A Gucci handbag may sell for US$60 in Italy and US$240 in the United States. Why? Gucci faces a *price escalation* problem. It must add the cost of transportation, tariffs, importer margin, wholesaler margin, and retailer margin to its factory price. Depending on these added costs, the product may have to sell for two to five times as much in another country to make the same profit.

To overcome this problem when selling to less-affluent consumers in developing countries, many companies make simpler or smaller versions of their products that can be sold at lower prices. For example, in China and other emerging markets, Dell sells its simplified Dell EC280 model for US$340 dollars, and P&G sells everything from shampoo to toothpaste in less costly formulations and smaller packages at more affordable prices.

Communication adaptation
A global communication strategy of fully adapting advertising messages to local markets.

The Internet is making global price difference more obvious, forcing companies toward more standardized international pricing.

Another problem involves setting a price for goods that a company ships to its foreign subsidiaries. If the company charges a foreign subsidiary too much, it may end up paying higher tariff duties even while paying lower income taxes in that country. If the company charges its subsidiary too little, it can be charged with *dumping*. Dumping occurs when a company either charges less than its costs or less than it charges in its home market. For example, U.S. nail makers accused foreign nail makers—especially those in China and the United Arab Emirates—of dumping excess supplies of nails in the United States, hurting the domestic steel nail market. Over three years, imports of nails from the two countries had grown 70 percent, forcing U.S. manufacturers to close facilities and lay off workers. The U.S. International Trade Commission agreed, and the U.S. Commerce Department imposed duties as high as 118 percent on steel nail imports from the offending countries.[41] Various governments are always watching for dumping abuses, and they often force companies to set the price charged by other competitors for the same or similar products.

Recent economic and technological forces have had an impact on global pricing. For example, the Internet is making global price differences more obvious. When firms sell their wares over the Internet, customers can see how much products sell for in different countries. They can even order a given product directly from the company location or dealer offering the lowest price. This is forcing companies toward more standardized international pricing.

Distribution Channels

Whole-channel view

Designing international channels that take into account the entire global supply chain and marketing channel, forging an effective global value delivery network.

The international company must take a **whole-channel view** of the problem of distributing products to final consumers.  Figure 16.4 shows the two major links between the seller and the final buyer. The first link, *channels between nations*, moves company products from points of production to the borders of countries within which they are sold. The second link, *channels within nations*, moves the products from their market entry points to the final consumers. The whole-channel view takes into account the entire global supply chain and marketing channel. It recognizes that to compete well internationally, the company must effectively design and manage an entire *global value delivery network*.

Channels of distribution within countries vary greatly from nation to nation. There are large differences in the numbers and types of intermediaries serving each country market, and in the transportation infrastructure serving these intermediaries. For example, whereas large-scale retail chains dominate the U.S. scene, much retailing in other countries is done by many small, independent retailers. In India, millions of retailers operate tiny shops or sell in open markets. Thus, in its efforts to sell rugged, affordable phones to Indian consumers, Nokia has had to forge its own distribution structure.[42]

In India, Nokia estimates there are 90,000 points-of-sale for its phones, ranging from modern stores to makeshift kiosks. That makes it difficult to control how products

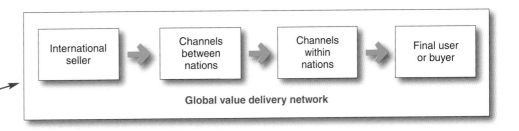

FIGURE | 16.4

Whole-Channel Concept for International Marketing

Distribution channels between and within nations can vary dramatically around the world. For example, in the United States, Nokia distributes phones through a network of sophisticated retailers. In rural India, it maintains a fleet of Nokia-branded vans that prowl the rutted country roads.

International seller → Channels between nations → Channels within nations → Final user or buyer

Global value delivery network

Distribution channels vary greatly from nation to nation. In its efforts to sell durable, affordable phones to Indian consumers, Nokia forged its own distribution structure, including a fleet of distinctive blue Nokia-branded vans that prowl rutted country roads to visit remote villages.

are displayed and pitched to consumers. "You have to understand where people live, what the shopping patterns are," says a Nokia executive. "You have to work with local means to reach people—even bicycles or rickshaws." To reach rural India, Nokia has outfitted its own fleet of distinctive blue Nokia-branded vans that prowl the rutted country roads. Staffers park these advertisements-on-wheels in villages, often on market or festival days. There, with crowds clustering around, Nokia reps explain the basics of how the phones work and how to buy them. Nokia has extended the concept to minivans, which can reach even more remote places.

Similarly, Coca-Cola adapts its distribution methods to meet local challenges in global markets. For example, in rural China, an army of more than 10,000 Coca-Cola sales reps make regular visits to small retailers, often on foot or bicycle. To reach the most isolated spots, the company even relies on teams of delivery donkeys. In Montevideo, Uruguay, where larger vehicles are challenged by traffic, parking, and pollution difficulties, Coca-Cola recently purchased 30 small, efficient three-wheeled ZAP alternative transportation trucks. The little trucks average about one-fifth the fuel consumption and move around congested city streets with greater ease. If the model works well in Montevideo, Coca-Cola may adopt it in other congested urban areas that pose similar challenges.[43]

In the Arab world, there is a trend for hypermarkets and shopping malls, which companies can reach easily to distribute their products efficiently and profitably. However, some countries such as Egypt have large rural areas, and companies targeting masses with relatively low prices in these locations canface serious challenges reaching consumers.

Author Comment | Many large companies, regardless of their 'home country,' now think of themselves as truly global organizations. They view the entire world as a single borderless market.

Deciding on the Global Marketing Organization (pp 488–489)

Companies manage their international marketing activities in at least three different ways: most companies first organize an export department, then create an international division, and finally become a global organization.

A firm normally gets into international marketing by simply shipping out its goods. If its international sales expand, the company organizes an *export department* with a sales manager and a few assistants. As sales increase, the export department can expand to include various marketing services so that it can actively go after business. If the firm moves into joint ventures or direct investment, the export department will no longer be adequate.

Many companies get involved in several international markets and ventures. A company may export to one country, license to another, have a joint ownership venture in a third, and own a subsidiary in a fourth. Sooner or later it will create *international divisions* or subsidiaries to handle all its international activity.

International divisions are organized in a variety of ways. An international division's corporate staff consists of marketing, manufacturing, research, finance, planning, and personnel specialists. It plans for and provides services to various operating units, which can be organized in one of three ways. They can be *geographical organizations*, with country managers who are responsible for salespeople, sales branches, distributors,

Boeing is headquartered in Chicago, but is as comfortable selling planes to Lufthansa and Air China as to American Airlines.

and licensees in their respective countries. Or the operating units can be *world product groups*, each responsible for worldwide sales of different product groups. Finally, operating units can be *international subsidiaries*, each responsible for its own sales and profits. Many firms have passed beyond the international division stage and become truly *global organizations*. For example, well over half of Boeing's airplane sales are made outside the United States. Although headquartered in Chicago, the company employs more than 159,300 people in 70 countries. Boeing is as comfortable selling planes to Lufthansa or Air China as to American Airlines.

Global organizations stop thinking of themselves as national marketers who sell abroad and start thinking of themselves as global marketers. The top corporate management and staff plan worldwide manufacturing facilities, marketing policies, financial flows, and logistical systems. The global operating units report directly to the chief executive or executive committee of the organization, not to the head of an international division. Executives are trained in worldwide operations, not just domestic *or* international operations. The company recruits management from many countries, buys components and supplies where they cost the least, and invests where the expected returns are greatest.

Today, major companies must become more global if they hope to compete. As foreign companies successfully invade their domestic markets, companies must move more aggressively into foreign markets. They will have to change from companies that treat their international operations as secondary to companies that view the entire world as a single borderless market.

REVIEWING Objectives AND KEY Terms

Companies today can no longer afford to pay attention only to their domestic market, regardless of its size. Many industries are global industries, and firms that operate globally achieve lower costs and higher brand awareness. At the same time, global marketing is risky because of variable exchange rates, unstable governments, protectionist tariffs and trade barriers, and several other factors. Given the potential gains and risks of international marketing, companies need a systematic way to make their global marketing decisions.

OBJECTIVE 1 Discuss how the international trade system and the economic, political-legal, and cultural environments affect a company's international marketing decisions. (pp 468–479)

A company must understand the *global marketing environment*, especially the international trade system. It must assess each foreign market's *economic*, *political-legal*, and *cultural characteristics*. The company must then decide whether it wants to

go abroad and consider the potential risks and benefits. It must decide on the volume of international sales it wants, how many countries it wants to market in, and which specific markets it wants to enter. This decision calls for weighing the probable rate of return on investment against the level of risk.

OBJECTIVE 2 Describe three key approaches to entering international markets. (pp 479–482)

The company must decide how to enter each chosen market—whether through *exporting*, *joint venturing*, or *direct investment*. Many companies start as exporters, move to joint ventures, and finally make a direct investment in foreign markets. In *exporting*, the company enters a foreign market by sending and selling products through international marketing intermediaries (indirect exporting) or the company's own department, branch, or sales representative or agents (direct exporting). When establishing a *joint venture*, a company enters foreign markets by joining with foreign companies to produce or market a product or service. In *licensing*, the company enters a foreign market by contracting with a licensee in the foreign market, offering the right to use a manufacturing process, trademark, patent, trade secret, or other item of value for a fee or royalty.

OBJECTIVE 3   Explain how companies adapt their marketing mixes for international markets. (pp 482–488)

Companies must also decide how much their products, promotion, price, and channels should be adapted for each foreign market. At one extreme, global companies use *standardized global marketing* worldwide. Others use an *adapted global marketing*, in which they adjust the marketing strategy and mix to each target market, bearing more costs but hoping for a larger market share and return. However, global standardization is not an all-or-nothing proposition. It's a matter of degree. Most international marketers suggest that companies should 'think globally but act locally'—that they should seek a balance between standardization and adaptation.

OBJECTIVE 4   Identify the three major forms of international marketing organization. (pp 488–489)

The company must develop an effective organization for international marketing. Most firms start with an *export department* and graduate to an *international division*. A few become *global organizations*, with worldwide marketing planned and managed by the top officers of the company. Global organizations view the entire world as a single, borderless market.

KEY Terms

OBJECTIVE 1

Global firm (p 469)
Economic community (p 471)
Countertrade (p 474)

OBJECTIVE 2

Exporting (p 480)
Joint venturing (p 480)

Licensing (p 480)
Contract manufacturing (p 481)
Management contracting (p 481)
Joint ownership (p 481)
Direct investment (p 481)

OBJECTIVE 3

Standardized global marketing (p 482)

Adapted global marketing (p 482)
Straight product extension (p 484)
Product adaptation (p 484)
Product invention (p 484)
Communication adaptation (p 486)
Whole-channel view (p 487)

DISCUSSING & APPLYING THE Concepts

Discussing the Concepts

1. Explain what is meant by the term *global firm* and list the six major decisions involved in international marketing.

2. Identify examples of economic communities and discuss their roles in international trade.

3. Name and define the four types of country industrial structures.

4. Discuss different forms of countertrade and explain why it is a growing practice.

5. Discuss the three ways to enter foreign markets. Which is the best?

6. Discuss the possible product strategies used for adapting to a global market.

Applying the Concepts

1. Visit the website of the Brazilian Embassy in Washington D.C. in the United States, at www.brasilemb.org. What do you learn about doing business in Brazil?

2. From time to time, certain countries fall foul of the international community and sanctions are imposed on them, either by the United Nations, other international organizations, or specific countries. At the UN what group is responsible for applying sanctions? Choose a country that has had sanctions applied to it and identify what kind of sanctions are being used and why.

3. Visit the Central Intelligence Agency's *World Factbook* at http://www.cia.gov/library/publications/the-world-factbook/index.html. In a small group select a country (not your own) and describe the information provided about that country on this site. How is this information useful to marketers?

FOCUS ON Technology

Most small to midsize businesses have small or nonexistent information technology departments, but to remain competitive, all need cutting-edge computing capabilities. The global market for these IT needs is estimated at US$500 billion, so

IBM, a goliath company that does not yet serve this market, is developing a Global Applications Marketplace (also called Blue Business Platform) for small businesses. Through this platform, a small business can search and purchase software applications from independent software vendors around the world. However, local IBM partners will install and manage the applications for the business. When businesses enter information and receive recommendations through the Global Applications Marketplace, they receive product reviews along with access to an online IBM advisor. IBM is setting up hundreds of local vendor partners—called 'innovation centers'—around the world, several of them in emerging markets. The Global Applications Marketplace is designed much like Apple's iTunes—customers will need an IBM server to use the system, just like consumers must have iPods to purchase music and movies from iTunes. While IBM is making the world available to small businesses, IBM's local channel partners bring it to their doorstep.

1. Read more about this initiative at www-03.ibm.com/press/us/en/pressrelease/24111.wss. Explain how IBM is delivering value for small to midsize businesses. How is it delivering value to independent software vendors?

2. Who will be IBM's competitors in this market space? What advantage does IBM offer over these competitors?

FOCUS ON Ethics

Advertising agency TBWA Worldwide came under fire in the months leading up to the 2008 Summer Olympics held in China for showing two sides of China in unrelated advertisements. On one side, ads developed for Adidas by TBWA's Beijing office showed athletes being lifted up by thousands of fans to depict Chinese pride. On the other side, ads developed by the agency's Paris office for Amnesty International depicted China's dark human rights side by showing Chinese athletes being tortured by authorities with the copy, "After the Olympic Games, the fight for human rights must go on." This second side is the one that Chinese authorities did not want the world to see, and it was the one that marketers supporting the games were tip-toeing around. Protests arose in cities around the world where the Olympic torch traveled—the route was even secretly altered in San Francisco amid fears of violent protests. China's Lenovo, the world's fourth largest PC firm, spent more than US$100 million on Olympics sponsorship and related marketing activities in hopes of boosting sales in major markets. Other companies, such as Coca-Cola, McDonald's, and Samsung, were major sponsors of the Olympics, but fear of a worldwide backlash for supporting China remains.

1. Was it right for businesses to sponsor the Olympic Games held in a country known for human rights violations?

2. Did sponsorship of the China Olympic Games help or harm businesses supporting them?

MARKETING BY THE Numbers

Apple agreed to allow Hutchinson Telecommunications International (also known as Hong Kong 3) to sell its iPhone in Hong Kong beginning in 2008. Consumers there can purchase an 8GB iPhone for nearly US$400 with a 24-month service contract for about US$25 per month or receive a free iPhone with a 24-month service contract for about US$65 per month. The first plan offers 5,000 MB of voice and data, and the second provides 2,200 minutes of airtime and unlimited data. For more discussion of the financial and quantitative implications of marketing decisions, see Appendix 2, Marketing by the Numbers.

1. Determine the total revenue generated by a customer over the life of each 24-month contract option. Which one generates more revenue for Hong Kong 3?

2. Using a currency conversion website such as www.xe.com/ucc, convert the revenue generated by both plans to your own currency. Compare this with iPhone plans available in your own country. Do consumers pay more or less?

VIDEO Case

Nivea

In 1911, German company Nivea introduced the revolutionary Nivea Crème in a simple blue tin. Today, that Crème is the centerpiece of a wide range of personal care products. The product line includes everything from soap, shampoo, and shaving products to baby care products, deodorant, and sunscreen. From small beginnings, the company's products are sold today in more than 150 countries worldwide.

But despite this global presence, most Nivea consumers believe that the products they buy are produced and marketed locally. Why? Although Nivea looks for commonalities between consumers around the globe, the company's marketers also recognize the differences between consumers in different markets. So Nivea adapts its marketing mix to reach local consumers while keeping its message consistent everywhere products are sold. This globally consistent, locally customized marketing strategy has sold more than 11 billion tins of the traditional Nivea Crème.

After viewing the video featuring Nivea, answer the following questions about the company and the global marketplace:

1. Which of the five strategies for adapting products and promotion for the global market does Nivea employ? How does it do so?

2. Visit Nivea's website, www.nivea.com, and tour the sites for several different countries. How does Nivea market its products differently in different countries? How does the company maintain the consistency of its brand?

3. How is Nivea's consistent brand message relevant to different target markets?

COMPANY Case

B-Tech: A Successful Regional Brand

Until the mid-1990s in Egypt, public sector companies such as Omar Effendi dominated most of the activities in the household appliances retail market. From this time, private retailers were given the chance to prove themselves in the market. Olympic Group, the established Egyptian manufacturer of household appliances, identified three major market trends which led to it considering vertical integration by expanding its activities into retail services. (Vertical integration refers to the growth of the business into a new set of products or services that fall within the production cycle of its original products or service line; for example, a clothes manufacturer can vertically integrate downward and operate a fashion retailing business, or it can vertically integrate upward into manufacturing fabrics or buttons.)

First, Olympic Group feared entrance into its sector by both local and international competitors, looking to take advantage of gaps in the Egyptian household retail industry market. Secondly, there was a need for better credit (*takseet*) terms when selling household appliances. At that time banks were the only players providing credit to customers, but their application procedures were considered onerous by many customers. Olympic saw this inconvenience as an opportunity for itself and its competitors to provide a more accessible service appealing to more customers. Finally, a number of private retailers in the household appliance market had fragmented and had non-unified management structures. An example was El Ogail, a renowned distributor of household appliances. While enjoying a wide market reach, its stores were managed individually—therefore, manufacturers had difficulties making consistent agreements with each store. These three market trends led to the creation of Olympic Stores in 1997.

B-TECH ESTABLISHMENT

The Olympic Stores chain began with three stores. By 2010, it had established itself as a major presence in the Egyptian household appliance market, with a total of 57 stores in 21 governorates. The stores not only sold a wide range of Olympic brands, but also appliances produced by many international brands, such as Sony, Ariston, Philips, and Daewoo. The chain had enjoyed a great deal of success up to this point, yet Dr Mahmoud Khattab, its chairman and CEO, was ambitious for more expansion. To kick-start its growth, the Olympic Group decided to make a number of major changes, even to the name of the stores themselves. "Olympic Stores was a name associated with sports more than what we

really do," Khattab said. It is fair to say that Olympic Stores was considered a retailer of Olympic-branded products rather than a place to purchase appliances produced by international manufacturers, and this was perceived as having a possible negative effect on sales. Following detailed research, in 2003, Khattab decided to go with the name 'B-Tech'—a generic name, meaning simply 'be technological.' The intention was to foster the idea that B-Tech is a retailer of a wide range of electronic and household brands.

B-TECH'S COMPETITIVE ADVANTAGE

In 2005, B-Tech had two main arms: retail services and sole selling agencies. Its retail arm continued to sell different brands, and in addition, it acted as a sole selling agent for many international brands, including Sony, Ariston, Philips, Daewoo, and Haier. It even distributed these brand's products to other retailers operating in Egypt, such as Carrefour and El Ogail.

The company has a number of competitive edges that are difficult for its rivals to match. Khattab points out that B-Tech does not consider its competitors, but rather the customer: "That does not mean that we disregard competitors, however, our main focus is on the customer... We seek to even exceed customers' expectations." That was evident in 2003, after seven years of operations, when B-Tech was 'Recognized for Excellence' by the European Foundation for Quality Management (EFQM). B-Tech was the first non-European company to be recognized in this way. The chain received the certification based on its excellence and focus on customer service after assessments were made of B-Tech sites and employees.

The early establishment of B-Tech stores has enabled it to develop know-how in many areas, especially customer service. In addition, it now offers more attractive credit sales terms to its customers than those offered by its competitors. Another competitive advantage is its wide geographic presence with 57 branches in 21 governorates. Traffic congestion is a major problem in Cairo, and proximity to a store often counted a key part of the retail service. Many customers first went to B-Tech because it was the closest and most convenient store, and subsequently became loyal customers after experiencing high levels of customer service.

Another key advantage is the company's role as the sole agent to 11 major international electronic and household goods manufacturers. It also acts as supplier of those brands to its competitors. Due to the fact that B-Tech stores follow a single management structure, its suppliers, including Sony and Ariston, have one management contact point. In contrast, its competitors stores often have different owners, which can lead to difficulties when dealing with suppliers. Furthermore, B-Tech is focused on selling electronic and household equipment only, while other big retailers such as Carrefour and Spinneys do not have a focus on onetype of product.

B-TECH'S GROWING STRATEGY

Khattab says that, "B-Tech is going to proceed with its success through following its mission and vision, which entail learning all the way." It has core values that it is committed to, and they are, "Trust, Love, Excellence, Empowerment, Innovation, Fun and Efficiency... [B-Tech] is the no. 1 retailer [in the household market] and this is because we meet our promises." The company enjoys an 8 percent market share in the industry, and it is seeking further growth. In March 2010, it introduced the idea of household appliance megastores, which are three times the size of other existing stores, stocking a wider variety of products. One megastore is now open, and the company intends to open more in the future.

THE FUTURE

The major question facing the company is whether it should continue to focus on the Egyptian market alone or whether it should consider expanding into regional and international markets. It is now well established and has attracted a large number of international brands. It is trusted by consumers and its business model has proven to be successful. Khattab believes that local knowledge has been a critical factor in its success, and he is therefore reluctant to expand abroad. The company has undoubtedly been successful, but going international is a challenging process, and the ability to successfully translate the company's strategies and core values outside of Egypt would be critical to success in a new market.

Questions for Discussion

1. What are the major reasons for B-Tech's success in the Egyptian market?

2. Would you recommend the company to go international? If yes, then why? Which countries to start with and why?

3. What would be the critical factors that would ensure B-Tech's international success?

4. Is there a threat from sticking to local markets?

Source: Personal Interview with Dr Mahmoud Khattab, chairman and CEO of B-Tech.

Copyright: El-Khazindar Business Research and Case Center (KCC), the American University in Cairo.

Chapter 17

Part 1   Defining Marketing and the Marketing Process (Chapters 1, 2)
Part 2   Understanding the Marketplace and Consumers (Chapters 3, 4, 5, 6)
Part 3   Designing a Customer-Driven Strategy and Mix (Chapters 7, 8, 9, 10, 11, 12, 13, 14)
Part 4   Extending Marketing (Chapters 15, 16, 17)

Sustainable Marketing
Social Responsibility and Ethics

Chapter
PREVIEW
In this final chapter, we'll examine the concepts of sustainable marketing, meeting the needs of consumers, businesses, and society—now and in the future—through socially and environmentally responsible marketing actions. We'll start by defining sustainable marketing and then look at some common criticisms of marketing as it impacts individual consumers and businesses. Next, we'll examine consumerism, environmentalism, and other citizen and public actions that promote sustainable marketing. Finally, we'll see how companies themselves can benefit from proactively pursuing sustainable marketing practices that bring value, not just to individual customers but to society as a whole. You'll see that sustainable marketing actions are more than just the right thing to do; they're also good for business.

First, let's look at how businesses in the Arab world are taking corporate social responsibility more and more seriously and recognizing that it is an integral part of today's business environment. Numerous initiatives are being set up by businesses and governments across the region.

CSR Middle East is a nonprofit platform that promotes corporate social responsibility (CSR) in the Arab world. The organization has a network of professionals who advocate CSR and thus, are helping to shape modern-day business practices.

CSR Middle East collects and disseminates information, news, and reports on CSR and sustainability in the Arab world. The group has a broad membership that includes nongovernmental organizations (NGOs) and other agencies which strongly believe in corporate citizenship, sustainability, and socially responsible initiatives. In the broadest terms, the group focuses on diversity, philanthropy, socially responsible investment, the environment, human rights, workplace issues, business ethics, community development, and transparent corporate governance. CSR Middle East has had some marked successes, including some key initiatives enacted not only by Middle Eastern businesses, but also by multinational corporations operating in the region.

In May 2008 at the World Economic Forum (WEF) held in Egypt's Sharm El-Sheikh, Mohammed Alshaya, executive chairman of the Alshaya retail group, which has some 1,400 stores in the region, made an address entitled 'Does Arab Business Care?' It was Alshaya's contention that CSR would play an important role in ensuring that the Middle East continues to grow and thrive in economic terms. Alshaya noted that many companies (in the Middle East and beyond) are not adverse to CSR but their involvement in CSR tends to be as part of one-off projects rather than an integral part of operations. Many businesses still use CSR as a publicity gimmick, knowing that charitable donations, for example, usually result in useful press coverage. Alshaya explained, "In the Middle East, CSR is still in its infancy, it is very much associated with 'giving' through charitable donations. There is much more we can do in partnership with governments and NGOs to tackle deeper issues like unemployment, lack of quality education, and carbon footprint reduction."

Alshaya was not the only speaker at the forum to make it plain that CSR was to the advantage of businesses and the economy of the Middle East. King Abdullah of Jordan pointed out that businesses should make more effort to welcome young people into the workplace environment by becoming involved in active training programs. He highlighted the Egyptian Education Initiative for particular praise in this respect.

Sheikh Mohammed bin Rashid Al Maktoum of Dubai had made the major announcement at the previous year's WEF in Jordan that Dubai was investing US$10 billion

> The World Economic Forum (WEF) has worked with businesses and governments in the Middle East to promote corporate social responsibility in the region.

in its attempts to help bridge the perceived gap in education and knowledge in the Middle East compared with the West. The Dubai Cares project also initiated a drive to encourage Dubai businesses to make charitable donations to the foundation, which aims to educate one million children in poor countries.

In his speech, Alshaya noted, "Regional corporations should place more emphasis on their social responsibilities, as consumers and governments are becoming increasingly conscious of ethical and environmental issues. Businesses not committing to CSR will not only risk their reputations but also give up the opportunity to contribute to the growth of this region, or successfully expand outside it."

Alshaya's comments were echoed by Neville Isdell, the now former CEO of Coca-Cola: "There has been a societal change, businesses and governments have to be partners not just in business development but in societal development. Unless we do that the legitimacy of our economic model will be jeopardized." Fadi Ghandour, CEO of Aramex, a major transportation and logistics company in the Middle East, added, "Businesses have to invest in society. Invest being the keyword here; it's not CSR; it's not charity. It's an investment in society."

Alshaya certainly practices what he preaches; his own group has launched a training program for some 1,000 students in Kuwait. Alshaya also made the point that many CSR projects are reactive rather than proactive at present. In other words, a government will announce an initiative and then ask for business support, rather than the businesses taking CSR as a driving force and leading the way.[1]

Another business taking CSR seriously is TAQA, which operates in the Abu Dhabi energy sector. TAQA was established in 2005 and has become a global energy business with assets valued at US$21 billion and investments all over the world. According to Shayma Majed, the company's manager in charge of CSR, diversity, and inclusion, TAQA's CSR objectives are "[To] implement programs of ethical, environmental, and social benefit to all of the company's stakeholders, which include employees, shareholders, regulators, bondholders, the environment, and the community."

In drafting any CSR policy, according to Majed, it is vital that external experts are included in the conversations and that internal departments of the organization are consulted: "A company pursues CSR at its peril if it has not consulted widely with external stakeholders such as NGOs, analysts, academics, and, of course, its customers and partners. We need to check periodically that what we have assumed internally will stand up externally."

Transparency is vital for any organization in its efforts to ensure that CSR is working and effective. TAQA uses external auditing to ensure that progress and tangible benefits are being made.

Leading political and business figures speak at the 2008 World Economic Forum on the Middle East in Sharm El-Sheikh, Egypt.

The external auditing is carried out by the ethical trading initiative Forum for the Future and the business-led charity-Business in the Community. Each of the groups "regularly has firsthand experiences with TAQA's actions and outputs and challenge us to continually improve our performance."

TAQA has introduced a code of business ethics that focuses on employee conduct both in the organization and in external dealings, specifically when an employee or manager is acting on behalf of the organization. An integral part of the diversity and inclusion aspect of the CSR policy is that the company has to appreciate that it and its employees and managers operate in some 38 different countries. Majed explained, "TAQA recognizes that its workforce consists of a diverse population of people, and it believes that harnessing these differences helps to create a productive environment where people feel valued, where they feel that their talents are fully utilized, and in which the organizational goals are being met."

Since environmental issues are also of concern in the CSR field for the company, TAQA has joined the 3C initiative, a group of business leaders that aim to set global limits for temperature increases and which has identified emission reduction targets. As part of this initiative, TAQA offers its employees an opportunity to buy a hybrid low-emissions car. Majed explained why this is so important: "TAQA believes changing individual behavior is the first step towards changing societies, and we have begun this journey together with our employees."[2]

> **CSR Middle East is an organization in the region that aims to promote corporate social responsibility. "In the Middle East, CSR is still in its infancy. It is very much associated with 'giving' through charitable donations,"** says Mohammed Alshaya, the executive chairman of a major Middle Eastern retail group. Other initiatives, such as Dubai Cares and company-specific projects, aim to create a code of business ethics.

Responsible marketers discover what consumers want and respond with market offerings that create value for buyers in order to capture value in return. The *marketing concept* is a philosophy of customer value and mutual gain. Its practice leads the economy by an invisible hand to satisfy the many and changing needs of millions of consumers.

Not all marketers follow the marketing concept, however. In fact, some companies use questionable marketing practices that serve their own rather than consumers' interests.

Objective Outline

Moreover, even well-intended marketing actions that meet the current needs of some consumers may cause immediate or future harm to other consumers or the larger society. Responsible marketers must consider whether their actions are *sustainable* in the long term.

Consider the sale of sport utility vehicles (SUVs). These large vehicles meet the immediate needs of many drivers in terms of capacity, power, and utility. However, SUV sales involve larger questions of consumer safety and environmental responsibility. For example, in accidents, SUVs are more likely to kill both their occupants and the occupants of other vehicles. Research shows that SUV occupants are three times more likely to die from their vehicle rolling than are occupants of sedans.[3] Moreover, gas-guzzling SUVs use more than their fair share of the world's energy and other resources and contribute disproportionately to pollution and congestion problems, creating costs that must be carried by both current and future generations.[4]

This chapter examines *sustainable* marketing and the social and environmental effects of private marketing practices. First, we address the question: What is sustainable marketing and why is it important?

> **Author Comment** | Marketers must think beyond immediate customer satisfaction and business performance toward strategies that preserve the world for future generations.

Sustainable Marketing (pp 496–498)

Sustainable marketing calls for meeting the present needs of consumers and businesses while also preserving or enhancing the ability of future generations to meet their needs. Figure 17.1 compares the sustainable marketing concept with other marketing concepts we studied in earlier chapters.[5]

The *marketing concept* recognizes that organizations thrive from day to day by determining the current needs and wants of target group customers and fulfilling those needs and wants more effectively and efficiently than the competition. It focuses on meeting the company's short-term sales, growth, and profit needs by giving customers what they want now. However, satisfying consumers' immediate needs and desires doesn't always serve the future best interests of either customers or the business.

For example, McDonald's early decisions to market tasty but fat- and salt-laden fast foods created immediate satisfaction for customers and sales and profits for the company.

Sustainable marketing

Marketing that meets the present needs of consumers and businesses while also preserving or enhancing the ability of future generations to meet their needs.

FIGURE | 17.1
Sustainable Marketing

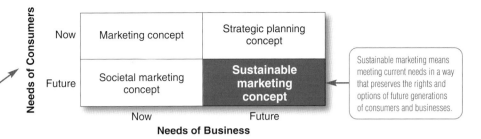

Sustainable marketing means meeting current needs in a way that preserves the rights and options of future generations of consumers and businesses.

The marketing concept means meeting the current needs of both customers and the company. But that can sometimes mean compromising the future of both.

However, critics assert that McDonald's and other fast-food chains contributed to a longer-term obesity epidemic, damaging consumer health and burdening health systems. In turn, many consumers began looking for healthier eating options, causing a slump in the fast-food industry. Beyond issues of ethical behavior and social welfare, McDonald's was also criticized for the sizable environmental footprint of its vast global operations, everything from wasteful packaging and solid waste creation to inefficient energy use in its stores. Thus, McDonald's strategy was not sustainable in terms of either consumer or company benefit.

Whereas the *societal marketing concept* identified in **Figure 17.1** considers the future welfare of consumers and the *strategic planning concept* considers future company needs, the *sustainable marketing concept* considers both. Sustainable marketing calls for socially and environmentally responsible actions that meet both the immediate and future needs of customers and the company.

For example, in recent years, McDonald's has responded with a more sustainable 'Plan to Win' strategy of diversifying into salads, fruits, grilled chicken, low-fat milk, and other healthy fare. Also, after a seven-year search for healthier cooking oil, McDonald's phased out traditional artery-clogging trans fats without compromising the taste of its French fries. And the company launched a major multifaceted education campaign—called "It's what I eat and what I do... I'm lovin' it"—to help consumers better understand the keys to living balanced, active lifestyles.

The 'Plan to Win' strategy also addresses environmental issues. For example, it calls for food-supply sustainability, reduced and environmentally sustainable packaging, reuse and recycling, and more responsible store designs. McDonald's has even developed an environmental scorecard that rates its suppliers' performance in areas such as water use, energy use, and solid waste management.

McDonald's more sustainable strategy is benefiting the company as well as its customers. Since announcing its 'Plan to Win' strategy, McDonald's sales have increased by 57 percent and profits have nearly tripled. And for the past three years, the company has been included in the Dow Jones Sustainability Index, recognizing its commitment to sustainable economic, environmental, and social performance. Thus, McDonald's is well positioned for a sustainably profitable future.[6]

Another example of sustainable marketing is the continuous input that telecom service providers in Egypt give as part of their social responsibility. Vodafone Egypt co-operated with Alashanek Ya Balady, an Egyptian NGO, in funding and implementing a development project called 'Qariaty.' The project aimed to create youth employment opportunities and provide mobile technology services in remote areas of Egypt.[7]

CSR initiatives were also employed by several companies in Egypt at the time of the Aswan floods that occurred in Upper Egypt in 2010. There are several examples of aid being offered by many big companies in Egypt. Vodafone, for example, provided

Large companies in the Arab world have recognized the importance of corporate social responsibility, and co-operated with NGOs in order to positively affect their societies. In this image, Aramex employees load trucks with relief supplies for flood victims.

food, blankets, and clothes for up to 500 families affected by the floods. Vodafone employees even assisted NGOs in distributing the aid. Moreover, the company assisted victims in re-building their damaged houses. Other companies, such as Aramex, encouraged their employees to help in the process of loading trucks with emergency supplies. Mobinil, the Egyptian-based mobile operator, distributed 2,000 bundles of cellphones and telephone lines to victims for free.[8]

Truly sustainable marketing requires a smooth-functioning marketing system in which consumers, companies, public policymakers, and others work together to ensure socially responsible and ethical marketing actions. Unfortunately, however, the marketing system doesn't always work smoothly. The following sections examine several sustainability questions: What are the most frequent social criticisms of marketing? What steps have private citizens taken to curb marketing ills? What steps have legislators and government agencies taken to promote sustainable marketing? What steps have enlightened companies taken to carry out socially responsible and ethical marketing that creates sustainable value for both individual customers and society as a whole?

> **Author Comment** | In most ways, we all benefit greatly from marketing activities. However, like most other human endeavors, marketing has its flaws. Here, we present both sides of some of the most common criticisms of marketing.

Social Criticisms of Marketing (pp 498–506)

Marketing receives much criticism. Some of this criticism is justified; much is not. Social critics claim that certain marketing practices hurt individual consumers, society as a whole, and other business firms.

Marketing's Impact on Individual Consumers

Consumers have many concerns about how well various approaches to marketing serve their interests. Surveys usually show that consumers hold mixed or even slightly unfavorable attitudes toward marketing practices. Consumer advocates, government agencies, and other critics have accused marketing of harming consumers through high prices, deceptive practices, high-pressure selling, low-quality or unsafe products, planned obsolescence (products which are not designed to last very long, forcing consumers to replace them), and poor service to disadvantaged consumers. Such questionable marketing practices are not sustainable in terms of long-term consumer or business welfare.

High Prices

The American marketing system has always been a model to look to for new creative marketing ideas. The tools used are often new to the Arab world and provide a wealth of stimuli. Nevertheless, many critics charge that the American marketing system causes prices to be higher than they would be under more 'sensible' systems, such as the economically-scaled Chinese system, which does not have a lot of creative marketing tools, yet has taken the world by storm with cheap products and simple yet effective marketing systems. They point to three factors—*high costs of distribution*, *high advertising and promotion costs*, and *excessive markups*.

High Costs of Distribution. A long-standing charge is that greedy channel intermediaries mark up prices beyond the value of their services. Critics charge that there are too many intermediaries, that intermediaries are inefficient, or that they provide unnecessary or duplicate services. As a result, distribution costs too much, and consumers pay for these excessive costs in the form of higher prices.

How do resellers answer these charges? They argue that intermediaries do work that would otherwise have to be done by manufacturers or consumers. Markups reflect services that consumers themselves want—more convenience, larger stores and assortments, more service, longer store hours, return privileges, and others. In fact, they argue, retail competition is so intense that margins are actually quite low. For example, after taxes, supermarket chains are typically left with barely 1 percent profit on their sales. If some resellers try to charge too much relative to the value they add, other resellers will step in with lower prices. Low-price stores such as Carrefour and other discounters put pressure on their competitors to operate efficiently and keep their prices down.

A heavily promoted brand of aspirin sells for much more than a virtually identical nonbranded or store-branded product. Critics charge that promotion adds only psychological value to the product rather than functional value.

High Advertising and Promotion Costs.   Modern marketing is also accused of pushing up prices to finance heavy advertising and sales promotion. For example, a few dozen tablets of a heavily promoted brand of pain reliever sell for the same price as 100 tablets of less-promoted brands. Differentiated products—cosmetics, detergents, toiletries—include promotion and packaging costs that can amount to 40 percent or more of the manufacturer's price to the retailer. Critics charge that much of the packaging and promotion adds only psychological value to the product rather than functional value.

Marketers respond that advertising does add to product costs. But it also adds value by informing potential buyers of the availability and merits of a brand. Brand name products may cost more, but branding gives buyers assurances of consistent quality. Moreover, consumers can usually buy functional versions of products at lower prices. However, they *want* and are willing to pay more for products that also provide psychological benefits—that make them feel wealthy, attractive, or special. Also, heavy advertising and promotion may be necessary for a firm to match competitors' efforts—the business would lose 'share of mind' if it did not match competitive spending. At the same time, companies are cost conscious about promotion and try to spend their money wisely.

Excessive Markups.   Critics also charge that some companies mark up goods excessively. They point to the drug industry, where a pill costing five cents to make may cost the consumer US$2 to buy. They point to the high charges for auto repair and other services once a customer already has a product that they need fixing.

Marketers respond that most businesses try to deal fairly with consumers because they want to build customer relationships and repeat business. Most consumer abuses are unintentional. When shady marketers do take advantage of consumers, they should be reported to Better Business Bureaus and appropriate government agencies. Marketers also respond that consumers often don't understand the reasons for high markups. For example, pharmaceutical markups must cover the costs of purchasing, promoting, and distributing existing medicines plus the high research and development costs of formulating and testing new medicines. As pharmaceuticals company GlaxoSmithKline states in its ads, "Today's medicines finance tomorrow's miracles."

Deceptive Practices

Marketers are sometimes accused of deceptive practices that lead consumers to believe they will get more value than they actually do. Deceptive practices fall into three groups: pricing, promotion, and packaging. *Deceptive pricing* includes practices such as falsely advertising 'factory' or 'wholesale' prices or a large price reduction from a phony high retail list price. *Deceptive promotion* includes practices such as misrepresenting the product's features or performance or luring the customers to the store for a bargain that is out of stock. *Deceptive packaging* includes exaggerating package contents through subtle design, using misleading labeling, or describing size in misleading terms.

Deceptive practices have led to legislation and other consumer-protection actions. For example, in 1938 the U.S. government reacted to such blatant deceptions as Fleischmann's Yeast's claim to straighten crooked teeth. The U.S. government has published several guidelines listing deceptive practices. Despite new regulations, some critics argue that deceptive claims are still the norm. Consider the glut of 'environmental responsibility' claims marketers are now making:

Are you a victim of 'greenwashing?' Biodegradable, eco-friendly, recycled, green, carbon neutral, carbon offsets, made from sustainable resources—such phrases are popping up more and more on products worldwide, leading many to question their validity. For example, there are several companies claiming to sell fresh organic food products in the Arab world. Even though the products are free of pesticides, they were still planted in land that was fertilized using non-organic fertilizers. That makes the products not totally chemical-free. Nevertheless, there has been no attempt from the governments of the region to audit or enforce proper communication to the consumer about the meaning of the word 'organic' and the truth about the products they buy. In fact, there is very little regulation against marketing claims in the Arab world, and existing regulations are not very well implemented.

Recently, the Ministry of Trade and Industry in Egypt established the Consumer Protection Agency (CPA), which introduced a new law on consumer protection. The law aims to regulate the "unbalanced consumer–trader relations, by monitoring trade transactions and enforcing consumer/trader binding laws and regulations." The CPA aims to raise awareness about the new law, and to enable consumers to protect their rights in case they face any problems when purchasing a product.[9]

The toughest problem is defining what is 'deceptive.' For instance, an advertiser's claim that its powerful laundry detergent "makes your washing machine 10 feet tall," showing a surprised homemaker watching her appliance burst through her laundry room ceiling, isn't intended to be taken literally. Instead, the advertiser might claim, it is an innocent exaggeration for effect. One noted marketing thinker, Theodore Levitt, once claimed that advertising exaggerations are bound to occur—and that they may even be desirable: "There is hardly a company that would not go down in ruin if it refused to provide fluff, because nobody will buy pure functionality.... Worse, it denies...people's honest needs and values. Without distortion, exaggeration, and elaboration, life would be dull...and at its existential worst."[10]

However, others claim that such exaggeration can harm consumers in subtle ways. For example, the popular and long-running MasterCard Priceless commercials paint pictures of consumers fulfilling their priceless dreams despite the costs. Similarly, Visa invites consumers to "Enjoy life's opportunities." Both suggest that your credit card can make it happen. But critics charge that such imagery by credit card companies encourages a spend-now-pay-later attitude that causes many consumers to *over* use their cards. The critics point to statistics showing the large proportion of people carrying a continuing balance on their credit cards.[11]

Marketers argue that most companies avoid deceptive practices. Because such practices harm their business in the long run, they simply aren't sustainable. Profitable customer relationships are built upon a foundation of value and trust. If consumers do not get what they expect, they will switch to more reliable products. In addition, consumers usually protect themselves from deception. Most consumers recognize a marketer's selling intent and are careful when they buy, sometimes to the point of not believing completely true product claims.

High-Pressure Selling

Salespeople are sometimes accused of high-pressure selling that persuades people to buy goods they had no intention of buying. It is often said that insurance, real estate, and used cars are *sold*, not *bought*. Salespeople are trained to deliver smooth, prepared talks to entice purchase. They sell hard because sales contests promise big prizes to those who sell the most.

But in most cases, marketers have little to gain from high-pressure selling. Such tactics may work in one-time selling situations for short-term gain. However, most selling involves building long-term relationships with valued customers. High-pressure or deceptive selling can do serious damage to such relationships. For example, imagine a Unilever account manager trying to put pressure on a Tesco buyer, or an IBM salesperson trying to pester a General Electric information technology manager. It simply wouldn't work.

Poor Quality, Harmful, or Unsafe Products

Another criticism concerns poor product quality or function. One complaint is that, too often, products are not made well and services are not performed well. A second complaint is that many products deliver little benefit, or that they might even be harmful.

For example, think again about the fast-food industry. Many critics blame the plentiful supply of fat-laden, high-calorie fast-food fare for the rapidly growing obesity epidemic. Studies show that some 66 percent of American adults, for example, and 17 percent of American children are overweight or obese. The number of people in the United States alone who are 100 pounds or more overweight increased by 500 percent between 2000 and 2005, from 1 adult in 200 to 1 in 40. This weight increase comes despite repeated medical studies showing that excess weight brings increased risks of heart disease, diabetes, and other maladies, even cancer.[12]

Similarly, there is a significant increase in obesity in the Arab world. In Bahrain, 83 percent of women are obese or overweight (compared with 62 percent of American women), according to the International Obesity Task Force, a London-based think tank. Furthermore, 74 percent and 75 percent of women are obese or overweight in the United Arab Emirates and Lebanon respectively. Further, according to the World Health Organization, childhood obesity in the Arab world has quickly increased in recent years.

The critics are quick to fault what they see as greedy food marketers who are cashing in on vulnerable consumers. Some food marketers are looking pretty much guilty as charged. Take the U.S. fast-food restaurant Hardee's, for example:[13]

> At a time when other fast-food chains such as McDonald's, Wendy's, and Subway were getting 'leaner,' Hardee's introduced the decadent Thickburger, featuring a third of a pound of Angus beef. It followed up with the *Monster* Thickburger: two-thirds of a pound of Angus beef, four strips of bacon, and three slices of American cheese, all nestled in a buttered sesame-seed bun slathered with mayonnaise! The Monster Thickburger weighs in at a whopping 1,410 calories and 107 grams of fat, far greater than the government's recommended fat intake for an entire day. Surely, you say, Hardee's made a massive blunder here. Not so! Since introducing the Thickburger, Hardee's has experienced healthy sales increases and even fatter profits.

So, should Hardee's hang its head in shame? Is it being socially irresponsible by aggressively promoting overindulgence to ill-informed or unwary consumers? Or is it simply practicing good marketing, creating more value for its customers by offering a big juicy burger that clearly appeals to their taste buds and letting them make their own choices? Critics claim the former; industry defenders claim the latter. Hardee's diligently targets young men aged 18 to 34, consumers capable of making their own decisions about health and well-being. And Hardee's certainly isn't hiding the nutritional facts. Here's how it describes Thickburgers on its website:

> There's only one thing that can slay the hunger of a young guy on the move: the Thickburger line at Hardee's. With nine cravable varieties, including the classic Original Thickburger and the monument to decadence, the Monster Thickburger, quick-service goes premium with 100% Angus beef and all the fixings.... If you want to indulge in a big, delicious, juicy burger, look no further than Hardee's.

Hardee's even offers a nutrition calculator on its website showing the calories, fat, and other content of all its menu items. In this case, as in many matters of social responsibility, what's right and wrong may be a matter of opinion.

A third complaint concerns product safety. Product safety has been a problem for several reasons, including company indifference, increased product complexity, and poor quality control. For years, Consumers Union in the U.S.—the nonprofit testing and information organization that publishes the *Consumer Reports* magazine and website—has reported various hazards in tested products: electrical dangers in appliances, carbon monoxide poisoning

Harmful products: Is Hardee's being socially irresponsible or simply practicing good marketing by giving customers a big juicy burger that clearly pings their taste buds? Judging by the nutrition calculator at its website, the company certainly isn't hiding the nutritional facts.

from room heaters, injury risks from lawn mowers, and faulty automobile design, among many others. The organization's testing and other activities have helped consumers make better buying decisions and encouraged businesses to eliminate product flaws.

However, most manufacturers *want* to produce quality goods. The way a company deals with product quality and safety problems can damage or help its reputation. Companies selling poor-quality or unsafe products risk damaging conflicts with consumer groups and regulators. Unsafe products can result in product liability suits and large awards for damages. More fundamentally, consumers who are unhappy with a firm's products may avoid future purchases and talk other consumers into doing the same. Thus, quality missteps can have severe consequences and are not consistent with sustainable marketing. Today's marketers know that good quality results in customer value and satisfaction, which in turn creates sustainable customer relationships.

Planned Obsolescence

Critics also have charged that some companies practice planned obsolescence, causing their products to become obsolete (unusable or out of date) before they actually should need replacing. They accuse some producers of using materials and components that will break, wear, rust, or rot sooner than they should. One writer put it this way: "The marvels of modern technology include the development of a soda can which, when discarded, will last forever—and a...car, which, when properly cared for, will rust out in two or three years."[14]

Others are charged with continually changing consumer concepts of acceptable styles to encourage more and earlier buying. An obvious example is constantly-changing clothing fashions. Still others are accused of introducing planned streams of new products that make older models obsolete. Critics claim that this occurs in the consumer electronics and computer industries. For example, consider this writer's tale about an aging mobile phone:[15]

> Today, most people, myself included, are all amazed at the wondrous outpouring of new technology, from cellphones to iPods, iPhones, laptops, BlackBerries, and on and on. Even though I am techno-incompetent and like to think I shun these new devices, I actually have a drawer filled with the remains of yesterday's hottest product, now reduced to the status of fossils. I have video cameras that use tapes no longer available, laptops with programs incompatible with anything on today's market, portable CD players I no longer use, and more. But what really upsets me is how quickly some still-useful gadgets become obsolete, at least in the eyes of their makers.
>
> I recently embarked on an epic search for a cord to plug into my wife's cellphone to recharge it. We were traveling and the poor phone kept bleating that it was running low and the battery needed recharging. So, we began a search—from big-box technology superstores to smaller suppliers and the cellphone companies themselves—all to no avail. Finally, a salesperson told my wife, "That's an old model, so we don't stock the charger any longer." "But I only bought it last year," she sputtered. "Yeah, like I said, that's an old model," he replied without a hint of irony or sympathy. So, in the world of insanely rapid obsolescence, each successive model is incompatible with the previous one it replaces. The proliferation and sheer waste of this type of practice is mind-boggling.

Planned obsolescence: Almost everyone, it seems, has a drawer filled with the remnants of yesterday's hottest product, now reduced to the status of fossils.

Marketers respond that consumers *like* style changes; they get tired of the old goods and want a new look in fashion. Or they *want* the latest high-tech innovations, even if older models still work. No one has to buy the new product, and if too few people like it, it will simply fail. Finally, most companies do not design their products to break down earlier, because they do not want to lose customers to other brands. Instead, they seek constant improvement to ensure that products will consistently meet or exceed customer expectations. Much of the so-called planned obsolescence is the working of the competitive and technological forces in a free society—forces that lead to ever-improving goods and services.

Poor Service to Disadvantaged Consumers

Finally, the marketing system has been accused of serving disadvantaged consumers poorly. For example, critics claim that the urban poor often have to shop in smaller stores that carry inferior goods and charge higher prices. The presence of large national chain stores in low-income neighborhoods would help to keep prices down. However, the critics accuse major chain retailers of 'redlining,' drawing a red line around disadvantaged neighborhoods and avoiding placing stores there.

Similar redlining charges have been leveled at the insurance, consumer lending, banking, and health care industries. Banks have been accused of offering lower credit options to poorer people. The banks build their loaning policy on the total proven revenue of the applicants. The fact is, the lower one's income, the more one needs loans or credit. Banks defend their methods by saying that the loans or credit facilities offered are based on the ability of the applicant to pay back.

Recently, small and medium enterprises have complained that they get higher interest rates than large organizations. The access they get to liquidity and bank facilities remains well below what a large organization gets. The larger the organization, the higher its loan ability becomes, when developing a balanced business environment and allowing organizations to grow dictates equal opportunity and access to loans.

Redlining is practiced in many developing countries, specially in rural areas. Large chain stores such as Carrefour and H&M locate themselves in the capital cities and avoid areas where the population has a lower income, when positioning themselves as very price-competitive and very affordable.

Marketers often deliver value to disadvantaged consumers; and in many cases, they profitably target them.

Clearly, better marketing systems must be built to service disadvantaged consumers. In fact, many marketers profitably target such consumers with legitimate goods and services that create real value. In cases where marketers do not step in to fill the void, the government likely will. For example, the U.S. Federal Trade Commission has taken action against sellers who advertise false values, wrongfully deny services, or charge disadvantaged customers too much.

Marketing's Impact on Society as a Whole

The marketing system has been accused of adding to several 'evils' in society at large. Advertising has been a special target—specifically, advertisers have been accused of misleading consumers. Recently, Brand Power campaigns have been advertised to position top brands as a better generic option for the consumer.[16]

False Wants and Too Much Materialism

Critics have charged that the marketing system urges too much interest in material possessions, and that consumers' love affair with worldly possessions is not sustainable. In many societies, people are judged by what they *own* rather than by who they *are*. In the Gulf states and other countries such as Lebanon, the cars people drive define their social status. In Egypt, owning multiple beach houses on the north coast and Ain Sokhna city defines a level of social class. In the U.S., this drive for wealth and possessions hit new highs in the 1980s and 1990s, when phrases such as 'greed is good' and 'shop till you drop' seemed to characterize the times.

The critics do not view this interest in material things as a natural state of mind but rather as a matter of false wants created by marketing. Businesses hire ad agencies to stimulate people's desires for goods, and the ad agencies use the mass media to create materialistic models of the good life. People work harder to earn the necessary money. Their purchases increase the output of industry, and industry in turn uses the agencies to stimulate yet more desire for the industrial output.

Thus, marketing is seen as creating false wants that benefit industry more than they benefit consumers. "In the world of consumerism, marketing is there to promote consumption," says one marketing critic. It is "inevitable that marketing will promote overconsumption, and from this, a psychologically, as well as ecologically, unsustainable world."[17]

Such criticisms overstate the power of business to create needs. People have strong defenses against advertising and other marketing tools. Marketers are most effective when they appeal to existing wants rather than when they attempt to create new ones. Furthermore, people seek information when making important purchases and often do not rely on single sources. Even minor purchases that may be affected by advertising messages lead to repeat purchases only if the product delivers the promised customer value. Finally, the high failure rate of new products shows that companies are not able to control demand.

On a deeper level, our wants and values are influenced not only by marketers but also by family, peer groups, religion, cultural background, and education. If people are highly materialistic, these values arise out of basic socialization processes that go much deeper than business and mass media could produce alone.

Too Few Social Goods

Business has been accused of overselling private goods at the expense of public goods. As private goods increase, they require more public services that are usually not forthcoming. For example, an increase in automobile ownership (private good) requires more highways, traffic control, parking spaces, and police services (public goods). The overselling of private goods results in 'social costs.' For cars, some of the social costs include traffic congestion, gasoline shortages, and air pollution. For example, people lose billions of hours a year in traffic jams. In the process, they waste billions of gallons of fuel and emit millions of tons of greenhouse gases.[18]

A way must be found to restore a balance between private and public goods. One option is to make producers bear the full social costs of their operations. The government could require automobile manufacturers to build cars with more efficient engines and better pollution-control systems. Automakers would then raise their prices to cover the extra costs. If buyers found the price of some cars too high, however, the producers of these cars would disappear. Demand would then move to those producers that could support the sum of the private and social costs.

A second option is to make consumers pay the social costs. For example, many cities around the world are starting to charge congestion tolls in an effort to reduce traffic congestion. To unclog its streets, the city of London now levies a congestion charge of US$16 per day per car to drive in an eight-square-mile area in the city centre. The charge has not only reduced traffic congestion within the zone and increased cycling by 43 percent; it also raises money to shore up London's public transportation system.[19]

Based on London's success, some U.S. cities such as San Diego, Houston, Seattle, and Denver have turned some of their HOV (high-occupancy vehicle) lanes into HOT (high-occupancy toll) lanes for drivers carrying too few passengers. Regular drivers can use the HOT lanes, but they must pay tolls ranging from US$0.50 off-peak to US$9 during rush hour. The

Balancing private and public goods: In response to lane-clogging traffic congestion like that above, London now levies a congestion charge. The charge has reduced congestion and raised money to shore up the city's public transport system.

U.S. government has also proposed a bill rush-hour fees in congested urban areas across the country. If the costs of driving rise high enough, the government hopes consumers will travel at nonpeak times or find alternative transportation modes, ultimately helping to curb America's oil addiction.[20]

Cultural Pollution

Critics charge the marketing system with creating *cultural pollution*. Our senses are being constantly assaulted by marketing and advertising. Television adverts interrupt serious programs; pages of printed adverts obscure magazines; billboards mar beautiful scenery; spam fills our inboxes. These interruptions continually pollute people's minds with messages of materialism, power, or status.[21] As a result, several campaigns were developed to preserve cultural virtues. **Real Marketing 17.1** discusses Al Baraka BelShbab campaign, which emphasizes the importance of cultural and Islamic virtues.

Marketers answer the charges of 'commercial noise' with these arguments: First, they hope that their ads reach primarily the target audience. But because of mass-communication channels, some ads are bound to reach people who have no interest in the product and are therefore bored or annoyed. People who buy magazines addressed to their interests—such as *Vogue* or *Fortune*—rarely complain about the ads because the magazines advertise products of interest.

Secondly, ads make much of television and radio free to users and keep down the costs of magazines and newspapers. Many people think commercials are a small price to pay for these benefits. Consumers find many television commercials entertaining and sometimes seek them out. Finally, today's consumers have alternatives. For example, they can delete television commercials on recorded programs or avoid them altogether on many paid cable or satellite channels. Thus, to hold consumer attention, advertisers are making their ads more entertaining and informative.

Marketing's Impact on Other Businesses

Critics also charge that a company's marketing practices can harm other companies and reduce competition. Three problems are involved: acquisitions of competitors, marketing practices that create barriers to entry, and unfair competitive marketing practices.

Critics claim that firms are harmed and competition reduced when companies expand by acquiring competitors rather than by developing their own new products. The large number of acquisitions and the rapid pace of industry consolidation over the past several decades have caused concern that vigorous young competitors will be absorbed and that competition will be reduced. In virtually every major industry—retailing, entertainment, financial services, utilities, transportation, automobiles, telecommunications, health care—the number of major competitors is shrinking.

Acquisition is a complex subject. Acquisitions can sometimes be good for society. The acquiring company may gain economies of scale that lead to lower costs and lower prices. A well-managed company may take over a poorly managed company and improve its efficiency. An industry that was not very competitive might become more competitive after the acquisition. But acquisitions can also be harmful and, therefore, are closely regulated by the government.

Critics have also charged that marketing practices bar new companies from entering an industry. Large marketing companies can use patents and heavy promotion spending or tie up suppliers or dealers to keep out or drive out competitors. Those concerned with anti-trust regulation recognize that some barriers are the natural result of the economic advantages of doing business on a large scale. Other barriers could be challenged by existing and new laws. For example, some critics have proposed a progressive tax on advertising spending to reduce the role of selling costs as a major barrier to entry.

Finally, some firms have in fact used unfair competitive marketing practices with the intention of hurting or destroying other firms. They may set their prices below costs, threaten to cut off business with suppliers, or discourage the buying of a competitor's products. Various laws work to prevent such predatory competition. It is difficult, however, to prove that the intent or action was really predatory.

In recent years, Wal-Mart has been accused of using predatory pricing in selected market areas to drive smaller retailers out of business. Wal-Mart has become an object for protests by citizens in dozens of towns who worry that the mega-retailer's unfair practices will choke out local businesses. However, whereas critics charge that Wal-Mart's actions are predatory, others assert that its actions are just the healthy competition of a more efficient company against less efficient ones.

For instance, when Wal-Mart recently began a program to sell generic drugs at US$4 a prescription, local pharmacists complained of predatory pricing. They charged that at those low prices, Wal-Mart must be selling under cost to drive them out of business. But Wal-Mart claimed that, given its substantial buying power and efficient operations, it could make a profit at those prices. The US$4 pricing program was not aimed at putting competitors out of business. Rather, it was simply a good competitive move that served customers better and brought more of them in the door.

| **Author Comment** | Sustainable marketing isn't the province of only businesses and governments. Through consumerism and environmentalism, consumers themselves can play an important role. |

Consumer Actions to Promote Sustainable Marketing (pp 506–513)

Sustainable marketing calls for more responsible actions by both businesses and consumers. Because some people view business as the cause of many economic and social ills, grassroots movements have arisen from time to time to keep business in line. The two major movements have been *consumerism* and *environmentalism*.

Consumerism

Some of the major consumer movements have originated in the U.S. The first consumer movement took place in the early 1900s. It was fueled by rising prices, author Upton Sinclair's writings on conditions in the meat industry, and scandals in the drug industry in that country. The second consumer movement, in the mid-1930s, was sparked by an upturn in consumer prices during the Great Depression and another drug scandal.

The third movement began in the 1960s. Consumers had become better educated, products had become more complex and potentially hazardous, and people were unhappy with American institutions. U.S. consumer advocate Ralph Nader appeared on the scene to force many issues, and other well-known writers accused big business of wasteful and unethical practices. U.S. President John F. Kennedy declared that consumers had the right to safety and to be informed, to choose, and to be heard. The U.S. government investigated certain industries and proposed consumer-protection legislation. Since then, many consumer groups have been organized and several consumer laws have been passed. The consumer movement has spread internationally and has become very strong in Europe.

But what is the consumer movement? **Consumerism** is an organized movement of citizens and government agencies to improve the rights and power of buyers in relation to sellers. Traditional *sellers' rights* include:

Consumerism
An organized movement of citizens and government agencies to improve the rights and power of buyers in relation to sellers.

- The right to introduce any product in any size and style, provided it is not hazardous to personal health or safety; or, if it is, to include proper warnings and controls

- The right to charge any price for the product, provided no discrimination exists among similar kinds of buyers

- The right to spend any amount to promote the product, provided it is not defined as unfair competition

- The right to use any product message, provided it is not misleading or dishonest in content or execution

- The right to use any buying incentive programs, provided they are not unfair or misleading.

Real Marketing 17.1

Improving Society Via Cultural and Islamic Virtues

An interesting example of a social responsibility campaign is Al Baraka BelShbab (Blessed Be the Youth), carried out by MBC, the Saudi-managed multi-channel company. The MBC channels broadcast entertainment programs including Hollywood movies and Arabic and Turkish soap operas. These widely watched 'free-to-air' channels are available across different countries in the Arab world.

The Al Baraka BelShbab campaign aims to promote regional cultural virtues. The campaign's messages include helping each other and fostering good behavior. For example, one advert shows a tourist couple asking for directions and being misled by someone, before a man suddenly shows up to guide the tourists in the right direction. Another cultural virtue is exhibited in an advert about repressing revenge when in a position of power. One man comes to fight another man after being provoked, but he holds himself back. In the end, the first man is revealed as a martial arts hero. Another type of behavior that is promoted is obedience and respect for one's parents, a principle mentioned in several Qur'anic verses. The advert shows a young man who is angry with his fatherafter a disagreement about the profession he wants to go into. His friends talk to him and convince him to go for a decision that satisfies both parties.

This is not the only way MBC has delivered messages that preach the good manners promoted by Islam. For example, MBC broadcast an advert to remind Muslims about prayers. This advert featured a man running through shopping malls, school classes, his house, and crowds, when he hears an *Athan* (the call for prayer). He stops to pray, then returns to his daily life. It is clear that this collection of adverts was targeted at a young audience, appealing to them to maintain the principles of Islam while at the same time interacting and being open to society.

The promotion of Islamic rituals has also been the aim of many social responsibility programs of big companies. For example, Etisalat, the large telecommunication operator, provided a number which people could use to

MBC's Al Baraka BelShbab campaign is aimed at young people in the Arab world, and uses television adverts to promote social values.

send their *Zakah* on mobile phones. Abu Dhabi Islamic Bank (ADIB) enabled donors to pay the Zakah to the Zakat Fund, a UAE-based organization dedicated to Islamic charities, by the use of an ATM. Zakah is usually paid in mosques at the end of the month of Ramadan; ADIB just made the process easier.

His Excellency Abdullah bin Aqeeda Al Muhairi, secretary general of Zakat Fund, noted: "Co-operating with such a reputed bank like ADIB reflects the success of our operating plans, programs and strategies which aim at facilitating the collection, calculation and disbursement of Zakat money through collaborating with various social establishments and authorities in the country." Those practices, providing more flexible means of payment, certainly helped more donors to pay the Zakah. "We highly appreciate the interest of ADIB's management and their efforts in activating the services of collecting Zakat money from its customers, the thing which would eventually help increase Zakat Fund revenues," added Al Muhairi.

Trad Mahmoud, CEO of ADIB, stated that: "ADIB is very interested in co-ordinating with Zakat Fund to collect Zakat money from our clients…responding to Islamic teachings that [place emphasis] on helping people doing charitable deeds."

Corporate social responsibility has been used in various other appeals to promote Islamic values. One of the most popular campaigns, which became wide spread throughout Egypt and other Arab countries, is *Hemaya* (Protection) against drugs addiction, led by one of *Time* magazine's 100 most influential people, the Muslim televangelist Amr Khaled. This campaign to end drugs abuse was a collaboration between the United Nations Office on Drugs and Crime (UNODC), Right Start Foundation, and the Dubai Police, among other Arab government representatives. In the first phase of the project, the aim was to raise awareness of the campaign logo and what it stood for, with three million posters and stickers being distributed. The campaign aimed to reach 5,000 drug addicts, and in the second phase of the project, 2,300 addicts were to be given proper rehabilitation. The main goal of the campaign was to encourage young people to volunteer in the quest to improve society.

Such impressive initiatives indicate the need to promote good behavior in order to improve society. Linking good behavior to Islamic principles is appealing and accepted, and linking such principles to modern life is considered the best way to ensure the right impact is made on Arab societies.

Sources: Information at MBC website, www.mbc.net; "Zakat Fund Collaborates with Abu Dhabi Islamic Bank to Collect Zakat Money," press release accessed at Zawya, August 22, 2010, www.zawya.com; Dalia Rabie, "Preacher, Teacher or Social Worker, Amr Khaled Is a Man on a Mission," *Daily News Egypt,* March 28, 2008, www.dailystaregypt.com.

Traditional *buyers' rights* include:

- The right not to buy a product that is offered for sale
- The right to expect the product to be safe
- The right to expect the product to perform as claimed.

Comparing these rights, many believe that the balance of power lies on the seller's side. True, the buyer can refuse to buy. But critics feel that the buyer has too little information, education, and protection to make wise decisions when facing sophisticated sellers. Consumer advocates call for the following additional consumer rights:

- The right to be well informed about important aspects of the product
- The right to be protected against questionable products and marketing practices
- The right to influence products and marketing practices in ways that will improve the 'quality of life'
- The right to consume now in a way that will preserve the world for future generations of consumers.

Each proposed right has led to more specific proposals by consumerists. The right to be informed includes the right to know the true interest on a loan (truth in lending), the true cost per unit of a brand (unit pricing), the ingredients in a product (ingredient labeling), the nutritional value of foods (nutritional labeling), product freshness (open dating), and the true benefits of a product (truth in advertising). Proposals related to consumer protection include strengthening consumer rights in cases of business fraud, requiring greater product safety, ensuring information privacy, and giving more power to government agencies. Proposals relating to quality of life include controlling the ingredients that go into certain products and packaging and reducing the level of advertising 'noise.' Proposals for preserving the world for future consumption include promoting the use of sustainable ingredients, recycling and reducing solid wastes, and managing energy consumption.

Sustainable marketing is up to consumers as well as to businesses and governments. Consumers have not only the *right* but also the *responsibility* to protect themselves instead of leaving this function to someone else. Consumers who believe they got a bad deal have several remedies available, including contacting the company or the media; contacting government agencies; and going to small-claims courts. Consumers should also make good consumption choices, rewarding companies that act responsibly while punishing those that don't.

Consumer desire for more information led to labels with useful facts, from ingredients and nutrition facts to recycling and country of origin information.

Environmentalism

Environmentalism
An organized movement of concerned citizens and government agencies to protect and improve people's current and future living environment.

Whereas consumerists consider whether the marketing system is efficiently serving consumer wants, environmentalists are concerned with marketing's effects on the environment and with the environmental costs of serving consumer needs and wants. **Environmentalism** is an organized movement of concerned citizens, businesses, and government agencies to protect and improve people's current and future living environment.

Environmentalists are not against marketing and consumption; they simply want people and organizations to operate with more care for the environment. The marketing system's goal, they assert, should not be to maximize consumption, consumer choice, or consumer satisfaction, but rather to maximize life quality. And 'life quality' means not only the quantity and quality of consumer goods and services, but also the quality of the environment. Environmentalists want current and future environmental costs included in both producer and consumer decision making.

The ideas of environmentalism are relatively new to the Arab world. With oil wealth so great in the period up to the 1990s, governments, planners, and ordinary citizens could ignore the toxic chemicals, air pollutants, and other waste products generated by oil-related processes.

An event that caused a dramatic shift in thinking during the 1990s was the destruction of Kuwaiti oil wells during Iraq's retreat in the 1991 war. The clouds of acrid smoke and the oil slicks from damaged tankers gradually passed down the Gulf. All governments in the region were forced to adopt environmental protection policies. Environmental protection legislation now exists, or is being developed, in virtually all MENA countries.

The primary motive for this is to maintain clean beaches and safe drinking water. But governments are also trying to work out their response to other environmental issues. For example, how they can manage the explosive growth in their working age populations? In some countries the working-age population is rising at over five per cent per year. Many are considering tourism and other environment-sensitive industries as a way to generate greatly needed jobs.

There is also environmental pressure linked to traditional industries like fisheries and agriculture. All of these are looking for better environmental standards in order to maximize productivity. In particular, there is pressure on the petrochemical sector to take a more environmentally sound approach to handling toxic waste.[22]

The first two environmentalism waves have now merged into a third and stronger wave in which companies are accepting more responsibility for doing no harm to the environment. They are shifting from protest to prevention, and from regulation to responsibility. More and more companies are adopting policies of **environmental sustainability**. Simply put, environmental sustainability is about generating profits while helping to save the planet. Environmental sustainability is a crucial but difficult societal goal.

Some companies have responded to consumer environmental concerns by doing only what is required to avert new regulations or to keep environmentalists quiet. Enlightened companies, however, are taking action not because someone is forcing them to, or to reap short-run profits, but because it is the right thing to do—for both the company and for the planet's environmental future.

◀ **Figure 17.2** shows a grid that companies can use to gage their progress toward environmental sustainability. It includes both internal and external 'greening' activities that will pay off for the firm and environment in the short run, and 'beyond greening' activities that will pay off in the longer term. At the most basic level, a company can practice *pollution prevention*. This involves more than pollution control—cleaning up waste after it has been created. Pollution prevention means eliminating or minimizing waste before it is created. Companies emphasizing prevention have responded with internal 'green marketing' programs—designing and developing ecologically safer products, recyclable and biodegradable packaging, better pollution controls, and more energy-efficient operations.

For example, the UAE made a significant 'greening' move in 2006. It published plans for a 6 kilometer-square eco-city called *Masdar* ('the source' in Arabic). In the words of Associate Project Director Dr Nawal Al Hosany, its aim is "to be the world's centre for

---

Environmental sustainability

A management approach that involves developing strategies that both sustain the environment and produce profits for the company.

◀ **FIGURE | 17.2**

The Environmental Sustainability Portfolio

Source: Stuart L. Hart, "Innovation, Creative Destruction, and Sustainability," *Research Technology Management*, September–October 2005, pp. 21–27.

	Today: Greening	**Tomorrow: Beyond Greening**
Internal	**Pollution prevention** Eliminating or reducing waste before it is created	**New clean technology** Developing new sets of environmental skills and capabilities
External	**Product stewardship** Minimizing environmental impact throughout the entire product life cycle	**Sustainability vision** Creating a strategic framework for future sustainability

How does 'environmental sustainability' relate to 'marketing sustainability'? Environmental sustainability involves preserving the natural environment, whereas marketing sustainability is a broader concept that involves both the natural and social environments—pretty much everything in this chapter.

Masdar's vision is to make Abu Dhabi the preeminent source of renewable energy knowledge, development, and implementation and the world's benchmark for sustainable development.

future energy solutions." The 81 billion Dhs plan (US$22 billion) has two main purposes: to foster sustainable development in the UAE and to encourage economic diversification through development of the alternative energy sector.

The eco-city is being built on principles of efficiency in the use of energy and other resources. For example, electricity is to be generated by solar panels, and water consumption will be significantly reduced by irrigating landscaping with treated waste water. The city is being designed to enable and encourage walking and cycling, but the city's estimated 1,500 businesses and 40,000 residents will be served by over 3,000 automated passenger vehicles, or Personal Rapid Transits (PRTs).

Overall, the radical Masdar initiative aims to be carbon neutral, car-free, and result in zero waste. It will also host the Institute of Science and Technology and the International Renewable Energy Agency (IRENA), in the hope that Abu Dhabi will become a hub of global knowledge for environmental protection.[23]

Other examples include Nike, which produces PVC-free shoes, recycles old sneakers, and educates young people about conservation, reuse, and recycling. General Mills shaved 20 percent off the paperboard packaging for its Hamburger Helper product, resulting in 500 fewer distribution trucks on the road each year. Sun Microsystems created its Open Work program that gives employees the option to work from home, preventing nearly 29,000 tons of CO_2 emissions, while at the same time saving US$67.8 million in real-estate costs and increasing worker productivity by 34 percent. And UPS continues to develop a 'green fleet' of alternative-fuel vehicles to replace its old fleet of diesel delivery trucks. In 2009 it deployed 200 new next-generation hybrid electric delivery vehicles to join the roughly 2,000 low-carbon, hybrid and compressed natural gas vehicles already in use. The hybrid vehicles produce 45 percent better fuel economy and a dramatic decrease in vehicle emissions.[24]

At the next level, companies can practice *product stewardship*—minimizing not just pollution from production and product design but all environmental impacts throughout the full product life cycle, and all the while reducing costs. Many companies are adopting *design for environment (DFE)* and *cradle-to-cradle* practices. This involves thinking ahead to design products that are easier to recover, reuse, recycle, or safely return to nature after usage, becoming part of the ecological cycle. DFE and cradle-to-cradle practices not only help to sustain the environment, they can also be highly profitable for the company.

An example is Xerox Corporation's Equipment Remanufacture and Parts Reuse Program, which converts end-of-life office equipment into new products and parts. Equipment returned to Xerox can be remanufactured reusing 70 to 90 percent by weight of old machine components, while still meeting performance standards for equipment made with all new parts. The program creates benefits for both the environment and for the company. So far, it has diverted nearly two billion pounds of waste from landfills. And it reduces the amount of raw material and energy needed to produce new parts. Energy savings from parts reuse total an estimated 320,000 megawatt hours annually—enough energy to light more than 250,000 homes for a year.[25]

Today's 'greening' activities focus on improving what companies already do to protect the environment. The 'beyond greening' activities identified in **Figure 17.2** look to the future. First, internally, companies can plan for *new clean technology*. Many organizations that have made good sustainability headway are still limited by existing technologies.

New clean technologies: Coca-Cola is investing heavily to build a state-of-the-art plastic-bottle-to-bottle recycling plant. It's also researching new alternatives such as bottles made from corn or bioplastics.

To create fully sustainable strategies, they will need to develop innovative new technologies. For example, Coca-Cola is investing heavily in research addressing many sustainability issues:[26]

From a sustainability viewpoint, for Coca-Cola, an aluminum can is an ideal package. Aluminum can be recycled indefinitely. Put a Coke can in a recycling bin, and the aluminum finds its way back to a store shelf in about six weeks. The trouble is, people prefer clear plastic bottles with screw-on tops. Plastic bottles account for nearly 50 percent of Coke's global volume, three times more than aluminum cans. And they are not currently sustainable. They're made from oil, a finite resource. Most end up in landfill sites or, worse, as roadside trash. They can't be recycled indefinitely because the plastic discolors. To attack this waste problem, Coca-Cola will invest about US$44 million to build the world's largest state-of-the-art plastic-bottle-to-bottle recycling plant. As a more permanent solution, the company is researching new ideas such as bottles made from corn or bioplastics.

Coke is also investing in new clean technologies to solve other environmental issues. For example, about ten million or so vending machines and refrigerated coolers use potent greenhouse gases called HFCs to keep Cokes cold. To eliminate them, the company invested US$40 million in research and formed a refrigeration alliance with McDonald's and even competitor PepsiCo. Coca-Cola has also promised to become 'water neutral' by researching ways to help its bottlers waste less water and ways to protect or replenish watersheds around the world.

Finally, companies can develop a *sustainability vision*, which serves as a guide to the future. It shows how the company's products and services, processes, and policies must evolve and what new technologies must be developed to get there. This vision of sustainability provides a framework for pollution control, product stewardship, and new environmental technology for the company and others to follow.

Most companies today focus on the upper-left quadrant of the grid in **Figure 17.2**, investing most heavily in pollution prevention. Some forward-looking companies practice product stewardship and are developing new environmental technologies. Few companies have well-defined sustainability visions. However, emphasizing only one or a few quadrants in the environmental sustainability grid can be shortsighted. Investing only in the left half of the grid puts a company in a good position today but leaves it vulnerable in the future. In contrast, a heavy emphasis on the right half suggests that a company has good environmental vision but lacks the skills needed to implement it. Thus, companies should work at developing all four dimensions of environmental sustainability.

Wal-Mart, for example, is doing just that. Through its own environmental sustainability actions and its impact on the actions of suppliers, Wal-Mart has emerged in recent years as the world's super 'eco-nanny.' Alcoa, the world's leading producer of aluminum, is also setting a high sustainability standard. For four years running it has been named one of the most sustainable corporations in the annual Global 100 Most Sustainable Corporations in the World ranking:

Alcoa has distinguished itself as a leader through its sophisticated approach to identifying and managing the material sustainability risks that it faces as a company. From pollution prevention via greenhouse gas emissions reduction programs to engaging stakeholders over new environmental technology, such as controversial hydropower projects, Alcoa has the sustainability strategies in place needed to meld its profitability objectives with society's larger environmental protection goals.... Importantly, Alcoa's approach to sustainability is firmly rooted in the idea that sustainability programs can indeed add financial value. Perhaps the best evidence is the company's efforts to promote the use of aluminum in transportation, where aluminum—with its excellent strength-to-weight ratio—is making inroads as a material of choice that allows automakers to build low-weight, fuel-efficient vehicles that produce fewer tailpipe emissions. This kind of forward-thinking strategy of supplying the market with the products that will help solve pressing global environmental problems shows a company that sees the future, has plotted a course, and is aligning its business accordingly. Says CEO Alain Belda, "Our values require us to think and act not only on the present challenges, but also with the legacy in mind that we leave for those who will come after us...as well as the commitments made by those that came before us."[27]

Environmentalism creates some special challenges for global marketers. As international trade barriers come down and global markets expand, environmental issues are having an ever-greater impact on international trade. Countries in western Europe, North America, and other developed regions are generating strict environmental standards. The European Union has passed 'end-of-life' regulations affecting automobiles and consumer electronics products. And the EU's Eco-Management and Audit Scheme (EMAS) provides guidelines for environmental self-regulation. In the United States, more than two dozen major pieces of environmental legislation have been enacted since 1970, and recent events suggest that more regulation is on the way. A side accord to the North American Free Trade Agreement (NAFTA) set up the Commission for Environmental Cooperation resolving environmental matters. From 2011, following U.S. National Emissions Standards for Hazardous Air Pollutants (NESHAP) regulations, GCC has implemented an environmental surcharge of US$7.00 per ton on all bulk cement and US$0.50 per bag. These regulations relate to all of the U.S. cement industry and will cause significant ongoing increases in production costs. The GCC has responded by applying the surcharge, and is gradually committing to make investments to lead the private–public partnership toward a more environmental approach to the building industry.[28]

However, environmental policies still vary widely from country to country. Countries such as Denmark, Germany, Japan, and the United States have fully developed environmental policies and high public expectations. But major countries such as China, India, Brazil, Russia and most of the countries of the Arab world are in only the early stages of developing such policies. Moreover, environmental factors that motivate consumers in one country may have no impact on consumers in another. For example, PVC soft-drink bottles cannot be used in Switzerland or Germany. However, they are preferred in France, which has an extensive recycling process for them. Thus, international companies have found it difficult to develop standard environmental practices that work around the world. Instead, they are creating general policies and then translating these policies into tailored programs that meet local regulations and expectations.

Public Actions to Regulate Marketing

Citizens' concerns about marketing practices will usually lead to public attention and legislative proposals. New bills will be debated—many will be defeated, others will be modified, and a few will become workable laws.

Many of the laws that affect marketing are listed in Chapter 3. The task is to translate these laws into the language that marketing executives understand as they make decisions about competitive relations, products, price, promotion, and channels of distribution. ◀ **Figure 17.3** illustrates the major legal issues facing marketing management.

◣FIGURE | 17.3
Major Marketing Decision Areas
that May Be Called Into Question
Under the Law

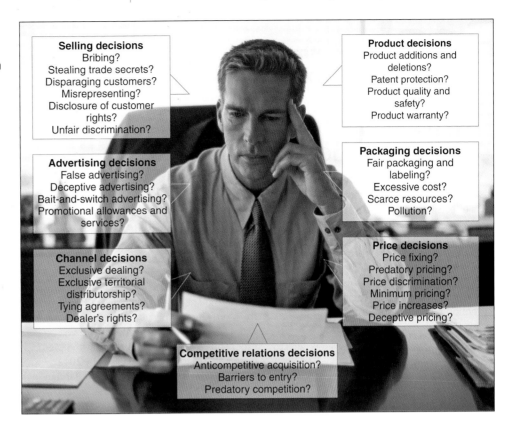

◣FIGURE | 17.3
Major Marketing Decision Areas
that May Be Called Into Question
Under the Law

Selling decisions
Bribing?
Stealing trade secrets?
Disparaging customers?
Misrepresenting?
Disclosure of customer
rights?
Unfair discrimination?

Product decisions
Product additions and
deletions?
Patent protection?
Product quality and
safety?
Product warranty?

Advertising decisions
False advertising?
Deceptive advertising?
Bait-and-switch advertising?
Promotional allowances and
services?

Packaging decisions
Fair packaging and
labeling?
Excessive cost?
Scarce resources?
Pollution?

Channel decisions
Exclusive dealing?
Exclusive territorial
distributorship?
Tying agreements?
Dealer's rights?

Price decisions
Price fixing?
Predatory pricing?
Price discrimination?
Minimum pricing?
Price increases?
Deceptive pricing?

Competitive relations decisions
Anticompetitive acquisition?
Barriers to entry?
Predatory competition?

Author Comment | In the end, marketers themselves must take responsibility for sustainable marketing. That means operating in a responsible and ethical way to bring immediate and future value to customers.

Business Actions Toward Sustainable Marketing (pp 513–517)

At first, many companies opposed consumerism, environmentalism, and other elements of sustainable marketing. They thought the criticisms were either unfair or unimportant. But by now, most companies have grown to embrace the new consumer rights, at least in principle. They might oppose certain pieces of legislation as inappropriate ways to solve specific consumer problems, but they recognize the consumer's right to information and protection. Many of these companies have responded positively to sustainable marketing as a way to create greater immediate and future customer value and to strengthen customer relationships.

Sustainable Marketing Principles

Under the sustainable marketing concept, a company's marketing should support the best long-run performance of the marketing system. It should be guided by five sustainable marketing principles: *consumer-oriented marketing*, *customer-value marketing*, *innovative marketing*, *sense-of-mission marketing*, and *societal marketing*.

Consumer-Oriented Marketing

Consumer-oriented marketing
The philosophy of sustainable marketing that holds that the company should view and organize its marketing activities from the consumer's point of view.

Consumer-oriented marketing means that the company should view and organize its marketing activities from the consumer's point of view. It should work hard to sense, serve, and satisfy the needs of a defined group of customers, both now and in the future. All of the good marketing companies that we've discussed in this text have had this in common: an all-consuming passion for delivering superior value to carefully chosen customers. Only by seeing the world through its customers' eyes can the company build lasting and profitable customer relationships. An example of this for Muslim communities is explored in **Real Marketing 17.2**.

Real Marketing 17.2

Takaful:
A True Customer-Driven Product

We are at risk of some type of loss from unforeseen events. To minimize this risk, or its effects, insurance has existed since at least 215 BC. Insurance is defined as the equitable transfer of the risk of a loss, from one entity to another, in exchange for payment.

Insurance, as a concept, is not accepted in the Islamic world owing to several factors. Five important differences distinguish conventional insurance from its Islamic alternative, Takaful:

1. Conventional insurance inevitably involves some element of uncertainty (*gharar*) in the contract of insurance.
2. Insurance can be seen to be gambling (*maysir*) on the consequences of uncertainty in future outcomes.
3. Conventional insurance companies gain interest (*riba*) from their investment activities.
4. Conventional insurance companies are motivated by needing to make a profit to satisfy their shareholders.
5. The conventional system of insurance can be exploited. For example, an insurance company (especially in a monopolistic situation) can charge an excessively high premium, with the resulting profit going to the company.

Many Islamic scholars forbid the purchase of traditional insurance. According to the European Council for Fatwa and Research, "Commercial insurance is originally *Haram* as agreed upon by most contemporary scholars. It is well known that in most non-Islamic countries there are co-operative and mutual insurance companies. There is no harm from the Shari'ah point of view to participate in these services. So, it is unlawful for a Muslim living in a country where there is such a co-operative insurance company to make an agreement with a commercial insurance company. But, if a co-operative insurance company is not found one may enter into a contract with a commercial insurance company only by way of necessity. If a person is forced by law to insurance or by way of need, it is obligatory for him to be content with the minimum proportion of insurance that covers his need or to the minimum of such transaction he's being forced to carry out."

The Islamic concept of insurance is Shari'ah-compliant. Known as *Takaful* (an Arabic word meaning 'guaranteeing each other'), it is an arrangement of mutual risk transfer which involves participants and operators. Takaful differs from conventional insurance in how the risk is assessed and handled, and in how the Takaful fund is managed. There are also differences in the relationship between the operator (the insurer) and the participants (the insured or the assured). In risk assessment (underwriting) and handling, Takaful does not allow what is called *Gharar*, *Maisir*, and *Riba*.

The Takaful industry in 2007 was broadly estimated to be worth over US$3.5 billion, for both life and nonlife business cover. The industry is growing 20 percent year on year, but with careful management the growth will be exponential—estimates indicate that the premiums are set to top US$10 billion by 2012.

Consider the Central Bank of Bahrain (CBB). This bank was named Best Financial Centre at the second annual International Takaful Awards in 2009, ahead of the Dubai International Financial Centre and the Malaysia International Islamic Finance Centre. 2008 witnessed the expansion of Bahrain's Takaful sector, with overall gross premiums reaching US$72.2 million, up from US$41.7 million in 2007—a 73 percent increase, building on the 58 percent increase from 2006 to 2007.

Recognizing the huge market demand, American International Group (AIG), the world's largest insurer, opened a unit in Bahrain, becoming the latest company to offer policies that comply with Islamic principles in an attempt to capture some of the market share of 1.6 billion Muslims. The global market for Takaful is estimated to reach US$14 billion by 2015, according to HSBC. Charles Bouloux, the AIG unit's chairman, said, "There are about 300 million Muslims we think could become new insurance buyers if the right products, ones that fit their beliefs, are actively sold to them." AIG Takaful, also known as *Enaya*, or 'solidarity' in English, started in 2006 with

US$15 million of capital which, according to Bouloux, "will expand significantly as our capability grows.... For a small capital commitment AIG is gaining a platform to sell a whole range of products." Premium rates are rising between 12 and 15 percent a year in the Middle Eastern and South Asian markets, compared with an average 9 percent decline in non-life premium rates outside the United States in 2006.

Outside the GCC, AIG stepped up to become the first company to offer Islamic homeowners Takaful in the U.S. with plans to expand into auto and other insurance products. In the U.S. Takaful is issued through AIG's underwriting subsidiary, Risk Specialist Companies, and through Lexington Insurance. New York-based Islamic financial services firm Zayan Finance is the exclusive broker for the product, which is currently offered in 13 states. "We hope to be in every state by the end of the year," said Nasser Nubani, spokesman for Zayan Finance, who expects to substantially improve on the several hundred policies that have so far been sold. "We are pleased to offer socially responsible solutions to this segment of the domestic market," said Matthew F. Power, president of Risk Specialist Companies.

T'azur, a Bahrain-based company, has launched a new Takaful product, which it claims is the world's first charitable insurance product, called *Sadaqah*. The Sadaqah plan is a form of donation which t'azur invests in Shari'ah-compliant funds over a fixed number of years. When the product matures, the fund is donated to a charity chosen by the donor. If unforeseen circumstances prevent the donor from making charitable donations (perhaps because of disability or critical illness) t'azur will continue to make regular donations on the donor's behalf. This ensures that the charity will receive the intended donation whatever unforeseen event may have occurred. "The Sadaqah Plan is to our knowledge the world's first insured charitable savings plan," said Nikolaus Frei, t'azur's chief executive.

Sources: Quotes from the European Council for Fatwa and Research, cited at "About Takaful Insurance," ICMIF Takaful, www.takaful.coop; "AIG Enters Islamic Insurance Market," *The Royal Gazette*, October 3, 2010; Shahzad Chaudhary, "IslamicInsurance Gains Toehold in U.S.," Medill Reports Chicago, August 26, 2009, http://news.medill.northwestern.edu/chicago/news.aspx?id=139219; Chelsea Schilling, "Bailed-out AIG Offers Islamic Insurance to U.S.," WorldNetDaily, December 5, 2008, www.wnd.com; "T'azur Launches First Charitable Islamic Insurance Product of Its Kind," *AME Info*, September 2, 2009, www.ameinfo.com/208353.html; additional information from the Institute of Islamic Banking and Insurance, www.islamic-banking.com; Suzanne White, "Islamic Insurance Markets and the Structure of Takaful," *Qfinance*, www.qfinance.com; Buby Kubursi, "Challenges for New Growth," *Islamic Banking & Finance,* January 1, 2009; "About Us," Chartis website, www.chartisinsurance.com; and various regional news outlets.

This case was provided by Mohamed Radwan, adjunct faculty member at the American University in Cairo and managing director for Platinum Partners.

Customer-Value Marketing

Customer-value marketing

A principle of sustainable marketing that holds that a company should put most of its resources into customer-value-building marketing investments.

According to the principle of **customer-value marketing**, the company should put most of its resources into customer-value-building marketing investments. Many things marketers do—one-shot sales promotions, cosmetic packaging changes, direct-response advertising—may raise sales in the short run but add less *value* than would actual improvements in the product's quality, features, or convenience. Enlightened marketing calls for building long-run consumer loyalty and relationships by continually improving the value consumers receive from the firm's market offering. By creating value *for* consumers, the company can capture value *from* consumers in return.

Innovative Marketing

Innovative marketing

A principle of sustainable marketing that requires that a company seek real product and marketing improvements.

The principle of **innovative marketing** requires that the company continuously seek real product and marketing improvements. The company that overlooks new and better ways to do things will eventually lose customers to another company that has found a better way. An excellent example of an innovative marketer is Nintendo:[29]

After Sony and Microsoft kicked the Mario out of Nintendo's GameCube in the Video Game War of 2001, the smallest of the three game platform makers needed a new plan. "Nintendo took a step back from the technology arms race and chose to focus on [customers and] the fun of playing, rather than cold tech specs," says the president of Nintendo of America. The resulting Wii system, with its intuitive motion-sensitive controller and interactive games, appealed not only to teen boys typically targeted by the game industry but also to their sisters, moms, dads, and even grandparents. The result: the perpetually sold-out Wii system quickly outsold both the PlayStation 3 and Xbox 360. But get this: Unlike its competitors—which lose money on each console and earn it back on software—Nintendo actually turns a profit on its consoles, makes more selling games, then takes in still more in licensing fees. "Not to sound too obvious," says the Nintendo executive, "but it makes good business sense to make a profit on the products you sell." Wall Street thinks so too. The company's stock has more than doubled over the past year. Nintendo's upset is doing more than attracting new gamers and bruising Sony and Microsoft. Says the president of Sega of America, "It has opened doors of creativity throughout the video-game business."

Innovative marketing: Nintendo's customer-focused innovation not only attracted new gamers and bruised competitors Sony and Microsoft, "it has opened doors of creativity throughout the video-game business."

Sense-of-Mission Marketing

Sense-of-mission marketing

A principle of sustainable marketing that holds that a company should define its mission in broad social terms rather than narrow product terms.

Sense-of-mission marketing means that the company should define its mission in broad *social* terms rather than narrow *product* terms. When a company defines a social mission, employees feel better about their work and have a clearer sense of direction. Brands linked with broader missions can serve the best long-run interests of both the brand and consumers. For example, Dove wants to do more than just sell its beauty care products. It's on a mission to discover "real beauty" and to help women be happy just the way they are:[30]

It all started with a Unilever study that examined the impact on women of images seen in entertainment, in advertising, and on fashion runways. The startling result: Only 2 percent of 3,300 women and girls surveyed in 10 countries around the world considered themselves beautiful. Unilever's conclusion: It's time to redefine beauty. So in 2004, Unilever launched the global Dove Campaign for Real Beauty, with ads that featured candid and confident images of real women of all types (not actresses or models) and headlines that made consumers ponder their perceptions of beauty.

The Dove Campaign for Real Beauty quickly went digital, with a campaign for real beauty .com website and award-winning viral videos with names such as "Evolution" and "Onslaught" that attacked damaging beauty stereotypes. As the campaign has taken off, so have sales of Dove products. But the people behind the Dove brand and the Campaign for Real Beauty have noble motives beyond sales and profits. According to a Unilever executive, Dove's bold and compelling mission to redefine beauty and reassure women ranks well above issues of dollars and cents. "You should see the faces of the people working on this brand now," he says. "There is a real love for the brand."

Societal Marketing

Following the principle of **societal marketing**, a company makes marketing decisions by considering consumers' wants and interests, the company's requirements, and society's long-run interests. The company is aware that neglecting consumer and societal long-run interests is a disservice to consumers and society. Alert companies view societal problems as opportunities.

Sustainable marketing calls for products that are not only pleasing but also beneficial. The difference is shown in **Figure 17.4**. Products can be classified according to their degree of immediate consumer satisfaction and long-run consumer benefit. **Deficient products**, such as bad-tasting and ineffective medicine, have neither immediate appeal nor long-run benefits. **Pleasing products** give high immediate satisfaction but may hurt consumers in the long run. Examples include cigarettes and junk food. **Salutary products** have low immediate appeal but may benefit consumers in the long run; for instance, bicycle helmets or some insurance products. **Desirable products** give both high immediate satisfaction and high long-run benefits, such as a tasty *and* nutritious breakfast food.

Examples of desirable products abound. GE's Energy Smart compact fluorescent light bulb provides good lighting at the same time that it gives long life and energy savings. Toyota's hybrid Prius gives both a quiet ride and fuel efficiency. Maytag's front-loading Neptune washer provides superior cleaning along with water savings and energy efficiency. And Haworth's Zody office chair is not only attractive and functional but also environmentally responsible:

Chances are, your chair is made of a horrible mix of polyvinyl chloride and hazardous chemicals that drift into your lungs each time you shift your weight. It was likely produced in a fossil-fuel-swilling factory that in turn spews toxic pollution and effluents. And it's ultimately destined for a landfill or incinerator, where it will emit carcinogenic dioxins and endocrine-disrupting phthalates, the kind of hormone-mimicking nasties that give male fish female genitalia and small children cancer (or is it the other way around?). Now, envision what you might be sitting on in 2016. Actually, never mind: Office-furniture outfit Haworth already built it. It's called the Zody, and

---

Societal marketing
A principle of sustainable marketing that holds that a company should make marketing decisions by considering consumers' wants, the company's requirements, consumers' long-run interests, and society's long-run interests.

Deficient products
Products that have neither immediate appeal nor long-run benefits.

Pleasing products
Products that give high immediate satisfaction but may hurt consumers in the long run.

Salutary products
Products that have low appeal but may benefit consumers in the long run.

Desirable products
Products that give both high immediate satisfaction and high long-run benefits.

FIGURE | 17.4
Societal Classification of Products

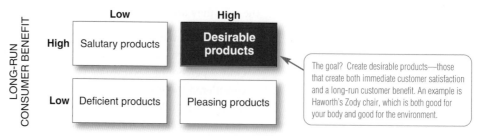

Desirable products: Haworth's Zody office chair is not only attractive and functional but also environmentally responsible.

it's made without PVC, CFCs, chrome, or any toxic materials. Ninety-eight percent of it can be recycled; some 50 percent of it already has been. The energy used in the manufacturing process is completely offset by wind-power credits, and when the chair is ready to retire, the company will take it off your hands and reuse its components. And the award-winning Zody's not just good for the environment, it's also good for your body. It was the first chair to be endorsed by the American Physical Therapy Association.[31]

Companies should try to turn all of their products into desirable products. The challenge posed by pleasing products is that they sell very well but may end up hurting the consumer. The product opportunity, therefore, is to add long-run benefits without reducing the product's pleasing qualities. The challenge posed by salutary products is to add some pleasing qualities so that they will become more desirable in consumers' minds.

Marketing Ethics (pp 517–519)

Good ethics is a cornerstone of sustainable marketing. In the long run, unethical marketing harms customers and society as a whole. Further, it eventually damages a company's reputation and effectiveness, jeopardizing the company's very survival. Thus, the sustainable marketing goals of long-term consumer and business welfare can be achieved only through ethical marketing conduct.

Conscientious marketers face many moral dilemmas. The best thing to do is often unclear. Because not all managers have fine moral sensitivity, companies need to develop *corporate marketing ethics policies*—broad guidelines that everyone in the organization must follow. These policies should cover distributor relations, advertising standards, customer service, pricing, product development, and general ethical standards.

The finest guidelines cannot resolve all the difficult ethical situations the marketer faces. ● **Table 17.1** lists some difficult ethical issues marketers could face during their careers. If marketers choose immediate sales-producing actions in all these cases, their marketing behavior might well be described as immoral or even amoral. If they refuse to go along with *any* of the actions, they might be ineffective as marketing managers and unhappy because of the constant moral tension. Managers need a set of principles that will help them figure out the moral importance of each situation and decide how far they can go in good conscience.

But *what* principle should guide companies and marketing managers on issues of ethics and social responsibility? One philosophy is that such issues are decided by the free market and legal system. Under this principle, companies and their managers are not responsible for making moral judgments. Companies can in good conscience do whatever the market and legal systems allow.

A second philosophy puts responsibility not on the system but in the hands of individual companies and managers. This more enlightened philosophy suggests that a company should have a 'social conscience.' Companies and managers should apply high standards of ethics and morality when making corporate decisions, regardless of 'what the system allows.' History provides an endless list of examples of company actions that were legal but highly irresponsible.

Each company and marketing manager must work out a philosophy of socially responsible and ethical behavior. Under the societal marketing concept, each manager must look beyond what is legal and allowed and develop standards based on personal integrity, corporate conscience, and long-run consumer welfare. A clear and responsible philosophy will help the company deal with knotty issues such as the one faced by 3M:

In late 1997, a powerful new research technique for scanning blood kept turning up the same odd result: Tiny amounts of a chemical 3M had made for nearly 40 years

● **TABLE | 17.1** Some Morally Difficult Situations in Marketing

1. You work for a cigarette company. Public policy debates over the past many years leave no doubt in your mind that cigarette smoking and cancer are closely linked. Although your company currently runs an 'If you don't smoke, don't start' promotion campaign, you believe that other company promotions might encourage young (although legal age) nonsmokers to pick up the habit. What would you do?

2. Your R&D department has changed one of your products slightly. It is not really 'new and improved,' but you know that putting this statement on the package and in advertising will increase sales. What would you do?

3. You have been asked to add a stripped-down version of a product to your line that could be advertised to pull customers into the store. The product won't be very good, but salespeople will be able to switch buyers up to higher-priced units. You are asked to give the green light for the stripped-down version. What would you do?

4. You are thinking of hiring a product manager who has just left a competitor's company. She would be more than happy to tell you all the competitor's plans for the coming year. What would you do?

5. One of your top dealers in an important territory recently has had family troubles, and his sales have slipped. It looks like it will take him a while to straighten out his family trouble. Meanwhile you are losing many sales. Legally, on performance grounds, you can terminate the dealer's franchise and replace him. What would you do?

6. You have a chance to win a big account that will mean a lot to you and your company. The purchasing agent hints that a ' gift' would influence the decision. Your assistant recommends sending a big-screen HDTV to the buyer's home. What would you do?

7. You have heard that a competitor has a new product feature that will make a big difference in sales. The competitor will demonstrate the feature in a private dealer meeting at the annual trade show. You can easily send a snooper to this meeting to learn about the new feature. What would you do?

8. You have to choose between three ad campaigns outlined by your agency. The first (a) is a soft-sell, honest, straight-information campaign. The second (b) uses emotional appeals and exaggerates the product's benefits. The third (c) involves a noisy, somewhat irritating commercial that is sure to gain audience attention. Pretests show that the campaigns are effective in the following order: c, b, and a. What would you do?

9. You are interviewing a capable female applicant for a job as salesperson. She is better qualified than the men just interviewed. Nevertheless, you know that in your industry some important customers prefer dealing with men, and you will lose some sales if you hire her. What would you do?

---

were showing up in blood drawn from people living all across the United States. If the results held up, it meant that virtually all Americans may be carrying some minuscule amount of the chemical, called perfluorooctanesulfonate (PFOS), in their systems. Even though at the time they had yet to come up with a definitive answer as to what harm the chemical might cause, the company reached a drastic decision. In mid-2000, although under no mandate to act, 3M voluntarily phased out products containing PFOS and related chemicals, including its popular Scotchgard fabric protector. This was no easy decision. Since there was as yet no replacement chemical, it meant a potential loss of US$500 million in annual sales. 3M's voluntary actions drew praise from regulators. "3M deserves great credit for identifying the problem and coming forward," says an Environmental Protection Agency administrator. "It took guts," comments another government scientist. "The fact is that most companies…go into anger, denial, and the rest of that stuff. [We're used to seeing] decades-long arguments about whether a chemical is really toxic." For 3M, however, it wasn't all that difficult a decision—it was simply the right thing to do. The company has since introduced reformulated Scotchgard products that it claims work even better than the original formula—and sell just as well.[32]

As with environmentalism, the issue of ethics presents special challenges for international marketers. Business standards and practices vary a great deal from one country to the next. For example, whereas bribes and kickbacks are illegal for U.S. firms, they are standard business practice in many South American countries. One recent study found that companies from some nations were much more likely to use bribes when seeking contracts in emerging-market nations. The most flagrant bribe-paying firms were from India, Russia, and China. Other countries where corruption is common include Myanmar, Haiti, and Iraq. Transparency International's Corruption Perceptions Index 2010 measured the perceived levels of public sector corruption in 178 countries around the world. It ranked Iraq at 175, making it the fourth highest country for perceived levels of corruption. Other Arab world countries with a high perceived corruption index were Yemen and Libya (ranked at 146), Syria and Lebanon (127), and Egypt (98). Some of the Arab world countries with the lowest perceived corruption index were Qatar (ranked at 19) and the UAE (ranked 28 countries from the top spot).[33]

The question arises as to whether a company must lower its ethical standards to compete effectively in countries with lower standards. The answer: No. Companies should make a commitment to a common set of shared standards worldwide. For example, John Hancock Mutual Life Insurance Company operates successfully in Southeast Asia, an area that by Western standards has widespread questionable business and government practices. Despite warnings from locals that Hancock would have to bend its rules to succeed, the company set out strict guidelines. "We told our people that we had the same ethical standards, same procedures, and same policies in these countries that we have in the United States, and we do," says Hancock Chairman Stephen Brown. "We just felt that things like payoffs were wrong—and if we had to do business that way, we'd rather not do business." Hancock employees feel good about the consistent levels of ethics. "There may be countries where you have to do that kind of thing," says Brown. "We haven't found that country yet, and if we do, we won't do business there."[34]

Many industrial and professional associations have suggested codes of ethics, and many companies are now adopting their own codes. For example, the American Marketing Association, an international association of marketing managers and scholars, developed the code of ethics shown in ● **Table 17.2**. Companies are also developing programs to teach managers about important ethics issues and to help them find the proper responses. They hold ethics workshops and seminars and set up ethics committees. Furthermore, most major U.S. companies have appointed high-level ethics officers to champion ethics issues and to help resolve ethics problems and concerns facing employees.

PricewaterhouseCoopers (PwC) is a good example. In 2002, PwC established a global ethics office and comprehensive ethics program, headed by a high-level global ethics officer. The ethics program begins with a code of conduct, called 'The Way We Do Business.' PwC employees learn about the code of conduct and about how to handle thorny ethics issues in comprehensive ethics training programs, which start when the employee joins the company and continue through the employee's career. The program also includes an ethics help line and regular communications at all levels. "It is obviously not enough to distribute a document," says PwC's CEO, Samuel DiPiazza. "Ethics is in everything we say and do."[35]

Still, written codes and ethics programs do not ensure ethical behavior. Ethics and social responsibility require a total corporate commitment. They must be a component of the overall corporate culture. According to PwC's DiPiazza, "I see ethics as a mission-critical issue...deeply imbedded in who we are and what we do. It's just as important as our product development cycle or our distribution system....It's about creating a culture based on integrity and respect, not a culture based on dealing with the crisis of the day.... We ask ourselves every day, 'Are we doing the right things?'"[36]

The Sustainable Company (pp 519–521)

At the foundation of marketing is the belief that companies that fulfill the needs and wants of customers will thrive. Companies that fail to meet customer needs or that intentionally or unintentionally harm customers, others in society, or future generations will decline. Sustainable companies are those that create value for customers through socially, environmentally, and ethically responsible actions.

● **TABLE** | **17.2** American Marketing Association Code of Ethics

ETHICAL NORMS AND VALUES FOR MARKETERS PREAMBLE

The American Marketing Association commits itself to promoting the highest standard of professional ethical norms and values for its members. Norms are established standards of conduct that are expected and maintained by society and/or professional organizations. Values represent the collective conception of what people find desirable, important and morally proper. Values serve as the criteria for evaluating the actions of others. Marketing practitioners must recognize that they not only serve their enterprises but also act as stewards of society in creating, facilitating and executing the efficient and effective transactions that are part of the greater economy. In this role, marketers should embrace the highest ethical norms of practicing professionals and the ethical values implied by their responsibility toward stakeholders (e.g., customers, employees, investors, channel members, regulators and the host community).

GENERAL NORMS

1. Marketers must do no harm. This means doing work for which they are appropriately trained or experienced so that they can actively add value to their organizations and customers. It also means adhering to all applicable laws and regulations and embodying high ethical standards in the choices they make.
2. Marketers must foster trust in the marketing system. This means that products are appropriate for their intended and promoted uses. It requires that marketing communications about goods and services are not intentionally deceptive or misleading. It suggests building relationships that provide for the equitable adjustment and/or redress of customer grievances. It implies striving for good faith and fair dealing so as to contribute toward the efficacy of the exchange process.
3. Marketers must embrace, communicate and practice the fundamental ethical values that will improve consumer confidence in the integrity of the marketing exchange system. These basic values are intentionally aspirational and include honesty, responsibility, fairness, respect, openness and citizenship.

ETHICAL VALUES

Honesty—to be truthful and forthright in our dealings with customers and stakeholders.

- We will tell the truth in all situations and at all times.
- We will offer products of value that do what we claim in our communications.
- We will stand behind our products if they fail to deliver their claimed benefits.
- We will honor our explicit and implicit commitments and promises.

Responsibility—to accept the consequences of our marketing decisions and strategies.

- We will make strenuous efforts to serve the needs of our customers.
- We will avoid using coercion with all stakeholders.
- We will acknowledge the social obligations to stakeholders that come with increased marketing and economic power.
- We will recognize our special commitments to economically vulnerable segments of the market such as children, the elderly and others who may be substantially disadvantaged.

Fairness—to try to balance justly the needs of the buyer with the interests of the seller.

- We will represent our products in a clear way in selling, advertising and other forms of communication; this includes the avoidance of false, misleading and deceptive promotion.
- We will reject manipulations and sales tactics that harm customer trust.
- We will not engage in price fixing, predatory pricing, price gouging or 'bait-and-switch' tactics.
- We will not knowingly participate in material conflicts of interest.

Respect—to acknowledge the basic human dignity of all stakeholders.

- We will value individual differences even as we avoid stereotyping customers or depicting demographic groups (e.g., gender, race, sexual orientation) in a negative or dehumanizing way in our promotions.
- We will listen to the needs of our customers and make all reasonable efforts to monitor and improve their satisfaction on an ongoing basis.
- We will make a special effort to understand suppliers, intermediaries and distributors from other cultures.
- We will appropriately acknowledge the contributions of others, such as consultants, employees and coworkers, to our marketing endeavors.

(continued)

Openness—to create transparency in our marketing operations.

- We will strive to communicate clearly with all our constituencies.
- We will accept constructive criticism from our customers and other stakeholders.
- We will explain significant product or service risks, component substitutions or other foreseeable eventualities that could affect customers or their perception of the purchase decision.
- We will fully disclose list prices and terms of financing as well as available price deals and adjustments.

Citizenship—to fulfill the economic, legal, philanthropic, and societal responsibilities that serve stakeholders in a strategic manner.

- We will strive to protect the natural environment in the execution of marketing campaigns.
- We will give back to the community through volunteerism and charitable donations.
- We will work to contribute to the overall betterment of marketing and its reputation.
- We will encourage supply chain members to ensure that trade is fair for all participants, including producers in developing countries.

IMPLEMENTATION

Finally, we recognize that every industry sector and marketing subdiscipline (e.g., marketing research, e-commerce, direct selling, direct marketing, advertising) has its own specific ethical issues that require policies and commentary. An array of such codes can be accessed through links on the AMA website. We encourage all such groups to develop and/or refine their industry and discipline-specific codes of ethics to supplement these general norms and values.

Source: Reprinted with permission of the American Marketing Association.

Sustainable marketing goes beyond caring for the needs and wants of today's customers. It means having concern for tomorrow's customers in assuring the survival and success of the business, shareholders, employees, and the broader world in which they all live. Sustainable marketing provides the context in which companies can build profitable customer relationships by creating value *for* customers in order to capture value *from* customers in return, now and in the future.

REVIEWING Objectives AND KEY Terms

Well—here you are at the end of your introductory marketing journey! In this chapter, we've closed with many important *sustainable marketing* concepts related to marketing's sweeping impact on individual consumers, other businesses, and society as a whole. You learned that sustainable marketing requires socially, environmentally, and ethically responsible actions that bring value not just to present-day consumers and businesses, but also to future generations and to society as a whole. Sustainable companies are those that act responsibly to create value for customers in order to capture value from customers in return, now and in the future.

OBJECTIVE 1 Define *sustainable marketing* and discuss its importance. (pp 496–498)

Sustainable marketing calls for meeting the present needs of consumers and businesses while still preserving or enhancing the ability of future generations to meet their needs. Whereas the marketing concept recognizes that companies thrive by fulfilling the day-to-day needs of customers, sustainable marketing calls for

socially and environmentally responsible actions that meet both the immediate and future needs of customers and the company. Truly sustainable marketing requires a smooth-functioning marketing system in which consumers, companies, public policy makers, and others work together to ensure responsible marketing actions.

OBJECTIVE 2 Identify the major social criticisms of marketing. (pp 498–506)

Marketing's *impact on individual consumer welfare* has been criticized for its high prices, deceptive practices, high-pressure selling, shoddy or unsafe products, planned obsolescence, and poor service to disadvantaged consumers. Marketing's *impact on society* has been criticized for creating false wants and too much materialism, too few social goods, and cultural pollution. Critics have also criticized marketing's *impact on other businesses* for harming competitors and reducing competition through acquisitions, practices that create barriers to entry, and unfair competitive marketing practices. Some of these concerns are justified; some are not.

OBJECTIVE 3 Define *consumerism* and *environmentalism* and explain how they affect marketing strategies. (pp 506–513)

Concerns about the marketing system have led to *citizen action movements*. *Consumerism* is an organized social movement intended to strengthen the rights and power of consumers relative to sellers. Alert marketers view it as an opportunity to serve consumers better by providing more consumer information, education, and protection. *Environmentalism* is an organized social movement seeking to minimize the harm done to the environment and quality of life by marketing practices. The first wave of modern environmentalism was driven by environmental groups and concerned consumers, whereas the second wave was driven by government, which passed laws and regulations governing industrial practices impacting the environment. The first two environmentalism waves are now merging into a third and stronger wave in which companies are accepting responsibility for doing no environmental harm. Companies now are adopting policies of *environmental sustainability*—developing strategies that both sustain the environment and produce profits for the company. Both consumerism and environmentalism are important components of sustainable marketing.

OBJECTIVE 4 Describe the principles of sustainable marketing. (pp 513–517)

Many companies originally opposed these social movements and laws, but most of them now recognize a need for positive consumer information, education, and protection. Under the sustainable marketing concept, a company's marketing should support the best long-run performance of the marketing system. It should be guided by five sustainable marketing principles: *consumer-oriented marketing*, *customer-value marketing*, *innovative marketing*, *sense-of-mission marketing*, and *societal marketing*.

OBJECTIVE 5 Explain the role of ethics in marketing. (pp 517–521)

Increasingly, companies are responding to the need to provide company policies and guidelines to help their managers deal with questions of *marketing ethics*. Of course, even the best guidelines cannot resolve all the difficult ethical decisions that individuals and firms must make. But there are some principles that marketers can choose among. One principle states that such issues should be decided by the free market and legal system. A second, and more enlightened principle, puts responsibility not on the system but in the hands of individual companies and managers. Each firm and marketing manager must work out a philosophy of socially responsible and ethical behavior. Under the sustainable marketing concept, managers must look beyond what is legal and allowable and develop standards based on personal integrity, corporate conscience, and long-term consumer welfare.

KEY Terms

OBJECTIVE 1

Sustainable marketing (p 496)

OBJECTIVE 3

Consumerism (p 506)
Environmentalism (p 508)
Environmental sustainability (p 509)

OBJECTIVE 4

Consumer-oriented marketing (p 513)
Customer-value marketing (p 515)
Innovative marketing (p 515)
Sense-of-mission marketing (p 515)

Societal marketing (p 516)
Deficient products (p 516)
Pleasing products (p 516)
Salutary products (p 516)
Desirable products (p 516)

DISCUSSING & APPLYING THE Concepts

Discussing the Concepts

1. What is sustainable marketing? Explain how the sustainable marketing concept differs from the marketing concept and the societal marketing concept.

2. Marketing's impact on individual consumers has been criticized. Discuss the issues relevant to this impact.

3. Discuss the types of harmful impact that marketing practices can have on competition and the associated problems.

4. Can an organization focus on both consumerism and environmentalism at the same time? Explain.

5. Describe the five sustainable marketing principles and explain how companies benefit from adhering to them.

6. Good ethics is the cornerstone of sustainable marketing. Explain what this means and discuss how companies practice good ethics.

Applying the Concepts

1. The Federal Republic of Germany is a member state of the European Union, and is bound by EU consumer protection directives. In 2002 a large amount of this legislation became part of the German Civil Code. Who is the federal cabinet minister responsible and which court handles consumer protection in Germany?

2. In a small group, discuss each of the morally difficult situations in marketing presented in **Table 17.1**. Which philosophy is guiding your decision in each situation?

3. The Virtual Global Taskforce (http://www.virtualglobaltaskforce. com) is made up of the Australian Federal Police, the Child Exploitation and Online Protection Centre in the United Kingdom, the Italian Postal and Communication Police Service, the Royal Canadian Mounted Police, the U.S. Department of Homeland Security, and Interpol. What are its goals and how might marketers have to be aware when they design online marketing activities?

FOCUS ON Technology

Do you share video files with others on the Internet? If you do, you're taking up a huge hunk of bandwidth, which can cause degraded service for other customers. As a result, Internet service providers may be blocking or slowing down Internet traffic of some customers—a practice referred to as network management. According to AT&T, Internet metering, which would make customers pay for the amount of bandwidth used, is inevitable. Under this practice, the Internet service provider would track the bandwidth use and then charge high-traffic customers more. A customer would select a service package with a flat rate including a specified amount of downloads and then pay an additional fee if he or she exceeds that limit.

1. Which type of Internet users is Internet metering aimed at?

2. How might Internet metering affect the business model for online companies?

3. What are the Internet penetration figures for Argentina, Brazil, Chile, and Mexico? How do they compare with the United States and the United Kingdom?

FOCUS ON Ethics

1st Place is a product placement agency based in the United Kingdom. It has worked on getting its customers' products and services featured in television shows and other media. The company's clients include Olympus, Volkswagen, and Sony.

The agency offers clients a full range of product placement opportunities:

- In television (branded integration and product placement)
- In film (with promotional campaigns, film festivals, branded content, and product placement)
- In digital content (branded integration and product placement)

- In music videos, live concerts, streaming video, and web pages
- In live theater productions
- In events with sponsorship and product launches
- In gaming (in-game placements)
- Using celebrities to endorse and be seen with the product.

1. What is meant by brand integration?

2. Find some examples of product placement and brand integration in your country. How effective are they?

MARKETING BY THE Numbers

Initially, you may pay US$30,000 for a car, but then the price suddenly drops to US$27,000. As a consequence of this, the demand for the new car jumps by 40 percent because the demand for the product is highly elastic. This means that when the percentage change in price (10 percent) is smaller than the corresponding percentage change in demand (40 percent), the demand is elastic.

1. A product is sold initially for US$100 in the first three months of its release and has an average demand per month of 12,000 units. After the third month, the price drops to US$80, and the average demand rises to 18,000 units per month. Is the demand elastic?

2. Suggest examples of products or services available in your country that have featured this kind of pricing policy. Apart from trying to increase demand, what other reasons might a business have for deciding to drop a product's price?

VIDEO Case

Land Rover

The automotive industry has seen better days. Many auto companies are now facing declining revenues and negative profits. Additionally, because of its primary dependence on products that consume petroleum, the auto industry has a big environmental black eye, especially companies that primarily make gas-guzzling trucks and SUVs.

During the past few years, however, Land Rover has experienced tremendous growth in revenues and profits. It is currently selling more vehicles than ever worldwide. How is this possible for a company that only sells SUVs? One of the biggest reasons is Land Rover's strategic focus on social responsibility and environmentalism. Land Rover believes that it can meet consumer needs for luxury all-terrain vehicles while at the same time providing a vehicle that is kinder to the environment. As a corporation, it is also working feverishly to reduce its carbon emissions, reduce waste, and

reduce water consumption and pollution. With actions like this, Land Rover is successfully repositioning its brand away from the standard perceptions of SUVs as environmental enemies.

After viewing the video featuring Land Rover, answer the following questions about the company's efforts toward social responsibility:

1. Make a list of social criticisms of the automotive industry. Discuss all of the ways that Land Rover is combating those criticisms.

2. By the textbook's definition, does Land Rover practice 'sustainable marketing'?

3. Do you believe that Land Rover is sincere in its efforts to be environmentally friendly? Is it even possible for a large SUV to be environmentally friendly? Present support for both sides of these arguments.

COMPANY Case

ExxonMobil: Social Responsibility in a Commodity Market

One fine spring day in 2008, Joe Tyler watched the numbers on the petrol pump speedily climb higher and higher as he filled up his 2002 Toyota at the neighborhood Exxon station. When his tank was full, what he saw shocked him right down to the core of his wallet. It had just cost him US$43.63 to fill up his economy car. How could this be? Sure, the tank was completely empty and took almost 11 gallons. And, yes, petrol prices were on the rise. But at US$4.04 per gallon, this was the first time that a fill-up had cost him more than US$40.

In the past, Joe hadn't usually looked at his petrol receipts. Even though petrol prices had risen dramatically over the past few years, it had still been relatively cheap by world standards; still cheaper than bottled water. Until now, Joe didn't think that his petrol expenses were affecting his budget all that much. But crossing the US$40 line gave him a wake-up call. Although it was far less than the US$100 fill-ups he'd heard about for SUV drivers in places like Los Angeles, where prices were among the highest in the United States, it didn't seem that long ago that he'd routinely filled his tank for not much more than US$10. In fact, he remembered paying around US$1.20 a gallon to fill this same car when it was new in early 2002. Now, he was starting to feel the frustration expressed by so many other buyers. What had happened?

Not long before Joe's epiphany about petrol prices, a man named Lee Raymond was retiring after 13 years as the chairman and CEO of ExxonMobil. He probably wasn't too concerned about how much it cost him to fill up his own car—or his jet for that matter. Including all his pension payoffs and stock options, Raymond's retirement package was valued at a mind-boggling US$400 million. And why not? While at the helm of the giant oil company, Raymond had kept ExxonMobil in one of the top three spots on *Fortune*'s 500

list year after year. By the end of 2007, ExxonMobil had been the most profitable company in America, setting a new record every year. While Joe and other consumers were going through pain at the pumps, Exxon had racked up US$40 billion in profits on US$372 billion in sales. ExxonMobil's fourth-quarter revenues alone exceeded the annual gross domestic product of some major oil-producing nations, including the United Arab Emirates and Kuwait.

Was it just a coincidence that ExxonMobil and the other major oil companies were posting record numbers at a time when consumers were getting hit so hard? Most consumers didn't think so—and they cried 'foul.' In an effort to calm irate consumers, politicians and consumer advocates were calling for action. Maria Cantwell was one of four U.S. senators who backed legislation that would give the U.S. government more oversight of oil, petrol, and electricity markets. "Right now excuses from oil companies on why petrol prices are so high are like smoke and mirrors," Senator Cantwell said. "The days of Enron taught us the painful lesson that fierce market manipulation does happen and I don't want American consumers to have to experience that again." In a hearing in 2008, U.S. Congresswoman Maxine Waters even threatened the CEOs of the largest oil companies with nationalizing their companies if things did not change.

Several state attorney generals also launched investigations. Even the George W. Bush administration demanded an investigation into petrol pricing. In a speech to the country, President Bush said, "Americans understand by and large that the price of crude oil is going up and that [petrol] prices are going up, but what they don't want and will not accept is manipulation of the market, and neither will I." But no investigation into the pricing activities of U.S. oil companies had ever produced any evidence of substantial wrongdoing. The Federal Trade Commission (FTC) had found isolated examples of price gouging, as in the wake of 2005 hurricanes Katrina and Rita. But most of those were explainable and the FTC had never found evidence of widespread market manipulation.

DEMAND AND SUPPLY: IS IT REALLY THAT SIMPLE?

Although the many parties disagree on where to place the blame for skyrocketing petrol prices, there is a high level of consistency among economists and industry observers. They agree that crude oil and even petrol are commodities. Like corn and pork bellies, there is little if any differentiation in the products producers are turning out. And even though ExxonMobil has tried hard to convince customers that its petrol differs from other brands based on a proprietary cocktail of detergents and additives, consumers do not generally perceive a difference. Thus, the market treats all offerings as the same.

Walter Lukken, a member of the U.S. Commodity Futures Trading Commission, has stated publicly what many know to be true about the pricing of commodities. In testimony before Congress on the nature of petrol prices, Mr Lukken said, "The commission thinks the markets accurately reflect tight world energy supplies and a pickup in growth and demand this year." But is it really as simple as demand and supply?

Let's look at demand. In the early 2000s, when oil was cheap, global demand was around 70 million barrels a day (mbd). Eight years later, world consumption had risen to 87 mbd. Many environmentalists point the finger at the driving habits of North Americans and their petrol-swilling SUVs—and with good reason. The United States continues to be one of the world's leading petroleum consumers, with an appetite that grows every year. And as much as U.S. consumers cry about high petrol prices, they've done little to change how much petrol they consume.

However, although the United States consumes more petrol than any other country, this consumption has grown only moderately. Over the past decade, the rise in global demand for oil has been much more the result of the exploding needs of emerging economies. The biggest contributors are China and India, which together account for 37 percent of the world's population. Both countries have a growing appetite for oil that reflects their rapid economic growth. With manufacturing and production increasing and with more individuals trading in bicycles for cars, China and India have the fastest growing economies in the world, with annual growth rates of 10 percent and 8 percent, respectively.

Now, let's look at supply. Recent spikes in the global price of crude are occurring at a time when rising demand coincides with constrained supply. Supply constraints exist at various levels of production, including drilling, refining, and distributing. In past decades, oil companies have had little incentive to invest in exploration and to expand capacity. Oil has been cheap, and environmental regulations created more constraints. Oil-producing countries claim that they are producing at or near capacity. Many analysts support this, noting that global consumption of oil is pressing up against the limits of what the world can produce.

Similar constraints place limits on other stages of the supply chain. For example, U.S. refineries no longer have the capacity to meet the country's demand for petroleum-based fuels. Not only has no new refinery been built in over 30 years, but the total number of refineries has actually shrunk. Many point to government regulation and public resistance as the reasons for this. And as regulations dictate more petrol blends for different regions, refineries feel an even greater pinch, and distribution lines experience bottlenecks.

But as much as supply and demand account for fluctuations in petrol prices, there is a third factor. At a time when supply is stretched so tightly across a growing level of demand, price volatility may result more from the global petroleum futures trading than from anything else. Modern futures markets function on speculation. When factors point to a rise in prices, traders buy futures contracts in hopes of profiting. When oil seems overvalued, they sell. The net effect of all the buying and selling is a constant tweaking of oil prices, which reflects both the fundamental supply–demand situation as well as the constantly changing risk of a major political crisis or natural disaster.

Some policy makers and consumer advocates have pointed to speculative futures trading as a cause of high gas prices. But according to Walter Lukken, "Blaming the futures markets for high commodity prices is like blaming a thermometer for it being hot outside." Although it is true that the oil futures trading can artificially inflate prices in the short term, economists have found that such activities have more of a stabilizing effect in the long run. Speculators absorb risk, often stepping in when nobody else wants to buy or sell. In fact, as with other commodities, the more traders in a given commodity market, the smaller the gap between the buying and selling price for petroleum. This reduces costs for companies at all stages of the value chain, which should ultimately lower prices for customers. Accordingly, if not for the global oil futures market, price spikes and crashes would probably be even bigger and occur more frequently.

THE ANATOMY OF THE PRICE OF A GALLON OF GAS

Consumers like Joe Tyler wonder not only what makes the price of petrol go up, but also just how much of the price of each gallon they buy goes into Big Oil's coffers. They might be surprised to learn the breakdown on the price of a gallon of petrol. Roughly 58 percent of the retail price of gas covers the cost of crude. In 2004, the price of crude was only about US$35 a barrel. That price nearly quadrupled by 2008. Thus, it should come as no surprise that petrol prices have risen in tandem.

Of course, there are other costs that contribute to the price of a gallon of gas. Distribution and marketing swallow 10 percent. Refining costs are good for another 8.5 percent. And then there are taxes. In the United States, the excise tax on petrol varies from state to state. But on average, state and federal sales taxes account for 15 percent of the retail price.

This leaves less for oil companies than most consumers might imagine. In 2007, the oil industry as a whole made a net profit of about 8.5 percent. Although this was higher than the average for all industries, it was less than half the profit margins for health care, financial services, and pharmaceuticals. Still, the absolute profits for big oil companies are among the highest of all industries. ExxonMobil representatives are quick to point out a simple reason: scale. ExxonMobil had the highest profits in 2007 because it had the highest revenues. And when a company like General Motors (number four on the *Fortune* 500) actually loses US$38 billion, ExxonMobil's US$40 billion net profit really stands out.

WHAT TO DO?

If petrol prices are determined in the way that so many experts say, it seems odd that so many people point the finger of scandal. Yet, given the impact of petrol prices on personal budgets and national economies, it is understandable that people want answers. But even if the investigations were to actually produce evidence of wrongdoing, many experts believe that this would only distract from examining the real factors that govern the price of oil.

Proposed solutions for petrol price woes span a very broad spectrum. At one end, some call for extreme government intervention and regulation. On the other end are those who suggest that no action be taken. "I don't think the government should be involved, trying to change the supply-and-demand equation here," said Evan Smith, a fund manager with U.S. Global Investors in the U.S. state of Texas. "I really don't think anything they might do will [make] much of a difference anyway." In a time of such turmoil, ExxonMobil must consider not only how it might help alleviate the problem, but also how actions by others might impact its operations.

Questions for Discussion

1. Consider and discuss the impact of the rising price of petrol on as many other products and services as possible.

2. How does the information in this case relate to the common criticism that marketing causes prices to be higher than they normally would?

3. Is ExxonMobil acting responsibly with respect to pricing its product? Can it keep its prices stable (or even lower them) when the market price is increasing? Should it even try?

4. From the perspective of social responsibility, what role does the consumer play in the price of petrol?

5. How would you 'fix' the problem of rising petrol prices? Consider solutions for different groups, including governments, corporations, nonprofit groups, and consumers. What are the advantages and disadvantages of your proposed solutions?

Sources: Peter Coy, "First Housing, Now Oil," *BusinessWeek*, June 9, 2008, accessed at www.businessweek.com; "A Primer on Gasoline Prices," brochure from the Energy Information Administration, May 2008, accessed at www.eia.doe.gov; Patricia Hill, "Market Fuel Prices Drop, Relief Ahead as Demand Slows and Supplies Rise," *Washington Times*, April 28, 2006, p. A01; Katherine Reynolds Lewis, "Oil Market Is Running on Fear," *New Orleans Times-Picayune*, May 6, 2006, p. M1; "High Gasoline Prices Not Due to Manipulation, Regulators Say," *Calgary Herald*, April 28, 2006, p. E5; and "High Oil Prices Drive Up Exxon Mobil's Profit," *Associated Press*, May 3, 2006, accessed at www.msnbc.com</ulink.

Marketing Plan

The Marketing Plan: An Introduction (pp A1–A2)

As a marketer, you'll need a good marketing plan to provide direction and focus for your brand, product, or company. With a detailed plan, any business will be better prepared to launch a new product or build sales for existing products. Nonprofit organizations also use marketing plans to guide their fund-raising and outreach efforts. Even government agencies put together marketing plans for initiatives such as building public awareness of proper nutrition and stimulating area tourism.

The Purpose and Content of a Marketing Plan

Unlike a business plan, which offers a broad overview of the entire organization's mission, objectives, strategy, and resource allocation, a marketing plan has a more limited scope. It serves to document how the organization's strategic objectives will be achieved through specific marketing strategies and tactics, with the customer as the starting point. It is also linked to the plans of other departments within the organization. Suppose that a marketing plan calls for selling 200,000 units annually. The production department must gear up to make that many units, the finance department must arrange funding to cover the expenses, the human resources department must be ready to hire and train staff, and so on. Without the appropriate level of organizational support and resources, no marketing plan can succeed.

Although the exact length and layout will vary from company to company, a marketing plan usually contains the sections described in Chapter 2. Smaller businesses may create shorter or less formal marketing plans, whereas corporations frequently require highly structured marketing plans. To guide implementation effectively, every part of the plan must be described in considerable detail. Sometimes a company will post its marketing plan on an internal Web site, which allows managers and employees in different locations to consult specific sections and collaborate on additions or changes.

The Role of Research

Marketing plans are not created in a vacuum. To develop successful strategies and action programs, marketers need up-to-date information about the environment, the competition, and the market segments to be served. Often, analysis of internal data is the starting point for assessing the current marketing situation, supplemented by marketing intelligence and research investigating the overall market, the competition, key issues, and threats and opportunities issues. As the plan is put into effect, marketers use a variety of research techniques to measure progress toward objectives and identify areas for improvement if results fall short of projections.

Finally, marketing research helps marketers learn more about their customers' requirements, expectations, perceptions, and satisfaction levels. This deeper understanding provides a foundation for building competitive advantage through well-informed segmentation, targeting, differentiation, and positioning decisions. Thus, the marketing plan should outline what marketing research will be conducted and how the findings will be applied.

The Role of Relationships

The marketing plan shows how the company will establish and maintain profitable customer relationships. In the process, however, it also shapes a number of internal and external relationships. First, it affects how marketing personnel work with each other and with other departments to deliver value and satisfy customers. Second, it affects how the company works with suppliers, distributors, and strategic alliance partners to achieve the objectives listed in the plan. Third, it influences the company's dealings with other stakeholders, including government regulators, the media, and the community at large. All of these relationships are important to the organization's success, so they should be considered when a marketing plan is being developed.

From Marketing Plan to Marketing Action

Companies generally create yearly marketing plans, although some plans cover a longer period. Marketers start planning well in advance of the implementation date to allow time for marketing research, thorough analysis, management review, and coordination between departments. Then, after each action program begins, marketers monitor ongoing results, compare them with projections, analyze any differences, and take corrective steps as needed. Some marketers also prepare contingency plans for implementation if certain conditions emerge. Because of inevitable and sometimes unpredictable environmental changes, marketers must be ready to update and adapt marketing plans at any time.

For effective implementation and control, the marketing plan should define how progress toward objectives will be measured. Managers typically use budgets, schedules, and performance standards for monitoring and evaluating results. With budgets, they can compare planned expenditures with actual expenditures for a given week, month, or other period. Schedules allow management to see when tasks were supposed to be completed—and when they were actually completed. Performance standards track the outcomes of marketing programs to see whether the company is moving toward its objectives. Some examples of performance standards are market share, sales volume, product profitability, and customer satisfaction.

Sample Marketing Plan for Sonic (pp A2–A10)

This section takes you inside the sample marketing plan for Sonic, a hypothetical start-up company. The company's first product is the Sonic 1000, a multimedia, cellular/Wi-Fi-enabled smartphone. Sonic will be competing with Apple, Nokia, Research in Motion, Motorola, and other well-established rivals in a crowded, fast-changing marketplace for smartphones that combine communication, entertainment, and storage functionality. The annotations explain more about what each section of the plan should contain and why.

Executive summary

This section summarizes the main goals, recommendations, and points as an overview for senior managers who will read and approve the marketing plan. A table of contents usually follows this section, for management convenience.

Executive Summary

Sonic is preparing to launch a new multimedia, dual-mode smartphone, the Sonic 1000, in a mature market. Our product offers a competitively unique combination of advanced features and functionality at a value-added price. We are targeting specific segments in the consumer and business markets, taking advantage of opportunities indicated by higher demand for easy-to-use smartphones with expanded communications, entertainment, and storage functionality.

The primary marketing objective is to achieve first-year U.S. sales of 500,000 units. The primary financial objectives are to achieve first-year sales revenues of $75 million, keep first-year losses to less than $8 million, and break even early in the second year.

Current marketing situation

In this section, marketing managers discuss the overall market, identify the market segments that they will target, and provide information about the company's current situation.

Current Marketing Situation

Sonic, founded 18 months ago by two entrepreneurs with experience in the PC market, is about to enter the maturing smartphone market. Multifunction cell phones, e-mail devices, and wireless communication devices have become commonplace for both personal and professional use. Research shows that the United States has 262 million wireless phone subscribers, and 85 percent of the population owns a cell phone.

Competition is therefore more intense even as demand flattens, industry consolidation continues, and pricing pressures squeeze profitability. Worldwide, Nokia is the smartphone leader, holding 45 percent of the global market. The runner-up is Research in Motion, maker of the BlackBerry, with 13 percent of the global market. In the U.S. market, BlackBerry is the market leader (with a 42 percent share) and Apple, maker of the iPhone, is the runner-up (with a 20 percent share). To gain market share in this dynamic environment, Sonic must carefully target specific segments with features that deliver benefits valued by each customer group.

Market description

Describing the targeted segments in detail provides context for the marketing strategies and detailed action programs discussed later in the plan.

Benefits and product features

Table A1.1 clarifies the benefits that product features will deliver to satisfy the needs of customers in each targeted segment.

Market Description

Sonic's market consists of consumers and business users who prefer to use a single device for communication, information storage and exchange, and entertainment on the go. Specific segments being targeted during the first year include professionals, corporations, students, entrepreneurs, and medical users. ● **Table A1.1** shows how the Sonic 1000 addresses the needs of targeted consumer and business segments.

Buyers can choose between models based on several different operating systems, including systems from Microsoft, Symbian, and BlackBerry, plus Linux variations. Sonic licenses a Linux-based system because it is somewhat less vulnerable to attack by hackers and viruses. Hard drives and removable memory cards are popular smartphone options. Sonic is equipping its first entry with an ultra-fast 20-gigabyte removable memory card for information and entertainment storage. This will also allow users to transfer photos and other data from the smartphone to a home or office computer. Technology costs are decreasing even as capabilities are increasing, which makes value-priced models more appealing to consumers and to business users with older devices who want to trade up to new, high-end multifunction units.

● TABLE | A1.1   Segment Needs and Corresponding Features/Benefits of Sonic

Targeted Segment	Customer Need	Corresponding Feature/Benefit
Professionals (consumer market)	• Stay in touch conveniently and securely while on the go • Perform many functions hands-free without carrying multiple gadgets	• Built-in cell phone and push-to-talk to communicate anywhere at any time; wireless e-mail/Web access from anywhere; Linux-based operating system less vulnerable to hackers • Voice-activated applications are convenient; GPS function, camera add value
Students (consumer market)	• Perform many functions hands-free without carrying multiple gadgets • Express style and individuality	• Compatible with numerous applications and peripherals for convenient, cost-effective communication and entertainment • Wardrobe of smartphone cases
Corporate users (business market)	• Security and adaptability for proprietary tasks • Obtain driving directions to business meetings	• Customizable to fit corporate tasks and networks; Linux-based operating system less vulnerable to hackers • Built-in GPS allows voice-activated access to directions and maps
Entrepreneurs (business market)	• Organize and access contacts, schedule details, business and financial files • Get in touch fast	• Hands-free, wireless access to calendar, address book, information files for checking appointments and data, connecting with contacts • Push-to-talk instant calling speeds up communications
Medical users (business market)	• Update, access, and exchange medical records • Photograph medical situations to maintain a visual record	• Removable memory card and hands-free, wireless information recording reduces paperwork and increases productivity • Built-in camera allows fast and easy photography, stores images for later retrieval

Product Review

Our first product, the Sonic 1000, offers the following standard features with a Linux OS:

- Built-in dual cell phone/Internet phone functionality and push-to-talk instant calling

- Digital music/video/television recording, wireless downloading, and playback

- Wireless Web and e-mail, text messaging, instant messaging

- Three-inch color screen for easy viewing

- Organizational functions, including calendar, address book, synchronization

- Global positioning system for directions and maps

- Integrated 4-megapixel digital camera

- Ultra-fast 20-gigabyte removable memory card with upgrade potential

- Interchangeable case wardrobe of different colors and patterns

- Voice recognition functionality for hands-free operation

First-year sales revenues are projected to be $75 million, based on sales of 500,000 Sonic 1000 units at a wholesale price of $150 each. During the second year, we plan to introduce the Sonic 2000, also with Linux OS, as a higher-end smartphone product offering the following standard features:

- Global phone and messaging compatibility

- Translation capabilities to send English text as Spanish text (other languages to be offered as add-on options)

- Integrated 8-megapixel camera with flash

Competitive Review

The emergence of lower-priced smartphones, including the Apple iPhone, has increased competitive pressure. Competition from specialized devices for text and e-mail messaging, such as BlackBerry devices, is a major factor, as well. Key competitors include the following:

- *Nokia.* The market leader in smartphones, Nokia offers a wide range of products for consumers and professionals. It recently purchased the maker of the Symbian operating system and made it into a separate foundation dedicated to improving and promoting this mobile software platform. Many of Nokia's smartphones offer full keyboards, similar to Research in Motion models, but stripped-down models are available for users who do not require the full keyboard and full multimedia capabilities.

- *Apple.* The stylish, popular iPhone 3G has a 3.5-inch color screen and is well-equipped for music, video, and Web access, as well as having communication, calendar, contact management, and file management functions. Its global positioning system technology can pinpoint a user's location. Also, users can erase data with a remote command if the smartphone is lost or stolen. However, AT&T is the only U.S. network provider. The iPhone is priced at $199 and up, with a two-year service contract.

- *RIM.* Research in Motion makes the lightweight BlackBerry wireless multifunction products that are especially popular among corporate users. RIM's continuous innovation and solid customer service support clearly strengthen its competitive standing as it introduces smartphones with enhanced features and communication capabilities. RIM's newer smartphones come equipped with the BlackBerry OS.

- *Motorola.* Motorola, a global giant, has been losing U.S. market share to Apple and Research in Motion, in particular, because it has slowed the pace of new product introduction. One of its top smartphone models is the slender, lightweight quad-band Q, which incorporates e-mail and text message functions, photo caller identification, a full keyboard, camera with flash, removable memory, updated multimedia audio/video/image capabilities, dual stereo speakers, and more. After rebate, the Q is priced at $149.99 with a two-year AT&T Wireless contract, although the retail price without a contract is considerably higher.

- *Samsung.* Value, style, function: Samsung is a strong competitor, offering a variety of smartphones for consumer and business segments. Some of its smartphones are available for specific telecommunications carriers and some are "unlocked," ready for any compatible telecommunications network. Its Instinct is a smartphone with features similar to the iPhone. Like the iPhone, service agreements are only available through one provider—Sprint. After a mail-in rebate of $100, the Instinct's introductory price is $129.99 with a two-year contract.

Despite this strong competition, Sonic can carve out a definite image and gain recognition among the targeted segments. Our voice-recognition system for completely hands-off operation is a critical point of differentiation for competitive advantage. Also, offering GPS as a standard feature gives us a competitive edge compared with similarly priced smartphones. Moreover, our product is speedier than most and runs the Linux OS, which is an appealing alternative for customers concerned about security. ● **Table A1.2** shows a sample of competitive products and prices.

Channels and logistics review

In this section, marketers list the most important channels, provide an overview of each channel arrangement, and identify developing issues in channels and logistics.

Channels and Logistics Review

Sonic-branded products will be distributed through a network of retailers in the top 50 U.S. markets. Among the most important channel partners being contacted are

- *Office supply superstores.* Office Max and Staples will both carry Sonic products in stores, in catalogs, and online.
- *Computer stores.* Independent computer retailers in major cities will carry Sonic products.
- *Electronics specialty stores.* Circuit City and Best Buy will feature Sonic products.
- *Online retailers.* Amazon.com will carry Sonic products and, for a promotional fee, will give Sonic prominent placement on its home page during the introduction.

Initially, our channel strategy will focus on the United States; according to demand, we plan to expand into Canada and beyond, with appropriate logistical support.

● TABLE | A1.2   Sample of Competitive Products and Pricing

Competitor	Model	Features	Price
Nokia	E61i	Quad-band for worldwide phone, e-mail, and Internet access, backlit keyboard, corporate and personal e-mail integration, 2.8-inch screen, 2-megapixel camera, memory card, Symbian OS.	$355 without phone contract
Apple	iPhone 3G	Sleek styling, big screen, fast Internet functions, one-touch calling, GPS navigation, integrated personal and corporate e-mail, open and edit Microsoft Office files, 2-megapixel camera, no keyboard, Apple Mac operating system.	$199 with phone contract
RIM	BlackBerry Curve	Phone, wireless e-mail and Internet access, 2-megapixel camera, built-in maps and GPS, audio and video recording, expandable |memory, keyboard, case color options, BlackBerry OS.	$149.99 with rebate, phone contract
Motorola	Q	Extremely thin and light, with keyboard, quad-band functionality for worldwide use, integrated camera including flash, e-mail and texting functions, Bluetooth connections, multimedia capabilities, voice-activated dialing, Windows OS.	$449.99 without phone contract
Samsung	Instinct	Phone plus e-mail and speedy Internet access, voice-guided GPS, 3.1-inch touch-screen, expandable memory, 2-megapixel camera, live TV, video recording and transmission, FM radio, no keyboard, proprietary operating system.	$129.99 with rebate, phone contract

Strengths, Weaknesses, Opportunities, and Threat Analysis

Sonic has several powerful strengths on which to build, but our major weakness is lack of brand awareness and image. The major opportunity is demand for multimedia smartphones that deliver a number of valued benefits, eliminating the need for customers to carry more than one device. We also face the threat of ever-higher competition from consumer electronics manufacturers, as well as downward pricing pressure. ● **Table A1.3** summarizes Sonic's main strengths, weaknesses, opportunities, and threats.

Strengths

Strengths are internal capabilities that can help the company reach its objectives.

Strengths

Sonic can build on three important strengths:

1. *Innovative product.* The Sonic 1000 offers a combination of features that would otherwise require customers to carry multiple devices: speedy, hands-free dual-mode cell/Wi-Fi telecommunications capabilities, GPS functions, and digital video/music/TV program storage/playback.

2. *Security.* Our smartphone uses a Linux-based operating system that is less vulnerable to hackers and other security threats that can result in stolen or corrupted data.

3. *Pricing.* Our product is priced lower than competing multifunction models—none of which offer the same bundle of features—which gives us an edge with price-conscious customers.

Weaknesses

Weaknesses are internal elements that may interfere with the company's ability to achieve its objectives.

Weaknesses

By waiting to enter the smartphone market until some consolidation of competitors has occurred, Sonic has learned from the successes and mistakes of others. Nonetheless, we have two main weaknesses:

1. *Lack of brand awareness.* Sonic has no established brand or image, whereas Apple and others have strong brand recognition. We will address this issue with aggressive promotion.

2. *Physical specifications.* The Sonic 1000 is slightly heavier and thicker than most competing models because it incorporates multiple features, offers sizable storage capacity, and is compatible with numerous peripheral devices. To counteract this weakness, we will emphasize our product's benefits and value-added pricing, two compelling competitive strengths.

Opportunities

Opportunities are external elements that the company may be able to exploit to its advantage.

Opportunities

Sonic can take advantage of two major market opportunities:

1. *Increasing demand for multimedia smartphones with multiple functions.* The market for multimedia, multifunction devices is growing much faster than the market for single-use

● **TABLE | A1.3** Sonic's Strengths, Weaknesses, Opportunities, and Threats

Strengths	Weaknesses
• Innovative combination of functions in one portable, voice-activated device • Security due to Linux-based operating system • Value pricing	• Lack of brand awareness and image • Heavier and thicker than most competing models
Opportunities	**Threats**
• Increased demand for multimedia, multifunction smartphones • Cost-efficient technology	• Intense competition • Downward pricing pressure • Compressed product life cycle

devices. Growth will accelerate as dual-mode capabilities become mainstream, giving customers the flexibility to make phone calls over cell or Internet connections. Smartphones are already commonplace in public, work, and educational settings, which is boosting primary demand. Also, customers who bought entry-level models are replacing older models with more advanced models.

2. *Cost-efficient technology.* Better technology is now available at a lower cost than ever before. Thus, Sonic can incorporate advanced features at a value-added price that allows for reasonable profits.

Threats

We face three main threats at the introduction of the Sonic 1000:

1. *Increased competition.* More companies are entering the U.S. market with smartphone models that offer some but not all of the features and benefits provided by Sonic's product. Therefore, Sonic's marketing communications must stress our clear differentiation and value-added pricing.

2. *Downward pressure on pricing.* Increased competition and market-share strategies are pushing smartphone prices down. Still, our objective of seeking a 10 percent profit on second-year sales of the original model is realistic, given the lower margins in this market.

3. *Compressed product life cycle.* Smartphones have reached the maturity stage of their life cycle more quickly than earlier technology products. We have contingency plans to keep sales growing by adding new features, targeting additional segments, and adjusting prices as needed.

Objectives and Issues

We have set aggressive but achievable objectives for the first and second years of market entry.

First-Year Objectives

During the Sonic 1000's initial year on the market, we are aiming for unit sales volume of 500,000.

Second-Year Objectives

Our second-year objectives are to sell a combined total of one million units of our two models and to achieve breakeven early in this period.

Issues

In relation to the product launch, our major issue is the ability to establish a well-regarded brand name linked to a meaningful positioning. We will have to invest heavily in marketing to create a memorable and distinctive brand image projecting innovation, quality, and value. We also must measure awareness and response so we can adjust our marketing efforts as necessary.

Marketing Strategy

Sonic's marketing strategy is based on a positioning of product differentiation. Our primary consumer target is middle- to upper-income professionals who need one portable device to coordinate their busy schedules, communicate with family and colleagues, get driving directions, and be entertained on the go. Our secondary consumer target is high school, college, and graduate students who want a multimedia, dual-mode device. This segment can be described demographically by age (16–30) and education status.

Our primary business target is mid- to large-sized corporations that want to help their managers and employees stay in touch and input or access critical data when out of the office. This segment consists of companies with more than $25 million in annual sales and more than 100 employees. We are also targeting entrepreneurs and small business owners as well as medical users who want to update or access patients' medical records while reducing paperwork.

Positioning

Using product differentiation, we are positioning the Sonic as the most versatile, convenient, value-added smartphone for personal and professional use. Our marketing will focus on the hands-free operation of multiple communication, entertainment, and information capabilities differentiating the Sonic 1000.

Product Strategy

The Sonic 1000, including all the features described in the earlier Product Review section, will be sold with a one-year warranty. We will introduce a more compact, powerful high-end model (the Sonic 2000) during the following year. Building the Sonic brand is an integral part of our product strategy. The brand and logo (Sonic's distinctive yellow thunderbolt) will be displayed on the product and its packaging, and reinforced by its prominence in the introductory marketing campaign.

Pricing Strategy

The Sonic 1000 will be introduced at $150 wholesale/$199 estimated retail price per unit. We expect to lower the price of this first model when we expand the product line by launching the Sonic 2000, to be priced at $175 wholesale per unit. These prices reflect a strategy of (1) attracting desirable channel partners and (2) taking share from Nokia, Research in Motion, and other established competitors.

Distribution Strategy

Our channel strategy is to use selective distribution, marketing Sonic smartphones through well-known stores and online retailers. During the first year, we will add channel partners until we have coverage in all major U.S. markets and the product is included in the major electronics catalogs and Web sites. We will also investigate distribution through cell-phone outlets maintained by major carriers such as Verizon Wireless. In support of our channel partners, Sonic will provide demonstration products, detailed specification handouts, and full-color photos and displays featuring the product. Finally, we plan to arrange special payment terms for retailers that place volume orders.

Marketing Communications Strategy

By integrating all messages in all media, we will reinforce the brand name and the main points of product differentiation. Research about media consumption patterns will help our advertising agency choose appropriate media and timing to reach prospects before and during product introduction. Thereafter, advertising will appear on a pulsing basis to maintain brand awareness and communicate various differentiation messages. The agency will also coordinate public relations efforts to build the Sonic brand and support the differentiation message. To create buzz, we will host a user-generated video contest on our Web site. To attract, retain, and motivate channel partners for a push strategy, we will use trade sales promotions and personal selling. Until the Sonic brand has been established, our communications will encourage purchases through channel partners rather than from our Web site.

Marketing Research

Using research, we are identifying the specific features and benefits that our target market segments value. Feedback from market tests, surveys, and focus groups will help us develop the Sonic 2000. We are also measuring and analyzing customers' attitudes toward competing brands and products. Brand awareness research will help us determine the effectiveness and efficiency of our messages and media. Finally, we will use customer satisfaction studies to gauge market reaction.

Positioning

A positioning built on meaningful differentiation, supported by appropriate strategy and implementation, can help the company build competitive advantage.

Marketing tools

These sections summarize the broad logic that will guide decisions made about the marketing tools to be used during the period covered by the plan.

Marketing research

This section shows how marketing research will be used to support development, implementation, and evaluation of strategies and action programs.

Marketing organization

The marketing department may be organized by function, as in this sample, by geography, by product, or by customer (or some combination).

Action programs

Action programs should be coordinated with the resources and activities of other departments, including production, finance, purchasing, and so on.

Marketing Organization

Sonic's chief marketing officer, Jane Melody, holds overall responsibility for all of the company's marketing activities. 🔖 **Figure A1.1** shows the structure of the eight-person marketing organization. Sonic has hired Worldwide Marketing to handle national sales campaigns, trade and consumer sales promotions, and public relations efforts.

Action Programs

The Sonic 1000 will be introduced in February. Following are summaries of the action programs we will use during the first six months of next year to achieve our stated objectives.

January We will launch a $200,000 trade sales promotion campaign and exhibit at the major industry trade shows to educate dealers and generate channel support for the product launch in February. Also, we will create buzz by providing samples to selected product reviewers, opinion leaders, influential bloggers, and celebrities. Our training staff will work with retail sales personnel at major chains to explain the Sonic 1000's features, benefits, and advantages.

February We will start an integrated print/radio/Internet campaign targeting professionals and consumers. The campaign will show how many functions the Sonic smartphone can perform and emphasize the convenience of a single, powerful handheld device. This multimedia campaign will be supported by point-of-sale signage as well as online-only ads and video tours.

March As the multimedia advertising campaign continues, we will add consumer sales promotions such as a contest in which consumers post videos to our Web site, showing how they use the Sonic in creative and unusual ways. We will also distribute new point-of-purchase displays to support our retailers.

April We will hold a trade sales contest offering prizes for the salesperson and retail organization that sells the most Sonic smartphones during the four-week period.

May We plan to roll out a new national advertising campaign this month. The radio ads will feature celebrity voices telling their Sonic smartphones to perform functions such as initiating a phone call, sending an e-mail, playing a song or video, and so on. The stylized print and online ads will feature avatars of these celebrities holding their Sonic smartphones.

🔖**FIGURE** │ **A1.1**
Sonic's Marketing Organization

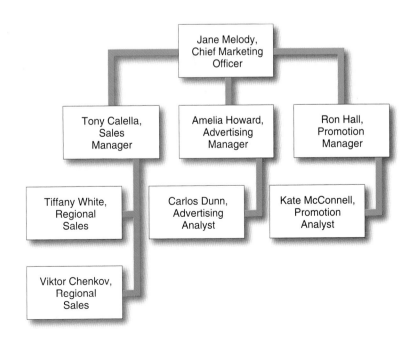

June Our radio campaign will add a new voice-over tag line promoting the Sonic 1000 as a graduation gift. We will also exhibit at the semiannual electronics trade show and provide channel partners with new competitive comparison handouts as a sales aid. In addition, we will tally and analyze the results of customer satisfaction surveys for use in future promotions and to provide feedback for product and marketing activities.

Budgets

Managers use budgets to project profitability and plan for each marketing program's expenditures, scheduling, and operations.

Budgets

Total first-year sales revenue for the Sonic 1000 is projected at $75 million, with an average wholesale price of $150 per unit and variable cost of $100 per unit for a unit sales volume of 500,000. We anticipate a first-year loss of up to $8 million on the Sonic 1000 model. Break-even calculations indicate that the Sonic 1000 will become profitable after the sales volume exceeds 650,000, early in the product's second year. Our break-even analysis of Sonic's first smartphone product assumes per-unit wholesale revenue of $150 per unit, variable cost of $100 per unit, and estimated first-year fixed costs of $32,500,000. Based on these assumptions, the break-even calculation is

$$\frac{32,500,000}{\$150 - \$100} = 650,000 \text{ units}$$

Controls

Controls help management assess results after the plan is implemented, identify any problems or performance variations, and initiate corrective action.

Controls

We are planning tight control measures to closely monitor quality and customer service satisfaction. This will enable us to react very quickly in correcting any problems that may occur. Other early warning signals that will be monitored for signs of deviation from the plan include monthly sales (by segment and channel) and monthly expenses. Given the market's volatility, we are developing contingency plans to address fast-moving environmental changes such as new technology and new competition.

Marketing Plan Tools

Pearson Prentice Hall offers two valuable resources to assist you in developing a marketing plan:

- *The Marketing Plan Handbook* by Marian Burk Wood explains the process of creating a marketing plan, complete with detailed checklists and dozens of real-world examples.

- *Marketing Plan Pro* is an award-winning software package that includes sample plans, step-by-step guides, an introductory video, help wizards, and customizable charts for documenting a marketing plan.

Sources: Background information and market data adapted from Laura M. Holson, "Phone Giants Fight to Keep Subscribers," *New York Times,* July 23, 2008, p. C1; Olga Kharif and Roger O. Crockett, "Motorola's Market Share Mess," *BusinessWeek,* July 10, 2008, www.businessweek.com; "Follow the Leader," *Economist,* June 14, 2008, pp. 78–80; Chris Nutall et al., "Apple Set to Slash iPhone Prices to Lift Sales," *Financial Times,* June 10, 2008, p. 20; Walter S. Mossberg, "Samsung Instinct Doesn't Ring True as an iPhone Clone," *Wall Street Journal,* June 12, 2008, p. D1; "Smartphones Get Smarter, Thanks in Part to the iPhone," *InformationWeek,* July 21, 2007; "Hospital Uses PDA App for Patient Transport," *Health Data Management,* June 2007, p. 14.

Marketing by the Numbers

Marketing managers are facing increased accountability for the financial implications of their actions. This appendix provides a basic introduction to measuring marketing financial performance. Such financial analysis guides marketers in making sound marketing decisions and in assessing the outcomes of those decisions.

The appendix is built around a hypothetical manufacturer of high-definition consumer electronics products—HDInhance. In the past, HDInhance has concentrated on making high-definition televisions for the consumer market. However, the company is now entering the accessories market. Specifically, HDInhance is introducing a new product—a Blu-ray high-definition optical disc player (DVD) that also plays videos streamed over the Internet. In this appendix, we will discuss and analyze the various decisions HDInhance's marketing managers must make before and after the new product launch.

The appendix is organized into *three sections*. The *first section* introduces pricing, break-even, and margin analysis assessments that will guide the introduction of HDInhance's new product. The *second section* discusses demand estimates, the marketing budget, and marketing performance measures. It begins with a discussion of estimating market potential and company sales. It then introduces the marketing budget, as illustrated through a *pro forma* profit-and-loss statement followed by the actual profit-and-loss statement. Next we discuss marketing performance measures with a focus on helping marketing managers to better defend their decisions from a financial perspective. In the *third section*, we analyze the financial implications of various marketing tactics, such as increasing advertising expenditures, adding sales representatives to increase distribution, lowering price, or extending the product line.

Each of the three sections ends with a set of quantitative exercises that provide you with an opportunity to apply the concepts you learned to situations beyond HDInhance.

Pricing, Break-Even, and Margin Analysis (pp A11–A16)

Pricing Considerations

Determining price is one of the most important marketing mix decisions, and marketers have considerable leeway when setting prices. The limiting factors are demand and costs. Demand factors, such as buyer-perceived value, set the price ceiling. The company's costs set the price floor. In between these two factors, marketers must consider competitors' prices and other factors such as reseller requirements, government regulations, and company objectives.

Current competing high-definition DVD/Internet streaming products in this relatively new product category were introduced in 2007 and sell at retail prices between $500 and $1,200. HDInhance plans to introduce its new product at a lower price in order to expand the market and to gain market share rapidly. We first consider HDInhance's pricing decision from a cost perspective. Then we consider consumer value, the competitive environment, and reseller requirements.

Fixed costs

Costs that do not vary with production or sales level.

Variable costs

Costs that vary directly with the level of production.

Total costs

The sum of the fixed and variable costs for any given level of production.

Cost-plus pricing (or markup pricing)

A standard markup to the cost of the product.

Relevant costs

Costs that will occur in the future and that will vary across the alternatives being considered.

Break-even price

The price at which total revenue equals total cost and profit is zero.

Return on investment (ROI) pricing (or target-return pricing)

A cost-based pricing method that determines price based on a specified rate of return on investment.

Determining Costs

Recall from Chapter 10 that there are different types of costs. **Fixed costs** do not vary with production or sales level and include costs such as rent, interest, depreciation, and clerical and management salaries. Regardless of the level of output, the company must pay these costs. Whereas total fixed costs remain constant as output increases, the fixed cost per unit (or average fixed cost) will decrease as output increases because the total fixed costs are spread across more units of output. **Variable costs** vary directly with the level of production and include costs related to the direct production of the product (such as costs of goods sold—COGS) and many of the marketing costs associated with selling it. Although these costs tend to be uniform for each unit produced, they are called variable because their total varies with the number of units produced. **Total costs** are the sum of the fixed and variable costs for any given level of production.

HDInhance has invested $10 million in refurbishing an existing facility to manufacture the new product. Once production begins, the company estimates that it will incur fixed costs of $20 million per year. The variable cost to produce each device is estimated to be $250 and is expected to remain at that level for the output capacity of the facility.

Setting Price Based on Costs

HDInhance starts with the cost-based approach to pricing discussed in Chapter 10. Recall that the simplest method, **cost-plus pricing (or markup pricing)**, simply adds a standard markup to the cost of the product. To use this method, however, HDInhance must specify expected unit sales so that total unit costs can be determined. Unit variable costs will remain constant regardless of the output, but *average unit fixed costs* will decrease as output increases.

To illustrate this method, suppose HDInhance has fixed costs of $20 million, variable costs of $250 per unit, and expects unit sales of 1 million units. Thus, the cost per unit is given by the following:

$$\text{Unite cost} = \text{variable cost} + \frac{\text{fixed costs}}{\text{unit sales}} = \$250 + \frac{\$20{,}000{,}000}{1{,}000{,}000} = \$270$$

Note that we do *not* include the initial investment of $10 million in the total fixed cost figure. It is not considered a fixed cost because it is not a *relevant* cost. **Relevant costs** are those that will occur in the future and that will vary across the alternatives being considered. HDInhance's investment to refurbish the manufacturing facility was a one-time cost that will not reoccur in the future. Such past costs are *sunk costs* and should not be considered in future analyses.

Also notice that if HDInhance sells its product for $270, the price is equal to the total cost per unit. This is the **break-even price**—the price at which unit revenue (price) equals unit cost and profit is zero.

Suppose HDInhance does not want to merely break even, but rather wants to earn a 25% markup on sales. HDInhance's markup price is as follows:[1]

$$\text{Markup price} = \frac{\text{unite cost}}{(1 - \text{desired return on sales})} = \frac{\$270}{1 - .25} = \$360$$

This is the price that HDInhance would sell the product to resellers such as wholesalers or retailers to earn a 25% profit on sales.

Another approach HDInhance could use is called **return on investment (ROI) pricing (or target-return pricing)**. In this case, the company *would* consider the initial $10 million investment, but only to determine the dollar profit goal. Suppose the company wants a 30% return on its investment. The price necessary to satisfy this requirement can be determined by the following:[2]

$$\text{ROI price} = \text{unitcost} + \frac{\text{ROTI} \times \text{investment}}{\text{unitsales}} = \$270 + \frac{0.3 \times \$10{,}000{,}000}{1{,}000{,}000} = \$273$$

That is, if HDInhance sells its product for $273, it will realize a 30% return on its initial investment of $10 million.

In these pricing calculations, unit cost is a function of the expected sales, which were estimated to be 1 million units. But what if actual sales were lower? Then the unit cost would be higher because the fixed costs would be spread over fewer units, and the realized percentage markup on sales or ROI would be lower. Alternatively, if sales are higher than the estimated 1 million units, unit cost would be lower than $270, so a lower price would produce the desired markup on sales or ROI. It's important to note that these cost-based pricing methods are *internally* focused and do not consider demand, competitors' prices, or reseller requirements. Because HDInhance will be selling this product to consumers through wholesalers and retailers offering competing brands, the company must consider markup pricing from this perspective.

Setting Price Based on External Factors

Whereas costs determine the price floor, HDInhance also must consider external factors when setting price. HDInhance does not have the final say concerning the final price to consumers—retailers do. So it must start with its suggested retail price and work back. In doing so, HDInhance must consider the markups required by resellers that sell the product to consumers.

Markup
The difference between a company's selling price for a product and its cost to manufacture or purchase it.

In general, a dollar **markup** is the difference between a company's selling price for a product and its cost to manufacture or purchase it. For a retailer, then, the markup is the difference between the price it charges consumers and the cost the retailer must pay for the product. Thus, for any level of reseller

$$\text{Dollar markup} = \text{selling price} - \text{cost}$$

Markups are usually expressed as a percentage, and there are two different ways to compute markups—on *cost* or on *selling price*:

$$\text{Marke up percentage on cost} = \frac{\text{dollar markup}}{\text{cost}}$$

$$\text{Markup percentage on selling price} = \frac{\text{dollar markup}}{\text{selling price}}$$

To apply reseller margin analysis, HDInhance must first set the suggested retail price and then work back to the price at which it must sell the product to a wholesaler. Suppose retailers expect a 30% margin and wholesalers want a 20% margin based on their respective selling prices. And suppose that HDInhance sets a manufacturer's suggested retail price (MSRP) of $599.99 for its product.

Value-based pricing
Offering just the right combination of quality and good service at a fair price.

Recall that HDInhance wants to expand the market by pricing low and generating market share quickly. HDInhance selected the $599.99 MSRP because it is lower than most competitors' prices, which can be as high as $1,200. And the company's research shows that it is below the threshold at which more consumers are willing to purchase the product. By using buyers' perceptions of value and not the seller's cost to determine the MSRP, HDInhance is using **value-based pricing.** For simplicity, we will use an MSRP of $600 in further analyses.

Markup chain
The sequence of markups used by firms at each level in a channel.

To determine the price HDInhance will charge wholesalers, we must first subtract the retailer's margin from the retail price to determine the retailer's cost ($600 − ($600 × 0.30) = $420). The retailer's cost is the wholesaler's price, so HDInhance next subtracts the wholesaler's margin ($420 − ($420 × 0.20) = $336). Thus, the **markup chain** representing the sequence of markups used by firms at each level in a channel for HDInhance's new product is as follows:

Suggested retail price:	$600
minus retail margin (30%):	−$180
Retailer's cost/wholesaler's price:	$420
minus wholesaler's margin (20%):	−$ 84
Wholesaler's cost/HDInhance's price:	$336

By deducting the markups for each level in the markup chain, HDInhance arrives at a price for the product to wholesalers of $336.

Break-Even and Margin Analysis

The previous analyses derived a value-based price of $336 for HDInhance's product. Although this price is higher than the break-even price of $270 and covers costs, that price assumed a demand of 1 million units. But how many units and what level of dollar sales must HDInhance achieve to break even at the $336 price? And what level of sales must be achieved to realize various profit goals? These questions can be answered through break-even and margin analysis.

Determining Break-Even Unit Volume and Dollar Sales

Based on an understanding of costs, consumer value, the competitive environment, and reseller requirements, HDInhance has decided to set its price to wholesalers at $336. At that price, what sales level will be needed for HDInhance to break even or make a profit? **Break-even analysis** determines the unit volume and dollar sales needed to be profitable given a particular price and cost structure. At the break-even point, total revenue equals total costs and profit is zero. Above this point, the company will make a profit; below it, the company will lose money. HDInhance can calculate break-even volume using the following formula:[3]

Break-even analysis
Analysis to determine the unit volume and dollar sales needed to be profitable given a particular price and cost structure.

$$\text{Break-even volume} = \frac{\text{fixed costs}}{\text{price} - \text{unit variable cost}}$$

The denominator (price – unit variable cost) is called **unit contribution** (sometimes called contribution margin). It represents the amount that each unit contributes to covering fixed costs. Break-even volume represents the level of output at which all (variable and fixed) costs are covered. In HDInhance's case, break-even unit volume is as follows:

Unit contribution
The amount that each unit contributes to covering fixed costs—the difference between price and variable costs.

$$\text{Break-even volume} = \frac{\text{fixed cost}}{\text{price} - \text{variable cost}} = \frac{\$20,000,000}{\$336 - \$250} = 232,558.1 \text{ units}$$

Thus, at the given cost and pricing structure, HDInhance will break even at 232,559 units.

To determine the break-even dollar sales, simply multiply unit break-even volume by the selling price:

$$\text{BE}_{sales} = \text{BE}_{vol} \times \text{price} = 232,559 \times \$336 = \$78,139,824$$

Another way to calculate dollar break-even sales is to use the percentage contribution margin (hereafter referred to as **contribution margin**), which is the unit contribution divided by the selling price:

Contribution margin
The unit contribution divided by the selling price.

$$\text{Contribution margin} = \frac{\text{price} - \text{variable cost}}{\text{price}} = \frac{\$336 - \$250}{\$336} = 0.256 \text{ or } 25.6\%$$

Then,

$$\text{Break-even sales} = \frac{\text{fixed costs}}{\text{contribution margin}} = \frac{\$20,000,000}{0.256} = \$78,125,000$$

Note that the difference between the two break-even sales calculations is due to rounding.

Such break-even analysis helps HDInhance by showing the unit volume needed to cover costs. If production capacity cannot attain this level of output, then the company should not launch this product. However, the unit break-even volume is well within HDInhance's capacity. Of course, the bigger question concerns whether HDInhance can sell this volume at the $336 price. We'll address that issue a little later.

Understanding contribution margin is useful in other types of analyses as well, particularly if unit prices and unit variable costs are unknown or if a company (say, a retailer) sells many products at different prices and knows the percentage of total sales variable costs represent. Whereas unit contribution is the difference between unit price and unit variable costs, total contribution is the difference between total sales and total variable costs. The overall contribution margin can be calculated by the following:

$$\text{Contribution margin} = \frac{\text{total sales} - \text{total variable costs}}{\text{total sales}}$$

Regardless of the actual level of sales, if the company knows what percentage of sales is represented by variable costs, it can calculate contribution margin. For example, HDInhance's unit variable cost is $250, or 74% of the selling price ($250 ÷ $336 = 0.74). That means for every $1 of sales revenue for HDInhance, $0.74 represents variable costs, and the difference ($0.26) represents contribution to fixed costs. But even if the company doesn't know its unit price and unit variable cost, it can calculate the contribution margin from total sales and total variable costs or from knowledge of the total cost structure. It can set total sales equal to 100% regardless of the actual absolute amount and determine the contribution margin:

$$\text{Contribution margin} = \frac{100\% - 74\%}{100\%} = \frac{1 - 0.74}{1} = 1 - 0.74 = 0.26 \text{ or } 26\%$$

Note that this matches the percentage calculated from the unit price and unit variable cost information. This alternative calculation will be very useful later when analyzing various marketing decisions.

Determining "Breakeven" for Profit Goals

Although it is useful to know the break-even point, most companies are more interested in making a profit. Assume HDInhance would like to realize a $5 million profit in the first year. How many units must it sell at the $336 price to cover fixed costs and produce this profit? To determine this, HDInhance can simply add the profit figure to fixed costs and again divide by the unit contribution to determine unit sales:[4]

$$\text{Unit volume} = \frac{\text{fixed cost} - \text{profit goal}}{\text{price} - \text{variable cost}} = \frac{\$20,000,000 + \$5,000,000}{\$336 - \$250} = 290,697.7 \text{ units}$$

Thus, to earn a $5 million profit, HDInhance must sell 290,698 units. Multiply by price to determine dollar sales needed to achieve a $5 million profit:

$$\text{Dollar sales} = 290,698 \text{ units} \times \$336 = \$97,674,528$$

Or use the contribution margin:

$$\text{Sales} = \frac{\text{fixed cost} + \text{profit goal}}{\text{contribution margin}} = \frac{\$20,000,000 + \$5,000,000}{0.256} = \$97,656,250$$

Again, note that the difference between the two break-even sales calculations is due to rounding.

As we saw previously, a profit goal can also be stated as a return on investment goal. For example, recall that HDInhance wants a 30% return on its $10 million investment. Thus, its absolute profit goal is $3 million ($10,000,000 × 0.30). This profit goal is treated the same way as in the previous example:[5]

$$\text{Unit volume} = \frac{\text{fixed cost} + \text{profit goal}}{\text{price} - \text{variable cost}} = \frac{\$20,000,000 + \$3,000,000}{\$336 - \$250} = 267,442 \text{ units}$$

$$\text{Dollar sales} = 267,442 \text{ units} \times \$336 = \$89,860,512$$

Or

$$\text{Dollar sales} = \frac{\text{fixed cost} + \text{profit goal}}{\text{contribution margin}} = \frac{\$20,000,000 + \$3,000,000}{0.26} = \$89,843,750$$

Finally, HDInhance can express its profit goal as a percentage of sales, which we also saw in previous pricing analyses. Assume HDInhance desires a 25% return on sales. To determine the unit and sales volume necessary to achieve this goal, the calculation is a little different from the previous two examples. In this case, we incorporate the profit goal into the unit contribution as an additional variable cost. Look at it this way: If 25% of each sale must go toward profits, that leaves only 75% of the selling price to cover fixed costs. Thus, the equation becomes:[6]

$$\text{Unit volume} = \frac{\text{fixed cost}}{\text{price} - \text{variable cost} - (0.25 \times \text{price})} \text{ or } \frac{\text{fixed cost}}{(0.75 \times \text{price}) - \text{variable cost}}$$

So,

$$\text{United volume} = \frac{\$20,000,000}{(0.75 \times \$336) - \$250} = 10,000,000 \text{ units}$$

$$\text{Dollar sales necessary} = 10,000,000 \text{ units} \times \$336 = \$3,360,000,000$$

Thus, HDInhance would need more than $3 billion in sales to realize a 25% return on sales given its current price and cost structure! Could it possibly achieve this level of sales? The major point is that although break-even analysis can be useful in determining the level of sales needed to cover costs or to achieve a stated profit goal, it does not tell the company whether it is *possible* to achieve that level of sales at the specified price. To address this issue, HDInhance needs to estimate demand for this product.

Before moving on, however, let's stop here and practice applying the concepts covered so far. Now that you have seen pricing and break-even concepts in action as they related to HDInhance's new product, here are several exercises for you to apply what you have learned in other contexts.

Marketing by the Numbers Exercise Set One

Now that you've studied pricing, break-even, and margin analysis as they relate to HDInhance's new-product launch, use the following exercises to apply these concepts in other contexts.

1.1 Sanborn, a manufacturer of electric roof vents, realizes a cost of $55 for every unit it produces. Its total fixed costs equal $2 million. If the company manufactures 500,000 units, compute the following:

a. Unit cost

b. Markup price if the company desires a 10% return on sales

c. ROI price if the company desires a 25% return on an investment of $1 million

1.2 An interior decorator purchases items to sell in her store. She purchases a lamp for $125 and sells it for $225. Determine the following:

a. Dollar markup

b. Markup percentage on cost

c. Markup percentage on selling price

1.3 A consumer purchases a toaster from a retailer for $60. The retailer's markup is 20%, and the wholesaler's markup is 15%, both based on selling price. For what price does the manufacturer sell the product to the wholesaler?

1.4 A vacuum manufacturer has a unit cost of $50 and wishes to achieve a margin of 30% based on selling price. If the manufacturer sells directly to a retailer who then adds a set margin of 40% based on selling price, determine the retail price charged to consumers.

1.5 Advanced Electronics manufactures DVDs and sells them directly to retailers who typically sell them for $20. Retailers take a 40% margin based on the retail selling price. Advanced's cost information is as follows:

DVD package and disc	$2.50/DVD
Royalties	$2.25/DVD
Advertising and promotion	$500,000
Overhead	$200,000

Calculate the following:

a. Contribution per unit and contribution margin

b. Break-even volume in DVD units and dollars

c. Volume in DVD units and dollar sales necessary if Advanced's profit goal is 20% profit on sales

d. Net profit if 5 million DVDs are sold

Demand Estimates, the Marketing Budget, and Marketing Performance Measures (pp A17–A18)

Market Potential and Sales Estimates

HDInhance has now calculated the sales needed to break even and to attain various profit goals on its new product. However, the company needs more information regarding demand in order to assess the feasibility of attaining the needed sales levels. This information is also needed for production and other decisions. For example, production schedules need to be developed and marketing tactics need to be planned.

Total market demand

The total volume that would be bought by a defined consumer group, in a defined geographic area, in a defined time period, in a defined marketing environment, under a defined level and mix of industry marketing effort.

The **total market demand** for a product or service is the total volume that would be bought by a defined consumer group, in a defined geographic area, in a defined time period, in a defined marketing environment, under a defined level and mix of industry marketing effort. Total market demand is not a fixed number but a function of the stated conditions. For example, next year's total market demand for high-definition DVD/Internet streaming devices will depend on how much Samsung, Sony, LG, and other producers spend on marketing their brands. It also depends on many environmental factors, such as government regulations, economic conditions, and the level of consumer confidence in a given market. The upper limit of market demand is called **market potential.**

Market potential

The upper limit of market demand.

One general but practical method that HDInhance might incorporate for estimating total market demand uses three variables: (1) the number of prospective buyers, (2) the quantity purchased by an average buyer per year, and (3) the price of an average unit. Using these numbers, HDInhance can estimate total market demand as follows:

$$Q = n \times q \times p$$

where

Q = total market demand
n = number of buyers in the market
q = quantity purchased by an average buyer per year
p = price of an average unit

Chain ratio method

Estimating market demand by multiplying a base number by a chain of adjusting percentages.

A variation of this approach is the **chain ratio method.** This method involves multiplying a base number by a chain of adjusting percentages. For example, HDInhance's product is designed to play high-definition DVD movies on high-definition televisions as well as play videos streamed from the Internet. Thus, consumers who do not own a high-definition television will not likely purchase this player. Additionally, only households with broadband Internet access will be able to use the product. Finally, not all HDTV households will be willing and able to purchase the new product. HDInhance can estimate U.S. demand using a chain of calculations like the following:

Total number of U.S. households

× The percentage of U.S. households owning a high-definition television

× The percentage of U.S. households with broadband Internet access

× The percentage of these households willing and able to buy this device

ACNielsen, the television ratings company, estimates that there are almost 113 million TV households in the United States. Experts estimate that 38% of TV households will own HDTVs by the end of 2008.8 Research also indicates that 50% of U.S. households have broadband Internet access.9 Finally, HDInhance's own research indicates that 87% of HDTV households possess the discretionary income needed and are willing to buy a device such as this. Then, the total number of households willing and able to purchase this product is

113 million households × 0.38 × 0.50 × 0.87 = 18.7 million households

Because HDTVs are relatively new and expensive products, most households have only one of these televisions, and it's usually the household's primary television.10 Thus, consumers who buy a high-definition DVD player/Internet streaming device will likely buy only one per household. Assuming the average retail price across all brands is $750 for this product, the estimate of total market demand is as follows:

$$18.7 \text{ million house holds} \times 1 \text{ drvice per household} \times \$750 = \$14 \text{ billion}$$

This simple chain of calculations gives HDInhance only a rough estimate of potential demand. However, more detailed chains involving additional segments and other qualifying factors would yield more accurate and refined estimates. Still, these are only *estimates* of market potential. They rely heavily on assumptions regarding adjusting percentages, average quantity, and average price. Thus, HDInhance must make certain that its assumptions are reasonable and defendable. As can be seen, the overall market potential in dollar sales can vary widely given the average price used. For this reason, HDInhance will use unit sales potential to determine its sales estimate for next year. Market potential in terms of units is 18.7 million (18.7 million households × 1 device per household).

Assuming that HDInhance wants to attain 2% market share (comparable to its share of the HDTV market) in the first year after launching this product, then it can forecast unit sales at 18.7 million units × 0.02 = 374,000 units. At a selling price of $336 per unit, this translates into sales of $125,664,000 (374,000 units × $336 per unit). For simplicity, further analyses will use forecasted sales of $125 million.

This unit volume estimate is well within HDInhance's production capacity and exceeds not only the break-even estimate (232,559 units) calculated earlier, but also the volume necessary to realize a $5 million profit (290,698 units) or a 30% return on investment (267,442 units). However, this forecast falls well short of the volume necessary to realize a 25% return on sales (10 million units!) and may require that HDInhance revise expectations.

To assess expected profits, we must now look at the budgeted expenses for launching this product. To do this, we will construct a pro forma profit-and-loss statement.

The Profit-and-Loss Statement and Marketing Budget (pp A18–A19)

Pro forma (or projected) profit-and-loss statement (or income statement or operating statement)
A statement that shows projected revenues less budgeted expenses and estimates the projected net profit for an organization, product, or brand during a specific planning period, typically a year.

All marketing managers must account for the profit impact of their marketing strategies. A major tool for projecting such profit impact is a **pro forma** (or projected) **profit-and-loss statement** (also called an **income statement** or **operating statement**). A pro forma statement shows projected revenues less budgeted expenses and estimates the projected net profit for an organization, product, or brand during a specific planning period, typically a year. It includes direct product production costs, marketing expenses budgeted to attain a given sales forecast, and overhead expenses assigned to the organization or product. A profit-and-loss statement typically consists of several major components (see
● **Table A2.1**):

- *Net sales*—gross sales revenue minus returns and allowances (for example, trade, cash, quantity, and promotion allowances). HDInhance's net sales for 2008 are estimated to be $125 million, as determined in the previous analysis.

- *Cost of goods sold* (sometimes called *cost of sales*)—the actual cost of the merchandise sold by a manufacturer or reseller. It includes the cost of inventory, purchases, and other costs associated with making the goods. HDInhance's cost of goods sold is estimated to be 50% of net sales, or $62.5 million.

- *Gross margin (or gross profit)*—the difference between net sales and cost of goods sold. HDInhance's gross margin is estimated to be $62.5 million.

● TABLE | A2.1   Pro Forma Profit-and-Loss Statement for the 12-Month Period Ended December 31, 2008

			% of Sales
Net Sales		$125,000,000	100%
Cost of Goods Sold		62,500,000	50%
Gross Margin		$ 62,500,000	50%
Marketing Expenses			
Sales expenses	$17,500,000		
Promotion expenses	15,000,000		
Freight	12,500,000	45,000,000	36%
General and Administrative Expenses			
Managerial salaries and expenses	$ 2,000,000		
Indirect overhead	3,000,000	5,000,000	4%
Net Profit Before Income Tax		$ 12,500,000	10%

- *Operating expenses*—the expenses incurred while doing business. These include all other expenses beyond the cost of goods sold that are necessary to conduct business. Operating expenses can be presented in total or broken down in detail. Here, HDInhance's estimated operating expenses include *marketing expenses* and *general and administrative expenses*.

Marketing expenses include sales expenses, promotion expenses, and distribution expenses. The new product will be sold though HDInhance's sales force, so the company budgets $5 million for sales salaries. However, because sales representatives earn a 10% commission on sales, HDInhance must also add a variable component to sales expenses of $12.5 million (10% of $125 million net sales), for a total budgeted sales expense of $17.5 million. HDInhance sets its advertising and promotion to launch this product at $10 million. However, the company also budgets 4% of sales, or $5 million, for cooperative advertising allowances to retailers who promote HDInhance's new product in their advertising. Thus, the total budgeted advertising and promotion expenses are $15 million ($10 million for advertising plus $5 million in co-op allowances). Finally, HDInhance budgets 10% of net sales, or $12.5 million, for freight and delivery charges. In all, total marketing expenses are estimated to be $17.5 million + $15 million + $12.5 million = $45 million.

General and administrative expenses are estimated at $5 million, broken down into $2 million for managerial salaries and expenses for the marketing function and $3 million of indirect overhead allocated to this product by the corporate accountants (such as depreciation, interest, maintenance, and insurance). Total expenses for the year, then, are estimated to be $50 million ($45 million marketing expenses + $5 million in general and administrative expenses).

- *Net profit before taxes*—profit earned after all costs are deducted. HDInhance's estimated net profit before taxes is $12.5 million.

In all, as Table A2.1 shows, HDInhance expects to earn a profit on its new product of $12.5 million in 2008. Also note that the percentage of sales that each component of the profit-and-loss statement represents is given in the right-hand column. These percentages are determined by dividing the cost figure by net sales (that is, marketing expenses represent 36% of net sales determined by $45 million ÷ $125 million). As can be seen, HDInhance projects a net profit return on sales of 10% in the first year after launching this product.

Marketing Performance Measures

(pp A20–A24)

Profit-and-loss statement (or income statement or operating statement)
A statement that shows actual revenues less expenses and net profit for an organization, product, or brand during a specific planning period, typically a year.

Now let's fast-forward a year. HDInhance's product has been on the market for one year and management wants to assess its sales and profit performance. One way to assess this performance is to compute performance ratios derived from HDInhance's **profit-and-loss statement** (or **income statement** or **operating statement**).

Whereas the pro forma profit-and-loss statement shows *projected* financial performance, the statement given in ● **Table A2.2** shows HDInhance's *actual* financial performance based on actual sales, cost of goods sold, and expenses during the past year. By comparing the profit-and-loss statement from one period to the next, HDInhance can gauge performance against goals, spot favorable or unfavorable trends, and take appropriate corrective action.

The profit-and-loss statement shows that HDInhance lost $1 million rather than making the $12.5 million profit projected in the pro forma statement. Why? One obvious reason is that net sales fell $25 million short of estimated sales. Lower sales translated into lower variable costs associated with marketing the product. However, both fixed costs and the cost of goods sold as a percentage of sales exceeded expectations. Hence, the product's contribution margin was 21% rather than the estimated 26%. That is, variable costs represented 79% of sales (55% for cost of goods sold, 10% for sales commissions, 10% for freight, and 4% for co-op allowances). Recall that contribution margin can be calculated by subtracting that fraction from one $(1 - 0.79 = 0.21)$. Total fixed costs were $22 million, $2 million more than estimated. Thus, the sales that HDInhance needed to break even given this cost structure can be calculated as follows:

$$\text{Break-even sales} = \frac{\text{fixed costs}}{\text{contribution margin}} = \frac{\$22,000,000}{0.21} = \$104,761,905$$

If HDInhance had achieved another $5 million in sales, it would have earned a profit.

Although HDInhance's sales fell short of the forecasted sales, so did overall industry sales for this product. Overall industry sales were only $2.5 billion. That means that HDInhance's **market share** was 4% ($100 million ÷ $2.5 billion = 0.04 = 4%), which was higher than forecasted. Thus, HDInhance attained a higher-than-expected market share but the overall market sales were not as high as estimated.

Market share
Company sales divided by market sales.

Analytic Ratios

Operating ratios
The ratios of selected operating statement items to net sales.

The profit-and-loss statement provides the figures needed to compute some crucial **operating ratios**—the ratios of selected operating statement items to net sales. These ratios let marketers compare the firm's performance in one year to that in previous years (or with

● **TABLE | A2.2** Profit-and-Loss Statement for the 12-Month Period Ended December 31, 2008

			% of Sales
Net Sales		$100,000,000	100%
Cost of Goods Sold		55,000,000	55%
Gross Margin		$ 45,000,000	45%
Marketing Expenses			
Sales expenses	$15,000,000		
Promotion expenses	14,000,000		
Freight	10,000,000	39,000,000	39%
General and Administrative Expenses			
Managerial salaries and expenses	$ 2,000,000		
Indirect overhead	5,000,000	7,000,000	7%
Net Profit Before Income Tax		($1,000,000)	(1%)

industry standards and competitors' performance in that year). The most commonly used operating ratios are the *gross margin percentage,* the *net profit percentage,* and the *operating expense percentage.* The *inventory turnover rate* and *return on investment (ROI)* are often used to measure managerial effectiveness and efficiency.

The **gross margin percentage** indicates the percentage of net sales remaining after cost of goods sold that can contribute to operating expenses and net profit before taxes. The higher this ratio, the more a firm has left to cover expenses and generate profit. HDInhance's gross margin ratio was 45%:

Gross margin percentage
The percentage of net sales remaining after cost of goods sold—calculated by dividing gross margin by net sales.

$$\text{Gross margin percentage} = \frac{\text{gross margin}}{\text{net sales}} = \frac{\$45,000,000}{\$100,000,000} = 0.45 = 45\%$$

Note that this percentage is lower than estimated, and this ratio is seen easily in the percentage of sales column in **Table A2.2.** Stating items in the profit-and-loss statement as a percent of sales allows managers to quickly spot abnormal changes in costs over time. If there was previous history for this product and this ratio was declining, management should examine it more closely to determine why it has decreased (that is, because of a decrease in sales volume or price, an increase in costs, or a combination of these). In HDInhance's case, net sales were $25 million lower than estimated, and cost of goods sold was higher than estimated (55% rather than the estimated 50%).

Net profit percentage
The percentage of each sales dollar going to profit—calculated by dividing net profits by net sales.

The **net profit percentage** shows the percentage of each sales dollar going to profit. It is calculated by dividing net profits by net sales:

$$\text{Net profit percentage} = \frac{\text{net profit}}{\text{net sales}} = \frac{-\$1,000,000}{\$100,000,000} = -0.01 = -1.0\%$$

This ratio is easily seen in the percent of sales column. HDInhance's new product generated negative profits in the first year, not a good situation given that before the product launch, net profits before taxes were estimated at more than $12 million. Later in this appendix, we will discuss further analyses the marketing manager should conduct to defend the product.

Operating expense percentage
The portion of net sales going to operating expenses—calculated by dividing total expenses by net sales.

The **operating expense percentage** indicates the portion of net sales going to operating expenses. Operating expenses include marketing and other expenses not directly related to marketing the product, such as indirect overhead assigned to this product. It is calculated by

$$\text{Operating expense percentage} = \frac{\text{total expenses}}{\text{net sales}} = \frac{\$46,000,000}{\$100,000,000} = 0.46 = 46\%$$

This ratio can also be quickly determined from the percent of sales column in the profit-and-loss statement by adding the percentages for marketing expenses and general and administrative expenses (39% + 7%). Thus, 46 cents of every sales dollar went for operations. Although HDInhance wants this ratio to be as low as possible, and 46% is not an alarming amount, it is of concern if it is increasing over time or if a loss is realized.

Inventory turnover rate (or stockturn rate)
The number of times an inventory turns over or is sold during a specified time period (often one year)—calculated based on costs, selling price, or units.

Another useful ratio is the **inventory turnover rate** (also called **stockturn rate** for resellers). The inventory turnover rate is the number of times an inventory turns over or is sold during a specified time period (often one year). This rate tells how quickly a business is moving inventory through the organization. Higher rates indicate that lower investments in inventory are made, thus freeing up funds for other investments. It may be computed on a cost, selling price, or unit basis. The formula based on cost is as follows:

$$\text{Inventory turnover rate} = \frac{\text{cost of goods solid}}{\text{average inventory at cost}}$$

Assuming HDInhance's beginning and ending inventories were $30 million and $20 million, respectively, the inventory turnover rate is as follows:

$$\text{Inventory turnover rate} = \frac{\$55,000,000}{(\$30,000,000 + \$20,000,000)/2} = \frac{\$55,000,000}{\$25,000,000} = 2.2$$

That is, HDInhance's inventory turned over 2.2 times in 2008. Normally, the higher the turnover rate, the higher the management efficiency and company profitability. However, this rate should be compared to industry averages, competitors' rates, and past performance to determine if HDInhance is doing well. A competitor with similar sales but a higher inventory turnover rate will have fewer resources tied up in inventory, allowing it to invest in other areas of the business.

Companies frequently use **return on investment (ROI)** to measure managerial effectiveness and efficiency. For HDInhance, ROI is the ratio of net profits to total investment required to manufacture the new product. This investment includes capital investments in land, buildings, and equipment (here, the initial $10 million to refurbish the manufacturing facility) plus inventory costs (HDInhance's average inventory totaled $25 million), for a total of $35 million. Thus, HDInhance's ROI for this product is as follows:

Return on investment (ROI)

A measure of managerial effectiveness and efficiency—net profit before taxes divided by total investment.

$$\text{Return on investment} = \frac{\text{net profit be for taxes}}{\text{inverstment}} = \frac{-\$1,000,000}{\$35,000,000} = -0.286 = -2.86\%$$

ROI is often used to compare alternatives, and a positive ROI is desired. The alternative with the highest ROI is preferred to other alternatives. HDInhance needs to be concerned with the ROI realized. One obvious way HDInhance can increase ROI is to increase net profit by reducing expenses. Another way is to reduce its investment, perhaps by investing less in inventory and turning it over more frequently.

Marketing Profitability Metrics

Given the above financial results, you may be thinking that HDInhance should drop this new product. But what arguments can marketers make for keeping or dropping this product? The obvious arguments for dropping the product are that first-year sales were well below expected levels and the product lost money, resulting in a negative return on investment.

So what would happen if HDInhance did drop this product? Surprisingly, if the company drops the product, the profits for the total organization will decrease by $4 million! How can that be? Marketing managers need to look closely at the numbers in the profit-and-loss statement to determine the *net marketing contribution* for this product. In HDInhance's case, the net marketing contribution for the product is $4 million, and if the company drops this product, that contribution will disappear as well. Let's look more closely at this concept to illustrate how marketing managers can better assess and defend their marketing strategies and programs.

Net Marketing Contribution

Net marketing contribution (NMC)

A measure of marketing profitability that includes only components of profitability controlled by marketing.

Net marketing contribution (NMC), along with other marketing metrics derived from it, measures *marketing* profitability. It includes only components of profitability that are controlled by marketing. Whereas the previous calculation of net profit before taxes from the profit-and-loss statement includes operating expenses not under marketing's control, NMC does not. Referring back to HDInhance's profit-and-loss statement given in Table A2.2, we can calculate net marketing contribution for the product as follows:

$$\text{NMC} = \text{net sales} - \text{cost of goods sold} - \text{marketing expenses}$$

$$= \$100 \text{ million} - \$55 \text{ million} - \$41 \text{ million} = \$4 \text{ million}$$

The marketing expenses include sales expenses ($15 million), promotion expenses ($14 million), freight expenses ($10 million), and the managerial salaries and expenses of the marketing function ($2 million), which total $41 million.

Thus, the product actually contributed $4 million to HDInhance's profits. It was the $5 million of indirect overhead allocated to this product that caused the negative profit. Further, the amount allocated was $2 million more than estimated in the pro forma profit-and-loss statement. Indeed, if only the estimated amount had been allocated, the product would have earned a *profit* of $1 million rather than losing $1 million. If HDInhance drops the product, the $5 million in fixed overhead expenses will not disappear—it will simply have to be allocated elsewhere. However, the $4 million in net marketing contribution *will* disappear.

Marketing Return on Sales and Investment

To get an even deeper understanding of the profit impact of marketing strategy, we'll now examine two measures of marketing efficiency—*marketing return on sales* (marketing ROS) and *marketing return on investment* (marketing ROI).[11]

Marketing return on sales (or marketing ROS)

The percent of net sales attributable to the net marketing contribution—calculated by dividing net marketing contribution by net sales.

Marketing return on sales (or **marketing ROS**) shows the percent of net sales attributable to the net marketing contribution. For our product, ROS is as follows:

$$\text{Marketing ROS} = \frac{\text{net marketing contribution}}{\text{net sales}} = \frac{\$4,000,000}{\$100,000,000} = 0.04 = 4\%$$

Thus, out of every $100 of sales, the product returns $4 to HDInhance's bottom line. A high marketing ROS is desirable. But to assess whether this is a good level of performance, HDInhance must compare this figure to previous marketing ROS levels for the product, the ROSs of other products in the company's portfolio, and the ROSs of competing products.

Marketing return on investment (or marketing ROI)

A measure of the marketing productivity of a marketing investment—calculated by dividing net marketing contribution by marketing expenses.

Marketing return on investment (or **marketing ROI**) measures the marketing productivity of a marketing investment. In HDInhance's case, the marketing investment is represented by $41 million of the total expenses. Thus, marketing ROI is as follows:

$$\text{Marketing ROI} = \frac{\text{net marketing contribution}}{\text{net marketing expenses}} = \frac{\$4,000,000}{\$41,000,000} = 0.0976 = 9.76\%$$

As with marketing ROS, a high value is desirable, but this figure should be compared with previous levels for the given product and with the marketing ROIs of competitors' products. Note from this equation that marketing ROI could be greater than 100%. This can be achieved by attaining a higher net marketing contribution and/or a lower total marketing expense.

In this section, we estimated market potential and sales, developed profit-and-loss statements, and examined financial measures of performance. In the next section, we discuss methods for analyzing the impact of various marketing tactics. However, before moving on to those analyses, here's another set of quantitative exercises to help you apply what you've learned to other situations.

Marketing by the Numbers Exercise Set Two

2.1 Determine the market potential for a product that has 50 million prospective buyers who purchase an average of 3 units per year and price averages $25. How many units must a company sell if it desires a 10% share of this market?

2.2 Develop a profit-and-loss statement for the Westgate division of North Industries. This division manufactures light fixtures sold to consumers through home improvement and hardware stores. Cost of goods sold represents 40% of net sales. Marketing expenses include selling expenses, promotion expenses, and freight. Selling expenses include sales salaries totaling $3 million per year and sales commissions (5% of sales). The company spent $3 million on advertising last year, and freight costs were 10% of sales. Other costs include $2 million for managerial salaries and expenses for the marketing function and another $3 million for indirect overhead allocated to the division.

a. Develop the profit-and-loss statement if net sales were $20 million last year.

b. Develop the profit-and-loss statement if net sales were $40 million last year.

c. Calculate Westgate's break-even sales.

2.3 Using the profit-and-loss statement you developed in question 2.2b, and assuming that Westgate's beginning inventory was $11 million, ending inventory was $7 million, and total investment was $20 million (including inventory), determine the following:

a. Gross margin percentage

b. Net profit percentage

c. Operating expense percentage

d. Inventory turnover rate

e. Return on investment (ROI)

       f. Net marketing contribution

       g. Marketing return on sales (marketing ROS)

       h. Marketing return on investment (marketing ROI)

       i. Is the Westgate division doing well? Explain your answer.

Financial Analysis of Marketing Tactics (pp A24–A28)

Although the first-year profit performance for HDInhance's new product was less than desired, management feels that this attractive market has excellent growth opportunities. Although the sales of HDInhance's product were lower than initially projected, they were not unreasonable given the size of the current market. Thus, HDInhance wants to explore new marketing tactics to help grow the market for this product and increase sales for the company.

For example, the company could increase advertising to promote more awareness of the new product and its category. It could add salespeople to secure greater product distribution. HDInhance could decrease prices so that more consumers could afford its product. Finally, to expand the market, HDInhance could introduce a lower-priced model in addition to the higher-priced original offering. Before pursuing any of these tactics, HDInhance must analyze the financial implications of each.

Increase Advertising Expenditures

Although most consumers understand DVD players, they may not be aware of high-definition DVD players that also stream video from the Internet. Thus, HDInhance is considering boosting its advertising to make more people aware of the benefits of this device in general and of its own brand in particular.

What if HDInhance's marketers recommend increasing national advertising by 50% to $15 million (assume no change in the variable cooperative component of promotional expenditures)? This represents an increase in fixed costs of $5 million. What increase in sales will be needed to break even on this $5 million increase in fixed costs?

A quick way to answer this question is to divide the increase in fixed cost by the contribution margin, which we found in a previous analysis to be 21%:

$$\text{Increase in sales} = \frac{\text{increase in fixed cost}}{\text{contribution margin}} = \frac{\$5{,}000{,}000}{0.21} = \$23{,}809{,}524$$

Thus, a 50% increase in advertising expenditures must produce a sales increase of almost $24 million to just break even. That $24 million sales increase translates into an almost 1 percentage point increase in market share (1% of the $2.5 billion overall market equals $25 million). That is, to break even on the increased advertising expenditure, HDInhance would have to increase its market share from 4% to 4.95% ($123,809,524 ÷ $2.5 billion = 0.0495 or 4.95% market share). All of this assumes that the total market will not grow, which might or might not be a reasonable assumption.

Increase Distribution Coverage

HDInhance also wants to consider hiring more salespeople in order to call on new retailer accounts and increase distribution through more outlets. Even though HDInhance sells directly to wholesalers, its sales representatives call on retail accounts to perform other functions in addition to selling, such as training retail salespeople. Currently, HDInhance employs 60 sales reps who earn an average of $50,000 in salary plus 10% commission on sales. The product is currently sold to consumers through 1,875 retail outlets. Suppose HDInhance wants to increase that number of outlets to 2,500, an increase of 625 retail outlets. How many additional salespeople will HDInhance need, and what sales will be necessary to break even on the increased cost?

Workload method
An approach to determining sales force size based on the workload required and the time available for selling.

One method for determining what size sales force HDInhance will need is the **workload method.** The workload method uses the following formula to determine the sales force size:

$$NS = \frac{NC \times FC \times LC}{TA}$$

where

NS = number of salespeople

NC = number of customers

FC = average frequency of customer calls per customer

LC = average length of customer call

TA = time an average salesperson has available for selling per year

HDInhance's sales reps typically call on accounts an average of 20 times per year for about 2 hours per call. Although each sales rep works 2,000 hours per year (50 weeks per year × 40 hours per week), they spent about 15 hours per week on nonselling activities such as administrative duties and travel. Thus, the average annual available selling time per sales rep per year is 1,250 hours (50 weeks × 25 hours per week). We can now calculate how many sales reps HDInhance will need to cover the anticipated 2,500 retail outlets:

$$NS = \frac{2,500 \times 20 \times 2}{1,250} = 80 \text{ salespeople}$$

Therefore, HDInhance will need to hire 20 more salespeople. The cost to hire these reps will be $1 million (20 salespeople × $50,000 salary per sales person).

What increase in sales will be required to break even on this increase in fixed costs? The 10% commission is already accounted for in the contribution margin, so the contribution margin remains unchanged at 21%. Thus, the increase in sales needed to cover this increase in fixed costs can be calculated by

$$\text{Increase in sales} = \frac{\text{increase in fixed cost}}{\text{contribution margin}} = \frac{\$1,000,000}{0.21} = \$4,761,905$$

That is, HDInhance's sales must increase almost $5 million to break even on this tactic. So, how many new retail outlets will the company need to secure to achieve this sales increase? The average revenue generated per current outlet is $53,333 ($100 million in sales divided by 1,875 outlets). To achieve the nearly $5 million sales increase needed to break even, HDInhance would need about 90 new outlets ($4,761,905 ÷ $53,333 = 89.3 outlets), or about 4.5 outlets per new rep. Given that current reps cover about 31 outlets apiece (1,875 outlets ÷ 60 reps), this seems very reasonable.

Decrease Price

HDInhance is also considering lowering its price to increase sales revenue through increased volume. The company's research has shown that demand for most types of consumer electronics products is elastic—that is, the percentage increase in the quantity demanded is greater than the percentage decrease in price. It has also been found that when the price of HDTVs goes down, the quantity of accessory products like DVD players demanded increases because they are complementary products.

What increase in sales would be necessary to break even on a 10% decrease in price? That is, what increase in sales will be needed to maintain the total contribution that HDInhance realized at the higher price? The current total contribution can be determined by multiplying the contribution margin by total sales:[12]

$$\text{Current total Contribution} = \text{contribution margin} \times \text{sales} = .21 \times \$100 \text{ million} = \$21 \text{ million}$$

Price changes result in changes in unit contribution and contribution margin. Recall that the contribution margin of 21% was based on variable costs representing 79% of sales. Therefore, unit variable costs can be determined by multiplying the original price by this percentage: $336 \times 0.79 = $265.44 per unit. If price is decreased by 10%, the new price is $302.40. However, variable costs do not change just because price decreased, so the contribution and contribution margin decrease as follows:

	Old	**New (reduced 10%)**
Price	$336	$302.40
– Unit variable cost	$265.44	$265.44
= Unit contribution	$ 70.56	$ 36.96
Contribution margin	$ 70.56/$336 = 0.21 or 21%	$ 36.96/$302.40 = 0.12 or 12%

So a 10% reduction in price results in a decrease in the contribution margin from 21% to 12%.13 To determine the sales level needed to break even on this price reduction, we calculate the level of sales that must be attained at the new contribution margin to achieve the original total contribution of $21 million:

$$\text{New contribution margin} \times \text{new sales level} = \text{original total contribution}$$

So,

$$\text{New sales level} = \frac{\text{original contribution}}{\text{new contribution margin}} = \frac{\$21,000,000}{0.12} = \$175,000,000$$

Thus, sales must increase by $75 million ($175 million – $100 million) just to break even on a 10% price reduction. This means that HDInhance must increase market share to 7% ($175 million ÷ $2.5 billion) to achieve the current level of profits (assuming no increase in the total market sales). The marketing manager must assess whether or not this is a reasonable goal.

Extend the Product Line

As a final option, HDInhance is considering extending its product line by offering a lower-priced model. Of course, the new, lower-priced product would steal some sales from the higher-priced model. This is called **cannibalization**—the situation in which one product sold by a company takes a portion of its sales from other company products. If the new product has a lower contribution than the original product, the company's total contribution will decrease on the cannibalized sales. However, if the new product can generate enough new volume, it is worth considering.

To assess cannibalization, HDInhance must look at the incremental contribution gained by having both products available. Recall that in the previous analysis we determined that unit variable costs were $265.44 and unit contribution was just over $70. Assuming costs remain the same next year, HDInhance can expect to realize a contribution per unit of approximately $70 for every unit of the original product sold.

Assume that the first model offered by HDInhance is called HD1 and the new, lower-priced model is called HD2. HD2 will retail for $400, and resellers will take the same markup percentages on price as they do with the higher-priced model. Therefore, HD2's price to wholesalers will be $224 as follows:

Retail price:	$400
minus retail margin (30%):	– $120
Retailer's cost/wholesaler's price:	$280
minus wholesaler's margin (20%):	– $ 56
Wholesaler's cost/HDInhance's price	$224

Cannibalization

The situation in which one product sold by a company takes a portion of its sales from other company products.

If HD2's variable costs are estimated to be $174, then its contribution per unit will equal $50 ($224 − $174 = $50). That means for every unit that HD2 cannibalizes from HD1, HDInhance will *lose* $20 in contribution toward fixed costs and profit (that is, contribution$_{HD2}$ − contribution$_{HD1}$ = $50 − $70 = − $20). You might conclude that HDInhance should not pursue this tactic because it appears as though the company will be worse off if it introduces the lower-priced model. However, if HD2 captures enough *additional* sales, HDInhance will be better off even though some HD1 sales are cannibalized. The company must examine what will happen to *total* contribution, which requires estimates of unit volume for both products.

Originally, HDInhance estimated that next year's sales of HD1 would be 600,000 units. However, with the introduction of HD2, it now estimates that 200,000 of those sales will be cannibalized by the new model. If HDInhance sells only 200,000 units of the new HD2 model (all cannibalized from HD1), the company would lose $4 million in total contribution (200,000 units × −$20 per cannibalized unit = −$4 million)—not a good outcome. However, HDInhance estimates that HD2 will generate the 200,000 of cannibalized sales plus an *additional* 500,000 unit sales. Thus, the contribution on these additional HD2 units will be $25 million (i.e., 500,000 units × $50 per unit = $25 million). The net effect is that HDInhance will gain $21 million in total contribution by introducing HD2.

The following table compares HDInhance's total contribution with and without the introduction of HD2:

	HD1 only	HD1 and HD2
HD1 contribution	600,000 units × $70 = $42,000,000	400,000 units × $70 = $28,000,000
HD2 contribution	0	700,000 units × $50 = $35,000,000
Total contribution	$42,000,000	$63,000,000

The difference in the total contribution is a net gain of $21 million ($63 million − $42 million). Based on this analysis, HDInhance should introduce the HD2 model because it results in a positive incremental contribution. However, if fixed costs will increase by more than $21 million as a result of adding this model, then the net effect will be negative and HDInhance should not pursue this tactic.

Now that you have seen these marketing tactic analysis concepts in action as they related to HDInhance's new product, here are several exercises for you to apply what you have learned in this section in other contexts.

Marketing by the Numbers Exercise Set Three

3.1 Kingsford, Inc., sells small plumbing components to consumers through retail outlets. Total industry sales for Kingsford's relevant market last year were $80 million, with Kingsford's sales representing 10% of that total. Contribution margin is 25%. Kingsford's sales force calls on retail outlets and each sales rep earns $45,000 per year plus 1% commission on all sales. Retailers receive a 40% margin on selling price and generate average revenue of $10,000 per outlet for Kingsford.

a. The marketing manager has suggested increasing consumer advertising by $300,000. By how much would dollar sales need to increase to break even on this expenditure? What increase in overall market share does this represent?

b. Another suggestion is to hire three more sales representatives to gain new consumer retail accounts. How many new retail outlets would be necessary to break even on the increased cost of adding three sales reps?

c. A final suggestion is to make a 20% across-the-board price reduction. By how much would dollar sales need to increase to maintain Kingsford's current contribution? (See endnote 13 to calculate the new contribution margin.)

d. Which suggestion do you think Kingsford should implement? Explain your recommendation.

3.2 PepsiCo sells its soft drinks in approximately 400,000 retail establishments, such as supermarkets, discount stores, and convenience stores. Sales representatives call on each retail account weekly, which means each account is called on by a sales rep 52 times per year. The average length of a sales call is 75 minutes (or 1.25 hours). An average salesperson works 2,000 hours per year (50 weeks per year $\times$ 40 hours per week) , but each spends 10 hours a week on nonselling activities, such as administrative tasks and travel. How many salespeople does PepsiCo need?

3.3 Hair Zone manufactures a brand of hair-styling gel. It is considering adding a modified version of the product—a foam that provides stronger hold. Hair Zone's variable costs and prices to wholesalers are as follows:

	Current Hair Gel	**New Foam Product**
Unit selling price	2.00	2.25
Unit variable costs	.85	1.25

Hair Zone expects to sell 1 million units of the new styling foam in the first year after introduction, but it expects that 60% of those sales will come from buyers who normally purchase Hair Zone's styling gel. Hair Zone estimates that it would sell 1.5 million units of the gel if it did not introduce the foam. If the fixed cost of launching the new foam will be $100,000 during the first year, should Hair Zone add the new product to its line? Why or why not?

Careers in Marketing

Now that you have completed this course in marketing, you have a good idea of what the field entails. You may have decided you want to pursue a marketing career because it offers constant challenge, stimulating problems, the opportunity to work with people, and excellent advancement opportunities. But you still may not know which part of marketing best suits you—marketing is a very broad field offering a wide variety of career options.

This appendix helps you discover what types of marketing jobs best match your special skills and interests, shows you how to conduct the kind of job search that will get you the position you want in the company of your choice, describes marketing career paths open to you, and suggests other information resources.

Marketing Careers Today (pp A29–A30)

Marketing salaries may vary by company, position, and region, and salary figures change constantly. In general, entry-level marketing salaries usually are only slightly below those for engineering and chemistry but equal or exceed starting salaries in economics, finance, accounting, general business, and the liberal arts. Moreover, if you succeed in an entry-level marketing position, it's likely that you will be promoted quickly to higher levels of responsibility and salary. In addition, because of the consumer and product knowledge you will gain in these jobs, marketing positions provide excellent training for the highest levels in an organization.

Overall Marketing Facts and Trends

In conducting your job search, consider the following facts and trends that are changing the world of marketing.

Focus on customers: More and more, companies are realizing that they win in the marketplace only by creating superior value for customers. To capture value from customers, they must first find new and better ways to solve customer problems and improve customer brand experiences. This increasing focus on the customer puts marketers at the forefront in many of today's companies. As the primary customer-facing function, marketing's mission is to get all company departments to "think customer."

Technology: Technology is changing the way marketers work. For example, price coding allows instantaneous retail inventorying. Software for marketing training, forecasting, and other functions is changing the ways we market. And the Internet is creating new jobs and new recruiting rules. Consider the explosive growth in new media marketing. Whereas advertising firms have traditionally recruited "generalists" in account management, "generalist" has now taken on a whole new meaning—advertising account executives must now have both broad and specialized knowledge.

Diversity: The number of women and minorities in marketing continues to rise. They also are rising rapidly into marketing management. For example, in the U.S., women now outnumber men by nearly two to one as advertising account executives. As marketing becomes more global, the need for diversity in marketing positions will continue to increase, opening new opportunities.

Global: Companies such as Coca-Cola, McDonald's, IBM, Wal-Mart, and Procter & Gamble have become multinational, with manufacturing and marketing operations in hundreds of countries. Indeed, such companies often make more profit from sales outside the United States than from within. And it's not just the big companies that are involved in international marketing. Organizations of all sizes have moved into the global arena. Many new marketing opportunities and careers will be directly linked to the expanding global marketplace. The globalization of business also means that you will need more cultural, language, and people skills in the marketing world of the twenty-first century.

Not-for-profit organizations: Increasingly, colleges, arts organizations, libraries, hospitals, and other not-for-profit organizations are recognizing the need for effectively marketing their "products" and services to various publics. This awareness has led to new marketing positions—with these organizations hiring their own marketing directors and marketing vice presidents or using outside marketing specialists.

Looking for a Job in Today's Marketing World (pp A30–A36)

To choose and find the right job, you will need to apply the marketing skills you've learned in this course, especially marketing analysis and planning. Follow these eight steps for marketing yourself: (1) Conduct a self-assessment and seek career counseling, (2) examine job descriptions, (3) explore the job market and assess opportunities, (4) develop search strategies, (5) prepare a résumé, (6) write a cover letter and assemble supporting documents, (7) interview for jobs, and (8) follow-up.

Conduct a Self-Assessment and Seek Career Counseling

If you're having difficulty deciding what kind of marketing position is the best fit for you, start out by doing some self-testing or get some career counseling. Self-assessments require that you honestly and thoroughly evaluate your interests, strengths, and weaknesses. What do you do well (your best and favorite skills) and not so well? What are your favorite interests? What are your career goals? What makes you stand out from other job seekers?

The answers to such questions may suggest which marketing careers you should seek or avoid. For help in making an effective self-assessment, look for the following books: Shoya Zichy, *Career Match: Connecting Who You Are with What You Love to Do* (AMACOM Books, 2007) and Richard Bolles, *What Color Is Your Parachute 2008?* (Ten Speed Press, 2007). Many Web sites also offer self-assessment tools, such as the Keirsey Temperament Theory and the Temperament Sorter, a free but broad assessment available at AdvisorTeam. com. For a more specific evaluation, CareerLeader.com offers a complete online business career self-assessment program designed by the Directors of MBA Career Development at Harvard Business School. You can use this for a fee.

For help in finding a career counselor to guide you in making a career assessment, Richard Bolles's *What Color Is Your Parachute 2008?* contains a useful state-by-state sampling. CareerLeader.com also offers personal career counseling. (Some counselors can help you in your actual job search, too.) You can also consult the career counseling, testing, and placement services at your college or university.

Examine Job Descriptions

After you have identified your skills, interests, and desires, you need to see which marketing positions are the best match for them. Two U.S. Labor Department publications (available in your local library or online)—the *Occupation Outlook Handbook* (www.bls.gov/oco) and the *Dictionary of Occupational Titles* (www.occupationalinfo.org)—describe the duties involved in various occupations, the specific training and education needed, the availability of jobs in each field, possibilities for advancement, and probable earnings.

Your initial career shopping list should be broad and flexible. Look for different ways to achieve your objectives. For example, if you want a career in marketing management, consider the public as well as the private sector, and local and regional as well as national and international firms. Be open initially to exploring many options, then focus on specific industries and jobs, listing your basic goals as a way to guide your choices. Your list might include "a job in a start-up company, near a big city in the UAE, doing new-product planning with a computer software firm."

Explore the Job Market and Assess Opportunities

At this stage, you need to look at the market and see what positions are actually available. You do not have to do this alone. Any of the following may assist you.

Career Development Centers

Your college's career development center is an excellent place to start. In addition, find out everything you can about the companies that interest you by consulting business magazines, Web sites, annual reports, business reference books, faculty, career counselors, and others. Try to analyze the industry's and the company's future growth and profit potential, advancement opportunities, salary levels, entry positions, travel time, and other factors of significance to you.

Job Fairs

Career development centers often work with corporate recruiters to organize on-campus job fairs. You might also use the Internet to check on upcoming career fairs in your region. For example, visit Monster Career Fairs at www.nationalcareerfairs.com/monster. You may find other opportunities at online career fairs such as The Wall Street Journal Virtual Career Fair at www.wsj-classified.com/vcf.

Networking

Networking—asking for job leads from friends, family, people in your community, and career centers—is one of the best ways to find a marketing job. Studies estimate that 60 to 90 percent of jobs are found through networking. The idea is to spread your net wide, contacting anybody and everybody.

The phone book is another effective way to job search. Check out employers in your field of interest in whatever region you want to work, then call and ask if they are hiring for the position of your choice.

Cooperative Education and Internships

According to a survey by CBcampus.com, CareerBuilder.com's college job search site, employers on average give full-time employment offers to about 61 percent of students who have had internships with their companies. Many company Internet sites have separate internship areas. For example, check out InternshipPrograms.com, MonsterTRAK. com, CampusCareerCenter.com (www.campuscareercenter.com/students/intern.asp), InternJobs.com, and InternAbroad.com. If you know of a company for which you wish to work, go to that company's corporate Web site, enter the human resources area, and check for internships. If none are listed, try e-mailing the human resources department, asking if internships are offered.

The Internet

A constantly increasing number of sites on the Internet deal with job hunting. You can also use the Internet to make contacts with people who can help you gain information on companies and research companies that interest you. The Riley Guide offers a great introduction to what jobs are available (www.rileyguide.com). CareerBuilder.com, Monster.com, and Yahoo! HotJobs (http://hotjobs.yahoo.com) are good general sites for seeking job listings.

Most companies have their own Web sites on which they post job listings. This may be helpful if you have a specific and fairly limited number of companies that you are keeping your eye on for job opportunities. But if this is not the case, remember that to find out what interesting marketing jobs the companies themselves are posting, you may have to visit hundreds of corporate sites.

Professional Networking Sites

Many companies have now begun to take advantage of social networking sites to find talented applicants. From Facebook to LinkedIn, social networking has become professional networking. For example, Ernst & Young has a career page on Facebook (www.facebook.com/ernstandyoungcareers) to find potential candidates for entry-level positions. For job seekers, online professional networking offers more efficient job targeting and reduces costs associated compared with traditional interaction methods such as traveling to job fairs and interviews, printing résumé, and other expenses.

However, although the Internet offers a wealth of resources for searching for the perfect job, be aware that it constitutes a two-way street. Just as job seekers can search the Web to find job opportunities, employers can search for information on job candidates. A recent Execunet survey found that a growing number of job searches are being derailed by "digital dirt"—information mined from online social networking sites that reveals unintended or embarrassing anecdotes and photos. Web searches also can sometimes reveal inconsistencies and résumé inflation. According to the Execunet survey, 77 percent of recruiters interviewed use search engines to learn more about candidates. Some 35 percent said they've eliminated a candidate based on information that they uncovered.[1]

Develop Search Strategies

Once you've decided which companies you are interested in, you need to contact them. One of the best ways is through on-campus interviews. But not every company you are interested in will visit your school. In such instances, you can write, e-mail, or phone the company directly or ask marketing professors or school alumni for contacts.

Prepare Résumés

A résumé is a concise yet comprehensive written summary of your qualifications, including your academic, personal, and professional achievements, that showcases why you are the best candidate for the job. Since an employer will spend an average of 15 to 20 seconds reviewing your résumé, you want to be sure that you prepare a good one.

In preparing your résumé, remember that all information on it must be accurate and complete. Résumés typically begin with the applicant's full name, telephone and fax numbers, and mail and e-mail addresses. A simple and direct statement of career objectives generally appears next, followed by work history and academic data (including awards and internships), and then by personal activities and experiences applicable to the job sought.

The résumé sometimes ends with a list of references the employer may contact (at other times, references may be listed separately). If your work or internship experience is limited, nonexistent, or irrelevant, then it is a good idea to emphasize your academic and nonacademic achievements, showing skills related to those required for excellent job performance.

There are three types of résumés. Reverse *chronological* résumés, which emphasize career growth, are organized in reverse chronological order, starting with your most recent job. They focus on job titles within organizations, describing the responsibilities required for each job. *Functional* résumés focus less on job titles and work history and more on assets and achievements. This format works best if your job history is scanty or discontinuous. *Mixed*, or *combination*, résumés take from each of the other two formats. First, the skills used for a specific job are listed, then the job title is stated. This format works best for applicants whose past jobs are in other fields or seemingly unrelated to the position.

Your local bookstore or library has many books that can assist you in developing your résumé. Popular guides are Brenda Greene, *Get the Interview Every Time: Fortune 500 Hiring Professionals' Tips for Writing Winning Résumés and Cover Letters* (Dearborn Trade, 2004) and Susan Britton Whitcomb's *Résumé Magic: Trade Secrets of a Professional Résumé Writer* (JIST Works, 2006). Computer software programs, such as *RésuméMaker* (ResumeMaker.com), provide hundreds of sample résumés and ready-to-use phrases while guiding you through the résumé preparation process. America's Career InfoNet (www.acinet.org/acinet/resume/resume_intro.asp) offers a step-by-step résumé tutorial, and Monster (http://content.monster.com/resume/home.aspx) offers résumé advice and writing services. Finally, you can even create your own personalized online résumé at sites such as optimalresume.com.

Electronic Résumés

Use of the Internet as a tool in the job search process is increasing, so it's a good idea to have your résumé ready for the online environment. You can forward an electronic résumé to networking contacts or recruiting professionals through e-mail. You can also post it in online databases with the hope that employers and recruiters will find it.

Successful electronic résumés require a different strategy than paper résumés. For instance, when companies search résumé banks, they search key words and industry buzz words that describe a skill or core work required for each job, so nouns are much more important than verbs. Two good resources for preparing electronic résumés are Susan Ireland's Electronic Résumé Guide (http://susanireland.com/eresumeguide) and The Riley Guide (www.rileyguide.com/eresume.html).

After you have written your electronic résumé, you need to post it. The following sites may be good locations to start: Monster.com (www.monster.com) and Yahoo! HotJobs (http://hotjobs.yahoo.com). However, use caution when posting your résumé on various sites. In this era of identity theft, you need to select sites with care so as to protect your privacy. Limit access to your personal contact information and don't use sites that offer to "blast" your résumé into cyberspace.

Résumé Tips

- Communicate your worth to potential employers in a concrete manner, citing examples whenever possible.

- Be concise and direct.

- Use active verbs to show you are a doer.

- Do not skimp on quality or use gimmicks. Spare no expense in presenting a professional résumé.

- Have someone critique your work. A single typo can eliminate you from being considered.

- Customize your résumé for specific employers. Emphasize your strengths as they pertain to your targeted job.

- Keep your résumé compact, usually one page.

- Format the text to be attractive, professional, and readable. Times New Roman is often the font of choice. Avoid too much "design" or gimmicky flourishes.

Write Cover Letter, Follow Up, and Assemble Supporting Documents

Cover Letter

You should include a cover letter informing the employer that a résumé is enclosed. But a cover letter does more than this. It also serves to summarize in one or two paragraphs the contents of the résumé and explains why you think you are the right person for the position. The goal is to persuade the employer to look at the more detailed résumé. A typical cover letter is organized as follows: (1) the name and position of the person you are contacting; (2) a statement identifying the position you are applying for, how you heard of the vacancy, and the reasons for your interest; (3) a summary of your qualifications for the job; (4) a description of what follow-ups you intend to make, such as phoning in two weeks to see if the résumé has been received; (5) an expression of gratitude for the opportunity of being a candidate for the job. America's Career InfoNet (www.acinet.org/acinet/resume/resume_intro.asp) offers a step-by-step tutorial on how to create a cover letter, and Susan Ireland's Web site contains more than 50 cover letter samples (http://susanireland.com/coverletterindex.htm).

Follow-Up

Once you send your cover letter and résumé to perspective employers via the method they prefer—e-mail, their Web site, fax, or regular mail—it's often a good idea to follow up. In today's market, job seekers can't afford to wait for interviews to find them. A quality résumé and an attractive cover letter are crucial, but a proper follow-up may be the key to landing an interview. However, before you engage your potential employer, be sure to research the company. Knowing about the company and understanding its place in the industry will help you shine. When you place a call, send an e-mail, or mail a letter to a company contact, be sure to restate your interest in the position, check on the status of your résumé, and ask the employer about any questions they may have.

Letters of Recommendation

Letters of recommendation are written references by professors, former and current employers, and others that testify to your character, skills, and abilities. Some companies may request letters of recommendation, to be submitted either with the résumé or at the interview. Even if letters of recommendation aren't requested, it's a good idea to bring them with you to the interview. A good reference letter tells why you would be an excellent candidate for the position. In choosing someone to write a letter of recommendation, be confident that the person will give you a good reference. In addition, do not assume the person knows everything about you or the position you are seeking. Rather, provide the person with your résumé and other relevant data. As a courtesy, allow the reference writer at least a month to complete the letter and enclose a stamped, addressed envelope with your materials.

In the packet containing your résumé, cover letter, and letters of recommendation, you may also want to attach other relevant documents that support your candidacy, such as academic transcripts, graphics, portfolios, and samples of writing.

Interview for Jobs

As the old saying goes, "The résumé gets you the interview; the interview gets you the job." The job interview offers you an opportunity to gather more information about the organization, while at the same time allowing the organization to gather more information about you. You'll want to present your best self. The interview process consists of three parts: before the interview, the interview itself, and after the interview. If you pass through these stages successfully, you will be called back for the follow-up interview.

Before the Interview

In preparing for your interview, do the following:

1. Understand that interviewers have diverse styles, including the "chitchat," let's-get-to-know-each-other style; the interrogation style of question after question; and the tough-probing "why, why, why" style, among others. So be ready for anything.

2. With a friend, practice being interviewed and then ask for a critique. Or, videotape yourself in a practice interview so that you can critique your own performance. Your college placement service may also offer "mock" interviews to help you.

3. Prepare at least five good questions whose answers are not easily found in the company literature, such as "What is the future direction of the firm?" "How does the firm differentiate itself from competitors?" "Do you have a new-media division?"

4. Anticipate possible interview questions, such as "Why do you want to work for this company?" or "Why should we hire you?" Prepare solid answers before the interview. Have a clear idea of why you are interested in joining the company and the industry to which it belongs. (See Susan Ireland's site for additional interview questions: http://susanireland.com/interviewwork.html)

5. Avoid back-to-back interviews—they can be exhausting and it is unpredictable how long they will last.

6. Prepare relevant documents that support your candidacy, such as academic transcripts, letters of recommendation, graphics, portfolios, and samples of writing. Bring multiple copies to the interview.

7. Dress conservatively and professionally. Be neat and clean.

8. Arrive 10 minutes early to collect your thoughts and review the major points you intend to cover. Check your name on the interview schedule, noting the name of the interviewer and the room number. Be courteous and polite to office staff.

9. Approach the interview enthusiastically. Let your personality shine through.

During the Interview

During the interview, do the following:

1. Shake hands firmly in greeting the interviewer. Introduce yourself, using the same form of address that the interviewer uses. Focus on creating a good initial impression.

2. Keep your poise. Relax, smile when appropriate, and be upbeat throughout.

3. Maintain eye contact, good posture, and speak distinctly. Don't clasp your hands or fiddle with jewelry, hair, or clothing. Sit comfortably in your chair. Do not smoke, even if it's permitted.

4. Along with the copies of relevant documents that support your candidacy, carry extra copies of your résumé with you.

5. Have your story down pat. Present your selling points. Answer questions directly. Avoid either one-word or too-wordy answers.

6. Let the interviewer take the initiative but don't be passive. Find an opportunity to direct the conversation to things about yourself that you want the interviewer to hear.

7. To end on a high note, make your most important point or ask your most pertinent question during the last part of the interview.

8. Don't hesitate to "close." You might say, "I'm very interested in the position, and I have enjoyed this interview."

9. Obtain the interviewer's business card or address and phone number so that you can follow up later.

A tip for acing the interview: Before you open your mouth, find out *what it's like* to be a brand manager, sales representative, market researcher, advertising account executive, or other position for which you're interviewing. See if you can find a "mentor"—someone in a position similar to the one you're seeking, perhaps with another company. Talk with this mentor about the ins and outs of the job and industry.

After the Interview

After the interview, do the following:

1. After leaving the interview, record the key points that arose. Be sure to note who is to follow up and when a decision can be expected.

2. Analyze the interview objectively, including the questions asked, the answers to them, your overall interview presentation, and the interviewer's responses to specific points.

3. Immediately send a thank-you letter or e-mail, mentioning any additional items and your willingness to supply further information.

4. If you do not hear within the specified time, write, e-mail, or call the interviewer to determine your status.

Follow-Up Interview

If your first interview takes place off-site, such as at your college or at a job fair, and if you are successful with that initial interview, you will be invited to visit the organization. The in-company interview will probably run from several hours to an entire day. The organization will examine your interest, maturity, enthusiasm, assertiveness, logic, and company and functional knowledge. You should ask questions about issues of importance to you. Find out about the working environment, job role, responsibilities, opportunities for advancement, current industrial issues, and the company's personality. The company wants to discover if you are the right person for the job, whereas you want to find out if it is the right job for you. The key is to determine if the right *fit* exists between you and the company.

Marketing Jobs (pp A36–A40)

This section describes some of the key marketing positions.

Advertising

Advertising is one of today's hottest fields in marketing. In fact, *Money* magazine lists a position in advertising as among the 50 best jobs in America.

Job Descriptions

Key advertising positions include copywriter, art director, production manager, account executive, and media planner/buyer.

- *Copywriters* write advertising copy and help find the concepts behind the written words and visual images of advertisements.

- *Art directors,* the other part of the creative team, help translate the copywriters' ideas into dramatic visuals called "layouts." Agency artists develop print layouts, package designs, television layouts (called "storyboards"), corporate logotypes, trademarks, and symbols. *Production managers* are responsible for physically creating ads, in-house or by contracting through outside production houses.

- *Account development executives* research and understand clients' markets and customers and help develop marketing and advertising strategies to impact them.

- *Account executives* serve as liaisons between clients and agencies. They coordinate the planning, creation, production, and implementation of an advertising campaign for the account.

- *Account planners* serve as the voice of the consumer in the agency. They research consumers to understand their needs and motivations as a basis for developing effective ad campaigns.

- *Media planners (or buyers)* determine the best mix of television, radio, newspaper, magazine, digital, and other media for the advertising campaign.

Skills Needed, Career Paths, and Typical Salaries

Work in advertising requires strong people skills in order to interact closely with an often-difficult and demanding client base. In addition, advertising attracts people with strong skills in planning, problem solving, creativity, communication, initiative, leadership, and presentation. Advertising involves working under high levels of stress and pressure created by unrelenting deadlines. Advertisers frequently have to work long hours to meet deadlines for a presentation. But work achievements are very apparent, with the results of creative strategies observed by thousands or even millions of people.

Because they are so sought after, positions in advertising sometimes require an MBA. But there are many jobs open for business, graphics arts, and liberal arts undergraduates. Advertising positions often serve as gateways to higher-level management. Moreover, with large advertising agencies opening offices all over the world, there is the possibility of eventually working on global campaigns.

Starting advertising salaries are relatively low compared to some other marketing jobs because of strong competition for entry-level advertising jobs. You may even want to consider working for free to break in. Compensation will increase quickly as you move into account executive or other management positions. For more facts and figures, see the Web pages of *Advertising Age*, a key ad industry publication (www.adage.com, click on the Job Bank link), and the American Association of Advertising Agencies (www.aaaa.org).

Brand and Product Management

Brand and product managers plan, direct, and control business and marketing efforts for their products. They are involved with research and development, packaging, manufacturing, sales and distribution, advertising, promotion, market research, and business analysis and forecasting.

Job Descriptions

A company's brand management team consists of people in several positions.

- *Brand managers* guide the development of marketing strategies for a specific brand.
- *Assistant brand managers* are responsible for certain strategic components of the brand.
- *Product managers* oversee several brands within a product line or product group.
- *Product category managers* direct multiple product lines in the product category.
- *Market analysts* research the market and provide important strategic information to the project managers.
- *Project directors* are responsible for collecting market information on a marketing or product project.
- *Research directors* oversee the planning, gathering, and analyzing of all organizational research.

Skills Needed, Career Paths, and Typical Salaries

Brand and product management requires high problem-solving, analytical, presentation, communication, and leadership skills, as well as the ability to work well in a team. Product management requires long hours and involves the high pressure of running large projects. In consumer goods companies, the newcomer—who usually needs an MBA—joins a brand team as an assistant and learns the ropes by doing numerical analyses and watching senior brand people. This person eventually heads the team and later moves on to manage a larger brand, then several brands.

Many industrial goods companies also have product managers. Product management is one of the best training grounds for future corporate officers. Product management also offers good opportunities to move into international marketing. Product managers command relatively high salaries. Because this job category encourages or requires a master's degree, starting pay tends to be higher than in other marketing categories such as advertising or retailing.

Sales and Sales Management

Sales and sales management opportunities exist in a wide range of profit and not-for-profit organizations and in product and service organizations, including financial, insurance, consulting, and government organizations.

Job Descriptions

Key jobs include consumer sales, industrial sales, national account manager, service support, sales trainers, sales management, and telesellers.

- *Consumer* sales involves selling consumer products and services through retailers.

- *Industrial sales* involves selling products and services to other businesses.

- *National account managers (NAM)* oversee a few very large accounts.

- *Service support* personnel support salespeople during and after the sale of a product.

- *Sales trainers* train new hires and provide refresher training for all sales personnel.

- *Sales management* includes a sequence of positions ranging from district manager to vice president of sales.

- The *teleseller* (not to be confused with the home consumer telemarketer) offers service and support to field salespeople.

Salespeople enjoy active professional lives, working outside the office and interacting with others. They manage their own time and activities. And successful salespeople can be very well paid. Competition for top jobs can be intense. Every sales job is different, but some positions involve extensive travel, long workdays, and working under pressure. You can also expect to be transferred more than once between company headquarters and regional offices. However, most companies are now working to bring good work–life balance to their salespeople and sales managers.

Skills Needed, Career Paths, and Typical Salaries

Selling is a people profession in which you will work with people every day, all day long. In addition to people skills, sales professionals need sales and communication skills. Most sales positions also require strong problem-solving, analytical, presentation, and leadership abilities as well as creativity and initiative. Teamwork skills are increasingly important.

Career paths lead from salesperson to district, regional, and higher levels of sales management and, in many cases, to the top management of the firm. Today, most entry-level sales management positions require a college degree. Increasingly, people seeking selling jobs are acquiring sales experience in an internship capacity or from a part-time job before graduating. Sales positions are great springboards to leadership positions, with more CEOs starting in sales than in any other entry-level position. This possibly explains why competition for top sales jobs is intense.

Starting base salaries in sales may be moderate, but compensation is often supplemented by significant commission, bonus, or other incentive plans. In addition, many sales jobs include a company car or car allowance. Successful salespeople are among most companies' highest paid employees.

Other Marketing Jobs

Retailing

Retailing provides an early opportunity to assume marketing responsibilities. Key jobs include store manager, regional manager, buyer, department manager, and salesperson. *Store managers* direct the management and operation of an individual store. *Regional managers* manage groups of stores across several states and report performance to headquarters. *Buyers* select and buy the merchandise that the store carries. The *department manager* acts as store manager of a department, such as clothing, but on the department level. The *salesperson* sells merchandise to retail customers. Retailing can involve relocation, but generally there is little travel, unless you are a buyer. Retailing requires high people and sales skills because retailers are constantly in contact with customers. Enthusiasm, willingness, and communication skills are very helpful for retailers, too.

Retailers work long hours, but their daily activities are often more structured than some types of marketing positions. Starting salaries in retailing tend to be low, but pay increases as you move into management or some retailing specialty job.

Marketing Research

Marketing researchers interact with managers to define problems and identify the information needed to resolve them. They design research projects, prepare questionnaires and samples, analyze data, prepare reports, and present their findings and recommendations to management. They must understand statistics, consumer behavior, psychology, and sociology. A master's degree helps. Career opportunities exist with manufacturers, retailers, some wholesalers, trade and industry associations, marketing research firms, advertising agencies, and governmental and private nonprofit agencies.

New-Product Planning

People interested in new-product planning can find opportunities in many types of organizations. They usually need a good background in marketing, marketing research, and sales forecasting; they need organizational skills to motivate and coordinate others; and they may need a technical background. Usually, these people work first in other marketing positions before joining the new-product department.

Marketing Logistics (Physical Distribution)

Marketing logistics, or physical distribution, is a large and dynamic field, with many career opportunities. Major transportation carriers, manufacturers, wholesalers, and retailers all employ logistics specialists. Increasingly, marketing teams include logistics specialists, and marketing managers' career paths include marketing logistics assignments. Coursework in quantitative methods, finance, accounting, and marketing will provide you with the necessary skills for entering the field.

Public Relations

Most organizations have a public relations staff to anticipate problems with various publics, handle complaints, deal with media, and build the corporate image. People interested in public relations should be able to speak and write clearly and persuasively, and they should have a background in journalism, communications, or the liberal arts. The challenges in this job are highly varied and very people-oriented.

Not-for-Profit Services

The key jobs in not-for-profits include marketing director, director of development, event coordinator, publication specialist, and intern/volunteer. The *marketing director* is in charge of all marketing activities for the organization. The *director of development* organizes, manages, and directs the fund-raising campaigns that keep a not-for-profit in existence. An *event coordinator* directs all aspects of fund-raising events, from initial planning through implementation. The *publication specialist* oversees publications designed to promote awareness of the organization.

Although typically an unpaid position, the *intern/volunteer* performs various marketing functions, and this work can be an important step to gaining a full-time position. The not-for-profit sector is typically not for someone who is money-driven. Rather, most not-for-profits look for people with a strong sense of community spirit and the desire to help others. Therefore, starting pay is usually lower than in other marketing fields. However, the bigger the not-for-profit, the better your chance of rapidly increasing your income when moving into upper management.

Other Resources (p A40)

Professional marketing associations and organizations are another source of information about careers. Marketers belong to many such societies. You may want to contact some of the following in your job search:

Advertising Women of New York, 25 West 45th Street, New York, NY 10036. (212) 221-7969 (www.awny.org)

American Advertising Federation, 1101 Vermont Avenue, NW, Suite 500, Washington, DC 2005. (800) 999-2231 (www.aaf.org)

American Marketing Association, 311 South Wacker Drive, Suite 5800, Chicago, IL 60606. (800) AMA-1150 (www.marketingpower.com)

Market Research Association, 110 National Drive, 2nd Floor, Glastonbury, CT 06033. (860) 682-1000 (www.mra-net.org)

National Association of Sales Professionals, 37577 Newburgh Park Circle, Livonia, MI 48152. (877) 800-7192 (www.nasp.com)

National Management Association, 2210 Arbor Boulevard, Dayton, OH 45439. (937) 294-0421 (www.nma1.org)

National Retail Federation, 325 Seventh Street NW, Suite 1100, Washington, DC 20004 (800) 673-4692 (www.nrf.com)

Product Development and Management Association, 15000 Commerce Parkway, Suite C, Mount Laurel, NJ 08054. (800) 232-5241 (www.pdma.org)

Public Relations Society of America, 33 Maiden Lane, Eleventh Floor, New York, NY 10038. (212) 460-1400 (www.prsa.org)

Sales and Marketing Executives International, PO Box 1390, Sumas, WA 98295-1390. (312) 893-0751 (www.smei.org)

The Association of Women in Communications, 3337 Duke Street, Alexandria, VA 22314. (703) 370-7436 (www.womcom.org)

References

CHAPTER 1

1. See "Mannai Automotive Opens New Showroom at Umm Al Afaee," *AME Info*, June 24, 2008, www.ameinfo.com/161480.html.

2. See "Markets: Since Launch of First Generation of iPod, Apple Inc. Has Sold More Than 88.7 Million Units Worldwide," *Associated Press Financial Wire*, March 14, 2007; Adam L. Penenberg, "All Eyes on Apple," *Fast Company*, December 2007–January 2008, pp. 83–91.

3. See "Introduction," Dubai Cares website, accessed at www.dubaicares.ae/Introduction, June 24, 2008.

4. As quoted in Carolyn P. Neal, "From the Editor," *Marketing Management*, January–February 2006, p. 3.

5. The American Marketing Association offers the following definition: "Marketing is the activity, set of institutions, and processes for creating, communicating, delivering, and exchanging offerings that have value for customers, clients, partners, and society at large." Accessed at http://www.marketingpower.com/AboutAMA/Pages/DefinitionofMarketing.aspx, June 2011. Also see, Lisa M. Keefe, "Marketing Defined," *Marketing News*, January 15, 2008, pp. 28–29.

6. Information from "Destination Oman," accessed at www.destinationoman.com, 2009.

7. See Theodore Levitt's classic article, "Marketing Myopia," *Harvard Business Review*, July–August 1960, pp. 45–56. For more recent discussions, see Yves Doz, Jose Santos, and Peter J. Williamson, "Marketing Myopia Re-Visited: Why Every Company Needs to Learn from the World," *Ivey Business Journal*, January–February 2004, p. 1; "What Business Are You In?" *Harvard Business Review*, October 2006, pp. 127–137; and John D. Nicholson and Philip J. Kitchen, "The Development of Regional Marketing—Have Marketers Been Myopic?" *International Journal of Business Studies*, June 2007, pp. 107–125.

8. Information from "Yas Marina Circuit," accessed at www.yasmarinacircuit.com, 2011.

9. Information from a recent "The Computer Is Personal Again" advertisement and www.hp.com/personal, August 2008.

10. See "Best Brands at Best Prices at Jashanmal," *AME Info*, February 8, 2009, www.ameinfo.com/184145.html.

11. *Marketing: An Introduction for Education Management Corporation*, 10th ed. Pearson Learning Solutions 6.4.5.1).

12. See John Parnell, "Bucking the Trend," *Arabian Business*, December 22, 2009, accessed at www.arabianbusiness.com/575686-bucking-the-trend.

13. See Ben Elgin, "How 'Green' Is That Water?" *BusinessWeek*, August 13, 2007, p. 68.

14. See Larry Edwards, et al., "75 Years of Ideas," *Advertising Age*, February 14, 2005, p. 14; "America's Most Admired Companies," *Fortune*, accessed at http://money.cnn.com/magazines/fortune/mostadmired/2007/index.html, August 2007; "The Top 10 PR Endeavors," *PR News*, October 30, 2006, p.1; and www.jnj.com/our_company/our_credo/index.htm, December 2008.

15. "Burj Al Arab," Jumeirah company website, accessed at www.jumeirah.com/en/hotels-and-resorts/Destinations/Dubai/Burj-Al-Arab, 2011; "Burj Al Arab," Trip Advisor hotel review from customer, accessed at www.tripadvisor.in/ShowUserReviews-g295424-d302457-r52322674-Burj_Al_Arab-Dubai.html, December 20, 2009.

16. For more on how to measure customer satisfaction, see D. Randall Brandt, "For Good Measure," *Marketing Management*, January–February 2007, pp. 21–25.

17. See "Dubai Residents Vote Etisalat's Customer Service—Best in Dubai," Etisalat's e-Vision, accessed at www.evision.ae, June 2, 2009.

18. "Logistics: OptiLog," news item, Aramex company website. Accessed at www.aramex.com/news/Default.aspx?id=462, March 24, 2009.

19. "Aramex supply chain management," Aramex company website. Accessed at www.aramex.com/logistics/aramex_supply_chain_management.aspx, 2011.

20. Andrew Walmsley, "The Year of Consumer Empowerment," *Marketing*, December 20, 2006, p. 9.

21. Walmsley, "The Year of Consumer Empowerment," p. 9; and "Who's in Control?" *Advertising Age*, January 28, 2008, p. C9.

22. Helen Coster, "Crowd Control," *Forbes*, November 26, 2007, pp. 38–39; and "Top 100 Global Marketers," *Advertising Age*, November 19, 2007, p. 4.

23. Adapted from information in Jonathan Birchall, "Just Do It, Marketers Say," *Los Angeles Times*, April 30, 2007, accessed at http://articles.latimes.com/2007/apr/30/business/ft-brands30. Other facts and information from Louise Story, "New Advertising Outlet: Your Life," *New York Times*, October 14, 2007; Nicholas Casey, "Nike, New Coach Chase Serious Runners," *Wall Street Journal*, December 6, 2007, p. B7; and "Consumer Experiences: Nike," *Fast Company*, March 8, 2008, pp. 94–95.

24. "Nike Elite Football Training Dubai," Dubai City Guide. Accessed at www.dubaicityinfo.com/cityguide/press_news_6829.aspx, February 18, 2010.

25. Matthew Creamer, "John Doe Edges Out Jeff Goodby," *Advertising Age*, January 8, 2007, pp. S4–S5. Also see Karen E. Klein, "Should Your Customers Make Your Ads?" *BusinessWeek*, January 2, 2008, www.businessweek.com.

26. Philip Kotler and Kevin Lane Keller, *Marketing Management*, 13th ed. (Upper Saddle River, NJ: Prentice Hall, 2009), p. 11.

27. For more on the relationship between customer satisfaction, loyalty, and company performance, see Fred Reichheld, *The Ultimate Question: Driving Good Profits and True Growth* (Boston: Harvard Business School Press, 2006); Bruce Cooil, et al., "A Longitudinal Analysis of Customer Satisfaction and Share of Wallet: Investigating the Moderating Effects of Customer Characteristics," *Journal of Marketing*, January 2007, pp. 67–83; Murali Chandrahsekaran, Kristin Rotte, Stephen S. Tax, and Rajdeep Grewal, "Satisfaction, Strength, and Customer Loyalty," *Journal of Marketing Research*, February 2007, pp. 153–163; and Leonard L. Berry, Lewis P. Carbone, "Build Loyalty Through Experience Management," *Quality Progress*, September 2007, pp. 26+.

28. "Stew Leonard's," *Hoover's Company Records*, July 15, 2007, pp. 104–226, and www.stew-leonards.com/html/about.cfm, November 2007.

29. For interesting discussions on assessing and using customer life-time value, see Rajkumar Venkatesan, V. Kumar, and Timothy Bohling, "Selecting Valuable Customers Using a Customer Lifetime Value Framework," Marketing Science Institute, Report No. 05–121, 2005; Sunil Gupta, et al., "Modeling Customer Lifetime Value," *Journal of Service Research*, November 2006, pp. 139–146; "Determining 'CLV' Can Lead to Making Magical Marketing Decisions," *BtoB*, May 7, 2007, p. 18; and Detlef Schoder, "The Flaw in Customer Lifetime Value," *Harvard Business Review*, December 2007, p. 26.

30. Erick Schonfeld, "Click Here for the Upsell," *Business 2.0*, July 11, 2007, accessed at http://cnnmoney.com; and "Getting Shoppers to Crave More," *Fortune Small Business*, August 24, 2007, p. 85.

31. Don Peppers and Martha Rogers, "Customers Don't Grow on Trees," *Fast Company*, July 2005, pp. 26.

32. See Roland T. Rust, Valerie A. Zeithaml, and Katherine A. Lemon, *Driving Customer Equity* (New York: Free Press 2000); Robert C. Blattberg, Gary Getz, and Jacquelyn S. Thomas, *Customer Equity* (Boston, MA: Harvard Business School Press, 2001); Rust, Lemon, and Zeithaml, "Return on Marketing: Using Customer Equity to Focus Marketing Strategy," *Journal of Marketing*, January 2004, pp. 109–127; Rust, Zeithaml, and Lemon, "Customer-Centered Brand Management," *Harvard Business Review*, September 2004, p. 110; Robert P. Leone, et al., "Linking Brand Equity to Customer Equity," *Journal of Service Marketing*, November 2006, pp. 125–138; Julian Villanueva and Dominique Hanssens, *Customer Equity: Measurement, Management and Research Opportunities* (Hanover, MA: Now Publishers Inc., 2007); and Roland T. Rust, "Seeking Higher ROI? Base Strategy on Customer Equity," *Advertising Age*, September 10, 2007, pp. 26–27.

33. This example is adapted from information in Rust, Lemon, and Zeithaml, "Where Should the Next Marketing Dollar Go?" *Marketing Management*, September–October 2001, pp. 24–28. Also see David Welch and David Kiley, "Can Caddy's Driver Make GM Cool?" *BusinessWeek*, September 20, 2004, pp. 105–106; and Jean Halliday, "Comeback Kid Cadillac Stalls after Shop Swap," *Advertising Age*, September 24, 2007, p. 1.

34. Werner Reinartz and V. Kumar, "The Mismanagement of Customer Loyalty," *Harvard Business Review*, July 2002, pp. 86–94. For more on customer equity management, see Michael D. Johnson and Fred Selnes, "Customer Portfolio Management: Toward a Dynamic Theory of Exchange Relationships," *Journal of Marketing*, April 2004, pp. 1–17; Sunil Gupta and Donald R. Lehman, *Managing Customers as Investments* (Philadelphia: Wharton School Publishing, 2005); Roland T. Rust, Katherine N. Lemon, and Das Narayandas, *Customer Equity Management* (Upper Saddle River, NJ: Prentice Hall, 2005); and Kathy Stevens, "Using Customer Equity Models to Improve Loyalty and Profits," *Journal of Consumer Marketing*, vol. 23, 2006, p. 379.

35. Brian Morrissey, "Is Social Media Killing the Campaign Micro-Site?" November 12, 2007, accessed at www.mediaweek.com.

36. See Allison Enright, "Get Clued In: Mystery of Web 2.0 Resolved," *Marketing News*, January 15, 2007, pp. 20–22. Also see Jessica Tsai, "Power to the People," *Customer Relationship Management*, December 2007, pp. 28+.

37. "JupiterResearch Forecasts Online Retail Spending Will Reach $144 Billion in 2010, a CAGR of 12% from 2005," February 6, 2006, accessed at www.jupitermedia.com/corporate/releases/06.02.06-newjupresearch.html.

38. See Kerry Capell, "The Arab World Wants Its MTD," *BusinessWeek*, October 22, 2007, pp. 79–81; and Tom Lowry, "The Game's the Thing at MTV Networks," *BusinessWeek*, February 18, 2008, p. 51. Additional information from annual reports and other information found at www.mcdonalds.com, www.viacom.com, and www.nikebiz.com, October 2008.

39. Adapted from information in Don Frischmann, "Nothing Is Insignificant When It Comes to Brand Fulfillment," *Advertising Age*, January 21, 2008, p. 16.

40. See Egyptian Biodynamic Association at SEKEM company website, 2011, www.sekem.com/english/cultural/EBDA.aspx?PageID=1.

41. For examples, and for a good review of nonprofit marketing, see Philip Kotler and Alan R. Andreasen, *Strategic Marketing for Nonprofit Organizations*, 6th ed. (Upper Saddle River, NJ: Prentice Hall, 2003); Philip Kotler and Karen Fox, *Strategic Marketing for Educational Institutions* (Upper Saddle River, NJ: Prentice Hall, 1995); Philip Kotler, John Bowen, and James Makens, *Marketing for Hospitality and Tourism*, 3rd ed. (Upper Saddle River, NJ: Prentice Hall, 2003); and Philip Kotler and Nancy Lee, *Marketing in the Public Sector A Roadmap for Improved Performance* (Philadelphia: Wharton School Publishing, 2007).

42. "Hospital 57357 Story: The Need for a Specialized Children's Cancer Hospital," 57357 website, www.57357.com/Default.aspx?tabid=869, 2010.

43. "Hospital 57357 Story: More Than Just a Children's Hospital," 57357 website, www.57357.com/Default.aspx?PageContentID=196&tabid=869, 2010.

44. "57357 Friends," 57357 website, online comment, September 29, 2009, www.57357.com/Default.aspx?tabid=885&mid=1173&newsid1173=1428&

45. Hospital 57357 website, www.57357.com, 2010.

CHAPTER 2

1. For more on mission statements, see Joseph Peyrefitte and Forest R. David, "A Content Analysis of Mission Statements of United States Firms in Four Industries," *International Journal of Management*, June 2006, pp. 296–301; Jeffrey Abrahams, *101 Mission Statements from Top Companies* (Berkeley, CA: Ten Speed Press, 2007); and Jack and Suzy Welch, "State Your Business," January 14, 2008, p. 80.

2. "About Us," Microsoft website, www.microsoft.com/about/en/us/default.aspx.

3. "Our World," Spinneys' company website, 2011, www.spinneys dubai.com/ourworld.htm.

4. Jack and Suzy Welch, "State Your Business; Too Many Mission Statements Are Loaded with Fatheaded Jargon. Play It Straight," *BusinessWeek*, January 14, 2008, p. 80.

5. "Our Foundation," Procter & Gamble website, 2011, www.pg.com/en_US/company/purpose_people/pvp.shtml.

6. "Mission to Lead," Zain company website, 2011, www.zain.com/muse/obj/lang.default/portal.view/content/About%20us/Corporate%20Philosophy/Mission.

7. The following discussion is based in part on information found at www.bcg.com/publications/files/Experience_Curve_IV_Growth_Share_Matrix_1973.pdf, December 2008.

8. For an interesting discussion on managing growth, see Matthew S. Olson, Derek van Bever, and Seth Verry, "When Growth Stalls," *Harvard Business Review*, March 2008, pp. 51–61.

9. H. Igor Ansoff, "Strategies for Diversification," *Harvard Business Review*, September–October 1957, pp. 113–124.

10. Michael E. Porter, *Competitive Advantage: Creating and Sustaining Superior Performance* (New York: Free Press, 1985); and Michel E. Porter, "What Is Strategy?" *Harvard Business Review*, November–December 1996, pp. 61–78; Also see "The Value Chain," accessed at www.quickmba.com/strategy/value-chain, July 2008; and Philip Kotler and Kevin Lane Keller, *Marketing Management*

(Upper Saddle River, NJ: Prentice Hall, 2009) pp. 35–36 and pp. 252–253.

11. Kotler, *Kotler on Marketing* (New York: The Free Press, 1999), pp. 20–22; and Marianne Seiler, "Transformation Trek," *Marketing Management*, January–February 2006, pp. 32–39.

12. "McDonald's Fetes 50th Birthday, Opens Anniversary Restaurant," *Knight Ridder Tribune Business News*, April 15, 2005, p. 1; and information from www.mcdonalds.com/corp.html, September 2008.

13. Quotes and other information from Jeffery K. Liker and Thomas Y. Choi, "Building Deep Supplier Relationships," *Harvard Business Review*, 2004, pp. 104–113; Lindsay Chappell, "Toyota Aims to Satisfy Its Suppliers," *Automotive News*, February 21, 2005, p. 10; "Toyota Recognizes Top Suppliers for 2007," *PR Newswire*, March 4, 2008; and www.toyotasupplier.com, November 2008.

14. Jack Trout, "Branding Can't Exist Without Positioning," *Advertising Age*, March 14, 2005, p. 28.

15. "100 Leading National Advertisers," special issue of *Advertising Age*, June 23, 2008, p. 10.

16. The four Ps classification was first suggested by E. Jerome McCarthy, *Basic Marketing: A Managerial Approach* (Homewood, IL: Irwin, 1960). For the 4Cs, other proposed classifications, and more discussion, see Robert Lauterborn, "New Marketing Litany: 4P's Passé C-Words Take Over," *Advertising Age*, October 1, 1990, p. 26; Don E. Schultz, "New Definition of Marketing Reinforces Idea of Integration," *Marketing News*, January 15, 2005, p. 8; and Phillip Kotler, "Alphabet Soup," *Marketing Management*, March–April 2006, p. 51.

17. For more discussion of the CMO position, see Pravin Nath and Vijay Mahajan, "Chief Marketing Officers: A Study of Their Presence in Firms' Top Management Teams," *Journal of Marketing*, January 2008, pp. 65–81; and Philip Kotler and Kevin Lane Keller, *Marketing Management*, (Upper Saddle River: NJ: Prentice Hall, 2009), pp. 11–12.

18. For more on brand and product management, see Kevin Lane Keller, *Strategic Brand Management*, 3rd ed. (Upper Saddle River, NJ: Prentice Hall, 2008).

19. Adapted from Diane Brady, "Making Marketing Measure Up," *BusinessWeek*, December 13, 2004, pp. 112–113; with information from "Kotler Readies World for One-on-One," *Point*, June 2005, p. 3. Also see Darryl E. Owens, "Champion ROI to Prove Worth," *Marketing News*, March 1, 2007, pp. 13, 22.

20. Mark McMaster, "ROI: More Vital Than Ever," *Sales & Marketing Management*, January 2002, pp. 51–52. Also see Gordon A. Wyner, "Beyond ROI," *Marketing Management*, June 2006, pp. 8–9; James Lenskold, "Unlock Profit Potential," *Marketing Management*, May–June, 2007, pp. 26–31; Steven H. Seggie, Erin Cavusgil, and Steven Phelan, "Measurement of Return on Marketing Investment: A Conceptual Framework and the Future of Marketing Metrics," *Industrial Marketing Management*, August 2007, pp. 834–841.

21. See David Skinner and Doug Brooks, "Move from Metrics Overload to Actionable Insights," *Advertising Age*, May 28, 2007, pp. 14–15; and Gregor Harter, Edward Landry, and Andrew Tipping, "The New Complete Marketer," *Strategy + Business*, Autumn 2007, pp. 79–87.

22. For more discussion, see Bruce H. Clark, Andrew V. Abela, and Tim Ambler, "Behind the Wheel," *Marketing Management*, May–June 2006, pp. 19–23; Christopher Hosford, "Driving Business with Dashboards," *BtoB*, December 11, 2006, p. 18; and Allison Enwright, "Measure Up: Create a ROMI Dashboard That Shows Current and Future Value," *Marketing News*, August 15, 2007, pp. 12–13.

23. For a full discussion of this model and details on customer centered measures of return on marketing investment, see

24. Deborah L. Vence, "Return on Investment," *Marketing News*, October 15, 2005, pp. 13–14.

25. "Mission and Vision," Olympic Group, 2011, www.olympicgroup.com/innerpages/missionandvision.aspx.

CHAPTER 3

1. "A Short History of Dubai Property," *AME Info*, May 27, 2004, www.ameinfo.com/40570.html.

2. "Dubai Property Prices to Fall in Q4 2008," *AME Info*, December 4, 2008, www.ameinfo.com/178047.html.

3. Emaar Properties website, 2011, www.emaar.com.

4. "Dubai's Property Market Still in 'Downward Phase of the Cycle'," *AME Info*, October 8, 2009, www.ameinfo.com/211673.html.

5. "Emaar Properties Records Revenue of Dhs5,429m in First Nine Months of 2009,"*AME Info*, October 22, 2009, www.ameinfo.com/213432.html; "Emaar Properties Records Net Operating Profit of AED 2.343 billion (US$638 million) in First Nine Months of 2010," Emaar Properties press release, October 27, 2010, www.emaar.com/index.aspx?page=press-release-details&id=1116.

6. "Emaar Properties Records Revenue of AED 5,429 million," Emaar press release, October 22, 2009, www.emaar.com.

7. "Emaar Properties Records Net Operating Profit of Dhs2.343bn in First Nine Months of 2010," *AME Info*, October 27, 2010, www.ameinfo.com/246964.html.

8. "Walk the Talk Says BurJuman," *AME Info*, October 12, 2006, www.ameinfo.com/98884.html

9. "Union Co-op Boycotts Danish Products," *Arabian Business*, March 15, 2008, www.arabianbusiness.com/union-co-op-boycotts-danish-products-52401.html.

10. World POPClock, U.S. Census Bureau, accessed online at www.census.gov, September 2008. This website provides continuously updated projections of the U.S. and world populations.

11. See from Frederik Balfour, "Educating the 'Little Emperors': There's a Big Market for Products That Help China's Coddled Kids Get Ahead," *BusinessWeek*, November 10, 2003, p. 22; Clay Chandler, "Little Emperors," *Fortune*, October 4, 2004, pp. 138–150; and "Hothousing Little Tykes," *Beijing Review*, May 5, 2005, accessed at www.bjreview.cn/EN/En-2005/05-18-e/china-5.htm; and "China's 'Little Emperors,'" *Financial Times*, May 5, 2007, p. 1.

12. Adapted from information in Janet Adamy, "Different Brew: Eyeing a Billion Tea Drinkers, Starbucks Pours It On in China," *Wall Street Journal*, November 29, 2006, p. A1. Also see "Where the Money Is," *Financial Times*, May 12, 2007, p. 8; and Loretta Chao, "Politics and Economics: China to Retain Its One-Child Policy," *Wall Street Journal*, March 11, 2008, p. A7.

13. Janet Adamy, "Different Brew: Eyeing a Billion Tea Drinkers, Starbucks Pours It On in China," *Wall Street Journal*, November 29, 2006, p. A1.

14. "Middle East," The World Factbook, Central Intelligence Agency, 2011, www.cia.gov/library/publications/the-world-factbook/wfbExt/region_mde.html.

Roland T. Rust, Katherine N. Lemon, and Valerie A. Zeithaml, "Return on Marketing: Using Customer Equity to Focus Marketing Strategy," *Journal of Marketing*, January 2004, pp. 109–127; Roland T. Rust, Katherine N. Lemon, and Das Narayandas, *Customer Equity Management* (Upper Saddle River, NJ: Prentice Hall, 2005); David Tiltman, "Everything You Know Is Wrong," *Marketing*, June 13, 2007, pp. 28–29; Roland T. Rust, "Seeking Higher ROI? Base Strategy on Customer Equity," *Advertising Age*, September 10, 2007, pp. 26–27; and Valerie P. Valente, "Redefining ROI," *Advertising Age*, January 28, 2008, p. C7.

15. Jack Neff, "Unilever Resuscitates the Demo Left for Dead," *Advertising Age*, May 28, 2007, pp. 1, 26; and Judann Pollack, "Boomers Don't Want Your Pity, but They Do Demand Your Respect," *Advertising Age*, October 8, 2007, p. 24.

16. "Income Builder Plan," Emirates NBD company website, 2011, www.emiratesbank.ae/personalBanking/bancassurance/incomeBuilderPlan.cfm.

17. "Al Aslami Takaful Programme," Dubai Islamic Bank, 2011, www.dib.ae/en/privatebanking_takafulprogramme.htm.

18. John Jullens, "Marketers: Meet the Millennial Generation," *Strategy + Business*, Spring 2007, pp. 16–18. Also see "Generation Y Research: What Makes 'y' Tick," *Brand Strategy*, February 5, 2007, p. 38.

19. www.traderscity.com/abcg/cultur11.htm.

20. "Middle East," The World Factbook, Central Intelligence Agency, 2011, www.cia.gov/library/publications/the-world-factbook/wfbExt/region_mde.html.

21. "Labour Migration To The GCC Countries," Prof. Baqer Al-Najjar, University of Bahrain, Kingdom of Bahrain, June 2006.

22. "Gulf States Told to Protect Migrant Workers," *France 24*, December 5, 2010, www.france24.com/en/20101205-gulf-states-told-protect-migrant-workers.

23. The March 2010 findings of the GCC Unemployment: Sustainable Economies report, published by recruitment company TalentRepublic.net.

24. Shane McGinley, "GCC Unemployment Forecast to Hit 10.5% in 2010," March 21, 2010, www.arabianbusiness.com.

25. "Middle East," The World Factbook, Central Intelligence Agency, 2011, www.cia.gov/library/publications/the-world-factbook/wfbExt/region_mde.html.

26. "UAE Population to Rise to 6.1m in 2020," UAE Interact, December 26, 2010, www.uaeinteract.com.

27. "Background Note: United Arab Emirates," U.S. Department of State, March 16, 2011, www.state.gov/r/pa/ei/bgn/5444.htm.

28. Trevor Lloyd-Jones, "Western Union refines ethnic marketing and brings mobile remittances to the Middle East," *Business Intelligence Middle East*, March 13, 2008, www.bi-me.com.

29. Gavin Rabinowitz, "Carmaker in India Unveils $2,500 Car," *USA Today*, January 10, 2008, accessed at www.usatoday.com; Gavin Rabinowitz, "India's Tata Motors Unveils $2,500 Car, Bringing Car Ownership Within Reach of Millions," *Associated Press*, January 10, 2008; and Mark Phelan, "Automaker Tata's Presence Already Felt in Detroit Area," *McClatchy-Tribune Business News*, March 17, 2008.

30. See Arik Hesseldahl, "What's Eating Apple?" *BusinessWeek*, February 25, 2008, p. 36; and "Not-So-Big Spenders," *Marketing Management*, January/February 2008, p. 5.

31. Mark Dolliver, "How the Rise of Inequality Fosters a New Culture of Antagonism," *Adweek*, December 17, 2007, pp. 30–31, 37.

32. Andrew Zolli, "Business 3.0," *Fast Company*, March 2007, pp. 64–70.

33. "Environment," *Qatar News Agency*, www.qnaol.net/QNAEn/Main_Sectors/Environment/Pages/default.aspx.

34. "About Us," Environmental Agency Abu Dhabi, 2009, www.ead.ae/en/en-us/about.us.aspx.

35. Steve Bronstein, "50 Ways to Green Your Business (and Boost Your Bottom Line)," *Fast Company*, November 2007, pp. 90–99.

36. Adapted from Lorraine Woellert, "HP Wants Your Old PC Back," *BusinessWeek*, April 10, 2006, pp. 82–83; with information from "HP Recycles Nearly 250 Million Pounds of Products in 2007—50 Percent Increase Over 2006," February 5, 2008, accessed at www.hp.com/hpinfo/newsroom/press/2008/080205a.html.

37. See "RFID Market Nears $7B," *Journal of Commerce Online Edition*, July 9, 2007; Scott Denne, "After Being Overhyped, RFID Starts to Deliver," *Wall Street Journal*, November 7, 2007, p. 5F; "Wal-Mart Expands RFID Requirements," *McClatchy-Tribune Business News*, January 30, 2008; "Sam's Club Gets Serious about RFID," *Modern Materials Handling*, March 2008, p. 18; and information accessed online at www.autoidlabs.org, September 2008.

38. "UAE Ministry of Economy to Introduce New Laws to Enhance Business Competitiveness," *AME Info*, April 10, 2010, www.ameinfo.com/229201.html.

39. Galadari & Associates, "Consumer Protection Law of UAE," January 24, 2008, www.hg.org/article.asp?id=4999.

40. "Press Releases," Ikea Dubai, www.ikeadubai.com/content/press.asp.

41. "Dubai Chamber Hosts Cause Marketing Workshop," *AME Info*, August 28, 2008, www.ameinfo.com/167299.html.

42. Adapted from descriptions found at www.yankelovich.com/products/lists.aspx, November 2006.

43. Ronald Grover, "Trading the Bleachers for the Couch," *BusinessWeek*, August 22, 2005, p. 32. Also see, "Examine the Impact Cocooning Is Having on Consumer Markets," *Business Wire*, February 22, 2007; and Paul Kagan, "Home Theatre 101," *Boxoffice*, January 2008, pp. 52–53.

44. "Decked Out," *Inside*, Spring 2006, pp. 76–77. See also "Meet Me at the Oasis; From Saunas to Spas, People Are Turning Their Homes into a Personal Paradise," *Ottawa Citizen*, April 18, 2007, p. E8.

45. "Tycoon Took Cash to Live the High Life," *7 Days*, June 7, 2010, www.7days.ae.

46. "UAE Embraces Growing Trend for Organic Foods," Hotelier Middle East, January 19, 2009, www.hoteliermiddleeast.com/3271-uae_embraces_growing_trend_for_organic_foods.

47. "UAE Embraces Growing Trend for Organic Foods," Hotelier Middle East, January 19, 2009, www.hoteliermiddleeast.com/3271-uae_embraces_growing_trend_for_organic_foods.

48. See Philip Kotler, *Kotler on Marketing* (New York: Free Press, 1999), p. 3; and Kotler, *Marketing Insights from A to Z* (Hoboken, NJ: John Wiley & Sons, 2003), pp. 23–24.

CHAPTER 4

1. "Maktoob Research Unveils Arab World's First Interactive Online Consumer Community," press release, November 5, 2009, available at: www.zawya.com/story.cfm/sidZAWYA20091105085525?en.

2. "Yahoo! Maktoob Research," company website, www.maktoob-research.com/company?lang=en; "About Research Panel," *Arab Eye*, www.arab-eye.com/en/mngmnt.php.

3. Mohanbir Sawhney, "Insights into Customer Insights," *CRMProject.com*, accessed 2011 at http://mthink.com/revenue/sites/default/files/legacy/crmproject/content/pdf/CRM5_wp_sawhney.pdf. The Apple iPod example is also adapted from this article.

4. Michael Fassnacht, "Beyond Spreadsheets," *Advertising Age*, February 19, 2007, p. 15.

5. Quotes from Mohanbir Sawhney, "Insights into Customer Insights," p. 3; and Robert Schieffer and Eric Leininger, "Customers at the Core," *Marketing Management*, January/February 2008, pp. 31–37.

6. Mohanbir Sawhney, "Insights into Customer Insights," accessed at http://mthink.com/revenue/sites/default/files/legacy/crmproject/content/pdf/CRM5_wp_sawhney.pdf, 2011, p. 2.

7. For more discussion, see Robert Schieffer and Eric Leininger, "Customers at the Core," *Marketing Management,* January/February 2008, pp. 31–37.

8. See Steve Wills and Sally Webb, "Measuring the Value of Insight—It Can and Must Be Done," *International Journal of Market Research,* vol. 49, no. 2, 2007, pp. 155–165.

9. "The Star Awards Program," Mobinil website, 2011, www.mobinil.com/Star/Loyaltyprograms.aspx#Star_Awards.

10. "What is Vodafone One?," Vodafone website, 2011, www.vodafone.com.eg/en/Personal/LoyaltyPrograms/VodafoneOne/WhatisVodafoneOne/index.htm.

11. See Jean Halliday, "Car Talk: Ford Listens in on Consumers' Online Chatter," *Advertising Age,* February 5, 2007, pp. 3, 34. Also see Sean Hargrave, "Measuring Buzz: Ears to the Ground," *New Media Age,* January 17, 2008, p. 21.

12. See Richard L. Wilkins, "Competitive Intelligence: The New Supply Chain Edge," *Supply Chain Management Review,* January/February 2007, pp. 18–27.

13. For more on research firms that supply marketing information, see Jack Honomichl, "Honomichl Top 50," special section, *Marketing News,* June 15, 2008, pp. H1–H67. Other information from www.infores.com; www.smrb.com; www.acnielsen.com; and www.yankelovich.com/products/monitor.aspx, August 2008.

14. Example adapted from information in Rhys Blakely, "You Know When It Feels Like Somebody's Watching You… " *Times,* May 14, 2007, p. 46; and Nandini Lakshman, "Nokia: It Takes a Village to Design a Phone for Emerging Markets," *BusinessWeek,* September 10, 2007, p. 12.

15. "The Science of Desire," *BusinessWeek,* June 5, 2006, www.businessweek.com/magazine/content/06_23/b3987083.htm.

16. Cited in Rhys Blakely, "You Know When it Feels Like Somebody's Watching You…," *The Times,* May 14, 2007, http://business.timesonline.co.uk/tol/business/industry_sectors/telecoms/article1784881.ece.

17. David Kiley, "Shoot the Focus Group," *BusinessWeek,* p. 120. Also see Peter Noel Murray, "Focus Groups Are Valid When Done Right," *Marketing News,* September 1, 2006, pp. 21, 25.

18. Adam Woods, "Get to the Truth with Web 2.0," *Revolution,* December 2007, p. 39.

19. Gelb, "Online Options Change Biz a Little—and a Lot," *Marketing News,* November 1, 2006, p. 23.

20. Johnson, "Forget Phone and Mail: Online's the Best Place to Administer Surveys," p. 23. See also, "Get to the Truth with Web 2.0," *Revolution,* December 4, 2007, p. 40.

21. "The Nielsen Company and Facebook Form Strategic Alliance," *AMEInfo,* September 24, 2009, www.ameinfo.com/210160.html.

22. John B. Horrigan and Aaron Smith, "Home Broadband Adoption 2007," Pew Internet & American Life Project, June 2007, www.pewinternet.org/pdfs/PIP_Broadband%202007.pdf.

23. For more on Internet privacy, see Jessica E. Vascellaro, "They've Got Your Number (and a Lot More), *Wall Street Journal,* March 13, 2007, pp. D1–D2; "Comment: Do Consumers Really Want Their Privacy?" *New Media Age,* December 13, 2007, p. 12; and Jim Puzzanghera, "Internet; Tough Cookies for Web Surfers Seeking Privacy," *Los Angeles Times,* April 19, 2008, p. C1.

24. Michael Krauss, "At Many Firms, Technology Obscures CRM," *Marketing News,* March 18, 2002, p. 5. Also see William Boulding et al., "A Customer Relationship Management Roadmap: What Is Known, Potential Pitfalls, and Where to Go," *Journal of Marketing,* October 2005, pp. 155–166; Deborah L. Vence,

"CRM: You Know What It Stands for, but Do You Know What It Means?" *Marketing News,* September 15, 2007, p. 12; and "Study: Marketers Stink When It Comes to CRM," *Brandweek,* April 14, 2008, p. 7.

25. See Darell K. Rigby and Vijay Vishwanath, "Localization: The Revolution in Consumer Markets," *Harvard Business Review,* April 2006, pp. 82–92; and information found at www.partnersonline.com, September 2008.

26. Zimmerman, "Small Business; Do the Research," *Wall Street Journal,* May 9, 2005, p. R3.

27. Industrial Modernisation Centre website, 2011, www.imc-egypt.org.

28. For some good advice on conducting market research in a small business, see "Marketing Research…Basics 101," accessed at www.sba.gov/starting_business/marketing/research.html, August 2008; and "Researching Your Market," U.S. Small Business Administration, accessed at www.sba.gov/idc/groups/public/documents/sba_homepage/pub_mt8.pdf, November 2008.

29. "2008 Honomichl Top 50," *MarketingNews,* June 15, 2008, www.marketingpower.com/ResourceLibrary/publications/MarketingNews/2008/42/11/Hono50-08.pdf.

30. James Verrinder, "Global Research Turnover Down 4.6%, Says Esomar Report," Research, September 6, 2010, accessed at www.research-live.com/news/financial/global-research-turnover-down-46-says-esomar-report/4003529.article.

31. See Nielsen International Research website, accessed at www2.acnielsen.com/company/where.php, September 2008.

32. Abbey Klaassen and Ira Teinowitz, "An Ad App You'll Love (and Privacy Groups Will Hate)," *Advertising Age,* November 5, 2007, pp. 3–4; Thomas Claburn, "Call Off the Wolves," *InformationWeek,* November 12, 2007, pp. 69+; and Anick Jesdanun, "Study: Online Privacy Concerns Increase," *Associated Press,* January 16, 2008.

33. Jaikumar Vijayan, "Disclosure Laws Driving Data Privacy Efforts, Says IBM Exec," *Computerworld,* May 8, 2006, p. 26. Also see Thornton A. May, "The What and Why of CPOs," *Computerworld,* November 27, 2006, p. 18.

34. Information accessed at www10.americanexpress.com/sif/cda/page/0,1641,14271,00.asp, July 2008.

35. Shaimaa Hussien and Yasmin Heshmat, "Determinants of Happiness and Life Satisfaction in Egypt: An Empirical Study using the World Values Survey – Egypt 2008 " *The Egyptian Cabinet - IDSC,* May 2009, www.idsc.gov.eg; www.worldvaluessurvey.org.

CHAPTER 5

1. Inas Mazhar, "Across the Barricades," *Al-Ahram Weekly,* 2004, http://weekly.ahram.org.eg/2004/2010/sc84.htm.

2. "The Offside Game", *Islam Story,* November 22, 2009, http://en.islamstory.com/offside-game.html.

3. "Zain Sponsors Soccer Excellence in KSA," Zain press release, October 11, 2009, www.sa.zain.com/autoforms/portal/home/corporate/press-releases/soccerexcellence?AF_language=en.

4. Information from "Saudi Football Fans Unite," *Arab News,* August 2, 2007, www.arabnews.com/?page=21&section=0&article=99214&d=7&m=8&y=2007; "Saudi Arabia Football," 2011, www.saudiarabiafootball.com.

5. GDP figures from *The World Fact Book,* February 7, 2008, accessed at www.cia.gov/library/publications/the-world-factbook/index.html. Population figures from the World POPClock, U.S. Census Bureau, www.census.gov, September 2008. This website

provides continuously updated projections of the U.S. and world populations.

6. "Geert Hofstede Cultural Dimensions: Arab World," Itim International, 2009, www.geert-hofstede.com/hofstede_arab_world.shtml.

7. Abbas J. Ali, Mohammed Al-Shakhis, (1990) "Multinationals and the Host Arab Society: A Managerial Perspective", *Leadership & Organization Development Journal*, vol. 11, no. 5, pp.17–21.

8. Abbas J. Ali, Mohammed Al-Shakhis, (1990) "Multinationals and the Host Arab Society: A Managerial Perspective", *Leadership & Organization Development Journal*, vol. 11, no. 5, pp.17–21.

9. "Emke Group," LinkedIn company profile, 2011, www.linkedin.com/companies/emke-group.

10. "United Arab Emirates," *Every Culture*, www.everyculture.com/To-Z/United-Arab-Emirates.html.

11. "United Arab Emirates," *Every Culture*, www.everyculture.com/To-Z/United-Arab-Emirates.html.

12. For a discussion of influencers, see Clive Thompson, "Is the Tipping Point Toast?" *Fast Company*, February 2008, pp. 75–105; Edward Keller and Jonathan Berry, *The Influentials* (New York: The Free Press, 2003); and Daniel B. Honigman, "Who's on First?" *Marketing News* November 1, 2007, pp. 14–17. The study results and quotes are from Kenneth Hein, "Report Explores What Influences the Influencers," *Brandweek*, February 5, 2007, p. 13; Ryan McConnell, "Spread the News: Word-Of-Mouth Worth $1 Billion," *Advertising Age*, November 15, 2007, p. 4; and Megan Mcilroy, "Family, Friends Most Influential on Shoppers," *Advertising Age*, April 9, 2008, accessed at www.adage.com.

13. Extract adapted from Robert Berner, "I Sold It Through the Grapevine," *BusinessWeek*, May 29, 2006, pp. 32–34; and Melanie Wells, "Kid Nabbing," *Forbes*, February 2, 2004, p. 84. Also see Jack Neff, "P&G, Unilever Are Ready to Clutter," *Advertising Age*, June 11, 2007, p. 4. Data on Vocalpoint from www.vocalpoint.com, July 2008.

14. Clayton Collins, "Marketers Tap Chatty Young Teens, and a Hit a Hot Button," Christian Science Monitor, March 30, 2005, www.csmonitor.com/2005/0330/p11s01-lifp.html.

15. See Yuval Rosenberg, "Building a New Nest," *Fast Company*, April 27, 2007, p. 48; and "About Us," Capessa website, October 2008, http://capessa.com/members/aboutus.aspx.

16. "Statistics," *Online Women In Politics*, updated April 2009, www.onlinewomeninpolitics.org/Statistics.htm.

17. Brian Whitaker, "Saudi Arabia: Women and Employment," Women Living Under Muslim Laws website, February 21, 2006, www.wluml.org/node/2771.

18. Jennifer Aaker, "Dimensions of Measuring Brand Personality," *Journal of Marketing Research*, August 1997, pp. 347–356. Also see Aaker, "The Malleable Self: The Role of Self Expression in Persuasion," *Journal of Marketing Research*, May 1999, pp. 45–57; and Audrey Azoulay and Jean-Noel Kapferer, "Do Brand Personality Scales Really Measure Brand Personality?" *Journal of Brand Management*, November 2003, p. 143.

19. See Mark Tadajewski, "Remembering Motivation Research: Toward an Alternative Genealogy of Interpretive Consumer Research," *Marketing Theory*, December 2006, pp. 429–466; and Leon G. Schiffman and Leslie L. Kanuk, *Consumer Behavior*, 9th ed. (Upper Saddle River, NJ: Prentice Hall, 2007), chapter 4.

20. See Abraham H. Maslow, "A Theory of Human Motivation," *Psychological Review*, 50 (1943), pp. 370–396. Also see Maslow, *Motivation and Personality*, 3rd ed. (New York: HarperCollins Publishers, 1987); and Barbara Marx Hubbard, "Seeking Our Future Potentials," *Futurist*, May 1998, pp. 29–32.

21. Louise Story, "Anywhere the Eye Can See, It's Likely to See an Ad," *New York Times*, January 15, 2007, accessed at www.nytimes.com; and Matthew Creamer, "Caught in the Clutter Crossfire: Your Brand," *Advertising Age*, April 1, 2007, p. 35.

22. Bob Garfield, "'Subliminal' Seduction and Other Urban Myths," *Advertising Age*, September 18, 2000, pp. 4, 105; and Lewis Smith, "Subliminal Advertising May Work, but Only If You're Paying Attention," *Times*, March 9, 2007. For more on subliminal advertising, see Alastair Goode, "The Implicit and Explicit Role of Ad Memory in Ad Persuasion: Rethinking the Hidden Persuaders," *International Journal of Marketing Research*, vol. 49, no. 2, 2007, pp. 95–116; Don E. Shultz, "Subliminal Ad Notions Still Resonate Today," *Marketing News*, March 15, 2007, p. 5; Cynthia Crossen, "For a Time in the 50s, a Huckster Fanned Fears of an Ad 'Hypnosis,'" *Wall Street Journal*, November 5, 2007, p. B1; and Beth Snyder Bulik, "This Brand Makes You More Creative," *Advertising Age*, March 24, 2008, p. 4.

23. Quotes and information from "Ogilvy Public Relations Worldwide and BzzAgent Forge Strategic Alliance to Offer Clients More Word-of-Mouth Communications Solutions," *PR Newswire*, January 10, 2008; Duglas Pruden and Terry G. Vavra, "Controlling the Grapevine," *Marketing Management*, July–August 2004, pp. 25–30; and Yubo Chen and Jinhong Xie, "Online Consumer Review: Word-of-Mouth as a New Element of Marketing Communication Mix," *Management Science*, March 2008, pp. 477–491.

24. See Leon Festinger, *A Theory of Cognitive Dissonance* (Stanford, CA: Stanford University Press, 1957); Schiffman and Kanuk, *Consumer Behavior*, pp. 219–220; "Cognitive Dissonance and the Stability of Service Quality Perceptions," *Journal of Services Marketing*, 2004, p. 433+; Cynthia Crossen, "'Cognitive Dissonance' Became a Milestone in the 1950s Psychology," *Wall Street Journal*, December 12, 2006, p. B1; and Mohammed N. Nadeem, "Post-Purchased Dissonance: the Wisdom of the Repeat Purchases," *Journal of Global Business Issues*, Summer 2007, pp. 183–194.

25. The following discussion draws from the work of Everett M. Rogers. See his *Diffusion of Innovations*, 5th ed. (New York: Free Press, 2003).

26. Nick Grande, "The Silver Bullet for MENA HDTV," *Digital Production Middle East*, April 12, 2009, www.digitalproductionme.com/article-1138-the-silver-bullet-for-mena-hdtv/.

CHAPTER 6

1. "Overview, Vision and Mission," Advanced Electronics Company website, 2011, http://careers.aecl.com/aec/page.aspx?pageid=9501.

2. "Advanced Electronics Company," The International Symposium on Air Defence 2020+, 2011, www.isad2020.org.sa/english/industry_partners.php.

3. "Advanced Electronics Company," Elite Saudi Careers, http://saudi.eliteic.net/en/participating-companies/aec/.

4. "Overview, Vision and Mission," Advanced Electronics Company website, 2011, http://careers.aecl.com/aec/page.aspx?pageid=9501.

5. Chris Whyatt, "Acer Spies Major Saudi Contract with PC Plant," *Arabian Business*, February 12, 2006, www.arabianbusiness.com.

6. See Kerry Capell, "How the Swedish Retailer Became a Global Cult Brand," *BusinessWeek*, November 14, 2005, p. 103; Greta Guest, "Inside IKEA's Formula for Global Success," *Detroit Free Press*, June 3, 2006; IKEA, *Hoover's Company Records*, April 1, 2008, p. 42925; "IKEA Group Stores," accessed www.ikea-group.ikea.com/?ID=11, April 2008; and "Our Vision: A Better Everyday Life," accessed at www.ikea.com, December 2008.

7. Patrick J. Robinson, Charles W. Faris, and Yoram Wind, *Industrial Buying Behavior and Creative Marketing* (Boston: Allyn & Bacon, 1967). Also see James C. Anderson and James A. Narus, *Business Market Management,* 2nd ed. (Upper Saddle River, NJ: Prentice Hall, 2004), chapter 3; and James C. Anderson, James A. Narus, and Wouter van Rossum, "Customer Value Propositions in Business Markets," *Harvard Business Review,* March 2006, pp. 91–99; and Philip Kotler and Kevin Lane Keller, *Marketing Management,* 13th ed. (Upper Saddle River, NJ: Prentice Hall, 2009), chapter 7.

8. "Aramex Provides Logistics Solutions to Nuqul Group's ABC4Office Enterprise," Aramex press release, May 26, 2009, www.aramex.com/news.

9. See Frederick E. Webster Jr. and Yoram Wind, *Organizational Buying Behavior* (Upper Saddle River, NJ: Prentice Hall, 1972), pp. 78–80. Also see James C. Anderson and James A. Narus, *Business Market Management: Understanding, Creating and Delivering Value* (Upper Saddle River NJ: Prentice Hall, 2004), chapter 3; Jorg Brinkman and Markus Voeth, "An Analysis of Buying Center Decisions Through the Sales Force," *Industrial Marketing Management,* October 2007, p. 998; and Philip Kotler and Kevin Lane Keller, *Marketing Management,* 13th ed. (Upper Saddle River, NJ: Prentice Hall, 2009), pp. 188–191.

10. Jennifer Lawinski, "Good Checkup—Avent's HealthPath University Puts VARs in Touch with How Things Work at a Hospital," *CRN,* August 20, 2007, p. 57.

11. See Frederick E. Webster, Jr., and Yoram Wind, *Organizational Buying Behavior,* (Upper Saddle River, NJ: Prentice Hall, 1972) pp. 33–37.

12. Robinson, Faris, and Wind, *Industrial Buying Behavior,* (Boston: Allyn & Bacon, 1967) p. 14.

13. For this and other examples, see Kate Maddox, "10 Great Web Sites," *BtoB Online,* September 11, 2006; accessed at www.btobonline.com; and Karen J. Bannan, "10 Great Web Sites," September 10, 2007, accessed at www.btobonline.com. Other information from www.sun.com, September 2008.

14. Michael A. Verespej, "E-Procurement Explosion," *Industry Week,* March 2002, pp. 25–28. For more information on e-procurement, see Amit Gupta, "E-Procurement Trials and Triumphs," *Contract Management,* January 2008, pp. 28–35; and Christian Tanner, et al., "Current Trends and Challenges in Electronic Procurement: an Empirical Study," *Electronic Markets,* February 2008, pp. 6–18.

15. Information from www.shrinershq.org/Hospitals/Hospitals_for_Children/Facts; and www.tenethealth.com, October 2008.

16. "The Medical Device Market: Saudi Arabia," Espicom Business Intelligence Ltd., Markets and Research, February 2011, www.researchandmarkets.com/reportinfo.asp?report_id=300728.

17. See "About Food Away from Home," accessed at www.fafh.com, April 2008.

18. "Saudi Arabia," Office of the United States Trade Representative, Executive Office of the President, 2008 report, www.ustr.gov/sites/default/files/uploads/reports/2009/NTE/asset_upload_file856_15503.pdf.

19. V. M. Satish, "Saudi's Huge Investment in IT to Create Opportunity for Global Firms," Emirates 24/7, October 25, 2009.

20. Ari Vidali, President of Envisage Technologies, personal communication, July 6, 2006.

21. "Dubai Municipality Bags Best Middle East e-Government Portal Award," *AME Info,* May 26, 2005, www.ameinfo.com/61105.html.

22. See "GSA Organization Overview," accessed at www.gsa.gov, December 2008; and VA Office of Acquisition & Material Management, accessed at www1.va.gov/oamm, December 2008.

CHAPTER 7

1. "About Damas: Overview," Damas company website, www.mydamas.com/Info.aspx?Info_Id=1.

2. "Damas Luxury Week Kicks Off Successfully," *AME Info,* November 7, 2009, www.ameinfo.com/215039.html.

3. "Damas Launches Roberto Coin Jewellery Collection," *AME Info,* January 5, 2009, www.ameinfo.com/180184.html.

4. "Damas Launches Roberto Coin Jewellery Collection," *AME Info,* January 5, 2009, www.ameinfo.com/180184.html.

5. "Damas Launches Roberto Coin Jewellery Collection." *AME Info,* January 5, 2009, www.ameinfo.com/180184.html.

6. Quote from Sarah Marquer, "In Depth: GPS Ban Removed," *Business Monthly,* American Chamber of Commerce in Egypt, June 2009, www.amcham.org.eg; also see "Geo-Marketing," Protrac Online, www.protraconline.com/.

7. See Beth Snyder Bulik, "Forget the Parents: HP Plans to Target Teenagers Instead," *Advertising Age,* July 30, 2007, p. 8.

8. "Middle East Telcos Face Stiff Growth Challenges in Emerging African and South Asian Markets," *BI-ME,* May 13, 2009, www.bi-me.com/main.php?id=36248&t=1.

9. Kate MacArthur, "BK Rebels Fall in Love with King," *Advertising Age,* May 1, 2006, pp. 1, 86; Kenneth Hein, "BK 'Lifestyle' Goods Aim for Young Males," *Adweek,* June 12, 2006, p. 8; and Janet Adamy, "Man Behind the Burger King Turnaround: Chidsey Says Identifying His Restaurant's Superfan Helped Beef Up Its Offerings," *Wall Street Journal,* April 2, 2008, p. B1.

10. See Manish Bhatt and Raghu Bhat, "Building a Brand, Creating a Cult," *LiveMint.com,* February 12, 2008, accessed at www.livemint.com/2008/02/12231611/Building-a-brand-creating-a-c.html; Chris Maxcer, "A Menagerie of Mac Fanatic Must-Haves," *MacNewsWorld,* November 19, 2007, www.macnewsworld.com/story/60367.html; and Asher Moses, "Doco Puts Macheads Under the Microscope," *Sydney Morning Herald,* February 19, 2008, accessed at www.smh.com.au.

11. Asher Moses, "Doco Puts Macheads Under the Microscope," *Sydney Morning Herald,* February 19, 2008, accessed at www.smh.com.au.

12. "Merchants," Visa corporate website, 2011, www.visacemea.com/ac/ais/ais_merchants.jsp#Merchant Levels.

13. See Thomas L. Powers and Jay U. Stirling, "Segmenting Business-to-Business Markets: A Micro-Macro Linking Methodology," *Journal of Business & Industrial Marketing,* April 15, 2008, pp. 170–177.

14. Raed Rafei, "Cola Makers Target Mideast," Los Angeles Times, February 4, 2008, accessed at www.latimes.com; "Uganda; Carol Mgasha Is MTV VJ," Africa News, September 17, 2007; "Music on the Coke Side of Life," September 18, 2007, accessed at www.coke-music.com.mt/subsites/news.htm; and Charles R. Taylor, "Lifestyle Matters Everywhere," Advertising Age, May 19, 2008, p. 24.

15. See Michael Porter, *Competitive Advantage* (New York: Free Press, 1985), pp. 4–8, 234–236. For more recent discussions, see Stanley Slater and Eric Olson, "A Fresh Look at Industry and Market Analysis," *Business Horizons,* January–February 2002, p. 15–22; Kenneth Sawka and Bill Fiora, "The Four Analytical Techniques Every Analyst Must Know: 2. Porter's Five Forces Analysis," *Competitive Intelligence Magazine,* May–June 2003, p. 57; and Philip Kotler and Kevin Lane Keller, *Marketing Management,* 13th ed. (Upper Saddle River, NJ: Prentice Hall, 2009), pp. 342–343.

16. See Arundhati Parmar, "On the Map," *Marketing News*, February 15, 2008, pp. 13–15; and information from http://mysbuxinteractive .com, accessed July 2008.

17. See "Reported Dollar Loss from Internet Crime Reaches All-Time High," April 3, 2008, accessed at www.ic3.gov/ media/2008/080403.htm.

18. Jack Trout, "Branding Can't Exist Without Positioning," *Advertising Age*, March 14, 2005, p. 28.

19. Adapted from a positioning map prepared by students Brian May, Josh Payne, Meredith Schakel, and Bryana Sterns, University of North Carolina, April 2003. SUV sales data furnished by WardsAuto. com, June 2008. Price data from www.edmunds.com, June 2008.

20. "Introduction," Al Baraka Banking Group, 2011, www.albaraka.com.

21. "eeZee Unlimited," Zain company website, Offers & Exclusives, 2011, www.kw.zain.com/kw/.

22. See Bobby J. Calder and Steven J. Reagan, "Brand Design," in Dawn Iacobucci, ed. *Kellogg on Marketing* (New York: John Wiley & Sons, 2001) p. 61. Also see Philip Kotler and Kevin Lane Keller, *Marketing Management*, 13th ed. (Upper Saddle River, NJ: Prentice Hall, 2009), pp. 315–316.

23. For a fuller discussion, see Philip Kotler and Kevin Lane Keller, *Marketing Management*, 13th ed. (Upper Saddle River, NJ: Prentice Hall, 2009), chapter 10.

CHAPTER 8

1. Case study written by Mike Lewicki. Sources include Bahrain Islamic Bank company website, www.bisb.com, accessed 2011; and published BisB product brochures.

2. "Al Rostamani: Superbrands 2010, UAE's Choice," Al Rostamani Group website, www.alrostamanigroup.ae/en/Documents/ Superbrands_2010.pdf.

3. "Nancy Ajram Becomes the Ambassador of Sony Ericsson," *AME Info*, February 12, 2009, www.ameinfo.com/184671.html.

4. Neesha C. Salian, "Star Power Sells," *Gulf News*, May 1, 2007, http:// gulfnews.com/in-focus/jewellery/star-power-sells-1.27633.

5. "Dubai Launches New Tourism Campaign," *Project Mena*, March 7, 2009, www.projectmena.com/article.aspx?id=3447.

6. Accessed online at www.social-marketing.org/aboutus.html, August 2008.

7. D. Eddy and G. Garb, "Stay Tuned Next Week. The Power of Social Marketing: How Egypt Learned about ORS," *World Education Reports*, 1986 Summer, no. 25, pp. 4–7. Accessed at www.ncbi.nlm.nih.gov/pubmed/12281150.

8. See Rob Gould and Karen Gutierrez, "Social Marketing Has a New Champion," *Marketing News*, February 7, 2000, p. 38. Also see Alan R. Andreasen, *Social Marketing in the 21st Century* (Thousand Oaks, CA: Sage Publications, 2006); Philip Kotler and Nancy Lee, *Social Marketing: Improving the Quality of Life*, 3rd ed. (Thousand Oaks, CA: Sage Publications, 2008); and www.social-marketing .org, November 2008.

9. Quotes and definitions from Philip Kotler, *Kotler on Marketing* (New York: Free Press, 1999), p. 17; and www.asq.org, July 2008.

10. "Dyson and Jumbo Electronics Team Up to Launch the Dyson Airblade at Dubai's Hotel Show," *AME Info*, June 3, 2007, www .ameinfo.com/122256.html.

11. See "Supermarket facts," accessed at www.fmi.org/facts_ figs/?fuseaction=superfact, April 2008; and "Wal-Mart Facts," accessed at www.walmartfacts.com/StateByState/?id=2, April 2008.

12. Sonja Reyes, "Ad Blitz, Bottle Design Fuel Debate over Heinz's Sales," *Brandweek*, February 12, 2007, accessed at www

.brandweek.com/bw/news/recent_display.jsp?vnu_content _id=1003544497.

13. David Williams, "UAE Establishes Arabic Labeling Requirements for Food Products," FAIRS Subject Report, USDBA Foreign Agricultural Service, March 4, 2008, www.fas.usda.gov/ gainfiles/200803/146293857.pdf.

14. See the HP Total Care site at http://h71036.www7.hp.com/hho/ cache/309717-0-0-225-121.html, accessed 2011.

15. Information accessed online at www.marriott.com, August 2007.

16. See "McAtlas Shrugged," *Foreign Policy*, May–June 2001, pp. 26–37; and Philip Kotler and Kevin Lane Keller, *Marketing Management*, 13th ed. (Upper Saddle River, NJ: Prentice Hall, 2009), p. 254.

17. See Jack Trout, "'Branding' Simplified," *Forbes*, April 19, 2007, accessed at www.forbes.com.

18. Keller, Kevin (2008), *Strategic Brand Management*, Third Edition.

19. For more on Y&R's Brand Asset Valuator, see "Brand Asset Valuator," Value Based Management.net, www.valuebasedmanagement.net/ methods_brand_asset_valuator.html, accessed February 2008; W. Ronald Lane, Karen Whitehill King, and J. Thomas Russell, *Kleppner's Advertising Procedure*, 17th ed. (Upper Saddle River, NJ: Prentice Hall, 2008), p. 105; and Chelsea Greene, "Using Brands to Drive Business Results," Landor, accessed at www.wpp.com/WPP/ Marketing/ReportsStudies/Usingbrandstodrivebusinessresults .htm, March 2008.

20. Al Ehrbar, "Breakaway Brands," *Fortune*, October 31, 2005, pp. 153–170. Also see "DeWalt Named Breakaway Brand," *Snips*, January 2006, p. 66.

21. See Millward Brown Optimor, "BrandZ Top 100 Most Powerful Brands 2008," accessed at www.brandz.com/output, July 2008.

22. See Scott Davis, *Brand Asset Management*, 2nd ed. (San Francisco: Jossey-Bass, 2002). For more on brand positioning, see Philip Kotler and Kevin Lane Keller, *Marketing Management*, 13th ed. (Upper Saddle River, NJ: Prentice Hall, 2009), chapter 10.

23. Adapted from information found in Geoff Colvin, "Selling P&G," *Fortune*, September 17, 2007, pp. 163–169; and "For P&G, Success Lies in More Than Merely a Dryer Diaper," *Advertising Age*, October 15, 2007, p. 20.

24. See Nirmalya Kumar and Jan-Benedict E. M. Steenkamp, *Private Label Strategy* (Boston, MA: Harvard Business School Press, 2007), pp. 1–12; Vanessa L. Facenda, "A Swift Kick to the Privates," *Brandweek*, September 3, 2007, pp. 24+; and Janet Groeber, "Emphasizing Quality, Price and Value, Supermarkets Say Goodbye to Generics and Hello to Proprietary Programs," *Stores*, February 2008, accessed at www.stores.org/Current_Issue/2008/02/Edit1.asp.

25. See Noreen O'Leary, "New and Improved Private Label Brands," *Adweek*, October 22, 2007, pp.16+; and Teresa F. Lindeman, "Store Brands Get a Boost," *McClatchy-Tribune Business News*, May 21, 2008.

26. Noreen O'Leary, "New and Improved Private Label Brands," *Adweek*, October 22, 2007, pp. 16+.

27. Nirmalya Kumar and Jan-Benedict E. M. Steenkamp, *Private Label Strategy* (Boston, MA: Harvard Business School Press, 2007), p. 5.

28. "Nick Puts Muscle Behind everGirl; Network Makes a New Foray Into Non-TV Branding," *TelevisionWeek*, January 5, 2004; "Dora the Explorer Takes the Lead as Sales Growth Elevates Property to Megabrand Status as Number-One Toy License in 2006," *PR Newswire*, February 8, 2007; Clint Cantwell, "$187 Billion Global Licensing Industry Comes to Life at Licensing International Expo 2008," *Business Wire*, June 6, 2008; and "Nickelodeon Expands Product Offerings and Debuts New Properties for Kids and Teens at Licensing 2008 International Show," June 10, 2008, accessed at http://biz.yahoo.com/prnews/080610/nytu056.html?.v=101.

29. Quote from Sony Ericsson Facebook page, www.facebook.com/group.php?gid=55254717595; and from www.apple.com/ipod/nike, August 2008.

30. Quote from www.apple.com/ipod/nike, August 2008.

31. Gabrielle Solomon, "Cobranding Alliances: Arranged Marriages Made by Marketers," *Fortune*, October 12, 1998, p. 188; "Martha Stewart Upgrading from Kmart to Macys," *FinancialWire*, April 26, 2006, p. 1; and James Mammerella, "Martha Stewart Narrows Loss," *Home Textiles Today*, November 7, 2007, p. 28.

32. For more examples of good and bad brand extensions, see Kenneth Hein, "Line Extensions to Cross the Line and '07," *Brandweek*, December 10, 2007, p. 4. For more discussion on the use of line and brand extensions and consumer attitudes toward them, see Philip Kotler and Kevin Lane Keller, *Marketing Management* (Upper Saddle River, NJ: Prentice Hall, 2009), p. 262.

33. "100 Leading National Advertisers," *Advertising Age*, June 25, 2007, accessed at http://adage.com/article?article_id=118648.

34. Quotes from Stephen Cole, "Value of the Brand," *CA Magazine*, May 2005, pp. 39–40; and Lawrence A. Crosby and Sheree L. Johnson, "Experience Required," *Marketing Management*, July/August 2007, pp. 21–27.

35. www.guardian.co.uk/world/2003/aug/10/stephenkhan.theobserver

36. The World Factbook, Central Intelligence Agency, 2011, www.cia.gov/library/publications/the-world-factbook; and information from the Bureau of Labor Statistics, www.bls.gov, accessed August 2008.

37. "Emaar's First Healthcare Facility, The Dubai Mall Medical Centre Opens to Offer World-class Medical Care," AME Info, October 3, 2009, www.ameinfo.com/210923.html.

38. "About US," EHL Management Services, www.ehl.ae/PageContent.aspx?pageid=1&groupid=1.

39. See James L. Heskett, W. Earl Sasser Jr., and Leonard A. Schlesinger, *The Service Profit Chain: How Leading Companies Link Profit and Growth to Loyalty, Satisfaction, and Value* (New York: Free Press, 1997); Heskett, Sasser, and Schlesinger, *The Value Profit Chain: Treat Employees Like Customers and Customers Like Employees* (New York: Free Press, 2003); and John F. Milliman, Jeffrey M. Ferguson, and Andrew J. Czaplewski, "Breaking the Cycle," *Marketing Management*, March–April 2008, pp. 14–17.

40. William C. Johnson and Larry G. Chiagouris, "So Happy Together," *Marketing Management*, March–April 2006, pp. 47–50.

41. Adapted from information in Jeffrey M. O'Brien, "A Perfect Season," *Fortune*, pp. 62–66.

42. O'Brien, "A Perfect Season," p. 66.

43. "Service Customer Affairs (CSA)," The Emirates Group Careers Centre, www.emiratesgroupcareers.com/english/Careers_Overview/commercial/serv_cust_affairs.aspx.

CHAPTER 9

1. Steve Maich, "Nowhere to go but Down," *Macleans*, May 6, 2005, www.macleans.ca.

2. Brent Schendler, Source unknown.

3. Brent Schendler, "How Big Can Apple Get?" *Fortune*, February 21, 2005, http://money.cnn.com/magazines/fortune/fortune_archive/2005/02/21/8251769/index.htm.

4. "'Crazy' Demand as Apple iPad Arrives in Dubai," *Arabian Business,* April 7, 2010, www.arabianbusiness.com/585483-crazy-demand-as-ipad-arrives-in-dubai.

5. Betsy Morris, "What Makes Apple Golden?" *Fortune*, March 17, 2008, pp. 68–74. Additional information from "Apple," BusinessWeek, March 26, 2007, p. 84; "The World's Most Innovative Companies," *BusinessWeek*, May 14, 2007, p. 55; Adam L. Penenberg, "All Eyes on Apple," *Fast Company*, December 2007/January 2008, pp. 83+; financial reports and other information accessed at www.apple.com, April 2008; "iPad set to go Down a Storm in Mideast—Survey," *Arabian Business*, February 17, 2010, www.arabianbusiness.com/581777-ipad-set-to-go-down-a-storm-in-mideast--survey.

6. Calvin Hodock, "Winning the New-Products Game," *Advertising Age*, November 12, 2007, p. 35.

7. "Mansour Distribution Co.," Ministry of Industry & Foreign Trade, Egyptian International Trade Point, www.tpegypt.gov.eg/Eng/ProDetails.aspx?ID=1302&Code=1439.

8. Information from Arma company website, www.arma.com.eg.

9. "IBM Taps Into Its Workers' Bright Ideas," *Irish Times*, October 27, 2006, p. 12; and Luke Collins, "Embedding Innovation into the Firm," Research Technology Management, March–April, 2007, pp. 5–6.

10. John Peppers and Martha Rogers, "The Buzz on Customer-Driven Innovation," *Sales & Marketing Management*, June 2007, p. 13.

11. See Rik Kirkland, "Cisco's Display of Strength," *Fortune*, November 12, 2007, pp. 90–100; and "Cisco on Cisco: Web 2.0 in the Enterprise," accessed at www.cisco.com, September 2008.

12. Cliff Saran, "Wake Up to the Dawn of Web 2.0," *Computer Weekly*, June 5, 2007.

13. Based on quotes and information from Robert D. Hof, "The Power of Us," *BusinessWeek*, June 20, 2005, pp. 74–82. See also Robert Weisman, "Firms Turn R&D on Its Head, Looking Outside for Ideas," *Boston Globe*, May 14, 2006, p. E1.

14. "Bill Invites Customers to Share Ideas and Original Video via Dell IdeaStorm and StudioDell," February 16, 2007, accessed at www.dell.com. Also see www.ideastorm.com.

15. Information accessed online at www.avon.com, August 2008.

16. Quotes from Robert Gray, "Not Invented Here," *Marketing*, May 6, 2004, pp. 34–37; and Betsy Morris, "What Makes Apple Golden?" *Fortune*, March 17, 2008, pp. 68–74.

17. See George S. Day, "Is It Real? Can We Win? Is It Worth Doing?" *Harvard Business Review*, December 2007, pp. 110–120.

18. Information for this example obtained from www.teslamotors.com, April 2008; and Alan Pierce, "Seeing Beyond Gasoline Powered Vehicles," *Tech Directions*, April 2008, pp. 10–11.

19. "Soft Drinks in Morocco," *Euromonitor International,* July 2010, www.euromonitor.com/soft-drinks-in-morocco/report.

20. "KFC Fires Up Grilled Chicken," March 23, 2008, accessed at www.money.cnn.com.

21. Jack Neff, "Is Testing the Answer?" *Advertising Age*, July 9, 2001, p. 13; and Dale Buss, "P&G's Rise," *Potentials*, January 2003, pp. 26–30. For more on test marketing, see Philip Kotler and Kevin Lane Keller, *Marketing Management*, 13th ed. (Upper Saddle River, NJ: Prentice Hall, 2008), pp. 587–590.

22. Example developed from information found in Allison Enright, "Best Practices: Frito-Lay Get Real Results from a Virtual World," *Marketing News*, December 15, 2006, p. 20; and "Decision Insight: Simushop," accessed at www.decisioninsight.com, September 2008.

23. See Steve McClellan, "Unilever's Sunsilk Launch Goes Far Beyond the Box," *Adweek*, August 21–28, 2006, p. 9.

24. See Beth Snyder Bulik, "$500 Million for Vista? Wow," *Advertising Age*, January 29, 2007, pp. 1, 30.

25. Robert G. Cooper, "Formula for Success," *Marketing Management*, March–April 2006, pp. 19–23; and Barry Jaruzelski and Kevin Dehoff, "The Global Innovation of 1000," *Strategy + Business*, Issue 49, fourth quarter, 2007, pp. 68–83.

26. "Juhayna Food Industries: Get Ready, Get Set, Grow," *EFG Hermes Investment Research*, July 29, 2010, http://xa.yimg.com/kq/groups/21139192/1408736674/name/Juhayna; "Bekhiro Milk," Juhayna company website, 2011, www.juhayna.com/Bekhiromilk.html; "Juhayna Food Industries: Shifting Gear," NBK Capital, January 23, 2011, www.nbkcapital.com/BR/Research/MER/FoodBeverageSectore/Egypt/Juhayna/NBK%20Capital-Juhayna%20Initiation%20of%20Coverage-23January2011.pdf; Tarek H. Selim, "The Egyptian Food Processing Industry: Formalization versus Informalization within the Nation's Food Security Policy," Industry Studies Association, May 2009, www.industrystudies.pitt.edu/chicago09/docs/Selim%203.1.pdf.

27. Lawrence A. Crosby and Sheree L. Johnson, "Customer-Centric Innovation," *Marketing Management*, March–April 2006, pp. 12–13.

28. Teressa Iezzi, "Innovate, But Do It for Customers," *Creativity*, September 2006, pp. 8–11.

29. Portions adapted from Chuck Salter, "Google: The Faces and Voices of the World's Most Innovative Company," *Fast Company*, March 2008, pp. 74–88.

30. This definition is based on one found in Bryan Lilly and Tammy R. Nelson, "Fads: Segmenting the Fad-Buyer Market," *Journal of Consumer Marketing*, vol. 20, no. 3, 2003, pp. 252–265.

31. Youngme Moon, "Break Free from the Product Life Cycle," *Harvard Business Review*, May 2005, pp. 87–94.

32. For a more comprehensive discussion of marketing strategies over the course of the product life cycle, see Philip Kotler and Kevin Lane Keller, *Marketing Management*, 13th ed. (Upper Saddle River, NJ: Prentice Hall, 2008), pp. 278–290.

33. Example based on information provided by Nestlé Japan Ltd., May 2008; with additional information from http://en.wikipedia.org/wiki/Kit_Kat and the Japanese Wikipedia discussion of Kit Kat at http://ja.wikipedia.org, accessed November 2008.

34. See www.HSBC.com.

35. See "2007 Global Powers of Retailing," *Stores*, January 2007, accessed at www.stores.org; "Wal-Mart International Operations," accessed at www.walmartstores.com, April 2008; and information accessed at www.carrefour.com/english/groupecarrefour/profil.jsp, July 2008.

CHAPTER 10

1. "Carrefour to Open Four New Hypermarkets in Saudi Arabia," MENA FN, August 5, 2007, www.menafn.com/qn_news_story_s.asp?StoryId=1093161941.

2. "Carrefour to Open Four New Hypermarkets in Saudi Arabia," MENA FN, August 5, 2007, www.menafn.com/qn_news_story_s.asp?StoryId=1093161941.

3. Javid Hassan, "Price War Between Supermarkets Benefits Consumers," *Arab News*, November 8, 2004, http://archive.arabnews.com/?page=9&section=0&article=54152&d=8&m=11&y=2004; with additional information from the Carrefour Group website, www.carrefour.com/cdc/group/our-group/.

4. George Mannes, "The Urge to Unbundle," *Fast Company*, February 27, 2005, pp. 23–24. Also see Stuart Elliott, "Creative Spots, Courtesy of a Stalled Economy," *New York Times*, April 11, 2008.

5. Linda Tischler, "The Price Is Right," *Fast Company*, November 2003, pp. 83–91. See also Elizabeth A. Sullivan, "Value Pricing: Smart Marketers Know Cost-Plus Can Be Costly," January 15, 2008, p. 8.

6. John Tayman, "The Six-Figure Steal," *Business 2.0*, June 2005, pp. 148–150.

7. These and other examples found at Stuart Elliott, "Creative Spots, Courtesy of a Stalled Economy," *New York Times*, April 11, 2008; and www.vw.com/rabbit/en/us/#, April 2008.

8. Here accumulated production is drawn on a semilog scale so that equal distances represent the same percentage increase in output.

9. The arithmetic of markups and margins is discussed in Appendix 2, Marketing by the Numbers.

10. Joshua Rosenbaum, "Guitar Maker Looks for a New Key," *Wall Street Journal*, February 11, 1998, p. B1; and information accessed online at www.gibson.com, September 2008.

11. See Nagle and Hogan, *The Strategy and Tactics of Pricing*, chapter 7.

12. Comments from www.yelp.com/biz/annie-blooms-books-portland, accessed May, 2008.

13. See Robert J. Dolan, "Pricing: A Value-Based Approach," *Harvard Business School Publishing*, 9-500-071, November 3, 2003.

14. Andy Sambridge, "Retailers Warned Over Ramadan Price Hikes," *Arabian Business*, June 3, 2010, www.arabianbusiness.com/retailers-warned-over-ramadan-price-hikes-272123.html.

15. Andrew White, "Bahrain Warning Over Ramadan Prices," *Arabian Business*, August 25, 2008, www.arabianbusiness.com/bahrain-warning-over-ramadan-prices-44548.html.

16. Mohamed Abdel Salam, "Egypt: Conflicting Ramadan Food Prices," *Bikyamasr*, August 29, 2009, http://bikyamasr.com/wordpress/?p=2611.

17. Elsa Baxter, "Fruit and Veg Doubled in Price During Ramadan," *Arabian Business*, August 23, 2009, www.arabianbusiness.com/fruit-veg-doubled-in-price-during-ramadan-14444.html.

18. See Philip Kotler and Kevin Lane Keller, *Marketing Management*, 13th ed. (Upper Saddle River, NJ: Prentice Hall, 2008), pp. 383–384; and Chris Tribbey, "HDTV Prices Projected to Drop 15% in 2008," *Home Media Magazine*, January 20–January 26, 2008, p. 10.

19. "At Sharaf DG, Big Is Beautiful," Sharaf Group website, January 26, 2009, www.sharafs.ae/news.php?id=69; additional information from "Sharaf DG Makes Foray Into Bahrain," press release, December 18, 2008, www.1888pressrelease.com.

20. See Nagle and Hogan, *The Strategy and Tactics of Pricing*, pp. 244–247; Bram Foubert and Els Gijsbrechts, "Shopper Response to Bundle Promotions for Packaged Goods," *Journal of Marketing Research*, November 2007, pp. 647–662; Roger M. Heeler, et al., "Bundles = Discount? Revisiting Complex Theories of Bundle Effects," *Journal of Product & Brand Management*, vol. 16, no. 7, 2007, pp. 492–500; and Timothy J. Gilbride, et al., "Framing Effects in Mixed Price Bundling," *Marketing Letters*, June 2008, pp. 125–140.

21. Susan Greco, "Small Businesses: Are Your Prices Right?" Inc., Jan 1, 1997, www.inc.com/magazine/19970101/1155.html.

22. Based on information from Eric Anderson and Duncan Simester, "Mind Your Pricing Cues," *Harvard Business Review*, September 2003, pp. 96–103. Also see Heyong Min Kim and Luke Kachersky, "Dimensions of Price Salience: A Conceptual Framework for Perceptions of Multi-Dimensional Prices," *Journal of Product and Brand Management*," 2006, vol. 15, no. 2, pp. 139–147; and Monika Kukar-Kinney, et al, "Consumer Responses to Characteristics of Price-Matching Guarantees," *Journal of Retailing*, April 2007, p. 211.

23. Cleofe Maceda, "Ramadan Promotions Bring Bargains to Dubai Shoppers," *Gulf News*, August 24, 2009, http://gulfnews.com.

24. "Suzuki's 'Beat Any Offer' Ramadan Promotion," Dubai Savers, September 21, 2009, www.dubaisavers.com/Dubai-Deal/suzukis-beat-any-offer-ramadan-promotion.

25. Karyn McCormack, "Price War Leaves AMD Reeling," *BusinessWeek Online*, January 25, 2007, p. 4; and Chris Nuttall, "AMD Suffers Further Losses Amid Price War with Rival Intel," *Financial Times*, October 19, 2007, p. 18.

26. "Souq.com launches its Egypt portal," *AME Info*, April 12, 2010, www.ameinfo.com/229413.html.

CHAPTER 11

1. "Unilever Launches Pond's Age Miracle, New Age in Anti-Ageing Technology, in Middle East," *AME Info*, March 10, 2009, www.ameinfo.com/187859.html; Unilever Middle East website, www.unileverme.com.

2. The first four of these definitions are adapted from Peter D. Bennett, *The AMA Dictionary of Marketing Terms*, 2nd ed. (New York: McGraw-Hill, 1995). Other definitions can be found at www.marketingpower.com/_layouts/Dictionary.aspx, accessed December 2008.

3. Bob Garfield, "The Chaos Scenario," *Advertising Age*, April 4, 2005, pp. 1, 57+; and Garfield, "The Chaos Scenario 2.0: The Post-Advertising Age," *Advertising Age*, March 26, 2007, pp. 1, 12–13.

4. Chase Squires and Dave Gussow, "The Ways in Which We Watch TV Are Changing Right Before Our Eyes," *St. Petersburg Times*, April 27, 2006; and Geoff Colvin, "TV Is Dying? Long Live TV!" *Fortune*, February 5, 2007, p. 43.

5. Brian Steinberg and Suzanne Vranica, "As 30-Second Spot Fades, What Will Advertisers Do Next?" *Wall Street Journal*, January 3, 2006, p. A15; Warren Berger, "A Hard Sell," *Business 2.0*, May 2007, pp. 91–96; and Megan Mcilroy, "Serving Other Media with TV Ups Appetite for Products," *Advertising Age*, June 2, 2008, accessed at http://adage.com/print?article_id127454.

6. TV advertising stats from "Lisa Snedeker, "Ad Spending Goes Limp as 2007 Ends," *Media Life*, March 28, 2008, www.medialifemagazine.com/artman2/publish/Media_economy_57/Ad_spending_goes_limp_as_2007_ends.asp. Quotes from Mike Shaw, "Direct Your Advertising Dollars Away from TV at Your Own Risk," *Advertising Age*, February 27, 2006, p. 29; and Bob Liodice, "TV Make Strides While Marketers Experiment Widely, *Advertising Age*, March 24, 2008, pp. 16–17.

7. Bob Garfield, "Lee Chow on What's Changed Since '1984,'" *Advertising Age*, June 11, 2007, p. 3.

8. "Flip Media Launches Online Campaign for Mercedes' New CLS Model," *AME Info*, October 14, 2004, www.ameinfo.com/47381.html.

9. Dan Hill, "CMOs, Win Big by Letting Emotions Drive Advertising," *Advertising Age*, August 27, 2007, p. 12.

10. "Brand Design: Cracking the Colour Code," *Marketing Week*, October 11, 2007, p. 28.

11. "Word of Mouth is Most Trusted in UAE-Nielsen Survey," *AME Info*, August 1, 2009, www.ameinfo.com/205297.html.

12. Jonah Bloom, "The Truth Is: Consumers Trust Fellow Buyers Before Marketers," *Advertising Age*, February 13, 2006, p. 25.

13. "Catch Brings First-of-a-Kind Online BuzzMarketing to Middle East," *AME Info*, July 14, 2008, www.ameinfo.com/163435.html.

14. For more on advertising spending by company and industry, see http://adage.com/datacenter/datapopup.php?article_id=119881, accessed September 2008.

15. For more on setting promotion budgets, see W. Ronald Lane, Karen Whitehill King, and J. Thomas Russell, *Kleppner's Advertising Procedure*, 17th ed. (Upper Saddle River, NJ: Prentice Hall, 2008), chapter 6.

16. Based on Matthew P. Gonring, "Putting Integrated Marketing Communications to Work Today," *Public Relations Quarterly*, Fall 1994, pp. 45–48. Also see Philip Kotler and Kevin Lane Keller, *Marketing Management*, 13th ed. (Upper Saddle River, NJ: Prentice Hall, 2009), pp. 491–493.

17. For more on the legal aspects of promotion, see Lane, King, and Russell, *Kleppner's Advertising Procedure*, chapter 25; and William L. Cron and Thomas E. DeCarlo, *Dalrymple's Sales Management*, 9th ed. (New York: Wiley, 2006), chapter 10.

CHAPTER 12

1. "Winner & Shortlists: Agency of the Year," Dubai Lynx Awards website, 2010, www.dubailynx.com/winners/2010/special/.

2. "TBWA Factsheet 2010," TBWA website, p. 2, http://open.mytbwa.com/tbwadotcom/TBWA_Facts_Sheet_2010.pdf.

3. "PARC analyzes advertising spending for year 2010," *MediaMe*, January 24, 2011, http://mediame.com/tags/parc/parc_analyzes_advertising_spending_year_2010. Data on U.S. and global advertising spending obtained at http://adage.com/datacenter/#top_marketers;_adspend_stats, accessed September 2008.

4. For more on advertising budgets, see Ronald Lane, Karen King, and Thomas Russell, *Kleppner's Advertising Procedure*, 17th ed. (Upper Saddle River, NJ: Prentice Hall, 2008), chapter 6.

5. For more discussion, see John Consoli, "Heavy Lifting," *MediaWeek*, March 3, 2008.

6. "Growth in Arab World's FTA Satellite TV Channels Slows Down in 2009/2010," *AME Info*, June 8, 2010, www.ameinfo.com/234722.html.

7. Louise Story, "Anywhere the Eye Can See, It's Likely to See an Ad," *New York Times*, January 15, 2007, accessed at www.nytimes.com; and Matthew Creamer, "Caught in the Clutter Crossfire: Your Brand," *Advertising Age*, April 1, 2007, pp. 1, 35.

8. John Consoli, "Broadcast, Cable Ad Clutter Continues to Rise," *MediaWeek*, May 4, 2006, accessed at www.mediaweek.com.

9. See Steve McKee, Advertising: Less Is Much More," *BusinessWeek Online*, May 10, 2006, accessed at www.businessweek.com; Stewart Elliott, "Now, the Clicking Is to Watch the Ads, Not Skip Them," *New York Times*, August 17, 2007, accessed at www.nytimes.com; and Theresa Howard, "'Viral' Advertising Spreads Through Marketing Plans," *USA Today*, June 23, 2005, accessed at www.usatoday.com/money/advertising/2005-06-22-viral-usat_x.htm.

10. For this and other examples, see Wendy Tanaka, "D.I.Y Ads," *Red Herring*, January 29, 2007, accessed at www.redherring.com/Article.aspx?a=20955&hed=D.I.Y.+Ads; and Lee Gomes, "Tips from Web Greats on Becoming a Legend in Your Spare Time," *Wall Street Journal*, November 14, 2007, p. B1.

11. Tanaka, "D.I.Y Ads," p. 3; and Laura Petrecca, "Madison Avenue Wants You! (Or at Least Your Videos)," *USA Today*, June 21, 2007, p. 1B.

12. Allison Enright, "Let Them Decide," *Marketing News*, June 1, 2006, pp. 10–11.

13. Enright, "Let Them Decide," pp. 10–11; and "Who's in Control?" *Advertising Age*, January 28, 2008, p. C1.

14. Stuart Elliot, "New Rules of Engagement," *New York Times*, March 21, 2006, p. C7; Abbey Klaassen, "New Wins Early Battle in Viewer-Engagement War," *Advertising Age*, March 20, 2006, p. 1; Mike DiFranza, "Rules of Engagement," *MediaWeek*, January 15, 2007, p. 9; Andrew Hampp, "Water Cooler," *Advertising Age*, April 16, 2007, p. 32; Megan McIlroy, "So Much for Engagement; Buys Are Still Based on Eyes," *Advertising Age*, January 14, 2008, p. 1; and Betsy Cummings, "Marketers Size Up New Metric System," *Brandweek*, April 6, 2008, accessed at www.brandweek.com.

15. For these and other examples and quotes, see Chris Walsh, "Ads on Board," *Rocky Mountain News*, February 27, 2007; David Kiley, "Rated M for Mad Ave," *BusinessWeek*, February 26, 2006, pp. 76–77; Cliff Peale, "Advertising Takes Many Forms," *Cincinnati Enquirer*, December 3, 2006, accessed at http://news.enquirer.com; Louise Story, "Anywhere the Eye Can See, It's Likely to See an Ad," *New York Times*, January 15, 2007, p. A12; and Adam Remson, "School Buses Latest Victim of Ad Creep," *Brandweek*, February 4, 2008, p. 4.

16. Adapted from information found in Claudia Wallis, "The Multitasking Generation," *Time*, March 27, 2006, accessed at www.time.com; Curtis L. Taylor, "Teens' Balancing Act: New Study Shows Young People Are Spending More Time Multitasking," *Knight Ridder Tribune Business News*, December 16, 2006, p. 1; John Harlow, "How We Squeeze 31 Hours into a Day," *Times* (London), April 13, 2008, p. 8; and Tanya Irwin, "Study: Kids Are Master Multitaskers on TV, Web, Mobile," *MediaPost Publications*, March 10, 2008, accessed at www.mediapostpublications.com.

17. *Newsweek* and *BusinessWeek* cost and circulation data accessed online at http://mediakit.businessweek.com and www.newsweekmediakit.com, September 2008.

18. See Stuart Elliot, "How Effective Is This Ad, in Real Numbers? Beats Me," *New York Times*, July 20, 2005, p. C8; Jack Neff, "Half Your Advertising Isn't Wasted—Just 37.3 Percent," *Advertising Age*, August 7, 2006, pp. 1, 32; Ben Richards and Faris Yakob, "The New Quid pro Quo," *Adweek*, March 19, 2007, p. 17; and Kate Maddox, "ROI Takes Center Stage at CMO Summit," *BtoB*, February 11, 2008, p. 3.

19. David Tiltman, "Everything You Know Is Wrong," *Marketing*, June 13, 2008, pp. 28+.

20. Stuart Elliot, "How Effective Is This Ad, in Real Numbers? Beats Me," p. C8; and "Taking Measure of Which Metrics Matter," *BtoB*, May 5, 2008.

21. Information on advertising agency revenues from "Top 10 Worldwide Ad Agencies," *Advertising Age*, May 5, 2008, accessed at http://adage.com/datacenter/datapopup.php?article_id=126731; and "World's Top 50 Agency Companies," May 5, 2008, accessed at http://adage.com/datacenter/datapopup.php?article_id=126706.

22. Adapted from information in Geoffrey A. Fowler, Brian Steinberg, and Aaron O. Patrick, "Mac and PC's Overseas Adventures," *Wall Street Journal*, March 1, 2007, p. B1.

23. See Alexandra Jardine and Laurel Wentz, "It's a Fat World After All," *Advertising Age*, March 7, 2005, p. 3; George E. Belch and Michael A. Belch, *Advertising and Promotion*, (New York: McGraw-Hill/Irwin, 2004), pp. 666–668; Jonathan Cheng, "China Demands Concrete Proof of Ads," *Wall Street Journal*, July 8, 2005, p. B1; Cris Prystay, "India's Brewers Cleverly Dodge Alcohol-Ad Ban," *Wall Street Journal*, June 15, 2005, p. B1; Dean Visser, "China Puts New Restrictions on Cell Phone, E-Mail Advertising," *Marketing News*, March 15, 2006, p. 23; Steve Inskeep, "Ban Thwarts 'Year of the Pig' Ads in China," *National Public Radio*, February 6, 2007; Maxine Frith, "It Worked in Canada to Ban Junk Food Ads and Now the Call Is on TV in Australia," *Sun Herald* (Sydney), March 16, 2008, p. 14.

24. Adapted from Scott Cutlip, Allen Center, and Glen Broom, *Effective Public Relations*, 9th ed. (Upper Saddle River, NJ: Prentice Hall, 2006), chapter 1.

25. See Jeff Manning and Kevin Lane Keller, "Got Advertising That Works?" *Marketing Management*, January–February 2004, pp. 16–20; Alice Z. Cuneo, "Now Even Cellphones Have Milk Mustaches," *Advertising Age*, February 26, 2007, p. 8; "Got Milk? Campaign Searches for America's First-Ever 'Chief Health Officer,'" *Business Wire*, May 6, 2008; and information from www.bodybymilk.com and www.whymilk.com, September 2008.

26. "GolinHarris Wins Mepra Award," *Trade Arabia*, December 13, 2010, www.tradearabia.com/news/MEDIA_190359.html.

27. Al Ries and Laura Ries, "First Do Some Publicity," *Advertising Age*, February 8, 1999, p. 42. Also see Al Ries and Laura Ries, *The Fall of Advertising and the Rise of PR* (New York: HarperBusiness, 2002). For points and counterpoints and discussions of the role of public relations, see O. Burtch Drake, "'Fall' of Advertising? I Differ," *Advertising Age*, January 13, 2003, p. 23; David Robinson. "Public Relations Comes of Age," *Business Horizons*, May–June 2006, pp. 247+; and Noelle Weaver, "Why Advertising and PR Can't Be Separated," *Advertising Age*, May 14, 2007, accessed at www.adage.com.

28. Aveeno case study, accessed at www.ogilvypr.com/case-studies/aveeno.cfm, October 2008; and see www.youtube.com/watch?v=hfn8Dz_13Ms.

29. Maktoob website, www.maktoob.com.

30. Paul Holmes, "Senior Marketers Are Sharply Divided about the Role of PR in the Overall Mix," *Advertising Age*, January 24, 2005, pp. C1–C2.

31. Based on information in Jennifer J. Salopek, "Bye, Bye, Used Car Guy," *T+D*, April 2007, pp. 22–25. Also see "Prepare to Win," *Selling Power*, April 2008, p. 27.

32. For more on 'salesperson-owned loyalty,' see Robert W. Palmatier, et al. "Customer Loyalty to Whom? Managing the Benefits and Risks of Salesperson-Owned Loyalty," *Journal of Marketing Research*, May 2007, pp. 185–199.

33. This extract and strategies that follow are based on Philip Kotler, Neil Rackham, and Suj Krishnaswamy, "Ending the War Between Sales and Marketing," *Harvard Business Review*, July–August 2006, pp. 68–78. Also see Timothy Smith, Srinath Gopalakrishna, and Rabikar Chatterjee, "A Three-Stage Model of Integrated Marketing Communications at the Marketing-Sales Interface," *Journal of Marketing Research*, November 2006, pp. 564–579; and Christian Homburg, Ove Jensen, and Harley Krohmer, "Configurations of Marketing and Sales: a Taxonomy," *Journal of Marketing*, March 2008, pp. 133–154.

34. "Selling Power 500," accessed at www.sellingpower.com/sp500/index.asp, October 2007.

35. See Aphidas website at www.lotustrain.com.

36. For more on this and other methods for determining sales force size, see Mark W. Johnston and Greg W. Marshall, *Sales Force Management*, 9th ed. (Boston: McGraw-Hill Irwin, 2009), pp. 152–156.

37. Theodore Kinni, "The Team Solution," *Selling Power*, April 2007, pp. 27–29.

38. Jennifer J. Salopek, "Bye, Bye, Used Car Guy," *T+D*, April 2007, pp. 22–25; and William F. Kendy, "No More Lone Rangers," *Selling Power*, April 2004, pp. 70–74. Also see Michelle Nichols, "Pull Together—Or Fall Apart," *BusinessWeek Online*, December 2, 2005, accessed at www.businessweek.com; and Theodore Kinni, "The Team Solution," *Selling Power*, April 2007, pp. 27–29.

39. "Customer Business Development," accessed at www.pg.com/jobs/jobs_us/work_we_offer/advisor_overview.jhtml?sl=jobs_advisor_business_development, November 2008.

40. "Renkus-Heinz Appoints Norbert Bau as Middle East Sales Representative," *PR Log* (press release), March 5, 2010, www.prlog

.org/10562007-renkus-heinz-appoints-norbert-bau-as-middle-east-sales-representative.html.

41. For more information and discussion, see Benson Smith, *Discover Your Strengths: How the World's Greatest Salespeople Develop Winning Careers* (New York: Warner Business Books, 2003); Kevin McDonald, "Therapist, Social Worker or Consultant?" *CRN*, December 2005–January 2006, p. 24; Tom Reilly, "Planning for Success," *Industrial Distribution*, May 2007, p. 25; Dave Kahle, "The Four Characteristics of Successful Salespeople," *Industrial Distribution*, April 2008, p. 54; and www.gallup.com/consulting/1477/Sales-Force-Effectiveness.aspx, accessed October 2008.

42. Geoffrey James, "The Return of Sales Training," *Selling Power*, May 2004, pp. 86–91. See also Rebecca Aronauer, "Tracking Your Investment," *Sales & Marketing Management*, October 2006, p. 13; Geoffrey James, "Training: A Wise Choice," *Selling Power*, January–February 2007, pp. 88–90; and James, "Return on Your Sales Training Investment," *Selling Power*, October 2007, p. 102. Also see Ashraf M. Attia, et al., "Global Sales Training: in Search of Antecedent, Mediating, and Consequence Variables," *Industrial Marketing Management*, April 2008, pp. 181+.

43. David Chelan, "Revving Up E-Learning to Drive Sales," *EContent*, March 2006, pp. 28–32. Also see "E-Learning Evolves into Mature Training Tool," *T+D*, April 2006, p. 20; Rebecca Aronauer, "The Classroom vs. E-Learning," *Sales & Marketing Management*, October 2006, p. 21; and Harry Sheff, "Agent Training Beyond the Classroom," *Call Center Magazine*, April 2007, p. 18.

44. See Henry Canady, "How to Increase the Times Reps Spend Selling," *Selling Power*, March 2005, p. 112; George Reinfeld, "8 Tips to Help Control the Hand of Time," *Printing News*, January 9, 2006, p. 10; and David J. Cichelli, "Plugging Sales 'Time Leaks,'" *Sales & Marketing Management*, April 2006, p. 23; Rebecca Aronauer, "Time Well Spent," *Sales & Marketing Management*, January–February 2007, p. 7; and Dave Bradford, "Finding More Time for Selling," *Electrical Wholesaling*," April 2007, pp. 66–67.

45. See Gary H. Anthes, "Portal Powers GE Sales," *Computerworld*, June 2, 2003, pp. 31–32. Also see Betsy Cummings, "Increasing Face Time," *Sales & Marketing Management*, January 2004, p. 12; David J. Cichelli, "Plugging Sales 'Time Leaks,'" *Sales & Marketing Management*, April 2006, p. 23; and Henry Canaday, "How to Boost Sales Productivity and Save Valuable Time," *Agency Sales*, November 2007, p. 20.

46. Based on information from Thomaselli, "Pharma Replacing Reps," *Advertising Age*, January 2005, p. 50; and Matthew Arnold, "Is There a Doctor on the Web?" *Medical Marketing and Media*, 2008, pp. 10–11. Also see Mary M. Long, Thomas Tellefsen, and J. David Lichtenthal, "Internet Integration into the Industrial Selling Process: A Step-By-Step Approach," *Industrial Marketing Management*, July 2007, pp. 676–689.

47. Quotes from Bob Donath, "Delivering Value Starts with Proper Prospecting," *Marketing News*, November 10, 1997, p. 5; and Bill Brooks, "Power-Packed Prospecting Pointers," *Agency Sales*, March 2004, p. 37. Also see Gerhard Gschwandtner, "The Basics of Successful Selling," *Selling Power*, 25th anniversary issue, 2007, pp. 22–26; and Maureen Hrehocik, "Why Prospecting Gets No Respect," *Sales & Marketing Management*, October 2007, p. 7.

48. Quotes in this paragraph from Lain Ehmann, "Prepare to Win," *Selling Power*, April 2008, pp. 27–29.

49. See ESRI Northeast Africa website, www.esrinea.com.

50. Betsy Cummings, "Listening for Deals," *Sales & Marketing Management*, August 2005, p. 8. Also see Michele Marchetti, "Listen to Me!" *Sales and Marketing Management*, April 2007, p. 12.

51. Adapted from Izabella Iizuka, "Not Your Father's Presentation," *Sales & Marketing Management*, March/April 2008, pp. 33–35.

52. See "Savings for All Ages," September 6, 2007, accessed at www.pmalink.org/press_releases/default.asp?p=pr_09062007; and "CMS Reports Annual Coupon Distribution to 286 Billion," accessed at www.couponinfonow.com/Couponing/2007trendsoverview.cfm, May 2008.

53. See "2007 Promotion Products Fact Sheet," at Promotion Products Association International Web site, www.ppai.org, accessed May 2008.

54. Adapted from information found in Betsey Spethmann, "Doritos Experiments with Sampling and Sweeps," *Promo*, June 19, 2007, accessed at http://promomagazine.com/contests/news/doritos_experiments_sampling_sweeps_061907.

55. "Exclusive PQ Media Research: Branded Entertainment Defies Slowing Economy," February 12, 2008, accessed at www.pqmedia.com/about-press-20080212-bemf.html.

56. *Shopper-Centric Trade: The Future of Trade Promotion* (Wilton, CT: Cannondale Associates, October 2007), p. 15.

CHAPTER 13

1. Quotes and other information from Josh Quittner, "The Charmed Life of Amazon's Jeff Bezos," *CNNMoney.com*, April 15, 2008, accessed at www.cnnmoney.com; Joe Nocera, "Putting Buyers First? What a Concept," *New York Times*, January 5, 2008; Jena McGregor, "Bezos: How Frugality Drives Innovation," *BusinessWeek*, April 28, 2008, p.64; and annual reports and other information found at www.amazon.com, accessed October 2008.

2. "Arab Direct Marketing Association Launched," *AME Info*, April 21, 2009, www.ameinfo.com/193380.html.

3. Roy Chitwood, "Making the Most out of Each Outside Sales Call," February 4, 2005, accessed at http://seattle.bizjournals.com/seattle/stories/2005/02/07/smallb3.html; and "The Cost of the Average Sales Call Today Is More Than $400," *Business Wire*, February 28, 2006.

4. Daniel Lyons, "Too Much Information," *Forbes*, December 13, 2004, p. 110; Mike Freeman, "Data Company Helps Wal-Mart, Casinos, Airlines Analyze Data," *Knight Ridder Business Tribune News*, February 24, 2006, p. 1; and Mary Hayes Weier, "HP Data Warehouse Lands in Wal-Mart's Shopping Cart," *InformationWeek*, August 6, 2007, p. 31.

5. Direct Marketing Association, *The Power of Direct Marketing: 2007–2008 Edition*, June 2008.

6. David Ranii, "Compact Discs, DVDs Get More Use as Promotional Tool," *Knight Ridder Tribune Business News*, May 5, 2004, p. 1; "DVD & CD Serious Cardz Increase Response Rate Over 1000% Over Traditional Direct Marketing," *Market Wire*, January 10, 2007, p.1; and Emily Maltby, "A Marketing Tool That Fits in Your Wallet," *FSB*, April 2007, p. 76.

7. Direct Marketing Association, *The Power of Direct Marketing: 2007–2008 Edition*, June 2008.

8. Teinowitz, "'Do Not Call' Does Not Hurt Direct Marketing," p. 3.

9. Steve McLellan, "For a Whole New DRTV Experience, Call Now," *Adweek*, September 5, 2005, p. 10; Jack Neff, "What Procter & Gamble Learned from Veg-O-Matic," p. 1; and "Analysis: Can DRTV Really Build Brands Better than Image Ads?" *Precision Marketing*, February 9, 2007, p. 11.

10. "Interactive: Ad Age Names Finalists," *Advertising Age*, February 27, 1995, pp. 12–14.

11. See http://interactivetouchscreenkiosk.blogspot.com/ and www.kis-kiosk.com/public/archives/000092.html.

12. Stephanie Kang, "Consumers Come Calling, Literally, for the Holidays," *Wall Street Journal*, November 16, 2007, p. B5; Daniel B. Honigman, "On the Verge: Mobile Marketing Will Make Strides," *Marketing News*, January 15, 2008, pp. 18–21; and "Nielsen Says Mobile Ads Growing, Consumers Respond," *Reuters*, March 5, 2008, accessed at www.reuters.com.

13. Alice Z. Cuneo, "Scramble for Content Drives Mobile," *Advertising Age*, October 24, 2005, p. S6; "Where Are Those Mobile Ads?" *International Herald Tribune*, May 4, 2008; and CTIA: The Wireless Association, June 2008, accessed at www.ctia.org.

14. Alice Z. Cuneo, "So Just What Is Mobile Marketing?" *Advertising Age*, March 17, 2008, p. 36.

15. For this and other examples, see Alice Z. Cuneo, "Marketers Get Serious About the "Third Screen," *Advertising Age*, July 11, 2005, p. 6; Louise Story, "Madison Avenue Calling," *New York Times*, January 20, 2007, accessed at www.nytimes.com; and Stephanie Kang, "Retailers Come Calling, Literally, for the holidays," *Wall Street Journal*, November 30, 2007, p. B5.

16. See Davidson, "Ad Campaigns for Your Tiny Cellphone Screen Get Bigger," p. 2; Julie Schlosser, "Get Outta My Phone," *Fortune*, February 10, 2007, p. 20; Emily Burg, "Acceptance of Mobile Ads on the Rise," *MediaPost Publications*, March 16, 2007, accessed at http://publications.mediapost.com; Steve Miller and Mike Beirne, "The iPhone Effect," *Adweek.com*, April 28, 2008; and Spencer E. Ante, "The Call for a Wireless Bill of Rights," *BusinessWeek*, March 31, 2008, pp. 80–81.

17. Evie Nagy, "Podding Along," *Billboard*, May 10, 2008, p. 14.

18. Shahnaz Mahmud, "Survey: Viewer Crave TV Ad Fusion," *Adweek.com*, January 25, 2008.

19. Adapted from Alice Z. Cuneo, "Nike Setting the Pace in Interactive-TV Race" *Advertising Age*, August 13, 2007, p. 3. For other information and examples, see Cliff Edwards, "I Want My iTV," *BusinessWeek*, November 19, 2007, pp. 54–63; and Suzanne Vranica, "Unilever Bets on Interactivity; Company Steps up iTV Ads in a Bid to Engage Viewers," *Wall Street Journal*, May 14, 2008, p. B13.

20. For these and other statistics on Internet usage, see "Nielsen Online reports," www.internetworldstats.com/stats.htm.

21. See "America's Top Ten Retail Businesses," accessed at www.internetretailer.com/top500/list.asp, August 2008.

22. See Tom Sullivan, "A Lot More Than Paper Clips," *Barron's*, April 16, 2007, pp. 23–25; and information from www.officedepot.com, September 2008.

23. See Shop.org, Forrester Research Inc., *The State of Retailing Online 2007*, accessed at www.forrester.com/SORO; and Jen Haberkorn, "Web Sales May Hit $204 Billion," *Washington Times*, April 8, 2008, p. C8.

24. "JupiterResearch Forecasts Online Retail Spending Will Reach $144 Billion in 2010, a CAGR of 12% from 2005," February 6, 2006, accessed at www.jupitermedia.com/corporate/releases/06.02.06-newjupresearch.html; and "Online Sales to Climb Despite Struggling Economy," National Retail Federation, April 8, 2008, accessed at www.nrf.com/modules.php?name=News&op=viewlive&sp_id=499.

25. Information for this example accessed at http://quickenloans.quicken.com, September 2008.

26. Information for this example accessed at www.dell.com/html/us/segments/pub/premier/tutorial/users_guide.html, August 2008.

27. See "eBay Inc.," *Hoover's Company Records*, June 1, 2008, p. 56307; and facts from eBay annual reports and other information accessed at www.ebay.com, September 2008.

28. Beth Snyder Bulik, "Who Blogs?" *Advertising Age*, June 4, 2007, p. 20.

29. Adapted from "Max Colchester, "Nescafé Brews Buzz via Blogs," *Wall Street Journal*, November 23, 2007, p. B3.

30. See David Ward, "GM Blog Keeps Everyone Up to Speed," *PRWeek*, April 3, 2006, p. 7; "Welburn: Calm Down, Camaro Complainers," *Automotive News*, January 14, 2008, p. 42; and Michelle Martin, "GM Keeps Pace with Customers Through Blogs," *Crain's Detroit Business*, May 12, 2008, p. 35.

31. Pete Blackshaw, "Irrational Exuberance? I Hope We're Not Guilty," *Barcode Blog*, August 26, 2005, accessed at www.barcodefactory.com/wordpress/?p=72.

32. Laurie Peterson, "When It Comes to Blogs, It Pays to Listen," *MediaPost Publications*, September 29, 2006, accessed at www.publications.com; and Michael Bush, "Starbucks Gets Web 2.0 Religion, But Can It Convert Nonbelievers?" *Advertising Age*, March 24, 2008, p. 1.

33. Carolyn Kepcher, "Bad Service? Point, Click, Complain," *New York Daily News*, May 12, 2008; and Kermit Pattison, "Does a New Website Hold the Secret to Great Customer Service?" *Fast Company*, April 2008, www.fastcompany.com/articles/2008/04/interview-muller.html.

34. Adapted from Jack Neff, "Media Owners Take Heed: P&G's Staid Old Web Site Has you Licked," *Advertising Age*, December 4, 2007, pp. 1, 38.

35. Jeffrey F. Rayport and Bernard J. Jaworski, *e-Commerce* (New York: McGraw-Hill, 2001), p. 116. Also see Goutam Chakraborty, "What Do Customers Consider Important in B2B Websites?" *Journal of Advertising*, March 2003, p. 50; and "Looks Are Everything," *Marketing Management*, March/April 2006, p. 7.

36. Adapted from Brooks Barnes, "In Overhaul, Disney.com Seeks a Path to More Fun," *New York Times*, June 25, 2008.

37. Internet Advertising Bureau, *IAB Internet Advertising Revenue Report*, May 2008, accessed at www.iab.net/insights_research/iab_news_article/299656.

38. Internet Advertising Bureau, *IAB Internet Advertising Revenue Report*, May 2008, accessed at www.iab.net/insights_research/iab_news_article/299656.

39. Danielle Sacks, "Down the Rabbit Hole," *Fast Company*, November 2006, pp. 86–93.

40. Chaddus Bruce, "Big Biz Biddies Up to Gen Y," *Wired*, December 20, 2006, accessed at www.wired.com; "Masterclass: The Revolution Masterclass on Social Networking Sites," *Revolution*, January 25, 2007, accessed at www.brandrepublic.com.

41. See "U.S. E-Mail Marketing Spending and User Data," *Digital Marketing and Media Fact Pack*, supplement to *Advertising Age*, April 23, 2007, p. 44; Alex Moskalyuk, "E-mail Marketing Spending to Reach $2.1 Bln by 2012," *ZDNet.com*, January 7, 2008, http://blogs.zdnet.com/ITFacts/?p=13581.

42. Jon Swartz, "Despite Filters, Tidal Wave of Spam Bears Down on e-Mailers," *USA Today*, November 23, 2008, p. 6B; "Spam Turns 30 and Never Looked Healthier," *TechWeb*, May 2, 2008; and Symantec, *The State of Spam, A Monthly Report—May 2008*, accessed at www.symantec.com/business/theme.jsp?themeid=state_of_spam.

43. William Hupp, "E-Mail," *Advertising Age*, March 17, 2008, p. 48.

44. "Sweepstakes Groups Settles with States," *New York Times*, June 27, 2001, p. A14; "PCH Reaches $34 Million Sweepstakes Settlement with 26 States," *Direct Marketing*, September 2001, p. 6; and Steve Higgins, "Reader's Digest Will Pay Up in Connecticut Sweepstakes Settlement," *Knight Ridder Tribune Business News*, March 29, 2005, p. 1.

45. See Internet Crime Complaint Center, "Internet Crime Report 2007," accessed at www.ic3.gov/media/annualreport/2007 _IC3Report.pdf.

46. "Jon Swartz, "Despite Filters, Tidal Wave of Spam Bears Down on e-Mailers," *USA Today*, November 23, 2008, p. 6B.

47. See "Consumer Security Fears Continue to Rise in Banking Industry," *Business Wire*, December 14, 2006; and Tom Wright, "Online Card Use Stirs Fears Despite Relatively Low Fraud," *Cards and Payments*, April 2007, p. 16.

48. "Net Threats," *Consumer Reports*, September 2007, p. 28. Excerpt adapted from Ben Elgin, "The Plot to Hijack Your Computer," *BusinessWeek*, July 17, 2006, p. 40. Also see Joseph Menn, "Online Tunes are More Risky than Web Porn," *Los Angeles Times*, June 4, 2007, p. C3.

49. "Net Threats," *Consumer Reports*, September 2007, p. 28.

50. See Damon Darlin, "Don't Call. Don't Write. Let Me Be," *New York Times*, January 20, 2007; Ira Tenowitz and Ken Wheaton, "Do Not Call," *Advertising Age*, March 12, 2007, pp. 1, 44; Louise Story, "FTC to Review Online Ads and Privacy," *New York Times*, November 1, 2007; and Saul Hansell, "Is Google Violating a California Privacy Law?" *New York Times*, May 30, 2008.

51. Information on the DMA Privacy Promise obtained at www .dmaconsumers.org/privacy.html, November 2008.

52. See Tom Sullivan, "A Lot More Than Paper Clips," *Barron's*, April 16, 2007, pp. 23–25; and information from www.officedepot.com, September 2008.

53. See Shop.org, Forrester Research Inc., *The State of Retailing Online 2007*, accessed at www.forrester.com/SORO; and Jen Haberkorn, "Web Sales May Hit $204 Billion," *Washington Times*, April 8, 2008, p. C8.

54. "JupiterResearch Forecasts Online Retail Spending Will Reach $144 Billion in 2010, a CAGR of 12% from 2005," February 6, 2006, accessed at www.jupitermedia.com/corporate/releases/06.02.06-newjupresearch.html; and "Online Sales to Climb Despite Struggling Economy," National Retail Federation, April 8, 2008, accessed at www .nrf.com/modules.php?name=News&op=viewlive&sp_id=499.

55. Information for this example accessed at http://quickenloans .quicken.com, September 2008.

56. See "eBay Inc.," *Hoover's Company Records*, June 1, 2008, p. 56307; and facts from eBay annual reports and other information accessed at www.ebay.com, September 2008.

57. Beth Snyder Bulik, "Who Blogs?" *Advertising Age*, June 4, 2007, p. 20.

58. Adapted from "Max Colchester, "Nescafé Brews Buzz via Blogs," *Wall Street Journal*, November 23, 2007, p. B3.

59. See David Ward, "GM Blog Keeps Everyone Up to Speed," *PRWeek*, April 3, 2006, p. 7; "Welburn: Calm Down, Camaro Complainers," *Automotive News*, January 14, 2008, p. 42; and Michelle Martin, "GM Keeps Pace with Customers Through Blogs," *Crain's Detroit Business*, May 12, 2008, p. 35.

60. Pete Blackshaw, "Irrational Exuberance? I Hope We're Not Guilty," *Barcode Blog*, August 26, 2005, accessed at www.barcodefactory.com/wordpress/?p=72.

61. Laurie Peterson, "When It Comes to Blogs, It Pays to Listen," *MediaPost Publications*, September 29, 2006, accessed at www.publications.com; and Michael Bush, "Starbucks Gets Web 2.0 Religion, But Can It Convert Nonbelievers?" *Advertising Age*, March 24, 2008, p. 1.

62. Carolyn Kepcher, "Bad Service? Point, Click, Complain," *New York Daily News*, May 12, 2008; and Kermit Pattison, "Does a New Website Hold the Secret to Great Customer Service?" *Fast Company*, April 2008, www.fastcompany.com/articles/2008/04/interview-muller.html.

63. Adapted from Jack Neff, "Media Owners Take Heed: P&G's Staid Old Web Site Has you Licked," *Advertising Age*, December 4, 2007, pp. 1, 38.

64. Jeffrey F. Rayport and Bernard J. Jaworski, *e-Commerce* (New York: McGraw-Hill, 2001), p. 116. Also see Goutam Chakraborty, "What Do Customers Consider Important in B2B Websites?" *Journal of Advertising*, March 2003, p. 50; and "Looks Are Everything," *Marketing Management*, March/April 2006, p. 7.

65. Adapted from Brooks Barnes, "In Overhaul, Disney.com Seeks a Path to More Fun," *New York Times*, June 25, 2008.

66. Internet Advertising bureau, *IAB Internet Advertising Revenue Report*, May 2008, accessed at www.iab.net/insights_research/iab_news_article/299656.

67. Internet Advertising Bureau, *IAB Internet Advertising Revenue Report*, May 2008, accessed at www.iab.net/insights_research/iab_news_article/299656.

68. Danielle Sacks, "Down the Rabbit Hole," *Fast Company*, November 2006, pp. 86–93.

69. Chaddus Bruce, "Big Biz Buddies Up With Gen Y," *Wired*, December 20, 2006, accessed at www.wired.com; "Masterclass: The Revolution Masterclass on Social Networking Sites," *Revolution*, January 25, 2007, accessed at www.brandrepublic.com.

70. See "U.S. E-Mail Marketing Spending and User Data," *Digital Marketing and Media Fact Pack*, supplement to *Advertising Age*, April 23, 2007, p. 44; Alex Moskalyuk, "E-mail Marketing Spending to Reach $2.1 Bln by 2012," *ZDNet.com*, January 7, 2008, http://blogs.zdnet.com/ITFacts/?p=13581.

71. Jon Swartz, "Despite Filters, Tidal Wave of Spam Bears Down on e-Mailers," *USA Today*, November 23, 2008, p. 6B; "Spam Turns 30 and Never Looked Healthier," *TechWeb*, May 2, 2008; and Symantec, *The State of Spam, A Monthly Report—May 2008*, accessed at www .symantec.com/business/theme.jsp?themeid=state_of_spam.

72. William Hupp, "E-Mail," *Advertising Age*, March 17, 2008, p. 48.

73. "Sweepstakes Groups Settles with States," *New York Times*, June 27, 2001, p. A14; "PCH Reaches $34 Million Sweepstakes Settlement with 26 States," *Direct Marketing*, September 2001, p. 6; and Steve Higgins, "Reader's Digest Will Pay Up in Connecticut Sweepstakes Settlement," *Knight Ridder Tribune Business News*, March 29, 2005, p. 1.

74. See Internet Crime Complaint Center, "Internet Crime Report 2007," accessed at www.ic3.gov/media/annualreport/2007 _IC3Report.pdf.

75. "Jon Swartz, "Despite Filters, Tidal Wave of Spam Bears Down on e-Mailers," *USA Today*, November 23, 2008, p. 6B.

76. See "Consumer Security Fears Continue to Rise in Banking Industry," *Business Wire*, December 14, 2006; and Tom Wright, "Online Card Use Stirs Fears Despite Relatively Low Fraud," *Cards and Payments*, April 2007, p. 16.

77. "Net Threats," *Consumer Reports*, September 2007, p. 28. Excerpt adapted from Ben Elgin, "The Plot to Hijack Your Computer," *BusinessWeek*, July 17, 2006, p. 40. Also see Joseph Menn, "Online Tunes are More Risky than Web Porn," *Los Angeles Times*, June 4, 2007, p. C3.

78. "Net Threats," *Consumer Reports*, September 2007, p. 28.

CHAPTER 14

1. "Distributors," Zaytoun company website, www.zaytoun.org/distribution/distributors.

2. "Suppliers," Zaytoun company website, www.zaytoun.org/products/suppliers.

3. See "No Time to Rest for Goodyear," *Tire Business*, February 13, 2006, p. 8; Kevin Kelleher, "Giving Dealers a Raw Deal," *Business 2.0*, December 2004, pp. 82–84; Jim MacKinnon, "Goodyear Tire & Rubber Company," *Knight Ridder Tribune Business News*, April 8, 2007, p. 1; and Jim MacKinnon, "Goodyear Boasts of Bright Future," *McClatchy-Tribune Business News*, April 9, 2008.

4. Abu Dhabi National Oil Company website, www.adnoc.ae/default.aspx.

5. "Middle East Franchise Market to Grow by 25%,"*AME Info*, May 14, 2008, www.ameinfo.com/156782.html.

6. "Middle East Franchise Market to Grow by 25%," *AME Info*, May 14, 2008, www.ameinfo.com/156782.html.

7. Information accessed at www.mind-advertising.com/ch/nestea_ch.htm, September 2007.

8. "Retail Network," Aftron Electronics website, www.aftron.com/RetailNetwork/tabid/73/Default.aspx.

9. See Paolo Del Nibletto, "Dell Stuck in the Middle," *Computer Dealer News*, March 21, 2008, p. 12.

10. Quotes and information from Normandy Madden, "Two Chinas," *Advertising Age*, August 16, 2004, pp. 1, 22; Russell Flannery, "China: The Slow Boat," *Forbes*, April 12, 2004, p. 76; Jeff Berman, "U.S. Providers Say Logistics in China on the Right Track," *Logistics Management*, March 2007, p. 22; and Jamie Bolton, "China: The Infrastructure Imperative," *Logistics Management*, July 2007, p. 63.

11. Nanette Byrnes, "Avon Calls. China Opens the Door," *BusinessWeek Online*, February 28, 2006, p. 19; Mei Fong, "Avon's Calling, but China Opens Door Only a Crack," *Wall Street Journal*, February 26, 2007, p. B1; "Direct-Selling Giants to Dig Chinese Market," *SinoCast China Business Daily News*, August 3, 2007, p. 1; and "Cosmetic Changes in China Market," www.Chinadaily.com.cn, October 11, 2007.

12. " CouncilRejects Sole Dealership for Expats; Critics Slam Stand," *The Peninsula*, May 11, 2011, www.thepeninsulaqatar.com.

13. Ari Natter, "Freight Costs Rising," *Traffic World*, April 14, 2008; Neil Shister, "Redesigned Supply Chain Positions Ford for Global Competition," *World Trade*, May 2005, pp. 20–26; and supply chain facts from www.cscmp.org/Website/AboutCSCMP/Media/FastFacts.asp; July 2008.

14. Gail Braccidiferro, "One Town's Rejection Is Another's 'Let's Do Business,'" *New York Times*, June 15, 2003, p. 2; Dan Scheraga, "Wal-Smart," *Chain Store Age*, January 2006 supplement, pp. 16A–21A; and facts from www.walmart.com, October 2008.

15. See "A Worldwide Look at RFID," *Supply Chain Management Review*, April 2007, pp. 48–55; Owen Davis, "Time to Roll with RFID," *Supply & Demand Chain Executive*, February–March 2007, p. 56; and "Wal-Mart Says Use RFID Tags or Pay Up," *Logistics Today*, March 2008, p. 4.

16. Transportation percentages and other figures in this section are from Bureau of Transportation Statistics, "Freight in America," January 2006, accessed at www.bts.gov/publications; and Bureau of Transportation Statistics, "Pocket Guide to Transportation 2008," February 2008, accessed at www.bts.gov/publications/pocket_guide_to_transportation/2008.

17. See Laurie Sullivan, "Hey, Wal-Mart, A New Case of Pampers Is on the Way," *InformationWeek*, January 23, 2006, p. 28; Connie Robbins Gentry, "No More Holes at Krispy Kreme," *Chain Store Age*, July 2006, pp. 64–65; "Collaborative Supply Chain Practices and Evolving Technological Approaches," *Supply Chain Management*, May 2007, pp. 210–220; and Yuliang Yao and Martin Dresner, "The Inventory Value of Information Sharing, Continuous Replenishment, and Vendor-Managed Inventory," *Transportation Research*, May 2008, p. 361+.

18. See "The 2007 Supply & Demand Chain Executive 100," *Supply & Demand Chain Executive*, May 2007; accessed at www.sdcexec.com/print/Supply-and-Demand-Chain-Executive/2007-Supply-and-Demand-Chain-Executive-100/1$9672; and David Blanchard, "Sterling Commerce Shifts from EDI to the Supply Chain," *Supply Chain and Logistics*, December 2007, p. 50.

19. "Whirlpool: Outsourcing Its National Service Parts Operation Provides Immediate Benefits," accessed at www.ryder.com/pdf/MCC633_Whirlpool_single.pdf, October 2008.

20. Kristy Barnes, "UAE's First Pharma 3PL Provider Springs Up," *Outsourcing Pharma*, January 28, 2008, www.outsourcing-pharma.com/Commercial-Services/UAE-s-first-pharma-3PL-provider-springs-up.

21. John Paul Quinn, "3PLs Hit Their Stride," *Logistics Management/Supply Chain Management Review*, July 2006, pp. 3T–8T; and "U.S. and Global Third-Party Logistics (3PL) Market Analysis Is Released," *PR Newswire*, April 12, 2007.

22. Quotes from "Ogilvy Gets Activated," *MediaPost Publications*, January 8, 2007, accessed at publications.mediapost.com/index.cfm?fuseaction=Articles.showArticle&art_aid=53477; and "OgilvyAction Takes Regional Marketers to the Last Mile," January 23, 2008, accessed at www.entrepreneur.com/tradejournals/article/173710015.html. Retail sales statistics from "Annual Revision of Monthly Retail and Food Services: Sales and Inventories—January 1992–2007," U.S. Census Bureau, March 2007, p. 3; and www.census.gov/mrts/www/mrts.html, accessed May 2008.

23. For more on shopper marketing, see Grocery Manufacturers Association and Deloitte Consulting, *Shopper Marketing: Capturing a Shopper's Mind, Heart, and Wallet*, 2007; Jack Neff, "What's in Store: The Rise of Shopper Marketing," *Advertising Age*, October 1, 2007, pp. 1, 42; and Bob Holston, "Avoid Shopper Marketing Pitfalls," *Advertising Age*, March 31, 2008, pp. 20–21.

24. "Convenience Store Industry Sales Top $569 Billion, NACS Reports," April 11, 2007, accessed online at www.nacsonline.com.

25. Elizabeth Woyke, "Buffett, the Wal-Mart Shopper," *BusinessWeek*, May 14, 2007, pp. 66–67.

26. Company information from www.subway.co.uk/business/franchise/facts_and_history.aspx and www.aboutmcdonalds.com/mcd/our_company.html.

27. "About Landmark Group—Retail," Landmark Group website, www.cplmg.com/our-brands/landmark-retail/centrepoint/24/15/1/index.html.

28. "Givori Launches Partnership with Harvey Nichols in Riyadh," *AME Info*, July 6, 2010, www.ameinfo.com/237150.html.

29. For definitions of these and other types of shopping centers, see "Dictionary of Marketing Terms," American Marketing Association, accessed at www.marketingpower.com/mgdictionary.php, September 2007.

30. "MADI International, P&G Finalize Deal for Distribution of Wella Professionals Products," Yahoo! Maktoob, February 24, 2010, http://en.news.maktoob.com.

31. "Cisco StrengthensPresenceThroughThreeNew Distribution Partners," *AME Info*, October 6, 2004, www.ameinfo.com/46877.html.

32. "Cops Raid Karama," *Daiji World*, May 15, 2007, www.daijiworld.com/news/.

CHAPTER 15

1. Information from Bahrain Polytechnic website, www.polytechnic.bh.

2. Logitech annual report, accessed at http://ir.logitech.com/annuals.cfm, June 2008.

3. For more on Encyclopaedia Britannica competitive positioning, see Paula Berinstein, "Wikipedia and Britannica: The Kid's All Right (And So's the Old Man)," *Searcher*, March 2006, pp. 16–27; "Encyclopedia Britannica, Inc.," *Hoover's Company Records*, May 1, 2008, p. 40871; and http://corporate.britannica.com, accessed October 2008.

4. Adapted from Taylor Clark, "Who's Afraid of the Big Bad Starbucks?" *The Week*, January 18, 2008, p. 46.

5. See Michael Porter, *Competitive Advantage: Creating and Sustaining Superior Performance* (New York: Free Press, 1998), chapter 6.

6. Based on Devin Leonard, "The Player," *Fortune*, March 20, 2006, p. 54; "The Slow Death of Digital Rights," *The Economist*, October 13, 2007; and information from www.apple.com, accessed May 2008.

7. Adapted from information found in "Blue Ocean Strategy: Making the Competition Irrelevant," accessed at www.blueoceanstrategy.com/resources/press.php, June 2008; and W. Chan Kim and Renée Mauborgne, *Blue Ocean Strategy* (Boston: Harvard Business School Press, 2005).

8. Michael E. Porter, *Competitive Strategy: Techniques for Analyzing Industries and Competitors* (New York: Free Press, 1980), chapter 2; and Porter, "What Is Strategy?" *Harvard Business Review*, November–December 1996, pp. 61–78. Also see Richard Allen and others, "A Comparison of Competitive Strategies in Japan and the United States," *S.A.M. Advanced Management Journal*, Winter 2006, pp. 24–36; and Stefan Stern, "May the Force Be with You and Your Plans for 2008," *Financial Times*, January 8, 2008, p. 14.

9. See Michael Treacy and Fred Wiersema, "Customer Intimacy and Other Value Disciplines," *Harvard Business Review*, January–February 1993, pp. 84–93; Michael Treacy and Mike Wiersema, *The Discipline of Market Leaders: Choose Your Customers, Narrow Your Focus, Dominate Your Market* (New York: Perseus Press, 1997); Fred Wiersema, *Customer Intimacy: Pick Your Partners, Shape Your Culture, Win Together* (Santa Monica, CA: Knowledge Exchange, 1998); Wiersema, *Double-Digit Growth: How Great Companies Achieve It—No Matter What* (New York: Portfolio, 2003); and Edward M. Hindin, "Learning from Leaders: Questions to Ask and Rules to Follow," *Health Care Strategic Management*, August 2006, pp. 11–13.

10. For more discussion, see Philip Kotler and Kevin Lane Keller, *Marketing Management*, 13th ed. (Upper Saddle River, NJ: Prentice Hall, 2009), chapter 11.

11. See "Consumers Can Get More Camera for Less Money," *USA Today*, January 30, 2008, p. 8B; and Betsy McKay, "Soft-Drink Sales Volume Slipped Faster Last Year," *Wall Street Journal*, March 13, 2008, p. B6.

12. Hyper One company website, www.hyperone.com.eg, accessed 2011.

13. Adapted from David J. Bryce and Jeffrey H. Dyer, "Strategies to Crack Well-Guarded Markets," *Harvard Business Review*, May 2007, pp. 84–91.

14. "Corporate Events," Arabian Adventures company website, www.arabian-adventures.com/CorporateEvents/CorporateEvents.Asp?nav=3&sub=0.

CHAPTER 16

1. Quotes and other information from: Janet Adamy, "Steady Diet: As Burgers Boom in Russia, McDonald's Touts Discipline," *Wall Street Journal*, October 16, 2007, p. A1; Fern Glazer, "NPD: QSR Chains Expanding Globally Must Also Act Locally," *Nation's Restaurant News*, October 22, 2007, p. 18; and information from www.mcdonalds.com/corp, accessed September 2008.

2. Data from Michael V. Copeland, "The Mighty Micro-Multinational," *Business 2.0*, July 28, 2006, accessed at http://cnnmoney.com; "Fortune 500," *Fortune*, May 5, 2008, pp. F1–F2; and "List of Countries by GDP," *Wikipedia*, accessed at http://en.wikipedia.org/wiki/List_of_countries_by_GDP_%28nominal%29, July 2008.

3. "Trade Growth to Ease in 2011 But Despite 2010 Record Surge, Crisis Hangover Persists," World Trade Organization press release, April 7, 2011, www.wto.org/english/news_e/pres11_e/pr628_e.htm; "Trade to Expand by 9.5% in 2010 After a Dismal 2009, WTO Reports," World Trade Organization press release, March 26, 2010, www.wto.org/english/news_e/pres10_e/pr598_e.htm; "Global GDP to Rise 2.9–3.3% in 2010–2011—World Bank," *RiaNovosti*, June 6, 2010, en.rian.ru/news/20100610/159368868.html; *Global Economic Prospects, 2007*, World Bank, June 3, 2005, accessed at www.worldbank.org; CIA, *The World Factbook*, accessed at http://www.cia.gov/library/publications/the-world-factbook/, June 2008.

4. Information from www.michelin.com/corporate, www.jnj.com, and www.caterpillar.com, October 2008.

5. Steve Hamm, "Borders Are So 20th Century," *BusinessWeek*, September 22, 2003, pp. 68–73; and "Otis Elevator Company," *Hoover's Company Records*, June 15, 2008, p. 56332.

6. Adapted from information in Brian Bremner and Dexter Robests, "How Beijing Is Keeping Banks at Bay," *BusinessWeek*, October 2, 2006, p. 42. Also see GeJianguo, WTO and Revision of China's Foreign Banking Regulations," *Banking Law Journal*, June 2007, p. 536.

7. "What Is the WTO?" accessed at www.wto.org/english/thewto_e/whatis_e/whatis_e.htm, September 2008.

8. See *WTO Annual Report 2005*, accessed at www.wto.org, September 2007; and World Trade Organization, "10 Benefits of the WTO Trading System," accessed at www.wto.org/english/thewto_e/whatis_e/whatis_e.htm, September 2008.

9. Peter Coy, "Why Free-Trade Talks Are in Free Fall," *BusinessWeek*, May 22, 2006, p. 44; and "EU Officials Still Hopes for Doha Meeting in May," *Journal of Commerce*, April 25, 2008.

10. "Gulf Cooperation Council," www.globalsecurity.org/military/world/gulf/gcc.htm; "GCC Population Gains Over 1.7 Million in Two Years," *Emirates 24/7*, March 26, 2009, accessed at www.zawya.com; Andy Sambridge, "GCC Population Seen Growing to 53m by 2020," *Arabian Business*, November 16, 2009, www.arabianbusiness.com.

11. Paul Holdsworth, "Nominal GDP in the GCC to Increase by $133 Billion This Year," Gulf Jobs Market News, December 5, 2010, http://news.gulfjobsmarket.com.

12. "The EU at a Glance," accessed online at http://europa.eu/abc/index-en.htm, September 2008.

13. "Economy of the European Union," www.wikipedia.org. See David J. Bailey, "Misperceiving Matters: Elite Ideas and the Failure of the European Constitution," *Comparative European Politics*, April 2008, pp. 33+; and CIA, *The World Factbook*, accessed at http://www.cia.gov, June 2008.

14. Statistics and other information from CIA, *The World Factbook*, accessed at http://www.cia.gov, June 2008; and "NAFTA Analysis 2007" and "NAFTA—A Success for Trade," Office of the United States Trade Representative, October 2007, accessed at www.ustr.gov/Trade_Agreements/Regional/NAFTA/Section_Index.html.

15. See Angela Greiling Keane, "Counting on CAFTA," *Traffic World*, August 8, 2005, p. 1; "Integrating the Americas: FTAA and Beyond," *Journal of Common Market Studies*," June 2005, p. 430; Alan M. Field, "Spinning Its Wheels," *Journal of Commerce*, December 3, 2007; CIA, *The World Factbook*, accessed at http://www.cia.gov, June 2008; "Foreign Trade Statistics," accessed at www.census.gov, June 2008.

16. "UNASUR pushes for consolidation, expansion in Latin America," *UPI.com*, March 11 2011, www.upi.com/Top_News/Special/2011/03/11/UNASUR-pushes-for-consolidation-expansion-

in-Latin-America/UPI-33621299877191/#ixzz1sʏwbᴏᴅ1v; and "Union of South American Nations," *Wikipedia*, accessed at http://en.wikipedia.org/wiki/South_American_Community_of_Nations, July 2008.

17. Adapted from information found in Clay Chandler, "China Deluxe," *Fortune*, July 26, 2004, pp. 148–156; "Brand Strategy in China: Luxury Looks East," *Brand Strategy*, June 12, 2007, p. 56; and "More Academic Focus on Luxury Product Craze," *Chinadaily.com .cn*, January 22, 2008.

18. "Egyptian Stock Market Reopens," *CNC World*, March 24, 2010, www.cncworld.tv/news/v_show/13508_Egyptian_stock_market _reopens_.shtml; also see "Venezuelan Financial Analyst Says Inflation Could Spark Political Instability," *BBC Worldwide Monitoring*, January 24, 2008; and "Venezuela," www.buyusa.gov, accessed May 2008.

19. Ricky Griffin and Michael Pustay, *International Business*, 5th ed. (Upper Saddle River, NJ: Prentice Hall, 2008), pp. 522–523.

20. "GCC Perfume Market 'Worth $3 billion,'" *Trade Arabia*, March 15, 2010, http://www.tradearabia.com/news/RET_176424.html.

21. For other examples, see Emma Hall, "Do You Know Your Rites? BBDO Does," *Advertising Age*, May 21, 2007, p. 22.

22. For other examples and discussion, see www.executiveplanet.com, December 2008; *Dun & Bradstreet's Guide to Doing Business Around the World* (Upper Saddle River, NJ: Prentice Hall, 2000); Richard Pooley, "When Cultures Collide," *Management Services*, Spring 2005, pp. 28–31; Terri Morrison and Wayne A. Conaway, *Kiss, Bow, or Shake Hands* (Avon, MA: Adams Media, 2006); and Helen Deresky, *International Management*, 6th ed. (Upper Saddle River, NJ: Prentice Hall, 2008).

23. See Elizabeth Esfahani, "Thinking Locally, Succeeding Globally," *Business 2.0*, December 2005, pp. 96–98, Evan Ramstas, "LG Electronics' Net Surges 91 Percent as Cell Phone Margins Improve," *Wall Street Journal*, January 25, 2006, p. B2; and www.lge.com, October 2008.

24. Adapted from Mark Rice-Oxley, "In 2,000 Years, Will the World Remember Disney or Plato?" *Christian Science Monitor*, January 15, 2004, p. 16.

25. Thomas L. Friedman, *The Lexus and the Olive Tree: Understanding Globalization* (New York: Anchor Books, 2000).

26. Elizabeth Rosenthal, "Beijing Journal; Buicks, Starbucks and Fried Chicken. Still China?" *Wall Street Journal*, February 22, 2002, www.nytimes.com.

27. "The 100 Most Powerful Brands 2008," www.millwardbrown.com/Sites/optimor/Content/KnowledgeCenter/BrandzRanking.aspx, accessed June 2008.

28. Eric Ellis, "Iran's Cola War," *Fortune*, March 5, 2007, pp. 35–38. Also see Robert Berner and David Kiley, "Global Brands," *BusinessWeek*, August 1, 2005, pp. 86–94.

29. Portions adapted from information found in Mark Rice-Oxley, "In 2,000 Years, Will the World Remember Disney or Plato?" *Christian Science Monitor*, January 15, 2004, p. 16. See also, Liz Robbins, "The NBA and China Hope They've Found the Next Yao," *New York Times*, June 25, 2007, accessed at www.nytimes.com; and Fara Warner, "Hidden Dragons," *Brandweek*, July 2, 2007, p. 18.

30. See Paulo Prada and Bruce Orwall, "A Certain 'Je Ne Sais Quoi' at Disney's New Park—Movie-Themed Site Near Paris Is Multilingual, Serves Wine—and Better Sausage Variety," *Wall Street Journal*, March 12, 2002, p. B1; and "Euro Disney S. C. A.," *Hoover's Company Records*, May 15, 2008, p. 42391. Hong Kong Disneyland faced similar problems. See Merissa Marr and Geoffrey A. Fowler, "Chinese Lessons for Disney," *Wall Street Journal*, June 12, 2006, p. B1; and Benjamin Scent, "Double-Digit Percentage Gain in Disneyland Attendance," *The Standard*, May 8, 2008.

31. Lisa LaMotta, "McDonald's Golden in International Markets," *Forbes*, February 8, 2008, accessed at www.forbes.com.

32. See Noreen O'Leary, "Bright Lights, Big Challenge," *Adweek*, January 15, 2007, pp. 22–28; and Dexter Roberts, "Scrambling to Bring Crest to the Masses," *BusinessWeek*, June 25, 2007, p. 72.

33. Habib Toumi, "Kuwait to Abolish Sponsorship System," *Gulf News*, October 7, 2009, http://gulfnews.com; "Abolishing Sponsorship System," *The Peninsula*, May 3, 2010, www .thepeninsulaqatar.com.

34. Bruce Einhorn and NandiniLakshman, "PC Makers Are Racing to India," *BusinessWeek*, October 1, 2007, p. 48.

35. Quotes from PankajGhemawat, "Regional Strategies for Global Leadership," *Harvard Business Review*, December 2005, pp. 97–108; Ben Laurance, "Unilever Learns to Join the Dots," *Sunday Times*, March 18, 2007, p. B1; Laurel Wentz, "Far-flung units connected," *Advertising Age*, April 7 2003, http://adage.com/article/news/flung-units-connected/49857. Also see Ghemawat, "Managing Differences," *Harvard Business Review*, March 2007, pp. 59–68.

36. Warren J. Keegan, *Global Marketing Management*, 7th ed. (Upper Saddle River, NJ: Prentice Hall, 2002), pp. 346–351. Also see Phillip Kotler and Kevin Lane Keller, *Marketing Management*, 13th ed. (Upper Saddle River, NJ: 2009), pp. 596–615.

37. Adapted from Jack Ewing, "First Mover in Mobile: How It's Selling Cell Phones to the Developing World," *BusinessWeek*, May 14, 2007, p. 60.

38. See Douglas McGray, "Translating Sony into English," *Fast Company*, January 2003, p. 38; James Coates, "Chicago Tribune Binary Beat Column," *Chicago Tribune*, January 9, 2005, p. 1; and http://vaio-online.sony.com/prod_info/vgn-u8g/index.html, accessed June 2008.

39. Kate MacArthur, "Coca-Cola Light Employs Local Edge," *Advertising Age*, August 21, 2000, pp. 18–19; "Case Studies: Coke Light Hottest Guy," Advantage Marketing, msn India, accessed at http://.advantage.msn.co.in, March 15, 2004; and www.youtube .com/watch?v=Tu5dku6YkHA, accessed June 2008.

40. See Alicia Clegg, "One Ad One World?" *Marketing Week*, June 20, 2002, pp. 51–52; Ira Teinowitz, "International Advertising Code Revised," *Advertising Age*, January 23, 2006, p. 3; George E. Belch and Michael A. Belch, *Advertising and Promotion: An Integrated Marketing Communications Perspective*, 7th ed. (New York: McGraw Hill, 2007), chapter 20; and Shintero Okazaki and Charles R. Taylor, "What Is SMS Advertising and Why Do Multinationals Adopt it?" *Journal of Business Research*, January 2008, pp. 4–12.

41. Bill Addison, "Nail Dumping Tariffs Approved," *Home Channel News*, February 11, 2008, pp. 4–5.

42. Adapted from Jack Ewing, "First Mover in Mobile: How It's Selling Cell Phones to the Developing World," *BusinessWeek*, May 14, 2007, p. 60.

43. See Leslie Chang, Chad Terhune, and Betsy McKay, "A Global Journal Report; Rural Thing—Coke's Big Gamble in Asia," *Wall Street Journal*, August 11, 2004, p. A1; and "Coca-Cola Rolls Out New Distribution Model with ZAP," www.zapworld.com/zap-coca-cola-truck, January 23, 2008.

CHAPTER 17

1. "CSR 'is Not Charity,'" *AME Info*, May 29, 2008, www.ameinfo .com/158575.html.

2. "Taqa CRS—AWork in Progress," *AME Info*, February 11, 2008, www.ameinfo.com/146441.html; additional information from CSR Middle East, www.csrmiddleeast.org; CSR Summit, www

.thecsrsummit.com; Business and Human Rights Resource Centre, www.business-humanrights.org; World Economic Forum, www.weforum.org; Alshaya Group, www.alshaya.com; His Highness Sheikh Mohammed Bin Rashid Al Maktoum, www.sheikhmohammed.co.ae; Coca-Cola, www.coca-cola.com; Aramex, www.aramex.com; and TAQA, www.taqa.ae.

3. For lots of information on SUV safety, see www.citizen.org/autosafety/suvsafety, accessed December 2008.

4. For lots of information on SUV safety and environmental performance, see www.citizen.org/autosafety/suvsafety, accessed July 2008.

5. The figure and the discussion in this section are adapted from Philip Kotler, Gary Armstrong, Veronica Wong, and John Saunders, *Principles of Marketing: European Edition*, 5th ed. (London: Pearson Publishing, 2009), chapter 2.

6. McDonald's financial information and other facts from www.mcdonalds.com/corp/invest.html and www.mcdonalds.com/corp/about/factsheets.html, accessed September 2008.

7. Vodafone Egypt press releases, www.vodafone.com/content/index/press/local_press_releases/egypt.html.

8. Information in press releases from Aramex, Vodafone Egypt, and Mobinil.

9. Consumer Protection Agency, www.cpa.gov.eg/english/index.htm.

10. Theodore Levitt, "The Morality (?)of Advertising," *Harvard Business Review*, July–August 1970, pp. 84–92. For counterpoints, see Heckman, "Don't Shoot the Messenger," *Marketing News*, May 24, 1999, pp. 1, 9.

11. "Elizabeth Warren on the Credit Card Industry," NRP's *Fresh Air*, March 27, 2007, accessed at www.npr.org/templates/story/story.php?storyId=9156929; and Jennifer Levitz, "Hi, My Name Is Fred, And I'm Addicted to Credit Cards," *Wall Street Journal*, June 10, 2008, p. A1.

12. See Rand Health, "Obesity and Disability: The Shape of Things to Come," 2007, accessed at www.rand.org/pubs/research_briefs/2007/RAND_RB9043-1.pdf.

13. Based on information from www.hardees.com/menu, accessed September 2008.

14. Cliff Edwards, "Where Have All the Edsels Gone?" *Greensboro News Record*, May 24, 1999, p. B6. Tim Cooper, "Inadequate Life? Evidence of Consumer Attitudes to Product Obsolescence," *Journal of Consumer Policy*, December 2004, pp. 421–448; David Hunter, "Planned Obsolescence Well Entrenched in Society," *Knoxville News-Sentinel*, August 15, 2005, p. B5; AtsuoUtaka, "Planned Obsolescence and Social Welfare," *Journal of Business*, January 2006, pp. 137–147; and Jessica Harbert and Caleb Pari Heeringga, "Camp Out for Days to Be First to Buy Apple iPhones," *Knight Ridder Tribune Business News*, June 30, 2007, p. 1.

15. Adapted from David Suzuki, "We All Pay for Technology," *Niagara Falls Review*, March 15, 2007, p. A4.

16. "What is Brand Power?" Brand Power website, www.brandpower.com/uae/what_is_brand_power.asp.

17. Oliver James, "It's More ThanEnough to Make You Sick," *Marketing*, January 23, 2008.

18. See Michael Kanellos, "A Nationwide Map of Traffic Jams," *CNET News.com*, September 11, 2007, accessed at http://news.cnet.com/8301-10784_3-9776535-7.html.

19. See www.tfl.gov.uk/roadusers/congestioncharging/6710.aspx, accessed July 2008.

20. See John D. McKinnon, "Politics & Economics: Bush Plays Traffic Cop in Budget Request," *Wall Street Journal*, February 5, 2007, p. A6; "A Rush-Hour Tax on Urban Drivers," *Christian Science Monitor*,

February 7, 2007; and Rich Saskal, "Washington: First HOT Lane Opens Up," *Bond Buyer*, May 9, 2008, p. 9.

21. See Allison Linn, "Ads Inundate Public Places," *MSNBC.com*, January 22, 2007; and Bob Garfield, "The Chaos Scenario 2.0: The Post-Advertising Age," *Advertising Age*, March 26, 2007, pp. 1, 12–13.

22. Josh Martin, "Arab Environmentalism Creates New Market," *The Middle East*, June 1999.

23. Information from Masdar website and press releases, www.masdar.ae.

24. For these and other examples, see Mark Borden et al., "50 Ways to Green Your Business," *Fast Company*, November 2007, pp. 90–99; and "UPS Places Largest Order Ever for Hybrid Electric Trucks," UPS press release, May 13, 2008, accessed at www.pressroom.ups.com.

25. Information from "Because We Can't Remanufacture the Earth…," March 2005, accessed at www.xerox.com/downloads/usa/en/e/ehs_remanufacture_2005.pdf; "Environmental Solutions That Work," April 2007, accessed at www.xerox.com/downloads/usa/en/e/Environmental_Overview.pdf; and "Nurturing a Greener World Through Sustainable Innovation and Development," *2007 Report on Global Citizenship*, accessed at www.xerox.com/Static_HTML/citizenshipreport/2007/nurturing-page9-2.html.

26. Based on information from Marc Gunther, "Coca-Cola's Green Crusader," *Fortune*, April 28, 2008, p. 150.

27. Adapted from "The Top 3 in 2005," *Global 100*, accessed at www.global100.org, July 2005; and "Alcoa Named One of the Top Three Most Sustainable Corporations in the World," *Business Wire*, January 28, 2005, www.businesswire.com. See also "Alcoa Again Named One of the World's Most Sustainable Companies at Davos," January 1, 2008, accessed at www.aloca.com; and information from www.global100.org, August 2008. For further information on Alcoa's sustainability program, see Alcoa's Sustainability Report, found at www.alcoa.com.

28. "2011 Environmental Surcharge Announcement," GCC website, October 12, 2010, http://gccusa.com; "EMAS: What's New?" accessed at http://europa.eu.int/comm/environment/emas, August 2008; "Special Report: Free Trade on Trial—Ten Years of NAFTA," *The Economist*, January 3, 2004, p. 13; Daniel J. Tschopp, "Corporate Social Responsibility: A Comparison Between the United States and Europe," *Corporate Social-Responsibility and Environmental Management*, March 2005, pp. 55–59; "Three Countries Working Together to Protect our Shared Environment," Commission for Environmental Cooperation, accessed at www.cec.org/who_we_are/index.cfm?varlan=english, August 2007.

29. Chuck Salter, "Fast 50 the World's Most Innovative Companies," *Fast Company*, March 2008, pp. 73+.

30. See Todd Wasserman, "Positioning: Getting Comfy In Their Skin," *Brandweek*, December 19, 2005; Laurel Wentz, "'Evolution' Win Marks Dawn of New Cannes Era," *Advertising Age*, June 25, 2007, p. 1; Theresa Howard, "Ad Campaign Tells Women to Celebrate How They Are," *USA Today*, August 7, 2005, accessed at www.usatoday.com; "Beyond Stereotypes: Rebuilding the Foundation of Beauty Beliefs," February 2006, accessed at www.campaignforrealbeauty.com; "Cause: Conscience Marketing. You Stand for Something. Shouldn't Your Brand?" *Strategy*, June 2007, p. 22; Maeve Hosea, "Case Study—Dove: Beneath the Skin," *Brand Strategy*, May 8, 2008, p. 20; and information found at www.campaignforrealbeauty.com, September 2008.

31. Adapted from Chip Giller and David Roberts, "Resources: The Revolution Begins," *Fast Company*, March 2006, pp. 73–78. Also see Joseph Ogando, "Green Engineering," *Design News*, January 9,

2006, p. 65; and information accessed online at www.haworth.com, October 2008.

32. Joseph Webber, "3M's Big Cleanup," *BusinessWeek*, June 5, 2000, pp. 96–98. Also see "3M to Phase Out Perfluorooctanylsulfonate (PFOS)," United States Environmental Protection Agency press release, May 16, 2000; and "What You Should Know About 3M's "Next Generation" Scotchgard Protector Products," accessed at http://solutions.3m.com/wps/portal/3M/en_US/Scotchgard/Home/Resources/Environmental, August 2008.

33. "Corruption Perception Index 2010 Results," www.transparency .org/policy_research/surveys_indices/cpi/2010/results. See *Global Corruption Report 2008*, Transparency International, accessed at www.transparency.org/publications/gcr/download _gcr#download.

34. John F. McGee and P. TanganathNayak, "Leaders' Perspectives on Business Ethics," *Prizm*, first quarter, 1994, pp. 71–72. Also see Adrian Henriques, "Good Decision—Bad Business?" *International Journal of Management & Decision Making*, 2005, p. 273; and Marylyn Carrigan, SvetlaMarinova, and Isabelle Szmigin, "Ethics and International Marketing: Research Background and Challenges," *International Marketing Review*, 2005, pp. 481–494.

35. See Samuel A. DiPiazza, "Ethics in Action," *Executive Excellence*, January 2002, pp. 15–16; Samuel A. DiPiazza, Jr., "It's All Down to Personal Values," accessed online at www.pwcglobal.com, August 2003; and "Code of Conduct: The Way We Do Business," accessed at www.pwc.com/ethics, December 2008. [PricewaterhouseCoopers (www.pwc.com) provides industry-focused assurance, tax, and advisory services to build public trust and enhance value for its clients and their stakeholders. More than 130,000 people in 148 countries across its network share their thinking, experience, and solutions to develop fresh perspectives and practical advice. "PricewaterhouseCoopers" refers to the network of member firms of PricewaterhouseCoopers International Limited, each of which is a separate and independent legal entity.]

36. DiPiazza, "Ethics in Action," p. 15.

APPENDIX 2

1. This is derived by rearranging the following equation and solving for price: Percentage markup = (price – cost) ÷ price.

2. The equation is derived from the basic profit = total revenue − total cost equation. Profit is set to equal the return on investment times the investment (ROI × I), total revenue equals price times quantity (P × Q), and total costs equals quantity times unit cost (Q × UC): ROI × I = (P × Q) − (Q × UC). Solving for P gives P = ((ROI × I) ÷ Q) + UC.

3. The break-even volume equation can also be derived from the basic profit = total revenue − total cost equation. At the break-even point, profit is equal to zero, and it is best to separate fixed and variable costs: 0 = (P × Q) − TFC − (Q × UVC). Solving for Q gives Q = TFC ÷ (P − UVC).

4. As in the previous note, this equation is derived from the basic profit = total revenue − total cost equation. However, unlike the break-even calculation, in which profit was set to equal zero, we set the profit equal to the dollar profit goal: Dollar profit goal = (P × Q) − TFC − (Q × UVC). Solving for Q gives Q = (TFC + dollar profit goal) ÷ (P − UVC).

5. Again, using the basic profit equation, we set profit equal to ROI × I: ROI × I = (P × Q) − TFC − (Q × UVC). Solving for Q gives Q = (TFC + (ROI × I)) ÷ (P − UVC).

6. Again, using the basic profit equation, we set profit equal to 25% of sales, which is 0.25 × P × Q: 0.25 × P × Q = (P × Q) − TFC − (Q × UVC). Solving for Q gives Q = TFC ÷ (P − UVC − (0.25 × P)) or TFC ÷ ((0.75 × P) − UVC).

7. "US Television Households Increase 1.3% for 2007–2008," www .marketingcharts.com/television/us-television-households-increase-13-for-2007-2008-season-1385, accessed August 25, 2008.

8. "HDTV Penetration and Sales Figures," www.parksassociates .blogspot.com/2008/02/hdtv-penetration-and-sales-figures.html, accessed August 25, 2008.

9. "Broadband Internet to Reach 77 Percent of Households by 2012," www.tmcnet.com/voip/ip-communications/articles/35393-gart ner-broadband-internet-reach-77-percent-households-2012.htm, accessed August 25, 2008.

10. Daisy Whitney, "'06 HDTV Sales to Outpace Analog," *Television Week*, October 31, 2005, pp. 19–24.

11. See Roger J. Best, *Market-Based Management*, 4th ed. (Upper Saddle River, NJ: Prentice Hall, 2005).

12. Total contribution can also be determined from the unit contribution and unit volume: Total contribution = unit contribution × unit sales. Total units sold were 297,619 units, which can be determined by dividing total sales by price per unit ($100 million ÷ $336). Total contribution = $70 contribution per unit × 297,619 units = $20,833,330 (difference due to rounding).

13. Recall that the contribution margin of 21% was based on variable costs representing 79% of sales. Therefore, if we do not know the price, we can set it equal to $1.00. If the price equals $1.00, 79 cents represents variable costs and 21 cents represents unit contribution. If the price is decreased by 10%, the new price is $0.90. However, variable costs do not change just because the price decreased, so the unit contribution and contribution margin decrease as follows:

	Old	New (reduced 10%)
Price	$1.00	$0.90
– Unit variable cost	$0.79	$0.79
= Unit contribution	$0.21	$0.11
Contribution margin	$0.21/$1.00 = 0.21 or 21%	$0.11/$0.90 = 0.12 or 12%

APPENDIX 3

1. See "Companies Give 'Web Search' a New Meaning," *CFO.com*, April 21, 2008, accessed at http://backwww.CFO.com.

Glossary

Adapted global marketing | التسويق العالمي المعدل حسب كل سوق
An international marketing strategy for adjusting the marketing strategy and mix elements to each international target market, bearing more costs but hoping for a larger market share and return.

Administered VMS | نظام التسويق الرأسي المحكم
A vertical marketing system that coordinates successive stages of production and distribution, not through common ownership or contractual ties, but through the size and power of one of the parties.

Adoption process | عملية تبني فكرة جديدة
The mental process through which an individual passes from first hearing about an innovation to final adoption.

Advertising | الدعاية
Any paid form of nonpersonal presentation and promotion of ideas, goods, or services by an identified sponsor.

Advertising agency | وكالة إعلانات
A marketing services firm that assists companies in planning, preparing, implementing, and evaluating all or portions of their advertising programs.

Advertising budget | ميزانية الدعاية
The dollars and other resources allocated to a product or company advertising program.

Advertising media | وسائل الإعلان
The vehicles through which advertising messages are delivered to their intended audiences.

Advertising objective | الهدف الإعلاني
A specific communication *task* to be accomplished with a specific *target* audience during a specific period of *time*.

Advertising strategy | استراتيجية الدعاية
The strategy by which the company accomplishes its advertising objectives. It consists of two major elements: creating advertising messages and selecting advertising media.

Affordable method | ميزانية دعاية يمكن تحملها
Setting the promotion budget at the level management thinks the company can afford.

Age and life-cycle segmentation | التقسيم وفقا للفئة العمرية والدورة الحياتية
Dividing a market into different age and life-cycle groups.

Alternative evaluation | التقييم البديل
The stage of the buyer decision process in which the consumer uses information to evaluate alternative brands in the choice set.

Approach | المقابلة الأولى (في عملية البيع)
The step in the selling process in which the salesperson meets the customer for the first time.

Attitude | موقف
A person's consistently favorable or unfavorable evaluations, feelings, and tendencies toward an object or idea.

Baby boomers | مواليد ما بعد الحرب العالمية الثانية وحتى عام 1964
The 78 million people born during the baby boom following World War II and lasting until 1964.

Basing-point pricing | اسناد نقطة التسعير
A geographical pricing strategy in which the seller designates some city as a basing point and charges all customers the freight cost from that city to the customer.

Behavioural segmentation | التقسيم على أساس السلوك
Dividing a market into groups based on consumer knowledge, attitudes, uses, or responses to a product.

Belief | الاعتقاد
A descriptive thought that a person holds about something.

Benchmarking | المقارنة المرجعية
The process of comparing the company's products and processes to those of competitors or leading firms in other industries to identify "best practices" and find ways to improve quality and performance.

Benefit segmentation | تقسيم السوق وفقا للفائدة التي يسعى إليها المستهلك
Dividing the market into groups according to the different benefits that consumers seek from the product.

Brand equity | قيمة العلامة التجارية
The differential effect that knowing the brand name has on customer response to the product or its marketing.

Brand extension | توسيع استخدام العلامة التجارية
Extending an existing brand name to new product categories.

Brand personality | سمات العلامة التجارية
The specific mix of human traits that may be attributed to a particular brand.

Brand | العلامة التجارية
A name, term, sign, symbol, design, or a combination of these that identifies the products or services of one seller or group of sellers and differentiates them from those of competitors.

Break-even pricing (target profit pricing) | التسعير على أساس نقطة التعادل (التسعير على أساس الربح المستهدف)
Analysis to determine the unit volume and dollar sales needed to be profitable given a particular price and cost structure.

Business analysis | تحليل الأنشطة التجارية
A review of the sales, costs, and profit projections for a new product to find out whether these factors satisfy the company's objectives.

Business buyer behaviour | سلوك مشتري منتجات أو خدمات الأنشطة التجارية
The buying behavior of the organizations that buy goods and services for use in the production of other products and services or to resell or rent them to others at a profit.

Business buying process | عملية شراء الخدمات والسلع التجارية
The decision process by which business buyers determine which products and services their organizations need to purchase, and then find, evaluate, and choose among alternative suppliers and brands.

Business portfolio | مجموع الاعمال التجارية و المنتجات التي تتكون منها و تقدمها الشركة
The collection of businesses and products that make up the company.

Business promotions | العروض الترويجية للنشاط التجاري
Sales promotion tools used to generate business leads, stimulate purchases, reward customers, and motivate salespeople.

Business-to business (B2B) online marketing | التسويق الإلكتروني فيما بين المؤسسات التجارية
Businesses using B2B Web sites, e-mail, online catalogs, online trading networks, and other online resources to reach new business customers, serve current customers more effectively, and obtain buying efficiencies and better prices.

Business-to-consumer (B2C) online marketing | التسويق الإلكتروني بين الشركات والعملاء
Businesses selling goods and services online to final consumers.

Buyer-readiness stages | المراحل التي يمر خلالها المستهلك قبل عملية إتخاذ قرار الشراء

The stages consumers normally pass through on their way to purchase, including awareness, knowledge, liking, preference, conviction, and purchase.

Buyers | المشترين

The people in the organization's buying center who make an actual purchase.

Buying center | مركز الشراء

All the individuals and units that play a role in the purchase decision making process.

Buzz marketing | التسويق بلفت الانتباه

Cultivating opinion leaders and getting them to spread information about a product or service to others in their communities.

By-product pricing | تسعير المنتجات الفرعية

Setting a price for by-products in order to make the main product's price more competitive.

Captive-product pricing | تسعير المنتجات المساندة

Setting a price for products that must be used along with a main product, such as blades for a razor and film for a camera.

Causal research | البحث التسويقي الاعتيادي الذى يختبر الفرضيات حول العلاقة بين السبب والتأثير

Marketing research to test hypotheses about cause-and-effect relationships.

Chain stores | متاجر متعددة الفروع (سلسلة متاجر)

Two or more outlets that are commonly owned and controlled.

Channel conflict | الصراع بين القنوات التسويقية

Disagreement among marketing channel members on goals and roles—who should do what and for what rewards.

Channel level | مستوى التوزيع

A layer of intermediaries that performs some work in bringing the product and its ownership closer to the final buyer

Click-and-mortar companies | شركات تقوم بتسويق منتجاتها بالطرق التقليدية بالإضافة إلى الإنترنت

Traditional brick-and-mortar companies that have added online marketing to their operations.

Click-only companies | شركات تقوم بتسويق منتجاتها عبر الإنترنت فقط

The so-called dotcoms, which operate only online without any brick-and-mortar market presence.

Closing | اتمام عملية البيع

The step in the selling process in which the salesperson asks the customer for an order.

Co-branding | علامة تجارية مشتركة

The practice of using the established brand names of two different companies on the same product.

Cognitive dissonance | الشعور بعدم الرضا بعد شراء المنتج

Buyer discomfort caused by postpurchase conflict.

Commercial online databases | قواعد البيانات التجارية على الإنترنت

Computerized collections of information available from online commercial sources or via the Internet.

Commercialization | تقديم منتج جديد للسوق

Introducing a new product into the market.

Communication adaptation | موائمة الإعلانات التجارية للاسواق المحلية المختلفة

A global communication strategy of fully adapting advertising messages to local markets.

Competitive advantage | الميزة التنافسية

An advantage over competitors gained by offering greater customer value, either through lower prices or by providing more benefits that justify higher prices.

Competitive marketing strategies | استراتيجيات التسويق التنافسية

Strategies that strongly position the company against competitors and that give the company the strongest possible strategic advantage.

Competitive-parity method | طريقة التماثل التنافسية

Setting the promotion budget to match competitors' outlays.

Competitor analysis | تحليل الجهة المنافسة

The process of identifying key competitors; assessing their objectives, strategies, strengths and weaknesses, and reaction patterns; and selecting which competitors to attack or avoid.

Competitor-centered company | شركة تركز على المنافس

A company whose moves are mainly based on competitors' actions and reactions.

Complex buying behaviour | سلوك الشراء المعقد

Consumer buying behavior in situations characterized by high consumer involvement in a purchase and significant perceived differences among brands.

Concentrated (niche) marketing | التسويق المركز (متخصص)

A market coverage strategy in which a firm goes after a large share of one or a few segments or niches.

Concept testing | اختبار المفاهيم

Testing new-product concepts with a group of target consumers to find out if the concepts have strong consumer appeal.

Consumer buyer behaviour | سلوك المستهلك الشرائي

The buying behavior of final consumers—individuals and households that buy goods and services for personal consumption.

Consumer market | سوق المستهلك

All the individuals and households who buy or acquire goods and services for personal consumption.

Consumer product | منتج استهلاكي

A product bought by final consumer for personal consumption.

Consumer promotions | العروض الترويجية للعميل

Sales promotion tools used to boost short-term customer buying and involvement or to enhance longterm customer relationships.

Consumer-generated marketing | تسويق يقوم به المستهلك للسلعة

Marketing messages, ads, and other brand exchanges created by consumers themselves—both invited and uninvited.

Consumerism | حماية المستهلك

An organized movement of citizens and government agencies to improve the rights and power of buyers in relation to sellers.

Consumer-oriented marketing | التسويق الموجه للمستهلك

The philosophy of sustainable marketing that holds that the company should view and organize its marketing activities from the consumer's point of view.

Consumer-to-business (C2B) online marketing | التسويق الإلكتروني فيما بين المستهلكين والمؤسسات التجارية

Online exchanges in which consumers search out sellers, learn about their offers, and initiate purchases, sometimes even driving transaction terms.

Consumer-to-consumer (C2C) online marketing | التسويق الإلكتروني فيما بين المستهلكين

Online exchanges of goods and information between final consumers.

Contract manufacturing | التسويق الإلكتروني فيما بين المستهلكين

A joint venture in which a company contracts with manufacturers in a foreign market to produce the product or provide its service.

Contractual VMS | نظام التسويق الرأسي التعاقدي

A vertical marketing system in which independent firms at different levels of production and distribution join together through contracts to obtain more economies or sales impact than they could achieve alone.

Convenience product | منتج سهل المنال (ميسّر)

A consumer product that customers usually buy frequently, immediately, and with a minimum of comparison and buying effort.

Convenience store | متاجر صغيرة
A small store, located near a residential area, that is open long hours seven days a week and carries a limited line of high-turnover convenience goods.

Conventional distribution channel | قنوات التوزيع التقليدية
A channel consisting of one or more independent producers, wholesalers, and retailers, each a separate business seeking to maximize its own profits even at the expense of profits for the system as a whole.

Corporate (or brand) website | الموقع الإلكتروني للشركة (أو العلامة التجارية)
A website designed to build customer goodwill, collect customer feedback, and supplement other sales channels, rather than to sell the company's products directly.

Corporate VMS | نظام التسويق الرأسي للشركات
A vertical marketing system that combines successive stages of production and distribution under single ownership—channel leadership is established through common ownership.

Cost-based pricing | التسعير القائم على التكلفة
Setting prices based on the costs for producing, distributing, and selling the product plus a fair rate of return for effort and risk.

Cost-plus pricing | التسعير على أساس اجمالي التكلفة والربح
Adding a standard markup to the cost of the product.

Countertrade | التجارة عن طريق تبادل السلع بدلا من المال (المقايضة)
International trade involving the direct or indirect exchange of goods for other goods instead of cash.

Creative concept | مفهوم الإبداع
The compelling "big idea" that will bring the advertising message strategy to life in a distinctive and memorable way.

Cultural environment | البيئة الثقافية
Institutions and other forces that affect society's basic values, perceptions, preferences, and behaviors.

Culture | الثقافة
The set of basic values, perceptions, wants, and behaviors learned by a member of society from family and other important institutions.

Customer database | قواعد بيانات العملاء
An organized collection of comprehensive data about individual customers or prospects, including geographic, demographic, psychographic, and behavioral data.

Customer equity | قيمة العميل
The total combined customer lifetime values of all of the company's customers.

Customer insights | رؤى العملاء
Fresh understandings of customers and the marketplace derived from marketing information that become the basis for creating customer value and relationships.

Customer lifetime value | القيمة الدائمة للعميل
The value of the entire stream of purchases that the Customer would make over a lifetime of patronage.

Customer relationship management | إدارة علاقات العملاء
Managing detailed information about individual customers and carefully managing customer "touch points" in order to maximize customer loyalty.

Customer sales force structure | هيكل قوى البيع للعملاء
A sales force organization under which salespeople specialize in selling only to certain customers or industries.

Customer satisfaction | رضا المستهلك
The extent to which a product's perceived performance matches a buyer's expectations.

Customer value analysis | تحليل الفوائد التى يعتبرها العميل قيمة
Analysis conducted to determine what benefits target customers value and how they rate the relative value of various competitors' offers.

Customer-centered company | شركة تركز على العميل
A company that pays balanced attention to both customers and competitors in designing its marketing strategies.

Customer-centered new-product development | تطوير منتجات جديدة لإيجاد حلول استهلاكية مناسبة
New-product development that focuses on finding new ways to solve customer problems and create more customer satisfying experiences.

Customer-perceived value | القيمة المدركة للمستهلك
The customer's evaluation of the difference between all the benefits and all the costs of a marketing offer relative to those of competing offers.

Customer relationship management (CRM) | ادارة علاقات المستهلكين
Managing detailed information about individual customers and carefully managing customer 'touch points' in order to maximize customer loyalty.

Customer-value marketing | قيمة المستهلك التسويقية
A principle of sustainable marketing that holds that a company should put most of its resources into customer value-building marketing investments.

Deciders | أصحاب القرار
People in the organization's buying center who have formal or informal power to select or approve the final suppliers.

Decline stage | مرحلة التدهور
The product life-cycle stage in which a product's sales decline.

Deficient products | المنتجات المعيبة
Products that have neither immediate appeal nor long-run benefits

Demand curve | منحنى الطلب
A curve that shows the number of units the market will buy in a given time period, at different prices that might be charged.

Demands | المتطلبات
Human wants that are backed by buying power.

Demographic segmentation | التقسيم الديموغرافي
Dividing the market into groups based on variables such as age, gender, family size, family life cycle, income, occupation, education, religion, race, generation, and nationality.

Demography | الديمغرافيا (علم دراسة السكان)
The study of human populations in terms of size, density, location, age, gender, race, occupation, and other statistics.

Department store | متاجر كبرى
A retail organization that carries a wide variety of product lines—each line is operated as a separate department managed by specialist buyers or merchandisers.

Derived demand | الطلب الاشتقاقي
Business demand that ultimately comes from (derives from) the demand for consumer goods.

Descriptive research | البحث الوصفي
Marketing research to better describe marketing problems, situations, or markets, such as the market potential for a product or the demographics and attitudes of consumers.

Desirable products | المنتجات المرغوبة
Products that give both high immediate satisfaction and high longrun benefits.

Differentiated (segmented) marketing | التسويق المتنوع (المجزأ)
A market-coverage strategy in which a firm decides to target several market segments and designs separate offers for each.

Differentiation | المفاضلة
Actually differentiating the market offering to create superior customer value.

Differentiation | المفاضلة
Actually differentiating the market offering to create superior customer value.

Direct investment | استثمار مباشر
Entering a foreign market by developing foreign-based assembly or manufacturing facilities.

Direct marketing | التسويق المباشر
Direct connections with carefully targeted individual consumers to both obtain an immediate response and cultivate lasting customer relationships—the use of direct mail, the telephone, direct response television, e-mail, the Internet, and other tools to communicate directly with specific consumers.

Direct marketing channel | قنوات التسويق المباشر
A marketing channel that has no intermediary levels.

Direct-mail marketing | التسويق المباشر عبر البريد
Direct marketing by sending an offer, announcement, reminder, or other item to a person at a particular physical or virtual address.

Direct-response television marketing |
التسويق بالاستجابة المباشرة عبر التليفزيون
Direct marketing via television, including *direct-response television advertising* (or *infomercials*) and *home shopping channels*.

Discount | الخصم
A straight reduction in price on purchases during a stated period of time.

Discount store | معرض للسلع المخفضة
A retail operation that sells standard merchandise at lower prices by accepting lower margins and selling at higher volume.

Disintermediation | حذف الوسطاء
The cutting out of marketing channel intermediaries by product or service producers, or the displacement of traditional resellers by radical new types of intermediaries.

Dissonance-reducing buying behavior |
سلوك المشتري عند شراء منتج باهظ الثمن مع وجود بضعة اختلافات بين الماركات
Consumer buying behaviour in situations characterized by high involvement but few perceived differences among brands.

Distribution center | مركز توزيع
A large, highly automated warehouse designed to receive goods from various plants and suppliers, take orders, fill them efficiently, and deliver goods to customers as quickly as possible.

Diversification | التنويع
A strategy for company growth through starting up or acquiring businesses outside the company's current products and markets.

Downsizing | التقليص
Reducing the business portfolio by eliminating products of business units that are not profitable or that no longer fit the company's overall strategy.

Dynamic pricing | التسعير الديناميكي
Adjusting prices continually to meet the characteristics and needs of individual customers and situations.

Economic community | المجتمع الاقتصادي
A group of nations organized to work toward common goals in the regulation of international trade.

Economic environment | المناخ الاقتصادي
Factors that affect consumer buying power and spending patterns.

Engel's laws | قوانين انجل
Differences noted over a century ago by Ernst Engel in how people shift their spending across food, housing, transportation, health care, and other goods and services categories as family income rises.

Environmental sustainability | الاستدامة البيئية
A management approach that involves developing strategies that both sustain the environment and produce profits for the company.

Environmental sustainability | الاستدامة البيئية
A management approach that involves developing strategies that both sustain the environment and produce profits for the company.

Environmentalism | حماية البيئة
An organized movement of concerned citizens and government agencies to protect and improve people's current and future living environment.

E-procurement | الشراء الإلكتروني
Purchasing through electronic connections between buyers and sellers—usually online.

Ethnographic research | البحث الإثنوغرافي
A form of observational research that involves Sending trained observers to watch and interact with consumers in their "natural habitat."

Event marketing | تسويق الحدث
Creating a brand marketing event or serving as a sole or participating sponsor of events created by others.

Exchange | تبادل
The act of obtaining a desired object from someone by offering something in return.

Exclusive distribution | التوزيع الحصري
Giving a limited number of dealers the exclusive right to distribute the company's products in their territories.

Exclusive distributor | الموزع الحصري
A representative who buys, stocks, and sells the products ofaforeign company to a retailer and wholesaler in his or her territory.

Execution style | أسلوب التنفيذ
The approach, style, tone, words, and format used for executing an advertising message.

Experience curve (learning curve) | منحنى الخبرة (منحنى التعلم)
The drop in the average per-unit production cost that comes with accumulated production experience.

Experimental research | البحث التجريبي
Gathering primary data by selecting matched groups of subjects, giving them different treatments, controlling related factors, and checking for differences in group responses.

Exploratory research | البحث الاستكشافي
Marketing research to gather preliminary information that will help define problems and suggest hypotheses.

Exporting | التصدير
Entering a foreign market by selling goods produced in the company's home country, often with little modification.

Factory outlet | منافذ بيع المصنع
An off-price retailing operation that is owned and operated by a manufacturer and that normally carries the manufacturer's surplus, discontinued, or irregular goods.

Fad | زيادة مؤقتة فى المبيعات نتيجة لشهرة منتج أو علامة تجارية ما
A temporary period of unusually high sales driven by consumer enthusiasm and immediate product or brand popularity.

Fashion | موضة
A currently accepted or popular style in a given field.

Fixed costs (overhead) | التكاليف الثابتة (المباشرة)
Costs that do not vary with production or sales level.

FOB-origin pricing | التسعير على أساس مكان التسليم
A geographical pricing strategy in which goods are placed free on board a carrier; the customer pays the freight from the factory to the destination.

Focus group interviewing |
مقابلة تضم مجموعة من الأفراد تركز على موضوع ما بشكل معمق
Personal interviewing that involves inviting six to ten people to gather for a few hours with a trained interviewer to talk about a product, service, or organization. The interviewer "focuses" the group discussion on important issues.

Follow-up | المتابعة
The last step in the selling process in which the salesperson follows up after the sale to ensure customer satisfaction and repeat business.

Franchise | الامتياز
A contractual association between a manufacturer, wholesaler, or service organization (a franchiser) and independent businesspeople (franchisees) who buy the right to own and operate one or more units in the franchise system.

Franchise organization | منظمة الامتياز
A contractual vertical marketing system in which a channel member, called a franchiser, links several stages in the production-distribution process.

Freight-absorption pricing | التسعير على أساس تحمل قيمة الشحن
A geographical pricing strategy in which the seller absorbs all or part of the freight charges in order to get the desired business.

Gatekeepers | منسقي تداول المعلومات
People in the organization's buying center who control the flow of information to others.

Gender segmentation | التجزئة على أساس الجنس
Dividing a market into different groups based on gender.

General need description | الوصف العام للحاجات
The stage in the business buying process in which the company describes the general characteristics and quantity of a needed item.

Generation X | جيل إكس
The 45 million people born between 1965 and 1976 in the "birth dearth" following the baby boom.

Geographic pricing | التسعير الجغرافي
Setting prices for customers located in different parts of the country or world.

Geographic segmentation | التجزئة الجغرافية
Dividing a market into different geographical units such as nations, states, regions, counties, cities, or neighborhoods.

Global firm | شركة دولية
A firm that, by operating in more than one country, gains R&D, production, marketing, and financial advantages in its costs and reputation that are not available to purely domestic competitors.

Good-value pricing | التسعير المبني على قيمة المنتج
Offering just the right combination of quality and good service at a fair price.

Government market | السوق الحكومي
Governmental units— federal, state, and local—that purchase or rent goods and services for carrying out the main functions of government.

Group | فئة
Two or more people who interact to accomplish individual or mutual goals.

Growth stage | مرحلة النمو
The product life-cycle stage in which a product's sales start climbing quickly.

Growth-share matrix | مصفوفة حصة النمو
A portfolio-planning method that evaluates a company's strategic business units in terms of its market growth rate and relative market share. SBUs are classified as stars, cash cows, question marks, or dogs.

Habitual buying behavior | السلوك المعتاد في الشراء
Consumer buying behavior in situations characterized by low-consumer involvement and few significantly perceived brand differences.

Handling objections | معالجة الاعتراض على الشراء
The step in the selling process in which the salesperson seeks out, clarifies, and overcomes customer objections to buying.

Horizontal marketing system | نظام التسويق الأفقي
A channel arrangement in which two or more companies at one level join together to follow a new marketing opportunity.

Hypermarket | محل تجاري ضخم
Very large stores traditionally aimed at meeting consumers' total needs for routinely purchased food and nonfood items. Includes combined supermarket and discount stores, and *category killers*, which carry a deep assortment in a particular category and have a knowledgeable staff.

Idea generation | توليد الأفكار
The systematic search for new-product ideas.

Idea screening | تصفية الأفكار
Screening new-product ideas in order to spot good ideas and drop poor ones as soon as possible.

Income segmentation | تقسيم الدخل
Dividing a market into different income groups.

Independent off-price retailer | بائع تجزئة مستقل للسلع المخفضة
An off-price retailer that is either independently owned and run or is a division of a larger retail corporation.

Indirect marketing channel | قنوات التسويق غير المباشرة
Channel containing one or more intermediary levels.

Individual marketing | التسويق الفردي
Tailoring products and marketing programs to the needs and preferences of individual customers—also labeled "one-to-one marketing," "customized marketing," and "markets-of-one marketing."

Industrial product | منتج صناعي
A product bought by individuals and organizations for further processing or for use in conducting a business.

Influencers | أصحاب التأثير
People in an organization's buying center who affect the buying decision; they often help define specifications and also provide information for evaluating alternatives.

Information search | البحث عن المعلومات
The stage of the buyer decision process in which the consumer is aroused to search for more information; the consumer may simply have heightened attention or may go into an active information search.

Innovative marketing | التسويق المبتكر
A principle of sustainable marketing that requires that a company seek real product and marketing improvements.

Inside sales force | قوى البيع الداخلية
Inside salespeople who conduct business from their offices via telephone, the Internet, or visits from prospective buyers.

Institutional market | السوق المؤسسي
Schools, hospitals, nursing homes, prisons, and other institutions that provide goods and services to people in their care.

Integrated logistics management | الإدارة المتكاملة للإمدادات
The logistics concept that emphasizes teamwork, both inside the company and among all the marketing channel organizations, to maximize the performance of the entire distribution system.

Integrated marketing communications (IMC) | الاتصالات التسويقية المتكاملة
Carefully integrating and coordinating the company's many communications channels to deliver a clear, consistent, and compelling message about the organization and its products.

Intensive distribution | توزيع مكثف
Stocking the product in as many outlets as possible.

Interactive marketing | التسويق التفاعلي
Training service employees in the fine art of interacting with customers to satisfy their needs.

Intermarket segmentation | تقسيم المستهلكين طبقا لتشابه متطلباتهم الشرائية رغم اختلاف بلادهم
Forming segments of consumers who have similar needs and buying behavior even though they are located in different countries.

Intermodal transportation | النقل متعدد الوسائط
Combining two or more modes of transportation.

Internal databases | قواعد البيانات الداخلية
Electronic collections of consumer and market information obtained from data sources within the company network.

Internal marketing | التسويق الداخلي
Orienting and motivating customer-contact employees and supporting service people to work as a team to provide customer satisfaction.

Introduction stage | مرحلة تقديم المنتج إلى السوق
The product life-cycle stage in which the new product is first distributed and made available for purchase.

Joint ownership | ملكية مشتركة
A joint venture in which a company joins investors in a foreign market to create a local business in which the company shares joint ownership and control.

Joint venturing | المشروع المشترك
Entering foreign markets by joining with foreign companies to produce or market a product or service.

Learning | التعلم
Changes in an individual's behavior arising from experience.

Licensing | الترخيص
A method of entering a foreign market in which the company enters into an agreement with a licensee in the foreign market, offering the right to use a manufacturing process, trademark, patent, trade secret, or other item of value for a fee or royalty.

Lifestyle | نمط المعيشة
A person's pattern of living as expressed in his or her activities, interests, and opinions.

Line extension | توسيع خط الإنتاج
Extending an existing brand name to new forms, colors, sizes, ingredients, or flavors of an existing product category.

Local agents | وكلاء محليين
Act as brokers between the local buyer and the foreign company

Local marketing | التسويق المحلي
Tailoring brands and promotions to the needs and wants of local customer groups—cities, neighborhoods, and even specific stores.

Macroenvironment | البيئة الكلية
The larger societal forces that affect the microenvironment—demographic, economic, natural, technological, political, and cultural forces.

Madison & Vine | ماديسون وفين
A term that has come to represent the merging of advertising and entertainment in an effort to break through the clutter and create new avenues for reaching consumers with more engaging messages.

Management contracting | التعاقد الإداري
A joint venture in which the domestic firm supplies the management knowhow to a foreign company that supplies the capital; the domestic firm exports management services rather than products.

Market | السوق
The set of all actual and potential buyers of a product or service.

Market challenger | منافس قوي في السوق
A runner-up firm that is fighting hard to increase its market share in an industry.

Market development | تنمية الأسواق
A strategy for company growth by identifying and developing new market segments for current company products.

Market follower | شركة تابعة في السوق
A runner-up firm that wants to hold its share in an industry without rocking the boat.

Market leader | شركة رائدة في السوق
The firm in an industry with the largest market share.

Market nicher | شركة متخصصة تعمل في سوق لا يتنافس فيه الكثير
A firm that serves small segments that the other firms in an industry overlook or ignore.

Market offering | الطرح في الأسواق
Some combination of products, services, information, or experiences offered to a market to satisfy a need or want.

Market penetration | النفاذ إلى الأسواق
A strategy for company growth by increasing sales of current products to current market segments without changing the product.

Market segment | الشريحة السوقية
A group of consumers who respond in a similar way to a given set of marketing efforts.

Market segmentation | تجزئة السوق
Dividing a market into distinct groups of buyers who have different needs, characteristics, or behaviors, and who might require separate products or marketing programs.

Market targeting (targeting) | استهداف السوق (أو الاستهداف)
The process of evaluating each market segment's attractiveness and selecting one or more segments to enter.

Market-centered company |
الشركة التي تعين اهتماما متساويا لعملائها ومنافسيها
A company that pays balanced attention to both customers and competitors in designing its marketing strategies.

Marketing | التسويق
The process by which companies create value for customers and build strong customer relationships in order to capture value from customers in return.

Marketing channel (distribution channel) |
قناة التسويق (قناة التوزيع)
A set of interdependent organizations that help make a product or service available for use or consumption by the consumer or business user.

Marketing channel design | تصميم قناة تسويقية
Designing effective marketing channels by analyzing consumer needs, setting channel objectives, identifying major channel alternatives, and evaluating them.

Marketing channel management | إدارة قنوات التسويق
Selecting, managing, and motivating individual channel members and evaluating their performance over time.

Marketing concept | مفهوم التسويق
The marketing management philosophy that holds that achieving organizational goals depends on knowing the needs and wants of target markets and delivering the desired satisfactions better than competitors do.

Marketing control | الرقابة التسويقية
The process of measuring and evaluating the results of marketing strategies and plans and taking corrective action to ensure that objectives are achieved.

Marketing environment | المناخ التسويقي
The actors and forces outside marketing that affect marketing management's ability to build and maintain successful relationships with target customers.

Marketing implementation | التنفيذ التسويقي
The process that turns marketing strategies and plans into marketing actions in order to accomplish strategic marketing objectives.

Marketing information system (MIS) | نظام المعلومات التسويقية
People and procedures for assessing information needs, developing the needed information, and helping decision makers to use the information to generate and validate actionable customer and market insights.

Marketing intelligence | الاستخبارات التسويقية
The systematic collection and analysis of publicly available
information about consumers, competitors, and developments in the
marketing environment.

Marketing intermediaries | الوسطاء التسويقيين
Firms that help the company to promote, sell, and distribute its goods
to final buyers.

Marketing logistics (physical distribution) |
الإمدادات التسويقية-التوزيع المادي
Planning, implementing, and controlling the physical flow of
materials, final goods, and related information from points of origin to
points of consumption to meet customer requirements at a profit.

Marketing management | إدارة التسويق
The art and science of choosing target markets and building profitable
relationships with them.

Marketing mix | المزيج التسويقي
The set of controllable tactical marketing tools—product, price, place,
and promotion—that the firm blends to produce the response it wants
in the target market.

Marketing myopia | قصر النظر التسويقي
The mistake of paying more attention to the specific products a
company offers than to the benefits and experiences produced by
these products.

Marketing research | البحث التسويقي
The systematic design, collection, analysis, and reporting of data
relevant to a specific marketing situation facing an organization.

Marketing strategy | استراتيجيه التسويق
The marketing logic by which the business unit hopes to create
customer value and achieve profitable customer relationships.

Marketing strategy development | تطوير استراتيجيات التسويق
Designing an initial marketing strategy for a new product based on
the product concept.

Marketing Website | موقع الكتروني للتسويق
A website that engages consumers in interactions that will move them
closer to a direct purchase or other marketing outcome.

Market-penetration pricing |
وضع سعر منخفض لمنتج جديد بغية جذب عدد كبير من المشتركين و الحصول على
حصة كبيرة من السوق
Setting a low price for a new product in order to attract a large
number of buyers and a large market share.

Market-skimming pricing |
وضع سعر أعلى لزبائن معيينين يرغبون بدفع قيمة أعلى مقابل الحصول على امتياز
الحصول على المنتج أولا
Setting a high price for a new product to skim maximum revenues
layer by layer from the segments willing to pay the high price; the
company makes fewer but more profitable sales.

Maturity stage | مرحلة النضوج
The product life-cycle stage in which sales growth slows or
levels off.

Microenvironment | البيئة التسويقية الجزئية
The actors close to the company that affect its ability to serve its
customers—the company, suppliers, marketing intermediaries,
customer markets, competitors, and publics.

Micromarketing | التسويق الجزئي - تسويق ضيق النطاق
The practice of tailoring products and marketing programs to the
needs and wants of specific individuals and local customer groups—
includes *local marketing and individual marketing.*

Millennials (Generation Y) | جيل الألفية (جيل واي)
The 83 million children of the baby boomers, born between 1977 and
2000.

Mission statement | مهمة الشركة
A statement of the organization's purpose—what it wants to
accomplish in the larger environment.

Modified rebuy | إعادة الشراء بعد تعديل المنتج
A business buying situation in which the buyer wants to modify
product specifications, prices, terms, or suppliers.

Motive (drive) | حافز (دافع)
A need that is sufficiently pressing to direct the person to seek
satisfaction of the need.

Multichannel distribution system | نظام التوزيع متعدد القنوات
A distribution system in which a single firm sets up two or more
marketing channels to reach one or more customer segments.

Natural environment | العوامل الطبيعية
Natural resources that are needed as inputs by marketers or that are
affected by marketing activities.

Need recognition | الشعور بالحاجة
The first stage of the buyer decision process, in which the consumer
recognizes a problem or need.

Needs | الاحتياجات
States of felt deprivation

New product | منتج جديد
A good, service, or idea that is perceived by some potential customers
as new.

New task | مهمة جديدة
A business buying situation in which the buyer purchases a product or
service for the first time.

New-product development | تطوير المنتج الجديد
The development of original products, product improvements,
product modifications, and new brands through the firm's own
product development efforts.

Nonpersonal communication channels | قنوات الاتصال غير الشخصية
Media that carry messages without personal contact or feedback,
including major media, atmospheres, and events.

Objective-and-task method | طريقة الهدف والمهمة
Developing the promotion budget by (1) defining specific
objectives; (2) determining the tasks that must be performed to
achieve these objectives; and (3) estimating the costs of performing
these tasks. The sum of these costs is the proposed promotion
budget.

Observational research | البحث القائم على الملاحظة
Gathering primary data by observing relevant people, actions, and
situations.

Occasion segmentation | التجزئة على أساس المناسبات
Dividing the market into groups according to occasions when buyers
get the idea to buy, actually make their purchase, or use the

Online advertising | الإعلان على الإنترنت
Advertising that appears while consumers are surfing the Web,
including display ads, search-related ads, online classifieds, and other
forms.

Online focus groups | إعداد مجموعات نقاش مركزة على الإنترنت
Gathering a small group of people online with a trained moderator
to chat about a product, service, or organization and gain qualitative
insights about consumer attitudes and behavior.

Online marketing | التسويق الإلكتروني
Company efforts to market products and services and build customer
relationships over the Internet.

Online marketing research | بحث التسويق عبر الإنترنت
Collecting primary data online through Internet surveys, online
focus groups, Web-based experiments, or tracking consumers' online
behavior.

Online social networks | الربط الإجتماعي عبر الإنترنت
Online social communities—blogs, social networking Web sites, or even virtual worlds—where people socialize or exchange information and opinions.

Opinion leader | قادة الرأي
Person within a reference group who, because of special skills, knowledge, personality, or other characteristics, exerts social influence on others.

Optional-product pricing | تسعير المنتجات غير الضرورية
The pricing of optional or accessory products along with a main product.

Order-routine specification | المواصفات الروتينية للطلبيات
The stage of the business buying process in which the buyer writes the final order with the chosen supplier(s), listing the technical specifications, quantity needed, expected time of delivery, return policies, and warranties.

Outside sales force (field sales force) | قوى البيع الخارجية (موظفو البيع الميدانيين)
Outside salespeople who travel to call on customers in the field.

Packaging | التعبئة والتغليف
The activities of designing and producing the container or wrapper for a product.

Partner relationship management | إدارة العلاقات مع الشركاء
Working closely with partners in other company departments and outside the company to jointly bring greater value to customers.

Percent-of-sales method | تحديد ميزانية الدعاية على أساس نسبة معينة من المبيعات
Setting the promotion budget at a certain percentage of current or forecasted sales or as a percentage of the unit sales price.

Perception | الإدارك
The process by which people select, organize, and interpret information to form a meaningful picture of the world.

Performance review | مراجعة الأداء
The stage of the business buying process in which the buyer assesses the performance of the supplier and decides to continue, modify, or drop the arrangement.

Personal communication channels | قنوات الاتصال الشخصي
Channels through which two or more people communicate directly with each other, including face to face, on the phone, through mail or e-mail, or even through an Internet "chat."

Personal selling | البيع الشخصي
Personal interactions between a customers and the firm's sales force for the purpose of making sales and building customer relationships.

Personality | الشخصية
The unique psychological characteristics that lead to relatively consistent and lasting responses to one's own environment.

Pleasing products | منتجات ذات قيمة امتاعية مؤقتة
Products that give high immediate satisfaction but may hurt consumers in the long run.

Political environment | البيئة السياسية
Laws, government agencies, and pressure groups that influence and limit various organizations and individuals in a given society.

Portfolio analysis | تحليل الحقيبة الاستثمارية (العمل المؤسسي)
The process by which management evaluates the products and businesses that make up the company.

Positioning | التمركز
Arranging for a product to occupy a clear, distinctive, and desirable place relative to competing products in the minds of target consumers.

Positioning statement | بيان التمركز
A statement that summarizes company or brand positioning— it takes this form: *To (target segment and need) our (brand) is (concept) that (point-of-difference).*

Postpurchase behaviour | سلوك ما بعد الشراء
The stage of the buyer decision process in which the consumers take further action after purchase, based on their satisfaction or dissatisfaction.

Pre approach | التحضير المسبق
The step in the selling process in which the salesperson or company identifies qualified potential customers.

Presentation | عرض المنتج
The step in the selling process in which the salesperson tells the "value story" to the buyer, showing how the company's offer solves the customer's problems.

Price | السعر
The amount of money charged for a product or service, or the sum of the values that customers exchange for the benefits of having or using the product or service.

Price elasticity | المرونة السعرية
A measure of the sensitivity of demand to changes in price.

Primary data | بيانات أولية
Information collected for the specific purpose at hand.

Problem recognition | إدراك المشكلة
The first stage of the business buying process in which someone in the company recognizes a problem or need that can be met by acquiring a good or a service.

Product | المنتج
Anything that can be offered to a market for attention, acquisition, use, or consumption that might satisfy a want or need.

Product adaptation | موائمة المنتج
Adapting a product to meet local conditions or wants in foreign markets.

Product bundle pricing | التسعير على أساس حزم المنتجات
Combining several products and offering the bundle at a reduced price.

Product concept | مفهوم المنتج
A detailed version of the new-product idea stated in meaningful consumer terms.

Product development | تطوير المنتج من فكرة إلى منتج فعلي
Developing the product concept into a physical product in order to ensure that the product idea can be turned into a workable market offering.

Product development | تطوير منتجات الشركة لتساهم في نموها
A strategy for company growth by offering modified or new products to current market segments.

Product invention | اختراع المنتج
Creating new products or services for foreign markets.

Product life cycle | دورة حياة المنتج
The course of a product's sales and profits over its lifetime. It involves five distinct stages: product development, introduction, growth, maturity, and decline.

Product line pricing | تسعير خط الإنتاج
Setting the price steps between various products in a product line based on cost differences between the products, customer evaluations of different features, and competitors' prices.

Product line | خط الإنتاج
A group of products that are closely related because they function in a similar manner, are sold to the same customer groups, are

marketed through the same types of outlets, or fall within given price ranges.

Product mix (product portfolio) | المنتجات المتنوعة المعروضة للبيع (قائمة المنتجات)
The set of all product lines and items that a particular seller offers for sale.

Product position | مركز المنتج
The way the product is defined by consumers on important attributes—the place the product occupies in consumers' minds relative to competing products.

Product quality | جودة المنتج
The characteristics of a product or service that bear on its ability to satisfy stated or implied customer needs.

Product sales force structure | هيكل قوى بيع جزء من منتجات الشركة للعملاء
A sales force organization under which salespeople specialize in selling only a portion of the company's products or lines

Product specification | مواصفات المنتج
The stage of the business buying process in which the buying organization decides on and specifies the best technical product characteristics for a needed item.

Product/market expansion grid | شبكة توسيع حجم المنتج/السوق
A portfolio-planning tool for identifying company growth opportunities through market penetration, market development, product development, or diversification.

Production concept | مفهوم الإنتاج
The idea that consumers will favor products that are available and highly affordable and that the organization should therefore focus on improving production and distribution efficiency.

Promotion mix (marketing communications mix) | مزيج ترويجي (مزيج الاتصالات التسويقية)
The specific blend of advertising, sales promotion, public relations, personal selling, and direct-marketing tools that the company uses to persuasively communicate customer value and build customer relationships.

Promotional pricing | التسعير الترويجي
Temporarily pricing products below the list price, and sometimes even below cost, to increase short-run sales.

Proposal solicitation | طلب العروض
The stage of the business buying process in which the buyer invites qualified suppliers to submit proposals.

Prospecting | البحث عن العملاء
The step in the selling process in which the salesperson or company identifies qualified potential customers.

Psychographic segmentation | التجزئة السيكوغرافية
Dividing a market into different groups based on social class, lifestyle, or personality characteristics.

Psychological pricing | التسعير السيكولوجي
A pricing approach that considers the psychology of prices and not simply the economics; the price is used to say something about the product.

Public | الجمهور
Any group that has an actual or potential interest in or impact on an organization's ability to achieve its objectives.

Public relations | العلاقات العامة
Building good relations with the company's various publics by obtaining favorable publicity, building up a good corporate image, and handling or heading off unfavorable rumors, stories, and events.

Pull strategy | استراتيجيه السحب
A promotion strategy that calls for spending a lot on advertising and consumer promotion to induce final consumers to buy the product,

creating a demand vacuum that "pulls" the product through the channel.

Purchase decision | قرار الشراء
The buyer's decision about which brand to purchase.

Push strategy | استراتيجيه الدفع
A promotion strategy that calls for using the sales force and trade promotion to push the product through channels. The producer promotes the product to channel members who in turn promote it to final consumers.

Reference prices | الأسعار المرجعية
Prices that buyers carry in their minds and refer to when they look at a given product.

Retailer | بائع التجزئة
A business whose sales come primarily from retailing.

Retailing | البيع بالتجزئة
All activities involved in selling goods or services directly to final consumers for their personal, non-business use.

Return on advertising investment | العائد من الاستثمار الإعلاني
The net return on advertising investment divided by the costs of the advertising investment.

Return on marketing investment | عائد استثمار التسويق
The net return from a marketing investment divided by the costs of the marketing investment.

Sales force management | إدارة قوى البيع
The analysis, planning, implementation, and control of sales force activities. It includes designing sales force strategy and structure and recruiting, selecting, training, supervising, compensating, and evaluating the firm's salespeople.

Sales promotion | الترويج للمبيعات
Short-term incentives to encourage the purchase or sale of a product or service.

Sales quota | حصة المبيعات
A standard that states the amount a salesperson should sell and how sales should be divided among the company's products.

Salesperson | مندوب مبيعات
An individual representing a company to customers by performing one or more of the following activities: prospecting, communicating, selling, servicing, information gathering, and relationship building.

Salutary products | المنتجات المفيدة (منتجات ضئيله الجاذبية بالنسبة للعملاء، ولكنها مفيدة لهم على المدى البعيد)
Products that have low appeal but may benefit consumers in the long run.

Sample | عينة
A segment of the population selected for marketing research to represent the population as a whole.

Secondary data | بيانات ثانوية
Information that already exists somewhere, having been collected for another purpose.

Segmented pricing | التسعير المجزئ
Selling a product or service at two or more prices, where the difference in prices is not based on differences in costs.

Selective distribution | التوزيع الانتقائي
The use of more than one, but fewer than all, of the intermediaries who are willing to carry the company's products.

Selling concept | مفهوم البيع
The idea that that consumers will not buy enough of the firm's products unless it undertakes a large-scale selling and promotion effort.

Selling process | عملية البيع
The steps that the salesperson follows when selling, which include prospecting and qualifying, preapproach, approach, presentation and demonstration, handling objections, closing, and follow-up.

Sense-of-mission marketing |
التسويق المبني على مبادىء المسؤولية الاجتماعية
A principle of sustainable marketing that holds that a company should define its mission in broad social terms rather than narrow product terms.

Service | الخدمات
Any activity or benefit that one party can offer to another that is essentially intangible and does not result in the ownership of anything.

Service inseparability | تلازم الخدمات
A major characteristic of services—they are produced and consumed at the same time and cannot be separated from their providers.

Service intangibility | الخدمات غير الملموسة
A major characteristic of services—they cannot be seen, tasted, felt, heard, or smelled before they are bought.

Service perishability | عدم قابلية تخزين الخدمة
A major characteristic of services—they cannot be stored for later sale or use.

Service retailer | (بائع تجزئة (خدمات
A retailer whose product line is actually a service, including hotels, airlines, banks, colleges, and many others.

Service variability | تنوع الخدمات
A major characteristic of services—their quality may vary greatly, depending on who provides them and when, where, and how.

Service-profit chain | سلسلة ربحية الخدمة
The chain that links service firm profits with employee and customer satisfaction.

Share of customer | حصة العميل
The portion of the customer's purchasing that a company gets in its product categories.

Shopping center | مركز تسوق
A group of retail businesses planned, developed, owned, and managed as a unit.

Shopping product | منتج شرائي
A consumer product that the customer, in the process of selection and purchase, usually compares on such bases as suitability, quality, price, and style.

Social class | طبقة إجتماعية
Relatively permanent and ordered divisions in a society whose members share similar values, interests, and behaviors.

Social marketing | التسويق الاجتماعي
The use of commercial marketing concepts and tools in programs designed to influence individuals' behavior to improve their well-being and that of society.

Societal marketing | التسويق المجتمعي
A principle of sustainable marketing that holds that a company should make marketing decisions by considering consumers' wants, the company's requirements, consumers' longrun interests, and society's long-run interests.

Societal marketing concept | مفهوم التسويق المجتمعي
The idea that a company's marketing decisions should consider consumers' wants, the company's requirements, consumers' long-run interests, and society's long-run interests.

Spam | البريد غير المرغوب
Unsolicited, unwanted commercial e-mail messages

Specialty product | منتج خاص
A consumer product with unique characteristics or brand identification for which a significant group of buyers is willing to make a special purchase effort.

Specialty store | متجر الصناعات المتخصصة
A retail store that carries a narrow product line with a deep assortment within that line.

Standardized global marketing | التسويق العالمي الموحد
An international marketing strategy for using basically the same marketing strategy and mix in all the company's international markets.

Store brand (private brand) |
(علامة تجارية مملوكة لتاجر(علامة تجارية خاصة
A brand created and owned by a reseller of a product or service

Straight product extension |
توسيع نطاق تسويق المنتج دون إحداث اي تغيير فيه
Marketing a product in a foreign market without any change.

Straight rebuy | إعادة الشراء المباشر
A business buying situation in which the buyer routinely reorders something without any modifications.

Strategic group | المجموعة الإستراتيجية
A group of firms in an industry following the same or a similar strategy.

Strategic planning | التخطيط الاستراتيجي
The process of developing and maintaining a strategic fit between the organization's goals and capabilities and its changing marketing opportunities.

Style | نمط
A basic and distinctive mode of expression.

Subculture | الجماعة الفرعية
A group of people with shared value systems based on common life experiences and situations.

Supermarket | السوبر ماركت
A large, low-cost, low-margin, high-volume, self-service store that carries a wide variety of grocery and household products.

Supplier development | تطوير أداء الموردين
Systematic development of networks of supplier partners to ensure an appropriate and dependable supply of products and materials for use in making products or reselling them to others.

Supplier search | البحث عن مورّد
The stage of the business buying process in which the buyer tries to find the best vendors.

Supplier selection | اختيار المورد
The stage of the business buying process in which the buyer reviews proposals and selects a supplier or suppliers.

Supply chain management | إدارة سلسلة الإمداد
Managing upstream and downstream value-added flows of materials, final goods, and related information among suppliers, the company, resellers, and final consumers.

Survey research | البحث المسحي
Gathering primary data by asking people questions about their knowledge, attitudes, preferences, and buying behavior.

Sustainable marketing | التسويق المستدام
A principle of sustainable marketing that holds that a company should make marketing decisions by considering consumers' wants, the company's requirements, consumers' longrun interests, and society's long-run interests.

SWOT analysis | (تحليل سوت (نقاط القوة والضعف والفرص والتهديدات
An overall evaluation of the company's strengths (S), weaknesses (W), opportunities (O), and threats (T).

Systems selling (solutions selling) | (بيع الأنظمة (بيع الحلول
Buying a packaged solution to a problem from a single seller, thus avoiding all the separate decisions involved in a complex buying situation.

Target costing | التكاليف المستهدفة
Pricing that starts with an ideal selling price, then targets costs that will ensure that the price is met.

Target market | السوق المستهدفة
A set of buyers sharing common needs or characteristics that the company decides to serve.

Team selling |
البيع من خلال عدة أقسام من الموظفين (المبيعات، المالية، التسويق...الخ)
Using teams of people from sales, marketing, engineering, finance, technical support, and even upper management to service large, complex accounts.

Team-based new-product development |
تطوير منتج جديد بالاعتماد على فريق العمل
An approach to developing new products in which various company departments work closely together, overlapping the steps in the product development process to save time and increase effectiveness.

Technological environment | البيئة التكنولوجية
Forces that create new technologies, creating new product and market opportunities.

Telephone marketing | التسويق عن طريق التليفون
Using the telephone to sell directly to customers.

Territorial sales force structure |
الهيكل التنظيمي لمندوبي المبيعات في مناطق جغرافية مختلفة
A sales force organization that assigns each salesperson to an exclusive geographic territory in which that salesperson sells the company's full line.

Test marketing | الإختبار التسويقي
The stage of new-product development in which the product and marketing program are tested in realistic market settings.

Third-party logistics (PL) provider | مقدم الخدمات اللوجستية المستقل
An independent logistics provider that performs any or all of the functions required to get its client's product to market.

Total costs | التكاليف الإجمالية
The sum of the fixed and variable costs for any given level of production.

Trade promotions | العروض الترويجية التجارية
Sales promotion tools used to persuade resellers to carry a brand, give it shelf space, promote it in advertising, and push it to consumers.

Undifferentiated (mass) marketing | التسويق المفتوح (الموسَّع)
A market-coverage strategy in which a firm decides to ignore market segment differences and go after the whole market with one offer.

Uniform-delivered pricing | التسعيرة الموحدة للتوصيل
A geographical pricing strategy in which the company charges the same price plus freight to all customers, regardless of their location.

Unsought product | منتج غير مطلوب
A consumer product that the consumer either does not know about or knows about but does not normally think of buying.

Users | المستخدمون
Members of the buying organization who will actually use the purchased product or service.

Value chain | سلسلة الإمدادات؛ سلسلة الأنشطة المضيفة للقيمة
The series of departments that carry out value-creating activities to design, produce, market, deliver, and support a firm's products.

Value delivery network | شبكة توفير القيمة
The network made up of the company, suppliers, distributors, and ultimately customers who "partner" with each other to improve the performance of the entire system in delivering customer value.

Value proposition | قيمة المنتج
The full positioning of a brand—the full mix of benefits upon which it is positioned.

Value-added pricing | التسعير القائم على القيمة المضافة
Attaching value added features and services to differentiate a company's offers and charging higher prices.

Value-based pricing | التسعير المبني على القيمة
Setting price based on buyers' perceptions of value rather than on the seller's cost.

Variable costs | التكاليف المتغيرة
Costs that vary directly with the level of production.

Variety-seeking buying behaviour | سلوك الشراء المتسم بالتنوع
Consumer buying behavior in situations characterized by low consumer involvement but significant perceived brand differences.

Vertical marketing system (VMS) | نظام التسويق الرأسي
A distribution channel structure in which producers, wholesalers, and retailers act as a unified system. One channel member owns the others, has contracts with them, or has so much power that they all cooperate

Viral marketing | تسويق المنتج عبر التناقل الالكتروني
The Internet version of word-of-mouth marketing—Web sites, videos, e-mail messages, or other marketing events that are so infectious that customers will want to pass them along to friends.

Wants | الرغبات
The form human needs take as shaped by culture and individual personality.

Whole-channel view | المنظور الكامل لقنوات التسويق
Designing international channels that take into account the entire global supply chain and marketing channel, forging and effective global value delivery network.

Wholesaler | تاجر الجملة
A firm engaged primarily in wholesaling activities.

Wholesaling | البيع بالجملة
All activities involved in selling goods and services to those buying for resale or business use.

Word-of-mouth influence | تأثير الكلمة المنطوقة
Personal communication about a product between target buyers and neighbors, friends, family members, and associates.

Zone pricing | التسعير حسب المناطق
A geographical pricing strategy in which the company sets up two or more zones. All customers within a zone pay the same total price; the more distant the zone, the higher the price.

Index

Credits

We are grateful to the following for permission to reproduce copyright material:

FIGURES

Figure 1.5 from "Mismanagement of Customer Loyalty", *Harvard Business Review*, p. 93 (Relnartz, W., and Kumar, V., July 2002), copyright © by the president and fellows of Harvard College; all rights reserved; Figure 2.2 adapted from 'The BCG Portfolio Matrix' from the *Product Portfolio Matrix*, copyright © 1970, The Boston Consulting Group; Figure 2.8 adapted from "Return on Marketing: Using Consumer Equity to Focus Marketing Strategy", *Journal of Marketing*, p. 112 (Rust, R.T., Lemon, K.N., and Zeithaml, V.A., 2004), copyright © American Marketing Association. Permission conveyed through Copyright Clearance Center; Figure 5.4 from *Motivation and Personality*, 3rd edition (Maslow, A. H., Eds Frager, R.D., and Fadiman, J.) copyright © 1987. Printed and Electronically reproduced by permission of Pearson Education, Inc., Upper Saddle River, New Jersey; Figure 5.5 adapted from *Consumer Behavior and Marketing Action*, Boston: Kent Publishing Company (Assael, H., 1987) copyright © 1987 by Wadsworth, Inc. Reprinted by permission of Kent Publishing Company, a division of Wadsworth, Inc.; Figure 5.7 from *Diffusion of Innovations, Fifth edition*, Free Press, a Division of Simon & Schuster (Rogers, E.M., 2003) copyright © 2003 Everett M. Rogers. All rights reserved. With the permission of The Free Press, a Division of Simon & Schuster, Inc.; Figure 12.3 'How Salespeople Spend Their Time' from Alexander Proudfoot. Data used with permission, www.alexanderproudfoot.com; Figures U13.1 to U13.5 'Internet Penetration and Number of Users in Egypt, 2000–2008', 'Internet Users in Egypt', 'Expansion of the Egyptian Retail Industry', 'Elsou2.com's Online Orders Supply Chain', and 'Elsou2.com's Forecasted Income Statement' published at El-Khazindar Business Research & Case Center and reproduced with permission; Figure 13.4 from 'Facebook Usage Growth in the Arab World', http://www.insidenetwork.com, copyright © INSIDENETWORK INC. All Rights Reserved. Reprinted with permission; Figure 15.2 adapted from "Can You Say What Your Strategy Is?", *Harvard Business Review*, p. 89 (Collins, D.J., and Rukstad, M.G., 2008), copyright © 2008 by the President and Fellows of Harvard College; all rights reserved. Figure 17.2 'The Environmental Sustainability Portfolio' from "Innovation, Creative Destruction, and Sustainability", *Research Technology Management*, Vol 48 (5), pp. 21–27, September-October 2005 (Hart, S.L.), copyright © Industrial Research Institute, Inc.

SCREENSHOTS

Screenshot 1.2 from BBK, www.bbkonline.com, reproduced with permission; Screenshot 1.6 from 'The societal marketing concept: Johnson & Johnson's credo stresses putting people before profits', www.jnj.com. Courtesy of Johnson & Johnson. Reprinted with permission; Screenshot 2.9 from Toyota, copyright © 2008 Toyota Motor Sales. All rights reserved. Used with permission; Screenshot 3.15 from First National Bank, http://fnb.com.lb, reproduced with permission; Screenshot 4.10b from Neilsen Germany, http://de.nielsen.com/site/index.shtml, copyright © The Nielsen Company; Screenshot 4.12 from Bill of Rights from Council for Marketing and Opinion Research website, http://cmoresearch.com/, copyright © Marketing Research Association; Screenshot 4.12 from Bill of Rights from Council for Marketing and Opinion Research website, http://cmoresearch.com/, copyright © Marketing Research Association; Screenshot 7.7 from Anything Left Handed, http://www.anythinglefthanded.co.uk/, copyright ©

Anything Left Handed; Screenshot 13.8 from www.officedepot.co.uk. Courtesy of Office Depot; Screenshot 13.9 from Nefsak, http://www.nefsak.com/books. Reproduced with permission; Screenshot 14.12 from www.logility.com, © 2008 Logility, Inc. All rights reserved. Used with permission; Screenshot 15.4 from Johnson & Johnson Acuvue website. Courtesy of Johnson & Johnson. Used with permission. Screenshot 15.6 of restaurant menu and text, www.wildpeeta.com, copyright © Wild Peeta.

TABLES

Table 4.4 from 'Internet Penetration in Arab Countries', www.internetworldstats.com, Copyright © 2000–2011, Miniwatts Marketing Group. All rights reserved; Table 5.1 from "Social Networking Explodes Worldwide as Sites Increase their Focus on Cultural Relevance" press release, 12 August 2008, www.comscore.com/Press_Events/Press_Releases/2008/08/Social_Networking_World_Wide, source: comScore; Table 9.2 from *Marketing Management*, 13th edition (Kotler, P., and Keller, K.) p.288, copyright © 2009. Printed and Electronically reproduced by permission of Pearson Education, Inc., Upper Saddle River, New Jersey; Table 17.2 from 'American Marketing Association Code of Ethics', Reprinted with permission of the American Marketing Association.

TEXT

Extract on page 4 after "Introduction", 2011 www.dubaicares.ae, reproduced with permission of Dubai Cares; Extract on page 13 from "The Top 10 PR Endeavors," PR News, 30 October 2006, p. 1, www.jnj.com. Courtesy of Johnson & Johnson. Reprinted with permission. All rights; Extract on page 14 from "Burj Al Arab," Jumeirah company website, 2011, www.jumeirah.com, reproduced with permission; Extract on page 14 from "Burj Al Arab," TripAdvisor, hotel review from customer, 20 December 2009, www.tripadvisor.com, copyright © 2011, TripAdvisor, LLC. All rights Reserved. Used with Permission; Extract on page 19 from "Advertising Trends in the Middle East - A Look Towards 2009," by Imran Jaffrey, *Business Insights*, Worldwide Partners Inc., www.worldwidepartners.com, copyright © Imran Jaffrey; Extract on page 28 from "57357 Friends" September 2009, www.57357.com, reproduced by kind permission of Children's Cancer Hospital Foundation 57357; Extract on page 39 after "The future of mobile marketing in the Middle East: trends and opportunities", *AMEInfo*, 29/09/2004, copyright © www.ameinfo.com; Case Study on pages 34–35 by May M. Kamal from El-Khazindar Business Research and Case Center (KCC), School of Business, The American University in Cairo. Reproduced by permission; Extract on page 41 from "Mission to lead" 2011, www.zain.com, copyright © Zain; Extract on page 44 from "Actis announces a significant investment in Mo'men, a leading Egyptian consumer business," Actis company press release, 30 July 2008, www.act.is. Reproduced with permission; Extract on page 63 from "Bahrain Bay - a $1.5 billion urban development set to change the face of Manama" *AMEInfo*, 10/12/2005 (Bahrain Bay Development B.S.C.© (Bahrain Bay BSC), Press Release), source: www.ameinfo.com; Extract on page 64 from "Bahrain Bay supports Busaiteen football club" *AMEInfo*, 16/01/2008 (Bahrain Bay Press Release), source: www.ameinfo.com; Extract on page 117 from "Global survey shows luxury is a lifestyle in UAE", *AMEInfo*, 22/12/2009 (Synovate Press Release), source: www.ameinfo.com; Adapted Case Study on pages 121–123 by